ECONOMICS

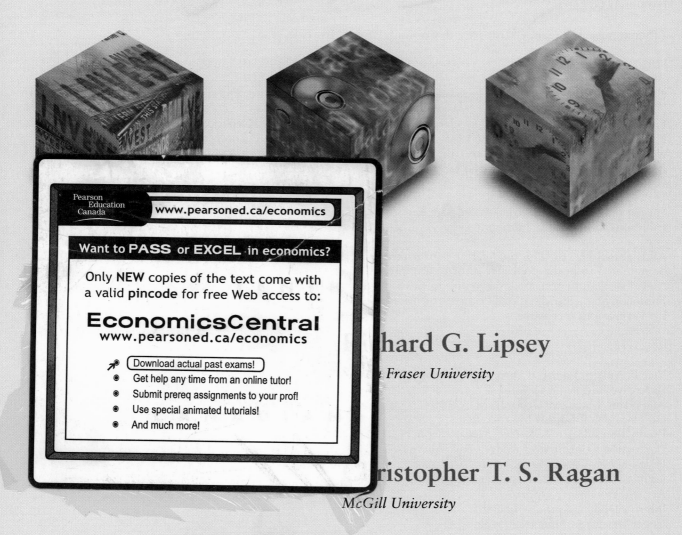

hard G. Lipsey

Fraser University

ristopher T. S. Ragan

McGill University

EDITION

Toronto

National Library of Canada Cataloguing in Publication

Lipsey, Richard G., 1928-
        Economics / Richard G. Lipsey, Christopher T.S. Ragan, Paul N. Courant. –
10th Canadian ed., study ed.

ISBN 0-321-12591-6

1. Economics. I. Ragan, Christopher II. Courant, Paul N. III. Title.

HB171.5.L733 2003   330   C2002-901956-7

Special thanks to Ingrid Kristjanson, Sam Fefferman, and Scott Cawfield for their contributions to this Study Edition.

0-321-12591-6

Vice President, Editorial Director: Michael J. Young
Executive Editor: Dave Ward
Marketing Manager: Deborah Meredith
Developmental Editor: Maurice Esses
Production Editor: Mary Ann McCutcheon
Production Coordinator: Andrea Falkenberg
Page Layout: Carol Magee
Permissions and Photo Research: Susan Wallace-Cox
Art Director: Mary Opper
Interior Design: Anthony Leung
Cover Design and Image: Artville LLC

1 2 3 4 5   07 06 05 04 03

Printed and bound in United States.

BRIEF CONTENTS

CONTENTS

LIST OF BOXES

Applying Economic Concepts

Extensions in Theory

Lessons from History

TO THE INSTRUCTOR

Economics is a living discipline, changing and evolving in response to developments in the world economy and in response to the research of many thousands of economists throughout the world. Through ten editions, *Economics* has evolved with the discipline. Our purpose in this edition, as in the previous nine, is to provide students with an introduction to the major issues facing the world's economies, to the methods that economists use to study those issues, and to the policy problems that those issues create. Our treatment is everywhere guided by three important principles:

1. Economics is *scientific,* in the sense that it progresses through the systematic confrontation of theory by evidence. Neither theory nor data alone can tell us much about the world, but combined they tell us a great deal.

2. Economics is *useful* and it should be seen by students to be so. An understanding of economic theory combined with knowledge about the economy produces many important insights about economic policy. Although we stress these insights, we are also careful to point out cases where too little is known to support strong statements about public policy. Appreciating what is not known is as important as learning what is known.

3. We strive always to be *honest* with our readers. Although we know that economics is not always easy, we do not approve of glossing over difficult bits of analysis without letting readers see what is happening and what has been assumed. We take whatever space is needed to explain why economists draw their conclusions, rather than just asserting the conclusions. We also take pains to avoid simplifying matters so much that students would have to unlearn what they have been taught if they continue their study beyond the introductory course. In short, we have tried to follow Albert Einstein's advice:

Everything should be made as simple as possible, but not simpler.

Current Economic Issues

In writing the tenth edition of *Economics*, we have tried to reflect the major economic issues that we face as we begin the twenty-first century.

Globalization

Enormous changes have occurred throughout the world over the last few decades. Flows of trade and investment between countries have risen so dramatically that it is now common to speak of the "globalization" of the world economy. Today it is no longer possible to study any economy without taking into account developments in the rest of the world.

What is true for most countries is also true for Canada. Economic relations between Canada and the rest of the world have a significant impact on most of the major "domestic" issues in the news.

For example, some observers believe that the difficulties faced by Canadian farmers in recent years is caused partly by subsidies that U.S. and European governments provide to their farmers. Students should know how subsidies to foreign farmers affect farmers in Canada. They should also be able to discuss the overall costs and benefits to Canada from agricultural income-support policies, whether they are subsidies or supply-management schemes. We address these issues in some detail in Chapter 5.

In recent years, many Canadians have begun worrying about a possible "brain drain" to the United States. The fear is that Canada's "best and brightest" are leaving in increasing numbers, in pursuit of greater employment prospects, lower income taxes, and higher living standards available south of the border. How mobile is labour across international borders? Does such labour mobility imply that Canada's policies cannot diverge significantly from those in other countries? We explore these issues at various points throughout the book, especially in Chapters 13, 14, and 18.

Another example of the importance of globalization for domestic policy is related to the Asian economic crisis that began in the summer of 1997 and lasted into 1999. The Asian crisis represented both a negative demand shock and a positive supply shock for Canada. The importance of the open economy appears throughout the macroeconomics half of the book—we place a greater emphasis on the importance of exchange rates than we have in past editions.

The forces of globalization are with us to stay. In this tenth edition of *Economics*, we have done our best to ensure that students are made aware of the world outside Canada and of how events elsewhere in the world affect the Canadian economy.

Transition and Development

Over the past decade, the century-long ideological conflict between capitalism and communism has virtually ended. The most powerful communist economy in the world, the Soviet Union, has disappeared, both as a nation and as a planned economy. Mixed capitalism, the system of economic organization that has long prevailed in much of the industrialized world, now prevails in virtually all of it. Many of the developing economies are also moving in this direction. The reasons for the failure of the planned economies of Eastern Europe and the Soviet Union are discussed in Chapter 1 as a contrast to the reasons for the relative success of mixed capitalism.

Developing countries face many of the same problems being experienced by the transition economies of Eastern Europe and the former Soviet Union. Countries in the developing world have been trying—some for many years—to make the difficult transformation from agricultural-based economies to industrialized ones. In many cases, they lack the same institutions that the centrally planned economies had failed to develop. Thus the "development" challenges faced by these economies are very similar to the "transition" challenges faced by the formerly centrally planned economies. We discuss the challenges faced by the developing economies in Chapter 33, which builds on the more fundamental discussion of long-term economic growth in Chapter 32.

The Role of Government

The political winds appear to have shifted in Canada, the United States, and many other countries over the past two decades. Political parties that once advocated a greater role for government in the economy now argue the benefits of proscribed government. But has the fundamental role of government really changed? In order to understand the role of government in the economy, students must understand the benefits of free markets as well as the situations that cause markets to fail. They must also understand that governments often intervene in the economy for reasons related more to equity than to efficiency.

In this tenth edition of *Economics*, we continue to incorporate the discussion of government policy as often as possible. Here are but a few of the many examples that we explore:

- the effects of payroll taxes (in Chapter 4)
- the effects of minimum wages (in Chapter 5)
- the disincentive effects of income taxes (in Chapters 6 and 18)
- economic regulation and competition policy (in Chapter 12)
- pay equity policy (in Chapter 13)
- environmental policies (in Chapter 17)
- fiscal policy (in Chapters 23 and 25)
- the importance of debt and deficits (in Chapter 31)
- monetary policy (in Chapters 27, 28, and 29)
- policies that affect the economy's long-run unemployment rate (in Chapter 30)
- policies related to the economy's long-run growth rate (in Chapters 32 and 33)
- trade policies (in Chapter 35)
- policies related to the exchange rate (in Chapter 36)

The Book

Globalization, growth and development, and the role of government are pressing issues of the day. Much of our study of economic principles and the Canadian economy has been shaped by these issues. In addition to specific coverage of growth and internationally oriented topics, growth and globalization appear naturally throughout the book in the treatment of many topics once thought to be entirely "domestic."

Most chapters of *Economics* contain some discussion of economic policy. We have two main goals in mind when we present these discussions:

1. We aim to give students practice in using economic theory, because applying theory is both a wonderfully effective teaching method and a reliable test of students' grasp of theory.

2. We want to introduce students to the major policy issues of the day and to let them discover that few policy debates are as "black and white" as they often appear in the press.

Both goals reflect our view that students should see economics as useful in helping us to understand and deal with the world around us.

Microeconomics: Structure and Coverage

Beginning Part 1, Chapter 1 presents the market as an instrument of coordination. We introduce the issues of scarcity and choice and then briefly discuss alternative economic systems. The problems of converting command economies to market economies will be with us for some time, and comparisons with command economies help to establish what a market economy is *by showing what it is not*. Chapter 2 makes the important distinction between positive and normative inquiries and goes on to an introductory discussion of the construction and testing of economic theories. We also discuss graphing in detail.

Part 2 deals with demand and supply. After introducing price determination and elasticity in Chapters 3 and 4, we apply these tools in Chapter 5. The case studies are designed to provide practice in applying the tools rather than a full coverage of each case.

Part 3 presents the foundations of demand and supply. The theory of consumer behaviour is developed via marginal utility theory in Chapter 6, which also provides an introduction to consumer surplus and an intuitive discussion of income and substitution effects. The Appendix to Chapter 6 covers indifference curves, budget lines, and the derivation of demand curves using indifference theory. Chapter 7 introduces the firm as an institution and develops short-run costs. Chapter 8 covers long-run costs and the principle of substitution, and goes on to consider shifts in cost curves due to technological change. The latter topic is seldom, if ever, covered in the micro part of elementary textbooks, yet applied work on firms' responses to changing economic signals shows it to be extremely important.

The first two chapters of Part 4, Chapters 9 and 10, present the standard theories of perfect competition and monopoly with some discussion of international cartels. Chapter 11 deals with monopolistic competition and oligopoly, which are the market structures most commonly found in Canadian industries. Strategic behaviour plays a central part in the analysis of this chapter. The first half of Chapter 12 deals with the efficiency of competition and the inefficiency of monopoly. The last half of the chapter deals with regulation and competition policy.

Part 5 begins in Chapter 13 by discussing the general principles of factor pricing and how factor prices are influenced by factor mobility. Chapter 14 then examines the operation of labour markets, addressing issues such as wage differentials, discrimination, labour unions, and the "good jobs/bad jobs" debate. Chapter 15 discusses capital and nonrenewable resources.

The first chapter of Part 6 (Chapter 16) provides a general discussion of market success and market failure, introduces social choice theory, and outlines the arguments for and against government intervention in a market economy. Chapter 17 deals with environmental regulation. In addition to providing current applications of microeconomic theory to policymaking, it contains a boxed discussion of the U.S. experience with tradable emissions permits for sulfur dioxide. Chapter 18 analyzes taxes, public expenditure, and the main elements of Canadian social policy. These three chapters expand on the basics of microeconomic analysis by providing current illustrations of the relevance of economic theory to contemporary policy situations.

Macroeconomics: Structure and Coverage

Our treatment of macroeconomics is divided into five parts: an introduction to macroeconomics; national income and fiscal policy; money, banking, and monetary policy; macroeconomic problems and policies; and international economics. The themes of internationalization and economic growth are interwoven throughout all five parts.

The first macro chapter, Chapter 19, identifies economic growth and the level of potential national income as the major determinants of a society's material standard of living. The discussion of national income accounting in Chapter 20 provides a thorough treatment of the distinction between real and nominal GDP, the distinction between GDP and GNP, and a discussion of what measures of national income *do not measure*. Chapter 21 presents a brief discussion of the important distinction between the short run and the long run in macroeconomics.

In Part 8, the core macro chapters (22–25) develop what has become the standard aggregate-demand-aggregate-supply approach. We start with a detailed exposition of the fixed-price (Keynesian cross) model of the determination of equilibrium income in Chapters 22 and 23. In Chapter 22 we consider a simplified economy, one with no international sector or government, in order to make the concepts of equilibrium income and the multiplier as teachable as possible. In Chapter 23 we add government and the international sector, thus opening our model economy to international trade at an early point.

In Chapter 24 we develop the aggregate demand (AD) curve and the short-run aggregate supply (SRAS) curve. Since we discuss the role of wealth in the consumption function in Chapter 22 and the international sector in Chapter 23, there is no mystery about why the AD curve slopes down—unlike other treatments where the AD curve is introduced prior to discussing these issues. Chapter 25 completes the core model by deriving the vertical long-run aggregate supply curve, which allows us to discuss the different effects of AD shifts in the short and long run. This leads directly to an introduction to fiscal policy and a discussion of business cycles in which both stabilization and growth are treated.

Part 9 focuses on the role of money and financial systems. Chapter 26 discusses the nature of money, various components of the money supply, the commercial banking system, and the Bank of Canada. In

Chapter 27 we review the determinants of the demand for money. We then turn to a detailed discussion of the link between the money supply and other economic variables such as interest rates, the exchange rate, national income, and the price level. This chapter builds directly on the material in Chapters 24 and 25, with an emphasis on the distinction between short-run and long-run effects. In Chapter 28 we discuss the Bank of Canada's monetary policy. The chapter ends with a review of Canadian monetary policy over the past 20 years. This provides some important historical context for policy discussions in later parts, as well as an opportunity to draw some general conclusions about the operation of monetary policy.

Part 10 deals with some of today's most pressing macroeconomic policy issues. It contains separate chapters on inflation, unemployment, budget deficits, economic growth, and growth in the developing countries. Chapter 29 on inflation examines the central role of expectations in determining inflation, and the importance of credibility on the part of the central bank. Chapter 30 on unemployment examines the determinants of frictional and structural unemployment and discusses likely reasons for increases in the NAIRU over the past few decades. Chapter 31 on budget deficits stresses the effect of deficits on national saving and long-term economic growth. Chapter 32 provides a comprehensive summary of what is and is not currently known about the causes of economic growth. Although some of the discussion ties directly into the emphasis of previous chapters on national saving, much of it examines current research on induced technological innovation and technological diffusion. Our treatment of economic growth—which we regard as one of the most important macroeconomic issues facing Canada and the world today—goes beyond the coverage in most other introductory texts. Chapter 33 continues the growth theme by providing a summary of current views about economic growth in the developing countries.

Virtually every macroeconomic chapter contains at least some discussion of international issues. However, the final part of *Economics* focuses primarily on international economics. Chapter 34 gives the basic treatment of international trade, developing both the traditional theory of static comparative advantage and newer theories based on imperfect competition and dynamic comparative advantage. Chapter 35 discusses both the positive and normative aspects of trade policy, as well as the GATT and WTO and prospects for regional free-trade areas. There is also a detailed discussion of NAFTA and a box on Canada-U.S. trade disputes. Chapter 36 introduces the balance of payments and examines exchange-rate determination. Here we also discuss three "hot" policy issues: the de-

sirability of current-account deficits or surpluses, whether there is a "right" value for the Canadian exchange rate, and the costs and benefits of Canada's adopting a fixed exchange rate.

We hope you find this menu both attractive and challenging; and we hope students find the material stimulating and enlightening. Many of the messages of economics are complex—if economic understanding were only a matter of common sense and simple observation, there would be no need for professional economists and no need for textbooks like this one. To understand economics, one must work hard. Working at this book should help readers gain a better understanding of the world around them and of the policy problems faced by all levels of government. Furthermore, in today's globalized world, the return to education is large. We like to think that we have contributed in some small part to the understanding that increased investment in human capital by the next generation is necessary to restore incomes to the rapid growth paths that so benefited our parents and our peers. Perhaps we may even contribute to some income-enhancing accumulation of human capital by some of our readers.

Substantive Changes to This Edition

We have done a major revision and update of the entire text with guidance from an extensive series of reviews and feedback from both users and nonusers of the previous editions of this book. As always, we have strived very hard to improve the teachability and readability of the book. We have shortened the overall length by two chapters (from 38 to 36) and by roughly 10 percent in terms of the number of words. There are two entirely new chapters, and several chapters have been completely rewritten. In the following subsections, we summarize the major changes that we have made for this edition. Later, in a separate section, we will describe the important new features that we have added in order to better accommodate the needs of both instructors and students.

Changes in Microeconomics

Here is a brief description of the major changes in the microeconomics portion of the textbook.

Part 1 What Is Economics?

- Chapter 1 has been completely rewritten, incorporating some material from the previous Chapter 3 (which has been removed). The chapter now begins with a discussion about how market economies are self-organizing entities that coordinate the decisions of decentralized agents. This is not an analytical section, but rather an easy introductory discussion. The chapter then goes on to discuss resources, scarcity, opportunity cost, the economy's decision makers, specialization, the division of labour, money, and globalization.
- Chapter 2 is a new chapter that examines how economists think. We begin by discussing normative and positive advice. We then go on to describe theories and models. The section on graphing appears in the main text (rather than the appendix) and shows how economists think about data and how they test their theories. The result is a discussion of graphing that is livelier than in the previous edition.

Part 2 An Introduction to Demand and Supply

- Chapter 3, on demand and supply, has been streamlined but its basic structure is unchanged. In the section on price determination we have added an initial discussion on the concept of a market in which we provide a rough definition of competitive markets. We have added a brief discussion of the 1998 Quebec ice storm in a box. We have also added a new box discussing technical progress and falling computer chip prices.
- Chapter 4 on elasticity has been restructured. We have put the section on supply elasticity as the second section. After discussing supply elasticity, we then go straight into an examination of tax incidence as an important example of why elasticity matters. We have added a new box on the incidence of payroll taxes.
- Chapter 5 begins with an entirely new section on market linkages. We introduce the distinction between partial and general equilibrium, and we go on to consider several ways that seemingly unrelated markets are nonetheless connected. We then discuss administered prices, a section that we have streamlined from the previous edition. We have added a new box on minimum wages. The section on agricultural policies has been updated, and we have added a brief discussion about opposition to the Wheat Board. The section on international trade has been moved to the trade chapter (34).

Part 3 Consumers and Producers

- Chapter 6, on consumer theory, is largely unchanged from the previous edition. We have eliminated the section on free and scarce goods, but have added a small discussion of how information from consumer surveys can easily be misinterpreted because of the failure to distinguish total from marginal value. In the section on income and substitution effects, we have added a box applying the idea to the disincentive effects of income taxation.
- Chapter 7, the first on the theory of the firm, has been extensively rewritten. We begin by discussing the organization and financing of firms, which leads to a new box on debt instruments. We address Coase's ideas regarding why firms exist, and the role of transactions costs. We then go on to discuss production, costs, and profits, explicitly introducing a production function. In the section on short-run production relationships, we have used new numbers in the table and have plotted these values for the diagrams. This should improve the message for the student. We also plot the associated cost data when we discuss the short-run cost curves. Finally, we have a new appendix that explores the issue of whether firms really do maximize profits, and how the market for corporate control places limits on the behaviour of non-profit-maximizing firms. This appendix includes a discussion of the principal-agent problem as applied to the firm's owners and managers.
- Chapter 8 deals with firms in the long run and very long run. It is largely unchanged from the previous edition. The focus on the long run is the cost-minimizing choice of factor mix. The focus on the very long run is how the firm responds to technological change. The chapter's appendix contains a detailed treatment of isoquants, isocosts, and cost minimization.

Part 4 Markets, Pricing, and Efficiency

- Chapter 9 on competitive markets is substantially unchanged from the previous edition, though we have tried to streamline and clarify wherever possible. The box on the seaside inn has been brought forward to the middle of the chapter where it fits naturally as an example of a firm that continues to operate even though it is not covering its total costs. The section of the appeal of perfect competition has been removed.
- Chapter 10 examines monopoly. The figure on elasticity and revenue has been deleted. We have added a new discussion on the comparison of monopoly

and competition, introducing the reader to the idea of allocative efficiency (which we explain in detail in Chapter 12). In our discussion of entry barriers we have added a new box showing how legislation has created local monopoly power for Irish pubs. We have added a discussion and figure to explain how firms price discriminate among markets; this adds to a current example dealing with Levi jeans.

- Chapter 11, on imperfect competition, has been shortened. There is less emphasis on the concentration ratio. We have added new examples of co-operation (diamonds and coffee cartels) and have also updated the OPEC box to include some of the recent political frictions that have contributed to OPEC's inability to restrict output.

- Chapter 12, which deals with efficiency, has been updated. The discussion of productive and allocative efficiency has been clarified, and we have added a diagram to emphasize the importance of equating marginal cost across firms. We have streamlined the discussion of regulation, in part by deleting the box on hydro authorities. The section on competition policy has been updated. We discuss the challenge of weighing a merger's efficiency gains against the reduction in competition. The importance of entry barriers is illustrated in an example regarding the 1998 proposed bank mergers. There is a new box on the U.S. antitrust case against Microsoft and some discussion of the Air Canada merger with Canadian Airlines.

Part 5 Factor Markets

- In Chapter 13, we have shortened the opening discussion of income distribution. We have a new figure on earnings distribution, and have both pre-tax and after-tax Lorenz curves. The box on backward-bending labour supply has been removed. We have added a new box on labour mobility—using current data on Canadian-U.S. migration patterns that has recently been the focus of the "brain drain" debate. We have removed the discussions of regional income equalization and of Canadian interprovincial labour mobility. We now give examples of rent to help the student better understand this important concept.

- Chapter 14 deals with labour markets. It has been shortened considerably from the previous edition. We get more quickly through the section on competitive wage differentials, in which we have incorporated a shortened discussion of discrimination. We have a new figure for education and earnings. We have added a new figure for union membership,

and have added discussion of some of the things that we *don't* know about unions, especially their effect on productivity. The "good jobs—bad jobs" debate remains, but we have added a figure showing the long-term changes in employment.

- Chapter 15 deals with capital and nonrenewable resources and is largely unchanged from the previous edition. We have improved the discussions of present value and of the firm's demand for capital. The box on interest rates and inflation has been shortened.

Part 6 Government in the Market Economy

- Chapter 16 examines market failures and government intervention. It has been significantly modified from the previous edition. The opening section on market coordination has been removed, since much of this appears in Chapter 1. We have added a new diagram in the discussion of externalities, as well as a discussion of transactions costs in the discussion of the Coase theorem. We have added an extensive discussion about excludability and rivalry, which then leads to the discussion of public goods. This includes a brief discussion of congestion on roads and road pricing. We have added two new boxes on common property resources. Finally, we have emphasized that the government has other motives for intervention (such as altering the income distribution) that are not based on market failures.

- Chapter 17 is devoted to environmental policy. The discussion in the previous edition on health and safety regulation has been removed. We have added a diagram to remind students about the basic economics of externalities. We then go through direct controls, emissions taxes and tradable emissions permits. The old box on resistance to market-based schemes now appears as an expanded final section entitled "the politics of pollution control".

- Chapter 18 covers taxation and public expenditure. It has been significantly shortened and rewritten from the previous edition. The first section on taxes has been shortened considerably, but we have spent more time discussing progressivity. In the second section we have added a figure to help explain direct and excess burdens. We have also shortened the section on expenditures. There is a brief review of Canadian social policy and the recent reforms, including the challenges facing the Canada Pension Plan and the concerns surrounding reforms that may lead to a two-tiered health-care system.

Changes in Macroeconomics

Here is a brief description of the major changes in the macroeconomics portion of the textbook.

Part 7 An Introduction to Macroeconomics

- Chapter 19 offers the student an introduction to important macroeconomic variables and issues. There are no major changes in this chapter from the previous edition, though we have streamlined it, especially the section on inflation. We have also removed the final section "trends and cycles" from this chapter; this material now reappears in an entirely new Chapter 21.
- Chapter 20, on measuring GDP, is mostly unaltered. We have modified the discussion of the income approach to match the way Statistics Canada presents the data. We have replaced the discussion of "net domestic income" with one on "net national income at factor cost." The box on real and nominal GDP has been expanded to include a discussion of how the choice of the base year slightly affects the results, depending on relative price movements.
- Chapter 21 is a completely new chapter. The purpose is to provide some flexibility for those instructors who want to discuss some aspects of the long run before discussing the short run. But this chapter contains no formal modelling, and so can be covered whenever the instructor chooses. We begin with two interesting discussions of why the short run is different from the long run. We present a simple accounting identity that decomposes all changes in GDP into changes in factor supplies, factor utilization, and productivity. We then present Canadian data to show that factor supplies and productivity change considerably over the long run but very little over the short run, whereas factor utilization changes a great deal over the short run but very little over the long run.

Part 8 National Income and Fiscal Policy

- Chapter 22 develops the simple income-expenditure model with a fixed price level and no government or foreign trade. We have tried to lighten what many instructors thought was a heavy chapter. We have added a new diagram explaining consumption smoothing. We have also added some data on investment volatility in Canada. In the discussion of the saving-investment approach to equilibrium, we have added some simple algebra to show that the difference between Y and AE is always equal to the difference between S and I.
- Chapter 23 adds government and foreign trade to the simple income-expenditure model. The saving-investment approach is now covered more efficiently. We have added some simple algebra to prove that the two approaches are equivalent. We have also rewritten the final section to highlight that the assumption of fixed prices is related to the assumption of demand-determined output.
- Chapter 24 introduces the AD/AS framework and is structurally the same as in the previous edition. We have completely removed the discussion of inside/outside assets and have rewritten the section describing the effect of a change in the price level on private-sector wealth. We have removed the subsection on "points off the AD curve." The old box on the shape of the $SRAS$ curve has been eliminated, and the material on the *increasing* slope has been incorporated into the text. There is now greater emphasis on the role of aggregate supply shocks. In the final section we have added a discussion on why some economic events embody *both* demand and supply shocks. This leads to a new box on the Asian crisis and its effects on the Canadian economy.
- Chapter 25 takes the AD/AS model to the long run, with factor-price adjustment returning actual GDP to potential GDP. We now explicitly hold technology and productivity constant during the analysis. We have also brought the simple Phillips curve into this chapter (and stress that it describes the adjustment process from output gaps to factor-price changes). In the section on shocks, we have added a detailed discussion of aggregate supply shocks. The box on anticipated demand shocks has been removed. We have expanded the box on fiscal policy in the Great Depression by adding some data on GDP, prices and unemployment.

Part 9 Money, Banking, and Monetary Policy

- Chapter 26 is the first chapter on money. We now include an international scatter-plot on inflation and money growth so students can see the long-run relationship. The box on the globalization of financial markets now has a brief discussion of the recent drive for Canadian bank mergers. In the discussion of deposit creation, we have added a little algebra to clarify the point. We have also rewritten the discussion of cash drains.

- Chapter 27 puts money into the *AD/AS* model. We have streamlined the discussions of financial assets and of money demand. In the section on the transmission mechanism, we have emphasized the role of the exchange rate, thus eliminating a box that was difficult for many students. This new discussion ends with a diagram showing the open-economy transmission mechanism. We have removed the material on how increases in the money supply frustrate the adjustment process.

- Chapter 28 reviews the details of Canadian monetary policy. The basic structure of the chapter is unchanged, but there are many changes from the previous edition. The box on the bank rate has been updated, as has the discussion of negative and positive balances at the Bank of Canada. The open economy now figures more prominently in the chapter, both in the review of the transmission mechanism and in the review of recent policy. We have added a discussion and figure of how the need for a forward-looking monetary policy sometimes puts the Bank into awkward political situations, tightening monetary policy even though *current* inflation is low. The discussion of recent monetary history now begins with the 1981 recession. We have added brief discussions of the Asian crisis, the stock market, and the possible costs of low inflation as issues that the Bank had to face in the late 1990s. Finally, we have restored and rewritten the appendix on the stock market that existed in earlier editions of the book.

Part 10 Macroeconomic Problems and Policies

- Chapter 29 deals with inflation. We have reorganized this chapter somewhat, and have also shortened it and updated with some current debates. We have incorporated the box on constant inflation into the first section of the chapter. This way the student sees immediately how sustained inflation can be incorporated into the model. We then go on to the issue of demand and supply shocks. We have removed the discussion of "isolated versus repeated" shocks which many reviewers found confusing—in this section all shocks are one-time, permanent shocks. In the section on reducing inflation, we have now included a discussion and figure for the sacrifice ratio. In the final section on Canadian inflation policy we have added two current debates: Is inflation dead? Is inflation too low?

- Chapter 30 discusses unemployment. After the section discussing the New Classical and New Keynesian theories of cyclical unemployment, we have added a brief discussion of why these differences really only apply in the short run—both classes of models agree that the long-run effect of monetary policies are the same. We have added a new figure showing different unemployment rates by demographic group. In the final section we have added a new box on the Canada-U.S. unemployment gap.

- Chapter 31 deals with government deficits and debt. There is now more emphasis on surpluses since federal deficits appear to have been eliminated. The basic analysis of the effects of deficits is unchanged; but we have now added a final short section, which also acts as a review, in which we predict the effects of ongoing surpluses. The discussion of Ricardian equivalence has been reworked and we have also added a diagram to help the student visualize the lifetime effects on wealth from a tax reduction. The box on the "myths" of debt has been rewritten.

- Chapter 32 is on long-term economic growth. There are some noteworthy changes from the previous edition. We have shortened the introductory section and have added a figure to show the opportunity cost of growth. We have added some OECD data on cross-country investment and growth rates. In our discussion of technological change, we now go to a new box on whether workers should be afraid of technical change. We have added a discussion on measuring technical change in which we briefly discuss Solow's method of growth accounting. The section on new growth theories has been slightly streamlined, as has the final section on the limits to growth. The box on the Brundtland Commission has been removed.

- Chapter 33 addresses growth in the developing countries. It has been streamlined considerably. We have added some new data on the external debts of the Highly Indebted Poor Countries. We have also sharpened the discussion of the "new" view of development and the Washington Consensus. The box on South Korea has been removed.

Part 11 International Economics

- Chapter 34 examines the gains from trade. We have added a figure in the introduction showing the growth of trade relative to GDP. We have considerably shortened the first section on comparative and absolute advantage and have also added a figure to show the production possibilities boundary for two countries. We then go on to a section that formerly appeared in Chapter 6—showing the imports and exports of internationally traded goods with a simple demand-and-supply apparatus. This section should help students see that what is desirable as given by comparative advantage is also largely what happens with actual trade.

- Chapter 35 provides a discussion of trade policy. We have significantly shortened the theoretical discussion of strategic trade policy, but we have added a brief discussion of the Bombardier/Embraer dispute over subsidization. We have removed the section on nominal versus effective protection. The box on VERs has been removed, although the discussion in the text has been expanded slightly. There is a new discussion about the WTO and some of its recent political opposition. We have also added a new box on the Multilateral Agreement on Investment. In the discussion of NAFTA results, we have added a new box on Canadian wine as a surprising success story. We have also updated the box on "headline" Canada-U.S. trade disputes.

- Chapter 36 deals with exchange rates and the balance of payments. It has been entirely rewritten and brings in some material from the old Chapter 38 (which has now been removed). We have rewritten why the balance of payments must always balance. There is a new box showing an individual's balance of payments with the rest of the world. The section on the foreign-exchange market is roughly the same. The final section now examines three "hot" policy issues. The first is whether current account deficits are a problem. Here we bring in some of the material on "twin deficits" from the old Chapter 38. The second is whether there is a "right" value for the Canadian dollar. This gets us into the issue of PPP, revised from the previous edition. The final issue is whether Canada should adopt a fixed exchange rate. We explore flexible rates as shock absorbers and fixed rates as a means of reducing foreign-exchange risk. This naturally leads to a new box on the idea of optimal currency areas.

Using the Book

Needs of students differ: Some want material that goes beyond the average class level, but others have gaps in their backgrounds. To accommodate the former we have included more material than we would assign to every student. Also, because there are many different kinds of first-year economics courses in colleges and universities, we have included more material than normally would be included in any single course.

Although instructors can best design their own courses, it may help if we indicate certain views of our own as to how this book might be adapted to different courses.

The choice of whether to study macro first or micro first is partly a personal one that cannot be decided solely by objective criteria. We believe that there are excellent reasons for preferring the micro-macro order. The thrust over the last 25 years has been to examine the micro underpinnings of macro functions and to erect macroeconomics on a firmer base of micro behavioural relations. Virtually every current macro controversy turns on some micro underpinning. For "micro-firsters" this poses no problem. For "macro-firsters" it is often hard to explain what is at issue.

Changes occur not only in economic theory but also in the problems that excite students. Many of today's problems that students find most challenging—mergers and takeovers, foreign direct investment, poverty, pollution—are microeconomic in character. The micro-macro order, moreover, reflects the historical evolution of the subject. A century of Classical and Neoclassical development of microeconomics preceded the Keynesian development of macroeconomics.

For those who prefer the macro-micro order, we have attempted to make reversibility easy. The first four chapters provide a solid foundation for studying either microeconomics (Chapter 5–18) or macroeconomics (Chapters 19–36).

TO THE STUDENT

A good course in economics will give you insight into how an economy functions and into some currently debated policy issues. Like all rewarding subjects, economics will not be mastered without effort. A book on economics must be worked at. It cannot be read like a novel.

You must develop your own technique for studying, but the following suggestions may prove helpful. Begin by carefully considering the Learning Objectives at the beginning of a chapter. Read the chapter itself relatively quickly in order to get the general run of the argument. At this first reading, you may want to skip the boxes and any footnotes. Then, after reading the Chapter Summary and the Key Concepts (both at the end of each chapter), reread the chapter more slowly, making sure that you understand each step of the argument.

With respect to the figures and tables, be sure you understand how the conclusions that are stated in boldface at the beginning of each caption have been reached. You must not skip the captions. They provide the core of economic reasoning. You should be prepared to spend time on difficult sections; occasionally, you may spend an hour on only a few pages. Paper and pencil are indispensable equipment in your reading. It is best to follow a difficult argument by building your own diagram while the argument unfolds rather than by relying on the finished diagram as it appears in the book.

The end-of-chapter Study Exercises require you to practise using some of the concepts that you learned in the chapter. These will be excellent preparation for your exams. The Discussion Questions require you to apply what you have studied. We advise you to outline answers to some of the questions. In short, you should seek to understand economics, not to memorize it.

The bracketed boldface numbers in the text itself refer to a series of mathematical notes that are found starting on page M-1 at the end of the book. For those of you who like mathematics or prefer mathematical argument to verbal or geometric exposition, these may prove useful. Others may disregard them.

A time line, which runs from the mid 1600s to the mid 1900s, follows the mathematical notes. Along this time line we have placed brief descriptions of the life and works of some great economists, most of whom you will encounter in the textbook. So that you have a better appreciation of *when* these economists did their work, the time line also lists some major world events. We hope this will improve your sense of history and your sense of who these great economists are.

In this edition of the book, we have incorporated many elements to help you review material and prepare for examinations. Pay special attention to the learning objectives, the important concepts highlighted in red, the key terms that are boldfaced and restated in the margins, the captions that accompany the features and tables, the lists of key concepts, and the chapter summaries. A brief description of all the features in this book is given in the separate section that follows.

This new Study Edition provides you with the original content of the textbook plus additional resources at no additional cost. By using the resources provided in this edition, you will be able to sharpen the skills required to succeed in economics. The first new section, Study Skills Tips, provides invaluable advice for organizing your studying and preparing for tests. The second new section, Self-Test Questions, provides 10 multiple choice questions for each chapter to reinforce important concepts. You can check your learning by consulting the explanations that are given in the answer section. Finally, the third new section, Practice Exams, provides samples of examinations (with answers). By working through these questions on your own, you will be better prepared to succeed in your course.

We hope you will find the book rewarding and stimulating. Students who used earlier editions made some of the most helpful suggestions for revision, and we hope that you will carry on the tradition. If you are moved to write to us (and we hope that you will be!), please do. You can send any comments or questions regarding the text (or any of the supplementary material, such as the *Study Guide*) to:

Christopher Ragan
Department of Economics
McGill University
855 Sherbrooke St. West
Montreal, Quebec
H3A 2T7

Or, if you prefer to communicate through e-mail, send your comments to:

ragan@leacock.lan.mcgill.ca

FEATURES OF THIS EDITION

We have made a careful effort with this edition to incorporate features that will facilitate the teaching and learning of economics.

- **A new single-column design** has been created for the book, making it more accessible to today's reader.
- A new set of **Learning Objectives** at the beginning of each chapter clarify the skills and knowledge to be learned in each chapter. These same learning objectives are used in the chapter summaries, as well as in the *Test Item File* and the *Study Guide*.

- **Major ideas** are highlighted in red in the text.
- **Key terms** are boldfaced where they are defined in the body of the text and they are restated with their definitions in the margins. In the Index at the back of the book, each key term and the page reference to its definition are boldfaced.
- **Weblinks** to useful Internet addresses are given in the margins. Each weblink presents a URL address, along with a brief description of the material available there. Some links are to government home pages where much data can be obtained. Other links are to organizations such as OPEC, the UN, and the WTO. We have also included links to selected articles from *World Economic Affairs* that we have posted on the Companion Web Site for this textbook.
- **Study Guide** references in the margin direct students to appropriate questions in the *Study Guide* that reinforce the topic being discussed in the text.

- **Applying Economic Concepts** boxes demonstrate economics in action, providing examples of how theoretical material relates to issues of current interest.

- **Lessons from History** boxes contain discussions of a particular policy debate or empirical finding that takes place in a historical context.

- **Extensions in Theory** boxes provide a deeper treatment of a theoretical topic that is discussed in the text.

- **A caption for each Figure and Table** summarizes the underlying economic reasoning. Each caption begins with a boldfaced statement of the relevant economic conclusion.
- A **new colour scheme for Figures** has been established to make the use of colour in the graphs consistent. Curves of a particular type are now always presented in the same colour. For example, all demand curves are blue, whereas all supply curves are red.
- **Photographs with short captions** are now interspersed throughout the chapters to illustrate some of the arguments.

- **Chapter Summaries** are organized using the same main heading as found in the body of the chapter. And the relevant learning objectives (LO) numbers are given in red next to each heading in the chapter summary

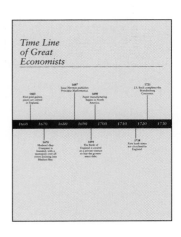

- **Key Concepts** are listed near the end of each chapter.
- A new set of **Study Exercises** has been created for each chapter. These quantitative exercises require the student to analyze problems by means of computations or graphs.
- A set of **Discussion Questions** is also provided for each chapter. These questions require the student to synthesize and generalize. They are designed especially for discussion in class.

- A set of **Mathematical Notes** is presented in a separate section near the end of the book. Because mathematical notation and derivations are not necessary to understand the principles of economics but are more helpful in advanced work, this seems to be a sensible arrangement. References in the text to these mathematical notes are given by means of boldfaced numbers in square brackets.
- A **Time Line of Great Economists**, running from the mid seventeenth century to the mid twentieth century, is presented near the end of the book. Along this time line we have placed brief descriptions of the life and works of some great economists, most of whom the reader will encounter in the textbook. Along this time line we have also listed some major world events in order to give readers an appreciation for when these economists did their work.
- **Economists on Record,** given on the inside of the back cover, quotes some classic excerpts that are relevant to the study and practice of economics.
- For convenience, a list of the **Common Abbreviations Used in the Text** is given on the inside of the front cover.

SUPPLEMENTS

The following supplements have been carefully prepared to accompany the new edition:

- A **Study Guide**, written by E. Kenneth Grant and William J. Furlong, is designed for use either in the classroom or by students on their own. The *Study Guide* offers additional study support and reinforcement for each text chapter. It reuses the same learning objectives that appear in the textbook. For each chapter, it provides a prose Overview, a Chapter Review consisting of multiple-choice questions, Exercises, Extension Exercises, and a Practice Multiple-Choice Test. The *Study Guide* is available as a cumulative volume or as split volumes for microeconomics and macroeconomics.

- An **Instructor's Manual**, written by Christopher Ragan, provides for each text chapter an overview (with teaching suggestions), solutions to the Study Exercises, and suggested answers to the Discussion Questions.

- A **Test Item File**, written by Greg Flanagan and Mike Fellows, contains more than 3300 multiple-choice questions. For each question, the authors have identified the relevant learning objective from the textbook, and they have classified each question by difficulty type (i.e., definitions, using definitions, key concepts, and applying one or more concepts).

- A **Computerized Version of the Test Item File** will enable instructors to edit existing questions, create new questions, generate tests, and administer tests on line over a variety of networks. It also includes a powerful grading system that combines a powerful database with analytical capabilities so that instructors can generate a full set of statistics.

- **Transparency Masters** of all the Figures and Tables in the textbook are available to instructors.

- **Electronic Transparencies** of all the Figures and Tables in the textbook are also available to instructors.

- A special **Companion Web Site** has been created for this book at **www.pearsoned.ca/lipsey**. It includes, among other elements, self-test questions for students, CBC Video Cases, hotlinks to the home pages of governments and other organizations that provide much current data, and the posting of articles from *World Economic Affairs* that are cited in the text.

ACKNOWLEDGEMENTS

It would be impossible to acknowledge here by name all the teachers, colleagues, and students who contributed to the development and improvement of this book over its previous nine editions. Hundreds of users have written to us with specific suggestions, and much of the credit for the improvement of the book over the years belongs to them. We can no longer list them individually but we thank them all sincerely.

For the development of this tenth edition, we are grateful to the many people who offered informal suggestions. We would also like to thank the following instructors who provided us with formal reviews of the textbook:

- Panos C. Afxentiou (University of Calgary)
- Jeremiah Allen (University of Lethbridge)
- F. Michael Bradfield (Dalhousie University)
- Rosilyn G. Coulson (Douglas College)
- Melvin L. Cross (Dalhousie University)
- Martin Dooley (McMaster University)
- Paul Geddes (Columbia College)
- Jack Guthrie (Camosun College)
- Cheryl Jenkins (John Abbott College)
- Eric Kam (York University)
- Susan Kamp (University of Alberta)
- Nargess Kayhani (Mount Saint Vincent University)
- Robert R. Kerton (University of Waterloo)
- Ralph Kolinski (University of Windsor)
- Irwin Lipnowski (The University of Manitoba)
- Rocky M. Mirza (Langara College)
- Robin Neill (University of Prince Edward Island)
- Victor C. Olshevski (The University of Winnipeg)
- Dan Otchere (Concordia University)
- Ian Parker (Scarborough College, University of Toronto)
- Arne Paus-Jenssen (University of Saskatchewan)
- Laurie Craig Phipps (Camosun College)
- Don Reddick (Kwantlen College)
- Charlene Richter (British Columbia Institute of Technology)
- Gary E. Riser (Memorial University)
- James Sentance (University of Prince Edward Island)
- Larry Smith (University of Waterloo)
- Bertram A. Somers (John Abbott College)

In addition, we would like to thank the following instructors for providing formal reviews for some of the supplements that accompany this tenth edition;

- Peter R. Burrell (University of Windsor)
- David M. Cape (Ryerson Polytechnic University)
- Michael F. Charette (University of Windsor)
- Greg L. Flanagan (Saint Mary's University)
- Paul A. R. Hobson (Acadia University)
- Cheryl Jenkins (John Abbott College)
- Eva Lau (University of Waterloo)
- Charlene Richter (British Columbia Institute of Technology)
- Larry Smith (University of Waterloo)
- Donna J. Tibbett (University of Lethbridge)

We would like to acknowledge the work of David Gray (University of Ottawa), who performed a technical review of the textbook.

We would also like to express our thanks to the many people at Pearson Education Canada who spent long hours editing and producing this text.

Our special thanks go to Ingrid Kristjanson, who did a tremendous amount of editing and also carefully reviewed all changes made to this edition. Her comments led to many improvements. For her diligence and hard work we are especially grateful.

Your Internet companion to the most exciting, state-of-the-art educational tools on the Web!

The Pearson Education Canada Companion Website is easy to navigate and is organized to correspond to the chapters in this textbook. The Companion Website is comprised of four distinct, functional features:

1) **Customized Online Resources**

2) **Online Study Guide**

3) **Reference Material**

4) **Communication**

Explore the four areas in this Companion Website. Students and distance learners will discover resources for indepth study, research, and communication, empowering them in their quest for greater knowledge and maximizing their potential for success in the course.

A NEW WAY TO DELIVER EDUCATIONAL CONTENT

1) Customized Online Resources

Our Companion Websites provide instructors and students with a range of options to access, view, and exchange content.

- **Syllabus Builder** provides *instructors* with the option to create online classes and construct an online syllabus linked to specific modules in the Companion Website.

- **Mailing lists** enable *instructors* and *students* to receive customized promotional literature.

- **Preferences** enable *students* to customize the sending of results to various recipients, and also to customize how the material is sent, e.g., as html, text, or as an attachment.

- **Help** includes an evaluation of the user's system and a tune-up area that makes updating browsers and plug-ins easier. This new feature will enhance the user's experience with Companion Websites.

www.pearsoned.ca/lipsey

Pearson Education

COMPANION WEBSITE

2) Online Study Guide

An Interactive Study Guide forms the core of the student learning experience in the Companion Website. Multiple Choice modules, organized by text chapter, provide students with the ability to send answers to our grader and receive instant feedback on their progress through our Results Reporter. Students can check suggested answers after submitting their problems.

3) Reference Material

Reference material broadens text coverage with up-to-date resources for learning. We have posted more than 35 journal articles from *World Economic Affairs*. Each article is cited by a special icon in the margin of the textbook. Special **CBC Video Case Studies** provide instructors and students with interesting video segments and stimulating cases for discussion. **Web Destinations** provides direct links to websites relevant to the subject matter in each chapter. **Net News (Internet Newsgroups)** are a fundamental source of information about a discipline, containing a wealth of brief, opinionated postings. **Net Search** simplifies key term search using Internet search engines.

4) Communication

Companion Websites contain the communication tools necessary to deliver courses in a **Distance Learning** environment. **Message Board** allows users to post messages and check back periodically for responses. **Live Chat** allows users to discuss course topics in real time, and enables professors to host online classes.

Communication facilities of Companion Websites provide a key element for distributed learning environments. There are two types of communication facilities currently in use in Companion Websites:

- **Message Board** – this module takes advantage of browser technology, providing the users of each Companion Website with a national newsgroup to post and reply to relevant course topics.

- **Live Chat** – enables instructor-led group activities in real time. Using our chat client, instructors can display Website content while students participate in the discussion.

Companion Websites are currently available for numerous Pearson Education Canada books, including

- Case, Fair, Strain, and Veall, *Principles of Microeconomics and Macroeconomics*, First Canadian Edition
- Miller and Clegg, *Economics Today*, First Canadian Edition
- Brown, Chambers, and Currie, *Personal Finance for Canadians*, Sixth Edition

Note: CW content will vary slightly from site to site depending on discipline requirements.

The Companion Website can be found at:

www.pearsoned.ca/lipsey

PEARSON EDUCATION CANADA

26 Prince Andrew Place
Don Mills, Ontario M3C 2T8

To order:
Call: 1-800-567-3800
Fax: 1-800-263-7733

For samples:
Call: 1-800-850-5813
Fax: (416) 447-2819
E-mail: phcinfo.pubcanada@pearsoned.com

ISBN 0-13-065088-9

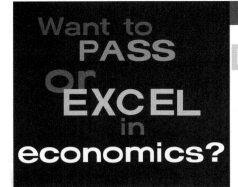

Don't Throw This Out!

This is your Online Resource Access Code for

EconomicsCentral

Welcome to **EconomicsCentral**, *Pearson Education Canada's online resource for economics students! You'll want to bookmark this site, because you'll find* **actual past exams**, **tutorials** *for difficult topics, an* **online tutor** *to help you with those tough questions, dynamic* **Weblinks**, *and much more, all right here.*

What do you do with this access code?

1. Locate the Site:
Launch your web browser and type **www.pearsoned.ca/economics** into the location area.

2. Use your Pearson Education Canada access code:
The first time you access the site, you will be required to register using this access code. Type in the access code on this page (one word per box) and follow the steps indicated. During registration, you will choose a personal User ID and password for logging into the site. Your access code can be used only once to establish your subscription, which is non-transferable. Once your registration has been confirmed, you need to enter only your personal User ID and password each time you enter the site. **This code is valid for 8 months of access to** *EconomicsCentral*.

Warning: Once you enter your access code, registration processing may take up to 3 minutes to complete. If you do not wait for confirmation before proceeding, the access code will become invalid.

3. Log onto the site:
Once your registration is confirmed, follow the **EconomicsCentral** link to log on with your newly-established User ID and Password.

CSBYT-CRYPT-EYING-COWED-GUSTO-DICES

This pincode is only valid with the purchase of a new book.
For help using this access code, please e-mail us at

online.support@pearsoned.com

PART ONE

What Is Economics?

Have you ever noticed that, when you go to a store to buy something, the product you seek is almost always available? Or, have you noticed that you rarely see either large numbers of people lined up waiting to buy goods or large amounts of unsold goods with nobody to buy them? What is it about a modern market economy that produces these remarkably coordinated outcomes in which the amount of something available is roughly equal to the amount that people want? What is the study of economics all about, and why will it help you to understand how today's economies function? How do economists do their job of analysing and explaining economic outcomes? What are economic models, and why are some models more sensible than others? Why is it that economists appear to disagree so much, or is this just an illusion? These are questions that you will be able to answer after reading the following two chapters.

Chapter 1 begins by talking about the self-organizing economy, and introduces Adam Smith's famous idea of an invisible hand. Here we see why markets made up of self-interested consumers and producers automatically produce the sort of coordination that we observe. We then examine the important concepts of scarcity, choice, and opportunity cost, three ideas that are central to all economic systems. We then introduce the various decision-makers in a typical market economy, including individual consumers, producers, and governments, and we see how their interactions can be represented by a circular flow of income and expenditure. Finally, we consider alternative economic systems, ranging from a pure market system to a centrally planned system in which a government planning authority makes all the decisions regarding who produces what and who consumes what. Canada, like all economies, is a mixed system, containing elements of both free markets and government intervention.

Chapter 2 discusses the study of economics itself. We consider the distinction between positive and normative statements, a distinction upon which the progress of economics as a social science is based. We then examine the role of theory in economics, and why economists—like physicists or chemists—build models to help them think about the complex world they are trying to understand. Finally, we will explain the way economists test their theories by confronting the predictions of their theories with the available evidence. Here we will also discuss graphing—a central tool for economists and one that is used extensively throughout this book—and you will see how different types of graphs can be used to present very different types of information.

CHAPTER 1

Economic Issues and Concepts

🔟 *LEARNING OBJECTIVES*

❶ View the market economy as a self-organizing entity in which order emerges from a large number of decentralized decisions.

❷ Understand the importance of scarcity, choice, and opportunity cost, and how all three concepts are illustrated by the production possibilities boundary.

❸ Explain the circular flow of income and expenditure.

❹ Recognize that there are several types of pure economic systems, but that all actual economies are mixed systems, having elements of free markets, tradition, and government intervention.

If you want a litre of milk, you go to your local grocery store and buy it. It probably does not occur to you that farmers may have stopped producing milk or that dairies may have stopped delivering it to stores. When the grocer needs more milk, he orders it from the distributor, who in turn gets it from the dairy, which in its turn gets it from the dairy farmer. The dairy farmer buys cattle feed and electric milking machines, and gets power to run all his equipment by putting a plug into a wall outlet where the electricity is supplied as he needs it. The milking machines are made from parts manufactured in several different places in Canada, the United States, and overseas. The parts themselves are made from materials mined and smelted in a dozen or more different countries.

As it is with the milk you drink, so it is with everything else that you buy. When you go to the appropriate store, what you want is normally on the shelf. Those who make these products find that all the required components and materials are available when they need them—even though these things typically come from many different parts of the world and are made by people who have no direct dealings with each other.

The Complexity of the Modern Economy

The sales and purchases in which you are involved are only a small part of the remarkably complex set of transactions that take place every day in a modern society. Shipments arrive daily at our ports, railway terminals, and airports. These shipments include raw materials, such as iron ore, logs and oil; parts, such as automobile engines, transistors, and circuit boards; tools, such as screwdrivers, lathes, and digging equipment; perishables, such as fresh flowers, coffee beans, and fruits; and all kinds of manufactured goods, such as washing machines, personal computers, and TV sets. Railways and trucking lines receive and dispatch these goods to thousands of different destinations within Canada. Some go directly to consumers. Others are used by local firms to manufacture their products—some of which will be sold domestically and some exported.

Most people who want to work can find work. They spend their working days engaging in the activities just described. In doing so, they earn incomes which they then spend on what they, and others like them, produce. Other people own firms that employ workers to assist in the many activities described above, such as importing, making, transporting, and selling things. They earn their incomes as profits from these enterprises.

The Self-Organizing Economy

Economics began when thoughtful observers asked themselves how such a complex set of dealings gets organized. Who coordinates the whole set of efforts? Who makes sure that all the activities fit together, providing jobs to produce the things that people want and delivering those things to where they are wanted? The answer is no one!

The great insight of the early economists was that an economy based on free-market transactions is *self-organizing.*

By following their own self-interest, doing what seems best and most profitable for themselves, and responding to the incentives of prices determined in open markets, people produce a spontaneous social order. In that order, literally thousands of millions of transactions and activities fit together to produce the things that people want within the constraints set by the resources that are available to the nation.

The great Scottish economist and political philosopher Adam Smith (1723-1790)[1], who was the first to develop this insight fully, put it this way:

> *It is not from the benevolence of the butcher, the brewer, or the baker, that we expect our dinner, but from their regard to their own interest. We address ourselves, not to their humanity but to their self-love, and never talk to them of our own necessities but of their advantages.*

Smith is not saying that benevolence is unimportant. Indeed, he praises it in many passages. He is saying, however, that the massive number of economic interactions that characterize a modern economy cannot all be motivated by benevolence. Although benevolence does motivate some of our actions, often the very dramatic ones, the vast majority of our everyday actions are motivated by self-interest. Self-interest, not benevolence, is therefore the foundation of economic order.

Efficient Organization

Another great insight, which was hinted at by Smith and fully developed over the next century and a half, was that this spontaneously generated social order is relatively *efficient.* Loosely speaking, efficiency means that the resources available to a nation are organized in such a way as to produce the maximum possible total output.

---

[1]Throughout this book we encounter many great economists from the past whose ideas shaped the discipline of economics. At the back of the book you will find a timeline, beginning in the 1600s, that contains brief discussions of many of these thinkers and places them in their historical context.

Smith said that a society whose economy is organized by free markets produces ordered behaviour that makes it appear as if people are guided by an *invisible hand*. He did not literally mean that a supernatural presence guides economic affairs. Instead, he referred to the amazing order that emerges out of so many independent decisions. The key to the explanation is that all individuals respond to the same set of prices, which are determined in markets that respond to overall conditions of national scarcity or plenty. Much of economics is devoted to a detailed elaboration of how this market order is generated.

A Planned Alternative

A century after Adam Smith, another great economist and political philosopher, Karl Marx (1818–1883), argued that although such a market system would produce high total output, it would distribute that output in such a way that, over time, the rich would get richer and the poor poorer. He went on to argue that when societies became rich enough, they should dispense with the spontaneous social order. They should then replace it by a consciously created system, called a *command economy*, or *communism*, in which the government plans all of the transactions we have just described and, in so doing, creates a more equal and socially just distribution of the total output.

Beginning with the Soviet Union in the early 1920s, many nations listened to Marx and established systems in which conscious government *central planning* largely replaced the spontaneous order of the free market. For much of the twentieth century two systems, the centrally planned and the market, competed with each other for the favour of undecided governments. Then, within the last two decades of the century, governments of one communist country after another abandoned their central planning apparatus. More and more economic transactions and activities were then left to be regulated by the self-organizing system of the market.

Lessons From History 1-1 elaborates on some of the reasons for the failure of the centrally planned economies. We hasten to add that Marx was right about many things, including the importance of technological change in raising living standards over the centuries (which is also a theme we discuss in this book). Where experience has shown him wrong, however, was in believing that central planning could successfully replace the market as a way of organizing all of a nation's economic activities.

In contrast to the failures of the command economies, the performance of the largely free-market economies is impressive. One theme of this book is *market success*—how the price system works to coordinate with relative efficiency the decentralized decisions made by private consumers and producers. However, doing things better does not necessarily mean doing things perfectly. Another theme of this book is *market failure*— how and why the unaided price system sometimes fails to produce efficient results and fails to take account of social values that cannot be expressed through the marketplace.

Today, as in the time of Adam Smith, economists seek to understand the self-organizing forces of a market economy, how well they function, and how governments may intervene to improve (but not to replace) their workings in specific situations.

Main Characteristics of Market Economies

What then are the main characteristics of market economies that produce this spontaneous self-ordering?

- Individuals pursue their own self-interest, buying and selling what seems best for themselves and their families.
- People respond to incentives. Other things being equal, sellers seek high prices and buyers seek low prices.
- Prices are determined in open markets in which would-be sellers compete to sell their wares to would-be buyers.
- People earn their incomes by selling their labour services, things they have produced, the services of the land, or buildings that they own to those who wish to buy them.
- All of these activities are governed by a set of institutions largely created by the state. The most important are private property and freedom of contract. The nature of private property and contractual obligations are defined by the legislature and enforced by the police and the courts.

Resources and Scarcity

All of the issues discussed so far would not matter much if we lived in an economy of such plenty that there was enough to satisfy all of everyone's wants. "Ask and you shall receive" would be the motto of such an imaginary world. In contrast, the motto of any real economy is closer to "Work for it and you may get at least some of it."

Why is the economy of plenty impossible? The short answer is "Because we live in a world of scarcity." Compared to the known desires of individuals for such products as better food, clothing, housing, education, holidays, health care, and entertainment, the existing supplies of resources are clearly inadequate. They are sufficient to produce only a small fraction of the goods and services that people desire. This gives rise to the basic economic problem of choice under conditions of scarcity. If we cannot have everything we want, we must choose what we will and will not have.

One definition of *economics* comes from the great economist Alfred Marshall (1842–1924), whom we will encounter at several points in this book: "Economics is a study of mankind in the ordinary business of life." A more penetrating definition is the following:

Economics is the study of the use of scarce resources to satisfy unlimited human wants.

Scarcity is inevitable and is central to economic problems. What are society's resources? Why is scarcity inevitable? What are the consequences of scarcity?

Resources

A society's resources consist of natural endowments such as land, forests, and minerals; human resources, both mental and physical; and manufactured aids to production such as tools, machinery, and buildings. Economists call such resources **factors of production** because they are used to produce the outputs that people desire. We divide these outputs into goods and services. **Goods** are tangible (e.g., cars and shoes), and **services** are intangible (e.g., haircuts and education).

People use goods and services to satisfy many of their wants. The act of making them is called **production**, and the act of using them to satisfy wants is called **consumption**. Goods are valued for the services they provide. An automobile, for example, helps to satisfy its owner's desires for transportation, mobility, and possibly status.

factors of production Resources used to produce goods and services; frequently divided into the basic categories of land, labour, and capital.

goods Tangible commodities, such as cars or shoes.

services Intangible commodities, such as haircuts or medical care.

production The act of making goods or services.

consumption The act of using goods or services to satisfy wants.

LESSONS FROM HISTORY 1-1

The Failure of Central Planning

In 1989, communism collapsed throughout Central and Eastern Europe, and the economic systems of formerly communist countries began the transition from centrally planned to market economies. Although political issues surely played a role in these events, the economic changes generally confirmed the superiority of a market-oriented price system over central planning as a method of organizing economic activity. The failure of central planning had many causes, but four were particularly significant.

The Failure of Coordination

In centrally planned economies, a body of planners tries to coordinate all the economic decisions about production, investment, trade, and consumption that are likely to be made by producers and consumers throughout the country. Without the use of prices to signal relative scarcity and abundance, central planning generally proved impossible to do with any reasonable degree of success. Bottlenecks in production, shortages of some goods, and gluts of others plagued the Soviet economy for decades. For example, for years there was an ample supply of black-and-white television sets but severe

shortages of toilet paper and soap. In 1989, much of a bumper harvest rotted because of shortages of storage and transportation facilities.

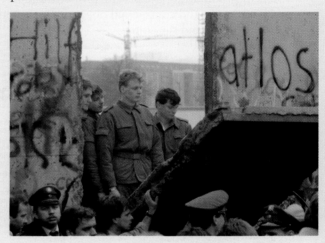

The fall of the Berlin Wall in November 1989 was the beginning of the end of the Soviet system of central planning.

Scarcity

For each of the world's six billion people, scarcity is real and ever present. As we said above, relative to people's desires, existing resources are inadequate; there are enough to produce only a fraction of the goods and services that are wanted.

But are not the advanced industrialized nations rich enough that scarcity is nearly banished? After all, they have been characterized as affluent societies. Whatever affluence may mean, however, it does not mean the end of the problem of scarcity. Most households that earn $100 000 per year (a princely amount by world standards) have no trouble spending it on things that seem useful to them and they would certainly have no trouble convincing you that their resources are scarce relative to their desires.

Choice

Because resources are scarce, all societies face the problem of deciding what to produce and how much each person will consume. Societies differ in who makes the choices and how they are made, but the need to choose is common to all. Just as scarcity implies the need for choice, so choice implies the existence of cost. A decision to have

Failure of Quality Control

Central planners can monitor the number of units produced by any factory and reward plants that exceed their production targets and punish ones that fall short. Factory managers operating under these conditions will meet their quotas by whatever means are available, and once the goods pass out of their factory, what happens to them is someone else's headache.

In market economies, poor quality is punished by low sales, and retailers soon give a signal to factory managers by shifting their purchases to other suppliers. The incentives that obviously flow from such private-sector purchasing discretion are generally absent from command economies, where purchases and sales are planned centrally and prices and profits are not used to signal customer satisfaction or dissatisfaction.

Misplaced Incentives

In market economies, relative wages and salaries provide incentives for labour to move from place to place, and the possibility of losing one's job provides an incentive to work diligently. This is a harsh mechanism that punishes losers with loss of income (although social programs provide floors to the amount of economic punishment that can be suffered). In planned economies, workers usually have complete job security. Industrial unemployment is rare, and even when it does occur, new jobs are usually found for all who lose theirs. Although the high level of security is attractive to many peo-

ple, it proved impossible to provide sufficient incentives for reasonably hard and efficient work under such conditions. In the words of Oxford historian Timothy Garton Ash, who wrote eyewitness chronicles of the developments in Eastern Europe from 1980 to 1990, the social contract between the workers and the government in the Eastern European countries was "We pretend to work, and you pretend to pay us."

Environmental Degradation

Fulfilling production plans became the all-embracing goal in planned economies, to the exclusion of most other considerations, including the environment. As a result, environmental degradation occurred in the Soviet Union and the countries of Eastern Europe on a scale unknown in advanced Western nations. A particularly disturbing example (only one of many) occurred in central Asia where high quotas for cotton output led to indiscriminate use of pesticides and irrigation. Birth defects are now found in nearly one child in three, and the vast Aral Sea has been half drained, causing major environmental effects.

This failure to protect the environment stemmed from the pressure to fulfill production plans and the absence of a "political marketplace" where citizens could express their preferences for the environment versus economic gain. Imperfect though the system may be in democratic market economies—and in some particular cases it has been quite poor—their record of environmental protection has been vastly better than that of the command economies.

---

more of something requires a decision to have less of something else. The less of "something else" can be thought of as the cost of having the more of "something."

Scarcity implies that choices must be made, and making choices implies the existence of costs.

Opportunity Cost

To see how choice implies cost, we look first at a trivial example and then at one that vitally affects all of us; both examples involve precisely the same fundamental principles.

Consider the choice that must be made by your little sister who has 50 cents to spend and who is determined to spend it all on candy. For your sister there are only two kinds of candy in the world: bubblegums, which sell for 5 cents each, and lollipops, which sell for 10 cents each. Your sister would like to buy 10 bubblegums and 10 lollipops but soon discovers that this is not possible: It is not an *attainable combination,* given her scarce resources. However, several combinations are attainable: 8 bubblegums and 1 lollipop, 4 bubblegums and 3 lollipops, 2 bubblegums and 4 lollipops, and so on. Some of these combinations leave money unspent, and she is not interested in them. Only six combinations, as shown in Figure 1-1, are both attainable and use the entire 50 cents.

FIGURE 1-1 A Choice Between Bubblegums and Lollipops

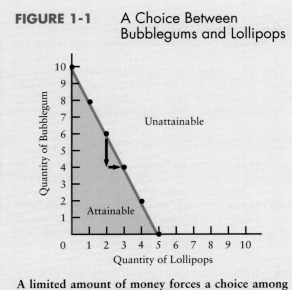

A limited amount of money forces a choice among alternatives. Six combinations of bubblegums and lollipops are attainable and use all of the child's money. The negatively sloped line provides a boundary between attainable and unattainable combinations. The arrows show that the opportunity cost of 1 more lollipop is 2 bubblegums.

opportunity cost
The cost of using resources for a certain purpose, measured by the benefit given up by not using them in their best alternative use.

After careful thought, your sister has almost decided to buy 6 bubblegums and 2 lollipops, but at the last moment she decides that she simply must have 3 lollipops. What will it cost to get this extra lollipop? One answer is 2 bubblegums. As seen in the figure, this is the number of bubblegums the child must forgo to get the extra lollipop. Economists describe the 2 bubblegums as the *opportunity cost* of the third lollipop.

Another answer is that the cost of the third lollipop is 10 cents. But this answer is less revealing than the first one. Though the real choice is one between more of this and more of that, the cost of "this" is usefully viewed in terms of what one cannot have of "that."

The idea of opportunity cost is one of the central insights of economics. Here is a precise definition. The **opportunity cost** of using resources for a certain purpose is defined to be *the benefit given up by not using them in the best alternative way.* That is, it is the cost measured in terms of other goods and services that could have been obtained instead. If, for example, resources that could have produced 20 km of road are best used instead to produce two small hospitals, the opportunity cost of a hospital is 10 km of road; looked at the other way round, the opportunity cost of 1 km of road is one-tenth of a hospital.

Every time a choice is made, opportunity costs are incurred.

See *Applying Economic Concepts 1-1* for an example of opportunity cost that should seem quite familiar to you—the opportunity cost of getting a university degree.

Production Possibilities

Although your sister's choice between bubblegums and lollipops may seem to be a trivial consumption decision, the essential nature of the decision is the same whatever the choice being made. Consider, for example, the choice that any country must face between producing military and civilian goods.

If resources are fully and efficiently employed, it is not possible to have more of both. However, as the government cuts defence expenditures, resources needed to produce civilian goods will be freed up. The opportunity cost of increased civilian goods is therefore the forgone military output. (Or, if we were considering an increase in military output, the opportunity cost of military output would be the forgone civilian goods.)

The choice is illustrated in Figure 1-2. Because resources are limited, some combinations—those that would require more than the total available supply of resources for their production—cannot be attained. The negatively sloped curve on the graph divides the combinations that can be attained from those that cannot. Points above and to the right of this curve cannot be attained because there are not enough resources; points below and to the left of the curve can be attained without using all of the available resources; and points on the curve can just be attained if all the available resources are used efficiently. The

APPLYING ECONOMIC CONCEPTS 1-1

The Opportunity Cost of Your University Degree

As discussed in the text, the opportunity cost of choosing one thing is what must be given up as the best alternative. Computing the opportunity cost of a college or university education is a good example to illustrate which factors are included (and which are excluded) from the computation of opportunity cost. You may also be surprised to learn how expensive your university degree really is!*

Suppose that a Bachelor's degree requires four years of study and that each year you spend $3500 for tuition fees—approximately the average at Canadian universities in 2000—and a further $1500 per year for books and materials. Does this mean that the cost of a university education is only $20 000? Unfortunately not; the true cost of a university degree is much higher.

The key point is that the opportunity cost of a university education does not just include the out-of-pocket expenses on tuition and books. You must also take into consideration *what you are forced to give up* by choosing to attend university. Of course, if you were not studying you could have been doing any one of a number of things, but the relevant one is *the one you would have chosen instead*—your best alternative to attending university.

Suppose that your best alternative to attending university was to get a job. In this case, the opportunity cost of your university degree must include the earnings that you would have received had you taken that job. Suppose that your (after-tax) annual earnings would have been $18 000 per year, for a total of $72 000 if you stayed at that job for four years. To the direct expenses of $20 000, we must therefore add $72 000 for the earnings that you gave up by not taking a job. This brings the true cost of your university degree—the opportunity cost—up to $92 000!

Notice that the cost of food, lodging, clothing, and other living expenses did not enter the calculation of the opportunity cost in this example. The living expenses must be incurred in either case—whether you attend uni-

versity or get a job. Of course, it is possible that your total living expenses as a student are different from what they would have been had you taken the job. In this case, the calculation of opportunity cost would need to be adjusted. For example, perhaps the job you would have taken *required* you to spend $3000 for clothes (over the 4 years) so that you could look presentable to customers. In contrast, you find that your university classmates and professors are pretty relaxed about fashion and that your old jeans are more than adequate. In this case, the opportunity cost of your university degree would be only $89 000 because by attending university you "saved" $3000 that you otherwise would have had to spend on clothes.

If the opportunity cost of a degree is so high, why do students choose to go to university? The simple answer is that they believe that they are better off by going to university than by not going (otherwise they would not go). Maybe the students simply enjoy learning, and thus are prepared to incur the high cost to be in the university environment. Or maybe they believe that a university degree will significantly increase their future earning potential. In this case, they are giving up four years of earnings at one salary so that they can invest in their own skills in the hopes of enjoying many more years in the future at a considerably higher salary.

Whatever the case, the recognition that a university degree is very expensive should convince students to make the best use of their time while they are there. Read on!

The opportunity cost to an individual completing a university degree in Canada is very large. It includes the direct cost of tuition and books as well as the earnings forgone while attending university.

---

* This box considers only the cost *to the student* of a university degree. For reasons that will be discussed in detail in Part 6 of this book, the government heavily subsidizes post-secondary education in Canada. Because of this subsidy, the cost *to society* of a university degree is generally much higher than the cost to an individual student.

production possibility boundary   A curve that shows which alternative combinations of commodities can just be attained if all available resources are used; it is thus the boundary between attainable and unattainable output combinations.

Practise with Study Guide Chapter 1, Exercise 2.

curve is called the **production possibility boundary** or *production possibility curve*. It has a negative slope because when all resources are being used efficiently, producing more of one kind of good requires producing less of the other kind.

A production possibility boundary illustrates three concepts: scarcity, choice, and opportunity cost. Scarcity is indicated by the unattainable combinations outside the boundary; choice, by the need to choose among the alternative attainable points along the boundary; and opportunity cost, by the negative slope of the boundary.

The shape of the production possibility boundary in Figure 1-2 implies that an increasing amount of civilian production must be given up to achieve equal successive increases in military production. This shape, referred to as *concave* to the origin, indicates that the opportunity cost of either good increases as we increase the amount of it that is produced. A straight-line boundary, as in Figure 1-1, indicates that the opportunity cost of one good in terms of the other stays constant, no matter how much of it is produced.

The concave shape in Figure 1-2 is the way that economists usually draw a country's production possibilities boundary. The shape occurs because each factor of production is not equally useful in producing all goods. To see why differences among factors of production are so important, suppose we begin at a point where all resources are devoted to the production of military goods, and then consider gradually shifting more and more resources toward the production of civilian goods. The first resources we shift might be, just to take an example, nutrient-rich land that is particularly well suited to growing wheat. This land may not be very useful for making military equipment, but it is very useful for making certain civilian goods (like bread). This shift of resources will therefore lead to a very small reduction in military ouptut but a substantial increase in civilian output. Thus the opportunity cost of producing the first unit of civilian goods, which is equal to the forgone military output, is very small. But as we shift more and more resources toward the production of civilian goods, we must shift more and more resources that are actually quite well suited to the production of military output, like aerospace engineers or the minerals needed to make gunpowder. As we produce more and more civilian goods (by having more and more resources devoted to producing them), the amount of military output that must be forgone to produce one *extra* unit of civilian goods rises. That is, the opportunity cost of producing one good rises as more of that good is produced.

FIGURE 1-2   A Production Possibility Boundary

The negatively sloped boundary shows the combinations that are just attainable when all of the society's resources are efficiently employed. The production possibility boundary separates the attainable combinations of goods, such as *a*, *b*, and *c*, from unattainable combinations, such as *d*. Points *a* and *b* represent full and efficient use of society's resources. Point *c* represents either inefficient use of resources or failure to use all the available resources.

Four Key Economic Problems

Modern economies involve thousands of complex production and consumption activities. Although this complexity is important, many of the basic kinds of decisions that must be made are not very different from those made in primitive economies in which people work with few tools and barter with their neighbours. Whatever the economic system, most problems studied by economists can be grouped under four main headings.

What Is Produced and How?

The allocation of scarce resources among alternative uses, called **resource allocation,** determines the quantities of various goods that are produced. What determines which goods get produced? Choosing to produce a particular combination of goods means choosing a particular allocation of resources among the industries or regions producing the goods.

resource allocation
The allocation of an economy's scarce resources of land, labour, and capital among alternative uses.

Further, because resources are scarce, it is desirable that they be used efficiently. Hence it matters which of the available methods of production is used to produce each of the goods. What determines which methods of production get used and which ones do not?

In terms of Figure 1-2, these questions relate to where the economy will produce. Will the economy be inside the production possibility boundary because resources are used inefficiently? If resources are used efficiently, then at which point on the boundary will production take place?

What Is Consumed and by Whom?

What is the relationship between an economy's production of goods and the consumption enjoyed by its citizens? Economists seek to understand what determines the distribution of a nation's total output among its people. Who gets a lot, who gets a little, and why?

If production takes place on the production possibility boundary, then how about consumption? Will the economy consume exactly the same goods that it produces? Or will the country's ability to trade with other countries permit the economy to consume a different combination of goods?

Questions relating to what is produced and how, and what is consumed and by whom, fall within the realm of microeconomics. Microeconomics is the study of the allocation of resources as it is affected by the workings of the price system and government policies that seek to influence it.

Why Are Resources Sometimes Idle?

When an economy is in a recession, many workers who would like to have jobs are unable to find employers to hire them. At the same time, the managers and owners of offices and factories would like to operate at a higher level of activity—that is, they would like to produce more goods and services. Similarly, during recessions raw materials are typically available in abundance. For some reason, however, these resources—labour, factories and equipment, and raw materials—are idle. Thus, in terms of Figure 1-2, the economy is operating within its production possibility boundary.

Why are resources sometimes idle? Should governments worry about such idle resources, or is there some reason to believe that such occassional idleness is appropriate in a well-functioning economy? Is there anything that the government can do to reduce such idleness?

Is Productive Capacity Growing?

The capacity to produce goods and services grows rapidly in some countries, expands slowly in others, and actually declines in others. Growth in productive capacity can be represented by an outward shift of the production possibility boundary, as shown in

FIGURE 1-3   The Effect of Economic Growth on the Production Possibility Boundary

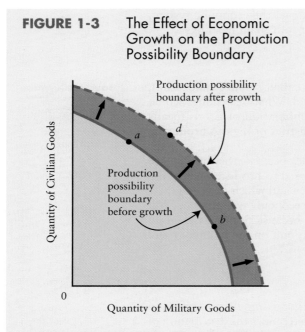

Production possibility boundary after growth

Production possibility boundary before growth

Quantity of Civilian Goods

Quantity of Military Goods

0

Economic growth shifts the boundary outward and makes it possible to produce more of all products. Before growth in productive capacity, points *a* and *b* were on the production possibility boundary and point *d* was an unattainable combination. After growth, as shown by the dark shaded band, point *d* and many other previously unattainable combinations are attainable.

Figure 1-3. If an economy's capacity to produce goods and services is growing, combinations that are unattainable today will become attainable tomorrow. Growth makes it possible to have more of all goods. What are the determinants of growth? Can governments do anything to increase economic growth?

Questions relating to the idleness of resources during recessions, and the growth of productive capacity, fall within the realm of macroeconomics. Macroeconomics is the study of the determination of economic aggregates such as total output, total employment, the price level, and the rate of economic growth.

Who Makes the Choices and How?

So choices have to be made, but who makes them and how are they made?

The Flow of Income and Expenditure

Figure 1-4 shows the basic decision makers and the flows of income and expenditure that they set up. Individuals own factors of production, including themselves. They sell the services of these factors to producers and receive payments in return. These are their incomes. Producers use the factor services that they buy to make goods and services for consumption. They sell these to individuals, receiving payments in return. These are the incomes of producers. These basic flows of income and expenditure pass through markets. Individuals sell the services of the factor that they own in what are collectively called *factor markets*. Producers sell their outputs of goods and services in what are collectively called *goods markets*.

The prices that are determined in these markets determine the incomes that are earned and the purchasing power of those incomes. People who get high prices for their factor services earn high incomes; those who get low prices earn low incomes. The income each person earns expressed as a fraction of all incomes that are earned in the nation shows the share of total income that each person can command. The *distribution of income* refers to how the nation's total production is distributed among its citizens. This is largely determined by the price that each type of factor service can command in factor markets.

Maximizing Decisions

The basic decision makers in a market economy are individual consumers and producers. To these two groups we will shortly add a third, the government. The most important thing about how these two groups make their decisions is that everyone tries to do as well as possible for themselves. In the jargon of economics, they are *maximizers*.

When individuals decide how many factor services to sell to producers and how many products to buy from them, they make choices designed to maximize their well-being, or *utility*. When producers decide how many factor services to buy from individuals and how many goods to produce and sell to them, they make choices designed to maximize their profits.

Marginal Decisions

The second key point about these choices is that they are all made *at the margin*. Let us see what this means. When you vote in a Canadian federal election, you have only one vote and you must support one party over the others. When you do, you vote for everything that party stands for, even though you may prefer to pick and choose elements from that party's political platform. You cannot say "I vote for the Liberals on issue A and for the Conservatives on issue B." You must make a total choice.

In contrast, when you spend your income, you do not have to decide which product to spend your entire income on. You can, and do, decide to spread your expenditure among many products. Furthermore, having decided to buy some CDs, you do not have to buy a large number or none at all. You can buy any number you wish and, as your circumstances change, you can vary the number you buy each month, raising it or lowering it a bit. These are *marginal* decisions—decisions to buy a bit more or a bit less.

Maximizing consumers and producers are constantly making marginal decisions, whether to buy or sell a bit more or less of each of the things that they buy and sell.

FIGURE 1-4   The Circular Flow of Income and Expenditure

The green line shows the flows of goods and services while the blue line shows the payments made to purchase these. Factor services flow from individuals who own the factors (including their own labour) through factor markets to firms that use them to make goods and services. These goods and services then flow through goods markets to those who consume them. Money payments flow from firms to individuals through factor markets. These payments become the income of individuals. When they spend this income buying goods and services, money flows through goods markets back to producers.

Production Choices

Producers decide what to produce and how to produce it. Production is a very complex process in any modern economy. A typical car manufacturer assembles a product out of thousands of individual parts. It makes some of these parts itself. Most are subcontracted to parts manufacturers and many of the major parts manufacturers subcontract some of their work out to smaller firms. This kind of production displays two characteristics noted long ago by Adam Smith—*specialization* and the *division of labour*.

Specialization

In ancient hunter–gather societies, and in modern subsistence economies, most people make most of the things they need for themselves. However, from the time that people first engaged in settled agriculture and some of them began to live in towns, people have specialized in doing particular jobs. Artisans, soldiers, priests, and government officials were some of the earliest specialized occupations. Economists call this allocation of different jobs to different people the **specialization of labour**. There are two fundamental reasons why specialization is extraordinarily efficient compared with universal self-sufficiency.

specialization of labour   The specialization of individual workers in the production of particular goods or services.

First, individual abilities differ, and specialization allows each person to do what he or she can do relatively well while leaving everything else to be done by others. Even when people's abilities are unaffected by the act of specializing, production is greater with specialization than with self-sufficiency. This is one of the most fundamental principles in economics. It is called the principle of *comparative advantage*. A much fuller discussion of comparative advantage is found in Chapter 34 where we discuss the gains from international trade.

The second reason concerns changes in people's abilities that occur *because* they specialize. A person who concentrates on one activity becomes better at it than could a jack-of-all-trades. This is called *learning by doing*. It was a factor much stressed by early economists. Modern research into what are called *learning curves* shows that learning by doing is important in many modern industries.

The Division of Labour

Throughout most of history each artisan who was specialized in making some product made the whole of that product. Over the last several hundred years many technical advances in production methods have made it efficient to organize agriculture and manufacturing into large-scale firms organized around what is called the **division of labour.** This term refers to specialization *within* the production process of a particular product.

Mass Production.   In a mass-production factory work is divided into highly specialized tasks using specialized machinery. Each individual repeatedly does one small task that is a small fraction of those necessary to produce any one product. This is an extreme case of the division of labour.

Artisans and Flexible Manufacturing.   Two very recent changes have significantly altered the degree of specialization found in many modern production processes. First, individual artisans have recently reappeared in some lines of production. They are responding to a revival in the demand for individually crafted, rather than mass-produced, products. Second, many manufacturing operations are being reorganized along new lines called "lean production" or "flexible manufacturing," which was pioneered by Japanese car manufacturers in the mid 1950s. It has led back to a more craft-based form of organization within the factory. In this technique employees work as a team; each employee is able to do every team member's job rather than one very specialized task at one point on the assembly line.

Globalization

Market economies constantly change, largely as a result of the development of new technologies. Many of the recent changes are referred to as *globalization*, a term often used very loosely to mean the increased importance of international trade. International trade, however, is an old phenomenon—just think of the ancient trading routes created largely by the spice trade. But the usual pattern over most of the last two hundred years was manufactured goods being sent from Europe and North America to the rest of the world, with raw materials and primary products being sent in return. What is new in the last few decades is the globalization of manufacturing.

Underlying the modern notion of globalization is the rapid reduction in transportation costs and the revolution in information technology that have occurred in the last half of the twentieth century. The cost of moving products around the world has fallen

division of labour
The breaking up of a production process into a series of specialized tasks, each done by a different worker.

greatly in recent decades owing to containerization and the increasing size of ships. Our ability to transmit and to analyze data has been increasing even more dramatically, while the costs of doing so have been decreasing, equally dramatically. For example, today $2000 buys a computer that fits into a briefcase and has the same computing power as one that in 1970 cost $10 million and filled a large room. This revolution in information and communication technology (ICT) has made it possible to coordinate economic transactions around the world in ways that were difficult and costly fifty years ago and quite impossible a hundred years ago.

Fifty years ago, if a car was to be assembled in Oshawa, all the parts had to be made nearby. Today it is possible to make parts anywhere in the world and get them to Oshawa just as they are required. As a result, manufacturing, which was formerly concentrated in the advanced industrial countries of Europe and North America, now takes place all over the world. A typical CD player, TV set, or car contains components made in dozens of different countries. We still know where a product is assembled, but it is becoming increasingly difficult to say where it is *made*.

Globalization is as important for consumers as it is for producers. For example, as some tastes become universal to young people, spread by ever-increasing access to foreign television stations and global internet chat lines, we can see the same clothes and hear the same music in virtually all big cities. And as tastes become more universal, many *corporations* are globalizing, as they become what economists call **transnational corporations**. These are massive firms with a physical presence in many countries and an increasingly decentralized management structure. McDonald's restaurants are as visible in Moscow or Beijing as in London, New York, Vancouver, or Montreal. Many other brands are also known around the world, such as Calvin Klein, Nike, Coca Cola, Kelloggs, Heinz, Nestlé, Molson, Toyota, Rolls-Royce, Sony, and Mitsubishi.

The revolution in computer technology has drastically reduced communication and transportation costs. This reduction in costs lies at the heart of globalization.

Today no country can take an isolationist economic stance and hope to take part in the global economy where an increasing share of jobs and incomes are created.

transnational corporations (TNCs) Firms that have operations in more than one country. Also called *multinational enterprises (MNEs)*.

Markets and Money

People who specialize in doing only one thing, whether they are artisans, factory workers, or computer programmers, must satisfy most of their wants by consuming things made by other people. In early societies the exchange of goods and services took place by simple mutual agreement among neighbours. In the course of time, however, trading became centred on particular gathering places called *markets*. For example, the French markets or trade fairs of Champagne were well-known throughout Europe as early as the eleventh century AD. Even now, many small towns in Canada have regular market days. Today, however, the term *market* has a much broader meaning. We use the term *market economy* to refer to a society in which people specialize in productive activities and meet most of their material wants through exchanges voluntarily agreed upon by the contracting parties.

Specialization must be accompanied by trade. People who produce only one thing must trade most of it to obtain all of the other things they require.

barter   An economic system in which goods and services are traded directly for other goods and services instead of for money.

Early trading was by means of **barter,** the trading of goods directly for other goods. But barter is costly in terms of time spent searching out satisfactory exchanges. If a farmer has wheat but wants a hammer, he must find someone who has a hammer and wants wheat. A successful barter transaction thus requires what is called a *double coincidence of wants*.

Money eliminates the cumbersome system of barter by separating the transactions involved in the exchange of products. If a farmer has wheat and wants a hammer, he does not have to find someone who has a hammer and wants wheat. He merely has to find someone who wants wheat. The farmer takes money in exchange. Then he finds a person who wishes to sell a hammer and gives up the money for the hammer.

Money greatly facilitates specialization and trade.

Is There an Alternative to the Market Economy?

The answer to the question in the above heading is no in one sense and yes in another. We answer no because the modern economy has no *practical* alternative to reliance on market determination. We answer yes because it is possible to identify other types of economic systems.

An economic system is a distinctive method of providing answers to the basic economic questions discussed above, such as who produces what, and who consumes what. All such systems are complex. They include producers of every sort—public and private, domestic and foreign. They include consumers of every sort—young and old, rich and poor, working and nonworking. They include laws—such as those relating to property rights—rules, regulations, taxes, subsidies, and everything else that governments use to influence what is produced, how it is produced, and who gets it. They also include customs of every conceivable kind and the entire range of contemporary mores and values.

Types of Economic Systems

Although every economy is in some ways unique, it is helpful to distinguish three pure types, called *traditional, command,* and *market* economies. These economies differ in the way in which economic decisions are coordinated. But no actual economy fits neatly into one of these three categories—all real economies contain some elements of each type.

Traditional Systems

traditional economy
An economy in which behaviour is based mostly on tradition, custom, and habit.

A **traditional economy** is one in which behaviour is based primarily on tradition, custom, and habit. Young men follow their fathers' occupations. Women do what their mothers did. There is little change in the pattern of goods produced from year to year, other than those imposed by the vagaries of nature. The techniques of production also follow traditional patterns, except when the effects of an occasional new invention are felt. Finally, production is allocated among the members according to long-established traditions. In short, the answers to the economic questions of what to produce, how to produce, and how to distribute are determined by traditions.

Such a system works best in an unchanging environment. Under such static conditions, a system that does not continually require people to make choices can prove effective in meeting economic and social needs.

Traditional systems were common in earlier times. The feudal system, under which most people in medieval Europe lived, was a largely traditional society. Peasants, artisans, and most others living in villages inherited their positions in that society. They also usually inherited their specific jobs, which they handled in traditional ways.

Command Systems

In command systems, economic behaviour is determined by some central authority, usually the government, which makes most of the necessary decisions on what to produce, how to produce it, and who gets it. Such economies are characterized by the *centralization* of decision making. Because centralized decision makers usually lay down elaborate and complex plans for the behaviour that they wish to impose, the terms **command economy** and *centrally planned economy* are usually used synonymously.

The sheer quantity of data required for central planning of an entire economy is enormous, and the task of analysing it to produce a fully integrated plan can hardly be exaggerated. Moreover, the plan must be continually changing to take account not only of current data but also of future trends in labour supplies, technological developments, and people's tastes for various goods and services. Doing so involves the planners in *forecasting*. This is a notoriously difficult exercise, not least because of the unavailability of all essential, accurate, and up-to-date information.

Fifteen years ago, more than one third of the world's population lived in countries that relied heavily on central planning to deal with the basic economic questions. Today, the number of such countries is small. Even in countries where planning is the proclaimed system, as in China or Cuba, increasing amounts of market determination are being quietly permitted.

command economy
An economy in which the decisions of a centralized planning authority exert the major influence over the allocation of resources.

Free-Market Systems

In the third type of economic system, the decisions about resource allocation are made without any central direction. Instead, they result from innumerable independent decisions made by individual producers and consumers. Such a system is known as a **free-market economy** or, more simply, a *market economy*. In such an economy, decisions relating to the basic economic issues are *decentralized*. Despite the absence of a central plan, these many decentralized decisions are nonetheless coordinated. The main coordinating device is the set of market-determined prices—which is why free-market systems are often called *price systems*.

In a pure market economy, all of these decisions, without exception, are made by buyers and sellers acting through unhindered markets. The state provides the background of defining property and protecting rights against foreign and domestic enemies but, beyond that, markets determine all resource allocation and income distribution.

free-market economy
An economy in which the decisions of individual households and firms exert the major influence over the allocation of resources.

Mixed Systems

Economies that are fully traditional or fully centrally planned or wholly free-market are pure types that are useful for studying basic principles. When we look in detail at any real economy, however, we discover that its economic behaviour is the result of some mixture of central control and market determination, with a certain amount of traditional behaviour as well.

mixed economy   An economy in which some decisions about the allocation of resources are made by firms and households and some by the government.

In practice, every economy is a **mixed economy** in the sense that it combines significant elements of all three systems in determining economic behaviour.

Furthermore, within any economy, the degree of the mix varies from sector to sector. For example, in some planned economies, the command principle was used more often to determine behaviour in heavy-goods industries, such as steel, than in agriculture. Farmers were often given substantial freedom to produce and sell what they wished in response to varying market prices.

When economists speak of a particular economy as being centrally planned, we mean only that the degree of the mix is weighted heavily toward the command principle. When we speak of one as being a market economy, we mean only that the degree of the mix is weighted heavily toward decentralized decision making in response to market signals. It is important to realize that such distinctions are always matters of degree and that almost every conceivable mix can be found across the spectrum of the world's economies.

Although no country offers an example of either system working alone, some economies, such as those of Canada, the United States, France, and Hong Kong, rely much more heavily on market decisions than others, such as the economies of China, North Korea, and Cuba. Yet even in Canada, the command principle has some sway. Crown corporations, legislated minimum wages, rules and regulations for environmental protection, quotas on some agricultural outputs, and restrictions on the import of some items are the obvious examples.

See Chapter 1 of www.pearsoned.ca/lipsey for an excellent discussion of Cuba's recent economic reforms: Archibald Ritter, "Is Cuba's Economic Reform Process Paralysed?" *World Economic Affairs.*

Ownership of Resources

We have seen that economies differ as to the principle used for coordinating their economic decisions. They also differ as to *who owns* their productive resources. Who owns a nation's farms and factories, its coal mines and forests? Who owns its railways, streams, and golf courses? Who owns its houses and hotels?

In a private-ownership economy, the basic raw materials, the productive assets of the society, and the goods produced in the economy are predominantly privately owned. By this standard, Canada has primarily a private-ownership economy. However, even in Canada, public ownership extends beyond the usual basic services such as schools and local transportation systems to include other activities such as housing projects, forest and range land, and electric power utilities.

In contrast, a public-ownership economy is one in which the productive assets are predominantly publicly owned. This was true of the former Soviet Union, and it is true to a significant extent in present-day China and in Cuba. In China, however, private ownership exists in many sectors, including the rapidly growing part of the manufacturing sector that is foreign owned, mainly by Japanese and by Chinese from Taiwan and Singapore.

Command Versus Market Determination

For over a century, a great debate raged on the relative merits of the command principle versus the market principle for coordinating economic decisions. The former Soviet Union, the countries of Eastern Europe, and China were command economies for much of this century. Canada, the United States, and most of the countries of Western Europe were, and still are, primarily market economies. The apparent successes of the Soviet Union and China in the early stages of industrialization suggested to many observers that the command principle was at least as good for organizing economic behaviour as the market principle, if not better. Over the long run, however, planned economies proved a failure of such disastrous proportions that they seriously depressed the living standards of their citizens. (Some of the reasons for this failure were examined in *Lessons from History 1-1*.)

Still Room for Disagreement

The failure of centrally planned economies suggests the superiority of decentralized markets over centrally planned ones as mechanisms for allocating an economy's scarce resources. Put another way, it demonstrates the superiority of mixed economies with substantial elements of market determination over fully planned command economies. However, it does *not* demonstrate, as some observers have asserted, the superiority of completely free-market economies over mixed economies.

There is no guarantee that completely free markets will, on their own, handle such urgent matters as controlling pollution or providing public goods (like national defence). Indeed, as we shall see in later chapters, much economic theory is devoted to explaining why free markets often fail to do these things. Mixed economies, with significant elements of government intervention, are needed to do these jobs.

Furthermore, acceptance of the free market over central planning does not provide an excuse to ignore a country's pressing social issues. Acceptance of the benefits of the free market still leaves plenty of scope to debate the kinds, amounts, and directions of government interventions into the workings of our market-based economy that will help to achieve social goals.

It follows that there is still considerable room for disagreement about the degree of the mix of market and government determination in any modern mixed economy—room enough to accommodate such divergent views as could be expressed by conservative, liberal, and modern social democratic parties. People can accept the free market as an efficient way of organizing economic affairs and still disagree about many things. A partial list includes: the optimal amount and types of government regulation of various parts of the economy; the types of measures needed to protect the environment; whether health care should be provided by the public or the private sector; and the optimal amount and design of social services and other policies intended to redistribute income from more to less fortunate citizens.

So, the first answer to the question posed at the outset of this section is no. There is no practical alternative to a mixed system with major reliance on markets but a substantial government presence in most aspects of the economy. The second answer is yes. Within the framework of a mixed economy there are substantial alternatives among many different and complex mixes of free-market and government determination of economic life.

Government in the Modern Mixed Economy

Market economies in today's advanced industrial countries are based primarily on voluntary transactions between individual buyers and sellers. Private individuals have the right to buy and sell what they wish, to accept or refuse work that is offered to them, and to move to where they want when they want.

Key institutions are private property and freedom of contract, both of which must be maintained by active government policies. The government creates laws of ownership and contract and then provides the institutions to enforce these laws.

In modern mixed economies governments go well beyond these important basic functions. They intervene in market transactions to correct what economists call *market failures*. These are well-defined situations in which free markets do not work well. Resources such as fishing grounds and common pastureland tend to be overexploited to the point of destruction under free-market conditions. Some products, called *public goods*, are not provided at all by markets because, once produced, no one can be prevented from using them. So their use cannot be restricted to those who are willing to pay for them. Defence and police protection are public goods. In other cases private transactors impose costs called *externalities* on those who have no say in the transaction. This is the case when factories pollute the air and rivers. The public is harmed but has no part in the producer's decisions about what to make and how to make it. These are some of the reasons why free markets sometimes fail to function as we would like them to. They explain why citizens wish governments to intervene and alter the allocation of resources that would otherwise result from leaving everything to the market.

Also, there are important equity issues that arise from letting free markets determine people's incomes. Some people lose their jobs because firms are reorganizing to become more efficient in the face of new technologies. Others keep their jobs, but the market places so little value on their services that they face economic deprivation. The old and the chronically ill may suffer if their past circumstances did not allow them to save enough to support themselves. For many reasons of this sort we accept government intervention to redistribute income by taking from the "haves" and giving to the "have-nots." Almost everyone supports some redistribution of incomes. Care must be taken, however, not to kill the goose that lays the golden egg. By taking too much from the haves, we risk eliminating their incentive to work hard and produce income, some of which is to be redistributed to the have-nots.

Governments also play a part in influencing the overall level of prices and in attempting to stabilize the economy against extreme fluctuations in income and employment. A stable price level and full employment are two major goals of the government's *macroeconomic* policy. These are dealt with in the second half of this book.

These are some of the reasons all modern economies are mixed economies. Throughout most of the twentieth century in advanced industrial societies the mix had been altering towards more and more government participation in decisions about the allocation of resources and the distribution of income. In the last two decades of the century, however, there has been a worldwide movement to reduce the degree of government participation. The details of this shift in the market/government mix, and the reasons for it, are some of the major issues that will be studied in this book.

S U M M A R Y

The Complexity of the Modern Economy   ⓛⓞ①

- A market economy is self-organizing in the sense that when individual consumers and producers act independently to pursue their own self-interest, responding to prices determined in open markets, the collective outcome is coordinated and relatively efficient.

- An alternative economic system requires a central planning authority to make the decisions of who consumes and who produces which goods. The experience of those countries that adopted central planning was that such planning was extremely difficult and quite inefficient in allocating resources.

Resources and Scarcity (LO)(2)

- Scarcity is a fundamental problem faced by all economies. Not enough resources are available to produce all the goods and services that people would like to consume. Scarcity makes it necessary to choose. All societies must have a mechanism for choosing what goods and services will be produced and in what quantities.
- The concept of opportunity cost emphasizes the problem of scarcity and choice by measuring the cost of obtaining a unit of one product in terms of the number of units of other products that could have been obtained instead.

- A production possibility boundary shows all of the combinations of goods that can be produced by an economy whose resources are fully and efficiently employed. Movement from one point to another along the boundary shows a shift in the amounts of goods being produced, which requires a reallocation of resources.
- Four basic questions must be answered in all economies: What is produced and how? What is consumed and by whom? Why are resources sometimes idle? Is productive capacity growing?

Who Makes the Choices and How? (LO)(3)

- The interaction of consumers and producers through goods and factor markets is illustrated by the circular flow of income and expenditure. Individual consumers sell factor services to producers and, by doing so, earn their income. Similarly, producers earn their income by selling goods and services to individual consumers.
- Individual consumers make their decisions in an effort to maximize their well-being or utility. Producers' decisions are designed to maximize their profits.

- Modern economies are based on the specialization and division of labour, which necessitate the exchange (trade) of goods and services. Exchange takes place in markets and is facilitated by the use of money.
- Driven by the ongoing revolution in transportation and communications technology, the world economy is rapidly globalizing. National and regional boundaries are becoming less important with the rise of transnational corporations.

Is There an Alternative to the Market Economy? (LO)(4)

- We can distinguish three pure types of economies: traditional, command, and free-market. In practice, all economies are mixed economies in that their economic behaviour responds to mixes of tradition, government command, and price incentives.
- In the late 1980s, events in Eastern Europe and the Soviet Union led to the general acceptance that the system of fully centrally planned economies had failed to produce minimally acceptable living standards for its citizens. All of these

countries are now moving toward greater market determination and less state command in their economies.
- Governments play an important role in modern mixed economies. They create and enforce important background institutions such as private property and freedom of contract. They intervene to correct situations where markets do not effectively perform their coordinating function. They also redistribute income and wealth in the interests of equity.

K E Y   C O N C E P T S

The self-organizing economy
Scarcity and the need for choice
Choice and opportunity cost
Production possibility boundary
Resource allocation

Growth in productive capacity
Specialization
Comparative advantange
The division of labour
Globalization

Traditional economies
Command economies
Pure market economies
Mixed economies

STUDY EXERCISES

For Questions 1-4, consider the following description of a mythical economy called Choiceland.

Choiceland has 250 workers and produces only two goods, X and Y. Labour is the only factor of production, but some workers are better suited to producing X than Y (and vice versa). The table below shows the maximum levels of output of each good possible from various levels of labour input.

Number of Workers Producing X	Annual Production of X	Number of Workers Producing Y	Annual Production of Y
0	0	250	1300
50	20	200	1200
100	45	150	900
150	60	100	600
200	70	50	350
250	75	0	0

1. Draw the production possibility boundary for Choiceland on a scale diagram.

2. Explain why the PPB is shaped concave to the origin.

3. Compute the opportunity cost of producing an extra 10 units of X if the economy is initially producing 60 units of X and 600 units of Y. How does this compare to the opportunity cost if the economy were initially producing 70 units of X?

4. Suppose now that the technology associated with producing good Y improves, so that the maximum level of Y that can be produced from any given level of labour input increases by 10 percent. Explain (or show in a diagram) what happens to the production possibilities curve.

5. Explain why a technological improvement in the production of one good means that a country can now produce more of *other* goods than it did previously.

6. Consider the decision you face when deciding whether to go skiing for the weekend. Suppose that transportation, lift tickets, and accommodation for the weekend costs $300. Suppose also that restaurant food for the weekend will cost $75. Finally, suppose that you have a weekend job that you will have to miss if you go skiing, a job that pays you $120 (after tax) for the one weekend day that you work. What is the opportunity cost of going skiing? Is there any other information that you need before computing the opportunity cost?

7. Suppose that you and a friend go wilderness camping for a week and must find your own food to survive. From past experience, you know that you and your friend have different abilities in fishing and hunting. If each of you were to work for one day either catching fish or trapping rabbits, the number of fish and rabbits that you could catch is given in the following table:

	Fish	Rabbits
You	6	3
Your friend	8	2

You and your friend decide that you should allocate the duties so that you get the most food for the least amount of work effort.

a. What is the opportunity cost for you to catch an additional rabbit? What is your friend's opportunity cost for catching an extra rabbit?

b. What is the allocation of tasks that maximizes total output for the least amount of work effort?

c. Suppose that you both decide to work for two days according to the allocation in part **b**. What is the total amount of output? What would it have been if you had decided the reverse allocation of tasks?

DISCUSSION QUESTIONS

1. What is the difference between scarcity and poverty? If everyone in the world had enough to eat, could we say that food was no longer scarce?

2. Evidence accumulates that the use of chemical fertilizers, which increases agricultural production greatly, damages water quality. Analyse the choice between more food and cleaner water involved in using such fertilizers. Use a production possibility curve with agricultural output on the vertical axis and water quality on the horizontal axis. In what ways does this production possibility curve reflect scarcity, choice, and opportunity cost? How would an improved fertilizer that increased agricultural output without further worsening water quality affect the curve? Suppose that a pollution-free fertilizer were developed; would this mean that there would no longer be any opportunity cost in using it?

3. Discuss the following statement by a leading U.S. economist: "One of the mysteries of semantics is why the government-managed economies ever came to be called planned and the market economies unplanned. It is the former that are in chronic chaos, in which buyers stand in line hoping to buy some toilet paper or soap. It is the latter that are in reasonable equilibrium—where if you want a cake of soap or a steak or a shirt or a car, you can go to the store and find that the item is magically there for you to buy. It is the liberal economies that reflect a highly sophisticated planning system, and the government-managed economies that are primitive and unplanned."

4. Consider the market for physicians' services. In what way has this market taken advantage of the specialization of labour?

5. "It is not from the benevolence of the butcher, the brewer, or the baker, that we expect our dinner, but from their regard to their own interest. We address ourselves, not to their humanity but to their self-love, and never talk to them of our own necessities but of their advantages." Do you agree with this quotation from Adam Smith's classic, *The Wealth of Nations*? How are "our dinner" and "their self-interest" related to the price system? What does Smith assume to be the motives of firms and households?

CHAPTER 2

How Economists Work

LO *LEARNING OBJECTIVES*

1. Recognize the difference between positive and normative statements.

2. Understand how theorizing and model-building help economists think about the economy.

3. Explain the interaction between economic theories and empirical observation.

4. Understand why testing theories about human behaviour usually requires studying large numbers of individuals.

5. Recognize several types of economic data, including index numbers, time-series and cross-section data, and scatter diagrams.

6. Understand that economic theories involve relations between variables and that such relations can be expressed in words, equations, or graphs.

7. Recognize that the slope of a relation between X and Y is interpreted as the marginal response in Y to a unit change in X.

In Chapter 1 we discussed the basic question whose answer gave rise to the study of economics. How do millions of producers and consumers, acting independently in their own self-interest, somehow become organized into a coherent system that delivers the goods and services where and when they are wanted and in the approximate quantities they are wanted? Economists study how this is done by the mixed market economies in which we live. Economists also identify situations in which markets fail to perform as well as they might. In such cases they ask whether specific markets may be able to perform more effectively. Usually this involves government intervention of one form or another. Economists then seek to evaluate the efficiency with which governments achieve their goals.

Having sought to understand what is happening in the mixed economy, the next step is often to give policy advice. Indeed, economists give advice on a wide variety of policy topics. If you read a newspaper, watch television, or listen to the radio you will often notice some economist's opinions being reported. Perhaps it is on unemployment, the exchange rate, or interest rates; on some new tax; on the case for privatization or regulation of an industry; or on the possible reforms to Canada's health-care system.

Economics is regarded as a social science. Unlike a training in chemsitry or physics, however, many economists would say that a training in economics provides the student more with a "way of thinking" than with a collection of facts. This does not mean that facts are unimportant to the economist—quite the contrary. It means only that facts are typically harder to establish in economics than in the "hard" sciences and often economists do not know which facts are important without first having a way to organize their thinking.

Central to the economist's way of thinking is the distinction between *positive statements* and *normative statements*. Also of crucial importance to the economist is the role of *theory* and, in particular, the use of economic *models* to provide a framework for thinking about complex issues. Such models can be used to generate *testable hypotheses*.

In this chapter, we explore what it means to be "scientific" in the study of human behaviour and to establish criteria for evaluating how well economics succeeds in meeting that goal.

Positive and Normative Advice

Economists give two broad types of advice, called *normative* and *positive*. They sometimes advise that the government ought to try harder to reduce unemployment or to preserve the environment. When they say such things they are giving normative advice. They may be using their expert knowledge to come to conclusions about the costs of various unemployment-reducing or environment-saving schemes. But when they say that the government *ought* to do something, they are making judgements about the value of the various things that the government could do with its limited resources. Advice that depends on a value judgement is normative—it tells others what they *ought* to do.

Another type of advice is illustrated by the statement "If the government wants to reduce unemployment, reducing unemployment-insurance benefits is an effective way of doing so." This is positive advice. It does not rely on a judgement about the value of reducing unemployment. Instead the expert is saying, "If this is what you want to do, here is a way to do it."

The distinction between positive and normative is fundamental to any rational inquiry. Much of the success of modern science depends on the ability of scientists to separate their views on *what does happen* in the world, from their views on *what they would like to happen*. For example, until the eighteenth century almost everyone believed that the Earth was only a few thousand years old. Evidence then began to accumulate that the Earth was billions of years old. This evidence was hard for most people to accept since it ran counter to a literal reading of many religious texts. Many did not want to believe the evidence. Nevertheless, scientists, many of whom were religious, continued their research because they refused to allow their feelings about what they wanted to believe to affect their scientific search for the truth. Eventually, all scientists came to accept that the Earth is about 4 billion years old.

Distinguishing what is true from what we would like to be, or what we feel ought to be, requires distinguishing between positive and normative statements.

Normative statements depend on value judgements. They involve issues of personal opinion, which cannot be settled by recourse to facts. In contrast, **positive statements** do not involve value judgements. They are statements about what is, was, or will be—that is, statements that are about matters of fact.

Examples of both types of statement are given in Table 2-1. All five positive statements in the table assert things about the nature of the world in which we live. In contrast, the five normative statements involve value judgements.

Notice two things about the positive/normative distinction. First, positive statements need not be true. Statement D is almost certainly false. Yet it is positive, not normative. Second, the inclusion of a value judgement in a statement does not necessarily make the statement normative. Statement E is about the value judgements that people

normative statement
A statement about what ought to be as opposed to what actually is.

positive statement
A statement about what actually is (was or will be), as opposed to what ought to be.

TABLE 2-1   Positive and Normative Statements

Positive		Normative	
A	Raising interest rates encourages people to save.	F	People should be encouraged to save.
B	High rates of income tax encourage people to evade paying taxes.	G	Governments should arrange taxes so that people cannot avoid paying them.
C	Raising wage rates causes people to work harder.	H	Firms should raise wage rates to provide a just reward for hard work.
D	Lowering the price of tobacco causes people to smoke less.	I	The government should raise the tax on tobacco to discourage people from smoking.
E	The majority of the population would prefer a policy that reduced unemployment to one that reduced inflation.	J	The government ought to be more concerned with reducing unemployment than inflation.

hold. We could, however, check to see if people really do prefer low unemployment to low inflation. We can ask them and we can observe how they vote. There is no need for the economist to introduce a value judgement in order to check the validity of the statement itself.

We leave you to analyse the remaining eight statements to decide precisely why each is either positive or normative. Remember to apply the two tests. First, is the statement only about actual or alleged facts? If so, it is a positive one. Second, are value judgements necessary to assess the truth of the statement? If so, it is normative.

Economic Theories and Models

Economists seek to understand the world by developing *theories* and *models* that explain some of the things that have been seen and to predict some of the things that will be seen. What is a theory and what is a model?

Theories

Theories are constructed to explain things. For example, what determines the number of eggs sold in Winnipeg in a particular week? As part of the answer to this question and ones like it, economists have developed theories of demand and supply—theories that we will study in detail in the next three chapters. Any theory is distinguished by its definitions, assumptions, and predictions.

Definitions

The basic elements of any theory are its variables. A **variable** is a magnitude that can take on different possible values.

In our theory of the egg market, the variable *quantity of eggs* might be defined as the number of cartons of 12 grade-A eggs. The variable *price of eggs* is the amount of money that must be given up to purchase each carton of eggs. The particular values taken on by

variable Any well-defined item, such as the price or quantity of a commodity, that can take on various specific values.

those two variables might be 2000 cartons at a price of $1.80 on July 1, 1998; 1800 cartons at a price of $1.95 on July 1, 1999; and 1950 cartons at a price of $1.85 on July 1, 2000.

For a theory of the egg market we define the variable *demand* as the number of cartons of eggs consumers wish to purchase over a particular time-period. We define the variable *supply* as the number of cartons of eggs producers want to sell over the same time-period.

There are two broad categories of variables that are important in any theory. An **endogenous variable** is one whose value is determined within the theory. An **exogenous variable** influences the endogenous variables but is itself determined by factors outside the theory. To illustrate the difference, the quantity of eggs is an endogenous variable in our theory of the egg market—our theory is designed to explain it. The state of the weather, however, is an exogenous variable. It may well affect the number of eggs consumers demand or producers supply but we can safely assume that the state of the weather is not influenced by the market for eggs.[1]

Assumptions

A theory's assumptions concern motives, physical relations, directions of causation, and the conditions under which the theory is meant to apply.

Motives.   The theories we study in this book make the fundamental assumption that everyone pursues their own self-interest when making economic decisions. People are assumed to know what they want, and to know how to go about getting it within the constraints set by the resources at their command.

Physical Relations.   If egg producers buy more chicks and use more labour, land, and chicken feed, they will produce more eggs. This is an example of one of the most important physical relations in the theory of markets. It concerns assumptions about how the amount of output is related to the quantities of factors of production used to produce it. This relation is specified in what is called a *production function*.

Conditions of Application.   Assumptions are often used to specify the conditions under which a theory is meant to hold. For example, a theory that assumes there is "no government" usually does not mean literally the absence of government, but only that the theory is meant to apply when governments are not significantly affecting the situation being studied.

Direction of Causation.   When economists assume that one variable is related to another, they are assuming some causal link between the two. For example, when the amount of eggs that producers want to supply is assumed to increase when the cost of their chicken feed falls, the causation runs from the price of chicken feed to the supply of eggs. Producers supply more eggs because the price of chicken feed has fallen; they do not get cheaper chicken feed because of their decision to supply more eggs.

Although assumptions are an essential part of all theories, students are often concerned about those that seem unrealistic. An example will illustrate some of the issues involved. Much of the theory that we are going to study in this book uses the assumption that owners of firms attempt to maximize their profits. The assumption of profit maximization allows economists to make predictions about the behaviour of firms. They

endogenous variable
A variable that is explained within a theory. Sometimes called an *induced variable* or a *dependent variable*.

exogenous variable
A variable that influences endogenous variables but is itself determined by factors outside the theory. Sometimes called an *autonomous variable* or an *independent variable*.

---

[1]Other words are sometimes used to make the same distinction. One frequently used pair is *induced* for endogenous and *autonomous* for exogenous. Another pair is *dependent* for endogenous and *independent* for exogenous.

A key assumption in economics is that firms make decisions with the goal of maximizing their profits.

study how firms' profits are affected by the choices firms make. They then predict that the alternative that produces the most profits will be the one selected.

Profit maximization may seem like a rather crude assumption. Surely, for example, the managers of firms sometimes choose to protect the environment rather than pursue certain highly polluting but profitable opportunities. Does this not discredit the assumption of profit maximization by showing it to be unrealistic?

The answer is no; to make successful predictions, the theory does not require that managers be solely and unwaveringly motivated by the desire to maximize profits. All that is required is that profits be a sufficiently important consideration that a theory based on the assumption of profit maximization will lead to explanations and predictions that are substantially correct.

This illustration shows that it is not always appropriate to criticize a theory because its assumptions seem unrealistic.

All theory is an abstraction from reality. If it were not, it would merely duplicate the world in all its complexity and would add little to our understanding of it.

A good theory abstracts in a useful way; a poor theory does not. If a theory has ignored some genuinely important factors, its predictions will be contradicted by the evidence—at least where an ignored factor exerts an important influence on the outcome.

Predictions

A theory's predictions are the propositions that can be deduced from it. They are often called *hypotheses*. For example, a prediction from our theory of the demand and supply for eggs is that "if the price of chicken feed falls, producers will supply more eggs." A prediction concerning a different market, the market for labour services, is "if the hourly wage paid to workers increases, the amount of labour employed will fall."

Models

economic model
A term used in several related ways: sometimes as a synonym for theory, sometimes for a specific quantification of a general theory, sometimes for the application of a general theory to a specific context, and sometimes for an abstraction designed to illustrate some point but not meant as a full theory on its own.

Economists often proceed by constructing what they call **economic models**. This term has several different but related meanings.

Sometimes the term "model" is used as a synonym for a theory, as when economists speak of the model of the determination of national income. Sometimes it may refer to a particular subset of theories, such as the Keynesian model or the Neoclassical model of income determination.

More often, a model means a specific quantitative formulation of a theory. In this case, specific numbers are attached to the mathematical relationships defined by the theory, the numbers often being derived from observations of the economy. The specific form of the model can then be used to make precise predictions about, say, the behaviour of prices in the potato market, or the course of national income and total employment. Forecasting models used by the Bank of Canada and the International Monetary Fund (IMF) are of this type.

The term "model" is often used to refer to an application of a general theory in a specific context. So if we take the theory of consumer demand and apply it to the egg market in Winnipeg we might speak of a model of the Winnipeg egg market.

Finally, a model may be an illustrative abstraction, not meant to be elaborate enough to generate testable hypotheses. The circular flow of income and expenditure in Chapter 1 is a model of this sort. By illustrating how income and payments flow between consumers and producers, it helps us to understand how decisions of these two groups influence each other through factor markets and goods markets. However, the actual flows in any real economy are vastly more complex than the simple flows shown in the figure. The model helps us to understand what is going on without being detailed enough to yield specific testable predictions about real-world behaviour. In some ways, a model of this sort is like a political caricature. Its value is in the insights it provides that help us to understand key features of a complex world.

Testing Theories

Economists make much use of evidence or, as they usually call it, empirical observation. Such observations can be used to test a specific prediction of some theory and to provide observations to be explained by theories.

A theory is tested by confronting its predictions with evidence. Are events of the type contained in the theory followed by the consequences predicted by the theory? For example, is a decrease in the price of chicken feed followed by an increase in the amount of eggs producers want to sell? Generally, theories tend to be abandoned when they are no longer useful. A theory ceases to be useful when it cannot predict better than an alternative theory. When a theory consistently fails to predict better than an available alternative, it is either modified or replaced.

The old question, "Which came first: the chicken or the egg?", is often raised when discussing economic theories. In the first instance, it was observation that preceded economic theories. People were not born with economic theories embedded in their minds; instead, economic theories first arose when people observed the coordination of market behaviour and asked themselves how such coordination occurred. But, once economics was established, theories and evidence interacted with each other. It has now become impossible to say that one precedes the other. In some cases, empirical evidence may suggest inadequacies that require the development of better theories. In other cases, an inspired guess may lead to a theory that has little current empirical support but is subsequently found to explain many observations. This interaction between theory and empirical observation is illustrated in Figure 2-1.

Theories About Human Behaviour

So far we have talked about theories in general. But what about theories that purport to explain and predict human behaviour? A scientific study of human behaviour is only possible if humans respond in predictable ways to things that affect them. Is it reasonable to expect such predictability? After all, we humans have free will and can behave in capricious ways if the spirit moves us.

Think, however, of what the world would be like if human behaviour were really unpredictable. Neither law, nor justice, nor airline timetables would be more reliable than the outcome of a single spin of a roulette wheel. A kind remark could as easily provoke fury as sympathy. Your landlady might evict you tomorrow or let you off the rent. One cannot really imagine a society of human beings that could work like this. In fact, we live

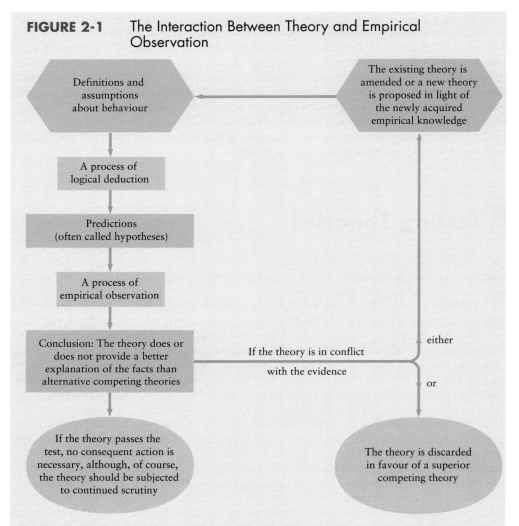

FIGURE 2-1   The Interaction Between Theory and Empirical Observation

Definitions and assumptions about behaviour

The existing theory is amended or a new theory is proposed in light of the newly acquired empirical knowledge

A process of logical deduction

Predictions (often called hypotheses)

A process of empirical observation

Conclusion: The theory does or does not provide a better explanation of the facts than alternative competing theories

If the theory is in conflict with the evidence

either

or

If the theory passes the test, no consequent action is necessary, although, of course, the theory should be subjected to continued scrutiny

The theory is discarded in favour of a superior competing theory

Theory and observation are in continuous interaction. Starting (at the top left) with the assumptions of a theory and the definitions of relevant terms, the theorist deduces by logical analysis everything that is implied by the assumptions. These implications are the predictions or the hypotheses of the theory. The theory is then tested by confronting its predictions with evidence. If the theory is in conflict with facts, it will usually be amended to make it consistent with those facts (thereby making it a better theory); or it will be discarded, to be replaced by a superior alternative. The process then begins again: The new or amended theory is subjected first to logical analysis and then to empirical testing.

in a world that is a mixture of the predictable for "most of the people most of the time" with the haphazard or random.

How is it that human behaviour can show stable responses even though we can never be quite sure what one individual will do? Successful predictions about the behaviour of large groups are made possible by the statistical "law" of large numbers. Very roughly, this "law" asserts that random movements of a large number of items tend to offset one another.

For example, we might wonder if there is a relationship between highway speed limits and road accidents. When the speed limit is actually lowered, it will be almost impossible to predict in advance what changes will occur in any single individual's driving record. One individual whose record had been good may have a series of accidents after the speed limit is lowered because of deterioration in his physical or emotional health. Another person may have an improved accident record for reasons not associated with the change in the speed limit—for example, because she purchases a more reliable car. Yet others may have altered driving records for no reasons that we can discern—we may have to put it down to an exercise of unpredictable free will.

If we study only a few individuals, we will learn nothing about the effects of the altered speed limit, since we will not know the importance of all the other causes that are at work. But, if we observe 1,000 individuals, the effects of the change in the speed limit— if such effects do exist—will tend to show up in the *average* responses. If a reduced speed limit does discourage accidents, the group as a whole will have fewer accidents even though some individuals have more. Individuals may do peculiar things that, as far as we can see, are inexplicable, but the group's behaviour will nonetheless be predictable, precisely because the odd things that one individual does will tend to cancel out the odd things that some other individual does.

Because the unusual behaviour of one individual often offsets the unusual behaviour of someone else, it is much easier to accurately predict the average behaviour in large groups of people.

Testing theories about human behaviour requires studying large numbers of people—to take advantage of the "law" of large numbers.

Why Economists Disagree

When all their theories have been constructed and all their evidence has been collected, economists still disagree with each other on many issues. If you hear a discussion among economists on the evening news or if you read about their debates in the daily press or weekly magazines, you will find that economists frequently disagree with each other. What should we make of this disagreement? Here are five of the many possible sources of disagreement.

First, different economists may be using different benchmarks. For example, inflation may be up compared with last year but down compared with 1990. When this sort of thing happens the disagreement is more apparent than real, although it can be confusing to observers.

Second, economists often fail to make it clear to their audience whether they are talking about short-term or long-term consequences. For example, one economist may be noting that a tax cut will stimulate consumption at the cost of lowering saving in the short run while another is pointing out that it will stimulate investment and saving in the long run. Here, again, the disagreement is more apparent than real, since both these short-run and long-run effects command much agreement among economists.

Third, economists often fail to acknowledge the full extent of their ignorance. There are many things on which economists know little, and even more on which the evidence is far from conclusive. Informed judgements are then required before an economist takes a position on even a purely positive question. If two economists' judgements differ, the disagreement is real. Evidence is not sufficient, and different people can come to different conclusions on the basis of a given set of evidence. What a responsible economist will do in such cases is to make clear the extent to which informed judgement is involved in any position he or she is taking.

Fourth, different economists have different values, and these normative views play a large part in most public discussions of policy. Many economists stress the importance of individual responsibility, while others stress the need for collective action to deal with certain issues. Different policy advice may stem from such differences in value judgements about what is socially important. The responsible economist will make it clear which part of her advice is normative and which part is positive.

A fifth reason for disagreement lies in the desire of the media to cover both sides of any contentious issue. As a result the public will usually hear one or two economists on each side of a debate, regardless of whether the profession is divided right down the middle or is nearly unanimous in its support of one side. Thus, the public will not know that in one case a reporter could have chosen from dozens of economists to present each side, whereas in another case the reporter had to spend three days finding someone willing to take a particular side because nearly all the economists supported the other side. In their desire to show both sides of all cases, however, the media tend to present the public with the appearance of a profession equally split over all matters.

Anyone seeking to discredit some particular economist's advice by showing that there is disagreement among economists will have no trouble finding evidence of some disagreement. But those who wish to know if there is a majority view, or even a strong consensus, will find one on a surprisingly large number of issues.

Because the world is complex and because no issue can be settled beyond any doubt, economists are never in unanimous agreement on any issue. Nonetheless, the methods we have been discussing in this chapter have produced an impressive amount of agreement on many aspects of how the economy works and what happens when governments intervene to alter its workings. A survey published in the *American Economic Review*, perhaps the most influential economics journal, showed strong agreement among economists on many propositions, including "Rent control leads to a housing shortage" (85 percent yes), "tariffs usually reduce economic welfare" (93 percent yes), and "large government budget deficits have adverse effects on the economy" (83 percent yes). Other examples of these areas of agreement will be found in countless places throughout this book.

Economic Data

For data on the Canadian economy and many other aspects of Canadian life, see Statistics Canada's website: www.statcan.ca.

Economists seek to explain events that they see in the world. Why, for example, did the price of wheat rise last year even though the wheat crop increased? Explaining such observations typically requires an understanding of how the economy works, an understanding based in part on the insights economists derive from their models.

Economists also use real-world observations to test their theories. For example, did the amount that people saved last year rise—as the theory predicts it should have—when a large tax cut increased after-tax incomes? To test this prediction we need reliable data for people's incomes and their savings.

Political scientists, sociologists, anthropologists, and psychologists all tend to collect the data they use to formulate and test their theories. Economists are unusual among social scientists in mainly using data collected by others, often government statisticians. In economics there is a division of labour between collecting data and using it to generate and test theories. The advantage is that economists do not need to spend much of their scarce research time collecting the data they use. The disadvantage is that they are often not as well informed about the limitations of the data collected by others as they would be if they collected the data themselves.

Once data are collected they can be displayed in various ways, many of which we will see later in this chapter. They can be laid out in tables. They can be displayed in various types of graphs. And where we are interested in relative movements rather than absolute ones, the data can be expressed in index numbers. We begin with a discussion of index numbers.

index number An average that measures change over time of such variables as the price level and industrial production; conventionally expressed as a percentage relative to a base period, which is assigned the value 100.

Index Numbers

The top part of Table 2-2 shows how the prices of gold and silver varied over an eight-year period from 1992 to 1999. How do these two sets of prices compare in volatility? It is difficult to tell from the table because the two prices fluctuate around different levels. It is easier to compare the series if we concentrate on relative rather than absolute price changes. (The absolute change is the dollar value of the change in price; the relative change is the change in the price expressed in relation to some base price.)

Index Numbers as Relative Magnitudes

Comparisons of relative changes can be made by expressing each price series as a set of **index numbers**. To do this we take the price at some point of time as the base to which prices in other periods will be compared. We call this the base period. In the present example we choose 1992 as the base period for both series. The price in that year is given a value of 100. We then take the price of gold in each subsequent year, called the given year, and divide it by the price in the base year, and then multiply the result by 100. This gives us an index number of gold prices. We then do the same for silver. The details of the calculations for gold are shown in the middle part of Table 2-2.

The results, which are shown in the bottom part of Table 2-2, allow us to compare the relative fluctuations in the two series, even though their absolute values are quite different. It is apparent from the figures that silver prices have shown significantly more percentage variability than have gold prices.

The formula of any index number is:

$$\frac{\text{Value of index}}{\text{in given period}} = \frac{\text{absolute value at given period}}{\text{absolute value in base period}} \times 100$$

An index number merely expresses the value of some series in any given period as a percentage of its value in the base period. Thus, the 1999 index of gold prices of 81.0 tells us that the 1999 price of gold was 81.0 percent of the 1992 price. By subtracting 100 from any index we get the change from the base to the given year, expressed as a percentage of the base year. So, in the above case, the price of gold in 1999 was 19.0 percent lower than in 1992. To take a second example, the silver index

TABLE 2-2   Indexes for Gold and Silver Prices

Average January Price, US dollars per troy ounce

Year	Gold	Silver
1992	$354.83	$4.13
1993	329.78	3.68
1994	386.21	5.10
1995	378.81	4.78
1996	400.28	5.50
1997	351.01	4.78
1998	290.51	5.90
1999	287.41	5.16

Constructing an Index of Gold Prices (Base Year 1992)

Year	Procedure	Index
1992	(354.83/354.83) × 100	= 100.0
1993	(329.78/354.83) × 100	= 92.9
1994	(386.21/354.83) × 100	= 108.8
1995	(378.81/354.83) × 100	= 106.8
1996	(400.28/354.83) × 100	= 112.8
1997	(351.01/354.83) × 100	= 98.9
1998	(290.51/354.83) × 100	= 81.9
1999	(287.41/354.83) × 100	= 81.0

Index numbers are calculated by dividing the given price by the base-year price and multiplying the result by 100. For example, the given price of gold in 1998 of $290.51 is divided by the base-year price of $354.83 and multiplied by 100 to yield an index value for 1998 of 81.9.

Constructed Indexes of Gold and Silver Prices

Year	Gold	Silver
1992	100.0	100.0
1993	92.9	89.1
1994	108.8	123.5
1995	106.8	115.7
1996	112.8	133.2
1997	98.9	115.7
1998	81.9	142.9
1999	81.0	124.9

(*Source:* The BCA Research Group.)

of 124.9 in 1999 tells us that the 1999 price of silver was 124.9 percent of the 1992 price—or, the price had increased by 24.9 percent between those two years.

Index Numbers as Average Magnitudes

Practise with Study Guide Chapter 2, Exercise 3.

Index numbers are particularly useful if we wish to combine several different series into some average. Say, for example, that we want an index of precious metal prices and gold and silver are the only two commodities we need to worry about.

An Unweighted Index.   For any one year we could add the price indexes for gold and silver and average them. This would give us a precious metals index. But the index would give the two prices equal weight in determining the value of the overall index. Such an index is often called an unweighted index, but that name is misleading. Actually, it is an equal-weight index. It would be sheer luck if this were the appropriate thing to do.

A Proportional-Weights Index.   In practice, we need to weight each price by some measure of its relative importance, letting the more important prices have more weight than the less important prices in determining what happens to the overall index. In the present example, we take the value of the outputs of each metal as the appropriate weights. In the base year, gold and silver outputs were $25.4 billion and $2.6 billion respectively. In order to make the new index still have a value in the base period equal to 100, the weights are all expressed as decimal fractions that sum to 1. To do this we express each value as a fraction of the total value of $28.0 billion. This gives us weights of 0.907 for gold and 0.093 for silver. In other words, since the value of silver is only about one-tenth of the value of gold, silver prices will be given only one-tenth the influence of gold prices in determining the overall index of precious metal prices. To get our weighted index of precious metal prices, we multiply each index value in the bottom part of Table 2-2 by that metal's weight and sum the two to obtain the final index. The results are shown in Table 2-3. The quite different behaviour of the two indexes shows the importance of the choice of weights. When both prices are given equal weight, the index rises in 1998, reflecting the sharp rise in the price of silver that year. But when gold is weighted by its importance in production, the precious metals index falls in that year (because the price of gold fell in that year).

An index that averages changes in several series is the weighted average of the indexes for the separate series, where the weights should reflect the relative importance of each series.

Table 2-3   Two Indexes of Precious Metals Prices

	Equal Weights	Proportional Weights
1992	100.0	100.0
1993	91.0	92.6
1994	116.2	110.2
1995	111.3	107.6
1996	123.0	114.7
1997	107.3	100.5
1998	112.4	87.5
1999	103.0	85.1

Weights really matter! The equal-weight index is calculated for each year by adding the gold and silver price indexes from Table 2-2 and dividing by two (a simple average). The proportional-weights index is calculated for each year by taking a weighted average of the price indexes from Table 2-2, where the weights are .907 for gold and .093 for silver. These weights reflect the proportion of the total value of sales of gold and silver (in the base year) accounted for by each precious metal.

Price Indexes.   Economists make frequent use of indexes of the price level which cover a broad group of prices across the whole economy. One of the most important of these is the consumer price index, CPI, which covers goods and services that individuals buy. This is described in detail in Chapter 19.

All price indexes are calculated using the same procedure. First, the relevant prices are collected. Then a base year is chosen. Then each price series is converted into index numbers, just as was done in Table 2-2. Finally, the index numbers are combined to create a weighted average index series where the weights indicate the relative importance of each price series, as done in Table 2-3. For example, in any consumer price index the price of sardines would be given a much smaller weight than the price of living accommodation, because what happens to the price of accommodation is much more important to consumers, all of whom spend much more on accommodation than on sardines.

Graphing Economic Data

A single economic variable such as unemployment or GDP can come in two basic forms.

Cross-Section and Time-Series Data

The first is called **cross-sectional data**, which means a number of different observations on one variable all taken in different places at the same point in time. Figure 2-2 shows an example. The variable in the figure is unemployment as a percentage of the labour force. It is shown for each of the ten Canadian provinces in September 1999.

The second type of data is called **time-series data**. It refers to observations taken on one variable at successive points in time. The data in Figure 2-3 show the unemployment rate for Canada from 1978 to 1999. (Note that the Canadian unemployment

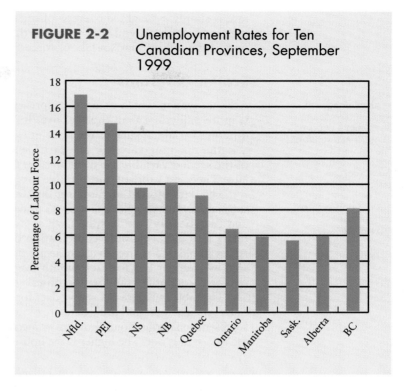

FIGURE 2-2   Unemployment Rates for Ten Canadian Provinces, September 1999

cross-sectional data
A set of measurements or observations made at the same time across several different units (such as households, firms, or countries).

time-series data
A set of measurements or observations made repeatedly at successive periods (or moments) of time.

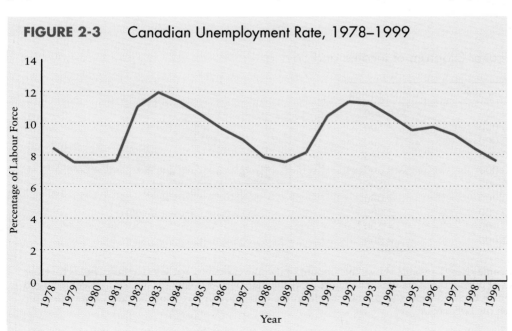

FIGURE 2-3   Canadian Unemployment Rate, 1978–1999

rate is simply a weighted average of the ten provincial unemployment rates, where the weight for each province is the size of that province's labour force expressed as a fraction of the total Canadian labour force.)

Scatter Diagrams

Another way in which data can be presented is in a **scatter diagram**. This type of chart is more analytical than those above. It is designed to show the relation between two different variables, such as the price of eggs and the quantity of eggs purchased. To plot a scatter diagram, values of one variable are measured on the horizontal axis and values of the second variable are measured on the vertical axis. Any point on the diagram relates a specific value of one variable to a corresponding specific value of the other.

The data plotted on a scatter diagram may be either cross-sectional data or time-series data. An example of a cross-sectional scatter diagram is a scatter of the price of eggs and the quantity sold in July 1999 at two dozen different places in Canada. Each dot refers to a price–quantity combination observed in a different place at the same time. An example of a scatter diagram using time-series data is the price and quantity of eggs sold in Thunder Bay for each month over the last ten years. Each of the 120 dots refers to a price–quantity combination observed at the same place in one particular month.

The table in Figure 2-4 shows data for the income and the savings of ten households in one particular year and these data are plotted on a scatter diagram. Each point in the figure represents one household, showing its income and its saving. The positive relation between the two stands out. The higher is the household's income, the higher its saving tends to be.

Graphing Economic Theories

Theories are built on assumptions about relationships between variables. For example, the quantity of eggs demanded is assumed to fall as the price of eggs rises. Or, the total amount an individual saves is assumed to rise as his or her income rises. How can such re-

Figure 2-4   A Scatter Diagram of Income and Saving

Household	Annual Income	Annual Saving
1	$70 000	$10 000
2	30 000	2 500
3	100 000	12 000
4	60 000	3 000
5	80 000	8 000
6	10 000	500
7	20 000	2 000
8	50 000	2 000
9	40 000	4 200
10	90 000	8 000

Saving tends to rise as income rises. The table shows the amount of income earned by ten selected households together with the amount they saved during the same year. The figure plots the income and saving for the ten households listed in the table. The number on each dot refers to the household in the corresponding row of the table. (Note that the scales are not the same on the two axes.)

lations be expressed? Here we introduce the concept of a *function* which is really just a special type of relation. When one variable, *X*, is related to another variable, *Y*, in such a way that to every value of *X* there is only one possible value of *Y*, we say that *Y* is a *function* of *X*.[2] When we write this relation down, we are expressing a *functional relation* between the two variables.

A functional relation can be expressed in words, in a numerical schedule, in mathematical equations, or in graphs.

To illustrate, we take a specific example of a relation between a family's annual income, which we denote by the symbol *Y*, and the total amount it spends on goods and services during that period, which we denote by the symbol *C*.

Verbal Statement.   When income is zero, the family will spend $800 a year (either by borrowing the money or by consuming past savings), and for every $1 of income that it obtains it will increase its expenditure by 80 cents.

Schedule.   This shows selected values of the family's income and the amount it spends on consumption.

Annual income	Consumption	Reference letter
$ 0	$ 800	*p*
2 500	2 800	*q*
5 000	4 800	*r*
7 500	6 800	*s*
10 000	8 800	*t*

Mathematical (Algebraic) Statement.   *C* = $800 + 0.8*Y* is the equation of the relation just described in words. As a check, you can first see that when *Y* is zero, *C* is $800. Then you can substitute any two values of *Y* that differ by $1, multiply each by 0.80, and add 800, and see that the corresponding two values of consumption differ by $0.80.

Graphical Statement.   Figure 2-5 shows both the points from the preceding schedule and the line representing the equation given in the previous paragraph.

Comparison of the values on the graph with the values in the schedule, and with the values derived from the equation just stated, shows that these are alternative expressions of the same relation between *C* and *Y*. All four of these modes of expression refer to the same relation between total consumption expenditure and total income.

FIGURE 2-5   Income and Consumption

Consumption expenditure rises as income rises. The figure graphs the schedule and the equation for the consumption function discussed in the text.

---

[2]For those who find this statement difficult to understand, here is a more detailed explanation. When a relationship between two variables, *X* and *Y*, is such that for any value of *X* there is one and only one value of the variable *Y*, then *Y* is said to be a function of *X*. For example, in the relation, $Y = a + bX + cX^2$, *Y* is a function of *X* because each value of *X* gives rise to one and only one value of *Y*. It is worth noting that *Y* being a function of *X* does not necessarily imply that *X* is a function of *Y*. For example, in the equation given in this footnote, *X* cannot be expressed as a *function* of *Y* because to many values of *Y* there correspond not one but two values of *X*. Though this distinction between relations and functions (a specific type of relation) is important in much of mathematics, it is not a distinction that will play a role in this book, where we confine ourselves to functions.

Functions

Let us look in a little more detail at the algebraic expression of this relation between income and consumption expenditure. To state the expression in general form, detached from the specific numerical example above, we use a symbol to express the dependence of one variable on another. Using "f" for this purpose, we write

$$C = f(Y) \qquad (2\text{-}1)$$

This is read, "C is a function of Y." Spelling this out more fully, we would say, "The amount of consumption expenditure depends upon the household's income."

The variable on the left-hand side is the dependent variable, since its value depends on the value of the variable on the right-hand side. The variable on the right-hand side is the independent variable, since it can take on any value. The letter "f" tells us that a functional relation is involved. This means that a knowledge of the value of the variable (or variables) within the parentheses on the right-hand side allows us to determine the value of the variable on the left-hand side. Although in this case we have used "f" (as a memory-aid for "function"), any convenient symbol can be used to denote the existence of a functional relation.

Functional notation can seem intimidating to those who are unfamiliar with it. But it is helpful. Since the functional concept is basic to all science, the notation is worth mastering.

Functional Forms

The equation $C = f(Y)$ states that C is related to Y. It says nothing about the *form* that this relation takes. The term *functional form* refers to the specific nature of the relation between the variables in the function. The example above gave one specific functional form for this relation:

$$C = \$800 + 0.8\,Y \qquad (2\text{-}2)$$

Equation 2-1 expresses the general assumption that consumption expenditure depends on the consumer's income. Equation 2-2 expresses the more specific assumption that C rises by 80 cents for every \$1 that Y rises. An alternative form for the function in Equation 2-1 would be $C = \$600 + 0.9Y$. You should be able to say in words the behaviour implied in this relation. There is no reason why either of these assumptions must be true; indeed, neither may be consistent with the facts. But that is a matter for testing. What we do have in each equation is a concise statement of a particular assumption.

Graphing Functional Relations

Practise with Study Guide Chapter 2, Exercise 4.

Different functional forms have different graphs, and we will meet many of these in subsequent chapters. Figure 2-5 is an example of a relation in which the two variables move together. When income goes up consumption goes up. In such a relation the two variables are *positively related* to each other.

Figure 2-6 gives an example of variables that move in opposite directions. As the amount spent on abating smoke pollution goes up, the amount of pollution goes down. In such a relation the two variables are *negatively related* to each other.

Both of these graphs are straight lines. In such cases the variables are *linearly related* to each other (either positively or negatively).

The Slope of a Straight Line

Slopes are important in economics. They show you how much one variable changes as the other changes. The slope is defined as the amount of change in the variable measured on the vertical or y-axis per unit change in the variable measured on the horizontal or x-axis. In the case of Figure 2-6 it tells us how many tons of smoke pollution, symbolized by P, are removed per dollar spent on pollution control, symbolized by E. As the figure shows, if we spend $2000 more we get 1000 tons less pollution. This is 0.5 tons per dollar spent. On the graph the extra $2000 is indicated by ΔE, the arrow indicating that E rises by 2000. The 1000 tons of pollution reduction is indicated by ΔP, the arrow showing that pollution falls by 1000. (The Greek uppercase letter delta, Δ, stands for a change in something.) To get the amount of abatement per dollar of expenditure we merely divide one by the other. In symbols this is $\Delta P / \Delta E$.

If we let X stand for whatever variable is measured on the horizontal axis and Y for whatever variable is measured on the vertical axis, the slope of a straight line is $\Delta Y / \Delta X$. [1][3]

In Figure 2-5 the two variables change in the same direction, so both changes will always be either positive or negative. As a result their ratio, which is the slope of this line, is positive. In Figure 2-6 the two variables change in opposite directions; when one increases the other decreases. So the two Δs will always be of opposite sign. As a result their ratio, which is the slope of the line, is always negative.

Notice also that straight lines have the same slope no matter where on the line you measure that slope. This tells us what inspection of the chart reveals: that the change in one variable in response to a unit change in the other is the same anywhere on the line. We get 0.5 tons of additional pollution abatement for every additional $1 that we spend on abatement no matter how much we are already spending.

Nonlinear Functions

Although it is sometimes convenient to simplify a real relation between two variables by assuming them to be linearly related, this is seldom the case over their whole range. Nonlinear relations are much more common than linear ones. In the case of pollution abatement

FIGURE 2-6   Linear Pollution Abatement

Pollution falls linearly as expenditure on abatement rises. The slope of the line indicates the marginal reduction in pollution for every increase of $1 of abatement expenditure. It is constant at -0.5, indicating that every extra $1 spent on abatement reduces pollution by half a ton.

FIGURE 2-7   Nonlinear Pollution Abatement

Pollution falls nonlinearly as abatement expenditure rises. When pollution is 8000 tons per year, an additional expenditure of $3000 reduces pollution by 2000 tons. The marginal return for $1 additional expenditure is $\Delta P / \Delta E$ or $-2000/3000$, which is two-thirds of a ton of pollution reduced per $1 spent on abatement. However, when pollution has already been reduced to 3000 tons, an extra $3000 spent on abatement reduces pollution by only 500 tons. The marginal return for $1 of additional expenditure, $\Delta P / \Delta E$, is now only $-500/3000$ or one-sixth of a ton of pollution reduced per $1 spent.

---

[3]Numbers in square brackets indicate mathematical notes that are found in a separate section at the back of the book.

FIGURE 2-8   Navigation Aids

Safe passages increase at an increasing rate as navigation aids are increased. The figure shows the number of safe passages varying positively with the amount spent on navigation aids. Because of network externalities, the number of safe passages increases at an increasing rate as more is spent on navigation aids. An increase in expenditure on navigation aids by $3000 when expenditure is $6000 raises safe passages by 500 from 3500 to 4000. The marginal return to $1 extra spent on navigation aids is then 500/3000 or 0.167. In other words it takes $6 to get one more safe passage (3000/500). When $14 000 is already being spent, a further increase of $3000 increases safe passages by 2000 from 6000 to 8000.The marginal return from $1 spent on aids is now 2000/3000 or 0.667. In other words, it takes only $1.50 extra spending to get one more safe passage (3000/2000).

it is usually quite cheap to eliminate the first units of pollution. Then, as the smoke gets cleaner and cleaner, the cost of further abatement tends to increase because more and more sophisticated and expensive methods need to be used. As a result, the graph relating expenditure on abatement and amount of pollution usually looks more like Figure 2-7 than Figure 2-6. Inspection of Figure 2-7 shows that as more and more is spent, the benefit in terms of extra abatement for an additional $1 of abatement expenditure gets smaller and smaller. This is shown by the diminishing slope of the curve as we move rightward along it. As the figure shows, an extra $1 of expenditure yields two-thirds of a ton of pollution reduction when pollution is 8000 tons ($\Delta Y/\Delta X = -2000/3000$) but only one-sixth of a ton of pollution reduction when pollution is 3000 tons ($\Delta Y/\Delta X = -500/3000$).

Economists call the change in abatement when a bit more or a bit less is spent on abatement the *marginal* change. The figure shows that the slope of the curve at each point measures this marginal change. It also shows that, in the type of curve illustrated, the marginal return per dollar spent is diminishing as abatement proceeds. There is always a payoff to more expenditure over the range shown in the figure, but the return diminishes as more is spent. This relation can be described as *diminishing marginal response*. We will meet such relations many times in what follows, so we emphasize now that diminishing marginal response does not mean that the *total* response is diminishing. In the figure the total amount of pollution continues to fall as more and more is spent on abatement. But diminishing marginal response does mean that the amount of abatement obtained for each additional unit of expense is diminishing as more and more pollution is abated.

Figure 2-8 shows a graph where the marginal return is increasing. It relates expenditure on navigational aids to the number of safe passages. At low levels of expenditure the curve is nearly flat. An additional unit of expenditure does not yield much additional protection. But as more and more is spent, it becomes possible to employ more efficient navigation aids that work together as a whole system. Each extra unit of expenditure yields more additional protection than each previous unit. In this case we have what economists call increasing marginal response. The reason is that navigation aids encounter what are called *network externalities*. They are most effective not as single stand-alone bits, such as one lighthouse, but as an integrated whole. Each aid becomes more effective the more complex and interrelated is the whole system of which it is a part.

Functions with Maxima and Minima

So far, all the graphs we have shown have had either a positive or negative slope over their entire range. But many relations change direction as the independent variable increases. Figures 2-9 and 2-10 extend our navigation and pollution examples over a larger range of the independent variables. We find that as more and more is spent on navigation aids, not only does the marginal contribution of each additional $1 spent begin to decline, but eventually the *total* safety begins to decline. The reason is that the signals begin to interfere with each other and confuse rather than aid navigators. So, as expenditure on navigation aids increases, eventually the safety reaches a maximum and then begins to decline.

At the maximum point the curve is flat—it has a zero slope. Up to that point each $1 spent does increase safety—it has a positive marginal contribution. But after that point each additional $1 spent reduces safety—it has a negative marginal contribution. At the maximum point the marginal contribution is zero.

Now look at Figure 2-10, which extends the pollution abatement example. Here we see that each $1 spent on pollution control adds to abatement up to the amount E_1, but after that abatement begins to decline. The reason in this case may be that the regulations become so costly that firms find ways of evading them and total enforcement gets less effective. Pollution reaches a minimum when E_1 is spent but rises thereafter. Notice that up to E_1 the curve has a negative slope, indicating that more expenditure is associated with less pollution, but that after E_1 the curve has a positive slope, indicating that more expenditure is associated with more pollution. At the point of minimum pollution the tangent to the curve shown by the line T has a slope of zero.

These two cases illustrate an important point, which we will see over and over in what follows:

At either a minimum or a maximum value of a function, its marginal value is zero.

FIGURE 2-9   Aid Saturation

Increases in expenditure on navigation aids eventually serve to reduce the number of safe passages. Up to E_1, expenditure on navigation aids encounters increasing marginal returns. Each additional $1 of expenditure allows a larger increase in safe passages than each previous $1 of expenditure. As expenditure approaches E_2, it encounters decreasing marginal returns. Each additional $1 spent increases the number of safe passages by less than the previous $1 of expenditure. At E_2, safe passages reach a maximum of S_2. Further expenditure encounters negative marginal returns. Each additional $1 spent lowers the number of safe passages. At the maximum point the slope of the tangent T (the straight line that just touches the curve at that point) is zero. At that point the number of safe passages shows no response to small changes in expenditure on navigation aids.

A Final Word

We have done much in this chapter. We have discussed why economists use theory and how they build economic models. We have discussed how they test their theories and how there is a continual back-and-forth process between empirical testing of predictions and refining the theoretical model. Finally, we have devoted considerable time and space to exploring the many ways that data can be displayed in graphs and how economists use graphs to illustrate their theories.

FIGURE 2-10   Abatement Saturation

Beyond a certain point additional abatement expenditure increases pollution. Up to E_1, each additional \$1 of expenditure reduces pollution, but at a diminishing amount for each \$1. At expenditure E_1, pollution reaches a minimum of P_1. If further amounts are spent, pollution actually rises. At the minimum point the slope of the tangent line T is zero. At that point, pollution shows no response to small changes in abatement expenditure.

Many students find themselves intimidated when they are first confronted with all of the details about graphing. But try not to worry. You may not yet be a master of all the graphing techniques that we have discussed in this chapter, but you will be surprised at how quickly it all falls into place. And, as is true for most skills, there is no substitute for practice. In the next three chapters we will encounter many graphs. But we will start simply and then slowly attempt more complicated cases. We are confident that in the process of learning some basic economic theories you will get enough practice in graphing that you will very soon look back at this chapter and realize how straightforward it all is.

S U M M A R Y

Positive and Normative Advice

- A key to the success of scientific inquiry lies in separating positive questions about the way the world works from normative questions about how one would like the world to work.

Economic Theories and Models

- Theories are designed to explain and predict what we see. A theory consists of a set of definitions of the variables to be employed, a set of assumptions about how things behave, and the conditions under which the theory is meant to apply.
- A theory provides conditional predictions of the type "if one event occurs, then another event will also occur."

- The term "model" has a number of meanings, including (a) a synonym for theory, (b) a precise realization of a general theory, with a specific numerical relation in place of each general relation posited by the theory, (c) an application of a general theory to a specific case, and (d) a simplified set of relations designed to study one specific force in isolation.

Testing Theories

- Theories are tested by checking their predictions against evidence. In some sciences, these tests can be conducted under laboratory conditions in which only one thing changes at a time. In economics, testing must be done using the data produced by the world of ordinary events.
- The fact that people sometimes act strangely, even capriciously, does not destroy the possibility of scientific study of group behaviour. The odd and inexplicable things that one person does will tend to cancel out the odd and inexplicable things that another person does. The law of large numbers thus means that group behaviour is often easier to predict than individual behaviour.
- The progress of any science lies in finding better explanations of events than are now available. Thus in any developing science, one must expect to discard some existing theories and replace them with demonstrably superior alternatives.

Economic Data

- Index numbers express economic series in relative form. Values in each period are expressed in relation to the value in the base period, which is given a value of 100.
- Economic data may be graphed in three different ways. Cross-section graphs show observations taken at the same time. Time-series graphs show observations on one variable taken over time. Scatter diagrams show many points, each one of which refers to specific observations on two different variables.

Graphing Economic Theories

- A functional relation can be expressed in words, in a schedule giving specific values, in a mathematical equation, or in a graph.
- A graph of two variables has a positive slope when they both increase or decrease together and a negative slope when they move in opposite directions.
- The marginal value of a variable gives the amount it changes in response to a change in a second variable. When the variable is measured on the vertical axis of a diagram, its marginal value at a specific point on the curve is measured by the slope of the line tangent to that point.

KEY CONCEPTS

Positive and normative statements
Endogenous and exogenous variables
Theories and models
Variables, assumptions, and predictions

Economic data
Functional relations
Positive and negative relations between variables

Positive and negatively sloped curves
Marginal values
Maximum and minimum values

STUDY EXERCISES

1. Suppose that the relationship between the government's tax revenue (T) and national income (Y) is represented by the following equation: $T = 10 + 0.25Y$. Plot this relationship on a scale diagram, with Y on the horizontal axis and T on the vertical axis. Interpret the equation.

2. Consider the following three specific functional forms for a functional relation between X and Y:
   i) $Y = 50 + 2X$
   ii) $Y = 50 + 2X + 0.05X^2$
   iii) $Y = 50 + 2X - 0.05X^2$

a. For the values of X of 0, 10, 20, 30, 40 and 50, plot X and Y on a scale diagram for each specific functional form. Connect these points with a smooth line.

b. For each functional form, state whether the slope of the line is constant, increasing or decreasing as the value of X increases.

c. Describe for each functional form how the marginal change in Y depends on the value of X.

3. Suppose you want to create a price index for the price of pizza across several Canadian university campuses, as of March 1, 2000. The data are as follows:

University	Price per Pizza
Dalhousie	$6.50
Laval	5.95
McGill	6.00
Queen's	8.00
Waterloo	7.50
Manitoba	5.50
Saskatchewan	5.75
Calgary	6.25
UBC	7.25
Victoria	7.00

a. Using Calgary as the "base university," construct the Canadian university pizza price index.

b. At which university is pizza the most expensive, and by what percentage is the price higher than in Calgary?

c. At which university is pizza the least expensive, and by what percentage is the price lower than in Calgary?

d. Are the data listed above time-series or cross-section data? Explain why.

4. For each of the functional relations listed below, plot the relations on a scale diagram (with X on the horizontal axis and Y on the vertical axis) and compute the slope of the line.

i) $Y = 10 + 3X$
ii) $Y = 20 + 4X$
iii) $Y = 30 + 5X$
iv) $Y = 10 + 5X$

5. Suppose we divide Canada into three regions—the West, the Centre, and the East. Each region has an unemployment rate, defined as the number of people unemployed, expressed as a fraction of that region's labour force. The table that follows shows each region's unemployment rate and the size of its labour force.

Region	Unemployment Rate	Labour Force
West	5.5%	5.3 million
Centre	7.2%	8.4 million
East	12.5%	3.5 million

a. Compute an unemployment rate for Canada using a simple (equal weights) average of the rates in the three regions. Is this the "right" unemployment rate for Canada as a whole? Explain why or why not.

b. Now compute an unemployment rate for Canada using weights which reflect the size of that region's labour force as a proportion of the overall Canadian labour force. Explain the difference in this unemployment rate from the one in part a. Is this a "better" measure of Canadian unemployment? Explain why.

6. Draw three graphs in which the dependent variable increases at an increasing rate, at a constant rate, and at a diminishing rate. Then draw three graphs in which it decreases at an increasing, constant, and diminishing rate. For each of these graphs state a real relation that might be described by it—other than the ones given in the text of this chapter.

DISCUSSION QUESTIONS

1. What are some of the positive and normative issues that lie behind the disagreements in the following cases?

a. Economists disagree on whether the Government of Canada should try to stimulate the economy in the next six months.

b. European and North American negotiators disagree over the desirability of reducing European farm subsidies.

c. Economists argue about the merits of a voucher system that allows parents to choose the schools their children will attend.

d. Economists debate the use of a two-tier medical system in Canada (whereby health care continues to be publicly provided, but individuals are permitted to be treated by doctors who bill the patient directly— "extra billing").

2. Much recent public debate has centred on the pros and cons of permitting continued unrestricted sale of cigarettes. Proposals for the control of cigarettes range from increasing excise taxes to the mandatory use of plain packaging to an outright ban on their sale. Discuss the positive and normative assumptions that underlie the national mood to reduce the consumption of tobacco products.

3. Economists sometimes make each of the following assumptions when they construct models. Discuss some situations in which each of these assumptions might be a useful simplification in order to think about some aspect of the real world.

   a. The earth is flat.
   b. There are no differences between men and women.
   c. There is no tomorrow.
   d. There are only two periods—this year and next year.
   e. A country produces only two types of goods.
   f. People are wholly selfish.

4. What may at first appear to be untestable statements can often be reworded so that they can be tested by an appeal to evidence. How might you do this for each of the following assertions?

   a. Free-market economic systems are the best in the world.
   b. Unemployment insurance is eroding the work ethic and encouraging people to become wards of the state rather than productive workers.
   c. Robotics ought to be outlawed because it will destroy the future of working people.
   d. Laws requiring equal pay for work of equal value will make women better off.
   e. Free trade improves the welfare of a country's citizens.

5. There are hundreds of eyewitnesses to the existence of flying saucers and other UFOs. There are films and eyewitness accounts of Nessie, the Loch Ness monster. Are you convinced of their existence? If not, what would it take to persuade you? If so, what would it take to make you change your mind?

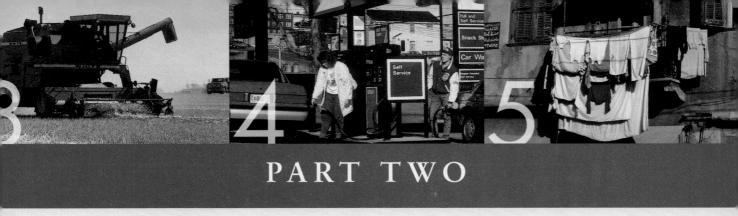

PART TWO

An Introduction to Demand and Supply

In January 1998, a massive ice storm hit Quebec and parts of Ontario and the northeastern United States, causing unprecedented stoppages in electric power. Did the ice storm cause the increase in price of portable electric generators that happened within a few days, or was this just a coincidence? In the summer of 1994, Brazil experienced a frost that severely damaged that country's coffee crop. Did it cause the large increase in the price of coffee that occurred almost immediately, or was that also a coincidence? Is the current housing shortage in Toronto related to the Ontario government's policy of rent controls, and if so, what is the connection? What determines the prices of specific products? What determines whether there will be a lot produced or only a little? These are the types of questions that you will be able to answer after reading the next three chapters.*

Chapter 3 introduces the basic concepts of demand and supply. We will see that the prices of goods in free markets are determined by the interaction of demand and supply. We will learn the meaning of equilibrium, and how equilibrium prices and quantities change in response to changes to either demand or supply. With this apparatus in place, we will look briefly at the 1998 ice storm and at Brazil's damaged coffee crop (the price increases were not coincidences!).

Chapter 4 then introduces the important idea of elasticity—the sensitivity of one variable to a change in some other variable. This concept is central to an understanding of whether a change in the demand or supply of some commodity primarily affects quantity or price. As an application of the concept of elasticity, we will examine the important policy issue of who bears the burden of commodity taxes. Do firms pay such taxes, or do consumers, or do both? How does elasticity affect the answer?

In Chapter 5 you get some practice in using what you learned in Chapters 3 and 4. We start with a discussion of how various markets interact with each other, so that events in one market lead not only to changes in that market but to changes in other markets as well. We then go on to explore two examples of government-controlled prices. The first is rent controls—you will see that the policy of rent controls produces some unusual outcomes in the rental-housing markets of Toronto, New York, and many other cities. The second is agricultural price-support policies—you will see what effects such policies have, both on farmers' incomes and on the allocation of resources.

---

*Chapter 5 does not appear in *Macroeconomics*.

CHAPTER 3

Demand, Supply, and Price

LO ***LEARNING OBJECTIVES***

❶ Understand what determines "quantity demanded," the amount of some product that households want to purchase.

❷ Distinguish between a shift in a demand curve and a movement along a demand curve.

❸ Understand what determines "quantity supplied," the amount of some product that firms want to sell.

❹ Distinguish between a shift in a supply curve and a movement along a supply curve.

❺ Recognize the forces that drive market price to equilibrium.

❻ Understand the four "laws" of demand and supply.

How do individual markets work? We are now ready to study this important question. The answer leads us to what are called the laws of supply and demand. And though there is much more to economics than just demand and supply (as many following chapters will illustrate), this is an essential starting point for understanding how a market, and thus a market economy, functions.

As a first step, we need to understand what determines the demand for and the supply of particular products. Then we can see how demand and supply together determine the prices of products and the quantities that are bought and sold. Finally, we examine how the price system allows the economy to respond to the many changes that impinge on it. Demand and supply help us to understand the price system's successes and failures, and the consequences of many government policies.

This chapter deals with the basic elements of demand, supply and price. In the next two chapters we use the demand-and-supply apparatus to discuss such issues as cigarette taxes, legislated minimum wages, price controls on rental housing, the burden of payroll taxes, and agricultural income-support policies.

Demand

What determines the demand for any given product? How did Canadian consumers react to the large increases in fuel prices in the 1970s? How did they respond to the more recent declines in the prices of personal computers and cellular telephones? We start by developing a theory designed to explain the demand for some typical product.

What Is "Quantity Demanded"?

The total amount of any particular good or service that consumers wish to purchase in some time period is called the **quantity demanded** of that product. It is important to notice two things about this concept.

First, quantity demanded is a *desired* quantity. It is the amount that consumers wish to purchase when faced with a particular price of the product, other prices, their incomes, their tastes, and everything else that might matter. It may be different from the amount that consumers actually succeed in purchasing. If sufficient quantities are not available, the amount that consumers wish to purchase may exceed the amount that they actually purchase. To distinguish these two concepts, the term *quantity demanded* is used to refer to desired purchases, and a phrase such as *quantity actually bought* or *quantity exchanged* is used to refer to actual purchases.

Second, quantity demanded refers to a *flow* of purchases. It must therefore be expressed as so much per period of time: 1 million units per day, 7 million per week, or 365 million per year. For example, being told that the quantity of new television sets demanded (at current prices) in Canada is 50 000 means nothing unless you are also told the period of time involved. Fifty thousand TVs demanded per day would be an enormous rate of demand; 50 000 per year would be a very small rate. The important distinction between *stocks* and *flows* is discussed in *Extensions in Theory 3-1*.

The amount of some product that consumers wish to buy in a given time period is influenced by the following important variables: [2]

- Product's own price
- Average household income
- Prices of other products
- Tastes
- Distribution of income
- Population
- Expectations about the future

It is difficult to determine the separate influence of each of these variables if we consider what happens when everything changes at once. Instead, we consider the influence of the variables one at a time. To do this, we hold all but one of them constant. Then we let the selected variable vary and study how it affects quantity demanded. We can do the same for each of the other variables in turn, and in this way we can come to understand the importance of each. We can then combine the separate influences of the variables to discover what happens when several things change at the same time—as they often do.

Holding all other influencing variables constant is often described by the expressions "other things being equal," "other things given," or the equivalent Latin phrase, *ceteris paribus*. When economists speak of the influence of the price of eggs on the quantity of eggs demanded, *ceteris paribus*, they refer to what a change in the price of eggs would do to the quantity of eggs demanded *if all other variables that influence the demand for eggs did not change*.

quantity demanded
The amount of a commodity that consumers wish to purchase in some time period.

Quantity Demanded and Price

We are interested in developing a theory of how prices are determined. To do this, we need to study the relationship between the quantity demanded of each product and that product's price. This requires that we hold all other influences constant and ask, "How will the quantity demanded of a product change as its price changes?"

EXTENSIONS IN THEORY 3-1

The Distinction Between Stocks and Flows

One important conceptual issue that arises frequently in economics is the distinction between stock and flow variables. Economic theories use both, and it takes a little practice to keep them straight.

As noted in the text, a flow variable has a time dimension—it is so much *per unit of time*. For example, the quantity of Grade A large eggs purchased in Edmonton is a flow variable. No useful information is conveyed if we are told that the number purchased was 2000 dozen eggs unless we are also told the period of time over which these purchases occurred. Two thousand dozen eggs per hour would indicate a much more active market in eggs than would 2000 dozen eggs per month.

In contrast, a stock variable is a variable whose value has meaning *at a point in time*. Thus the number of eggs in the egg producer's warehouse on a particular day—for example, 20 000 dozen eggs on September 3, 1999—is a stock variable. All those eggs are there at one time, and they remain there until something happens to change the stock held in the warehouse. The stock variable is just a number at a point in time, not a rate of flow of so much per unit of time.

The terminology of stocks and flows can be understood in terms of an analogy to a bathtub. At any moment, the tub holds so much water. This is the *stock,* and it can be measured in terms of the volume of water, say, 100 litres. There might also be water flowing into the tub from the tap; this *flow* is measured as so much water per unit time, say, 500 litres per hour.

The distinction between stocks and flows is important. Failure to keep them straight is a common source of confusion and even error. Note, for example, that because they have different dimensions, a stock variable and a flow variable cannot be added together without specifying some time period for which the flow persists.

We cannot add the stock of 100 litres of water in the tub to the flow of 500 litres per hour to get 600 litres. The new stock of water will depend on how long the flow persists; if it lasts for half an hour, the new stock will be 350 litres; if the flow persists for two hours, the new stock will be 1100 litres (or the tub will overflow!).

The amount of income earned is a flow; there is so much per year or per month or per hour. The amount of a consumer's expenditure is also a flow—so much spent per week or per month or per year. The amount of money in a bank account or a miser's hoard (earned, perhaps, in the past but unspent) is a stock—just so many thousands of dollars. The key test is always whether a time dimension is required to give the variable meaning. Other variables are neither stocks nor flows, but just numbers; for example, the price of one dozen eggs.

The amount of water behind the dam at any time is the stock of water; the amount moving through the gate is the flow, which is measured per unit of time.

A basic economic hypothesis is that the price of a product and the quantity demanded are related negatively, other things being equal. That is, the lower the price, the higher the quantity demanded; and the higher the price, the lower the quantity demanded.

The British economist Alfred Marshall (1842–1924) called this fundamental relation the "law of demand." In Chapter 6, we will derive the law of demand as a prediction that follows from more basic assumptions about consumer behaviour. For now, let's simply ask "why might this be so?" Products are used to satisfy desires and needs, and there is almost always more than one product that will satisfy any desire or need. Hunger may be alleviated by meat or vegetables; a desire for green vegetables can be satisfied by broccoli or spinach. The desire for a vacation may be satisfied by a trip to the ocean or to the mountains; the need to get there may be satisfied by different airlines, a bus, a car, or a train. For any general desire or need, there are many different products that will satisfy it.

Now consider what happens if income, tastes, population, and the prices of all other products remain constant and the price of only one product changes. As the price goes up, that product becomes an increasingly expensive way to satisfy a desire. Some consumers will stop buying it altogether; others will buy smaller amounts; still others may continue to buy the same quantity. Because many consumers will switch wholly or partly to other products to satisfy the same desire, less will be demanded of the product whose price has risen. As meat becomes more expensive, for example, consumers may to some extent switch to meat substitutes; they may also forgo meat at some meals and eat less meat at others.

Conversely, as the price goes down, the product becomes a cheaper method of satisfying a desire. Households will demand more of it. Consequently, they will buy less of similar products whose prices have not fallen and as a result have become expensive *relative* to the product in question. When the price of tomatoes falls, shoppers switch to tomatoes and cut their purchases of many other vegetables that now look relatively more expensive.

Demand Schedules and Demand Curves

A **demand schedule** is one way of showing the relationship between quantity demanded and the price of a product, other things being equal. It is a numerical tabulation showing the quantity that is demanded at certain prices.

The table in Figure 3-1 shows a hypothetical demand schedule for carrots. It lists the quantity of carrots that would be demanded at various prices, given the assumption that all other variables are held constant. We should note in particular that average

demand schedule
A table showing the relationship between the quantity of a commodity that buyers wish to purchase (per period of time) and the price of that commodity, other things being equal.

FIGURE 3-1   The Demand for Carrots

	Price Per Ton ($)	Quantity Demanded When Average Household Income Is $50 000 Per Year (thousands of tons per year)
U	20	110.0
V	40	90.0
W	60	77.5
X	80	67.5
Y	100	62.5
Z	120	60.0

Both the table and the graph show the quantity of carrots that would be demanded at various prices, *ceteris paribus*. For example, row *W* indicates that if the price of carrots were $60 per ton, consumers would desire to purchase 77 500 tons of carrots per year, given the values of the other variables that affect quantity demanded. The demand curve, labelled *D*, relates quantity of carrots demanded to the price of carrots; its negative slope indicates that quantity demanded increases as price falls.

household income is fixed at $50 000 because later we will want to see what happens when income changes. The table gives the quantities demanded for six selected prices, but in fact a separate quantity would be demanded at each possible price from 1 cent to several hundreds of dollars.

A second method of showing the relationship between quantity demanded and price is to draw a graph. The six price-quantity combinations shown in the table are plotted in Figure 3-1. Price is plotted on the vertical axis, and quantity is plotted on the horizontal axis.

demand curve   The graphical representation of the relationship between the quantity of a commodity that buyers wish to purchase (per period of time) and the price of that commodity, other things being equal.

The smooth curve drawn through these points is called a **demand curve.** It shows the quantity that purchasers would like to buy at each price. The negative slope of the curve indicates that the quantity demanded increases as the price falls. Each point on the demand curve indicates a single price-quantity combination. The demand curve as a whole shows something more.

The demand curve represents the relationship between quantity demanded and price, other things being equal.

When economists speak of demand in a particular market, they are referring not just to the particular quantity being demanded at the moment (i.e., not just to one point on the demand curve) but to the entire demand curve—to the relationship between desired purchases and all the possible prices of the product.

demand   The entire relationship between the quantity of a commodity that buyers wish to purchase (per period of time) and the price of that commodity, other things being equal.

Thus, the term **demand** refers to the entire relationship between the quantity demanded of a product and the price of that product (as shown, for example, by the demand curve in Figure 3-1). In contrast, a single point on a demand schedule or curve is the quantity demanded at that point. This distinction between "demand" and "quantity demanded" is an extremely important one and we will examine it more closely later in this chapter.

Shifts in the Demand Curve

The demand schedule is drawn with the assumption that everything except the product's own price is being held constant. But what if other things change, as surely they do? For example, consider an increase in household income while price remains constant. If households increase their purchases of the product, the new quantity demanded cannot be represented by a point on the original demand curve. It must be represented on a new demand curve that is to the right of the old curve. Thus, the rise in consumer income shifts the demand curve to the right, as shown in Figure 3-2. This shift illustrates the operation of an important general rule.

A demand curve is drawn with the assumption that everything except the product's own price is held constant. A change in any of the variables previously held constant will shift the demand curve to a new position.

A demand curve can shift in two important ways. In the first case, more is bought at each price—the demand curve shifts rightward so that each price corresponds to a higher quantity than it did before. In the second case, less is bought at each price—the demand curve shifts leftward so that each price corresponds to a lower quantity than it did before.

We can assess the influence of changes in variables other than price by determining how changes in each variable shift the demand curve. Any change will shift the demand curve to the right if it increases the amount that households wish to buy, other things remaining equal. It will shift the demand curve to the left if it decreases the amount that households wish to buy, other things remaining equal.

FIGURE 3-2   An Increase in the Demand for Carrots

Price Per Ton ($) p	Quantity Demanded When Average Household Income Is $50 000 Per Year (thousands of tons per year) D_0		Quantity Demanded When Average Household Income Is $60 000 Per Year (thousands of tons per year) D_1	
20	110.0	U	140.0	U′
40	90.0	V	116.0	V′
60	77.5	W	100.8	W′
80	67.5	X	87.5	X′
100	62.5	Y	81.3	Y′
120	60.0	Z	78.0	Z′

An increase in average household income increases the quantity demanded at each price. This is shown by the rightward shift in the demand curve, from D_0 to D_1. When average income rises from $50 000 to $60 000 per year, quantity demanded at a price of $60 per ton rises from 77 500 tons per year to 100 800 tons per year. A similar rise occurs at every other price.

Average Household Income.   If consumers receive more income on average, they can be expected to purchase more of most products even though product prices remain the same.[1] We therefore expect that a rise in average consumer income shifts the demand curve for most products to the right, indicating that more will be demanded at any given price. Such a shift is illustrated in Figure 3-2.

Prices of Other Goods.   We saw that the negative slope of a product's demand curve occurs because the lower its price, the cheaper the product becomes relative to other products that can satisfy the same needs or desires. These other products are called **substitutes.** Another way for the same change to come about is that the price of the substitute product rises. For example, carrots can become cheap relative to broccoli either because the price of carrots falls or because the price of broccoli rises. Either change will increase the amount of carrots that consumers wish to buy as consumers substitute away from broccoli and toward carrots. Thus a rise in the price of a substitute for a product shifts the demand curve for the product to the right. More will be demanded at each price.

substitutes Goods that can be used in place of another good to satisfy similar needs or desires.

Complements are products that tend to be used jointly. Cars and gasoline are complements; so are CD players and speakers, golf clubs and golf balls, electric stoves and electricity, and airplane flights to Calgary and ski-lift tickets in Banff. Because complements tend to be consumed together, a fall in the price of one will increase the quantity demanded of *both* products. Thus, a fall in the price of a complement for a product will shift that product's demand curve to the right. More will be demanded at each price.

complements Goods that tend to be used jointly.

---

[1]Such products are called *normal goods*. Products for which the quantity demanded falls as income rises are called *inferior goods*. These concepts are defined and discussed in Chapter 4.

For example, a fall in the price of airplane trips to Calgary will lead to a rise in the demand for ski-lift tickets in Banff, even though the price of those lift tickets is unchanged. (So the demand curve for ski-lift tickets will shift to the right.)

Tastes. Tastes have an effect on people's desired purchases. A change in tastes may be long-lasting, such as the shift from fountain pens to ballpoint pens or from typewriters to computers; or it may be a short-lived fad such as CB radios (a fad in the late 1970s and early 1980s) and many toys such as Pogs and Beanie Babies. In either case, a change in tastes in favour of a product shifts the demand curve to the right. More will be demanded at each price.

Distribution of Income. If a constant total of income is distributed differently among the population, demands may change. A change in the distribution of income, therefore, will cause an increase in the demand for products bought most by households whose incomes increase and a decrease in the demand for products bought most by households whose incomes decrease. If, for example, the government increases the deductions that may be taken for children on income-tax returns and compensates by raising basic tax rates, income will be transferred from households without children to households with children. Demands for products more heavily bought by childless persons will decline, while demands for products more heavily bought by households with children will increase.

Population. Population growth does not create new demand unless the additional people have the means to purchase goods—that is, unless they have purchasing power. If there is an increase in population with purchasing power—for example, the immigration of wealthy foreigners—the demands for all the products purchased by the new people will rise. Thus, we expect that an increase in population will shift the demand curves for most products to the right, indicating that more will be demanded at each price.

Expectations about the Future. Our discussion has so far focused on how changes in the current value of variables may change demand. But it is also true that changes in people's *expectations about future values* of variables may change demand. For example, suppose that you are thinking about buying a house in a small town in Nova Scotia and you have learned that in the near future a large high-tech firm will be moving its head office and several hundred employees to this same small town. Since their future movement into your town will surely increase the demand for housing and thus will drive up the *future* price of houses, this expectation will lead you (and others like you) to increase your demand *today* so as to make the purchase before the price rises. Thus, the demand curve for houses will shift to the right today in anticipation of a future event.

Figure 3-3 summarizes the reasons that demand curves shift.

FIGURE 3-3 Shifts in the Demand Curve

A rightward shift in the demand curve from D_0 to D_1 indicates an increase in demand; a leftward shift from D_0 to D_2 indicates a decrease in demand. An increase in demand means that more is demanded at each price. Such a rightward shift can be caused by a rise in income, a rise in the price of a substitute, a fall in the price of a complement, a change in tastes that favours that product, an increase in population, a redistribution of income toward groups that favour the product, or the anticipation of a future event that will increase the price.

A decrease in demand means that less is demanded at each price. Such a leftward shift can be caused by a fall in income, a fall in the price of a substitute, a rise in the price of a complement, a change in tastes that disfavours the product, a decrease in population, a redistribution of income away from groups that favour the product, or the anticipation of a future event that will decrease the price.

Movements Along the Curve Versus Shifts of the Whole Curve

Suppose that you read in today's newspaper that a sharp increase in the price of carrots has been caused by an increased demand for carrots. Then tomorrow you read that the rising price of carrots is reducing the typical consumer's purchases of carrots, as shoppers switch to potatoes, yams, and peas. The two stories appear to contradict each other. The first associates a rising price with rising demand; the second associates a rising price with declining demand. Can both statements be true? The answer is yes—because they refer to different things. The first describes a shift in the demand curve; the second describes a movement along a demand curve in response to a change in price.

Consider first the statement that the increase in the price of carrots has been caused by an increased demand for carrots. This statement refers to a shift in the demand curve for carrots—in this case, a shift to the right, indicating more carrots demanded at each price. This shift, as we will see later in this chapter, will increase the price of carrots.

Now consider the second statement—that fewer carrots are being bought because carrots have become more expensive. This refers to a movement along the new demand curve and reflects a change between two specific quantities demanded, one before the price increased and one afterward.

Possible explanations for the two stories are:

1. A change in tastes is shifting the demand curve for carrots to the right as more carrots are demanded at each price. This, in turn, raises the price of carrots (for reasons we will soon study in detail). This was the first newspaper story.

2. The rising price of carrots is causing each individual household to cut back on its purchase of carrots. The cutback is represented by an upward movement to the left along any particular demand curve for carrots. This was the second newspaper story.

To prevent the type of confusion caused by our two newspaper stories, economists use a specialized vocabulary to distinguish between shifts of curves and movements along curves.

We have seen that demand refers to the *entire* demand curve, whereas quantity demanded refers to the quantity that is demanded at a specific price, as indicated by a particular *point* on the demand curve. In Figure 3-1, for example, demand is given by the curve D; at a price of $40 per ton, the quantity demanded is 90 000 tons, as indicated by the point V.

Economists reserve the term **change in demand** to describe a change in the quantity demanded at *every* price. That is, a change in demand refers to a shift of the entire demand curve. The term **change in quantity demanded** refers to a movement from one point on a demand curve to another point, either on the same demand curve or on a new one.

A change in quantity demanded can result from a shift in the demand curve with the price constant; from a movement along a given demand curve due to a change in the price; or from a combination of the two. [3]

We consider these three possibilities in turn.

An increase in demand means that the whole demand curve shifts to the right; a decrease in demand means that the whole demand curve shifts to the left. At a given price, an increase in demand causes an increase in quantity demanded, whereas a decrease in demand causes a decrease in quantity demanded. For example, in Figure 3-2, the shift in the demand curve from D_0 to D_1 represents an increase in demand, and at a price of $40 per ton, quantity demanded increases from 90 000 tons to 116 000 tons, as indicated by the move from V to V'.

change in demand
A change in the quantity demanded at each possible price of the commodity, represented by a shift in the whole demand curve.

change in quantity demanded   A change in the specific quantity of the good demanded, represented by a change from one point on a demand curve to another point, either on the original demand curve or on a new one.

FIGURE 3-4   Shifts of and Movements Along the Demand Curve

An increase in demand means that the demand curve shifts to the right, and hence quantity demanded will be higher at each price. A rise in price causes an upward movement to the left along the demand curve, and hence quantity demanded will fall. The demand curve is originally D_0 and price is p_0, which means that quantity demanded is q_0. Suppose that demand increases to D_1, which means that at any particular price, there is a larger quantity demanded; for example, at p_0, quantity demanded is now q_1. Now suppose that the price rises above p_0. This causes a movement up and to the left along D_1, and quantity demanded falls below q_1.

The net effect of these two changes can be either an increase or a decrease in the quantity demanded. In this figure, a rise in price to p_2 means that the quantity demanded q_2 is still in excess of the original quantity demanded q_0; a rise in price to p_3 means that the final quantity demanded q_3 is below the original quantity demanded q_0.

A movement down and to the right along a demand curve represents an increase in quantity demanded; a movement up and to the left along a demand curve represents a decrease in quantity demanded. For example, in Figure 3-2, with demand given by the curve D_1, an increase in price from $40 to $60 per ton causes a movement along D_1 from V' to W', and quantity demanded decreases from 116 000 tons to 100 800 tons.

When there is a change in demand *and* a change in the price, the overall change in quantity demanded is the net effect of the shift in the demand curve and the movement along the new demand curve. Figure 3-4 shows the combined effect of an increase in demand, shown by a rightward shift in the whole demand curve, and an upward movement to the left along the new demand curve due to an increase in price. The increase in demand causes an increase in quantity demanded at the initial price, whereas the movement along the demand curve causes a decrease in the quantity demanded. Whether quantity demanded rises or falls overall depends on the relative magnitudes of these two changes.

Supply

What determines the supply of any given product? Why do Canadian oil producers extract and market more oil when the price of oil is high? Why do Canadian cattle ranchers sell more beef when the price of cattle-feed (mostly grain) falls? We start by developing a theory designed to explain the supply of some typical product.

What Is "Quantity Supplied"?

quantity supplied
The amount of a commodity that producers wish to sell in some time period.

The amount of a product that firms wish to sell in some time period is called the **quantity supplied** of that product. Quantity supplied is a flow; it is so much per unit of time. Note also that quantity supplied is the amount that firms are willing to offer for sale; it is not necessarily the amount that they succeed in selling, which is expressed by *quantity actually sold* or *quantity exchanged*.

The quantity supplied of a product is influenced by the following variables: [4]

- Product's own price
- Prices of inputs
- Technology
- Number of suppliers

The situation with supply is the same as that with demand: There are several influencing variables, and we will not get far if we try to discover what happens when they all change at the same time. Again, we use the convenient *ceteris paribus* assumption to study the influence of the variables one at a time.

Quantity Supplied and Price

We begin by holding all other influences constant and ask, "How do we expect the quantity of a product supplied to vary with its own price?"

A basic hypothesis of economics is that the price of the product and the quantity supplied are related *positively*, other things being equal. That is, the higher the product's own price, the more its producers will supply; and the lower the price, the less its producers will supply.

In later chapters we will derive this hypothesis as a prediction from more basic assumptions about the behaviour of firms. But now we simply ask "why might this be so?" Firms will supply more because the profits that can be earned from producing a product will increase if the price of that product rises, whereas the costs of inputs used to produce it will remain unchanged. As a result, firms, which are in business to earn profits, will wish to produce more of the product whose price has risen.

Supply Schedules and Supply Curves

A rise in the price of wheat, other things being equal, will lead farmers to plant less of other crops and plant more wheat.

The general relationship just discussed can be illustrated by a **supply schedule,** which shows the relationship between quantity supplied of a product and the price of the product, other things being equal. A supply schedule is analogous to a demand schedule; the former shows what producers would be willing to sell, whereas the latter shows what households would be willing to buy, at alternative prices of the product. The table in Figure 3-5 presents a hypothetical supply schedule for carrots.

A **supply curve,** the graphical representation of the supply schedule, is illustrated in Figure 3-5. Each point on the supply curve represents a specific price-quantity combination; however, the whole curve shows something more.

The supply curve represents the relationship between quantity supplied and price, other things being equal; its positive slope indicates that quantity supplied increases when price increases.

When economists make statements about the conditions of supply, they are not referring just to the particular quantity being supplied at the moment—that is, not to just one point on the supply curve. Instead, they are referring to the entire supply curve, to the complete relationship between desired sales and all possible prices of the product.

Supply refers to the entire relationship between the quantity supplied of a product and the price of that product, other things being equal. A single point on the supply curve refers to the *quantity supplied* at that price.

supply schedule
A table showing the relationship between the quantity of some commodity that producers wish to sell (per period of time) and the price of that commodity, other things being equal.

supply curve   The graphical representation of the relationship between the quantity of some commodity that producers wish to sell (per period of time) and the price of that commodity, other things being equal.

supply   The entire relationship between the quantity of some commodity that producers wish to sell (per period of time) and the price of that commodity, other things being equal.

FIGURE 3-5   The Supply of Carrots

	Price Per Ton ($)	Quantity Supplied (thousands of tons per year)
u	20	5.0
v	40	46.0
w	60	77.5
x	80	100.0
y	100	115.0
z	120	122.5

Both the table and the graph show the quantities that producers wish to sell at various prices, *ceteris paribus.* For example, row *w* indicates that if the price of carrots were $60 per ton, producers would want to sell 77 500 tons per year. The supply curve, labelled *S*, relates quantity of carrots supplied to the price of carrots; its positive slope indicates that quantity supplied increases as price increases.

Shifts in the Supply Curve

A shift in the supply curve means that at each price a quantity different from the previous one will be supplied. An increase in the quantity supplied at each price is shown in Figure 3-6. This change appears as a rightward shift in the supply curve. In contrast, a decrease in the quantity supplied at each price appears as a leftward shift. For supply, as for demand, there is an important general rule:

A change in any of the variables (other than the product's own price) that affects the quantity supplied will shift the supply curve to a new position.

Let's consider the effect of changes in several variables.

Price of Inputs.   All things that a firm uses to produce its outputs, such as materials, labour, and machines, are called the firm's *inputs*. Other things being equal, the higher the price of any input used to make a product, the less will be the profit from making that product. We expect, therefore, that the higher the price of any input used by a firm, the less the firm will produce and offer for sale at any given price of the product. A rise in the price of inputs therefore shifts the supply curve to the left, indicating that less will be supplied at any given price; a fall in the cost of inputs shifts the supply curve to the right.

Technology.   At any time, what is produced and how it is produced depend on what is known. Over time, knowledge changes; so do the quantities of individual products supplied. The enormous increase in production per worker that has been going on in industrial societies for about 200 years is due largely to improved methods of production. The Industrial Revolution is more than a historical event; it is a present reality. Discoveries in chemistry have led to lower costs of production for well-established products, such as

FIGURE 3-6   An Increase in the Supply of Carrots

Price Per Ton ($) p	Quantity Supplied Before Cost-Saving Innovation (thousands of tons per year) S_0		Quantity Supplied After Innovation (thousands of tons per year) S_1	
20	5.0	u	28.0	u'
40	46.0	v	76.0	v'
60	77.5	w	102.0	w'
80	100.0	x	120.0	x'
100	115.0	y	132.0	y'
120	122.5	z	140.0	z'

A cost-saving innovation increases the quantity supplied at each price. This is shown by the rightward shift in the supply curve, from S_0 to S_1. As a result of a cost-saving innovation, the quantity that is supplied at a price of $100 per ton rises from 115 000 to 132 000 tons per year. A similar rise occurs at every price.

paints, and to a large variety of new products made of plastics and synthetic fibers. Such inventions as silicon chips have radically changed products such as computers, televisions, and telephones, and the consequent development of smaller computers has revolutionized the production of countless other nonelectronic products.

Any technological innovation that decreases production costs will increase the profits that can be earned at any given price of the product. Because increased profitability leads to increased willingness to produce, this change shifts the supply curve to the right.

Number of Suppliers.   For given prices and technology, the total amount of any product supplied depends on the number of firms producing that product and offering it for sale. For example, in Chapter 9 we will examine the situation where profits made by existing firms producing a particular good attract other firms to enter the industry in pursuit of those profits. The effect of this increase in the number of suppliers is to shift the supply curve to the right. Similarly, if the existing firms are losing money, they will eventually leave the industry; such a reduction in the number of suppliers shifts the supply curve to the left.

Movements Along the Curve Versus Shifts of the Whole Curve

As with demand, it is important to distinguish movements along supply curves from shifts of the whole curve. Economists reserve the term **change in supply** to describe a shift of the whole supply curve—that is, a change in the quantity that will be supplied at every price. The term **change in quantity supplied** refers to a movement from one point on a supply curve to another point, either on the same supply curve or a new one. In other words, an increase in supply means that the whole supply curve has shifted to the right, so that the quantity supplied at any given price has increased; a movement up and to the right along a supply curve indicates an increase in the quantity supplied in response to an increase in the price of the product.

Practise with Study Guide Chapter 3, Exercise 6.

change in supply
A change in the quantity supplied at each possible price of the commodity, represented by a shift in the whole supply curve.

change in quantity supplied   A change in the specific quantity supplied, represented by a change from one point on a supply curve to another point, either on the original supply curve or on a new one.

A change in quantity supplied can result from a change in supply, with the price constant; from a movement along a given supply curve due to a change in the price; or from a combination of the two.

The Determination of Price

So far we have considered demand and supply separately. We now come to a key question: how do the two forces of demand and supply interact to determine price?

The Concept of a Market

Originally the term "market" designated a physical place where products were bought and sold. We still use the term this way to describe places such as Granville Island Market in Vancouver, Kensington Market in Toronto, or Jean Talon Market in Montreal. Once developed, however, theories of market behaviour were easily extended to cover products such as wheat or oil, which can be purchased anywhere in the world at a price that tends to be uniform the world over. The concepts of "the wheat market" or "the oil market" extend our viewpoint well beyond the idea of a single place to which the consumer goes to buy something.

market Any situation in which buyers and sellers can negotiate the exchange of goods or services.

For present purposes a **market** may be defined as existing in any situation (a physical place or an electronic medium) in which buyers and sellers negotiate the exchange of some product or related group of products. It must be possible, therefore, for buyers and sellers to communicate with each other and to make meaningful deals over the whole market.

Individual markets differ in the degree of *competition* among the various buyers and sellers. In the next few chapters we will confine ourselves to examining markets in which the number of buyers and sellers is sufficiently large that no one of them has any appreciable influence on the market price. This is a very rough definition of what economists call *perfectly competitive markets*. Starting in Chapter 10, we will consider the behaviour of markets in which there are small numbers of either sellers or buyers. But our initial theory of markets will actually be a very good description of the markets for such things as wheat, pork, newsprint, coffee, copper, and many other commodities.

Graphical Analysis of a Market

The table in Figure 3-7 brings together the demand and supply schedules from Figure 3-1 and 3-5. The quantities of carrots demanded and supplied at each price may now be compared.

excess demand A situation in which, at the given price, quantity demanded exceeds quantity supplied.

excess supply A situation in which, at the given price, quantity supplied exceeds quantity demanded.

There is only one price, $60 per ton, at which the quantity of carrots demanded equals the quantity supplied. At prices less than $60 per ton, there is a shortage of carrots because the quantity demanded exceeds the quantity supplied. This is a situation of **excess demand.** At prices greater than $60 per ton, there is a surplus of carrots because the quantity supplied exceeds the quantity demanded. This is a situation of **excess supply.** This same story can also be told in graphical terms. The quantities demanded and supplied at any price can be read off the two curves; the excess supply or excess demand is shown by the horizontal distance between the curves at each price.

FIGURE 3-7   Determination of the Equilibrium Price of Carrots

Price Per Ton ($) p	Quantity Demanded (thousands of tons per year) D	Quantity Supplied (thousands of tons per year) S	Excess Demand (+) or Excess Supply (−) (thousands of tons per year) $D - S$
20	110.0	5.0	+105.0
40	90.0	46.0	+44.0
60	77.5	77.5	0.0
80	67.5	100.0	−32.5
100	62.5	115.0	−52.5
120	60.0	122.5	−62.5

The equilibrium price corresponds to the intersection of the demand and supply curves. Equilibrium is indicated by E, which is point W on the demand curve and point w on the supply curve. At a price of $60, quantity demanded equals quantity supplied. At prices above equilibrium, there is excess supply and downward pressure on price. At prices below equilibrium, there is excess demand and upward pressure on price.

To examine the determination of market price, let's suppose first that the price is $100 per ton. At this price, 115 000 tons are offered for sale, but only 62 500 tons are demanded. There is an excess supply of 52 500 tons per year. Sellers are then likely to cut their prices to get rid of this surplus. And purchasers, observing the stock of unsold carrots, will begin to offer less money for the product. In other words, *excess supply causes downward pressure on price.*

Now consider the price of $20 per ton. At this price, there is excess demand. The 5000 tons produced each year are snapped up quickly, and 105 000 tons of desired purchases cannot be made. Rivalry between would-be purchasers may lead them to offer more than the prevailing price to outbid other purchasers. Also, sellers may begin to ask a higher price for the quantities that they do have to sell. In other words, *excess demand causes upward pressure on price.*

Finally, consider the price of $60. At this price, producers wish to sell 77 500 tons per year, and purchasers wish to buy that same quantity. There is neither a shortage nor a surplus of carrots. There are no unsatisfied buyers to bid the price up, nor are there unsatisfied sellers to force the price down. Once the price of $60 has been reached, therefore, there will be no tendency for it to change.

Equilibrium implies a state of rest, or balance, between opposing forces. The **equilibrium price** is the one toward which the actual market price will tend. It will persist, once established, unless it is disturbed by some change in market conditions which shifts the demand curve, the supply curve, or both.

equilibrium price
The price at which quantity demanded equals quantity supplied. Also called the market-clearing price.

The price at which the quantity demanded equals the quantity supplied is called the equilibrium price, or the market-clearing price. [5]

disequilibrium price
A price at which quantity demanded does not equal quantity supplied.

disequilibrium
A situation in a market in which there is excess demand or excess supply.

Any price at which the market does not "clear"—that is, quantity demanded does not equal quantity supplied—is called a **disequilibrium price.** Whenever there is either excess demand or excess supply in a market, that market is said to be in a state of **disequilibrium,** and the market price will be changing.

Figure 3-7 makes it clear that the equilibrium price occurs where the demand and supply curves intersect. Below that price, there is excess demand and hence upward pressure on the existing price. Above that price, there is excess supply and hence downward pressure on the existing price.

The Laws of Demand and Supply

Changes in any of the variables, other than price, that influence quantity demanded or supplied will cause a shift in the supply curve, the demand curve, or both. There are four possible shifts: an increase in demand (a rightward shift in the demand curve), a decrease in demand (a leftward shift in the demand curve), an increase in supply (a rightward shift in the supply curve), and a decrease in supply (a leftward shift in the supply curve).

comparative statics
The derivation of predictions by analysing the effect of a change in some exogenous variable on the equilibrium.

To discover the effects of each of the possible curve shifts, we use the method known as **comparative statics.**[2] With this method, we derive predictions by analysing the effect on the equilibrium of some change in which we are interested. We start from a position of equilibrium and then introduce the change to be studied. We then determine the new equilibrium position and compare it with the original one. The difference between the two positions of equilibrium must result from the change that was introduced because everything else has been held constant.

Each of the four possible curve shifts causes changes that are described by one of the four "laws" of demand and supply. Each of the laws summarizes what happens when an initial position of equilibrium is disturbed by a shift in either the demand curve or the supply curve. By using the term "law" to describe what happens, economists do not mean that they are absolutely certain of the outcome. The term "law" in science is used to describe a theory that has stood up to substantial testing. The laws of demand and supply are thus hypotheses that predict certain kinds of behaviour in certain situations, and the predicted behaviour occurs sufficiently often that economists continue to have confidence in the underlying theory.

The four laws of demand and supply are derived in Figure 3-8. Study the figure carefully. Previously, we had given the axes specific labels, but because it is now intended to apply to any product, the horizontal axis is simply labelled "Quantity." This means quantity per period in whatever units output is measured. "Price," the vertical axis, means the price measured as dollars per unit of quantity for the same product.

The four laws of demand and supply are as follows:

1. An increase in demand causes an increase in both the equilibrium price and the equilibrium quantity exchanged.

2. A decrease in demand causes a decrease in both the equilibrium price and the equilibrium quantity exchanged.

---

[2]The term *static* is used because we are not concerned with the actual path by which the market goes from the first equilibrium position to the second or with the time taken to reach the second equilibrium. Analysis of these movements would be described as *dynamic analysis.*

FIGURE 3-8   The Four "Laws" of Demand and Supply

(i) The effect of shifts in the demand curve

(ii) The effect of shifts in the supply curve

The effects on equilibrium price and quantity of shifts in either demand or supply are known as the laws of demand and supply.

A rise in demand. In part (i), suppose that the original demand and supply curves are D_0 and S, which intersect to produce equilibrium at E_0, with a price of p_0 and a quantity of q_0. An increase in demand shifts the demand curve to D_1, RIGHT taking the new equilibrium to E_1. Price rises to p_1 and quantity rises to q_1.

A fall in demand. In part (i), the original demand and supply curves are D_1 and S, which intersect to produce equilibrium at E_1, with a price of p_1 and a quantity of q_1. A decrease in demand shifts the demand curve to D_0, taking the new equilibrium to E_0. Price falls to p_0, and quantity falls to q_0. LEFT

A rise in supply. In part (ii), the original demand and supply curves are D and S_0, which intersect to produce equilibrium at E_0, with a price of p_0 and a quantity of q_0. An increase in supply shifts the supply curve to S_1, taking the new equilibrium to E_1. Price falls to p_1, and quantity rises to q_1. RIGHT

A fall in supply. In part (ii), the original demand and supply curves are D and S_1, which intersect to produce equilibrium at E_1, with a price of p_1 and a quantity of q_1. A decrease in supply shifts the supply curve to S_0, taking the new equilibrium to E_0. Price rises to p_0, and quantity falls to q_0. LEFT

3. An increase in supply causes a decrease in the equilibrium price and an increase in the equilibrium quantity exchanged.

4. A decrease in supply causes an increase in the equilibrium price and a decrease in the equilibrium quantity exchanged.

Demonstrations of these laws are given in the caption to Figure 3-8. The intuitive reasoning behind each is as follows:

1. An increase in demand creates a shortage at the initial equilibrium price, and the unsatisfied buyers bid up the price. This rise in price causes a larger quantity to be supplied with the result that at the new equilibrium, more is exchanged at a higher price.

2. A decrease in demand creates a glut at the initial equilibrium price, and the unsuccessful sellers bid the price down. As a result, less of the product is supplied and offered for sale. At the new equilibrium, both price and quantity exchanged are lower than they were originally.

3. An increase in supply creates a glut at the initial equilibrium price, and the unsuccessful suppliers force the price down. This drop in price increases the quantity demanded, and the new equilibrium is at a lower price and a higher quantity exchanged.

4. A decrease in supply creates a shortage at the initial equilibrium price that causes the price to be bid up. This rise in price reduces the quantity demanded, and the new equilibrium is at a higher price and a lower quantity exchanged.

Practise with Study Guide Chapter 3, Exercise 3.

In this chapter, we have studied many forces that can cause demand or supply curves to shift. By combining this analysis with the four laws of demand and supply, we can link many real-world events that cause demand or supply curves to shift with changes in market prices and quantities. *Applying Economic Concepts 3-1* shows how we can use demand-and-supply analysis to examine two real-world shocks: the effects of Brazil's 1994 coffee-crop failure and the effects of the 1998 ice storm in Eastern Canada. *Applying Economic Concepts 3-2* examines the effect of ongoing technological improvement on the price of computer chips.

The theory of the determination of price by demand and supply is beautiful in its simplicity. Yet as we shall see throughout this book, it is powerful in its wide range of applications.

Prices and Inflation

The theory we have developed explains how individual prices are determined by the forces of demand and supply. To facilitate matters, we have made *ceteris paribus* assumptions. Specifically, we have assumed the constancy of all prices except the one we are studying. Does this mean that our theory is inapplicable to an inflationary world in which all prices are rising at the same time? Fortunately, the answer is no.

absolute price   The amount of money that must be spent to acquire one unit of a commodity. Also called *money price*.

The price of a product is the amount of money that must be spent to acquire one unit of that product. This is called the **absolute price** or *money price*. A **relative price** is the ratio of two absolute prices; it expresses the price of one good in terms of (relative to) another.

We have been reminded several times that what matters for demand and supply is the price of the product in question *relative to the prices of other products;* that is, what matters is the relative price.

relative price   The ratio of the money price of one commodity to the money price of another commodity; that is, a ratio of two absolute prices.

In an inflationary world, we are often interested in the price of a given product as it relates to the average price of all other products. If, during a period when all prices were increasing by an average of 10 percent, the price of oranges rose by 30 percent, then the price of oranges rose relative to the prices of other goods as a whole. Oranges became *relatively* expensive. However, if oranges had risen in price by 30 percent when other prices increased by 40 percent, then the relative price of oranges would have fallen. Although the money price of oranges rose substantially, oranges became *relatively* cheap.

It has been convenient in this chapter to analyse changes in particular prices in the context of a constant price level. We can easily extend the analysis to an inflationary period by remembering that any force that raises the price of one product when other prices remain constant will, given general inflation, raise the price of that product faster than the price level is rising. For example, a change in tastes in favour of carrots that would raise their price by 5 percent when other prices were constant would raise their price by 8 percent if, at the same time, the general price level were rising by 3 percent. In each case, the price of carrots rises 5 percent *relative to the average of all prices*.

In microeconomics, whenever we refer to a change in the price of one product, we mean a change in that product's relative price; that is, a change in the price of that product relative to the prices of all other goods.

If the price level is constant, an increase in the product's relative price requires only a rise in the money price of the product. If the price level itself is rising, an increase in the product's relative price requires that the money price of the product rise faster than the price level.

APPLYING ECONOMIC CONCEPTS 3-1
Ice Storms, Droughts, and Economics

Here are two simple examples of the demand and supply apparatus in action. Both examples show how the weather—something that changes in unpredictable and often dramatic ways—can have significant effects on either the demand or the supply of various products, with obvious implications for the observed market price.

The Weather and a Demand Shock

In January of 1998, Quebec, eastern Ontario, and parts of the northeastern United States were hit by a massive ice storm. So unprecedented was this storm in its magnitude that many electric power systems were devastated. Homes and businesses in the Montreal area went without power for as long as four weeks.

This electric power shortage had many economic effects, including lost factory production, damage to much capital stock, the death of farm livestock, and the displacement of thousands of people, especially elderly people, into shelters where they could be fed and cared for. Another effect of the power shortage, as soon as it became clear that it would last for more than just a few hours, was a sudden and substantial increase in the demand for portable gas-powered electric generators. Within just a couple of days, all stores in the greater Montreal area were sold out of such generators, and the prices for newly ordered units had increased.

Furthermore, the shortages and price increases for electric generators were not confined to the area directly hit by the ice storm. As it became clear that there was an excess demand for generators in Quebec, sellers in other parts of the country began to divert their supply toward Quebec. This reduction in supply caused shortages, and thus price increases, in other parts of the country, as far away as Edmonton.

The Weather and a Supply Shock

Brazil, which produces one-third of the world's coffee, experienced unusually severe weather in 1994. Two killing frosts in June and July and a period of drought thereafter severely damaged the next year's crop. Some experts estimated that the frosts had destroyed as much as 45 percent of Brazil's 1995 harvest.

This crop damage meant that the world's supply curve of coffee shifted in—upward and to the left. Without a change in price, there would have been excess demand for coffee, with more people wanting to buy than wanting to sell. Predictably, the market forces reacted swiftly, and coffee prices soared by nearly 100 percent on the wholesale commodity market on July 14. Consumers also felt the impact of the supply shock, with retail prices climbing by about $5 per kilogram.

This severe weather hurt coffee growers in Brazil, reducing their incomes considerably. But coffee growers elsewhere—such as Colombia, Costa Rica and Kenya—actually benefited from Brazil's misfortune. They sold their normal-size crop at the elevated world price and thus enjoyed unusually high incomes.

The Quebec ice storm in January 1998 decimated the electricity distribution system. The demand for portable electricity generators (and many other emergency products) increased sharply as a result.

APPLYING ECONOMIC CONCEPTS 3-2

Technological Progress and the Market for Computer Chips

According to a June 1996 article in the *Financial Times*,

It is only nine months since the world semiconductor industry was forging ahead. Demand for chips was so great that there was a shortage, analysts were forecasting record growth and manufacturers were unveiling plans for dozens of $1 billion chip factories....

The euphoria has been short-lived. The shortage rapidly turned into surplus, and the price of dynamic random access memory (D-RAM) chips—the basic memory chips for PCs—has dropped by about 65 percent over the past six or seven months....

Commodity chip prices normally fall by 20 percent to 30 percent each year as manufacturing costs fall. But with manufacturers scrambling to protect market share, international spot market prices have fallen below the break-even point of some Asian manufacturers.

The newspaper story points to key aspects of this market. First, the technology of producing computer chips is evolving rapidly. This causes the market supply curve to shift continually to the right. Second, the demand curve has a negative slope, and shifts in some periods.

The trend decline of "20 percent to 30 percent each year" is clearly shown in the accompanying figure. So is the abnormal period between 1992 and 1995 when chip prices actually rose slightly before falling back sharply in 1996, as discussed above. What is the explanation?

In "normal" times the primary influence is that the ongoing technological improvement causes the supply curve to shift to the right along a nearly stationary demand curve. Chip prices fall and quantity demanded increases. In the 1992–95 period, however, the demand curve shifted sharply to the right. This increase in demand was due to the increased availability (and reduced prices) of such complementary software products as multimedia games and educational programs. By 1996, the demand curve had stopped shifting to the right but the supply curve had continued to shift, since the technolog-

ical improvements continued to occur. Hence prices returned to their "usual" downward trend.

Notice that the price rises associated with the temporary boom in demand between 1992 and 1995 would have increased the quantity supplied on each rightward-shifting supply curve because the high profitability of chip production encouraged higher production at each level of capacity. The fall in price in 1996 no doubt reduced the quantity supplied along the supply curve that existed at the time. However, despite the fall in price, the supply curve continued to shift to the right in successive periods as technological progress continued to reduce the costs of production.

S U M M A R Y

Demand   LO 1 2

- The amount of a product that consumers wish to purchase is called *quantity demanded.* It is a flow expressed as so much per period of time. It is determined by tastes, average household income, the product's own price, the prices of other products, the size of the population, the distribution of income among consumers, and expectations about the future.
- The relationship between quantity demanded and price is represented graphically by a demand curve that shows how much will be demanded at each market price. Quantity demanded is assumed to increase as the price of the product falls, other things held constant. Thus, demand curves are downward sloping.

- A shift in a demand curve represents a change in the quantity demanded at each price and is referred to as a *change in demand.* The demand curve shifts to the right (an increase in demand) if average income rises, if population rises, if the price of a substitute rises, if the price of a complement falls, or if there is a change in tastes in favour of the product. The opposite changes shift the demand curve to the left (a decrease in demand).
- It is important to make the distinction between a movement along a demand curve (caused by a change in the product's price) and a shift of a demand curve (caused by a change in any of the other determinants of demand).

Supply   LO 3 4

- The amount of a product that firms wish to sell is called *quantity supplied.* It is a flow expressed as so much per period of time. It depends on the product's own price, the costs of inputs, the number of suppliers, and the state of technology.
- The relationship between quantity supplied and price is represented graphically by a supply curve that shows how much will be supplied at each market price. Quantity supplied is assumed to increase as the price of the product increases, other things held constant. Thus, supply curves are upward sloping.

- A shift in the supply curve indicates a change in the quantity supplied at each price and is referred to as a *change in supply.* The supply curve shifts to the right (an increase in supply) if the costs of producing the product fall or if, for any reason, producers become more willing to produce the product. The opposite changes shift the supply curve to the left (a decrease in supply).
- It is important to make the distinction between a movement along a supply curve (caused by a change in the product's price) and a shift of a supply curve (caused by a change in any of the other determinants of supply).

The Determination of Price   LO 5 6

- The *equilibrium price* is the price at which the quantity demanded equals the quantity supplied. At any price below equilibrium, there will be excess demand; at any price above equilibrium, there will be excess supply. Graphically, equilibrium occurs where the demand and supply curves intersect.

- Price rises when there is excess demand and falls when there is excess supply. Thus the actual market price will be pushed toward the equilibrium price. When it is reached, there will be neither excess demand nor excess supply, and the price will not change until either the supply curve or the demand curve shifts.

- Using the method of *comparative statics,* we can determine the effects of a shift in either demand or supply. An increase in demand raises both equilibrium price and equilibrium quantity; a decrease in demand lowers both. An increase in supply raises equilibrium quantity but lowers equilibrium price; a decrease in supply lowers equilibrium quantity but raises equilibrium price. These are called the laws of demand and supply.

- The absolute price of a product is its price in terms of money; its relative price is its price in relation to other products. In an inflationary period, a rise in the *relative price* of one product means that its absolute price rises by more than the price level; a fall in its relative price means that its absolute price rises by less than the price level.

K E Y   C O N C E P T S

"Ceteris paribus" or "other things being equal"

Quantity demanded and quantity actually bought

Demand schedule and demand curve

Change in quantity demanded versus change in demand

Quantity supplied and quantity actually sold

Supply schedule and supply curve

Change in quantity supplied versus change in supply

Equilibrium, equilibrium price, and disequilibrium

Comparative statics

Laws of supply and demand

Relative price

S T U D Y   E X E R C I S E S

1. Consider households' demand for chicken meat. For each of the events listed below, state and explain the likely effect on the demand for chicken. How would each event be illustrated in a diagram?

   a. A medical study reports that eating chicken meat reduces the likelihood of suffering from particular types of heart problems.
   b. A widespread bovine disease leads to an increase in the price of beef.
   c. An increase in average household income.

2. Consider the world market for a particular quality of coffee beans. The following table shows the demand and supply schedules for this market.

Price (per kg)	Quantity Demanded	Quantity Supplied
	(millions of kg per year)	
$2.00	28	10
$2.40	26	12
$3.10	22	13.5
$3.50	19.5	19.5
$3.90	17	22
$4.30	14.5	23.5

   a. Plot the demand and supply schedules on a scale diagram.
   b. Identify the amount of excess demand or supply associated with each price.
   c. Identify the equilibrium price in this market.
   d. Suppose that government (or a collection of national governments) were somehow able to set a minimum price for coffee equal to $3.90 per kg. Explain the outcome in the world coffee market.

3. Consider the supply for grade-A beef. As the price of beef rises, ranchers will tend to sell more cattle to the slaughter houses. Yet, a central prediction from the supply-and-demand model of this chapter is that an increase in the supply of beef reduces the equilibrium price. Reconcile the apparent contradiction. Use a diagram to do so.

4. Consider the world market for wheat. Suppose there is a major failure in Russia's wheat crop due to a severe drought. Explain the likely effect on the equilibrium price and quantity in the world wheat market. Also explain why North American wheat farmers certainly benefit from Russia's drought. Draw a diagram to carefully describe and analyse the situation.

5. The *New York Times* recently stated:

   > *While the world's appetite for chocolate grows more voracious each year, cocoa farms around the globe are failing, under siege from fungal and viral diseases and insects....Researchers predict a shortfall in beans from the cacao tree, the raw material from which chocolate is made, in as little as five to ten years.*

   Describe in terms of the supply-and-demand apparatus what is described in the quote. What is the implied prediction for the equilibrium price of chocolate? What is the implied prediction for the equilibrium quantity of chocolate?

6. This is a challenging question intended for those students who like mathematics. It requires you to solve a supply-and-demand model as a system of *simultaneous equations* (meaning simply that both equations apply at the same time). Letting p be the price of the product, suppose the demand and supply functions for some product are given by

   $$Q^D = 100 - 3p$$
   $$Q^S = 10 + 2p$$

   a. Plot both the demand curve and the supply curve.
   b. What is the condition for equilibrium in this market?
   c. By imposing the condition for equilibrium, solve for the equilibrium price.
   d. Substitute the equilibrium price into either the demand or supply function to solve for the equilibrium quantity. Check to make sure you get the same answer whether you use the demand function or the supply function.
   e. Now suppose there is an increase in demand so that the new demand function is given by

   $$Q^D = 180 - 3p.$$

   Compute the new equilibrium price and quantity. Is your result consistent with the "law" of demand?
   f. Now suppose that, with the new demand curve in place, there is an increase in supply so that the new supply function is given by $Q^S = 90 + 2p$. Compute the new equilibrium price and quantity. Is your result consistent with the "law" of supply?

DISCUSSION QUESTIONS

1. Recently, a government economist predicted that this spring's excellent weather would result in larger crops of wheat and canola than farmers had expected. But the economist warned consumers not to expect prices to decrease because the cost of production was rising and foreign demand for Canadian crops was increasing. "The classic pattern of supply and demand won't work this time," the economist said. Discuss his observation.

2. What would be the effect on the equilibrium price and quantity of marijuana if its sale and consumption were legalized?

3. Classify the effect of each of the following as (i) a decrease in the demand for fish or (ii) a decrease in the quantity of fish demanded. Illustrate each diagrammatically.

   a. The government of Canada closes the Atlantic cod fishery.
   b. People buy less fish because of a rise in fish prices.
   c. The Catholic Church relaxed its ban on eating meat on Fridays.

   d. The price of beef falls and, as a result, consumers buy more beef and less fish.
   e. Fears of mercury pollution lead locals to shun fish caught in nearby lakes.
   f. It is generally alleged that eating fish is better for one's health than eating meat.

4. Predict the effect on the price of at least one product of each of the following events:

   a. Winter snowfall is at a record high in the interior of British Columbia, but drought continues in Quebec ski areas.
   b. A recession decreases employment in Oshawa automobile factories.
   c. The French grape harvest is the smallest in 20 years.
   d. The province of Ontario cancels permission for citizens to cut firewood in provincial camp grounds.

5. Are the following two observations inconsistent? (a) Rising demand for housing causes prices of new homes to soar. (b) Many families refuse to buy homes as prices become prohibitive for them.

CHAPTER 4

Elasticity

🔟 *LEARNING OBJECTIVES*

1 Understand the measurement of price elasticity of demand, and know its determinants.

2 Understand the measurement of price elasticity of supply, and know its determinants.

3 Explain how an excise (or sales) tax affects the producer price and the consumer price.

4 Recognize that the incidence of a sales tax depends on relative demand and supply elasticities.

5 Understand the effect of income on quantity demanded, and how this elasticity defines normal and inferior goods.

6 Recognize the difference between substitute and complement goods, and how the degree of substitutability can be measured by the cross elasticity of demand.

The laws of demand and supply predict the *direction* of changes in price and quantity in response to various shifts in demand and supply. However, it usually is not enough to know merely whether price and quantity simply rise or fall; it is also important to know by *how much* each changes.

In the previous chapter we discussed the coffee-crop failure in Brazil and how this drove up the world coffee price. But what did this crop failure do to the incomes of Brazilian coffee growers? If the world price increased by more (in percentage terms) than their crop shrank, their incomes would have actually *increased*; that is, the crop failure actually would have made them, as a group, better off. On the other hand, if the price increased by less than the crop shrank, their incomes would have fallen.

Measuring and describing the extent of the responsiveness of quantities to changes in prices and other variables are often essential if we are to understand the significance of these changes. Such measurement is accomplished with the concept of *elasticity*.

Price Elasticity of Demand

Suppose there is an increase in the supply of some farm crop—that is, a rightward shift in the supply curve. We saw in Figure 3-8 when we examined the laws of supply and demand that such an increase in supply will cause the equilibrium price to fall and the equilibrium quantity to rise. But by how much will each change? The answer depends on what is called the *price elasticity of demand*.

Loosely speaking, demand is said to be *elastic* when quantity demanded is quite responsive to changes in price. When quantity demanded is quite unresponsive to changes in price, demand is said to be *inelastic*.

The meaning of elasticity is illustrated in the two parts of Figure 4-1. The two parts of the figure have the same initial equilibrium, and that equilibrium is disturbed by the same leftward shift in the supply curve. But, because the demand curves are different in the two parts of the figure, the new equilibrium position is different, and hence the magnitude

FIGURE 4-1   The Effect of the Shape of the Demand Curve

(i) Relatively elastic demand   (ii) Relatively inelastic demand

The more responsive the quantity demanded is to changes in price, the less the change in price and the greater the change in quantity resulting from any given shift in the supply curve. Both parts of the figure are drawn to the same scale. They show the same initial equilibrium and the same shift in the supply curve. In each part, initial equilibrium is at price p_0 and output q_0 and the new equilibrium is at p_1 and q_1. In part (i), the effect of the shift in supply from S_0 to S_1 is a slight rise in the price and a large decrease in quantity. In part (ii), the effect of the identical shift in the supply curve from S_0 to S_1 is a large increase in the price and a relatively small decrease in quantity.

of the effects of the increase in supply on equilibrium price and quantity are different. The demand curve in part (i) is more elastic than the demand curve in part (ii).

A shift in supply will have different quantitative effects, depending on the shape of the demand curve. The difference may be significant for government policy. Suppose the market being depicted in Figure 4-1 is the market for cigarettes, and that the government imposes a tax on each pack of cigarettes sold (as the federal government and all Canadian provincial governments do). As we will see later in this chapter, the effect of such a tax is to shift the supply curve of cigarettes upward by the amount of the tax—a reduction in supply.

Part (i) of Figure 4-1 illustrates a case in which the quantity that consumers demand is relatively responsive to price changes—that is, demand is relatively elastic. The reduction in supply pushes up the price, but, because the quantity demanded is quite responsive, only a small change in price is necessary to restore equilibrium. Thus, the effect of the government's policy is to achieve a large decrease in the production (and consumption) of cigarettes and only a small increase in price.

Part (ii) of Figure 4-1 shows a case in which the quantity demanded is relatively unresponsive to price changes—that is, demand is relatively inelastic. As before, the decrease in supply at the original price causes a shortage that increases the price. However, this time the quantity demanded by consumers does not fall much in response to the rise in price. The result is that equilibrium price rises more, and equilibrium quantity falls less, than in the first case. The effect of the government's policy is to achieve a large increase in the price of cigarettes but only a small decrease in the quantity purchased.

In both of the cases shown in Figure 4-1, the government's policy has exactly the same effectiveness as far as the producers' willingness to supply the commodity is concerned—the shifts of the supply curve are identical. The magnitude of the effects on the equilibrium price and quantity, however, is different because of the different elasticities of demand.

If the objective of the government's policy is to decrease the quantity of cigarettes consumed, the policy will be more successful if the demand curve is similar to the one shown in part (i) of Figure 4-1 than if it is similar to the one shown in part (ii). If, however, the goal of the policy is to achieve a large increase in the price of cigarettes, the policy will be less successful if demand is as shown in part (i) than if it is as shown in part (ii).

The Measurement of Price Elasticity

In Figure 4-1, we were able to say that the curve in part (i) showed a demand that was more responsive to price changes than the curve in part (ii) because two conditions were fulfilled. First, both curves were drawn on the same scale. Second, the initial equilibrium prices and quantities were the same in both parts of the figure. Let us see why these conditions matter.

First, by drawing both figures on the same scale, the curve that looked steeper actually did have the larger absolute slope. (The slope of a demand curve tells us the number of dollars by which price must change to cause a unit change in quantity demanded.)

		Increase in
	Reduction in Price	Quantity Demanded
Commodity	(cents)	(per month)
Cheese	40 per kilogram	7500 kilograms
T-shirts	40 per shirt	5000 shirts
CD players	40 per CD player	100 CD players

TABLE 4-1   Price Reductions and Corresponding Increases in Quantity Demanded for Three Products

The data show, for each of the three products, the change in quantity demanded resulting from the same absolute fall in price. The data are fairly uninformative about the responsiveness of demand to price because they do not tell us either the original price or the original quantity demanded.

If we had drawn the two curves on different scales, we could have concluded nothing about the relative price changes needed to get a unit change in quantity demanded by comparing their appearances on the graph.

Second, because we started from the same price-quantity equilibrium in both parts of the figure, we did not need to distinguish between *percentage* changes and *absolute* changes. If the initial prices and quantities are the same in both cases, the larger absolute change is also the larger percentage change. However, when we wish to deal with different initial price-quantity equilibria, we need to decide whether we are interested in absolute or percentage changes. To see which is relevant, let's suppose that we have the information shown in Table 4-1. Should we conclude that the demand for portable CD players is not as responsive to price changes as the demand for cheese? After all, price cuts of 40 cents cause quite a large increase in the quantity of cheese demanded but only a small increase in the quantity demanded of CD players.

It should be obvious that a reduction in the price of 40 cents will be a large price cut for a low-priced product and an insignificant price cut for a high-priced product. All of the price reductions listed in Table 4-1 represent price reductions of 40 cents, but they are clearly different proportions of the respective prices. It is usually more revealing to know the *percentage* change in the prices of the various products. For similar reasons knowing the quantity by which demand changes is not very revealing unless the initial level of demand is also known. An increase of 7500 kilograms is quite a significant reaction to demand if the quantity formerly bought was 15 000 kilograms, but it is insignificant if the quantity formerly bought was 10 million kilograms.

Table 4-2 shows the original and new levels of price and quantity. Changes in price and quantity expressed as percentages of the *average* prices and quantities are shown in columns (1) and (2) of Table 4-3. The **price elasticity of demand,** the measure of responsiveness of quantity of a product demanded to a change in that product's price, is symbolized by the Greek letter eta, η. It is defined as follows:

price elasticity of demand (η) A measure of the responsiveness of quantity demanded to a change in the commodity's own price.

$$\eta = \frac{\text{percentage change in quantity demanded}}{\text{percentage change in price}}$$

This measure is called the price elasticity of demand, or simply *demand elasticity.* Because the variable causing the change in quantity demanded is the product's own price, the term *own-price elasticity of demand* is also used.

TABLE 4-2   Price and Quantity Information Underlying Data of Table 4-1

Product	Unit	Original Price ($)	New Price ($)	Average Price ($)	Original Quantity	New Quantity	Average Quantity
Cheese	kg	3.40	3.00	3.20	116 250	123 750	120 000
T-shirts	shirt	16.20	15.80	16.00	197 500	202 500	200 000
CD players	player	80.20	79.80	80.00	9 950	10 050	10 000

These data provide the appropriate context for the data given in Table 4-1. The table relates the 40-cent-per-unit price reduction of each product to the actual prices and quantities demanded.

TABLE 4-3 Calculation of Demand Elasticities

Product	(1) Percentage Decrease in Price	(2) Percentage Increase in Quantity	(3) Elasticity of Demand (2) ÷ (1)
Cheese	12.5	6.25	0.5
T-shirts	2.5	2.50	1.0
CD players	0.5	1.00	2.0

Elasticity of demand is the percentage change in quantity demanded divided by the percentage change in price. The percentage changes are based on average prices and quantities shown in Table 4-2. For example, the 40-cent-per-kilogram decrease in the price of cheese is 12.5 percent of $3.20. A 40-cent change in the price of CD players is only 0.5 percent of the average price per CD player of $80.00.

The Use of Average Price and Quantity in Computing Elasticity

The caption in Table 4-3 stresses that the demand elasticities are computed using changes in price and quantity measured in terms of the *average* values of each. Averages are used to avoid the ambiguity caused by the fact that when a price or quantity changes, the change is a different percentage of the original value than it is of the new value. For example, the 40-cent change in the price of cheese shown in Table 4-2 represents an 11.8 percent change of the original price of $3.40 but a 13.3 percent change of the new price of $3.00.

Using average values for price and quantity means that the measured elasticity of demand between any two points on the demand curve, call them A and B, is independent of whether the movement is from A to B or from B to A. In the example of cheese in Tables 4-2 and 4-3, the 40-cent change in the price of cheese is unambiguously 12.5 percent of the average price of $3.20, and that percentage applies to a price increase from $3.00 to $3.40 or for a price decrease from $3.40 to $3.00.

The implications of using average values for price and quantity for calculating elasticity are as follows. Consider a change from an initial price of p_0 and quantity of q_0 to a new price of p_1 and quantity of q_1. The formula for elasticity is then

$$\eta = \frac{(q_1 - q_0)/q}{(p_1 - p_0)/p} \qquad (4\text{-}1)$$

where p and q are the average price and average quantity, respectively. Thus

$$p = (p_1 + p_0)/2 \quad \text{and} \quad q = (q_1 + q_0)/2.$$

We can substitute these expressions for p and q in Equation 4-1 and, after dividing out the factors of 2, we get

$$\eta = \frac{(q_1 - q_0)/(q_1 + q_0)}{(p_1 - p_0)/(p_1 + p_0)} \qquad (4\text{-}2)$$

which provides a convenient formula for calculating demand elasticity. For example, for the case of cheese in Tables 4-2 and 4-3, we have

$$\eta = \frac{7500/240\,000}{0.40/6.40} = \frac{0.03125}{0.0625} = 0.5$$

which is as in Table 4-3. There is further discussion of the use of averages to calculate elasticity and of alternative methods in the appendix to this chapter. [6]

Interpreting Numerical Elasticities

Because demand curves have negative slopes, an increase in price is associated with a decrease in quantity demanded, and vice versa. Because the percentage changes in price and quantity have opposite signs, demand elasticity is a negative number. However, we will follow the usual practice of ignoring the negative sign and speak of the measure as a positive number, as we have done in the illustrative calculations in Table 4-3. Thus the more responsive the quantity demanded (for example, CD players relative to cheese), the greater the elasticity of demand and the higher the measure (e.g., 2.0 compared with 0.5).

The numerical value of demand elasticity can vary from zero to infinity. Elasticity is zero when quantity demanded does not respond at all to a price change. As long as the percentage change in quantity demanded is less than the percentage change in price, the elasticity of demand has a value of less than one (economists sometimes say less than *unity*). When the two percentage changes are equal, elasticity is equal to one. When the percentage change in quantity demanded exceeds the percentage change in price, the elasticity of demand is greater than one.

When the percentage change in quantity demanded is less than the percentage change in price (elasticity less than 1), there is said to be **inelastic demand**. When the percentage change in quantity is greater than the percentage change in price (elasticity greater than 1), there is said to be **elastic demand**. This important terminology is summarized in part A of *Extensions in Theory 4-1*, which is found toward the end of the chapter.

A demand curve need not, and usually does not, have the same elasticity over every part of the curve. Figure 4-2 shows that a negatively sloped straight-line demand curve does not have a constant elasticity, even though it does have a constant slope. A straight-line demand curve has constant elasticity only when it is vertical or horizontal. Figure 4-3 illustrates these two cases, in addition to a third case of a particular *nonlinear* demand curve that also has a constant elasticity.

FIGURE 4-2   Elasticity Along a Straight-Line Demand Curve

Moving down a straight-line demand curve, elasticity falls continuously. On this straight-line demand curve, a reduction in price of $0.20 always leads to the same increase (1000 units) in quantity demanded.

Near the upper end of the curve, where price is $3.80 and quantity demanded is 1000 units, a reduction in price of $0.20 (from $3.90 to $3.70) is just slightly more than a 5 percent reduction, but the 1000-unit increase in quantity demanded is a 100 percent increase. Here, elasticity is 19.

Near the lower end, at a price of $1.00 and a quantity of 15 000 units, a price reduction of $0.20 (from $1.10 to $0.90) leads to the same 1000-unit increase in quantity demanded. However, the $0.20 price reduction represents a 20 percent fall, whereas the 1000-unit increase in quantity demanded represents only a 6.67 percent increase. Here, elasticity is 0.33.

What Determines Elasticity of Demand?

The main determinant of demand elasticity is the availability of substitutes. Some products, such as margarine, broccoli, lamb, and Toyota cars, have quite close substitutes—butter, other green vegetables, beef, and Mazda cars. A change in the prices of these products, *with the prices of the substitutes remaining constant,* can be expected to cause much substitution. A fall in price leads consumers to buy more of the product and less of the substitutes, and a rise in price leads consumers to buy less of the product and more of the substitutes. Products defined more broadly, such as *all* foods or *all* clothing or *all* methods of transportation, have many fewer satisfactory substitutes. A rise in their prices can be expected to cause a smaller fall in quantities demanded than would be the case if close substitutes were available.

A product with close substitutes tends to have an elastic demand; a product with no close substitutes tends to have an inelastic demand.

inelastic demand The situation in which, for a given percentage change in price, there is a smaller percentage change in quantity demanded; elasticity less than one.

elastic demand The situation in which, for a given percentage change in price, there is a greater percentage change in quantity demanded; elasticity greater than one.

FIGURE 4-3   Three Demand Curves with Constant Elasticity

Each of these demand curves has a constant elasticity. D_1 has zero elasticity: The quantity demanded is equal to q_0, independent of the price. D_2 has infinite elasticity at the price p_0: A small price increase from p_0 decreases quantity demanded from an indefinitely large amount to zero. D_3 has unit elasticity: A given percentage increase in price brings an equal percentage decrease in quantity demanded at all points on the curve; it is a rectangular hyperbola for which price times quantity demanded is a constant.

Demand elasticity depends on the availability of substitutes. The availability of a product's substitutes, in turn, depends on how the product is defined and on the time period being considered. We explore these aspects next.

Definition of the Product

For food taken as a whole, demand is inelastic over a large price range. It does not follow, however, that any one food, such as white bread or peanut butter, is a necessity in the same sense. Individual foods can have quite elastic demands, and they frequently do.

Clothing provides a similar example. Clothing as a whole has a less elastic demand than do individual kinds of clothes. For example, when the price of wool sweaters rises, many households may buy cotton sweaters or down vests instead of buying an additional wool sweater. Thus, although purchases of wool sweaters fall, total purchases of clothing do not.

Any one of a group of related products will have a more elastic demand than the group as a whole.

Short Run and Long Run

Because it takes time to develop satisfactory substitutes, a demand that is inelastic in the short run may prove to be elastic when enough time has passed. Perhaps the most dramatic example of this principle occurred in 1973 when the Organization of Petroleum Exporting Countries (OPEC) shocked the world with its sudden and large increase in the price of oil. At that time, the short-run demand for oil proved to be highly inelastic. Large price increases were met in the short run by very small reductions in quantity demanded. In this case, the short run lasted for several years. Gradually, however, the high price of petroleum products led to such adjustments as the development of smaller, more fuel-efficient cars, economizing on heating oil by installing more efficient insulation, and replacement of fuel oil in many industrial processes with such other power sources as coal and hydroelectricity. The long-run elasticity of demand, relating the change in price to the change in quantity demanded after all adjustments were made, turned out to have an elasticity of well over unity, although the long-run adjustments took as much as a decade to work out.

The response to a price change, and thus the measured price elasticity of demand, will tend to be greater the longer the time span.

For such products as cornflakes and pillowcases, the full response to a price change occurs quickly, and there is little reason to make the distinction between short-run and long-run effects. But other products are typically used in connection with highly durable appliances or machines. A change in the price of, say, electricity and gasoline may not have its major effect until the stock of appliances and machines using these products has been adjusted. This adjustment may take several years to occur.

For products for which substitutes are developed over a period of time, it is helpful to identify two kinds of demand curves. A *short-run demand curve* shows the response of quantity demanded to a change in price for a given structure of the durable goods that use the product and for the existing sets of substitute products. A different short-run demand curve will exist for each such structure. The *long-run demand curve* shows the response of quantity demanded to a change in price after enough time has passed to ensure that all adjustments to the changed price have occurred.

The long-run demand for a product is more elastic than the short-run demand.

Figure 4-4 shows the short-run and long-run effects of an increase in supply. In the short run, the supply increase leads to a movement down the relatively inelastic short-run demand curve; it thus causes a large fall in price but only a small increase in quantity. In the long run, demand is more elastic; thus long-run equilibrium has price and quantity above those that prevailed in short-run equilibrium.

This pattern is often referred to as *overshooting* of the price. The overshooting of price that is evident in the figure is the way in which markets clear when demand is less elastic in the short run than in the long run. Note also that there is *undershooting* of quantity—that is, the equilibrium quantity rises by less in the short run than in the long run.

Elasticity and Total Expenditure

We know that quantity demanded increases as price falls, but what happens to the total expenditure on that product? It turns out that the response of total expenditure depends on the price elasticity of demand.

To see the relationship between the elasticity of demand and total expenditure, we begin by noting that total expenditure is equal to price times quantity:

$$\text{Total Expenditure} = \text{Price} \times \text{Quantity}$$

Because price and quantity move in opposite directions along a demand curve, one falling when the other rises, the change in total expenditure appears to be ambiguous. It is easily shown, however, that the direction of change in total expenditure depends on the relative percentage changes in the price and quantity. If the percentage change in price exceeds the percentage change in quantity, the price change will dominate, and total expenditure will change in the same direction as the price changes; this is the case where elasticity is less than unity. If the percentage change in the price is less than the percentage change in the quantity demanded (elasticity exceeds unity), the quantity change will dominate, and total expenditure will

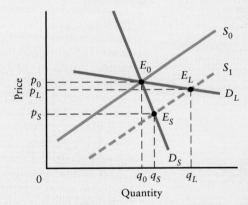

Because most people cannot easily or quickly change their method of transportation, the demand for gasoline is much less elastic in the short run than in the long run.

FIGURE 4-4   Short-Run and Long-Run Equilibrium Following an Increase in Supply

The magnitude of the changes in the equilibrium price and quantity following a shift in supply depends on the time allowed for demand to adjust. The initial equilibrium is at E_0, with price p_0 and quantity q_0. Supply then increases such that the supply curve shifts from S_0 to S_1.

On impact, the relevant demand curve is the short-run curve D_S, and the new equilibrium immediately following the supply shock is E_S. Price falls sharply to p_S, and quantity rises only to q_S. In the long run, the demand curve is the more elastic one given by D_L, and equilibrium is at E_L. The long-run equilibrium price is p_L (greater than p_S), and quantity is q_L (greater than q_S).

FIGURE 4-5   Total Expenditure and Quantity Demanded

Price ($)	Quantity Demanded	Expenditure ($)
3.80	1 000	3 800
3.00	5 000	15 000
2.50	7 500	18 750
2.00	10 000	20 000
1.50	12 500	18 750
1.00	15 000	15 000

The change in total expenditure on a product in response to a change in price depends on the elasticity of demand. The table and graph are based on the demand curve shown in Figure 4-2. For quantities demanded that are less than 10 000, elasticity of demand is greater than one, and hence any increase in quantity demanded will be proportionately larger than the fall in price that caused it. In that range, total expenditure is increasing. For quantities greater than 10 000, elasticity of demand is less than one, and hence any increase in quantity demanded will be proportionately smaller than the fall in price that caused it. In that range, total expenditure is decreasing. The maximum of total expenditure occurs where the elasticity of demand equals one.

Practise with Study Guide Chapter 4, Exercises 3 and 5.

For information on OPEC and its activities, see www.opec.org.

change in the same direction as quantity changes. If the two percentage changes are equal, total expenditure is unchanged—this is the case of unit elasticity.

Figure 4-5 illustrates the relationship between elasticity of demand and total expenditure; it is based on the straight-line demand curve in Figure 4-2. Total expenditure at each of a number of points on the demand curve is calculated in the table, and the general relationship between total expenditure and quantity demanded is shown by the plotted curve. In the figure we see that expenditure reaches its maximum when elasticity is equal to 1. [7]

The following example uses this relationship between elasticity, price and total expenditure. When a bumper potato crop recently sent prices down 50 percent (a rightward shift in the supply curve), the quantity purchased increased by only 15 percent. Demand was clearly inelastic, and the result of the bumper crop was that total expenditure on potatoes *fell* sharply. Potato farmers, therefore, experienced a sharp fall in income.

A second example relates to the OPEC oil shock in the early 1970s. As the OPEC countries acted together to restrict supply and push up the world price of oil, quantity demanded fell, but only by a small percentage—much smaller than the percentage increase in price. World demand for oil (at least in the short run) was very inelastic, and the result was that total expenditure on oil *increased* dramatically. The OPEC oil producers, therefore, experienced an enormous increase in income.

Price Elasticity of Supply

price elasticity of supply (η_S)   A measure of the responsiveness of quantity supplied to a change in the commodity's own price.

The concept of elasticity can be applied to supply as well as to demand. **Price elasticity of supply** measures the responsiveness of the quantity supplied to a change in the product's price. It is denoted η_S and defined as follows:

$$\eta_s = \frac{\text{percentage change in quantity supplied}}{\text{percentage change in price}}$$

This is often called *supply elasticity*. The supply curves considered in this chapter all have positive slopes: An increase in price causes an increase in quantity supplied. Such supply curves all have positive elasticities because price and quantity change in the same direction.

There are important special cases. If the supply curve is vertical—the quantity supplied does not change as price changes—then elasticity of supply is zero. A horizontal supply curve has an infinite elasticity of supply: A small drop in price will reduce the quantity that producers are willing to supply from an indefinitely large amount to zero. Between these two extremes, elasticity of supply varies with the shape of the supply curve. Loosely speaking, steeper supply curves imply a smaller quantity response for a given change in price, and thus a lower elasticity.

Note, however, that a steeper supply curve does *not always* reflect less elastic supply. There is an important special case worth remembering. Students are quite often surprised to learn that straight-line supply curves *that pass through the origin* have a particular characteristic.

Any positively sloped straight-line supply curve through the origin has a price elasticity equal to one.

Such a supply curve is shown in Figure 4-6. To see that the price elasticity is equal to one, consider two triangles in the figure. The first has the sides p, q, and the S curve; the second has the sides Δp, Δq, and the S curve. These are similar triangles. It follows that the ratios of their sides are equal. That is,

$$p/q = \Delta p/\Delta q$$

From our earlier discussion, elasticity of supply is defined as

$$\eta_s = (\Delta q/\Delta p) \times (p/q)$$

which, by substitution, gives

$$\eta_s = (q/p) \times (p/q) = 1$$

FIGURE 4-6   A Straight-Line Supply Curve Through the Origin

At every point on the supply curve, p/q equals $\Delta p/\Delta q$; hence supply elasticity equals unity at every point.

Determinants of Supply Elasticity

Because much of the treatment of demand elasticity carries over to supply elasticity, we can cover the main points quickly.

Substitution and Production Costs

The ease of substitution can vary in production as well as in consumption. If the price of a product rises, how much more can be produced profitably? This depends in part on how easy it is for producers to shift from the production of other products to the one whose price has risen. If agricultural land and labour can be readily shifted from one crop to another, the supply of any one crop will be more elastic than if they cannot. Or, if machines used to produce coats can be easily modified to produce pants (and vice versa), then the supply of both pants and coats will be more elastic than if the machines cannot be so easily modified.

Supply elasticity depends to a great extent on how costs behave as output is varied. If the costs of producing a unit of output rise rapidly as output rises, then the stimulus to expand production in response to a rise in price will quickly be choked off by increases in costs. In this case, supply will tend to be rather inelastic. If, however, the costs of producing a unit of output rise only slowly as production increases, a rise in price that raises profits will elicit a large increase in quantity supplied before the rise in costs puts a halt to the expansion in output. In this case, supply will tend to be rather elastic.

Short Run and Long Run

As with demand, length of time for response is important. It may be difficult to change quantities supplied in response to a price increase in a matter of weeks or months but easy to do so over a period of years. An obvious example is the planting cycle of crops. An increase in the price of wheat that occurs in mid-summer may lead wheat farmers to be more careful (and less wasteful) in their harvesting this fall, but it occurs too late to influence how much wheat gets planted for this years' crop. But if the high price persists, it will surely influence how much wheat gets planted next spring. Also, new oil fields can be discovered, wells drilled, and pipelines built over a period of years but not in just a few months. Thus the elasticity of oil supply is much greater over five years than over one year.

As with demand, it is useful to make the distinction between the short-run and the long-run supply curve. The *short-run supply curve* shows the response of quantity supplied to a change in price given producers' current capacity to produce the good. The *long-run supply curve* shows the response of quantity supplied to a change in price after enough time has passed to allow producers to adjust their productive capacity.

The long-run supply for a product is more elastic than the short-run supply.

Figure 4-7 illustrates the short-run and long-run effects of an increase in demand. The short-run overshooting of price and the undershooting of quantity that are evident in the figure are analogous to that shown in Figure 4-4 when we examined the short-run and long-run effects following a shift in supply. Here it arises following a shift in demand and is the market-clearing response when supply is less elastic in the short run than in the long run.

FIGURE 4-7   Short-Run and Long-Run Equilibrium Following an Increase in Demand

The size of the changes in the equilibrium price and quantity following a shift in demand depends on the time frame of the analysis. The initial equilibrium is at E_0, with price p_0 and quantity q_0. Demand then increases such that the demand curve shifts from D_0 to D_1.

On impact, the relevant supply curve is the short-run curve S_S, so that the new equilibrium immediately following the demand shock is at E_S. Price rises sharply to p_S, and quantity rises only to q_S. In the long run, the supply curve is the more elastic one given by S_L. The long-run equilibrium is at E_L; price is p_L (less than p_S) and quantity is q_L (greater than q_S).

An Important Example Where Elasticity Matters

So far, this chapter has been fairly tough going. We have spent much time examining price elasticity (of both demand and supply) and how to measure it. But who cares? In this section we explore the important concept of *tax incidence* and show that elasticity is crucial to determining whether consumers or producers (or both) end up being harmed by excise taxes.

The federal and provincial governments levy special sales taxes (called **excise taxes**) on many goods such as cigarettes, alcohol, and gasoline. All such taxes work in the following way. At the point of sale of the product, the sellers collect the tax on behalf of the government and then periodically remit the tax collections.

When the sellers write their cheques to the government, these firms feel—with some justification—that they are the ones paying the tax. Consumers, however, argue—again, with some justification—that *they* are the ones who are shouldering the burden of the tax because the tax causes the price of the product to rise.

The question of who *bears the burden* of a tax is called the question of **tax incidence**. A straightforward application of demand-and-supply analysis will show that tax incidence has nothing to do with whether the government collects the tax directly from consumers or from firms.

> The burden of a sales (or excise) tax is distributed between consumers and sellers in a manner that depends on the relative elasticities of supply and demand.

At the beginning of this chapter we considered a government that taxed the sale of cigarettes. Let's examine that possibility again in a little more detail. We begin with Figure 4-8. To simplify the problem, we analyse the case where there is initially no tax. The equilibrium without taxes is illustrated by the solid supply and demand curves. What happens when a sales tax of t per pack of cigarettes is introduced? A sales tax means that the price paid by the consumer, called the *consumer price*, and the price received by the seller, called the *seller price*, must now differ by the amount of the tax, t.

In terms of the figure, we can analyse the effect of the tax by considering a new supply curve S' that is above the original supply curve S by the amount of the tax, t. To understand this new curve, let's consider the firm's situation at the original equilibrium quantity q_0. To supply that quantity, producers must receive p_0 per pack of cigarettes sold. However, for producers to receive p_0 when there is a tax on cigarettes, the consumer must pay a total price of $p_0 + t$—whether the consumer "pays the tax directly" by giving p_0 to the firm and t to the government or whether the consumer pays the total $p_0 + t$ to the firm and the firm then remits the tax t to

excise tax   A tax on the sale of a particular commodity.

tax incidence   The location of the burden of a tax; that is, the identity of the ultimate bearer of the tax.

FIGURE 4-8   The Effect of a Cigarette Excise Tax

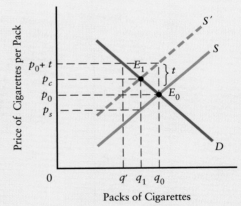

The burden of an excise tax is shared by consumers and producers. The original supply and demand curves for cigarettes are given by the solid lines S and D; equilibrium is at E_0 with price p_0 and quantity q_0. When a sales tax of t per pack is imposed, the supply curve shifts up to the dashed line S', which lies above the original supply curve by the amount of the tax t. The tax increases the consumer price and reduces the seller price. It also reduces the equilibrium quantity exchanged.

the government. Either way, the total amount that consumers must pay to obtain a given quantity from firms has increased by the amount of the tax t.

This upward shift in the supply curve for cigarettes is depicted in Figure 4-8 as the dashed curve, S'. This shift in the supply curve, caused by the tax, will generally also cause a movement *along* the demand curve, reducing the equilibrium quantity.

Consider the situation at the consumer price of $p_0 + t$. Firms will still be willing to sell the original quantity, but households will demand less because the price has risen; there is excess supply and hence pressure for the consumer price to fall.

The new equilibrium after the imposition of the sales tax occurs at the intersection of the original demand curve D with the tax-shifted supply curve S'. At this new equilibrium, E_1, the consumer price rises to p_c (greater than p_0), the seller price falls to p_s (less than p_0), and the equilibrium quantity falls to q_1.

Note that the quantity demanded *at the consumer price* is equal to the quantity supplied *at the seller price*, a condition that is required for equilibrium. As shown in the figure, compared to the original equilibrium, the consumer price is higher and the seller price is lower, although in each case the change in price is less than the full extent of the sales tax.

After the imposition of a sales tax, the difference between the consumer and seller prices is equal to the tax. In the new equilibrium, the quantity exchanged is less than that exchanged prior to the imposition of the tax.

The role of the relative elasticities of supply and demand in determining the incidence of the sales tax is illustrated in Figure 4-9. In part (i), demand is inelastic relative to

FIGURE 4-9   Elasticity and the Incidence of an Excise Tax

(i) Inelastic demand

(ii) Inelastic supply

The distribution of the burden of a sales tax between consumers and producers depends on the relative elasticities of supply and demand. In both parts of the figure, the initial supply and demand curves are given by S and D; the initial equilibrium is at E_0 with equilibrium price p_0 and quantity q_0. A tax of t per pack of cigarettes is imposed, causing the supply curve to shift up by the amount of the tax to S'. The new equilibrium is at E_1. The consumer price rises to p_c, the seller price falls to p_s, and the quantity falls to q_1. Sellers bear little of the burden of the tax in the first case (and consumers bear a lot), whereas consumers bear little of the burden in the second case (and sellers bear a lot).

supply; as a result, the fall in quantity is quite small, whereas the price paid by consumers rises by almost the full extent of the tax. Because neither the price received by sellers nor the quantity sold changes very much, sellers bear little of the burden of the tax. In part (ii), supply is inelastic relative to demand; in this case, consumers can more easily substitute away from cigarettes. There is little change in the price, and hence they bear little of the burden of the tax, which falls mostly on suppliers. Notice in Figure 4-9 that the size of the upward shift in supply is the same in the two cases, indicating the same tax increase in both cases.

When demand is inelastic relative to supply, consumers bear most of the burden of excise taxes. When supply is inelastic relative to demand, producers bear most of the burden.

Now we can examine who really pays for cigarette tax increases (or tax increases on gasoline and alcohol). The demand for cigarettes is inelastic both overall and relative to supply, suggesting that a cigarette-tax increase would be borne more by consumers than by producers. Thus, the large *reductions* in cigarette taxes which took place in the summer of 1994 in Ontario and Quebec benefited consumers more than producers. The demand for gasoline is also inelastic, but much more so in the short run than in the long run. (In the long run, drivers can change their driving routines and improve the efficiency of their vehicles, but in the short run such changes are very costly.) The supply of gasoline, given world trade in petroleum and petroleum products, is elastic relative to demand. The relatively inelastic demand and elastic supply imply that the burden of gasoline taxes falls mostly on consumers.

Applying Economic Concepts 4-1 discusses another important example of the issue of tax incidence—this time involving the burden of payroll taxes, such as the premiums that firms and workers pay for employment insurance and the Canada Pension Plan.

Practise with Study Guide Chapter 4, Exercise 9.

Other Demand Elasticities

The price of the product is not the only important variable determining demand for that product. Income and other prices also matter, and elasticity is a useful concept in measuring their effects.

Income Elasticity of Demand

One of the most important determinants of demand is the income of the customers. The responsiveness of demand to changes in income is termed the **income elasticity of demand** and is symbolized η_Y.

$$\eta_Y = \frac{\text{percentage change in quantity demanded}}{\text{percentage change in income}}$$

For most goods, increases in income lead to increases in demand—their income elasticity is positive. These are called **normal goods.** Goods for which demand decreases in response to a rise in income have negative income elasticities and are called **inferior goods.**

The income elasticity of normal goods can be greater than unity (elastic) or less than unity (inelastic), depending on whether the percentage change in the quantity

income elasticity of demand (η_Y)
A measure of the responsiveness of quantity demanded to a change in income.

normal good
A good for which quantity demanded rises as income rises—its income elasticity is positive.

inferior good
A good for which quantity demanded falls as income rises—its income elasticity is negative.

APPLYING ECONOMIC CONCEPTS 4-2

Who Really Pays for Payroll Taxes?

Some social programs in Canada are financed by **payroll taxes**—taxes collected from both firms and workers, computed as a proportion of workers' earnings. For example, the Employment Insurance program (formerly known as Unemployment Insurance) is financed by premiums paid by both firms and workers. The Canada Pension Plan is financed the same way.

When the federal government determines that such payroll taxes need to be increased (for reasons that we will discuss in Chapter 18 when we examine many aspects of Canadian social policy), an immediate question comes to the fore of the public debate: Should workers or firms be required to pay the extra taxes? There appears to be a great deal at stake in the resolution of this question. After all, neither workers nor firms want to bear the burden of extra taxes. Strikingly, however, *there is no economic difference between imposing payroll taxes on firms and imposing them on workers*. This proposition can be established by using the

same supply-and-demand analysis that we used to examine the incidence of sales taxes.

The accompanying figure illustrates a model of the labour market. The figure shows a standard demand-and-supply apparatus except that the axes have been relabelled as "Employment" and "Hourly Wage Rate."* Firms represent the demand for labour services. As the wage falls, it is profitable for firms to hire more workers (and to produce more output). Thus the demand curve for labour has a negative slope. Workers represent the supply of labour services. As the wage rises, the opportunity cost of *not working* rises, and thus workers substitute away from other activities and supply more labour services. Thus the supply curve for labour has a positive slope. The supply curve is shown to be relatively inelastic, in keeping with a considerable amount of empirical evidence showing that the quantity of labour supplied to the economy is quite unresponsive to changes in the wage rate. In the absence of any payroll taxes, the equilib-

---

payroll taxes Taxes paid by the firm and worker, computed as a percentage of the worker's total earnings.

demanded is greater or less than the percentage change in income that brought it about. It is also common to use the terms *income-elastic* and *income-inelastic* to refer to income elasticities of greater or less than unity. (See *Extensions in Theory 4-1* for a summary of the different elasticity concepts.)

The reaction of demand to changes in income is extremely important. We know that in most Western countries, economic growth caused the level of income to double every 20 to 30 years over a sustained period of at least a century. This rise in income has been shared to some extent by most citizens. As they found their incomes increasing, they increased their demands for most products, but the demands for some products, such as food and basic clothing, did not increase as much as the demands for other products. In developing countries the demand for durable goods is increasing most rapidly as household incomes rise, while in North America and Western Europe, the demand for services has risen most rapidly. The uneven impact of the growth of income on the demands for different products has important economic effects, which are studied at several points in this book.

What Determines Income Elasticity of Demand?

The variations in income elasticities shown in Table 4-4 suggest that the more basic a product, the lower its income elasticity. Food as a whole has an income elasticity of 0.2, consumer durables of 1.8. In Canada, starchy roots such as potatoes are inferior goods; their quantity demanded falls as income rises.

rium wage is w_0 and the equilibrium level of employment is E_0.

As in the analysis of excise taxes, the effect of the payroll tax is to drive a wedge between the wage paid by the firm (w_F) and the wage received by the worker (w_W). With a payroll tax of t dollars per hour, w_F rises above w_0 and w_W falls below w_0. Employment falls from E_0 to E_1. As the supply curve is drawn in the figure, however, almost all of the burden of the tax falls on workers. The lower right-hand bracket shows the amount by which the workers' take-home wage falls. The upper right-hand bracket shows the amount by which the employers' total payment per worker rises. Together, these add up to the payroll tax, shown by the left-hand bracket. Were the supply curve *perfectly* inelastic, the entire burden would fall on workers.

Quite apart from how the burden of the tax is apportioned between workers and firms, the figure also shows why many economic commentators refer to payroll taxes as "job killers"—by increasing the total cost that firms must pay for each unit of labour services, payroll taxes naturally lead firms to hire fewer workers.

The burden of payroll taxes would be shared more by firms if the supply of labour were more elastic (or if the demand were less elastic). But, as is the case with excise taxes that we discussed in the text, it is the shapes of the supply and demand curves that determine who bears the burden of payroll taxes.

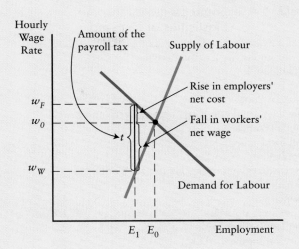

* This analysis assumes that the labour market is reasonably competitive—meaning that there are a large number of both workers and firms, none of which have the power to influence the market wage. Though this is usually a good description of the labour market, there are some situations that are not well modelled by a simple supply-and-demand apparatus. We discuss the role of labour unions, for example, in Chapter 14.

The more basic is an item in the consumption pattern of consumers, the lower is its income elasticity.

Income elasticities for any one product also vary with the level of a consumer's income. When incomes are low, consumers may eat almost no green vegetables and consume lots of starchy foods such as bread and potatoes; when incomes are higher, they may eat cheap cuts of meat and more green vegetables along with their bread and potatoes; when incomes are higher still, they are likely to eat higher quality and prepared foods of a wide variety.

The distinction between luxuries and necessities helps to explain differences in income elasticities. The case of restaurant meals is one example. Such meals are almost always more expensive, calorie for calorie, than meals prepared at home. It would thus be expected that at lower ranges of income, restaurant meals would be regarded as an expensive luxury but that the demand for them would expand substantially as consumers became richer. This is actually what happens.

What is true of individual consumers is also true of countries. Empirical studies show that for different countries at comparable stages of economic development, income elasticities are similar. However, the countries of the world are at various stages of economic development and thus have widely different income elasticities for the same products. Notice in Table 4-4 the different income elasticity of poultry in the United States, where it is a standard item of consumption, and in Sri Lanka, where it is a luxury good.

TABLE 4-4	Some Estimated Income Elasticities of Demand	
Inferior goods (η_Y less than zero)		
Whole milk		−0.5
Pig products		−0.2
Starchy roots		−0.2
Inelastic normal goods (η_Y between zero and one)		
Wine (France)		0.1
All food		0.2
Poultry		0.3
Elastic normal goods (η_Y greater than one)		
Gasoline		1.1
Wine		1.4
Consumer durables		1.8
Poultry (Sri Lanka)		2.0
Restaurant meals (U.K.)		2.4

Income elasticities vary widely across commodities and sometimes across countries. The basic source of food estimates by country is the Food and Agriculture Organization of the United Nations, but many individual studies have been made. (For the United States except where noted.)

Another example of the luxury-necessity distinction is shown in Table 4-4 by the different income elasticities for wine in France and the United States. In France, wine is a much more basic part of the meal than is the case in the United States, where wine is regarded as more of a luxury. As a result, increases in income lead to much smaller increases in the demand for wine in France than in the United States.

Graphical Representation of Income Elasticity

Increases in income shift the demand curve to the right for a normal good and to the left for an inferior good. Figure 4-10 shows a different kind of graph, an *income-consumption curve*. The curve resembles an ordinary demand curve in one respect: It shows the relationship of quantity demanded to one other variable, *ceteris paribus*. The other variable is not price, however, but household income. (An increase in the price of the product, holding income constant, would shift the curves in Figure 4-10 downward.)[1]

The figure shows three different patterns of income elasticity. Goods that consumers regard as necessities will generally have income elasticities that fall as income rises. The obvious reason is that as incomes rise, it becomes possible for consumers to devote a smaller proportion of their incomes to meeting basic needs and a larger proportion to buying things that they previously could not afford. At high levels of income some of the necessities may even become inferior goods. So-called luxury goods will not tend to be purchased at low levels of income but will have high income elasticities once incomes rise enough to permit consumers to sample the better things of life now available to them.

Cross Elasticity of Demand

cross elasticity of demand (η_{XY})
A measure of the responsiveness of the quantity of one commodity demanded to changes in the price of another commodity.

The responsiveness of demand to changes in the price of *another* product is called the **cross elasticity of demand**. It is denoted η_{XY} and defined as follows:

$$\eta_{XY} = \frac{\text{percentage change in quantity demanded of good } X}{\text{percentage change in price of good } Y}$$

The change in the price of good Y causes the *demand curve* for good X to shift. If X and Y are substitutes, an increase in the price of Y leads to an increase in the demand for

---

[1]In Figure 4-10, in contrast to the ordinary demand curve, quantity demanded is on the vertical axis. This placement follows the usual practice of putting the variable to be explained (the dependent variable) on the vertical axis and the explanatory variable (the independent variable) on the horizontal axis. It is the ordinary demand curve that has the axes "backward." The explanation is buried in the history of economics and dates to Alfred Marshall's *Principles of Economics* (1890). [8] For better or worse, Marshall's scheme is now used by everybody, although mathematicians never fail to wonder at this example of the odd ways of economists.

FIGURE 4-10   Income-Consumption Curves of Different Products

(i) Normal good: income inelastic

(ii) Normal good: income elastic beyond I_1

(iii) Inferior good beyond I_2

Different shapes of the curve relating quantity demanded to income correspond to different ranges of income elasticity. Normal goods have upward-sloping curves; inferior goods have downward-sloping curves. The good in part (i) is a typical normal good that is a necessity (the income elasticity declines as income rises). The good in part (ii) is a luxury good that is income elastic beyond income I_1. The good in part (iii) is a necessity (normal) at low incomes but becomes an inferior good at incomes beyond I_2.

X. If X and Y are complements, an increase in the price of Y leads to a reduction in demand for X. In either case, we are holding the price of X constant. We therefore measure the change in the quantity demanded of X (at its unchanged price) by measuring the shift of the demand curve for X.

Cross elasticity can vary from minus infinity to plus infinity. Complementary products, such as cars and gasoline, have negative cross elasticities. A large rise in the price of gasoline will lead to a decline in the demand for cars, as some people decide to do without a car and others decide not to buy an additional car. Substitute products, such as cars and public transport, have positive cross elasticities. A large rise in the price of cars (relative to public transport) will lead to a rise in the demand for public transport as some people shift from cars to public transport. (See *Extensions in Theory 4-1* for a summary of elasticity terminology.)

The positive or negative sign of cross elasticities tell us whether goods are substitutes or complements.

Measures of cross elasticity sometimes prove helpful in defining whether producers of similar products are in competition with each other. For example, glass bottles and tin cans have a high cross elasticity of demand. The producer of bottles is thus in competition with the producer of cans. If the bottle company raises its price, it will lose substantial sales to the can producer. In contrast, men's shoes and women's shoes have a low cross elasticity and thus a producer of men's shoes is not in close competition with a producer of women's shoes. If the former raises its price, it will not lose many sales to the latter. Knowledge of cross elasticity can be important in matters of *competition policy* in which the issue is whether a firm in one industry is or is not competing with firms in another industry. We discuss competition policy in more detail in Chapter 12.

Substitute products have a positive cross elasticity; an increase in the price of one leads to an increase in demand for the other.

EXTENSIONS IN THEORY 4-1

The Terminology of Elasticity

Term	Symbol	Numerical Measure of Elasticity	Verbal Description
A. Price elasticity of demand (supply)	η (η_S)		
Perfectly or completely inelastic		Zero	Quantity demanded (supplied) does not change as price changes.
Inelastic		Between zero and one	Quantity demanded (supplied) changes by a smaller percentage than does price.
Unit elastic		One	Quantity demanded (supplied) changes by exactly the same percentage as does price.
Elastic		Greater than one but less than infinity	Quantity demanded (supplied) changes by a larger percentage than does price
Perfectly, completely, or infinitely elastic		Infinity	Purchasers (sellers) are prepared to buy (sell) all they can at some price and none at all at a higher (lower) price.
B. Income elasticity of demand	η_Y		
Inferior good		Negative	Quantity demanded decreases as income increases.
Normal good		Positive	Quantity demanded increases as income increases:
Income-inelastic		Less than one	Less than in proportion to income increase
Income-elastic		Greater than one	More than in proportion to income increase
C. Cross elasticity of demand	η_{XY}		
Substitute		Positive	Price increase of a substitute leads to an increase in quantity demanded of this good.
Complement		Negative	Price increase of a complement leads to a decrease in quantity demanded of this good.

Practise with Study Guide Chapter 4, Exercise 1.

S U M M A R Y

Price Elasticity of Demand

LO 1

- *Price elasticity of demand*, also called *elasticity of demand*, is a measure of the extent to which the quantity demanded of a product responds to a change in its price. Represented by the symbol η, it is defined as

$$\eta = \frac{\text{percentage change in quantity demanded}}{\text{percentage change in price}}$$

The percentage changes are usually calculated as the change divided by the *average* value. Elasticity is defined to be a positive number, and it can vary from zero to infinity.

- When the numerical measure of elasticity is less than unity, demand is *inelastic*—the percentage change in quantity demanded is less than the percentage change in price that brought it about. When the numerical measure exceeds unity, demand is *elastic*—the percentage change in quantity demanded is greater than the percentage change in price that brought it about.

- The main determinant of the price elasticity of demand is the availability of substitutes for the product. Any one of a group of close substitutes will have a more elastic demand than will the group as a whole. Items that have few substitutes in the short run tend to develop many substitutes when consumers and producers have time to adapt.

- Since price elasticities are larger in the long run than in the short run, a shift in supply will lead to a larger change in price and a smaller change in quantity in the short run than in the long run.

- Elasticity and total expenditure are related in the following way: If elasticity is less than unity, total expenditure is positively related with price; if elasticity is greater than unity, total expenditure is negatively related with price; and if elasticity is unity, total expenditure does not change as price changes.

Price Elasticity of Supply

LO 2

- *Elasticity of supply* measures the extent to which the quantity supplied of some product changes when the price of that product changes. Represented by the symbol η_S, it is defined as

$$\eta_S = \frac{\text{percentage change in quantity supplied}}{\text{percentage change in price}}$$

- Supply tends to be more elastic in the long run than in the short run because it usually takes time for producers to alter their productive capacity in response to price changes.

An Important Example Where Elasticity Matters

LO 3 4

- The distribution of the burden of a sales tax between consumers and producers is independent of who actually remits the tax to the government. Rather, it depends on the relative elasticities of the supply and the demand for the product.

- The less elastic that demand is relative to supply, the more of the burden of an excise tax falls on the consumers.

Other Demand Elasticities

- *Income elasticity of demand* is a measure of the extent to which the quantity demanded of some product changes as income changes. Represented by the symbol η_Y, it is defined as

$$\eta_Y = \frac{\text{percentage change in quantity demanded}}{\text{percentage change in income}}$$

The income elasticity of demand for a product will usually change as income varies. For example, a product that has a high income elasticity at a low income (because increases in income bring it within reach of the typical household) may have a low or negative income elasticity at higher incomes (because with further rises in incomes, it is gradually replaced by a superior substitute).

- *Cross elasticity of demand* is a measure of the extent to which the quantity demanded of one product changes when the price of a different product changes. Represented by the symbol η_{XY}, it is defined as

$$\eta_{XY} = \frac{\text{percentage change in quantity demanded of good } X}{\text{percentage change in price of good } Y}$$

It is used to define products that are substitutes for one another (positive cross elasticity) and products that are complements for one another (negative cross elasticity).

K E Y   C O N C E P T S

Price elasticity of demand
Inelastic and perfectly inelastic demand
Elastic and infinitely elastic demand
Relationship between demand elasticity and total expenditure
The burden of a sales (or excise) tax

Consumer price and seller price
Income elasticity of demand
Income-elastic and income-inelastic demands
Normal goods and inferior goods

Cross elasticity of demand
Substitutes and complements
Elasticity of supply
Short-run and long-run responses to shifts in demand and supply

---

S T U D Y   E X E R C I S E S

1. What would you predict about the *relative* price elasticity of demand for each of the following items? Explain your reasoning.

   a. food
   b. vegetables
   c. leafy vegetables (such as spinach and lettuce)
   d. leafy vegetables sold at your local supermarket
   e. leafy vegetables sold at your local supermarket on Wednesdays

2. Suppose a stamp collector buys the only two existing copies of a stamp at an auction. After the purchase, the collector goes to the front of the room and burns one of the stamps in front of the shocked audience. What must the collector believe in order for this to be a wealth-maximizing action? Explain with a demand-and-supply diagram.

3. For each of the following events, state the relevant elasticity concept. Then compute the measure of elasticity. Where appropriate, use average prices and quantities in your calculations. In all cases, assume that these are *ceteris paribus* changes.

   a. When the price of theatre tickets is reduced from $14.00 to $11.00, ticket sales increase from 1200 to 1350.
   b. As average household income in Canada increases by 10 percent, annual sales of Toyota Camrys increase from 56 000 to 67 000.
   c. After a major failure of Brazil's coffee crop sent coffee prices up from $3.00 per kg to $4.80 per kg, sales of tea in Canada increased from 7500 kg per month to 8000 kg per month.
   d. An increase in the world demand for pulp (used in producing newsprint) increases the price by 14

percent. Annual Canadian production increases from 8 million tons to 11 million tons.

4. The following table shows the demand schedule for denim jeans.

	Price (per unit)	Quantity Demanded (per year)	Total Expenditure
A	$30	400 000	
B	35	380 000	
C	40	350 000	
D	45	320 000	
E	50	300 000	
F	55	260 000	
G	60	230 000	
H	65	190 000	

a. Compute total expenditure for each row in the table.
b. Plot the demand curve and the total expenditure curve.
c. Compute the price elasticity of demand between points A and B, B and C, C and D, and so on.
d. Over what range of prices is the demand for denim jeans elastic? Explain.
e. Over what range of prices is the demand for denim jeans inelastic? Explain.

5. Consider the following straight-line supply curves. In each case, p is the price (measured in $ per unit) and Q^S is the quantity supplied of the product (measured in thousands of units per month).

i) $p = 2Q^S$
ii) $p = 4Q^S$
iii) $p = 5Q^S$
iv) $p = 10Q^S$

a. Plot each supply curve on a scale diagram. In each case, plot point A (which corresponds to price equal to $20) and point B (which corresponds to price equal to $40).
b. For each supply curve, compute the price elasticity of supply between points A and B.
c. Explain why the *slope* of a supply curve is not the same as the *elasticity* of supply.

6. This is a challenging question intended for those students who like mathematics. It will help you work through the issue of tax incidence. Consider the market for gasoline. Suppose the market demand and supply curves are as given below. In each case, quantity refers to millions of litres of gasoline per month; price is the price per litre (in cents).

$$\text{Demand: } p = 80 - 5Q^D$$

$$\text{Supply: } p = 24 + 2Q^S$$

a. Plot the demand and supply curves on a scale diagram.
b. Compute the equilibrium price and quantity.
c. Now suppose the government imposes a tax of 14 cents per litre. Show how this affects the market equilibrium. What is the new "consumer price" and what is the new "producer price"?
d. Compute the total revenue raised by the gasoline tax. What share of this tax revenue is "paid" by consumers, and what share is "paid" by producers? (Hint: if the consumer price were unchanged from the pre-tax equilibrium, we would say that consumers pay none of the tax.)

DISCUSSION QUESTIONS

1. From the following quotations, what, if anything, can you conclude about elasticity of demand?

a. "Good weather resulted in record wheat harvests and sent wheat prices tumbling. The result has been disastrous for many wheat farmers."

b. "Ridership always went up when bus fares came down, but the increased patronage never was enough to prevent a decrease in overall revenue."

c. "As the price of CD players fell, producers found their revenues soaring."

d. "Coffee to me is an essential good—I've just gotta have it no matter what the price."

e. "The soaring price of condominiums does little to curb the strong demand in Vancouver."

2. Home computers were a leader in sales appeal through much of the 1990s. But per capita sales are much lower in Mexico than in Canada, and lower in Newfoundland than in Alberta. Manufacturers are puzzled by the big differences. Can you offer an explanation in terms of elasticity?

3. What elasticity measure or measures would be useful in answering the following questions?

a. Will cheaper transport into the central city help to keep downtown shopping centres profitable?

b. Will raising the bulk postage rate increase or decrease the revenues for Canada Post?

c. Are producers of toothpaste and mouthwash in competition with each other?

d. What effect will rising gasoline prices have on the sale of cars that use propane gas?

4. Interpret the following statements in terms of the relevant elasticity concept.

a. "As fuel for tractors has become more expensive, many farmers have shifted from plowing their fields to no-till farming. No-till acreage increased dramatically in the past 20 years."

a. "Fertilizer makers brace for dismal year as fertilizer prices soar."

c. "When farmers are hurting, small towns feel the pain."

d. "The development of the Hibernia oil field may bring temporary prosperity to Newfoundland merchants."

5. When the New York City Opera faced a growing deficit, it cut its ticket prices by 20 percent, hoping to attract more customers. At the same time, the New York Transit Authority raised subway fares to reduce its growing deficit. Was one of these two opposite approaches to reducing a deficit necessarily wrong?

More Details About Demand Elasticity

The definition of elasticity used in the text may be written symbolically in the following form:[1]

$$\eta = \frac{\Delta q}{\text{average } q} \div \frac{\Delta p}{\text{average } p}$$

where the averages are over the range, or *arc*, of the demand curve being considered. Rearranging terms, we can write

$$\eta = \frac{\Delta q}{\Delta p} \times \frac{\text{average } p}{\text{average } q}.$$

This is called *arc elasticity*, and it measures the average responsiveness of quantity to price over an interval of the demand curve.

Most theoretical treatments use a slightly different concept called *point elasticity*. This is the measure of responsiveness of quantity demanded to price *at a particular point* on the demand curve. The precise definition of point elasticity uses the concept of a derivative, which is drawn from differential calculus.

In this appendix, we first study arc elasticity, which we can regard as an approximation of point elasticity. Then we study point elasticity.

Before proceeding, we should note one further change. In the text of Chapter 4, we reported our price elasticities as positive values and thus implicitly multiplied all our calculations by -1. In theoretical work, it is more convenient to retain the concept's natural sign. Hence, normal demand elasticities have negative signs, and statements about "more" or "less" elasticity refer to the absolute, not the algebraic, value of demand elasticity.

---

[1]The following notation is used throughout this appendix.

$\eta \equiv$ elasticity of demand
$q \equiv$ initial quantity
$\Delta q \equiv$ change in quantity
$p \equiv$ initial price
$\Delta p \equiv$ change in price

Arc Elasticity as an Approximation of Point Elasticity

Point elasticity is a precise measure of elasticity at a particular price-quantity point. Without using calculus, however, we can only approximate this point elasticity. We do this by measuring the responsiveness of quantity demanded to a change in price *over a small range* of the demand curve, starting from that price-quantity point. For example, in Figure 4A-1, we can measure the elasticity at point 1 by the responsiveness of quantity demanded to a change in price that takes price and quantity from point 1 to point 2. The algebraic formula for this elasticity concept is

$$\eta = \frac{\Delta q}{\Delta p} \times \frac{p}{q} \qquad (4A\text{-}1)$$

This is similar to the definition of arc elasticity above except that, because elasticity is being measured at a

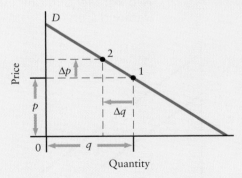

FIGURE 4A-1 A Straight-Line Demand Curve

Because p/q varies with $\Delta q/\Delta p$ constant, the elasticity varies along this demand curve; it is high at the left and low at the right.

point, the p and q corresponding to that point are used (rather than the average p and q over an arc of the curve).

Equation 4A-1 splits elasticity into two parts. The first part, $\Delta q/\Delta p$, is related to the *slope* of the demand curve. In fact, it is the *reciprocal* of the slope. The second part, p/q, is related to the *point* on the curve at which the measurement is made.

Although point elasticity of demand refers to a price-quantity point on the demand curve, the first term in Equation 4A-1 still refers to changes over an arc of the curve. This is the part of the formula that involves approximation, and, as we shall see, it has some unsatisfactory results. Nonetheless, we can derive some interesting results by using this formula as long as we confine ourselves to straight-line demand curves.

The elasticity of a downward-sloping straight-line demand curve varies from zero at the quantity axis to infinity at the price axis.

First, notice that because a straight line has a constant slope, the ratio $\Delta p/\Delta q$ is the same everywhere on the line. Therefore, its reciprocal, $\Delta q/\Delta p$, must also be constant. The changes in η can now be inferred by inspecting the ratio p/q. Where the line cuts the quantity axis, price is zero, so the ratio p/q is zero; thus $\eta = 0$. Moving up the line, p rises and q falls, so the ratio p/q rises; thus elasticity rises. Approaching the top of the line, q approaches zero, so the ratio becomes very large. Thus elasticity increases without limit as the price axis is approached.

Where there are two straight-line demand curves of the same slope, the one farther from the origin is less elastic at each price than the one closer to the origin.

Figure 4A-2 shows two parallel straight-line demand curves. Compare the elasticities of the two curves at any price, say, p_0. Because the curves are parallel, the ratio $\Delta q/\Delta p$ is the same on both curves. Because elasticities at the same price are being compared on both curves, p is the same, and the only factor left to vary is q. On the curve farther from the origin, quantity is larger (i.e., $q_1 > q_0$) and hence p_0/q_1 is smaller than p_0/q_0; thus η is smaller.

It follows that parallel shifts of a straight-line demand curve reduce elasticity (at each price) when the line shifts outward and increase elasticity when the line shifts inward.

For two intersecting straight-line demand curves the steeper curve is the less elastic.

In Figure 4A-3, there are two intersecting curves. At the point of intersection, p and q are common to both curves, and hence the ratio p/q is the same. Therefore, η varies only with $\Delta q/\Delta p$. On the steeper

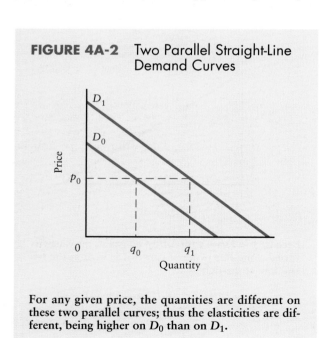

FIGURE 4A-2   Two Parallel Straight-Line Demand Curves

For any given price, the quantities are different on these two parallel curves; thus the elasticities are different, being higher on D_0 than on D_1.

FIGURE 4A-3   Two Intersecting Straight-Line Demand Curves

Elasticities are different at the point of intersection of these demand curves because the slopes are different, being higher on D_0 than on D_1. Therefore, D_1 is more elastic than D_0 at p_0.

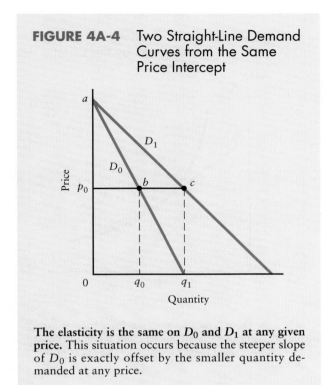

FIGURE 4A-4   Two Straight-Line Demand Curves from the Same Price Intercept

The elasticity is the same on D_0 and D_1 at any given price. This situation occurs because the steeper slope of D_0 is exactly offset by the smaller quantity demanded at any price.

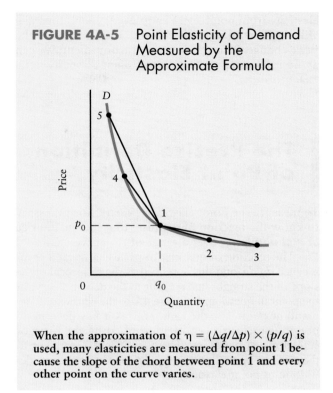

FIGURE 4A-5   Point Elasticity of Demand Measured by the Approximate Formula

When the approximation of $\eta = (\Delta q/\Delta p) \times (p/q)$ is used, many elasticities are measured from point 1 because the slope of the chord between point 1 and every other point on the curve varies.

curve, $\Delta q/\Delta p$ is smaller than on the flatter curve, so elasticity is lower.

If the slope of a straight-line demand curve changes while the price intercept remains constant, elasticity at any given price is unchanged.

This case is interesting for at least two reasons. First, when more customers having similar tastes to those already in the market enter the market, the demand curve pivots outward in this way. Second, when more firms enter a market that is shared proportionally among all firms, each firm's demand curve shifts inward in this way.

Consider in Figure 4A-4 the elasticities at point b on demand curve D_0 and at point c on demand curve D_1. We shall focus on the two triangles abp_0 on D_0 and acp_0 on D_1 formed by the two straight-line demand curves emanating from point a and by the price p_0. The price p_0 is the line segment $0p_0$. The quantities q_0 and q_1 are the line segments p_0b and p_0c, respectively. The slope of D_0 is $\Delta p/\Delta q = ap_0/p_0b$, and the slope of D_1 is $\Delta p/\Delta q = ap_0/p_0c$. From Equation 4A-1 we can

represent the elasticities of D_0 and D_1 at the points b and c, respectively, as

$$\eta \text{ at point } b = (p_0b/ap_0) \times (0p_0/p_0b) = (0p_0/ap_0)$$
$$\eta \text{ at point } c = (p_0c/ap_0) \times (0p_0/p_0c) = (0p_0/ap_0)$$

Because the distance corresponding to the quantity demanded at p_0 appears in both the numerator and the denominator and thus cancels out, the two values of the elasticity are the same. Put differently, if the straight-line demand curve D_0 is twice as steep as D_1, it has half the quantity demanded at p_0. Therefore, in Equation 4A-1 the steeper slope (a smaller Δq for the same Δp) is exactly offset by the smaller quantity demanded (a smaller q for the same p).

The demand elasticity measured from any point, according to Equation 4A-1, depends on the direction and magnitude of the change in price and quantity.

Except for a straight line (for which the slope does not change), the ratio $\Delta q/\Delta p$ will not be the same over different ranges of a curve. Figure 4A-5 shows a demand curve that is not a straight line. To measure the elasticity from point 1, the ratio $\Delta q/\Delta p$—and thus η—will vary according to the size and the direction of the price change. This result is very inconvenient; we can avoid it by using the concept of point elasticity in its exact form.

The Precise Definition of Point Elasticity

To measure the point elasticity *exactly*, it is necessary to know the reaction of quantity to a change in price *at that point*, not over a range of the curve.

The reaction of quantity to price change at a point is called dq/dp, and this is defined as the reciprocal of the slope of the straight line tangent to the demand curve at the point in question. In Figure 4A-6, the elasticity of demand at point 1 is the ratio p/q (as it has been in all previous measures), now multiplied by the ratio of $\Delta q/\Delta p$ measured along the straight line T, tangent to the curve at point 1, that is, by dq/dp. Thus the exact definition of point elasticity is

$$\eta = \frac{dq}{dp} \times \frac{p}{q} \qquad (4A\text{-}2)$$

The ratio dq/dp, as defined, is in fact the differential calculus concept of the *derivative* of quantity with respect to price.

This definition of point elasticity is the one normally used in economic theory. Equation 4A-1 is mathematically only an approximation of this expression. In Figure 4A-6, the measure of arc elasticity will come

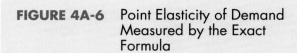

FIGURE 4A-6   Point Elasticity of Demand Measured by the Exact Formula

When the exact definition $\eta = (dq/dp) \times (p/q)$ is used, only one elasticity is measured from point 1 because there is only one tangent to the demand curve at that point.

closer to the measure of point elasticity as a smaller price change is used to calculate the arc elasticity. The $\Delta q/\Delta p$ in Equation 4A-1 is the reciprocal of the slope of the chord connecting the two points being compared. As the chord becomes shorter, its slope gets closer to that of the tangent T. (Compare the chords connecting point 1 to b' and b'' in Figure 4A-6.) Thus the error in using Equation 4A-1 as an approximation of Equation 4A-2 tends to diminish as the size of Δp diminishes.

CHAPTER 5

Markets in Action

Over the past two chapters, we have developed the model of demand and supply that you can now use to analyse individual markets. A full understanding of the basic theory, however, comes only with practice. This chapter is designed to give you such practice by examining some cases drawn from real-world experience. We explore the effects of legislated minimum wages, rent controls, and agricultural income-support policies.

Before examining these cases, however, we begin the chapter by discussing how various markets are related to each other. In Chapters 3 and 4, we used the simple demand-and-supply model to describe a single market, ignoring what was going on in other markets. For example, when we examined the market for carrots, we made no mention of the markets for inline skates, milk, or CD players. In other words, we viewed the market for carrots in isolation from all other markets. But this was only a simplification. In this chapter's opening section we note that the economy should *not* be viewed as a series of isolated markets. Rather, the economy is a complex system of interlocking markets. The implication of this complex structure is that events that lead to changes in one market typically lead to changes in other markets as well.

The Interaction Among Markets

Suppose there is an advance made in the methods for extracting natural gas. This technological improvement would be represented as a rightward shift in the supply curve for natural gas. The equilibrium price of natural gas would fall and there would be an increase in the equilibrium quantity exchanged.

How would other markets be affected? As natural-gas firms expand their production, they would increase their demand for the entire range of goods and services necessary for the extraction, processing, pumping, and distribution of natural gas. This increase in demand would raise the prices of those items, and lead the producers of those goods to devote more resources to their production. The natural-gas firms would also increase their demand for labour, since more workers would be required to drill for and extract more natural gas. The increase in demand for labour would tend to push wages up. Firms that hire similar workers in other industries would have to pay higher wages to retain their workers, and the profits of those firms would fall.

There also would be a direct effect on consumers. The reduction in the equilibrium price of natural gas would generate some substitution away from other fuels, such as oil or propane, and toward the now-lower-priced natural gas. Such reductions in demand would tend to push down the price of oil and propane, and producers of those fuels would devote fewer resources to their production.

In short, a technological improvement in the natural gas industry would have effects in many other markets. But there is nothing special about the natural gas industry. The same would be true about a change in almost any market you can think of.

No market or industry exists in isolation from the economy's many other markets.

Partial and General Equilibrium

As we have just seen, a change in one market will lead to changes in many other markets. But the induced changes in these other markets will, in turn, lead to changes in the first market. This is what economists call *feedback*. In the example of the natural gas industry, we argued that the reduction in the price of natural gas would lead consumers to reduce their demand for oil and propane, thus driving down the prices of these other fuels. But when we consider the demand and supply curves for natural gas, we assume that the *prices of all other goods are constant*. So, when the prices of oil and propane fall, the feedback effect on the natural gas market is to shift the demand curve for natural gas to the left (because natural gas is a substitute for both oil and propane).

Predicting the precise size of this feedback effect is difficult, and the analysis of the natural gas industry—or any other industry—would certainly be much easier if we could ignore it. But we cannot always ignore such feedback effects. Economists make a distinction between cases where the feedback effects are small enough that they can safely be ignored, and cases where the feedback effects are large enough that ignoring them would significantly change the analysis.

Partial-equilibrium analysis is the analysis of a single market in situations where the feedback effects from other markets are ignored. This is the type of analysis that we have used so far in this book, and it is the most common type of analysis in microeconomics. For example, when we examined the market for cigarettes at the end of Chapter 4, we ignored any potential feedback effects that could have come from the market for alcohol, coffee, or many other goods or services. In this case, we used partial-equilibrium analysis, focusing only on the market for cigarettes, because we assumed that the changes in the cigarette market would produce small enough changes on the other markets that the feedback effects from the other markets would, in turn, be sufficiently diffused that we could safely ignore them. This suggests the general rule for when partial-equilibrium analysis is a legitimate method of analysis.

If a specific market is quite small relative to the entire economy, changes in the market will have relatively small effects on other markets. The feedback effects on the original

partial-equilibrium analysis The analysis of a single market in isolation, taking as given the outcomes in all other markets.

market will, in turn, be very diffuse. In such cases, partial-equilibrium analysis can successfully be used to analyse the original market.

When economists study all markets together, rather than a single market in isolation, they use what is called **general-equilibrium analysis**. This is naturally more complicated than partial-equilibrium analysis because the economist must consider not only what is happening in each individual market but also must take into account how events in each market affect all the other markets.

General-equilibrium analysis is the study of how all markets function together, taking into account the various relationships and feedback effects between individual markets.

If you go on to take advanced courses in economics, especially at the graduate level, you will study general-equilibrium analysis in considerable detail. In this section of the chapter, however, we limit the discussion to one simple but important message: when events lead to changes in one market, there are typically changes caused in other markets as well. We examine three broad reasons that markets may be connected—*regional* linkages, *input-output* linkages, and linkages through a *resource constraint*.

> **general-equilibrium analysis**   The analysis of all the economy's markets simultaneously, recognizing the interactions among the various markets.

Regional Linkages

How are geographically separate markets connected? We examine two different linkages. In the first, *mobile supply* is what links the markets; in the second, the linkage is provided by *mobile demand*.

Mobile Supply

By mobility of supply we mean the ease with which suppliers can move their products from one market to another. This mobility depends on the product in question and the distance between the two markets. If the product is very costly to transport (like gravel or cement) and the markets are far apart (like British Columbia and Nova Scotia) then the two markets will be separate. But if the product is inexpensive to transport (like computer chips or leather gloves) and the markets are close together (like Ottawa and Toronto) then the two markets will be closely linked. Consider the following example that illustrates how mobile supply can link regional markets.

In August 1992, Hurricane Andrew struck the Florida coast and caused a great deal of damage to buildings and houses. As soon as the hurricane was over, the process of rebuilding began. This caused a sharp increase in the demand for plywood for rebuilding roofs and covering windows. The predicted excess demand and price increase occurred in Florida almost immediately.

But the economic effects of the hurricane were not confined to Florida. As the price of plywood soared in Florida, suppliers from other regions of the country directed their plywood shipments toward high-price Florida. This reduction in supply in the other regions caused shortages and led to price increases. Builders across the country were forced to adjust to more expensive plywood—prices increased by 18 percent in just two weeks. This situation is illustrated in Figure 5-1.

Mobile Demand

Now consider a situation in which it is prohibitively expensive to transport a product (immobile supply) but demand can move relatively easily. This would be the case, for example, in the housing market in two residential neighbourhoods that are close together.

FIGURE 5-1   Regional Linkages with Mobile Supply

Quantity of Plywood in Florida   Quantity of Plywood in Region A

When the supply of a product is mobile between regions, prices in regional markets tend to move together. The initial equilibrium in Florida is p_0^F and Q_0^F; in some other region, denoted Region A, it is p_0^A and Q_0^A. The hurricane leads to an increase in demand for plywood in Florida and thus drives prices in Florida up to p_1^F. The supply curve in Region A, however, is drawn *for a given price of plywood in Florida* since supplying to Florida is a substitute to supplying Region A. The increase in p^F therefore reduces the supply in Region A. This reduction in supply (the shift from S_A to S_A') shows up as part of the increase in quantity supplied in Florida (the movement along S_F). The supply reduction in Region A increases price to p_1^A. The two markets are linked through the mobility of supply, and the prices in the two markets move together.

It is obviously very expensive to move a house from one neighbourhood to another, and it is not easy to build new houses in the short run. So we can think of these two neighbourhoods as each having very inelastic short-run supplies of housing. Demand, in contrast, may be relatively mobile between the two neighbourhoods since living in one neighbourhood may be viewed as a reasonable substitute to living in the other.

Suppose that Neighbourhood A experiences a substantial increase in demand for housing, perhaps because its schools are widely reported to be of very high quality. Further, suppose that the increase in demand for housing in Neighbourhood A comes from families currently living in faraway neighbourhoods. This increase in demand will naturally create an excess demand and thus raise housing prices in Neighbourhood A. As prices rise there, however, some of the potential homeowners get crowded out by the price increases and they begin to look more favourably at houses in nearby Neighbourhood B, where prices are not rising. The shift in demand toward Neighbourhood B then creates excess demand and so prices rise there as well. Figure 5-2 illustrates this example.

Practise with Study Guide Chapter 5, Exercise 1.

The Role of Substitution

In both of the previous examples, *substitution* plays a key role in linking the regional markets. Indeed, substitution is just another word for the *mobility* of demand and supply. In

FIGURE 5-2   Regional Linkages with Mobile Demand

When demand for a product is mobile between regions, prices in regional markets tend to move together. The initial equilibrium in Neighbourhood A is Q_0^A and p_0^A; the equilibrium in Neighbourhood B is Q_0^B and p_0^B. Demand increases in Neighbourhood A to D_A' (coming from faraway neighbourhoods, not including B) and raises the price to p_1^A. As price increases in Neighbourhood A, some of the new demand gets crowded out and switches over to the houses in nearby Neighbourhood B. The reduction in quantity demanded along D_A' becomes the increase in Neighbourhood B's demand curve to D_B'. The regional markets are linked and the prices in the two markets move together.

the plywood example, firms viewed selling plywood in Florida as a substitute for selling plywood in other regions. In the housing example, consumers viewed buying houses in Neighbourhood B as a substitute for buying houses in Neighbourhood A.

Linkages between regional markets are determined by substitutability, either in demand or supply. The degree of substitutability, in turn, is determined by transport costs and the nature of the products.

In the plywood example, the degree of substitutability of supply—and thus the extent of the linkage between markets—is determined by the cost of transporting the plywood relative to its price. The more costly it is to transport, the less willing firms will be to move the plywood between regions. At some high level of transport costs, it will no longer pay suppliers to move the plywood, and the regional markets will not be linked together.

In the housing example, the degree of substitutability of demand—and thus the extent of the linkage between markets—is determined by the attributes of the housing in each neighbourhood (and by the characteristics of the neighbourhoods themselves). If living in Neighbourhood A is viewed by consumers as being very similar to living in Neighbourhood B, then the markets will be linked. If the two neighbourhoods are viewed as offering completely different living experiences, the markets will not be linked together.

Input-Output Linkages

We have considered cases where regional markets of the same product are linked through the mobility of supply or demand. Now think about linkages between markets of very different products. For instance, is the market for anchovies linked in any way to the beef market? Is the market for glass linked to the market for cars? The answer in both cases is yes. The linkages arise because some products (like anchovies and glass) are used as *inputs* to the production of other products (like beef and cars, respectively).

Anything that significantly increases the price of cattle feed will also increase the price of beef.

Changes in the price of one product lead to similar changes in the prices of goods that use that product as an input.

Consider the following example dealing with anchovies and cattle that is illustrated in Figure 5-3. One important use of anchovies (besides being used in Caesar salads and as a topping for pizza) is as a protein supplement for livestock, especially beef cattle. In 1973, partly as a result of the unusual weather associated with the cyclical recurrence of El Niño, there was a sharp reduction in the Peruvian anchovy catch. Since Peru was a large producer of anchovies, the decline in Peru's catch led to a significant decline in the world's supply of anchovies, which then pushed up anchovy prices. The higher price of anchovies, in turn, sharply increased the price of cattle-feed. The increased cost of the cattle-feed then led to a reduction in the supply of beef cattle. Prices for beef increased. The anchovy market and beef markets were linked, with the prices of the two products moving together.

FIGURE 5-3   Input-Output Market Linkages

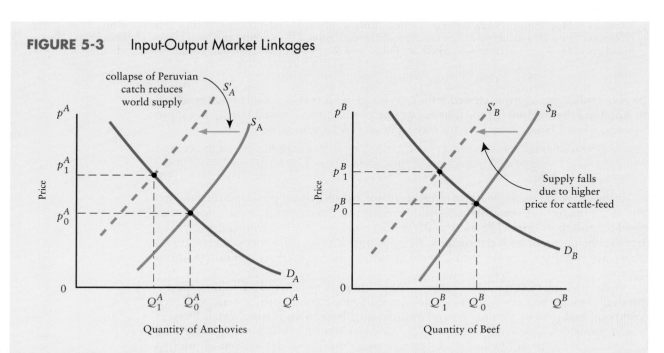

Changes in the price of inputs lead to similar changes in the prices of outputs. The initial equilibrium is Q_0^A and p_0^A in the anchovy market, and Q_0^B and p_0^B in the beef market. When El Niño leads to a reduction in the Peruvian anchovy catch, the world supply of anchovies shifts from S_A to S'_A. The shortage pushes anchovy prices up to p_1^A. The supply curve for beef is drawn for a given price of cattle-feed. As the price of cattle-feed rises (because it includes anchovies), the supply of beef shifts from S_B to S'_B. This reduction in the supply of beef causes beef shortages and price increases.

This example may seem like an unusual one but the principle involved is very general. An increase in the price of one product generally leads to price increases for all goods using that product as an input. Through such input-output linkages, we can better understand co-movements in the prices of many products, including electricity and aluminum, wheat and poultry, rubber and running shoes, fertilizer and agricultural crops, and steel and automobiles.

Linkages Through Resource Constraints

Are the markets for restaurant meals and clothing linked in any way? How about the markets for corporate jets and automobiles? In both cases, the products are clearly different and there are no obvious input-output linkages. Even though there may be none of the obvious regional or input-output linkages that we have been discussing, these seemingly unrelated markets are indeed linked, though the nature of the linkage is subtle.

Even seemingly unrelated markets are linked through resource constraints.

There are two ways to think of the resource constraints linking markets. The first is a demand-side constraint, the second is a supply-side constraint.

Demand-Side Resource Constraints

Consumers have only so much income they can spend. Even if they decide to borrow (so that they can spend in excess of their income) they must divide their total expenditure between housing, food, clothing, education, travel, entertainment, and so on. Thus, an extra $100 spent on restaurant meals must imply a reduction in spending on something else. As we saw in Chapter 1, this need for the consumer to make choices exists because of scarcity.

The scarcity faced by consumers implies that many apparently unrelated markets are actually linked together. If consumers with a constant amount of income increase their demand for chicken, they are probably decreasing their demand for beef or pork. If they increase their demand for movie tickets, they are probably reducing their demand for concerts or other forms of entertainment. If they increase their demand for airplane tickets, they are likely reducing their demand for railway or bus tickets. These linked demand changes will have effects on prices and resource allocation that you should by now be able to analyse.

Supply-Side Resource Constraints

Restaurants and theatres compete against each other for the consumer's entertainment dollar. But how about products that are arguably not in competition with each other? Surely consumers do not view corporate jets as a substitute for automobiles, or hospitals as a substitute for bridges. Though it may be true that consumers view the degree of substitutability between such products as negligible, the markets for these goods are still linked through supply-side resource constraints.

In an economy with fully employed resources, devoting more resources to producing one product must imply devoting fewer resources to producing other products.

In other words, for a given level of technology and a given amount of resources, an increase in the supply of one product must imply a reduction in the supply of some other product. This is nothing more than a restatement of what we first encountered in Chapter 1 when we described a country's production possibilities boundary. But it is surprising how often this fundamental point is either ignored or forgotten in public debate.

One of the best examples of how this supply-side constraint is ignored in public debate is the often-heard government claim that a specific program in one industry—such as a subsidy or a tax incentive—has "created jobs." The alleged proof of the claim is that the level of employment in the assisted industry is higher after the subsidy than before. But where did these new jobs come from?

Figure 5-4 shows how this situation can be analysed. The basic story is as follows. Suppose the government chooses to subsidize firms in the aerospace industry (as they have in Canada for many years). A government subsidy to aerospace firms leads those firms to expand production and increase their demand for workers. Employment in the aerospace industry will therefore increase. But those workers must come from somewhere. In particular, those workers must be drawn away from other industries, and the way this happens is through an increase in wages. The increase in demand for labour in the subsidized aerospace industry drives up the wage in that industry. As the wage rises, workers in other industries are attracted to the aerospace industry (this is the movement along the labour supply curve for the aerospace industry). But as these workers move toward the aerospace industry, there is a reduction in the supply of labour to all other industries. Thus the "created jobs" in the subsidized aerospace industry are only possible

FIGURE 5-4   Supply-Side Resource Constraints

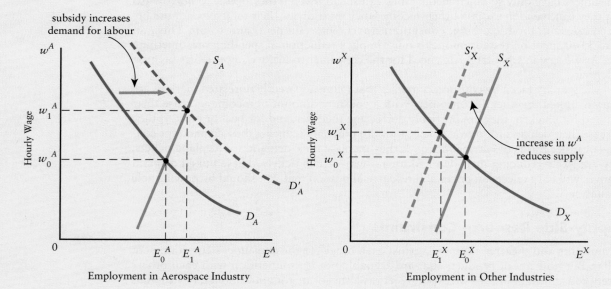

With given total supply of labour, an increase in employment in one industry must be matched by a decrease in other industries. The figure shows the two labour markets, one for the aerospace industry and the other for all other industries combined. The initial equilibrium is E_0^A and w_0^A in the aerospace industry and E_0^X and w_0^X in the other industries. When the government subsidizes firms in the aerospace industry, the demand for labour increases from D_A to D'_A. This pushes up wages in the aerospace industry and attracts workers from other industries. But, as workers move to the aerospace industry, the supply of labour to other industries falls from S_X to S'_X. This raises wages and leads to a reduction in employment in other industries. The jobs that are "created" in the aerospace industry are matched by "destroyed" jobs in other industries.

because of the "destroyed jobs" in other industries. Jobs do get created in the aerospace industry, but no new jobs get created *in the economy as a whole.*

We have just suggested that government efforts to stimulate total employment by assisting particular industries are ineffective, since the economy's resource constraint implies that any job gains in one part of the economy must be matched by job losses elsewhere. Keep in mind, however, that we have been considering an economy in which resources are fully employed, so that the economy is on the production possibility boundary. But this is not always the case. When you go on to study macroeconomics, you will learn that the economy is sometimes *inside* the production possibilities boundary because it has idle resources, the most important of which is probably unemployed labour. In such cases, government efforts to "create jobs" might have the intended effect since some of the newly employed workers in the assisted industry could come from the pool of unemployed workers. But even in such cases, this supply-side resource constraint is important. Except in extreme situations, the increase in employment in the assisted industries will overstate the increase in *total* employment because *some* of the new workers will come from other industries.

See Chapter 5 of www.pearsoned.ca/lipsey for an interview with Laurent Beaudoin, the Chairman of Bombardier, Canada's leading aerospace firm: "Trade and Subsidies in the Air," *World Economic Affairs.*

A Final Word

We began this section of the chapter by noting the difference between *partial-equilibrium analysis*, which is the study of one market in isolation, and *general-equilibrium analysis*, which is the study of all markets together. We then went on to examine how markets are linked together. By this point you should be fairly comfortable thinking about how various markets might relate to each other. Though we did not go all to way to developing formal general-equilibrium analysis, the basic point of this section has been both useful and simple: when changes occur in one market, there are generally related changes occurring in other markets.

As you go on to learn more microeconomics in this and later chapters, you will encounter mostly partial-equilibrium analysis. The book is written this way intentionally—it is easier to learn about the basic ideas of monopoly, competition policy, labour unions, and environmental policy (as well as many other topics) by restricting our attention to a single market. But keep in mind what we have seen in this section—there are many other markets "behind the scenes" that are linked in various ways to the individual markets we choose to study.

We now go on to examine the effects of government-controlled prices. These appear prominently in labour markets, rental housing markets, and agricultural markets.

Government-Controlled Prices

In a number of important cases, governments fix the price at which a product must be bought and sold in the domestic market. Here we examine the general consequences of such policies. Later, we look at some specific examples.

The equilibrium price in a free market occurs at the price at which quantity demanded equals quantity supplied. Government *price controls* are policies that attempt to hold the price at some disequilibrium value. Some controls hold the market price below its equilibrium value, thus creating a shortage at the controlled price. Other controls hold price above the equilibrium price, thus creating a surplus at the controlled price.

Disequilibrium Prices

When controls hold price at some disequilibrium value, what determines the quantity *actually traded* on the market? This is not a question we have to ask when examining a free market because the price adjusts to equate quantity demanded with quantity supplied. But this adjustment cannot take place if the government is controlling the price. So, in this case, what determines the quantity actually exchanged?

The key to the answer is the fact that any *voluntary* market transaction requires both a willing buyer and a willing seller. So, if quantity demanded is less than quantity supplied, demand will determine the amount actually exchanged, while the rest of the quantity supplied will remain in the hands of the unsuccessful sellers. Conversely, if quantity demanded exceeds quantity supplied, supply will determine the amount actually exchanged, while the rest of the quantity demanded will represent unsatisfied demand of unsuccessful buyers. This argument is spelled out in more detail in Figure 5-5, which establishes the following general conclusion:

At any disequilibrium price, quantity exchanged is determined by the *lesser* of quantity demanded or quantity supplied.

Price Floors

Governments sometimes establish a *price floor*, which is the minimum permissible price that can be charged for a particular good or service. A price floor that is set at or below the equilibrium price has no effect because the free-market equilibrium remains attainable. If, however, the price floor is set above the equilibrium, it will raise the price, in which case it is said to be *binding* or *effective*.

Price floors may be established by rules that make it illegal to sell the product below the prescribed price, as in the case of a legislated minimum wage. Or the government may establish a price floor by announcing that it will guarantee a certain price by buying any excess supply. Such guarantees are a feature of many agricultural support policies.

The effects of a binding price floor are illustrated in Figure 5-6, which establishes the following key result:

Effective price floors lead to excess supply. Either an unsold surplus will exist, or someone (usually the government) must enter the market and buy the excess supply.

FIGURE 5-5 The Determination of Quantity Exchanged in Disequilibrium

In disequilibrium, quantity exchanged is determined by the lesser of quantity demanded and quantity supplied. At p_0, the market is in equilibrium, with quantity demanded equal to quantity supplied. For prices below p_0, the quantity exchanged will be determined by the supply curve. For prices above p_0, the quantity exchanged will be determined by the demand curve. Thus the darker portions of the S and D curves show the actual quantities exchanged at different disequilibrium prices.

FIGURE 5-6 A Binding Price Floor

A binding price floor leads to excess supply. The free-market equilibrium is at E, with price p_0 and quantity q_0. The government now establishes an effective (binding) price floor at p_1. The result is excess supply equal to q_1q_2.

and selling only to customers of their own choosing. When sellers decide to whom they will and will not sell their scarce supplies, allocation is said to be by **sellers' preferences.**

If the government dislikes these allocation systems, it can choose to ration the product. To do so, it prints only enough ration coupons to match the quantity supplied at the price ceiling and then distributes the coupons to would-be purchasers, who then need both money and coupons to buy the product. The coupons may be distributed equally among the population or on the basis of some criterion such as age, family status, or occupation. Rationing of this sort was used by Canada and many other countries during both the First and Second World Wars.

Black Markets

Price ceilings usually give rise to black markets. A **black market** is any market in which goods are sold illegally at prices that violate a legal price control.

Effective price ceilings create the potential for a black market because a profit can be made by buying at the controlled price and selling at the black-market price.

Figure 5-7 illustrates the extreme case in which all the available supply is sold on a black market. We say this case is extreme because there are law-abiding people in every society and because governments ordinarily have at least *some* power to enforce their price ceilings. Although some of a product subject to an effective price ceiling will be sold on the black market, it is unlikely that all of that product will be.

Does the existence of a black market mean that the goals sought by imposing price ceilings have been thwarted? The answer depends on what the goals are. A government might have three main goals for imposing a price ceiling.

1. To restrict production (perhaps to release resources for other uses, such as wartime military production)

2. To keep specific prices down

3. To satisfy notions of equity in the consumption of a product that is temporarily in short supply

When price ceilings are accompanied by a black market, only the first objective is achieved. Black markets clearly frustrate the second objective. Effective price ceilings on manufacturers in addition to an extensive black market at the retail level may produce the opposite of the third goal. There will be less to go around than if there were no controls, and the available quantities will tend to go to the people with the most money or the least social conscience.

Rent Controls: A Case Study of Price Ceilings

For long periods over this century, rent controls have existed in London, Paris, New York, and many other large cities. In Sweden and Britain, where rent controls on apartments existed for decades, shortages of rental accommodations were chronic. When rent controls were initiated in Ontario in 1975 and Rome in 1978, severe housing shortages developed, especially in those areas where demand was rising.

Rent controls provide a vivid illustration of the short- and long-term effects of this type of market intervention. Note, however, that the specifics of rent-control laws vary

sellers' preferences
Allocation of commodities in excess demand by decisions of the sellers.

black market
A situation in which goods are sold illegally at prices that violate a legal price control.

Practise with Study Guide Chapter 5, Exercise 3.

greatly and have changed significantly since they were first imposed many decades ago. In particular, current laws often permit exemptions for new buildings and allowances for maintenance costs and inflation. Moreover, in many countries rent controls have evolved into a "second generation" of legislation that focuses more on *regulating* the rental housing market than simply *controlling the price* of rental accommodation.

In this section, we confine ourselves to an analysis of rent controls that are aimed primarily at holding the price of rental housing below the free-market equilibrium value. It is this "first generation" of rent controls which produced serious results in cities like London, Paris, New York, and Toronto.

The Predicted Effects of Rent Controls

Binding rent controls are a specific case of price ceilings and therefore Figure 5-7 can be used to predict some of their effects:

1. There will be a housing shortage in the sense that quantity demanded will exceed quantity supplied. Since rents are held below their free-market levels, the available quantity of rental housing will be less than if free-market rents had been charged.

2. The shortage will lead to alternative allocation schemes. Landlords may allocate by sellers' preferences, or the government may intervene, often through security-of-tenure laws, which protect tenants from eviction and thereby give them priority over prospective new tenants.

3. Black markets will appear. For example, landlords may require large "entrance fees" from new tenants, which reflect the difference in value between the free-market and the controlled rents. In the absence of security-of-tenure laws, landlords may force tenants out when their leases expire in order to extract a large entrance fee from new tenants.

The unique feature of rent controls, however, as compared to price controls in general, is that they are applied to a highly *durable good* that provides services to consumers for a long period of time. Once built, an apartment can be used for decades. As a result, the immediate effects of rent control are typically quite different from the long-term effects.

The short-run supply response to the imposition of rent controls is quite limited. Some conversions of apartment units to condominiums (that are not covered by the rent-control legislation) may occur but the quantity of apartments does not change much. The short-run supply curve for rental housing is therefore quite *inelastic*.

In the long run, however, the supply response to rent controls can be quite dramatic. If the expected return from building new rental housing falls significantly below what can be earned on comparable investments, funds will go elsewhere. New construction will be halted, and old buildings will be converted to other uses, or will simply be left to deteriorate. Thus the long-run supply curve of rental accommodations is highly *elastic*.

Figure 5-8 illustrates the housing shortage that worsens as time passes under rent control. Because the short-run supply of housing is inelastic, the controlled rent causes only a moderate housing shortage in the short run. Indeed, most of the shortage comes from an increase in the quantity demanded rather than from a reduction in quantity supplied. As time passes, however, fewer new apartments are built, more conversions take place, and older buildings are not replaced (and not repaired) as they wear out. As a result, the quantity supplied shrinks steadily.

Along with the growing housing shortage comes an increasingly inefficient use of rental accommodation space. Existing tenants will have an incentive to stay where they are even though their family size, location of employment, or economic circumstances may change. Since they cannot move without giving up their low-rent accommodation, some may accept lower-paying jobs nearby to avoid the necessity for moving. Thus a situation will arise in which existing tenants will hang on to accommodation even if it is poorly suited to their needs while new individuals and families will be unable to find any rental accommodation except at black-market prices.

The province of Ontario instituted rent controls in 1975 and tightened them on at least two subsequent occasions. The controls permitted significant increases in rents only where these were needed to pass on cost increases. As a result, the restrictive effects of rent controls were felt mainly in areas where demand was increasing rapidly (as opposed to areas where only costs were increasing rapidly).

During the mid and late 1990s, the population of Ontario grew substantially but the stock of rental housing did not keep pace. A shortage developed in the rental-housing market, and was especially acute in Metro Toronto. This growing housing shortage led the Ontario government in 1997 to loosen rent controls, in particular by allowing landlords to increase the rent as much as they saw fit *but only as tenants vacated the apartment.* Not surprisingly, this policy had both critics and supporters. Supporters argued that a loosening of controls would encourage the construction of apartments and thus help to reduce the housing shortage. Critics argued that landlords would harass existing tenants, forcing them to move out so that rents could be increased for incoming tenants. (Indeed, this exact behaviour happened in rent-controlled New York City where a landlord pleaded guilty in January 1999 to hiring a "hit man" to kill tenants and set fires to scare them out so that rents could be increased!)

FIGURE 5-8   The Short-Run and Long-Run Effects of Rent Controls

Rent control causes housing shortages that worsen as time passes. The controlled rent of r_c forces rents below their free-market equilibrium value of r_1. The short-run supply of housing is shown by the perfectly inelastic curve S_S. Thus quantity supplied remains at q_1 in the short run, and the housing shortage is q_1q_2. Over time, the quantity supplied shrinks, as shown by the long-run supply curve S_L. In the long run, there are only q_3 units of rental accommodations, fewer than when controls were instituted. The long-run housing shortage of q_3q_2 is larger than the initial shortage of q_1q_2.

Who Gains and Who Loses?

Existing tenants in rent-controlled accommodations are the principal gainers from a policy of rent control. As the gap between the controlled and the free-market rents grows, those who are lucky enough to be tenants gain more and more.

Landlords suffer because they do not get the return that they had expected on their investments. Some landlords are large companies, and others are wealthy individuals. Neither one of these groups attracts great public sympathy, even though the rental companies' stockholders are not all rich. But some landlords are people of modest means who have put their retirement savings into a small apartment block or a house or two. They find that the value of their savings is diminished, and sometimes they find themselves in the ironic position of subsidizing tenants who are far better off than they are.

The other important group of people who suffer from rent controls are *potential future* tenants. The housing shortage hurts them because the rental housing they will require will not exist in the future. These people, who wind up living elsewhere, farther from their places of employment and study, are invisible in debates over rent control because they cannot obtain housing in the rent-controlled jurisdiction. Thus rent control is often stable politically even when it causes a long-run housing shortage. The current tenants benefit, and the potential tenants, who are harmed, are nowhere to be seen or heard.

Temporary Versus Permanent Increases in Demand

We have seen that the effects of binding rent controls are more serious in the long run than in the short run because it is only over the long run that the quantity supplied of rental housing falls significantly. This suggests that a policy of rent controls *imposed only for a short time* may have few costs. Here we consider the distinction between temporary and permanent increases in housing demand, and the effects of rent controls in each case.

When Rent Controls Can Work: Short-Term Shortages

Pressure for rent controls is strongest when prices are rising most rapidly. The case for stemming the rapid rise of rents is strongest when the forces causing the rent increase are short-lived, as would be the case, for example, when people move temporarily into an area in response to a major construction project or significant international event, such as a World Exposition or the Olympic Games. When a temporary population floods in, market rents will rise. New construction of apartments will not occur, however, because investors recognize that the rise in demand for rental accommodation is only temporary. In such a situation, rent controls may stop existing landlords from making large profits and may result in few harmful supply effects because a long-run supply response is not expected in any case. After the boom is over, demand will fall, and free-market equilibrium rents will fall. Rent controls may then be removed with little further effect. This situation is illustrated in Figure 5-9.

Although the rent controls have no long-run adverse effect under these circumstances, they will still have some disadvantages. At controlled rents, there will be a severe housing shortage but no *price incentive* for existing tenants to economize on housing or for potential suppliers to find ways to convert existing space into short-run accommodations, as would occur if rents were allowed to rise. Even though the supply of permanent apartments does not change, the supply of temporary accommodations can increase (mobile homes, and the renting of bedrooms, for example). Such reactions are encouraged by the signal of rising rents but are inhibited by rent controls.

FIGURE 5-9   Rent Controls in Response to Increasing Demand

Rent controls prevent a temporary skyrocketing of rents when demand rises but also prevent the long-term supply adjustment where it is required.

Temporary demand fluctuations. The short-run supply curve S_S applies. In the free market, a temporary shift in demand from D_0 to D_1 and then back to D_0 will change rents from r_0 to r_1 and back to r_0. Rent control would hold rents at r_0 throughout. There would be a housing shortage of q_0q_1 because of excess demand, as long as demand was D_1, but rent control would not affect the quantity of housing supplied.

Permanent changes in demand. The long-run supply curve S_L applies. A permanent rise in demand from D_0 to D_1 would cause free-market rents to rise temporarily from r_0 to r_1 and then to fall to r_2 as the quantity of accommodations supplied grows from q_0 to q_2. But controlling the rent at r_0 produces a *permanent* housing shortage of q_0q_1.

When Rent Controls Fail: Long-Term Shortages

Now consider what happens when there is a long-term increase in the demand for rental accommodations. This has occurred most recently in Vancouver, Calgary, and Toronto where rapidly increasing populations have created local housing shortages and have forced rents to increase. Such increases in rents give the signal that apartments are highly profitable investments. A consequent building boom will lead to increases in the quantity supplied, and it will continue as long as profits can be earned on rental housing.

If rent controls are imposed in the face of such long-term increases in demand, they will prevent landlords from earning (temporarily) high profits, but they will also prevent the needed long-run construction boom from occurring. Thus, binding controls will convert a temporary shortage into a permanent one, as shown in Figure 5-9.

Policy Alternatives

Most rent controls today are meant to protect lower-income tenants, not only against "profiteering" by landlords in the face of severe local shortages but also against the steadily rising cost of housing. The market solution is to let rents rise sufficiently to cover the rising costs. If people decide that they cannot afford the market price of apartments and will not rent them, construction will cease. Given what we know about consumer behaviour, however, it is more likely that people will make agonizing choices, both to economize on housing and to spend a higher proportion of total income on it, which mean consuming less housing and less of other things as well.

If governments do not wish to accept this market solution, there are many things they can do, but they cannot avoid the fundamental fact that the opportunity cost of good housing is high. Binding rent controls create housing shortages. The shortages can be removed only if the government, at taxpayer expense, either subsidizes housing production or produces public housing directly.

Alternatively, the government can make housing more affordable to lower-income households by providing income-assistance to these households, allowing them access to higher-quality housing than they could otherwise afford. Whatever policy is adopted, it is important to recognize that providing greater access to rental accommodations has a resource cost. The costs of providing additional housing cannot be voted out of existence; all that can be done is to transfer the costs from one set of persons to another.

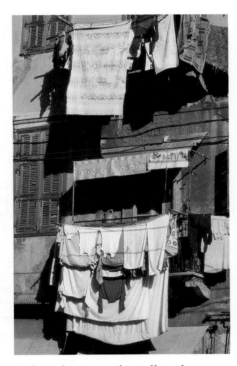

Perhaps the most striking effect of rent control is the long-term decline in the quality of rental housing.

Agriculture and the Farm Problem

For over 80 years, policymakers in many western countries, including Canada, have been challenged and frustrated by what is often called the "farm problem." There are actually two separate farm problems, and supply-and-demand analysis can help to make it clear why they are so challenging.

Long-Term and Short-Term Problems

The first problem is that there is a long-run tendency for farm incomes to fall below urban incomes. The second problem is that agricultural prices fluctuate substantially from year to year, causing a great deal of variability in farm incomes. The farm policies implemented by most Western countries are nominally directed at *stabilizing* farm incomes. However, the underlying long-term trend of declining farm incomes also puts pressure on governments to implement policies that *raise* farm incomes.

Long-Term Trends

Agriculture's long-term problems arise from both the demand and the supply sides of agricultural markets.

Increasing Supply.   Since 1900, the output per worker in Canadian agriculture has increased tenfold, roughly twice as much as the increase in manufacturing productivity. In 1900, one farm worker could produce enough food to feed about 2 1/2 people. Currently, the figure is approximately 65 people! Similar growth in farm productivity has occurred in Europe and the United States. Moreover, increases in supply—especially in Europe—have resulted from very generous agricultural subsidies under the European Union's Common Agricultural Policy (CAP). The combination of productivity growth and aggressive subsidization has caused the supply curves for agricultural products—both in Canada and abroad—to shift rapidly to the right.

Lagging Demand.   The overall growth of output throughout the entire Canadian economy has resulted in a rising trend for the real income of the average Canadian family during the last 150 years. However, at the levels of income existing in Canada and in other advanced industrial nations, most foodstuffs have low income elasticities of demand because most people are already well fed. Thus as incomes in Canada and other countries grow, the demand for agricultural goods also grows, but less rapidly.

Explosive growth of world population in the past half century has provided an expanding demand for foodstuffs, which, over much of the period, translated into a growing export market for North American produce. This tended to alleviate somewhat the domestic pressures just discussed. Beginning in the 1970s, however, many developing countries succeeded in dramatically increasing their own food production, thus reducing their demand for other countries' agricultural products.

Excess Supply.   Both the demand and the supply curves in typical agricultural markets have been shifting to the right over the whole of this century, with the demand curve shifting more slowly than the supply curve. As a result, there is a continuing tendency for an excess supply of agricultural produce to develop at existing market prices. This naturally tends to depress world prices for agricultural products.

To see the significance of these developments, note the change in the *real* crop prices received by North American farmers over the past two decades. Between 1975 and 1998, average crop prices in Canada and the United States increased by just over 27 percent. But over the same period, average prices in the economy increased by over 200 percent. This difference represents an enormous decline in the real prices received by farmers (roughly a 60 percent decline). And since most agricultural products tend to have price elasticities of demand less than one, the decline in prices tends to depress agricultural incomes.

Resource Reallocation.   Depressed prices, wages, and farm incomes signal the need for resources to move out of agriculture and into other sectors. However necessary they may be, adjustments of this kind prove to be painful to those who live and work on farms, especially when resources move slowly in response to depressed incomes. It is one thing for farmers' sons and daughters to move to the city; it is quite another for existing farmers and their parents to be displaced.

The magnitude of the required supply response has been enormous. In 1900, over 45 percent of the Canadian labour force worked in agriculture; by 1930 it was down to 29 percent, and by 1998 the number had fallen below 3 percent.

Short-Term Fluctuations

The second part of the farm problem is the short-term price volatility that is typical of many agricultural markets. Such volatility occurs for two basic reasons, both of which are beyond the farmers' control.

First, in markets that are mainly domestic, such as some fresh fruit and vegetables, changes in growing conditions—mostly due to changes in weather—can lead to sharp changes in the supply of these products. Such changes in supply, combined with a typically inelastic domestic demand, lead to large fluctuations in price. As we learned in Chapter 4, price fluctuations with inelastic demand imply that income and price fluctuate in the same direction. Thus, large supply fluctuations in such markets generate large fluctuations in farmers' incomes.

Second, in markets that are mainly international, such as wheat and other grains, changes in the *world* demand and supply lead to changes in the world price of these products. Such changes in the world price lead to significant fluctuations in the income of Canadian farmers. For example, in 1997 several countries in Southeast Asia entered into a significant recession. As incomes in these countries fell sharply, so too did their demand for many commodities, including agricultural products. This reduction in demand contributed to an ongoing decline in the world prices of such products. The implication for Canadian farmers was severe; total Canadian farm income fell by 53 percent from 1996 to 1997, even though growing conditions within Canada were approximately normal.

We discuss these two general situations and others in more detail in the next section, in which we examine the effects of agricultural stabilization and income-support policies.

The Theory of Agricultural Policy

Because of the long-term trends and the short-term fluctuations that we have just discussed, governments throughout the world intervene in agricultural markets in attempts both to stabilize agricultural incomes and to raise average farm incomes. We deal with three cases that are relevant to much of Canadian agriculture. The first two cases deal purely with the stabilization of farm income—first, the production of commodities mainly for export and, second, the production of commodities mainly for domestic consumption. The third case deals with price supports above the free-market equilibrium price. In what follows, we assume that all supply curves refer to *planned* production per year but that actual production fluctuates around that level for reasons beyond the control of farmers.

Production for Export Markets

When Canadian production is sold on world markets, the prices are largely independent of the amount sold by Canadian producers because they contribute only a small proportion of total world supply. In these markets, domestic producers face a perfectly

FIGURE 5-10   Production at a Given World Price

A country that exports only a small portion of the world's supply of some product faces a perfectly elastic demand because the world price is not affected by its own sales. The given world price is p_w. The domestic supply curve shows that planned output is q_0 at that price. Unplanned fluctuations cause output between q_1 and q_2. When output is q_1 (a partial crop failure), farm income is given by the shaded area. When output is q_2 (a bumper crop), farm income is given by the total of the bordered areas.

elastic demand curve, indicating that they can sell all that they wish at the given world price. A government stabilization policy then faces two key problems: first, how to cope with short-term supply fluctuations at home and, second, how to react to fluctuations in world prices.

Output Fluctuations at Given World Prices. Figure 5-10 illustrates sales at a given world price when domestic output fluctuates. In years of bumper crops, sales will rise and thus incomes will rise. In years of poor crops, sales will fall and thus incomes will fall. In neither case do the fluctuations in domestic output affect the world price.

When domestic farmers sell at a given world price, their incomes fluctuate in the same direction as their short-term fluctuations in output.

The incomes of farmers who produce nonperishable crops could be stabilized if the government developed a scheme allowing farmers to store their outputs in years of bumper crops and to sell from their accumulated stocks in years of poor crops. Effectively, sales would always be equal to planned output (q_0 in Figure 5-10). Any unplanned excess of production would be stored, and any shortfall would be made up out of sales from stocks. But storage costs money and postpones the receipt of revenue until the sales occur. A simpler alternative would be for the farmer to sell all the crop each year and then save the extra money received in good years to spend in bad years. This is something that farmers can do on their own without assistance from the government.

Fluctuations in World Prices.   Now consider a situation in which domestic supply curve is stable but the world price is fluctuating. When the domestic farmers see an increase in the world price they will increase production, though the quantity response is quite limited in the short run. Domestic farmers benefit from increases in the world price since they sell all of their output at a higher price. On the other hand, a decrease in the world price harms them because they sell all of their output at a lower price.

When domestic farmers sell their products at the world price, their incomes fluctuate in the same direction as the fluctuations in the world price.

For example, in the late summer of 1998 the Russian economy began a significant recession. As Russia is the world's largest importer of meat, its recession had a dramatic effect on the world price of meat. This contributed to the already low meat prices—especially pork—that were driven by the reductions in demand from the recession-hit Southeast Asian economies (which consume large amounts of pork). The result was a 60 percent fall in hog prices over just a few months, with the expected dramatic effect on the incomes of Canadian hog farmers. In some reported cases, farmers were losing so much money on each animal sold that it made more sense to slaughter the animals simply to get rid of them rather than to keep feeding them at considerable expense.

To stabilize farmers' incomes when the world price fluctuates, the government could create a scheme whereby they effectively guarantee farmers a price for their product equal to the *average* of the fluctuating world price. In low-price years, farmers would receive the low world price plus a supplement from the government. In high-price years, the farmers would receive the high world price but would make a payment to the government. The guaranteed price could be computed so that over time there would be a net balance between the government and the farmers—payments received by farmers in low-price years could balance the payments made by farmers in high-price years. In this way, farmers would have a smooth income stream; their income would be *as if* the world price were constant.

One problem with such a policy involves the computation of the guaranteed price. If the guaranteed price actually does equal the average of the fluctuating world price, then the payments from the farmers in the high-price years will indeed finance their income supplements in the low-price years. But if the guaranteed price is set too high, then the scheme will incur losses that must be financed from general tax revenues. Such financing, of course, involves a redistribution from taxpayers to farmers.

Production for Domestic Markets

Quite a few Canadian agricultural goods are sold mainly on the domestic market. The difference between this case and the one just considered is that the demand curve facing domestic producers is now negatively sloped and typically inelastic. In this case, increases in domestic supply (bumper crops) lead to large price reductions and declines in farm incomes, whereas decreases in supply (crop failures) lead to large price increases and increases in farm incomes. Can farm income be stabilized in this case?

Price Stabilization.   Suppose that the government enters the market, buying and thereby adding to its own stocks when there is a bumper crop, and selling and thereby reducing its stocks when there is a crop failure. If it had enough storage facilities, and if its support price were set at a realistic level, the government could stabilize *prices* indefinitely. But this action would not stabilize farmers' incomes, which would be high with bumper crops and low with poor crops. In effect, the government policy that we just described imposes a demand curve that is perfectly elastic (horizontal) at the support price. The situation is then analogous to the one analysed in Figure 5-10: The product can be sold at a given price, and income fluctuates in the same direction as output.

When domestic supply is fluctuating, a policy that stabilizes farm prices will not stabilize farm incomes.

Income Stabilization.   When the government does not intervene at all in domestic agricultural markets, farm income fluctuates in the *opposite* direction as farm output (because of inelastic demand). If the government intervenes to stabilize price, then farm income fluctuates in the *same* direction as farm output. This line of argument suggests that there must exist *some* government buying-and-selling policy that is able to stabilize farmers' incomes. What are the characteristics of such a policy? As has been seen, too much price stability causes incomes to vary directly with production, and too little price stability causes receipts to vary inversely with production. Thus it appears that the government could aim at some intermediate degree of price stability to stabilize farmers' incomes. If the government allows prices to vary in inverse proportion to variations in production, incomes will be stabilized. A 10 percent rise in production could be met by a 10 percent fall in price, and a 10 percent fall in production by a 10 percent rise in price.

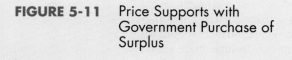

FIGURE 5-11   Price Supports with Government Purchase of Surplus

The price support becomes a price floor, and the government must purchase the excess supply at that price. *Average* annual demand and supply are D and S, respectively. The free-market equilibrium is at E_0. If the government will buy any quantity at p_s, the demand curve becomes the light blue curve D_1 and equilibrium changes to E_1. The *average* addition to storage is the quantity q_1q_2. The government's purchases, financed by the taxpayer, add to farmers' incomes, but also add to the stocks of unsold output.

To stabilize farmers' incomes, the government must make the effective demand curve unit elastic. It must buy in periods of high output and sell in periods of low output, but only enough to let prices change in inverse proportion to farmers' output.

Supporting Prices Above Equilibrium

Actual stabilization plans, whether they fix prices completely or merely dampen free-market fluctuations, often maintain an average price above the average free-market equilibrium level. This is because stabilization is not the only goal; governments aim to *raise* farm incomes as well as stabilize them.

The government buys in periods of high output and sells in periods of low output, but, as shown in Figure 5-11, it buys much more on average than it sells, with the result that unsold surpluses accumulate. Taxpayers will generally be paying farmers for producing goods that no one is willing to purchase—at least, not at prices that come near to covering costs.

We have just seen that when the government directly supports the price above the free-market equilibrium there is an accumulation of unsold output. An alternative method of supporting the price that partially avoids this problem is through the use of output *quotas*. Under this system, no one can produce the product without having a government-issued quota. Sufficient quotas are issued to hold production at any desired level below the free-market output. This action drives prices above their free-market level. A quota system, which is analysed in Figure 5-12, has the advantage of not causing the accumulation of massive unsold surpluses. It is widely used in Canada.

The quota system, which is called *supply management* in Canada, affects both the short-term and the long-term behaviour of agricultural markets. Consider short-term fluctuations first. There will still be natural disturbances, such as outbreaks of crop disease, that will cause short-term reductions in output. A shortfall of output below the quota will drive price upward. Farmers with no crop to sell will lose, but farmers whose outputs fall proportionally less than the price rise will gain. Since most agricultural products have inelastic demands, the typical farmer's income must increase—the percentage increase in market price will exceed the percentage fall in the aggregate crop.

What about bumper crops that result from favourable conditions? The farmer is allowed to sell only the amount covered by the quota. The rest must be either destroyed or sold on some secondary market not covered by the quota system.

A quota system guarantees that farmers will receive income at least equal to the quota output times the market price at that restricted level of output. In bad years, when output is less than the quota amount, inelastic demand ensures that farmers' incomes will be even higher.

Now let's consider the long term. We have seen that the quota drives price above its free-market level by restricting output. For purposes of illustration, let's suppose that the quota is for milk. Those who are producing milk when the quota system is first instituted must gain. Since production falls, total costs must fall; since demand is inelastic, total revenue must rise. Therefore, milk producers find their profits rising, since they spend less to earn more revenue. No wonder quotas are popular among the original producers!

But do quotas really increase the profitability of farming in the long run? Because people leave the industry for such reasons as death and retirement and new people must enter to replace them, existing quota holders are allowed to transfer their quotas to new would-be milk producers. But the quota is valuable, since it confers the right to produce milk and earn a large profit as a result of the supply restriction. Therefore, the quota commands a market price that naturally reflects the current value of the extra future profits that ownership of the quota allows.

The free-market price of a quota to produce any good will be such that the profitability of that good's production will, after deducting the cost of the quota, be no more than the profitability of other lines of activity carrying similar risks.

In other words, the entire extra profitability created by the quota system becomes embodied in the price of the quota. The extra profits created by the quota will just provide an acceptable return on the money invested in buying the quota—if it provided more, the price of the quota would be bid up; if it provided less, the price of the quota would fall.

For this reason, *new entrants* to the industry will earn no more than the return available in other lines of production. Since that would also be the case under market-determined prices and outputs, the quota does not raise the long-run profitability of farm production. What it does do is reduce some of the uncertainty due to unexpected short-term fluctuations of output. Farming becomes a somewhat less risky operation than before.

FIGURE 5-12   Price Support Through the Use of Quotas

The quota below the free-market equilibrium quantity maintains the price above the free-market equilibrium level without generating surpluses. If the total quota of q_1 is enforced, the price will rise to p_2. Since the supply curve indicates that in a free market producers would be willing to sell the quantity q_1 at the price p_1, the effect of the quota is to increase the revenues (by the shaded area) to those producers who hold quota.

Practise with Study Guide Chapter 5, Exercise 5.

Agricultural Policy in Canada

The main tools of agricultural stabilization in Canada are marketing boards and income supplement programs. Sales through marketing boards account for about half of all farm cash receipts.

Marketing Boards

There are essentially two types of government marketing boards. The first seeks to influence prices by controlling supply. The second takes prices as given and acts as a selling agency for producers.

Supply Management.   The supply-management schemes typically are provincially administered systems that restrict output of commodities sold in the Canadian market through quotas issued by provincial marketing boards. They vary from province to province but often cover milk, eggs, cheese, butter, and poultry. The farm profits created by these schemes are enormous and are reflected by the high prices farmers must pay to purchase quotas.

Schemes of this type, analysed in Figure 5-12, are successful in reducing short-term fluctuations. However, they also greatly increase the cost of becoming a producer, because a quota must be purchased in addition to the physical capital needed for production. The schemes are popular among farmers because they reduce risk in the short term and because the value of the quotas often rises over the long term. The gains to farmers and food importers are paid for by consumers in the form of higher prices.

The high domestic prices caused by supply management would normally lead to a flood of lower-priced imports. To prevent this, the federal government used to impose quotas on imports of goods subject to supply management. Under the Uruguay Round of the General Agreement on Tariffs and Trade (the GATT), Canada agreed to replace these quotas in 1994 with tariffs which had an equivalent effect. In some cases the tariff rates exceeded 300 percent! The slow speed at which these tariff rates are to be reduced under the GATT will allow the effects of supply management to persist for many years. Consumers will have to wait for future tariff reductions before they get real relief from the high-price effects of Canadian marketing boards.

Marketing Agencies.   The prime example of a marketing agency is the Canadian Wheat Board, which sells Canadian wheat at prices set on the world wheat market. Canadian wheat farmers are *required* to sell their crops to the Wheat Board at a pre-specified price. Each year, the Board estimates the average price at which it expects the wheat crop to be sold. Seventy-five percent of that price is then paid to each farmer on delivery of the wheat. After the Board sells the wheat, any proceeds in excess of the initial payments are distributed to the producers in proportion to the amount of wheat supplied by each.

The primary goal of the Wheat Board is not to influence world prices (since even the large amount of wheat sold by the Board is small relative to the total size of the world wheat market). Instead, by paying farmers 75 percent of the estimated average selling price over the year, the Board provides farmers with a secure cash flow early in the selling period. The Board also serves to secure farmers' incomes against intrayear fluctuations in wheat prices. It does this by pooling all of its receipts and paying them out to farmers according to the amount of wheat delivered by each farmer but irrespective of the date within the year of that delivery. So the farmer is relieved of worry about what the spot price of wheat may be on the day of delivery.

All wheat grown in Canada must be marketed through the Canadian Wheat Board.

In the last few years, the Canadian Wheat Board has come under attack by many prairie wheat farmers who see little value in their being restricted to sell their crops to the Board. They prefer to have the flexibility to sell their own crops to whomever they choose. Other critics of the Wheat Board point out that in recent years taxpayers have actually been supporting wheat farmers through the Board because the final selling price has been below the initial price paid to farmers (in which case, the Wheat Board does not require repayments from the farmers). Defenders of the Board argue that it is an effective means of reducing the costs associated with finding buyers and completing transactions, and that there is no evidence that the Wheat Board receives lower prices than those available to farmers acting individually.

For information on the Canadian Wheat Board, go to www.cwb.ca.

Income Supplements

The current system of income supplements to farmers includes the Net Income Stabilization Account (NISA) and the Gross Revenue Insurance Plan (GRIP). These two programs, combined with a system of crop insurance (and other companion programs) make up what might be called the "safety net programs" for Canadian farmers.

NISA is a voluntary program designed to help producers set aside money in good years to be used in bad years; producers' contributions of up to 2 percent of their net sales are matched by contributions from the federal and relevant provincial governments. Thus, although part of this program involves the individual producers saving their own financial resources, there is also a considerable portion of taxpayers' money being used to supplement farmers' incomes.

GRIP offers producers protection from revenue loss due to output or price changes beyond their control. It provides producers with a guaranteed target revenue. Though GRIP is essentially just an insurance program, it also has an income-support component. This comes from the fact that two-thirds of the insurance premiums are paid by the federal and relevant provincial governments.

All in all, the level of direct financial assistance to farmers is quite considerable, especially when seen relative to total farm income. In 1994 (an approximately typical year in the 1990s for Canadian farming), net cash income to Canadian farmers totalled $5.9 billion. In that same year, direct cash payments to farmers equalled $1.7 billion; thus direct financial assistance to farmers represented roughly 30 percent of their net cash income.

For information on Canada's agricultural sector, and Canadian agricultural policy, go to Agriculture Canada's website: www.agr.ca. Click on "Finances and Economics in Agriculture."

The Future of Agricultural Policy

A central dilemma arises whenever government intervention is designed to protect some people from economic hardship created by long-run shifts in demand and supply. Canadian farm policy reflects this dilemma. By intervening in the market—either with price supports or quotas— government farm policy impedes the reallocation of resources that is required in a changing economy. Most economists—and many politicians—believe that Canadian farm policies have been unnecessarily expensive and wasteful and that they have impeded the long-run adjustments required by changing tastes and technology.

The full benefit of increases in agricultural productivity, that permit the same farm output to be produced with fewer resources, will be felt only when resources flow out of the agricultural sector and begin producing valuable goods and services in other sectors.

Most economists believe that a more efficient system would assist farm workers to change occupations and farm producers to change products rather than subsidize them to stay where they are not needed and to produce products that cannot be marketed profitably. Such assistance would require significant outlays—as do the present schemes— but would allow the market to do the job of allocating resources to agriculture.

There is no doubt that a policy of allowing agricultural prices and outputs to be determined on free markets would avoid surplus production, but the human and political costs of this policy have been judged to be unacceptable. The challenge has been to respond to the real hardships of the farm population without intensifying the long-term problems. Canadian farm policy has not always succeeded in doing so; the economic analysis in the previous sections helps us to understand why.

S U M M A R Y

Linkages Between Markets

(LO) 1

- Partial-equilibrium analysis is the study of a single market in isolation, ignoring events in other markets. General-equilibrium analysis is the study of all markets together.
- Even markets that appear to be separate from each other are usually linked in one of three ways. Regional markets of the same product are linked, as long as there is mobile demand or supply.
- Markets for different products often have input-output linkages. In such cases, a change in the price of one prod-

uct leads to a similar change in the prices of all goods that use that product as an input.
- Seemingly unrelated markets are also linked through resource constraints. Consumers have only so much income to spend, so an increase in demand for one product must be matched by a decrease in demand for another product. Furthermore, if the economy's resources are fully employed, an increase in the supply of one product must imply a reduction in supply of some other product.

Government-Controlled Prices

(LO) 2 3

- Government price controls are policies that attempt to hold the price of some good or service at some disequilibrium value—a value that could not be maintained in the absence of the government's intervention. A binding price floor is set above the equilibrium price; a binding price ceiling is set below the equilibrium price.

- Effective price floors lead to excess supply. Either the potential seller is left with quantities that cannot be sold, or the government must step in and buy the surplus. Effective price ceilings lead to excess demand and provide a strong incentive for black marketeers to buy at the controlled price and sell at the higher free-market (illegal) price.

Rent Controls: A Case Study of Price Ceilings

(LO) 4 5

- Rent controls are a widespread form of price ceiling. The major consequence of effective rent controls is a shortage of rental accommodations that gets worse over time because of a decline in the quantity of rental housing supplied.

- Rent controls can be an effective response to temporary situations in which there is a ban on building or a transitory increase in demand. They usually fail when they are introduced as a response to a long-run increase in demand.

Agriculture and the Farm Problem

(LO) 6

- Agricultural markets are subject to wide fluctuations that cause variability in farmers' incomes. They occur because of year-to-year unplanned fluctuations in supplies combined with inelastic demands (domestic markets), and because of fluctuations in prices (world markets).

- To stabilize farm incomes, the government should not stabilize prices. Instead, it should buy and sell just enough to allow prices to vary in proportion to changes in quantity, thus causing the elasticity of demand for the product to be unity.

- Agricultural prices and incomes are depressed by chronic surpluses in agricultural markets. Government policies to protect farm incomes have included buying farmers' output at above free-market prices, limiting production and acreage through quotas, and paying farmers to leave crops unproduced. Such policies tend to inhibit the reallocation mechanism.

- Canadian farm policy illustrates that government intervention to prevent the working of the market mechanisms affects resource allocation and requires alternative allocative mechanisms. Although farm policy has protected farmers from certain hardships, it has slowed the required outflow of resources that would otherwise solve the problem of chronic excess supply.

KEY CONCEPTS

Partial-equilibrium analysis
General-equilibrium analysis
Regional linkages between markets
Input-output linkages between markets
Linkages through resource constraints
Price controls: floors and ceilings

Allocation by sellers' preferences and by black markets
Rent controls
Short-run and long-run supply curves of rental accommodations

The farm problem: short-run fluctuations and long-run trends
Price stabilization versus income stabilization
Quotas and price-support schemes

STUDY EXERCISES

1. Consider the market for some product X that is represented below in the demand-and-supply diagram.

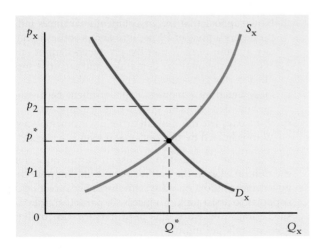

   a. Suppose the government decides to impose a price floor at p_1. Describe how this affects the market equilibrium.
   b. Suppose the government decides to impose a price floor at p_2. Describe how this affects the market equilibrium.
   c. Suppose the government decides to impose a price ceiling at p_1. Describe how this affects the market equilibrium.
   d. Suppose the government decides to impose a price ceiling at p_2. Describe how this affects the market equilibrium.

2. Consider the market for rental housing in Yourtown. The demand and supply schedules for rental housing are given in the table.

Price ($ per month)	Quantity Demanded (thousands of units)	Quantity Supplied (thousands of units)
1100	40	80
1000	50	77
900	60	73
800	70	70
700	80	67
600	90	65
500	100	60

a. In a free market for rental housing, what is the equilibrium price and quantity?

b. Now suppose that the government in Yourtown decides to impose a ceiling on the monthly rental price. What is the highest level that such a ceiling could be, in order to have any effect on the market? Explain your answer.

c. Suppose that the maximum rental price is set equal to $500 per month. Describe the effect on the rental-housing market.

d. Suppose that a black market develops in the presence of these rent controls. What is the black-market price that would exist if all of the quantity supplied were supplied on the black market?

3. Explain and show in a diagram why the short-run effects of rent control are likely to be much less significant than the long-run effects.

4. Consider the situation faced by Canadian oil producers. The price of oil is determined in world markets and Canadian oil producers take that price as given. Letting p be the world price of oil (in dollars per barrel) and Q^S be the number of barrels (in millions per month) supplied by Canadian producers, suppose the domestic supply curve is given by:

Domestic Supply: $Q^S = 20 + 8p$

a. Plot the domestic supply curve for oil (between $p = \$8$ and $p = \$18$).

b. Explain why the supply curve is upward sloping. (That is, what are firms doing to increase quantity supplied in response to an increase in price?)

c. Now suppose that the world price is volatile. For simplicity, suppose it varies between a high value of $16 per barrel and a low value of $9 per barrel. How does such volatility affect the revenue of Canadian oil producers? Show this in a diagram.

5. Consider the situation of Canadian barley farmers, who face weather conditions largely independent of those faced by barley growers in other countries. The incomes earned by the Canadian farmers, however, are affected by what happens to barley farmers in other countries. The key point is that Canadian barley farmers sell their barley on the same *world market* as all other barley farmers.

a. Show in a diagram how a bumper crop of European barley will push down the world barley price.

b. Show in a diagram how a reduction in the world price of barley, *ceteris paribus*, will reduce the incomes of Canadian barley farmers.

c. Explain why Canadian barley farmers are made better off when there are crop failures in other parts of the world.

6. This is a challenging question designed for those students who like mathematics. Consider the market for milk in Saskatchewan. If p is the price of milk (cents per litre) and Q is the quantity of litres (in millions per month), suppose that the demand and supply curves for milk are given by:

Demand: $p = 225 - 15Q^D$
Supply: $p = 25 + 35Q^S$

a. Assuming there is no government form of price support in this market, what is the equilibrium price and quantity?

b. Now suppose that the government guarantees milk producers a price of $2 per litre and promises to buy any amount of milk that the producers cannot sell. What are the quantity demanded and quantity supplied at this guaranteed price?

c. How much milk would the government be buying (per month) with this system of price supports?

d. Who pays for the milk that the government buys? Who is helped by this policy and who is harmed?

7. This question is related to the use of output quotas in the milk market in the previous question. Suppose the government used a quota system instead of direct price supports to assist milk producers. In particular, they issued quotas to existing milk producers for 1.67 million litres of milk per month.

a. If milk production is exactly equal to the amount of quotas issued, what price do consumers pay for milk?

b. Compared to the direct price controls in the previous question, whose income is higher under the quota system? Whose is lower?

8. In 1994, the Quebec and Ontario governments significantly reduced their excise taxes on cigarettes, but Manitoba and Saskatchewan left theirs in place. This led to cigarette smuggling between provinces that linked the provincial markets.

a. Draw a simple demand-and-supply diagram for the "Eastern" market and a separate one for the "Western" market.

b. Suppose that cigarette taxes are reduced in the Eastern market. Show the immediate effects.

c. Now suppose that the supply of cigarettes is (illegally) mobile. Explain and show what happens.

d. What limits the extent of smuggling that will take place in this situation?

DISCUSSION QUESTIONS

1. "When an item is vital to everyone, it is easier to start controlling the price than to stop controlling it. Such controls are popular with consumers, regardless of their harmful consequences." Explain why it may be inefficient to have such controls, why they may be popular, and why, if they are popular, the government might nevertheless choose to decontrol these prices.

2. It is sometimes asserted that the rising costs of construction are putting housing out of the reach of ordinary citizens. Who bears the heaviest cost when rentals are kept down by (a) rent controls, (b) a subsidy to tenants equal to some fraction of their rent payments, and (c) low-cost public housing?

3. "This year the weather smiled on us, and we made a crop," says a wheat farmer near Minedosa in Manitoba. "But just as we made a crop, the economic situation changed." This quotation brings to mind the old saying, "If you are a farmer, the weather is always bad." Discuss the sense in which this saying might be true.

4. During the summer of 1993, severe floods swept through the American Midwest. Although many homes that flooded that year do not typically flood, for many people this was only one in a long string of floods. However, after the waters receded, most people rebuilt their homes, generally with low-interest loans and disaster relief grants from the federal government. Discuss how the policy of subsidizing the reconstruction of property following floods affects the market for real estate in flood-prone areas. Is the outcome more or less efficient in the long run with such government intervention?

5. Gary Storey, a professor of agricultural economics at the University of Saskatchewan, made the following statement: "One of the sad truths of the agricultural policies in Europe and the United States is that they do very little for the future generations of farmers. Most of the subsidies get capitalized into higher land prices, creating windfall gains for current landowners (i.e., gains that they did not expect). It creates a situation where the next generation of farmers require, and ask for, increased government support."

a. Explain why subsidies to farmers increase land values and generate windfall gains to current landowners.

b. As we have seen in this chapter, some Canadian agricultural policies are based on supply management, which involves the use of production quotas. Do such quota systems avoid the problem described by Professor Storey?

6. Soon after the Liberal government was elected in 1993, an "infrastructure" program was implemented that involved spending several billion dollars on bridges, highways, sewer systems, and so on. One of the alleged benefits of this program was to create thousands of jobs, not only in the construction industry but also elsewhere in the economy as construction workers spent their now-higher income on cars, clothing, entertainment, and so on. Discuss how such spending would create jobs in the construction industry. Is such a program likely to create jobs in the economy as a whole?

PART THREE

Consumers and Producers

Why does water, which is essential to life and which we all value dearly, have such a low price? And why do diamonds, a more-or-less unnecessary part of life, have such a high price? Does this paradox mean that the demand-and-supply apparatus that we have just studied is all wrong? What determines the cost of specific products, and why does the cost sometimes depend on how many units are produced? For example, why is the production cost of a widely used textbook significantly less than a similar textbook used only by a few universities? Why has the declining cost of computer-related equipment led some firms to reduce their number of employees? These are the sort of questions you will be able to answer after reading the next three chapters.

In Part 2, we saw that demand and supply are important for determining market prices and quantities. We also saw that the shapes of demand and supply curves influence the way prices and quantities respond to changes in income, technology, or excise taxes. In the next three chapters, we go "behind the scenes" of demand and supply to examine in more detail the behaviour of consumers and the behaviour of firms. This detail will give us a deeper understanding of what demand and supply are all about.

In Chapter 6, we explore the theory of consumer behaviour. There we see how economists think about the way consumers make decisions. We introduce the important concept of utility, as well as the distinction between marginal and total utility. It is this distinction that explains why water has a lower price than diamonds even though it is clearly more "valuable." We will also see how demand curves are derived from the underlying consumer behaviour, and that (except in some very unusual cases) demand curves are indeed negatively sloped.

Chapters 7 and 8 explore the theory of the firm. We consider profits and costs, and how these terms are used differently in economics than in everyday life. The important concepts of average cost and marginal cost will be developed, at which point it will be clear why 50,000 textbooks can be produced at a lower cost per book than can 10,000 textbooks. We will see how firms follow the principle of substitution, and how this explains why the falling cost of computers has led some firms to reduce their workforces (and increase their use of computers). Finally, we explore how changes in technology lead to changes in firms' behaviour.

CHAPTER 6

Consumer Behaviour

🔵 *LEARNING OBJECTIVES*

① Understand why marginal utility falls as the consumption of a product rises.

② Recognize that maximizing utility requires consumers to adjust expenditure until the marginal utility per dollar spent is equalized across all products.

③ View consumer surplus as the "bargain" the consumer gets by paying less for the product than he or she was willing to pay.

④ Understand the distinction between total value, marginal value, and market value.

⑤ Explain how any change in price generates both an income and a substitution effect on quantity demanded.

Imagine that you are walking down the aisle of a supermarket looking for something for your late-night snack (to have while you are studying!). With only a $5 bill in your pocket, you must choose how to divide this $5 between frozen burritos and cans of Coke. How do you make this decision? In this chapter, we see the way economists think about such problems—the theory of consumer behaviour. Not surprisingly, economists (being consumers themselves) think about consumers as caring both about the prices of the goods and the satisfaction they get from the goods.

Marginal Utility and Consumer Choice

Consumers make all kinds of decisions—they choose to drink coffee or tea (or neither), to go to the movies, to dine out, to buy excellent (or not so good) stereo equipment. As we discussed in Chapter 1, economists assume that in making their choices, consumers are motivated to maximize their **utility,** the total satisfaction that they derive from the goods and services that they consume.

utility The satisfaction or well-being that a consumer receives from consuming some good or service.

Utility cannot be measured directly. But our inability to measure something does not mean it is not real. You know that you derive satisfaction—or utility—from a good meal, listening to a CD, or taking a bicycle ride through a park. And even though we cannot measure the utility you derive from these things, we need some way to think about how you as a consumer make your decisions. As we will see in this chapter, it is possible to construct a useful theory of consumer behaviour based on utility maximization even though we cannot directly measure utility.

In developing our theory of consumer behaviour we begin by considering the consumption of a single product. It is useful to distinguish between the consumer's **total utility,** which is the full satisfaction resulting from the consumption of that product by a consumer, and the consumer's **marginal utility,** which is the *additional* satisfaction resulting from consuming one more unit of that product. For example, the total utility of consuming seven Cokes per week is the total satisfaction that those seven Cokes provide. The marginal utility of the seventh Coke consumed is the additional satisfaction provided by the consumption of that Coke.[1]

total utility The total satisfaction resulting from the consumption of a given commodity by a consumer in a period of time.

marginal utility The additional satisfaction obtained by a consumer from consuming one unit more of a good or service.

Diminishing Marginal Utility

The central hypothesis of utility theory, often called the *law of diminishing marginal utility,* is as follows:

The utility that any consumer derives from *successive* units of a particular product diminishes as total consumption of the product increases (if the consumption of all other products is unchanged).

Consider your utility from using clean water, either for drinking, bathing, washing your dishes or clothes, or some other purpose. Some minimum quantity is very important and you would, if necessary, give up a considerable sum of money to obtain that quantity of water. Thus, your marginal utility of that basic quantity of water is very high. You will, of course, consume more than this bare minimum, but your marginal utility of successive litres of water used over a period of time will decline steadily.

We will consider evidence for this hypothesis later, but you can convince yourself that it is at least reasonable by asking a few questions. How much money would be needed to induce you to reduce your consumption of water by one litre per week? The answer is: very little. How much would induce you to reduce it by a second litre? By a third litre? To only one litre consumed per week? The answer to the last question is: quite a bit. The fewer litres you are already using, the higher the marginal utility of one more litre of water.

Utility Schedules and Graphs

The hypothetical schedule in the table in Figure 6-1 illustrates the assumptions that have been made about utility, using Alison's movie attendance as an example. The table shows that Alison's total utility rises as she attends more movies per month. However, the utility that she gets from each *additional* movie per month is less than that of the previous one—that is, her marginal utility declines as the quantity she consumes rises. [10] The data are graphed in the two parts of Figure 6-1.

---

[1]Technically, *incremental* utility is measured over a discrete interval, such as from 6 to 7, whereas *marginal* utility is a rate of change measured over an infinitesimal interval. However, common usage applies the word marginal when the last unit is involved, even if a one-unit change is not infinitesimal. [9]

FIGURE 6-1   Alison's Total and Marginal Utility

Number of Movies Alison Attends Per Month	Alison's Total Utility	Alison's Marginal Utility
0	0	
		30
1	30	
		20
2	50	
		15
3	65	
		10
4	75	
		8
5	83	
		6
6	89	
		4
7	93	
		3
8	96	
		2
9	98	
		1
10	99	

Total utility rises, but marginal utility declines, as consumption increases. The marginal utility of 20, shown as the second entry in the third column, arises because Alison's total utility increases from 30 to 50—a difference of 20—with attendance at the second movie. To indicate that the marginal utility is associated with the change from one level of consumption to another, the figures in the third column are recorded between the rows of the figures in the second column.

Maximizing Utility

Economists assume that consumers try to make themselves as well off as they possibly can in the circumstances in which they find themselves. In other words, the members of a household seek to maximize their total utility.

The Consumer's Decision

How can a consumer adjust expenditure so as to maximize total utility? A simple answer is that the consumer should consume such that the marginal utility of each product is the same—that is, such that the last unit of each product consumed is valued equally. But this would make sense only if each product had the same price per unit. Suppose Alison is buying two goods that have prices per unit of $3 and $1. The first product would represent a poor use of money if the marginal utility of the two goods were equal.

Alison would be spending $3 to get utility equal to what she could have acquired for only $1 by buying the other good.

A consumer who is maximizing utility will allocate expenditures so that the utility obtained from the last dollar spent on each product is equal.

Imagine that Alison's utility from the last dollar spent on cashews is three times her utility from the last dollar spent on toffee. In this case, Alison can increase her total utility by switching a dollar of expenditure from toffee to cashews and by gaining the difference between the utilities of a dollar spent on each.

Alison will continue to switch her expenditure from toffee to cashews as long as her last dollar spent on cashews yields more utility than her last dollar spent on toffee. This switching, however, reduces the quantity of toffee consumed and, given the law of diminishing marginal utility, raises the marginal utility of toffee. At the same time, switching increases the quantity of cashews consumed and thereby lowers the marginal utility of cashews.

Eventually, the marginal utilities will have changed enough so that the utility of Alison's last dollar spent on cashews is just equal to the utility of her last dollar spent on toffee. At this point, she gains nothing from further switches. (In fact, switching further would *reduce* her total utility.)

So much for the simple example. Now, what can we say more generally about utility maximization? Suppose we denote the marginal utility of the last unit of product X by MU_X and its price by p_X. Let MU_Y and p_Y refer, respectively, to the marginal utility of a second product Y and its price. The marginal utility per dollar spent on X will be MU_X/p_X. For example, if the last unit of X increases utility by 30 and costs $2, its marginal utility per dollar is $30/2 = 15$.

The condition required for a consumer to be maximizing utility, for any pair of products, is

$$\frac{MU_X}{p_X} = \frac{MU_Y}{p_Y} \qquad (6\text{-}1)$$

This equation says that the consumer will allocate expenditure so that the utility gained from the last dollar spent on each product is equal.

This is the fundamental equation of marginal utility theory. A consumer demands each good up to the point at which the marginal utility per dollar spent on it is the same as the marginal utility per dollar spent on every other good. When this condition is met for all goods, the consumer cannot increase utility further by reallocating expenditure. That is, utility will be maximized.

Notice from our example that when Alison is deciding how much of a given product to purchase, she compares the utility from that product to the utility she could derive from spending the same money on other things. Thus, the idea of *opportunity cost* is central to our theory of consumer behaviour.

When expenditure is adjusted to maximize utility, the value to the consumer of consuming the marginal unit of some good is just equal to the opportunity cost—the value to the consumer of the money used to make the purchase.

An Alternative Interpretation

If we rearrange the terms in Equation 6-1, we can gain additional insight into consumer behaviour.

$$\frac{MU_X}{MU_Y} = \frac{p_X}{p_Y} \qquad\qquad (6\text{-}2)$$

The right side of this equation is the *relative* price of the two goods. It is determined by the market and is beyond Alison's control. She reacts to these market prices but is powerless to change them. The left side is the *relative* ability of the two goods to add to Alison's utility. This is within her control because in determining the quantities of different goods to buy, she also determines their marginal utilities. (If you have difficulty seeing why, look again at Figure 6-1.)

If the two sides of Equation 6-2 are not equal, Alison can increase her total utility by rearranging purchases. To see this, suppose that the price of a unit of X is twice the price of a unit of Y ($p_X/p_Y = 2$) and that the marginal utility of a unit of X is three times that of a unit of Y ($MU_X/MU_Y = 3$). Under these conditions, it is worthwhile for Alison to buy more of X and less of Y. For example, if she reduces purchases of Y by two units, enough purchasing power is freed for her to buy one unit of X. Because one extra unit of X yields 1½ times the utility of two units of Y forgone, the switch is worth making. What about a further switch of X for Y? As Alison buys more of X and less of Y, the marginal utility of X falls and the marginal utility of Y rises. Alison will go on rearranging purchases, reducing Y and increasing X, until (in this example) the marginal utility of X is only twice that of Y. At this point, Alison's total utility cannot be increased further by rearranging purchases between the two products.

Consider what Alison is doing. She is faced with a set of prices that she cannot change. She responds to these prices and maximizes her utility by adjusting the things that she *can* change—the quantities of the various goods that she purchases—until Equation 6-2 is satisfied for all pairs of products.

The Consumer's Demand Curve

To derive the consumer's demand curve for a product, it is only necessary to ask what happens when there is a change in the price of that product. As an example, let us derive Alison's demand curve for cashews. Consider Equation 6-2 and let X represent cashews and Y represent *all other products taken together*. In this case, the price of Y is interpreted as the average price of all other products. What will Alison do if, with all other prices remaining constant, there is an increase in the price of cashews? When the price of cashews rises, the right side of Equation 6-2 increases. But, until Alison adjusts consumption, the left side is unchanged. Thus, after the price changes but before Alison reacts, she will be in a position in which the following circumstance prevails:

$$\frac{MU \text{ of cashews}}{MU \text{ of } Y} < \frac{\text{price of cashews}}{\text{price of } Y}$$

What does Alison do to restore the equality? The hypothesis of diminishing marginal utility tells us that as she buys fewer cashews, the *marginal* utility of cashews will rise and thereby increase the ratio on the left side. Thus, in response to an increase in the price of cashews, with all other prices constant, Alison reduces her consumption of cashews until the marginal utility of cashews rises sufficiently that Equation 6-2 is restored.

This analysis leads to the basic prediction of demand theory:

A rise in the price of a product (with income and the prices of all other products held constant) leads each consumer to reduce the quantity demanded of the product.

Practise with Study Guide Chapter 6, Exercise 2.

If this is what each consumer does, it is also what all consumers taken together do. Thus the theory of consumer behaviour that we have considered here predicts a negatively sloped market demand curve in addition to a negatively sloped demand curve for each individual consumer. *Extensions in Theory 6-1* shows how we can obtain a market demand curve by adding up the demand curves of individual consumers.

Consumer Surplus

An instinctive appreciation for the difference between *total* utility and *marginal* utility is important for understanding the theory of consumer behaviour. The concept of *consumer surplus* helps make this difference clear.

EXTENSIONS IN THEORY 6-1
Market and Individual Demand Curves

Market demand curves show how much is demanded by all purchasers. For example, in Figure 3-1, the market demand for carrots is 90 000 tons when the price is $40 per ton. This 90 000 tons is the sum of the quantities demanded by millions of different consumers. The demand curve in Figure 3-1 also tells us that when the price rises to $60, the total quantity demanded falls to 77 500 tons per year. This quantity, too, can be traced back to individual consumers. Notice that we have now identified two points not only on the market demand curve but also on the demand curves of each of the millions of individual consumers.

The market demand curve is the horizontal sum of the demand curves of individual consumers. It is the horizontal sum because we wish to add quantities demanded at a given price, and quantities are measured in the horizontal direction on a conventional demand curve.

The figure illustrates aggregation over two consumers, Alison and Brenda. At a price of $3, Alison purchases 2 units and Brenda purchases 4 units; thus together they purchase 6 units, yielding one point on the market demand curve. No matter how many consumers are involved, the process is the same: Add the quantities demanded by all consumers at each price, and the result is the market demand curve.

(i) Alison   (ii) Brenda   (iii) Alison and Brenda

The Concept

Imagine yourself facing an either-or choice concerning some particular product, say, ice cream: You can have the amount you are now consuming, or you can have none of it. Suppose that you would be willing to pay as much as $100 per month for the 8 litres of gourmet ice cream that you now consume, rather than do without it. Further suppose that you actually buy those 8 litres for only $40 instead of $100. What a bargain! You have paid $60 less than the most you were willing to pay. Actually this sort of bargain occurs every day in any economy in which prices do the rationing. Indeed, it is so common that the $60 "saved" in this example has been given a name: *consumer surplus*. **Consumer surplus** is the difference between the total value that consumers place on all the units consumed of some product and the payment they must make to purchase that amount of the product.

Consumer surplus is a direct consequence of negatively sloped demand curves. To illustrate this connection, suppose that we have interviewed Mr. Jean Aulait and displayed the information from the interview in the table in Figure 6-2. Our first question to Jean is, "If you were getting no milk at all, how much would you be willing to pay for one glass per week?" With no hesitation he replies, "$3.00." We then ask, "If you had already consumed that one glass, how much would you be willing to pay for a second glass per week?" After a bit of thought, he answers, "$1.50." Adding one glass per

consumer surplus
The difference between the total value that consumers place on all units consumed of a commodity and the payment that they must make to purchase that amount of the commodity.

FIGURE 6-2   Jean's Consumer Surplus on Milk Consumption

Glasses of Milk Jean Consumes Per Week	Amount Jean Is Willing to Pay to Obtain This Glass	Jean's Consumer Surplus on Each Glass if Milk Costs 30 Cents Per Glass
First	$3.00	$2.70
Second	1.50	1.20
Third	1.00	0.70
Fourth	0.80	0.50
Fifth	0.60	0.30
Sixth	0.50	0.20
Seventh	0.40	0.10
Eighth	0.30	0.00
Ninth	0.25	—
Tenth	0.20	—

Consumer surplus on each unit consumed is the difference between the market price and the maximum price that the consumer is willing to pay to obtain that unit. The table shows the value that Jean puts on successive glasses of milk consumed each week. His negatively sloped demand curve shows that he would be willing to pay progressively smaller amounts for each additional unit consumed. If the market price is 30 cents per glass, Jean will buy eight glasses of milk per week and pay the amount in the dark shaded area. The total value he places on these eight glasses is the entire shaded area. His consumer surplus is the light shaded area.

week with each question, we discover that he would be willing to pay $1.00 to get a third glass per week and 80, 60, 50, 40, 30, 25, and 20 cents for successive glasses from the fourth to the tenth glass per week.

The sum of the values that he places on each glass of milk gives us the *total value* that he places on all 10 glasses. In this case, Jean Aulait values 10 glasses of milk per week at $8.55. This is the amount he would be willing to pay if he faced the either-or choice of 10 glasses or none. This is also the amount he would be willing to pay if he were offered the milk one glass at a time and charged the maximum he was willing to pay for each.

However, Jean does not have to pay a different price for each glass of milk he consumes each week; he can buy all he wants at the prevailing market price. Suppose that the price is 30 cents per glass. He will buy eight glasses per week because he values the eighth glass just at the market price but all earlier glasses at higher amounts. He does not buy a ninth glass because he values it at less than the market price.

Because Jean values the first glass at $3.00 but gets it for 30 cents, he makes a "profit" of $2.70 on that glass. Between his $1.50 valuation of the second glass and what he has to pay for it, he clears a "profit" of $1.20. He clears a "profit" of 70 cents on the third glass, and so on. This "profit," which is shown in the third column of the table, is Jean's consumer surplus on each glass.

We can calculate Jean's total consumer surplus of $5.70 per week by summing his surplus on each glass; we can calculate the same total by first summing what he would be willing to pay for all eight glasses, which is $8.10, and then subtracting the $2.40 that he actually does pay.

The value placed by each consumer on the total consumption of some product can be estimated in two ways: The valuation that the consumer places on each successive unit may be summed, or the consumer may be asked how much he or she would be willing to pay to consume the amount in question if the alternative were to have none of that product.

Consumer surplus is the difference between what the consumer is willing to pay for the product and what the consumer actually pays.

Although other consumers would put different numerical values into the table in Figure 6-2, the negative slope of the demand curve implies that the values in the second column would be declining for every consumer. Because any consumer will go on buying additional units until the value placed on the last unit equals the market price, it follows that there will be consumer surplus on every unit consumed except the last one.

The data in the first two columns of the table give Jean's demand curve for milk. It is his demand curve because he will go on buying glasses of milk as long as he values each glass at least as much as the market price he must pay for it. When the market price is $3.00 per glass, he will buy only one glass; when it is $1.50, he will buy two glasses; and so on. The total valuation is the area below his demand curve, and consumer surplus is the part of the area that lies above the price line. These areas are shown in Figure 6-2.

Figure 6-3 shows that the same relationship holds for the smooth market demand curve that indicates the total amount that all consumers would buy at each price. Figure 6-2 is a bar chart because we only allowed Jean Aulait to vary his consumption in discrete units of one glass at a time. Had we allowed him to vary his consumption of milk one drop at a time, we could have traced out a continuous curve similar to the one shown in Figure 6-3.

Practise with Study Guide Chapter 6,
Extension Exercise E-1.

Consumer surplus for the entire market is equal to the area under the market demand curve but above the price line.

Applications

Consumer surplus is an important and useful concept. It will prove useful in later chapters when we evaluate the performance—the *efficiency*—of the market system. For now, however, we discuss two examples where the concept of consumer surplus helps us to understand apparently paradoxical market outcomes. Central to both examples is the distinction between total value and marginal value.

The Paradox of Value

Early economists, struggling with the problem of what determines the relative prices of products, encountered what they called the *paradox of value*. Many necessary products, such as water, have prices that are low compared to the prices of luxury products, such as diamonds. Water is necessary to our existence, whereas diamonds are used mostly for frivolous purposes and could disappear from the face of the earth tomorrow without causing any real hardship. Does it not seem odd, then, that water is so cheap and diamonds are so expensive? As it took a long time to resolve this apparent paradox, it is not surprising that even today, analogous confusions cloud many policy discussions.

The key to resolving this apparent paradox lies in the important distinction between the total and marginal value of any product. We have seen already that the area under the demand curve is a measure of the *total value* placed on all of the units that the consumer consumes. For all consumers together, the total value of q_0 units is the entire shaded area (light and dark) under the demand curve in Figure 6-3.

What about the *marginal value* that each consumer places on one additional unit? This is given by the product's market price, which is p_0 in Figure 6-3. Facing a market price of p_0, each consumer buys all the units that he or she values at p_0 or greater but does not purchase any units valued at less than p_0. It follows that each consumer values the last unit consumed of any product at that product's price.

Now look at the total *market* value of the product. This is the amount that everyone spends to purchase it. It is price multiplied by quantity. In Figure 6-3, this is the dark shaded rectangle.

Because the market demand curve is negatively sloped, the total value that consumers place on a given amount of a product, as measured by the relevant area under the demand curve, is different from the total market value of a product, as given by the product's price multiplied by the quantity consumed. Not only are the two values different, but they are generally unrelated, except that the total area under the demand curve is always greater than the total market value. Figure 6-4 illustrates a case in which a good—like clean

FIGURE 6-3 Consumer Surplus for the Market

Price

Market price

p_0

D

0 q_0

Quantity Consumed Per Period

Total consumer surplus is the area under the demand curve and above the price line. The area under the demand curve shows the total valuation that consumers place on all units consumed. For example, the total value that consumers place on q_0 units is the entire shaded area under the demand curve up to q_0. At a market price of p_0, the amount paid for q_0 units is the dark shaded area. Hence consumer surplus is the light shaded area.

FIGURE 6-4   Total Value Versus Market Value

(i) Water

(ii) Diamonds

The market value of the amount of some product bears no necessary relationship to the total value that consumers place on that amount. The graph presents hypothetical demand curves for water and diamonds that are meant to be stylized versions of the real curves. The total value that consumers place on water, as shown by the area under the demand curve, is great. The total value that consumers place on diamonds is shown by the area under the demand curve for diamonds. This is clearly less than the total value placed on water.

The large supply of water makes water plentiful and makes water low in price, as shown by p_w in part (i) of the figure. Thus the total *market* value of water consumed, indicated by the dark shaded area, is low. The low supply of diamonds makes diamonds scarce and keeps diamonds high in price, as shown by p_d in part (ii) of the figure. Thus the total *market* value of diamonds sold, indicated by the light shaded area, is high.

water—has a high total value but a low market value, whereas a different good—like diamonds—has a low total value but a high market value.

The resolution of the paradox of value is that a good that is very plentiful, such as water, will have a low price and will thus be consumed to the point where all consumers place a low value on the last unit consumed, whether or not they place a high value on their *total* consumption of the product. By contrast, a product that is relatively scarce will have a high market price, and consumption will therefore stop at a point where consumers place a high value on the last unit consumed, regardless of the value that they place on their total consumption of the good.

Because the market price of a product depends on both demand and supply, there is nothing paradoxical in there being a product on which consumers place a high *total* value (such as water) selling for a low price and hence having a low *marginal* value.

Attitude Surveys

Attitude surveys often ask people which of several alternatives they prefer. Such questions reveal *total* rather than *marginal* utilities. Where the behaviour being predicted involves an either-or decision, such as to vote for the Liberal or the Conservative candidate, the total utility that is attached to each party or candidate will indeed be what matters, because the voter must choose one and reject the other. Where the decision is a marginal one regarding a little more or a little less, however, total utility is not what will determine behaviour. If one attempts to predict behaviour in these cases from knowledge of total utilities, even if the information is correct, one will make serious errors.

Here are two examples of how surveys can be misinterpreted. A Canadian market research survey asked people to name the household device they thought was most important. Though many appliances ranked highly, vacuum cleaners were judged by the most households as being the most important device. Suppliers of a new version of vacuum cleaner used the survey to predict demand but subsequently found that it had failed to accurately do so. A post-mortem revealed that most people did not respond to the sales promotion because they already had a vacuum cleaner and were unwilling to pay the advertised price for a second one. In other words, although the *total* utility they got from their vacuum cleaner was high, the utility they would get from an additional one—their *marginal* utility—was low.

For a second example, a political party in the U.K. conducted a survey to determine what types of public expenditure people thought most valuable. Unemployment benefits rated very high. The party was subsequently surprised when it aroused great voter hostility by advocating an increase in unemployment benefits. Although the party was surprised, there was nothing inconsistent or irrational in the voters' feeling that protection of the unemployed was a very good thing, providing a high total utility, but that additional payments were unnecessary, and therefore had a low marginal utility.

Income and Substitution Effects of Price Changes

In the first section of this chapter, we examined the relationship between the *law of diminishing marginal utility* and the slope of the consumer's demand curve for some product. In this section, we will consider an alternative method for thinking about the slope of an individual's demand curve. From the discussion in *Extensions in Theory 6-1*, this alternative method can also be used to think about the slope of a market demand curve.

Let's consider Tony, a college student who loves to eat ice cream. A fall in the price of ice cream affects Tony in two ways. First, it provides an incentive to buy more ice cream because it is cheaper. Second, because the price of ice cream has fallen, Tony has more *purchasing power* available to spend on all products. Suppose that the price of premium ice cream fell from $5.00 to $4.00 per litre and Tony was in the habit of eating half a litre of ice cream a day. In the course of a 30-day month, Tony could keep his ice cream habit unchanged but save $15.00, money that would be available for any purpose—more ice cream, video rentals, or photocopies of your economics notes.

real income Income expressed in terms of the purchasing power of money income, that is, the quantity of goods and services that can be purchased with the money income. It can be calculated as money income deflated by a price index.

The price fall generates an increase in Tony's **real income**, which is defined as the quantity of goods and services that can be purchased with a given amount of money income. This rise in real income in turn provides an incentive to buy more of all normal goods. (Recall from Chapter 4 that when real income rises, the consumer buys more of all normal goods and less of all inferior goods.)

In general, the *extent* of the rise in real income depends on the share of total expenditures that the consumer spends on each good. For example, consider the extreme case in which Tony spends all of his income on ice cream. If the price of ice cream falls by half, he would find that his real income has doubled because he can buy twice as much as before. At the other extreme, if Tony spent none of his income on ice cream and all of it on other things, he would find that his consumption opportunities are unchanged—he can still buy exactly what he bought before the price of ice cream fell. For intermediate cases where both ice cream and other goods are purchased, there will be some positive effect on real income when the price of ice cream falls.

The Substitution Effect

To isolate the effect of the change in relative price when the price of ice cream falls, we can consider what would happen if we also reduce Tony's money income to restore the original purchasing power. Suppose that Tony's uncle sends him a monthly allowance for ice cream, and that when the price of ice cream falls, the allowance is reduced so that Tony can buy just as much ice cream—and everything else—as he could before. Tony's purchasing power will be unchanged. If his behaviour remains unchanged, however, he will not be maximizing his utility. Recall that utility maximization requires that the ratio of marginal utility to price be the same for all goods. In our example, with no change in behaviour, the quantities (and hence marginal utilities) and the prices of all goods other than ice cream are unchanged. The quantity of ice cream is also unchanged, but the price has fallen. To maximize his utility, Tony must therefore increase his consumption (reduce his marginal utility) of ice cream and reduce his consumption of all other goods.

When purchasing power is held constant, the change in the quantity demanded of a good whose relative price changed is called the **substitution effect** of the price change.[2]

The substitution effect increases the quantity demanded of a good whose price has fallen and reduces the quantity demanded of a good whose price has risen.

substitution effect The change in the quantity of a good demanded resulting from a change in its relative price (holding real income constant).

The Income Effect

To examine the substitution effect, we reduced Tony's *money* income following the price reduction so that we could see the effect of the relative price change, holding purchasing power constant. Now we want to see the effect of the change in purchasing power, *holding relative prices constant at their new value.* To do this, suppose that after Tony has adjusted his purchases to the new price and his reduced income, he then calls his uncle and pleads to have his allowance restored to its original (higher) amount. Tony's uncle agrees, and Tony's money income is returned to its original level. If we assume that ice cream is a normal good, Tony will increase his consumption of ice cream. The change in the quantity of ice cream demanded as a result of Tony's reaction to increased real income is called the **income effect**.

income effect The change in the quantity of a good demanded resulting from a change in real income (holding relative prices constant).

---

[2]This measure, which isolates the substitution effect by holding the consumer's purchasing power constant, is known as the *Slutsky Effect.* A related but slightly different measure that holds the consumer's level of utility constant is discussed in the appendix to this chapter.

The income effect leads consumers to buy more of a product whose price has fallen, provided that the product is a normal good.

Notice that the size of the income effect depends on the amount of income spent on the good whose price changes and on the amount by which the price changes. In our example, if Tony were initially spending half of his income on ice cream, a reduction in the price of ice cream from $5 to $4 would be equivalent to a 10 percent increase in income (20 percent of 50 percent). Now consider a different case: The price of gasoline falls by 20 percent. For a consumer who was spending only 5 percent of income on gas, this is equivalent to only a 1 percent increase in purchasing power (20 percent of 5 percent).

The Slope of the Demand Curve

We have now divided Tony's reaction to a change in the price of ice cream into a substitution effect and an income effect. Of course, when the price changes, Tony moves directly from the initial consumption pattern to the final one; we do not observe any "halfway" consumption pattern. By breaking this movement into two parts for analytical purposes, however, we are able to study Tony's total change in quantity demanded as a response to a change in relative prices plus a response to a change in real income.

What is true for Tony is also true, in general terms, for all consumers. The substitution effect leads consumers to increase their demand for goods whose prices fall. The income effect leads consumers to buy more of all normal goods whose prices fall.

Putting the income and substitution effects together gives the following statement of the law of demand:

Because of the combined operation of the income and substitution effects, the demand curve for any normal commodity will be negatively sloped. Thus a fall in price will increase the quantity demanded.

For most inferior goods, the demand curve also has a negative slope. The theoretical possibility that demand curves might not have a negative slope is considered in *Extensions in Theory 6-2*.

Finally, note that the logic of breaking down a price change into the separate income and substitution effects is not limited to the analysis of demand. The same logic applies to supply. A particularly important example involves the labour market: How does a change in the market wage affect the quantity of work effort supplied by individuals? *Applying Economic Concepts 6-1* addresses the issue of how a change in income-tax rates—and thus a change in the after-tax wage—alters individuals' incentives to work.

EXTENSIONS IN THEORY 6-2

Can Demand Curves Have a Positive Slope?

The law of demand asserts that, other things being constant, the price and quantity demanded of a product are negatively related; that is, demand curves have a negative slope. Challenges to the law have taken various forms, focusing on Giffen goods and "conspicuous consumption" goods.

Giffen Goods

Great interest was attached to the apparent refutation of the law of demand by the English economist Sir Robert Giffen (1837–1910). He is alleged to have observed that when a rise in the price of imported wheat led to an increase in the price of bread, members of the British working class *increased* their consumption of bread, suggesting that their demand curve for bread was positively sloped.

Two things must be true in order for a good to be a so-called **Giffen good**. First, the good must be an inferior good, meaning that a reduction in real income leads households to purchase *more* of that good. Second, the good must take a large proportion of total household expenditure. Bread was indeed a dietary staple of the British working classes during the nineteenth century. A rise in the price of bread would therefore cause a large reduction in their real income. This could lead people to eat more bread (and less meat) in order to consume enough calories to stay alive. Though possible, such cases are all but unknown in the modern world, for in all but the poorest societies, typical households do not spend large proportions of their incomes on any single inferior good.

Conspicuous Consumption Goods

Thorstein Veblen (1857–1929), in *The Theory of the Leisure Class*, noted that some products were consumed not for their intrinsic qualities but because they had "snob appeal." He suggested that the more expensive such a commodity became, the greater might be its ability to confer status on its purchaser.

Consumers might value diamonds, for example, precisely because everyone knows they are expensive. Thus a fall in price might lead them to stop buying diamonds and to switch to a more satisfactory object of conspicuous consumption. They may behave in the same way with respect to luxury cars, buying them *because* they are expensive.

Two comments are in order. First, in a case where individuals appear to buy more goods at a higher price *because of the high price*, there is actually something else going on that explains the apparent violation of the law of demand. What really appeals to such individuals is that *other people think* they paid a high price—this is the basis for the "snob appeal." But such snobs would still buy more at a lower price (and hence still have negatively sloped demand curves) as long as they were absolutely sure that other people *thought* they had paid the high price. As one advertising slogan for a discount department store puts it: "Only you know how little you paid."

Second, even if such conspicuous consumers do exist, it is very unlikely that the *market* demand curve is positively sloped. The reason is easy to discover. The fact that countless lower-income consumers would be glad to buy diamonds or Cadillacs only if these commodities were sufficiently inexpensive suggests that positively sloped demand curves for a few individual wealthy households are much more likely than a positively sloped *market* demand curve for the same commodity.

Market Demand Curves

Even if some individual consumers exhibited one or both of the "exceptions" to the law of demand discussed here, in most cases their actions would be swamped by those of the many more consumers whose behaviour conformed to the law of demand. Thus the *market* demand curve would still be negatively sloped.

All in all, the mass of accumulated evidence confirms that demand curves generally have a negative slope. Exceptions are extremely rare.

Giffen good   An inferior good for which the negative income effect outweighs the substitution effect so that the demand curve is positively sloped.

APPLYING ECONOMIC CONCEPTS 6-1

Do Taxes Discourage Work Effort?

Although they sound highly abstract and "theoretical" when you first encounter them, the income and substitution effects turn out to be very useful tools. They help a great deal when thinking about many economic issues. One particularly important issue involves the effect that income taxes have on individuals' incentive to work. Would cutting the income-tax rate lead individuals to work more?

Policymakers frequently face such questions, and they are often surprised at the results produced by the market. In several countries, increases in income-tax rates (within a moderate range) have been found to be associated with people working more hours, rather than fewer. The surprise in such cases was the same. Simple intuition suggests that if you pay people a higher wage, they will work more hours. Experience, however, shows that the result is often the opposite.

The explanation of this surprising behaviour lies in distinguishing the income effect from the substitution effect of a change in the after-tax wage. Consider Luke starting with an endowment of 24 hours per day and deciding to consume some of that time as "leisure" (including sleep) and to trade the rest of the time for income by working. If Luke works 9 hours a day at an after-tax wage of $10 per hour, he earns $90. He is then "consuming" 15 hours a day of leisure and can use the $90 worth of income to buy goods and services.

Now suppose the government reduces the rate of income tax so that Luke's after-tax wage rises from $10 to $12. What does Luke do? His response to the increase in the after-tax wage will be made up by the income effect and the substitution effect.

The substitution effect works in the same away as does the simple intuition above. With a higher after-tax wage, Luke's opportunity cost of leisure increases. That is, Luke must now give up more income (and thus more other goods and services) for each hour of leisure that he enjoys. This simple change in relative prices (the price of leisure in terms of other goods) leads Luke to substitute

toward work and away from leisure. If the substitution effect were all that mattered, then the reduction in taxes would lead people to work harder.

But there is also an income effect, and this is where the surprise comes in. The rise in the after-tax wage increases Luke's purchasing power in the sense that Luke can now afford to have more goods and more leisure. For example, he could choose to reduce his daily work time from 9 hours to 8 hours and still increase his earnings from $90 (9 hours × $10 per hour) to $96 (8 hours × $12 per hour). In this case, Luke would have more leisure and he could purchase more goods and services. In fact, if leisure is a normal "good"—meaning that Luke demands more of it when his income rises—then the income effect taken by itself would lead Luke to work less in response to the tax reduction.

What is the total effect on Luke's work effort? We simply add together the income effect and the substitution effect. If the substitution effect dominates, then the tax reduction will lead Luke to work more hours. But if the income effect dominates, then the tax reduction will lead Luke to work fewer hours.

In general, we don't know exactly how any given individual will respond to such a tax reduction. If leisure is an *inferior* good, then the substitution and income effects work in the same direction, in which case a reduction in income-tax rates will surely lead people to work more. But most economists think that leisure is a normal good. Thus the substitution and income effects work in opposite directions; in this more likely case, the net effect depends on the individual's circumstances and preferences.

Given the possibilities, policymakers should not be surprised if they find that increases in income-tax rates sometimes lead people to work more. This result is not guaranteed, but it is certainly possible. The simple explanation is that leisure is a normal good and that the income effect of the tax change is stronger than the substitution effect.

S U M M A R Y

Marginal Utility and Consumer Choice

LO ① ②

- Marginal utility theory distinguishes between the total utility from the consumption of *all units* of some product and the incremental (or marginal) utility derived from consuming *one more unit* of the product.
- The basic assumption in marginal utility theory is that the utility that consumers derive from the consumption of successive units of a product diminishes as the number of units consumed increases.
- Consumers are assumed to make their decisions in a way that maximizes their utility. They thus make their choices such that the utility derived from the last dollar spent on

each product is equal. For two goods X and Y, utility will be maximized when

$$\frac{MU_X}{p_X} = \frac{MU_Y}{p_Y}$$

- Demand curves have negative slopes because when the price of one product, X, falls, each consumer responds by increasing purchases of X sufficiently to restore the ratio of that product's marginal utility to its now lower price (MU_X/p_X) to the same level achieved for all other products.

Consumer Surplus

LO ③ ④

- The total value that consumers place on some quantity of a product consumed is given by the area under the demand curve up to that quantity. The market value is given by an area below the market price up to that quantity. Consumer surplus is the difference between the two. In other words, consumer surplus is the difference between what the consumers would be *willing to pay* for some quantity of the good and what the consumers *actually pay* for that quantity of the good.
- Consumer surplus arises because a consumer can purchase every unit of a product at a price equal to the value placed on the last unit purchased. The negative slope of demand curves implies that the value that consumers

place on all other units purchased exceeds the value of the last unit purchased and hence that all but the last unit purchased yields consumer surplus.
- It is important to distinguish between total and marginal values because choices concerning a bit more and a bit less cannot be predicted from a knowledge of total values. The paradox of value involves a confusion between total value and marginal value.
- Price is related to the *marginal* value that consumers place on having a bit more or a bit less of some product; it bears no necessary relationship to the *total* value that consumers place on all of the units consumed of that product.

Income and Substitution Effects of Price Changes

LO ⑤

- A change in the price of a product generates both an income effect and a substitution effect. The substitution effect is the reaction of the consumer to the change in relative prices, with purchasing power held constant. The substitution effect leads the consumer to increase purchases of the product whose relative price has fallen.
- The income effect is the reaction of the consumer to the change in purchasing power that is caused by the price change, holding relative prices constant. A fall in one

price will lead to an increase in the consumer's purchasing power and thus to an increase in purchases of all normal goods.
- The combined income and substitution effects ensure that the quantity demanded of any normal good will increase when its money price falls, other things being equal. Normal goods, therefore, have negatively sloped demand curves.

KEY CONCEPTS

Total utility and marginal utility
Utility maximization
Equality of MU/p across different
  goods

Slope of the demand curve
Consumer surplus
The paradox of value

Income effect and substitution effect
Giffen goods and conspicuous
  consumption goods

STUDY EXERCISES

1. The table below shows how Brett's utility increases as the number of avocados he consumes (each month) increases. Brett's utility is measured in *utils*, a name that economists invented to describe units of utility.

Avocados	Total Utility (in utils)	Marginal Utility (in utils)
Zero	0	____
First	100	____
Second	185	____
Third	245	____
Fourth	285	____
Fifth	315	____
Sixth	335	____
Seventh	345	____
Eighth	350	____

   a. Plot Brett's total utility on a scale diagram, with utils on the vertical axis and the number of avocados (per month) on the horizontal axis.
   b. Compute the marginal utility for each avocado and fill in the table.
   c. Plot the marginal utility on a scale diagram, with utils on the vertical axis and the number of avocados (per month) on the horizontal axis. (Make sure to plot marginal utility at the midpoints between units.)
   d. Explain why it is reasonable that Brett's utility increases by smaller and smaller amounts for each successive avocado consumed.

2. In each of the cases listed below, identify how Claudia's expenditure should be changed to maximize her utility.

Case	Price of X ($)	Marginal Utility of X (units of utility)	Price of Y ($)	Marginal Utility of Y (units of utility)
A	10	2	5	3
B	12	4	4	2
C	3	1	6	2
D	4	2	4	2
E	8	4	4	3

3. Rupert really loves pizza, but he eventually tires of it. The table below shows the highest price that Rupert is willing to pay for each successive pizza per week.

Pizza	Rupert's Willingness to Pay
First	$18
Second	$16
Third	$13
Fourth	$9
Fifth	$4
Sixth	$0

   a. Suppose Rupert were to eat five pizzas per week. What is the total value Rupert would place on his five weekly pizzas?
   b. If the market price is $10 per pizza, how many pizzas will Rupert eat per week?
   c. If the market price is $10 per pizza, what is the weekly consumer surplus that Rupert gets from eating pizza?
   d. Can you state a generalization about the relationship between market price and consumer surplus?

4. Suppose there is a 10 percent increase in the prices of the following products. Explain whether you think the income effect in each case would be small or large, and why.

   a. salt
   b. blue jeans
   c. canned vegetables
   d. gasoline
   e. mini-vans
   f. rental apartments
   g. luxury cars

5. Consider the following supply-and-demand diagrams depicting the markets for X and Y, respectively. In the market for good X, supply is perfectly elastic, indicating that producers are prepared to supply any amount of X at price p_0.

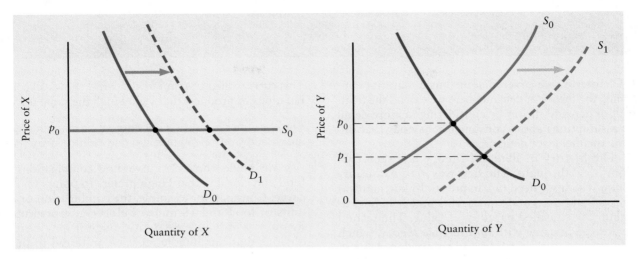

a. In the market for X, demand increases from D_0 to D_1. Explain what happens to the *total* value that consumers place on X.
b. Explain how the increase in demand for X alters the *marginal* value that consumers place on X.
c. In the market for Y, a technological improvement causes supply to increase from S_0 to S_1, causing price to fall from p_0 to p_1. Explain what happens to the total value that consumers place *on a given quantity* of Y.
d. Explain why the increase in supply leads consumers to reduce their *marginal* value of Y even though there has been no change in their preferences regarding Y (and thus no shift in the demand curve).

6. Consider the market for some product, X. The demand and supply curves for X are given by:

Demand: $p = 30 - 4Q^D$
Supply: $p = 6 + 2Q^S$

a. Plot the demand and supply curves on a scale diagram. Compute the equilibrium price (p^*) and quantity (Q^*).
b. Show in the diagram the total value that consumers place on Q^* units of the good.
c. What is the value that consumers place on an *additional* unit of the good?
d. Now suppose that production costs fall and so the market supply curve shifts to a new position given by: $p = 2 + 2Q^S$. How do consumers now value an additional unit of the good?
e. Explain why consumers' marginal value has fallen even though there has been no change in their preferences (and thus no change in the demand curve).

DISCUSSION QUESTIONS

1. Describe the difference in behaviour at a party at which drinks are free between someone who imbibes up to the point where the *marginal* value of more alcohol consumed is zero and someone who imbibes up to the point where the *average* value of alcohol consumed is zero.

2. Compare the consequences of the income effect of a drastic fall in food prices with the consequences of a rise in incomes when prices are constant.

3. Two U.S. economics professors, Jeff Biddle and Daniel Hamermesh, recently estimated that a 25 percent increase in wages will cause the average individual to reduce the time that he or she spends sleeping by about 1 percent. Interpret this finding in terms of the income and substitution effects of a wage change.

4. Consider the following common scenario. An economist is attending a conference in an unfamiliar city. She is in the mood for a high-quality dinner and wanders through the centre of the city looking for a restaurant. After narrowing her search to two establishments, she ultimately selects the restaurant with the higher prices. Because she is an economist, we know that she is rational. What might account for this behaviour?

5. Medical and hospital services in Canada are provided at zero cost to all Canadians and are paid for out of general government revenues. What will be the *marginal value* of such services consumed by each Canadian if the government provides funds to meet all demand?

Indifference Curves

In Chapter 6, we covered some basic material concerning the theory of demand; here we extend the treatment of demand theory by considering in more detail the assumptions about consumer behaviour that underlie the theory of demand.

The history of demand theory has seen two major breakthroughs. The first was *marginal utility theory,* which we used in Chapter 6. By distinguishing total and marginal values, this theory helped to explain the so-called paradox of value. The second breakthrough came with *indifference theory,* which showed that all that is required to develop demand theory is to assume that consumers can always say which of two consumption bundles they prefer without having to say *by how much* they prefer it.

Indifference Curves

Suppose Hugh currently has available some specific bundle of goods, say, 18 units of clothing and 10 units of food. Now offer him an alternative bundle of, say, 13 units of clothing and 15 units of food. This alternative combination of goods has 5 fewer units of clothing and 5 more units of food than the first one. Whether Hugh prefers this new bundle depends on the relative valuation that he places on 5 more units of food and 5 fewer units of clothing. If he values the extra food more than the forgone clothing, he will prefer the new bundle to the original one. If he values the extra food less than the forgone clothing, he will prefer the original bundle. If Hugh values the extra food the same as the forgone clothing, he is said to be *indifferent* between the two bundles.

Suppose that after much trial and error, we have identified several bundles between which Hugh is indifferent. In other words, each bundle gives him equal satisfaction or utility. They are shown in the table in Figure 6A-1.

Of course, there are combinations of the two products other than those enumerated in the table that will give Hugh the same level of utility. All of these combinations are shown in Figure 6A-1 by the smooth curve that passes through the points plotted from the table.

This curve, called an *indifference curve,* shows all combinations of products that yield Hugh the same utility.

The consumer is indifferent between the combinations indicated by any two points on one indifference curve.

Any points above the curve show combinations of food and clothing that Hugh prefers to points on the curve. Consider, for example, the combination of 20 units of food and 18 units of clothing, represented by point *g* in Figure 6A-1. Although it may not be obvious that this bundle must be preferred to bundle *a* (which has more clothing but less food), it is obvious that it will be preferred to bundle *c* because both less clothing and less food are represented at *c* than at *g*. Inspection of the graph shows that any point above the curve will be superior to some points on the curve in the sense that it will contain both more food and more clothing than those points on the curve. However, because all points on the curve are equal in Hugh's eyes, any point above the curve must be superior to all points on the curve. By a similar argument, all points below and to the left of the curve represent bundles that are inferior to bundles represented by points on the curve.

Any point above an indifference curve is preferred to any point along that same indifference curve; any point below an indifference curve is inferior to any point along the indifference curve.

Diminishing Marginal Rate of Substitution

How much clothing would Hugh be prepared to give up to get one more unit of food? The answer to this question measures what is called Hugh's marginal rate of substitution of clothing for food. The *marginal rate of substitution (MRS)* is the amount of one product that a consumer is prepared to give up to get one more unit of another product.

The first basic assumption of indifference theory is that the algebraic value of the *MRS* between two goods is always negative.

FIGURE 6A-1   Hugh's Indifference Curve

Alternative Bundles Giving Hugh Equal Utility

Bundle	Clothing	Food
a	30	5
b	18	10
c	13	15
d	10	20
e	8	25
f	7	30

This indifference curve shows combinations of food and clothing that yield equal utility and between which Hugh is indifferent. The smooth curve through the points is an indifference curve; each combination on it gives Hugh equal utility. Point *g* above the line is a preferred combination to any point on the line; point *h* below the line is an inferior combination to any point on the line. The slope of the line *T* gives the marginal rate of substitution at point *b*. Moving down the curve from *b* to *f*, the slope flattens, showing that the more food and the less clothing Hugh has, the less willing he is to sacrifice further clothing to get more food.

A negative *MRS* means that to increase consumption of one product, Hugh is prepared to decrease consumption of a second product. The negative value of the marginal rate of substitution is indicated graphically by the negative slope of indifference curves. (See, for example, the curve in Figure 6A-1.)

The second basic assumption of indifference theory is that the marginal rate of substitution between any two goods depends on the amounts of the goods currently being consumed.

Consider a case in which Hugh has a lot of clothing and only a little food. Common sense suggests that he might be willing to give up quite a bit of plentiful clothing to get one more unit of scarce food. It suggests as well that if Hugh had little clothing and a lot of food he would be willing to give up only a little scarce clothing to get one more unit of already plentiful food.

This example illustrates the hypothesis of *diminishing marginal rate of substitution*. The less of one product, *A*, and the more of a second product, *B*, that the consumer has already, the smaller the amount of *A*

that the consumer will be willing to give up to get one additional unit of *B*. The hypothesis says that the marginal rate of substitution changes when the amounts of two products consumed change. The graphical expression of this hypothesis is that any indifference curve becomes flatter as the consumer moves downward and to the right along the curve. In Figure 6A-1, a movement downward and to the right means that Hugh is consuming less clothing and more food. The decreasing steepness of the curve means that Hugh is willing to sacrifice less and less clothing to get each additional unit of food. [11]

The hypothesis of diminishing marginal rate of substitution is illustrated in Table 6A-1, which is based on the example in Figure 6A-1. The last column of the table shows the rate at which Hugh is prepared to sacrifice units of clothing per unit of food obtained. At first, Hugh will sacrifice 2.4 units of clothing to get 1 unit more of food, but as his consumption of clothing diminishes and his consumption of food increases, Hugh becomes less and less willing to sacrifice further clothing for more food.

TABLE 6A-1	Hugh's Marginal Rate of Substitution Between Clothing and Food		
	(1)	(2)	(3)
Movement	Change in Clothing	Change in Food	Marginal Rate of Substitution (1) ÷ (2)
From *a* to *b*	−12	5	−2.4
From *b* to *c*	−5	5	−1.0
From *c* to *d*	−3	5	−0.6
From *d* to *e*	−2	5	−0.4
From *e* to *f*	−1	5	−0.2

The marginal rate of substitution of clothing for food declines (in absolute value) as the quantity of food increases. This table is based on Figure 6A-1. When Hugh moves from *a* to *b,* he gives up 12 units of clothing and gains 5 units of food; he remains at the same level of overall utility. At point *a* Hugh is prepared to sacrifice 12 units of clothing for 5 units of food (i.e., 12/5 = 2.4 units of clothing per unit of food obtained). When he moves from *b* to *c,* he sacrifices 5 units of clothing for 5 units of food (a rate of substitution of 1 unit of clothing for each unit of food).

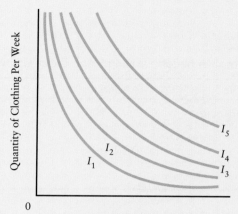

FIGURE 6A-2   Hugh's Indifference Map

Quantity of Clothing Per Week

I_5

I_2

I_1

I_4

I_3

0

Quantity of Food Per Week

An indifference map consists of a set of indifference curves. All points on a particular curve indicate alternative combinations of food and clothing that give Hugh equal utility. The farther the curve is from the origin, the higher is the level of utility it represents. For example, I_5 is a higher indifference curve than I_4, which means that all the points on I_5 give Hugh a higher level of utility than do the points on I_4.

The Indifference Map

So far, we have constructed only a single indifference curve for Hugh. However, starting at any other point in Figure 6A-1, such as *g,* there will be other combinations that will give Hugh equal utility. If the points indicating all of these combinations are connected, they will form another indifference curve. This exercise can be repeated many times, and we can thereby generate many indifference curves for Hugh. The farther any indifference curve is from the origin, the higher will be the level of Hugh's utility given by any of the points on the curve.

A set of indifference curves is called an *indifference map,* an example of which is shown in Figure 6A-2. It specifies the consumer's tastes by showing his rate of substitution between the two products for every possible level of current consumption of these products.

When economists say that a consumer's tastes are given, they do not mean that the consumer's current consumption pattern is given; rather, they mean that the consumer's entire indifference map is given.

The Budget Line

Indifference curves illustrate consumers' tastes. To develop a complete theory of their choices, we must also illustrate the alternatives available to them. These are shown as the solid line *ab* in Figure 6A-3. That line, called a *budget line,* shows all the combinations of food and clothing that Hugh can buy if he spends a fixed amount of money, in this case his entire money income of $720 per week, at fixed prices of the products (in this case, $12 per unit for clothing and $24 per unit for food).

Properties of the Budget Line

The budget line has several important properties:

1. Points on the budget line indicate bundles of products that use up the consumer's entire income. (Try, for example, the point 20C, 20F.)

FIGURE 6A-3   Hugh's Budget Line

The budget line shows the quantities of goods available to a consumer given money income and the prices of goods. Any point in this diagram indicates a combination (or bundle) of so much food and so much clothing. Point x_1, for example, indicates 40 units of clothing and 10 units of food per week.

With an income of $720 a week and prices of $24 per unit for food and $12 per unit for clothing, Hugh's budget line is ab. This line shows all the combinations of F and C available to him. He could spend all of this money income on clothing and obtain 60 units of clothing and zero food each week. Or he could go to the other extreme and purchase only food, buying 30 units of F and zero units of C. Hugh could also choose an intermediate position and consume some of both goods—for example, spending $240 to buy 10 units of F and $480 to buy 40 units of C (point x_1). Points above the budget line, such as x_2, are not attainable.

2. Points between the budget line and the origin indicate bundles of products that cost less than the consumer's income. (Try, for example, the point 20C, 10F.)

3. Points above the budget line indicate combinations of products that cost more than the consumer's income. (Try, for example, the point 30C, 40F.)

The budget line shows all combinations of products that are available to the consumer given his money income and the prices of the goods that he purchases.

We can also show Hugh's alternatives with an equation that uses symbols to express the information contained in the budget line. Let E stand for Hugh's money income, which must be equal to his total expenditure on food and clothing. If p_F and p_C represent the money prices of food and clothing, respectively, and F and C represent the quantities of food and clothing that Hugh chooses, then his spending on food is equal to p_F times F, and his spending on clothing is equal to p_C times C. Thus the equation for the budget line is

$$E = p_F \times F + p_C \times C$$

The Slope of the Budget Line

Look again at Hugh's budget line in Figure 6A-3. The vertical intercept is 60 units of clothing, and the horizontal intercept is 30 units of food. Thus the slope is equal to -2. The minus sign means that increases in Hugh's purchases of one of the goods must be accompanied by decreases in his purchases of the other. The numerical value of the slope indicates how much of one good must be given up to obtain an additional unit of the other; in our example, the slope of -2 means that Hugh must forgo the purchase of 2 units of clothing to acquire 1 extra unit of food.

Recall that in Chapter 3 we contrasted the *absolute*, or *money*, price of a product with its *relative* price, which is the ratio of its absolute price to that of some other product or group of products. One important point is that the relative price determines the slope of the budget line. In terms of our example of food and clothing, the slope of the budget line is determined by the relative price of food in terms of clothing, p_F/p_C; with the price of food (p_F) at $24 per unit and the price of clothing (p_C) at $12 per unit, the slope of the budget line (in absolute value) is 2. [12]

The significance of the slope of Hugh's budget line for food and clothing is that it reflects his *opportunity cost* of food in terms of clothing. To increase food consumption while maintaining expenditure constant, Hugh must move along the budget line and therefore consume less clothing; the slope of the budget line determines how much clothing he must give up to obtain an additional unit of food.

The opportunity cost of food in terms of clothing is measured by the (absolute value of the) slope of the budget line, which is equal to the relative price ratio, p_F/p_C.

In the example, with fixed income and with the relative price of food in terms of clothing (p_F/p_C) equal to 2, Hugh must forgo the purchase of 2 units of clothing to acquire 1 extra unit of food. The opportunity cost of a unit of food is thus 2 units of clothing. Notice that the relative price (in our example, $p_F/p_C = 2$) is consistent with an infinite number of absolute prices. If $p_F = \$40$ and $p_C = \$20$, it is still necessary to sacrifice 2 units of clothing to acquire 1 unit of food.[1] Thus relative, not absolute, prices determine opportunity cost.

The Consumer's Utility-Maximizing Choice

An indifference map describes the preferences of a consumer, and a budget line describes the possibilities available to a consumer. To predict what a consumer will actually do, both sets of information must be combined, as is done in Figure 6A-4. Hugh's budget line is shown by the straight line, and the curves from the indifference map are also shown. Any point on the budget line is attainable, but which point will Hugh actually choose?

Because Hugh wishes to maximize utility, he wishes to reach the highest attainable indifference curve. Inspection of Figure 6A-4 shows that if Hugh purchases any bundle on the budget line at a point cut by an indifference curve, he can reach a higher indifference curve. Only when the bundle purchased is such that the indifference curve is tangent to the budget line is it impossible for Hugh to reach a higher curve by altering his purchases.

The consumer's utility is maximized at the point where an indifference curve is tangent to the budget line. At that point, the consumer's marginal rate of substitution for the two goods is equal to the relative prices of the two goods.

The intuitive explanation for this result is that if Hugh values goods differently from the way the market does, there is room for profitable exchange. Hugh

FIGURE 6A-4 Hugh's Utility-Maximizing Choice

The consumer's utility is maximized at *E*, where an indifference curve is tangent to the budget line. Hugh has a money income of \$750 per week and faces money prices of \$25 per unit for clothing and \$30 per unit for food. A combination of units of clothing and food indicated by point *a* on I_1 is attainable but, by moving along the budget line, Hugh can reach higher indifference curves. The same is true at *b* on I_2 and at *c* on I_3. At *E*, however, where an indifference curve (I_4) is tangent to the budget line, Hugh cannot reach a higher curve by moving along the budget line.

can give up some of the good that he values relatively less than the market does and take in return some of the good that he values relatively more than the market does. When he is prepared to exchange goods at the same rate as they can be traded on the market, there is no further opportunity for him to raise utility by substituting one product for the other.

The theory thus proceeds by supposing that Hugh is presented with market prices that he cannot change and then analysing how he adjusts to these prices by choosing a bundle of goods such that, at the margin, his own subjective evaluation of the goods coincides with the valuations given by market prices.

We will now use this theory to predict the typical consumer's response to a change in income and in prices.

---

[1]Of course, with a given income, Hugh can afford much less of each at these higher money prices, but the opportunity cost of food in terms of clothing remains unchanged.

FIGURE 6A-5 Hugh's Income-Consumption Line

The income-consumption line shows how the consumer's purchases react to a change in money income with relative prices being held constant. Increases in Hugh's money income cause a parallel outward shift of his budget line, moving his utility-maximizing point from E_1 to E_2 to E_3. By joining all the utility-maximizing points, Hugh's income-consumption line is traced out.

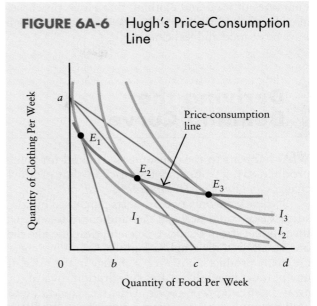

FIGURE 6A-6 Hugh's Price-Consumption Line

The price-consumption line shows how the consumer's purchases react to a change in one price with money income and other prices being held constant. Decreases in the price of food (with money income and the price of clothing held constant) pivot Hugh's budget line from ab to ac to ad. Hugh's utility-maximizing bundle moves from E_1 to E_2 to E_3. By joining all the utility-maximizing points, a price-consumption line is traced out, showing that Hugh purchases more food and less clothing as the price of food falls.

The Consumer's Reaction to a Change in Income

A change in Hugh's money income will, *ceteris paribus*, shift his budget line. For example, if Hugh's income doubles, he will be able to buy twice as much of both food and clothing compared with any combination on his previous budget line. His budget line will therefore shift out parallel to itself to indicate this expansion in his consumption possibilities. (The fact that it will be a parallel shift is established by the previous demonstration that the slope of the budget line depends only on the relative price of the two products.)

For each level of Hugh's income, there will be a utility-maximizing point at which an indifference curve is tangent to the relevant budget line. Each such utility-maximizing position means that Hugh is doing as well as possible at that level of income. If we move the budget line through all possible levels of income and if we join up all the utility-maximizing points, we will trace

out what is called an *income-consumption line*, an example of which is shown in Figure 6A-5. This line shows how Hugh's consumption bundle changes as his income changes, with relative prices being held constant.

The Consumer's Reaction to a Change in Price

We already know that a change in the relative price of the two goods changes the slope of the budget line. Given the price of clothing, for each possible price of food there is a different utility-maximizing consumption bundle for Hugh. If we connect these bundles, at a given money income, we will trace out a *price-consumption line*, as shown in Figure 6A-6. Notice that in this example, as the relative prices of food and clothing change, the relative quantities of food and clothing that Hugh purchases also change. In particular, as the price of food falls, Hugh buys more food and less clothing.

Deriving the Demand Curve

What happens to the consumer's demand for some product, say, gasoline, as the price of that product changes, *holding constant the prices of all other goods?*

If there were only two products purchased by consumers, we could derive a demand curve for one of the products from the price-consumption line like the one we showed for Hugh in Figure 6A-6. When there are many products, however, a change in the price of one product generally causes substitution toward (or away from) *all other goods*. Thus we would like to have a simple way of representing the individual's tastes in a world of many products.

In part (i) of Figure 6A-7, a new type of indifference map is plotted in which litres of gasoline per month are measured on the horizontal axis and the *value* of all other goods consumed per month is plotted on the vertical axis. We have in effect used "everything but gasoline" as the second product. The indifference curves in this figure then show the rate at which the consumer is prepared to substitute gasoline for money (which allows him to buy all other goods) at each level of consumption of gasoline and of all other goods.

To illustrate the derivation of demand curves, we use the numerical example shown in Figure 6A-7. The consumer is assumed to have an after-tax money income of $4000 per month. This level of money income is plotted on the vertical axis, showing that if the consumer consumes no gasoline, he can consume $4000 worth of other goods each month. When gasoline costs $1.50 per litre, the consumer could buy a maximum of 2667 litres per month. This set of choices gives rise to the innermost budget line. Given the consumer's tastes, utility is maximized at point E_0, consuming 600 litres of gasoline and $3100 worth of other products.

Next, let the price of gasoline fall to $1.00 per litre. Now the maximum possible consumption of gasoline is 4000 litres per month, giving rise to the middle budget line in the figure. The consumer's utility is maximized, as always, at the point where the new budget line is tangent to an indifference curve. At this point, E_1, the consumer is consuming 1200 litres of gasoline per month and spending $2800 on all other goods. Finally, let the price fall to 50 cents per

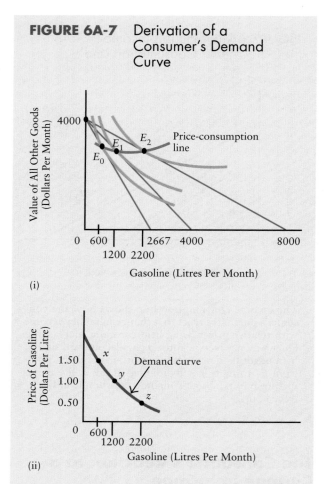

FIGURE 6A-7   Derivation of a Consumer's Demand Curve

Every point on the price-consumption line corresponds to both a price of the product and a quantity demanded; this is the information required for a demand curve. In part (i), the consumer has a money income of $4000 and alternatively faces prices of $1.50, $1.00, and $0.50 per litre of gasoline, choosing positions E_0, E_1, and E_2 at each price. The information for litres demanded at each price is then plotted in part (ii) to yield the consumer's demand curve. The three points x, y, and z in part (ii) correspond to the points E_0, E_1, and E_2 in part (i).

litre. The consumer can now buy a maximum of 8000 litres per month, giving rise to the outermost of the three budget lines. The consumer maximizes utility by consuming 2200 litres of gasoline per month and spending $2900 on other products.

If we let the price vary over all possible amounts, we will trace out a complete price-consumption line, as shown in Figure 6A-7. The points derived in the preceding paragraph are merely three points on this line.

We have now derived all that we need to plot the consumer's demand curve for gasoline, now that we know how much the consumer will purchase at each price. To draw the curve, we merely replot the data from part (i) of Figure 6A-7 onto a demand graph, as shown in part (ii) of Figure 6A-7.

Like part (i), part (ii) has quantity of gasoline on the horizontal axis. By placing one graph under the other, we can directly transcribe the quantity determined on the upper graph to the lower one. We first do this for the 600 litres consumed on the innermost budget line. We now note that the price of gasoline that gives rise to that budget line is $1.50 per litre. Plotting 600 litres against $1.50 in part (ii) produces the point x, derived from point E_0 in part (i). This is one point on the consumer's demand curve. Next we consider the middle budget line, which occurs when the price of gasoline is $1.00 per litre. We take the figure of 1200 litres from point E_1 in part (i) and transfer it to part (ii). We then plot this quantity against the price of $1.00 to get the point y on the demand curve. Doing the same thing for point E_2 yields the point z in part (ii): price 50 cents, quantity 2200 litres.

Repeating the operation for all prices yields the demand curve in part (ii). Note that the two parts of Figure 6A-7 describe the same behaviour. Both parts measure the quantity of gasoline on the horizontal axes; the only difference is that in part (i) the price of gasoline determines the slope of the budget line, whereas in part (ii) the price of gasoline is plotted explicitly on the vertical axis.

Income and Substitution Effects

The price-consumption line in part (i) of Figure 6A-7 indicates that as price decreases, the quantity of gasoline demanded increases, thus giving rise to the negatively sloped demand curve in part (ii). As we saw in Chapter 6, the key to understanding the negative slope of the demand curve is to distinguish between the income effect and the substitution effect of a change in price. We can make this distinction more precisely, and somewhat differently, using indifference curves.

In Chapter 6, we examined the substitution effect of a reduction in price by eliminating the income effect. We did this by reducing money income until the consumer could just purchase the original bundle of goods. We then examined how the change in relative prices affected the consumer's choices. In indifference theory, however, the income effect is removed by changing money income until the *original level of utility*—the original indifference curve—can just be achieved. This method results in a slightly different measure of the income effect, but the principle involved in separating the total change into an income

FIGURE 6A-8   The Income and Substitution Effects of a Price Change

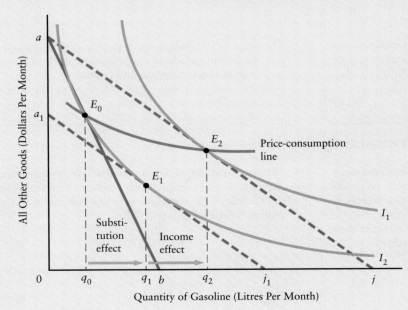

The substitution effect is defined by sliding the budget line around a fixed indifference curve; the income effect is defined by a parallel shift of the budget line. The original budget line is at ab, and a fall in the price of gasoline takes it to aj. The original utility-maximizing point is at E_0 with q_0 of gasoline being consumed, and the new utility-maximizing point is at E_2 with q_2 of gasoline being consumed. To remove the income effect, imagine reducing the consumer's money income until the original indifference curve is just attainable. We do this by shifting the line aj to a parallel line nearer the origin a_1j_1 that just touches the indifference curve that passes through E_0. The intermediate point E_1 divides the quantity change into a substitution effect q_0q_1 and an income effect q_1q_2.

effect and a substitution effect is exactly the same as in Chapter 6.

The separation of the two effects according to indifference theory is shown in Figure 6A-8. The figure shows in greater detail part of the price-consumption line first drawn in Figure 6A-7. Points E_0 and E_2 are on the price-consumption line for gasoline; E_0 is the consumer's utility-maximizing point at the initial price, whereas E_2 is the consumer's utility maximizing point at the new price.

We can think of the separation of the income and substitution effects as occurring in the following way. After the price of the good has fallen, we reduce money income *until the original indifference curve can just be obtained*. The consumer moves from point E_0 to an intermediate point E_1, and this response is defined as the substitution effect. Then, to measure the income effect, we restore money income. The consumer moves from the point E_1 to the final point E_2, and this response is defined as the income effect.

S U M M A R Y

Indifference Curves

- Indifference curves describe consumers' tastes or preferences. A single indifference curve joins combinations of products that give consumers equal utility and among which they are therefore indifferent. An indifference map is a set of indifference curves.

- The basic hypothesis about tastes is that of *diminishing marginal rate of substitution*. This hypothesis states that the less of one good and the more of another the consumer has, the less willing she will be to give up some of the first good to get an additional unit of the second. Thus indifference curves are downward sloping and convex to the origin.

The Budget Line

- The budget line shows all combinations of products that are available to a consumer with a given amount of money income who faces given prices of the products.

- The slope of the budget line is determined by the relative prices of the products; the position of the budget line is determined by both prices and income.

The Consumer's Utility-Maximizing Choice

- Given the constraint of the budget line, the consumer's utility is maximized by consuming a bundle of goods such that the indifference curve through that bundle is tangent to the budget line.
- The income-consumption line shows how quantity consumed changes as income changes with relative prices being held constant.

- The price-consumption line shows how quantity consumed changes when the price of one product changes. When prices change, the consumer will consume more of the product whose relative price falls.

Deriving the Demand Curve

- The price-consumption line relating the purchases of one particular product to all other products contains the same information as a conventional demand curve. The horizontal axis measures quantity, and the slope of the budget line measures price. Transferring this price-quantity information to a diagram whose axes represent price and quantity yields a demand curve.

- The effect of a change in price of one product, all other prices and money income being held constant, changes not only relative prices but also real incomes. A change in price affects consumption through both the substitution effect and the income effect.

STUDY EXERCISES

1. Consider Katie's preferences for videos and ice-cream cones. Several "consumption bundles" are shown in the table below.

Bundle	Ice-Cream Cones	Videos
a	9	0
b	7	2
c	6	2
d	5	3
e	4	4
f	4	3
g	3	4
h	2	6
i	0	6

a. On a scale diagram with the quantity of ice-cream cones on the vertical axis and the quantity of videos on the horizontal axis, plot the various bundles.

b. Suppose that Katie is indifferent between bundles c and i. She is also indifferent between bundles d, g, and h, but all three of these are preferred to c or i. Finally, suppose that, of the bundles shown in the table, bundle e is Katie's favourite. Draw three indifference curves showing this information.

c. Consider bundles e, f, and g. What can you conclude about how Katie would rank these bundles?

2. Continue with Katie from the previous question. Katie has a monthly allowance of $18 that she chooses to divide between rental videos and ice-cream cones. Videos rent for $3 each and ice-cream cones cost $2 each.

a. For each of the consumption bundles shown in the table, compute the total cost. Which ones can Katie afford, and which ones can't she afford?

b. Draw Katie's budget line. What is the slope of the line?

c. Given Katie's monthly budget constraint, which bundle does she choose to maximize her utility?

3. Debra travels to Mexico and enjoys both burritos and Coronas. The diagram shows her utility-maximizing choices.

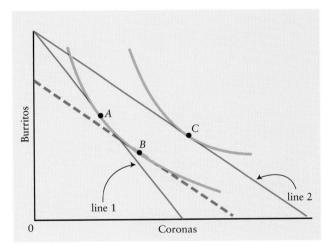

a. If the budget line is Line 1, describe why point A is Debra's utility-maximizing choice.

b. What event can explain why the budget line moves to Line 2?

c. What is the meaning of point B in the figure?

d. Suppose Coronas are a normal good for Debra. What does this restriction imply about the location of point C? Is this restriction satisfied in the diagram?

DISCUSSION QUESTIONS

1. We have all seen people who consume too much alcohol at parties. Often, even though these individuals are quite sick, they continue to drink. Draw an indifference curve for alcohol for a person who has begun to get ill but still continues to drink. Explain your representation.

2. Figure 6A-5 shows the behaviour of a hypothetical consumer as income increases. Do you think that such responses would hold globally? How might the response differ if the individual has $10 000 in income versus $1 million in income? Would there ever be a time when a person might exhibit no response to an increase in income? If so, what would the indifference map look like in that case?

3. Consider your sets of indifference curves for

   i) Coke and chips
   ii) Coke and Pepsi.

   Explain why these sets of indifference curves are likely to look different. Illustrate with a diagram. What does this difference imply about the magnitude of the substitution effects in response to changes in the price of Coke?

CHAPTER 7

Producers in the Short Run

LO *LEARNING OBJECTIVES*

1 Know the different forms of business organization and understand the various ways that firms can be financed.

2 Explain why firms sometimes make goods or services "in house" but other times purchase them from other firms.

3 Distinguish between accounting profits and economic profits.

4 Understand the relationships between total product, average product, and marginal product.

5 Explain the law of diminishing marginal returns.

6 Recognize that short-run production relationships have their counterparts in terms of short-run costs.

7 Understand the differences between fixed and variable costs, and know the relationships between total costs, average costs, and marginal costs.

In Chapter 6 we went behind the demand curve to understand how it is determined by the behaviour of consumers. In this chapter and the next we go behind the supply curve to understand how it is determined by the behaviour of firms.

We begin by comparing the firms that we see in the real world with those that appear in economic theory. Next we introduce the concepts of costs, revenues, and profits and outline the key role that profits play in determining the allocation of the nation's resources. To determine the most profitable amount for a firm to produce and supply to the market, we need to see how its costs vary with its output.

When examining the relationship between output and cost, *time* plays an important role. In this chapter, the focus is on the short run, where a firm can change only some of its inputs, and output is governed by the famous "law of diminishing returns." In the next chapter we examine the firm's behaviour in the long run—when all the firm's factors are variable—and in the very long run—when the state of technology changes. There we encounter scale economies and firms' incentives for research and development.

Firms as Agents of Production

We start by taking a brief look at the basic unit of production, the firm. After briefly studying firms as we see them in the real world, we go on to see how firms are treated in economic theory.

Firms in Practice

How are firms organized? How are firms financed? What are their goals?

Organization

single proprietorship
A form of business organization in which the firm has one owner who makes all the decisions and is personally responsible for all of the firm's actions and debts.

ordinary partnership
A form of business organization in which the firm has two or more joint owners, each of whom takes part in the management of the firm and is personally responsible for all of the firm's actions and debts.

limited partnership
A form of business organization in which the firm has two classes of owners: general partners, who take part in managing the firm and are personally liable for all of the firm's actions and debts, and limited partners, who take no part in the management of the firm and risk only the money that they have invested.

corporation   A form of business organization in which the firm has a legal existence separate from that of the owners, and ownership and financial responsibility are divided, limited, and shared among any number of individual and institutional shareholders.

crown corporations
Firms that are owned by the government.

transnational corporations (TNCs)
Firms that have operations in more than one country. Also called multinational enterprises (MNEs).

A firm can be organized in any one of five different ways. A **single proprietorship**, or sole trader, has one owner-manager who is personally responsible for everything that is done. An **ordinary partnership** has two or more joint owners, each of whom is personally responsible for all of the partnership's debts. The **limited partnership**, which is less common than ordinary partnerships, provides for two types of partner. *General partners* take part in the running of the business and are liable for all the firm's debts. *Limited partners* take no part in the running of the business, and their liability is limited to the amount they actually invest in the enterprise. A **corporation** is a firm regarded in law as having an identity of its own; its owners are not personally responsible for anything that is done in the name of the firm, though its directors may be. The shares of a *private* corporation are not traded on any stock exchange (such as the Toronto or New York Stock Exchanges) whereas the shares of a *public* corporation are. A *state-owned enterprise* is set up to run a nationalized industry. It is owned by the state but is usually under the direction of a more or less independent, state-appointed board. Although its ownership differs, the organization and legal status of a state-owned enterprise are similar to those of a corporation. In Canada, such state-owned enterprises are called **crown corporations**.

A sixth method of organizing production differs from all the others in that the output is not sold. Instead, it is provided to consumers free (or at a nominal price), while costs of production are paid from tax revenue (in the case of government production) or charitable donations (in the case of private production). Important examples found in all countries are government agencies providing defence, roads, and education. In Canada we must add health-care services and post-secondary education to this list (though in recent years the prices charged for post-secondary education have been increasing significantly).

Firms that have locations in more than one country are often called *multinational enterprises (MNEs)*, although the United Nations officially designates them as **transnational corporations (TNCs)**. Their numbers and importance have increased greatly over the last few decades. They are discussed in more detail in *Applying Economic Concepts 7-1*.

Financing

The money a firm raises for carrying on its business is sometimes called its financial capital, as distinct from its real capital, which is the firm's physical assets such as factories, machinery, offices, and stocks of materials and finished goods. Although the use of the term "capital" to refer to both an amount of money and a quantity of goods can be confusing, it will usually be clear from the context which sense is being used.

APPLYING ECONOMIC CONCEPTS 7-1
Transnational Corporations

Over the past half century the concept of a *national* economy has become less precise as firms have produced what they require in more than one country. Such firms used to be called *multinational corporations*, but the United Nations now officially calls them *transnational corporations* (TNCs). TNCs encourage global competition as well as the transfer of technological know-how among countries. Their number has been increasing steadily over the years. Although large firms still dominate the TNC scene, the role of medium-size and small TNCs is significant and growing.

At the beginning of the 1990s there were about 37 000 TNCs in the world and they controlled about 170 000 foreign affiliates. Ninety percent of these TNCs are headquartered in developed countries; the five major home countries being France, Germany, Japan, the United Kingdom, and the United States. About 60 percent of all parent TNCs are in manufacturing, 37 percent are in services, and 3 percent are in primary production such as forestry and mining.

The main way in which firms used to develop foreign operations was foreign direct investment (FDI), which means acquiring the controlling interest in foreign production facilities either by purchasing existing facilities or by building new ones. More recently, however, other methods have become more common. The most important of these are joint ventures with domestic firms located in countries where the TNCs wish to develop an interest, and licensing arrangements whereby a domestic firm produces a TNC's product locally.

There are many reasons for a company to transfer some of its production beyond its home base (thus becoming a TNC) rather than producing everything at home and then exporting the output. First, products become more sophisticated and differentiated; locating production in large local markets allows more flexible responses to local needs than can be achieved through centralized

production back home. Second, trade barriers make location in large foreign markets, such as the United States and the European Union, less risky than sending exports from the home base. Third, many TNCs are in the rapidly developing service industries such as advertising, marketing, public management, accounting, law, and financial services, where a physical presence is needed to produce a service in any country. Fourth, the computer and communications revolutions have allowed production to be "disintegrated" on a global basis. Components of any one product are often manufactured in many countries, each component being made where its production is cheapest.

Other reasons for a transnational corporation to locate production away from its home base have led some observers to be critical of TNCs. First, the TNC's internal accounting practices may allow it to report most of its revenues in low-tax countries and most of its costs in high-tax countries, thereby reducing the total tax it pays and avoiding altogether the paying of tax in some countries. Second, the TNC may threaten to remove its production away from its home base in an attempt to secure "friendly" tax policies from the government of that country. Third, the TNC may relocate its production in order to produce in countries with less stringent environmental standards.

On balance, however, most economists believe that the globalization of production—much of which has occurred through the spread of TNCs—has brought benefits to most countries. This includes developing countries, which have gained increasing employment at wages that are low by world standards but high by their own. TNCs now account for a large proportion of the foreign trade of many developed countries. As the United Nations puts it, "This dynamic aspect of the growth of TNCs is one of the major channels by which economic change is spread throughout the world."

The basic types of financial capital used by firms are *equity* and *debt*. Equity is the capital provided by the owners of the firm. Debt is the funds borrowed from creditors outside the firm.

Equity.   In individual proprietorships and partnerships, one or more owners provide much of the required funds. A corporation acquires funds from its owners in return for stocks, shares, or equities (as they are variously called). These are basically ownership certificates. The money goes to the company and the shareholders become owners of the firm, risking the loss of their money, and gaining the right to share in the firm's profits. Profits that are paid out to shareholders are called **dividends.**

One easy way for an established firm to raise money is to retain current profits rather than paying them out to shareholders. Financing investment from such *undistributed profits* has become an important source of funding in modern times. Reinvested profits add to the value of the firm, and hence raise the market value of existing shares; they are capital provided by owners.

Debt.   The firm's creditors are not owners; they have loaned money in return for some form of loan agreement, or IOU. There is a bewildering array of such agreements, which are collectively called *debt instruments* in the business world and **bonds** in economic theory. Each has its own set of characteristics and its own name, and some types are discussed in *Applying Economics Concepts 7-2.* Two characteristics are, however, common to all debt instruments issued by firms. First, they carry an obligation to repay the

dividends   Profits paid out to shareholders of a corporation. Sometimes called distributed profits.

bond   A debt instrument carrying a specified amount and schedule of interest payments and (usually) a date for redemption of its face value.

APPLYING ECONOMIC CONCEPTS 7-2
Kinds of Debt Instruments

Most debt instruments can be grouped into three broad classes. First, some debt is in the form of *loans* from financial institutions such as chartered banks. These are private agreements between the firm and the bank usually calling for the periodic payment of interest and repayment of the principal, either at a stipulated future date or "on demand," meaning whenever the bank requests repayment.

Second, *bills* and *notes* are commonly used for short-term loans of up to a year. They carry no fixed interest payments, only a principal value and a redemption date. Interest arises because the borrowing firm sells the new bills that it issues at a price below their redemption value. If, for example, a bill promising to pay $1000 in one year's time is sold to a lender for $950, this gives the lender an interest payment of $50 in one year's time when the bill that he bought for $950 is redeemed for $1000. This makes an interest rate of 5.26 percent per year ((50/950) x 100). Bills are *negotiable*, which means they can be bought and sold. So if I buy a 90-day bill from some firm and want my money back 30 days later, I can sell the bill on the open market. The purchaser must be prepared to assume the loan to the firm for the 60 days that it still has to run.

The third type of instrument carries a fixed redemption date, as does a bill, and the obligation to make periodic interest payments, as do most loans. These instruments have many different details and correspondingly many different names, such as *bonds* and *debentures*. They are commonly used for long-term loans—up to 20 or 30 years. A firm that issues a 7 percent 30-year instrument of this sort with redemption value of $1000 is borrowing money now and promising to pay $70 a year for 30 years and then to pay $1000 on the redemption date. All such instruments are negotiable. This is important, because few people would be willing to lend money for such long periods of time if there were no way to get it back before the redemption date.

Many large firms borrow money by issuing long-term bonds, like this one issued by MacMillan Bloedel, a large Canadian forestry products firm.

amount borrowed, called the *principal* of the loan. Second, they carry (explicitly or implicitly) an obligation to make some form of payment to the lender called *interest*. The time at which the principal is to be repaid is called the *redemption date* of the debt. The amount of time between the issue of the debt and its redemption date is called its *term*.

Goals

Firms are in business to make profits, which they do by making and selling goods and services. They must pay all their costs of production. The cost of labour includes wages, pensions, and other payments that must be made whenever labour is employed. The cost of borrowed capital is the interest they pay to those who have lent them money. The cost of intermediate goods and services covers the inputs they buy from other firms. The cost of rented inputs covers whatever they rent rather than own, often land and buildings. Firms must also *impute* costs for using their own capital equipment such as buildings, machinery, and office equipment. This cost, which is called *depreciation*, is measured by the reduction in the value of the assets that will occur if the firm uses them over the period in question. After deducting all these costs, the remainder is what firms call their profits. It is the return to their owners' capital. Some of this may be distributed to the shareholders in the form of dividends while the rest is retained for reinvestment. If the investments are sound, the value of the firm increases and this adds to the owners' capital.

Firms in Theory

In economic theory, the concept of the firm includes all types of business organization, from the single proprietorship to the corporation. It also covers the whole variety of business sizes and methods of financing, from the single investor operating in his garage and financed by whatever he can extract from a reluctant bank manager, to vast undertakings with many thousands of shareholders and customers.

The Boundaries of the Firm

If firms require something, either a specific input such as a specialized part, or a service such as cleaning their shop floor, they have two options. Either they can do it themselves—making the part and providing their own service—or they can buy what they need from some other firms. The boundary between what firms do for themselves and what they buy from outside differs among firms and changes over time. Why is is this so?

One answer was provided by British-born economist Ronald Coase, who received the 1991 Nobel Prize in economics for this, and other, path-breaking work. His analysis is based on the concept of **transaction costs**, which are the costs associated with all market transactions. For example, when a firm purchases some good or service, it must identify the market and then find what different quantities and qualities are available at what prices. This takes time and money, and it usually involves some uncertainty. When the firm decides to do the job itself "in house," it uses the *command principle*: it orders the product to be made, or the service to be performed, to its desired specifications. When the firm produces the product itself, the market transaction costs are avoided. But the advantages of buying in a competitive market are also lost.

transaction costs
Costs incurred in effecting market transactions (such as negotiation costs, billing costs, and bad debts).

All firms must choose when to transact internally and when to transact through the market. For example, a car manufacturer must decide whether to purchase a certain component from an independent parts manufacturer or to produce the component itself. Most firms do both, buying many of their components from other firms and producing others for themselves.

Coase's insight was to see the firm as an institution that economizes on transaction costs. The market works best when transaction costs are low. When transaction costs are high, there is an incentive for the firm to avoid these by using the internal mechanisms of the command principle in place of market transactions.

Firms exist as an alternative to a pure market structure of transactions. Inside a firm there is a command economy. Managers of firms must decide which activities should be done inside the firm and which should be obtained in the market from other suppliers.

Changes in technology alter the relative advantages of these two types of activity. For example, the modern information and communications revolution, centred on the computer, has greatly reduced the transactions costs associated with many market activities. So the costs of obtaining things through the market have fallen relative to the costs of doing them in house. As a result, firms do many fewer things in house than they used to do. Instead, they "contract out" both the production of many parts and the performance of many services. Large firms are then able to concentrate on what they call their "core competencies," the main things they do. Smaller firms that specialize in producing single services, such as elevator maintenance, office cleaning, accounting, and product design, are often able to perform these services more efficiently than can a large multi-purpose firm.

Goals

The theory of the firm that we study in this book is called *Neoclassical*. It is based on two key assumptions. First, all firms are profit-maximizers, seeking to make as much profit for their owners as is possible. Second, each firm is regarded as a single, consistent decision-making unit.

The desire to maximize profits is assumed to motivate all decisions made within a firm, and such decisions are assumed to be unaffected by the peculiarities of the persons making the decisions and by the organizational structure in which they work.

These assumptions allow the theory to ignore the firm's internal organization and its financial structure, although the firm must still decide on the boundary between what it provides internally and what it obtains through the market. Using these assumptions, economists can predict the behaviour of firms. To do this, they first study the choices open to the firm, establishing the effect that each choice would have on the firm's profits. They then predict that the firm will select the alternative that produces the largest profits.

The appendix to this chapter considers some limitations of theories that are based on these simple but powerful assumptions. In particular, we examine why firms may in some situations choose to have an objective *other than* profit maximization. In such settings, however, a firm that is not maximizing profits becomes a potential target for takeover by other firms.

Production, Costs, and Profits

We must now specify a little more precisely the concepts of production, costs, and profits that are used by economists.

Production

In order to produce the goods or services that it sells, each firm needs inputs. Hundreds of inputs enter into the production of any specific output. Among the many inputs entering into car production, for example, are steel, rubber, spark plugs, electricity, the site of the factory, machinists, accountants, spray-painting machines, forklift trucks, painters, and managers. These can be grouped into four broad categories:

- inputs to the car firm which are outputs to some other firm, such as spark plugs, electricity, and steel;
- inputs that are provided directly by nature, such as land;
- inputs that are provided directly by people, such as the services of workers and managers; and
- inputs that are provided by the factories and machines used for manufacturing cars.

The items that make up the first group of inputs, goods and services produced by other firms, are called **intermediate products**. For example, one firm mines iron ore and sells it to a steel manufacturer. Iron ore is an intermediate product: an output of the mining firm and an input for the steel plant. These appear as inputs only because the stages of production are divided among different firms. If these intermediate products are traced back to their sources, all production can be accounted for by the services of the other three kinds of input which we first discussed in Chapter 1, and which are called *factors of production*. These are the gifts of nature, such as soil and raw materials called *land*; physical and mental efforts provided by people, called *labour*; and factories, machines, and other man-made aids to production, called *capital*.

intermediate products All outputs that are used as inputs by other producers in a further stage of production.

The **production function** relates inputs to outputs. It describes the technological relationship between the inputs that a firm uses and the output that it produces. Remember that production is a flow: it is so many units per period of time. For example, when we say that production rises from 100 to 101 units, we do not mean 100 units are produced this month and 1 unit next month. Instead we mean that the rate of production has risen from 100 units each month to 101 units each month.

production function A functional relation showing the maximum output that can be produced by each and every combination of inputs.

In terms of functional notation, a simplified production function is written as

$$q = f(L,K)$$

where q is the level of output per period, K is the flow of capital services, and L is the flow of labour services. "f" is the production function itself. Changes in the firm's technology, which alter the relationship between inputs and output, are reflected by changes in the function f.

Costs and Profits

The production function specifies the amount of output that can be obtained from any given amounts of inputs. We have seen that firms arrive at what they call profits by taking the revenues they obtain from selling their output and deducting all the costs associated with their inputs, including depreciation of their own capital. When all costs have been correctly deducted the resulting profits are the return to the owners' capital.

Economic Profits

Compared with accountants, economists use somewhat different concepts of costs and profits. They add the opportunity cost of the owners' capital, both the pure return and the risk premium, to the firm's other costs. This is not just the depreciation of the capital, but an estimate of what the capital, and any other special advantages owned by the firm, could have earned in their best alternative uses. When this larger set of costs is deducted from revenues, the remainder is called **economic profits** (sometimes called pure profit). Where there is no room for ambiguity, economists just use the term profit.

What is the opportunity cost of the financial capital that the owner has tied up in a firm? The answer is best broken into two parts. First, ask what could be earned by lending this amount to someone else in a *riskless* loan. The owners could have purchased a government bond, which has no significant risk of default. Say the return on this is 6 percent per year. This amount is called the pure return, or risk-free rate of return on capital. It is clearly an opportunity cost, since the firm could close down operations, lend out its money, and earn a 6 percent return. Next, ask what the firm could earn in addition to this amount by lending its money to another firm where risk of default was equal to the firm's own risk of loss. Say this is an additional 4 percent. This is called the risk premium and it is clearly also a cost. If the firm does not expect to earn this much in its own operations, it could close down and lend its money out to some equally risky firm and earn 10 percent (6 percent pure return plus 4 percent risk premium).

Next suppose a firm owns a valuable patent or a highly desirable location, or produces a product with a popular brand name such as Kodak, Labatt, Corel, or Gap. Each of these involves an opportunity cost to the firm in production (even if it was acquired free), because if the firm did not choose to use the special advantage itself, *it could sell or lease it to others*. The firm must, therefore, charge itself for using the special advantage if it chooses to do so.

Table 7-1 compares the concepts of costs and profits as used by firms in practice and by economists in their theories. (Notice that Table 7-1 divides the firm's costs between those that vary with output, called *variable costs,* and those that do not, called *fixed costs,* a distinction that is considered in detail later in this chapter.)

What firms call profit is the return to the owners' capital. Economists deduct from this the opportunity cost of the owners' capital (and any marketable special advantages owned by the firm) to obtain their concept of economic profits.

Since there are two different concepts it would be better if two different terms were used. What firms call their profits might be referred to as the return to owners' capital. But firms do call these "profits." So when there is any possibility of confusion, economists speak of economic or pure profits. But since this is always what economists mean when they are dealing with their own theories, they usually just use the word "profits" to mean the return to the firm over and above the opportunity costs of capital.

Note that firms may have positive *accounting* profits even though they have zero *economic* profits. If a firm's profits represent a return just equal to what is available if the owner's capital were used elsewhere, then the owner's capital is earning exactly its opportunity cost. In this case, there are zero *economic* profits, even though the firm's accountant will record positive profits.

Is one of these concepts better than the other? No. Firms are interested in the return to their owners, which is what they call profits. They must also conform with tax laws which define profits the way they do. In contrast, economists are interested in how profits affect resource allocation and their definition is best for that purpose.

Practise with Study Guide Chapter 7, Exercise 4.

Profits and Resource Allocation

When resources are valued by the opportunity-cost principle, their costs show how much these resources would earn if used in their best alternative uses. If the revenues of all the firms in some industry exceed opportunity cost, the firms in that industry will be earning pure or economic profits. Hence, the owners of factors of production will want to move resources into the industry, because the earnings potentially available to them are greater there than in alternative uses. If, in some other industry, firms are incurring economic losses, some or all of this industry's resources are more highly valued in other uses, and owners of the resources will want to move them to those other uses.

Economic profits and losses play a crucial signalling role in the workings of a free-market system.

Economic profits in an industry are the signal that resources can profitably be moved into the industry. Losses are the signal that the resources can profitably be moved elsewhere. Only if there are zero economic profits is there no incentive for resources to move into or out of an industry.

Profit-Maximizing Output

To develop a theory of supply, we need to determine the level of output that will maximize a firm's profit, to which we give the symbol π (the lowercase Greek letter pi). This is the difference between the revenue each firm derives from the sale of its output, R, and the cost of producing that output, C:

$$\pi = R - C.$$

Thus, what happens to profits as output varies depends on what happens to both revenues and costs. In the rest of this chapter we develop a theory of how costs vary with output when the firm has some inputs that are fixed. In the next chapter we allow all inputs to be variable. The theory that we develop about costs and output is common to all firms. In the chapters that follow we consider how revenue varies with output. Costs and revenues are then combined to determine the profit-maximizing choices for firms in various market situations. The resulting theory can then be used to predict the outcome of changes in such things as demand, costs, taxes, and subsidies. This may seem like quite a long route to get to a theory of supply, and it is, but the payoff when we get there is in being able to understand and evaluate a great deal of economic behaviour.

TABLE 7-1   Profit and Loss Statement for XYZ Company for the Year Ending December 31, 2000

Costs		Income	
Variable Costs			
Wages	$200 000	Revenue from sales	$1 000 000
Materials	300 000		
Other	100 000		
Total VC	$600 000		
Fixed Costs			
Rent	$ 50 000		
Managerial salaries	60 000		
Interest on loans	90 000		
Depreciation allowance	50 000		
Total FC	$250 000		
Total Costs	$850 000		
Accounting Profit			$150 000

Calculation of Economic Profits	
Profit as reported by the firm	$150 000
Opportunity cost of capital	
Pure return on the firm's capital	–100 000
Risk premium	–40 000
Pure or economic profit	$ 10 000

The profit-and-loss statement shows profits as defined by the firm. The table gives a simplified version of a real profit-and-loss statement. The total revenue earned by the firm, minus what it regards as costs, yields the accounting concept of profits. To arrive at the economist's definition of profit, the opportunity cost of capital—the return on a riskless investment plus any risk premium—must be deducted from the firm's definition of profit. What is left is economic profit.

We start with inputs. Suppose that a firm wishes to increase its rate of output. To do so, it must increase the inputs of one or more factors of production. For the rest of this chapter, we consider a very simple example relating to the production of some industrial product. We can best focus on essentials by dealing with only two inputs. The first is labour, to which we give the symbol L. The second is capital, to which we give the symbol K. Thus we are ignoring land and all intermediate inputs and dealing with the simplified production function introduced earlier in this chapter:

$$q = f(L,K),$$

where q is quantity of output per period of time, L is the flow of labour services employed in production, and K is the flow of capital services used. The letter f again stands for the relation that links the inputs to the output.

Time Horizons for Decision Making

Economists organize the decisions that firms make into three classes: (1) how best to employ existing plant and equipment—the *short run*; (2) what new plant and equipment and production processes to select, given known technical possibilities—the *long run*; and (3) how to encourage, or adapt to, the development of new techniques—the *very long run*.

The Short Run

short run A period of time in which the quantity of some inputs cannot be increased beyond the fixed amount that is available.

fixed factor An input whose quantity cannot be changed in the short run.

variable factor An input whose quantity can be changed in the short run.

The **short run** is a time period in which the quantity of some inputs, called **fixed factors,** cannot be increased (or can only be increased at extremely high cost). A fixed factor is usually an element of capital (such as plant and equipment), but it might be land, the services of management, or even the supply of skilled labour. Inputs that are not fixed but instead can be varied in the short run are called **variable factors.**

The short run does not correspond to a specific number of months or years. In some industries, it may extend over many years; in others, it may be a matter of months or even weeks. In the electric power industry, for example, it takes three or more years to acquire and install a steam turbine generator. An unforeseen increase in demand will involve a long period during which the extra demand must be met with the existing capital equipment. In contrast, a machine shop can acquire new equipment in a few weeks. An increase in demand will have to be met with the existing stock of capital for only a brief time, after which it can be adjusted to the level made desirable by the higher demand.

The short run is the length of time over which some of the firm's factors of production are fixed.

The Long Run

long run A period of time in which all inputs may be varied but the basic technology of production cannot be changed.

The **long run** is a time period in which all inputs may be varied but in which the basic technology of production cannot be changed. Like the short run, the long run does not correspond to a specific length of time.

The long run corresponds to the situation the firm faces when it is planning to go into business, to expand the scale of its operations, to branch out into new products or new areas, or to change its method of production. The firm's *planning decisions* are long-run decisions because they are made from given technological possibilities but with freedom to choose from a variety of production processes that will use factor inputs in different proportions.

The long run is the length of time over which all of the firm's factors of production can be varied, but its technology is fixed.

The Very Long Run

Unlike the short run and the long run, the **very long run** is a period of time in which the technological possibilities available to a firm will change. Modern industrial societies are characterized by continuously changing technologies that lead to new and improved products and production methods.

Some of these technological advances are made by the firm's own research and development efforts. For example, much of the innovation in computer hardware and software has been made by IBM, Apple, Microsoft, and Intel. Some firms adopt technological changes developed by others. For example, liquid crystal displays and microprocessor chips have revolutionized dozens of industries that had nothing to do with developing them. Firms must regularly decide how much to spend in efforts to change technology either by developing new techniques or by adapting techniques that have been developed by others.

The very long run is the length of time over which all the firm's factors of production and its technology can be varied.

For the remainder of this chapter, we consider costs and production in the short run. We consider a simplified situation in which there are only two factors of production—labour and capital. We will assume that capital is the fixed factor whereas labour is the variable factor. In the next chapter we explore the firm's decisions in the long run and the very long run.

Production in the Short Run

Suppose that a firm starts with a fixed amount of capital and contemplates applying various amounts of labour to it. The table in Figure 7-1 shows three different ways of looking at how output varies with the quantity of the variable factor.

Total, Average, and Marginal Products

Total product *(TP)* is the total amount that is produced during a given period of time. Total product will change as more or less of the variable factor is used in conjunction with the given amount of the fixed factor. This variation is shown in columns 1 and 2 of the table in Figure 7-1. Part (i) of Figure 7-1 plots the schedule from the table. (The shape of the curve will be discussed shortly.)

Average product *(AP)* is the total product divided by the number of units of the variable factor used to produce it. If we let the number of units of labour be denoted by L, the average product is given by

$$AP = \frac{TP}{L}$$

very long run
A period of time that is long enough for the technological possibilities available to a firm to change.

total product (*TP*)
Total amount produced by a firm during some time period.

average product (*AP*)
Total product divided by the number of units of the variable factor used in its production.

FIGURE 7-1   Total, Average, and Marginal Products in the Short Run

Quantity of Labour (L)	Total Product (TP)	Average Product (AP) $\left(= \dfrac{TP}{L} \right)$	Marginal Product (MP) $\left(= \dfrac{\Delta TP}{\Delta L} \right)$
(1)	(2)	(3)	(4)
0	0	0	
1	43	43	43
2	160	80	117
3	351	117	191
4	600	150	249
5	875	175	275
6	1152	192	277
7	1372	196	220
8	1536	192	164
9	1656	184	120
10	1750	175	94
11	1815	165	65
12	1860	155	45

(i) Total product

(ii) Average and marginal product

The relation of output to changes in the quantity of the variable factor can be looked at in three different ways. As the quantity of labour increases, the rate of total output increases, as shown in column (2). The average product in column (3) is found by dividing the total product in column (2) by the labour requirement shown in the corresponding row of column (1). The marginal product is shown between the rows because it refers to the change in output from one level of labour input to another. The curves are plotted from the data in the table. In part (i) the *TP* curve shows the total product steadily rising, first at an increasing rate, then at a decreasing rate. This causes both the average and the marginal product curves in part (ii) to rise at first and then decline. Where *AP* reaches its maximum, *MP* = *AP*.

---

point of diminishing average productivity
The level of factor use at which average product reaches a maximum.

marginal product (MP) The change in total output that results from using one more unit of a variable factor. Also called *incremental product* and *marginal physical product* (*MPP*).

Notice in column 3 of the table that as more of the variable factor is used, average product first rises and then falls. The level of output at which average product reaches a maximum (1372 units of output in the example) is called the **point of diminishing average productivity**. Up to that point, average product is increasing; beyond that point, average product is decreasing.

Marginal product (MP), sometimes called *incremental product* or *marginal physical product (MPP)*, is the change in total product resulting from the use of one additional unit of the variable factor. [13] Recalling that the Greek letter Δ (delta) means "the change in," marginal product is given by:

$$MP = \frac{\Delta TP}{\Delta L}$$

Computed values of marginal product are shown in column 4 of the table in Figure 7-1. The values in this column are placed between the other rows of the table to stress that the concept refers to the *change* in output caused by the *change* in quantity of the variable factor. For example, the increase in labour from 3 to 4 units ($\Delta L = 1$) raises output from 351 to 600 ($\Delta TP = 249$). Thus the *MP* equals 249, and it is recorded between 3 and 4 units of labour. Note that the *MP* in the example first rises and then falls as output increases. The level of output at which marginal product reaches a maximum (between 875 and 1152 units in this example) is called the **point of diminishing marginal productivity.**

Part (ii) of Figure 7-1 plots the average product and marginal product curves from the table. Although three different curves are shown in Figure 7-1, they are all aspects of the same single relationship described by the production function. As we vary the quantity of labour, with capital being fixed, output changes. Sometimes it is interesting to look at total product, sometimes at average product, and sometimes at the marginal product.

point of diminishing marginal productivity   The level of factor use at which marginal product reaches a maximum.

Diminishing Marginal Product

The variations in output that result from applying more or less of a variable factor to a given quantity of a fixed factor are the subject of a famous economic hypothesis, referred to as the **law of diminishing returns.**

The law of diminishing returns states that if increasing amounts of a variable factor are applied to a given quantity of a fixed factor, (holding the level of technology constant) eventually a situation will be reached in which the marginal product of the variable factor declines.

law of diminishing returns   The hypothesis that if increasing quantities of a variable factor are applied to a given quantity of fixed factors, the marginal product and average product of the variable factor will eventually decrease.

Notice in Figure 7-1 that the marginal product curve rises at first and then begins to fall with each successive increase in the quantity of labour.

The commonsense explanation of the law of diminishing returns is that as output is increased in the short run, more and more of the variable factor is combined with a given amount of the fixed factor. As a result, each unit of the variable factor has less and less of the fixed factor to work with. When the fixed factor is capital and the variable factor is labour, each unit of labour gets a declining amount of capital to assist it as the total output grows. It is not surprising, therefore, that sooner or later, equal increases in labour eventually begin to add less and less to total output.

To illustrate the concept, consider the use of workers in a manufacturing operation. If there is only one worker, that worker must do all the tasks, shifting from one to another and becoming competent at each. As a second, third, and subsequent workers are added, each can specialize in one task, becoming expert at it. This process, as we noted in Chapter 1, is called the *division of labour.* If additional workers allow more efficient divisions of labour, marginal product will rise: Each newly hired worker will add more to total output than each previous worker did. However, according to the law of diminishing returns, the scope for such increases must eventually disappear, and sooner or later the marginal products of additional workers must decline. When the decline takes place, each additional worker will increase total output by less than did the previous worker.

Eventually, as more and more of the variable factor is employed, marginal product may reach zero and even become negative. It is not hard to see why if you consider the extreme case, in which there would be so many workers in a limited space, that additional workers would simply get in the way, thus reducing the total output.

The Average-Marginal Relationship

We have so far examined the concept of diminishing *marginal* returns; but *average* returns are also expected to diminish. The *law of diminishing average returns* states that if increasing quantities of a variable factor are applied to a given quantity of fixed factors, the average product of the variable factor will eventually decrease. [14]

Notice that in part (ii) of Figure 7-1, the *MP* curve cuts the *AP* curve at the *AP*'s maximum point. This is not a matter of luck or the way the artist just happened to draw the figure. Rather, it illustrates a fundamental property of the relationship between average and marginal product curves, one that is very important to understand.

The average product curve slopes upward as long as the marginal product curve is *above* it; whether the marginal product curve is itself sloping upward or downward is irrelevant. If an additional worker is to raise the average product of all workers, that additional worker's output must be greater than the average output of the other workers. It is immaterial whether the new worker's contribution to output is greater or less than the contribution of the worker hired immediately before; all that matters is that the new worker's contribution to output exceeds the *average* output of all workers hired previously. [15]

Any batter will improve his batting average if his "marginal hit" (his next time at bat) is better than his "average hit" (his current average).

The relationship between marginal and average measures is very general. If the marginal is greater than the average, the average must be rising; if the marginal is less than the average, the average must be falling. For example, if you have a 3.6 cumulative grade point average (GPA) through last semester and in this (marginal) semester you get only a 3.0 GPA, your cumulative GPA will fall. To increase your cumulative GPA, you must score better in this (marginal) semester than you have on average in the past—that is, to increase the average, the marginal must be greater than the average.

The Significance of Diminishing Returns

Empirical confirmation of both diminishing marginal and diminishing average returns occurs frequently. Some examples are illustrated in *Applying Economic Concepts 7-3*. But one might wish that it were not so. There would then be no reason to fear a food crisis caused by the population explosion in developing countries. If the marginal product of additional workers applied to a fixed quantity of land were constant, food production could be expanded in proportion to population growth merely by keeping a constant fraction of the population on farms. With fixed techniques, however, diminishing returns dictate an inexorable decline in the marginal product of each additional worker because an expanding population must work with a fixed supply of agricultural land.

Thus, were it not for the steady improvement in the techniques of production, continuous population growth would bring with it, according to the law of diminishing returns, declining average living standards and eventually widespread famine. This gloomy prediction of the English economist Thomas Malthus (1766–1834) is discussed further in the next chapter.

Costs in the Short Run

We now shift our attention from production to costs. The majority of firms cannot influence the prices of the inputs that they employ; instead they must pay the going market price for their inputs. For example, a shoe factory in Montreal, a metals manufacturer in

APPLYING ECONOMIC CONCEPTS 7-3
Some Examples of Diminishing Returns

- British Columbia's Campbell River, a noted sport-fishing area, has long been the centre of a thriving, well-promoted tourist trade. As sport-fishing has increased over the years, the total number of fish caught has steadily increased, but the number of fish *per person fishing* has decreased and the average hours fished for each fish caught has increased.*

- When Southern California Edison was required to modify its Mojave power plant to reduce the amount of pollutants emitted into the atmosphere, it discovered that a series of filters applied to the smokestacks could do the job. A single filter eliminated one-half of the discharge. Five filters in series reduced the discharge to the 3 percent allowed by law. When a state senator proposed a new standard that would permit no more than 1 percent of the pollutant to be emitted, the company brought in experts who testified that this would require at least 15 filters per stack and would triple the cost. In other words, increasing the number of filters leads to diminishing marginal returns in pollution reduction.

- Public opinion pollsters, as well as all students of statistics, know that you can use a sample to estimate characteristics of a large population. Even a relatively small sample can provide a useful estimate—at a tiny fraction of the cost of a complete enumeration of the population. However, sample estimates are subject to sampling error. If, for example, 38 percent of a sample approves of a certain policy, the percentage of the population that approves of it is likely to be close to 38 percent, but it might well be anywhere from 36 to 40 percent. The theory of statistics shows that the size of the expected sampling error can be reduced by increasing the sample size. However, the theory also shows that successive reductions in the sampling error require ever larger increases in the sample size. Suppose that the original sample was 400; if quadrupling the sample to 1600 would halve the chance of an error of any given size from occurring, then to halve it again, the new sample would have to be quadrupled again—to 6400. In other words, increasing the sample size leads to diminishing marginal returns in terms of accuracy.

- During the early days of World War II, so few naval ships were available that each North Atlantic convoy had only a few escort vessels to protect it from German submarines. The escorts dashed about from one side of the convoy to the other and ended up sinking very few submarines. As the construction program made more ships available, the escorts could stay in one position in the convoy: some could close in on the various flanks; others could hunt farther afield. Not only did the total number of submarines sunk per convoy crossing rise, but also the number of submarines sunk per escort vessel rose. Still later in the war, as each successive convoy was provided with more and more escort vessels, the number of submarines sunk per convoy crossing continued to rise, but the number of submarines sunk *per escort vessel* began to fall sharply. Total output (submarines sunk) increased, but marginal output fell.

*For a *given stock of fish* and increasing numbers of boats, this example is a good illustration of the law of diminishing returns. But in recent years the story has become more complicated as overfishing has depleted the stock of fish. We examine the reasons for overfishing in Chapter 16.

Sarnia, a rancher in Red Deer, and a boat builder in Prince Rupert are each too small a part of the total demand for the factors that they use to be able to influence their prices significantly. The firms must pay the going rent for the land that they need, the going wage rate for the labour that they employ, and the going interest rate that banks charge for loans; so it is with most other firms.[1] Given these prices and the physical returns summarized by the product curves, the costs of different levels of output can be calculated.

---

[1]The firm that is a large enough employer of labour or user of land or capital to affect the prices of its factor services is the exception rather than the rule. We examine the case of such *monopsony power* in Chapter 14.

Cost Concepts Defined

total cost (TC) The total cost to the firm of producing any given level of output; it can be divided into *total fixed costs* and *total variable costs*.

total fixed cost (TFC) All costs of production that do not vary with the level of output.

total variable cost (TVC) Total costs of production that vary directly with the level of output.

average total cost (ATC) Total cost of producing a given output divided by the number of units of output; it can also be calculated as the sum of average fixed costs and average variable costs. Also called *unit cost* or *average cost*.

average fixed cost (AFC) Total fixed costs divided by the number of units of output.

average variable cost (AVC) Total variable costs divided by the number of units of output.

marginal cost (MC) The increase in total cost resulting from raising the rate of production by one unit. Also called *incremental cost*.

Practise with Study Guide Chapter 7, Exercise 6.

The following definitions of several cost concepts are closely related to the product concepts just introduced.

Total cost *(TC)* is the full cost of producing any given level of output. Total cost is divided into two parts, *total fixed cost* and *total variable cost*. **Total fixed cost** *(TFC)* does not vary with the level of output; it is the same whether output is 1 unit or 1 million units. Such a cost is also referred to as an *overhead cost*. A cost that varies directly with output is called a **total variable cost** *(TVC)*. In the example in Figure 7-1, labour is the variable factor of production, and wages are therefore a variable cost.

Average total cost *(ATC)* is the total cost of producing any given number of units of output divided by that number of units. Average total cost is therefore the average cost *per unit of output*. ATC can be separated into **average fixed costs** *(AFC)*, fixed cost divided by the quantity of output, and **average variable costs** *(AVC)*, variable cost divided by the quantity of output.

Although average variable costs may rise or fall as production is increased, average fixed costs decline continuously as output increases. A doubling of output always leads to a halving of fixed costs *per unit of output*. This is a process known as spreading one's overhead.

Marginal cost *(MC)* is the increase in total cost resulting from increasing the level of output by one unit. Because fixed costs do not vary with output, marginal fixed costs are always zero. Therefore, marginal costs are necessarily marginal *variable* costs, and a change in fixed costs will leave marginal costs unaffected. For example, the marginal cost of producing a few more potatoes by farming a given amount of land more intensively is not affected by the rent paid for the land. [16]

See Table 7-2 for a summary of the firm's short-run cost concepts.

Short-Run Cost Curves

Using the production relationships found in Figure 7-1, suppose that the price of labour is $20 per unit and the price of capital is $10 per unit. The cost schedules that result from these values are shown in the table in Figure 7-2.

Figure 7-2 plots the cost curves for the data in the table. Notice that the MC curve cuts the ATC curve and the AVC curve at their lowest points. This is another example of the relationship between a marginal and an average curve. The ATC curve, for example, slopes downward as long as the MC curve is below it; it is upward sloping whenever MC is above it.

We consider these various cost curves one at a time.

Short-Run Average Costs

In part (ii) of Figure 7-2, the average variable cost (AVC) curve reaches a minimum and then rises. For given factor prices, when average product per worker is at a maximum, average variable cost is at a minimum. [17] Each additional worker adds the same amount to cost but a different amount to output; thus, when output per worker rises, the cost per unit of output must fall, and vice versa.

Eventually diminishing average productivity implies eventually increasing average variable costs.

The average fixed cost (*AFC*) curve in Figure 7-2 declines steadily as output rises. This decline reflects the spreading of overhead costs over more units of output.

Since average total cost is simply the sum of average variable cost and average fixed cost, it follows that the average total cost (*ATC*) curve is obtained by vertically adding the *AVC* and *AFC* curves. The result is usually a U-shaped *ATC* curve, as shown in Figure 7-2. This shape reflects the assumption that average productivity increases when output is low but that at some level of output, average productivity begins to fall fast enough so that average variable costs increase faster than average fixed costs are falling. When this happens, *ATC* increases.

Marginal Cost

In part (ii) of Figure 7-2, the marginal cost (*MC*) curve declines, reaches a minimum, and then rises. This is the reverse of the shape of the marginal product curve in part (ii) of Figure 7-1. The reason for the reversal is as follows: If extra units of a variable factor result in increasing quantities of output (marginal *product* rising), the cost per unit of extra output must be falling (marginal *cost* falling). However, if marginal product is falling, marginal cost will be rising. [18]

The law of eventually diminishing marginal product implies eventually increasing marginal cost.

Capacity

The level of output that corresponds to the minimum short-run average total cost is often called the *capacity* of the firm. In this sense, capacity is the largest output that can be produced without encountering rising average costs per unit. In part (ii) of Figure 7-2, capacity output is about 1600 units, but higher outputs can be achieved, provided that the firm is willing to accept the higher per-unit costs that accompany any level of output that is "above capacity." A firm that is producing at an output less than the point of minimum average total cost is said to have *excess capacity*.

The technical definition gives the word *capacity* a meaning that is different from the one used in everyday speech, in which it often means an upper limit that cannot be exceeded. The technical definition is, however, a useful concept in economic and business discussions.

TABLE 7-2   Short-Run Cost Concepts

Total Costs:

$$TC = TFC + TVC$$

Total Cost (*TC*) is the total cost to the firm of producing a given level of output.

Total Fixed Cost (*TFC*) is the sum of all costs of production that do not vary with the level of output. Also called overhead costs.

Total Variable Cost (*TVC*) varies directly with the level of output; it rises as more output is produced and falls as less output is produced.

Average Costs:

$$(ATC) = (AFC) + (AVC)$$

Average Total Cost (*ATC*) is the total cost per unit of output: $ATC = \dfrac{TC}{Q}$.

Average Fixed Cost (*AFC*) is the total fixed cost per unit of output: $AFC = \dfrac{TFC}{Q}$.

Average Variable Cost (*AVC*) is the total variable cost per unit of output: $AVC = \dfrac{TVC}{Q}$.

Marginal Costs:

$$MC = \dfrac{\Delta TC}{\Delta Q}$$

Marginal Cost (*MC*) is the change in total cost (ΔTC) per unit change in output (ΔQ).

FIGURE 7-2   Total, Average and Marginal Cost Curves

(i) Total cost curves

(ii) Marginal and average cost curves

Costs with Capital Fixed and Labour Variable

Inputs		Output	Total Cost			Average Cost			Marginal Cost
Capital (K) (1)	Labour (L) (2)	(q) (3)	Fixed (TFC) (4)	Variable (TVC) (5)	Total (TC) (6)	Fixed (AFC) (7)	Variable (AVC) (8)	Total (ATC) (9)	(MC) (10)
10	1	43	$100	$20	$120	$2.326	$0.465	$2.791	$0.456
10	2	160	100	40	140	0.625	0.250	0.865	0.171
10	3	351	100	60	160	0.285	0.171	0.456	0.105
10	4	600	100	80	180	0.167	0.133	0.300	0.080
10	5	875	100	100	200	0.114	0.114	0.228	0.073
10	6	1152	100	120	220	0.087	0.104	0.191	0.072
10	7	1372	100	140	240	0.073	0.102	0.175	0.091
10	8	1536	100	160	260	0.065	0.104	0.169	0.122
10	9	1656	100	180	280	0.060	0.109	0.169	0.167
10	10	1750	100	200	300	0.057	0.114	0.171	0.213
10	11	1815	100	220	320	0.055	0.121	0.176	0.308
10	12	1860	100	240	340	0.054	0.129	0.183	0.444

The relation of cost to the rate of output can be looked at in several different ways. These cost schedules are computed from the product curves of Figure 7-1, given the price of capital of $10 per unit and the price of labour of $20 per unit. Marginal cost (in column 10) is shown between the lines of total cost because it refers to the *change* in cost divided by the *change* in output that brought it about. Marginal cost is calculated by dividing the increase in costs by the increase in output when one additional unit of labour is used. This gives the increase in cost per unit of output over that range of output. For example, the MC of $0.08 is the increase in total cost of $20 (from $160 to $180) divided by the 249 unit increase in output (from 351 to 600). This tells us that when output goes from 351 to 600 (because labour inputs go from 3 to 4), the increase in costs is $0.08 per unit of output. In constructing a graph, marginal costs should be plotted midway in the interval over which they are computed. The MC of $0.08 would thus be plotted at output 475.5.

The curves are plotted from the table. Total fixed cost does not vary with output. Total variable cost and the total of all costs (TC = TVC + TFC) rise with output, first at a decreasing rate, then at an increasing rate. The total cost curves in (i) give rise to the average and marginal curves in (ii). Average fixed cost (AFC) declines as output increases. Average variable cost (AVC) and average total cost (ATC) fall and then rise as output increases. Marginal cost (MC) does the same, intersecting the ATC and AVC curves at their minimum points. Capacity output is at the minimum point of the ATC curve, which is an output of about 1600 in this example.

Shifts in Short-Run Cost Curves

So far, we have seen how costs vary as output varies, with input prices being held constant. Figure 7-3 shows the effect on a firm's cost curves of a change in the price of any variable input. A rise in the price of any input used by the firm must raise the price of producing any given quantity of output. A fall in the price of any input has the opposite effect.

A change in the price of any variable input used by the firm will shift its marginal and average cost curves—upward for a price increase and downward for a price decrease.

Thus, there is a set of average and marginal cost curves that correspond to each price of the variable factor.

A short-run cost curve shows how costs vary with output for a given quantity of the fixed factor, say, a given size of plant. But what happens when the amount of the fixed factor changes?

There is a different short-run cost curve for each given quantity of the fixed factor.

A small plant that manufactures nuts and bolts will have its own short-run cost curve. A medium-size plant and a large plant will each have its own short-run cost curve. If a firm expands and replaces its small plant with a medium-size plant, it will move from one short-run cost curve to another. This change from one plant size to another is a long-run change, which brings us to the next chapter, in which we discuss how short-run cost curves for plants of different sizes are related to each other.

FIGURE 7-3   The Effect of an Increase in Input Prices

A change in any input price shifts the average total cost curve and the marginal cost curve. The original average total cost and marginal cost curves are shown by ATC_0 and MC_0. A rise in the price of a variable input—for example, the wage rate—raises the cost of producing each level of output. As a result, the average total cost curve and the marginal cost curve shift upward to ATC_1 and MC_1.

S U M M A R Y

Firms as Agents of Production

- Production is organized either by private-sector firms, which take four main forms—single proprietorships, ordinary partnerships, limited partnerships, and corporations—or by state-owned enterprises.
- Modern firms finance themselves by selling shares, reinvesting their profits, or borrowing from lenders such as banks.

- A firm's profit is the difference between its total revenue and its total costs.
- The boundaries of firms are determined by the relation between the costs of making transactions in the market and the costs of producing what is required within the firm.

Production, Costs, and, Profits

- The production function relates inputs of factor services to output.
- In addition to what firms count as their costs, economists include the opportunity costs of owners' capital. This includes the pure return (the amount that could be earned on a riskless investment) and a risk premium (the amount that could be earned over the pure return on an equally risky investment). Economic profits are the difference between revenues and all these costs.

- Economic profits play a key role in resource allocation. Positive economic profits attract resources into an industry; negative economic profits induce resources to move elsewhere.
- A firm's production decisions can be classified into three groups. The short run involves decisions in which one or more factors of production are fixed. The long run involves decisions in which all factors are variable but technology is unchanging. The very long run involves decisions in which technology can change.

Production in the Short Run

- The theory of short-run costs is concerned with how output varies as different amounts of the variable factors are combined with given amounts of the fixed factors. The concepts of total, average, and marginal product represent alternative relationships between output and the quantity of the variable factors of production.

- The law of diminishing returns asserts that if increasing quantities of a variable factor are combined with given quantities of fixed factors, the marginal and the average products of the variable factor will eventually decrease. For given factor prices, this hypothesis implies that marginal and average costs will eventually rise.

Costs in the Short Run

- Short-run average total cost curves are often U-shaped because average productivity increases at low levels of outputs but eventually declines sufficiently and rapidly to offset advantages of spreading overheads. The output corresponding to the minimum point of a short-run average total cost curve is called the plant's capacity.
- Changes in factor prices shift the short-run cost curves—upward when prices rise and downward when prices fall.

Thus there is a whole family of short-run cost curves, one for each set of factor prices.
- Changes in the quantity of the fixed factor also shift the short-run cost curves. An increase in the amount of capital increases the productivity of labour and thus shifts the *MC* and *AVC* curves down.

K E Y   C O N C E P T S

Forms of business organization
Methods of financing modern firms
Profit maximization
Inputs and factors of production
Alternative definitions of profits

Profits and resource allocation
Short run, long run, and very long run
Total product, average product, and
  marginal product
The law of diminishing returns

The relationship between productivity
  and cost
Total cost, marginal cost, and average
  cost
Short-run cost curves
Capacity

STUDY EXERCISES

1. Consider the revenues and costs in 1999 for Spruce Decor Inc., an Alberta-based furniture company entirely owned by Mr. Harold Buford.

Furniture Sales	$645 000
Catalogue Sales	$ 12 000
Labour Costs	$325 000
Materials Costs	$157 000
Advertising Costs	$ 28 000
Debt-Service Costs	$ 32 000

   a. What would accountants determine Spruce Decor's profits to be in 1999?
   b. Suppose Mr. Buford has $400 000 of capital invested in Spruce Decor. Also suppose that equally risky enterprises earn a 16% rate of return on capital. What is the opportunity cost for Mr. Buford's capital?
   c. What are the *economic* profits for Spruce Decor in 1999?
   d. If Spruce Decor's economic profits were typical of furniture makers in 1999, what would you expect to happen in this industry? Explain.

2. Consider an example of a production function that relates the monthly production of widgets to the monthly inputs of capital and labour. Suppose the production function takes the following specific algebraic form:

$$q = KL - (0.1) L^2$$

where q is the output of widgets, K is the input of capital services, and L is the input of labour services.

   a. Suppose that, in the short run, K is constant and equal to 10. Fill in the following table.

K	L	q
10	5	—
10	10	—
10	15	—
10	20	—
10	25	—
10	30	—
10	40	—
10	50	—

   b. Using the values from the table, plot the values of q and L on a scale diagram, with q on the vertical axis and L on the horizontal axis.
   c. Now suppose that K increases to 20 because the firm increases the size of its widget factory. Re-compute the value of q for each of the alternative values of L. Plot the values of q and L on the same diagram as in **b**.

   d. Explain why an increase in K increases the level of q (for any given level of L).

3. The following table shows how the total output of skates (per month) changes when the quantity of the variable input (labour) changes. The firm's amount of capital is fixed.

Hours of Labour	Pairs of Skates	Average Product	Marginal Product
100	200	—	—
120	260	—	—
140	350	—	—
160	580	—	—
180	720	—	—
200	780	—	—
220	800	—	—
240	810	—	—

   a. Compute the average product of labour for each level of output and fill in the table. Plot the *AP* curve on a scale diagram.
   b. Compute the marginal product of labour for each interval (that is, between 100 and 120 hours, between 120 and 140 hours, and so on). Fill in the table and plot the *MP* curve on the same diagram. Remember to plot the value for *MP* at the midpoint of the intervals.
   c. Is the "law of diminishing marginal returns" satisfied?
   d. Explain the relationship between the marginal product of labour and the average product of labour.

4. Consider the table below which shows the total fixed costs (*TFC*) and variable costs (*TVC*) for producing specialty bicycles in a small factory with a fixed amount of capital.

Output per year (thousands of bicycles)	TFC	TVC	AFC	AVC	ATC
		(thousands of dollars)			
1	200	40	—	—	—
2	200	70	—	—	—
3	200	105	—	—	—
4	200	120	—	—	—
5	200	135	—	—	—
6	200	155	—	—	—
7	200	185	—	—	—
8	200	230	—	—	—
9	200	290	—	—	—
10	200	350	—	—	—
11	200	425	—	—	—

a. Compute average fixed costs (*AFC*) for each level of output.

b. Compute average variable costs (*AVC*) for each level of output.

c. Compute average total cost (*ATC*) for each level of output. What level of output (per year) is the firm's "capacity"?

d. Plot the *AFC*, *AVC* and *ATC* curves on a scale diagram with dollars on the vertical axis and the level of output on the horizontal axis.

5. This is a challenging question that requires you to understand the relationship between total product, average product, and marginal product. Each of the diagrams below shows how total product (*TP*) changes as the quantity of the variable input (which we call *L*) changes. These reflect four *different* production functions.

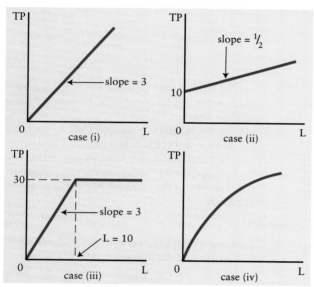

a. In each case, describe in words how total output depends on the amount of variable input.

b. In each case, draw a diagram showing the average product (*AP*) curve. (Recall that *AP* is given by total output divided by total variable input. The value of *AP* is also equal to the slope of a straight line from the origin to the *TP* curve.)

c. On the same diagram, draw the marginal product (*MP*) curve. (Recall that *MP* is given by the *change* in total output divided by the *change* in the variable input. The value of *MP* is also equal to the slope of a tangent line to the *TP* curve.)

d. Is the relationship between *AP* and *MP* discussed in the text satisfied by each of the production functions?

6. In 1921, a classic set of experiments with chemical fertilizers was performed at the Rothampsted Experimental Station, an agricultural research institute in Hertfordshire, England. Researchers applied different amounts of a particular fertilizer to 10 apparently identical quarter-acre plots of land. The results for one test, using identical seed grain, are listed in the following table. Compute the average and marginal product of fertilizer, and identify the (approximate) points of diminishing average and marginal productivity.

Plot	Fertilizer Dose	Yield Index*
1	15	104.2
2	30	110.4
3	45	118.0
4	60	125.3
5	75	130.2
6	90	131.4
7	105	131.9
8	120	132.3
9	135	132.5
10	150	132.8

* Yield without fertilizer = 100.

DISCUSSION QUESTIONS

1. Which concept of profits—accounting or economic—is implied in the following quotations?

   a. "Profits are necessary if firms are to stay in business."

   b. "Profits are signals for firms to expand production and investment."

   c. "Accelerated depreciation allowances reduce profits and thus benefit the company's owners."

2. Does the short run consist of the same number of months for increasing output as for decreasing it? Must the short run in an industry be the same length for all firms in the industry? Under what circumstances might the short run actually involve a longer time span than the very long run for one particular firm?

3. Indicate whether each of the following conforms to the hypothesis of diminishing returns and, if so, whether it refers to marginal returns, average returns, or both.

   a. "The bigger they are, the harder they fall."

   b. "As more and more of the population receives chicken pox vaccinations, the reduction in the chicken pox disease rate for each additional 100 000 vaccinations becomes smaller."

c. "Five workers produce twice as much today as 10 workers did 40 years ago."

d. "Diminishing returns set in last year when the rising rural population actually caused agricultural output to fall."

4. Consider the education of a person as a process of production. Regard years of schooling as one variable factor of production. What are the other factors? What factors are fixed? At what point would you expect diminishing returns to set in? For an Einstein, would diminishing returns set in during his lifetime?

5. A carpenter quits his job at a furniture factory to open his own cabinetmaking business. In his first two years of operation, his sales average $100 000 and his operating costs for wood, workshop and tool rental, utilities, and miscellaneous expenses average $70 000. Now his old job at the furniture factory is again available. Should he take it or remain in business for himself? How would you make this decision?

6. The point of minimum average cost is referred to as the capacity of the firm. Yet we draw the average cost curve extending both to the left and to the right of this point. Obviously, a firm can operate below capacity, but how can a firm operate above capacity? Are there any types of firms for which it may be desirable to have a capacity below the level at which the firm may have to produce occasionally or even relatively frequently? Explain.

Do Firms Really Maximize Profits?

In the text, we said that the Neoclassical theory of the firm is based on two key assumptions. First, firms strive to maximize their profits. Second, firms act as if they are a single consistent decision maker. These assumptions rule out two potentially interesting questions regarding actual firm behaviour. First, do firms ever have a goal other than profit maximization? Second, doesn't it matter who is actually making the decisions inside the firm? These issues are explored in this appendix. As we will see, they are related to each other: the decisions actually made by a firm may depend on who is making them.

The Separation of Ownership From Control

One hundred years ago, the single-proprietor firm, whose manager was its owner, was common in many branches of industry. In such firms, the single-minded pursuit of profits would be expected. Today, however, ownership is commonly diversified among thousands of stockholders, and the firm's managers are rarely its owners. Arranging matters so that managers always act in the best interests of stockholders is, as we shall see, anything but straightforward. Thus there is potential for managers to maximize something other than profits.

In corporations, the stockholders elect directors, and those directors then appoint managers. Directors are supposed to represent stockholders' interests and to determine broad policies that the managers will carry out. To conduct the complicated business of running a large firm, a full-time professional management group must be given broad powers of decision making. Although managerial decisions can be reviewed from time to time, they cannot be closely monitored on a day-to-day basis. The links between the directors and the managers are typically weak enough so that top management often truly controls the corporation over long periods of time.

As long as directors have confidence in the managerial group, they accept and ratify their proposals. Stockholders in turn elect and reelect directors who are proposed to them. If the managerial group does not satisfy the directors' expectations, it may be replaced.

Within fairly broad limits, then, effective control of the corporation's activities generally resides with the managers. Although the managers are legally employed by the stockholders, they remain largely independent of them. Indeed, the management group typically asks for, and gets, the *proxies* of enough stockholders to elect directors who will reappoint it, and thus it perpetuates itself in office. (A proxy authorizes a person who is attending a stockholders' meeting to cast a stockholder's vote.) In the vast majority of cases, nearly all votes cast are in the form of proxies.

None of these factors matter unless the managers pursue different interests from those of the stockholders. Do the interests of the two groups diverge? To study this question, we need to look at what is called principal-agent theory.

Principal-Agent Theory

If you (the *principal*) hire a girl down the block (your *agent*) to mow your lawn while you are away, all you can observe is how the lawn looks when you come back. She could have mowed it every week, as you agreed, or she could have waited until two days before you were due home and mowed it only once. By prevailing on a friend or a neighbour to *monitor* your agent's behaviour, you could find out what she actually did, but only at some cost.

When you visit a doctor for a diagnosis and for treatment of your lower back pain, it is almost impossible for you to monitor the doctor's effort and diligence on your behalf. You have not been to medical school, and much of what the doctor does will be a mystery to you.

This latter situation is close to the principal-agent relationship that exists between stockholders and managers. The managers have information and expertise that the stockholders do not have—indeed, that is why they are the managers. The stockholders can observe profits, but they cannot directly observe the managers' efforts. To complicate matters further, even when the managers' behaviour can be observed, the stockholders do not generally have the expertise to evaluate whether that behaviour was the most appropriate. Everyone can see how well the firm performs, but it takes very detailed knowledge of the firm and the industry to know how well it *could have performed*.

Boards of directors, who represent the firm's stockholders, can acquire some of the relevant expertise and monitor managerial behaviour, but, again, such monitoring is costly.

These examples illustrate the *principal-agent problem*—the problem of designing mechanisms that will induce agents to act in their principals' interests. In general, unless there is close monitoring of the agent's behaviour, the problem cannot be completely solved. Hired managers (like hired gardeners) will generally wish to pursue their own goals. They cannot ignore profits because if they perform badly enough, they will lose their jobs. Just how much latitude they have to pursue their own goals at the expense of profits will depend on many things, including the degree of competition in the industry and the possibility of takeover by more profit-oriented management.

Principal-agent analysis shows that when a firm's ownership and control are separated, the self-interest of agents will tend to make profits lower than in a world in which principals act as their own agents.

Managers' Motives

In the case of firms, the principals (the stockholders) are interested in maximizing profits. What different motives might their agents (the managers) have, and what market forces might limit their ability to act on these motives?

Sales Maximization

If managers do not maximize profits, what do they do? One alternative is that they seek to maximize *sales*. Suppose that the managers need to make some minimum level of profits to keep the stockholders satisfied. Beyond this, they are free to maximize their firm's sales revenue. This might be a sensible policy on the part of management because salary, power, and prestige all rise with the size of a firm as well as with its profits. Generally, the manager of a large, normally profitable corporation will earn a salary that is considerably higher than the salary earned by the manager of a small but highly profitable corporation.

The sales-maximization hypothesis says that managers of firms seek to maximize their sales revenue, subject to a profit constraint.

Sales maximization subject to a profit constraint leads to the prediction that a firm's managers will sac-

FIGURE 7A-1 Output of the Firm Under Profit Maximizing, Sales Maximizing, and Satisficing Behaviour

The "best" level of output depends on the motivation of the firm's managers. The curve shows the level of profits associated with each level of output. The shape of the curve reflects the fact that the firm generally has a unique level of output that maximizes its profits.

A profit-maximizing firm produces output q_m and earns profit π_m. A sales-maximizing firm, with a minimum profit constraint of π_t, produces the output q_1. A satisficing firm with a target level of profits of π_t is willing to produce any output between q_0 and q_1. Thus, satisficing allows a range of outputs on either side of the profit-maximizing level, whereas sales maximization results in a higher output than profit maximization.

rifice some profits by producing more output than the profit-maximizing level. Figure 7A-1 demonstrates this point.

Failure to Minimize Costs

It is also possible that firms will produce their chosen output at greater than minimum cost. Why would a firm's managers fail to minimize costs?

The most straightforward answer is that minimizing costs can demand a great deal of detailed managerial attention, and if management can avoid doing so, it would prefer not to make the necessary effort. A second reason managers may not minimize costs is that they may benefit from some higher-than-necessary expenditures. For example, lavish offices, in-house fitness centres, and subsidized cafeterias may all increase the pleasure of the job. And though *some* spending of this type may also be good for the employees' morale and productivity—and thus be good for the company overall—managers may prefer to spend much more generously than is necessary.

As with sales maximization, however, pressure from profit-minded stockholders will limit the extent to which such inefficiencies can persist. Also relevant is the threat of takeover—to which we now turn.

The Market for Corporate Control

Managers who stray too far from profit maximization face the risk that their firms will be taken over by more profit-oriented ownership. *Mergers* and *takeovers* can be interpreted as transactions in a *market for corporate control*. This market, like any other, has both buyers (people who would acquire the rights to control a firm) and sellers (the current stockholders of the firm). As in other markets, the expected outcome is that the assets being exchanged will wind up in the hands of the parties who value them most—usually those who can come closest to maximizing the firm's profits.

A takeover begins when the management of the acquiring firm makes a *tender offer* to the stockholders of the target firm. Tender offers are promises to purchase stock at a specified price for a limited period of time, during which the acquiring firm hopes to gain control of the target company. Typically, the prices offered are considerably higher than the prevailing stock-market price, reflecting the belief by the acquiring firm that the assets of the target firm would be worth more if they were better managed. A takeover is called a *hostile takeover* when the current management of the target firm opposes it.

Are takeovers beneficial for the economy as a whole? The main argument in their favour is that after a takeover, the new management can make more efficient use of the target firm's assets. The acquiring firm should be able to exploit profit opportunities that the target management is not exploiting. This can be done by such means as operating the target firm more efficiently, providing funds that the target firm could not obtain, or providing access to markets that would be too expensive for the target firm to open up on its own.

Most economists believe that the threat of takeovers provides a useful discipline that helps to restrain managers from acting in non-profit-maximizing ways. Such discipline helps to improve the allocation of resources as managers are under pressure to use the assets under their management in the most efficient way.

Nonmaximizing Theories

Many students of corporate behaviour, particularly economists based in business schools, criticize the profit-maximization assumption from a perspective different from that given by principal-agent theory. They argue that there are other reasons for doubting that modern corporations are "simple profit-maximizing computers." They believe that corporations are *profit-oriented* in the sense that, other things being equal, more profits are preferred to less profits. They do not believe, however, that corporations are profit *maximizers*.

A major group of critics of profit maximization develop their argument as follows: Firms operate in highly uncertain environments. Their long-term success or failure is determined largely by their ability to administer innovation and change. But the risks of innovation are large, and the outcomes are highly uncertain. Rational firms therefore tend to be quite risk-averse. They develop routines of behaviour that they follow as long as they are successful. Only when profits fall low enough to threaten their survival do they significantly change their course of action.

Supporters of this view argue that firms simply cannot handle the task of scrutinizing all possibilities, calculating the probable outcomes, and then choosing among these so as to maximize their expected profits. Instead, firms carry on with existing routines as long as these produce satisfactory profits, and only when profits fall to unacceptably low levels do the firms search for new ways of doing old things or new lines of activity.

One way of formalizing these views is the *theory of satisficing*. It was first put forward by Herbert Simon of Carnegie-Mellon University, who was awarded the Nobel Prize in Economics in 1978 for his work on the behaviour of firms. He wrote, "We must expect the firm's goals to be not maximizing profits but attaining a certain level or rate of profit, holding a certain share of the market or a certain level of sales." In general, a firm is said to be *satisficing* if it does not change its behaviour, provided that a *satisfactory* (rather than optimal) level of performance is achieved.

According to the satisficing hypothesis, firms could produce any one of a range of outputs that produce profits at least equal to the target level. This contrasts with the unique output that is predicted by profit-maximizing theory. Figure 7A-1 compares satisficing behaviour with sales- and profit-maximizing behaviour.

The theory of satisficing predicts not a unique level of output but a range of possible outputs that includes the profit-maximizing output.

The Importance of Nonmaximizing Behaviour

What would be the implications if nonmaximizing theories were accepted as being better theories of the behaviour of firms than the "standard model," which is based on the assumption of profit maximization?

The Implications of Nonmaximizing Behaviour

To the extent that existing non-profit-maximizing theories are accurate, the economic system does not perform with the delicate precision that follows from profit maximization. Firms will not always respond quickly and precisely to changes in market signals from either the private sector or government policy.

The nonmaximizing theories imply that in many cases, firms' responses to small changes in market signals will be of uncertain speed and direction.

According to all existing theories, maximizing and nonmaximizing, firms will tend to sell more when demand increases and less when it decreases. They will also tend to alter their prices and their input mixes when they face sufficiently large changes in input prices. (This is an aspect of firm behaviour we will examine in detail in the next chapter.) Moreover, there are limits to the extent to which the nonmaximizing behaviour can survive in the marketplace. Failure to respond to profit opportunities can lead to takeover by a more profit-oriented management. Although this threat of takeover does not mean that profits are being precisely maximized at all times, it does put real limits on the extent to which firms can ignore profits.

Profits are a potent force in the life and death of firms. The resilience of profit-maximizing theory and its ability to predict the economy's reactions to many major changes (such as the dramatic decline in computer prices that have occurred over the past two decades) suggest that firms are at least strongly motivated by the pursuit of profits.

Over the past two decades, the question of how firms behave in detail has received renewed attention from both economists and organization theorists. Almost everyone in the field agrees that firms do not *exactly* maximize profits at all times and in all places. At the same time, almost everyone agrees that firms cannot stray too far from the goal of profit maximization. Just how far is too far depends on the circumstances in which firms operate and the mechanisms that firms' owners can use to influence managers. These areas are at the frontier of current economic research.

Profit Maximization as an Evolutionary Equilibrium

U.S. economist Armen Alchian has suggested that firms will evolve over time to become profit maximizers. The basic argument is based on the principle of *survival of the fittest*. In a competitive environment, firms that pursue goals or adopt rules that are inconsistent with profit maximization will be unable to stay in business; firms that either choose or happen upon rules that are closer to profit maximization will displace those that do not. Eventually, only the profit-maximizing firms will survive in the marketplace.

A similar kind of argument can be applied to firms that operate in markets with fewer competitors (such as oligopolistic markets that we examine in Chapter 11). Here it is not competition in the product market that forces the firm toward profit maximization in the long run but competition in the market for corporate control. A firm that does not maximize profits will be less valuable than one that does maximize profits. Thus, the non-profit-maximizing firm can be bought by profit-maximizing managers, who will increase its value as they increase its profits.

Alchian's argument suggests the following conclusion:

Even if no firm starts out with the intention of maximizing profits, in the long run the firms that survive in the marketplace will tend to be the profit maximizers.

This view provides an apparent synthesis of maximizing and evolutionary theories of the firm. The distinction between the theories is not so stark as it might seem.

CHAPTER 8

Producers in the Long Run

🔵 LEARNING OBJECTIVES

1 Understand why cost minimization requires firms to equate the marginal product per dollar spent for all factors.

2 Explain the principle of substitution, and why it implies that firms will use more of factors whose prices have fallen (and use less of factors whose prices have increased).

3 Recognize the relationship between short-run and long-run cost curves.

4 Understand that changes in the economic environment often lead firms to innovate to improve their technology.

In the first part of this chapter, we look at the long run, in which firms are free to vary all factors of production. Picking up from the end of Chapter 7, the choice that a firm faces in the long run is *which* of the several short-run cost curves it should be on. Remember that a different short-run average total cost (*SRATC*) curve exists for each possible amount of the fixed factor. Some firms use a great deal of capital and only a small amount of labour. Others use less capital and more labour. Here we examine the effects that these choices have on firms' costs, and we look at the conditions that determine these choices.

In the second part of the chapter, we examine the very long run, in which technology changes. The discussion concerns the improvements in technology and productivity that have dramatically increased output and incomes in all industrial countries over centuries. Firms are among the most important economic actors that cause technological advances to take place. Evidence shows that the hypotheses of profit maximization and cost minimization can help us to understand technological changes. Here, as in the short and long run, firms respond to events such as changes in factor prices. But in the very long run, firms often respond by innovating—that is, by developing *new* technologies.

Throughout this chapter, we should remember that the lengths of the various runs under consideration are defined by the kinds of changes that can take place, not by calendar time. Thus we would expect actual firms in any given time period to minimize costs in the short run, as described in Chapter 7; to choose among alternative short-run cost curves in the long run, as described in the first part of this chapter; and to change technologies in the very long run as described in the latter part of this chapter.

The Long Run: No Fixed Factors

In the short run, in which at least one factor is fixed, the only way to produce a given output is to adjust the input of the variable factors. In the long run, in which all factors can be varied, there are numerous ways to produce any given output. For example, the firm could use a lot of capital and few workers, or little capital and many workers. Thus, firms in the long run must choose the type and amount of plant and equipment and the size of their labour force.

In making these choices, the firm tries to be **technically efficient** by using no more of all inputs than necessary—that is, the firm does not want to waste any of its valuable inputs. Technical efficiency is not enough, however. To be *economically* efficient, the firm must choose from among the many technically efficient options the one that produces a given level of output at the lowest possible cost. (The distinction between various types of efficiency sometimes causes confusion, particularly when engineers and economists are involved in the same decision-making process. *Applying Economic Concepts 8-1* elaborates on this important distinction.)

Long-run planning decisions are important. A firm that decides to build a new steel mill and invest in the required machinery will choose among many alternatives. Once installed, that equipment is fixed for a long time. If the firm makes a wrong choice, its survival may be threatened; if it estimates correctly, it may be rewarded with large profits.

technical efficiency
When a given number of inputs are combined in such a way as to maximize the level of output.

Profit Maximization and Cost Minimization

Any firm that is trying to maximize its profits in the long run should select the economically efficient method of production, which is the method that produces its output at the lowest possible cost. As we noted in the previous chapter, this implication of the hypothesis of profit maximization is called **cost minimization**: From the alternatives open to it, the profit-maximizing firm will choose the least costly way of producing whatever level of output it chooses.

cost minimization
An implication of profit maximization that firms choose the production method that produces any given level of output at the lowest possible cost.

Long-Run Cost Minimization

If it is possible to substitute one factor for another to keep output constant while reducing total cost, the firm is currently not using the least costly combination of factors. In such a situation, the firm should substitute one factor for another factor as long as the marginal product of the one factor *per dollar spent on it* is greater than the marginal product of the other factor *per dollar spent on it*. The firm is not minimizing its costs whenever these two magnitudes are unequal. For example, if an extra dollar spent on labour produces more output than an extra dollar spent on capital, the firm can reduce costs by spending less on capital and more on labour.

If we use K to represent capital, L to represent labour, and p_L and p_K to represent the prices per unit of the two factors, the necessary condition for cost minimization is as follows:

Oil is a very important input in many industries. Increases in the price of oil will lead profit-maximizing firms to substitute away from oil toward other factors of production.

APPLYING ECONOMIC CONCEPTS 8-1
Different Concepts of Efficiency

In popular discussion, business decision making, and government policies, three different types of efficiency concepts are encountered. These are engineering, technical, and economic efficiency. Each is a valid concept, and each conveys useful information. However, the use of one concept in a situation in which another is appropriate is a frequent source of error and confusion.

Engineering efficiency refers to the physical amount of some *single key input* that is used in production. It is measured by the ratio of that input to output. For example, the engineering efficiency of an engine refers to the ratio of the amount of energy in the fuel burned by the engine to the amount of usable energy produced by the engine. The difference is in friction, heat loss, and other unavoidable sources of waste. Saying that a steam engine is 40 percent efficient means that 40 percent of the energy in the fuel that is burned in the boiler is converted into work that is done by the engine, while the other 60 percent is lost.

Technical efficiency is related to the physical amount of *all factors* used in the process of producing some product. A particular method of producing a given level of output is technically efficient if there are no other ways of producing the output that use less of at least one input while not using more of any others.

Economic efficiency is related to the *value* (rather than the physical amounts) of all inputs used in producing a given output. The production of a given output is economically efficient if there are no other ways of producing the output that use a smaller *total value* of inputs.

What is the relationship between economic efficiency and these other two concepts? We have seen that engineering efficiency measures the efficiency with which a single input is used. Although knowing the efficiency of

any given gasoline, electric, or diesel engine is interesting, increasing this efficiency is not necessarily economically efficient because doing so usually requires the use of other valuable resources. For example, the engineering efficiency of a gas turbine engine can be increased by using more and stronger steel in its construction. Raising the engineering efficiency of an engine saves on fuel, but at the cost of using more of other inputs. To know whether this is worth doing, the firm must compare the value of the fuel saved with the value of the other inputs used.

Technical efficiency is desirable as long as inputs are costly to the firm in any way. If a technically inefficient process is replaced by a technically efficient process, there is a saving of resources. We do not need to put a precise value on the cost of inputs to make this judgement. All we need to know is that inputs have a positive cost to the firm, so that saving on these costs is desirable.

Usually, however, any given output may be produced in any one of many alternative technically efficient ways. Achieving technical efficiency is clearly a *necessary* condition for producing any output at the least cost. The existence of technical inefficiency means that costs can be reduced by reducing some inputs and not increasing any others. Achieving technical efficiency, however, is not a *sufficient* condition for producing at the lowest possible cost. The firm must still ask which of the many technically efficient methods it should use. This is where the concept of economic efficiency comes in. The appropriate method is the one that uses the smallest *total value* of inputs. This ensures that the firm spends as little as possible producing its given output; in terms of opportunity cost, the firm sacrifices the least possible value with respect to other things that it might do with those inputs.

$$\frac{MP_K}{p_K} = \frac{MP_L}{p_L} \tag{8-1}$$

Whenever the ratio of the marginal product of each factor to its price is not equal for all factors, there are possibilities for factor substitutions that will reduce costs (for a given level of output).

To see why Equation 8-1 must be satisfied when costs are being minimized, consider an example where the equation is *not* satisfied. Suppose that the marginal product of capital is 40 units of output and the price of a unit of capital is $10, making the left side of Equation 8-1 equal to 4. Suppose also that the marginal product of labour is 20 units of output and the price of a unit of labour is $2, making the right side equal to 10. Thus the last dollar spent on capital adds only 4 units to output, whereas the last dollar spent on labour adds 10 units to output. In this case, it is possible for the firm to keep its output constant but reduce its costs by using more labour and less capital. Specifically, if the firm spent an additional $4 on labour, output would rise by 40 units; but then it could spend exactly $10 less on capital and output would fall back by 40 units. Making such a substitution of labour for capital would leave output unchanged but it would reduce costs by $6. Thus the original combination of factors was not a cost-minimizing one.[1]

By rearranging the terms in Equation 8-1, we can look at the cost-minimizing condition a bit differently.[2]

$$\frac{MP_K}{MP_L} = \frac{p_K}{p_L} \qquad (8\text{-}2)$$

The ratio of the marginal products on the left side compares the contribution to output of the last unit of capital and the last unit of labour. The right side shows how the cost of an additional unit of capital compares to the cost of an additional unit of labour. If the two sides of Equation 8-2 are the same, then the firm cannot make any substitutions between labour and capital to reduce costs (if output is held constant). However, with the marginal products and factor prices used in the example above, the left side of the equation equals 2 but the right side equals 5; the last unit of capital is twice as productive as the last unit of labour but it is five times as expensive. It will thus pay the firm to switch to a method of production that uses less capital and more labour. If, however, the ratio on the right side were less than the ratio on the left, then it would pay the firm to switch to a method of production that used less labour and more capital. Only when the ratio of marginal products is exactly equal to the ratio of factor prices does the firm have no incentive to change its production method.

Firms adjust the quantities of factors they use to the prices of the factors given by the market.

Practise with Study Guide Chapter 8, Exercise 2.

The Principle of Substitution

The preceding discussion suggests that cost-minimizing firms will react to changes in factor prices by changing their methods of production. This is referred to as the **principle of substitution**.

Suppose that a firm is currently meeting the cost-minimizing conditions and that the cost of capital decreases while the cost of labour remains unchanged. The least-cost method of producing any output will now use less labour and more capital than was required to produce the same output before the factor prices changed.

Methods of production will change if the relative prices of factors change. Relatively more of the cheaper factor and relatively less of the more expensive factor will be used.

The principle of substitution plays a central role in resource allocation because it relates to the way in which individual firms respond to changes in relative factor prices that are caused by the changing relative scarcities of factors in the economy as a whole.

principle of substitution   The principle that methods of production will change if relative prices of inputs change, with relatively more of the cheaper input and relatively less of the more expensive input being used.

---

[1]The argument in this paragraph assumes that the marginal products do not change when expenditure changes by a very small amount.
[2]The appendix to this chapter provides a graphical analysis of this condition, which is similar to the analysis of consumer behaviour in the appendix to Chapter 6.

Individual firms are motivated to use less of factors that become scarcer to the economy and more of factors that become more plentiful. Here are two examples of the principle of substitution in action.

In the past two decades, the price of both business computers and office software has fallen sharply relative to the wages of clerical workers. One result of this change has been the near demise of the form letter, beginning "Dear Sir or Madam." Nowadays, even total strangers send you letters that are customized by name and sometimes more. Twenty years ago, such customized attention would have required that a secretary look up the information in a file and type it into a letter. Now a basic mail-merge program can do the job at much lower cost, and we see the result every day. Here we see the substitution toward capital and away from labour as their relative prices change.

The principle of substitution can also explain why methods of producing the same product often differ across countries. In Canada, where labour is generally highly skilled and expensive, a farmer with a large farm may use elaborate machinery to economize on labour. In China, however, where labour is abundant and capital is scarce, a much less mechanized method of production is appropriate. The Western engineer who believes that the Chinese are inefficient because they are using methods long ago discarded in the West is missing the truth about efficiency in the use of resources: Where factor scarcities differ across nations, so will the economically efficient methods of production.

Long-Run Cost Curves

When all factors of production can be varied, there exists a least-cost method of producing any given level of output. Thus, with given factor prices, there is a minimum achievable cost for each level of output; if this cost is expressed in terms of dollars per unit of output, we obtain the long-run average cost of producing each level of output. When this minimum cost of producing each level of output is plotted on a graph, the result is called a **long-run average cost (*LRAC*) curve**. Figure 8-1 shows one such curve.

The *LRAC* cost curve is determined by the firm's current technology and by the prices of the factors of production. It is a "boundary" in the sense that points below it are unattainable; points on the curve, however, are attainable if sufficient time elapses for all inputs to be adjusted. To move from one point on the *LRAC* curve to another requires an adjustment in *all* factor inputs, which may, for example, require building a larger, more elaborate factory.

The *LRAC* curve is the boundary between cost levels that are attainable, with known technology and given factor prices, and those that are unattainable.

Just as the short-run cost curves discussed in Chapter 7 relate to the production function describing the physical relationship between factor inputs and output, so does the *LRAC* curve. The difference is that in deriving the *LRAC* curve, there are no fixed factors of production. Thus, since all costs are variable in the long run, we do not need to distinguish between *AVC*, *AFC*, and *ATC*, as we did in the short run; in the long run, there is only one *LRAC* for any given set of input prices.

The Shape of the Long-Run Average Cost Curve

The *LRAC* curve shown in Figure 8-1 first falls and then rises. This curve is often described as U-shaped, although empirical studies suggest it is often "saucer-shaped." Consider the three portions of any such saucer-shaped *LRAC* curve.

long-run average cost (*LRAC*) curve The curve showing the lowest possible cost of producing each level of output when all inputs can be varied.

FIGURE 8-1   A Long-Run Average Cost Curve

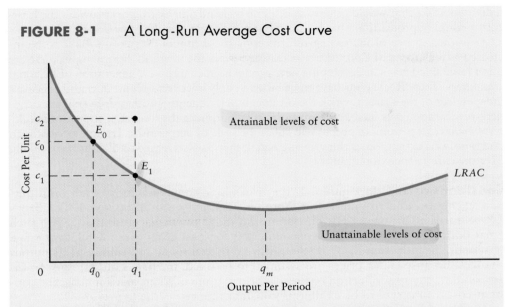

The long-run average cost *(LRAC)* curve is the boundary between attainable and unattainable levels of costs. If the firm wishes to produce output q_0, the lowest attainable cost level is c_0 per unit. Thus, point E_0 is on the *LRAC* curve. E_1 represents the lowest possible average cost of producing q_1. Suppose that a firm is producing at q_0 and desires to increase output to q_1. In the long run, a plant optimal for output q_1 can be built, and the cost of c_1 per unit can be attained. However, in the short run, it will not be able to vary all factors, and thus costs per unit will be above c_1, say, c_2. At output q_m, the firm attains its lowest possible per unit cost of production for the given technology and factor prices.

Decreasing Costs.   Over the range of output from zero to q_m, the firm has falling long-run average costs: An expansion of output permits a reduction of costs per unit of output. Technologies with this property exhibit **economies of scale**. Because the *LRAC* curve is drawn under the assumption of constant factor prices, the decline in long-run average cost occurs because output is increasing *more than* in proportion to inputs as the scale of the firm's production expands. Over this range of output, the decreasing-cost firm is often said to enjoy long-run **increasing returns**.[3]

Increasing returns may occur as a result of increased opportunities for specialization of tasks made possible by the division of labour. Even the most casual observation of the differences in production techniques used in large and small plants will show that larger plants use greater specialization. These differences arise because large, specialized equipment is useful only when the volume of output that the firm can sell justifies employment of that equipment. For example, assembly-line techniques and body-stamping machinery in automobile production are economically efficient only when individual operations are repeated thousands of times. Use of elaborate harvesting equipment (which combines many

economies of scale Reduction of average total costs resulting from an expansion in the scale of a firm's operations so that more of all inputs are being used.

increasing returns (to scale)   A situation in which output increases more than in proportion to inputs as the scale of a firm's production increases. A firm in this situation is a decreasing-cost firm.

---

[3] Economists shift back and forth between speaking in physical terms ("increasing returns") and cost terms ("decreasing costs"). As the text explains, the same relationship can be expressed either way.

individual tasks that would otherwise be done by hand and by tractor) provides the least-cost method of production on a big farm but not on one of only a few acres.

Another source of increasing returns consists of inputs that do not have to be increased as the output of a product is increased, even in the long run. For example, there are often large fixed costs in developing new products, such as a new generation of personal computers. These R&D costs have to be incurred only once for each product and hence are independent of the scale at which the product is subsequently produced. Even if the product's *production costs* increase in proportion to output in the long run, such *product development costs* per unit of output will fall as the scale of output rises. The influence of such one-time costs is that, other things being equal, they cause average total costs to be falling over the entire range of output.

constant returns (to scale) A situation in which output increases in proportion to inputs as the scale of production is increased. A firm in this situation is a constant-cost firm.

decreasing returns (to scale) A situation in which output increases less than in proportion to inputs as the scale of a firm's production increases. A firm in this situation is an increasing-cost firm.

Constant Costs.   In Figure 8-1, the firm's long-run average costs fall until output reaches q_m and rise thereafter. Another possibility should be noted. The firm's *LRAC* curve might have a flat portion over a range of output around q_m. With such a flat portion, the firm would be encountering constant costs over the relevant range of output, meaning that the firm's long-run average costs do not change as its output changes. Because factor prices are assumed to be fixed, the firm's output must be increasing *exactly in proportion to* the increase in inputs. When this happens, the constant-cost firm is said to be exhibiting **constant returns.**

Increasing Costs.   Over the range of outputs greater than q_m, the firm encounters rising long-run average costs. An expansion in production, even after sufficient time has elapsed for all adjustments to be made, is accompanied by a rise in average costs. If factor prices are constant, the firm's output must be increasing *less than* in proportion to the increase in inputs. When this happens, the increasing-cost firm is said to encounter long-run **decreasing returns.** Decreasing returns imply that the firm suffers some *diseconomies of scale.* As its scale of operations increases, diseconomies are encountered that increase its per-unit cost of production.

Such diseconomies may be associated with the difficulties of managing and controlling an enterprise as its size increases. For example, planning problems do not necessarily vary in direct proportion to size. At first, there may be scale economies as the firm grows and benefits from greater specialization. But, sooner or later, planning and coordination problems may multiply more than in proportion to the growth in size. If so, management costs per unit of output will rise.

Other sources of scale diseconomies are the possible alienation of the labour force as size increases; it becomes more difficult to provide appropriate supervision as more layers of supervisors and middle managers come between the person at the top and the workers on the shop floor. Control of middle-range managers may also become more difficult. As the firm becomes larger, managers may begin to pursue their own goals rather than devote all of their efforts to making profits for the firm. Much of the "reengineering" of large firms in the 1990s has been aimed at reducing the extent to which management difficulties increase with firm size, but the problem has not been, and probably cannot be, eliminated entirely.

FIGURE 8-2   *LRAC and SRATC Curves*

The *SRATC* curve is tangent to the *LRAC* curve at the output for which the quantity of the fixed factors is optimal. The particular *SRATC* curve shown is drawn for a plant size that minimizes costs for output q_0. For all other levels of output the plant is either too big or too small and *SRATC* therefore lies above *LRAC*. If some level of output other than q_0 is to be sustained, costs can be reduced to the level of the *LRAC* curve when sufficient time has elapsed to adjust the plant size.

Note that long-run decreasing returns differs from short-run diminishing returns. In the short run, at least one factor is fixed, and the law of diminishing returns ensures that returns to the variable factor will eventually diminish. In the long run, all factors are variable, and it is possible that physically diminishing returns will never be encountered—at least as long as it is genuinely possible to increase inputs of all factors.

The Relationship Between Long-Run and Short-Run Costs

The short-run cost curves from the previous chapter and the long-run curve studied in this chapter are all derived from the same production function. Each curve assumes given prices for all factor inputs. The long-run average cost *(LRAC)* curve shows the lowest cost of producing any output when all factors are variable. Each short-run average total cost *(SRATC)* curve shows the lowest cost of producing any output when one or more factors are fixed.

No short-run cost curve can fall below the long-run curve because the *LRAC* curve represents the lowest attainable cost for each possible output.

As the level of output is changed, a different-size plant is normally required to achieve the lowest attainable cost. Figure 8-2 shows the *SRATC* curve above the *LRAC* curve at all levels of output except q_0.

As we saw in the last chapter, any individual *SRATC* curve is just one of many such curves. The *SRATC* curve in Figure 8-2 shows how costs vary as output is varied, holding the plant size constant. Figure 8-3 shows a family of *SRATC* curves, along with a single *LRAC* curve. The *LRAC* curve is sometimes called an **envelope** because it encloses a series of *SRATC* cost curves by being tangent to them.

Practise with Study Guide Chapter 8, Exercise 4.

envelope Any curve that encloses, by being tangent to, a series of other curves. In particular, the envelope cost curve is the *LRAC* curve, which encloses the *SRATC* curves by being tangent to each without cutting any of them.

FIGURE 8-3 The Envelope Relationship Between the *LRAC* Curve and All of the *SRATC* Curves

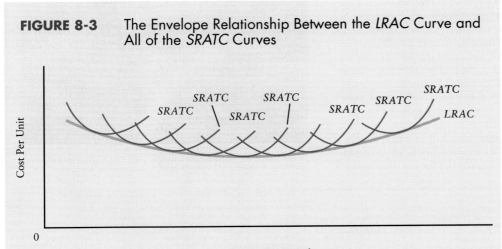

To every point on the *LRAC* curve, there is an associated *SRATC* curve tangent at that point. Each short-run curve is drawn for a given amount of fixed factors, and shows how costs vary if output varies. The level of output at the tangency between each *SRATC* curve and the *LRAC* curve shows the level of output for which the amount of the fixed factor is optimal.

LESSONS FROM HISTORY 8-1

Jacob Viner and the Clever Draftsman

Jacob Viner (1892–1970) was born in Montreal and studied economics at McGill University under Stephen Leacock (1869–1944). Viner was clearly an outstanding student and, according to some of his McGill classmates, knew much more about economics than did Leacock, who was actually better known as a humourist than an economist. Viner was such a good economist that he was the first person to work out the relationship between a firm's long-run average costs and its short-run average costs. He went on to teach economics at the University of Chicago and at Princeton University and became one of the world's leading economic theorists.

The student who finds the relationship between *SRATC* and *LRAC* hard to understand may take some comfort from the fact that when Jacob Viner first worked out this relationship, and published it in 1931, he made a crucial mistake. In preparing a diagram like Figure 8-3, he instructed his draftsman to draw the *LRAC* curve through the *minimum points* of all the *SRATC* curves, "but so as to never lie above" the *SRATC* curves. Viner later said of the draftsman: "He is a mathematician, however, not an economist, and he saw some mathematical objection to this procedure which I could not succeed in understanding. I could not persuade him to disregard his scruples as a craftsman and to follow my instructions, absurd though they might be."

Viner's mistake was to require that the draftsman connect all of the *minimum* points of the *SRATC* curves rather than to construct the curve that would be the *lower envelope* of all the *SRATC* curves. The former curve can of course be drawn, but it *is not* the *LRAC* curve. The latter curve *is* the *LRAC* curve, and is tangent to each *SRATC* curve.

Since Viner's article was published in 1931, generations of economics students have experienced great satisfaction when they finally figured out his crucial mistake.

Viner's famous article was often reprinted, for its fame was justly deserved, despite the importance of the mistake. But Viner always rejected suggestions that he correct the error because he did not wish to deprive other students of the pleasure of feeling one up on him.

The economic sense of the fact that tangency is *not* at the minimum points of *SRATC* rests on the subtle distinction between the least-cost method of utilizing *a given plant* and the least-cost method of producing *a given level of output*. The first concept defines the minimum of any given *SRATC* curve, whereas the second defines a point on the *LRAC* curve for any given level of output. It is the second concept that interests us in the long run. If bigger plants can achieve lower average costs, there will be a gain in building a bigger plant *and underutilizing it* whenever the gains from using the bigger plant are enough to offset the costs of being inefficient in the use of the plant. If there are gains from building bigger plants (i.e., if *LRAC* is declining), some underutilization is always justified.

Montreal-born Jacob Viner taught at Princeton and Chicago and was one of the world's leading economic theorists.

Each *SRATC* curve is tangent to the long-run average cost curve at the level of output for which the quantity of the fixed factor is optimal and lies above it for all other levels of output.

The relationship between the *LRAC* curve and the many different *SRATC* curves has a famous history in economics. The economist who is credited with first working out this relationship, Jacob Viner, initially made a serious mistake that ended up being published; *Lessons From History 8-1* explains his mistake and shows how it illustrates an important difference between short-run and long-run costs.

Shifts in Cost Curves

We saw in Chapter 7 how changes in either technological knowledge or factor prices will cause the entire family of short-run cost curves to shift. The same is true for long-run cost curves. Because loss of existing technological knowledge is rare, we focus on the effects of technological improvement. Improved ways of producing existing products make lower-cost methods of production available, thereby shifting cost curves downward.

Changes in factor prices can exert an influence in either direction. If a firm has to pay more for any factor that it uses, the cost of producing each level of output will rise; if the firm has to pay less for any factor that it uses, the cost of producing each level of output will fall.

A rise in factor prices shifts short-run and long-run average cost curves upward. A fall in factor prices or a technological improvement shifts average cost curves downward.

The Very Long Run: Changes in Technology

In the long run, profit-maximizing firms do the best they can to produce known products with the techniques and the resources currently available. Firms are therefore on, rather than above, their long-run cost curves. In the very long run, however, there are changes in the available techniques and resources. Such changes cause *shifts* in long-run cost curves.

The decrease in costs that can be achieved by choosing from among available factors of production, known techniques, and alternative levels of output is necessarily limited. Improvements by invention and innovation are potentially limitless, however, and hence sustained growth in living standards is critically linked to technological change.

Technological change refers to all changes in the available techniques of production. To measure its extent, economists use the notion of **productivity,** defined as a measure of output produced per unit of resource input. Two widely used measures of productivity are output per worker and output per hour of work. The rate of increase in productivity provides a measure of technological change. The significance of productivity growth is explored in *Applying Economic Concepts 8-2.*

technological change Any change in the available techniques of production.

productivity Output produced per unit of some input; frequently used to refer to labour productivity, measured by total output divided by the amount of labour used.

Technological Change

Technological change was once thought to be mainly a random process, brought about by inventions made by crackpots and eccentric scientists working in garages and scientific laboratories. As a result of recent research by economists, we now know better.

Changes in technology are often *endogenous responses* to changing economic signals; that is, they result from responses by firms to the same things that induce the substitution of one factor for another within the confines of a given technology.

In our discussion of long-run demand curves in Chapter 4, we looked at just such technological changes in response to rising relative prices when we spoke of the development, in the 1970s, of smaller, more fuel-efficient cars in the wake of rising gasoline prices. Similarly, much of the move to substitute capital for labour in manufacturing,

APPLYING ECONOMIC CONCEPTS 8-2

The Significance of Productivity Growth

Economics used to be known as the "dismal science" because some of its predictions were grim. Thomas Malthus (1766–1834) and other Classical economists predicted that the pressure of more and more people on the world's limited resources would cause a decline in output per person due to the law of diminishing returns. Human history would see more and more people living less and less well and the surplus population, which could not be supported, dying off from hunger and disease.

This prediction has proved wrong for the developed countries, for two main reasons. First, their populations have not expanded as rapidly as predicted by early economists, who were writing before birth-control techniques were widely used. Second, technological advances have been so important during the past 150 years that output has increased faster than the population. We have experienced sustained growth in productivity that has permitted increases in output per person. As the accompanying figure shows, real output per worker in Canada increased by 264 percent between 1926 and 1998, an average annual growth rate of 1.8 percent.

Even such small annual productivity increases are a powerful force for increasing living standards over many years. Our great-grandparents would have regarded today's standard of living in most industrialized countries as unattainable. An apparently modest rate of increase in productivity of 2 percent per year leads to a doubling of per capita output every 35 years.

During the 1970s, the rate of productivity growth in most industrialized countries dropped sharply below its historical trend. This slowdown was particularly acute in Canada and the United States. In recent years, annual productivity growth rates have increased somewhat, but are still below the high rates that existed in the 1950s and 1960s.

Due to the importance of productivity growth in raising long-run living standards, it is not surprising that explaining the sources of technological progress has become a very active area of research, among both academic and government economists.

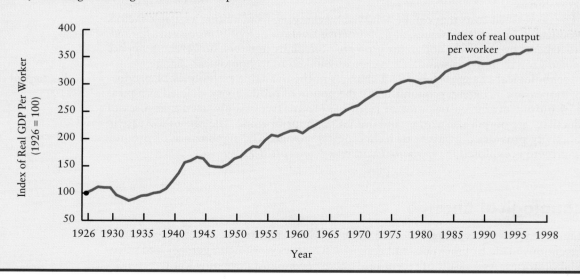

transportation, communications, mining, and agriculture in response to rising wage rates has taken the form of inventing new labour-saving methods of production.

Consider three kinds of change that influence production and cost in the very long run—*new techniques, new products,* and *improved inputs.*

New Techniques

Throughout the nineteenth and twentieth centuries, changes in the techniques available for producing existing products have been dramatic; this is called *process innovation*. About the same amount of coal is produced in North America today as was produced 50 years ago, but the number of coal miners is less than one-tenth what it was then. A century ago, roads and railways were built by gangs of workers who used buckets, spades, and draft horses. Today, bulldozers, giant trucks, and other specialized equipment have banished the workhorse completely from construction sites and to a great extent have displaced the pick-and-shovel worker.

Prior to the Second World War, electricity was generated either by burning fossil fuels or by harnessing the power of flowing water. With the rise of the atomic age immediately following the war, many countries developed large-scale nuclear generating capacity. Economies of scale in electricity production were significant. In recent years, however, the development of small-scale, gas-combustion turbines has permitted inexpensive construction of small generating stations that can produce electricity at a lower average cost than the much larger nuclear, hydro, or fossil-fuel-burning generating stations. The product—electricity—is absolutely unchanged, but the techniques of production have changed markedly over the past several decades.

New Products

New goods and services are constantly being invented and marketed; this is called *product innovation*. VCRs, personal computers, CD players, video disks, cellular phones, and many other current consumer products did not exist a mere generation ago. Other products have changed so dramatically that the only connection they have with the "same" product from the past is the name. Today's Ford automobile is very different from a 1920 Ford, and it is even different from a 1980 Ford in size, safety, and gasoline consumption. Modern jet airliners are revolutionary compared with the first passenger jet aircraft, which were in turn many times larger and faster than the DC–3, the workhorse of the airlines during the 1930s and 1940s. Beyond having wings and engines, the DC–3 itself bore little resemblance to the Wright brothers' original flying machine.

Improved Inputs

Improvements in health and education raise the quality of labour services. Today's workers and managers are healthier and better educated than their grandparents. Many of today's unskilled workers are literate and competent in arithmetic, and their managers are apt to be trained in methods of business management and computer science.

Similarly, improvements in material inputs are constantly occurring. For example, the type and quality of metals have changed. Steel has replaced iron, and aluminum substitutes for steel in a process of change that makes a statistical category such as "primary metals" seem unsatisfactory. Even for a given category, say, steel, today's product is lighter, stronger, and more flexible than the "same" product manufactured only 20 years ago.

Firms' Choices in the Very Long Run

Firms respond to signals that indicate changes in the economic environment. For example, consider the situation faced by Alcan—a major Canadian aluminum producer—when the price of electricity (a major input) increases and is expected to remain at the higher level for some time. How can Alcan respond to this change in the economic environment?

One option for Alcan is to make a long-run response by substituting away from the use of electricity by changing its production techniques within the confines of existing technology. Another option is to invest in research in order to develop new production techniques that innovate away from electricity. Of course, both responses could be adopted, but because both involve the use of costly resources, the responses are substitutes in the sense that Alcan may have to choose more of one at the cost of using less of the other.

Faced with increases in the price of an input, firms may either *substitute away* or *innovate away* from the input.

It is important to recognize that the two options can involve quite different actions and can ultimately have quite different implications for productivity.

For example, consider three different responses to an increase in Canadian labour costs. One firm reallocates its production activities to Mexico or Southeast Asia, where labour costs are relatively low and hence labour-intensive production techniques remain quite profitable. A second firm chooses to reduce its use of labour but increase its use of capital equipment. These two firms have, in different ways, chosen to *substitute away* from the higher-priced Canadian labour. A third firm devotes resources to developing new production techniques, perhaps using robotics or other new equipment. This firm has *innovated away* from higher-priced Canadian labour.

All three are possible reactions to the changed circumstances. The first two are largely well understood in advance and will lead to improved efficiency relative to continued reliance on the original production methods. The third response, depending on the often unpredictable results of the innovation, may reduce costs sufficiently to warrant the investment in research and development and may even lead to substantially more effective production techniques that allow the firm to maintain an advantage over its competitors for a number of years.

S U M M A R Y

The Long Run: No Fixed Factors

⑩①②③

- There are no fixed factors in the long run. Profit-maximizing firms choose from the available alternatives the least-cost method of producing any specific output. A long-run cost curve represents the boundary between attainable and unattainable costs for the given technology and given factor prices.
- The principle of substitution implies that, in response to changes in factor prices, firms will substitute toward the cheaper factors and substitute away from the more expensive factors.
- The shape of the *LRAC* curve depends on the relationship of inputs to outputs as the whole scale of a firm's operations changes. Increasing, constant, and decreasing re-

turns lead, respectively, to decreasing, constant, and increasing long-run average costs.
- The *LRAC* and *SRATC* curves are related. Every long-run cost corresponds to some quantity of each factor and is thus on some short-run cost curve. The short-run cost curve shows how costs vary when that particular quantity of a fixed factor is used to produce outputs greater than or less than the output for which it is optimal.
- Cost curves shift upward or downward in response to changes in the prices of factors or changes in technology. Increases in factor prices shift cost curves upward. Decreases in factor prices and technological advances shift cost curves downward.

The Very Long Run: Changes in Technology

LO 4

- Over the very long run, the most important influence on costs of production and on standards of living has been increases in output made possible by technological improvements.
- Changes in technology are often *endogenous responses* to changing economic signals; that is, they result from responses by firms to the same things that induce the substitution of one factor for another in a given technology.

- There are three important kinds of technological change—developments of new techniques, new products, and improved inputs.
- In trying to understand any industry's response to changes in its operating environment, it is important to consider the effects of endogenous innovations in technology as well as substitution based on changes in the use of existing technologies.

KEY CONCEPTS

The implication of cost minimization
The interpretation of $MP_K/MP_L = p_K/p_L$
The principle of substitution

Increasing, decreasing, and constant returns
Economies of scale
LRAC curve as an envelope of *SRATC* curves

Technological change and productivity growth
Changes in technology as endogenous responses

STUDY EXERCISES

1. Use the principle of substitution to predict the effect in each of the following situations.

   a. During the past 10 years, technological advances in the computer industry have led to dramatic reductions in the prices of personal and business computers. At the same time, real wages have increased slowly.

   b. The ratio of land costs to building costs is much higher in big cities than in small cities.

   c. Wages of textile workers and shoe machinery operators are higher in Canada than in the southern United States.

   d. A new collective agreement results in a significant increase in wages for pulp and paper workers.

2. The following table shows the marginal product of capital and labour for each of several methods of producing 1000 kilograms of flour per day.

Production Method	MP_K	MP_L
A	14	3
B	12	6
C	10	9
D	8	12
E	6	15
F	4	18
G	2	21

   a. As we move from *A* to *G*, are the production methods becoming more or less *capital intensive*? Explain.

   b. If capital costs $8 per unit and labour costs $4 per unit, which production method minimizes the cost of producing 1000 kg of flour?

   c. For each of the methods that are not cost minimizing (with the factor prices from part **b**), describe how the firm would have to adjust its use of capital and labour to minimize costs.

d. Now suppose that the price of capital falls to $4 per unit and the price of labour rises to $6 per unit. Which method now minimizes costs?

3. Consider the following diagram of *SRATC* and *LRAC* curves.

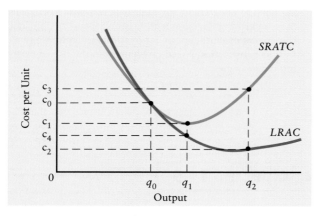

a. The *SRATC* curve is drawn for a given plant size. What is the level of output for which this plant size is optimal in the short run? What are unit costs in the short run at this level of output?
b. What is the level of output for which this plant size is optimal in the long run? What are unit costs in the short run at this level of output?
c. Explain the economics of why c_1 is greater than c_4.
d. Suppose the firm wants to increase output to q_2 in the short run. How is this accomplished, and what would unit costs be?
e. Suppose the firm wants to increase output to q_2 in the long run. How is this accomplished, and what would unit costs be?

4. In the text, we stated that the *LRAC* curve eventually slopes upward because of *diseconomies of scale*. In the previous chapter we saw that the *SRATC* curve eventually slopes upward because of *diminishing marginal product of the variable factor*.

a. Explain the difference between *diseconomies of scale and diminishing marginal product of the variable factor*. Why is one a short-run concept and the other a long-run concept?
b. Draw a diagram which shows short-run and long-run average cost curves that illustrates *for the same level of output* both diseconomies of scale and diminishing marginal product of the variable factor.

5. In the text, we stated that the *LRAC* curve initially slopes downward because of *economies of scale*. In the previous chapter we saw that the *SRATC* curve can initially slope downward because of *spreading overhead*.

a. Explain the difference between *economies of scale* and *spreading overhead*. Why is one a short-run concept and the other a long-run concept?
b. Draw a diagram which shows short-run and long-run average cost curves that illustrates *for the same level of output* both economies of scale and spreading overhead.

6. This question combines the various concepts from questions 4 and 5.

a. Draw a diagram which shows short-run and long-run average cost curves that illustrates *for the same level of output* economies of scale in the long run but diminishing marginal product for the variable factor in the short run.
b. Draw a diagram which shows short-run and long-run average cost curves that illustrates *for the same level of output* diseconomies of scale in the long run but falling average total costs in the short run.

7. This question relates to the material in the appendix. The following table shows several methods of producing 500 rubber tires per day. There are two factors, labour and capital, with prices per unit of $3 and $6, respectively.

Production Method	Units of Labour	Units of Capital	Total Cost
A	110	20	—-
B	90	25	—-
C	70	33	—-
D	50	43	—-
E	30	55	—-
F	10	70	—-

a. Compute the total cost for each production method and fill in the table.
b. Which production method minimizes costs for producing 500 tires?
c. Plot the isoquant for 500 tires.
d. Given the factor prices, draw the isocost line that corresponds to the cost-minimizing production method.
e. Now suppose that the price of labour rises to $5 per unit but the firm still wants to produce 500 tires per day. Explain how a cost-minimizing firm adjusts to this change (with no change in technology).

DISCUSSION QUESTIONS

1. In *The Competitive Advantage of Nations,* Michael Porter of Harvard University claimed: "Faced with high relative labor cost, . . . American consumer electronics firms moved to locate labor-intensive activities in . . . Asian countries, leaving the product and production process essentially the same. . . . Japanese rivals . . . set out instead to eliminate labor through automation. Doing so involved reducing the number of components which further lowered cost and improved quality. Japanese firms were soon building assembly plants in the United States, the place American firms had sought to avoid." Discuss these reactions in terms of changes over the long run and the very-long run.

2. Why must a profit-maximizing firm choose the least-cost method of producing any given output? Might a non-profit-maximizing organization such as a university, church, or government intentionally choose a method of production other than the least-cost one?

3. What is the interpretation of a move from one point on a long-run average cost curve to another point on the same curve? Contrast this with a movement along a short-run average total cost curve.

4. Each of the following is a means of increasing productivity. Discuss which groups in a society might oppose each one.

   a. A labour-saving invention that permits all goods to be manufactured with less labour than before
   b. Rapidly increasing population growth in the economy
   c. The removal of all government production safety rules
   d. A reduction in corporate income taxes
   e. A reduction in production of services and an increase in agricultural production

5. Policymakers and commentators often argue that the Canadian health-care system is more efficient than the U.S. health-care system. What sense of the term *efficiency* is being used in these arguments?

6. In December 1998, after a year in which Asian demand for B.C. lumber had fallen dramatically, an article in *The Globe and Mail* had the following headline: "Drastic Cost Reductions Needed to Save 13 B.C. Sawmills."

   a. Does the headline suggest that the B.C. lumber companies are not profit maximizers?
   b. If long-run unit costs are "too high," what is stopping the lumber companies from simply moving down their *LRAC* curves?

7. "Necessity is the mother of invention." Explain why this statement captures the essence of the view that firms often innovate their way around unfavourable changes in their economic environment.

The production function gives the relationship between the factor inputs that the firm uses and the output that it obtains. In the long run, the firm can choose among many different combinations of inputs that yield the same output. The production function and the long-run choices open to the firm can be represented graphically by using *isoquants*.

Isoquants

The table in Figure 8A-1 illustrates a hypothetical example in which several combinations of two inputs, labour and capital, can produce a given quantity of output. The data from the table are plotted graphically in Figure 8A-1. A smooth curve is drawn through the points to indicate that there are additional ways, which are not listed in the table, of producing the same output.

This curve is called an *isoquant*. It shows the whole set of technically efficient factor combinations for producing a given level of output. This is an example of graphing a relationship between three variables in two dimensions. It is analogous to the contour line on a map, which shows all points of equal altitude, and to an indifference curve (discussed in the Appendix to Chapter 6), which shows all combinations of products that yield the consumer equal utility.

As we move from one point on an isoquant to another, we are *substituting one factor for another* while holding output constant. If we move from point *b* to point *c,* we are substituting 1 unit of labour for 3 units of capital.

The marginal rate of substitution measures the rate at which one factor is substituted for another with output being held constant.

Sometimes the term *marginal rate of technical substitution* is used to distinguish this concept from the analogous one for consumer theory (the marginal rate of substitution) that we examined in Chapter 6.

Graphically, the marginal rate of substitution is measured by the slope of the isoquant at a particular point. We adopt the standard practice of defining the marginal rate of substitution as the negative of the

slope of the isoquant so that it is a positive number. The table in Figure 8A-1 shows the calculation of some marginal rates of substitution between various points on an isoquant. [19]

The marginal rate of substitution is related to the marginal products of the factors of production. To see how, consider an example. Suppose that at the present level of inputs of labour and capital, the marginal product of labour is 2 units of output and the marginal product of capital is 1 unit of output. If the firm reduces its use of capital and increases its use of labour to keep output constant, it needs to add only one-half unit of labour for 1 unit of capital given up. If, at another point on the isoquant with more labour and less capital, the marginal products are 2 for capital and 1 for labour, the firm will have to add 2 units of labour for every unit of capital it gives up. The general proposition is this:

The marginal rate of (technical) substitution between two factors of production is equal to the ratio of their marginal products.

Economists assume that isoquants satisfy two important conditions: They are downward sloping, and they are convex when viewed from the origin. What is the economic meaning of these conditions?

The downward slope indicates that each factor input has a positive marginal product. If the input of one factor is reduced and that of the other is held constant, output will be reduced. Thus if one input is decreased, production can be held constant only if the other factor input is increased.

To understand the convexity of the isoquant, consider what happens as the firm moves along the isoquant of Figure 8A-1 downward and to the right. Labour is being added and capital reduced to keep output constant. If labour is added in increments of exactly 1 unit, how much capital can be dispensed with each time? The key to the answer is that both factors are assumed to be subject to the law of diminishing returns. Thus the gain in output associated with each additional unit of labour added is *diminishing*, whereas the loss of output associated with each additional unit of capital forgone is *increasing*. Therefore, it takes ever-smaller reductions in capital to compensate for equal increases in labour. Viewed from the origin, therefore, the isoquant is convex.

FIGURE 8A-1   An Isoquant

Alternative Methods of Producing a Given Level of Output

Method	K	L	ΔK	ΔL	Marginal Rate of Substitution (absolute value of ΔK/ΔL)
a	18	2			
			−6	1	6.00
b	12	3			
			−3	1	3.00
c	9	4			
			−3	2	1.50
d	6	6			
			−2	3	0.67
e	4	9			
			−1	3	0.33
f	3	12			
			−1	6	0.17
g	2	18			

An isoquant describes the firm's alternative methods for producing a given level of output. Method *a* uses a great deal of capital *(K)* and very little labour *(L)*. As we move down the table, labour is substituted for capital in such a way as to keep output constant. Finally, at the bottom, most of the capital has been replaced by labour. The marginal rate of substitution between the two factors is calculated in the last three columns of the table. Note that as we move down the table, the marginal rate of substitution declines.

When the isoquant is plotted it is downward sloping and convex. The downward slope reflects the requirement of technical efficiency: keeping the level of output constant, a reduction in the use of one factor requires an increase in the use of the other factor. The convex shape of the isoquant reflects a diminishing marginal rate of (technical) substitution.

An Isoquant Map

The isoquant of Figure 8A-1 is for a given level of output. Suppose it is for 6 units. In this case, there is another isoquant for 7 units, another for 7000 units, and a different one for every other level of output. Each isoquant refers to a specific level of output and connects combinations of factors that are technically efficient methods of producing that output. If we plot a representative set of these isoquants from the same production function on a single graph, we get an *isoquant map* like that in Figure 8A-2. The higher the level of output along a particular isoquant, the farther the isoquant is from the origin.

Cost Minimization

Finding the *economically efficient* way of producing any output requires finding the least-cost factor com-

bination. To do this requires knowledge of the factor prices. Suppose that capital is priced at $4 per unit and labour at $1 per unit. An *isocost line* shows alternative combinations of factors that a firm can buy for a given total cost. Four different isocost lines appear in Figure 8A-3. The slope of each isocost line reflects *relative* factor prices. For given factor prices, a series of parallel isocost lines will reflect the alternative levels of expenditure on factor purchases that are available to the firm. The higher the level of expenditure, the farther the isocost line is from the origin.

In Figure 8A-4, the isoquant and isocost maps are brought together. Recall that economic efficiency requires any given level of output to be produced at minimum possible cost. Thus, the economically efficient method of production must be a point on an isoquant that just touches (is tangent to) an isocost line. If the isoquant cuts the isocost line, it is possible to move along the isoquant and reach a lower level of cost. Only at a point of tangency is a movement in either direction along the isoquant a movement to a higher cost level.

FIGURE 8A-2   An Isoquant Map

An isoquant map shows a set of isoquants, one for each level of output. Each isoquant corresponds to a specific level of output and shows factor combinations that are technically efficient methods of producing that output.

FIGURE 8A-3   Isocost Lines

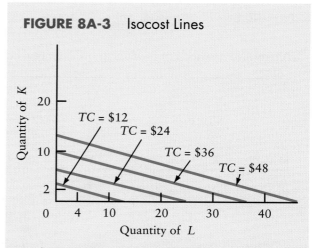

Each isocost line shows alternative factor combinations that require the same expenditure. The graph shows the four isocost lines that result when labour costs $1 per unit and capital $4 per unit and when expenditure (total cost, TC) is held constant at $12, $24, $36, and $48, respectively.

As shown in Figure 8A-4, the lowest attainable cost of producing 6 units is $24. This cost level can be achieved only by operating at point A, where the $24 isocost line is tangent to the 6-unit isoquant.

The least-cost position is given graphically by the tangency point between the isoquant and the isocost lines.

The slope of the isocost line is given by the ratio of the prices of the two factors of production. The slope of the isoquant is given by the ratio of their marginal products. When the firm reaches its cost-minimizing position, it has equated the price ratio (which is given to it by the market) with the ratio of the marginal products (which it can adjust by changing its usage of the factors). In symbols,

$$\frac{MP_L}{MP_K} = \frac{p_L}{p_K}$$

This is the same condition that we derived in the text (see Equation 8-2), but here we have derived it by using the isoquant analysis of the firm's decisions. [20]

Note the similarity of this condition for a cost-minimizing firm to Equation 6-2 where we saw how utility maximization for a consumer requires that the ratio of marginal utilities of consuming two products must equal the ratio of the two product prices. Both conditions reveal the basic principle that the decision makers (consumers or producers) face market prices beyond their control and so adjust quantities (consumption or factor inputs) until they are achieving their objective (utility maximization or cost minimization).

The Principle of Substitution

Suppose that with technology unchanged (that is, for a given isoquant map), the price of one factor changes. In particular, suppose that with the price of capital unchanged at $4 per unit, the price of labour rises from $1 to $4 per unit. Originally, the efficient factor combination for producing 6 units of output was 12 units of labour and 3 units of capital. Total cost was $24. To produce that same output in the same way would now cost $60 at the new factor prices. Figure 8A-5 shows why this is not economically efficient. The slope of the isocost line has changed, which makes it efficient to substitute the now relatively cheaper capital for the relatively more expensive labour. The change in slope of the isocost line illustrates the principle of substitution.

FIGURE 8A-4   Cost Minimization

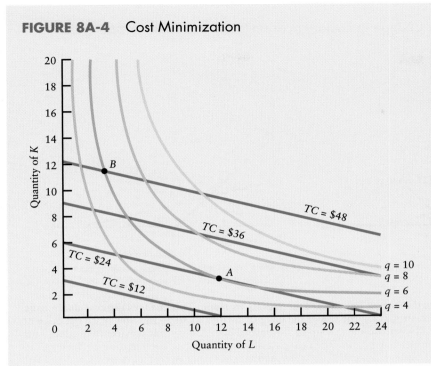

Cost minimization occurs at points of tangency between isoquant and isocost lines. The isoquant map of Figure 8A-2 and the isocost lines of Figure 8A-3 are brought together. Consider point A. It is on the 6-unit isoquant and the $24 isocost line. Thus it is possible to achieve the output $q = 6$ for a total cost of $24. There are other ways to achieve this output, for example, at point B, where $TC = 48. Moving along the isoquant from point A in either direction increases cost. Similarly, moving along the isocost line from point A in either direction lowers output. Thus either move would raise cost per unit.

Changes in relative factor prices will cause a partial replacement of factors that have become relatively more expensive by factors that have become relatively cheaper.

Of course, substitution of capital for labour cannot fully offset the effects of a rise in the cost of labour, as Figure 8A-5(i) shows. Consider the output attainable for $24. In the figure, there are two isocost lines representing $24 of outlay—at the old and new prices of labour. The new isocost line for $24 lies inside the old one (except where no labour is used). The $24 isocost line must therefore be tangent to a lower isoquant. Thus, if production is to be held constant, higher costs must be accepted. However, because of substitution, it is not necessary to accept costs as high as those that

would accompany an unchanged factor proportion. In the example, 6 units can be produced for $48 rather than the $60 that would be required if no change in factor proportions were made.

This analysis leads to the following predictions:

A rise in the price of one factor with all other factor prices held constant will (1) shift the cost curves of products that use that factor upward and (2) lead to a substitution of factors that are now relatively cheaper for the factor whose price has risen.

Both of these predictions were stated in Chapter 8; now they have been derived formally by the use of isoquants and isocost lines.

FIGURE 8A-5   The Effects of a Change in Factor Prices on Costs and Factor Proportions

(i) The effect on the isocost line of an increase in the price of labour

(ii) Substitution of capital for labour resulting from an increase in the price of labour

An increase in the price of labour pivots the isocost line inward, increasing its slope. This changes the cost-minimizing method of producing any level of output. In part (i), the rise in the price of L from \$1 to \$4 per unit (with the price of K being held constant at \$4) pivots the \$24 isocost line inward to the dashed line. Any output previously produced for \$24 will cost more at the new prices if it uses any labour. The new cost of using the factor combination at A rises from \$24 to \$60. In part (ii), the steeper isocost line is tangent to the $q = 6$ isoquant at C, not A, so that more capital and less labour is used. Costs at C are \$48, higher than they were before the price increase but not as high as they would be if the factor substitution had not occurred.

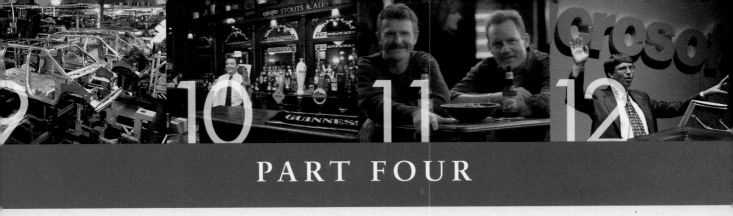

PART FOUR

Markets, Pricing, and Efficiency

Do wheat farmers in Saskatchewan and Manitoba compete with each other in the same way that Nike competes with Reebok? How would the Saskatchewan farmer respond to an improvement in techniques used by the Manitoba farmer? How would Nike respond to a price reduction by Reebok? Why do some firms, such as airlines, charge different prices to different consumers for the same product? Why did the Canadian government prevent the merger of the Royal Bank and the Bank of Montreal in 1998? These are the types of questions you will be able to answer after reading the next four chapters.

Chapter 9 discusses the theory of perfect competition. This theory describes markets in which a very large number of firms produce very similar products, like the wheat farmers in Saskatchewan and Manitoba. The chapter introduces the important concept of price taking. We will discuss how the existence of profits in such an industry leads to the entry of new firms, and why such entry leads to the dissipation of those profits. Similarly, we will see why losses lead existing firms to exit, and why this increases the profits of the remaining firms.

Chapter 10 examines monopoly—a situation in which there is only a single seller of a product. We will see that monopolies typically produce less output and have higher prices than do firms under perfect competition. We will discuss why several firms often try to join together to form a cartel, in which case they act as if they were a monopoly seller. We will also see why such cartels often break down.

Imperfect competition, which describes markets that are between the polar cases of perfect competition and monopoly, is discussed in Chapter 11. We will learn about industries with many firms but differentiated products, and also about industries with very few firms, in which strategic behaviour between the firms is important. It is here that you will see how economists use simple game theory to think about Nike's likely response to Reebok's price reduction.

The concept of allocative efficiency is examined in Chapter 12. We will consider why perfectly competitive markets are more efficient than monopolized markets. This difference in efficiency explains economists' long-held wariness of monopoly and why economists typically advocate competition over monopoly. Canadian competition policy, as we will see, is designed to encourage competition and discourage monopoly.

CHAPTER 9

Competitive Markets

🔵 LEARNING OBJECTIVES

① Distinguish between competitive markets and competitive firm behaviour.

② Know the key assumptions of the theory of perfect competition.

③ Explain the difference between an individual firm's demand curve and the industry demand curve for a perfectly competitive market.

④ Understand the rules for profit-maximizing behaviour.

⑤ Identify whether firms are making losses or profits in the short run.

⑥ Explain the role that entry and exit play in a competitive industry's long-run equilibrium.

⑦ Understand how competitive industries respond to long-run changes in demand.

Does PetroCanada compete with Esso in the sale of gasoline? Does American Express compete with Visa? Does a wheat farmer from Biggar, Saskatchewan compete with a wheat farmer from Brandon, Manitoba? If we use the ordinary meaning of the word compete, the answer to the first two questions is plainly yes, and the answer to the third question is no.

PetroCanada and Esso both advertise extensively to persuade consumers to buy their products. All sorts of things, from free dishes to performance-enhancing gasoline additives, are used to tempt drivers to buy one brand of gasoline rather than another. A host of world travellers in various tight spots attest on television or in magazines to the virtues of American Express, while other happy faces advise us that only with a Visa card can their pleasures be ours.

When we shift our attention to wheat farmers, however, we see that there is nothing that the Saskatchewan farmer can do to affect either the sales or the profits of the Manitoba farmer. Even if the Saskatchewan farmer could do something to influence the profits of the Manitoba farmer, there would be no point in doing so, since changes in the profits of the Manitoba farmer would not affect the Saskatchewan farmer.

To sort out the questions of who is competing with whom and in what sense, it is useful to distinguish between the behaviour of individual firms and the type of market in which they operate. Economists are interested in two different concepts—*competitive behaviour* and *competitive market structure*.

Market Structure and Firm Behaviour

The term **market structure** refers to all the features that may affect the behaviour and performance of the firms in a market, such as the number of firms in the market or the type of product that they sell.

market structure   All features of a market that affect the behaviour and performance of firms in that market, such as the number and size of sellers, the extent of knowledge about one another's actions, the degree of freedom of entry, and the degree of product differentiation.

Competitive Market Structure

The competitiveness of the market is the extent to which individual firms have power to influence market prices or the terms on which their product is sold.

The less power an individual firm has to influence the market in which it sells its product, the more competitive is that market's structure.

The extreme form of competitive market structure occurs when each firm has zero market power. In such a case, there are so many firms in the market that each must accept the price set by the forces of market demand and market supply. The firms perceive themselves as being able to sell as much as they choose at the prevailing market price and as having no power to influence that price. If the firm charged a higher price, it would make no sales; so many other firms would be selling at the market price that buyers would take their business elsewhere.

This extreme is called a *perfectly competitive market structure* or, more simply, a *perfectly competitive market*. In such a market there is no need for individual firms to compete actively with one another because none has any power over the market. One firm's ability to sell its product does not depend on the behaviour of any other firm. For example, the Saskatchewan and Manitoba wheat farms operate in a perfectly competitive market over which they have no power. Neither can change the market price for its wheat by altering its own behaviour.

Competitive Behaviour

In everyday language, the term *competitive behaviour* refers to the degree to which individual firms actively vie with one another for business. For example, PetroCanada and Esso clearly engage in competitive behaviour. It is also true, however, that both companies have some real power over their market. Each has the power to decide the price that people will pay for their gasoline and oil, within limits set by buyers' tastes and the prices of competing products. Either firm could raise its prices and still continue to attract some customers. Even though they actively compete with each other, they do so in a market that does not have a perfectly competitive structure.

In contrast, the Saskatchewan and Manitoba wheat farmers do not engage in competitive behaviour because the only way they can affect their profits is by changing their own outputs of wheat or their own production costs.

The distinction that we have just made between behaviour and structure explains why firms in perfectly competitive markets (e.g., the Saskatchewan and Manitoba wheat producers) do not compete actively with each other, whereas firms that do compete actively with each other (e.g., PetroCanada and Esso) do not operate in perfectly competitive markets.

The Significance of Market Structure

When the managers of a firm make their production and sales decisions, they need to know what quantity of a product their firm can sell at various prices. That is, they need to know the demand curve for their *own firm's* output. If they know the demand curve that their own firm faces, they know the sales that their firm can make at each price it might charge, and thus they know its potential revenues. If they also know their firm's costs for producing the product, they can calculate the profits that would be associated with each rate of output. With this information, they can choose the output that maximizes profits.

Note that the demand curve for the firm's output may not be the same as the demand curve for the industry as a whole. Indeed, this is where *market structure* enters the picture. Recall that economists define market structure as the characteristics that affect the behaviour and performance of firms that sell in that market. These characteristics determine, among other things, the relationship between the market demand curve for the industry's product and the demand curve that each firm in that industry faces. One thing that we will see in this chapter is that in a perfectly competitive market, an individual firm faces a very different demand curve than that faced by the industry as a whole.

To reduce the analysis of market structure to manageable proportions, economists focus on four theoretical market structures that cover most actual cases: *perfect competition, monopoly, monopolistic competition,* and *oligopoly.* Perfect competition will be dealt with in the rest of this chapter, the other structures in the chapters that follow.

The Theory of Perfect Competition

perfect competition
A market structure in which all firms in an industry are price takers and in which there is freedom of entry into and exit from the industry.

The perfectly competitive market structure—usually referred to simply as **perfect competition**—applies directly to a number of markets. It also provides an important benchmark for comparison with other market structures.

The Assumptions of Perfect Competition

The theory of perfect competition is built on a number of key assumptions relating to each firm and to the industry as a whole.

homogeneous product   In the eyes of purchasers, every unit of the product is identical to every other unit.

1. All the firms in the industry sell an identical product. Economists say that the firms sell a **homogeneous product.**

2. Customers know the nature of the product being sold and the prices charged by each firm.

3. The level of a firm's output at which its long-run average cost reaches a minimum is small relative to the *industry's* total output. (This is the precise way of saying that the firm is small relative to the size of the industry.)

4. The industry is characterized by *freedom of entry and exit;* that is, any new firm is free to enter the industry and start producing if it so wishes, and any existing firm is free to cease production and leave the industry. Existing firms cannot bar the entry of new firms, and there are no legal prohibitions or other artificial barriers to entering or exiting the industry.

The first three assumptions imply that each firm in a perfectly competitive industry is a **price taker.** This means that the firm can alter its rate of production and sales without affecting the market price of its product. Thus a firm operating in a perfectly competitive market has no power to influence that market through its own individual actions. It must passively accept whatever happens to be the market price, but it can sell as much as it wants at that price.

The Saskatchewan and Manitoba wheat farmers we considered earlier provide us with good illustrations of firms that are operating in a perfectly competitive market. Because each individual wheat farmer is just one of a very large number of producers who are all growing the same product, one firm's contribution to the industry's total production is a tiny drop in an extremely large bucket. Each firm will correctly assume that variations in its output have no significant effect on the price of wheat. Thus, each firm, knowing that it can sell as much or as little as it chooses at that price, adapts its behaviour to a given market price of wheat. Furthermore, there is nothing that any one farmer can do to stop another farmer from growing wheat, and there are no legal deterrents to becoming a wheat farmer. Anyone who has enough money to buy or rent the necessary land, labour, and equipment can become a wheat farmer.

The difference between the wheat farmers and PetroCanada is the *degree of market power.* Each firm that is producing wheat is an insignificant part of the whole market and thus has no power to influence the price of wheat. PetroCanada does have power to influence the price of gasoline because its own sales represent a significant part of the total Canadian sales of gasoline.

The Demand Curve for a Perfectly Competitive Firm

A major distinction between firms in perfectly competitive markets and firms in any other type of market is the shape of the firm's own demand curve.

Each firm in a perfectly competitive market faces a horizontal demand curve because variations in the firm's output have no noticeable effect on price.

The horizontal (perfectly elastic) demand curve does not indicate that the firm could actually sell an infinite amount at the going price. It indicates, rather, that the variations in production *that it will normally be possible for the firm to make* will leave price unchanged because their effect on total industry output will be negligible.

Figure 9-1 contrasts the market demand curve for the product of a competitive industry with the demand curve that a single firm in that industry faces. *Applying Economic Concepts 9-1* provides an example of the important difference between the firm's demand curve and the market demand curve. It shows a detailed calculation of why the demand curve facing any individual wheat farmer is very nearly perfectly elastic, even though the *market* demand for wheat is quite inelastic.

Total, Average, and Marginal Revenue

To study the revenues that firms receive from the sales of their products, economists define three concepts called *total, average,* and *marginal revenue.* These are the revenue counterparts of the concepts of total, average, and marginal cost that we considered in Chapter 7.

Total revenue *(TR)* is the total amount received by the seller from the sale of a product. If q units are sold at p dollars each, $TR = p \times q$.

price taker   A firm that can alter its rate of production and sales without significantly affecting the market price of its product.

total revenue (TR)   Total receipts from the sale of a product; price times quantity.

FIGURE 9-1   The Demand Curve for a Competitive Industry and for One Firm in the Industry

(i) Competitive industry's
demand curve

(ii) Competitive firm's
demand curve

The industry's demand curve is negatively sloped; the firm's demand curve is virtually horizontal. Notice the difference in the quantities shown on the horizontal scale in each part of the figure. The competitive industry has an output of 200 million tons when the price is $3. The individual firm takes that market price as given and considers producing up to, say, 6000 tons. The firm's demand curve in part (ii) is horizontal because any change in output that this single firm could manage would leave price virtually unchanged at $3. The firm's output variation has only a tiny percentage effect on industry output.

average revenue (AR)   Total revenue divided by quantity sold; this is the market price when all units are sold at the same price.

marginal revenue (MR)   The change in a firm's total revenue resulting from a change in its rate of sales by one unit. Also called *incremental revenue*.

Average revenue (AR) is the amount of revenue per unit sold. It is equal to total revenue divided by the number of units sold, and is thus equal to the price at which the product is sold: $AR = (p \times q)/q = p$.

Marginal revenue (MR), sometimes called *incremental revenue,* is the change in a firm's total revenue resulting from a change in its sales by 1 unit. Whenever output changes by more than 1 unit, the change in revenue must be divided by the change in output to calculate marginal revenue. For example, if an increase in output of 3 units is accompanied by an increase in revenue of $1500, the marginal revenue is $1500/3, or $500. [21]

To illustrate each of these revenue concepts, consider a firm that is selling barley in a perfectly competitive market at a price of $3 per bushel. Total revenue rises by $3 for every bushel sold. Because every bushel brings in $3, the average revenue per bushel sold is clearly $3. Furthermore, because each *additional* bushel sold brings in $3, the marginal revenue of an extra bushel sold is also $3. The table in Figure 9-2 shows calculations of these revenue concepts for a range of outputs between 10 and 13 bushels.

The important point illustrated in the table is that as long as the firm's own level of output cannot affect the price of the product it sells, then the firm's marginal revenue is equal to its average revenue (which is *always* equal to price). Thus, for a price-taking firm, $AR = MR = \text{price}$. Graphically, as shown in part (i) of Figure 9-2, average revenue and marginal revenue are the same horizontal line drawn at the level of market price. Because the firm can sell any quantity it chooses at this price, the horizontal line is also the *firm's demand curve;* it shows that any quantity the firm chooses to sell will be associated with this same market price.

If the market price is unaffected by variations in the firm's output, then the firm's demand curve, its average revenue curve, and its marginal revenue curve all coincide in the same horizontal line.

This result can be stated in a slightly different way that turns out to be important for our later study:

For a firm in perfect competition, price equals marginal revenue.

It follows, of course, that total revenue rises in direct proportion to output, as shown in part (ii) of Figure 9-2.

APPLYING ECONOMIC CONCEPTS 9-1

Demand Under Perfect Competition: Firm and Industry

Consider an individual wheat farmer and the market for wheat. Since products have negatively sloped market demand curves, any increase in the industry's output (caused by a shift in supply) will cause some fall in the market price. However, as the calculations made below show, any conceivable increase that one wheat farm could make in its output has such a negligible effect on the industry's price that the farmer correctly ignores it—the individual wheat farmer is thus a price taker. Although the arithmetic used in reaching this conclusion is unimportant, it is crucial to understand why an individual wheat farmer is a price taker.

Here is the argument that the calculations summarize. The *market* elasticity of demand for wheat is approximately 0.25. Thus, if the quantity of wheat supplied in the world were to increase by 1 percent, the price of wheat would have to fall by roughly 4 percent to induce the world's wheat buyers to purchase the extra wheat.

Even huge farms produce a very small fraction of the total world crop. In a recent year, one large farm produced 1750 metric tons of wheat. This was only 0.000 35 percent of that year's world production of 500 million metric tons. Suppose that the farmer decided in one year to produce nothing and in another year managed to produce twice the normal output of 1750 metric tons. This is an extremely large variation in one farm's output.

The increase in output from zero to 3500 metric tons represents a 200 percent variation measured around the farm's average output of 1750 metric tons. Yet the percentage increase in world output is only (3500 / 500 million) × 100 = 0.0007 percent. Given the demand elasticity of 0.25, this increase in output would lead to a decrease in the world price of 0.0028 percent. This price change, together with the 200 percent change in the farm's *own* output, implies that the farm's own demand curve has an elasticity of over 71 000. This enormous elasticity of demand means that the farm would have to increase its output by over 71 000 percent to bring about a 1 percent decrease in the price of wheat. Because the farm's output cannot be varied this much, it is not surprising that the farmer regards the price of wheat as unaffected by any change in output that he or she could conceiv-

ably make. For all intents and purposes, the individual farmer faces a perfectly elastic demand curve for its product and is thus a *price taker*.

Calculation of the Firm's Demand Elasticity

We begin by taking as given the world elasticity of demand ($\eta = 0.25$) and world output (500 million metric tons). A large farm with an average output of 1750 metric tons varies its output between 0 and 3500 tons. The variation of 3500 tons represents 200 percent of the farm's average output of 1750 metric tons. This causes world output to vary by only 0.0007 percent.

Step 1: Find the percentage change in world price. We know that the market elasticity is 0.25. This means that the percentage change in price must be *four* times as big as the percentage change in *quantity*. Since world quantity changes by 0.0007 percent, world price must change by 0.0028 percent.

Step 2: Find the firm's elasticity of demand. This is the percentage change in its *own output* divided by the resulting percentage change in the world price: 200 percent divided by 0.0028 percent. Clearly, the percentage change in quantity vastly exceeds the percentage change in price, making elasticity very high. Its precise value is 200 / 0.0028 = 71 429.

The demand for wheat is quite inelastic. But the demand for an individual farmer's wheat is almost perfectly elastic.

FIGURE 9-2   Revenue Curves for a Price-Taking Firm

Price p	Quantity q	$TR = p \times q$	$AR = TR/q$	$MR = \Delta TR/\Delta q$
$3	10	$30	$3	
3	11	33	3	$3
3	12	36	3	3
3	13	39	3	3

(i) Average and marginal revenue

(ii) Total revenue

When the firm is a price taker, $AR = MR = p$. Because price does not change as a result of the *firm* changing its output, neither marginal revenue nor average revenue varies with output. In the table, marginal revenue is shown between the rows because it represents the *change* in total revenues in response to a *change* in quantity. When price is constant, total revenue (which is price times quantity) is an upward-sloping straight line starting from the origin.

Short-Run Decisions

We learned in Chapters 7 and 8 how each firm's costs vary with its output. In the short run, the firm has one or more fixed factors, and the only way it can change its output is by using more or less of its variable factor inputs. Thus, the firm's short-run cost curves are relevant to its output decision.

Rules for All Profit-Maximizing Firms

We have just learned how the revenues of each price-taking firm vary with its output. The next step is to combine information about the firm's costs and revenues to determine the level of output that will maximize its profits. We start by stating two rules that apply to *all* profit-maximizing firms, whether or not they operate in perfectly competitive markets. The first rule determines whether the firm should produce at all, and the second determines how much it should produce.

Should the Firm Produce at All?

The firm always has the option of producing nothing. If it exercises this option, it will have an operating loss that is equal to its fixed costs. If it decides to produce, it will add the variable cost of production to its costs and the receipts from the sale of its product to its revenue. Therefore, since it must pay its fixed costs in any event, it will be worthwhile for the firm to produce as long as it can find some level of output for which revenue exceeds *variable* cost. However, if its revenue is less than its variable cost at every level of output, the firm will actually lose more by producing any level of output than by not producing at all.

Rule 1: A firm should not produce at all if for all levels of output, the total variable cost of producing that output exceeds the total revenue derived from selling it or, equivalently, if the average variable cost of producing the output exceeds the price at which it can be sold. [22]

The price at which the firm can just cover its average variable cost, and so is indifferent between producing and not producing, is called the **shut-down price.** Such a price is shown in part (i) of Figure 9-5. (We will return in a moment to Figures 9-3 and 9-4.) At the price of $2, the firm can just cover its average variable cost by producing q_0 units. At this price, any other output would not produce enough revenue to cover variable costs. For any price below $2, there is no output at which variable costs can be covered, and thus the firm will shut down. The price of $2 in part (i) is therefore the shut-down price.

shut-down price
The price that is equal to the minimum of a firm's average variable costs. At prices below this, a profit-maximizing firm will produce no output.

How Much Should the Firm Produce?

If a firm decides that, according to Rule 1, production is worth undertaking, it must then decide *how much* to produce. The key to understanding how much the firm should produce is to think about it on a unit-by-unit basis. If any unit of production adds more to revenue than it does to cost, producing and selling that unit will increase profits. However, if any unit adds more to cost than it does to revenue, producing and selling that unit will decrease profits. According to the terminology introduced earlier, a unit of production raises profits if the *marginal* revenue obtained from selling it exceeds the *marginal* cost of producing it; it lowers profits if the marginal revenue (*MR*) obtained from selling it is less than the marginal cost (*MC*) of producing it.

Now let a firm with some existing rate of output consider increasing or decreasing that output. If a further unit of production will increase the firm's revenues by *more* than it increases costs (*MR>MC*), the firm should expand its output. However, if the last unit produced increases revenues by *less* than it increases costs (*MR<MC*), the firm should reduce its output. From this it follows that the only time the firm should leave its output unaltered is when the last unit produced adds the same amount to revenues as it does to costs (*MR = MC*).

FIGURE 9-3   Profit-Maximization for a Competitive Firm

The firm chooses the output for which $p = MC$ above the level of *AVC*. When $p = MC$, as at q^*, the firm would decrease its profits if it changed its output. At any point to the left of q^*, price is greater than the marginal cost, and it is worthwhile for the firm to increase output (as indicated by the arrow on the left). At any point to the right of q^*, price is less than the marginal cost, and it is worthwhile for the firm to reduce output (as indicated by the arrow on the right).

Rule 2: If it is worthwhile for the firm to produce at all, the firm should produce the output at which marginal revenue equals marginal cost. [23]

The two rules that we have stated refer to each firm's own costs and revenues, and they apply to all profit-maximizing firms, whatever the market structure in which they operate.

FIGURE 9-4   Profit-Maximization Using Total Cost and Revenue Curves

The firm chooses the output for which the gap between the total revenue and the total cost curves is the largest. At each output, the vertical distance between the *TR* and the *TC* curves shows the amount by which total revenue exceeds total cost. In the figure, the gap is largest at output q^*, which is thus the profit-maximizing output.

Practise with Study Guide Chapter 9, Exercise 1.

Rule 2 Applied to Price-Taking Firms

Rule 2 tells us that any profit-maximizing firm that produces at all will produce at the point where marginal cost equals marginal revenue. However, we have already seen that for price-taking firms, marginal revenue is the market price. Combining these two results gives us an important conclusion:

A firm that is operating in a perfectly competitive market will produce the output that equates its marginal cost of production with the market price of its product (as long as price exceeds average variable cost).

In a perfectly competitive industry, the market determines the price at which the firm sells its product. The firm then picks the quantity of output that maximizes its profits. We have seen that this is the output for which price equals marginal cost. When the firm has reached a position where its profits are maximized, it has no incentive to change its output. Therefore, unless prices or costs change, the firm will continue to produce this output because it is doing as well as it can do, given the market situation. This profit-maximizing behaviour is illustrated in Figures 9-3 and 9-4.

The perfectly competitive firm adjusts its level of output in response to changes in the market-determined price.

Figure 9-3 shows the profit-maximizing choice of the firm using average cost and revenue curves. We can, if we wish, show the same result using total cost and revenue curves, as in Figure 9-4. Figure 9-4 combines the total cost curve first drawn in Figure 7-2 with the total revenue curve first shown in Figure 9-2. It shows the profit-maximizing output as the output with the largest positive difference between total revenue and total cost. This, of course, is the same output as the one we located in Figure 9-3 by equating marginal cost and marginal revenue.

Short-Run Supply Curves

We have seen that in a perfectly competitive market, the firm responds to a price that is set by the forces of demand and supply. By adjusting the quantity it produces in response to the current market price, the firm helps to determine the market supply. The link between the behaviour of the firm and the behaviour of the competitive market is provided by the market supply curve. But, before we can derive the supply curve for the market, we need to derive the supply curve for each of the firms in that market.

The Supply Curve for One Firm

The competitive firm's supply curve is derived in part (i) of Figure 9-5, which shows a firm's marginal cost curve and four alternative prices. The horizontal line at each price is the firm's demand curve when the market price is at that level. The firm's marginal cost curve gives the marginal cost corresponding to each level of output. What we are trying

FIGURE 9-5   The Derivation of the Supply Curve for a Competitive Firm

(i) Marginal cost and average variable
     cost curves

(ii) Supply curve

The supply curve of the competitive firm, shown in part (ii), is the same as its *MC* curve, shown in part (i). For prices below
$2, output is zero because there is no output at which *AVC* can be covered. The point *A*, where the price of $2 is just equal
to *AVC*, is the point at which the firm will shut down. As price rises to $3, $4, and $5, the profit-maximizing point changes
to *B*, *C*, and *D*, taking output to q_1, q_2, and q_3. At any of these prices, the firm's revenue exceeds its variable costs of production. An example of the excess is shown in part (i) of the figure by the shaded area associated with price p_1 and output
q_1. This amount is available to help cover fixed costs and, once these are covered, to provide a profit.

to derive is a supply curve that shows the quantity of output that the firm will supply at
each price. For prices below average variable cost, the firm will supply zero units (Rule
1). For prices above average variable cost, the competitive firm will equate price and
marginal cost (Rule 2). This behaviour leads to the following conclusion:

A competitive firm's supply curve is given by its marginal cost curve for those levels of
output for which marginal cost exceeds average variable cost.

The Supply Curve for an Industry

Figure 9-6 shows the derivation of an industry supply curve for an industry containing
only two firms. The general result is as follows:

In perfect competition, the industry supply curve is the horizontal sum of the marginal
cost curves (above the level of average variable cost) of all firms in the industry.

Each firm's marginal cost curve shows how much that firm will supply at each given
market price, and the industry supply curve is the sum of what each firm will supply.
     This supply curve, based on the short-run marginal cost curves of all the firms in the
industry, is the industry's supply curve that we first encountered in Chapter 3. We have now
established the profit-maximizing behaviour of individual firms that lies behind that curve.
It is sometimes called a **short-run supply curve** because it is based on the short-run, profit-
maximizing behaviour of all the firms in the industry. It should not be confused with the
long-run industry supply curve, which relates quantity supplied to the price that exists
when the industry is in long-run equilibrium (which we will study later in this chapter).

Practise with Study Guide Chapter 9,
Exercise 4.

**short-run supply
curve**   A curve showing
the relationship between
quantity supplied and
market price, with one or
more fixed factors; it is the
horizontal sum of marginal
cost curves (above the
level of average variable
costs) of all firms in a
perfectly competitive
industry.

FIGURE 9-6   The Derivation of the Supply Curve of a Competitive Industry

(i) Firm A's Supply Curve   (ii) Firm B's Supply Curve   (iii) Industry Supply Curve

The industry's supply curve is the horizontal sum of the supply curves of each of the firms in the industry. At a price of $3, Firm A would supply 4 units and Firm B would supply 3 units. Together, as shown in part (iii), they would supply 7 units. If there are hundreds of firms, the process is the same. In this example, because Firm B does not enter the market at prices below $2, the supply curve S_{A+B} is identical to S_A up to price $2 and is the horizontal sum of S_A and S_B above $2.

Short-Run Equilibrium in a Competitive Market

The price of a product sold in a perfectly competitive market is determined by the interaction of the industry's short-run supply curve and the market demand curve. Although no single firm can influence the market price significantly, the collective actions of all firms in the industry (as shown by the industry supply curve) and the collective actions of households (as shown by the market demand curve) together determine the equilibrium price. This occurs at the point where the market demand and supply curves intersect.

short-run equilibrium For a competitive industry, the price and output at which industry demand equals short-run industry supply, and all firms are maximizing their profits. Either profits or losses for individual firms are possible.

When a perfectly competitive industry is in **short-run equilibrium,** each firm is producing and selling a quantity for which its marginal cost equals price. No firm is motivated to change its output in the short run. Because total quantity demanded equals total quantity supplied, there is no reason for market price to change in the short run.

When an industry is in short-run equilibrium, quantity demanded equals quantity supplied, and each firm is maximizing its profits given the market price.

However, we do not know *how large* these profits are. It is one thing to know that a firm is doing as well as it can, given its particular circumstances; it is another thing to know *how well* it is doing.

Figure 9-7 shows three possible positions for a firm when the industry is in short-run equilibrium. In all cases, the firm is maximizing its profits by producing where price equals marginal cost, but in part (i) the firm is suffering losses, in part (ii) it is just covering all of its costs (breaking even), and in part (iii) it is making profits because price exceeds average total cost. In all three cases, the firm is doing as well as it can, given its costs and the market price.

FIGURE 9-7   Alternative Short-Run Profits of a Competitive Firm

(i) Losses

(ii) Zero profit

(iii) Positive profit

When the industry is in short-run equilibrium, a competitive firm may be suffering losses, breaking even, or making profits. The diagrams show a firm with given costs that faces three alternative prices p_1, p_2, and p_3. In each part of the figure, $MC = MR$ = price. Because in all three cases price exceeds AVC, the firm produces positive output in each case.

In part (i), price is p_1 and the firm is suffering losses, shown by the shaded area, because price is below average total cost. Because price exceeds average variable cost, it is worthwhile for the firm to keep producing, but it is not worthwhile for it to replace its capital equipment as it wears out. In part (ii), price is p_2 and the firm is just covering its total costs. It is worthwhile for the firm to replace its capital as it wears out, since it is covering the full opportunity cost of its capital. In part (iii), price is p_3 and the firm is earning profits, shown by the shaded area.

Applying Economic Concepts 9-2 discusses an interesting example of a firm that remains in operation even though it is not covering its full costs—that is, even though it is making losses as in part (i) of Figure 9-7. You have probably seen many firms like this one as you drive through small towns in any part of Canada.

Long-Run Decisions

Although Figure 9-7 shows three possible positions for a typical firm when the industry is in short-run equilibrium, not all of them are possible outcomes in the long run.

Entry and Exit

The key difference between a perfectly competitive industry in the short run and in the long run is the entry or exit of firms. We have seen that firms may be making profits, suffering losses, or just breaking even when the industry is in short-run equilibrium. Because costs include the opportunity cost of capital, firms that are just breaking even are doing as well as they could do by investing their capital elsewhere. Hence there will be no incentive

APPLYING ECONOMIC CONCEPTS 9-2

The Parable of the Seaside Inn

Why do some resort hotels stay open during the off-season, even though to do so they must offer bargain rates that do not even cover their "full costs"? Why do the managers of other hotels allow them to fall into disrepair even though they are able to attract enough customers to stay in business? Are the former being overly generous, and are the latter being irrational penny-pinchers?

To illustrate what is involved, consider an imaginary resort hotel called the Seaside Inn. Its revenues and costs of operating during the four months of the high-season and during the eight months of the off-season are shown in the accompanying table. When the profit-maximizing price for its rooms is charged in the high-season, the hotel earns revenues of $58 000 and incurs variable costs equal to $36 000. Thus there is an "operating profit" of $22 000 during the high-season. This surplus goes toward meeting the hotel's annual fixed costs of $24 000. Thus, $2000 of the fixed costs are not yet paid.

If the Seaside Inn were to charge the same rates during the off-season, it could not attract enough customers even to cover its costs of maids, bellhops, and managers. However, the hotel discovers that by charging lower rates during the off-season, it can rent some of its rooms and earn revenues of $20 000. Its costs of operating (variable costs) during the off-season are $18 000. So, by operating at reduced rates in the off-season, the hotel is able to contribute another $2000 toward its annual fixed costs, thereby eliminating the shortfall.

Therefore, the hotel stays open during the whole year by offering off-season bargain rates to grateful guests. Indeed, if it were to close during the off-season, it would not be able to cover its total fixed and variable costs solely through its high-season operations.

We have not yet discussed firms' long-run decisions in the chapter, but you can get a feel for the issues by considering the following situation. Suppose that the off-season revenues fall to $19 000 (everything else remaining the same). The short-run condition for staying open, that total revenue (TR) must exceed total variable cost (TVC), is met both for the high-season and for the off-season. However, since the TR over the whole year of $77 000 is less than the total costs of $78 000, the hotel is now making losses for the year as a whole. The hotel will remain open as long as it can do so with its present capital—it will produce in the short run. However, it will not be worthwhile for the owners to replace the capital as it wears out.

If the reduction in revenues persists, the hotel will become one of those run-down hotels about which guests ask, "Why don't they do something about this place?"—but the owners are behaving quite sensibly. They are operating the hotel as long as it covers its variable costs, but they are not putting any more investment into it because it cannot cover its fixed costs. Sooner or later, the fixed capital will become too old to be run, or at least to attract customers, and the hotel will be closed.

The Seaside Inn: Total Costs and Revenues ($)

Season	Total Revenue (TR)	Total Variable Cost (TVC)	Contribution to Fixed Costs (TR-TVC)	Total Fixed Costs
High-Season	58 000	36 000	22 000	
Off-Season	20 000	18 000	2 000	
Total	78 000	54 000	24 000	24 000

Hotels and other resorts often charge low prices in the off-season, low enough that they do not cover their total costs, but as long as the price covers the variable costs, it is better than shutting down during the off-season.

for such firms to leave the industry. Similarly, if new entrants expect just to break even, there will be no incentive for firms to enter the industry, because capital can earn the same return elsewhere in the economy. If, however, existing firms are earning revenues in excess of all costs, including the opportunity cost of capital, new capital will enter the industry to share in these profits. Conversely, if existing firms are suffering losses, capital will leave the industry because a better return can be obtained elsewhere in the economy. Let us now consider this process in a little more detail.

An Entry-Attracting Price

First, suppose that there are 100 firms in a competitive industry, all making positive profits like the firm shown in part (iii) of Figure 9-7. New firms, attracted by the profitability of existing firms, will enter the industry. Suppose that in response to the high profits, 20 new firms enter. The market supply curve that formerly added up the outputs of 100 firms must now add up the outputs of 120 firms. At any price, more will be supplied because there are more producers. This entry of new firms into the industry implies a rightward shift in the industry supply curve.

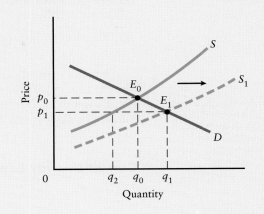

FIGURE 9-8   The Effect of New Entrants

New entrants shift the supply curve to the right and reduce the equilibrium price. Initial equilibrium is at E_0. The entry of new firms shifts the supply curve to S_1. Equilibrium price falls to p_1, while output rises to q_1. Before the entry of new firms, only q_2 would have been produced had the price been p_1. The extra output is supplied by the new firms.

With an unchanged market demand curve, this shift in the short-run industry supply curve means that the previous equilibrium price will no longer prevail. The shift in supply will reduce the equilibrium price, and both new and old firms will have to adjust their output to this new price, as illustrated in Figure 9-8. New firms will continue to enter, and the equilibrium price will continue to fall, until all firms in the industry are just covering their total costs. All firms will then be in the position of the firm shown in part (ii) of Figure 9-7, which is called a *zero-profit equilibrium*. The entry of new firms then ceases.

Profits in a competitive industry are a signal for the entry of new firms; the industry will expand, pushing price down until profits fall to zero.

An Exit-Inducing Price

Now suppose that all of the firms in the industry are making losses, like the firm shown in part (i) of Figure 9-7. Although the firms are covering their variable costs, the return on their capital is less than the opportunity cost of capital. They are not covering their total costs. This is a signal for the exit of firms. Old plants and equipment will not be replaced as they wear out. As a result, the industry's short-run supply curve eventually shifts leftward, and the market price rises. Firms will continue to exit, and the market price will continue to rise, until the remaining firms can cover their total costs—that is, until they are all in the zero-profit equilibrium illustrated in part (ii) of Figure 9-7. The exit of firms then ceases.

Losses in a competitive industry are a signal for the exit of firms; the industry will contract, driving the market price up until the remaining firms are just covering their total costs.

Practise with Study Guide Chapter 9, Exercise 5.

Long-Run Equilibrium

Because firms exit when they are making losses and enter in pursuit of profits, we get the following conclusion:

The long-run equilibrium of a competitive industry occurs when firms are earning zero profits.

When a perfectly competitive industry is in long-run equilibrium, each firm will be like the firm in part (ii) of Figure 9-7. For such firms, the price p_2 is sometimes called the **break-even price**. It is the price at which all costs, including the opportunity cost of capital, are being covered. The firm is just willing to stay in the industry. It has no incentive to leave, nor do other firms have an incentive to enter.

break-even price
The price at which a firm is just able to cover all of its costs, including the opportunity cost of capital.

Conditions for Long-Run Equilibrium

The previous discussion suggests four conditions for a competitive industry to be in long-run equilibrium.

1. Existing firms must be maximizing their profits, given their existing capital. Thus short-run marginal costs of production must be equal to market price.

2. Existing firms must not be suffering losses. If they are suffering losses, they will not replace their capital and the size of the industry will decline over time.

3. Existing firms must not be earning profits. If they are earning profits, then new firms will enter the industry and the size of the industry will increase over time.

4. Existing firms must not be able to increase their profits by changing the size of their production facilities. Thus each existing firm must be at the minimum point of its *long-run* average cost (*LRAC*) curve.

This last condition is new to our discussion. Figure 9-9 shows that if the condition does not hold—that is, if the firm is *not* at the minimum of its *LRAC* curve—a firm can increase its profits. Although the firm is maximizing its profits with its existing production facilities, there are unexploited economies of scale. By building larger plants, the firm can move down its *LRAC* curve and reduce its average cost. Because in its present position, average cost is just equal to the market price, any reduction in average cost must yield profits.

For a competitive firm to be maximizing its long-run profits, it must be producing at the minimum point on its *LRAC* curve.

FIGURE 9-9 Short-Run Versus Long-Run Profit Maximization for a Competitive Firm

A competitive firm that is not at the minimum point on its *LRAC* curve is not maximizing its long-run profits. A competitive firm with short-run cost curves *SRATC* and *MC* faces a market price of p_0. The firm produces q_0, where *MC* equals price and total costs are just being covered. However, the firm's long-run average cost curve lies below its short-run curve at output q_0. The firm could produce output q_0 at cost c_0 by building a larger plant so as to take advantage of economies of scale. Profits would rise, because average total costs of c_0 would then be less than price p_0. The firm cannot be maximizing its long-run profits at any output below q_m because, with any such output, average total costs can be reduced by building a larger plant. The output q_m is the *minimum efficient scale* of the firm.

The level of output at which *LRAC* reaches a minimum is known as the firm's **minimum efficient scale** *(MES)*.

When each firm in the industry is producing at the minimum point of its long-run average cost curve and just covering its costs, as in Figure 9-10, the industry is in long-run equilibrium. Because marginal cost equals price, no firm can improve its profits by varying its output in the short run. Because each firm is at the minimum point on its *LRAC* curve, there is no incentive for any existing firm to alter the scale of its operations. Because there are neither profits nor losses, there is no incentive for entry into or exit from the industry.

In long-run competitive equilibrium, each firm's average cost of production is the lowest attainable, given the limits of known technology and factor prices.

The Long-Run Industry Supply Curve

Consider a competitive industry that is in long-run equilibrium. Now suppose that the market demand for the industry's product increases. The reactions to this demand shift should by now be a familiar story. First, price will rise and, in response, existing firms will increase their outputs and earn profits. New firms then enter the industry, attracted by the profits. As new firms enter the industry, the industry supply curve will shift to the right, driving down the market price. This process continues until profits have been eliminated. At that time, existing firms once again will be just covering their full costs. Note that in *both* of the long-run equilibrium positions just discussed—the one before and the one after the change in demand—all firms in the industry are producing at the lowest point on their *LRAC* curves.

This is now familiar ground, but there is one further question that we could ask. When all the dust has settled, will the new long-run equilibrium price be higher than, lower than, or the same as the price at the initial long-run equilibrium? We could make a similar analysis for a fall in demand, and could ask the same question.

The adjustment of a competitive industry to the types of changes that we have just discussed is shown by what is sometimes called the **long-run industry supply** *(LRS)* **curve.** This curve shows the relationship between the market price and the quantity produced in a competitive industry *when it is in long-run equilibrium.* Note that the curve is drawn on the assumption that technological knowledge is constant. Figure 9-11 shows the derivation of this curve and its possible shapes.

Horizontal Long-Run Supply Curve.
In part (i) of the figure, the *LRS* curve is horizontal. An industry with a horizontal *LRS* curve is said to be a **constant-cost industry.** This situation occurs when the long-run expansion of the industry, due to the entry of new firms, leaves the long-run cost curves of existing firms unchanged. Because new firms have access to the same technology and face the same factor prices as existing firms, their cost curves will be the same as those of existing firms. It follows that the cost curves of all firms, new or old, will be unaffected by expansion or contraction of the

FIGURE 9-10   A Typical Competitive Firm When the Industry is in Long-Run Equilibrium

In long-run competitive equilibrium, each firm is operating at the minimum point on its *LRAC* curve. In long-run equilibrium, each firm must be (1) maximizing short-run profits, *MC* = *p*; (2) earning profits of zero on its existing plant, *SRATC* = *p*; and (3) unable to increase its profits by altering the scale of its operations. These three conditions can be met only when the firm is at *E*, the minimum point on its *LRAC* curve, with price *p** and output *q_m*.

minimum efficient scale (MES)   The smallest output at which long-run average cost reaches its minimum; all available economies of scale in production and distribution have been realized at this point.

long-run industry supply (LRS) curve   A curve showing the relationship between the market price and the quantity supplied by a competitive industry when all the firms in that industry are at the minimum of their *LRAC* curves.

constant-cost industry   An industry in which costs of the most efficient size firm remain constant as the entire industry expands or contracts in the long run.

FIGURE 9-11   Long-Run Industry Supply Curves

(i) Constant-cost industry   (ii) Increasing-cost industry   (iii) Declining-cost industry

The long-run industry supply curve may be horizontal, positively sloped, or negatively sloped. In all three parts, the initial curves are at D_0 and S_0, yielding equilibrium at E_0, with price p_0 and output q_0. A rise in demand shifts the demand curve to D_1, taking the short-run equilibrium to E_1. New firms now enter the industry, shifting the supply curve to the right, pushing down price until profits are no longer being earned. At this point, the supply curve is S_1 and the new equilibrium is E_2, with price at p_2 and output q_2.

In part (i), price returns to its original level, making the long-run industry supply curve horizontal. In part (ii), a new long-run equilibrium is achieved at a price higher than p_0. This gives the LRS curve a positive slope. In part (iii), the price falls below its original level before profits are eliminated, giving the LRS curve a negative slope.

industry. Thus long-run equilibrium can be reestablished only when price returns to its original level. In other words, because cost curves are unaffected by the expansion or contraction of the industry, each firm must start from, and return to, the long-run position shown in Figure 9-10—*which means that market price must also do the same.*

Upward-Sloping Long-Run Supply Curve.   When an increase in demand for an industry's product leads that industry to expand, more of its inputs will be needed. The increase in demand for these inputs tends to bid up their prices.

If costs rise with increasing levels of industry output, so too must the price at which the producers are able to cover their costs. As the industry expands, the short-run supply curve shifts outward, but the firms' *SRATC* curves shift upward because of rising factor prices. The expansion of the industry comes to a halt when price is equal to minimum *LRAC* for existing firms. Because costs have risen, this new equilibrium must occur at a higher price than prevailed before the expansion began, as illustrated in part (ii) of Figure 9-11. A competitive industry with an upward-sloping *LRS* curve is called an **increasing-cost industry.**

increasing-cost industry   An industry in which costs of the most efficient size firm rise as the entire industry expands in the long run.

Downward-Sloping Long-Run Supply Curve.   So far in our discussion the long-run supply curve has been flat or upward sloping. Could it ever be downward sloping, thereby indicating that higher outputs are associated with lower prices in long-run equilibrium?

It is tempting to answer yes because of the opportunities of more efficient scales of operation using greater mechanization and more effective specialization of labour.

However, this answer would not be correct for perfectly competitive industries because in long-run equilibrium each firm must already be at the lowest point on its *LRAC* curve. If a firm could lower its costs by building a larger, more mechanized plant, it would be profitable to do so without waiting for an increase in demand.

The scale economies that we have just considered are within the control of the firm; they are said to be **internal economies of scale.** A perfectly competitive industry might, however, have a downward-sloping long-run supply curve if industries that supply its inputs have increasing returns to scale. Such effects are outside the control of the perfectly competitive firm and are called **external economies of scale.** Whenever expansion of an industry leads to a fall in the prices of some of its inputs, the individual firms will find their cost curves shifting downward.

As an illustration of how the expansion of one industry could cause the prices of some of its inputs to fall, consider the early stages of the growth of the automobile industry. As the output of automobiles increased, the industry's demand for tires grew greatly. This increased the demand for rubber and tended to raise its price, but it also provided the opportunity for tire manufacturers to build larger plants that exploited the scale economies available in tire production. These economies were large enough to offset any factor price increases, and tire prices charged to automobile manufacturers fell. Thus automobile costs fell because of lower prices of an important input. This case is illustrated in part (iii) of Figure 9-11. An industry that has a downward-sloping *LRS* curve is called a **declining-cost industry.**

Notice in this example that although the economies of scale were *external* to the automobile industry, they were *internal* to the tire industry. This, in turn, requires that the tire industry *not* be perfectly competitive; if it were, all of its scale economies would already have been exploited as firms locate at the minimum of their *LRAC* curves in the long run. So this case refers to a perfectly competitive industry that uses an input produced by a non-perfectly-competitive industry whose own scale economies have not yet been fully exploited because demand is insufficient.

We can now use our long-run theory to understand the behaviour of firms in two commonly encountered but often misunderstood situations—changes in technology and declining industries.

internal economies of scale   Scale economies that result from the firm's own actions and hence are available to it by raising its own output.

external economies of scale   Scale economies that cause the firm's costs to fall as industry output rises but are external to the firm and so cannot be obtained by the firm's increasing its own output.

declining-cost industry   An industry in which costs of the most efficient size firm decline as the entire industry expands in the long run.

Changes in Technology

Consider a competitive industry in long-run equilibrium. Because the industry is in long-run equilibrium, each firm must be earning zero profits. Now suppose that some technological development lowers the cost curves *of newly built plants.* Because price is just equal to the average total cost *for the existing plants,* new plants will be able to earn profits, and some of them will now be built. The resulting expansion in capacity shifts the short-run supply curve to the right and drives price down.

The expansion in industry output and the fall in price will continue until price is equal to the short-run average total cost of the *new* plants. At this price, old plants will not be covering their long-run costs. As long as price exceeds their average variable cost, however, such plants will continue in production. As the outmoded plants wear out, they will gradually be closed. Eventually, a new long-run equilibrium will be established in which all plants will use the new technology.

New plants are usually built with the latest technology. This often results in new plants having lower unit costs (and thus higher profits) than the existing plants built with older technology.

FIGURE 9-12   Plants of Different Vintages in an Industry with Continuous Technological Progress

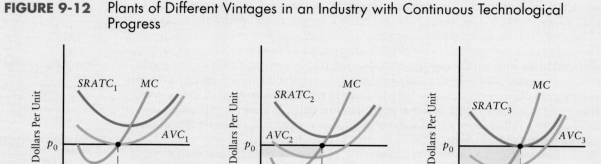

(i) Plant 1: High costs   (ii) Plant 2: Medium costs   (iii) Plant 3: Low costs

Entry of progressively lower-cost firms forces price down, but older plants with higher costs remain in the industry as long as price covers average variable cost. Plant 3 is the newest plant with the lowest costs. Long-run equilibrium price will be determined by the average total costs of plants of this type because entry will continue as long as the owners of the newest plants expect to earn profits from them. Plant 1 is the oldest plant in operation. It is just covering its AVC, and if the price falls any further, it will be closed down. Plant 2 is a plant of intermediate age. It is covering its variable costs and earning some contribution toward its fixed costs. In parts (ii) and (iii), profits are shown by the shaded area.

What happens in a competitive industry in which technological change does not occur as a single isolated event but instead happens more or less continuously? Plants built in any one year will tend to have lower costs than plants built in any previous year. This common occurrence is illustrated in Figure 9-12.

Industries that are subject to continuous technological change have three common characteristics. The first is that plants of different ages and with different costs exist side by side. This characteristic is dramatically illustrated by the many different vintages of farm equipment found in the agricultural sector; some farms have much newer and better equipment than others. Indeed, even any individual farm that has been established for a long time will have various vintages of equipment, all of which are in use. Older models are not discarded as soon as a better model comes on the market.

Critics who observe the continued use of older, higher-cost plants and equipment often urge that something be done to "eliminate these wasteful practices." These critics miss the point of economic efficiency. If the plant or piece of equipment is already there, it can be profitably operated as long as its revenues more than cover its *variable* costs. As long as a plant or equipment can produce goods that are valued by consumers at an amount above the value of the resources currently used up for their production (variable costs), the value of society's total output is increased by using it.

In industries with continual technological improvement, low-cost firms will exist side by side with older high-cost firms. The older firms will continue operating as long as their revenue covers their variable costs.

A second characteristic of a competitive industry that is subject to continuous technological improvement is that price is eventually governed by the minimum ATC of the *lowest-cost* plants. Firms will enter the industry until plants of the newest vintage are just expected to earn normal profits over their lifetimes. The benefits of the new technology are passed on to consumers because all of the units of the product, whether produced by new or old plants, are sold at a price that is related solely to the *ATC*s of the new plants. Owners of older plants find that their returns over variable costs fall steadily as newer plants drive the price of the product down.

A third characteristic is that old plants are discarded (or "mothballed") when the price falls below their *AVC*s. This may occur well before the plants are physically worn out. In industries with continuous technological progress, capital is usually discarded because it is *economically obsolete,* not because it is physically worn out. Old capital is obsolete when the market price of output does not even cover its average variable cost of production. Thus a steel mill that is still fully capable of producing top-quality steel may be shut down for perfectly sensible reasons; if the price of steel cannot cover the average variable cost of the steel produced, then profit-maximizing firms will shut down the plant.

Declining Industries

What happens when a competitive industry in long-run equilibrium experiences a continual decrease in the demand for its product? One example of this might be a long-term change in tastes that leads households to substitute away from red meat and toward fish and poultry. As market demand for red meat declines, market price falls, and firms that were previously covering average total costs are no longer able to do so. They find themselves suffering losses instead of breaking even; the signal for the exit of capital is given, but exit takes time.

The Response of Firms

The economically efficient response to a steadily declining demand is to continue to operate with existing equipment as long as its variable costs of production can be covered. As equipment becomes obsolete because the firm cannot cover even its variable cost, it will not be replaced unless the new equipment can cover its total cost. As a result, the capacity of the industry will shrink. If demand keeps declining, capacity must keep shrinking.

Declining industries typically present a sorry sight to the observer. Revenues are below long-run total costs and, as a result, new equipment is not brought in to replace old equipment as it wears out. The average age of equipment in use thus rises steadily. The untrained observer, seeing the industry's plight, is likely to blame it on the old equipment.

The antiquated equipment in a declining industry is often the effect rather than the cause of the industry's decline.

The Response of Governments

Governments are often tempted to support declining industries because they are worried about the resulting job losses. Experience suggests, however, that propping up genuinely declining industries only delays their demise—at significant national cost. When the government finally withdraws its support, the decline is usually more abrupt and, hence, the required adjustment is more difficult than it would have been had the industry been allowed to decline gradually under the natural market forces.

Once governments recognize the decay of certain industries and the collapse of certain firms as an inevitable aspect of economic growth, a more effective response is to provide retraining and income-support schemes that cushion the impacts of change. These can moderate the effects on the incomes of workers who lose their jobs and make it easier for them to transfer to expanding industries. Intervention that is intended to increase mobility while reducing the social and personal costs of mobility is a viable long-run policy; trying to freeze the existing industrial structure by shoring up an inevitably declining industry is not.

SUMMARY

Market Structure and Firm Behaviour

LO 1

- A competitive market structure is one in which individual firms have no power to influence the market in which they sell their product.

- Competitive behaviour exists when firms actively compete against one another, responding directly to other firms' actions. Perfectly competitive firms *do not* have competitive behaviour.

The Theory of Perfect Competition

LO 2 3

- Four key assumptions of the theory of perfect competition are as follows:

    1. All firms produce a homogeneous product.
    2. Purchasers know the nature of the product and the price charged for it.
    3. Each firm's minimum efficient scale occurs at a level of output that is small relative to the industry's total output.
    4. The industry displays freedom of entry and exit.

- Any profit-maximizing firm will produce at a level of output at which (a) price is at least as great as average variable cost and (b) marginal cost equals marginal revenue. In perfect competition, firms are price takers, so marginal revenue is equal to price. Thus, a profit-maximizing competitive firm equates marginal cost to price.

Short-Run Decisions

LO 4 5

- If a profit-maximizing firm is to produce at all, it must be able to cover its variable costs. However, such a firm may be suffering losses (price is less than average total cost), making profits (price is greater than average total cost), or just breaking even (price is equal to average total cost).

- Under perfect competition, each firm's short-run supply curve is identical to its marginal cost curve above average variable cost. The perfectly competitive industry's short-run supply curve is the horizontal sum of the supply curves of the individual firms.

Long-Run Decisions

LO 6 7

- In the long run, profits or losses will lead to the entry or the exit of firms into or out of the industry. This pushes any competitive industry to a long-run, zero-profit equilibrium and moves production to the level that minimizes average cost.

- The long-run response of an industry to steadily changing technology is the gradual replacement of less efficient plants by more efficient ones. Older plants will be discarded and replaced by more modern ones only when price falls below average variable cost.

- The long-run response of a declining industry will be to continue to satisfy demand by employing its existing plants as long as price exceeds short-run average variable cost. Despite the antiquated appearance that results, this response is the correct one.

KEY CONCEPTS

Competitive behaviour and competitive market structure
Perfect competition
Price taking and a horizontal demand curve

Average revenue, marginal revenue, and price under perfect competition
Rules for maximizing profits
The relationship of supply curves to marginal cost curves
Short-run and long-run equilibrium of competitive industries

Entry and exit in achieving long-run equilibrium
Long-run industry supply curves
Constant, increasing, and decreasing cost industries

STUDY EXERCISES

1. In Figure 9-1 in the chapter, we explain the difference between the demand curve for a competitive industry and the demand curve facing an individual firm in that industry. Review that figure now and then answer the following questions.

   a. Explain what would happen if the individual firm tried to charge a higher price for its product.
   b. Explain why the individual firm has no incentive to charge a lower price for its product.
   c. Explain why the demand curve for an individual firm is horizontal at the current market price.

2. Consider the following table showing the various revenue concepts for DairyTreat Inc., a perfectly competitive firm that sells milk by the litre. Suppose the firm faces a constant market price of $2 per litre.

Price (p)	Quantity	Total Revenue (TR)	Average Revenue (AR)	Marginal Revenue (MR)
$2	150	—	—	—
2	175	—	—	—
2	200	—	—	—
2	225	—	—	—
2	250	—	—	—

   a. Compute total revenue for each level of output. Fill in the table.
   b. Compute average and marginal revenue for each level of output. Fill in the table. (Remember to compute marginal revenue *between* successive levels of output.)
   c. Explain why for a perfectly competitive firm, $AR = MR = p$.
   d. Plot the TR, MR, and AR curves on a scale diagram. What is the slope of the TR curve?

3. The diagram below shows the various short-run cost curves for a perfectly competitive firm.

   a. Based on the diagram above, and the assumption that the firm is maximizing its profit, fill in the following table. The last three columns require only a "yes" or "no."

Market Price ($)	Firm's Output	Is price >ATC?	Is price >AVC?	Are Profits Positive?
$3	—	—	—	—
4	—	—	—	—
5	—	—	—	—
6	—	—	—	—
7	—	—	—	—
8	—	—	—	—
9	—	—	—	—
10	—	—	—	—

   b. At which price will this firm shut down? Explain.
   c. What is this firm's supply curve? Explain.

4. Consider the table below showing the supply schedules for three competitive firms, each producing honey by the kilogram. These three firms make up the entire industry.

Market Price ($ per kg)	Output (kg)			
	Firm A	Firm B	Firm C	Industry
2.50	100	0	0	—-
3.00	125	0	0	—-
3.50	150	100	0	—-
4.00	175	150	0	—-
4.50	200	200	100	—-
5.00	225	250	175	—-
5.50	250	300	250	—-
6.00	275	350	325	—-

   a. Compute the total industry supply at each price and fill in the table.
   b. On a scale diagram similar to Figure 9-6, plot the supply curve for each firm and for the industry as a whole.

   c. Explain the economics of why Firm B produces no output at prices $3 and lower (or for why Firm C produces no output at prices $4 and lower).

5. Consider the perfectly competitive barley industry. It is initially in long-run equilibrium at quantity Q_0 and price p_0.

   a. Draw a supply-and-demand diagram for the barley market, showing the initial long-run equilibrium.
   b. Draw a diagram for a typical firm when the industry is in its initial long-run equilibrium, showing its *MC, ATC,* and *LRAC* curves. Are there any profits being earned by the typical barley farmer?
   c. Now suppose there is an increase in demand (caused by an increase in demand for beer, which uses barley as an input). Price rises to p_1. In your diagram, show the typical firm's response to the increase in market price from p_0 to p_1. Show the typical firm's profits at this new price.
   d. Explain how this industry adjusts to its new long-run equilibrium. Illustrate this adjustment both in the demand-and-supply diagram and in the diagram of the typical firm. (You may assume that the barley industry is a constant-cost industry.)

6. A major theme of this chapter is the role that *free entry and exit* play in determining a competitive industry's long-run equilibrium. Keeping this theme in mind, think of the following statement:

In industry X, demand and supply do determine price in the short run, but in the long run, only supply matters.

   a. Assuming that Industry X is a constant-cost industry, use a demand-and-supply diagram to illustrate why the statement is exactly correct.
   b. Now, assuming that Industry X is an increasing-cost industry, show in a demand-and-supply diagram why the statement is not quite correct.

DISCUSSION QUESTIONS

1. Discuss the common allegation that when all firms in an industry are charging the same price, this indicates the absence of competition and the presence of some form of price-setting agreement.

2. Which of the following observed facts about an industry are inconsistent with its being a perfectly competitive industry?

   a. Different firms use different methods of production.
   b. The industry's product is extensively advertised by a trade association.
   c. Individual firms devote a large fraction of their sales receipts to advertising their own product brands.
   d. There are 24 firms in the industry.
   e. The largest firm in the industry makes 40 percent of the sales, and the next largest firm makes 20 per-

cent of the sales, but the products are identical, and there are 61 other firms.

f. All firms made large profits last year.

3. In which of the following sectors of the Canadian economy might you expect to find competitive behaviour? In which might you expect to find industries that are classified as operating under perfectly competitive market structures?

a. Manufacturing
b. Agriculture
c. Transportation and public utilities
d. Wholesale and retail trade
e. Illegal drugs

4. Today's typical office contains personal computers of various vintages, with the newest machines having the largest output per unit of cost. There are also old machines that, though still able to function, are not in use at all. What determines the secondhand price of the older machines? What is the economic value of the machines that are no longer used?

5. What, if anything, does each one of the following tell you about ease of entry into or exit from an industry?

a. Profits have been very high for two decades.
b. No new firms have entered the industry for 20 years.
c. The average age of the firms in the 40-year-old industry is less than 7 years.
d. Most existing firms are using obsolete equipment alongside newer, more modern equipment.
e. Profits are low or negative; many firms are still producing, but from steadily aging equipment.

6. Explain why perfectly competitive agricultural industries may have external economies of scale—and thus may be declining-cost industries—arising from the behaviour of the farm machinery industry. Is it relevant that the farm machinery industry is dominated by a small number of very large firms?

CHAPTER 10

Monopoly

🔵 LEARNING OBJECTIVES

❶ Explain why marginal revenue is less than price for a profit-maximizing monopolist.

❷ Recognize the importance of entry barriers in allowing monopolists to maintain positive profits in the long run.

❸ Understand how firms can form a cartel in which they restrict industry output and increase price and profits.

❹ Explain the different forms and consequences of price discrimination.

monopoly A market containing a single firm.

monopolist A firm that is the only seller in a market.

Perfect competition is at one end of the spectrum of market structures. At the other end is **monopoly**. Economists say that a monopoly occurs when the output of an entire industry is produced and sold by a single firm, called a **monopolist** or a *monopoly firm*. Examples of monopoly are rare at the national level but are much more common for smaller geographical areas. The company that supplies electric power to your home is almost certainly a monopoly, as is the firm that provides local (but not long-distance) telephone service and cable television. Because monopoly is the market structure that allows for the maximum possible exercise of market power on the part of the firm, monopoly markets and perfectly competitive markets provide two extremes of behaviour that are useful for economists in their study of market structure.

In this chapter we examine how a profit-maximizing monopolist determines its price and quantity. We begin by considering a monopolist that sells all of its output at a single price. We then consider *cartels*—the attempt by several firms to band together and behave like a monopolist. We end the chapter by examining situations in which a firm is able to charge different prices to its different customers—something you have probably observed with airlines, movie theatres, and even your local grocery store.

A Single-Price Monopolist

We look first at a monopolist that charges a single price for its product. This firm's profits, like those of all firms, will depend on the relationship between its production costs and its sales revenues.

Cost and Revenue in the Short Run

We saw in Chapter 7 that U-shaped short-run cost curves are a consequence of the law of diminishing returns. Because this law applies to the conditions under which goods are produced rather than to the market structure in which they are sold, monopolists have U-shaped short-run cost curves for the same reasons as do perfectly competitive firms.

Because a monopolist is the sole producer of the product that it sells, its demand curve is simply the market demand curve for that product. The market demand curve, which shows the total quantity that buyers want to purchase at each price, also shows the quantity that the monopolist will be able to sell at each price.

The monopolist, unlike the perfectly competitive firm, faces a negatively sloped demand curve.

A monopolist therefore faces a tradeoff between the price it charges and the quantity it sells. For a monopolist, sales can be increased only if price is reduced, and price can be increased only if sales are reduced.

Average Revenue

Starting with the market demand curve, we can readily derive the monopolist's average and marginal revenue curves. When the monopolist charges the same price for all units sold, its total revenue (TR) is simply equal to the single price times the quantity sold,

$$TR = p \times q$$

Since average revenue is total revenue divided by quantity, it follows that average revenue is equal to the price,

$$AR = TR/q = (p \times q)/q = p$$

And since the price is given by the position of the demand curve, it follows that the demand curve is also the monopolist's average revenue curve.

Marginal Revenue

Now let's consider the monopolist's *marginal revenue*—the revenue resulting from the sale of an additional (or marginal) unit of production. Because its demand curve is negatively sloped, the monopolist must reduce the price that it charges on *all* units in order to sell an extra unit. It follows that the addition to its revenue resulting from the sale of an extra unit is less than the price that it receives for that unit. It is less by the amount that it loses as a result of cutting the price on all the units that it was selling already.

The monopolist's marginal revenue is less than the price at which it sells its output. Thus the monopolist's *MR* curve is below its demand curve. [24]

The relationship between marginal revenue and price for an example is shown in detail in Figure 10-1. Consider the table first. Notice that the numbers in columns (4) and (5) are plotted between the rows that refer to specific prices, because the figures refer to what happens when the price is changed between the amounts shown in two adjacent

FIGURE 10-1   A Monopolist's Average and Marginal Revenue Curves

(1) Price (Average Revenue)	(2) Quantity Sold	(3) Total Revenue ($p \times q$)	(4) Change in Total Revenue (ΔTR)	(5) Marginal Revenue ($\Delta TR/\Delta q$)
10	0	0		
9	10	90	90	9
8	20	160	70	7
7	30	210	50	5
6	40	240	30	3
5	50	250	10	1
4	60	240	−10	−1
3	70	210	−30	−3
2	80	160	−50	−5
1	90	90	−70	−7
0	100	0	−90	−9

Marginal revenue is less than price because the price at which existing units are sold must be reduced in order to sell more units. The data show that every time the firm lowers its price by $1, its sales increase by 10 units. Column 3 gives the total revenue associated with each price, which is that price multiplied by the quantity sold. Column 4 gives the change in total revenue as the price is altered by $1. To calculate the change in revenue associated with a unit change in quantity, we must divide the change in column 4 by 10 to get the change in revenue *per unit change in quantity*. The result is recorded in column 5, which is the marginal revenue.

rows. The method of calculating marginal revenue shown in the table involves subtracting the total revenue associated with one price from the total revenue associated with another price and then dividing this change by the change in the number of units sold.

Now look at the figure. It plots the entire demand curve that gave rise to the individual figures for price and quantity shown in the table. It also plots the entire marginal revenue curve and locates the specific points on it that were calculated in the table. For purposes of illustration, a straight-line demand curve has been chosen.[1]

Notice that marginal revenue is positive up to 50 units of sales, indicating that reductions in price between $10 and $5 increase total revenue. Notice also that marginal revenue is negative for sales greater than 50 units, indicating that reductions in price below $5 cause total revenue to fall.

The figure also illustrates the two opposing forces that are present whenever the price is changed. As an example, consider the reduction in price from $6 to $5. First, the

[1]When drawing these curves, note that if the demand curve is a negatively sloped straight line, the *MR* curve also has a negative slope but is twice as steep. Its price intercept (where $q = 0$) is the same as that of the demand curve, and its quantity intercept (where $p = 0$) is one-half that of the demand curve. [25]

40 units that the firm was already selling bring in less money at the new lower price than at the original higher price. This loss in revenue is the amount of the price reduction multiplied by the number of units already being sold (40 units × $1 per unit = $40). This is shown as the green shaded area in the figure. The second force, operating in the opposite direction, is that new units are sold, which brings in more revenue. This gain in revenue is given by the number of new units sold multiplied by the price at which they are sold (10 units × $5 = $50). This is shown as the purple shaded area. The *net change* in total revenue is the *difference* between these two amounts ($10). In the example shown in the figure, the increase resulting from the sale of new units exceeds the decrease resulting from existing sales now being made at a lower price. Marginal revenue is thus positive. Furthermore, the change in total revenue is $10 whereas the change in the number of units sold is 10 units. Thus marginal revenue, given by $\Delta TR/\Delta q$, is equal to $10/10 = $1.

The proposition that marginal revenue is always less than price provides an important contrast with perfect competition. Recall that in perfect competition, the firm's marginal revenue from selling an extra unit of output is equal to the price at which that unit is sold. The reason for the difference is not difficult to understand. The perfectly competitive firm is a price taker; it can sell all it wants at the given market price. In contrast, the monopolist faces a negatively sloped demand curve; it must reduce the market price to increase its sales.

If you plot the data on *TR* from Figure 10-1 you will notice that *TR* rises (*MR* is positive) as price falls, reaching a maximum where *p* = $5 and *MR* = 0. Then, as price continues to fall, *TR* falls (*MR* is negative). Using the relationship between elasticity and total revenue that we first saw in Chapter 4, it follows that demand is elastic ($\eta > 1$) when *MR* is positive and demand is inelastic ($\eta < 1$) when *MR* is negative. The value of η declines steadily as we move down the demand curve. As we will see shortly, a profit-maximizing monopolist will always produce on the elastic portion of its demand curve (that is, where *MR* is positive).

Short-Run Profit Maximization

To show the profit-maximizing position of a monopolist, we bring together information about its revenues and its costs and then apply the two rules developed in Chapter 9: (1) The firm should not produce at all unless there is some level of output for which price is at least equal to average variable cost, and (2) if the firm does produce, its output should be set at the point where marginal cost equals marginal revenue.

When the monopolist equates marginal cost with marginal revenue, its situation is as shown in Figure 10-2. The profit-maximizing level of output is where marginal cost equals marginal revenue. The price is read off the demand curve, which shows the price corresponding to that output.

Notice that because marginal revenue is always less than price for the monopolist, when marginal revenue is equated with marginal cost, both are less than price.

When a monopolist is maximizing its profit, its marginal cost is always less than the price it charges for its output.

Monopoly Profits

The fact that a monopolist produces the output that maximizes its profits tells us nothing about *how large* these profits will be or even whether there will be any profits at all. The monopolist may earn positive profits or may suffer losses, depending on the position of the *ATC* curve. Figure 10-2 shows the possibilities. Nothing guarantees that

FIGURE 10-2   Short-Run Profit Maximization for a Monopolist

The profit-maximizing output is q_0, where $MR = MC$; price is p_0, which is above MC at that output. The rules for profit maximization require $MR = MC$ and $p > AVC$. (AVC is not shown in the graph, but it must be below ATC.) Whether profits at q_0 are positive or negative (or zero) depends on the position of the ATC curve. If average total cost is ATC_1, then unit costs at q_0 are given by c_1 and the monopolist makes positive profits shown by the light shaded area. If average cost is ATC_2, the monopolist breaks even because the price p_0 exactly equals average total costs, c_2. If average total cost is ATC_3, unit costs at q_0 are given by c_3 and the monopolist makes losses shown by the dark shaded area.

a monopolist will make profits in the short run, but if it suffers persistent losses, it will eventually go out of business.

No Supply Curve for a Monopolist

In describing the monopolist's profit-maximizing behaviour, we did not introduce the concept of a supply curve, as we did in the discussion of perfect competition. In perfect competition, the industry short-run supply curve depends only on the marginal cost curves of the individual firms, because under perfect competition, profit-maximizing firms equate marginal cost with price. Given marginal costs, it is possible to know how much will be supplied at each price. This is not the case, however, with a monopolist.

For a monopolist, there is no unique relationship between market price and quantity supplied.

To prove this point to yourself, draw a monopolist's marginal cost curve and any marginal revenue curve to intersect the MC curve at some output that you call q^*. Now draw as many other different MR curves as you like, all of which intersect MC at q^*. All of these curves give rise to profit-maximizing output of q^*, but because each MR curve is different, each must be associated with a different demand curve and hence a different price at which q^* is sold. This exercise shows that a given quantity may be associated with many different prices, depending on the slope of the demand curve that the monopolist faces.

Firm and Industry

Because the monopolist is the only producer in an industry, there is no need for separate theories about the firm and the industry, as is necessary with perfect competition. The monopolist *is* the industry. Thus, the short-run, profit-maximizing position of the firm, as shown in Figure 10-2, is also the short-run equilibrium of the industry.

Competition and Monopoly Compared

The comparison of monopoly with perfect competition is important. For a perfectly competitive industry, the equilibrium is determined by the intersection of the industry demand and supply curves. Since the industry supply curve is simply the sum of the individual firms' marginal cost curves, the equilibrium output in a perfectly competitive industry is such that price equals marginal cost. For the monopolist, in contrast, equilibrium output is such that price is greater than marginal cost. And since demand curves are downward sloping and MC curves are typically upward sloping, the gap between price and marginal cost implies one thing: the level of output in a monopolized industry is less than the level of output that would be produced if the industry were instead made up of many price-taking firms.

A perfectly competitive industry produces a level of output such that price equals marginal cost. A monopolist produces a lower level of output, with price exceeding marginal cost.

In Chapter 12 we will discuss the important concept of *allocative efficiency* and will see that a perfectly competitive industry achieves allocative efficiency whereas a monopolist does not. The full explanation is fairly involved, but for now a simple explanation will suffice. Since price exceeds marginal cost for a monopolist, society as a whole would benefit by reallocating resources so as to produce more of the monopolist's product—because the gain to society of additional output, as reflected in the marginal value (price) of the product, exceeds the marginal cost of producing the additional output. In contrast, a perfectly competitive industry has price equal to marginal cost. Thus the marginal value (price) to society of additional output is equal to the marginal cost of producing it, and there is no scope to improve the outcome.

We will return in detail to the topic of allocative efficiency in Chapter 12, where we will compare perfect competition, monopoly, and other market structures. For now, we go on to discuss the long-run equilibrium for monopoly.

Long-Run Equilibrium

In a monopolized industry, as in a perfectly competitive one, losses and profits provide incentives for exit and entry. If the monopoly is suffering losses in the short run, it will continue to operate as long as it can cover its variable costs. In the long run, however, it will leave the industry unless it can find a scale of operations at which its full opportunity costs can be covered. If the monopoly is making profits, other firms will wish to enter the industry in order to earn more than the opportunity cost of their capital. If such entry occurs, the monopoly's position will change and the firm will cease to be a monopoly. Instead of facing the entire market demand curve, the (former) monopolist will have to compete with the new firms and thus will capture only part of the overall market demand.

In order for positive monopoly profits to lead to the entry of new firms into the industry, however, these new firms must *be able* to enter the industry. This observation leads us to a discussion of *entry barriers*.

Entry Barriers

Impediments that prevent entry are called **entry barriers**; they may be either natural or created.

If monopoly profits are to persist in the long run, the entry of new firms into the industry must be prevented by effective entry barriers.

entry barrier Any natural barrier to the entry of new firms into an industry, such as a large minimum efficient scale for firms, or any firm-created barrier, such as a patent.

Natural Entry Barriers.   Natural barriers most commonly arise as a result of economies of scale. When the long-run average cost curve is negatively sloped over a large range of output, big firms have significantly lower average total costs than small firms.

Recall from Chapter 9 that the *minimum efficient scale (MES)* is the smallest-size firm that can reap all of the economies of large-scale production. It occurs at the level of output where the firm's long-run average cost curve reaches a minimum.

To see how economies of scale can act as an entry barrier, suppose that the technology of an industry is such that one firm's *MES* would be 10 000 units per week at an average total cost of $10 per unit. Further suppose that at a price of $10, the quantity demanded in the entire market is 11 000 units per week. Under these circumstances, only one firm can operate at or near its *MES*. Any potential entrant would have unit costs higher than those of the existing firm and so could not compete successfully.

A **natural monopoly** occurs when the industry's demand conditions allow no more than one firm to cover its costs while producing at its minimum efficient scale. Electrical power transmission is a natural monopoly—with current technology it is cheaper to have only one set of power lines (rather than two or more) serving a given region.

Another type of natural barrier is *setup cost*. If a firm could be catapulted fully grown into the market, it might be able to compete effectively with the existing monopolist. However, the cost to the new firm of entering the market, developing its products, and establishing such things as its brand image and its dealer network may be so large that entry would be unprofitable.

natural monopoly
An industry characterized by economies of scale sufficiently large that one firm can most efficiently supply the entire market demand.

Created Entry Barriers.   Many entry barriers are created by conscious government action. Patent laws, for instance, may prevent entry by conferring on the patent holder the sole legal right to produce a particular product for a specific period of time.

Patent protection has led to a major and prolonged battle among nations fought out in international organizations that seek to enforce conditions for fair trade and investment. The major developed countries, where much of the research and development is done, have sought to extend patent rights to other countries. They argue that without the temporary monopoly profits that a patent creates, the incentive to develop new products will be weakened. The developing countries have sought to maintain weak or nonexistent patent laws. This allows them to produce new products under more competitive conditions and thus to avoid paying monopoly profits to the original patent holders in developed countries.

A firm may also be granted a charter or a franchise that prohibits competition by law. Canada Post, for example, has a government-sanctioned monopoly on the delivery of first-class mail. In other cases the regulation and/or licensing of firms severely restricts entry. Professional organizations for dentists or engineers, for example, might restrict the number of places in accredited dental or engineering schools, and thus restrict entry into those industries.

Other barriers can be created by the firm or firms already in the market. In extreme cases, the threat of force or sabotage can deter entry. The most obvious entry barriers of this type are encountered in organized crime, where operation outside of the law makes available an array of illegal but potent barriers to new entrants. But law-abiding firms must use legal tactics in an attempt to increase a new entrant's setup costs. Such tactics range from the threat of price cutting—designed to impose unsustainable losses on a new entrant—to heavy brand-name advertising. (These and other created entry barriers will be discussed in more detail in Chapter 11.)

The Significance of Entry Barriers

Because there are no entry barriers in perfect competition, profits cannot persist in the long run. In monopolized industries, however, profits can persist in the long run whenever there are effective barriers to entry.

In competitive industries, profits attract entry, and entry erodes profits. In monopolized industries, entry barriers permit positive profits to remain in the long run.

Applying Economic Concepts 10-1 discusses an interesting example from Ireland where government regulations, by restricting entry, have led local pubs to have considerable monopoly power. At a time when Irish pubs are becoming a popular trend in many countries, it is ironic to see how a booming Irish economy combined with government regulation has caused a shortage of Irish pubs in Ireland itself!

APPLYING ECONOMIC CONCEPTS 10-1

The Economics of Irish Pubs

In recent years, the Irish economy has been booming—so much that many economists refer to it as the "Celtic Tiger," putting it in the same category as the Asian tigers of Taiwan, Singapore, Hong Kong, and South Korea. As the Irish economy has boomed, however, line-ups and prices in many Irish pubs have skyrocketed. The shortage of pubs has been so severe that some pub operators have implemented their own rationing schemes by turning away young people, bachelor parties, and sloppy dressers. In some cases, publicans have even threatened to expel anyone who starts to sing, a long-standing tradition in Irish pubs.

So what is going on in the pub industry in Ireland? Ordinarily, as demand increases and profits rise, new pubs would be established. This entry of new pubs would keep the existing pubs from earning high profits.

The problem in Ireland is that the issuance of pub licences is governed by a 1902 law that froze the number of licences at the level in place at that time. As incomes grew over time and the demand for pubs increased, the entry of new pubs was prevented. It is therefore no surprise that prices in pubs have been rising and that existing pubs are extremely profitable. This profitability is reflected in the high purchase prices of the pubs themselves. Currently, pubs sell for about two and a half times their annual sales. Twenty years ago, well before the shortages developed, pubs sold for a price roughly equal to their annual sales.

Another aspect of the 1902 legislation that has caused local pub shortages is that pub owners are prevented from transferring licences across county lines. As the population has increasingly moved from small towns to larger cities over the past several decades, small towns are left with too many pubs while neighbourhoods in the larger cities have far too few. The legislation therefore acts as *both* a barrier to entry and a barrier to exit (though closing down the pub is still permitted).

Who gains from this legislation, and who loses? The clear losers are the pubs' customers (especially in growing towns and cities) who are faced with higher prices and longer lineups. The clear gainers are the current owners of the pubs in areas where demand is strong. It is no surprise, therefore, that Ireland's powerful pub lobby continues to fight efforts by the government to review pub legislation.

Government legislation in Ireland has restricted the entry of new pubs and has therefore permitted existing pubs to earn high profits without the threat of competition.

Based on "Barred: Ireland Faces a Shortage of Pubs" in *The Globe and Mail*, March 17, 1999.

The Very Long Run and Creative Destruction

In the very long run, technology changes. New ways of producing old products are invented, and new products are created to satisfy both familiar and new wants. These are related to the concept of entry barriers; a monopoly that succeeds in preventing the entry of new firms capable of producing its product will sooner or later find its barriers circumvented by innovations. One firm may be able to use new processes that avoid some patent or other barrier that the monopolist relies on to bar entry of competing firms. Another firm may compete by producing a somewhat different product that satisfies the same need as the monopolist's product. Yet another firm might get around a natural monopoly by inventing a technology that produces at a low minimum efficient scale and ultimately allows several firms to enter the market and still cover costs.

The distinguished economist, Joseph Schumpeter (1883–1950), took the view that entry barriers were not a serious problem in the very long run. He argued that monopoly profits provide one of the major incentives for people who risk their money by financing inventions and innovations. In his view, the short-run profits of a monopoly provide a strong incentive for others to try to usurp some of these profits for themselves. If a frontal attack on the monopolist's entry barriers is not possible, the barriers will be circumvented by such means as the development of similar products against which the monopolist will not have entry protection.

Schumpeter called the replacement of one monopolist by another through the invention of new products or new production techniques the *process of creative destruction*. "Creative" referred to the rise of new products; "destruction" referred to the demise of the existing monopoly. Some everyday examples of creative destruction are presented in *Applying Economic Concepts 10-2*.

Schumpeter argued that this process of creative destruction reflects new firms' abilities to circumvent entry barriers that would otherwise permit monopolists to earn profits in the long run. He also argued that because creative destruction thrives on innovation, the existence of monopoly profits is a major incentive to economic growth. A key part of his argument appears in the following words:

> *What we have got to accept is that it [monopoly] has come to be the most powerful engine of progress and in particular of the long-run expansion of total output not only in spite of, but to a considerable extent through, this strategy [of creating monopolies], which looks so restrictive when viewed in the individual case and from the individual point of time.*[2]

Schumpeter was writing at a time when the two dominant market structures studied by economists were perfect competition and monopoly. His argument easily extends, however, to any market structure that allows profits to exist in the long run. Today, pure monopolies are few, but there are many industries in which profits can be earned for long periods of time. Such industries, which are called *oligopolies,* are candidates for the operation of the process of creative destruction. We study these industries in detail in Chapter 11.

Cartels as Monopolies

To learn more about OPEC, see its website at www.opec.org.

cartel   An organization of producers who agree to act as a single seller in order to maximize joint profits.

So far in our discussion, a monopoly has meant that there is only one firm in an industry. A second way a monopoly can arise is for many firms in an industry to agree to cooperate with one another, to behave as if they were a single seller, in order to maximize joint profits, eliminating competition among themselves. Such a group of firms is called a **cartel**. The firms can agree among themselves to restrict their total output to the level that maximizes their joint profits.

The most famous example of a successful cartel is the Organization of Petroleum Exporting Countries (OPEC), which successfully raised the world price of oil in 1973 and again in 1979. In recent years, however, its members have had difficulty agreeing among themselves regarding the appropriate level of output restrictions.

A less well-known example, but one that has been more successful over many years, is the diamond cartel, controlled by the South African company, DeBeers. DeBeers produces roughly half of the world's annual production of diamonds but also purchases a

---

[2]Joseph Schumpeter, *Capitalism, Socialism, and Democracy,* 3rd ed. (New York: Harper & Row, 1950), p. 106.

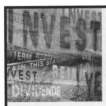

APPLYING ECONOMIC CONCEPTS 10-2

Some Everyday Examples of Creative Destruction

Creative destruction, the elimination of one product by a superior product or one production process by a superior process, is a major characteristic of all advanced countries. It eliminates the strong market position of the firms and workers who make the threatened product or operate the threatened process.

The steel-nibbed pen eliminated the quill pen with its sharpened bird's feather nib. The fountain pen eliminated the steel pen and its accompanying ink well. The ballpoint pen virtually eliminated the fountain pen. Who knows what will come next in writing implements?

The silent films eliminated vaudeville. The talkies eliminated silent films and colour films have all but eliminated black and white. Television seriously reduced the demand for films (and radio) while not eliminating either of them. Cable greatly reduced the demand for direct TV reception by offering better pictures and a more varied selection. The satellite is threatening to eliminate cable by offering much more selection.

For long-distance passenger travel by sea, the steamship eliminated the sailing vessel around the beginning of the twentieth century. The airplane eliminated the ocean liner in the 1950s and 1960s. For passenger travel on land, the train eliminated the stage coach while the bus competed with the train without eliminating it. The airplane wiped out the passenger train in most of North America while leaving the bus still in a low-cost niche used mainly for short and medium distances.

The above examples all involve the elimination of a product by the development of a new, better product. But creative destruction also occurs with the development of better *processes*. The laborious hand-setting of metal type for printing was replaced by the linotype that allowed the type to be set by a keyboard operator but that still involved a costly procedure for making corrections. The linotype was swept away by computer typesetting and much of the established printing shop operations have been replaced by desktop publishing.

Masses of assembly-line workers, operating highly specialized and inflexible machines, replaced craftsmen when Henry Ford perfected the techniques of mass production. A smaller number of less specialized flexible manufacturing workers, operating sophisticated and less specialized machinery, have replaced the assembly line workers who operated the traditional factory.

These cases all illustrate the same general message. Technological change transforms the products we consume, how we make those products, and how we work. It continually sweeps away positions of high income and economic power established by firms that were in the previous wave of technological change and by those who work for them. It is an agent of dynamism in our economy, an agent of change and economic growth, but it is not without its dark side in terms of the periodic loss of privileged positions on the part of the replaced firms and their workers.

---

considerable amount from smaller producers worldwide. The result is that roughly 70 percent of the world's annual diamond supply is marketed through the DeBeers-controlled Central Selling Organization (CSO). In years when demand is slack, DeBeers restricts the output of diamonds through the CSO to keep prices from falling.

Notice in both examples that there are firms *outside* of the cartel. There are many oil producers that are not part of OPEC; similarly, there are many diamond mines that are not owned or controlled by DeBeers (one of which is Canada's first diamond mine, the Ekati mine in the North West Territories). Indeed, this type of cartel is much more common than the type in which *all* firms successfully band together to form a cartel.

In this chapter, however, we simplify the analysis by considering the case in which *all* firms in the industry form a cartel. This is the easiest setting in which to see the central point—that cartels are inherently unstable.

DeBeers controls 70 percent of the world's supply of diamonds through its Central Selling Organization.

FIGURE 10-3   The Effect of Cartelizing a Competitive Industry

Cartelization of a competitive industry can always increase that industry's profits. Equilibrium for a competitive industry occurs at E_0, where the supply and the demand curves intersect. Equilibrium price and output are p_c and q_c. Because the industry demand curve is negatively sloped, marginal revenue is less than price.

If the industry is cartelized, profits can be increased by reducing output. All units between q_m and q_c add less to revenue than to cost—the MR curve lies below the MC curve. (Recall from Figure 9-6 that the industry's supply curve is the sum of the supply curves, and hence of the marginal cost curves, of each of the firms in the industry.) If the units between q_m and q_c are not produced, output is reduced to q_m and price rises to p_m. This price-output combination maximizes the industry's profits because it is where industry marginal revenue equals industry marginal cost.

The Effects of Cartelization

Because perfectly competitive firms are price takers, they accept the market price as given and increase their output until their marginal cost equals price. In contrast, a monopolist knows that increasing its output will depress the market price. Taking account of this, the monopolist increases its output only until marginal cost equals marginal revenue. If all the firms in a competitive industry form a cartel, they too will be able to take account of the effect of their *joint output* on price. They can agree to restrict industry output to the level that maximizes their joint profits (where the industry's marginal cost is equal to the industry's marginal revenue). The incentive for firms to form a cartel lies in the cartel's ability to restrict output, thereby raising price and increasing profits.

When a competitive industry is cartelized, the firms can agree to restrict their joint output to the joint-profit-maximizing level. One way to do this is to establish a quota for each firm's output. For example, suppose that the joint-profit-maximizing output is two-thirds of the perfectly competitive output. When the cartel is formed, each firm could be given a quota equal to two-thirds of its competitive output.

The cartelization of a competitive industry will reduce output and raise price from the perfectly competitive levels.

The effect of cartelizing a competitive industry is shown in more detail in Figure 10-3.

Problems That Cartels Face

Cartels encounter two characteristic problems. The first is ensuring that members follow the behaviour that will maximize the cartel members' *joint* profits. The second is preventing these profits from being eroded by the entry of new firms.

Enforcement of Output Restrictions

The managers of any cartel want the industry to produce its profit-maximizing output. Their job is made more difficult if individual firms either stay out of the cartel or join the cartel and then cheat on their output quotas. Any one firm, however, has an incentive to do just this—to be either the one that stays out of the organization or the one that enters and then cheats on its output quota. For the sake of simplicity, assume that all firms enter the cartel; thus enforcement problems are concerned strictly with cheating by its members.

If Firm X is the only firm to cheat, it is then in the best of all possible situations. All other firms restrict output and hold the industry price up near its monopoly level. They earn profits but only by restricting output. Firm X can then reap the full benefit of the other firms' output restraint and sell some additional output at the high price that has been set by the cartel's actions. However, if all of the firms cheat, the price will be pushed back to the competitive level, and all of the firms will return to their competitive position.

This conflict between the interests of the group as a whole and the interests of each individual firm is the cartel's main dilemma. Provided that enough firms cooperate in restricting output, all firms are better off than they would be if the industry remained perfectly competitive. Any one firm, however, is even better off if it remains outside or if it enters and cheats. However, if all firms act on this incentive, all will be worse off than if they had joined the cartel and restricted output.

Cartels tend to be unstable because of the incentives for individual firms to violate the output quotas needed to sustain the monopoly price.

The conflict between the motives for cooperation and for independent action is analysed in more detail in Figure 10-4. In Chapter 11, we will consider an explicit theory, called *game theory,* that economists use to analyse conflicts of this kind.

Cartels and similar output-restricting arrangements have a long history. For example, schemes to raise farm incomes by limiting crops bear ample testimony to the accuracy of the predicted instability of cartels. Industry agreements concerning crop restriction

Practise with Study Guide Chapter 10, Exercise 5.

FIGURE 10-4   A Cartel Member's Incentive to Cheat

(i) Market equilibrium

(ii) Firm incentives

Cooperation leads to the monopoly price, but individual self-interest leads to production in excess of the monopoly output. Market conditions are shown in part (i), and the situation of a typical firm is shown in part (ii). (The change of scale between the two graphs is reflected by the upper case Q in part (i) and the lower case q in part (ii).) Initially, the market is in competitive equilibrium with price p_0 and quantity Q_0. The individual firm is producing output q_0 and is just covering its total costs.

The cartel is formed and then enforces quotas on individual firms that are sufficient to reduce the industry's output to Q_1, the output where industry MR equals industry MC. Q_1 is thus the output that maximizes the joint profits of the cartel members. Price rises to p_1 as a result. The typical firm's quota in part (ii) is q_1. The firm's profits rise from zero to the amount shown by the gray shaded area in part (ii). Once price is raised to p_1, however, the individual firm would like to increase output to q_2, where marginal cost is equal to the price set by the cartel. This would allow the firm to earn profits, shown by the diagonally striped area. However, if all firms increase their outputs above their quotas, industry output will increase beyond Q_1, and the resulting fall in price will reduce the joint profits of the cartel.

often break down, and prices fall as individual farmers exceed their quotas. This is why most crop restriction plans are now operated by governments rather than by private cartels. Government marketing boards of the type discussed in Chapter 5, backed by the full coercive power of the state, can force monopoly behaviour on existing producers and can effectively bar the entry of new ones.

Restricting Entry

A cartel must not only police the behaviour of its members but must also be able to prevent the entry of new producers. An industry that is able to support a number of individual firms presumably has no overriding natural entry barriers. Thus, if it is to maintain its profits in the long run, a cartel of many separate firms must create barriers that prevent the entry of new firms that are attracted by the cartel's profits. Successful cartels are often able to license the firms in the industry and to control entry by restricting the number of licences. This practice is often used by professionals, from physicians to beauticians. At other times, the government has operated a quota system and has given it the force of law. If no one can produce without a quota and the quotas are allocated among existing producers, entry is successfully prevented.

As we mentioned earlier, DeBeers has been somewhat successful at preventing the entry of new diamond producers and has been able to control 70 percent of the world's annual diamond sales through its Central Selling Organization (CSO). But recently, restricting entry into the diamond industry has been a bit more challenging. In the diamond industry, of course, "entry" means the development of new diamond mines. In 1998, Canada's first diamond mine (the Ekati mine in the North West Territories) began production. At production levels of roughly $500 million per year, the Ekati mine alone accounts for roughly 7 percent of the world's total annual production. The owners of the Ekati mine, however, have stated that they will market the diamonds independently rather than going through the CSO. With entries such as this, combined with some Russian and Australian producers leaving the CSO to sell their diamonds independently, DeBeers is faced with the challenge of keeping diamond prices supported above competitive levels. Time and further developments will determine how successful DeBeers will be in maintaining their dominant position in the industry.

A Multiprice Monopolist: Price Discrimination

So far in this chapter, we have assumed that the monopolist charges the same price for every unit of its product, no matter where or to whom it sells that product. But as we shall soon see, a monopolist finds it profitable to sell different units of the same product at different prices whenever it gets the opportunity. Because this practice is prevalent both for monopoly and for markets in which there are a few large sellers, the range of examples we will discuss cover both types of market structure.

Airlines often charge less to people who stay over a Saturday night than to those who come and go within the week. Raw milk is often sold at one price when it is to be used as fluid milk but at a lower price when it is to be used to make ice cream or cheese. In countries where medical services are provided by the market, physicians in private practice often charge for their services according to the incomes of their patients. Movie theatres often have lower admission prices for children than for adults, and typically also have lower prices for seniors. Electric companies sell electricity at one rate to homes and at a different rate to firms.

Price discrimination occurs when a producer charges different prices for different units of the same product *for reasons not associated with differences in cost.* Not all price differences represent price discrimination. Quantity discounts, differences between whole-sale and retail prices, and prices that vary with the time of day or the season of the year may not represent price discrimination because the same product sold at a different time, in a different place, or in different quantities may have different costs. An excellent example is electricity. If an electric power company has unused capacity at certain times of the day, it may be cheaper for the company to provide service at those hours than at peak demand hours.

If price differences reflect cost differences, they are not discriminatory. When a price difference is based on different buyers' valuations of the same product, it is discriminatory.

It does not cost a movie-theatre operator less to fill seats with children than with adults, but it is worthwhile for the movie theatre to let the children in at a discriminatory low price if few of them would attend at the full adult fare and if they take up seats that would otherwise be empty. Similarly, it does not cost an airline any less to sell a ticket to a student than to a non-student. But since few students may be inclined to buy airline tickets at the full price, it is profitable for the airline to attract more students with a lower price and, in that manner, fill up seats that would otherwise be empty.

price discrimination
The sale by one firm of different units of a commodity at two or more different prices for reasons not associated with differences in cost.

Different Forms of Price Discrimination

Why should a firm want to sell some units of its output at a price that is below the price that it receives for other units of its output? The simple answer is because it is profitable to do so. Why should it be profitable?

Persistent price discrimination is profitable either because different buyers are willing to pay different amounts for the same product or because one buyer is willing to pay different amounts for different units of the same product. The basic point about price discrimination is that in either of these circumstances, sellers may be able to capture some of the consumer surplus that would otherwise go to buyers. (Review the discussion of consumer surplus in Chapter 6.) We first discuss how each type of discrimination takes place; we then examine its implications.

Discrimination Among Units of Output

Look back to Figure 6-2, which shows the consumer surplus received by one consumer when buying eight glasses of milk at a single price. If the firm could sell the consumer each glass separately, it could capture this consumer surplus. It would sell the first unit for $3.00, the second unit for $1.50, the third unit for $1.00, and so on until the eighth unit was sold for 30 cents. The firm would get total revenues of $8.10 rather than the $2.40 obtained from selling eight units at the single price of 30 cents each. In this example, the firm is able to discriminate perfectly and to extract all of the consumer surplus.

Perfect price discrimination occurs when the entire consumer surplus is obtained by the firm. This usually requires that each unit be sold at a different price. In practice, perfect discrimination is seldom possible. Suppose, however, that the firm could charge two different prices, one for the first 4 glasses sold and one for the next 4 glasses sold. If it sold each of the first 4 glasses of milk for 80 cents and each of the next 4 glasses for 30 cents, it would receive $4.40—less than it would receive if it could discriminate perfectly but more than it would receive if it sold all glasses at 30 cents.

Discrimination Among Buyers

Think of the demand curve in a market that is made up of individual buyers, each of whom has indicated the maximum price that he or she is prepared to pay for a single unit. Suppose, for the sake of simplicity, that there are only four buyers for the product; the first is prepared to pay up to $4 for one unit of the good, the second is prepared to pay up to $3, the third up to $2, and the fourth up to $1. Suppose that the product has a marginal cost of production of $1 per unit for all units. If the selling firm is limited to a single price, we know it will maximize its profits by setting marginal revenue equal to marginal cost. It will thus charge $3, sell 2 units, and earn profits of $4. (You can compute for yourself the firm's marginal revenue schedule.)

However, if the seller is able to discriminate among the buyers, it could charge the first buyer $4 and the second $3, thus increasing its profits from the first 2 units to $5. Moreover, it could also sell the third unit for $2, thus increasing its profits to $6. It would be indifferent about selling a fourth unit because the price would just cover marginal cost.

Price discrimination among buyers is quite common. Discounted prices charged for seniors at movie theatres or for students on airlines are both examples of this practice.

Discrimination Among Markets

Practise with Study Guide Chapter 10, Exercise 4.

Suppose now that the monopolist sells its product in two different markets. For example, it might be the only seller in a tariff-protected home market while in foreign markets it sells in competition with so many other firms that it is a price taker. In this case, the firm would equate its marginal cost to the price in the foreign market but to marginal revenue in the domestic market. As a result, it would charge a higher price on sales in the home market than on sales abroad.

Figure 10-5 shows in more detail how a firm might discriminate among markets. Profit maximization requires that marginal cost be set equal to marginal revenue *in each market*. Examine Figure 10-5 to see that the market with the less elastic demand will be the market with the higher price. For a very elastic demand curve, the vertical distance between the demand curve and the marginal revenue curve is small. In contrast, this distance is larger for an inelastic demand curve. Thus, when the firm equates *MC* and *MR* in each market, the price is higher in the market with inelastic demand.

Price discrimination between markets results in higher prices in those markets with less elastic demand.

FIGURE 10-5   Price Discrimination Among Markets

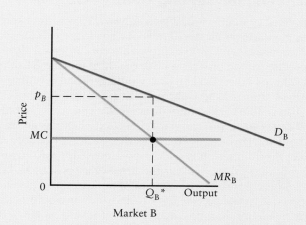

Market A

Market B

Price discrimination among markets leads firms to charge higher prices in those markets where demand is less elastic. Market A has less elastic demand than Market B. The *MC* curve for each firm is horizontal, indicating that all units have the same marginal cost. Profit maximization requires that *MC* = *MR* in each market, thus determining Q_A^* and Q_B^*. Since Market A has less elastic demand than Market B, p_A exceeds p_B.

Price discrimination is quite common among markets for the same product in different countries. In these cases, distance and transport costs or government regulation help to keep the markets separate. For example, Levi Strauss, the manufacturer of jeans, actively discriminates in its pricing of Levi 501s (and other products). The price in France is more than twice that in the United States. Ordinarily, we would expect importers in France to import inexpensive 501s from the United States and sell them in France, thus pushing down the price. In this case, however, the price discrimination is made possible by European Union legislation barring the import of less expensive brand-name goods from outside the European Union. French consumers understandably don't like this price discrimination, but their less elastic demand combined with the EU legal barriers leads Levi Strauss to sensibly charge much more in France than in the United States.

Price Discrimination in General

Demand curves have a negative slope because different units are valued differently, either by one individual or by different individuals. This fact, combined with a single price for a product, gives rise to consumer surplus.

The ability to charge multiple prices gives a seller the opportunity to capture some (or, in the extreme case, all) of the consumer surplus.

FIGURE 10-6   Price Discrimination

(i) Two prices charged

(ii) Four prices charged

Multiple prices permit a seller to capture consumer surplus. Suppose in either graph that if a single price were charged, it would be the price p_0. Quantity q_0 would be sold, and consumer surplus would be the entire area above p_0 and below the demand curve. The seller's revenue is the cross-hatched area.

Part (i) assumes that the market can be segregated in such a way that two prices are charged: p_1 for the first q_1 units and p_0 for the remaining q_1q_0 units. Consumer surplus is reduced to the two light blue triangles, and the seller's revenue is increased by the dark shaded area.

Part (ii) assumes that the market can be segregated in such a way that four prices are charged: p_2 for the first q_2 units, p_1 for the units between q_2 and q_1, and so on. Consumer surplus is reduced to the four light blue triangles, and the seller's revenue is increased by the dark shaded area. At the extreme, if a different price could be charged for each unit, producers could extract every bit of the consumer surplus, and the price discrimination would be perfect.

In general, the larger the number of different prices it can charge, the greater the firm's ability to increase its revenue at the expense of consumers. This is illustrated in Figure 10-6.

It follows that if a selling firm is able to discriminate through price, it can increase revenues received (and thus also profits) from the sale of any given quantity. However, price discrimination is not always possible, even if there are no legal barriers to its use.

When Is Price Discrimination Possible?

Discrimination *among units of output* sold to the same buyer requires that the seller be able to keep track of the units that a buyer consumes in each period. Thus the tenth unit purchased by a given buyer in a given month can be sold at a price that is different from the fifth unit *only* if the seller can keep track of each consumer's purchases. This can be done by an electric company through its meter readings or by a magazine publisher by distinguishing between renewals and new subscriptions. Another familiar example is the coffee-cards that are handed out at coffee shops such as Second Cup. For each coffee purchased, the consumer's card gets hole-punched. After 6 hole-punches, the consumer is entitled to one free coffee. The coffee-card is the way that the seller keeps track of the consumer's purchases.

Discrimination *among buyers* is possible only if the buyers who face the low price cannot resell the goods to the buyers who face the high price. However, even though the local butcher might like to charge the banker twice as much for steak as he charges the taxi driver, he cannot succeed in doing so. The banker can always shop for meat in the supermarket, where her occupation is not known. Even if the butcher and the supermarket agreed to charge her twice as much, she could hire the taxi driver to shop for her. The surgeon, however, may succeed in discriminating (especially if other reputable surgeons do the same) because it will not do the banker much good to hire the taxi driver to have her operation for her.

Price discrimination is possible if the seller can either distinguish individual units bought by a single buyer or separate buyers into groups such that resale between groups is impossible.

The ability to prevent resale tends to be associated with the nature of the product or the ability to classify buyers into readily identifiable groups. Services are less easily resold than goods; goods that require installation by the firm (e.g., heavy equipment or cable TV service) are less easily resold than movable goods such as household appliances. In general, transportation costs, tariff barriers, and import quotas are among the factors that separate groups of buyers geographically and may make discrimination possible.

Of course, it is not enough to be able to separate different buyers or different units into separate groups. The seller must also be able to control the supply going to each group. For example, there is no point in asking more than the competitive price from some buyers if they can simply go to other firms who sell the good at the competitive price.

The Consequences of Price Discrimination

The consequences of price discrimination are summarized in the following two propositions.

For any given level of output, the most profitable system of discriminatory prices will provide higher profits to the firm than the profit-maximizing single price.

This first proposition, which was illustrated in Figure 10-6, requires only that the demand curve have a negative slope. To see that the proposition is correct, remember that a monopolist with the power to discriminate could produce exactly the same quantity as a single-price monopolist and charge everyone the same price. Therefore, it need never receive less revenue, and it can do better if it can raise the price on even one unit sold, so long as the price need not be reduced on any other.

A monopolist that price discriminates among units will produce more output than will a single-price monopolist.

To understand this second proposition, remember that a monopolist that must charge a single price for a product will produce less than would all the firms in a perfectly competitive industry. It produces less because it knows that selling more depresses the price. Price discrimination allows it to reduce this disincentive. To the extent that the firm can sell its output in separate blocks, it can sell another block without spoiling the market for blocks that are already sold. In the case of perfect price discrimination, in which every unit of output is sold at a different price, the profit-maximizing monopolist will produce every unit for which the price charged is greater than or equal to its marginal cost. A perfect-price-discriminating monopolist will therefore produce the same quantity of output as would all firms combined in a perfectly competitive industry.

Normative Aspects of Price Discrimination

Two quite separate issues are involved in evaluating any particular example of price discrimination. One is the effect of price discrimination on the level of output, and the other is the effect of discrimination on the distribution of income.

As we saw in the second proposition above, a monopolist that is able to price discriminate among units will produce more output than will a single-price monopolist. This has implications for *allocative efficiency*, a concept we briefly introduced earlier in the chapter.

Recall from this earlier discussion that a single-price monopolist produces at a level of output where price exceeds marginal cost. Thus society would benefit from having more of the good produced because the marginal value of the good to society (as reflected by its price) exceeds the marginal cost of the good. This gap between price and marginal cost reflects the allocative *inefficiency* of monopoly.

For a monopolist that price discriminates among units, however, there are several prices rather than just a single price. As Figure 10-6 shows, the more prices the discriminating monopolist is able to charge, the more output is produced, and the lower the price becomes *on the marginal units*. Thus the gap between price and marginal cost is lower for a price-discriminating monopolist than for a single-price monopolist. The smaller gap between price and marginal cost implies that a price-discriminating monopolist is more efficient (or less inefficient) than a single-price monopolist.

Efficiency, however, is only one of the normative aspects of price discrimination. Often it is the effects on income distribution that lead to people's strong emotional reactions to it. But one's view will depend on who wins and who loses.

For instance, when railroads discriminate against small farmers, the results arouse public anger. It seems acceptable to many people, however, that doctors practise price discrimination in countries where medical services are provided by the market, charging lower prices to poor patients than to wealthy ones. Not everyone disapproves when airlines discriminate by giving senior citizens and vacationers lower fares than business travellers.

By increasing the seller's profits, price discrimination transfers income from buyers to sellers. When buyers are poor and sellers are rich, this transfer may seem undesirable. However, as in the case of doctor's fees and senior citizens' discounts, discrimination sometimes allows lower-income people to buy a product that they would otherwise be unable to afford if it were sold at the single price that maximized the producer's profits.

S U M M A R Y

A Single-Price Monopolist

- Monopoly is a market structure in which an entire industry is supplied by a single firm. The monopolist's own demand curve is identical to the market demand curve for the product. The market demand curve is the monopolist's average revenue curve, and its marginal revenue curve always lies below its demand curve.
- A single-price monopolist is maximizing its profits when its marginal revenue is equal to marginal costs. Since marginal costs are positive, profit maximization means that marginal revenue is positive. Thus, in turn, elasticity of demand is greater than unity at the monopolist's profit-maximizing level of output.
- A monopolist produces such that price exceeds marginal cost, whereas in a perfectly competitive industry price equals marginal cost. Output in a monopolized industry is less than if the industry were made up of many competitive price-taking firms.
- The profits that a monopoly earns may be positive, zero, or negative in the short run, depending on the relationship between demand and cost.
- For monopoly profits to persist in the long run, there must be effective barriers to the entry of other firms. Entry barriers can be natural or created.
- Monopoly power is limited by the presence of substitute products, the development of new products, and the entry of new firms. In the very long run, it is difficult to maintain entry barriers in the face of the process of creative destruction—the invention of new processes and new products to attack the entrenched position of existing monopolies.

Cartels as Monopolies

- A group of firms may form a cartel by agreeing to restrict their joint output to the monopoly level. Cartels tend to be unstable because of the strong incentives for each individual firm to cheat by producing more than its quota allows.

A Multiprice Monopolist: Price Discrimination

- A price-discriminating monopolist can capture some of the consumer surplus that exists when all of the units of a product are sold at a single price. Successful price discrimination requires that the firm be able to control the supply of the product offered to particular buyers and to prevent the resale of the product.
- A firm that discriminates between different markets will equate MC and MR in each market. The market with the less elastic demand will have the higher price.
- A profit-maximizing monopolist that can enforce discriminatory prices will produce higher output and earn larger profits than will a single-price monopolist.

K E Y   C O N C E P T S

The relationship between price and
  marginal revenue for a monopolist
Short-run monopoly profits
Natural and created entry barriers

The process of creative destruction
Cartels as monopolies
The instability of cartels
Price discrimination among units or
  buyers or markets

The causes and consequences of price
  discrimination
Perfect price discrimination

STUDY EXERCISES

1. The following table shows data for a monopolist. The first two columns provide all the data necessary to plot the monopolist's demand curve.

Price	Quantity Demanded	Total Revenue (TR)	Average Revenue (AR)	Marginal Revenue (MR)
$20	100	—	—	—
18	125	—	—	—
16	150	—	—	—
14	175	—	—	—
12	200	—	—	—
10	225	—	—	—
8	250	—	—	—
6	275	—	—	—
4	300	—	—	—

a. Compute total and average revenue for each level of output and fill in the third and fourth columns in the table. Explain why average revenue is equal to price.

b. Compute marginal revenue for each successive *change* in output and fill in the last column. Explain why *MR* is less than price.

c. On a scale diagram, plot the demand (average revenue) curve and the marginal revenue curve.

d. On a second scale diagram, with $ on the vertical axis and output on the horizontal axis, plot the *TR* curve. What is the value of *MR* when *TR* reaches its maximum?

2. The diagram below shows a monopolist's *MC* and *ATC* curves as well as the industry demand and *MR* curves.

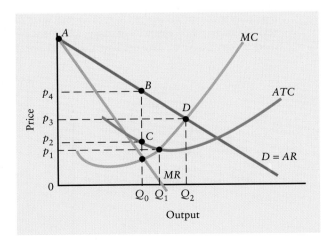

a. What is the profit-maximizing price and level of output for the monopolist?

b. What area in the figure shows the level of profits for the monopolist? Are profits positive or negative?

c. What area shows consumer surplus in this case?

d. Now suppose that the industry is made up of many small, price-taking firms (with the same technology). What are the equilibrium price and level of output in this case?

e. What area shows consumer surplus in this case?

3. Imagine a monopolist that has fixed costs but no variable costs (thus there are no marginal costs, so $MC = 0$). For example, consider a firm that owns a spring of water that can produce indefinitely once it installs certain pipes in an area where no other source of water is available.

a. Draw a downward-sloping demand curve for water, its associated *MR* curve, and the monopolist's *MC* curve.

b. On your diagram, show the monopolist's profit-maximizing price and level of output.

c. What is the marginal value of this good to society, and how does it compare to the marginal cost? What do you conclude about the *allocative efficiency* of this outcome?

4. Consider the market for corn. Suppose this is a competitive industry, made up of many price-taking farmers. We begin in a situation where market price is p_0, industry output is Q_0, and the typical farm is earning zero profit.

a. Draw two diagrams like the ones on the next page.

b. Now suppose that the farmers in this industry form a cartel and collectively agree to restrict the industry output of corn to the level that a monopolist would produce. Call this level of output Q^c and call the new price p^c. Show this outcome in the two diagrams.

c. Show how the cartel raises the profits for the typical farmer.

d. Now consider the incentives for an individual farm to cheat on its fellow cartel members. Would it be profitable to produce an extra unit and sell it at the cartel price? How is this shown in your diagram?

e. Show how the typical farm's profits would rise if it were the only farm to cheat. What level of output would the cheating farm produce?

f. Explain what would happen if *all* farms tried to cheat in this way.

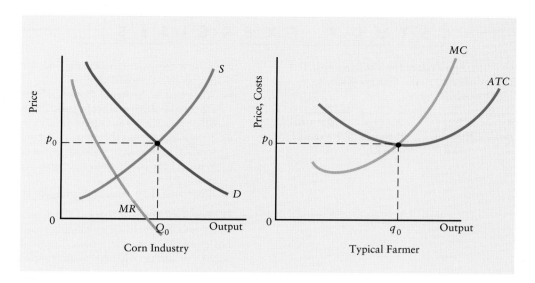

Corn Industry | Typical Farmer

5. Consider each of the following examples where a firm sells the same product to different customers at different prices. Identify in each case whether price discrimination is likely to be taking place. If there is unlikely to be price discrimination occurring, what explains the different prices?

   a. Weekend airline fares that are less than mid-week fares.
   b. Business-class airline fares that are 50% higher than economy-class fares. (Recognize that two business class seats take the same space inside the plane as three economy-class seats.)
   c. Discounts on furniture negotiated from "suggested retail price" for which sales personnel are authorized to bargain and to get as much in each transaction as the customer is prepared to pay.
   d. Higher tuition for law students than for graduate students in economics.

6. In the text we mentioned how Levi Strauss price discriminates between the European and American markets. This question is designed to help you analyse this situation. The equations below are hypothetical demand curves for Levi 501s in Europe and in America. We have expressed the price in dollars in both markets, and quantity is thousands of units per year.

   | European Demand: | $Q^D_E = 150 - p$ |
   | American Demand: | $Q^D_A = 250 - 4p$ |

   a. On two separate scale diagrams, one for Europe and one for America, plot the two demand curves.
   b. Now, recalling that a straight-line demand curve has an associated MR curve that has twice its slope, plot the two MR curves.
   c. Now suppose that Levi Strauss has a constant marginal cost of $15 per unit. Plot the MC curve in both diagrams.
   d. What is the profit-maximizing price in each market? Explain why profit maximization requires that MC be equated to MR *in each market*.
   e. Compute the price elasticity of demand (at the profit-maximizing points) in each market. (You may want to review Chapter 4 on elasticity at this point.) Does the market with less elastic demand have the higher price?

DISCUSSION QUESTIONS

1. Suppose that only one professor teaches economics at your university. Would you say that this professor is a monopolist who can exact any "price" from students in the form of readings assigned, tests given, and material covered? Suppose now that two additional professors have been hired. Has the original professor's market power been decreased? What if the three professors form a cartel agreeing on common reading lists, workloads, and the like?

2. Which of these industries—licorice candy, copper wire, outboard motors, coal, or the local newspaper—would it be most profitable to monopolize? Why? Does your answer depend on several factors or on just one or two? Which would you as a consumer least like to have monopolized by someone else? If your answers to the two questions are different, explain why.

3. Aristotle Murphy owns movie theatres in two towns of roughly the same size, 100 kilometres apart. In Monopolia, he owns the only chain of theatres; in Competitia, there is no theatre chain, and he is only one of a number of independent theatre operators. Would you expect movie prices to be higher in Monopolia or in Competitia in the short run? In the long run? If differences occur in his prices, would Murphy be discriminating in price?

4. Airline fares to Europe are higher in summer than in winter. Some railroads charge lower fares during the week than on weekends. Electric companies charge consumers lower rates the more electricity they use. Are these all examples of price discrimination? What additional information would you like to have before answering this question?

5. Acme Department Store has a sale on luggage. It is offering $30 off any new set of luggage to customers who trade in an old suitcase. Acme has no use for the old luggage and throws it away at the end of each day. Is this price discrimination? Why or why not? Which of the conditions necessary for price discrimination are or are not met?

6. The world price of coffee has declined in real terms over the past 40 years. In 1950, coffee was priced at just under $3 per pound (in 1994 U.S. dollars), whereas by 1995 the world price had fallen to just over $1 per pound. On July 29, 1995, *The Economist* magazine reported that,

> On July 26 the Association of Coffee Producing Countries agreed in New York to limit exports to 60m bags for 12 months. The current level is 70m bags. . . . Coffee prices rallied a bit on the news, but few expect the pact to last: some big coffee producers such as Mexico have not signed up, and even those who have will probably cheat.

Explain why "few expect the pact to last," keeping in mind the two characteristic problems for cartels that were discussed in this chapter.

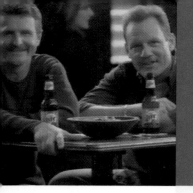

CHAPTER 11

Imperfect Competition

The two market structures that we have studied so far—perfect competition and monopoly—are polar cases; they define the two extremes of a firm's market power over an industry. Under perfect competition, firms are price takers, price is equal to marginal cost, and economic profits in the long run are zero. Under monopoly, the firm is a price setter, it sets price above marginal cost, and it may earn positive profits in the long run.

Although they provide important insights, these two polar cases are insufficient for understanding the behaviour of *all* firms. Indeed, most of the products that we easily recognize—computers, breakfast cereals, automobiles, cameras and fast food, to name a few—are produced by firms that have some market power but are neither perfect competitors nor monopolists.

This chapter is devoted to the discussion of industries that are neither perfectly competitive nor monopolistic. Before discussing the theory, however, we turn to a brief discussion of how prevalent this "intermediate" market structure is in the Canadian economy.

The Structure of the Canadian Economy

Along the spectrum of market structures, we can divide Canadian industries into two broad groups—those with a large number of relatively small firms and those with a small number of relatively large firms.

Industries with Many Small Firms

About two-thirds of Canada's gross domestic product is produced by industries made up of firms that are small relative to the size of the market in which they sell.

The perfectly competitive model does quite well in explaining the behaviour of some of these industries. These are the ones in which individual firms produce more-or-less identical products and so are price takers. Forest and fish products provide many examples. Agriculture also fits fairly well in most ways since individual farmers are clearly price takers. Many basic raw materials, such as iron ore, tin, and copper, are sold on world markets where most individual firms lack significant market power.

Other industries, however, are not well described by the perfectly competitive model, even though they contain many small firms. In retail trade and in services, for example, most firms have some influence over prices. Your local grocery stores, clothing shops, night clubs, and restaurants spend a good deal of money advertising on television and in newspapers—something they would not have to do if they faced perfectly elastic demand curves. Moreover, each store in these industries has a unique location that may give it some local monopoly power over nearby customers.

Industries with many relatively small firms can therefore be divided into two categories. In one category, the firms' behaviour can be explained by the perfectly competitive model; in the other category, the perfectly competitive model does not apply because the firms, though small, are not price takers. It is this second group of industries that we examine in this chapter.

Industries with a Few Large Firms

About one third of Canada's gross domestic product is produced by industries that are dominated by either a single firm or a few large ones.

The most striking cases of single-firm monopolies in today's economy are the electric utilities and the firms which provide local telephone and cable TV services. In the first case they are typically owned by provincial governments; in the second they are subject to government regulation (which we examine in Chapter 12). Other than these and similar cases in which government ownership or regulation play an important role, cases of single-firm monopoly are very rare in Canada today. However, there are some notable examples of monopoly (or near monopoly) from many years ago. For example, the Eddy Match Company was virtually the sole producer of wooden matches in Canada between 1927 and 1940, and Canada Cement Limited produced nearly all of the output of cement until the 1950s.

This type of market dominance by a single large firm is now a thing of the past. Most modern industries that are dominated by large firms contain several firms. Their names are part of the average Canadian's vocabulary: Canadian National and Canadian Pacific; Canadian Airlines and Air Canada; Banque National, Royal Bank, and Scotiabank; Imperial Oil, Petro Canada, and Irving; Stelco, Dofasco, and Alcan; Falconbridge and INCO; Abitibi-Consolidated and MacMillan Bloedel; Ford, Toyota, and GM; Sony, Mitsubishi, and Toshiba; and Nortel, Newbridge, and Corel. Many service industries that used to be dominated by small independent producers have in recent decades seen the development of large firms operating on a world-wide basis. In accounting, firms such as PricewaterhouseCoopers are enormous and clearly have some market power. SNC-Lavalin and Acres are two examples of very large engineering firms that have business contracts all over the world. In management consulting, McKinsey & Co., Boston Consulting Group, and Monitor are also very large firms with market power.

Industrial Concentration

An industry with a small number of relatively large firms is said to be highly *concentrated*. An industry with a large number of relatively small firms is less concentrated. A formal measure of such industrial concentration is given by the *concentration ratio*.

Concentration Ratios

For data on many aspects of Canadian industries, see Industry Canada's website: www.strategis.ic.gc.ca.

concentration ratio
The fraction of total market sales (or some other measure of market occupancy) controlled by a specified number of the industry's largest firms.

When we measure whether an industry has power concentrated in the hands of only a few firms or dispersed over many, it is not sufficient to count the number of firms. For example, an industry with one enormous firm and 29 very small ones is more concentrated in any meaningful sense than an industry with only five equally sized firms. One approach to this problem is to calculate what is called a **concentration ratio,** which shows the fraction of total market sales controlled by the largest sellers. Common types of concentration ratios cite the share of total market sales made by the largest four or eight firms.

Figure 11-1 shows the four-firm concentration ratios in several Canadian manufacturing industries. As is clear, the degree of concentration is quite varied across these industries. In the tobacco and petroleum industries, for example, the largest four firms account for over 80 percent of total sales. At the other extreme, the largest four firms in the furniture industry account for a paltry 7 percent of sales. These largest furniture firms may be large in some absolute sense, but the low concentration ratios suggest that they have quite limited market power.

Defining the Market

The main problem associated with using concentration ratios is to *define the market* with reasonable accuracy. On the one hand, the market may be much smaller than the whole country. For example, concentration ratios in national cement sales are low, but they understate the market power of cement companies because high transportation costs divide the cement *industry* into a series of regional *markets,* with each having relatively few firms. On the other hand, the market may be larger than one country. This is a particularly important consideration in a small trading country such as Canada.

Indeed, the globalization of competition brought about by the falling costs of transportation and communication has been one of the most significant developments in the world economy in recent decades. As the world has "become smaller" through the advances in communication technologies, the nature of domestic markets has changed dramatically. The presence of only a single firm in one industry in Canada in no way implies monopoly power when it is in competition with five foreign firms that can easily sell in the Canadian market. *Applying Economic Concepts 11-1* discusses how the communication revolution that has taken place in the past two decades has altered the nature of production and competition in Canada and around the world.

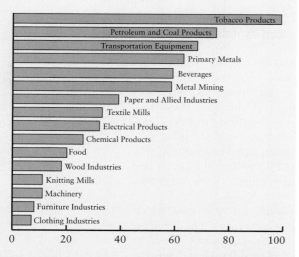

FIGURE 11-1   Concentration Ratios in Selected Canadian Industries

Concentration ratios vary greatly among manufacturing industries. These data show the share of total shipments (in dollar terms) accounted for by the four largest firms in the industry.

(*Source*: Douglas West, *Modern Canadian Industrial Organization*, HarperCollins 1994, p. 37.)

APPLYING ECONOMIC CONCEPTS 11-1

Globalization and the Communication Revolution

A mere 150 years ago, people and news travelled by sailing ship, and it took months to communicate across various parts of the world. Advances in the first 60 years of the twentieth century sped up both communications and travel. In the past few decades, the pace of change in communication technology has accelerated. The world has witnessed a communication revolution that has dramatically changed the speed with which business decisions are made and implemented.

Four decades ago, telephone links were labouriously and unreliably connected by operators, satellites were newfangled and not especially useful toys for rocket scientists, photocopying and telecopying were completely unknown, mail was the only way to send hard copy and getting it to overseas destinations often took weeks, computers were in their infancy, and jets were just beginning to replace the much slower and less reliable propeller aircraft. Today, direct dialing is available worldwide at a fraction of what long-distance calls cost 40 years ago. Faxes, satellite links, jet travel, computer networks, cheap courier services, and a host of other developments have made communication that is reliable and often instantaneous available throughout the world.

The communication revolution has been a major contributor to the development of what has become known as the "global village," a term first used by Canadian author Marshall McLuhan in his writing about the social implications of changes in communication technology. Three important characteristics of the global village are a globalization of production, an increase in competition, and a decline in the power of the nation-state.

Production

The communication revolution has allowed many large international companies, known as *transnational corporations (TNCs)*, to decentralize their production processes. They are now able to locate their research and development (R&D) where the best scientists are available. They can produce various components in dozens of places, locating each activity in a country where costs are cheapest for that type of production. They can then ship all the parts, as they are needed, to an assembly factory where the product is "made."

The globalization of production has brought employment, and rising real wages, to people in many developing countries. At the same time, it has put less-skilled labour in the developed countries under strong competitive pressures.

Competition

The communication revolution has also caused a globalization of competition in almost all industries. National markets are no longer protected for local producers by high costs of transportation and communication or by the ignorance of foreign firms. Walk into a local supermarket or department store today and you will have no trouble finding products representing most nations of the world.

Consumers gain by being able to choose from an enormous range of well-made, low-priced goods and services. Firms that are successful gain worldwide sales. Firms that fall behind even momentarily may, however, be wiped out by competition coming from many quarters. Global competition is fierce, and firms need to be fast on the uptake—of other people's new ideas or their own—if they are to survive.

Economic Policy

The international character of TNCs means that national economic policies have been seriously constrained. Much international trade takes place between segments of single TNCs. This gives them the opportunity, through their accounting practices, to localize their profits in countries where corporate taxes are lowest and to localize their costs in countries where cost write-offs are highest.

The globalization of production also allows TNCs to shift production around the world. Tough national policies in one country may lead firms to move production elsewhere. Generous policies that seek to attract production may succeed in attracting only small and specialized parts of it.

Globalization of production, and consequently of competition, places constraints on the way countries design and implement policies. In particular, government policies must take into account the heightened international mobility of labour and capital. Such mobility does not make governments powerless, but it forces them to recognize that policies implemented today may have different effects than the same policies would have had a mere generation ago.

However, the use of concentration ratios, adjusted appropriately to correctly define the relevant market, can give us useful information about the degree to which production in a given market is concentrated in the hands of a few firms.

The industries shown in Figure 11-1 are not monopolies, because there are several firms in the industry, and these firms engage in rivalrous behaviour. But neither do these firms operate in perfectly competitive markets. Often there are only a few major rival firms in an industry, but even when there are many, they are not price takers. Virtually all consumer goods are differentiated products, and any one firm will typically have several lines of a product that differ more or less from one another and from competing lines produced by other firms. To explain and predict behaviour in these markets, we must go beyond simple concentration ratios; we need to develop theories of the behaviour of firms in market structures other than monopoly and perfect competition.

Imperfectly Competitive Market Structures

The market structures that we are now going to study are called *imperfectly competitive*. The word *competitive* emphasizes that we are not dealing with monopoly, and the word *imperfect* emphasizes that we are not dealing with perfect competition (in which firms are price takers). What is referred to, then, is rivalrous competitive behaviour among firms that have some amount of market power.

Let's begin by noting a number of important characteristics of behaviour that are typical of imperfectly competitive firms. To help organize our thoughts, we classify these under two main headings. First, firms choose the *variety* of the product that they produce and sell. Second, firms choose the *price* at which they will sell that product.

Firms Choose Their Products

differentiated product   A group of commodities that are similar enough to be called the same product but dissimilar enough so that all of them do not have to be sold at the same price.

If a new farmer enters the wheat industry, the full range of products that the farmer can produce is already in existence. In contrast, if a new firm enters the snack food industry, that firm must decide on the characteristics of the new snacks that it is to produce. It will not produce snacks that are identical to those already in production. Rather, it will develop variations on existing snack foods or even a totally new food. Each of these will have its own distinctive characteristics. As a result, firms in the snack food industry sell an array of differentiated products, no two of which are identical.

The term **differentiated product** refers to a group of commodities that are similar enough to be called the same product but dissimilar enough that they can be sold at different prices. For example, although one brand of face soap is similar to most others, soaps differ from each other in chemical composition, colour, smell, softness, brand name, packaging, reputation, and a host of other characteristics that matter to customers. All face soaps taken together can be regarded as one differentiated product.

These breakfast cereals are different enough that they can each have their own price, but they are similar enough to be called the same product – they are a differentiated product.

Most firms in imperfectly competitive markets sell differentiated products. In such industries, the firm itself must decide on what characteristics to give the products that it will sell.

Firms Choose Their Prices

Because firms in perfect competition sell an identical product, they face a market price that they are unable to influence. In all other market structures, firms have negatively sloped demand curves and thus face a tradeoff between the price that they charge and the quantity that they sell.

Whenever different firms' products are not identical, each firm must decide on a price to set. For example, no market sets a single price for razor blades or television sets by equating overall demand with overall supply. What is true for razor blades and for television sets is true for virtually all consumer goods and many capital goods. Any one manufacturer will typically have several product lines that differ from each other and from the competing product lines of other firms. Each product has a price that must be set by its producer.

In such circumstances, economists say that firms *administer* their price. An **administered price** is a price set by the conscious decision of an individual firm rather than by impersonal market forces. Firms that administer their prices are said to be **price setters.**

Each firm has expectations about the quantity it can sell at each price that it might set. Unexpected demand fluctuations then cause unexpected variations in the quantities that are sold at the administered prices.

In market structures other than perfect competition, firms set their prices and then let demand determine sales. Changes in market conditions are signaled to the firm by changes in the firm's sales.

The changed sales may or may not then lead firms to change their prices.

One striking contrast between perfectly competitive markets and markets for differentiated products concerns the behaviour of prices. In perfect competition, prices change continually in response to changes in demand and supply. In markets where differentiated products are sold, prices often change less frequently. Manufacturers' prices for automobiles, TVs, and men's suits do not change with anything like the frequency that prices change in markets for wheat, oil, copper, and newsprint.

Modern firms that sell differentiated products typically have hundreds of distinct products on their price lists. Changing such a long list of administered prices at the same frequency that competitive market prices change would be extremely costly if not impossible. Even changing them only occasionally involves costs. These include the costs of printing new list prices and notifying all customers, the difficulty of keeping track of frequently changing prices for purposes of accounting and billing, and the loss of customer and retailer goodwill due to the uncertainty caused by frequent changes in prices.

Thus transitory fluctuations in demand may be met by changing output with prices constant, while changes in costs that accompany inflation are typically passed on through price increases. Because few firms expect inflationary price increases to be reversed, they know that they must raise their prices to cover them. Even in these cases, however, they do so periodically, rather than continuously, because of the costs incurred in making such changes.

Non-price Competition

Several other important aspects of the observed behaviour of firms in imperfect competition could not occur under either perfect competition or monopoly.

administered price
A price set by the conscious decision of the seller rather than by impersonal market forces.

price setter   A firm that faces a downward sloping demand curve for its product. It chooses which price to set.

First, many firms spend large sums of money on advertising. They do so in an attempt both to shift the demand curves for the industry's products and to attract customers from competing firms. A firm in a perfectly competitive market would not engage in advertising because the firm faces a perfectly elastic demand curve at the market price and so advertising would involve costs but would not increase the firm's revenues. A monopolist would see no benefit in advertising because it has no competitors in the industry. However, in some cases a monopolist will still advertise in an attempt to convince consumers to shift their spending away from other goods and toward the monopolist's product. An example is when DeBeers, the giant near-monopoly diamond producer, has lavish advertisements claiming that "A diamond is forever."

Second, many firms engage in a variety of other forms of non-price competition, such as offering competing standards of quality and product guarantees.

Third, firms in many industries engage in activities that appear to be designed to hinder the entry of new firms, thereby preventing existing pure profits from being eroded by entry. We will consider these activities in more detail later in the chapter.

Monopolistic Competition

monopolistic competition Market structure of an industry in which there are many firms and freedom of entry and exit but in which each firm has a product somewhat differentiated from the others, giving it some control over its price.

The theory of **monopolistic competition** was originally developed to deal with the phenomenon of product differentiation. This theory was first developed by the U.S. economist Edward Chamberlin in his 1933 pioneering book, *The Theory of Monopolistic Competition.*

This market structure is similar to perfect competition in that the industry contains many firms and exhibits freedom of entry and exit. It differs, however, in one important respect: Whereas firms in perfect competition sell an identical product and are price takers, firms in monopolistic competition sell a differentiated product and thus have some power over setting price.

Product differentiation leads to, and is enhanced by, the establishment of brand names and advertising, and it gives each firm a degree of monopoly power over its own product. Each firm can raise its price, even if its competitors do not, without losing all its sales. This is the *monopolistic* part of the theory. However, each firm's monopoly power is severely restricted in both the short run and the long run. The short-run restriction comes from the presence of similar products sold by many competing firms; this causes each firm's demand curve to be very elastic. The long-run restriction comes from free entry into the industry, which permits new firms to compete away the profits being earned by existing firms. These restrictions comprise the *competition* part of the theory.

The Assumptions of Monopolistic Competition

The theory of monopolistic competition is based on three key assumptions.

1. Each firm produces one specific variety, or brand, of the industry's differentiated product. Each firm thus faces a demand curve that, although negatively sloped, is highly elastic because competing firms produce many close substitutes.

2. The industry contains so many firms that each one ignores the possible reactions of its many competitors when it makes its own price and output decisions. In this re-

spect, firms in monopolistic competition are similar to firms in perfect competition. They make decisions based on their own demand and cost conditions and do not consider interdependence between their own decisions and those of the other firms in the industry.

3. There is freedom of entry and exit in the industry. If profits are being earned by existing firms, new firms have an incentive to enter. When they do, the demand for the industry's product must be shared among more brands.

Predictions of the Theory

Product differentiation, which is the *only* thing that makes monopolistic competition different from perfect competition, has important consequences for behaviour in both the short and the long run.

The Short-Run Decision of the Firm

In the short run, a firm that is operating in a monopolistically competitive market structure is similar to a monopoly. It faces a negatively sloped demand curve and maximizes its profits by equating marginal cost with marginal revenue. If the demand curve cuts the average total cost curve as shown in part (i) of Figure 11-2, the firm makes positive profits.

FIGURE 11-2   Profit Maximization for a Firm in Monopolistic Competition

(i) A typical firm in the short run

(ii) A typical firm when the industry is in long-run equilibrium

The short-run position for a monopolistically competitive firm is similar to that of a monopolist. In the long run, firms in a monopolistically competitive industry have zero profits and excess capacity. Note the very elastic demand curve—this reflects the fact that each firm produces a good for which there are many close (but not perfect) substitutes. Short-run profit maximization occurs in part (i) at E_S, the output for which $MR = MC$. Price is p_S and quantity is q_S. Profits may exist; in this example they are shown by the shaded area. Starting from the short-run position shown in part (i), entry of new firms shifts the firm's demand curve to the left and eliminates profits. In part (ii), point E_L, where demand is tangent to $LRAC$, is the position of each firm when the industry is in long-run equilibrium. Price is p_L and quantity is q_L. Price is greater and quantity is less than would exist in the long run if the industry were perfectly competitive (p_C and q_C). When the industry is in long-run equilibrium, each monopolistically competitive firm has excess capacity of $q_L q_C$.

Practise with Study Guide Chapter 11, Exercises 1 and 2.

The Long-Run Equilibrium of the Industry

Profits, as shown in part (i) of Figure 11-2, provide an incentive for new firms to enter the industry. As they do so, the total demand for the industry's product must be shared among this larger number of firms; thus, each gets a smaller share of the total market. Such entry shifts the demand curve for each existing firm's product to the left. Entry, and the consequent leftward shifting of the existing firms' demand curves, continues until profits are eliminated. When this has occurred, each firm is in the position shown in part (ii) of Figure 11-2. Its demand curve has shifted to the left until the curve is *tangent* to the average total cost curve. At this output, the firm is just covering all of its costs. At any other output, it would be suffering losses because average total costs would exceed average revenue.

To see why this "tangency solution" provides the only possible long-run equilibrium for the industry, consider the two possible alternatives. First, suppose that the firm's demand curve *nowhere touched* the ATC curve. There would then be no output at which costs could be covered, and exit would occur. The exit of firms from the industry would then lead each *remaining* firm's demand curve to shift to the right, until it eventually touched the ATC curve. Second, suppose that the demand curve *cut* the ATC curve. There would then be a range of output over which profits could be earned. These profits would lead firms to enter the industry, and this entry would shift each *remaining* firm's demand curve to the left until it was just tangent to the ATC curve.

The Excess-Capacity Theorem

Part (ii) of Figure 11-2 makes it clear that monopolistic competition results in a long-run equilibrium of zero profits, even though each individual firm faces a negatively sloped demand curve. It does this by forcing each firm into a position in which it has *excess capacity;* that is, each firm is producing an output less than that corresponding to the lowest point on its long-run average cost (LRAC) curve. If the firm were to increase its output, it would reduce its cost per unit, but it does not do so because selling more would reduce revenue by more than it would reduce cost. This result is often called the **excess-capacity theorem.**

In monopolistic competition, goods are produced at a point where average total costs are not at their minimum, in contrast to perfect competition, where they are produced at their lowest possible cost.

excess-capacity theorem The property of long-run equilibrium in monopolistic competition that firms produce on the falling portion of their long-run average cost curves. This results in excess capacity, measured by the gap between present output and the output that coincides with minimum average cost.

Evaluation of the Theory

The excess-capacity theorem once aroused passionate debate among economists because it seemed to show that all industries that sell differentiated products would produce them at a higher cost than was necessary. Because product differentiation is a characteristic of virtually all modern consumer goods industries, this theorem suggested that modern market economies were systematically inefficient.

Subsequent analysis by economists has shown that the charge of inefficiency has not been proved. The excess capacity of monopolistic competition does not necessarily indicate a waste of resources because some benefits accrue to consumers from the greater choice and variety of products.

Saying that consumers value variety is not saying that *each* consumer necessarily values variety. You might like only one of the many brands of tooth paste and be better off if only that one brand were produced and the price were lower. But other consumers would prefer one of the other brands. Thus, it is the differences in tastes *across many consumers* that gives rise to the social value of variety, and the price of that greater variety is the higher price per unit.

From society's point of view, there is a tradeoff between producing more brands to satisfy diverse tastes and producing fewer brands at a lower cost per unit.

Monopolistic competition produces a wider range of products but at a somewhat higher cost per unit than perfect competition. As consumers clearly value variety, the benefits of variety must be matched against the extra cost that variety imposes in order to find the *socially optimal* amount of product differentiation. Product differentiation is wasteful only if the costs of providing variety exceed the benefits conferred by providing that variety. Depending on consumers' tastes and firms' costs, monopolistic competition may result in too much, too little, or the optimal amount of product variety.

Empirical Relevance

A controversy raged for several decades as to the empirical relevance of monopolistic competition. Of course, product differentiation is pervasive in many industries. Nonetheless, many economists maintained that the monopolistically competitive market structure was almost never found in practice.

To see why, we need to distinguish between products and firms. Single-product firms are extremely rare in manufacturing industries. Typically, a vast array of differentiated products is produced by each of the few firms in the industry. Most of the vast variety of breakfast cereals, for example, is produced by only three firms (Kellogg's, Nabisco, and General Foods). Similar circumstances exist in soap, chemicals, cigarettes, and numerous other industries where many competing products are produced by a few very large firms. These industries are clearly not perfectly competitive and neither are they monopolies. Are they monopolistically competitive? The answer is no because they contain few enough firms for each to take account of the others' reactions when determining its own behaviour. Furthermore, these firms often earn large profits without attracting new entry (thereby violating the third assumption of monopolistic competition). In fact, they operate under the market structure called *oligopoly*, which we consider in the next section.

Although monopolistic competition is not applicable to differentiated products produced in industries with high concentration, some economists think that the theory is useful for analysing industries where concentration ratios are low and products are differentiated, as in the cases of restaurants, clothing stores, gas stations, dry cleaners, hair salons, and landscaping services. Indeed, many of the small stores and services that are located in or near your neighbourhood are monopolistically competitive firms.

Oligopoly

Industries that are made up of a small number of large firms have a market structure called *oligopoly*, from the Greek words *oligos polein*, meaning "few to sell." An **oligopoly** is an industry that contains two or more firms, at least one of which produces a significant portion of the industry's total output. Whenever there is a high concentration ratio for the firms that are serving one particular market, that market is oligopolistic. The market structures of oligopoly, monopoly, and monopolistic competition are similar in that firms in all of these markets face negatively sloped demand curves.

oligopoly   An industry that contains two or more firms, at least one of which produces a significant portion of the industry's total output.

In contrast to a monopoly (which has no competitors) and to a monopolistically competitive firm (which has many competitors), an oligopolistic firm faces only a few competitors. The number of competitors is small enough for each firm to realize that its competitors may respond to anything that it does and that it should take such possible responses into account. In other words, *oligopolists are aware of the interdependence among the decisions made by the various firms in the industry.*

Economists say that oligopolists exhibit **strategic behaviour,** which means that they take explicit account of the impact of their decisions on competing firms and of the reactions they expect competing firms to make. In contrast, firms in perfect competition or monopolistic competition engage in **nonstrategic behaviour,** which means they make decisions based on their own costs and their own demand curves without considering any possible reactions from their large number of competitors. Monopolists also do not engage in strategic behaviour—simply because they have no competitors to worry about.

In oligopolistic industries, prices are typically administered. Products are usually differentiated. The intensity and the nature of rivalrous behaviour vary greatly from industry to industry and from one period of time to another. This variety has invited extensive theorizing and empirical study.

Why Bigness?

There are several reasons why so many industries are dominated by a few large firms. Some are based on technology and some are based on firms' behaviour.

Economies of Scale

Much factory production uses the principle of the division of labour that we first studied in Chapter 1. The production of a commodity is broken up into hundreds of simple tasks. This type of division of labour is the basis of the assembly line, which revolutionized the production of many goods in the early twentieth century, and still underlies economies of large-scale production in many industries. Such division of labour is, as Adam Smith observed long ago, dependent on the size of the market. If only a few units of a product can be sold each day, there is no point in dividing its production into a number of tasks, each of which can be done in a few minutes. So big firms with large sales have an advantage over small firms with small sales whenever there are opportunities for economies based on an extensive division of labour.

Modern industries produce many differentiated products that give rise to a different type of scale economies. It is costly to develop and market a new product, and it may be only a matter of a few years before it is replaced by some superior version of the same basic product. These *fixed costs* of product development and marketing must be recovered in the revenues from sales of the product. The larger the firm's sales, the lower the fixed cost that has to be recovered from each unit sold and thus the lower the market price can be. With the enormous development costs of some of today's high-tech products, firms that can sell a large volume have a distinct pricing advantage over firms that sell a smaller volume.

Where size confers a cost advantage through economies of scale, there may be room for only a few firms, even when the total market is quite large. This cost advantage of size will dictate that the industry be an oligopoly unless government regulation prevents the firms from growing to their efficient size.

strategic behaviour
Behaviour designed to take account of the reactions of one's rivals to one's own behaviour.

nonstrategic behaviour   Behaviour that does not take account of the reactions of rivals to one's own behaviour.

See Chapter 11 of www.pearsoned.ca/lipsey for a discussion of business strategy by Hugh Courtney, "What Is Business Strategy?" *World Economic Affairs.*

Firm-Created Causes of Bigness

The number of firms in an industry may be decreased while the average size of the survivors rises because of strategic behaviour of the firms themselves. Firms may grow by buying out rivals or merging with them or by driving rivals into bankruptcy through extreme competitive practices. This process increases the size and market shares of the survivors and may, by reducing competitive behaviour, allow them to achieve larger profit margins.

The surviving firms must then be able to create and sustain barriers to entry where natural ones—based on economies of scale—do not exist. The industry will then be dominated by a few large firms only because they are successful in preventing the entry of new firms that would otherwise reduce the industry's concentration ratio.

Is Bigness Natural or Firm-Created?

Most observers would agree that bigness results from a mix of both natural and firm-created causes. Some industries have high concentration ratios because the efficient size of the firm is large relative to the overall size of the industry's market. Other industries may have high concentration ratios mainly because the firms are seeking enhanced market power through entry restriction. The issue that is debated is the relative importance of these two forces, the one coming from economies of scale and the other coming from the desire of firms to create market power by growing large. In Chapter 12 we will see that this debate lies at the heart of *competition policy*—the set of laws designed to promote competition among firms.

The Basic Dilemma of Oligopoly

Oligopoly behaviour is often strategic behaviour. It is dangerous for an oligopolist to neglect how its rivals might react to its actions. In deciding on strategies, oligopolists face a basic dilemma between *competing* and *cooperating*.

Oligopolistic firms will make more profits as a group if they cooperate; any one firm, however, may make more profits for itself if it defects while the others cooperate.

This result is similar to the one established in Chapter 10 for the incentives of an individual firm within a cartel. In a competitive industry with many firms, a cooperative outcome cannot be reached unless some central governing body is formed, by either themselves or the government, to force the necessary behaviour on all firms. In contrast, the few firms in an oligopolistic industry will themselves recognize the possibility of cooperating to avoid the loss of profits that will result from competitive behaviour.

Cooperative and Noncooperative Outcomes

If the firms in an oligopolistic industry cooperate to produce among themselves the monopoly output, they can maximize their joint profits. If they do this, they will reach what is called a **cooperative outcome**, which is the position that a single monopoly firm would reach if it owned all the firms in the industry.

If all the firms in an oligopolistic industry are at the cooperative outcome, it will usually be worthwhile for any one of them to cut its price or to raise its output, so long as the others do not do so. However, if everyone does the same thing, they will be worse off as a group and may all be worse off individually. An industry outcome that is reached

cooperative outcome
A situation in which existing firms cooperate to maximize their joint profits.

noncooperative outcome   An industry outcome reached when firms calculate their own best policy without considering competitors' reactions.

game theory   The theory that studies rational decision making in situations in which one must anticipate the reactions of one's competitors to the moves that one makes.

duopoly   An industry that contains only two firms.

Practise with Study Guide Chapter 11, Exercises 3 and 4.

when firms proceed by calculating only their own gains, without considering the reactions of others, is called a **noncooperative outcome.**

An Example from Game Theory

Game theory is used to study decision making in situations in which a number of players compete, each knowing that others will react to their actions and each taking account of others' expected reactions when making moves. For example, suppose that a firm is deciding whether to raise, lower, or maintain its price. Before arriving at an answer, it asks: "What will the other firms do in each of these cases, and how will their actions affect the profitability of whatever decision I make?"

When game theory is applied to oligopoly, the players are firms, their game is played in the market, their strategies are their price or output decisions, and the payoffs are their profits.

An illustration of the basic dilemma of oligopolists, to cooperate or to compete, is shown in Figure 11-3 for the case of a two-firm oligopoly, called a **duopoly.** In this simplified game there are only two strategies for each firm: to produce an output equal to either one-half of the monopoly output or two-thirds of the monopoly output. Even this simple game, however, is sufficient to illustrate several key ideas in the modern theory of oligopoly.

Figure 11-3 presents what is called a *payoff matrix.* The data in the matrix show that if both firms cooperate, *each* producing one-half of the monopoly output, they achieve the cooperative outcome and jointly earn the monopoly profits by *jointly* producing the output that a monopolist would produce. As a group, they can do no better.

Once the cooperative outcome is attained, the data in the figure show that if A cheats and produces more, its profits will increase. However, B's profits will be reduced: A's behaviour drives the industry's price down, so B earns less from its unchanged output. Because A's cheating takes the firms away from the joint-profit-maximizing monopoly output, their joint profits must fall. Thus B's profits fall by more than A's rise.

Similar considerations also apply to B. It is worthwhile for B to depart from the joint-profit-maximizing output, so long as A does not do so. Thus both A and B have an incentive to agree to cooperate to jointly produce the monopoly output and then to privately cheat by departing from that level of output.

Finally, Figure 11-3 shows that when either firm does depart from the cooperative outcome, the other has an incentive to do so as well. When each follows this "selfish" strategy, both reach the noncooperative outcome at which they jointly produce 1⅓ times as much as the monopolist would. Each then has lower profits than at the cooperative outcome.

Nash equilibrium
An equilibrium that results when each firm in an industry is currently doing the best that it can, given the current behaviour of the other firms in the industry.

Nash Equilibrium.   The noncooperative outcome shown in Figure 11-3 is called a **Nash equilibrium,** after the U.S. mathematician John Nash, who developed the concept in the 1950s and received the Nobel Prize in Economics in 1994 for this work. In a Nash equilibrium, each firm's best strategy is to maintain its present behaviour *given the present behaviour of the other firms.*

It is easy to see that there is only one Nash equilibrium in Figure 11-3. In the bottom-right cell, the best decision for each firm, given that the other firm is producing two-thirds of the monopoly output, is to produce two-thirds of the monopoly output itself. Between them, they produce a joint output of 1⅓ times the monopoly output. Neither firm has an incentive to depart from this position (except through cooperation with the other). In any other cell, each firm has an incentive to change its output *given the output of the other firm.*

The basis of a Nash equilibrium is rational decision-making in the absence of cooperation. Its particular importance in oligopoly theory is that it is the only type of self-policing equilibrium. It is self-policing in the sense that there is no need for group behaviour to enforce it. Each firm has a self-interest to maintain it because no move will improve its profits, given what other firms are currently doing.

If a Nash equilibrium is established by any means whatsoever, no firm has an incentive to depart from it by altering its own behaviour.

Strategic Behaviour.   We have seen how the Nash equilibrium in Figure 11-3 can be arrived at when both firms cheat on an agreement to reach the cooperative outcome. The same equilibrium will be attained if each firm behaves strategically by choosing its optimal strategy taking into account what the other firm may do. Let's see how this works.

Suppose that Firm A reasons as follows: "B can do one of two things; what is the best thing for me to do in each case? First, what if B produces one-half of the monopoly output? If I do the same, I receive a profit of 20, but if I produce two-thirds of the monopoly output, I receive 22. Second, what if B produces two-thirds of the monopoly output? If I produce one-half of the monopoly output, I receive a profit of 15, whereas if I produce two-thirds, I receive 17. Clearly, in either case my best strategy is to produce two-thirds of the monopoly output."

Firm B will reason in the same way. As a result, they end up producing 1⅓ times the monopoly output between themselves, and each earns a profit of 17. This type of game, in which the noncooperative equilibrium makes *both* players worse off than if they were able to cooperate, is called a *prisoners' dilemma*. The reason for this curious name is discussed in *Extensions in Theory 11-1.*

Cooperation or Competition?

We have seen that although oligopolists have an incentive to cooperate, they may be driven, through their own individual decisions, to produce more and earn less than they would if they cooperated. Our next step is to look in more detail at the types of cooperative and competitive behaviour that oligopolists may adopt. We can then go on to study the forces that influence the balance between cooperation and competition in actual situations.

FIGURE 11-3   The Oligopolist's Dilemma: To Cooperate or to Compete?

Cooperation to determine the overall level of output can maximize joint profits, but it leaves each firm with an incentive to cheat. The figure gives what is called a payoff matrix for a two-firm game. Only two levels of production are considered in order to illustrate the basic problem. A's production is indicated across the top, and its payoffs (profits in millions of dollars) are shown in the green circles within each square. B's production is indicated down the left side, and its payoffs are shown in the red circles within each square. For example, the top right square tells us that if B produces one-half while A produces two-thirds of the output that a monopolist would produce, A's profits will be 22, while B's will be 15.

If A and B cooperate, each produces one-half the monopoly output and receives a payoff of 20, as shown in the upper left box. However, at that position, known as the cooperative outcome, each firm can raise its profits by producing two-thirds of the monopoly output, provided that the other firm does not do the same.

Now suppose that A and B make their decisions noncooperatively. A reasons that whether B produces either one-half or two-thirds of the monopoly output, A's best output is two-thirds. B reasons similarly. In this case, they reach the noncooperative outcome, where each produces two-thirds of the monopoly output, and each makes less than it would if the two firms cooperated. In this example, the noncooperative outcome is a Nash equilibrium.

EXTENSIONS IN THEORY 11-1

The Prisoners' Dilemma

The game shown in Figure 11-3 is often known as a prisoners' dilemma game. This is the story that lies behind the name:

Two men, John and William, are arrested for jointly committing a crime and are interrogated separately. They know that if they both plead innocence, they will get only a light sentence, and if they both admit guilt they will both receive a medium sentence. Each is told, however, that if either protests innocence while the other admits guilt, the one who claims innocence will get a severe sentence while the other will be released with no sentence at all.

Here is the payoff matrix for that game:

		John's Plea	
		Innocent	Guilty
William's Plea	Innocent	J light sentence / W light sentence	J no sentence / W severe sentence
	Guilty	J severe sentence / W no sentence	J medium sentence / W medium sentence

John reasons as follows: William will plead either guilty or innocent. First assume that he pleads innocent. I get a light sentence if I also plead innocent but no sentence at all if I plead guilty, so guilty is my better plea. Now assume that he pleads guilty. I get a severe sentence if I plead innocent and a medium sentence if I plead guilty. So once again guilty is my preferred plea. William reasons in the same way and, as a result, they both plead guilty and get a medium sentence. Note, however, that if they had been able to communicate and coordinate their pleas, they could both have agreed to plead innocent and get off with a light sentence.

The prisoners' dilemma also arises in many situations of firm rivalry. Consider the case where two firms are making sealed bids on a contract. For simplicity, suppose that only two bids are permitted, either a high or a low price. The high price yields a profit of $10 million, whereas the low price yields a profit of $7 million. If the two firms put in the same price, they share the job, and each earns half the profits. If they give different bids, the firm submitting the lower bid gets the job and all the profits. You should have no trouble in drawing up the payoff matrix and determining the outcomes under noncooperative and cooperative behaviour. (See Study Exercises #5 at the end of the chapter for an example of this type.)

Types of Cooperative Behaviour

collusion An agreement among sellers to act jointly in their common interest, for example, by agreeing to raise prices. Collusion may be overt or covert, explicit or tacit.

When firms agree to cooperate in order to restrict output and raise prices, their behaviour is called **collusion**. Collusive behaviour may occur with or without an explicit agreement to collude. Where explicit agreement occurs, economists speak of *overt* or *covert collusion*, depending on whether the agreement is open or secret. Where no explicit agreement actually occurs, economists speak of *tacit collusion*. In this case, all firms behave cooperatively without an explicit agreement to do so. They merely understand that it is in their mutual interest to restrict output and to raise prices.

Explicit Collusion. The easiest way for firms to ensure that they will all maintain their joint-profit-maximizing output is to make an explicit agreement to do so. Such collusive agreements have occurred in the past, although they have been illegal among privately owned firms in Canada for a long time. When they are discovered today, they are rigorously prosecuted. We shall see, however, that such agreements are not illegal everywhere in the world, particularly when they are supported by national governments.

We saw in Chapter 10 that when a group of firms get together to act in this way, they create a *cartel*. Cartels show in stark form the basic conflict between cooperation and competition that we just discussed. Cooperation among cartel members allows them to restrict output and raise prices, thereby increasing the cartel members' profits. But it also presents each cartel member with the incentive to cheat. The larger the number of firms, the greater the temptation for any one of them to cheat. After all, cheating by one small firm may not be noticed because it will have a negligible effect on price. Conversely, a cartel made up of a small number of firms is more likely to persist because cheating by any one member is more difficult to conceal from the other members.

DeBeers is an example of a firm that has been able to assemble a cartel in the world's diamond industry. Through their own Central Selling Organization (CSO), DeBeers markets roughly 70 percent of the world's annual diamond production. With such influence over the market, they are able to manage the flow of output, in response to changes in world demand, to keep prices high. Another example of a cartel is the Association of Coffee Producing Countries, a collection of Central American countries that have attempted to restrict output in order to raise coffee prices in recent years.

For information on DeBeers and the diamond industry, see DeBeers' website: www.adiamondisforever.com.

But surely the most famous example of a cartel—and the one that has had the most dramatic effect on the world economy—is the Organization of Petroleum Exporting Countries (OPEC). OPEC's explicit cooperation is discussed in *Lessons from History 11-1*.

For more information on OPEC, check out their website: www.opec.org.

Tacit Collusion. Although collusive behaviour that affects prices is illegal, a small group of firms that recognize the influence that each has on the others may act without any explicit agreement to achieve the cooperative outcome. In such tacit agreements, the two forces that push toward cooperation and competition are still evident.

First, firms have a common interest in cooperating to maximize their joint profits at the cooperative solution. Second, each firm is interested in its own profits, and any one of them can usually increase its profits by behaving competitively.

Types of Competitive Behaviour

Although the most obvious way for a firm to violate the cooperative solution is to produce more than its share of the joint-profit-maximizing output, there are other ways in which rivalrous behaviour can occur.

Competition for Market Shares. Even if *joint* profits are maximized, there is the problem of market shares. How is the profit-maximizing level of sales to be divided among the colluding firms? Competition for market shares may upset the tacit agreement to hold to joint-profit-maximizing behaviour. Firms often compete for market shares through various forms of non-price competition, such as advertising and variations in the quality of their product. Such costly competition may reduce industry profits.

Covert Cheating. In an industry that has many differentiated products and in which sales are often by contract between buyers and sellers, covert rather than overt cheating may seem attractive. Secret discounts and rebates can allow a firm to increase its sales at the expense of its competitors while appearing to hold to the tacitly agreed price.

LESSONS FROM HISTORY 11-1

Explicit Cooperation in OPEC

The experience of the Organization of Petroleum Exporting Countries (OPEC) in the 1970s and 1980s illustrates the power of cooperative behaviour to create short-run profits, as well as the problems of trying to exercise long-run market power in an industry without substantial entry barriers.

OPEC did not attract worldwide attention until 1973, when its members voluntarily restricted their output by negotiating quotas among themselves. In that year, OPEC countries accounted for about 70 percent of the world's supply of crude oil. Although it was not a complete monopoly, the cartel came close to being one. By reducing output, the OPEC countries were able to drive up the world price of oil and to earn massive profits both for themselves and for non-OPEC producers, who obtained the high prices without having to limit their output. After several years of success, however, OPEC began to experience the typical problems of cartels.

Entry

Entry became a problem for the OPEC countries. The high price of oil encouraged the development of new supplies, and within a few years, new productive capacity was coming into use at a rapid rate in non-OPEC countries. The development of North Sea oil by the UK and the development of the Athabasca Tar Sands in Alberta, both in the late 1970s, are two examples of this new productive capacity.

Long-Run Adjustment of Demand

The short-run demand for oil proved to be highly inelastic. Over time, however, adaptations to reduce the demand for oil were made within the confines of existing technology. Homes and offices were insulated more efficiently, and smaller, more fuel-efficient cars became popular. This is an example of the distinction between the short-run and long-run demand for a commodity first introduced in Chapter 4.

Innovation further reduced the demand for oil in the very long run. Over time, technologies that were more efficient in their use of oil, as well as alternative energy sources, were developed. Had the oil prices stayed up longer than they did, major breakthroughs in solar and geothermal energy would surely have occurred.

This experience in both the long run and the very long run shows the price system at work, signaling the need for adaptation and providing the incentives for that adaptation. It also provides an illustration of Schumpeter's concept of creative destruction, which we first discussed in Chapter 10. To share in the profits generated by high energy prices, new technologies and new substitute products were developed, and these destroyed much of the market power of the original cartel.

Cheating

At first, there was little incentive for OPEC countries to violate quotas. Members found themselves with such undreamed-of increases in their incomes that they found it difficult to use all of their money productively. As the output of non-OPEC oil grew, however, OPEC's output had to be reduced to hold prices high. Furthermore, as the long-run adjustments in demand occurred, even larger output restrictions by OPEC were required to prop up the price of oil. Incomes in OPEC countries declined as a result.

Many OPEC countries had become used to their enormous incomes, and their attempts to maintain them in the face of falling output quotas brought to the surface the instabilities inherent in all cartels. In 1981, oil prices reached their peak of U.S. $35 per barrel. In real terms, this was about five times as high as the 1972 price, but production quotas were less than one-half of OPEC's capacity. Eager to increase their oil revenues, many individual OPEC members gave in to the pressure to cheat and produced in excess of their production quotas. In 1984, Saudi Arabia indicated that it would not tolerate further cheating by its partners and demanded

Very-Long-Run Competition.   As we first discussed in Chapter 10, very-long-run considerations may also be important. When technology and product characteristics change constantly, there may be advantages to behaving competitively. A firm that behaves competitively may be able to maintain a larger market share and earn larger profits than it would if it cooperated with the other firms in the industry, even though all the firms' joint profits are lower. In our world of constant change, a firm that thinks it can keep ahead of its rivals through innovation has an incentive to compete even if that

that others share equally in reducing their quotas yet further. However, agreement proved impossible. In December 1985, OPEC decided to eliminate production quotas and let each member make its own decisions about output.

After the Collapse

OPEC's collapse as an output-restricting cartel led to a major reduction in world oil prices. Early in 1986, the downward slide took the price to $20 per barrel, and it fell to $11 per barrel later in the year. Allowing for inflation, this was around the price that had prevailed just before OPEC introduced its output restrictions in 1973. Prices have been volatile since then, oscillating between about $10 per barrel, which is close to the perfectly competitive price, and $20 per barrel, which seems to be all that can be sustained under the modest output restrictions that can currently be obtained.

The Role of Politics

OPEC is also an excellent example of how politics affects economic outcomes. Especially during the 1990s, OPEC's inability to significantly restrict oil production has been largely a result of political frictions among the various OPEC members.

In OPEC's March 1999 meetings, for example, Iran was pushing for reductions in Saudi Arabia's oil production to compensate for Iraq's production increases. Iran argued that when Iraq's oil exports were prevented by a United Nations sanction (following the Persian Gulf War in 1990), Saudi Arabia received the lion's share of Iraq's production quota. Thus, in Iran's view, Iraq's subsequent increases in production should have been matched by a reduction in Saudia Arabia's. Saudia Arabia argued that their large share of OPEC production (roughly 30 percent) was justified on the grounds that it spent a lot of money in the Gulf War and invested considerably in production capacity when the war disrupted oil production.

Political frictions like these will not end anytime soon. Along with the basic economic incentives that individual OPEC members have to cheat on any output-restricting agreement, such political frictions only add to the already difficult task of forming and maintaining a cartel. Only time will tell if OPEC will be able to repeat their spectacular successes of the 1970s. By early in 2000, OPEC had succeeded in driving the world price of oil up to $30 per barrel. But will it last?

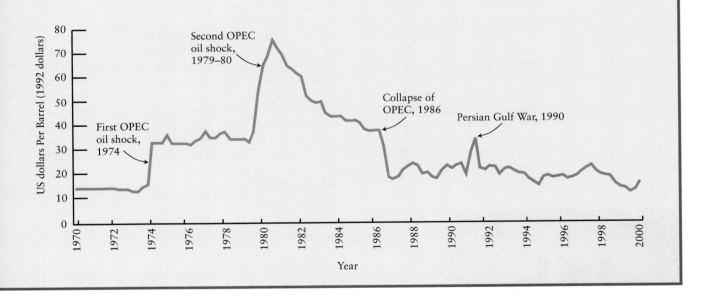

competition lowers the joint profits of the whole industry. Such competitive behaviour contributes to the long-run growth of living standards and may provide social benefits over time that outweigh any losses due to the restriction of output at any one point in time.

For these and other reasons, there are often strong incentives for oligopolistic firms to compete rather than to maintain the cooperative outcome, even when they understand the inherent risks to their joint profits.

The Importance of Entry Barriers

Suppose that firms in an oligopolistic industry succeed in raising prices above long-run average costs and earn substantial profits that are not completely eliminated by non-price competition. In the absence of significant entry barriers, new firms will enter the industry and erode the profits of existing firms, as they do in monopolistic competition. Natural barriers to entry were discussed in Chapter 10. They are an important part of the explanation of the persistence of profits in many oligopolistic industries.

Where such natural entry barriers do not exist, however, oligopolistic firms can earn profits in the long run only if they can *create* entry barriers. To the extent this is done, existing firms can move toward joint profit maximization without fear that new firms, attracted by the high profits, will enter the industry. We now discuss some types of *firm-created* entry barriers.

See Chapter 11 of www.pearsoned.ca/lipsey for an interesting discussion of how simple game theory can be used by managers: Hugh Courtney, "Games Managers Should Play," *World Economic Affairs*.

Brand Proliferation

By altering the characteristics of a differentiated product, it is possible to produce a vast array of variations on the general theme of that product. Think, for example, of automobiles with a little more or a little less acceleration, braking power, top speed, cornering ability, fuel efficiency, and so on, compared with existing models.

Although the multiplicity of existing brands is no doubt partly a response to consumers' tastes, it can have the effect of discouraging the entry of new firms. To see why, suppose that the product is the type for which there is a substantial amount of brand switching by consumers. In this case, the larger the number of brands sold by existing firms, the smaller the expected sales of a new entrant.

Suppose, for example, that an industry contains three large firms, each selling one brand of cigarettes, and say that 30 percent of all smokers change brands in a random fashion each year. If a new firm enters the industry, it can expect to pick up one-third of the smokers who change brands (a smoker who switches brands now has three *other* brands to choose between). The new firm would get 10 percent (one-third of 30 percent) of the total market the first year merely as a result of picking up its share of the random switchers, and it would keep increasing its share for some time thereafter. If, however, the existing three firms have five brands each, there would be 15 brands already available, and a new firm selling one new brand could expect to pick up only one-fifteenth of the brand switchers, giving it only 2 percent of the total market the first year, with smaller gains also in subsequent years. This is an extreme case, but it illustrates a general result.

The larger the number of differentiated products that are sold by existing oligopolists, the smaller the market share available to a new firm that is entering with a single new product. Brand proliferation therefore can be an effective entry barrier.

Many companies spend millions of dollars annually on lavish advertising campaigns. In addition to being informative, advertising can be an effective entry barrier.

Advertising

Advertising is one means by which existing firms can impose heavy costs on new entrants. Advertising, of course, serves purposes other than that of creating barriers to entry. Among them, it performs the useful function of informing buyers about their alternatives. Indeed, a new firm may find that advertising is essential, even when existing firms do not advertise at all, simply to call attention to its entry into an industry in which it is currently unknown.

Nonetheless, advertising can also operate as a potent entry barrier by increasing the costs of new entrants. Where heavy advertising has established strong brand images for existing products, a new firm may have to spend heavily on advertising to create its own brand images in consumers' minds. If the firm's sales are small, advertising costs *per unit* will be large, and price will have to be correspondingly high to cover those costs. Consider Nike, Reebok, and their competitors. They advertise not so much the quality of their athletic shoes as images that they wish consumers to associate with the shoes. The same is true for cosmetics, beer, cars, and many more consumer goods. The ads are lavishly produced and photographed. They constitute a formidable entry barrier for a new producer.

Figure 11-4 illustrates how heavy advertising can shift the cost curves of a firm with a low minimum efficient scale *(MES)* to make it one with a high *MES*. In essence, what happens is that a high *MES* of advertising is added to a low *MES* of production, with the result that the overall *MES* is raised.

A new entrant with small sales but large required advertising costs finds itself at a substantial cost disadvantage relative to its established rivals.

The combined use of brand proliferation and advertising as an entry barrier helps to explain one apparent paradox of everyday life—that one firm often sells multiple brands of the same product, which compete actively against one another as well as against the products of other firms. The soap and beer industries provide classic examples of this behaviour. Because all available scale economies can be realized by quite small plants, both industries have few natural barriers to entry. Both contain a few large firms, each of which produces an array of heavily advertised products. The numerous existing products make it harder for a new entrant to obtain a large market niche with a single new product. The heavy advertising, although directed against existing products, creates an entry barrier by increasing the average costs of a new product that seeks to gain the attention of consumers and to establish its own brand image.

Predatory Pricing

A firm will not enter a market if it expects continued losses after entry. One way in which an existing firm can create such an expectation is to cut prices below costs whenever entry occurs and to keep them there until the entrant goes bankrupt. The existing firm sacrifices profits while doing this, but it sends a discouraging message to potential future rivals, as well as to present ones. Even if this strategy is costly in terms of lost profits in the short run, it may pay for itself in the long run by creating *reputation effects* that deter the entry of new firms at other times or in other markets that the firm controls.

Predatory pricing is controversial. Some economists argue that pricing policies that appear to be predatory can be explained by other motives and that existing firms only hurt themselves when they engage

FIGURE 11-4 Advertising Cost as a Barrier to Entry

Large advertising costs can increase the minimum efficient scale *(MES)* of production and thereby increase entry barriers. The ATC_0 curve shows that the *MES* without advertising is at q_0. The curve *AAC* (for average advertising cost) shows that advertising cost per unit falls as output rises. Advertising increases average total cost to ATC_1, which is downward sloping over its entire range. The new *MES* is given by q_1. Advertising has given a scale advantage to large sellers and has thus created a barrier to entry.

in such practices instead of accommodating new entrants. Others argue that predatory pricing has been observed and that it is in the long-run interests of existing firms to punish the occasional new entrant even when it is costly to do so in the short run.

Canadian courts have taken the position that predatory pricing does indeed occur and a number of firms have been convicted of using it as a method of restricting entry.

Contestable Markets

We have been discussing the role played by entry barriers in determining the long-run characteristics of an oligopolistic industry. In general, we expect profits made by existing firms to lead new firms to enter the industry. Such entry will, in turn, reduce profits toward their competitive level. We now turn to a theory that emphasizes not the role of *actual* entry, but rather the role of *potential* entry in keeping industry profits near their competitive level.

The theory of *contestable markets* holds that markets do not have to contain many firms or experience *actual* entry for profits to be held near the competitive level. *Potential* entry can do the job just as well as actual entry, as long as (1) entry can be easily accomplished and (2) existing firms take potential entry into account when making price and output decisions.

The Theory of Contestable Markets

Entry is usually costly to the entering firm. It may have to build a plant, develop new versions of the industry's differentiated product, or advertise heavily to call attention to its product. These and many other initial expenses are often called *sunk costs of entry*. A sunk cost of entry is a cost that a firm must incur to enter the market and that *cannot be recovered if the firm subsequently exits*. For example, if an entering firm builds a product-specific factory that has no resale value, the new factory is a sunk cost of entry. However, the cost of a factory that is not product-specific and can be resold for an amount that is close to its original cost is not a sunk cost of entry.

contestable market
A market in which there are no sunk costs of entry or exit so that potential entry may hold profits of existing firms to low levels—zero in the case of perfect contestability.

A market in which new firms can enter and leave without incurring *any* sunk costs of entry is called a perfectly **contestable market.** But because all markets require at least some sunk costs of entry, contestability must be viewed along a continuum. The lower the sunk costs of entry, the more contestable the market.

In a contestable market, the existence of even temporary profits will attract entry. Firms will enter to gain a share of these profits and will then exit.

As an example, consider the market for air travel in the lucrative Toronto-Ottawa-Montreal triangle. This market would be quite contestable *if* counter and loading space were available to new entrants at the three cities' airline terminals. An airline that was not currently serving the cities in question could shift some of its existing planes to the market with small sunk costs of entry. Some training of personnel would be needed for them to become familiar with the route and the airport. This is a sunk cost of entry that could not be recovered if the cities in question were no longer to be served. However, most of the airline's costs are not sunk costs of entry. If it were to subsequently decide to leave a city, the rental of terminal space would stop and the airplanes and the ground equipment could be shifted to another location.

Sunk costs of entry constitute a barrier to entry, and the larger these are, the larger the profits of existing firms can be without attracting new entrants. The flip side of this argument is that firms operating in markets without large sunk costs of entry will not earn large profits. Strategic considerations will lead them to keep prices near the level that would just cover their total costs. They know that if they charge higher prices, firms will enter to capture the profits while they last and then exit.

Contestability, where it is possible, is a force that can limit the profits of existing oligopolists. Even if entry does not occur, the ease with which it can be accomplished may keep existing oligopolists from charging prices that would maximize their joint profits.

Contestability is just another example, in somewhat more refined form, of the key point that the possibility of entry is the major force preventing the exploitation of market power to restrict output and to raise prices. But, in practice, the degree of contestability is something to be measured rather than simply asserted. The higher the sunk costs of entry, the less contestable the market, and the higher the profits that existing firms can earn without attracting entry. Current evidence suggests that a high degree of contestability is quite rare in practice.

Oligopoly and the Economy

Oligopoly is found in many industries and in all advanced economies. It typically occurs in industries where both perfect and monopolistic competition are made impossible by the existence of major economies of scale. In such industries, there is simply not enough room for a large number of firms all operating at or near their minimum efficient scales.

Three questions are important for the evaluation of oligopoly. First, do oligopolistic firms respond to changes in market conditions very differently from the way perfectly competitive firms do? Second, in their short-run and long-run price-output behaviour, where do oligopolistic firms typically settle between the extreme outcomes of earning zero profits and earning the profits that would be available to a monopolist? Third, how much do oligopolists contribute to economic growth by encouraging innovative activity in the very long run? We consider each of these questions in turn.

Market Adjustment Under Oligopoly

We have seen that under perfect competition, prices are set by the impersonal forces of demand and supply, whereas firms in oligopolistic markets administer their prices. The market signaling system works slightly differently when prices are administered rather than being determined by the market. Changes in market conditions are signaled to the perfectly competitive firm by changes in the price of its product. Changes in market conditions for the oligopolist, however, are typically signaled by changes in the volume of sales at administered prices.

Increases in demand will cause the sales of oligopolistic firms to rise. Firms will then respond by increasing output, thereby increasing the quantities of society's resources that are allocated to producing that output. They will then decide whether or not to alter their administered prices.

The market system adjusts to changes in demands in roughly the same way under oligopoly as it does under perfect competition.

Profits Under Oligopoly

Some firms in some oligopolistic industries succeed in coming close to joint profit maximization in the short run. In other oligopolistic industries, firms compete so intensely among themselves that they come close to achieving competitive prices and outputs.

In the long run, those profits that do survive competitive behaviour among existing firms will tend to attract entry. These profits will persist only insofar as entry is restricted either by natural barriers, such as large minimum efficient scales for potential entrants, or by barriers created, and successfully defended, by the existing firms.

Very-Long-Run Competition

Once we allow for the effects of technological change, we need to ask which market structure is most conducive to the sorts of very-long-run changes that we discussed in Chapter 8. These are the driving force of the economic growth that has so greatly raised living standards over the past two centuries. They are intimately related to Schumpeter's concept of creative destruction, which we first encountered in our discussion of entry barriers in Chapter 10.

As we saw in Chapter 10, examples of creative destruction abound. In the nineteenth century, railways began to compete with wagons and barges for the carriage of freight. In the twentieth century, trucks operating on newly constructed highways began competing with trains. During the 1950s and 1960s, airplanes began to compete seriously with both trucks and trains. In recent years, fax machines and e-mail have eliminated the monopoly of the postal service in delivering hard-copy (printed) communications.

An important defence of oligopoly relates to this process of creative destruction. Some economists have adopted Schumpeter's concept of creative destruction to develop theories in which intermediate market structures, such as oligopoly, lead to more innovation than would occur in either perfect competition or monopoly. They argue that the oligopolist faces strong competition from existing rivals and cannot afford the more relaxed life of the monopolist. At the same time, however, oligopolistic firms expect to keep a good share of the profits that they earn from their innovative activity and thus have considerable incentive to innovate.

Everyday observation provides support for this view. Leading North American firms that operate in highly concentrated industries, such as Abitibi-Consolidated, Du Pont, Kodak, General Electric, Newbridge, Nortel, and Xerox, have been highly innovative over many years.

This observation is not meant to suggest that *only* oligopolistic industries are innovative. Much innovation is also done by very small new firms; and if today's new firms are successful in their innovation, they may become tomorrow's corporate giants. For example, Hewlett-Packard, Microsoft, and Intel, which are enormous firms today, barely existed two decades ago; their rise from new start-up firms to corporate giants reflects their powers of innovation.

Oligopoly is an important market structure in modern economies because there are many industries in which the minimum efficient scale is simply too large to support many competing firms. The challenge to public policy is to keep oligopolists competing, rather than colluding, and using their competitive energies to improve products and to reduce costs, rather than merely to erect entry barriers.

S U M M A R Y

The Structure of the Canadian Economy

- Most industries in the Canadian economy lie between the two extremes of monopoly and perfect competition. Within this spectrum of market structure we can divide Canadian industries into two broad groups—those with a large number of relatively small firms and those with a small number of relatively large firms. Such intermediate market structures are called imperfectly competitive.
- When measuring whether an industry has power concentrated in the hands of only a few firms or dispersed over many, it is not sufficient to count the number of firms. Instead, economists consider the concentration ratio, which shows the fraction of total market sales controlled by the largest group of sellers.
- One important problem associated with using concentration ratios is to define the market with reasonable accuracy. Since many goods produced in Canada compete with foreign-produced goods, the national concentration ratios overstate the degree of industrial concentration.

Imperfectly Competitive Market Structures

- Most firms operating in imperfectly competitive market structures sell differentiated products whose characteristics they choose themselves. They also administer their prices, do not change their prices as often as prices change in perfectly competitive markets, engage in non-price competition, and sometimes take actions designed to prevent the entry of new firms.

Monopolistic Competition

- Monopolistic competition is a market structure that has the same characteristics as perfect competition except that the many firms each sell a differentiated product rather than all selling a single homogeneous product. Firms face negatively sloped demand curves and may earn profits in the short run.
- As in a perfectly competitive industry, the long run in monopolistic competition sees new firms enter the industry whenever profits can be made. Long-run equilibrium in the industry requires that each firm earn zero profits. But unlike perfect competition, the long-run equilibrium in monopolistic competition has each firm producing less than its minimum-cost level of output. This is the excess-capacity theorem associated with monopolistic competition.
- Excess capacity in the long-run equilibrium of monopolistic competition does not necessarily result in inefficiency. Even though each firm produces at a cost that is higher than the minimum attainable cost, the resulting product choice is valued by consumers and so may be worth the extra cost.

Oligopoly

- Oligopolies are dominated by a few large firms that usually sell differentiated products and have significant market power. They can maximize their joint profits if they cooperate to produce the monopoly output. By acting individually, each firm has an incentive to depart from this cooperative outcome.
- Strategic behaviour, in which each firm chooses its best strategy in light of other firms' possible decisions, may lead to a Nash equilibrium. Economists use game theory to study strategic behaviour.
- Tacit cooperation is possible but often breaks down as firms struggle for market share, indulge in non-price competition, and seek advantages through the introduction of new technology.
- Oligopolistic industries will exhibit profits in the long run only if there are significant barriers to entry. Natural barriers relate to the economies of scale in production, finance and marketing, and also to large entry costs. Firm-created barriers can be created by proliferation of competing brands, heavy brand-image advertising, and the threat of predatory pricing when new entry occurs.

- The theory of contestable markets holds that *potential* entry may be sufficient to hold profits down and emphasizes the importance of sunk costs as an entry barrier.
- In the presence of major scale economies, oligopoly may be the best of the feasible alternative market structures.

Evaluation of oligopoly depends on how much inter-firm competition (a) drives the firms away from the co-operative, profit-maximizing solution and (b) leads to innovations in the very long run.

KEY CONCEPTS

Concentration ratios
Administered prices
Product differentiation
Monopolistic competition
The excess-capacity theorem

Oligopoly
Strategic behaviour
Cooperative and noncooperative out-
  comes
Game theory
Nash equilibrium

Explicit and tacit collusion
Natural and firm-created entry barriers
Contestable markets
Sunk costs of entry
The social benefits of oligopoly in the
  very long run

STUDY EXERCISES

1. The following table provides annual sales for the four largest firms in four hypothetical industries in Canada. Also provided are total Canadian and total world sales for the industry. (All figures are in millions of dollars.)

	Firm 1	Firm 2	Firm 3	Firm 4	Total Sales —Canada	Total Sales —World
Forestry products	185	167	98	47	550	1368
Chemicals	27	24	9	4	172	2452
Women's clothing	6	5	4	2	94	3688
Pharmaceuticals	44	37	22	19	297	2135

a. Suppose that Canada does not trade internationally any of the goods produced in these industries. Compute the 4-firm Canadian concentration ratio for each industry.

b. Rank the industries in order from the most concentrated to the least concentrated.

c. Now suppose that goods in these industries are freely traded around the world. Compute a new concentration ratio for each industry based on world sales.

2. The following figure shows the revenue and cost curves for a typical monopolistically competitive firm in the short run.

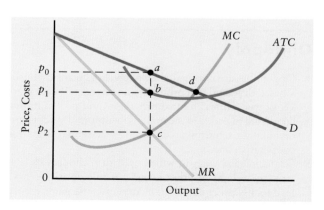

a. Note that the firm's demand curve is shown to be quite flat. Explain which assumption of monopolistic competition suggests a relatively elastic demand curve for each firm.

b. What is the profit-maximizing level of output for the firm?

c. At the profit-maximizing level of output, are profits positive or negative? What area in the diagram represents the firm's profits?

d. Will firms enter or exit the industry? Explain.

3. The diagram below shows a typical monopolistically competitive firm when the industry is in long-run equilibrium.

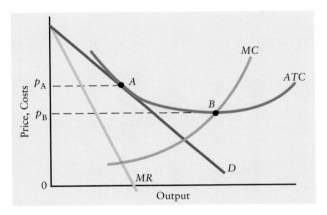

a. Explain why free entry and exit implies that the long-run equilibrium is at point A.

b. What is the significance of point B and price p_B?

c. Explain the sense in which long-run equilibrium in monopolistic competition is less efficient than in perfect competition.

4. In the text we argued that a key difference between monopolistic competition and oligopoly is that in the former firms do not behave *strategically* whereas in the latter they do. For each of the goods or services listed below, state whether the industries are likely to be best described by monopolistic competition or oligopoly. Explain your reasoning.

a. Car repair
b. Haircuts
c. Dry cleaning
d. Soft drinks
e. Breakfast cereals
f. Restaurant meals

5. The table below is the "payoff matrix" for a simple two-firm game. Firms A and B are bidding on a government contract, and each firm's bid is not known by the other firm. Each firm can bid either $10 000 or $5000. The cost of completing the project for each firm is $4000. The low-bid firm will win the contract at its stated price; the high-bid firm will get nothing. If the two bids are equal, the two firms will split the price and costs evenly. The payoffs for each firm under each situation are shown in the matrix.

	A bids $10 000	A bids $5000
B bids $10 000	Firms share the contract	A wins the contract
	Payoff to A = $3000	Payoff to A = $1000
	Payoff to B = $3000	Payoff to B = $0
B bids $5000	B wins the contract	Firms share the contract
	Payoff to A = $0	Payoff to A = $500
	Payoff to B = $1000	Payoff to B = $500

a. Recall from the text that a Nash equilibrium is an outcome in which each player is maximizing their own payoff *given the actions of the other players.* Is there a Nash equilibrium in this game?

b. Is there more than one Nash equilibrium? Explain.

c. If the two firms could cooperate, what outcome would you predict in this game? Explain.

DISCUSSION QUESTIONS

1. It is sometimes said that there are more drugstores and gasoline stations than are needed. In what sense might this be correct? Does the consumer gain anything from this plethora of retail outlets?

2. Do you think any of the following industries might be monopolistically competitive? Why or why not?

a. Textbook publishing (more than 12 elementary economics textbooks are in use on campuses in Canada this year)
b. Postsecondary education
c. Cigarette manufacturing
d. Restaurant operation
e. Automobile retailing

3. "The periods following each of the major OPEC price shocks proved to the world that there were many available substitutes for gasoline, among them bicycles, car pools, moving closer to work, cable TV, and Japanese cars." Discuss how each of these may be a substitute for gasoline.

4. Evidence suggests that the profits earned by all the firms in many oligopolistic industries are less than the profits that would be earned if the industry were monopolized. What are some reasons why this might be so?

5. What is the key difference between monopolistic competition and oligopoly? Assume that you are in an industry that is monopolistically competitive. What actual steps might you take to transform your industry into a more oligopolistic form?

6. Explain why an unregulated taxi industry is likely to be more contestable than an unregulated restaurant industry. What is the implication for prices and profits in the two industries?

Economic Efficiency and Public Policy

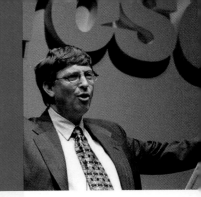

Monopoly has long been regarded with suspicion. In *The Wealth of Nations,* Adam Smith (1723–1790) developed a stinging attack on monopolists. Since then, most economists have criticized monopoly and advocated competition.

In this chapter, we first consider what economic theory has to say about the relevant advantages of the two polar market structures of monopoly and perfect competition. This discussion requires an understanding of *economic efficiency*. We then examine how economic regulations and competition policy are designed to promote economic efficiency.

Economic Efficiency

Economic efficiency requires that resources not be wasted. This requires that workers, machines, and land are not lying idle. In other words, economic efficiency requires that factors of production are fully employed. However, full employment of resources is not enough to prevent the waste of resources. Even when resources are fully employed, they may be used inefficiently. Here are three examples of inefficiency in the use of fully employed resources.

1. If firms do not use the least-cost method of producing their chosen outputs, they are being inefficient. For example, a firm that produces 30 000 pairs of shoes at a resource cost of $400 000 when it could have been done at a cost of only $350 000 is using resources inefficiently. The lower-cost method would allow $50 000 worth of resources to be transferred to other productive uses.

2. If the marginal cost of production is not the same for every firm in an industry, the industry is being inefficient. For example, if the cost of producing the last ton of steel is higher for some firms than for others, the industry's overall cost of producing steel is

higher than necessary. The same amount of steel could be produced at lower total cost if the total output were distributed differently among the various producers.

3. If too much of one product and too little of another product are produced, resources are being used inefficiently. To take an extreme example, suppose that so many shoes are produced that every consumer has all the shoes he or she could possibly want and thus places a zero value on obtaining an additional pair of shoes. Further suppose that fewer coats are produced relative to demand, so that each consumer places a positive value on obtaining an additional coat. In these circumstances, each consumer can be made better off if resources are reallocated from shoe production, where the last shoe produced has a low value in the eyes of each consumer, to coat production, where one more coat produced would have a higher value to each consumer.

These three examples illustrate inefficiency in the use of resources. But the *type* of inefficiency is different in each case. The first example considers the cost for a single firm producing some level of output. The second example is closely related, but the focus is on the total cost for all of the firms in an industry. The third example relates to the level of output of one product compared to another.

Productive and Allocative Efficiency

These examples suggest that we must refine our ideas about the waste of resources beyond the simple notion of ensuring that all resources are employed.

Productive Efficiency

Productive efficiency has two aspects, one concerning production within each firm and one concerning the allocation of production among the firms in an industry.

productive efficiency for the firm   When the firm chooses among all available technologies and produces a given level of output at the lowest possible cost.

Productive efficiency for the firm requires that the firm produce any given level of output at the lowest possible cost. In the short run, with only one variable factor, the choice of technique is not a problem for the firm. It merely uses enough of the variable factor to produce the desired level of output. In the long run, however, more than one method of production is available. Productive efficiency requires that the firm use the least costly of the available methods of producing any given output—that is, firms are located on, rather than above, their long-run average cost curves.

In Chapter 8, we studied the condition for productive efficiency within the firm:

Productive efficiency for the firm requires the firm to produce its given output by combining factors of production so that the ratios of the marginal products of each pair of factors equals the ratio of their prices.

If this were not so, the firm could reduce the resource costs of producing its given output by altering the quantities of each input it uses.

productive efficiency for the industry   When the industry is producing a given level of output at the lowest possible cost. This requires that marginal cost be equated across all firms in the industry.

Any firm that is not being productively efficient is producing at a higher cost than is necessary and thus will have lower profits. It follows that any profit-maximizing firm will seek to be productively efficient no matter which market structure it operates within—perfect competition, monopoly, oligopoly, or monopolistic competition.

Productive efficiency for the industry requires that the industry's total output is allocated among its individual firms in such a way that the total cost is minimized. If an industry is productively *inefficient,* it is possible to reduce the industry's total cost of producing any given output by reallocating production among the industry's firms.

Productive efficiency at the level of the industry requires that the marginal cost of production must be the same for each firm.

To see why marginal costs must be equated across firms, consider a simple example that is illustrated in Figure 12-1. Aslan Shoe Company has a marginal cost of $70 for the last shoe of some standard type it produces. Digory Shoes Inc. has a marginal cost of only $50 for the same type of shoe. If Aslan were to produce one fewer pair of shoes and Digory were to produce one more pair, total shoe production would be unchanged. Total industry costs, however, would be lower by $20.

Clearly, this cost saving can go on as long as the two firms have different marginal costs. However, as Aslan produces more shoes, its marginal cost rises, and as Digory produces fewer shoes, its marginal cost falls. Once marginal cost is equated across the two firms, there are no further cost savings to be obtained by reallocating production.

Figure 12-2 shows a production possibility curve of the sort that we first saw in Chapter 1. Productive *inefficiency* implies that the economy is at some point *inside* the production possibility curve. In such a situation, it is possible to produce more of some goods without producing less of others.

Productive efficiency implies being on, rather than inside, the economy's production possibility curve.

Allocative Efficiency

Allocative efficiency concerns the relative quantities of the products to be produced. It concerns the choice between alternative points on the production possibilities curve such as points *b, c,* and *d* in Figure 12-2. When the combination of goods produced is allocatively efficient, economists say that the economy is *Pareto efficient*, in honour of

allocative efficiency
A situation in which no reorganization of production or consumption could make anybody better off without making at least one person worse off.

FIGURE 12-1   Productive Efficiency for the Industry

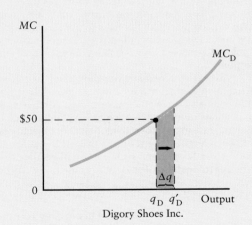

Productive efficiency for the industry requires that marginal costs be equated for all firms. At the initial levels of output, q_A and q_D, marginal costs are $70 for Aslan and $50 for Digory. If Digory increases output by Δq to q'_D and Aslan reduces output by the same amount, Δq, to q'_A, total output is unchanged. But total industry costs are lower by an amount equal to Aslan's shaded area minus Digory's shaded area. When marginal costs are equalized, no further reallocation of output can reduce costs—product efficiency will have been achieved.

FIGURE 12-2 Productive and Allocative Efficiency

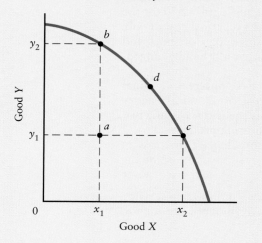

Any point on the production possibility curve is productively efficient; not all points on this curve are allocatively efficient. The curve shows all combinations of two goods X and Y that can be produced when the economy's resources are fully employed and being used with productive efficiency.

Any point inside the curve, such as *a*, is productively inefficient. If the inefficiency exists in industry X, then either some producer of X is productively inefficient or industry X as a whole is productively inefficient. In either case, it is possible to increase total production of X without using more resources, and thus without reducing the output of Y. This would take the economy from point *a* to point *c*. Similarly, if the inefficiency exists in industry Y, production of Y could be increased, moving the economy from point *a* to point *b*.

Allocative efficiency requires being at the most efficient point on the production possibility curve. Assessing allocative efficiency requires comparing various points on the curve, such as *b*, *c*, and *d*, and comparing marginal cost with price for each good. Allocative efficiency requires that *MC* = *p* for *each* good. Usually only one such point will be allocatively efficient (though all of them are productively efficient).

the nineteenth century Italian economist Vilfredo Pareto (1843–1923) who developed this concept of efficiency.

From an allocative point of view, resources are said to be used *inefficiently* when using them to produce a different bundle of goods makes it possible for at least one person to be better off while making no other person worse off. Conversely, resources are said to be used *efficiently* when it is impossible to produce a different bundle of goods that makes one person better off without making at least one other person worse off.

How do we find the efficient point on the production possibility curve? For example, how many shoes, dresses, and hats should be produced to achieve allocative efficiency? The answer is as follows:

The economy is allocatively efficient when, for each good produced, its marginal cost of production is equal to its price.

To understand the reasoning behind this answer, we need to recall a point that was established in our discussion of consumer surplus in Chapter 6. The price of any product indicates the value that consumers place on the last unit consumed of that product. Faced with the market price of some product, the consumer goes on buying units until the last one is valued exactly at its price. Consumer surplus arises because the consumer would be willing to pay more than the market price for all but the last unit that is bought. On the last unit bought (the marginal unit), however, the consumer only "breaks even" because the valuation placed on it is just equal to its price.

Now let us return to our shoe example. Suppose that shoes sell for $60 per pair but the marginal cost is $70. If one fewer pair of shoes were produced, the value that all households would place on the pair of shoes not produced would be $60. Using the concept of opportunity cost, however, we see that the resources that would have been used to produce that last pair of shoes could instead produce another good (say, a coat) valued at $70. If society can give up something that its members value at $60 and get in return something that its members value at $70, the original allocation of resources is inefficient. Someone can be made better off, and no one need be worse off.

This is easy to understand when the same consumer gives up the shoes and gets the coat, but the concept applies even when different consumers are involved. In this case, the market value of the gains to the household that gets the coat exceeds the market value of the loss to the household that gives up the shoes. The gaining household *could afford* to compensate the losing household and still come out ahead.

Suppose next that shoe production is cut back until the price of a pair of shoes rises from $60 to $65, while its marginal cost falls from $70 to $65. Efficiency is achieved in shoe production because $p = MC = \$65$. Now if one fewer pair of shoes were produced, $65 worth of shoes would be sacrificed, while at most, $65 worth of other products could be produced with the freed resources.

In this situation, it is not possible to change the allocation of resources to shoe production to make someone better off without making someone else worse off. If one household were to sacrifice one pair of shoes, it would give up goods worth $65 and would then have to obtain for itself all of the new production of the alternative commodity produced just to break even. It cannot gain without making another household worse off. The same argument can be repeated for every product, and it leads to the following conclusion:

The allocation of resources is efficient when each product's price equals its marginal cost of production.

There is one final point to make about allocative efficiency. Whereas an individual firm or an individual industry may be *productively efficient,* it does not make sense to say that a given firm or industry is *allocatively efficient.* Allocative efficiency is a property of the overall economy, concerning the relative outputs of its various industries, and it is achieved when price equals marginal cost in *all* industries simultaneously. Thus, if we were to observe price greater than marginal cost in an individual industry, we would know that the economy is not allocatively efficient because society as a whole would be made better off by producing more of that good and less of other goods. But if we were to see price equal to marginal cost in that one industry, we must still check *all* other industries before we know whether the economy is allocatively efficient.

Efficiency and Market Structure

We now know that for productive efficiency, marginal cost should be the same for all firms in any one industry, and that for allocative efficiency, marginal cost should be equal to price in each industry. Do the market structures that we have studied in earlier chapters lead to productive and allocative efficiency?

Perfect Competition

Productive Efficiency.   We saw in Chapter 9 that in the long run under perfect competition, each firm produces at the lowest point on its long-run average cost curve. Therefore, no one firm could reduce its costs by altering its own production. Every firm in perfect competition is therefore productively efficient.

We also know that in perfect competition, all firms in an industry face the same price of their product and they equate marginal cost to that price. It follows immediately that marginal cost will be the same for all firms. (Suppose, for example, that Aslan and Digory faced the same market price in Figure 12-1. Aslan would produce where $MC_A = p$ and Digory would produce where $MC_D = p$. It follows then that $MC_A = MC_D$.) Thus, in perfectly competitive industries, the industry as a whole is productively efficient.

Allocative Efficiency.   We have already seen that perfectly competitive firms maximize their profits by equating marginal cost to price. Thus, when perfect competition is the market structure for the whole economy, price is equal to marginal cost in each line of production, resulting in allocative efficiency.

Monopoly

Productive Efficiency. Monopolists have an incentive to be productively efficient because their profits will be maximized when they adopt the lowest-cost production method. Hence, profit-maximizing monopolists will operate on their *LRAC* curves.

Allocative Efficiency. Although a monopolist will be productively efficient, it will choose a level of output that is too low to achieve allocative efficiency. This result follows from what we saw in Chapter 10—that the monopolist chooses an output at which the price charged is *greater than* marginal cost. Such a choice violates the conditions for allocative efficiency because the amount that consumers pay for the last unit of output exceeds the opportunity cost of producing it.

Consumers would be prepared to buy additional units for an amount that is greater than the cost of producing these units. Some consumers could be made better off, and none need be made worse off, by shifting extra resources into production of the monopolized product, thus increasing the output of the product. From this follows the classic efficiency-based preference for competition over monopoly:

Monopoly creates allocative inefficiency because the monopolist's price always exceeds its marginal cost.

This result has important policy implications for economists and for policymakers, as we shall see later in this chapter.

Other Market Structures

Note that the result just stated extends beyond the case of a simple monopoly. Whenever a firm has any market power, in the sense that it faces a negatively sloped demand curve, its marginal revenue will be less than its price. Thus, when it equates marginal cost to marginal revenue, as all profit-maximizing firms do, marginal cost will also be less than price. This inequality implies allocative inefficiency. Thus, oligopoly and monopolistic competition are also allocatively inefficient.

Oligopoly is an important market structure in today's economy because in many industries the minimum efficient scale is simply too high to support a large number of competing firms. Although oligopoly does not achieve the conditions for allocative efficiency, it may nevertheless produce more satisfactory results than monopoly. We observed one reason why oligopoly may be preferable to monopoly in Chapter 11: Competition among oligopolists encourages very-long-run adaptations that result in both new products and cost-reducing methods of producing old ones.

An important defence of oligopoly as an acceptable market structure is that it may be the best of the available alternatives when minimum efficient scale is large. As we observed at the end of Chapter 11, the challenge to public policy is to keep oligopolists competing and using their competitive energies to improve products and to reduce costs rather than to restrict interfirm competition and to erect entry barriers. As we shall see later in this chapter, much public policy has just this purpose. What economic policymakers call *monopolistic practices* include not only output restrictions operated by firms with complete monopoly power but also anticompetitive behaviour among firms that are operating in oligopolistic industries.

Allocative Efficiency and Total Surplus

By using the concepts of price and marginal cost, we have established the basic points of productive and allocative efficiency. A different way of thinking about allocative efficiency—though completely consistent with the first approach—is to use the concepts of consumer and producer surplus.

Consumer and Producer Surplus

Recall from Chapter 6 that consumer surplus is the difference between the total value that consumers place on all the units consumed of some product and the payment that they actually make for the purchase of that product. Consumer surplus is shown once again in Figure 12-3.

Producer surplus is analogous to consumer surplus. It occurs because all units of each firm's output are sold at the same market price whereas, given an upward-sloping *MC* curve, each unit except the last is produced at a marginal cost that is less than the market price.

Producer surplus is defined as the price that producers receive for a product minus the lowest price that they would be prepared to accept for it (which is equal to the marginal cost). It is thus the difference between price and marginal cost. Since in perfect competition the industry supply curve is simply the horizontal sum of all firms' *MC* curves, producer surplus in a perfectly competitive market is the area above the supply curve and below the price line, as shown in Figure 12-3.

producer surplus
The difference between the amount that producers receive for a unit sold of a commodity and the marginal cost of producing that unit.

The Allocative Efficiency of Perfect Competition Revisited

Using the concepts of consumer and producer surplus, we can restate the condition for allocative efficiency.

Allocative efficiency occurs where the sum of consumer and producer surplus is maximized.

The allocatively efficient output occurs under perfect competition where the demand curve intersects the supply curve—that is, the point of equilibrium in a competitive market. This is shown in Figure 12-4. For any output that is less than the competitive output, the demand curve lies above the supply curve; thus the value that consumers place on the last unit of production exceeds its marginal cost of production. Suppose that the current output of shoes is such that consumers value at $70 an additional pair of shoes that adds $60 to costs. If it is sold at any price between $60 and $70, both producers and consumers gain; $10 of surplus will be divided between the two groups. In contrast, the last unit produced and sold in a competitive equilibrium adds nothing to either

FIGURE 12-3   Consumer Surplus and Producer Surplus

Consumer surplus is the area under the demand curve and above the market price line. Producer surplus is the area above the supply curve and below the market price line. The total value that consumers place on q_0 of the commodity is given by the sum of the three shaded areas. The amount they pay is the rectangle p_0q_0. The difference, shown as the dark blue shaded area is consumer surplus.

The receipts to producers from the sale of q_0 units are also p_0q_0. The area under the supply curve, the red shaded area, is the minimum amount producers require to supply the output. The difference, shown as the light blue shaded area, is producer surplus.

FIGURE 12-4   The Allocative Efficiency
of Perfect Competition

Competitive equilibrium is allocatively efficient because it maximizes the sum of consumer and producer surplus. The competitive equilibrium occurs at the price-output combination of p_0 and q_0. At this equilibrium, consumer surplus is the dark shaded area above the price line, while producer surplus is the light shaded area below the price line.

For any output that is less than q_0, the sum of the two surpluses is less than at q_0. For example, reducing the output to q_1 but keeping price at p_0 lowers consumer surplus by area 1 and lowers producer surplus by area 2.

For any output that is greater than q_0, the sum of the surpluses is also less than at q_0. For example, if producers are forced to produce output q_2 and to sell it to consumers, who are in turn forced to buy it at price p_0, producer surplus is reduced by area 3 while the amount of consumer surplus is reduced by area 4.

Practise with Study Guide Chapter 12, Exercise 4.

consumer or producer surplus because consumers value it at exactly its market price, and it adds the full amount of the market price to producers' costs.

If production were pushed beyond the competitive equilibrium, the sum of the two surpluses would fall. Suppose, for example, that firms were forced to produce and sell further units of output at the competitive market price and that consumers were forced to buy these extra units at that price. (Note that neither group would do so voluntarily.) Firms would lose producer surplus on those extra units because their marginal costs of producing the extra output would be above the price that they received for it. Purchasers would lose consumer surplus because the valuation that they placed on these extra units, as shown by the height of the demand curve, would be less than the price that they would have to pay.

The sum of producer and consumer surplus is maximized only at the perfectly competitive level of output. This is the only level of output that is allocatively efficient.

The Allocative Inefficiency of Monopoly Revisited

We have just seen in Figure 12-4 that the output in perfectly competitive equilibrium maximizes the sum of consumer and producer surplus. It follows that the lower monopoly output must result in a smaller total of consumer and producer surplus.

The monopoly equilibrium is not the outcome of a voluntary agreement between the one producer and the many consumers. Instead, it is imposed by the monopolist by virtue of the power it has over the market. When the monopolist chooses an output below the competitive level, market price is higher than it would be under perfect competition. As a result, consumer surplus is diminished, and producer surplus is increased. In this way, the monopolist gains at the expense of consumers. This is not the whole story, however.

When output is below the competitive level, there is always a *net loss* of total surplus: More surplus is lost by consumers than is gained by the monopolist. Some surplus is lost because output between the monopolistic and the competitive levels is not produced. This loss of surplus is called the *deadweight loss of monopoly*. It is illustrated in Figure 12-5.

It follows that there is a conflict between the private interest of the monopolist and the public interest of all the nation's consumers. This creates grounds for government intervention to prevent the formation of monopolies or at least to control their behaviour.

Allocative Efficiency and Market Failure

We have seen that perfect competition is allocatively efficient and that monopoly, in general, is not. Most of the remainder of the chapter presents ways in which public policy has attempted to deal with problems raised by monopoly. Before we go on, however, it is important to reemphasize that perfect competition is a theoretical ideal that exists in a small number of industries, is at best only approximated in many others, and is not even closely resembled in most. Hence, to say that perfect competition is allocatively efficient is not to say that real-world market economies are ever allocatively efficient.

In Chapter 16, we discuss the most important ways (other than monopoly) that market economies may fail to produce efficient outcomes. In Chapters 17 and 18, we discuss and evaluate the most important public policies that have been used to try to correct for these *market failures*. The most important problems arise when market transactions—production and consumption—impose costs or confer benefits on economic agents who are not involved in the transaction. Cases like these, which are called *externalities* because they involve economic effects that are external to the transaction, generally raise the possibility that market outcomes will be allocatively inefficient.

A simple example illustrates the problem. We know that markets for most agricultural commodities are highly competitive, with many relatively small producers who are unable to affect the price of the goods that they are producing. At the same time, the technology of agricultural production involves the extensive use of fertilizers that pollute nearby streams and rivers. This pollution in turn imposes costs on downstream fisheries and on households downstream who use the water for drinking and cleaning. Because these costs are not taken into account in the market for the agricultural products, they will be external to transactions in those markets. Generally, when production of a good or service causes pollution, the quantity produced in a perfectly competitive industry will exceed the efficient amount.

FIGURE 12-5   The Allocative Inefficiency of Monopoly

Monopoly is allocatively inefficient because it produces less than the competitive output and thus does not maximize the sum of consumer and producer surplus. If this market were perfectly competitive, price would be p_0, output would be q_0, and consumer surplus would be the sum of areas 1, 5, and 6. When the industry is monopolized, price rises to p_m and consumer surplus falls to area 5. Consumers lose area 1 because that output is not produced; they lose area 6 because the price rise has transferred it to the monopolist.

Producer surplus in a competitive equilibrium would be the sum of areas 7 and 2. When the market is monopolized and price rises to p_m, the surplus area 2 is lost because the output is not produced. However, the monopolist gains area 6 from consumers (6 is known to be greater than 2 because p_m maximizes profits).

Whereas area 6 is surplus that is transferred from consumers to producers by the price rise, areas 1 and 2 are lost altogether. They represent the deadweight loss resulting from monopoly and account for its allocative inefficiency.

One of the most important issues in public policy is whether, and under what circumstances, government action can increase the allocative efficiency of market outcomes.

As we will see later in this book, there are many circumstances in which there is room to increase the efficiency of market outcomes, but there are also many cases in which the cure is worse than the disease. In the remainder of this chapter we examine economic regulation and competition policy, both of which are designed to promote economic efficiency.

Economic Regulation to Promote Efficiency

To learn about the Canadian Radio-television and Telecommunications Commission (CRTC), see their website: www.crtc.gc.ca.

Monopolies, cartels, and price-fixing agreements among oligopolists, whether explicit or tacit, have met with public suspicion and official hostility for over a century. These and other noncompetitive practices are collectively referred to as *monopoly practices.* The laws and other instruments that are used to encourage competition and discourage monopoly practices make up *competition policy.* By and large, Canadian competition policy has sought to create more competitive market structures where possible, to discourage monopolistic practices, and to encourage competitive behaviour where competitive market structures cannot be established.

Federal, provincial, and local governments also employ *economic regulations,* which prescribe the rules under which firms can do business and in some cases determine the prices that businesses can charge for their output. Electric power, local telephone, and cable TV are examples of services that are subject to this kind of regulation.

The quest for allocative efficiency provides rationales both for competition policy and for economic regulation. Competition policy is used to promote allocative efficiency by increasing competition in the marketplace. Where effective competition is not possible (as in the case of a natural monopoly, such as an electric power company), public ownership or economic regulation of privately owned firms can be used as a substitute for competition. Consumers can then be protected from the high prices and reduced output that result from the use of monopoly power.[1]

In the remainder of this chapter, we look at a variety of ways in which policy-makers have chosen to intervene in the workings of the market economy using economic regulation and competition policy.

Regulation of Natural Monopolies

natural monopoly
An industry characterized by economies of scale sufficiently large that one firm can most efficiently supply the entire market demand.

The clearest case for public intervention arises with what is called a **natural monopoly**—an industry in which scale effects are so dominant that there is room for *at most* one firm to operate at the minimum efficient scale. (Indeed, scale effects could be so important that even a single firm could satisfy the entire market demand before reaching its minimum efficient scale.) In the past, there have been many natural monopolies. Today, they are found mainly in public utilities, such as electricity transmission, cable television, and local telephone service.

crown corporations
In Canada, business concerns owned by the federal or a provincial government.

One response to natural monopoly is for government to assume ownership of the single firm. In Canada, such government-owned firms are called **crown corporations.** In these cases, the government appoints managers and directors who are supposed to set prices in the national interest. Another response to the problem of natural monopoly is to allow private ownership but to *regulate* the monopolist's behaviour. In Canada, both government ownership (e.g., Canada Post and the provincial hydro authorities) and regulation (e.g., cable television and local telephone) are used actively. In the United States, with a few notable exceptions, regulation has been the preferred alternative.

Whether the government owns or merely regulates natural monopolies, the industry's pricing policy is determined by the government. The industry is typically required to fol-

---

[1] A second kind of regulation involves the legislated rules that require firms to consider the environmental and other consequences of their behaviour. Environmental regulation is discussed in Chapter 17.

low some pricing policy that conflicts with the goal of profit max-imization. We will see that such government intervention must deal with problems that arise in the short run, the long run, and the very long run.

Short-Run Price and Output

There are three general types of pricing policies for regulated nat-ural monopolies: *marginal-cost pricing, two-part tariffs,* and *av-erage-cost pricing.* We discuss each in turn.

Marginal-Cost Pricing.
Sometimes the government dictates that the natural monopoly sets prices equal to short-run marginal cost. In principle, this policy, called **marginal-cost pricing,** induces the allocatively efficient level of output. This is not, however, the profit-maximizing output, which is where marginal cost equals marginal revenue. Thus, marginal-cost pricing sets up a tension between the regulator's desire to achieve the allocatively efficient level of output and the monopolist's desire to maximize profits.

The CRTC regulates radio and television broad-casting as well as telecommunications rates and licensing.

Marginal-cost pricing creates different problems in each of two cases. In the first case, when producing the allocatively efficient level of output, the natural monopoly is operating on the downward-sloping portion of its *ATC* curve. In this case, marginal cost will be less than average total cost. It follows that when price is set equal to marginal cost, price will be less than average cost, and marginal-cost pricing will lead to losses. This result is shown in part (i) of Figure 12-6.

In the second case, demand is sufficient to allow the firm to produce a level of out-put beyond its minimum efficient scale and thus to operate on the upward-sloping por-tion of its *ATC* curve. At any such level of output, marginal cost exceeds average total cost. If the firm is required to equate price with marginal cost, it is clear that price will be above average total cost. Marginal-cost pricing will therefore lead the firm to earn pos-itive profits. This result is shown in part (ii) of the figure.

When a natural monopoly with falling average costs sets price equal to marginal cost, it will suffer losses. When a natural monopoly with rising average costs sets price equal to marginal cost, it will earn positive profits.

> **marginal-cost pricing**
> Setting price equal to marginal cost so that buyers for the last unit are just willing to pay the amount that it cost to make that unit.

Two-Part Tariff.
Though marginal-cost pricing achieves allocative efficiency, a natural monopoly with declining average costs cannot be expected to incur losses indefinitely. One way of trying to cover total costs in this case is to allow the firm to charge a **two-part tariff** in which customers pay one price to gain access to the product and a second price for each unit consumed. Consider the case of a regulated cable TV company. In principle, the hook-up fee covers fixed costs, and then each unit of output can be priced at marginal cost. Indeed, most new subscribers to cable TV are surprised at how high the hook-up fee is—clearly much higher than the cost of the cable guy's half-hour to complete the job! Yet, if this fee also includes that household's share of the firm's fixed costs (spread over many thousands of households), then the large hook-up fee is more understandable.

> **two-part tariff**
> A method of charging for a good or a service in which the consumer pays a flat access fee and a specified amount per unit purchased.

Average-Cost Pricing.
Another method of regulating a natural monopoly is to set prices just high enough to cover total costs, thus generating neither profits nor losses. The firm produces to the point where average revenue equals average total cost, which is where the demand curve cuts the *ATC* curve. Part (i) of Figure 12-6 shows that for a firm with declining average costs, this pricing policy requires producing at less than the

FIGURE 12-6   Pricing Policies for Natural Monopolies

(i) When average costs are falling   (ii) When average costs are rising

Marginal-cost pricing leads to profits or losses, whereas average-cost pricing violates the efficiency condition. In each part, the output at which marginal cost equals price is q_1 and price is p_1. In part (i), average costs are falling at output q_1, so marginal costs are less than the average cost c_1. There is an average loss of $c_1 - p_1$ on each unit, making a total loss equal to the shaded area. In part (ii), average cost c_1 is less than price at output q_1. There is an average profit of $p_1 - c_1$ on each unit sold, making a total profit equal to the shaded area.

In each part of the diagram, the output at which average cost equals price is q_2 and the associated price is p_2. In part (i), marginal cost is less than price at q_2, so output is below its allocatively efficient level. In part (ii), marginal cost exceeds price at q_2, so output is greater than its allocatively efficient level.

allocatively efficient output. The firm's financial losses that would occur under marginal-cost pricing are avoided by producing less output than what is socially optimal. Part (ii) shows that for a firm with rising average costs, the average-cost pricing policy requires producing at more than the allocatively efficient output. The profits that would occur under marginal-cost pricing are dissipated by producing more output than what is socially optimal.

Practise with Study Guide Chapter 12, Exercise 3.

Generally, average-cost pricing will not result in allocative efficiency because price will not equal marginal cost.

On what basis do we choose between marginal-cost pricing and average-cost pricing? Marginal-cost pricing generates allocative efficiency, but the firm may incur losses. In this case, the firm will eventually go out of business unless someone is prepared to cover the firm's costs. If the government is unwilling to do so, seeing no reason why taxpayers should subsidize the users of the product in question, then average-cost pricing is probably preferable. It provides the lowest price that can be charged and the largest output that can be produced, given the requirement that sales revenue must cover the total cost of producing the product.

Long-Run Investment

So far, we have examined the implications of different pricing policies in the short run. Recall that in the short run the level of the firm's capital is fixed. The allocatively efficient pricing policy sets price equal to short-run marginal cost. The position of the short-run marginal cost curve depends, however, on the amount of fixed capital that is currently available to be combined with the variable factors. What should determine the firm's long-run capital stock? In answering this question, we begin by assuming that the demand for the product is constant.

The efficient answer follows from comparing the current market price with the *long-run* marginal cost of producing the product. The current market price reflects the value consumers place on one additional unit of output. The long-run marginal cost reflects the full resource cost (including capital costs) of providing an extra unit of output. Thus, if the current price exceeds long-run marginal cost, then the natural monopoly should increase its capacity; if current price is less than long-run marginal cost, the natural monopoly should allow its capacity to decline as its capital wears out.

The previous paragraph assumed that demand was constant and so the *current* market price was relevant to the long-run investment decision. But what if demand is expected to increase in the future, and therefore consumers' marginal value of the product will rise? In this case, the appropriate comparison is between the future price and the long-run marginal cost, and so it may be efficient to increase capacity even if the current price is below the long-run marginal cost. Similarly, if demand is expected to fall in the future, then it may be efficient to decrease capacity even though the current price is above long-run marginal cost.

For given capacity in the short run, the allocatively efficient pricing system determines output by setting price equal to the short-run marginal cost of production. It also adjusts capacity in the long run until the long-run marginal cost of production is equal to the price.

Since marginal cost is generally different from average cost, average-cost pricing will generally lead to inefficient patterns of long-run investment. For example, consider a regulated utility that is operating on the downward-sloping portion of its *ATC* curve and is required to set price equal to average cost. Since price equals average cost, the firm will be just breaking even and thus it will have no incentive to increase its amount of fixed capital. Note, however, that the price in this case must exceed the short-run marginal cost (because marginal cost must be below average cost if average cost is falling). If the price also exceeds the long-run marginal cost, society would benefit by having a larger amount of fixed capital allocated to producing this good. But the regulated utility will not undertake this socially desirable investment.

Average-cost pricing generally leads to inefficient long-run investment decisions.

Very-Long-Run Innovation

Natural monopoly is a long-run concept—that is, given *existing technology,* there is room for only one firm to operate profitably. In the very long run, however, technology changes. Not only does today's competitive industry sometimes become tomorrow's natural monopoly, but today's natural monopoly often becomes tomorrow's competitive industry.

A striking example is found in the telecommunications industry. Thirty years ago, hard-copy message transmission was close to a natural monopoly belonging to the post office. Today, technological developments such as satellite transmission, electronic mail, fax machines, and the Internet have made this activity highly competitive.

Other examples of industries that used to be natural monopolies but are now much more competitive include airlines, long-distance telephone service, and the generation of electricity (the distribution of electricity continues to be a natural monopoly).

Practical Problems

Many practical problems arise with regulations designed to prevent natural monopolies from charging profit-maximizing prices. These problems begin with the fact that regulators do not have enough data to determine demand and cost curves precisely. In the absence of accurate data, regulators have tended to judge prices according to the level of the regulated firm's profits. Regulatory agencies tend to permit price increases only when profits fall below "fair" levels and require price reductions if profits exceed such levels. What started as price regulation becomes instead profit regulation, which is often called *rate-of-return regulation*. Concepts of marginal cost and economic efficiency are typically ignored in such regulatory decisions.

If average-cost regulation is successful, only a normal rate of return will be earned; that is, economic profits will be zero. Unfortunately, the reverse is not necessarily true. Profits can be zero for any of a number of reasons, including inefficient operation and misleading accounting. Thus, regulatory commissions that rely on rate of return as their guide to pricing must monitor a number of other aspects of the regulated firm's behaviour in order to limit the possibility of wasting resources. This monitoring itself requires a considerable expenditure of resources.

Regulation of Oligopolies

Governments have from time to time intervened in industries that were oligopolies (rather than natural monopolies), seeking to enforce the type of price and entry behaviour that was thought to be in the public interest. Such intervention has typically taken two distinct forms. In many European countries, it was primarily nationalization of whole oligopolistic industries such as railways, steel, and coal mining, which were then to be run by government-appointed boards. In the United States, firms such as airlines and railways were left in private hands, but their decisions were regulated by government-appointed bodies that set prices and regulated entry. As so often happens, Canada followed a mixture of British and American practices. Many Canadian crown corporations were set up, and many firms that remained in private hands were regulated. For example, in the regulated railway industry, Canadian Pacific was privately owned while Canadian National, until it was privatized in 1995, was a crown corporation.

Scepticism About Direct Control

Policymakers have become increasingly sceptical of their ability to improve the behaviour of oligopolistic industries by having governments control the details of their behaviour through either ownership or regulation. Three main experiences have been important in developing this scepticism.

Oligopolies and Economic Growth.   Oligopolistic market structures provided much of the economic growth in the twentieth century. New products and new ways of producing old products have followed each other in rapid succession, leading to higher living standards and higher productivity. Many of these innovations have been provided by firms in oligopolistic industries such as automobiles, agricultural implements, steel, petroleum refining, chemicals, electronics, computing, and telecommunications. As long as oligopolists continue to compete with each other, rather than cooperating to produce monopoly profits, most economists see no need to regulate such things as the prices at which oligopolists sell their products and the conditions of entry into oligopolistic industries.

Cross Subsidization.   Many regulatory bodies have imposed policies in which prices are not related to the cost of each of the services being priced. These prices involved what is called *cross subsidization,* whereby profits that are earned in the provision of one service are used to subsidize the provision of another service at a price below cost. For example, when they were in control, regulators typically required that long-distance telephone calls subsidize local calls, first-class mail subsidize third-class mail, and long-haul airline rates subsidize short-haul rates. These pricing policies forced users of the profitable service to subsidize users of the unprofitable service. But cross subsidization does not increase overall welfare. It reduces the sum of producer and consumer surplus because price exceeds marginal cost in some lines of output but is less than marginal cost in others.

Protection from Competition.   The record of postwar government intervention into regulated industries seemed poorer in practice than its supporters had predicted. Research by the University of Chicago Nobel Laureate George Stigler (1911–1991) and others established that in many industries, regulatory bodies were "captured" by the very firms that they were supposed to be regulating. As a result, the regulatory bodies that were meant to ensure competition often acted to enforce monopoly practices that would have been illegal if instituted by the firms themselves.

Airline regulation in Canada and the United States provides an obvious example. When airline routes and fares were first regulated, it was possible to argue that demand was too low to permit effective competition among many firms. Whatever the validity of that argument in earlier times, by the mid 1960s the regulation was plainly protecting the industry, allowing it to charge higher fares, earn higher profits, and pay higher wages than it would under more competitive conditions. For decades, Canadian and U.S. regulation of airline prices consistently prevented price competition. For example, until recently airlines other than Air Canada and Canadian Airlines were prevented from introducing cheap fares between Canada and Europe. This regulation could not be explained as protecting the interests of passengers against the predatory behaviour of the carriers.

Why did regulatory bodies shift from protecting consumers to protecting firms? One reason is that the regulatory commissions were gradually captured by the firms they were supposed to regulate. In part, this capture was natural enough. When regulatory bodies were hiring staff, they needed people who were knowledgeable in the industries they were regulating. Where better to go than to people who had worked in these industries? Naturally, these people tended to be sympathetic to firms in their own industries. Also, because many of them aspired to go back to those industries once they had gained experience within the regulatory bodies, they were not inclined to arouse the wrath of industry officials by imposing policies that were against the firms' interests.

Deregulation and Privatization

The 1980s witnessed the beginning of a movement in many advanced industrial nations to reduce the level of government control over industry. Various experiences in these countries have been pushing in this direction:

- The realization that regulatory bodies often sought to reduce, rather than increase, competition
- The dashing of the hopes that publicly owned industries would work better than privately owned firms in the areas of efficiency, productivity growth, and industrial relations

- The realization that replacing a private monopoly with a publicly owned one would not greatly change the industry's performance and that replacing privately owned oligopolists by a publicly owned monopoly might actually worsen the industry's performance
- The awareness that falling transportation costs and revolutions in data processing and communications exposed local industries to much more widespread international competition than they had previously experienced domestically

There were two natural outcomes from these revised views. The first was deregulation—intended to leave prices and entry free to be determined by private decisions. The second was privatization of publicly owned firms.

In the United States, where regulation rather than government ownership had been the adopted policy, many industries were deregulated. In Canada, hundreds of crown corporations that the government had acquired for a variety of reasons, but were neither natural monopolies nor operating in highly concentrated industries, were sold off. Many large crown corporations operating in oligopolistic industries, such as Air Canada, Petro Canada, and Canadian National, were privatized. Also, many industries, such as airlines and gas and oil, were deregulated. Prices were freed, to be set by the firms in the industries, and entry was no longer restricted by government policy.

Canadian Competition Policy

competition policy Policy designed to prohibit the acquisition and exercise of monopoly power by business firms.

combine laws Laws that prevent firms either from combining into one unit or from cooperating so as to behave monopolistically.

The least stringent form of government intervention is designed neither to force firms to sell at particular prices nor to regulate the conditions of entry and exit; it is designed, instead, to create conditions of competition by preventing firms from merging unnecessarily or from engaging in anticompetitive practices such as colluding to set monopoly prices. This is referred to as **competition policy.**

Laws designed for the purposes of preventing anticompetitive behaviour are called **combine laws** in Canada. They have provided the main thrust of Canadian competition policy since its inception in the nineteenth century. They prohibit monopolies, attempts to monopolize, and conspiracies in restraint of trade. Throughout the history of Canadian competition policy, legislation has been directed chiefly at the misuse of market power by single firms or groups of firms and only rarely at mergers per se.

This acceptance of the need for relatively large firms in the business sector was partly a function of the small size of the Canadian economy in the days when most production was solely for the domestic market. Firms that were large enough to exploit the available economies of scale were likely to be large in relation to the total market. This meant that there would be fewer firms in Canadian industries dominated by scale effects than would be found in similar industries in such relatively large economies as the United States.

See Chapter 12 of www.pearsoned.ca/lipsey for an excellent discussion of how economic theory has played a role in competition policy: Jerry Hausman and Greg Leonard, "Achieving Competition: Antitrust Policy and Consumer Welfare," *World Economic Affairs.*

The Evolution of Canadian Policy

The first Canadian combine laws were adopted in 1889 and 1890, when legislation made it an offence to combine, to agree to lessen competition unduly, or to restrain trade. Because the proscribed behaviour was illegal, an offence was a criminal act to be handled by the criminal justice system. The laws have been changed frequently since that time, but their basic procompetition stance still prevails in current legislation.

By the 1950s, Canadian anticombine laws had evolved to make illegal three broad classes of activity:

- combinations, such as price-fixing agreements that unduly lessen competition
- mergers or monopolies that may operate to the detriment of the public interest
- unfair trade practices

Many cases of unfair trade practices were successfully pursued under these laws, but few cases were brought against mergers, and none of those that were brought were successful. The reason most often cited for this lack of success was the inability of criminal legislation to cope with complex economic issues. Under criminal law, the government must prove *beyond a reasonable doubt* that the accused party has committed the offence. As an added complication, Canadian courts have been much less willing than American courts to assess economic evidence.

A major review of Canadian legislation was undertaken in the late 1960s by the now-disbanded Economic Council of Canada. Its recommendations formed the basis of the amendments to the Combines Investigation Act that are still in force. Of the recommendations that were accepted, some were put into effect in 1976 and the remainder in 1986.

The 1976 amendments included several provisions:

- extending the Combines Investigation Act to service industries
- allowing *civil* (rather than criminal) actions to be brought for damages resulting from contravention of the act
- strengthening legislation against misleading advertising

Claims about product quality must now be based on adequate tests. Advertising a product at a bargain price when the supplier does not supply the product in reasonable quantities is prohibited. Also prohibited is the supplying of a product at a price higher than the advertised price. In 1992, the court levied a record fine against one individual of $500 000 for seriously misleading advertising.

In 1986, the final set of amendments to the Combines Investigation Act were passed. The resulting Act—now called the Competition Act—has three central themes: economic efficiency, adaptability, and international trade. The new Act creates a specialized Competition Tribunal to deal with civil matters now that competition policy has been taken out of the sphere of the criminal law. The Act also gives the role of "watchdog" to the Director of Investigations who heads the Competition Bureau. This gives the Director of Investigations the responsibility for observing developments in the economy and evaluating the likely effects on competition of mergers and various trade practices.

Perhaps the most important of the 1986 amendments was the one which placed mergers under civil (rather than criminal) law—the statutory test being whether or not the merger "substantially lessens competition." For the first time in Canada, economic considerations are stated to be directly relevant in judging the acceptability of a merger. When reviewing a merger, the Competition Bureau is obliged to consider such things as effective competition after the merger, the degree of foreign competition, barriers to entry, the availability of substitutes, and the financial state of the merging firms.

The Competition Bureau also considers any efficiency gains that a merger might generate. Even in a situation where there are considerable entry barriers to an industry, a merger may bring benefits to consumers even though it raises the industry's measured concentration. If, by merging, two firms can achieve scale economies that were not achievable separately, then reductions in average total costs may get passed on to consumers in the form of lower prices.

This possibility presents a significant challenge to competition policy. The challenge is to prevent those mergers that mostly lead to less competition, producing only small efficiency gains, but to allow those mergers that mostly lead to efficiency gains, with only small reductions in competition. The practical problem for the authorities is to identify the likely effects of each merger.

Recent Developments

This new merger legislation has had some substantial effects on business mergers for the first time in the history of Canadian competition policy. Many firms have consulted with the Competition Bureau before concluding a merger. As a result, some proposed mergers have been amended, and a few have been abandoned. Many mergers that have gone forward have been investigated, and the terms of some have been substantially modified.

The most recent high-profile merger case in Canada occurred in the spring of 1998 when the Royal Bank and the Bank of Montreal announced their intentions to merge. This was followed almost immediately by a similar announcement by the CIBC and Toronto Dominion. These four large chartered banks argued that in order to compete effectively in the world market for financial services, they needed to achieve larger scale. In particular, they argued that the mergers would allow them to spread the enormous fixed costs of computing systems over a much larger customer base, thereby achieving cost reductions that would allow them to compete against foreign banks, especially those in the United States.

The Competition Bureau was not convinced. It concluded, after studying all relevant aspects of the financial-services industry, that the bank mergers would substantially lessen competition in many local personal banking markets, as well as in many banking markets for small and medium-sized businesses. An important part of the Competition Bureau's arguments was that, even if current legislation were changed to increase foreign firms' access to the Canadian market, the established network of bank branches represented a massive entry barrier. This barrier would permit the merged banks to have a stranglehold on the Canadian banking industry.

As it turned out, the Minister of Finance (who ultimately must make the decision on any mergers in the financial sector) disallowed the mergers. But spokespeople for Canada's banks continue to emphasize the need for mergers in order to compete successfully against foreign banks. They argue that the established network of branches is no longer a significant entry barrier in a world in which foreign banks can sell credit cards and mutual funds to Canadian households over the Internet.

The next few years will likely see some reforms in Canada's financial-services industry. The issue of bank mergers, though settled for the time being, is sure to come to the fore of public debate once again.

Another important merger is the one between Canadian Airlines and Air Canada. In April of 1999, Onex Corporation made an offer to purchase both airlines and merge them. Canadian Airlines, which had been losing money for some time, was receptive to the offer. In contrast, the management of Air Canada viewed Onex's offer as a hostile takeover attempt, and responded by making its own offer to purchase Canadian Airlines and operate it as an independent airline. In November, however, Onex withdrew its offer when a Quebec court ruled that the offer was illegal since it would result in more than 10 percent of Air Canada being owned by one party (a restriction on ownership put in place when Air Canada was privatized in the mid 1980s).

With the withdrawal of the Onex bid, however, Air Canada left its offer on the table. The Competition Bureau recommended allowing the merger provided that the Canadian market was opened up to foreign competition—the so-called open skies policy. This, in turn, would probably require that a 25 percent foreign-ownership restriction on Canadian airlines be either altered or removed altogether. As this book went to press in the late fall of 1999, the government appeared unwilling to open the doors to increased foreign ownership, but it also appeared unwilling to prevent the merger.

Without an increase in foreign competition, however, it is clear that a merger between Air Canada and Canadian Airlines will significantly lessen competition. However, there will also be some cost reductions as the two airlines consolidate their flights and, as a

To read the Competition Bureau's assessment of the proposed 1998 bank mergers, as well as other mergers, go to its website: www.ct-tc.gc.ca.

APPLYING ECONOMIC CONCEPTS 12-1

The U.S. Antitrust Case Against Microsoft

In May of 1998, the U.S. Department of Justice and 20 state attorneys-general launched what may well turn out to be the most important antitrust suit of the century. The target of the suit was Microsoft, the enormous software company that has dominated the market for operating systems of personal computers, first with DOS and more recently with Windows. The head of the Justice Department, in launching the suit, stated that "What cannot be tolerated—and what the antitrust laws forbid—is the barrage of anticompetitive practices that Microsoft uses to destroy its rivals and to avoid competition."

The focus of the ongoing suit concerns the way Microsoft has responded to competition in the market for Internet browsers. Netscape is the leading supplier of Internet browsers, with its flagship product called Navigator. Microsoft has a competing browser called Internet Explorer. Central to the case is that, while Microsoft is not the leader in the Internet browser market, it is the undisputed leader in the market for PC operating systems. But, as the Internet develops along with new programming languages such as Java, access to the Internet may end up being a substitute for the PC operating system. If this happens, Microsoft would end up being the dominant producer of largely redundant operating systems. And Netscape, as the leading supplier of browsers, would then be in a position of considerable dominance.

The Justice Department alleges that Microsoft initially tried to push Netscape into colluding with it, dividing up the market for browsers. When Netscape rejected the offer, Microsoft then tried to force PC manufacturers into installing its own Internet Explorer as a condition for receiving licences for Windows 95. Such "tied selling" is illegal under U.S. antitrust law. Microsoft argues that Internet Explorer is an integral part of the Windows operating system, and thus the tying of the sales of Internet Explorer to the sales of Windows is only natural. Furthermore, Microsoft argues that if it is prohibited from tying Internet Explorer to the Windows operating system, there will be fewer innovative developments from Microsoft and the ultimate losers will be the consumers.

In November of 1999, Thomas Penfield Jackson, the judge for the case, concluded that Microsoft was a monopolist and was guilty of business practices that had the effect of reducing the amount of competition. Judge Jackson said:

Most harmful of all is the message that Microsoft's actions have conveyed to every enterprise with the potential to innovate in the computer industry. Through its conduct toward Netscape, IBM, Compaq, Intel, and others, Microsoft has demonstrated that it will use its prodigious market power and immense profits to harm any firm that insists on pursuing initiatives that could intensify competition against one of Microsoft's core products.

Microsoft's sentence was not announced in November. Instead, the judge gave Microsoft time to meet with the plaintiffs in an attempt to reach an out-of-court settlement. As this book went to press, a settlement had yet to be reached. One possibility is to break Microsoft into three separate companies, one dealing with operating systems, a second for applications, and a third for its Internet operations. Critics of this proposal point out that each of these three companies would still be huge and would possess immense power in their respective markets. Others argue that much of Microsoft's market power comes from the linkage among these three areas and that severing the links will indeed lead to more competition. Look for the final outcome in the months and years to come!

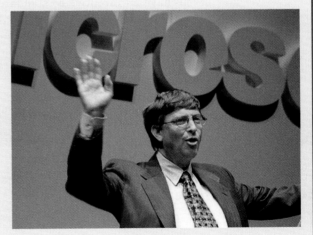

Bill Gates, chairman of Microsoft Corp., created Microsoft in the late 1970s and turned it into a multibillion-dollar company and in the process became the world's wealthiest person.

result, operate their planes with less excess capacity. Thus, while the reduction in competition will probably have the effect of raising prices, the reduction in excess capacity will reduce costs and tend to reduce prices. In this merger case, as in many others, the tradeoff between the reduction in competition and the reduction in costs is of central importance. Time will tell how this merger proceeds.

See *Applying Economic Concepts 12-1* for a brief discussion of an important antitrust case in the United States—the case against Microsoft.

Looking Forward

The 1986 Competition Act will not be the end of the evolution of Canadian competition policy, but it appears to have marked the end of a major chapter. Canadian legislation has for a long time provided substantial protection to consumers against the misuse of market power by large firms. For the first time, it now also seems to provide some substantial protection against the creation, through mergers, of market power that is not justified by gains to efficiency or international competitiveness.

What type of reforms might we expect in the years ahead? The ongoing process of globalization poses two challenges for Canadian competition policy. First, as the flow of goods and services across national boundaries increases, it becomes more important to define markets on an international basis rather than on national ones. For example, consider again the Canadian banking industry. With the continuing development of the Internet, it becomes possible for foreign-based banks to sell some financial services to Canadians without establishing a costly *physical* presence in Canada—such as a network of branches. In this case, the appropriate definition of the market (for the case of assessing the impact of a merger) is larger than just the one defined by Canada's borders.

The second challenge posed by globalization is the desirability of standardizing competition policy across countries. Firms that are mobile and have considerable market power may tend to locate their firms where competition policy is the most lax, exporting into other countries. To avoid such socially inefficient locational choices, countries have an incentive to standardize their competition policy—in this case, firms would choose their locations on the basis of economic rather than legal forces.

See Chapter 12 of www.pearsoned.ca/lipsey for an interview with the Royal Bank's John Cleghorn on the case for bank mergers: "A Case for Bank Mergers," *World Economic Affairs.*

S U M M A R Y

Economic Efficiency

LO 1 2

- Economists distinguish two main kinds of efficiency: productive and allocative.
- Productive efficiency exists for given technology when whatever output being produced is being produced at the lowest attainable cost. This outcome requires, first, that firms be on, rather than above, their relevant cost curves and, second, that all firms in an industry have the same marginal cost.

- Allocative efficiency is achieved when it is impossible to change the mix of production in such a way as to make someone better off without making someone else worse off. The allocation of resources will be efficient when each product's price equals its marginal cost.
- Perfect competition achieves both productive and allocative efficiency. Productive efficiency is achieved because

the same forces that lead to long-run equilibrium lead to production at the lowest attainable cost. Allocative efficiency is achieved because in competitive equilibrium, with quantity demanded equalling quantity supplied, price equals marginal cost for every product.

- The economic case against monopoly rests on its allocative inefficiency, which arises because profit maximization for a monopolist implies that price exceeds marginal cost. Oligopolistic industries are also allocatively inefficient since price exceeds marginal cost. But oligopoly also produces benefits. Empirical evidence suggests that technological change and innovation can, to a measurable extent, be traced to the efforts of large firms operating in oligopolistic industries.

Economic Regulation to Promote Efficiency

- Two broad types of policies are designed to promote allocative efficiency in imperfectly competitive markets. These can be divided into *economic regulations* and *competition policy*. Economic regulation is used both in the case of a natural monopoly and in the case of an oligopolistic industry. Competition policy applies more to the latter.
- Efficient operation of natural monopolies requires that price be set equal to short-run marginal cost and that investment be undertaken whenever that price exceeds the full long-run marginal cost of production. Average-cost pricing results in too little output in the short run and too little investment in the long run in falling-cost industries; it also leads to too much output and too much investment in rising-cost industries.
- Direct control of pricing and entry conditions of some key oligopolistic industries has been common in the past, but deregulation is reducing such control. The move to deregulation is largely the result of the experiences that oligopolistic industries are a major engine of growth, as long as their firms are encouraged to compete; that direct control of such industries has produced disappointing results in the past; and that forced cross subsidization can have serious consequences for some users.

Canadian Competition Policy

- Canadian combine laws have always recognized the need for firms that are large in relation to the domestic market if economies of scale are to be exploited. Such laws seek to restrict growth in size through mergers where the size is not justified by efficiencies and seek to prevent the unwarranted exploitation of market power.
- In 1976, such laws were removed from the criminal code, where enforcement proved difficult, and placed in the civil code, where enforcement appears to be easier.
- Since 1986, the Competition Bureau has modified its approach to mergers. Whereas in early years there was generally a presumption that a merger would reduce competition and thus be undesirable, there is now a view that efficiency gains may make some mergers desirable.

K E Y   C O N C E P T S

Productive and allocative efficiency	The inefficiency of monopoly	Regulation and effects on innovation
Consumer and producer surplus	Regulation of natural monopolies	Deregulation
The efficiency of competition	Marginal- and average-cost pricing	Canadian competition policy

STUDY EXERCISES

1. Summer Tees and Fancy Tees are two firms producing T-shirts. The table below shows the average and marginal cost of producing T-shirts for the two companies.

Summer Tees				Fancy Tees			
Quantity	ATC	TC	MC	Quantity	ATC	TC	MC
5	$8	—		5	$9	—	
			—				—
10	7	—		10	7	—	
			—				—
15	6	—		15	6	—	
			—				—
20	6	—		20	5	—	
			—				—
25	7	—		25	5.50	—	
			—				—
30	9	—		30	6.50	—	
			—				—
35	11	—		35	8	—	

a. Calculate *TC* and *MC* for both companies and fill in the table.

b. Draw, in two separate scale diagrams, the *ATC* and *MC* curves for each firm.

c. Summer Tees is initially producing 30 shirts; Fancy Tees is initially producing 15 shirts. What is the total industry production cost?

d. Now suppose that Summer Tees produces 10 fewer shirts. By how much do its costs fall?

e. Now suppose that Fancy Tees produces 10 more shirts. By how much do its costs rise?

f. If the two firms are to produce 45 shirts in total, what is the cost-minimizing way to allocate production between the two firms? (Assume that production must be changed by increments of 5 shirts, as shown in the table.)

2. Assume that the market for eggs is perfectly competitive. The diagram shows the demand and supply for eggs.

a. At the free-market equilibrium, p^* and Q^*, show what areas represent consumer and producer surplus.

b. Now suppose that the egg producers organize themselves and establish a system of quotas. Each farmer's output is restricted by an amount to keep aggregate output at Q^Q. What happens to industry price?

c. In the quota system in part **b**, what areas now represent consumer and producer surplus? Is the quota system allocatively efficient? Explain.

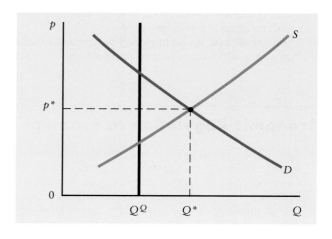

3. The diagram below shows supply and demand in the labour market.

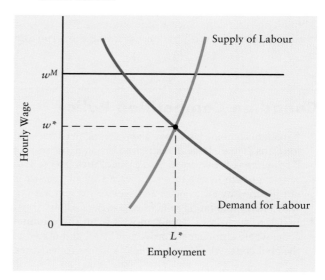

a. At the free-market equilibrium, w^* and L^*, show what areas represent consumer and producer surplus.

b. Now suppose that the government establishes a minimum wage at w^M. What is the outcome of this policy?

c. In the situation of part **b**, what areas now represent consumer and producer surplus? Is the outcome allocatively efficient? Explain.

4. The diagram below shows the production possibility boundary for a country that produces only two goods, limes and coconuts. Assume that resources are fully employed at points *A*, *B*, *C*, and *D*.

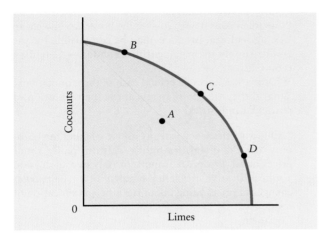

a. Suppose individual firms in the lime industry are not producing at their minimum possible cost. Which point(s) could represent this situation?
b. Suppose all firms and both industries are productively efficient. Which points could represent this situation?
c. Suppose point *B* occurs when the lime industry is monopolized but the coconut industry is perfectly competitive. Is point *B* allocatively efficient? Is it productively efficient?
d. Suppose point *D* occurs when the coconut industry is monopolized but the lime industry is perfectly competitive. Is point *D* allocatively efficient? Is it productively efficient?
e. Suppose point *C* is allocatively efficient. What do we know about each industry in this case?

5. The following diagram shows the *ATC* and *MC* curves for a natural monopoly—average costs are falling over the entire range of the demand curve.

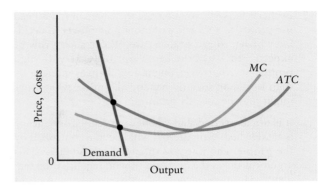

a. Identify what price and quantity would exist if the firm were required by regulators to set price equal average cost.
b. What would be the profits (or losses) in this case?
c. Would the outcome be allocatively efficient? Explain why or why not.
d. Suppose now that the firm were required by regulators to set price equal to marginal cost. What would be the price and quantity in this case?
e. In the diagram, show the profits (or losses) in this case.
f. Would the outcome be allocatively efficient? Explain why or why not.

6. One important factor that the Canadian Competition Bureau must consider when assessing the likely effects of a merger is the definition of the market. Discuss how geography is likely to affect the definition of the market for the following products:

a. fresh-baked breads and cakes
b. cement
c. gold jewellery
d. computer hardware

DISCUSSION QUESTIONS
---

1. Suppose that allocative inefficiency of some economy amounts to 5 percent of the value of production. What does this statement mean? If it is true, would consumers *as a whole* be better off if policy measures were suc-cessful in moving the economy to an allocatively efficient outcome? Would *every* consumer be better off if the economy moved to an allocatively efficient outcome?

2. Evaluate the wisdom of having the Competition Bureau use profits as a measure of monopoly power in deciding whether to prosecute a case. Would such a rule be expected to affect the behaviour of firms with high profits? In what ways might any changes induced by such a rule be socially beneficial, and in what ways might they be socially harmful?

3. It is often asserted that whenever a regulatory agency is established, ultimately it will become controlled by the people whom it was intended to regulate. (This argument raises the question of who regulates the regulators.) Can you identify why this phenomenon might happen? How might the integrity of regulatory boards be protected?

4. This chapter has identified several strategies for dealing with natural monopolies and their associated inefficiencies. Alternatively, assume that you are a regulator and that the monopoly you face is able to price discriminate—perhaps perfectly. Does this ability change the options you have for encouraging the efficient level of production? Would you choose to use this additional option? Why or why not?

5. "Canadian air travellers opting for U.S. carriers were [partly] responsible for Canadian airlines deregulation." —C. D. Howe Institute.
"Canadian consumers crossing the border to buy cheap U.S. agricultural products may be responsible for the end of supply management in Canada."—Canadian economist.
What market forces lie behind each of these quotations? What difficulties do they reveal for the regulation of particular industries?

6. "Allocative efficiency is really about whether the economy 'has the quantities right'—it is not really about prices at all. Prices are important only in a discussion about allocative efficiency because *in a free market* changes in prices bring about the efficient allocation of resources."
Comment.

PART FIVE

Factor Markets

Why do university professors typically get paid more than elementary-school teachers? Why does an acre of land outside Kamloops rent for less than an acre of land in downtown Vancouver? Are government attempts to equalize the earnings of people in different occupations ever successful? What do unions do? What are the effects of discrimination in the labour market? What is the connection between the interest rate and firms' investment in physical capital? These are the sort of questions you will be able to answer after reading the next three chapters.

In Chapter 13, we examine the way economists think about markets for factors of production. Not surprisingly, demand and supply play a key role. We will see several reasons for factor-price differentials. It is here that we see why the acre of land in Kamloops rents for less than the one in Vancouver. We will also discuss the importance of factor mobility, and why this mobility can thwart government efforts to establish pay equity.

Chapter 14 examines labour markets in detail. We explore how working conditions and human capital can combine to explain why some workers get paid more than others. We examine the effects of legislated minimum wages, the objectives of labour unions, and the important issue of discrimination in labour markets. Finally, we will discuss whether the decline of the manufacturing sector (and the rise of the service sector) is necessarily a bad thing.

Chapter 15 begins by discussing the market for physical capital. We will see why firms choose to buy less capital when the interest rate rises (and more when the interest rate falls). We will also examine how the equilibrium interest rate is determined, and how it is affected by changes in technology. The chapter then goes on to discuss the pricing of nonrenewable resources, such as oil, natural gas, or minerals. We will discuss how the market system works as a conservation mechanism—the idea that rising prices of nonrenewable resources encourage the conservation of these scarce resources.

CHAPTER 13

Factor Pricing and Factor Mobility

LEARNING OBJECTIVES

1. Understand the size and functional distributions of income.

2. Explain a profit-maximizing firm's demand for a factor.

3. Understand the determinants of the elasticity of factor demand.

4. Explain the role of factor mobility in determining factor supply.

5. Distinguish between temporary and equilibrium factor-price differentials.

6. Explain the concept of economic rent, and how it is related to factor mobility.

Most people spend a considerable amount of their time working. Some of those people are fortunate enough to earn good wages, and thus have good incomes that enable them to afford many of the "good things in life." Others are not so fortunate, and earn only low wages. What determines the wages that individuals earn? What explains why professors usually are paid more than high-school teachers, or why doctors are paid more than nurses? Labour is not the only factor of production, of course. Physical capital is also important, as are land and natural resources. What determines the payments that these factors earn? Why does an acre of farm land in northern Saskatchewan rent for much less than an acre of land in downtown Toronto? Not surprisingly, understanding why different factors of production earn different payments requires us to understand both demand-side and supply-side aspects of the relevant factor markets.

In this chapter we examine the issue of factor pricing and the closely related issue of factor mobility. Understanding what determines the payments to different factors of production will help us to understand the overall distribution of income in the economy. We begin with the distribution of income.

Income Distribution

The founders of Classical economics, Adam Smith (1723–1790) and David Ricardo (1772–1823), were concerned with the distribution of income among what were then the three great social classes: workers, capitalists, and landowners. They defined three factors of production as labour, capital, and land. The return to each factor was treated as the income of the respective social class.

Smith and Ricardo were interested in what determined the income of each class relative to the total national income. Their theories predicted that as society progressed, landlords would become relatively better off and capitalists would become relatively worse off. Karl Marx (1818–1883) had a different theory which predicted that as growth occurred, capitalists would become relatively better off and workers would become relatively worse off (until the whole capitalist system collapsed).

These nineteenth-century debates focused on what is now called the **functional distribution of income,** defined as the distribution of national income among the major factors of production. Modern economists, however, emphasize the **size distribution of income.** This refers to the distribution of income among different individuals without reference to the source of the income or the "social class" of the individual.

If we want to measure and understand the income inequality between individuals, the size distribution of income is a better indicator than is the functional distribution of income. The reason is that income classes often do not coincide with "social" classes. Many capitalists, such as the owners of small retail stores, are in the lower part of the income scale. Conversely, many wage earners, such as professional athletes, are in the upper income scale. Furthermore, it is becoming increasingly difficult to distinguish "workers" from "capitalists." Through employer-sponsored pension plans, workers now own much more of the country's capital than do the richer "non-working" capitalists.

Figure 13-1 shows that even among full-time, full-year workers, there was substantial inequality in the distribution of (pre-tax) income across individuals in 1996 (the most recent year for which these data are available). Another way to show the size distribution of income is found in Figure 13-2. Each of the curves in the figure is a Lorenz curve. A **Lorenz curve** shows how much of total income is accounted for by given proportions of the nation's families. If every family had the same income, then the Lorenz curve would lie exactly along the diagonal. The farther the curve bends away from the diagonal, the less equal the distribution of income. The curve farther from the diagonal in Figure 13-2 shows, for example, that in 1995 the bottom 20 percent of all Canadian

functional distribution of income   The distribution of national income among the major factors of production.

size distribution of income   The distribution of income among households, without regard to source of income or social class of households.

Lorenz curve   A graph showing the extent of inequality of income distribution.

FIGURE 13-1   Earnings of Full-Time, Full-Year Workers, 1996

There is considerable inequality in the distribution of (pre-tax) earned income, even among full-time workers who work the full year. Just over 12 percent of such workers earned more than $60 000 in 1996; 20.5 percent earned less than $20 000. Average earned income in 1996 was $37 465.

(Source: These data are available on Statistics Canada's website: www.statcan.ca.)

families received 2.1 percent of all pre-tax income. The curve closer to the diagonal, however, shows that Canada's tax-and-transfer system is effective at redistributing income; the same 20 percent of families receive 7.7 percent of after-tax income.

To understand the size distribution of income, we must first study how individual incomes are determined. Superficial explanations of differences in income, such as "People earn according to their ability," are inadequate. Incomes are distributed much more unequally than any *measured* index of ability, be it IQ, physical strength, or typing skill. The best professional sports players may only score twice as many points as the average players, but their salary is many times more than the average salary. Something other than simple ability is at work here. However, if answers that are couched in terms of ability are easily refuted, so are answers such as "It's all a matter of luck" or "It's just the system." In this chapter, we look beyond such superficial explanations.

A Glimpse of the Theory Ahead

In this chapter, we confine ourselves to factor markets that are perfectly competitive. As a result, the firms we study face a given price of each factor that they buy. Similarly, owners of factors face a given price for the factor services that they sell.

Dealing first with competitive factor markets allows us to study the principles of factor-price determination in the simplest context. Once these principles are understood, it is relatively easy to extend the theory to more complicated settings. This is done in Chapter 14.

The income that a factor earns depends on the price charged for its services and on the quantity that is employed. To determine factor incomes, therefore, we need to ask how markets determine these prices and quantities. The answer is that factor prices and quantities are determined in just the same way as the prices and quantities of goods—by the interaction of demand and supply. What is new about factor pricing arises from the *determinants* of factor demands and factor supplies.

FIGURE 13-2   Lorenz Curves of Family Income in Canada, 1995

The size of the shaded area between the Lorenz curve and the diagonal is a measure of the inequality of income distribution. If there were complete income equality, the bottom 20 percent of income receivers would receive 20 percent of the income, and so forth, and the Lorenz curve would coincide with the diagonal line.

The Lorenz curve farther from the diagonal is the one for pre-tax income. That Canada's tax-and-transfer system achieves some redistribution of income is shown by the Lorenz curve for after-tax income, which is closer to the diagonal.

(*Source:* Statistics Canada #13-210-XPB, 1996)

Events in goods markets have implications for factor markets. Firms' decisions on how much to produce and how to produce it imply specific demands for the various factors of production. These demands, together with the supplies of the factors of production (which are determined by the owners of the factors), come together in factor markets. Together they determine the quantities of the various factors of production that are employed, their prices, and the incomes earned by their owners.

There is a close relationship between the production and pricing of the goods produced by firms, on the one hand, and the pricing, employment, and incomes earned by the factors of production they hire, on the other hand. This relationship leads to one of the great insights of economics:

When demand and supply interact to determine the allocation of resources among various lines of production, they also determine the incomes of the factors that are used in producing the goods.

The rest of this chapter is an elaboration of this important theme. We first study the demand for factors, then their supply, and finally how demand and supply come together to determine factor prices and quantities.

The Demand for Factors

Firms require the services of land, labour, capital, and natural resources to be used as inputs. Firms also use as inputs the products of other firms, such as steel, legal services, computer software, and electricity.

Firms require inputs not for their own sake but as a means to produce goods and services. For example, the demand for computer programmers and technicians is growing as more and more computers are used. The demand for carpenters and building materials rises and falls as the amount of housing construction rises and falls. The demand for any input is therefore *derived from the demand* for the goods and services that it helps to produce; for this reason, the demand for a factor of production is said to be a **derived demand**.

Derived demand provides a link between goods markets and factor markets.

derived demand
The demand for a factor of production that results from the demand for the products that it is used to make.

The Firm's Marginal Decision on Factor Use

What determines whether an individual firm will choose to hire one extra worker, or whether the same firm will decide to use one extra machine, or an extra kilowatt-hour of electricity? Since we are considering whether the firm will use one extra unit of some factor, we refer to this as the firm's *marginal decision* on factor use.

As we have seen in earlier chapters, any profit-maximizing firm increases its output until its marginal cost equals its marginal revenue. Since producing more output requires hiring more factors of production, we can say this another way—the firm will increase its use of any factor of production until the last unit of the factor adds as much to revenue as it does to costs.

The addition to total cost resulting from employing one more unit of a factor is that factor's price. (Recall that the firm is assumed to buy its factors in competitive markets.) So, if one more worker is hired at a wage of $15 per hour, the addition to the firm's costs is $15.

The amount that one unit of a factor adds to revenue is called the factor's **marginal revenue product (MRP)**. The factor's *MRP* has two components—a *physical* component and a *dollar* component. The physical amount by which output increases when one more unit of the factor is employed is called the factor's **marginal physical product (MPP)**. This is the concept we learned about in Chapter 7 where we simply called it the factor's *marginal product*. The dollar amount by which total revenue changes when output increases by one unit is simply the firm's marginal revenue, *MR*.

The factor's marginal revenue product is simply the combination of this physical component and this dollar component—it is the change in output (*MPP*) times the firm's marginal revenue (*MR*). [26] For example, if the factor's marginal physical product is 2 units and the firm's marginal revenue is $7.50, the factor's *MRP* is $15 ($7.50×2).

We can now restate the condition for a firm to be maximizing its profits in two ways. First:

$$\text{Marginal Cost of the Factor} = \text{Marginal Revenue Product of the Factor} \qquad (13\text{-}1)$$

This equation holds for *any* firm and any factor, no matter what market structure applies. In the special case of competitive goods and factor markets, however, we can simplify the equation. In this case, the marginal cost of the factor is simply the factor's price, which we call w. Furthermore, since the firm's *MR* is just the product's price, p, the *MRP* is equal to $MPP \times p$. Thus, the condition for profit maximization becomes

$$w = MPP \times p \qquad (13\text{-}2)$$

To check your understanding of Equation 13-2, consider an example. Suppose that the factor is available to the firm at a cost of $10 per unit ($w = \$10$). Suppose also that employing another unit of the factor adds 3 units to output ($MPP = 3$). Suppose further that any amount of output can be sold for $5 per unit ($p = \$5$). Thus, the additional unit of the factor adds $15 to the firm's revenue but only $10 to its costs. In this case, the firm will increase profits by hiring more units of the factor.

Now suppose, however, that the last unit of the factor hired by the firm has a marginal physical product of 1 unit of output—it adds only one extra unit to output—and so adds only $5 to revenue. In this case, the firm can increase profits by reducing its use of the factor.

Finally, suppose that another unit of the factor taken on or laid off changes revenue by $10. Now the firm cannot increase its profits by altering its employment of the variable factor in either direction.

To maximize its profits, any firm must hire each factor to the point where the factor's marginal revenue product equals the factor's price.

In Chapters 9 and 10, we saw the firm varying its output until the marginal cost of producing another unit was equal to the marginal revenue derived from selling that unit. Now we see the same profit-maximizing behaviour in terms of the firm's varying its inputs until the marginal cost of another unit of input is just equal to the revenue derived from selling that unit's marginal product.

---

marginal revenue product (MRP) The extra revenue that results from using one unit more of a variable factor.

marginal physical product (MPP) The extra output that results from using one unit more of a variable factor.

The Firm's Demand Curve for a Factor

We now know what determines the quantity of a variable factor a firm will buy when facing some specific price of the factor and some specific price of its output. Next we wish to derive the firm's *entire* demand curve for a factor, which tells us how much of the factor the firm will buy at *each* price.

Practise with Study Guide Chapter 13, Exercise 1.

To derive a firm's demand curve for a factor, we start by considering the right-hand side of Equation 13-1, which tells us that the factor's marginal revenue product is composed of a physical component and a dollar component. We examine these two separate components in turn.

The Physical Component of *MRP: MPP*

As the quantity of the variable factor changes, output will change. The hypothesis of diminishing returns, first discussed in Chapter 7, predicts what will happen: As the firm adds further units of the variable factor to a given quantity of the fixed factor, the additions to output will eventually get smaller and smaller. In other words, the factor's marginal physical product declines as shown in part (i) of Figure 13-3.

The Dollar Component of *MRP: MR*

To convert the marginal physical product curve of Figure 13-3(i) into a curve showing the marginal revenue product of the variable factor, we need to know the dollar value of the extra physical product. Part (ii) of Figure 13-3 shows a marginal revenue product curve for labour on the assumption that the firm sells its product in a competitive market at a price of $5 per unit. The *MRP* curve represents *MPP* × *MR* for each additional unit of the factor. Since the *MR* for a firm in perfect competition is simply equal to the price of the product, the *MRP* curve has the same shape as the *MPP* curve.

Note, however, that if the firm were not perfectly competitive, then *MR* would not be equal to price. If *MR* declined as output increases (as it would if the firm were not a price taker), then the *MRP* curve would be steeper than the *MPP* curve—because the increase in output produced by the extra unit of the factor would lead to a fall in the price of the product.

From *MRP* to the Demand Curve

Equation 13-1 states that the profit-maximizing firm will employ additional units of the factor up to the point at which the *MRP* equals the price of the factor. For example, in Figure 13-3, if the price of hiring one worker were $2000 per month, the profit-maximizing firm would employ 60 workers. (There is no point in employing a sixty-first because that worker would add less than $2000 to revenue but a full $2000 to costs.) Thus, the profit-maximizing firm hires the quantity of the variable factor that equates the marginal revenue product with the price of the variable factor.

The *MRP* curve of the variable factor is the firm's (derived) demand curve for that variable factor.

Elasticity of Factor Demand

The elasticity of demand for a factor measures the *degree* of the response of the quantity demanded to a change in its price. The preceding sections have explained the *direction* of the response; that is, that quantity demanded is negatively related to price. But you

FIGURE 13-3 From Marginal Physical Product to Demand Curve

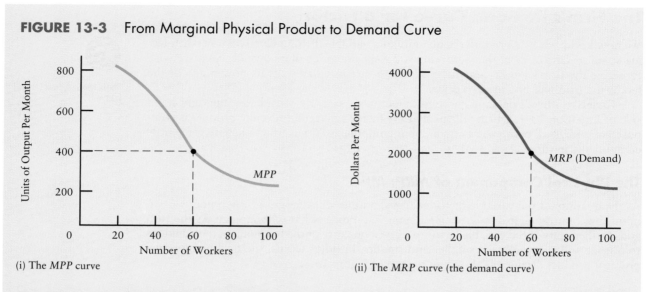

(i) The *MPP* curve

(ii) The *MRP* curve (the demand curve)

Each additional unit of the factor employed adds a certain amount to total product, as shown in part (i), and hence a certain amount to total revenue, as shown in part (ii). This determines the amount of the factor that firms will demand at each price. The firm is assumed to be a price taker in the goods market, facing a price of $5 per unit.

should not be surprised to hear that the magnitude of the response depends on the strength of various effects. For example, the extent of diminishing returns to labour, and the ability of the firm to substitute between labour and other factors of production, will both affect the firm's elasticity of demand for labour.

Diminishing Returns

The first influence on the slope of the demand curve for a factor is the diminishing marginal product of that factor. If marginal product declines rapidly as more of a variable factor is employed, a fall in the factor's price will not induce many more units to be employed. This is the case of a relatively steep *MPP* curve, and thus *MRP* curve, in Figure 13-3. Conversely, if marginal product falls only slowly as more of a variable factor is employed, there will be a large increase in quantity demanded as price falls. This is the case of a relatively flat *MPP* curve, and thus *MRP* curve, in Figure 13-3.

Substitution Between Factors

In the long run, all factors are variable. If one factor's price rises, firms will try to substitute relatively cheaper factors for it. (This is the *principle of substitution*, which we first encountered in Chapter 8.) For this reason, the slope of the demand curve for a factor is influenced by the ease with which other factors can be substituted for the factor whose price has changed.

The ease of substitution depends on the substitutes that are available and on the technical conditions of production. It is often possible to vary factor proportions in surprising ways. For example, in automobile manufacturing and in building construction, glass and steel can be substituted for each other simply by varying the dimensions of the windows. Another example is that construction materials can be substituted for maintenance labour in the case of most durable consumer goods. This is done by making the product more or less durable and more or less subject to breakdowns by using more or less expensive materials in its construction.

Importance of the Factor

Other things being equal, the more important is a factor in producing some good, the greater the elasticity of demand for that factor.

To see this, suppose that wages account for 50 percent of the costs of producing a good and raw materials account for 10 percent. A 20 percent rise in the price of labour raises the cost of producing the good by 10 percent (20 percent of 50 percent), but a 20 percent rise in the price of raw materials raises the cost of the good by only 2 percent (20 percent of 10 percent). The larger the increase in the cost of production, the larger the shift in the product's supply curve and hence the larger the decreases in quantities demanded of both the good and the factors used to produce it.

Elasticity of Demand for the Output

Other things being equal, the more elastic is the demand for the product that the factor is used to produce, the more elastic is the demand for the factor.

If an increase in the price of the product causes a large decrease in the quantity demanded—that is, if the demand for the product is highly elastic—there will be a large decrease in the quantity of a factor needed to produce it in response to a rise in the factor's price. However, if an increase in the price of a product causes only a small decrease in the quantity demanded—that is, if the demand for the product is inelastic—there will be only a small decrease in the quantity of the factor required in response to a rise in its price.

In *Extensions in Theory 13-1*, the forces affecting the elasticity of the derived demand curves are related more specifically to the market for the industry's output.

The Supply of Factors

When we consider the supply of any factor of production, we can consider supply at three different levels of aggregation:

- the amount supplied to the economy as a whole
- the amount supplied to a particular industry or occupation
- the amount supplied to a particular firm

The elasticity of supply of a factor will normally be different at each of these levels of aggregation for the simple reason that the amount of factor mobility is very different at these different levels of aggregation. A given factor of production is often very mobile between firms within a given industry, less mobile between different industries, and even less mobile from the perspective of the entire economy. As an example, an electrician may be very mobile between industries within a given city, and reasonably mobile between provinces, but it may be very difficult for that electrician to move to another country to find a job. In this section, we examine the relationship between factor mobility and the supply of factors of production. We start with the highest level of aggregation, the supply of each factor to the economy as a whole.

EXTENSIONS IN THEORY 13-1

The Principles of Derived Demand

Alfred Marshall (1842–1924) referred to the two propositions derived here as the principles of *derived demand*.

1. The larger the proportion of total costs accounted for by a factor, the more elastic the demand for it.

    Consider the figure on the left. The demand curve for the industry's product is D and, *given the factor's original price*, the industry supply curve is S_0. Equilibrium is at E_0 with output at q_0.

    Suppose that the factor's price then falls. If the factor accounts for a small part of the industry's total costs, each firm's marginal cost curve shifts downward by only a small amount. So also does the industry supply curve, as illustrated by the supply curve S_1. Output expands only a small amount to q_1, a change that implies only a small increase in the quantity of the factor demanded.

    If the factor accounts for a large part of the industry's total costs, each firm's marginal cost curve shifts downward a great deal. So also does the industry supply curve, as illustrated by the curve S_2. Output expands to q_2, a

change that implies a large increase in the quantity of the factor demanded.

2. The more elastic the demand curve for the product, the more elastic the demand for the factors that are used to make it.

    Now consider the figure on the right. The original demand and supply curves for the industry's product intersect at E_0 to produce an industry output of q_0. A fall in the price of a factor causes the industry supply curve to shift downward to S_1.

    When the demand curve is relatively inelastic, as shown by the curve D_i, industry output increases by only a small amount, to q_1. The quantity of the factor demanded increases by a correspondingly small amount.

    When demand for the product is relatively elastic, as shown by the curve D_e, industry output increases by a large amount to q_2. The quantity of the factor demanded then increases by a correspondingly large amount.

The Total Supply of Factors

At any one time, the total supply of each factor of production is given. For example, in each country, the labour force is of a certain size, so much arable land is available, and there is a given supply of discovered petroleum. However, these supplies can and do change in response to both economic and noneconomic forces. Sometimes the change is very gradual, as when a climatic change slowly turns arable land into desert or when medical advances reduce the rate of infant mortality and, hence, increase the rate of population growth, thereby eventually increasing the supply of adult labour. Sometimes the changes can be quite rapid, as when a boom in business activity brings retired persons back into the labour force or a rise in the price of agricultural produce encourages the draining of marshes to add to the supply of farmland.

Physical Capital

The supply of capital in a country consists of the stock of existing machines, plants, and equipment. Capital is a manufactured factor of production, and its total supply is in no sense fixed, although it changes only slowly. Each year, the stock of capital goods is diminished by the amount that becomes physically or economically obsolete and is increased by the amount that is newly produced. The difference between these is the net addition to (or net subtraction from) the capital stock. On balance, the trend has been for the capital stock to grow from decade to decade over the past few centuries. We will consider the determinants of investment in capital in Chapter 15.

Land

The total area of dry land in a country is almost completely fixed, but the supply of *fertile* land is not. Considerable care and effort are required to sustain the productive power of land. If farmers earn low incomes, they may not provide the necessary care, and the land's fertility may be destroyed within a short time. In contrast, high earnings from farming may provide the incentive to increase the supply of arable land by irrigation and other forms of reclamation.

Labour

The number of people willing to work is called the labour force; the total number of hours they are willing to work is called the **supply of labour.** The supply of labour depends on three influences: the size of the population, the proportion of the population willing to work, and the number of hours that each individual wishes to work. Each of these is partly influenced by economic forces.

supply of labour
The total number of hours of work that the population is willing to supply. Also called the *supply of effort.*

Population.   The population of a country varies over time, and these variations are influenced to some extent by economic forces. There is some evidence, for example, that the birthrate and the net immigration rate (immigration minus emigration) are higher in good times than in bad.

Labour-Force Participation.   The proportion of the total population that is willing to work is called the *labour-force participation rate.* Economists also define participation rates for subgroups, such as women or youths. Participation rates vary in response to many influences, including changes in attitudes and tastes. The enormous rise in female participation rates in the past four decades is one example. Another is a lowering of the retirement age, which has the effect of reducing the overall labour-force participation rate.

Forces other than tastes also play a role in determining the labour-force participation rate. For example, a rise in the demand for labour, and an accompanying rise in the wage, will lead to an increase in the proportion of the population willing to work. More women with children enter the labour force when wages are high. For the same reasons, the labour force tends to decline when earnings and employment opportunities decline.

These new births will eventually increase the labour force and thus the country's supply of labour.

Hours Worked.   The wage rate not only influences the number of people in the labour force, but it also affects the number of hours worked for each person. When workers sell their labour services to employers, they are giving up leisure in order to gain income with which to buy goods. They can therefore be thought of as trading leisure for goods. A rise in the wage implies a change in the relative price of goods and leisure. An increase in the wage means that leisure becomes more expensive relative to goods, because each hour of leisure consumed is at the cost of more goods forgone.

It is not necessarily the case, however, that an increase in the wage increases the amount of hours worked. In fact, an increase in the wage generates both income and substitution effects (see Chapter 6). As the wage rises, the substitution effect leads the individual to work more hours (consume less leisure) because leisure is now relatively more expensive. The income effect of a higher wage, however, leads the individual to work fewer hours (consume more leisure). Because the two effects work in the opposite direction we are, in general, unsure how a rise in the wage will affect the number of hours an individual chooses to work.

The Supply of Factors to a Particular Use

Most factors have many uses. A given piece of land can be used to grow any one of several crops, or it can be subdivided for a housing development. A computer programmer living in the Ottawa valley can work for one of several firms, for the government, or for Carleton University. A lathe can be used to make many different products, and it requires no adaptation when it is turned for one use or another.

One industry or occupation can attract a factor away from another industry or occupation, even though the total supply of that factor may be fixed. Thus, a factor's elasticity of supply to a particular use is larger than its elasticity of supply to the entire economy.

factor mobility   The ease with which factors can be transferred between uses.

When we consider the supply of a factor for a particular use, the most important concept is **factor mobility**. A factor that shifts easily between uses in response to small changes in incentives is said to be *mobile*. Its supply to any one use will be elastic because a small increase in the price offered will attract many units of the factor from other uses. A factor that does not shift easily from one use to another, even in response to large changes in remuneration, is said to be *immobile*. It will be in inelastic supply in any one use because even a large increase in the price offered will attract only a small inflow from other uses. Generally, a factor is less mobile in the short run than in the long run.

An important determinant of factor mobility is time: The longer the time interval, the easier it is for a factor to convert from one use to another.

Consider the factor mobility among particular uses of each of the three key factors of production.

Capital.   Some kinds of capital equipment—lathes, trucks, and computers, for example—can be shifted readily among uses; many others are comparatively unshiftable. A great deal of machinery is specific: Once built, it must be used for the purpose for which it was designed, or it cannot be used at all. Indeed, it is the immobility of much fixed capital equipment that makes the exit of firms from declining industries the slow and difficult process described in Chapter 9.

In the long run, however, capital is highly mobile. When capital goods wear out, a firm may replace them with identical goods, it may buy a newly designed machine to produce the same goods, or it may buy machines to produce totally different goods.

Land.   Land, which is physically the least mobile of factors, is one of the *most* mobile in an economic sense. Consider agricultural land. In a given year, one crop can be harvested and a totally different crop can be planted. A farm on the outskirts of a growing city can be sold for subdivision and development on short notice. Once land is built on, however, its mobility is much reduced.

Although land is highly mobile among alternative uses, it is completely immobile as far as location is concerned. There is only so much land within a given distance of the centre of any city, and no increase in the price paid can induce further land to be located within that distance. This locational immobility has important consequences, including high prices for desirable locations and the tendency to build tall buildings to economize on the use of scarce land, as in the centre of large cities.

Labour.   The supply of labour services often requires the physical presence of the person who supplies it. Absentee landlords, while continuing to live in the place of their choice, can obtain income from land that is located in remote parts of the world. Investment can be shifted from iron mines in South Africa to mines in Labrador while the owners commute between Calgary and Hawaii. The same is true for some workers, such as designers or bookkeepers, who can work in one location and submit their work to clients in other locations. But almost all workers involved in manufacturing and most of those involved in serving the public in stores, restaurants, and so on, must actually be present to supply their labour services to an employer. When a worker who is employed by a firm producing men's ties in Montreal decides instead to supply his or her labour services to a firm producing women's shoes in Winnipeg, the worker must physically travel to Winnipeg. This has an important consequence.

Because of the need for labour's physical presence when its services are provided for the production of many goods, nonmonetary considerations are much more important for the supply of labour than for other factors of production.

People may be satisfied with or frustrated by the kind of work that they do, where they do it, the people with whom they do it, and the social status of their occupations. Because these considerations influence their decisions about what they will do with their labour services, they will not always move just because they could earn a higher wage.

Nevertheless, labour is mobile among industries, occupations, and areas in response to changes in the signals provided by wages and opportunities for employment. The ease with which such mobility occurs depends on many forces. For example, it is not difficult for a secretary to shift from one company to another in order to take a job in Red Deer, Alberta, instead of Regina, Saskatchewan, but it can be difficult for a secretary to become an editor, a model, a machinist, or a doctor within a short period of time. Workers who lack ability, training, or inclination find certain kinds of mobility difficult or impossible.

Some barriers to movement may be virtually insurmountable once a person's training has been completed. For example, it may be impossible for a farmer to become a surgeon or for a truck driver to become a professional athlete, even if the relative wage rates change greatly. However, the children of farmers, doctors, truck drivers, and athletes, when they are deciding how much education or training to obtain, are not nearly as limited in their choices as their parents, who have already completed their education and are settled in their occupations.

The role of education in helping new labour-force entrants to adapt to available jobs is important. In a society like Canada's in which university and college education is available to most people at highly subsidized rates, it is possible to achieve large increases in the supply of any needed labour skill within just a few years. These issues are discussed at greater length in the first part of Chapter 14.

The labour force as a whole is mobile, even though many individual members in it are not.

The mobility of labour may sound like a pretty abstract topic—one that is hard to get excited about. You may not think so, however, when you find that jobs for which you are trained are abundant but only at the other end of the country. One particular case of labour mobility has become hotly debated in Canada in the past few years. Some economists and policymakers are concerned about the net flow of workers, especially highly skilled ones, from Canada to the United States—what has become known as Canada's "brain drain." *Applying Economic Concepts 13-1* discusses the recent mobility of labour between Canada and the United States, and outlines some of the central issues in the debate.

The Supply of Factors to a Particular Firm

Most firms usually employ a small proportion of the total supply of each factor that they use. As a result, they can usually obtain their factors at the going market price. This is true both in the case of less-skilled workers and in the case of highly skilled workers. For example, a firm of management consultants can usually augment its clerical staff by placing an ad in the local newspaper and paying the going rate for clerks. A university which is hoping to expand its economics department can similarly place an ad in *The Economist* or in a professional journal; it would also find itself paying the going rate for economics professors. In neither case will the employer's hiring actions affect the rate of pay earned by clerks (or professors) in its area.

Individual firms generally face perfectly elastic supply curves for factors, even though the supply for the economy as a whole may be quite inelastic.

FIGURE 13-4   The Determination of Factor Price and Income in a Competitive Factor Market

In competitive factor markets, demand and supply determine factor prices, quantities of factors used, and factor incomes. With demand and supply curves D_0 and S, the price of the factor will be p_0 and the quantity employed will be q_0. The total income earned by the factor is the light gray shaded area. A shift in demand from D_0 to D_1 raises equilibrium price and quantity to p_1 and q_1, respectively. The income earned by the factor rises by an amount equal to the dark gray shaded area.

The Operation of Factor Markets

Once you have mastered the basic analysis of demand and supply in Chapters 3 through 5, the determination of the price, quantity, and income of a factor in a single market poses no new problems. Figure 13-4 shows a competitive market for a factor. The intersection of the demand and the supply curve determine the factor's price and the quantity of it that is employed. The price times quantity is the factor's total income.

In this section, we explore three issues relating to factor pricing. First, what explains the differences in payments received by different units of the same factor? For example, why do some workers get paid more than others? Second, what is the effectiveness of policies designed to reduce these differences? Can policies that promote "pay equity" eliminate these differences? Finally, we explore the important concept of *economic rent*.

Differentials in Factor Prices

Why is it that airline pilots typically get paid more than auto mechanics? Why does an acre of land in downtown Calgary rent for much more than an acre of land 150 kilometres away in the Crowsnest Pass? Are such *factor-price differentials* to be expected in well-functioning markets?

If all workers were the same, if the attractiveness of all jobs were the same, and if workers moved freely among markets, the price of labour would be the same in all uses. Workers would move from low-priced jobs to high-priced ones. The quantity of labour supplied would diminish in low-wage occupations and the resulting labour shortage would tend to force those wages up. Conversely, the quantity of labour supplied would increase in high-wage occupations and the resulting surplus would force wages down. The movement would continue until there were no further incentives to change occupations—that is, until wages were equalized in all uses.

In fact, however, wage differentials commonly occur, as is clear from even the most cursory examination of the help-wanted ads in any newspaper. As it is with labour, so it is with other factors of production. If all units of any factor of production were identical and moved freely among markets, all units would receive the same remuneration in equilibrium. In fact, however, different units of any one factor receive different payments.

Factor-price differentials can be divided into two types: those that exist only temporarily and those that exist in long-run equilibrium.

Temporary factor-price differentials lead to, and are eroded by, factor mobility. Equilibrium differentials are not eliminated by factor mobility.

Let's see why this is the case.

Temporary Differentials

Some factor-price differentials reflect temporary disturbances in factor markets. They are brought about by circumstances such as the growth of one industry and the decline of another. The differentials themselves lead to reallocation of factors, and such reallocations in turn act to eliminate the differentials.

Consider the effect on factor prices of a rise in the demand for air transport and a decline in the demand for rail transport. The airline industry's demand for factors increases while the railroad industry's demand for factors decreases. Factor prices will go up in airlines and down in railroads. The differential in factor prices causes a net movement of factors away from the railroad industry and toward the airline industry, and this movement causes the differentials to lessen and eventually to disappear. How long this process takes will depend on how easily factors can be reallocated from one industry to the other—that is, on the degree of factor mobility.

The behaviour that causes the erosion of temporary differentials is summarized in the hypothesis of the *maximization of net advantage:* The owners of factors of production will allocate those factors to uses that maximize the net advantages to themselves, taking both monetary and nonmonetary rewards into consideration. If net advantages were higher

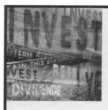

APPLYING ECONOMIC CONCEPTS 13-1

Is Canada Suffering a "Brain Drain"?

Thousands of United Empire Loyalists left the American colonies in the late 1770s and settled in what eventually became eastern and southern Ontario. A century later, thousands of Canadians moved to work in the rapidly expanding textile factories in Massachusetts and other New England states. Indeed, workers have been flowing in both directions across the 49th parallel for centuries. The close proximity of Canada and the United States, combined with a shared language and similar culture, makes moving between the two countries relatively easy. This movement of workers is an excellent example of labour mobility.

Recent Canada–U.S. Migration

The accompanying figure shows the annual total flows of migrants between Canada and the United States between 1982 and 1996. By migration, we mean people who move permanently between countries. In 1982, the two flows were about the same—approximately 3500 workers per year migrated in each direction. More recently, however, the flows out of Canada have grown substantially whereas the flows into Canada have gradually declined. By 1996, almost 7000 Canadian workers were migrating annually to the United States whereas only 1300 were coming in the opposite direction.

Note that these migration data understate the amount of worker mobility. Many workers move temporarily between the two countries, working for several months or even a few years before returning to their home country. There is some debate about the size of these flows of temporary workers, but based on research by John Helliwell at UBC, the annual flow of temporary workers from Canada to the United States appears to be roughly 10 000.

Two questions immediately come to mind regarding these data. First, who are these mobile workers? When the migration data are examined more closely, we see a net outflow from Canada of all broad categories of worker—professionals, managers, skilled workers and unskilled workers. The greatest outflow, however, occurs among the professionals and managers. For the temporary workers, the data are less clear, but roughly half of the annual outflow have university degrees.

Second, why are these people moving? This question is more difficult to answer precisely. Here are four possible an-

swers. First, U.S. immigration policy, especially toward Canadians, has loosened since the inception of the Canada-U.S. Free Trade Agreement (FTA) in 1989 and the North American Free Trade Agreement (NAFTA) in 1994. But this only tells us that it is easier to move than before—it doesn't tell us why people want to move in the first place. Second, job prospects for certain types of workers may be more promising in the United States than in Canada. This may be especially true for university researchers and workers in the health-care sector. As government budget cuts during the 1990s have hit these publicly funded areas sharply, highly trained workers may be led to seek better prospects in the United States. A third explanation is that relatively higher personal income-tax rates in Canada have been driving Canadians southward, seeking a smaller "tax bite." A fourth reason for Canadians to move to the United States is that average real incomes in the United States are significantly higher than in Canada—the gap was approximately 30 percent in 1997.

The "Brain Drain"

Many Canadian economists and policymakers have come to see this net outflow of Canadian workers—the "brain drain"—as an important problem. They argue that the brain drain generates both short-term and long-term costs. To the extent that education and skills are an important determinant of long-run economic growth, the departure of highly trained workers will harm Canada's long-run growth potential. This is the long-run cost.

The short-run cost is the effect on the government's fiscal budget. First, the departure of highly trained workers means that the Canadian government will no longer be able to tax their higher-than-average incomes. This is a direct reduction in government revenues. Second, the education and skills acquired by people in Canada before they move to the United States have, in general, been provided at publicly funded institutions. Thus, Canadian taxpayers are financing individuals to acquire education that is then used to generate benefits accruing to those in the United States—this is a transfer from Canadian taxpayers to U.S. residents.

Many who see the brain drain as a serious economic problem advocate "doing something" to either reduce or re-

in occupation A than in occupation B, factors would move from B to A. The increased supply in A and the reduced supply in B would drive factor earnings down in A and up in B until net advantages would be equalized, after which no further movement would occur. This analysis gives rise to the prediction of *equal net advantage:* In equilibrium, units of each verse this outflow of Canadian workers. But what can be done? The Canadian tax system is a straightforward policy tool that many economists and policymakers have advocated using. They propose reducing tax rates as a way of preventing both the short-run and long-run costs that a continuing brain drain would otherwise cause. Another option that is more directed at reducing the mobility of highly trained workers is to make students pay the full cost of their university education unless they remain in Canada for a specified number of years after graduation. This would both reduce the outflow of workers and, where such an outflow still existed, reduce the cost to Canadian taxpayers.

An Important Debate

Some economists suggest several reasons why the brain drain may not be so serious. They point to the large flow of temporary workers from Canada to the United Sates and note that as long as those workers return to Canada, there will be no permanent costs for the Canadian economy. But many economists fear that a large fraction of those large annual flows of "temporary" workers will quickly choose to remain in the United States where job prospects are better and real incomes are higher.

The second point is that the mobility between Canada and the United States is only part of the story. Equally important is the mobility of workers between Canada and other countries. Canada may be suffering a brain drain to the United States, but if this is more than made up by a "brain gain" from other countries, then perhaps there is no real

problem at all. Indeed, Helliwell's data suggest that over the past fifty years, total emigration from Canada has averaged only about 35 percent of total immigration to Canada. Others point out, however, that these workers from Asia, Eastern Europe or South America tend to be slightly less skilled than the workers we lose to the United States.

Finally, note that the annual flows of workers shown in the figure are actually small compared to the total Canadian labour force. In 1996, the Canadian labour force was 15.1 million workers. Thus, the outflow of 7000 workers was only 0.0004 percent of the labour force. Even if we add the full 10 000 temporary workers, the total is still only 0.001 percent of the labour force. Other economists, however, note that while this flow is small relative to the overall Canadian labour force, it is a much larger fraction of Canada's stock of highly skilled workers. And it is the loss of these workers that is at the heart of the issue.

So what is the conclusion? Is the brain drain an important enough problem that Canadian policymakers should be worried about the tax and expenditure implications, or the effects on Canada's long-run growth? It is too early for a consensus. More research will surely be done on this issue over the next few years, and perhaps then a consensus will emerge.

The migration data in this box are from D. DeVoretz and S. Laryea, "Canadian Human Capital Transfers: The United States and Beyond," C.D. Howe Institute Commentary No. 115, October 1998. See also John Helliwell, "Checking the Brain Drain: Evidence and Implications," UBC mimeo, June 1999.

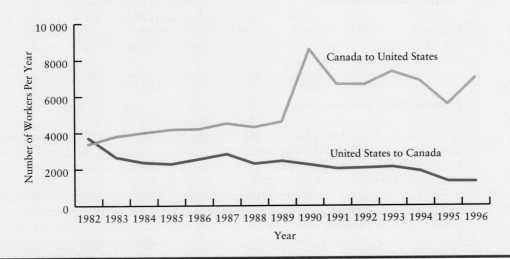

kind of factor of production will be allocated among alternative possible uses in such a way that the net advantages in all uses are equalized.

Although nonmonetary advantages are important in explaining differences in levels of pay for labour in different occupations, they tend to be fairly stable over time. As a result, monetary advantages, which vary with market conditions, lead to *changes* in net advantage.

A change in the relative price of a factor between two uses will change the net advantages of the uses. It will lead to a shift of some units of that factor to the use for which relative price has increased.

This shift implies an upward-sloping supply curve for a factor in any particular use. When the price of a factor rises in that use, more will be supplied to that use. This factor supply curve (like all supply curves) can also *shift* in response to changes in other variables. For example, an improvement in the safety record in a particular occupation improves the attractiveness of that occupation and thus shifts to the right the labour-supply curve to that occupation.

Equilibrium Differentials

Some factor-price differentials persist without generating any forces that eliminate them. These equilibrium differentials can be explained by intrinsic differences in the factors themselves and, for labour, by differences in the cost of acquiring skills and by different non-monetary advantages of different occupations. Because these factor-price differentials *compensate* for nonmonetary aspects of the job or the factor, they are commonly called **compensating differentials**; they were introduced into economics more than two hundred years ago by Adam Smith.

compensating differential
A difference in the financial payment to a factor of production (usually labour) across two jobs to compensate the factor for differences in non-monetary aspects of the two jobs.

Intrinsic Differences.   If various units of a factor have different characteristics, the price that is paid may differ among these units. If dexterity is required to accomplish a task, manually dexterous workers will earn more than less dexterous workers. If land is to be used for agricultural purposes, highly fertile land will earn more than poor land. These differences will persist even in long-run equilibrium.

Acquired Differences.   If the fertility of land can be increased by costly methods, then more fertile land must command a higher price than less fertile land. If it did not, landowners would not incur the costs of improving fertility. The same principle holds true for labour since it is costly to acquire most skills. For example, an engineer must train for some time, and unless the earnings of engineers remain sufficiently above what can be earned in less skilled occupations, people will not incur the cost of training.

Nonmonetary Advantages.   Whenever working conditions differ among various uses for a single factor, that factor will earn different equilibrium amounts in its various uses. The difference between a test pilot's wage and a chauffeur's wage is only partly a matter of skill; the rest is compensation to the worker for facing the higher risk of testing new planes as compared to driving a car. If both were paid the same, there would be an excess supply of chauffeurs and a shortage of test pilots.

Academic researchers commonly earn less than they could earn in the world of commerce and industry because of the substantial nonmonetary advantages of academic employment. If chemists were paid the same in both sectors, many chemists would prefer academic to industrial jobs. Excess demand for industrial chemists and excess supply of academic chemists would then force chemists' wages up in industry and down in academia until the two types of jobs seemed equally attractive on balance.

Equilibrium differentials also exist in the regional earnings of otherwise identical factors. People who work in remote logging or mining areas are paid more than are people who do jobs requiring similar skills in large cities. Without higher pay, not enough people would be willing to work at sometimes dangerous jobs in unattractive or remote locations. Similarly, because many people prefer living in the Maritimes to living in the Yukon, equilibrium wages in comparable occupations are lower in the Maritimes than in the Yukon.

Pay Equity

The distinction between temporary and equilibrium factor-price differentials raises an important consideration for policy. Trade unions, governments, and other bodies often have explicit policies about earnings differentials, sometimes seeking to eliminate them in the name of equity. The success of such policies depends to a great extent on the kind of differential that is being attacked. One general lesson here is the following: Policies that attempt to eliminate *equilibrium* differentials will encounter severe difficulties.

Some government legislation attempts to impose *equal pay for work of equal value,* or **pay equity.** Such policy is designed to eliminate the wage differentials that exist between workers *in different jobs* but who are deemed to have approximately the same skills and responsibilities. For example, a policy of pay equity might require that a nurse with 10 years of experience receive the same salary as a teacher with 10 years of experience. Whatever the social value of such laws, they run into trouble whenever they require equal pay for jobs that have different nonmonetary advantages.

To illustrate the nature of the problem encountered by such legislation, consider the following example. Suppose that two jobs demand equal skills, training, and everything else that is taken into account in a decision about what constitutes work of equal value but that, in a city with an unpleasant climate, one is an outside job and the other is an inside job. If legislation requires equal pay for both jobs, there will be a shortage of people who are willing to work outside and an excess of people who want to work inside. Employers will seek ways to attract outside workers. Higher pensions, shorter hours, and longer holidays may be offered. If these are allowed, they will achieve the desired result but will defeat the original purpose of equalizing the monetary benefits of the inside and outside jobs; they will also cut down on the number of outside workers that employers will hire because the total cost of an outside worker to an employer will have risen. If the jobs are unionized or if the government prevents such "cheating," the shortage of workers for outside jobs will remain.

In Chapter 14, we discuss the effects of race and sex discrimination on wage differentials. Although these effects can be important, it remains true that many factor-price differentials are a natural market consequence of supply and demand conditions that have nothing to do with inequitable treatment of different groups in the society.

Policies that seek to eliminate factor-price differentials without consideration of what causes them or how they affect the supply of the factor often have perverse results.

Economic Rent

One of the most important concepts in economics is that of *economic rent*.

A factor must earn a certain amount in its present use to prevent it from moving to another use—Alfred Marshall called this amount the factor's **transfer earnings.** If there were no nonmonetary advantages in alternative uses, as is typically the case for land and capital, the factor would have to earn its opportunity cost (what it could earn elsewhere) to prevent it from moving elsewhere.

pay equity
A government policy designed to eliminate the wage differentials between workers in different jobs who nonetheless appear to have similar levels of skills and responsibilities.

transfer earnings
The payment required by a factor in order to prevent it from leaving to other uses. Any payment in excess of the transfer earnings is economic rent.

For labour, however, the nonmonetary advantages of various jobs are very important. Labour must earn enough in each use to equate the total advantages—both monetary and nonmonetary—among various jobs. For example, in order to accept a job that is dirty or unsafe, workers will require a higher wage so that the total advantage of the unsafe job equals the total advantage of some alternative job.

Any excess that a factor earns over the minimum amount needed to keep it at its present use is called its **economic rent**. Economic rent is analogous to economic profit as a surplus over the opportunity cost of capital. Here are three examples:

economic rent   The surplus of total earnings over what must be paid to prevent a factor from moving to another use.

1. Consider a farmer who grows wheat and earns $1000 per acre. He has calculated that if his earnings fall to $900 per acre, he will switch to growing barley instead, his next best alternative. In this case, each acre of land is earning $100 of economic rent.

2. A famous actor earns $15 million per year. She decides that her next best alternative to acting is to promote shampoo in television commercials, in which case she would earn $2.5 million per year. She is earning $12.5 million per year of economic rent.

3. An individual has invested $300 000 of capital into a restaurant, and currently earns a 20 percent annual return—investment income of $60 000 annually. The next best alternative investment (with similar risk) can earn a 15 percent return, or $45 000 annually. The $300 000 of capital is thus earning economic rent equal to $15 000 per year. In this case, rent is just another name for profit in the economist's sense of the term.

The concept of economic rent is crucial in predicting the effects that changes in earnings have on the movement of factors among alternative uses. However, the terminology is confusing because economic rent is often called simply *rent,* which can of course also mean the price paid to hire something, such as a machine, a piece of land, or an apartment. How the same term came to be used for these two very different concepts is explained in *Lessons from History 13-1.*

FIGURE 13-5   The Determination of Rent in Factor Payments

The amount of rent in factor payments depends on the shape of the supply curve. A single demand curve is shown with three different supply curves. In each case, the competitive equilibrium price is $600, and 4000 units of the factor are hired. The total payment ($2.4 million) is represented by the entire shaded area.

When the supply curve is vertical (S_0), the whole payment is economic rent because a decrease in price would not lead any units of the factor to move elsewhere.

When the supply curve is horizontal (S_1), none of the payment is rent because even a small decrease in price offered would lead all units of the factor to move elsewhere.

When the supply curve is positively sloped (S_2), part of the payment is rent. As shown by the height of the supply curve, at a price of $600, the 4000th unit of the factor is receiving just enough to persuade it to offer its services in this market, but the 2000th unit, for example, is earning well above what it requires to stay in this market. The aggregate of economic rents is shown by the blue shaded area, whereas the aggregate of the factor's transfer earnings is shown by the red area.

How Much of Factor Earnings Is Rent?

In most cases, as in the three previous examples, economic rent makes up part of the factor's total earnings. From the definitions above, however, note that total earnings for any factor are the sum of its transfer earnings and its economic rent.

Practise with Study Guide Chapter 13, Exercises 3 and 5.

A factor's transfer earnings plus its economic rent equals its total earnings.

But *how much* of total earnings is economic rent? The distinction is easiest to see in two extreme examples. In the first, all of the factor's income is rent; in the second, none of the income is rent.

The possibilities are illustrated in Figure 13-5. When supply is perfectly inelastic, the same quantity is supplied whatever the price. Evidently, the quantity supplied does not decrease, no matter how low the price goes. This inelasticity indicates that the factor has no alternative use, and thus requires no minimum payment to keep it in its present use. In this case, there are no transfer earnings and so the whole of the payment is economic rent.

When supply is perfectly elastic, the factor is extremely mobile between various uses. In this case, all of the factor's income is transfer earnings and so none of it is economic rent. If any lower price is offered, nothing whatsoever will be supplied since all units of the factor will transfer to some other use.

The more usual situation is that of an upward-sloping supply curve. A rise in the factor's price serves the allocative function of attracting more units of the factor into the market in question, but the same rise provides additional economic rent to all units of the factor that are *already employed*. We know that the extra pay that is going to the units already employed is economic rent because the owners of these units were willing to

LESSONS FROM HISTORY 13-1

David Ricardo and "Economic Rent"

In the early nineteenth century, there was a public debate about the high price of wheat in England. The high price was causing great hardship because bread was a primary source of food for the working class. Some people argued that wheat had a high price because landlords were charging high rents to tenant farmers. In short, it was argued that the price of wheat was high because the rents of agricultural land were high. Some of those who held this view advocated restricting the rents that landlords could charge.

David Ricardo (1772–1823), a great British economist who was one of the originators of Classical economics, argued that the situation was exactly the reverse. The price of wheat was high, he said, because there was a shortage, caused by the Napoleonic Wars. Because wheat was profitable to produce, there was keen competition among farmers to obtain land on which to grow wheat. This competition in turn forced up the rental price of wheat land. Ricardo advocated removing the existing tariff on wheat so that imported wheat could come into the country. The increase in imports would then increase the supply of wheat in England and lower its price. This would then reduce the rent on land.

The essentials of Ricardo's argument were these: The supply of land was fixed. Land was regarded as having only one use, the growing of wheat. Nothing had to be paid to prevent land from transferring to a use other than growing wheat because it had no other use. No landowner would leave land idle as long as some return could be obtained by renting it out. Therefore, all the payment to land, that is, rent in the ordinary sense of the word, was a surplus over and above what was necessary to keep it in its present use.

Given a fixed supply of land, the price of land depended on the demand for land, which depended in turn on the demand for wheat (i.e., the demand for land was *derived from* the demand for wheat). Rent, the term for the payment for the use of land, thus became the term for a surplus payment to a factor over and above what was necessary to keep it in its present use.

Later, two facts were realized. First, land often had alternative uses, and, from the point of view of any one use, part of the payment made to land would necessarily have to be paid to keep it in that use. Second, factors of production other than land also often earned a surplus over and above what was necessary to keep them in their present use. This surplus is now called *economic rent*, whether the factor is land, labour, or a piece of capital equipment.

supply them at the lower price. The general result for a positively sloped supply curve is stated as follows.

If the demand for a factor in any of its uses rises relative to the supply available to that use, its price will rise in that use. This increase in price will serve the allocative function of attracting additional units into that use. It will also increase the economic rent to all units of the factor already in that use.

Various Perspectives on Economic Rent

The proportion of a given factor payment that is economic rent varies from situation to situation. We cannot point to a factor of production and assert that some fixed fraction of its income is always its economic rent. The proportion of its earnings that is rent depends on its alternatives.

Consider first a narrowly defined use of a given factor—say, its use by a particular firm. From that firm's point of view, the factor will be highly mobile, as it could readily move to another firm in the same industry. The firm must pay the going wage or risk losing that factor. Thus, from the perspective of the single firm, a large proportion of the payment made to a factor is needed to prevent it from transferring to another use. Thus, only a small portion of its payment is rent.

Now consider a more broadly defined use—for example, the factor's use in an entire industry. From the industry's point of view, the factor is less mobile because it would be more difficult for it to gain employment quickly outside the industry. From the perspective of the particular *industry* (rather than the specific *firm* within the industry), a larger proportion of the payment to a factor is economic rent.

From the even more general perspective of a particular *occupation*, mobility is likely to be even less, and the proportion of the factor payment that is economic rent is likely to be more. It may be easier, for example, for a carpenter to move from the construction industry to the furniture industry than to retrain to be a computer programmer.

As the perspective moves from a narrowly defined use of a factor to a broadly defined use of a factor, the mobility of the factor decreases; as mobility decreases, the share of the factor payment that is economic rent increases.

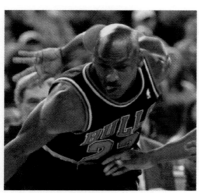

Whether Michael Jordan's immense salary with the Chicago Bulls was economic rent depends on the perspective. From the perspective of the entire NBA, most of his salary was economic rent.

Consider how this relationship applies to the often controversial large salaries that are received by some highly specialized types of labourers, such as recording stars and professional athletes. These performers have a style and a talent that cannot be duplicated, whatever the training. The earnings that they receive are mostly economic rent from the viewpoint of the occupation: These performers generally enjoy their occupations and would pursue them for much less than the high remuneration that they actually receive.

For example, Michael Jordan would probably have chosen basketball over other alternatives even at a much lower salary. However, because of Jordan's amazing skills as a basketball player, most NBA teams would have paid handsomely to have him on their rosters, and he was able to command a high salary from the team he did play for. From the perspective of the individual firm, the Chicago Bulls, most of Jordan's salary was required to keep him from switching to another team and hence was not economic rent. From the point of view of the basketball "industry," however, much of his salary was economic rent.

Notice also that Michael Jordan's salary was largely determined by the demand for his services. The supply was perfectly inelastic—no one else possessed his particular combination of skills. So the market-clearing price was determined by the position of the demand curve.

A Final Word

This chapter has examined the operation of factor markets. You should now be able to answer the questions that we posed in the opening paragraph. Here are some of the key points for two of those questions.

What explains why professors usually get paid more than high-school teachers? Part of the answer surely lies in the fact that to be a university professor typically requires nine years of university education (four for the bachelor's degree plus five for the completion of the master's degree and the doctorate) whereas to be a teacher usually requires only four or five years. Since that extra education is costly and time-consuming, it is not surprising that fewer people are willing to become university professors than teachers. This lower supply for professors, other things equal, leads to a higher wage.

Why does an acre of farm land in northern Saskatchewan rent for far less than an acre of land in downtown Toronto? To answer this, just think about the alternative uses for the farm land, and compare them to the alternative uses for the acre in downtown Toronto. The acre of farm land has very few alternative uses. Or, more correctly, it has many alternative uses, but there is little demand to use that particular piece of land to build a skyscraper, shopping mall, or baseball stadium. But one acre of land in downtown Toronto has many alternative uses—there always seems to be demand for additional space for parking garages, office buildings, retail stores, and many other things. Since the piece of farm land in Saskatchewan must stay where it is, its rental price is determined by demand. Since there is little demand for the land, its rental price is low. Similarly, the land in downtown Toronto cannot move anywhere, and so its rental price is determined by demand. And since there is lots of demand for an acre in downtown Toronto, its rental price is high.

Having learned about factor markets in general, we are now ready to examine some specific factor markets. In Chapter 14, we examine some details about labour markets, such as minimum wages, discrimination, and labour unions. In Chapter 15, we examine the pricing of physical capital and of nonrenewable resources.

S U M M A R Y

Income Distribution

- The functional distribution of income refers to the shares of total national income going to each of the major factors of production; it focuses on sources of income. The size distribution of income refers to the shares of total national income going to various groups of households; it focuses only on the amount of income, not its source.

- Canada has considerable inequality in the distribution of income. The poorest fifth of families currently receive 2.1 percent of aggregate pre-tax income; the richest fifth receives 44.6 percent. But Canada's tax-and-transfer system reduces the extent of inequality—the poorest fifth of families earn 7.7 percent of after-tax income.

- The income of a factor of production is composed of two elements: the price paid per unit of the factor and the quantity of the factor used. The determination of factor prices and quantities is an application of the same price theory that is used to determine product prices and quantities.

The Demand for Factors   (LO) ② ③

- The firm's decisions on how much to produce and how to produce it imply demands for factors of production, which are said to be derived from the demand for goods that they are used to produce.
- A profit-maximizing firm will hire units of a factor until the last unit adds as much to cost as it does to revenue. Thus, the marginal cost of the factor will be equated with that factor's marginal revenue product.
- When the firm is a price taker in input markets, the marginal cost of the factor is its price per unit. When the firm sells its output in a competitive market, the marginal revenue product is the factor's marginal physical product multiplied by the market price of the output.

- A price-taking firm's demand for a factor is negatively sloped because the law of diminishing returns implies that the marginal physical product of a factor declines as more of that factor is employed (with other inputs held constant).
- The industry's demand for a factor will be more elastic (a) the slower the marginal physical product of the factor declines as more of the factor is used, (b) the easier it is to substitute one factor for another, (c) the larger the proportion of total variable costs accounted for by the cost of the factor in question, and (d) the more elastic the demand for the good that the factor is used to produce.

The Supply of Factors   (LO) ④

- The total supply of each factor is fixed at any moment but varies over time. The supply of labour depends on the size of the population, the participation rate, and the number of hours that people want to work.
- A rise in the wage rate has a substitution effect, which tends to induce more work, and an income effect, which tends to induce less work (more leisure consumed).

- The supply of a factor to a particular industry or occupation is more elastic than its supply to the whole economy because one industry can bid units away from other industries. The elasticity of supply to a particular use depends on factor mobility, which tends to be greater the longer the time allowed for a reaction to take place.

The Operation of Factor Markets   (LO) ⑤ ⑥

- Factor-price differentials often occur in competitive markets. Temporary differentials in the earnings of different units of factors of production induce factor movements that eventually remove the differentials. Equilibrium differentials reflect differences among units of factors as well as nonmonetary benefits of different jobs; they can persist indefinitely.
- Equal net advantage is a theory of the allocation of the total supply of factors to particular uses. Owners of factors will choose the use that produces the greatest net advantage, allowing for both the monetary and nonmonetary advantages of a particular employment.
- Some amount must be paid to a factor to prevent it from transferring to another use. This amount is the factor's transfer earnings. Economic rent is the difference between that amount and a factor's actual earnings. Whenever the supply curve is positively sloped, part of the total payment going to a factor is needed to prevent it from transferring to another use, and part of it is rent. The more narrowly defined the use, the larger the fraction that is transfer earnings and the smaller the fraction that is economic rent.

KEY CONCEPTS

Functional distribution and size distribution of income

Derived demand for a factor

Marginal physical product *(MPP)*

Marginal revenue product *(MRP)*

The determinants of elasticity of factor demand

Factor mobility

Temporary versus equilibrium factor-price differentials

Equal net advantage

Transfer earnings

Economic rent

STUDY EXERCISES

1. The table below shows the size distribution of income for Fantasyland.

Household Income Rank	Percentage of Aggregate Income	Cumulative Total
Lowest fifth	6.8	—
Second fifth	14.1	—
Third fifth	21.5	—
Fourth fifth	26.2	—
Highest fifth	31.4	—

   a. Compute the cumulative percentage of total income. Fill in the table.

   b. On a scale diagram, with the percentage of households on the vertical axis and the percentage of aggregate income on the horizontal axis, plot the Lorenz curve for Fantasyland.

   c. How does the diagram show the extent of income inequality in Fantasyland?

   d. Now suppose that Fantasyland introduces a system which redistributes income from higher-income households to lower-income households. How would this affect the Lorenz curve?

2. Demands for the following goods and services are increasing rapidly. In each case, list two derived demands that you predict will be increasing as a result.

   a. Demand for natural gas

   b. Demand for medical services

   c. Demand for international travel

   d. Demand for children's computer games

3. The diagram below shows the market for fast-food workers in British Columbia.

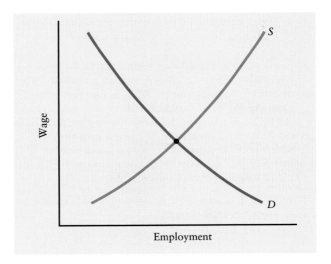

   a. The supply curve is upward sloping. If the wage in this industry rises, where do the extra workers come from?

   b. Suppose there is a significant decrease in demand for fast food. How is this likely to affect fast-food workers' earnings? Show this in the diagram.

   c. Now suppose that new legislation bans high-school students from doing any homework. As a result, more students look for jobs in the fast-food industry. How will this affect the labour market for fast-food workers? Show this in the diagram.

4. The three following diagrams show the supply of luxury ocean liners at three different levels of aggregation—the entire world, a particular country, and a particular firm.

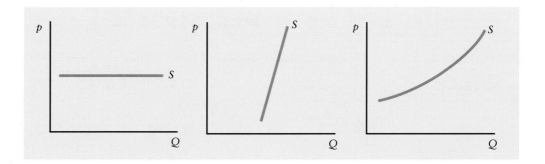

a. Which diagram shows the supply of ocean liners to the world as whole? Explain its elasticity.
b. Which diagram shows the supply of ocean liners to Canada? Explain its elasticity.
c. Which diagram shows the supply of ocean liners to an individual Canadian firm? Explain its elasticity.
d. What is the general relationship between factor mobility and the elasticity of factor supply?

5. In the text we argued that temporary factor-price differentials tend to be eroded by factor mobility. This question requires you to think about this process. Consider the two markets for sheet-iron workers and steel-pipe workers in the same region. Suppose both markets are competitive. We begin in a situation in which both sheet-iron workers and steel-pipe workers earn $20 per hour. Assume that workers can switch reasonably easily between the two jobs.

a. Draw diagrams showing the supply and demand for labour in each market.

b. Now suppose there is a sharp increase in the demand for steel pipe. Explain what happens in the market for steel-pipe workers.
c. If the employment of steel-pipe workers increased in part b, explain where the extra workers came from.
d. What effect does the event in part b have on the market for sheet-iron workers?
e. What is the long-run effect of the shock on the relative wages in the two types of jobs?

6. How much of the following payments for factor services is likely to be economic rent?

a. The $750 per month that a landlord receives for an apartment rented to students
b. The salary of the Canadian Prime Minister
c. The annual income of Tiger Woods or Shania Twain
d. The salary of a window cleaner who says, "It's dangerous work, but it beats driving a truck."

DISCUSSION QUESTIONS

1. Other things being equal, how would you expect each of the following events to affect the size distribution of after-tax income?

a. An increase in unemployment
b. Rapid population growth in an already crowded city
c. An increase in food prices relative to other prices
d. An increase in social insurance benefits and taxes
e. Elimination of the personal income-tax exemption for interest earned within an RRSP.

2. A labour dispute has broken out at a university between the faculty and the university's board of governors. One

of the issues is the faculty's complaint that summer school teaching salaries are below the regional average and hence too low. The trustees argue that considering that they have more professors asking to teach summer school at the current pay than they have courses for these faculty to teach, the pay is adequate. Comment.

3. This chapter introduced the Lorenz curve, which gives a graphical representation of the equality of income distribution. Many observers criticize Canadian policy because Canada's Lorenz curve is bent significantly off the diagonal. Can you provide an economically valid defence of this criticism? If you could pick a shape for

the nation's Lorenz curve, what would it be? Defend your choice using positive economic tools.

4. A recent *Wall Street Journal* article asks, "Why do baseball players earn millions of dollars a year for their negligible contribution to society while major contributors—such as schoolteachers, policemen, firemen, and ambulance drivers—earn barely enough to survive?" Can you offer an answer based on what was discussed in this chapter?

5. For most of the years in the past two decades, the unemployment rate in the province of Quebec has been higher than the Canadian average. It has also been higher than the unemployment rate in next-door Ontario. Given that there are almost no legal restrictions on the flow of labour across Canadian provincial boundaries, provide an explanation for how such a gap in unemployment rates can persist for so long.

CHAPTER 14

Labour Markets

LEARNING OBJECTIVES

1. Explain wage differentials in competitive labour markets.

2. Explain the wage differentials that arise in imperfectly competitive labour markets.

3. Understand the effects of legislated minimum wages.

4. Recognize the tradeoff that unions face between employment and wages.

5. Explain why the trend away from manufacturing jobs and toward service jobs is not necessarily a problem for the economy as a whole.

The competitive theory of factor-price determination, presented in Chapter 13, tells us a great deal about factor prices, factor movements, and the distribution of income. In this chapter, we apply this theory to the most important of factor markets, the labour market. In the process, we extend the theory to cover situations in which suppliers and demanders of labour have some market power in the labour market, and are thus not price takers. We also examine the effects of legislated minimum wages and the role of labour unions. The chapter closes with a discussion of the often-heard claim that Canada and other developed countries have been gaining "bad jobs" at the expense of "good jobs."

Wage Differentials

If all workers were identical, all jobs had the same working conditions, and labour markets were perfectly competitive, all workers would earn the same wage. In reality, however, wages vary enormously across workers and occupations. Generally, the more education and experience a worker has, the higher are his or her wages. Given equal education and experience, women on average earn less than men. Workers in highly unionized industries tend to get paid more than workers with similar skills and experience in nonunionized industries. Such differentials arise because workers are not all identical, jobs are not all identical, and because many important noncompetitive forces operate in labour markets. We now look more systematically at the reasons why different types of labour earn different wages.

Wage Differentials in Competitive Markets

Where there are many employers (buyers) and many workers (sellers), there is a competitive labour market of the kind discussed in Chapter 13. Under competitive conditions, the wage rate and level of employment are set by supply and demand. No worker or group of workers, and no firm or group of firms, is able to affect the market wage. In practice, however, there are many kinds of workers and many kinds of jobs. We can therefore think of a series of related labour markets rather than a single national market. Among these various labour markets, there are several reasons for wage differentials.

Working Conditions

Given identical skills, those working under relatively onerous or risky conditions earn more than those working in pleasant or safe conditions. For example, construction workers who work the "high iron," assembling the frames for skyscrapers, are paid more than workers who do similar work at ground level. The reason is simple: Risk and unpleasantness reduce the supply of labour, thus raising the wage above what it would otherwise be. Different working conditions in different jobs thus lead to wage differentials—these are equilibrium differentials as discussed in Chapter 13.

In competitive labour markets, supply and demand set the equilibrium wage, but the wage will differ according to the nonmonetary aspects of the job.

Inherited Skills

Large incomes will be earned by people who have scarce skills that cannot be taught and that are highly valued—for example, the physical ability to be an NBA basketball player. In this case, the combination of a small and inelastic supply and a large enough demand of the relevant kind of labour cause the market-clearing wage to be high. Wage differentials of this kind are equilibrium differentials.

Inherited skills, which are mostly beyond the individual's control, can have important effects on wages.

Human Capital

A machine is physical capital. It requires an investment of time and money to create it, and once created, it yields valuable services over a long time. In the same way, labour skills require an investment of time and money to acquire, and once acquired, they yield an increased income to their owner over a long time. Since investment in labour skills is similar to investment in physical capital, acquired skills are called **human capital.** The more costly it is to acquire the skill required for a particular job, the higher its pay must be to attract people to train for it.

human capital The capitalized value of productive investments in persons; usually refers to value derived from expenditures on education, training, and health improvements.

Investment in human capital is costly, and the return is usually in terms of higher future wages.

The two main ways in which human capital is acquired are through formal education and on-the-job training.

Formal Education. Compulsory education is an attempt to provide some minimum human capital for all citizens. Some people, either through luck or through their own efforts, acquire more human capital than others. Subsequent income differentials

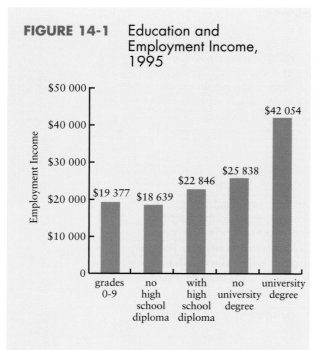

FIGURE 14-1   Education and Employment Income, 1995

There is a financial payoff to formal education, especially a university degree. The increase in employment income that can be expected from extra education is modest for levels of education below a university degree. But the payoff for completing a university degree is very substantial.

(*Source:* These data are available on Statistics Canada's website: www.statcan.ca.)

reflect these differences in human capital acquired in the early stages of education.

Those who decide to stay in school beyond the years of compulsory education, such as the people reading this book, are deciding to invest voluntarily in acquiring further human capital. The opportunity cost is measured by the income that could have been earned if the person had entered the labour force immediately, in addition to any out-of-pocket costs for such items as tuition fees and equipment. The return is measured by the higher income earned when a better job is obtained.

How large is the payoff to higher education? Figure 14-1 shows how average employment income varies with years of schooling. In 1995, the latest year for which census data are available, the average employment income for Canadians with a university degree was just over $42 000; in contrast, someone who had completed grade 9 or less had an average employment income of less than half this amount.

Evidence suggests that in recent years the demand for workers with more education has been rising relative to the demand for those with less education. As we would expect, this change in relative demand raises the relative wages of more-educated people, thereby increasing the payoff to their investment in education. Not surprisingly, students today find the completion of a university degree much more important than did students a generation ago.

Changes in demand and supply change the costs and benefits of acquiring human capital. Individuals respond according to their personal assessment of these costs and benefits.

On-the-Job Training.   Wage differentials according to experience are readily observable in most firms and occupations. To a significant extent, these differentials are a response to human capital acquired on the job. For example, a civil engineer with 20 years' experience in bridge design will generally earn more than a newly graduated civil engineer, even though they both have the same formal education.

On-the-job training is important in creating rising wages for employees and for making firms competitive. Evidence suggests that people who miss on-the-job training early in life are handicapped relative to others throughout much of their later working careers.

Wage differentials that are due to differences in human capital—either through formal education or on-the-job-training—are *temporary* differentials. In the long run, these wage differentials will affect the choices that individuals make about investing in human capital. These choices will, in turn, help to erode these differentials. For example, if university graduates earn more than high-school graduates, then more people will choose to attend university. This will eventually increase the supply of university graduates (and reduce the supply of people with only a high-school education) and thus reduce their wage relative to high-school graduates. Full adjustment in this process will clearly not occur immediately, and may take many years.

Wage differentials due to differences in human capital will eventually be eroded by the changing pattern of human-capital acquisition. But these wage differentials may persist for many years.

Gender and Race Discrimination

Crude statistics show that incomes vary by race and gender. For example, the average full-time female worker in Canada earns only about 75 percent of the wage of the average full-time male worker. More detailed studies suggest that a significant part of these differences can be explained by such considerations as the amount of human capital acquired through both formal education and on-the-job experience. When all such explanations are taken into account, however, there still appears to be some discrimination on the basis of both gender and race. The following is a simple model of labour-market discrimination.

To isolate the effects of discrimination, we begin by building a simplified picture of a nondiscriminating labour market and then introduce discrimination between two sets of equally qualified workers. The discussion here is phrased in terms of males and females but the analysis applies equally well to any situation in which workers are distinguished on grounds *other than* their ability, such as race or skin colour, citizenship, religion, sexual preference, or political beliefs.

FIGURE 14-2   The Effect of Discrimination on Wages

(i) Elite market (E)

(ii) Ordinary market (O)

If market E discriminates against one group and market O does not, the supply curve will shift to the left in E and to the right in O. Market E requires above-average skills, while market O requires only ordinary skills. When there is no discrimination, demand and supply are D_E and S_E in market E and D_O and S_O in market O. Initially, the wage rate is w_0 and employment is q_0 in each market. (w_0 in market E will be higher than w_0 in market O because the workers in E have higher skills than those in O.) When all women are barred from E occupations, the supply curve shifts to S'_E, and the wage earned by the remaining workers, all of whom are men, rises to w_1. Women put out of work in the E occupations now seek work in the O occupations. The resulting shift in the supply curve to S'_O brings down the wage to w_2 in the O occupations. Because all women are in O occupations, they have a lower wage rate than many men. The average male wage in the economy is higher than the average female wage.

Suppose that half of the people are male and the other half are female. Each group has the same proportion who are educated to various levels, identical distributions of talent, and so on. Suppose also that there are two occupations. Occupation E (*elite*) requires people of above-average education and skills, and occupation O (*ordinary*) can use anyone. Finally, suppose that the nonmonetary aspects of the two occupations are the same.

In the absence of discrimination, the theory of competitive factor markets that we have developed suggests that the wages in E occupations will be bid up above those in O occupations in order that the E jobs attract the workers of above-average skills. Men and women of above-average skill will take the E jobs, while the others, both men and women, will have no choice but to seek O jobs. Because skills are equally distributed among both sexes, each occupation will employ one-half men and one-half women.

Now suppose that discrimination enters in an extreme form. All E occupations are hereafter open only to men, but O occupations are open to either men or women. The immediate effect is to reduce by 50 percent the supply of job candidates for E occupations; candidates must now be *both* men and above average. The discrimination also increases the supply of applicants for O jobs by 50 percent; this group now includes all women and the below-average men.

As shown in Figure 14-2, wages rise in E occupations and fall in O occupations.

Discrimination, by changing supply, can decrease the wages and incomes of a group that is discriminated against.

In the longer run, further changes may occur. Notice that total employment in the E jobs falls. Employers may find ways to use slightly below average labour and thus lure the next best qualified men out of O occupations. Although this will raise O wages slightly, it will also make these occupations increasingly "female occupations." If discrimination has been in place for a sufficient length of time, women will learn that it does not pay to acquire above-average skills. Regardless of ability, women are forced by discrimination to work in unskilled jobs.

Now suppose that a long-standing discriminatory policy is reversed. Because they will have responded to discrimination by acquiring fewer skills than men, many women will be locked into the O occupations, at least for a time. Moreover, if both men and women come to expect that women will have less education than men, employers will tend to look for men to fill the E jobs. This will reinforce the belief of women that education does not pay. Such subtle discrimination can persist for a very long time, making the supply of women to O jobs higher than it would be in the absence of the initial discrimination, thereby depressing the wages of women and below-average men.

The kind of discrimination that we have considered in our model is extreme. It is similar to the South African apartheid system that was dismantled in the 1980s and 1990s, in which blacks were excluded by law from prestigious and high-paying occupations. In Canada and the United States, labour-market discrimination against a specific group usually occurs in somewhat less obvious ways. First, it may be difficult (but not impossible, as in our model) for members of the group to get employment in certain jobs. Second, members of groups subject to discrimination may receive lower pay for a given kind of work than members of groups not subject to discrimination.

Wage Differentials in Noncompetitive Markets

We have examined several explanations for why wage differentials exist in competitive labour markets. Another explanation for wage differentials is that the labour market may *not* be competitive. In Chapters 9 through 11, we distinguished different *structures* for the markets in which firms sell their outputs. The inputs that firms use are also bought in markets that can have different structures. Although some markets are perfectly competitive, many show elements of market power on either the demand or the supply side.

To study the influence of different labour-market structures on wages, consider the case of an industry that employs identical workers for only one kind of job. In this way, we eliminate the possibility that any wage differentials are caused by differences between workers or differences between jobs—we thus highlight the role of market structure.

Let's examine two general cases. The first is one in which workers form a group and exercise some market power over setting the wage; the second is one in which the firm does not have to compete with other firms to hire workers.

Monopoly: A Union in a Competitive Market

For the purposes of our discussion of labour markets, a **union** (or *labour union*) is an association that is authorized to represent workers in negotiations with their employers. We examine unions in greater detail later in this chapter. For now we take the simple view that when workers are represented by a labour union, there is essentially only a single supplier of labour.

Suppose that a union enters a competitive labour market to represent all of the workers. As the single seller of labour for many buyers, the union is a monopolist, and it can establish a wage below which no one will work, thus changing the supply curve of labour. The industry can hire as many units of labour as are prepared to work at the union wage but no one at a lower wage. Thus, the industry (and each firm) faces a supply curve that is horizontal at the level of the union wage up to the maximum quantity of labour that is willing to work at that wage.

If the union uses its monopoly power, it will negotiate a wage above the competitive level. This situation is shown in Figure 14-3, in which the intersection of this horizontal supply curve and the demand curve establishes a higher wage rate and a lower level of employment than the competitive equilibrium. In this case, there will be some workers who would like to work in the unionized industry or occupation but cannot. A conflict of interest has been created between serving the interests of the union's employed and unemployed members.

An alternative way to achieve the higher wage is to shift the supply curve to the left. The union may do this by restricting entry into the occupation by methods such as lengthening the required period of apprenticeship and reducing openings for trainees.

FIGURE 14-3 A Union in a Competitive Labour Market

A union can raise the wages of people who continue to be employed but only by reducing the number of people employed. The competitive equilibrium is at E_0, the wage is w_0, and employment is q_0. If a union enters this market and sets a wage of w_1, a new equilibrium will be established at E_1. The supply curve has become $w_1 x S_0$. At the new wage w_1, employment will be q_1, and there will be $q_1 q_2$ workers who would like to work but whom the industry will not hire.

The wage w_1 can be achieved without generating a pool of unemployed persons. To do so, the union must restrict entry into the occupation and thus shift the supply curve to the left to S_1. Employment will again be q_1.

This figure can also be used to illustrate the effect of the government imposing a minimum wage of w_1 on the market where the competitive equilibrium is at E_0. The q_1 workers who remain employed benefit by the wage increase. The $q_1 q_0$ workers who lose their jobs in this industry suffer to the extent that they fail to find new jobs at a wage of w_0 or more.

union An association authorized to represent workers in bargaining with employers. Also called *trade union* and *labour union*.

Practise with Study Guide Chapter 14, Exercise 1.

Alternatively, the union may shift the supply curve by persuading the government to impose restrictive licensing or certification requirements on people who wish to work.

By restricting entry into the occupation or industry, unions may drive the wage above the competitive level.

Raising wages by restricting entry is not limited to unions. It occurs, for example, with many professional groups, including doctors. Because professional standards have long been regarded as necessary to protect the public from incompetent practitioners, doctors have found it publicly acceptable to control supply by limiting entry into their profession. Physicians' incomes are among the highest of any profession partly because of barriers to entry, including the difficulties of getting into an approved medical school, the high costs of setting up new medical schools, and various certification requirements applying to students, schools, and practitioners.

Monopsony: A Single Buyer in the Market

monopsony
A market situation in which there is a single buyer.

A **monopsony** is a market in which there is only one buyer; monopsony is to the buying side of the market what monopoly is to the selling side. Although cases of monopsony are not very common, it does sometimes arise. Monopsony sometimes occurs in small towns that contain only one industry and often only one large plant or mine. For example, the towns of Iroquois Falls in Ontario and Pine Falls in Manitoba are small towns where the principal employer is a single firm (Abitibi-Consolidated) that operates a newsprint plant. Although both towns provide alternative sources of employment in retailing and service establishments, the large industrial employer has some monopsony power over the local labour market. In other cases, local labour markets may contain only a few large industrial employers. Individually, each has substantial market power, and if they all act together, either explicitly or tacitly, they can behave as if they were a single monopsonist. Our analysis applies whenever employers have substantial monopsony power, but for concreteness, we consider a case in which the few firms operating in one labour market form an employers' hiring association in order to act as a single buying unit. We therefore refer to a single monopsonist.

Monopsony Without a Union. Suppose there are many potential workers and they are not members of a union. The monopsonist can offer any wage rate that it chooses, and the workers must either accept employment at that rate or find a different job.

Suppose that the monopsonist decides to hire some specific quantity of labour. The labour supply curve shows the wage that it must offer. To the monopsonist, this wage is the *average cost* of labour. In deciding how much labour to hire, however, the monopsonist is interested in the *marginal cost* of hiring additional workers. The monopsonist wants to know how much its total costs will increase as it takes on additional units of labour.

FIGURE 14-4   Monopsony in a Labour Market

A monopsonist lowers both the wage rate and employment below their competitive levels. D and S are the competitive demand and supply curves, respectively. The competitive equilibrium is E_0. The marginal cost of labour (*MC*) to the monopsonist is above the average cost. The monopsonistic firm will maximize profits at E_1. It will hire only q_1 units of labour. At q_1, the marginal cost of the last worker is just equal to the amount that the worker adds to the firm's revenue, as shown by the demand curve. The wage that must be paid to get q_1 workers is only w_1.

Whenever the supply curve of labour slopes upward, the marginal cost of employing extra units will exceed the average cost.

The marginal cost exceeds the wage paid (the average cost) because the increased wage rate necessary to attract an extra worker must also be paid to *everyone already employed*. [27] For example, assume that 100 workers are employed at $8.00 per hour and that to attract an extra worker, the wage must be raised to $8.01 per hour. The marginal cost of the 101st worker is not the $8.01 per hour paid to the worker but $9.01 per hour—made up of the extra 1 cent per hour paid to the 100 existing workers and $8.01 paid to the new worker. Thus the marginal cost is $9.01, whereas the average cost is $8.01.

The profit-maximizing monopsonist will hire labour up to the point at which the marginal cost of labour just equals the amount that the firm is willing to pay for an additional unit of labour. That amount is determined by labour's marginal revenue product *(MRP)* and is shown by the demand curve illustrated in Figure 14-4.

Monopsony power in a labour market will result in a lower level of employment and lower wages than would exist in a competitive labour market.

The intuitive explanation is that the monopsonistic employer is aware that by trying to purchase more, it is responsible for driving up the wage. It will therefore stop short of the point that is reached when workers are hired by many separate firms, no one of which can exert a significant influence on the wage rate.

Bilateral Monopoly: Monopsony with a Union.

Suppose that the workers in this industry organize themselves under a single union so that the monopsonistic employer's organization now faces a monopoly union. This situation is often referred to as *bilateral monopoly* since both sides of the market have considerable market power. In this case, the two sides will settle the wage through a process known as *collective bargaining*. The outcome of this bargaining process will depend on each side's objective and on the skill that each has in bargaining for its objective. We have seen that, left to itself, the employer's organization will set the monopsonistic wage shown in Figure 14-4. To understand the possible outcomes for the wage after the monopoly union enters the market, let us ask what the union would do if it had the power to set the wage unilaterally. The result will give us insight into the union's objectives in the actual collective bargaining that does occur.

Suppose the union can set a wage below which its members will not work. Here, just as in the case of a wage-setting union in a competitive market, the union presents the employer with a horizontal supply curve (up to the maximum number of workers who will accept work at the union wage). As shown in Figure 14-5, if the union sets the

FIGURE 14-5   Bilateral Monopoly in the Labour Market

By presenting a monopsonistic employer with a fixed wage, the union can raise both wages and employment over the monopsonistic level. The monopsony position before the union enters is at E_1 (from Figure 14-4), with a wage rate of w_1 and q_1 workers hired. A union now enters and sets the wage at w_0. The supply curve of labour becomes w_0E_0S, and wages and employment rise to their competitive levels of w_0 and q_0 without creating a pool of unemployed workers. If the wage is raised further, say, to w_2, the supply curve will become w_2xS, the quantity of employment will fall below the competitive level to q_2, and a pool of unsuccessful job applicants of q_2q_3 will develop.

This figure can also be used to illustrate the effect of the government imposing a minimum wage of w_0 or w_2 on a monopsonistic labour market where the equilibrium wage was initially w_1.

Practise with Study Guide Chapter 14, Exercise 3.

wage above the monopsony wage but below the competitive wage, the union can raise *both* wages and employment above the monopsonistic level.

However, the union may not be content merely to neutralize the monopsonist's power. It may choose to raise wages further above the competitive level. If it does, the outcome will be similar to that shown in Figure 14-3. If the wage is raised above the competitive level, the employer will no longer wish to hire all the labour that is offered at that wage. The amount of employment will fall, and unemployment will develop. These changes are also shown in Figure 14-5.

We now know that the employers would like to set the monopsonistic wage (w_1) while the union would like a wage *no less than* the competitive wage (w_0). The union may target for a still higher wage, depending on how it trades off employment losses against wage gains. If the union is content with an amount of employment as low as would occur at the monopsonistic wage, it could target for a wage substantially higher than the competitive wage.

Simple demand and supply analysis can take us no further. The actual outcome will, as we have already observed, depend on such other things as what target wage the two sides actually set for themselves, their relative bargaining skills, how each side assesses the costs of concessions, and how serious a strike would be for each. We discuss unions in more detail in the next section of this chapter.

For interesting information on labour-market policies in Canada, see the website for Human Resources Development Canada: www.hrdc-drhc.gc.ca. Click on "Labour Program."

Legislated Minimum Wages

We have examined wage differentials arising in competitive and noncompetitive labour markets. Government policy can also affect observed wage differentials by legislating minimum wages. Governments in Canada and many other countries legislate specific **minimum wages,** which define the lowest wage rates that may legally be paid. In 1999, minimum wages ranged from $5.40 per hour in Newfoundland to $7.20 per hour in the Yukon.

minimum wages
Legally specified minimum rate of pay for labour.

For a large proportion of all employment covered by the law, the minimum wage is below the actual market wage, and thus in such cases the minimum wage is *not binding.* Some workers, however, are employed in industries in which the free-market wage would be below the legal minimum, and thus the legislated minimum wage is *binding.* It is only in these cases where the effects of minimum wages are of interest.

Although legislated minimum wages are now an accepted part of the labour scene in Canada and many other industrialized countries, economists are often sceptical about the benefits from such a policy. As our analysis in Chapter 5 indicated, a binding price floor in a competitive market leads to a market surplus of the product—in this case, an excess supply of labour, or unemployment. Thus, a policy that legislates minimum wages in an otherwise competitive market will benefit some workers only by hurting others.

The problem is more complicated than the analysis of Chapter 5 would suggest, however, because not all labour markets are competitive. In addition, those groups in the labour force that tend to have the lowest wages, such as youth and minorities, are affected more than the average worker by minimum wages.

Theoretical Effects of a Minimum Wage

Suppose that minimum-wage laws apply uniformly to all occupations. The occupations and the industries in which minimum wages are binding will be the lowest paying in the country; they usually involve unskilled or semiskilled labour. In most of them, the workers are not members of unions. Thus, the situations in which minimum wages are likely to be binding include competitive labour markets and those in which employers exercise some monopsony power. The effects on employment are different in the two cases.

Competitive Labour Markets. The consequences for employment of a binding minimum wage are unambiguous when the labour market is competitive. By raising the wage that employers must pay, minimum-wage legislation leads to a reduction in the quantity of labour that is demanded and an increase in the quantity of labour that is supplied. As a result, the actual level of employment falls, and unemployment rises. This situation is exactly analogous to the one that arises when a union succeeds in setting a wage above the competitive equilibrium wage, as illustrated in Figure 14-3. The excess supply of labour at the minimum wage also creates incentives for people to evade the law by working "under the table" at wages below the legal minimum wage.

Employers with Some Monopsony Power. The minimum-wage law can simultaneously increase both wages and employment in markets in which employers have some monopsony power. The circumstances in which this can occur are the same as those in which a union facing a monopsonistic employer is able to increase both the wage and the level of employment, as shown in Figure 14-5. Of course, if the minimum wage is raised above the competitive wage, employment will start to fall, as in the union case. When it is set at the competitive level, however, the minimum wage can protect workers against monopsony power and lead to *increases* in employment.

Evidence on the Effects of Minimum Wages

Empirical research on the effects of minimum-wage laws reflects these mixed theoretical predictions. There is some evidence that people who keep their jobs gain when the minimum wage is raised. There is some evidence that some groups suffer a decline in employment consistent with raising the wage in a fairly competitive market. At other times and places, there is evidence that both wages and employment rise when the minimum wage rises, consistent with labour markets in which employers have some monopsony power.

Several Canadian studies have examined the relationship between minimum wages and employment (or unemployment). Though the studies differ in their approaches and data used, there is a broad consensus that minimum wages decrease the level of employment (and raise unemployment), particularly for low-wage groups such as women and teenagers. In this sense, the Canadian results confirm the theoretical predictions of the effects of minimum wages in competitive labour markets.

Some widely discussed research in the United States, however, has produced different and hotly debated results. David Card, from Berkeley, and Alan Krueger, from Princeton University, traced the effects of minimum-wage increases in California during 1988 and New Jersey during 1992 and found that substantial rises in these states' minimum wages not only increased wages but were also associated with small employment *gains* for teenagers. Card and Krueger argue that these findings are inconsistent with a competitive labour market and thus take the results as evidence in support of the view that firms have some monopsony power in the labour market.

The Card and Krueger results, however, have come under heavy criticism from many other economists in the last few years. One criticism is that some of the data used by Card and Krueger are faulty, and that their conclusions are therefore suspect. Another relates to the short span of time covered by their study. The argument is that firms will not immediately reduce the level of employment in response to an increase in the minimum wage—they will instead choose *not to replace* workers who leave their jobs in the natural turnover process that occurs in labour markets. But workers who are receiving the minimum wage may be more reluctant to leave their job after an increase in their wage, thereby reducing this natural turnover. Thus, it is not surprising to see few employment losses (or slight gains) when one examines the labour market immediately before and

APPLYING ECONOMIC CONCEPTS 14-1

The Puzzle of Interindustry Wage Differentials in Canada

Differences in wages across industries have been observed for as long as information on wages has been collected. But only recently have economists examined carefully whether they can be explained by differences in skills, jobs, or market structure. In Canada, a study published by Surendra Gera and Gilles Grenier shows the extent of these wage differentials in 1986.*

The table shows results from their study for selected industries; for each industry, the number in the table shows the industry's *wage premium*—that is, the amount by which wages in each industry exceed the average after controlling for such factors as the worker's education, age, gender, occupation, union status, and so on. The challenge is to explain such wage premia.

Competitive Wage Differentials?

Following our discussion in the text, three possible explanations of these wage differentials are consistent with the labour market being competitive.

The first possibility is that these observed wage differentials for 1986 may reflect temporary shifts in the pattern of labour demand or supply across industries. For example, a large increase in the demand for labour in the forestry industry that occurs together with a large decline in the demand for labour in the textiles industry could account for some of the data in the table. To address this possible explanation, Gera and Grenier examine Canadian census data for 1970, 1980, and 1985. They find that the pattern of interindustry wage differentials is very similar across these three periods, suggesting that the observed wage differentials are not simply temporary phenomena.

*S. Gera and G. Grenier, "Interindustry Wage Differentials and Efficiency Wages: Some Canadian Evidence," *Canadian Journal of Economics*, 1994.

The second possibility is that the wage differentials can be explained by differences in the quality of the workers that are not observable to economists when conducting such a study. For example, they are not able to observe whether a worker is "highly motivated," "innovative," or "a good problem solver." But many of these characteristics *are* observable to potential employers, either by watching the individual work for a short period of time, or by asking previous employers who know the worker. To examine this explanation, Gera and Grenier examine the group of individuals in their sample that move from a job in one industry to a job in a different in-

Selected Industry Wage Premia in Canada (percentage above average wage)	
Tobacco Products	33.4
Mineral Fuels	25.5
Forestry	18.9
Electric Power, Gas, and Water Utilities	14.4
Paper and Allied Products	12.0
Communications	10.5
Transportation Equipment	7.0
Wholesale Trade	3.8
Electrical Products	2.6
Education and Related Services	−1.0
Food and Beverages	−3.5
Insurance and Real Estate Agencies	−4.1
Clothing	−8.1
Fishing and Trapping	−9.5
Personal Services	−16.7
Retail Trade	−11.1
Textiles	−19.0
Accommodation and Food Services	−20.3

See Chapter 14 of www.pearsoned.ca/lipsey for a discussion of the possible effects of legislating the length of the work week: Jan Olters, "Some Doubts About France's 35-Hour Week," *World Economic Affairs.*

immediately after the change in legislation. Proponents of this view argue that the total employment effects of minimum wages can only be detected by examining the data over longer periods of time.

Economists have not reached a definitive conclusion regarding the desirability or the effects of legislated minimum wages. Given its mixed economic effects, support for and opposition to the minimum wage might be understood as arising largely from political and sociological motives. Organized labour has consistently pressed for a broad, relatively high minimum wage. There is some economic reason for this, in that there is evidence that the minimum wage "trickles up" to higher-wage workers, both unionized and not. Arguably, however, the support dates back to the 1930s, when organized labour was still dustry. For example, if high wages to a particular worker in the tobacco industry are due to that worker's unobserved skills, then when that worker switches to the clothing industry, the high wage should persist. But Gera and Grenier find the opposite. A worker that moves from a high-wage industry to a low-wage industry tends to suffer a fall in wage; similarly, a worker that moves from a low-wage industry to a high-wage industry tends to experience a rise in the wage. This finding suggests that the observed wage differentials are not due mainly to unobserved labour quality.

The final possible explanation consistent with a competitive labour market is that the observed wage differentials reflect different characteristics of the *jobs*. Maybe the jobs in the high-wage industries are less pleasant jobs—longer hours, less job security, less safe—than those in the low-wage industries. Gera and Grenier offer two pieces of evidence against this explanation. First, they note that workers in *similar occupations* receive very different wages in different industries, and it is difficult to believe that working conditions for, say, a clerk are very different in the tobacco industry than in the textiles industry. Second, if the observed wage differentials reflect just different job characteristics, then in competitive equilibrium workers are indifferent between (pleasant) jobs in the low-wage industries and (unpleasant) jobs in the high-wage industries. Yet workers appear to quit jobs in the high-wage industries much less frequently than they quit jobs in the low-wage industries. In other words, workers *appear* to view the high-wage jobs as valuable relative to the low-wage jobs. This phenomenon, of course, suggests that the observed wage differentials are reflecting more than just differences in working conditions.

Other Explanations?

Maybe the explanation for these observed wage differentials lies in a noncompetitive market structure. Perhaps unions have a large presence in some industries and little or no presence in others. When Gera and Grenier examine this possibility, they find that the interindustry wage differentials are just as marked among unionized workers as they are among nonunionized workers.

If the observed wage differentials across Canadian industries cannot be explained by considering different characteris-

tics of the workers, jobs, or market structures, what is the explanation? One possible explanation is based on the theory of *efficiency wages*. According to this theory, firms in even a competitive labour market may *pay more than the competitive wage* to their workers. Firms do this because they perceive that a higher wage will make their workers more productive. Since workers are receiving more than is required to attract their services, they are earning *economic rents* (a concept that we examined in Chapter 13). The fact that workers are receiving rents, in turn, explains why they are reluctant to leave these good jobs—and thus their quit rates from such jobs are low.

Though the efficiency-wage theory offers one possible explanation for why some workers might earn rents, it does not directly offer an explanation for why these rents might be different across industries. In order for the efficiency-wage theory to explain the observed interindustry wage differentials, it must explain why firms' incentives to pay higher wages are greater in some industries than in others. So far, proponents of the theory have not come up with convincing reasons.

The efficiency-wage theory generates considerable disagreement among economists. But there is little debate that there exist significant wage differentials across industries, even after taking account of observable characteristics of workers and jobs. As more data become available, perhaps economists will find better explanations for the observed interindustry wage differentials.

Workers in the forestry industry receive wages roughly 20 percent higher than workers of similar ages and skills in the average industry.

fighting for its position in North American society. Enactment of a minimum wage was then a great political victory, and the minimum wage still has symbolic significance.

A Final Word

We have examined several explanations for why some workers get paid more than others. The explanations include differences in workers' educations and skills, differences in job characteristics, discrimination, and differences in the structure of the various labour markets. But this apparent abundance of explanations should not

FIGURE 14-6   Union Membership in Canada, 1921-1992

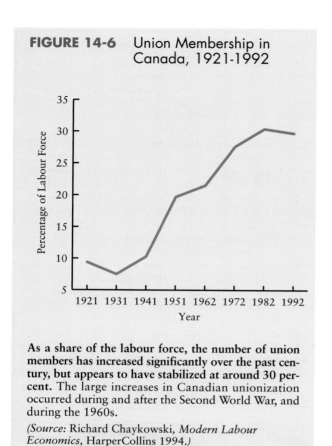

As a share of the labour force, the number of union members has increased significantly over the past century, but appears to have stabilized at around 30 percent. The large increases in Canadian unionization occurred during and after the Second World War, and during the 1960s.

(*Source:* Richard Chaykowski, *Modern Labour Economics*, HarperCollins 1994.)

lead you to believe that economists understand *all* wage differentials that are observed in the labour market. Recent studies, both in Canada and in the United States, have revealed significant differences in wages across industries that appear to defy explanations based on the sort of arguments we have examined. *Applying Economic Concepts 14-1* discusses the continuing puzzle of interindustry wage differentials in Canada.

Labour Unions

Unions currently represent fewer than 30 percent of the labour force in Canada. Of those workers employed in the public sector, however, approximately 80 percent are unionized. Figure 14-6 shows how union membership has changed in Canada over the past several decades. Table 14-1 shows unionization rates by industry. As is clear from the table, unionization is most common in the public and educational sectors and least common in agriculture, finance, and business services.

Despite the relatively low degree of unionization among Canada's private-sector workers, unions have a considerable influence in the private sector. One reason is the impact that union wage contracts have on other labour markets. When, for example, the Canadian Auto Workers negotiates a new contract with an automobile producer in Oshawa, its provisions set a pattern that directly or indirectly affects other labour markets, both in Ontario and in other provinces. A second reason is the major leadership role that unions have played in the past 50 years in the development of labour market practices and in lobbying for legislation that applies to all workers.

In this section, we discuss the process of *collective bargaining* and, in particular, examine the inherent conflict that unions face between striving for higher wages and for increasing employment. *Lessons from History 14-1* examines the historical development of labour unions in Canada.

Collective Bargaining

collective bargaining
The process by which unions and employers arrive at and enforce agreements.

The process by which unions and employers reach an agreement is known as **collective bargaining**. This process has an important difference from the theoretical models that we discussed in the previous section. In those models, we assumed that the union had the power to set the wage unilaterally; the employer then decided how much labour to hire. In actual collective bargaining, however, the firm and union typically bargain over the wage (as well as other aspects of the employment relationship). There is usually a substantial range over which an agreement can be reached, and the actual result in particular cases will depend on the strengths of the two bargaining parties and on the skill of their negotiators.

To see the possible outcomes, refer back to Figure 14-5. It may be that the firm wants the wage to be w_1 and the union wants the wage to be w_2. Depending on each side's market power, and on their bargaining tactics, the final agreed-upon wage may be anywhere in between. Note that while actual collective bargaining has the firm and union bargaining over the wage, it is typically the case that the firm retains the "right to manage"—meaning that the firm can decide how much labour it wants to employ at the bargained wage.

Wages Versus Employment

Unions seek many goals when they bargain with management. They may push for higher wages, higher fringe benefits, or less onerous working conditions. In recent years, unions in Canada have also emphasized the importance of "job security," meaning a commitment by the firm to not lay workers off in the event of a downturn in business conditions. Firms, however, are understandably reluctant to promise such security since reducing their workforce is an effective way to reduce costs when business conditions deteriorate.

Whatever unions' specific goals, unless they face a monopsonist across the bargaining table, they must deal with a fundamental dilemma.

There is an inherent conflict between the level of wages and the size of the union itself.

The more successful a union is in raising wages, the more management will reduce the size of its work force, substituting capital for labour. This will lead to lower union membership. However, if the union does not provide some wage improvement for its members, they will have little incentive to stay around.

TABLE 14-1   Unionization Rates by Industry

Industry	Membership as Percentage of Paid Workers
Agriculture	1.8
Forestry	58.8
Fishing & Trapping	33.4
Mining	28.4
Manufacturing	36.7
Construction	59.6
Transportation, Communication, and other Utilities	54.8
Trade	11.6
Finance, Real Estate, and Insurance	3.5
Services	
Business	3.1
Educational	77.0
Health and Social	50.8
Other	11.6
Public Administration	80.6
Total Canadian Economy	**34.7**

There is considerable variation across Canadian industries in the extent of unionization. The public sector and the educational services sector are the most unionized; agriculture, finance, and business services are the least unionized.

(*Source:* Richard Chaykowski, *Modern Labour Economics*, HarperCollins 1994.)

The Union Wage Premium

Despite the costs to unions (i.e., reduced membership) of pushing for higher wages, there is clear evidence in Canada of a *union wage premium*—that is, a higher wage attributed only to the union status of the job. It is not easy to measure this wage premium, however, because it is not appropriate simply to compare the average wage of unionized workers with the average wage of nonunionized workers. After all, unions may occur mainly in industries where workers have higher skills or where working conditions are less pleasant. And we know from the first section of this chapter that differences in skills or working conditions can lead to wage differentials. Economists have therefore been forced to use complicated statistical techniques to identify this union wage premium. The consensus appears to be that the union wage premium in Canada is somewhere between 10 and 15 percent—that is, unionized workers with a particular set of skills in particular types of jobs get paid 10 to 15 percent more than *otherwise identical workers* who are not members of unions.

For information on the Canadian labour movement, see the website for the Canadian Labour Congress: www.clc.org.

LESSONS FROM HISTORY 14-1

The Development of Unions in Canada

Early Canadian unionization was strongly dominated by the influence of international unions, which had their headquarters and an overwhelming proportion of their membership outside Canada. The creation of Canadian locals of American unions began in the 1860s. By 1911, 90 percent of Canadian workers who were union members belonged to international unions.

During the first half of the twentieth century, there was strong pressure: first, toward a single national federation; and second, to achieve autonomy from American unions. The issues became intertwined when conflicts in the United States arose between craft and industrial unions. Until the 1930s, *craft unions*—which cover persons in a particular occupation—were the characteristic form of collective action in the United States. In Canada, meanwhile, trade unionists were attracted to *industrial unions* that embraced unskilled workers as well as skilled craftsmen in one industry such as steel making.

Because of the impossibility of establishing bargaining strength by controlling the supply of unskilled workers, the rise of industrial unionism in Canada was associated with political action as an alternative means of improving the lot of the membership. In general, social and political reform were given much more emphasis by Canadian unionists than by their American counterparts. Political action here extended to the support for social democratic political parties: first, the Cooperative Commonwealth Federation (CCF), established in 1932, and later its successor, the New Democratic Party (NDP), formed in 1961.

The late Senator Eugene Forsey, a former director of research for the Canadian Labour Congress, viewed the unification of the bulk of Canadian unions under the CLC in 1956 as the beginning of virtual autonomy for Canadian locals from their U.S. head offices. Throughout the postwar period, the percentage of total Canadian union membership represented by international unions fell: In the mid 1950s, it was about 70 percent, and by the mid 1990s, it was just over 30 percent.

One factor in the increased share of national unions is the growth of membership in the two unions representing government workers, the Canadian Union of Public Employees and the Public Service Alliance. Another major component of noninternational union membership has arisen out of the distinct aspirations of French-Canadian workers. More recently, the formation of the Canadian Auto Workers, independent of the American Auto Workers, represented a significant further reduction of membership in international unions.

Rapid gains in union membership in Canada occurred in the years during World War II. This led to pressure for the rights of workers to organize and to elect an exclusive bargaining agent. These rights were established by provisions of the Wartime Labour Relations Regulations Act of 1944.

Government intervention in industrial disputes in Canada has a history dating back to the early years of the twentieth century. The earliest legislation applied only to public utilities and coal mining. It provided that before a strike or a lockout could be initiated, the parties were required to submit any dispute to a conciliation board. This system of compulsory conciliation and compulsory delay in work stoppage was extended to a much larger segment of the economy under special emergency powers adopted by the government of Canada during World War II. In the postwar period, jurisdiction over labour policy reverted to the provinces, but the principles established have been carried over into provincial legislation.

The Winnipeg General Strike of 1919 began a wave of increased unionism and militancy across Canada.

Unionized workers earn, on average, between 10 and 15 percent higher wages than nonunionized workers with similar characteristics.

There is also evidence that the size of this union wage premium differs across industries. Given that workers in different industries and with different occupations are often represented by different unions, this cross-industry difference in the union wage premium may simply reflect the differences in unions' preferences for higher wages versus higher employment.

Employment Effects of Unions

We said earlier that unions face an inherent conflict between the level of wages and the level of employment. This simply reflects the firm's profit-maximizing behaviour as embodied in its downward-sloping demand curve for labour. As the union pushes for higher wages, the firm naturally chooses to hire fewer workers.

What continues to puzzle economists, however, is how the clear evidence of a 10 to 15 percent union wage premium can be consistent with a second empirical result—the absence of any clear effect on employment. One possible explanation for the absence of an employment effect is that unions use the collective bargaining process to pressure firms to hire more workers than they otherwise would. This practice is known as *feather-bedding*, and for years was infamous in the railroads where union contracts required the railway to hire firemen (whose job it was to keep the coal fires burning) long after the widespread adoption of diesel locomotives.

If such feather-bedding is pervasive in unionized firms, it may well be the explanation for the absence of an observable union effect on employment. The employment reduction caused by the higher wage may be offset by the employment increase due to feather-bedding.

Unanswered Questions

Labour unions have played a significant role in the economies of Canada, the United States, and Europe for many years. Given this fact, it is surprising how little economists actually know about how unions influence economic outcomes and, in particular, how unions affect long-run productivity.

Unions may reduce long-run productivity through a process known as the *hold-up* of capital. Much physical capital, once it is installed, is very difficult to move or resell. For this reason, *installed* capital has a very inelastic supply and, following the discussion from Chapter 13, a large part of its factor payment takes the form of economic rent. The union may be able to extract these rents from the firm in the form of higher wages. That is, the union may be able to *hold up* the firm by forcing it to pay higher wages; the firm is stuck with its installed capital and thus pays the higher wages and, in turn, receives lower profits. If firms are forward-looking, however, they can anticipate this sort of behaviour from unions *before* making such investments in physical capital. The possibility of being held up by union wage demands reduces the expected profitability of investment and may result in a reduction in investment. This decision to invest less would likely have negative implications for productivity growth in the industry.

There is some empirical evidence that the presence of a union does reduce investment by firms. It is not yet clear, however, whether such reduced investment has long-term effects on productivity. This issue is currently unresolved.

The "Good Jobs–Bad Jobs" Debate

Figure 14-7 shows how the composition of Canadian employment has changed over the past century. In particular, the share of total employment in agriculture has fallen from 45 percent in 1891 to less than three percent today. In contrast, the share of total employment in services (including government) has increased from less than 10 percent in

FIGURE 14-7 One Hundred Years of Change in the Composition of Canadian Employment

Over the past century, major shifts in employment have taken place between sectors of the economy. In 1891, over 45 percent of Canadian employment was in agriculture, and only 9 percent in services (including government). One hundred years later, agriculture accounted for only 3 percent of employment, while services had increased to 41 percent. The share of employment in manufacturing and construction increased from 26 percent in 1891 to 32 percent just after the Second World War, and then declined back to 20 percent by 1991.

(*Source: Canadian Census*, various years, authors' calculations.)

1891 to over 40 percent today. The share in manufacturing and construction has been more variable, but has been on a clear downward trend over the past half-century, falling from about 35 percent in 1951 to about 20 percent today.

Similar changes have also occurred in the United States and in many other industrialized countries. This changing composition of the labour force has led to some concerns. The specific change that has received considerable attention is the decline in the share of total employment in the manufacturing sector since the Second World War, and the simultaneous increase in the share of total employment in the service sector.

Some people fear that productivity is lower and the opportunities for growth are much more limited in some service industries than in goods-producing industries. They argue that the possibilities for using more capital per unit of labour employed, which raises labour productivity, are less in the service sector than in the manufacturing sector. Another concern is that many of the "good jobs" in the manufacturing sector appear to have been replaced by "bad jobs" in the service sector, where such "bad jobs" are characterized by lower pay and less job security.

The reduction in manufacturing employment is partly the result of that sector's dynamism – more and more output can be produced with fewer and fewer workers.

Should these dramatic changes in the composition of employment worry us? Is there something undesirable about the fact that fewer workers are now producing manufactured goods than forty years ago? Or that more workers are working in the service sector than forty years ago? Are good jobs being replaced by bad jobs? This final section of the chapter addresses this contentious issue.

Four Observations

There are four reasons why the decline in the manufacturing sector—in Canada and elsewhere—may not reflect anything "wrong" with the economy. First, we need to keep a sense of perspective about the emergence of low-paying service jobs. As is apparent in Figure 14-7, the trend toward services has been going on for over a century. Yet real income per hour worked has been rising throughout this period; as a nation, we are getting wealthier, not poorer.

Second, to a considerable extent, the decrease in the share of manufacturing in total employment is a result of that sector's dynamism. More and more manufactured goods have been produced by fewer and fewer workers, leaving more workers to produce services. This movement is analogous to the one out of agriculture earlier in the century. At the turn of the century, nearly 45 percent of the Canadian labour force worked on farms. Today that number is less than 3 percent, yet they produce more total output than did the 45 percent in 1900. This movement away from agricultural employment freed workers to move into manufacturing, raising our living standards and transforming our way of life. In like manner, the movement away from manufacturing is freeing workers to move into services, and by replacing the grimy blue-collar jobs of the smokestack industries with more pleasant white-collar jobs in the service industries, it will once again transform our way of life.

Third, to a considerable extent, the decrease in the share of manufacturing in total employment also follows from consumers' tastes. Just as consumers in the first half of the century did not want to go on consuming more and more food products as their incomes rose, today's consumers do not wish to spend all of their additional income on manufactured products. Households have chosen to spend a high proportion of their increased incomes on services, thus creating employment opportunities in that sector. This simply reflects the fact that many products of the service sector—like restaurant meals, hotel stays, and airline flights—are products that have a high income elasticity of demand. Thus, as the income of the average Canadian household increases, so too does that household's demand for these products of the service sector.

Finally, it is easy to underestimate the scope for quality, quantity, and productivity increases in services. But these changes permit us to have a higher standard of living than we would otherwise have. As just one example of productivity increases, consider your ability to make an automatic cash withdrawal, at any time of the day or night, from your bank account in Truro, Nova Scotia, while you are on vacation in Brazil. Now compare that to the apprehension your parents faced twenty years ago when they had to get to the bank before 3:00 pm on a Friday afternoon to make sure that they had enough cash for the weekend. It would have been simply impossible for them to cash a cheque in Brazil without having made elaborate prior arrangements.

Also, many quality improvements in services go unrecorded. Today's hotel room is vastly more comfortable than a hotel room of 40 years ago, yet this quality improvement does not show up in our national income statistics. Measuring such technological improvements is even more difficult when they take the form of entirely new products. Airline transportation, telecommunication, fast-food chains, and financial services are prominent examples. The resulting increase in output is not always properly captured in existing statistics.

A Mixed Blessing?

It is easy to become concerned when looking at the official statistics, which show low wages earned in some service jobs. Indeed, the shift in employment toward services is, like most changes that hit the economy, a mixed blessing. It entails a significant increase in the number of "bad" service-sector jobs with low pay or low job security. Further, such transitions often generate temporary unemployment as workers get laid off from a contracting manufacturing sector and only slowly find jobs in the expanding service sector. Such transitions suggest a role for government policy to maintain the income of those workers temporarily unemployed (we will discuss unemployment insurance and other income-support programs in Chapter 18). However, if we focus on the *overall economy*, and consider the growth in the real living standards of the *average* Canadian household, we are reminded that average real income has continued to rise, not only throughout the shift from agriculture to manufacturing, but also throughout the shift from manufacturing to services. There is little reason to think that the continued growth of the service sector will stand in the way of this slow but steady improvement in Canadians' living standards.

S U M M A R Y

Wage Differentials
LO 1 2 3

- In a competitive labour market, wages are set by the forces of supply and demand. Differences in wages will arise because some skills are more valued than others, because some jobs are more onerous than others, because of varying amounts of human capital, and because of discrimination based on such factors as gender and race.

- A union entering a competitive market acts as a monopolist and can raise wages, but only at the cost of reducing employment.

- A monopsonistic employer entering a competitive labour market will reduce both the wage and the level of employment.

- A union in a monopsonistic labour market—a case of bilateral monopoly—may increase both employment and wages relative to the pure monopsony outcome. If the union sets wages above the competitive level, however, it will create a pool of workers who are unable to get the jobs that they want at the going wage.

- Governments set some wages above their competitive levels by passing minimum-wage laws. In competitive labour markets, these laws raise the incomes of many employees, and cause unemployment for some of those with the lowest levels of skills. In monopsonistic labour markets, a legislated minimum wage (as long as it is not too high) can raise both wages and employment.

Labour Unions
LO 4

- Labour unions seek many goals when they bargain with management. They may push for higher wages, higher fringe benefits, more stable employment, or less onerous working conditions. Whatever their specific goals, unless they face a monopsonist across the bargaining table, they must recognize the inherent conflict between the level of wages and the size of the union itself.

- Despite the costs to unions (i.e., reduced membership) of pushing for higher wages, there is clear evidence in Canada of a union wage premium. The union wage premium is somewhere between 10 and 15 percent—that is, unionized workers with a particular set of skills in particular types of jobs get paid 10 to 15 percent more than otherwise identical workers that are not members of unions.

The "Good Jobs–Bad Jobs" Debate

● The past half-century has witnessed an increase in the share of total employment in the service sector and a decline in the share of employment in manufacturing. Some people are concerned that "good" manufacturing jobs are being replaced by "bad" service jobs.

● Though the shift away from manufacturing and toward services involves some costs during the transition period, the ongoing growth in average per capita income (plus the hard-to-measure quality improvements) suggests that the shift is not a problem for the economy as a whole.

K E Y   C O N C E P T S

Wage differentials in competitive labour markets
Effects of discrimination on wages
Labour unions as monopolists

Single employer as monopsonist
Effects of legislated minimum wages
Collective bargaining

Union goals: wages versus employment
Union wage premium
"Good jobs" vs. "bad jobs"

S T U D Y   E X E R C I S E S

1. Suppose there were only two industries in the economy. All workers have the same skills and the same preferences. But the jobs in the two industries are different. In the Pleasant industry, working conditions are desirable (quiet, safe, clean, etc.). In the Grimy industry, working conditions are awful (noisy, unsafe, dirty, etc.).

   a. Draw supply-and-demand diagrams for the labour market in each industry.
   b. In which industry are wages higher? Why?
   c. Now suppose that the Grimy industry made its working conditions just as pleasant as in the Pleasant industry? Explain what happens in *both* labour markets.

2. Suppose there are two types of basketball players—black and white. Suppose also that, on average, black players are no better and no worse than white players. Furthermore, suppose there are only two types of basketball teams—good and bad. Good teams hire only good players; bad teams will hire both good and bad players. The two diagrams that follow show the initial outcomes in the labour markets for good teams and bad teams. Assume there is *no discrimination based on race.*

   a. As shown in the figures, the wage paid by good teams is higher than the wage paid by bad teams. What explains this wage differential?
   b. Do black players earn more or less than white players, on average? Explain.
   c. Now suppose that the good teams discriminate against white players—rightly or wrongly they *believe* that black players are better than white players. Show in your diagram what happens in both labour markets.
   d. In the situation in part c, what happens to the wage differential between good and bad teams?
   e. In the situation in part c, what happens to the average black-white wage differential?

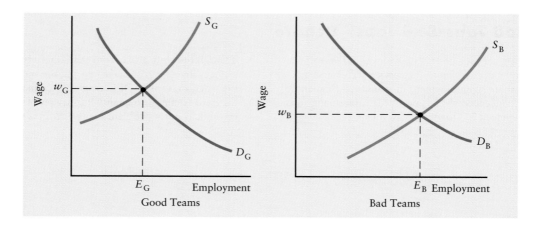

Good Teams   Bad Teams

3. Suppose *in the real world* you observe that black basketball players get paid more than white basketball players. Do you conclude that discrimination is present? Explain why or why not.

4. The table below shows how many workers are prepared to work at various hourly wages in the forestry industry. It also shows the workers' marginal revenue product (*MRP*).

Number of Workers	Wage ($)	Marginal Cost of Labour ($)	MRP ($)
50	10	—	50
100	12	14	40
150	14	18	30
200	16	—	24
250	18	—	22
300	20	—	20
350	22	—	18

a. On a scale diagram, draw the supply of labour curve and the demand for labour curve.
b. What is the equilibrium wage and level of employment if the labour market is competitive?
c. Now suppose there is only a single buyer for labour—a *monopsonist*. Compute the marginal cost of labour for each level of employment and fill in the table. (Recall that the *MC* of labour is the change in labour cost divided by the change in employment. The first two rows have been completed for you.)
d. What wage and level of employment would the monopsonist choose? Explain.

5. The diagram below shows the market for labour in a particular industry. It shows both the supply of labour (the average cost of labour) and the marginal cost of labour.

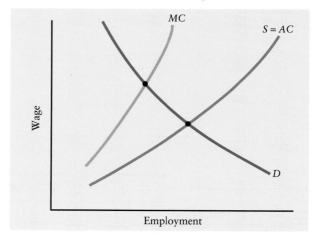

a. Suppose the labour market is competitive. What will be the equilibrium wage and level of employment (call them w^* and L^*)?
b. Now suppose the government imposes a minimum wage equal to $w^{min} > w^*$. Show what happens to wages and employment.
c. In the absence of a minimum wage, show the outcome if there is a monosony buyer of labour services. Call this wage w^p.
d. Beginning with the monopsony outcome, show what happens if the government imposes a minimum wage above w^p but lower than w^*.
e. Do minimum wages always reduce employment? Explain.

6. The following diagram shows the market for labour in a particular industry. It shows both the supply of labour

(the average cost of labour) and the marginal cost of labour. If the labour market were competitive, the outcome would be w^* and L^*.

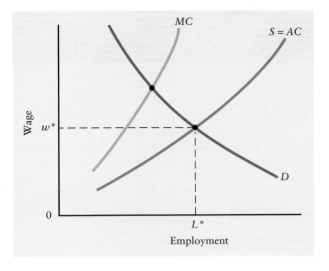

a. Suppose the workers in this industry form a union that is able to raise the wage above w^*. Show the expected outcome in the figure.
b. Now suppose there is no union, but there is a monopsony buyer of labour. Show the expected outcome in this market.
c. Now suppose there is both a union and a monopsony firm. What can you predict about the outcome in this case?

DISCUSSION QUESTIONS

1. "The great increase in the number of women entering the labour force for the first time means that relatively more women than men earn beginning salaries. It is therefore not evidence of discrimination that the average wage earned by females is less than that earned by males." Discuss.

2. Physicians are among the highest-paid of workers. However, in addition to a bachelor's degree, would-be physicians must attend four years of medical school, three years of residency, and up to seven additional years of residency to be specialists. How does this lengthy training change your perception with respect to how much physicians are paid? What additional information would you need to determine whether physicians' real pay is higher than that of other professionals?

3. In trying to measure the extent to which labour unions are responsible for increasing wages, economists use sophisticated statistical methods to compare the wages of unionized workers with those of nonunionized workers. Explain why it is not legitimate to simply compare the average wage across the two groups and attribute the difference to the effects of unionization.

4. "One can judge the presence or absence of discrimination by looking at the proportion of the population in different occupations." Does such information help? Does it suffice? Consider each of the following examples. Relative to their numbers in the total population, there are

a. Too many blacks and too few Jews among professional athletes
b. Too few male secretaries
c. Too few female judges
d. Too few female prison guards
e. Too few male school teachers
f. Too few female graduate students in economics.

5. "Equal pay for work of equal value" is a commonly held goal, but "equal value" is hard to define. What would be the consequences of legislation that enforces equal pay for what turns out to be work of unequal value?

6. There is clear evidence of a union wage premium of between 10 and 15 percent. There is also clear evidence that firms' demand curves are downward sloping. Reconcile these two "facts" with the third fact that there is *no* clear evidence that unions lead to employment reductions.

CHAPTER 15

Capital and Natural Resources

(LO) LEARNING OBJECTIVES

❶ Compute the present value of an asset that delivers a stream of future benefits.

❷ Explain why the demand for physical capital depends on the interest rate.

❸ Understand how the equilibrium interest rate is determined.

❹ Explain how competitive firms will determine the rate of extraction of a nonrenewable resource.

❺ Recognize the conservation role played by free-market prices for resources.

In this chapter, we discuss capital and nonrenewable natural resources. These are similar factors of production in that each is a stock of valuable things that gets used up in the process of producing goods and services. They are also similar in that the optimal level of capital used by firms and the optimal level of extraction of a nonrenewable resource depend on the interest rate. They are different in that capital can be replaced, whereas nonrenewable resources—by definition—cannot. A new machine can always be built to replace one that wears out, but a barrel of oil used represents a permanent reduction in the world's total stock of oil.

We begin the chapter by discussing how firms decide how much capital to purchase and how the market determines the price of capital. The interest rate plays an important role in both parts. We then go on to discuss how profit-maximizing firms decide how fast to extract a nonrenewable resource, and we also examine whether competitive markets produce the socially desirable rate of extraction. Here we see the price system behaving as a conservation mechanism, with the price of the resource rising as it becomes more scarce.

Capital and the Interest Rate

Capital is a produced factor of production. The nation's capital stock consists of all produced goods that are used in the production of other goods and services. Factories, machines, tools, computers, roads, bridges, and railroads are but a few of the many examples.

We begin our study of capital by exploring an important complication that arises because factors of production are durable—a machine lasts for years, a labourer for a lifetime, and land more or less forever. It is convenient to think of a factor's lifetime as being divided into the shorter periods that we refer to as *production periods*. The present time is the current period. Future time is one, two, three, and so on, periods hence.

The durability of factors makes it necessary to distinguish between the factor itself and the *flow of services* that it provides in a given production period. For example, we can rent a piece of land for use over some period of time, or we can buy the land outright. This distinction is just a particular instance of the general distinction between flows and stocks that we first encountered in Chapter 3.

Two Prices of Capital

If a firm hires a piece of capital equipment for use over some period of time—for example, one truck for one month—it pays a price for the privilege of using that piece of capital equipment. If the firm buys the truck outright, it pays a different (and higher) price for the purchase. Consider each of these prices in turn.

Rental Price

The *rental price of capital* is the amount that a firm pays to obtain the services of a capital good for a given period of time. The rental price of one week's use of a piece of capital is analogous to the weekly wage rate that is the price of hiring the services of labour.

A capital good may also be used by the firm that owns it. In this case, the firm does not pay out any rental fee. However, the rental price is the amount that the firm could charge if it leased its capital to another firm. The rental price is thus the *opportunity cost* to the firm of using the capital good itself. This rental price is the *implicit* price that reflects the value to the firm of the services of its own capital that it uses during the current production period.

Purchase Price

The price that a firm pays to buy a capital good is called the *purchase price of capital*. When a firm buys a capital good outright, it obtains the use of the good's services over the whole of that good's lifetime. The capital good contributes a flow of benefits over its lifetime. These benefits are the marginal revenue product (*MRP*) of capital in each production period. The price that the firm is willing to pay for the capital good, naturally enough, is related to the total value that it places now on this stream of *expected MRPs* over future time periods. The term *expected* emphasizes that the firm is usually uncertain about what the future *MRP*s will be.

In order to compute the value that the firm places on receiving a future stream of benefits, we must examine the concept of *present value*. The following discussion proceeds under the simplifying assumption that the firm knows the future *MRP*s with certainty. This allows us to develop the central insights about present value without dealing with the complications arising from uncertainty.

The distinction between the rental price and the purchase price applies to any durable factor of production, including land and labour. *Applying Economic Concepts 15-1* examines this distinction in the case of labour. We now turn to the computation of present value.

APPLYING ECONOMIC CONCEPTS 15-1

The Rental and Purchase Price of Labour

If you wish to farm a piece of land, you can buy it yourself, or you can rent it for a specific period of time. If you want to set up a small business, you can buy your office and equipment, or you can rent them. The same is true for all capital and all land; a firm often has the option of buying or renting.

Exactly the same would be true for labour if we lived in a slave society. You could buy a slave to be your assistant, or you could rent the services either of someone else's slave or of a free person. Fortunately, slavery is illegal throughout most of today's world. As a result, the labour markets that we know deal only in the *services* of labour; we do not go to a labour market to buy a worker, only to hire his or her services.

You can, however, hire the services of a labourer for a long period of time. In professional sports, multiyear contracts are common. Publishers sometimes tie up their authors in multibook contracts, and movie and television production firms often sign up their actors on long-term contracts. In all cases of such *personal-services contracts,* the person is not a slave, and his or her personal rights and liberties are protected by law. The purchaser of the long-term contract is nonetheless buying ownership of the factor's *services* for an extended period of time. The price of the contract will reflect the person's expected earnings over the contract's lifetime. If the contract is transferable, the owner can sell these services for a lump sum or rent them out for some period. As with land and capital goods, the price paid for this stock of labour services depends on the expected rental prices over the contract period.

For many years, Wayne Gretzky had a personal-service contract with Peter Pocklington, the former owner of the Edmonton Oilers.

The Present Value of Future Returns

Consider the stream of future benefits that is provided by a piece of capital equipment. How much is that stream worth *now?* How much would someone be willing to pay now to buy the right to receive that flow of future benefits? The answer is called the capital's *present value.* In general, present value (*PV*) refers to the value now of one or more payments to be received in the future.

The Present Value of a Single Future Payment

One Period in the Future.   How much would a firm be prepared to pay now to purchase a capital good that produces an *MRP* of $100 in one year's time, after which time the capital good will be useless? One way to answer this question is to ask a somewhat *opposite* question: How much would the firm have to *lend* now in order to have $100 a year from now? Suppose for the moment that the interest rate is 5 percent per annum, which means that $1.00 invested today will be worth $1.05 in one year's time.

If we use PV to stand for this unknown amount, we can write $PV \times (1.05) = \$100$. Thus, $PV = \$100/1.05 = \$95.24$. This tells us that the present value of $100 receivable in one year's time is $95.24 when the interest rate is 5 percent. Anyone who lends out $95.24 for one year at 5 percent interest will receive $95.24 back plus $4.76 in interest, or $100 in total. When we calculate this present value, the interest rate is used to *discount* (reduce to its present value) the $100 to be received in one year's time.

The actual present value that we have calculated depended on our assuming that the interest rate is 5 percent. What if the interest rate is 7 percent? At that interest rate, the present value of the $100 receivable in one year's time would be $100/1.07 = $93.46.

These examples are easy to generalize. In both cases, we have found the present value by dividing the sum that is receivable in the future by 1 plus the rate of interest.[1] In general, if the interest rate is i per year, then the present value of the MRP (in dollars) received one year hence is

$$PV = MRP/(1 + i)$$

Several Periods in the Future.   Now we know how to calculate the present value of a single sum that is receivable one year in the future. The next step is to ask what would happen if the sum were receivable at a later date. For example, what is the present value of $100 to be received *two* years hence when the interest rate is 5 percent? This is $100/[(1.05)(1.05)] = $90.70. We can check this by seeing what would happen if $90.70 were lent out for two years. In the first year, the loan would earn interest of $(0.05)(\$90.70) = \$4.54$, and hence after one year, the firm would receive $95.24. In the second year, the interest would be earned on this entire amount; interest earned in the second year would equal $(0.05)(\$95.24) = \$4.76$. Hence, in two years the firm would have $100.

In general, the present value of MRP dollars received t years in the future when the interest rate is i per year is

$$PV = MRP/(1 + i)^t$$

This formula simply discounts the MRP by the interest rate, repeatedly, once for each of the t periods that must pass until the MRP becomes available. If we look at the formula, we see that the higher is i or t, the higher is the whole term $(1 + i)^t$. This term, however, appears in the denominator, so PV is *negatively* related to both i and t.

The formula $PV = MRP/(1 + i)^t$ shows that the present value of a given sum payable in the future will be smaller the more distant the payment date and the higher the rate of interest.

The Present Value of a Stream of Payments

Now consider the present value of a stream of receipts that continues *forever*. This is closer to the situation we are interested in when examining the firm's decision to purchase a capital good since that capital good will typically generate a stream of benefits long into the future. At first glance, the PV in this case might seem very high because the total amount received grows without reaching any limit as time passes. The preceding section suggests, however, that people will not value the far-distant payments very highly.

To find the PV of $100 a year, payable forever, we ask: How much would you have to lend now, at an interest rate of i per year, to obtain $100 each year in interest earnings? This is simply $i \times PV = \$100$, where i is the interest rate and PV the sum required. Dividing through by i shows the present value of the stream of $100 per year forever:

$$PV = \$100/i$$

---

[1] In this type of formula, the interest rate i is expressed as a decimal fraction where, for example, 7 percent is expressed as 0.07, so that $1 + i$ equals 1.07.

For example, if the interest rate is 10 percent, the present value would be $1000. In other words, $1000 invested at 10 percent yields $100 of interest per year forever. Notice that, as in the preceding sections, *PV* is negatively related to the rate of interest: The higher the interest rate, the lower the present value of the stream of future payments.

Practise with Study Guide Chapter 15, Exercise 2.

Conclusions

Our discussion about present value can be summarized as follows:

1. The present value of a unit of capital is positively related to the *MRP*s it produces.

2. The present value of a unit of capital is negatively related to the interest rate.

3. The present value of a unit of capital is negatively related to the time the owner must wait to receive the future *MRP*s.

The Firm's Decision

An individual firm faces a given interest rate and a given purchase price of capital goods. The firm can vary the quantity of capital that it employs, and as a result, the marginal revenue product of its capital varies. The law of diminishing marginal returns tells us that the more capital the firm uses, the lower its *MRP*.

The Decision to Purchase a Unit of Capital

Consider a firm that is deciding whether or not to add to its capital stock and facing an interest rate of *i* at which it can borrow or lend money. The first thing the firm has to do is to estimate the expected stream of *MRP*s from the new piece of capital over its lifetime. Then it discounts this at the interest rate of *i* per year to find the present value of the stream of receipts the machine will generate. Having computed the *PV* of the stream of *MRP*s, the firm then compares this *PV* with the purchase price of the capital good. If the purchase price is less than the *PV*, then the firm buys the capital good; if *PV* is less than the purchase price, the firm will not buy the capital good.

Consider the following simple example. Suppose that a machine has an *MRP* of $1000 each period—that is, by buying this machine the firm can produce more and thereby achieve a net addition to its revenues of $1000 each period. Suppose further that the machine lasts for 3 periods—after that, the machine is completely worn out and worth nothing. Finally, suppose the interest rate is 10 percent per year. The *PV* of this stream of *MRP*s is then equal to

$$PV = \$1000 + \$1000/(1 + 0.10) + \$1000/(1 + 0.10)^2 = \$2735.53.$$

The present value, by its construction, tells us how much any flow of future receipts is worth now. If the firm can buy the machine for less than its *PV*—that is, for any amount less than $2735.53—then this machine is a good buy. If it must pay more, the machine is not worth its price.

It is worthwhile for a firm to buy another unit of capital whenever the present value of the stream of future *MRP*s provided by that unit exceeds its purchase price.

The Firm's Optimal Capital Stock

Because of the law of diminishing marginal returns, the *MRP* declines as the firm's capital stock rises. The firm will thus go on adding to its stock of capital until the present value of the stream of *MRP*s generated by the *last unit* added is equal to the purchase price of that unit.

The profit-maximizing capital stock of the firm is such that the present value of the flow of *MRP*s that is provided by the last unit of capital is equal to its purchase price.

Now suppose the firm has achieved its profit-maximizing stock of capital. What would then lead the firm to increase that stock? Given the price of the machines, anything that increases the present value of the flow of income that the machines produce will have that effect. Two things will do this. First, the *MRP*s of the capital may rise, as would happen if technological changes make capital more productive so that each unit produces more than before. (We will deal with this possibility later in the chapter.) Second, the interest rate may fall, causing an increase in the present value of any given stream of future *MRP*s. For example, suppose that next year's *MRP* is $1000. This has a *PV* of $909.09 when the interest rate is 10 percent and $952.38 when the interest rate falls to 5 percent.

Thus, when the interest rate falls, the firm will wish to add to its capital stock. It will go on doing so until the decline in the *MRP*s of successive additions to its capital stock, according to the law of diminishing marginal returns, reduces the present value of the *MRP* at the new lower rate of interest to the purchase price of the capital.

The size of a firm's desired capital stock increases when the rate of interest falls, and it decreases when the rate of interest rises.

This relationship is shown in Figure 15-1. It can be thought of as the firm's demand curve for capital where the relevant "price" is the interest rate. It shows how the desired stock of capital varies with the interest rate.

What would cause a firm's demand for capital to shift? First, suppose the firm's expectations about future demand for its product improve. This optimism leads the firm to expect an increase in the future stream of *MRP*s produced by capital. With higher expected *MRP*s, the firm is prepared to purchase more units of capital (at any interest rate). Thus the firm's demand curve for capital shifts to the right. Second, suppose an improvement in technology increases the future stream of *MRP*s. Again, the higher future *MRP*s leads to a higher demand for capital at any interest rate—a rightward shift in the firm's demand curve for capital.

Any event that increases the expected future stream of *MRP*s leads to an increase in the firm's demand for capital.

FIGURE 15-1   The Firm's Demand for Capital

Anything that increases the future stream of *MRP*s will increase the demand for capital

The lower the rate of interest, the larger is the firm's desired capital stock. The lower the interest rate, the higher is the present value of any given stream of *MRP*s and hence the more capital that the firm will wish to use.

An improvement in technology that increases the future stream of *MRP*s produced by the capital leads the firm to demand more units of capital at any interest rate—the demand curve shifts to *D'*.

FIGURE 15-2   The Equilibrium Interest Rate

In the short run, the interest rate fluctuates to equate the demand and supply of capital; in the long run, the interest rate falls as more capital is accumulated. The economy's desired capital stock is negatively related to the interest rate, as shown by the curve D. In the short run, the aggregate capital stock is given. When the capital stock is K_0, the equilibrium interest rate is i_0. Above that rate firms will not want to hold all of the available capital; below that rate firms will want to borrow and add to their capital. In the long run, as the capital stock grows to K_1, the equilibrium interest rate falls to i_1.

The Equilibrium Interest Rate

Because the aggregate or total demand for capital goods is simply the sum of all the individual firms' demands, the analysis that we have used for a single firm also applies for the entire economy. Thus the higher is the market interest rate, the lower will be the total quantity of capital goods demanded. Also, changes in technology that make each unit of capital more productive lead to an increase in the total demand for capital goods.

The important difference between the analysis of a single firm and the analysis of the entire economy is that, whereas any individual firm takes the market interest rate as given, the interest rate is determined *in equilibrium* for the economy as a whole. This is analogous to each competitive firm taking the product price as given, whereas the product's price is determined in equilibrium in the market as a whole.

Short-Run Equilibrium

In the short run, the economy's capital stock is given. Though any single firm can change its own capital stock relatively easily—by buying or selling capital goods to or from other firms—the economy as a whole adjusts its capital stock only slowly. To reduce the aggregate capital stock, firms must either scrap their existing capital (if it is no longer profitable to keep it) or allow their capital goods to wear out, or *depreciate*. To increase the aggregate capital stock, new capital goods must be built, some of which—like buildings, bridges, and factories—take a considerable time to complete.

Figure 15-2 shows the economy's fixed short-run supply of capital as well as the total demand for capital goods, which is negatively related to the interest rate. Since the aggregate capital stock is fixed in the short run, equilibrium is achieved through changes in the interest rate, as opposed to changes in the level of capital.[2]

For the economy as a whole, the condition that the present value of the *MRP*s should equal the price of capital goods determines the equilibrium interest rate.

Let us see how this comes about. If the price of capital is less than the present value of its stream of future *MRP*s, it would be worthwhile for all firms to borrow money to purchase capital. For the economy as a whole, however, the stock of capital cannot change quickly, so the effect of this demand for borrowing would be to push up the interest rate until the present value of the *MRP*s equals the price of a unit of capital goods. Conversely, if the price of capital is above its present value, no one would

---

[2]In the macroeconomics part of this textbook, we see that if prices are inflexible in the short run, then actions taken by the central bank can also affect the interest rate. For now, we continue our assumption that all prices (for goods and factors) rise or fall quickly to clear markets, so that the short-run equilibrium interest rate is determined only by the economy's marginal product of capital.

wish to borrow money to invest in capital, and the rate of interest would fall. These points are illustrated in Figure 15-2.

Changing Capital and Technology

In the long run, the economy's capital stock is free to change, but technology is constant. If capital is accumulated over time, then the MRP will fall, and the equilibrium interest rate will also fall. Conversely, if the aggregate capital stock is allowed to wear out, then the MRP will rise and so will the equilibrium interest rate. This is shown in Figure 15-2, where the aggregate capital stock changes between K_0 and K_1, holding the demand for capital goods constant.

In the very long run, however, technology changes. As a result, the capital stock becomes more productive as the old, obsolete capital is replaced by newer, more efficient capital. The resulting outward shift of the D curve tends to increase the equilibrium interest rate associated with any particular size of the capital stock. In contrast, the accumulation of capital moves the economy downward to the right along any given D curve, which reduces the interest rate. The net effect on the interest rate of both of these changes may be to raise it, to lower it, or to leave it unchanged, as shown in Figure 15-3.

In almost all industrialized countries, there have been enormous increases in the aggregate capital stock over the past century. Yet, there *have not* been large decreases in the interest rate over the same period. We can easily understand this fact by examining Figure 15-3. Technological change has improved the marginal productivity of capital goods and has thus led to increases in the aggregate demand for capital. Taken alone, such technological improvements would lead to increases in the equilibrium interest rate. Working in the other direction, however, is the continual accumu-

FIGURE 15-3 The Effect of Changing Technology and Capital Stock

Technological changes which increase the marginal product of capital, and changes in the capital stock itself, have opposite effects on the equilibrium interest rate. The original capital stock is K_0 and the original technology gives rise to the demand for capital given by D_0. Thus, the equilibrium interest rate is i_0. Technological changes which increase the marginal product of capital shift the demand curve to D_1 and, with a constant capital stock, would increase the interest rate to i_1. Alternatively, an increase in the capital stock to K_1, holding technology constant, lowers the interest rate to i_2. If technology improves *and* the capital stock increases, then the interest rate could rise or fall. In the figure, the two effects exactly offset each other so that the interest rate is unchanged at i_0.

lation of capital, which tends to push down the equilibrium interest rate. The observation that the aggregate capital stock has increased dramatically, combined with the absence of a clear trend in the interest rate, suggests that these forces are offsetting each other more or less equally. The very-long-run effects of changing technology, combined with a growing capital stock, are represented in greater detail in Chapter 32.

One final comment about capital and the interest rate. We have shown that changes in the interest rate lead to changes in the firm's desired capital stock. We have also said that changes in the economy's stock of capital lead to changes in the equilibrium interest rate. When you go on to study macroeconomics, however, you will learn that the presence of inflation requires economists to make a distinction between the *real* interest rate and the *nominal* interest rate. All of our discussion here has been about the real interest rate. See *Extensions in Theory 15-1* for a more detailed discussion of inflation and interest rates.

EXTENSIONS IN THEORY 15-1

Inflation and Interest Rates

Inflation means the prices of all goods in the economy are rising. More correctly, it means that the prices of goods are rising on *average*—some prices may be rising and others may be falling, but if there is inflation then the price of the average good is rising. Economists refer to the average price of all goods as the *price level*. When the price level is rising, inflation is positive; if prices are rising at a rate of 5 percent per year, the rate of inflation is 5 percent. When the price level is falling, inflation is negative. If prices are falling at a rate of 2 percent per year, the rate of inflation is −2 percent.

Real and Nominal Interest Rates

In the presence of inflation, it becomes very important to distinguish between the *real interest rate* and the *nominal interest rate*. The nominal interest rate is measured simply in dollars paid. If you pay me $7 interest for a $100 loan for one year, the nominal interest rate is 7 percent.

Consider further my one-year loan to you of $100 at the nominal rate of 7 percent. The real rate that I earn depends on what happens to the price level during the course of the year. If the price level remains constant over the year, then the real rate that I earn is also 7 percent— because I can buy 7 percent more real goods and services with the $107 that you repay me than with the $100 that I lent you. However, if the price level were to rise by 7 percent during the year, the real rate would be zero because the $107 you repay me will buy exactly the same quantity of real goods as did the $100 I gave up. If I were unlucky enough to have lent money at a nominal rate of 7 percent in a year in which prices rose by 10 percent, the real rate would be −3 percent. The real rate of interest concerns the ratio of the purchasing power of the money repaid to the purchasing power of the money initially borrowed, and it will be different from the nominal rate whenever inflation is not zero. *The real interest rate is the difference between the nominal interest rate and the rate of inflation.*

If lenders and borrowers are concerned with the real costs measured in terms of purchasing power, the nominal interest rate will be set at the real rate they require plus an amount to cover any expected rate of inflation. Consider a one-year loan that is meant to earn a real return to the lender of 3 percent. If the expected rate of inflation is zero, the nominal interest rate for the loan will also be 3 percent. If, however, a 10 percent inflation is expected, the nominal interest rate will have to be set at 13 percent in order that the real return be 3 percent.

This point is often overlooked, and as a result people are surprised at the high nominal interest rates that exist during periods of high inflation. But it is the real interest rate that matters more to borrowers and lenders. Inflation is currently quite low in Canada but it has not always been that way. For example, in 1976 the rate of inflation was 7.5 percent and the nominal interest rate to prime borrowers was 10.0 percent! The real interest rate was then 2.5 percent. By 1999, the rate of inflation had fallen to 1.5 percent and the nominal rate to prime borrowers had fallen to 6.5 percent; the real rate was then 5.0 percent. Thus, the period of higher nominal interest rates was actually the period of lower real interest rates.

Back to Capital

In this chapter, we have examined the firm's decision to buy capital stock, and we emphasized the importance of the interest rate to this decision. We also discussed how changes in the aggregate stock of capital affected the economy's equilibrium interest rate. Though the text did not say it explicitly, all of our discussion related to the *real* interest rate.

When you go on to study *macroeconomics*, you will learn more about what causes inflation, and thus what forces us to make the distinction between real and nominal interest rates. For now, however, keep in mind that in this chapter we are supposing that there is no inflation; thus, real and nominal interest rates are the same.

Nonrenewable Resources

So far, we have discussed the pricing of factors, such as labour and capital, that can be replaced as they wear out. As older people leave the labour force because of retirement or death, young persons, seeking their first jobs, enter. As an existing piece of capital equipment is retired because of depreciation or obsolescence, it is replaced by a new piece of equipment. Such resources are called **renewable resources.**

We now consider factors of production that are available in fixed amounts. For each such factor, the total stock is given, and every unit that is used today permanently reduces the stock that is available for future use. Such a factor is called a **nonrenewable resource** or an *exhaustible resource.*

In practice, few, if any, resources are completely nonrenewable. Although there is only a fixed stock of oil, coal, or iron ore that is known to exist at any given time, new discoveries add to the known stock, and extraction subtracts from it. However, it is possible to imagine exhausting all of the world's supplies of oil, natural gas, or coal. In this sense, they are nonrenewable resources.

The Extraction Rate of a Resource

To focus on the basic issues, it is easiest to think of a resource that is completely nonrenewable. Suppose for the moment that all of the oil in existence has been discovered so that every unit that is used permanently diminishes the available stock by one unit.

Suppose that many firms own the land that contains the oil supply. They have invested money in discovering the oil, drilling wells, and laying pipelines. Their current extraction costs are virtually zero; all they have to do is turn their taps on, and the oil flows at any desired rate to the oil markets. It is obviously a simplification to assume that current production costs are actually zero. But this assumption is actually not too far from reality in the case of such a resource as oil, where the fixed costs of discovery, extraction, and distribution account for the bulk of total costs.

Profit-Maximizing Firms

What should each firm do? It could extract all of its oil in a great binge of production this year, or it could save the resource for some future rainy day and produce nothing this year. In practice, it is likely to adopt some intermediate policy, producing and selling some oil this year and holding stocks of it in the ground for extraction in future years. But *how much* should it extract this year and *how much* should it carry over for future years? What will the decision imply for the price of oil over the years?

The firms that own land with oil underneath it are holding a valuable resource. These firms have two alternatives. First, they can extract the oil now and sell it at the current market price. Second, they can leave the oil in the ground and extract it at some later date. The firms, naturally, will choose the alternative that gives them the highest return. Their choice will depend on two key variables—the interest rate and the expected rate of increase in the price of oil. To see how the firms' decisions are made, consider two cases.

First, suppose that the price of oil is expected to rise by less than the interest rate. For example, suppose the interest rate is 10 percent per year but the price of oil is expected to increase by only 5 percent per year. Oil extracted and sold now will in this case have a higher value than oil left in the ground, since revenues from current sales could be earning 10 percent in a bank account. Firms will therefore extract more oil this year. Because the demand curve for oil has a negative slope, raising the extraction rate (increasing the current supply) will reduce this year's price. Production will rise, and the current price will fall until the expected price increase between this year and next year is equal to the interest rate. The firms will then be indifferent between producing another barrel this year and holding it for production next year.

Second, suppose that the price is expected to rise by more than the interest rate. Firms will in this case prefer to leave more oil in the ground, where they earn a higher return than they could earn by selling the oil this year and investing the proceeds at the current interest rate. Thus, firms will cut their rate of production for this year, which will reduce the current supply and therefore raise this year's price. When the current price has risen so that the gap between the current price and next year's expected price is equal to the interest rate, firms will value equally a barrel of oil extracted and one left in the ground.

In a competitive industry for a nonrenewable resource, equilibrium occurs when the last unit currently produced earns just as much for each firm as it would if it had been left in the ground for future sales.

If the current interest rate is greater than the expected rate of increase in the price of oil, a profit-maximizing firm will extract the oil today.

To illustrate this important idea, suppose that next year's price is expected to be $1.05 and that the rate of interest is 5 percent. Now suppose that the current price is $1.04 per barrel. It clearly pays to extract more oil now because the $1.04 that is earned by selling a barrel now can be invested to yield approximately $1.09 ($1.04 × 1.05), which is more than the $1.05 that the oil would be worth in a year's time if it is left in the ground.

Now suppose that the current price is $.90 cents per barrel. It pays to extract less oil because oil left in the ground will be worth 16.7 percent more next year [(1.05/0.90) × 100]. Extracting it this year and investing the money will produce a gain of only 5 percent.

Finally, suppose the current price is $1.00. Now oil producers make the same amount of money whether they leave $1.00 worth of oil in the ground to be worth $1.05 next year or they sell the oil for $1.00 this year and invest the proceeds at 5 percent interest.

Market Pricing

What we have established so far determines the *rate of increase* of prices over time: If stocks are given and unchanging, prices should rise over time at a rate equal to the rate of interest. But what about the *level* of prices? Will they start low and rise to only moderate levels over the next few years, or will they start high and then rise to even higher levels? The answer depends on the total stock of the resource that is available (and, where some new discoveries are possible, on the expected additions to that stock in the future). The scarcer the resource relative to the demand for it, the higher its market price at the outset.

A resource's price tends to rise over time at a rate equal to the rate of interest; the current price will depend on current demand.

Hotelling's Rule

Oil is a scarce resource, and the value to consumers of one more barrel produced now is the price that they would be willing to pay for it, which in our example is the current $1.00 market price of the oil. If the oil is extracted this year and the proceeds are invested at the rate of interest (5 percent), they will produce $1.05 worth of valuable goods next year. If that barrel of oil is not produced this year and is left in the ground for extraction next year, its value to consumers at that time will be next year's price of oil. It is not *socially optimal*, therefore, to leave the oil in the ground unless it will be worth at least $1.05 to consumers next year.

Hotelling's rule
Determines the optimal rate of extraction of a nonrenewable resource as one such that the price rises at a rate equal to the interest rate.

The answer to the question "How much of a nonrenewable resource should be consumed now?" was provided many years ago by the U.S. economist Harold Hotelling. His answer—now referred to as **Hotelling's Rule**—is very simple, yet it specifically determines the optimal pattern of prices over the years. It is interesting that the answer applies to *all* nonrenewable resources. It does not matter whether there is a large or a small demand or whether that demand is elastic or inelastic. In all cases the answer is the same:

The socially optimal rate of extraction of any nonrenewable resource is such that its price increases at a rate equal to the interest rate.

For example, if the rate of interest is 4 percent, the price of the resource should be rising 4 percent per year. If it is rising by more, there is too much current extraction; if it is rising by less, there is not enough current extraction. We have already seen that this is the rate of extraction that will be produced by a competitive industry.

A competitive industry produces the socially optimal rate of extraction of a nonrenewable resource.

The Rate of Extraction

Hotelling's Rule does not tell us exactly how many barrels of oil should be extracted each year. Instead, it only tells us that the year's extraction rate should be such that the market price rises at a rate equal to the interest rate. What then should the actual extraction rate be if the competitive market fulfills Hotelling's Rule for optimal extraction rates? The answer to this question *does* depend on market conditions. Specifically, it depends on the position and the slope of the demand curve. If the quantity demanded at all prices is small, the rate of extraction will be small. The larger the quantity demanded at each price, the higher the rate of extraction will tend to be.

Now consider the influence of the demand elasticity. A highly inelastic demand curve suggests that there are few substitutes and that purchasers are prepared to pay large sums rather than do without the resource. This inelasticity will produce a relatively even rate of extraction, with small reductions in each period being sufficient to drive up the price at the required rate. A relatively elastic demand curve suggests that people can easily find substitutes once the price rises. This will encourage a great deal of consumption now and a rapidly diminishing amount over future years because large reductions in consumption are needed to drive the price up at the required rate.

Figure 15-4 illustrates this working of the price mechanism with a simple example in which the whole stock of oil must be consumed in only two periods, this year and next year. The general point is this:

The more inelastic the demand curve, the more even the rate of extraction (and hence the rate of use) will be over time; the more elastic the demand curve, the more uneven the rate of extraction will be over time.

An elastic demand curve will lead to large consumption now and a rapid fall in consumption over the years. An inelastic demand curve will lead to lower consumption now and a less rapid fall in consumption over the years.

Practise with Study Guide Chapter 15, Exercise 6.

Conservation Through the Price System

In this discussion, we see the price system playing its now familiar role of coordinator. By following private profit incentives, firms are led to conserve the resource in a manner that is consistent with society's needs.

The Role of Rising Prices

We have seen that, from society's viewpoint, the optimal extraction pattern of a nonrenewable resource occurs when its price rises each year at a rate equal to the interest

FIGURE 15-4   The Extraction Rate for a Nonrenewable Resource

The shape of the demand curve determines the extraction pattern over time. In the example in this figure, the interest rate is assumed to be 10 percent, and there is a fixed supply of 200 000 barrels of oil that can be extracted from the ground at zero marginal cost. (All costs are fixed costs.) The oil is available for extraction either in the current period or in the next period, after which it spoils.

In part (i) of the figure, the demand curve is relatively flat. The two conditions—that the whole supply be used over two periods and that the price rise by 10 percent between the two periods—dictate that the quantities be 120 000 barrels in the first period, with a price of $1.00 per barrel, and 80 000 in the second period, with a price of $1.10 per barrel.

In part (ii), the demand curve is rather steep. The same two conditions now dictate that the quantities be 104 000 barrels in the first period, with a price of $1.50 per barrel, and 96 000 barrels in the second period, with a price of $1.65 per barrel.

rate. If the price is prevented from rising, the resource is depleted too quickly. The rising price fulfills a number of useful functions.

First, the rising price encourages conservation. As the resource becomes scarcer and its price rises, users will be motivated to be more economical in its use. Uses with low yields may be abandoned altogether, and uses with high yields will be pursued only as long as their value at the margin is enough to compensate for the high price.

Second, the rising price encourages the discovery of new sources of supply—at least in cases in which the world supply is not totally fixed and already known.

Third, the rising price encourages innovation. New products that will do the same job may be developed, as well as new processes that use alternative resources. For example, a rising price of oil encourages the development of alternative sources of energy, such as solar and wind power.

How Might the Price System Fail?

We now examine three basic ways in which the price system might fail to produce the optimal rate of resource extraction. First, private owners may not have sufficient information to determine the optimal extraction rate. Second, deficiencies in property rights may result in firms' having incentives to extract the resource too fast. Third, markets may not correctly reflect social values. We look at examples of each of these and ask if they justify government intervention. In looking at these examples in which the price system fails, we are anticipating what will be the major theme of Chapter 16.

Ignorance. Private owners might not have enough knowledge to arrive at the best estimate of the rate at which prices will rise. If they do not know the world stocks of their commodity and the current extraction rate, they may be unable to estimate the rate of the price rise and thus will not know when to raise or lower their current rates of extraction. For example, if all firms think that prices will rise only slowly in the future, but prices actually end up rising quickly, they will all produce too much now and conserve too little for future periods.

In this situation, however, there is no reason to think that the government could do any better, unless it has access to some special knowledge that private firms do not possess. If it does have such knowledge, the government can make it public; further intervention is unnecessary if a competitive industry is maximizing profits on the basis of the best information available to it. In practice, what knowledge does exist about both the proven reserves of nonrenewable resources and their current extraction rates is usually freely and openly available.

Inadequate Property Rights. Some nonrenewable resources have the characteristics of what is called *common property*. Such property cannot be exclusively owned and controlled by one person or firm. For example, one person's oil-bearing land may be adjacent to another person's, and the underground supplies may be interconnected. In such a case, if one firm holds off producing now, the oil may end up being extracted by the neighbour. In such cases, which are often encountered with oil, there is a tendency for a firm to extract the resource too fast because a firm's oil that has been left in the ground may not be available to that firm at a future date. (A similar issue arises with any common-property resource such as fishing grounds. We examine this further in Chapter 16.)

What is being described here is a problem of *inadequate property rights*. Because the resource will be worth more in total value when it is exploited at the optimal extraction rate than when small firms exploit it too quickly, there will be an incentive for individual owners to combine until each self-contained source of supply is owned by only one firm. After that, the problem of overexploitation will no longer arise. Government ownership is not necessary to achieve this result. What is needed, at most, is intervention to ensure that markets can work to provide the optimal size of individual units so that proper extraction management can be applied by the private owners.

Political uncertainty can be another source of inadequate property rights. For example, the owners of the resource may fear that a future election or a revolution will establish a government that will confiscate their property. They will then be motivated to exploit the resource too quickly, on the grounds that certain revenue now is more valuable than uncertain revenue in the future. The current rate of extraction will tend to increase until the expected rate of price rise exceeds the interest rate by a sufficient margin to compensate for the risks of future confiscation of supplies left in the ground.

Unequal Market and Social Values. In a competitive world, the market interest rate indicates the rate at which it is optimal to discount the future. Society's investments are beneficial if they earn at least the market rate of return; they are not beneficial if they earn less (because the resources could be used in other ways to produce more value to consumers). In certain circumstances, however, the government may have reasons to adopt a different discount rate. It is then said that the *social rate of discount*—the discount rate that is appropriate to the society as a whole—differs from the private rate, as indicated by the market rate of interest. In such circumstances, there is reason for the government to intervene to alter the rate at which the private firms would exploit the resource.

Critics are often ready to assume that profit-hungry producers will despoil most exhaustible resources by using them up too quickly. They argue for government intervention

For good information on fossil fuels, see the website for the U.S. Department of Energy: www.doe.gov. Click on "Fossil Fuel Lessons."

to conserve the resource by slowing its rate of extraction. Yet, unless the social rate of discount is below the private rate, there is no clear social gain in investing by holding resources in the ground where they will yield only, say, a 2 percent return, when perhaps 5 percent can be gained on other investments.

Because governments must worry about their short-term popularity and their chances of reelection, they may have a discount rate higher than either the social or market rate. Thus, there is no presumption that government intervention will slow the rate of extraction. Instead, governments might extract resources *faster* than would occur by private firms in the absence of intervention.

A good example is provided by the Hybernia oil field that lies off the coast of Newfoundland. When development began in the late 1970s, the cost of developing the field and extracting the oil exceeded the market value of the oil. It would therefore not have been extracted under free-market conditions. Instead, taxpayers' money was used to produce oil whose market value was less than its full costs of production. If left beneath the ocean floor, the oil would one day have developed a value sufficient for it to be extracted by private firms, either because of increases in the price of oil or improvements in technology that reduced the costs of extraction.

Actual Price Movements

Many nonrenewable resources do not seem to have the steadily rising prices predicted by Hotelling's Rule. The OPEC cartel restricted the supply of oil in the 1970s and thereby pushed its price up dramatically. But in the mid 1980s both the rate of extraction and the real price of oil returned approximately to their pre-OPEC levels. Since then the price of oil has increased only occasionally, whenever the producing countries have succeeded in intermittently enforcing some output restrictions. The price of coal has not soared; nor has the price of iron ore. In many cases, the reason lies in the discovery of new supplies, which have prevented the total known stocks of many resources from being depleted. In the case of oil, for example, the ratio of known reserves to one year's consumption is no lower now than it was two or even four decades ago. Furthermore, most industry experts believe that large quantities of undiscovered oil exist under both the land and the sea.

In other cases, the invention of new substitute products has reduced the demand for some of these resources and has thus prevented prices from rising as quickly as they otherwise would have. For example, plastics have replaced metals in many uses, and fiber optics have replaced copper wire in many types of message transmission.

In yet other cases, the reason is to be found in government pricing policy. An important example of this type is the use of nonrenewable water for irrigation in much of the United States. Though vast underground reserves of water lie in aquifers beneath many areas of the United States, they are being used up at a rate that will exhaust them in a matter of decades. The water is often supplied by government water authorities at a price that covers only a small part of the total extraction cost and that does not rise steadily to reflect the dwindling stocks. Current U.S. water policy will have strong effects on Canada, which controls a large *renewable* supply of fresh water from rivers and lakes.

Such a constant-price policy for *any* nonrenewable resource creates three characteristic problems. First, the resource will be exhausted much faster than if the price were to rise over time. Second, since the price is not allowed to rise, no signals go out to induce conservation, innovation, and exploration. Third, when the supply of the resource is finally exhausted, the adjustment will have to come all at once. If the price had risen steadily each year under free-market conditions, adjustment would have taken place little by little each year. The controlled price, however, gives no signal of the ever-diminishing stock of the resource until all at once the supplies run out. The required adjustment will then be much more painful than it would have been if it had been spread over time in response to steadily rising prices.

When governments intervene to keep the price of a nonrenewable resource below its free-market value, the current users of the resource are essentially obtaining a subsidy from future users, who, if the policy continues, will have to make many adjustments abruptly while paying much higher prices for the resource.

For lots of good information about various forms of energy, check out the Energy Information Administration's website: www.eia.doe.gov.

Currently, several of the western U.S. states are suffering severe water shortages. In spite of the shortages, water prices are being held well below what they would be in free markets. The low prices both encourage water uses that would not even be contemplated under free-market conditions and discourage conservation, thus leading to more rapidly growing shortages than would occur under rising free-market prices. For example, about 80 percent of California's water supply goes to farmers even though agriculture accounts for only one tenth of the state's economy. Throughout California's Central Valley, sprinklers irrigate cattle pastures and fields of alfalfa, cotton, and rice—crops more suited to monsoon lands than to the valley's dry climate. Alfalfa fields alone take up more water than that used by all the people in San Francisco and Los Angeles combined.

The dwindling water supplies under much of the continent would long ago have led to price increases close to those predicted by Hotelling's theory, and hence to a series of gradual adjustments, had the price been permitted to rise to reflect the growing scarcity of the resource.

SUMMARY

Capital and the Interest Rate

- Because capital goods are durable, it is necessary to distinguish between the stock of capital goods and the flow of services provided by them and thus between their purchase price and their rental price. The rental price is the amount that is paid to obtain the flow of services that a capital good provides for a given period. The purchase price is the amount that is paid to acquire ownership of the capital.

- To determine the purchase price of capital, it is necessary to compute the present value of the stream of benefits produced by the unit of capital. The present value will be lower when the benefits are more distant and the interest rate is higher.

- An individual firm will purchase capital as long as the present value of the stream of future net returns that is provided by another unit of capital exceeds its purchase price. For a single firm and for the economy as a whole, the profit-maximizing size of the capital stock varies negatively with the rate of interest.

- Whereas individual firms take the market interest rate as given, the interest rate is determined in equilibrium for the economy as a whole. Long-run increases in the aggregate capital stock, holding technology constant, lead to reductions in the equilibrium interest rate. Changes in technology that increase the marginal revenue product of capital lead to increases in the equilibrium interest rate.

Nonrenewable Resources

LO 4 5

- The socially optimal rate of extraction for a nonrenewable resource occurs when its price rises at a rate equal to the rate of interest. This is Hotelling's Rule. This rate of price increase is also the rate that will be established by profit-maximizing firms in a competitive industry.
- Resources for which the demand is highly elastic will have a high rate of extraction in the near future and a fairly rapid falloff over time. Resources for which the demand is highly inelastic will have a lower rate of extraction in the near future and a smaller falloff over time.
- Rising prices act as a conservation device by rationing consumption over time according to people's preferences.

As prices rise, conservation, discovery of new sources of supply, and innovation to reduce demand are all encouraged.
- The price system can fail to produce optimal results if (a) people lack the necessary knowledge, (b) property rights are inadequate to protect supplies left for future use by their owners, or (c) the social rate of discount differs significantly from the market rate.
- Controlling the price of an exhaustible resource at a constant level speeds up the rate of extraction and removes the price incentives to react to its growing scarcity.

KEY CONCEPTS

Rental price and purchase price
 of capital
Present value

A firm's demand for capital
The interest rate and the capital stock
The equilibrium interest rate

Hotelling's Rule
The conservation role of rising prices
 of nonrenewable resources

STUDY EXERCISES

1. The following table shows the stream of income produced by several different assets. In each case, P_1, P_2, and P_3 are the payments made by the asset in years 1, 2 and 3.

Asset	(i)	P_1	P_2	P_3	Present Value
A	8%	$1000	$0	$0	—-
B	7%	0	0	5000	—-
C	9%	200	0	200	—-
D	10%	50	40	60	—-

   a. For each asset, compute the asset's present value. (Note that the market interest rate, i, is not the same in each situation.)
   b. In each case, what is the most a firm would be prepared to pay to acquire the asset?
   c. Suppose the listed purchase price for an asset were less than its present value. What would you expect to observe?

2. The table below shows how the present value of the future MRPs produced by each unit of capital changes as the firm's total capital stock increases.

Units of Capital	PV of future MRPs
100	$10 000
101	9 000
102	8 000
103	7 000
104	6 000
105	5 000
106	4 000
107	3 000

a. Notice that the present value of the *MRP* declines as more capital is used. What economic principle accounts for this?

b. If a unit of capital can be purchased for $5000, how many will the firm purchase? Explain.

c. Suppose the market interest rate suddenly falls. Explain what happens to the *PV* of the stream of future *MRP*s. What happens to the firm's profit-maximizing level of capital?

3. The diagram below shows an individual firm's demand curve for capital. The market interest rate is i_0.

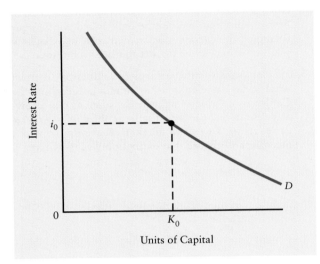

a. Explain why the firm's demand curve is downward sloping.

b. Suppose the firm now expects the market for its product to be especially good in the future. Explain what happens to its demand curve for capital.

c. Now suppose that some technical problem leads to a reduction in the future stream of *MRP*s produced by capital. How does this affect the firm's demand for capital?

4. The following diagram shows the economy's aggregate demand for capital as a function of the interest rate.

a. If the economy's stock of capital is currently K_0, what is the equilibrium interest rate? Explain.

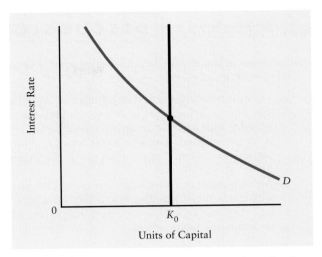

b. If firms experience an improvement in technology that increases the expected future *MRP* of each unit of capital, what is the effect on the equilibrium interest rate? Explain.

5. The table below shows a number of situations faced by Prairie Energy Inc., an Alberta-based oil company. The price of oil is given as dollars per barrel.

Case	Interest Rate (per annum)	Oil Price Now	Oil Price in One Year	Extract Now?
A	8%	$20	$25	—-
B	10%	15	18	—-
C	12%	10	8	—-
D	12%	10	12	—-
E	20%	15	18	—-

a. In each case, what rate of return would Prairie Energy earn *over the coming year* by leaving its oil in the ground and then extracting it and selling it in one years' time?

b. In each case, what rate of return would Prairie Energy earn on its alternative investment?

c. In each case, indicate whether it is beneficial for Prairie Energy to extract the oil now, or to wait until next year.

DISCUSSION QUESTIONS

1. How would you go about evaluating the present value of each of the following?

   a. The existing reserves of a relatively small oil company
   b. The total world reserves of an exhaustible natural resource with a known completely fixed supply
   c. A long-term bond, issued by a very unstable third-world government, that promises to pay the bearer $1000 per year forever
   d. A lottery ticket that your neighbour bought for $10, which was one of 1 million tickets sold for a drawing which will be held in one year's time paying $2 million to the single winner

2. Your parents argue that it makes more sense for you to take taxis and, on occasion, to rent a car while you are at university because you will be spending most of your time in the library and your need for a car should be minimal. Make an argument based on the rental price of transportation (not on the other advantages of having the car) that it may be cheaper for you to buy a car for use while you are at university.

3. Obtain annual data on the world price of oil over the past 30 years. Explain whether the observed path of prices appears to follow Hotelling's Rule. Can you explain any deviations? (For lots of energy-related data, check out www.eia.doe.gov.)

4. There are many examples of resources that are technically renewable—such as the stock of old-growth forests—but that may not be replenished within your lifetime if the current stock is depleted. Explain how you would expect the market to price such resources.

5. Species that are on the verge of extinction—beluga whales, African elephants, mountain gorillas, and the California condor—might be classified as nonrenewable resources; once they disappear, there will be no regeneration. Does the market create appropriate incentives to ensure that extinction will not occur?

PART SIX

Government in the Market Economy

When is there a role for government to intervene in the market economy? Is government action necessary to reduce sulphur dioxide emissions, or can the market economy handle that problem itself? Why doesn't the private sector provide things like national defence? What are tradable pollution permits and how do they work? How does the Canadian government raise the money it needs to finance its expenditures, and on what does the Canadian government spend? These are the kinds of questions you will be able to answer after reading the next three chapters.

Chapter 16 discusses the basic functions of governments and then reviews the case for free markets. We will see the reasons why economists often argue in favour of free markets and against government intervention. We then explore the case for government intervention based on the concept of a market failure—a situation in which the free market fails to produce the allocatively efficient outcome. It is here that we see why the free market typically cannot be relied upon to solve the problem of pollution; we will also learn why the private sector does not provide national defence. Next, we explore reasons for government intervention that are motivated by the pursuit of broad social goals. Finally, we examine the process of government intervention and the reasons for government failures.

In Chapter 17 we explore the economics of pollution. We examine the rationale for regulating pollution and various methods of pollution control, including tradable pollution permits—the most recent (and most controversial) method for dealing with pollution.

Chapter 18 then examines the taxation and expenditure patterns of Canadian governments. We discuss the Canadian tax system, and how to evaluate a tax system from the standpoints of both efficiency and equity. We then explore some of the most important spending programs and discuss some of the recent debates about reforming various elements of Canadian social programs.

CHAPTER 16

Market Failures and Government Intervention

LO *LEARNING OBJECTIVES*

1 Recognize that two basic functions of government are the protection of individuals from others and the establishment and enforcement of property rights.

2 Understand the ability of free markets to respond to change and to promote innovation.

3 Define an externality and explain why it leads to allocative inefficiency.

4 Define public goods, and explain why they will not be provided by private markets.

5 Understand why asymmetric information can lead to market failures.

6 Understand why free markets generally will not achieve some desirable social goals.

7 Explain the direct and indirect costs of government intervention.

8 Understand some of the important causes of government failure.

Most aspects of Canadian economic life are determined in free markets. Most of the goods and services that you buy are produced by privately owned profit-making firms, and the prices of those goods and services are determined in free markets. The incomes of most Canadian workers are also determined by free-market forces.

But government intervention and regulation are also pervasive. Canadian governments regulate the pricing of cable TV, local telephone service, and electricity. The Canadian government owns Canada Post, the Export Development Corporation, and many other crown corporations that sell goods or services to firms and households. And Canadian governments have extensive regulations regarding many aspects of our lives, including waste disposal, workplace safety, building codes, minimum wages, taxi service, and so on.

Which elements of the economy can be left to free markets and which elements require government intervention? Governments are necessary to provide law and order and to define and enforce property rights. But beyond these basic functions—ones that we all too often take for granted—what is the case for government intervention in otherwise free markets?

The general case for some reliance on free markets is that allowing decentralized decision making is more desirable than having all economic decisions made by a centralized planning body. The general case for some government intervention is that almost no one wants to let markets decide *everything* about our economic affairs. Most people believe that there are areas in which markets do not function well and in which government intervention can improve the general social good.

The operative choice is not between an unhampered free-market economy and a fully centralized command economy. It is rather the choice of *which mix* of markets and government intervention best suits people's hopes and needs.

In this chapter, we discuss the role of the government in market-based economies, making the case both for and against government intervention. We begin by examining the basic functions of government.

Basic Functions of Government

Governments are as old as organized economic activity. They arose shortly after the neolithic agricultural revolution turned people from hunter–gatherers into settled farmers. An institution that has survived that long must be doing something right! Over the intervening 100 centuries the functions undertaken by governments have varied enormously. But through all that time the function that has not changed is to provide what is called a *monopoly of violence*. Violent acts can be conducted by the military and the civilian police arms of government, and through its judicial system the government can deprive people of their liberty by incarcerating them or, in extreme cases, by executing them. This is a dangerous monopoly that is easily abused. For this reason satisfactory societies have systems of checks and balances designed to keep the government's monopoly directed to the general good rather than to the good of a narrow government circle.

The importance of having a monopoly of violence can be seen in those countries whose governments do not have it. Somalia in recent decades and China in the 1920s provide examples of countries in which individual warlords commanded armies that could not vanquish each other. Colombia, and to some extent Russia, provide examples of organized crime having substantial power to commit violence that the government cannot control. In extreme cases where many groups have almost equal ability to exert military violence, power struggles can create havoc with normal economic and social life. Life then becomes "nasty, brutish, and short"—to use the words of the seventeenth-century English political philosopher Thomas Hobbes (1588–1679).

The importance of having checks on the government's arbitrary use of its monopoly is seen in the disasters that ensue in the many dictatorships that misuse their power. The USSR under Stalin, Uganda under Idi Amin, Nigeria under Sanni Abacha, and Cambodia under Pol Pot are a few of the many modern-day examples.

When the government's monopoly of violence is secure and functions with restrictions against its arbitrary use, citizens can safely carry on their ordinary economic and social activities.

So governments are, as they always have been, institutions to which people accept a monopoly of violence in return for the enforcement of "law and order."

A related government activity is to provide security of property. Governments define and enforce property rights that give people a secure claim to the fruits of their own labour. These property rights include clear definition and enforcement of the rights and obligations of institutions such as corporations, banks, insurance companies, and stock exchanges.

As the founder of British classical economics, Adam Smith, put it a long time ago:

The first duty of the sovereign [is] that of protecting the society from the violence and invasion of other independent societies. . . . The second duty of the sovereign [is] that of protecting, as far as possible, every member of the society from the injustice or oppression of every other member of it.[1]

In a modern complex economy, providing these "minimal" government services is no simple task. Countries whose governments are not good at doing these things have seldom prospered economically.

The Case for Free Markets

Within a secure framework of law and order, and well-defined and enforced property rights, a modern economy can function at least moderately well without further government assistance. In this section we review the case for free markets. In subsequent sections we study government functions that arise when free markets fail to produce acceptable results.

Free markets are impressive institutions. Consumers' tastes and producers' costs help to generate price signals. These signals coordinate separate decisions taken by millions of independent agents, all pursuing their own self-interest and oblivious to national priorities. In doing so, they allocate the nation's resources without conscious central direction. Markets also determine the distribution of income by establishing prices of factors of production, which provide incomes for their owners. Furthermore, modern market economies, where firms compete to get ahead of each other by producing better goods more cheaply, generate the technological changes that have raised average living standards fairly steadily at least over the past two centuries.

In presenting the case for free markets economists have used two quite different approaches. The first of these may be characterized as the "formal defence," and is based on the concept of allocative efficiency, introduced in Chapter 12. The essence of the formal defence of free-market economies is that if all markets were perfectly competitive, and if governments allowed all prices to be determined by demand and supply, then resources would be allocated in the *optimal* manner. That is, prices would equal marginal cost for all products and thus the economy would be allocatively efficient.

The other defence of free markets—what might be called the "informal defence"—is at least as old as Adam Smith and is meant to apply to market economies whether or not they are perfectly competitive. It is based on the theme that markets are a very effective mechanism for coordinating the decisions of decentralized decision makers. The informal defence is intuitive in that it is not laid out in a formal model of an economy, but it does follow from some hard reasoning, and it has been subjected to much intellectual probing.

This informal defence of free markets is based on three central arguments.

1. Free markets provide automatic coordination of the actions of decentralized decision makers.

2. The pursuit of profits in free markets provides a stimulus to innovation and economic growth.

3. Free markets permit a decentralization of economic power.

---

[1]Adam Smith, *The Wealth of Nations* (1976; New York: Random House, 1937 edn., pp. 653, 669).

Automatic Coordination

Defenders of the market economy argue that, compared with the alternatives, the decentralized market system is more flexible and adjusts more quickly to changes.

Suppose, for example, that the price of oil rises. One household might prefer to respond by maintaining a high temperature in its house and economizing on its driving; another household might do the reverse. A third household might give up air-conditioning instead. This flexibility can be contrasted with centralized control, which would force the same pattern on everyone, say, by fixing the price, by rationing heating oil and gasoline, by regulating permitted temperatures, and by limiting air-conditioning to days when the temperature exceeded 27°C.

Furthermore, as conditions continue to change, prices in a market economy will continue to change, and decentralized decision makers can react continually. In contrast, government quotas, allocations, and rationing schemes are much more difficult to adjust. As a result, there are likely to be shortages and surpluses before adjustments are made. One great value of the market is that it provides automatic signals *as a situation develops* so that not all of the consequences of an economic change have to be anticipated and allowed for by a group of central planners. Millions of responses to millions of changes in thousands of markets are required every year, and it would be a herculean task to anticipate and plan for them all.

A market system allows for coordination *without anyone needing to understand how the whole system works.* As Professor Thomas Schelling put it:

> The dairy farmer doesn't need to know how many people eat butter and how far away they are, how many other people raise cows, how many babies drink milk, or whether more money is spent on beer or milk. What he needs to know is the prices of different feeds, the characteristics of different cows, the different prices . . . for milk . . . , the relative cost of hired labor and electrical machinery, and what his net earnings might be if he sold his cows and raised pigs instead.[2]

It is, of course, an enormous advantage that all the producers and consumers of a country collectively can make the system operate, yet not one of them, much less all of them, has to understand how it works.

Innovation and Growth

Technology, tastes, and resource availability are changing all the time, in all economies. Thirty years ago, there was no such thing as a personal computer or a digital watch. Front-wheel drive was a curiosity in North America. Students carried their books in briefcases or in canvas bags that were anything but waterproof. Manuscripts existed only as hard copy, not as electronic files in a computer. To change one word in a manuscript, one usually had to retype an entire page. Videocassettes did not exist, nor did compact discs, cell phones, or the Internet.

Digital watches, personal computers, front-wheel drive cars, and compact discs are all products that were invented or developed by individuals or firms in pursuit of profits. An entrepreneur who correctly "reads" the market and perceives that there may be a demand for some product will be inclined to develop it.

The next 20 years will also surely see changes great and small. Changes in technology may make an idea that is not practical today practical five years from now. New prod-

---

[2]Schelling, T.C. *Micro Motives and Macro Behavior* (New York: Norton, 1978).

ucts and techniques will be devised to adapt to shortages, gluts, and changes in consumer demands and to exploit new opportunities made available by new technologies.

In a market economy, individuals risk their time and money in the hope of earning profits. Though many fail, some succeed. New products and processes appear and disappear. Some are fads or have little impact; others become items of major significance. The market system works by trial and error to sort them out and allocates resources to what prove to be successful innovations.

In contrast, planners in more centralized systems have to guess which innovations will be productive and which goods will be strongly demanded. Central planning may achieve wonders by permitting a massive effort in a chosen direction, but central planners also may guess incorrectly about the direction and put too many eggs in the wrong basket or reject as unpromising something that will turn out to be vital. Perhaps the biggest failure of centrally planned economies was their inability to encourage the experimentation and innovation that have proved to be the driving forces behind long-run growth in advanced market economies. It is striking that the last decade has seen most centrally planned economies abandon their system in favour of a price system in one fell swoop while the only remaining large planned economy, China, is increasing the role of markets in most aspects of its economy.

Decentralization of Power

Another important part of the case for a free-market economy is that it tends to decentralize power and thus requires less coercion of individuals than any other type of economy. Of course, even though markets tend to diffuse power, they do not do so completely; large firms and large labour unions clearly have and exercise substantial economic power.

Though the market power of large corporations and unions is not negligible, it tends to be constrained both by the competition of other large entities and by the emergence of new products and firms. This is the process of creative destruction that was described by Joseph Schumpeter and that we examined in Chapter 10. In any case, say defenders of the free market, even such aggregations of private power are far less substantial than government power.

Governments must coerce if markets are not allowed to allocate people to jobs and goods to consumers. Not only will such coercion be regarded as arbitrary (especially by those who do not like the results), but the power creates major opportunities for bribery, corruption, and allocation according to the tastes of the central administrators. If, at the going prices and wages, there are not enough apartments or coveted jobs to go around, the bureaucrats can allocate some to those who pay the largest bribe, some to those with religious beliefs, or political views that they like, and only the rest to those whose names come up on the waiting list.

This line of reasoning has been articulated forcefully by the Nobel laureate and conservative economist Milton Friedman, who was for many years a professor of economics at the University of Chicago. Friedman argues that economic freedom—the ability to allocate resources through private markets—is essential to the maintenance of political freedom.[3] Other economists and social theorists have challenged this proposition.

---

[3]Milton Friedman, *Capitalism and Freedom* (Chicago: The University of Chicago Press: 1982).

Market Failures

Free markets do all of the good things that we have just discussed; yet there are many circumstances in which the free market does not produce the best outcomes. In these cases, economists say that markets have *failed*. The case for intervening in free markets turns in large part on identifying the conditions that lead to market failure. Much of the following discussion is devoted to this task.

We must be careful when using the expression *market failure* because the word *failure* may convey the wrong impression. Market failure does not mean that nothing good has happened. It means, instead, that the *best attainable outcome* has not been achieved. More precisely, **market failure** refers to a situation where private markets, in the absence of government intervention, fail to achieve allocative efficiency. In other words, in some market or markets, the marginal benefit of the good differs from its marginal cost.

Market failure describes a situation in which the free market, in the absence of government intervention, fails to achieve allocative efficiency.

It is useful to recall the distinction between normative and positive statements that we first encountered in Chapter 2. The statement that the economy is allocatively efficient (or not) is a *positive* statement. We can say that the economy has or has not achieved allocative efficiency without making any value judgement—the statement uses only an observation about the economy and the definition of allocative efficiency. It is important to note, however, that the allocatively efficient outcome may not be the most desirable outcome in a normative sense. For example, the economy may be allocatively efficient even though the distribution of income is judged by some to be undesirable. As we see later in the chapter, such concerns provide another motivation for government intervention.

We now examine five situations in which the free market fails to achieve allocative efficiency—*monopoly*, *externalities*, *non-rivalrous* and *non-excludable goods*, *asymmetric information* and *missing markets*. All of these market failures provide a justification, at least in principle, for government intervention in markets. We then discuss other reasons for government intervention that are not based on market failure—chief among these is intervention to achieve a desirable income distribution.

market failure
Failure of the unregulated market system to achieve allocative efficiency.

Market Power

As we discussed in Chapter 10, firms that face downward-sloping demand curves—whether they are monopolistic competitors or monopolists—will maximize profits at an output where price exceeds marginal cost, leading to allocative inefficiency. Although some market power is maintained through artificial barriers to entry, such power can also arise naturally because in some industries the least costly way to produce a good or a service is to have few producers relative to the size of the market. The standard government remedies are competition policy and regulation, which, as discussed in Chapter 12, present problems of their own.

Externalities

Recall from Chapter 12 that in order for the economy to be allocatively efficient, marginal benefit must equal marginal cost for all products. But whose benefits and costs are relevant? Firms that are maximizing their *own* profits are interested only in their own costs of production—they are not interested in any costs that their actions might impose on others. Similarly, individual consumers are interested in the benefits *they* receive from any given

externality An effect, either good or bad, on parties not directly involved in the production or use of a commodity. Also called *third-party effects*.

product—they usually ignore the benefits that might accrue to others. An **externality** occurs whenever actions taken by firms or consumers impose costs or confer benefits on *others that are not involved in the transaction*. When you smoke a cigarette in a restaurant, you might impose costs on others present; when you renovate your home, you might confer benefits on your neighbours by improving the general look of the neighbourhood. Externalities are also called *third-party effects* because parties other than the two primary participants in the transaction (the buyer and the seller) are affected.

Private and Social Costs

private cost The value of the best alternative use of resources used in production as valued by the producer.

social cost The value of the best alternative use of resources used in production as valued by society.

The foregoing discussion suggests the importance of the distinction between *private cost* and *social cost*. **Private cost** measures the cost faced by the private decision maker, including production costs, advertising costs, and so on. **Social cost** includes the private cost (since the decision maker is a member of society) but also includes any other costs imposed on third parties. There is a similar distinction between *private benefit* and *social benefit*. To simplify things, however, we will discuss all externalities in terms of the distinction between private and social cost. But this does not limit our discussion in any way. If we want to consider a situation where your listening to good music confers benefits to your nearby friends, we can think of your action as either increasing their benefits or, equivalently, as decreasing their costs. Similarly, your smoking of cigarettes can be viewed either as reducing their benefits or, equivalently, as increasing their costs. By expressing everything in terms of costs (rather than benefits), we merely simplify the discussion.

Discrepancies between private cost and social cost occur when there are externalities. The presence of externalities, even when all markets are perfectly competitive, leads to allocatively inefficient outcomes.

Externalities arise in many different ways, and they may be harmful or beneficial to the third parties. When they are harmful they are called *negative externalities;* when they are beneficial, they are called *positive externalities*. Figure 16-1 shows why an externality leads to allocative efficiency, even though the market is perfectly competitive. Here are two examples.

Consider the case of a firm whose production process for steel generates harmful smoke as a byproduct. Individuals who live and work near the firm bear real costs as they cope with breathing (or trying to avoid breathing) the harmful smoke. When the firm makes its decision concerning how much steel to produce, it ignores the costs that it imposes on other people. This is a negative externality. In this case, because the firm ignores those parts of social cost that are not its own private cost, the firm will produce too much steel relative to what is allocatively efficient.

Now consider what happens when an individual renovates her home and thus improves its external appearance. Such improvements enhance the neighbours' view and the value of their property. Yet the individual renovator ignores the benefits that her actions have on the neighbours. This is a positive externality. In this case, because the renovator ignores those parts of social benefits that are not her own private benefits, there will be too little home renovation done relative to what is allocatively efficient.

With a positive externality, a competitive free market will produce too little of the good. With a negative externality, a competitive free market will produce too much of the good.

The Importance of Property Rights

Economist and Nobel laureate Ronald Coase has argued that when property rights are well defined (for example, the law is clear on whether a polluter has rights to determine the emissions from a smokestack), third parties will be able to negotiate with the producers of externalities in order to ensure that the producers take all relevant valuations of their behaviour into account. In such cases, externalities would not be a source of allocative inefficiency because social marginal cost and social marginal benefit would be incorporated into the supply and demand decisions of the parties engaged in the externality-producing activity. Since social marginal cost and social marginal benefit would then be equalized, the free market would generate the allocatively efficient outcome.

An example will help to clarify this important idea—known as the **Coase Theorem.** Suppose a paper mill dumps toxic waste in a nearby river and there is a privately owned beach resort on the shore of the river downstream from the paper mill. Suppose further that for every ton of paper produced a barrel of toxic waste is dumped in the river, thereby imposing a $100 cost on the downstream resort owner. The social marginal cost per ton of paper produced is thus $100 more than the private marginal cost.

Coase's insight is that, *as long as property rights are clearly defined,* this situation need not result in allocative inefficiency. For example, if the owners of the paper mill also owned the river, then they would clearly have the "right" to dump their toxic waste there. However, the downstream resort owner would be prepared to pay $100 for every ton of paper that the paper mill *did not produce.* If the resort owner made such an offer, the paper mill would then face an incentive to reduce the output of paper. Indeed, since the paper mill would gain $100 for each ton *not produced* (in addition to the private costs not incurred), the paper mill's private marginal cost of production would equal the social marginal cost of production. The market outcome would therefore be allocatively efficient. (In terms of Figure 16-1, the offer by the downstream resort owner would shift the mill's *MC* curve up to MC_S^1, so the mill's output would fall.)

Note, however, that the efficient result does not

FIGURE 16-1   An Externality Leads to Allocative Inefficiency

When there is an externality, either too much or too little of the good is produced. The outcome is not allocatively efficient. If the market for this good is perfectly competitive and there is no government intervention, the equilibrium is shown by p^C and Q^C. If there is no externality, then social and private marginal cost are the same and so the outcome is allocatively efficient.

Now suppose the production or the consumption of the good imposes costs on third parties. This is a *negative* externality—social marginal costs are MC_S^1, above MC_P. The allocatively efficient quantity is now Q^1 where *MB* equals MC_S^1. But the free market will produce Q^C, too much of the good.

If the production or consumption of the good instead confers benefits on third parties, this is a positive externality—social marginal costs are MC_S^2, below MC_P. The allocatively efficient quantity is now Q^2 where *MB* equals MC_S^2. But the free market will produce Q^C, too little of the good.

require that ownership over the river is given to the paper mill. Perhaps the most striking part of the Coase Theorem is that the allocatively efficient outcome would also be achieved if the resort owner were awarded ownership over the river. To see this, note that if the resort owner owned the river, then he could force the paper mill to pay for the right to dump toxic waste in the river. If the resort owner charged the paper mill $100 per barrel of waste dumped in the river, then the paper mill would be forced to recognize the costs that its activities incur on the rest of society. That is, the paper mill's private marginal cost would now equal the social marginal cost, and hence the market outcome would be allocatively efficient. (In terms of Figure 16-1, the charge by the downstream resort owner would again shift the mill's *MC* curve up to MC_S^1.)

Coase theorem   The idea (originally put forward by Ronald Coase) that as long as property rights are clearly assigned, externalities need not result in allocative inefficiency.

If the two sides to an externality—the one causing it and the one suffering it—can bargain together, they will produce the allocatively efficient outcome. The externality will then not become a market failure.

High Transactions Costs

The practical application of the Coase Theorem depends in large part on the *number* of third parties affected. In cases where there is only one (or a few), as in the example above, it is plausible that careful definition of property rights would be sufficient to permit private markets to deal efficiently with the externality. When millions of third parties are affected, however, as often is the case with air pollution in urban areas, it is hard to see how such negotiations could proceed. This is because the *transactions costs* of the negotiations would be far too high. Another example is where the externalities cross international boundaries. The smokestack industries of the U.S. industrial midwest are commonly thought to be responsible for the problems of acid rain in Canada and New England. It is difficult to believe that any practical definition of property rights could eliminate the effects of these externalities.

In cases where property rights cannot be clearly assigned or transactions costs are excessive, there are only two possibilities. We may accept the externality and learn to live with it, or governments may intervene on our behalf to deal with it.

In the next chapter we will see how governments do indeed intervene on our behalf to control and regulate pollution in order to reduce the amount of environmental degradation. As we will see there, government intervention to achieve allocative efficiency is not always easy.

Non-Rivalrous and Non-Excludable Goods

rivalrous   A good or service is rivalrous if, when one person consumes one unit of it, there is one less unit available for others to consume.

excludable   A good or service is excludable if its owner can prevent others from consuming it.

Economists classify goods and services into four broad categories depending on the *rivalry* for the good and the *excludability* of the good. Table 16-1 shows these four types of goods.

A good or service is said to be **rivalrous** if one person's consumption of the good means that no one else can also consume it. For example, a chocolate bar is rivalrous because if you eat the entire bar, it cannot also be eaten by your friend. In contrast, a television signal is not rivalrous. You and your friend can sit in your separate living rooms and both receive the same signal, neither of you diminishing the amount available to the other.

A good is said to be **excludable** if people can be prevented from consuming it. A chocolate bar is excludable because you cannot eat it unless you buy it first. A regular TV signal is not excludable, but some speciality channels are because only those who pay for the special receivers can view them. Your access to clean air is also not excludable since nobody can effectively prevent you from breathing.

TABLE 16-1   Four Types of Goods

	Excludable	Non-Excludable
Rivalrous	*Ordinary Goods* VCRs A seat on an airplane An hour of legal advice	*Common Property* Fisheries Rivers and streams Wildlife
Non-Rivalrous (up to capacity)	Art galleries Roads Bridges	*Public Goods* National defence Public information Public protection

Free markets cope best with rivalrous and excludable goods—what we here call "ordinary" goods. The table gives examples of goods in each of four categories, depending on whether consumption of the good is rivalrous and whether one can be excluded from consuming the good.

Ordinary Goods

Most goods and services that you consume are both rivalrous and excludable. Your consumption of food, clothing, a rental apartment, a car, gasoline, CDs, airline tickets, and textbooks are only possible because you pay the seller for the right to own those goods or services. Furthermore, your consumption of those goods reduces the amount available for others. In Table 16-1 we simply refer to these goods as ordinary goods.

Goods that are both rivalrous and excludable pose no particular problem to public policy.

Common-Property Resources

Goods that are rivalrous but non-excludable pose an interesting challenge for public policy. Note in Table 16-1 that the examples of these goods include such things as fisheries, common grazing land, wildlife, rivers and streams, and so on. These are called **common-property resources**. My consumption of clean river water reduces the amount available for you, but there is no practical way that my access to the water can be controlled. And since my access to the water cannot be controlled, there is no practical way to make me pay for it. The result is that there is a zero price. The zero price leads to the obvious result that, in the absence of government intervention, private users will tend to *overuse* common-property resources. In other words, private users will use so much of these resources that the marginal cost to society of having one more user will exceed the marginal benefit to society of having one more user. Society would thus be better off if less of these resources were used.

The overuse of common-property resources is especially noticeable in such cases as the Atlantic cod and Pacific salmon fisheries where individual fishermen have a natural incentive to over-fish. After all, if they don't catch a particular fish, they will merely be leaving it to be caught by the next fisherman who comes along. It is this natural inclination to overuse the fisheries that have led the Canadian government over the years to develop a system of licences and quotas whereby individual fishermen must pay to have access to the common-property resource. *Applying Economic Concepts 16-1* examines the depletion of the world's fisheries.

Goods that are rivalrous and non-excludable are called common-property resources. They tend to be overused by private firms and consumers.

Applying Economic Concepts 16-2 examines other cases of common property, including North American buffalo a century ago and African elephants today.

Excludable But Non-Rivalrous Goods

Goods that are excludable but not rivalrous are also interesting, and many of the obvious examples of these—art galleries, roads, and bridges—are typically provided by government. The non-rivalry for these goods means that the marginal cost of providing the good to one extra person is zero. To see this, just ask yourself what it costs for an extra person to walk through the Canadian Museum of Civilization in Hull, given that it is already open but not many people are there. The answer is zero. But if the marginal cost to society of providing one more unit of the good is zero, then allocative efficiency requires that the price also be zero. Any positive price would prevent some people from using it, but this would be inefficient. As long as their marginal benefit exceeds the social marginal cost of providing the good (zero in this case), it is efficient for these people to use the good.

To avoid inefficient exclusion, the government often provides non-rivalrous but excludable goods and services.

For this reason, art galleries, museums, libraries, roads, bridges, and national parks are provided by various levels of government. In some cases, like libraries and roads, the price is usually zero. In others, like national parks and art galleries, there is usually some positive price.

common-property resource   A resource that is owned by nobody and may be used by anyone.

For information on Canada's policies for commercial fishing, and for data on the fisheries, see the website for the Department of Fisheries and Oceans: www.dfo-mpo.gc.ca.

APPLYING ECONOMIC CONCEPTS 16-1

The World's Endangered Fish

The fish in the ocean are a common-property resource, and theory predicts that such a resource will be overexploited if there is a high enough demand for the product and suppliers are able to meet that demand. In the past centuries there were neither enough people eating fish nor efficient enough fishing technologies to endanger stocks. Over the last fifty years, however, the population explosion has added to the demand for fish and advances in technology have vastly increased the ability to catch fish. Large boats, radar detection, and more murderous nets have tipped the balance in favour of the predator and against the prey. As a result, the overfishing prediction of common property theory has been amply borne out. Today, fish are a common-property resource; tomorrow, they could become no one's resource.

Since 1950 the world's catch has increased fivefold. The increase was sustained only by substituting smaller, less desirable fish for the diminishing stocks of the more desirable fish and by penetrating ever further into remote oceans. Today, all available stocks are being exploited, and now even the total tonnage is beginning to fall. The UN estimates that the total value of the world's catch could be increased by nearly $30 billion if fish stocks were properly managed by governments interested in the total catch, rather than exploited by individuals interested in their own catch.

The developed countries have so overfished their own stocks that Iceland and the European Union could cut their fleets by 40 per cent and catch as much fish as they do today. This is because more fish would survive to spawn, allowing each boat in a smaller fleet to catch about 40 per cent more than does each boat in today's large fishing fleet.

The problem has become so acute that Canada shut down its entire Atlantic cod fishing industry in 1993 and its Pacific salmon industry in 1998. Tens of thousands of Newfoundland residents lost their livelihoods in the demise of what had been the province's largest indus-

try—the catching, freezing, and canning of fish—an industry that had flourished for five centuries.

Canada and the European Union have since been in conflict over what Canada claims is predatory overfishing by EU boats just outside Canadian territorial waters. These tensions heightened in March 1995 when the Spanish fishing trawler Estai was fired at and forced into St. John's harbour by a Canadian fisheries-protection vessel for fishing turbot just outside Canada's 200-nautical-mile "economic zone." The EU (on behalf of Spain) accused Canada of piracy. Canada accused Spain of overfishing and depleting the value of Canada's turbot fishery.

Some developing countries are taking action to conserve their fish stocks but the majority are encouraging rapid expansion of their own fishing fleets with the all-too-predictable results that their domestic waters will soon be seriously overfished.

Worldwide action saved most species of whales. It remains to be seen how many types of fish will be caught to extinction and how many will recover as individual nations slowly learn the lesson of economic theory. Common-property resources need central management if they are not to be overexploited to an extent that risks extinction.

In July 1997, B.C. fishermen blockaded a U.S. ferry in Prince Rupert in protest over U.S. fishermen catching "Canadian" salmon.

The positive price in some of these cases can be explained by another feature of these goods. What happens in the Canadian Museum of Civilization on a summer Saturday morning? What happens on Highway 401 outside Toronto at rush hour? The answer is *crowds*. When congestion occurs on roads and bridges, or in art galleries and museums, it is no longer true that the marginal cost of providing the good to one more user is zero. By increasing the amount of congestion, providing the good to one more per-

APPLYING ECONOMIC CONCEPTS 16-2

Buffalos, Cows, and Elephants

For centuries, North American bison—commonly called buffalos—were a common-property resource for the Plains Indians, whose populations were small enough that they could kill all they needed without endangering the ability of the herds to reproduce themselves. In a little over a decade following the end of the American Civil War in 1865, white hunters decimated the herds. Buffalo Bill Cody may have been a folk hero, but he, and those like him, were the buffalo's executioners.

The buffalo was replaced by cattle, which did not follow the buffalo into extinction. The difference was that cattle were the private property of the rancher. Rustlers and other predators attacked the herds, but the self-interest of ranchers made it worthwhile for them to protect their cattle.

Many people, watching the decimation of wildlife in Africa and Asia, have argued that property rights should be used to turn these animals from the modern equivalent of the buffalo into the modern equivalent of cattle. Wildlife is a common-property resource. When it becomes endangered, laws are passed to prevent predatory hunting. But no one has any profit motive in enforcing these laws. Government officials are employed to do this

job, but they are often few in number and poorly paid. Some become corrupted by the large sums poachers are willing to pay to avoid enforcement. Others find the policing job impossible, given the inadequate resources that their governments devote to enforcement.

Some African governments have dealt with the problem by giving ownership of the wild animals to local villages and allowing them to use animals as a commercial asset. The animals are the subjects of camera safaris whose organizers pay the locals for the privilege. They are also prey for hunters who pay large sums for licences to kill a selected number of animals. Local tribesmen control poachers and keep the licenced kill rate below the reproduction rate because they have a profit motive in protecting what has become their very valuable property.

These schemes have many opponents as well as many supporters. Some opponents object to any permissible "sports hunting" and other commercial use of wild animals. They argue for more effective public enforcement of anti-poaching laws. Supporters counter that leaving the animals as common property is bound to result in their extinction. Farming them, they argue, is better than presiding over their extinction.

---

son imposes costs on those already using the good. If I enter an already-busy highway, I slow down all the existing traffic. If you visit an already-crowded museum, you make it that much less pleasant for everybody else. In these cases, a good that is non-rivalrous when uncongested becomes rivalrous when congested. At this point it appears much (in economic terms) like an ordinary good.

Governments who provide such goods often charge a price to help ration the good when rivalry becomes significant. An excellent example of this is the new toll highways that, with the aid of powerful cameras and computers, charge motorists a different amount per kilometre driven depending on how crowded the highway is. As the traffic slows down due to congestion, the price per kilometre increases to reflect the higher marginal cost. This higher price is indicated on electronic highway signs posted regularly along the highway. Drivers can then choose either to remain on the highway and pay the higher price or exit the highway and take another route to their destination.

See the website for the World Wildlife Fund to learn about one organization's efforts to protect endangered species: www.wwfcanada.org.

Public Goods

Finally, there are some goods that are neither excludable nor rivalrous. These are called **public goods** or sometimes *collective consumption goods*. The classic case of a public good is national defence. Increasing the population of Canada does not reduce

public goods Goods or services that can simultaneously provide benefits to a large group of people. Also called *collective consumption goods*.

the extent to which each individual is defended by a given size and quality of armed forces. Also, it would not be possible to provide national defence to some people and not to others.

Information is also often a public good. Suppose a certain food additive causes cancer. The cost of discovering this fact needs to be borne only once. The information is then of value to everyone who might have used the additive, and the cost of making the information available to one more consumer is essentially zero. Furthermore, once the information of the newly discovered carcinogen is available, it is impossible to prevent people from using that information. Other public goods include street-lighting, weather forecasts (a type of information), and police services.

All of these examples raise what is called the *free-rider problem,* which follows from the fact that it is difficult to prevent people from using public goods once they are produced. This in turn implies that the private market will generally not produce efficient amounts of the public good because once the good is produced, it is impractical (or impossible) to make people pay for its use. Indeed, free markets may fail to produce public goods at all. The obvious remedy in these cases is for the government to provide the good, financed from its tax revenues.

Practise with Study Guide Chapter 16, Exercise 2.

> Because of the free-rider problem, private markets will not provide public goods.

How much of a public good should the government provide? It should provide the public good up to the point where the *sum* of everyone's individual marginal benefit from the good is just equal to the marginal cost of providing the good. We add everyone's individual marginal benefit to get the total marginal benefit because a public good—unlike an ordinary private good—can be used simultaneously by everyone. It therefore generates value to more than one person at a time. Figure 16-2 shows the optimal provision of a public good in the simple case of only two individuals.

Consider a simple example. Suppose that Andrew, Brenda, Carol, and Dick are all thinking of renting a video. For each of them individually, a video rental is a private good. But for the four of them together, it is a public good because the cost will be the same no matter how many of them decide to watch. Suppose that each honestly expresses his or her value of watching the tape. Say it is worth $1.00 to Andrew, $2.00 each to Brenda and Carol, and 50 cents to Dick. If the rental charge for the tape is $5.50 or less, it is worth renting because the total value to all four consumers will be at least equal to the cost.

> Efficient provision of public goods requires that consumers pay the marginal cost of their consumption—zero. Private markets will never provide goods at a price of zero and thus will always underprovide public goods. Public goods are therefore left to be provided by government.

FIGURE 16-2   The Optimal Provision of a Public Good

Determining the optimal provision of a public good requires adding together the marginal benefits for each individual. The figure shows the demand curves (marginal benefit) for a public good by two individuals, Andrew and Brenda. By adding MB_A and MB_B *vertically* (that is, for any given quantity of the public good), we derive society's marginal benefit curve, MB_{A+B}. The marginal cost of providing the public good is shown by MC. The allocatively efficient level of the public good is Q^*, where the marginal cost to society is just equal to the marginal benefit to society.

Asymmetric Information

The role of information in the economy has received increasing attention from economists in recent years. Information is, of course, a valuable commodity, and markets for information and expertise are well developed, as every college student is aware. Markets for expertise are conceptually identical to markets for any other valuable service. They can pose special problems, however. One of these we have already discussed: Information is often a public good and thus will tend to be underproduced by a free market.

Even where information is not a public good, markets for expertise are prone to market failure. The reason for this is that one party to a transaction can often take advantage of special knowledge in ways that change the nature of the transaction itself. Situations where one party to a transaction has special knowledge are called situations of **asymmetric information.** The two important sources of market failure that arise from situations of asymmetric information are *moral hazard* and *adverse selection*.

asymmetric information
A situation in which one party to a transaction has more or better information about the transaction than the other party.

Moral Hazard

In general, **moral hazard** exists when one party to a transaction has both the *incentive* and the *ability* to shift costs onto the other party. Moral hazard problems often arise from insurance contracts. The classic example is the homeowner who does not bother to shovel snow from his sidewalk because he knows that his insurance will cover the cost if the mail carrier should fall and break a leg. The costs of the homeowner's lax behaviour will be borne largely by others, including the mail carrier and the insurance company.

Individuals and firms who are insured against loss will often take less care to prevent that loss than they would in the absence of insurance. They do so because they do not bear all of the marginal cost imposed by the risk, whereas they do bear all of the marginal cost of taking action to reduce the risk.

With moral hazard, the market failure arises because the action by the insured individual or firm raises total costs for society. In the first example above, the decision not to shovel the sidewalk reduces costs for the individual but, in the event of an accident, increases by much more the costs to other individuals and firms.

Insurance is not the only context in which moral hazard problems arise. Another example is professional services. Suppose that you ask a dentist whether your teeth are healthy or a lawyer whether you need legal assistance. The dentist and the lawyer both face moral hazard in that they both have a financial interest in giving you answers that will encourage you to buy their services, and it is difficult for you to find out if their advice is good. In both cases, one party to the transaction has special knowledge that he or she could use to change the nature of the transaction in his or her favour. Codes of professional ethics and licensing and certification practices, both governmental and private, are reactions to concerns about this kind of moral hazard.

moral hazard
A situation in which an individual or a firm takes advantage of special knowledge while engaging in socially uneconomic behaviour.

Adverse Selection

Adverse selection refers to the tendency for people who are more at risk than the average to purchase insurance and for those who are less at risk than the average to reject insurance. A person who is suffering from a heart condition may seek to increase his life insurance coverage by purchasing as much additional coverage as is available without a medical examination. People who buy insurance almost always know more about themselves as individual insurance risks than do their insurance companies. The company can try to limit the variation in risk by requiring physical examinations (for life or health insurance) and by setting up broad categories based on variables, such as age and occupation, over

adverse selection
Self-selection, within a single risk category, of persons of above-average risk.

which actuarial risk is known to vary. The rate charged is then different across categories and is based on the average risk in each category, but there will always be much variability of risk *within* any one category.

People who know that they are well above the average risk for their category are offered a bargain and will be led to take out more car, health, life, or fire insurance than they otherwise would. Their insurance premiums will also not cover the full expected cost of the risk that they are insuring against. Once again, their private cost is less than social cost. On the other side, someone who knows that she is at low risk and pays a higher price than the amount warranted by her risk is motivated to take out less insurance than she otherwise would. In this case, her private cost is more than the social cost.

In both cases, resources are allocated inefficiently because the marginal private benefit of the action (taking out insurance) is not equal to the marginal social cost.

More generally, whenever either party to a transaction lacks information that the other party has, or is deceived by claims made by the other party, market results will tend to be changed, and such changes may lead to inefficiency. Economically (but not legally), it is but a small step from such unequal knowledge to outright fraud. The arsonist who buys fire insurance before setting a building on fire and the business person with fire insurance who decides that a fire is preferable to bankruptcy are extreme examples of moral hazard.

Asymmetric information is involved in many other situations of market failure. The *principal-agent problem,* which we discussed in the appendix to Chapter 7, is one example. In its classic form, the firm's managers act as agents for the shareholders, who are the legal principals of the firm. The managers are much better informed than the principals are about what they do and what they can do. Indeed, the managers are hired for their special expertise. Given that it is expensive for the shareholders (principals) to monitor what the managers (agents) do, the managers have latitude to pursue goals other than maximizing the firm's profits. The private costs and benefits of their actions will thus be different from the social costs and benefits, with the usual consequences for the allocative efficiency of the market system.

A second example of market failure due to asymmetric information is the apparent overdiscounting of the prices of used cars because of the buyer's risk of acquiring a "lemon." See the discussion of this problem in *Applying Economic Concepts 16-3.*

Missing Markets

In the 1950s two American economists, Kenneth Arrow and Gerard Debreu, who were subsequently awarded Nobel Prizes in economics, studied necessary conditions for optimality in resource allocation. One of the conditions is that there must exist a separate market in which each good and service can be traded to the point where the social marginal benefit equals the social marginal cost. Missing markets are the final item in our list of causes of market failure.

Not only do markets not exist for such prominent things as public goods and common-property resources; they are also absent in a number of less obvious but equally important cases.

One important set of missing markets involves risk. You can insure your house against its burning down. This is because your knowledge of the probability of this occurrence is not much better than your insurance company's, and because the probability of your house burning down is normally independent of the probability of other houses burning down.

If you are a farmer, you cannot usually insure your crop against bad weather. This is because the probabilities of yours and your neighbour's crop suffering from bad weather are interrelated. If the insurance company has to pay you, chances are that it will also have to pay your neighbour and everyone else in the region—perhaps even through-

APPLYING ECONOMIC CONCEPTS 16-3

Used-Car Prices: The "Lemons" Problem

It is common for people to regard the large loss of value of a new car in the first year of its life as a sign that consumers are overly style-conscious and will always pay a big premium for the latest in anything. Professor George Akerlof of the University of California at Berkeley suggests a different explanation based on the proposition that the flow of services expected from a one-year-old car that is *purchased on the used-car market* will be lower than those expected from an *average* one-year-old car on the road. Consider his theory.

Any particular model year of automobiles will include a certain proportion of "lemons"—cars that have one or more serious defects. Purchasers of new cars of a certain year and model take a chance on their car turning out to be a lemon. Those who are unlucky and get a lemon are more likely to resell their car than those who are lucky and get a quality car. Hence, in the used-car market, there will be a disproportionately large number of lemons for sale. For example, there may be only one percent of all 1999 Toyota Corollas that have a particular defect and are thus lemons. But, in the market for used 1999 Toyota Corollas, 20 percent of them may be lemons.

Buyers of used cars are therefore right to be on the lookout for low-quality cars, while salespeople are quick to invent reasons for the high quality of the cars they are selling ("It was owned by a little old lady who drove it only on Sundays."). Because it is difficult to identify a lemon or a badly treated used car before buying it, the purchaser is prepared to buy a used car only at a price that is low enough to offset the increased probability that it is of poor quality.

This is a rational consumer response to uncertainty and may explain why one-year-old cars typically sell for a discount that is much larger than can be explained by the physical depreciation that occurs in one year in the *average* car of that model. The large discount reflects the lower services that the purchaser can expect from a used car because of the higher probability that it will be a lemon.

The market failure in this situation arises because of the asymmetric information between the buyers and the sellers. If there were perfect information, prices would better reflect the value of the used car. Good used cars would command higher prices than used cars known to be lemons. Buyers and sellers would then conduct more transactions, for two reasons. First, sellers of good used cars would be more likely to sell them since they know they will get a good price. In contrast, when information is poor, owners of good used cars are less inclined to sell their cars because the price of used cars reflects the average quality, which of course is diminished by the presence of the lemons. Second, when information is good consumers know precisely what it is they are buying. Consumers that wish to spend more on a good used car can do so; other consumers that want the bargain price on a car known to be a lemon can also be satisfied. A larger number of successful transactions between buyers and sellers means more surplus on both side of the market— that is, a more efficient outcome.

Owners have an incentive to keep good-quality used cars because it is difficult to convince buyers that a used car is not a "lemon." As a result, lemons represent a larger proportion of used-car sales than of the total car population.

out the country. An insurance company survives by pooling independent risks. It cannot survive if the same events affect all its clients in the same way. This is why income insurance for farmers is provided by the government (see Chapter 5) rather than by private insurance companies.

If you are in business, you cannot insure against bankruptcy. Here the problem is adverse selection. You know much better than does your would-be insurance company the chances that your business will fail. If insurance were offered against such failure, it would mainly be taken out by people whose businesses had recently developed a high chance of failure.

Another set of missing markets concerns future events. You can buy certain well-established and unchanging products, such as corn or oil, on future markets. But you cannot do so for most manufactured products, such as cars and TV sets, because no one knows the precise specifications of future models. Future markets for these products are missing, so there is no way that the costs and benefits of planned future expenditure on these products can be equated by economic transactions made today.

Summary

Our discussion about market failures has covered a lot of ground. Before we move on to explore some details of government intervention, it is worthwhile to briefly summarize what we have learned. The following five situations result in market failures and, in principle at least, provide a rationale for some government intervention.

1. Firms with market power will charge a price greater than marginal cost. The level of output in these cases is less than the allocatively efficient level.

2. When there are externalities, social and private marginal costs are not equal. If there is a negative externality, output will be greater than the allocatively efficient level. If there is a positive externality, output will be less than the allocatively efficient level.

3. Common-property resources will be overused by private firms and consumers. Public goods will be underprovided by private markets.

4. Situations in which there is asymmetric information—both moral hazard and adverse selection—can lead to allocative inefficiency.

5. Allocative efficiency requires that a separate market exist for each good or service. Missing markets results in allocative inefficiency.

These situations of market failure justify a role for government in a market economy. Let's now explore some reasons for government intervention that are *not* based on market failures.

Other Government Objectives

Suppose that the market did generate the allocatively efficient outcome. That is, suppose that all markets were perfectly competitive and that there were no problems of market power, externalities, public goods, asymmetric information or missing markets. In such an extreme world, does the achievement of allocative efficiency mean that the government would have no reason for intervening in free markets? The answer, in general, is no.

Even if there are no market failures, the government may choose to intervene in markets to achieve broader social goals.

It should not be surprising that even when the free-market system generates an allocatively efficient outcome, it may not always achieve broader social goals. Some of these goals (for example, the desire for an "equitable" income distribution) are basically economic. Some, especially notions that people in a given society should have shared values, such as patriotism or a belief in basic human rights, are clearly not economic. In either set of cases, however, markets are not very effective, precisely because the "goods"

Practise with Study Guide Chapter 16, Exercise 3.

in question are not of the kind that can be exchanged in decentralized transactions. (Indeed, if we stretch the definition a bit, these are public goods, and we have seen that markets tend to underproduce such goods.)

Income Distribution

As we saw in Chapter 13, an important characteristic of a market economy is the *distribution of income* that it determines. People whose services are in heavy demand relative to supply, such as good television anchors and outstanding hockey players, earn large incomes, whereas people whose services are not in heavy demand relative to supply, such as doctorates in classics and high-school graduates without work experience, earn much less.

The distribution of income produced by the market can be looked at in the long run or in the short run. In the long run, in an efficiently operating free-market economy, similar efforts of work or investment by similar people will tend to be similarly rewarded everywhere in the economy. Of course, dissimilar people, or people in dissimilar jobs, will be dissimilarly rewarded.

In the short run, however, similar people making similar efforts may be dissimilarly rewarded. People in declining industries, areas, and occupations suffer the "punishment" of low earnings through no fault of their own. Those in expanding sectors earn the "reward" of high earnings through no extra effort or talent of their own. But these differentials are likely to be temporary, eliminated by the mobility of workers across industries, occupations, or regions.

These rewards and punishments serve the important function of motivating people to adapt. The advantage of such a system is that individuals can make their own decisions about how to alter their behaviour when market conditions change; the disadvantage is that temporary rewards and punishments are dealt out as a result of changes in market conditions that are beyond the control of the affected individuals.

Moreover, even equilibrium differences in income may seem unfair. A free-market system rewards certain groups and penalizes others. Because the workings of the market may be stern, even cruel, society often chooses to intervene. Should heads of households be forced to bear the full burden of their misfortune if, through no fault of their own, they lose their jobs? Even if they lose their jobs through their own fault, should they and their families have to bear the whole burden, which may include starvation? Should the ill and the aged be thrown on the mercy of their families? What if they have no families? Both private charities and a great many government policies are concerned with modifying the distribution of income that results from such things as where one starts, how able one is, how lucky one is, and how one fares in the labour market.

We might all agree that it is desirable to have a more equal distribution of income than the one generated by the free market. We would probably also agree that the pursuit of allocative efficiency is a good thing. It is important to understand, however, that the goal of a more equitable distribution of income invariably conflicts with the goal of allocative efficiency. To understand why this is so, see *Extensions in Theory 16-1* which discusses Arthur Okun's famous analogy of the "leaky bucket."

Preferences for Public Provision

Police protection and justice could in principle be provided by private-market mechanisms. Security guards, private detectives, and bodyguards all provide policelike protection. Privately hired arbitrators, "hired guns," and vigilantes of the Old West represent private

EXTENSIONS IN THEORY 16-1

Arthur Okun's "Leaky Bucket"

Economists recognize that government actions can affect both the allocation of resources and the distribution of income. Resource allocation is easier to talk about simply because economists have developed precise definitions of *efficient* and *inefficient* allocations. Distribution is more difficult because we cannot talk about *better* or *worse* distributions of income without introducing value judgements.

To the extent that society chooses to redistribute income, it is generally the case that allocative efficiency will be reduced. Arthur Okun (1928–1980)—a noted economist at Yale University—developed the image of a "leaky bucket" to illustrate this problem. Suppose we have a well-supplied reservoir of water and we wish to get some water to a household that is not able to come to the reservoir. The only vessel available for transporting the water is a leaky bucket; it works, in that water is deliverable to the intended location, but it works at a cost, in that some of the water is lost on the trip. Thus, to get a litre of water to its destination, more than a litre of water has to be removed from the reservoir. It may be possible to design better or worse buckets, but all of them will leak somewhat.

The analogy to an economy is this: The act of redistribution (carrying the water) reduces the total value of goods and services available to the economy (by the amount of water that leaks on the trip). Getting a dollar to the poor reduces the resources available to everyone else by more than a dollar. Thus, pursuing social goals—like the redistribution of income—conflicts with the goal of allocative efficiency.

Why is the bucket always leaky? Because there is no way to redistribute income without changing the incentives that private households and firms face. For example, a tax-and-transfer system that takes from the rich and gives to the poor will reduce the incentives of both the rich and the poor to produce income. Thus, the redistribution of income will lead to less total income being generated. As another example, a policy of subsidizing goods that are deemed to be important, such as food, shelter, or oil, will cause the market prices of those goods to be lower than marginal costs, a result implying that resources used to produce those goods could be used to produce goods of higher value elsewhere in the economy.

Measuring the efficiency costs of redistribution is an important area of economic research. One result from this research is that some methods of redistribution are more efficient than others. For example, most economists agree that programs that directly redistribute income are more efficient (per dollar of resources made available to a given income group) than programs that subsidize the prices of specific goods. One reason for this is that price subsidies apply even when high-income households purchase the goods in question. These high-income households therefore benefit from the subsidy—an unintended (and perhaps undesirable) consequence of the program.

Redistribution virtually always entails some efficiency cost. However, this inefficiency does *not* imply that such programs should not be undertaken. (That buckets leak surely does not imply that they should not be used to transport water, given that we want to transport water and that the buckets we have are the best available tools.) Whatever the social policy regarding redistribution of income, economics has an important role to play in measuring the efficiency costs and distributional consequences of different programs of redistribution. Put another way, it has useful things to say about the design and deployment of buckets.

ways of obtaining "justice." Yet the members of society may believe that a public police force is *preferable* to a private one and that public justice is preferable to justice for hire. The question of the boundary between public and private provision of any number of goods and services became an important topic of debate during the late 1980s and early 1990s, and the debate shows no sign of waning. In Canada, the United States and Western Europe, the issue is framed as *privatization*. In the formerly socialist countries of Eastern Europe, the disposition of much of the productive capacity of entire countries is currently under dispute. In all of these cases, part of the debate is about the magnitude of the efficiency gains that could be realized by private organization, and part is about less tangible issues, such as changes in the nature and distribution of goods and services that may take place when production is shifted from one sector to the other.

Protecting Individuals from Others

People can use and even abuse other people for economic gain in ways that the members of society find offensive. Child labour laws and minimum standards of working conditions are responses to such actions. Yet direct abuse is not the only example of this kind of market failure. In an unhindered free market, the adults in a household would usually decide how much education to buy for their children. Selfish parents might buy no education, while egalitarian parents might buy the same education for all of their children, regardless of their abilities. The rest of society may want to interfere in these choices, both to protect the child of the selfish parent and to ensure that some of the scarce educational resources are distributed according to the ability and the willingness to use them rather than according to a family's wealth. All households are forced to provide a minimum of education for their children, and a number of inducements are offered—through public universities, scholarships, and other means—for talented children to consume more education than they or their parents might choose if they had to pay the entire cost themselves.

Paternalism

Members of society, acting through government, often seek to protect adult (and presumably responsible) individuals, not from others, but from themselves. Laws prohibiting the use of addictive drugs and laws prescribing the installation and use of seat belts are intended primarily to protect individuals from their own ignorance or shortsightedness. This kind of interference in the free choices of individuals is called **paternalism**. Whether such actions reflect the wishes of the majority in the society or whether they reflect the actions of overbearing governments, there is no doubt that the market will not provide this kind of protection. Buyers do not buy what they do not want, and sellers have no motive to provide it.

paternalism
Intervention in the free choices of individuals by others (including governments) to protect them against their own ignorance or folly.

Social Responsibility

In a free-market system, if you can pay another person to do things for you, you may do so. If you persuade someone else to clean your house in return for $35, presumably both parties to the transaction are better off (otherwise neither of you would have voluntarily conducted the transaction). Normally, society does not interfere with people's ability to negotiate mutually advantageous contracts.

Most people do not feel this way, however, about activities that are regarded as social responsibilities. For example, when military service is compulsory, contracts similar to the one between you and a housekeeper could also be negotiated. Some persons faced with the obligation to do military service could no doubt pay enough to persuade others to do their military service for them. Indeed, during the U.S. Civil War, it was common practice for a man to avoid the draft by hiring a substitute to serve in his place. Yet such contracts are usually prohibited by law. They are prohibited because there are values to be considered other than those that can be expressed in a market. In times when it is necessary, military service is usually held to be a duty that is independent of an individual's tastes, wealth, influence, or social position. It is felt that everyone *ought* to do this service, and exchanges between willing traders are prohibited.

Military service is not the only example of a social obligation. Citizens cannot buy their way out of jury duty or legally sell their voting rights to others, even though in many cases they could find willing trading partners.

See Chapter 16 of www.pearsoned.ca/lipsey for an excellent discussion of the government's evolving role in society: John Richards, "The Welfare State as a Valuable Work in Progress," *World Economic Affairs*.

Polices for Economic Growth

Over the long haul economic growth is the most powerful determinant of living standards. Whatever their policies concerning efficiency and equity, people who live in economies with rapid rates of growth find their living standards rising (on average) faster than those of people who live in countries with low rates of growth. Over a few decades these growth-induced changes tend to have much larger effects on living standards than any policy-induced changes in the efficiency of resource allocation or the distribution of income.

For the last half of the twentieth century most economists viewed growth mainly as a macroeconomic phenomenon related to total saving and total investment. Reflecting this view, most textbooks do not even mention growth in the chapters on microeconomic policy.

More recently there has been a shift back to the perspective of earlier economists, who saw technological change as the engine of growth, with the individual entrepreneurs and firms as the agents of innovation. This is a microeconomic perspective, which is meant to add to, not replace, the macroeconomic emphasis on total saving and total investment.

Although most basic textbooks have not yet caught up with the change to a microeconomic perspective on growth, governments have. Today few microeconomic policies escape being exposed to the question "Even if this policy achieves its main goal, will it have unfavourable effects on growth?" Answering yes is not a sufficient reason to abandon a specific policy. But it is a sufficient reason to think again. Is it possible to redesign the policy so that it can still achieve its main objective, while removing its undesirable side-effects on growth?

A General Principle

We have discussed how the free market may fail to achieve social goals that members of society deem to be desirable. This discussion suggests the following general principle:

Even if free markets generated allocatively efficient outcomes, they would be unlikely to generate outcomes consistent with most people's social goals. Furthermore, there is generally a tradeoff between achieving these social goals and achieving allocative efficiency.

Government Intervention

Private collective action can sometimes remedy the failures of private individual action. For example, volunteer fire departments can fight fires or insurance companies can guard against adverse selection by more careful classification of clients. However, by far the most common remedy for market failure is government intervention.

Since markets sometimes *do* fail, there is a potential scope for governments to intervene in beneficial ways. Whether government intervention is warranted in any particular case depends both on the magnitude of the market failure that the intervention is designed to correct and on the costs of the government action itself.

The benefits of some types of government intervention—such as a publicly provided justice system—are both difficult to quantify and potentially very large. Further, government intervention often imposes difficulties of its own. For many types of government activity, however, *cost-benefit analysis* can be helpful in considering the general question of when governments ought to intervene and to what extent.

The idea behind **cost-benefit analysis** is simple: Add up the (opportunity) costs of a given policy, then add up the benefits, and implement the policy only if the benefits outweigh the costs. In practice, however, cost-benefit analysis is usually quite difficult for three reasons. First, it may be difficult to ascertain what will happen when an action is undertaken. Second, many government actions involve costs and benefits that will occur only in the distant future; thus, they will be more complicated to assess. Third, some benefits and costs—such as the benefits of prohibiting actions that would harm members of an endangered animal species—are very difficult to quantify. Indeed, many people would argue that they cannot be and should not be quantified, as they involve values that are not commensurate with money. The practice then is to use cost-benefit analysis to measure the things that can be measured and to be sure that the things that cannot be measured are not ignored when collective decisions are made. By narrowing the range of things that must be determined by informal judgement, cost-benefit analysis can still play a useful role.

In this chapter, we have been working toward a cost-benefit analysis of government intervention. We have made a general case against government intervention, stressing that free markets are great economizers on information and coordination costs. We have also made a general case for government intervention, emphasizing that free markets fail to produce allocative efficiency when there are monopolies, public goods, externalities, information asymmetries or missing markets, and may also fail to achieve broader social goals. We now turn to the more specific questions of what governments do when they intervene, what the costs of government intervention are, and under which circumstances government interventions may fail to improve on imperfect private markets.

cost-benefit analysis
An approach for evaluating the desirability of a given policy, based on comparing total (opportunity) costs with total benefits.

The Tools of Government Intervention

The legal power of governments to intervene in the workings of the economy is limited only by the Charter of Rights (as interpreted by the courts), the willingness of legislatures to pass laws, and the willingness of the government to enforce them. There are numerous ways in which one or another level of government can prevent, alter, complement, or replace the workings of the unrestricted market economy.

Public Provision.   National defence, the criminal justice system, public schools, the highway system, and national parks are all examples of goods or services that are directly provided by governments in Canada. Public provision is the most obvious remedy for market failure to provide public goods, but it is also often used in the interest of redistribution (e.g., hospitals) and other social goals (e.g., public schools). We shall consider public spending in detail in Chapter 18.

Redistribution Programs.   Taxes and spending are often used to provide a distribution of income that is different from that generated by the free market. Government transfer programs affect the distribution of income in this way. We examine the distributive effects of the Canadian tax system in Chapter 18.

Regulation.   Government regulations are public rules that apply to private behaviour. In Chapter 12, we saw that governments regulate private markets to limit monopoly power. In Chapter 17, we will focus on regulations designed to deal with environmental quality. Among other things, government regulations prohibit minors from consuming alcohol, require that children attend school, penalize racial discrimination in housing and labour markets, and require that new automobiles have seatbelts.

See the Government of Canada's web page to see just how many various government departments and crown corporations exist: www.gc.ca.

Government regulation is used to deal with all of the sources of market failure that we have discussed in this chapter; it applies at some level to virtually all spheres of modern economic life.

Structuring Incentives.   Almost all government actions, including the kinds we have discussed here, change the incentives that consumers and firms face. If the government provides a park, people will have a weakened incentive to own large plots of land of their own. Fixing minimum or maximum prices (as we saw in the discussion of rent control and agriculture in Chapter 5) affects privately chosen levels of output. If the government taxes income, people may have a reduced incentive to work.

The government can adjust the tax system to provide subsidies to some kinds of behaviour and penalties to others. In the United States, for example, deductible mortgage interest makes owned housing relatively more attractive than other assets that a person might purchase. In Canada, tax exemptions for contributions to Registered Retirement Saving Plans (RRSPs) may lead individuals to increase their total saving. Such tax treatment sends the household different signals from those sent by the free market. Scholarships to students to become nurses or teachers may offset barriers to mobility into those occupations.

The Costs of Government Intervention

Consider the following argument: The market system produces an outcome that is deemed to be undesirable; government has the legal means to improve the situation; therefore, the public interest will be served by government intervention.

At first glance the argument is appealing. But it is deficient because it neglects three important considerations. First, government intervention is itself costly since it uses scarce resources; for this reason alone, not every market failure is worth correcting because the intervention itself may use up more resources than are being wasted in the (inefficient) free-market outcome. Second, government intervention is generally imperfect. Just as markets sometimes succeed and sometimes fail, so government interventions sometimes succeed and sometimes fail. Third, deciding what governments are to do and how they are to do it is also costly and intrinsically imperfect.

Large potential benefits do not necessarily justify government intervention, nor do large potential costs necessarily make it unwise. What matters is the balance between benefits and costs.

There are several different costs of government intervention. Economists divide these costs into two categories—*direct resource costs* and *indirect costs*.

Direct Resource Costs

Government intervention uses real resources that could be used elsewhere. Civil servants must be paid. Paper, photocopying, and other trappings of bureaucracy; the steel in the navy's ships; the fuel for the army's tanks; and the pilot of the Prime Minister's jet all have valuable alternative uses. The same is true of the accountants who administer the Canada Pension Plan, the economists who are employed by the Bureau of Competition Policy, and the educators who retrain displaced workers.

Similarly, when government inspectors visit plants to monitor compliance with federally imposed standards of health, industrial safety, or environmental protection, they are imposing costs on the public in the form of their salaries and expenses. When regulatory bodies develop rules, hold hearings, write opinions, or have their staff prepare research reports, they are incurring costs. The costs of the judges, clerks, and court reporters who hear, transcribe, and review the evidence are also imposed by government regulation. All these activities use valuable resources that could have provided very different goods and services.

All forms of government intervention use real resources and hence impose direct costs.

This type of cost is fairly easy to identify, as it almost always involves well-documented expenditures. Other costs of intervention are less apparent but no less real.

Indirect Costs

Most government interventions in the economy impose some costs on firms and households. The nature and the size of the extra costs borne by firms and households vary with the type of intervention. A few examples will illustrate what is involved.

Changes in Costs of Production.   Government safety and emission standards for automobiles have raised the costs of both producing and operating cars. These costs are much greater than the direct budgetary costs of administering the regulations. Taxes used to finance the provision of public goods must be paid by producers and consumers and often increase the cost of producing or selling goods and services.

Costs of Compliance.   Government regulation and supervision generate a flood of reporting and related activities that are often referred to collectively as *red tape*. The number of hours of business time devoted to understanding, reporting, and contesting regulatory provisions is enormous. Regulations dealing with occupational safety and environmental control have all increased the size of nonproduction payrolls. The legal costs alone of a major corporation sometimes can run into tens or hundreds of millions of dollars per year. While all this provides lots of employment for lawyers and economic experts, it is costly because there are other tasks these professionals could do that would add more to the production of consumer goods and services.

Households also bear compliance costs directly. A recent study found that the time and money cost of filling out individual income-tax returns was about eight percent of the total revenue that is collected. In addition to costs of compliance, there are costs borne as firms and households try to avoid regulation. There will be a substantial incentive to find loopholes in regulations. Resources that could be used elsewhere will be devoted to the search for such loopholes and then, in turn, by the regulators to counteracting such evasion.

Farmers in Canada often request government assistance to offset the effects of low crop prices or bad weather. This is one example of "rent seeking."

Rent Seeking.   A different kind of problem arises from the mere existence of government and its potential to use its tools in ways that affect the distribution of economic resources. This phenomenon has been dubbed **rent seeking** by economists because private firms, households, and business groups will use their political influence to seek *economic rents* from the government. These valuable rents can come in the form of favourable regulations, direct subsidies, and profitable contracts. Democratic governments are especially vulnerable to manipulation of this kind because they respond to well-articulated interests of all sorts.

rent seeking
Behaviour whereby private firms and individuals try to use the powers of the government to enhance their own economic well-being.

Rent seeking is endemic to mixed economies. Because of the many things that governments are called on to do, they have the power to act in ways that transfer resources among private entities. Because they are democratic, they are responsive to public pressures of various kinds. If a government's behaviour can be influenced, whether by voting, campaign contributions, lobbying, or bribes, real resources will be used in trying to do so.

In the aggregate, the indirect costs of government intervention are substantial. But they are difficult to measure and are usually dispersed across a large number of firms and households.

Government Failure

Our conceptual cost-benefit analysis of government intervention is almost complete. First, we identify each market failure. Then we make our best estimate of the expected benefits of a government intervention designed to correct that failure. Then we calculate the expected costs of the government intervention, as outlined in the preceding section. If the expected benefits exceed the expected costs, the intervention is warranted. Unfortunately, things are never this simple. For one thing, as we have already noted, many of the benefits of government intervention are extremely difficult to quantify. But even in the cases where the benefits and costs of intervention can be easily measured, governments, like private markets, are imperfect. Often they will fail, in the same sense that markets do, to achieve their potential.

The reason for government failure is not that public-sector employees are less able, honest, or virtuous than people who work in the private sector. Rather, the causes of government failure are inherent in government institutions, just as the causes of market failure stem from the nature of markets. Importantly, some government failure is an inescapable cost of democratic decision making.

Decision Makers' Objectives

By far the most important cause of government failure arises from the nature of the government's own objectives. Until recently, economists did not concern themselves greatly with the motivation of government. The theory of economic policy implicitly assumed that governments had no objectives of their own. As a result economists only needed to identify places where the market functioned well on its own, and places where government intervention could improve the market's functioning. Governments would then stay out of the former markets and intervene as necessary in the latter.

This model of government behaviour never fitted reality, and economists were gradually forced to think more deeply about the motivation of governments. Today economists no longer assume that governments are faceless robots doing whatever economic analysis shows to be in the social interest. Instead they are modelled just as are producers and consumers—as units with their own objectives, which they seek to maximize.

Governments undoubtedly do care about the social good to some extent, but public officials have their careers, their families, and their prejudices as well. As a result, public officials' own needs are seldom wholly absent from their consideration of the actions they will take. Similarly, their definition of the public interest is likely to be influenced heavily by their personal views of what policies are best. The resulting problems are similar to the principal-agent issues that we discussed in Chapter 7. In the present case the principals are the public; they want governments to do certain things. However, their agents—elected and appointed—are motivated by considerations that sometimes pull against what the public wishes.

Modelling governments as maximizers of their own welfare, and then incorporating them into theoretical models of the working of the economy, was a major breakthrough. One of the pioneers of this development was the American economist James Buchanan, who was awarded the 1986 Nobel Prize in economics for his work in this field. The theory that he helped to develop is called *public choice theory*. The key breakthrough was to view the government as just another economic agent engaging in its own maximizing behaviour.

Public Choice Theory

Full-blown public choice theory deals with three maximizing groups. Elected officials seek to maximize their votes. Civil servants seek to maximize their salaries (and their positions in the hierarchy). Voters seek to maximize their own utility. To this end, voters look to the government to provide them with goods and services and income transfers that raise their personal utility. No one cares about the general interest!

On the one hand, this surely is not a completely accurate characterization of motives. Elected statesmen have acted in what they perceive to be the public interest, hoping to be vindicated by history even if they know they risk losing the next election. Some civil servants have exposed inside corruption even though it cost them their jobs. And some high-income individuals vote for the political party that advocates the most, not the least, income redistribution.

On the other hand, the characterization is close to the mark in many cases. Most of us have read of politicians whose only principle is "What will get me the most votes?" And many voters ask only "What is in it for me?" This is why the theory can take us a long way in understanding what we see, even though real behaviour is more complex.

Here is one example that we discussed in Chapter 5. Why, in spite of strong advice from economists, have governments persisted in assisting agriculture for decades, until many governments now have major farm crises on their hands? Public choice theory looks at the gainers and the losers among the voters.

The gainers from agricultural supports are farmers. They are a politically powerful group, and are aware of what they will lose if farm supports are reduced. They would show their disapproval of such action by voting against any government that even suggests it. The losers are the entire group of consumers or taxpayers. Although they are more numerous than farmers, and although their total loss is large, each individual suffers only a small loss. Citizens have more important things to worry about, and so do not vote against the government just because it supports farmers. As long as the average voters are unconcerned about, and often unaware of, the losses they suffer, the vote-maximizing government will ignore the interests of the many and support the interests of the few. The vote-maximizing government will consider changing the agricultural policy only when the cost of agricultural support becomes so large that ordinary taxpayers begin to be concerned by the cost. What is required for a policy change, according to this theory, is that those who lose become sufficiently aware of their losses for this awareness to affect their voting behaviour.

Another example that we will see in Chapter 35 is the use of tariffs. When a tariff is imposed on an imported good, it increases the domestic price of the good. Tariffs therefore provide protection to the domestic firms producing competing products. This protection typically raises prices, profits, and wages in those firms. The costs of such tariffs are borne by a much larger number of consumers, each of whom is hurt a relatively small amount by the higher price. This concentration of benefits and the dispersion of costs explains to a large extent why tariffs, once in place, are so politically difficult to remove.

The ability of elected officials and civil servants to ignore the public interest is strengthened by a phenomenon called **rational ignorance**. Many policy issues are extremely complex. For example, even the experts are divided when assessing the pros and cons of Canada's maintaining a flexible exchange rate rather than pegging the value

rational ignorance When agents have no incentive to become informed about some government policy because the costs of becoming informed exceed the benefits of any well-informed action the agent might take.

of the Canadian dollar in terms of the U.S. dollar. Much time and effort is required for a layperson even to attempt to understand the issue. Similar comments apply to the evidence for and against capital punishment or lowering the age of criminal liability. Yet one person's vote has little influence on which party gets elected or on what they will really do about the issue in question once elected. So the costs are large, the benefits small. Thus a majority of rational, self-interested voters will choose to remain innocent of the complexities involved in most policy issues.

Who will be the informed minority? The answer is those who stand to gain or lose a lot from the policy, those with a strong sense of moral obligation, and those policy junkies who just like this sort of thing.

Inefficient Public Choices

At the core of most people's idea of democracy is that each citizen's vote should have the same weight. One of the insights of the theory of social choice is that resource allocation, based on the principle of one vote per person, will generally be inefficient because it fails to take into account the *intensity of preferences*. Consider three farmers, Albert, Bob, and Charlie, who are contemplating building access roads. Suppose that the road to Albert's farm is worth $7000 to him and that the road to Bob's farm is worth $7000 to him. Charlie's farm is on the main road, which already exists. Suppose that under the current tax rules, each road would cost each farmer $2000. It is plainly efficient to build both roads because each generates net benefits of $1000 ($7000 gross benefits to Albert and Bob minus $6000 total cost). But each road would be defeated 2-1 in a simple majority vote. (Bob and Charlie would vote against Albert's road; Albert and Charlie would vote against Bob's road.)

Now suppose that we allow Albert and Bob to make a deal: "I will vote for your road if you will vote for mine." Although such deals are often decried by political commentators, the deal enhances efficiency: Both roads now get 2–1 majorities, and both roads get built. However, such deals can just as easily reduce efficiency. If the gross value of each road were $5000 instead of $7000, and Albert and Bob again make their deal, each road will still command a 2–1 majority, but building the roads will now be inefficient. (The gross value of each road is now only $5000, but the cost is still $6000.) Albert and Bob will be using democracy to appropriate resources from Charlie while reducing economic efficiency.

The possibility of inefficient public choices stems in large part from the problems inherent to a democratic system. *Extensions in Theory 16-2* discusses Kenneth Arrow's famous result in the theory of social choice. Arrow's somewhat unsettling theorem is that there is very often a tradeoff between democracy and efficiency.

Governments as Monopolists

Governments face the same problems of cost minimization that private firms do but often operate in an environment where they are monopoly producers without stockholders. Large governments (provinces, big cities, the federal government) face all of the organizational problems faced by large corporations. They tend to use relatively rigid rules and hence to respond slowly to change. Building codes are an example of this type of problem. Most local governments have detailed requirements regarding the materials that must go into a new house, factory, or office. When technology changes, the codes often lag behind. For example, plastic pipe, which is cheaper and easier to use than copper pipe, was prohibited by building codes for decades after its use became efficient. Similarly, much antipollution regulation specifies the type of control equipment that must be em-

EXTENSIONS IN THEORY 16-2
The Problem with Democracy

Nobel laureate Kenneth Arrow from Stanford University has shown that it is generally impossible to construct a set of rules for making social choices that is at once comprehensive, democratic, efficient, and consistent. This striking idea—called Arrow's Impossibility Theorem—has led to decades of work on the part of economists, philosophers, and political scientists, who have tried to find conditions under which democracy can be expected to yield efficient allocations of resources. The news is generally not good. Unless individual preferences or their distribution in the population meet fairly unlikely criteria, either democracy or efficiency must be sacrificed in the design of social-choice mechanisms.

The Arrow theorem can be illustrated by a simple case, depicted in the following table.

| | Voter | | |
Density of Trees	A	B	C
Sparse (1)	3	1	2
Medium (2)	1	2	3
Thick (3)	2	3	1

Imagine that we have a society that consists of three voters who are choosing how many trees to plant in the local park. The three possibilities are as follows: (1) Plant very few trees in one corner. This would make the park suitable for playing Frisbee and soccer but not for walks in the woods. (2) Plant trees in moderate density throughout the park. In this case, the park would be nice for jogging but not usable for most sports. (3) Plant trees densely everywhere. This would make the park a pleasant place to get away from it all (for whatever reasons) but not a good place to jog. Voter A loves jogging, hates Frisbee, and likes walking in the woods. His ranking of the alternatives is 3–1–2. Voter B likes the wide open spaces. His ranking is 1–2–3. Voter C likes to play Frisbee, likes solitude even more, and has little taste for a park that provides neither. Her ranking is 2–3–1.

Now, suppose that the electorate gets to choose between alternatives that are presented two at a time. What does majority rule do? Unfortunately, there is no unique democratic outcome; the result of such voting depends on which two alternatives are presented. In a choice of 1 versus 2, 1 wins, getting votes from B and C. When the choice is between 2 and 3, 2 wins, getting votes from A and B. When 3 is pitted against 1, 3 wins with the support of A and C. Thus, the social-choice mechanism of majority rule is *inconsistent*. It tells us that 1 is preferred to 2, 2 is preferred to 3, and 3 is preferred to 1. There is no way to make a choice without arbitrarily—that is, undemocratically—choosing which set of alternatives to offer the electorate. This is the essence of Arrow's famous argument that, in general, democracy and efficiency cannot both be achieved in issues of social choice.

---

ployed. Changes in technology may make a regulation inefficient, but the regulation may stay in place for some time.

In the private sector, market forces often push the corporation into revising its view of the problem at hand, whereas there is ordinarily no market mechanism to force governments to use relatively efficient regulations. Put another way, much government failure arises precisely because governments do not have competitors and are not constrained by the "bottom line."

How Much Should Government Intervene?

Do governments intervene too little, or too much, in response to market failure? This question reflects one aspect of the continuing debate over the role of government in the economy. The theoretical principles for determining the optimal amount of government intervention are individually accepted by most economists. What they add up to, however, is more controversial. Moreover, the issue is often framed ideologically. Those on the "right wing" tend to compare heavy-handed government with a hypothetical and perfectly operating competitive market. In contrast, those on the "left wing" tend to compare hypothetical and ideal government intervention with a laissez-faire economy rife with market failures.

Evaluating the costs and the benefits of government intervention requires a comparison of the private economic system as it is working (not as it might work ideally) with the pattern of government intervention as it actually performs (not as it might perform ideally).

Over the last two decades in most of the advanced industrial countries the mix of free-market determination and government ownership and regulation has been shifting towards more market determination. No one believes that government intervention can, or should, be reduced to zero. Do we still have a long way to go in reversing the tide of big intrusive government that flowed through most of the twentieth century? Or perhaps we have gone too far and have given some things to the market that governments could do better? These will be some of the great social debates of the early decades of the twenty-first century.

The cases that we have made for and against government intervention are both valid, depending on time, place, and the values that are brought to bear. At this point, we turn to the issue of what government actually does, something that will perhaps illuminate the question of what it ought to do. In Chapter 12, we discussed government action that is designed to affect monopoly and competition. In the next two chapters, we will discuss in some detail three other important types of intervention in the Canadian economy today: environmental regulation, taxation, and public spending.

SUMMARY

Basic Functions of Government

- The government's monopoly of violence gives it the ability to enforce laws and protect its citizens. But restrictions on the government's power are required to ensure that the individual's rights are not violated.

The Case for Free Markets

- The case for free markets can be made in two different ways. The "formal defence" is based on the concept of allocative efficiency. This was the basis for the appeal of competitive markets as discussed in Chapter 12.
- The "informal defence" of free markets is not specifically based on the idea of allocative efficiency, and thus applies to market structures other than just perfect competition. The informal defence of free markets is based on three central arguments:

1. Free markets provide automatic coordination of the actions of decentralized decision makers.

2. The pursuit of profits which is central to free markets provides a stimulus to innovation and economic growth.

3. Free markets permit a decentralization of economic power.

Market Failures

- Market failure refers to situations in which the free market does not achieve allocative efficiency. Five main sources of market failure are

   1. monopoly

   2. externalities

   3. public goods

   4. information asymmetries

   5. missing markets

- Pollution is an example of an externality. A producer who pollutes the air or water does not pay the social cost

of the pollution and is therefore not motivated to avoid the costs. Private producers will therefore produce too much pollution relative to what is allocatively efficient.
- National defence is an example of a public good. Markets fail to produce public goods because the benefits of such goods are available to people whether they pay for them or not.
- Information asymmetries cause market failure when one party to a transaction is able to use personal expertise to manipulate the transaction in his or her own favour. Moral hazard and adverse selection are consequences of information asymmetries.

Other Government Objectives

- Changing the distribution of income is one of the roles for government intervention that members of a society may desire. Others include values that are placed on public pro-

vision for its own sake, on protection of individuals from themselves or from others, on recognition of social responsibilities, and on the promotion of economic growth.

Government Intervention

- Major tools of microeconomic policy include (a) public provision, (b) redistribution, (c) regulation, and (d) structuring incentives. (The first two are the subject of Chapter 18.) Regulation can take various forms. Incentives can be structured in a number of ways, including the use of fines, subsidies, taxes, and effluent charges (which are discussed in Chapter 17).
- The costs and benefits of government intervention must be considered in deciding whether, when, and how much in-

tervention is appropriate. Among the costs are the direct costs that are incurred by the government, the costs that are imposed on the parties who are regulated, directly and indirectly, and the costs that are imposed on third parties. These costs are seldom negligible and are often large.
- The possibility of government failure must be balanced against the potential benefits of removing market failure. It is neither possible nor efficient to correct all market failure; neither is it always efficient to do nothing.

KEY CONCEPTS

Market failure
Externalities
Private and social cost
Coase theorem
Excludable and non-excludable goods

Rivalrous and non-rivalrous goods
Common-property resource
Public goods
Information asymmetries
Missing markets

Moral hazard and adverse selection
Cost-benefit analysis
Rent seeking
Government failure
Public choice theory

STUDY EXERCISES

1. For each of the situations in the table below, indicate whether there is a positive or a negative externality. Indicate in each case whether social marginal cost (MC_S) is greater than or less than private marginal cost (MC_P).

	Positive or Negative Externality?	MC_S greater than or less than MC_P?
You smoke a cigarette and blow the smoke into others' faces.		
You cut your lawn early on a Sunday morning.		
A firm conducts R&D and generates useful "basic" knowledge that is freely available.		
A firm produces aluminum, but also produces toxic waste as a byproduct.		

2. Consider the following diagram showing the perfectly competitive market for newsprint. The demand curve shows the marginal benefit to society of consuming an extra unit of newsprint. The supply curve shows the firms' marginal costs of producing an extra unit of newsprint.

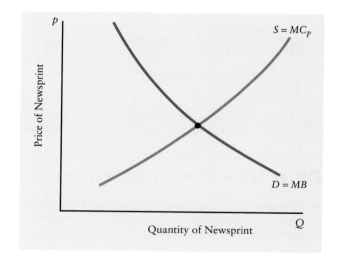

a. Describe the equilibrium in this competitive market.
b. Now suppose that, as a byproduct to producing newsprint, some nasty chemicals are also produced that get dumped in public streams and rivers. Suppose that for each unit of newsprint produced, one unit of nasty chemicals is also produced, imposing an external cost of $100. Show the social marginal cost curve in the diagram.
c. What is the allocatively efficient level of newsprint?

3. For each of the listed goods indicate whether they are rivalrous or non-rivalrous, and also indicate whether the use of them is excludable or non-excludable.

	Rivalrous?	Excludable?
CD player		
Clothing		
Library		
Lighthouse		
Medical services		
Published product safety information		
Pacific salmon		

Number of people	Value of park per person	Total
10	$1000	$10 000
30	500	15 000
30	200	6 000
20	50	1 000
10	0	0
100		$32 000

a. Which of the goods in the table are public goods? Explain.
b. Which are common-property resources? Explain.

4. Art galleries, museums, roads, and bridges are usually provided by the government.

a. Explain why uncrowded goods of this sort should have a price of zero if allocative efficiency is to be achieved.
b. Would allocative efficiency be achieved if private firms provided these goods? Explain.
c. What happens when access to these goods becomes congested? Does efficiency still require a zero price? Explain.

5. Consider a small town deciding whether to build a public park. The town council conducts a survey of its 100 residents and asks them how much they would each value the park. The survey results are as follows:

a. Suppose it costs $35 000 to build the park. Should the town do it?
b. Suppose the park costs only $20 000 to build. Should the town build the park? If so, how should the town pay for building the park?
c. Suppose the town builds the park but charges people $50 for an annual pass. Does this present a problem for efficiency? Explain.

6. In the text we discussed how rent seeking is one of the costs of government intervention. Consider a group of pig farmers who are lobbying the federal government for some form of financial assistance (as they did in 1998 when the world price of pork declined steeply).

a. Explain why economists call such lobbying "rent seeking."
b. Suppose the farmers spend $500 000 in their lobbying efforts but it has no effect on government policy. What is the cost to society of the rent seeking? Explain.
c. Suppose the $500 000 of lobbying *does* lead to a change in government policy. Now what is the social cost of the rent seeking?

DISCUSSION QUESTIONS

1. In each case, identify any divergence between social and private costs.

a. Cigarette smoking
b. Getting a university education
c. Private ownership of guns
d. Drilling for offshore oil

2. Consider the possible beneficial and adverse effects of each of the following forms of government intervention.

a. Charging motorists a tax for driving in the downtown areas of large cities and using the revenues to provide peripheral parking and shuttle buses
b. Prohibiting juries from awarding large malpractice judgements against doctors
c. Mandating no-fault automobile insurance, in which the automobile owner's insurance company is responsible for damage to his or her vehicle no matter who causes the accident

3. The president of Goodyear Tire and Rubber Company complained that government regulation had imposed $30 million per year in "unproductive costs" on his company, as listed here. How would one determine whether these costs were "productive" or "unproductive"?

a. Environmental regulation, $17 million
b. Occupational safety and health, $7 million
c. Motor vehicle safety, $3 million
d. Personnel and administration, $3 million

4. Your local government almost certainly provides a police department, a fire department, and a public library. What are the market imperfections, if any, that each of these seeks to correct? Which of these are closest to being public goods? Which are furthest?

5. Suppose that for $100, a laboratory can accurately assess a person's probability of developing a fairly rare disease that is costly to treat. What would be the likely effects of such a test on health-insurance markets?

6. What market failures do public support of higher education seek to remedy? How would you go about evaluating whether the benefits of this support outweigh the costs?

CHAPTER 17

Environmental Policy

For information about the new
Canadian Environmental Protection Act,
see Environment Canada's website:
www.ec.gc.ca.

🔵 *LEARNING OBJECTIVES*

❶ Explain how an externality can be internalized, and how this can lead to allocative efficiency.

❷ Understand why direct pollution controls are inefficient.

❸ Explain how market-based policies such as emissions taxes and tradable pollution permits can improve economic efficiency.

❹ Have a general understanding of some popular arguments against market-based environmental policies.

In almost everything we do, we are subject to some form of government regulation. The system of criminal law regulates our interactions with people and property. Local zoning ordinances regulate the ways in which the land that we own may be used. Insurance commissions must approve both the insurance contracts that we sign and the rates that we are charged. Regulatory commissions set rates for electricity, natural gas, local telephone service, and a host of other goods and services. Seat belts, brake lights, turn signals, air bags, internal door panels, bumpers, and catalytic converters are subjects of regulation—all in a single industry. The list goes on and on. A good case can be made that various governments in Canada have more effect on the economy through regulation than through taxing and spending.

The focus in this chapter is on a specific type of government regulation, one that has become increasingly important in the eyes of the public in recent years. In particular, we examine the negative externalities of pollution and the various government policies designed to address them. As we will see, policies intended to reduce the amount of environmental degradation do not always do so in an efficient manner. One of the central themes in this chapter is that the information available to the regulatory agencies, especially regarding firms' technologies for reducing pollution, is generally incomplete. This lack of good information leads to the result that *market-based* environmental regulations may be much more successful than methods based on the government's *direct control*.

The Economics of Pollution Control

Pollution is a negative externality. As a consequence of producing or consuming goods and services, "bads" are produced as well. Steel plants produce smoke in addition to steel. Farms produce chemical runoff as well as food. Logging leads to soil erosion which contaminates fish-breeding grounds. Households produce human waste and garbage as they consume goods and services. Individuals who smoke impose costs on nearby persons. In all of these cases, the technology of production and consumption automatically generates pollution. Indeed, there are few human endeavors that do not have negative pollution externalities.

The Economic Rationale for Regulating Pollution

When firms use resources that they do not regard as scarce, they fail to consider the cost of those resources. This is a characteristic of most examples of pollution. The valuable resource that polluting firms do not regard as scarce is a clean environment. When a paper mill produces newsprint for the world's newspapers, more people are affected than just its suppliers, employees, and customers. Its water-discharged effluent hurts the fishing boats that ply nearby waters, and its smog makes many resort areas less attractive, thereby reducing the tourist revenues that local motel operators and boat renters can expect. The profit-maximizing paper mill neglects these external effects of its actions because its profits are not directly affected by them.

As shown in Figure 17-1, allocative efficiency requires that the price (the value that consumers place on the marginal unit of output) be just equal to the marginal social cost (the value of the resources that society gives up to produce the marginal unit of output). When there are negative externalities, *social* marginal cost exceeds *private* marginal cost (the cost borne by the producer) because the act of production generates costs for society that are not faced by the producer.

By producing where price equals private marginal cost and thereby ignoring the externality, the firms are maximizing profits but producing too much output. The price that consumers pay just covers the private marginal cost but does not pay for the external damage. The *social benefit* of the last unit of output (the market price) is less than the social cost (private marginal cost plus the social cost imposed by the externality). Reducing output by one unit would increase allocative efficiency and thus make society as a whole better off.

Making polluting firms bear the entire social cost of their production is called **internalizing the externality.** This leads them to produce a lower level of output, as shown in Figure 17-1. Indeed, at the optimal output, where the externality is completely internalized, consumer prices would just cover all of the *social* marginal cost of production. We would have the familiar condition for allocative efficiency that marginal benefits to consumers are just equal to the marginal cost of producing these benefits. The difference here is that some of the social marginal cost takes the form of the externality.

FIGURE 17-1   A Pollution Externality in a Competitive Market

A negative externality implies that a competitive free market will produce more output than the allocatively efficient level. If the externality can be internalized, allocative efficiency can be achieved. A competitive free market will produce where the demand and supply curves intersect—that is, at Q^c and p^c. If each unit of output of this good also generates an external cost of EC, then social marginal cost is greater than private marginal cost by this amount. The allocatively efficient level of output is where marginal benefit equals *social* marginal cost—that is, at Q^*. The competitive free market therefore produces too much output.

If firms in this industry are now required to pay a tax of $\$EC$ per unit of output, then the private marginal cost curve, MC_P, shifts up to MC_S. The externality will thus be *internalized* because firms will now be forced to pay the full social cost of their production. The new competitive equilibrium will be p^*, Q^*, and allocative efficiency will be achieved.

internalizing the externality   A process that results in a producer or consumer taking account of a previously external effect.

Note that in order to successfully internalize the externality, it is necessary to be able to accurately measure the size of the externality. Looking at Figure 17-1, we must be able to measure the magnitude of the marginal external cost, *EC*. In practice, however, external costs are quite difficult to measure. This measurement is especially difficult in the case of air pollution, where the damage is often spread over hundreds of thousands of square kilometres and can affect millions of people. Another difficulty arises because the cost that is imposed by pollution—in addition to the water that it contaminates or the animals that it kills—depends on the mechanisms that are used to undo the damage that it causes. Pollution-control mechanisms are themselves costly, and their costs must also be counted as part of the social cost of pollution. Nevertheless, the basic analysis of Figure 17-1 applies to these more difficult cases.

The socially optimal level of output is at the quantity where all marginal costs, private plus external, equal the marginal benefit to society.

The Optimal Amount of Pollution Abatement

Notice from Figure 17-1 that the allocatively efficient outcome still has some pollution being generated. This is because the production of each unit of output in Figure 17-1 generates some pollution. And this is generally the case. It is simply impossible to produce goods and services without generating *some* environmental damage. The economic problem is then to determine how much environmental damage to allow—this is determined where the costs to society of further pollution reduction equal the benefits to society of further pollution reduction.

Zero environmental damage is generally not economically efficient.

FIGURE 17-2   The Optimal Amount of Pollution Abatement

The optimal amount of pollution abatement occurs where the marginal cost of reducing pollution is just equal to the marginal benefits from doing so. *MB* represents the marginal benefit that is achieved by pollution abatement in some activity. *MC* represents the marginal cost of abating pollution; it rises sharply as more and more pollution is prevented. The optimal level of pollution abatement is *q**, where *MB* = *MC*. *Notice that not all pollution is avoided.* For each unit up to *q**, the marginal benefit derived from pollution abatement exceeds the marginal cost. The total net benefit from the optimal amount of pollution abatement is given by the shaded area—the sum of the difference between marginal benefit and marginal cost at each level of abatement. Any further efforts to prevent pollution beyond *q** would add more to costs than to benefits.

The economics of determining how much pollution to prohibit, and therefore how much to allow, is summarized in Figure 17-2, which depicts the benefits and costs of pollution abatement (reduction). The analysis might be thought of as applying, for example, to water pollution in a specific watershed. It is drawn from the perspective of a public authority whose mandate is to maximize social welfare.

Note that the figure is drawn in terms of the amount of pollution that is prevented (or abated) rather than in terms of the total amount of pollution produced. We do this because pollution abatement (rather than pollution itself) is a "good" of economic value, and we are more familiar with applying the concepts of supply and demand for goods with positive values. If no pollution is abated, the watershed will be subjected to the amount of pollution that would occur in an unregulated market. The greater the amount of pollution abated, the smaller the amount of pollution that remains.

Pollution is an externality. Firms do not take the social costs of their pollution into account when they make their private profit-maximizing decisions.

The marginal cost of abating pollution is likely to be small at low levels but to rise steeply after some point. This is the upward-sloping line shown in Figure 17-2. There are two reasons for believing that this shape is generally accurate. First is the familiar logic behind increasing marginal costs. For each firm that pollutes, because there will be some antipollution measures that can be taken fairly easily, the first portion of pollution prevention will be cheap relative to later portions. In addition, it is likely that pollution prevention of any degree will be easier for some firms than for others. New facilities are likely to run cleaner than old ones, for example. Pollution abatement in a factory that was designed in the era of environmental concern may be much easier than obtaining similar abatement in an older factory. After some point, however, the easy fixes are exhausted, and the marginal cost of preventing pollution further rises steeply.

The downward-sloping curve in Figure 17-2 is the "demand" for pollution abatement, and reflects the marginal benefit of pollution reduction. The curve slopes downward for much the same reason that the typical demand curve slopes downward. Starting at any nonlethal level of pollution, people will derive some benefit from reducing the level of pollution, but the marginal benefit from a given amount of abatement will be lower, the lower the level of pollution (or the higher the level of abatement). Put another way, in a very dirty environment, a little cleanliness will be much prized, but in a very clean environment, a little more cleanliness will be of only small additional value.

The optimal amount of pollution abatement occurs where the marginal benefit is equal to the marginal cost—where "supply" and "demand" in Figure 17-2 intersect. In trying to reach this optimum, the pollution-control authority faces three serious problems.

First, although Figure 17-2 looks like a supply-demand diagram, we have already seen that the private sector will not by itself create a market in pollution control. Hence, the government must intervene in private-sector markets if the optimal level of control shown in Figure 17-2 is to be attained.

The second problem is that the optimal level of pollution abatement is not easily known because the marginal benefit and the marginal cost curves shown in Figure 17-2 are not usually observable. In practice, the government can only estimate these curves, and accurate estimates are often difficult to obtain, especially when the technology of pollution abatement is changing rapidly and the health consequences of various pollutants are not known.

The third problem is that the available techniques for regulating pollution are themselves imperfect. Even when the optimal level of pollution abatement is known, there are both technical and legal impediments to achieving that level through regulation.

Pollution-Control Policies

In what follows we examine three different types of policies designed to bring about the optimal amount of pollution abatement (or the optimal amount of pollution). These are *direct controls*, *emissions taxes*, and *tradable emissions permits*.

Direct Controls

Direct control is the form of environmental regulation that is used most often. Automobile emissions standards are direct controls that are familiar to most of us. The standards must be met by all new cars that are sold in Canada. They require that emissions per kilometre of a number of noxious chemicals and other pollutants be less than certain specified amounts. The standards are the same no matter where the car is driven. The marginal benefit of reducing carbon monoxide emissions in rural Saskatchewan, where there is relatively little air pollution, is certainly much less than the marginal benefit in Montreal, where there is already a good deal of carbon monoxide in the air. Yet the standard is the same in both places.

Direct controls also often require that specific *techniques* be used to reduce pollution. For example, coal-fired electric plants were sometimes required to use devices called "scrubbers" to reduce sulfur dioxide emissions, even in cases where other techniques could have achieved the same level of pollution abatement at lower cost.

Another form of direct control is the simple prohibition of certain polluting behaviours. For example, many cities and towns prohibit the private burning of leaves and other trash because of the air pollution problem that the burning would cause. A number of communities have banned the use of wood stoves. Similarly, the government gradually reduced the amount of lead allowed in leaded gasoline and then eliminated leaded gasoline altogether.

Problems with Direct Controls. Suppose that pollution of a given waterway is to be reduced by a certain amount. Regulators will typically apportion the required reduction among all of the polluters according to some roughly equitable criterion. The regulators might require that every polluter reduce its pollution by the same percentage. Alternatively, every polluter might be required to install a certain type of control device or to ensure that each litre of water that is dumped into the watershed meets certain quality criteria. Although any of these rules might seem reasonable, each of them will be inefficient.

Pollution is being abated efficiently when the marginal cost of abatement is the same for all firms.

When firms are required to abide by direct pollution controls, however, the marginal cost of pollution abatement is usually *not* equated across firms. To see this, consider two firms that face different costs of pollution abatement, as shown in Figure 17-3. Suppose that, for any level of pollution abatement, Firm A's marginal costs of abatement are lower than those for Firm B. A situation like this is quite likely because pollution comes from many different industries, and it may be easier for firms in one industry to cut back on the amount of pollution that they produce than it is for firms in another industry.

In this situation, consider a system of direct pollution controls that requires Firm A and Firm B to each reduce pollution by a given amount, say Q_R. As shown in Figure 17-3, Firm A's marginal cost at Q_R is less than Firm B's marginal cost. The total cost of abating this much pollution could be reduced by having the low-marginal-cost firm (Firm A) abate more pollution and having the high-marginal-cost firm (Firm B) abate less. As long as the two firms' marginal costs of abatement are not equal, it is possible to further reduce total costs. Only when marginal costs are equal across the two firms is the given level of pollution abatement being achieved at the lowest possible cost.

Direct pollution controls are inefficient because they do not minimize the cost of a given amount of pollution abatement.

Direct controls are also expensive to monitor and to enforce. The regulatory agency has to check, factory by factory, farm by farm, how many pollutants of what kinds are being emitted. It then also needs a mechanism for penalizing offenders. Accurate monitoring of all potential sources of pollution requires a level of resources that is much greater than has ever been made available to the relevant regulatory agencies. Moreover, the existing system of fines and penalties, in the view of many critics, is not nearly harsh

FIGURE 17-3   The Inefficiency of Direct Pollution Controls

Requiring equal amounts of pollution abatement from different polluters is inefficient when the different polluters have different technologies of pollution abatement. Firm A is able to reduce its emissions according to the marginal cost curve MC_A. Firm B, which operates at the same scale but in a different kind of factory, has a higher marginal cost of abatement, MC_B. Suppose that a regulatory authority requires that the two firms reduce pollution by the same amount, Q_R. Firm A will have a marginal cost of pollution abatement of C_A, whereas Firm B's marginal cost will be C_B, which is larger than C_A.

To see that this outcome is inefficient, consider what happens if Firm A reduces its pollution (increases its pollution abatement) by one unit while Firm B increases its pollution by one unit. Total pollution remains the same, but total costs fall. Firm A incurs added costs of C_A, and Firm B saves a greater amount, C_B. Because the total amount of pollution is unchanged, the total social cost of pollution and pollution abatement is lower.

enough to have much effect. A potential polluter, required to limit emissions of a pollutant to so many kilograms or litres per day, will take into account the cost of meeting the standard, the probability of being caught, and the severity of the penalty before deciding how to behave. If the chances of being caught and the penalties for being caught are small, the direct controls may have little effect.

Monitoring and enforcement of direct pollution controls are costly, and this costliness reduces the effectiveness of the controls.

Emissions Taxes

An alternative method of pollution control is to levy a tax on emissions at the source. The great advantage of such a procedure is that it internalizes the pollution externality so that decentralized decisions can lead to allocatively efficient outcomes. Again, suppose that Firm A can reduce emissions cheaply, while it is more expensive for Firm B to reduce emissions. If all firms are required to pay a tax of t for each unit of pollution they produce, then t is equal to each firm's marginal benefit of pollution reduction. The goal of profit maximization will then lead firms to reduce emissions to the point where the marginal cost of further reduction is just equal to t. Thus, Firm A will reduce emissions much more than Firm B and both will then have the same marginal cost of further abatement, which is required for allocative efficiency. Such a situation is illustrated in Figure 17-4.

FIGURE 17-4   The Efficiency of Emissions Taxes

Emission taxes can lead to efficient pollution abatement. As in Figure 17-3, Firm A faces a lower marginal cost of pollution abatement than does Firm B. Suppose that the regulatory authority imposes a tax of t dollars per unit of pollution. Since each firm must then pay t dollars for each unit of pollution it produces, t can be viewed as the firm's marginal benefit of pollution abatement—for each unit of pollution it *does not produce* it avoids paying taxes equal to t.

Firm A will choose to reduce its pollution by Q_A. Up to this point, the tax saved by reducing pollution exceeds the marginal cost of reducing pollution. If Firm A chooses not to reduce pollution at all, it would pay $t \times Q_{maxA}$ in pollution taxes, where Q_{maxA} is the firm's total pollution if it takes no action to prevent pollution. By abating its pollution by Q_A, Firm A saves an amount that is given by the shaded area in the panel on the left.

Firm B chooses to abate only a small amount of pollution, Q_B. Any further abatement would require that the firm incur costs along MC_B, which would be greater than the benefits of taxes saved.

Note that if the regulatory agency is able to obtain a good estimate of the marginal damage done by pollution, it could set the tax rate just equal to that amount. In such a case, polluters would be forced by the tax to internalize the full pollution externality and allocative efficiency would be achieved. In terms of Figure 17-1, the firms' private marginal cost curve would shift up by the full amount of the tax (set to equal the marginal external cost, EC) and thus the allocatively efficient level of output would be produced.

A second great advantage of using emissions taxes is that regulators are not required to specify anything about *how* polluters should abate pollution. Rather, polluters themselves can be left to find the most efficient abatement techniques. The profit motive will lead them to do so because they will want to avoid paying the tax.

Emissions taxes can perfectly internalize pollution externalities so that profit-maximizing firms will produce the allocatively efficient amount of pollution abatement.

Applying Economic Concepts 17-1 discusses a simple type of pollution tax that is becoming quite common in many U.S. cities—charging for household garbage by the bag.

Problems with Emissions Taxes.   Emissions taxes can work only if it is possible to measure emissions accurately. For some kinds of pollution-creating activities, this does not pose much of a problem, but for many other types of pollution, good

APPLYING ECONOMIC CONCEPTS 17-1
Charging for Garbage by the Bag

One of the most common forms of pollution is household garbage. The economic theory of pollution externalities discussed in the text suggests that a tax on household trash should reduce the volume of pollution. In a number of communities in the United States, per-bag charges on household garbage have led to reductions in the amount of trash generated. The waste that is not going into the costly bags is going into compost heaps and into recycling. Communities vary in the way that charges are assessed and in the degree of support that they provide for alternative uses of waste. Typically, the municipal garbage trucks will pick up trash only if the trash bag (or other type of garbage) carries a special sticker. The stickers are sold by the municipal authorities; the fewer a household uses, the less money it spends on having its trash picked up. Fees of $1 to $2 per bag are not uncommon. In one U.S. community (High Bridge, New Jersey), a fee of $1.25 per bag has led to a 25 percent reduction in the volume of garbage.

The externality in this case is the use of landfills. Especially in the more populated areas of the United States, landfills for solid waste are becoming scarce and, consequently, expensive. By charging residents something for use of the landfill, alternative means of dealing with waste are encouraged, and a solid waste facility of given size can last longer.

Even in this case, the problem of finding the optimal charge per bag of garbage poses serious technical difficulties. There are also enforcement problems: Rather than pay the charge, some households will illegally dump their trash, adding to environmental damage. However, the pollution itself is very easy to measure, and it is plain that the optimum charge is greater than zero.

Household garbage is costly to dispose of in landfills. Charging by the bag for garbage internalizes the disposal cost.

measuring devices that can be installed at reasonable cost do not exist. Obviously, in these cases, emissions taxes cannot work, and direct controls are the only feasible approach.

When there is good reason to prohibit a pollutant completely, direct controls are obviously better than taxes. Municipal bans on the burning of leaves fall in this category, as do the occasional emergency bans on some kinds of pollution that are invoked during an air pollution crisis in cities such as Los Angeles and Vancouver.

Another problem with emissions taxes involves setting the tax rate. Ideally, the regulatory agency would obtain an estimate of the marginal social damage caused per unit of each pollutant and set the tax equal to this amount. This ideal tax rate would perfectly internalize the pollution externality. However, the information that is needed to determine the marginal external cost (*EC*) shown in Figure 17-1 is often difficult to obtain. If society is currently far away from the optimum, it may be very difficult to estimate what the marginal external cost will be at the optimum. If the regulatory agency sets the tax rate too high, too many resources will be devoted to pollution control. If the tax is set too low, there will be too little pollution abatement and thus too much pollution.

A potentially serious problem with emissions taxes is that information necessary to determine the optimal tax rate is often unavailable.

Tradable Emissions Permits

One advantage of direct controls is that the regulators can set the standards to limit the total quantity of pollution in a given geographical area. They can do this without knowing the details of either the marginal benefits or the marginal costs in Figure 17-2. The advantage of emissions taxes is that they allow for decentralized decision making, providing firms with an incentive to internalize the negative externality of pollution. **Tradable emissions permits** can combine both of these advantages and thus have the potential for being superior to either direct controls or emissions taxes.

In Figure 17-3, we noted that direct pollution controls are generally inefficient because the marginal cost curves for pollution abatement vary across firms. Tradable permits can achieve efficiency despite differences in firms' marginal cost curves. To see this, we must first figure out how much pollution to allow. This involves reformulating the regulator's problem. Start with the same conditions as those in Figure 17-3, and permit each firm to pollute exactly the same amount as would be allowed by the direct controls. Now suppose that the firms are each allocated Q_R tradable pollution permits—each one being simply a "right to pollute" by one unit. These permits are tradable in that firms are allowed to buy and sell them among themselves, at whatever price the market determines. Trades among firms will lead to discovery of the lowest-cost means of achieving the permitted level of pollution.

To see how the outcome is changed in the presence of tradable emissions permits, note that at the initial allowed amounts of pollution (Q_R), the marginal cost of pollution abatement for Firm A is lower than that for Firm B. Since Firm B must pay C_B to reduce pollution by one unit, it would be willing to pay any amount *less than* C_B to purchase one more pollution permit (and thus avoid reducing that last unit of pollution at cost C_B). Firm A would be willing to sell one pollution permit for any amount *greater than* C_A. By doing so, it earns an amount greater than C_A in return for reducing one more unit of pollution and paying the cost C_A. If Firm A and Firm B made such a trade, Firm A would be selling one of its pollution permits to Firm B. Society would benefit from this transaction because pollution would end up being abated at a lower cost than previously. If such a trade were made, the total amount of pollution would be unchanged, the total cost of abating pollution would fall (by $C_B - C_A$), and both firms would be at least as well off as before. We would thus have a clear efficiency improvement.

See Chapter 17 of www.pearsoned.ca/lipsey for an excellent discussion of why tradable emissions permits may be good for developing countries: Georges Tanguay, "Will Kyoto Lead to World Trade in Pollution Permits?" *World Economic Affairs*.

Once firms engage in trading pollution permits, an equilibrium market price will quickly be established. Facing this market price for permits, firms will end up equating their marginal abatement costs. To see this, note that the market price for a pollution permit will be each firm's marginal benefit of abatement since reducing pollution by one unit means the firm needs to purchase one less pollution permit. Profit-maximizing firms will therefore choose the level of abatement (and thus the number of permits) that equate this marginal benefit with their marginal abatement costs. Therefore, as in the case of emissions taxes shown in Figure 17-4, the introduction of tradable pollution permits will equate firms' marginal abatement costs and thus minimize the total cost of any given amount of pollution abatement.

Practise with Study Guide Chapter 17, Exercise 3.

With tradable pollution permits, profit-maximizing firms will abate pollution until their marginal abatement costs equal the price of the pollution permit. This will minimize the total cost of any given amount of pollution abatement.

Note, however, that the use of tradable pollution permits requires less information on the part of the regulators than does the use of emissions taxes. With tradable pollution permits, regulators do not need to calculate the optimal pollution tax. Given the permitted quantity of pollution, the market in permits will calculate the equivalent to the tax through the voluntary trades of firms.

Problems with Tradable Emissions Permits.   Tradable permits pose some problems of implementation. Some of these involve technical difficulties in measuring pollution and in designing mechanisms to ensure that firms and households comply with regulations (some of these problems also exist for direct controls and emissions taxes). Furthermore, the potential efficiency gains arising from tradable permits cannot be realized if regulatory agencies are prone to change the rules under which trades may take place. Such changes have been a problem in the past, but they are a problem that can be corrected.

One problem with tradable permits is more political than economic, but it is certainly important in explaining why such policies are so rare. Opponents of tradable permits often argue that by providing permits, rather than simply outlawing pollution above some amount, the government is condoning crimes against society. Direct controls, according to this argument, have much greater normative force because they say that violating the standards is simply wrong. Emissions taxes and markets for pollution make violating the standards just one more element of cost for the firm to consider as it pursues its private goals.

Most economists find arguments of this kind unpersuasive. An absolute ban on pollution is impossible because any production of goods and services generates at least some pollution. In choosing how much pollution to allow, society must trade pollution abatement against other valuable things. Economic analysis has a good deal to say about how a society might minimize the cost of *any* degree of pollution abatement. By taking the moral attitude that pollution is wrong and pollution permits should not be allowed, the result is that *less* pollution gets abated for any given amount of society's scarce resources that are allocated toward this goal.

The creation of markets for pollution emissions may become one of the most promising strategies for efficiently overcoming the market failure that leads to environmental pollution.

Most experimentation with tradable pollution permits has so far been conducted in the United States. *Applying Economic Concepts 17-2* discusses how the U.S. Clean Air Act of 1990 created a national market in tradable permits for sulfur dioxide, the major cause of acid rain.

The Politics of Pollution Control

To see a copy of the Kyoto Protocol, go to the website for the United Nations Framework Convention on Climate Change: www.unfccc.de.

Tradable emissions permits increased in prominence after the December 1997 conference on global warming held in Kyoto, Japan. At this conference, representatives for 166 countries met to discuss the need for reducing the emissions of greenhouse gases—gases that many scientists believe are capable of trapping enough heat to significantly raise the earth's surface temperature. Thirty-eight countries eventually signed the "Kyoto Protocol," whereby the signing countries agreed to reduce their emissions of greenhouse gases. Central to the Protocol was the agreement in principle to use tradable emissions permits. Though many environmental groups applauded the agreement to reduce the emissions of greenhouse gases, there was widespread scepticism about the use of tradable emissions permits.

What is the basis for this scepticism? We consider, in turn, the views of producers, the public, and environmentalists.

APPLYING ECONOMIC CONCEPTS 17-2

A Market for SO₂ Emissions in the United States

Coal-burning electric power plants are the major cause of acid rain. They emit sulfur dioxide (SO_2) through their tall smokestacks, and the SO_2, which stays in the air for between two and five days, becomes acidic when it combines with moisture. Such emissions from the Ohio Valley and the Midwest, combined with prevailing winds from the southwest, provide a serious pollution problem for New England and parts of eastern Canada. Acid rain (or snow) harms the ability of lakes to sustain aquatic life and damages agricultural crops, forests, and even the surfaces of cars and buildings.

Much of the enthusiasm for tradable emissions permits, in the United States and elsewhere, comes from the success that the United States has had in reducing SO_2 emissions from electric utilities. The U.S. Clean Air Act of 1990 established targets for SO_2 emissions and implemented those targets by issuing (for free) a fixed number of "permits to pollute." Beginning in 1993, additional permits were auctioned to the highest bidder every year. Starting in 1995, the Environmental Protection Agency (EPA) implemented emissions trading, whereby emissions permits could be bought and sold at market-determined prices. The total number of emissions permits is controlled so that by the year 2000, emissions will be less than half the 1980 level. After 2000, the allowed emissions will be sharply reduced again.

Once firms receive their permits, either from the initial issuance or from the annual auction, they may use them or sell them as they please. But individual utilities are limited in their SO_2 emissions by the quantity of the permits that they own. For this system to be effective, monitoring of each firm's emissions is necessary; thus as part of the program all utilities subject to the new law are required to install continuous monitoring equipment. Each ton of emissions for which the polluter does not have a permit is subject to a $2000 fine. In addition, each such violation must be matched with an equivalent amount of underpollution (emissions less than the permitted amount) in the future.

Before the Clean Air Act was passed, utilities warned that annual compliance costs would be very large and that the emissions permits would be very expensive—ranging from $170 to $1000 per ton of emissions. By the end of the 1997, however, the market price was about $90 per ton. As technology for operating power plants with reduced SO_2 emissions improves, and thus the cost of emissions abatement falls, the price of the permits will also fall.

In addition to the utilities' participation in the market for emissions permits, several environmental groups have purchased permits, only to retire them from the market. By doing so, such groups can "put their money where their mouth is"—that is, they can express their preference for having a cleaner environment by purchasing the permits themselves and, by so doing, directly reduce the amount of SO_2 that can legally be produced.

Producers

Some firms object to the costs that they are asked to pay in terms of emissions taxes or the purchase prices of emissions permits. However, there is no reason why payments to government under any market-based scheme need to be an unjustified "tax grab." Emissions taxes need not be in excess of the costs imposed on society by the industry's activities. If government uses the introduction of a market-based scheme to raise general revenue—and thus levies emissions taxes in excess of the costs generated by the pollution—firms can oppose the extra tax burden without opposing the market-based scheme itself.

The introduction of market-based measures may signal the end of a free ride that producers have been taking at society's expense. If the firms in an industry were bearing none of the cost of their pollution, any efficient antipollution scheme will impose a burden on them—but only to the extent of forcing them to bear the costs of their own ac-

See Chapter 17 of www.pearsoned.ca/lipsey for an argument that stringent environmental standards may improve productivity: Georges Tanguay, "Environmental Standards and Industrial Competitiveness," *World Economic Affairs.*

tivities. The difference between direct controls and the market-based solution, however, is that the former will cost the average firm in the industry more than the market solution. (This difference just reflects the fact that direct controls are generally less efficient than emissions taxes or tradable emissions permits.)

Under market-based schemes (rather than direct controls), many firms feel a sense of unfairness because their competitors continue polluting while they must clean up. Their complaints ignore the fact that those firms that continue to pollute have paid for the right to do so, either by paying effluent taxes or by buying pollution rights, and that the complaining firm could do the same if it wished (it does not do so because cleaning up is cheaper for it than paying to pollute, as the competitors are doing).

These points make clear a key issue in assessing market-based solutions: Such solutions must not be judged relative to a "no action" policy. Given a government's decision to reduce pollution, the market solution must be compared with other alternatives that reduce pollution by the same amount. When such a comparison is made, much of the opposition from producers fades away.

Some firms argue that environmental protection reduces overall welfare because output and employment will fall if firms are required to pay emissions taxes or the price of pollution permits. This argument is misleading. It is surely true, as is clear in Figure 17-1, that firms required to pay for the external cost of the pollution they create will experience an increase in marginal cost—this is precisely how the externality gets internalized. It is also true that the level of output and employment in such firms will fall. But there is no tradeoff here between the environment and overall welfare. The environment is part of overall welfare. When we say that one unit of pollution generates an external cost of $100, we are measuring the cost imposed on the environment (or, equivalently, the amount of resources required to clean up that bit of environmental damage).

If steel-producing firms are required to pay the external cost of their pollution, the reduction in output and employment in those firms will indeed cause some pain. Profits will be lower, and some workers will be laid off. But this reduction in the amount of total resources devoted to the steel industry is part of the solution to the pollution externality. A negative externality in the steel industry means that too much steel is being produced. Thus it will improve overall welfare—not reduce it—to reduce the amount of resources in the steel industry. The resources that are no longer used in the steel industry are now free to be used in other industries, producing goods and services that society values more at the margin than an extra unit of steel.

The General Public

Some members of the general public have a moral opposition to selling anyone the right to pollute. Since it involves human survival, dealing in the right to pollute seems evil to many people. As we said earlier, however, it is not possible simply to ban pollution outright since all production invariably generates some pollution. The relevant question then becomes: How best can society reduce pollution by a given amount? Economic analysis suggests that tradable pollution permits are an efficient way of reducing pollution, and are much more efficient than direct pollution controls.

Opposition to the outcome where those who have the highest costs of cleaning up continue to pollute while those with the lowest costs do the cleaning up. Morality may dictate to many observers that the biggest polluters should do the cleaning up. Economists cannot show this reaction to be wrong; they can only point out the cost in terms of unnecessary resource use and less overall pollution abatement that follow from adopting such a position.

Environmentalists

Many environmentalists are sceptical about the efficiency and desirability of markets. Some do not understand economists' reasoning as to why markets can be, and often are, efficient mechanisms for allocating scarce resources. Others understand the economists' case but reject it, although few complete their argument by trying to demonstrate that direct government controls will be more effective.

Many environmentalists do not recognize that markets can be an efficient tool for protecting the environment.

Many environmentalists do not like the use of self-interest incentives to solve what they regard as "social" rather than "economic" issues. Economists who point to the voluminous evidence of the importance of self-interest incentives are often accused of ignoring higher motives such as social responsibility, self-sacrifice, and compassion. Although such motives are absent from the simple theories that try to explain the everyday behaviour of buyers and sellers, economists since Adam Smith have been aware that these higher motives often do exert strong influences on human behaviour.

Such higher motives are very powerful at some times and in some situations, but they do not govern many people's behaviour in the course of day-to-day living. If we want to understand how people behave in the aftermath of a flood, or an earthquake, or a war, we need motives in addition to self-interest; if we want to understand how people behave day after day in their buying and selling, we need little other than a theory of the self-interested responses to market incentives. Since control of the environment requires influencing the mass of small decisions, as well as a few large ones, the appeal to self-interest is the only currently known way to induce the required behaviour through voluntary actions.

Some environmentalists have the view that resources such as clean air and pure water are above mere monetary calculation and should thus be treated in special ways. The economist can point out that the use of this view to justify departing from market-based solutions ensures that measured material living standards will be lowered. If that is the understood and accepted price of regarding resources as special entities, then so be it!

Summary

This chapter has examined the main economic issues, and some of the political issues, associated with pollution control. The fact that pollution is a byproduct of some other production process means that pollution is a negative externality. Producers think about their own private costs but ignore the pollution costs that their production imposes on the rest of society. The efficient solution to this problem involves *internalizing the externality*—that is, making sure that the producers of the pollution are made to bear its full external cost. In the chapter we reviewed two ways of internalizing pollution externalities: emissions taxes and tradable pollution permits.

If properly designed, such market-based environmental policies can reverse the effects of the pollution externality. In terms of Figure 17-1, these policies have the effect of shifting the private marginal cost curve up by the full amount of the marginal external cost, thus equating private marginal cost with social marginal cost. When this occurs, firms will reduce the output of the goods that produce pollution as a byproduct, and the amount of pollution produced will also decline.

There is considerable opposition among environmentalists and the general public to market-based environmental policies. Tradable pollution permits, especially, appear to generate much scepticism among non-economists. Much of this scepticism has the same source as scepticism toward others policies that advocate the use of markets: *the lack of understanding of how markets work to allocate resources efficiently.* In response, economists can only continue to explain how markets work, illustrate what happens when markets are not permitted to operate, and present the costs and benefits of various environmental policies. Eventually, the message will get through.

S U M M A R Y

The Economics of Pollution Control

LO ❶ ❷ ❸

- Almost all economic activity is subject to at least some government regulation. Government regulation, of some form or another, is used to deal with every type of market failure—public goods, externalities, natural monopoly problems, and information asymmetries.
- Most pollution problems can be analysed as negative externalities. Polluting firms and households going about their daily business do harm to the environment and fail to take account of the costs that they impose on others.
- In a market that produces pollution as a byproduct, the external cost of the pollution implies that too much of the good is produced compared with what is allocatively efficient.
- The allocatively efficient level of pollution in any activity is generally not zero; it is the level where the marginal cost of further pollution reduction is just equal to the

marginal damage done by a unit of pollution. If a firm or a household faces incentives that cause it to internalize fully the costs that pollution imposes, it will choose the allocatively efficient level of pollution.
- Pollution can be regulated either directly or indirectly. Direct controls are used most often. Direct controls are often inefficient because they require that all polluters meet the same standard regardless of the benefits and costs of doing so.
- Market-based environmental controls, such as taxes on emissions, are more efficient; ideally, they cause firms to internalize perfectly the pollution externality. Tradable emissions permits could have the same effect as taxes without requiring regulators to know as much about the technology of pollution abatement.

The Politics of Pollution Control

LO ❹

- There is considerable opposition by the public to the use of market-based environmental policies—especially the use of tradable pollution permits.
- Many firms oppose having to pay for pollution permits. But the market-determined price of pollution permits will equal the marginal external cost of pollution, and thus firms will only pay the external cost that their production imposes on society.

- Some environmentalists and other members of the public oppose on moral grounds that firms should pay for the "right to pollute." These criticisms ignore the fact that pollution is an important economic problem, and a strong case can be made for wanting to minimize the total cost of any given level of pollution abatement.

Negative pollution externalities
Marginal external cost

Costs and benefits of pollution abatement
The efficient level of pollution

Direct pollution controls
Emissions taxes
Tradable emissions permits

S T U D Y   E X E R C I S E S

1. Consider the market for lumber, which we assume here to be perfectly competitive.

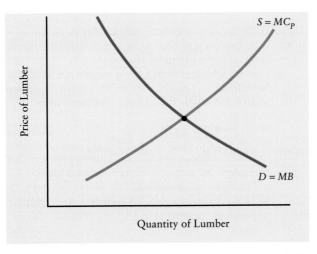

a. Suppose that for each unit of lumber produced, the firm also generates $10 of damage to the environment. Draw the social marginal cost curve in the diagram.
b. What is the allocatively efficient level of lumber output? Explain.
c. Describe and show the new market outcome if lumber producers are required to pay a tax of $10 per unit of lumber produced. Explain.
d. In part c, does the equilibrium price of lumber rise by the full $10 of the tax? Explain.

2. The following diagram shows society's marginal benefit and marginal cost for abating a particular type of pollution—say sulfur dioxide emissions.

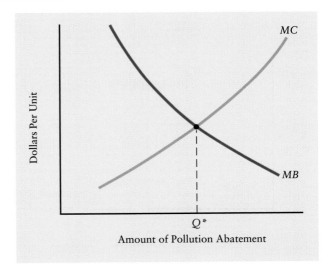

a. Explain why the marginal cost curve is upward sloping.
b. Explain why the marginal benefit curve is downward sloping.
c. At Q^*, are all sulfur dioxide emissions eliminated? Explain.
d. Is there an "optimal" level of sulfur dioxide emissions? Explain.

3. Suppose there are only two firms—Softies Inc. and Cuddlies Inc.—producing disposable diapers. Both firms are releasing dioxins into the same river. To reduce the pollution, the regulatory agency must choose between using direct controls and emissions taxes. The following diagrams show each firm's marginal cost of pollution abatement.

Abatement by Softies Inc.

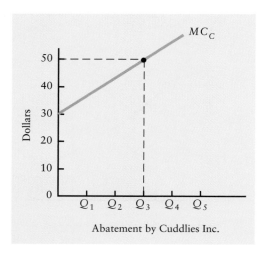

Abatement by Cuddlies Inc.

a. Suppose the regulatory agency requires that the two firms each abate Q_3 units of pollution. What is each firm's marginal abatement cost at Q_3?

b. Could the total cost of this amount of pollution abatement be reduced? Explain how.

c. Now suppose that the regulatory agency instead imposes an emissions tax of $40 per unit of emissions. Explain why this tax can be thought of as each firm's "marginal benefit of abatement".

d. In part c, how much pollution will each firm choose to abate?

e. Is it possible to reduce the total cost of the amount of abatement being done in part d?

4. Suppose that the government issues a fixed quantity of tradable pollution permits, each one permitting the emission of 1 ton of sulfur dioxide. In thinking about the market for pollution permits, think of the demand for permits as reflecting the marginal benefit to firms from being able to avoid costly pollution abatement.

a. If there is a competitive market for pollution permits, explain why the equilibrium price of the permit will equal the marginal abatement cost.

b. Explain why if polluting firms experience a technological improvement that reduces their marginal abatement costs, the equilibrium price of permits will fall.

c. What would happen if firms suffered a deterioration in their abatement technology?

d. One advantage of tradable pollution permits is that they allow the public to express their preferences for pollution reduction through the market. What happens if Greenpeace decides to buy a large number of pollution permits (and "retires" them)?

DISCUSSION QUESTIONS

1. "Pollution is wrong. When a corporation pollutes, it commits assault on the citizens of the country, and it should be punished." Comment on this statement in light of the discussion in this chapter.

2. Consider the following (alleged) facts about pollution control and indicate what influence they might have on policy determination.

   a. The cost of meeting government pollution requirements is about $300 per person per year.

   b. More than one-third of the world's known oil supplies lie under the ocean floor, and there is no known method of recovery that guarantees that large amounts of oil will not spill into the ocean.

   c. Sulfur-removal requirements and strip-mining regulations have led to the tripling of the cost of a ton of coal used in generating electricity.

   d. Every million dollars that is spent on pollution control creates 47 new jobs in the economy.

3. Suppose you were given the job of drafting a law to regulate water pollution over the entire length of some river.

a. How would you determine how much total pollution to permit?

b. What control mechanism would you use to regulate emissions into the river? Why?

c. Would you impose the same rules on cities as on farms?

d. Would your answer to parts **a, b,** or **c** depend on the quality of information that would be available to you? How and why?

4. The federal government has imposed many regulations aimed at reducing the pollution that is generated by driving. The more familiar regulations are direct—catalytic converters, fuel efficiency, and the like. Given the discussion in the chapter, why do you think the government opted for such direct controls? Can you think of any indirect controls currently in use to reduce automobile pollution?

CHAPTER 18

Taxation and Public Expenditure

LEARNING OBJECTIVES

1. Explain progressive, proportional, and regressive taxes.

2. Have a general knowledge of the main taxes used in Canada.

3. Explain how a tax generates both a direct and an excess burden.

4. Understand why high income taxes may act as a disincentive to work.

5. Understand why funds are transferred between various levels of government in Canada.

6. Describe a general outline of Canada's major social programs.

7. Be aware of some common pitfalls in evaluating government's role in the economy.

In Chapter 16, we saw some of the reasons why the scope of government is so extensive. Taxation is needed to raise money for public spending, and it can also play a policy role in its own right. Taxes can affect the distribution of income—some people get taxed more than others. Moreover, by taxing some activities heavily and others lightly or not at all, the tax system can influence the allocation of resources. In some cases, tax policy is carefully designed with such effects in mind; in other cases, the effects are unintentional by-products of policies pursued for other purposes.

In this chapter, we examine the various sources of government tax revenues and the various types of government expenditures. We ask how taxation and public expenditure affect the allocation of resources and the distribution of income, and to what extent they are effective tools of public policy. We examine the basis on which to evaluate a tax system, emphasizing the distinction between equity and efficiency. The types of public expenditures in Canada are examined along with the important concept of fiscal federalism. Finally, we describe the five pillars of Canadian social policy as well as some of the current pressures for reform of Canada's social programs.

Taxation in Canada

There is a bewildering array of taxes in Canada today. These are levied at the federal, provincial, and local levels. Some are highly visible, such as income taxes and the Goods and Services Tax (GST). Others are all but invisible to most people because they do not show up on income-tax forms or on receipts for purchases. For example, there are special taxes

For information on how Canada's tax system compares to those of other countries, see the website for the Canadian Tax Foundation: www.counsel.ca.

TABLE 18-1 Tax Revenues of Canadian Governments, 1997-98

	Billions of Dollars	Percent of GDP
Income taxes	$159.2	17.9
Consumption taxes	73.1	8.2
(GST, provincial sales taxes, and excise taxes)		
Property and related taxes	27.3	3.1
Other taxes	14.8	1.7
Health and social insurance premiums	27.1	3.0
Total tax revenues	$301.5	33.9
Non-tax revenues	44.7	5.0
(sales of goods and services, investment income)		
Total government revenues	$346.2	38.9

Canadian governments (at all levels) collect over $300 billion in various taxes, about one-third of the value of GDP. These data show total tax revenues for all levels of government combined. They *do not* include the mandatory contributions to the Canada and Quebec Pension Plans (which would increase the total by about $25 billion). Notice also that Canadian governments have considerable revenue, about $45 billion in 1998, from non-tax sources.

(*Source:* These data are available on Statistics Canada's website: www.statcan.ca)

tax expenditures
Tax provisions, such as exemptions and deductions from taxable income, that are designed to induce market responses considered to be desirable.

progressive tax
A tax that takes a larger percentage of income the higher the level of income.

proportional tax
A tax that takes a constant percentage of income at all levels of income and is thus neither progressive nor regressive.

levied on the sales of alcohol, cigarettes, and gasoline, but these taxes are levied directly on the producers (rather than the retailers) of these goods. People and firms are taxed on what they earn, on what they spend, and on what they own. Not only are taxes numerous, but taken together they raise a tremendous amount of revenue. Table 18-1 shows, for the federal, provincial, and local governments combined, the amount of revenue raised by the different types of taxes in 1998.

Canada lies roughly in the middle of other developed countries in terms of tax revenues as a share of GDP. Among the major industrialized countries, Denmark, Sweden, and the Netherlands collect roughly 50 percent of GDP in taxes. The lowest-tax industrialized country is Turkey, which collects about 25 percent of GDP in taxes. Canada is in the middle of the pack, collecting taxes equal to approximately 34 percent of GDP.

Some Definitions

Before discussing some details about the Canadian tax system, we examine two general concepts—*tax expenditures* and the *progressivity* of taxes.

Tax Expenditures

Sometimes taxes are used in ways that are similar to spending programs. For example, one way to deal with polluted rivers is to spend public funds to clean them up. An alternative, as we saw in Chapter 17, is to use taxes to penalize polluters or to give tax concessions to firms that install pollution-abating devices. Tax concessions that seek to induce market responses are called **tax expenditures**—tax revenue forgone to achieve purposes that the government believes are desirable.

The difference between a tax expenditure and an ordinary budgetary expenditure is that a tax expenditure represents *a reduction in tax revenue* whereas an ordinary expenditure represents *an increase in spending*. Because tax expenditures represent forgone earnings for the government, they are less visible than actual budgetary expenditures. They therefore usually receive little scrutiny from Parliament or the public. But this does not mean that they are small or unimportant. On the contrary, tax expenditures are very significant in the current Canadian economy. Personal income-tax expenditures alone, including such things as RRSP deductions, tuition fee credits, and child-care expense deductions, amount to over $75 billion annually.

Progressivity

When the government taxes one group in society more heavily than it taxes another, it influences the distribution of income. The effect of taxes on the distribution of income can be summarized in terms of *progressivity*. A **progressive tax** takes a larger percentage of income from high-income people than it does from low-income people. A **proportional tax** takes amounts of money from people in direct proportion to their income—

for example, every individual pays 10 percent of their income in taxes. A **regressive tax** takes a larger percentage of income from low-income people than it does from high-income people.

Note that the progressivity or regressivity of a tax is expressed in terms of *shares* of income rather than absolute dollar amounts. Thus a tax that collects $1000 from each individual clearly collects the same dollar amount from everybody, though it collects a higher share of income from low-income people than from higher-income people. A tax of this type—often called a **poll tax** or a *lump-sum tax*—is therefore a regressive tax.

Since a progressive tax takes a larger share of income from high-income people than it does from low-income people, progressive taxes reduce the inequality of income. A regressive tax increases the inequality of income.

A progressive tax involves an important distinction between the average tax rate and the marginal tax rate. The **average tax rate** is the percentage of income that the individual pays in taxes. The **marginal tax rate** is the percentage *of the next dollar* earned that the individual pays in taxes. Progressivity in the tax system requires an *average* tax rate that rises with income. As you may recall from Chapter 7, where we examined the relationship between average and marginal, a rising average product can be accomplished only by having the marginal product above the average product. This is also true for tax rates: the average tax rate can rise only if the marginal tax rate is above the average tax rate. Figure 18-1 shows the difference between progressive, proportional, and regressive income taxes.

For many families, day-care expenditures are tax deductible. The tax revenue forgone through such deductions are called "tax expenditures."

regressive tax   A tax that takes a lower percentage of income the higher the level of income.

poll tax   A tax that takes the same absolute amount from each person, independent of the level of their income. Also called a *lump-sum tax*.

average tax rate The ratio of total taxes paid to total income earned.

marginal tax rate The fraction of an additional dollar of income that is paid in taxes.

The Canadian Tax System

Taxes are collected by the federal government, by each of the provinces, and by thousands of cities, townships, and villages. Here is a brief guide to the most important of the various taxes.

Personal Income Taxes

Personal income taxes are paid directly to the government by individuals. The amount of tax any individual pays is the result of a fairly complicated series of calculations. All types of income are included in what is called total income, although certain types of income qualify for total or partial exemption. Then a number of allowable deductions are subtracted from total income to determine taxable income. Once taxable income is calculated, the amount of tax payable is then calculated by applying different tax rates to different levels of income. There are three federal personal income tax rates, each applying within what is called a tax bracket. In 1999, the three **tax brackets** were $0–$29 590; $29 590–$59 180; and greater than $59 180. The federal tax rates in these brackets were 17 percent, 26 percent, and 29 percent, respectively.

To see how this system of differential tax rates and tax brackets operates, consider Christine, who has a taxable income of $70 000. To the federal government, she pays at a rate of 17 percent on the first $29 590 ($5030), at a rate of 26 percent on the next $29 590 ($7693), and at a rate of 29 percent on all income *above* $59 180 (0.29 × $10 820 = $3138). Christine's total federal income tax payable is thus $15 861.

Recalling the definition of average and marginal tax rates, Christine's *average* tax rate is $15 861/$70 000, or 22.6 percent. Her *marginal* tax rate—the rate on an additional dollar of income—is 29 percent.

tax bracket   A range of income for which there is a constant marginal tax rate.

FIGURE 18-1   Alternative Income-Tax Systems

The relationship between income and taxes paid determines whether an income tax is progressive, proportional, or regressive. The average tax rate at any level of income, say $X, can be measured by computing the slope of a straight line from the origin to a point on the curve at income equal to $X. The slope of the curve at that point shows the marginal tax rate.

Along Curve A, the average tax rate rises as income rises. It shows a progressive income tax. The marginal tax rate also rises as income rises. Along Curve B, the average and marginal tax rate are equal to each other and are constant as income rises. This is a proportional tax system. Along Curve C, the average tax rate falls as income rises. This is a regressive tax system. The marginal tax rate is also falling as income rises.

The three federal personal income-tax rates do not represent the complete taxation of personal income in Canada, for two reasons. First, both the federal and many provincial governments have added more progressivity to the personal income tax by levying surcharges that kick in at various higher levels of income.

Second, the provincial governments also tax personal income. Quebec runs its own income-tax system, whereas the other nine provinces simply use the federal tax base (and federally distributed tax forms) and essentially "top up" federal taxes. Except for Quebec, taxpayers pay a single amount to Revenue Canada, which then distributes the total between the federal government and each province according to the amount collected from residents of that province.

The provincial taxation of income implies that Canada's highest marginal income-tax rate is not the federal rate, 29 percent. As of 1999, the highest marginal tax rates vary from a low of about 40 percent in Alberta to over 50 percent in Quebec and Newfoundland.

Corporate Taxes

The federal corporate income tax is, for practical purposes, a flat-rate (proportional) tax on profits as defined by the taxing authorities—which includes the return on capital as well as economic profits. In 1999, the rate was 28 percent.

Some corporate profits get distributed as dividends to shareholders. These dividends represent the shareholder's share of after-tax profits, and would ordinarily be taxed along with their other income. To avoid double taxation on this income, however, individual shareholders get a personal income-tax credit for the amount of corporate tax already paid by the firm. In this way, the corporate and personal income-tax systems are said to be *integrated*.

Excise and Sales Taxes

An excise tax is levied on a particular commodity. In many countries, commodities such as tobacco, alcohol, and gasoline are singled out for high rates of excise taxation. Because these commodities usually account for a much greater proportion of the expenditure of lower-income than higher-income groups, the excise taxes on them are regressive.

A sales tax applies to the sale of all or most goods and services. All provinces except Alberta impose a retail sales tax. Such a tax is mildly regressive, because poorer families tend to spend a larger proportion of their incomes than richer families.

Both excise and sales taxes are often referred to as "indirect" taxes to contrast them with income taxes, which are levied directly on the income of individuals or firms.

Since 1991, Canada has had a country-wide tax which applies at the same rate (7 percent) to the sale of all goods and services (with a few exceptions, such as basic groceries).

The Goods and Services Tax (GST) was introduced—despite enormous political controversy—for a number of reasons. First, it followed the modern trend in taxing expenditure rather than income. One problem with taxing income is that interest earnings from accumulated savings get counted as income and thus get taxed. Income taxes therefore discourage saving by lowering the after-tax rate of return to saving. In contrast, the GST only applies to the value of expenditure. Since the GST does not tax income (and therefore does not tax interest income) it does not discourage saving.

Second, the GST does not distort the relative prices of goods and services because it is applied at the same rate to all goods and services. Third, it followed the trend in almost all other developed nations (except the United States), which levy similar taxes; they are called *value added taxes* (VAT) in Europe.

In practice, the GST works by taxing a firm on the gross value of its output and then allowing a tax credit equal to the taxes paid on the inputs that were produced by other firms. Thus the GST taxes each firm's contribution to the value of final output—its value added. The result is the same as if each good and service bore a 7 percent tax when it was sold to its final user. Figure 18-2 shows how the GST is calculated at each stage from the mining of iron ore to the final retail sale of a washing machine.

Like sales and excise taxes, the GST is applied to expenditure rather than income. The GST taken alone would therefore be mildly regressive, because the proportion of income saved, and hence not taxed, rises with income. This regressivity is reduced by exempting food and, more importantly, by giving low- and middle-income people a refundable tax credit, which for the poor exceeds the value of GST that they would pay even if they spent all of their incomes on taxable commodities.

Property Taxes

The property tax is the most important Canadian tax that is based on wealth and is an important source of revenue for municipalities. It is different from any other important tax because it is not related directly to a current transaction. In contrast, income taxes are levied on the current payment to a factor of production (income) and sales taxes are levied on the value of a currently purchased good or service.

Taxing the value of existing property creates two problems. First, someone has to assess what the property is worth. Because the assessment is only an estimate, it is always subject to challenge. Second, sometimes owners of valuable property have low *incomes* (though considerable wealth) and thus have difficulty paying the tax.

The progressivity of the property tax has been studied extensively. It is obvious that the rich typically live in more expensive houses than the poor, and thus pay more in property taxes. But this does not mean

Practise with Study Guide Chapter 18, Exercise 4.

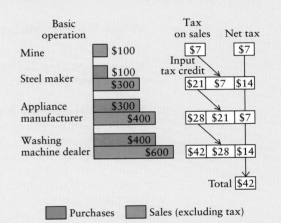

FIGURE 18-2   The Operation of the GST

A tax on value added is the same as a tax on the value of final goods with a credit allowed for the tax paid for purchased inputs. The example is for the stages involved as iron ore is mined and then sold to a steel maker, the steel then sold to an appliance manufacturer, and the washing machine sold to a retailer and then to a consumer. The example makes the simplifying assumption that no produced inputs are used in the mining operation (so that the value of the iron ore is all value added); at all further stages, however, the use of produced inputs makes the firm's value added less than the value of final output at that stage. The steel maker's value added is $200, and its tax is thus $14; $21 on the total value of its output less the $7 credit on the taxes already paid by the mine on the value of the iron ore. Total taxes paid equal $42, which is 7 percent of the $600 value of the final product; each firm pays 7 percent of its share in creating that $600 value.

that the rich pay more property taxes *as a fraction of their income* than the poor. Thus it is not readily apparent that property taxes are progressive. Indeed, most studies have shown that the proportion of income spent on housing tends to decrease with income—that is, the property tax is regressive.

For information about the Canadian tax system, see the website for the Canada Customs and Revenue Agency: www.ccra-adrc.gc.ca.

Evaluating the Tax System

What makes one tax system better or worse than another? Economists deal with this question by considering two aspects of taxation—equity and efficiency. We deal with equity first.

Taxation and Equity

Debate about income distribution and tax policy usually involves the important but hard-to-define concept of *equity*.

What Do We Mean By Equity?

Equity (or fairness) is a normative concept; what one group thinks is fair may seem outrageous to another. Two principles can be helpful in assessing equity in taxation: equity according to *ability to pay*, and equity according to *benefits received*.

The Ability-to-Pay Principle.   Most people view an equitable tax system as being based on people's ability to pay taxes. In considering equity that is based on ability to pay, two concepts need to be distinguished.

Vertical equity concerns equity *across* income groups; it focuses on comparisons between individuals or families with different levels of income. The concept of vertical equity is central to discussions of the progressivity of taxation. Proponents of progressive taxation argue as follows. First, taxes should be based on ability to pay. Second, the greater one's income, the greater the percentage of income that is available for goods and services beyond the bare necessities. It follows, therefore, that the greater one's income, the greater the proportion of income that is available to pay taxes. Thus, an ability-to-pay standard of vertical equity requires progressive taxation.

Horizontal equity concerns equity *within* a given income group; it is concerned with establishing just who should be considered equal to whom in terms of ability to pay taxes. Two households with the same income may have different numbers of children to support. One of the households may have greater dental expenses, leaving less for life's necessities and for taxes. One of the households may incur expenses that are necessary for earning income (e.g., requirements to buy uniforms or to pay union dues). There is no objective way to decide how much these and similar factors affect the ability to pay taxes. In practice, the income-tax law makes some allowance for factors that create differences in ability to pay by permitting taxpayers to exempt some of their income from tax. However, the corrections are rough at best.

The Benefit Principle.   According to the benefit principle, taxes should be paid in proportion to the benefits that taxpayers derive from public expenditure. From this perspective, the ideal taxes are *user charges*, such as those that would be charged if private firms provided the government services.

The benefit principle is the basis for the gasoline tax, since gasoline usage is closely related to the services obtained from using public roads. There is also a special airline ticket excise tax that is used for airport operations and airport security. Although there are other examples, especially at the local level, the benefit principle has historically played only a minor role in the design of the Canadian tax system. But its use is growing in Canada and elsewhere as governments seek new ways to finance many of their expenditures. For example, a decade ago Statistics Canada supplied data for free to anybody who wanted it. Now, Statistics Canada charges on a "cost recovery basis" for any data other than the most general data which they make available on their website.

The benefit principle can be easily applied to some government-provided goods and services. But it is difficult to see how the benefit principle could be applied to many of the most important categories of government spending. Who gets how much benefit from national defence or from interest on the public debt? It is even more difficult to imagine applying the benefit principle to government programs that redistribute income.

How Progressive Is the Canadian Tax System?

Although most public controversy over tax equity stresses the progressivity or regressivity of particular taxes, what matters in the end is the overall progressivity of the *entire tax system*. For a modern government to raise sufficient funds, many taxes must be used. We have already discussed personal and corporate income taxes, excise and provincial sales taxes, the Canada-wide GST, and municipal property taxes. Not all of them are equally progressive in design and each one has its own loopholes and anomalies. So, how high-, middle-, and low-income people are taxed relative to each other depends on how the entire tax system impacts on each group.

Assessing how the entire tax system affects the distribution of income is complicated by two factors. First, the progressivity of the system depends on the mix of the different taxes. Federal taxes tend to be somewhat progressive; the progressivity of the income-tax system and the use of a low-income tax credit more than offset the regressivity of the federal GST. Provincial and municipal governments rely heavily on property and sales taxes and thus have tax systems that are probably slightly regressive.

Second, income from different sources is taxed at different rates. For example, in the federal personal income tax, income from royalties on oil wells is taxed less than income from royalties on books, and profits from sales of assets (capital gains) are taxed less than wages and salaries. To evaluate progressivity, therefore, one needs to know the way in which different *levels* of income are related with different *sources* of income.

Many economists have concluded that the Canadian tax system is roughly proportional for middle-income classes and mildly progressive for low- and high-income persons. Thus the overall tax system is essentially redistributing income from high-income people to low-income people, and doing little redistribution among the middle-income people.

Taxation and Efficiency

The tax system influences the allocation of resources by altering such things as the relative prices of various goods and factors and the relative profitability of various industries.

Although it is theoretically possible to design a neutral tax system—one that leaves all relative prices unchanged—the conditions are too complex to be met in practice. As a result, any actual tax system, including Canada's, does alter the allocation of resources. The taxes change the relationship between prices and marginal costs and shift consumption and production toward goods and services that are taxed relatively lightly and away from those that are taxed more heavily. Usually, this alteration of free-market outcomes causes allocative inefficiency. In a world without taxes (and without other market imperfections), prices would equal marginal costs, and society's resources could be allocated efficiently.

Of course, in a world without taxes, there would be other problems—it would be impossible to pay for any government programs or public goods desired by society. In practise, then, the relevant objective for tax policy is to design a tax system that minimizes inefficiency, *holding constant the amount of revenue to be raised*. In designing such a tax system, a natural place to start would be with taxes that both raise revenue and enhance efficiency. An example of such a tax is the emissions tax that we discussed in Chapter 17. When taxes are imposed on negative externalities, marginal social benefit is moved closer to marginal social cost, *and* government revenue is raised. Unfortunately, such taxes cannot raise nearly enough revenue to finance all of government expenditure.

The Two Burdens of Taxation

In the absence of externalities, a tax normally does two things. It takes money from the taxpayers, and it changes their behaviour. Taxpayers are typically made worse off by both aspects of the tax. Economists call the revenue collected the **direct burden** of the tax. The additional cost that results from the induced changes in behaviour is called the **excess burden.**

> **direct burden**
> Amount of money for a tax that is collected from taxpayers.

> **excess burden** The amount that taxpayers would be willing to pay, over and above the direct burden of taxes, to abolish the taxes.

The direct burden of a tax is the amount paid by taxpayers. The excess burden of a tax is the amount of money that the taxpayers would have to be given, over and above the taxes paid, in order to be just as well off as they would be without the tax. The excess burden reflects the allocative inefficiency of the tax.

Figure 18-3 shows an example that illustrates this important distinction. Suppose that your provincial government imposes a $2 excise tax on the purchase of compact discs. Suppose further that you are a serious music lover and that this tax does not change your quantity demanded of CDs—that is, your demand for them is perfectly inelastic and hence you continue to buy your usual five CDs per month. In this case, you pay $10 in excise taxes per month, and you therefore have to reduce your consumption of other goods by $10 per month.

In this special case, the burden on you is not reflected by the change in your consumption of CDs (because there is no change), but rather by the change in your overall purchasing power. That is, if you were to be given an additional $10 a month in income, you would be exactly as well off as you were before the tax was imposed. Thus, the total burden on you is equal to the direct burden, $10 a month; there is no excess burden of this tax. The absence of any excess burden from this tax is just another way of saying that there is no allocative inefficiency; the cost of raising $10 a month for the province is just the $10 a month that you pay in taxes. In this case, the tax is *purely* a redistribution of resources from you to the government.

Now suppose that a friend of yours is also a music lover but is not quite so dedicated. The tax leads her to cut back on her consumption of CDs from two per month to none. In this case, your friend pays no taxes and therefore experiences no reduction in her overall purchasing power. The direct burden of the tax is therefore zero. However, your friend *is* worse off as a result of this tax—she has given up the satisfaction that she would have derived from two new CDs per month. She would have to be given some amount of money greater than zero (exactly her consumer surplus from buying two untaxed CDs per month) in order to make her as well off as she was before the tax was imposed. In this case, the direct burden is zero (because no tax is paid) but there *is* an excess burden. The excess burden is equal to her loss in consumer surplus from the two CDs per month that she no longer enjoys.

FIGURE 18-3   Direct and Excess Burdens of an Excise Tax

(i) You   (ii) Your friend   (iii) Entire market

The allocative inefficiency of a tax is measured by its excess burden. The excess burden is greater the more elastic is demand. Part (i) shows your demand for CDs. It is perfectly inelastic at five CDs per month. When the government imposes an excise tax of $2 per CD, the price rises from $15 to $17. Your quantity demanded is unchanged, and so you pay $10 per month in taxes ($2 tax per CD × 5 CDs). The direct burden of the tax is $10; but because your behaviour is unchanged, there is no excess burden.

Part (ii) shows your friend's demand. Her quantity demanded falls from two CDs per month to zero as a result of the tax. Since she pays no tax on CDs, she bears no direct burden of the tax. But because she has lost consumer surplus, she bears an excess burden from the tax.

Part (iii) shows the entire market demand. There is both a direct burden, the dark shaded area, and an excess burden, the light shaded area. The more elastic is the demand curve, the larger is the excess burden of the tax.

When a tax is imposed, some people behave like the music buff and do not change their consumption of the taxed good at all, others cease consuming the taxed good altogether, and most simply reduce their consumption. There will be an excess burden for those in the latter two groups. Thus, the revenue collected will understate the total cost to taxpayers of generating that revenue. Since our exercise in judging the efficiency of a tax system is to hold constant the total revenue raised, and thus to hold constant the direct burden generated by the tax system, *an efficient tax system will be one that minimizes the amount of excess burden.*

As the example above shows, the excess burden is minimized when taxes are imposed on goods with the lowest price elasticities of demand; the extreme case is illustrated by the music fan who has perfectly inelastic demand for CDs. A good with perfectly inelastic demand (one that has a vertical demand curve) can be taxed with no excess burden at all. Unfortunately, because many of life's necessities (such as food) have very price-inelastic demand curves, a tax system that taxed only goods that had inelastic demand curves would prove to be very regressive. This example illustrates an important general point:

Efficiency and equity are often competing goals in the design of tax systems. Improving efficiency often reduces equity; improving equity often reduces efficiency.

Disincentive Effects of Taxation

We have just shown how a tax can change consumers' behaviour. By raising the price of a good or service, the tax can lead consumers to purchase less of that good. What is true for consumers' demand for goods is also true for their demand for leisure. And their demand for leisure is simply the opposite of their supply of work effort. Thus,

Practise with Study Guide Chapter 18, Exercise 2.

FIGURE 18-4   A Laffer Curve

Increases in tax rates beyond some level will decrease rather than increase tax revenues. The curve relates the government's tax revenue to the tax rate. As drawn, revenue reaches a maximum level of R_0 at the tax rate r_0. If the tax rate were r_1, then *reducing* it to r_0 would increase the government's tax revenue from R_1 to R_0.

taxes can be expected to influence individuals' supply of work effort. In particular, an increase in the income-tax rate, by reducing after-tax earnings, may lead individuals to reduce their work effort. (It would be helpful to review the discussion of this point from *Applying Economic Concepts 6-1*.) This possibility leads to the paradoxical result that reducing income-tax rates may lead individuals to work and earn more, with the result that tax revenue actually *rises*. This possibility is illustrated in Figure 18-4, which shows what economists call a *Laffer Curve*.

The reasoning behind the general shape of the Laffer curve is as follows. At a zero tax rate, no revenue would be collected. As rates are raised above zero, some revenue will be gained. But as rates continue to rise, revenue will eventually fall because the very high tax rates will lead people to work less and less. At a tax rate of 100 percent, they will not bother to work at all (because all of their income would go to the government) and so tax revenue will be zero. It follows that there must be *some* tax rate, greater than zero and less than 100 percent, at which tax revenue reaches a maximum.

Figure 18-4 is drawn under the assumption that there is a steady increase in tax revenue as tax rates rise to r_0, and a steady decrease in tax revenues as tax rates continue to rise toward 100 percent. This particular shape—with a single peak in tax revenues—is not necessary. But the precise shape is beside the point. The key point is that there is *some* tax rate like r_0 that maximizes total tax revenue. And as long as this is true, then tax rates both above and below r_0 will raise less tax revenue than is raised at r_0.

Just where this maximum occurs—whether at average tax rates closer to 40 or to 70 percent—is currently unknown for either corporate or personal income taxes. Also, there will be a separate Laffer curve for each type of tax. The curve does, however, provide an important warning: Governments cannot increase their tax revenues to any desired level simply by increasing their tax rates. Sooner or later, further increases in the rates will reduce work incentives so much that total tax revenues will fall.

Public Expenditure in Canada

In recent years, spending by the consolidated public sector—which includes federal, provincial, and municipal governments—has equaled about 40 percent of Canadian GDP. Table 18-2 gives the distribution of consolidated government spending across a number of major *functions* for 1998. As can be seen, health care, education, and social services are very large items; collectively, they make up almost half of the total spending of $357 billion. Interest on the public debt is the largest single item, making up about one-quarter of total spending. The remaining quarter covers everything else, from police protection and sanitation to general administration of government, environmental protection, and foreign aid.

There are three broad categories of government expenditure. First, the government spends to provide goods and services to the public, as when the government pays for physicians' services, highway repair, primary and secondary education, and so on. Included in this category of expenditures are the salaries that the government pays to its employees. The second category of government expenditures is **transfer payments**. These are payments to individuals, firms, or other levels of government that are *not* made in exchange for a good or a service. For example, when the federal government pays employment insurance benefits to an unemployed individual, the government is not getting any good or service in return. Similarly, when the federal government transfers money to the provincial governments, it is not getting any good or service in return. The third category is actually expenditure on a particular type of service, but it is common to treat it separately—this is the interest the government pays on its outstanding stock of debt. Table 18-2, however, does not show a breakdown of expenditures between transfer payments and the provision of goods and services; instead, it shows the breakdown according to the broad area of spending.

transfer payment
A payment to a private person or institution that does not arise out of current productive activity.

Table 18-2 also does not show which of the three levels of government—federal, provincial, and municipal—actually do the spending. For example, of the $40.2 billion spent on education in 1998, the vast majority—over $36 billion—was spent by provincial and municipal governments. In contrast, expenditures on foreign affairs and foreign aid are made exclusively by the federal government. Expenditures on social services are about equally divided between the federal and provincial governments with only a small role played by the municipalities.

Fiscal Federalism

Canada is a federal state with governing powers divided between the central authority and the ten provinces and three territories. Municipalities provide a third level of government, whose powers are determined by the provincial legislatures. Understanding the fiscal interaction of the various levels of government is central to understanding the nature of government expenditure in Canada. In this section, we examine the concept of *fiscal federalism*; in the next section we examine how fiscal federalism affects the operation of Canada's social programs.

The Logic of Fiscal Federalism

The essence of fiscal federalism is the recognition that Canada is a country with many different fiscal authorities (federal, provincial, and municipal governments) that need a certain amount of coordination to be responsive to the needs and desires of the citizens—who are free to move from one area to another. We discuss four motivations for fiscal federalism.

TABLE 18-2 Expenditures by Canadian Governments, 1997–98

Category of Spending	Billions of Dollars	Percent of GDP
General government services	12.9	1.4
Protection of persons and property	28.5	3.2
Transportation and communication	19.4	2.2
Health	50.9	5.7
Social services	84.6	9.5
Education	40.2	4.5
Resource conservation, environment, and industrial development	23.5	2.6
Recreation and culture	9.0	1.0
Housing	4.9	0.5
Labour, employment, and immigration	2.0	0.2
Foreign affairs and international aid	4.0	0.4
Debt charges	72.9	8.2
Other expenditures	3.7	0.4
	356.5	39.8

Expenditures on health, social services, and education together make up almost half of total government expenditure. These data show the various categories of spending by all levels of government combined.

(*Source:* These data are available on the Statistics Canada website: www.statcan.ca.)

Differences in Tax Bases. The ten Canadian provinces vary considerably in terms of their average levels of prosperity. Newfoundland and Quebec have for many years lagged the national average in terms of per capita real incomes, whereas Alberta and Ontario have for many years exceeded the national average. In order to provide public goods such as highways and judicial systems, the provincial governments must levy various types of provincial taxes. Provinces that are more prosperous, and thus have larger tax bases, are able to provide a given amount of public goods while having relatively low tax rates. In contrast, less affluent provinces with smaller tax bases will be able to provide the same amount of public goods only by having higher tax rates.

Why don't we just let the more affluent provinces have lower tax rates than the less affluent provinces? The answer is that one of the guiding principles in Canada's system of fiscal federalism is that individuals, no matter where they live, should have approximately the same access to public goods and should face approximately the same tax rates to finance those public goods.

Since revenue sources do not always match revenue needs at each level, **intergovernmental transfers** are required. This is the underlying motivation behind Canada's system of *equalization payments*, which transfers resources from the richer provinces to the poorer ones. We examine this shortly.

intergovernmental transfer   A transfer of funds from one government to another.

Geographic Extent of Externalities.

Because the government of a province or a municipality is unlikely to be responsive to the needs of citizens outside its jurisdiction, public services that involve *geographic spillovers* may not be provided adequately unless responsibility for them is delegated to a higher level of government. For example, national defence is normally delegated to the central government for this reason. Control of pollution is another obvious case, since contamination of air and water often literally spills over provincial and municipal boundaries. At the other extreme is fire protection. If fire protection is to be effective, it is necessary that there be fire stations serving small geographic areas. Accordingly, responsibility for fire stations lies with municipal governments.

Regional Differences in Preferences.

The delegation of some functions to lower levels of government may provide a political process that is more responsive to regional differences in preferences for public versus private goods. Some people may prefer to live in communities with higher-quality schools and police protection, and they may be prepared to pay the high taxes required. Others may prefer lower taxes and lower levels of services. The differences in provincial tax rates that we noted earlier presumably reflect each provincial government's own view of the appropriate level of taxation.

Administrative Efficiency.

Administrative efficiency requires that duplication of the services provided at different levels of government be minimized and that related programs be coordinated. On the revenue side, it is desirable that a particular tax be collected by only one level of government. This consideration has led to the negotiation of federal-provincial tax agreements that provide for efficient tax collection and revenue sharing.

Intergovernmental Transfers

The foregoing discussion of fiscal federalism suggests a role for transfers between various levels of government. For example, if income taxes are paid to the federal government but spending on hospitals and highways is undertaken by provincial governments, then federal-provincial transfers must be made. In addition, if some provinces have large tax bases, while others have much smaller tax bases, there is also a role for transferring resources between provinces. Canada has three major programs of intergovernmental transfers.

Canada Health and Social Transfer.

A major reform of the system of federal-provincial transfers occurred in 1996 with the creation of the Canada Health and Social Transfer (CHST). The CHST is a block grant made by the federal government to each provincial government to help finance expenditures on health care, social assistance (welfare) and post-secondary education. Though the CHST transfer is described as being directed at these three categories of expenditure, there is no practical way to prevent the provincial governments from spending the money on whatever they deem to be appropriate. Thus, the CHST is received by the provinces with "no strings attached."

The CHST replaced two previous transfer programs. The first, Established Programs Financing (EPF), was directed at health care and post-secondary education. The second, the Canada Assistance Plan (CAP), was a transfer program in which the federal government financed 50 percent of the province's welfare system. Thus, until the creation of the CHST, the federal government was obliged to increase CAP funding to any province that chose to increase the generosity of its welfare program. The CHST therefore gives the federal government more control over its funding of provincially administered programs. Beginning in 2001–02, the CHST payment to each province is made on a per capita basis, equal to $960 for each resident of that province.

Equalization Payments.   With the object of ensuring that citizens in all regions of the country have access to a reasonable level of public services, **equalization payments** are made out of federal government general revenues to provinces with below-average tax capacity. Though this is not explicitly a revenue-sharing program (provinces with above-average tax capacity do not pay in), the richer provinces (typically British Columbia, Alberta, and Ontario) are, in effect, transferring resources via the federal government to the poorer provinces. The equalization payments are calculated by a complicated formula that involves 30 different revenue sources.

Equalization payments are a relatively new phenomenon in Canada, but they have exhibited rapid growth. From their inception with the 1957 Tax-Sharing Act to the time of the 1977 Fiscal Arrangements Act to their formal inclusion in the Constitution Act of 1982, they have expanded considerably. Equalization payments for the 1999–2000 fiscal year were approximately $9.3 billion.

Revenue Sharing.   Since the 1940s, most provinces have maintained **tax-rental arrangements**, whereby the federal government collects income taxes and makes a per capita payment to the provinces for that right. In 1999, with the exception of the Quebec personal income tax and the Ontario and Quebec corporate levies, all income taxes in Canada were collected by the federal government.

Outside Quebec, the provincial income tax is calculated as a percentage of the federal tax payable at rates determined by the individual provinces.[1] Federal income-tax rates are set at levels that allow substantial "tax room" to the provinces. That is, by keeping the federal income-tax rates relatively low the provinces can still raise considerable revenue by taxing income without generating extreme supply-side effects such as those discussed in Figure 18-4. A similar arrangement applies to the corporate income tax. The effect of these measures can be thought of in terms of the "value of tax points." Tax points reflect the taxes levied by the provinces, collected by the federal government, and then returned to the provinces as a transfer.

Canadian Social Policy

Canada has a wide variety of social programs, from unemployment insurance and the Canada Pension Plan to the systems of publicly provided health care and heavily subsidized

equalization payments   Transfers of tax revenues from the federal government to the low-income provinces to compensate them for their lower per capita tax yields.

tax-rental arrangements   An agreement by which the federal government makes a per capita payment to the provinces for the right to collect income taxes.

---

[1]In 1999, Alberta introduced a flat-rate provincial income tax of 11 percent. The tax is still collected by the federal government.

post-secondary education. Canadian governments—both federal and provincial—have been urged to reexamine and redesign these programs with the twin objectives of improving the benefits delivered to the intended beneficiaries and reducing costs wherever possible. It is not surprising that controversies over Canada's social programs have been major news items in recent years. Indeed, these controversies will likely continue well into the future.

Some social programs are universal, in the sense that they pay benefits to anyone meeting only such minimal requirements as age or residence. These are referred to as **demogrants.** Other programs are selective, in the sense that they pay benefits only to people who qualify by meeting specific conditions, such as by having young children or being unemployed. When these conditions are related to the individual's income, the term **income-tested benefits** is used. Some benefits are expenditure programs (including direct transfers to persons), while others are delivered through the tax system in the form of tax expenditures. Some programs are administered by the federal government, some by the provincial governments, and still others by the municipalities.

In this section we examine the five pillars of Canadian social policy: education, health care, income support, employment insurance, and retirement benefits. Each of these pillars, at various points in recent years, have been the focus of attention as financially strapped governments have explored new ways to provide what many perceive as vital social services.

Education

Public education, one of the earliest types of social expenditure in Canada, remains one of the most important. It has been supplemented over the years by numerous other programs aimed at developing human resources.

Basic Education.

Primary and secondary schools teach literacy and numeracy. These basic skills are needed in order to acquire further marketable skills. Canada has one of the world's highest per capita expenditures on basic education, yet Canadian students do relatively poorly on international comparisons that use standardized tests. Studies show that many Canadian adults (some estimates say as many as one-quarter) are functional illiterates—people who cannot comprehend simple written instructions well enough to carry them out. One educational target should be to reduce illiteracy and innumeracy, deficiencies that are lifetime handicaps.

Postsecondary Education.

Postsecondary education is a provincial responsibility in Canada. As discussed earlier in this chapter, however, the federal government makes large payments to the provinces to support postsecondary education as part of the Canada Health and Social Transfer (CHST).

In Canada, all universities are public institutions, and university education is heavily subsidized by government. In 1998, total revenues for universities and colleges was $17.7 billion, with 62 percent coming from various levels of government. Only 16 percent came from student tuition fees. (The remaining 22 percent comes from various other sources—maybe those overpriced shirts that you can't afford to buy from your campus bookstore!)

Two arguments can be advanced for subsidizing higher education; one is an efficiency argument, and the other concerns equity. The efficiency argument is based on the claim that there are positive externalities from higher education—that is, that the country as a whole benefits when a student receives higher education. In many cases these externalities cannot be internalized by the students receiving the education, so, left to their own maximizing decisions, students who had to pay the whole cost of their education would choose less than is socially optimal. The equity argument is that if students were forced to pay anything like the full cost of the services they receive, a university education would become prohibi-

demogrants   Social benefits paid to anyone meeting only minimal requirements such as age or residence; in particular, *not* income-tested.

income-tested benefits   Social benefits paid to recipients who qualify because their income is less than some critical level.

For data on the financial position of Canadian universities, see Statistics Canada's website: www.statcan.ca. Click on "Canadian Statistics" and then "Education."

tively expensive to low- and even middle-income families. Government subsidies help provide education according to ability rather than according to income.

Arguments to reduce the subsidy to higher education, and thus to finance a larger fraction of the costs of running universities from tuition fees, start with the observation that the value of many kinds of education is internalized and recaptured in higher incomes earned by the recipients later in their life. This is particularly true of professional training in such fields as law, medicine, dentistry, management, and computer science. Yet students in these fields typically pay a smaller part of their real education costs than students in the arts, where the argument for externalities is greatest. Also, subsidized education does represent a significant income transfer from taxpayers to students, even though the average taxpayer may have a lower income than the average student can expect to earn in the future.

Health Care

Taking federal and provincial payments into account, Canada's public health-care system is the country's single most expensive social program. In 1998, government expenditure on health care was $50.9 billion, about 15 percent of total government expenditure and 5.8 percent of GDP. Private spending on health care brought total spending up to about 10 percent of GDP. In other words, one out of every ten dollars in income produced in the Canadian economy gets spent on health care.

"Cost containment" in the health-care sector has become a priority for most provincial governments and the debate currently rages over what reforms are practicable and acceptable. Hospital and bed closures, nurse's strikes, and growing queues for non-critical treatments are part of the daily news. Most observers agree that some type of expenditure-controlling reform is urgently needed. Unfortunately, agreement stops here.

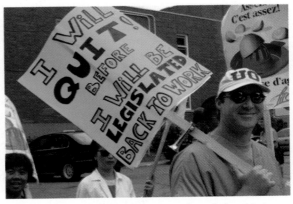

Budget cuts in the health-care sector have led to friction between provincial governments and health-care professionals, such as doctors and nurses.

Private Hospitals in a Public System. In 1999, the Alberta government announced its proposal to allow private, for-profit hospitals to exist within the publicly funded health-care system. According to this proposal, the provincial government would make the same payment to a private hospital for providing a given service as it would make to a public hospital. The Alberta government saw this proposal as one way to reduce waiting lists in the public health-care system without using scarce public funds to build new hospitals or expand existing ones.

The Alberta proposal has met with strong opposition, in part by the federal government. The main concern is that private hospitals may begin "extra billing" their patients. In this case there would develop a "two-tiered" health-care system in which individuals with higher incomes have better access to health care than do individuals with lower incomes. If extra billing becomes a feature of private hospitals, then only those individuals who can afford to pay the extra fees will be able to use the private hospitals. Furthermore, many nurses and doctors that are currently within the financially strapped public health-care system may move to the private hospitals if salaries or working conditions are better there. The overall concern, therefore, is that the introduction of private hospitals into the existing public health-care system, while reducing waiting lists and providing more health-care services overall, may result in a high-quality system for the wealthy and a low-quality system for lower-income people. Many people think that such a two-tiered health-care system would destroy the equity that the public system was initially designed to promote.

Advocates of private hospitals, on the other hand, argue that to a significant extent, Canada already has a two-tiered system. Many Canadians, frustrated by the long

See Chapter 18 of www.pearsoned.ca/lipsey for an excellent discussion of the government's evolving role in society: John Richards, "The Welfare State as a Valuable Work in Progress," *World Economic Affairs.*

waiting lists in the Canadian public health-care system, travel to the United States for medical treatment. Furthermore, these advocates argue that the lack of public funding in the Canadian health-care system has already caused many doctors and nurses to leave Canada and move to the United States (contributing to Canada's "brain drain" which we discussed in Chapter 13). In this view, the introduction of private hospitals to the Canadian system would not significantly increase the degree to which a two-tiered system already exists. Moreover, it would help stem the flow of nurses and doctors out of Canada, thereby *improving* Canada's overall health-care system.

In the late fall of 1999, the Alberta proposals were very new; only time will tell what will happen in Alberta's health-care system. Other provincial governments are watching Alberta closely.

Fee for Service.   One major possibility of cost containment that retains the public nature of the health-care system is to move away from the present system of "fee for service." In the system used in most of Canada, the physician and the hospital charge a prescribed fee for each service that is performed. Since under any provincial health scheme, the doctors and hospitals are assured of receiving these fees from the government, there is no reason for the provider of health services to economize on those services. Indeed, much research shows that the rate of elective surgery—operations that are not necessary for survival but may nonetheless be useful—rises with the ratio of physicians to the population. In areas where there are many physicians, the typical physician has time on his or her hands, and the rate of elective surgery goes up. In areas where doctors are in short supply, much less elective surgery is performed.

This illustrates a general point. The case for the free market is strongest when consumers are the best judges of their own needs. The case for market efficiency is greatly weakened when suppliers, such as physicians, can influence the demand for the product they supply. Thus, in the many cases where judgement is needed to decide among several courses of action, all of which have something to recommend them, the evidence is that doctors often create their own demand.

Health Maintenance Organizations.   Health maintenance organizations (HMOs) provide a possible way around this problem. Large hospitals and large groups of doctors work on what is called a *capitation* basis. This means that the HMO is paid an annual fee for each person registered with it. Since payment is on a per capita basis rather than on a services-rendered basis, there is no incentive to prescribe more care than is needed. Furthermore, to the extent that an individual registers with the same HMO for several years, there is little incentive for the HMO to scimp on necessary services, because scimping today (by ignoring a problem, for example) may mean that much more is spent in the future to correct the problem after it has gotten worse. Thus, one big advantage of HMOs is that each HMO has the incentive to keep its clients healthy *and* to keep costs down. The HMO at Sault Ste. Marie, pioneered by the steelworkers' union and their employers, was an early and successful Canadian example of such an organization.

Income-Support Programs

Canada has various programs that provide assistance for people in financial need—these programs constitute what is often called the "social safety net." The overriding objective of this safety net is to reduce poverty. Though nothing like the serious problem it was in Canada's past and still is in many other countries, poverty remains a matter of real concern to Canadian policy makers.

Statistics Canada defines the **poverty line** or *low-income cutoff* as the level of income below which the typical household spends more than 55 percent of its income on

poverty line   The official government estimate of the annual family income that is required to maintain a minimum adequate standard of living.

the three necessities of food, shelter, and clothing. According to Statistics Canada's definition, 17.5 percent of the Canadian population lives below the poverty line. There is considerable debate, however, about the methods used to measure poverty. Some studies find a higher poverty rate, others find a lower rate. But all experts agree that many Canadians live in poverty. Canada has several income-support programs designed to address this important problem.

Income-support programs can be divided into three types. The first is designed to provide income assistance to those individuals whose incomes are deemed to be too low to provide an adequate standard of living. The second is designed to assist specifically those individuals who are in financial need because of temporary job loss—employment insurance. The third is designed to provide income assistance specifically to the elderly. In this subsection, we examine the first type. The next two subsections discuss employment insurance and elderly benefits, respectively.

Welfare.   Social assistance for individuals below retirement age, usually called *welfare*, is mainly a provincial responsibility in Canada. The details of the programs vary considerably across the provinces even though they are partly financed by transfers received from the federal government under the Canada Health and Social Transfer (CHST).

Poverty and homelessness exist in Canada, though there is considerable disagreement about how widespread these problems are.

Suggested reforms to welfare take two main forms. First, most economists advocate reforms of the tax-and-transfer system in an effort to reduce what are called *poverty traps*. **Poverty traps** occur whenever the tax-and-transfer system results in individuals having very little incentive to increase their pre-tax income (by accepting a job, for example) because such an increase in their pre-tax income would make them ineligible for some benefits (such as welfare) and might even make them worse off overall. The presence of such poverty traps reflects a tax-and-transfer system that has been modified in many small steps over many years, the result of which is a plethora of programs often working at cross purposes. The elimination of such poverty traps requires that the tax-and-transfer system be examined in its entirety rather than on a piecemeal basis. *Applying Economic Concepts 18-1* discusses one possible reform of the tax-and-transfer system that maintains progressivity of the system while eliminating poverty traps. This is the idea of the negative income tax.

poverty trap   Occurs whenever individuals have little incentive to increase their pre-tax income because the resulting loss of benefits makes them worse off.

The second type of reform is designed to provide positive incentives to self-help by increasing benefits for recipients who accept work or training for work. A related (and quite contentious) proposal is referred to as *workfare*—the idea that welfare recipients should be required to put in some sort of work in order to be eligible for welfare benefits.[2] In 1997, Ontario reformed its welfare program so that single parents with school-aged children are now required to work in order to receive welfare payments.

Child Benefits.   The support system for families with children has been evolving quite rapidly over the years. Prior to the last change in 1993, the system was a combination of universal family allowance payments and tax credits. In 1993, universality was eliminated. A Child Tax Benefit is now paid according to the number of children in the family and varies according to family income, reaching zero at an income of $60 000.

[2]For a wide-ranging discussion of the issues involved in workfare, see John Richards and William Watson (eds.), *Helping the Poor: A Qualified Case for Workfare*, C. D. Howe Institute (Social Policy Challenge No. 5), Toronto, 1995.

APPLYING ECONOMIC CONCEPTS 18-1

Poverty Traps and the Negative Income Tax

A tax is negative when the government pays the taxpayer rather than the other way around. The *negative income tax (NIT)* is designed to increase progressivity by making taxes negative at very low incomes. Such a tax would increase progressivity at the very lowest incomes, and thus help to combat poverty. Furthermore, the NIT achieves its progressivity *without* a schedule of rising marginal income-tax rates and thus potentially avoids some of the extreme disincentive effects that are caused by very high marginal tax rates. Finally, by combining taxes and transfers into a single system, the negative income tax also avoids the occurrence of poverty traps.

The underlying principle of the NIT is that a family of a given size should be *guaranteed* a minimum annual income. The tax system must be designed, however, to guarantee this income without eliminating the household's incentive to be self-supporting.

As an example, consider a system in which each household is guaranteed a minimum annual income of $10 000 and the marginal tax rate is 40 percent. Money can be thought of as flowing in two directions; the government gives every household $10 000, and then every household remits 40 percent of any *earned* income back to the government. The *break-even* level of income in this example is $25 000. All households earning less than $25 000 pay negative taxes overall; they receive more money from the government than they remit in taxes. Households earning exactly $25 000 pay no net taxes—their $10 000 from the government exactly equals the taxes they remit to the government on their earned income. All households earning more than $25 000 pay more than $10 000 in taxes and so they are paying *positive* taxes overall.

The figure shows the operation of this scheme by relating earned income on the horizontal axis to after-tax income on the vertical axis. The 45° line shows what after-tax income would be if there were no taxes. The blue line shows after-tax income with a NIT. It starts at the guaranteed annual income of $10 000, rises by 60 cents for every one dollar increase in earned income, and crosses the 45° line at the break-even level of income, $25 000. The vertical distance between the two lines shows the net transfers between the household and the government.

Employment Insurance

Employment insurance (EI) is a federal program designed to provide temporary income support to workers who lose their jobs. Employers and employees remit EI premiums to the government equal to a small percentage of wages and salaries. These premiums then finance the EI payments to unemployed workers who qualify for the benefits. In boom times, when there is little unemployment, the EI premiums exceed the EI benefits; in times of high unemployment, the benefits exceed the premiums. As a result, the EI program is approximately self-financing over the duration of the average business cycle (6 to 7 years).

EI gives incentives to remain in seasonal jobs and in areas with poor employment prospects and to take EI-financed holidays. Saying that the EI system encourages behaviour that increases unemployment and reduces regional mobility does not say that the unemployed themselves are responsible for the "abuses" of the system that lead to these results. The responsibility lies with the people who designed the incentives and those who strive to preserve them. It is they who can alter the system to make it deliver the intended benefits with fewer incentives for undesired behaviour.

A number of changes have been made during the 1990s. Some respond to the criticisms noted above. For example, rules for qualifying to receive benefits have been tightened, and extended coverage and additional assistance provided for individuals attending approved training courses. Other changes worked in the opposite direction, by expanding coverage into areas some critics had argued were better handled outside of the EI program (for example, expanded parental and sickness benefits).

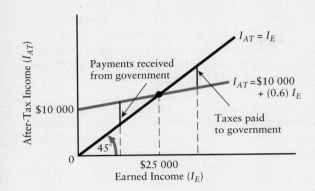

Note that the NIT is a progressive tax, despite the *constant* marginal income-tax rate. To see this, note that a household's *average* tax rate is equal to the total taxes paid divided by total earned income. If I_E is earned income, then

$$\text{Average Tax Rate} = \frac{(0.40) \times I_E - \$10\,000}{I_E}$$

$$= (0.40) - \frac{\$10\,000}{I_E}$$

Thus the average tax rate for the household rises as earned income rises, but the average tax rate is *always less* than the marginal tax rate (40 percent). That the average tax rate rises with earned income means that higher-income households pay a larger fraction of their income in taxes than is paid by lower-income households—that is, the NIT is progressive.

Supporters of the NIT believe that it would be an effective tool for reducing poverty. The NIT provides a minimum level of income as a matter of right, not of charity, and it does so without removing the work incentives for people who are eligible for payments; every dollar earned adds to the after-tax income of the family. Poverty traps are avoided.

One step toward the NIT was taken in 1987 when the personal income-tax system was reformed. In those reforms, many personal exemptions were replaced with tax credits. An exemption reduces an individual's taxable income, whereas a tax credit reduces taxes payable by the amount of the credit. At present, however, the tax credit is not refundable— the credit can be used to reduce taxes payable to zero, but cannot be used to reduce taxes payable to a negative number. Thus, if an individual has taxes payable equal to $5000 and then receives a $6000 tax credit, total taxes payable fall only to zero—any remaining credit ($1000) cannot be claimed back from the government. If the tax credit were fully refundable, however, someone whose taxes on earned income were less than the tax credit would receive the difference from the government. This would be a negative income tax.

Retirement Benefits

There are essentially three components of the system of retirement benefits. These are the Canada Pension Plan (CPP), retirement income support programs such as Old Age Security (OAS) and Guaranteed Income Supplement (GIS), and tax-assisted saving plans.

The Canada Pension Plan (CPP).   The CPP provides a basic level of retirement income for all Canadians who have contributed to it over their working lives. (A separate but similar scheme exists in Quebec, the Quebec Pension Plan or QPP.) Unlike some private programs, the pension provided by the CPP is portable—changing jobs does not cause any loss of eligibility. Crucial to understanding the problems faced by the CPP is recognizing that the payments to current retirees are financed by the contributions made by those currently working.

Given the "pay-as-you-go" nature of the Canada Pension Plan, it was inevitable that the CPP would encounter financing problems as the population aged. As the oldest members of the baby boom begin to retire around 2010, the ratio of retirees to contributors will rise rapidly. There will not be enough young workers contributing to the CPP fund to keep the benefits at the generous level received by the current generation of retirees. For young (and even middle-aged) workers today, the CPP is not the good "investment" that it was for people who retired in the past 20 years.

This inevitable financing crisis has led to a great deal of concern, expressed both by young workers and by politicians. By the middle of 1998, politicians of all stripes were discussing the problem. The solution is by no means clear. One alternative is to reduce

See Chapter 18 of
www.pearsoned.ca/lipsey to read Paul
Martin's arguments about reforming
the CPP: "Regaining Canada's Fiscal
Levers," *World Economic Affairs.*

See Chapter 18 of
www.pearsoned.ca/lipsey for an inter-
esting discussion of reforms in
Hungary's pension system: Antal
Deutsch, "Pension Reform for
Beginners: The Hungarian Case,"
World Economic Affairs.

benefit payments to retirees. This option, for obvious reasons, is opposed by elderly people who view their current benefits as a contractual obligation of the government. A second alternative is to raise workers' contributions to the CPP fund. The problem with this option, however, is that it worsens what is already a poor "investment" in the eyes of the current young workers. In 1998 the Canadian government introduced modest changes to the CPP, involving both slight reductions in benefit rates and slight increases in contribution rates. Many economists think that the 1998 changes will not be enough to save the CPP.

A third option, one that is getting increasing attention, is the movement toward "privatizing" the Canada Pension Plan. This could be accomplished by having working individuals contribute to privately managed accounts rather than to the CPP fund. In this way, the funds set aside by individuals during their working years would be used to directly finance their retirement—a so-called fully funded pension system. This option would largely solve the problem as seen by the current generation of workers, but it would still require someone (presumably the taxpayers) to finance the pensions of the current retirees and those in the near future.

Retirement Income-Support Programs.   The existing public benefits system for the elderly is in many ways analogous to the child benefits system. There are three parts to the system. First, a universal benefit called the Old Age Security (OAS) program, acts much like the family allowance. Under the OAS program, the government sends out monthly benefit cheques to each Canadian over the qualifying age of 65. Since 1989, however, OAS payments to relatively wealthy individuals have been recaptured by means of a tax "clawback."

Second, in calculating the personal nonrefundable tax credit, provisions available to the elderly serve to reduce their taxes payable. These include a credit available to anyone 65 or older and a pension income credit that offsets the taxes due on the first $1000 of pension income.

Third, an income-tested program, called the Guaranteed Income Supplement (GIS), provides benefits targeted to the low-income elderly. (In some provinces this is supplemented by further targeted assistance.) The GIS provides for most of the progressivity that arises in the elderly benefits system.

Tax-Assisted Saving Plans.   The CPP, OAS, and GIS are programs which involve direct spending on the part of the government. But the government has also introduced programs that require no direct government spending but instead rely on *tax expenditures* (i.e., tax reductions). These tax expenditures are designed to provide incentives for individuals to save more for their retirement. There are essentially two types of programs. The first is through Registered Retirement Savings Plans (RRSPs) and the second is through employer-sponsored Registered Pension Plans (RPPs).

RRSPs provide an incentive for individuals to provide for their own retirement, either because they are not covered by a company plan or because they wish to supplement their company plan. Funds contributed are deductible from taxable income but become fully taxable when they are withdrawn. It is thus a tax deferral plan, and as such it is more valuable the higher one's current taxable income and the lower one's expected future income.

Individuals without RRSPs may still receive some tax assistance for saving if their employer has a Registered Pension Plan. In this case, contributions to the company pension plan (which are often mandatory and are withdrawn directly from the regular paycheque) are tax deductible in a manner similar to an RRSP contribution.

Evaluating the Role of Government

Almost everyone agrees that the government has a major role to play in the economy because of the many sources of possible market failure. Yet there is no consensus that the present level of government intervention is the correct one.

Public Versus Private Sector

When the government raises money by taxation and spends it on an activity, it increases the spending of the public sector and decreases that of the private sector. Since the public sector and the private sector spend on different things, the government is changing the allocation of resources. Is this change good or bad? Should there be more schools and fewer houses or more houses and fewer schools?

For all goods that are produced and sold on the market, consumers' demand has a significant influence on the relative prices and quantities produced and thus on the allocation of the nation's resources. But no market provides relative prices for private houses versus public schools; thus, the choice between allowing money to be spent in the private sector and allowing it to be spent for public goods is a matter to be decided by Parliament and other legislative bodies.

John Kenneth Galbraith's 1958 bestseller, *The Affluent Society*, proclaimed that a correct assignment of marginal utilities would show them to be higher for an extra dollar's worth of public parks, clean water, and education than for an extra dollar's worth of television sets, shampoo, or automobiles. In Galbraith's view, the political process often fails to translate preferences for public goods into effective action; thus more resources are devoted to the private sector and fewer to the public sector than would be the case if the political mechanism were as effective as the market.

The alternative view has many supporters, who agree with Nobel Laureate James Buchanan that society has already reached a point where the value of the *marginal* dollar spent by government is less than the value of that dollar left in the hands of households or firms. These people argue that because bureaucrats are spending other people's money, they care very little about a few million or billion dollars here or there. They have only a weak sense of the opportunity cost of public expenditure and, thus, tend to spend beyond the point where marginal benefits equal marginal costs.

See Chapter 18 of www.pearsoned.ca/lipsey for an interview with John Kenneth Galbraith: "Unconventional Wisdom," *World Economic Affairs.*

Scope of Government Activity

One of the most difficult problems for the student of the Canadian economic system is to maintain the appropriate perspective about the scope of government activity in the market economy. On the one hand, there are tens of thousands of laws, regulations, and policies that affect firms and households. Many people believe that a general reduction in the role of government is both possible and desirable. On the other hand, private decision makers still have an enormous amount of discretion about what they do and how they do it.

One pitfall is to become so impressed (or obsessed) with the many ways in which government activity impinges on the individual that one fails to see that these only make changes—sometimes large, but often small—in market signals in a system that basically leaves individuals free to make their own decisions. It is in the private sector that most individuals choose their occupations, earn their living, spend their incomes, and live their lives. In this sector too, firms are formed, choose products, live, grow, and sometimes die.

A different pitfall is to fail to see that a significant share of the taxes paid by the private sector is used to buy goods and services that add to the welfare of individuals. By and large, the public sector complements the private sector, doing things the private sector would leave undone or would do differently. For example, Canadians pay taxes that are used to finance expenditures on health and education. But certainly Canadians would continue to use hospitals and attend schools even if the various levels of government did not provide these goods, and instead left more money in peoples' pockets. Thus, in many cases, the government is levying taxes to raise money to finance goods that people would have purchased anyway. To recognize that we often benefit directly from public expenditure in no way denies that there is often waste, and sometimes worse, in public expenditure.

Evolution of Policy

Public policies in operation at any time are not the result of a single master plan that specifies precisely where and how the public sector shall seek to complement or interfere with the workings of the market mechanism. Rather, as individual problems arise, governments attempt to meet them by passing appropriate legislation to deal with the problem. These laws stay on the books, and some become obsolete and unenforceable. This pattern is generally true of systems of law.

Many anomalies exist in our economic policies; for example, laws designed to support the incomes of small farmers have created some agricultural millionaires, and commissions created to ensure competition between firms often end up creating and protecting monopolies. Neither individual policies nor whole programs are above criticism.

In a society that elects its policy makers at regular intervals, however, the majority view on the amount of government intervention that is desirable will have some considerable influence on the amount of intervention that actually occurs. Fundamentally, a free-market system is retained because it is valued for its lack of coercion and its ability to do much of the allocating of society's resources better than any known alternative. But we are not mesmerized by it; we feel free to intervene in pursuit of a better world in which to live. We also recognize, however, that sometimes intervention has proved ineffective or even counterproductive.

SUMMARY

Taxation in Canada   ⓁⓄ①②

- Although the main purpose of the tax system is to raise revenue, tax policy is potentially a powerful device for income redistribution because the progressivity of different kinds of taxes varies greatly.
- The most important taxes in Canada are the personal income tax, the corporate income tax, excise and sales taxes (including the nation-wide GST), and property taxes.

- The progressivity of a tax is determined by how the average tax rate (taxes paid divided by income) changes as income changes. If the average tax rate rises as income rises, the tax is progressive. If the average tax rate falls as income rises, the tax is regressive.

Evaluating the Tax System

LO 3 4

- Evaluating the tax system involves evaluating the efficiency and progressivity of the entire system, rather than of individual taxes within the system. For a given amount of revenue to be raised, efficiency and progressivity can be altered by changing the mix of the various taxes used.
- The total Canadian tax structure is roughly proportional, except for very low-income and very high-income groups (where it is mildly progressive).
- Taxes often generate allocative inefficiency. The allocative inefficiency of a tax is measured by the excess burden.

The greater is the elasticity of demand, the greater will be the excess burden of an excise tax.

- There are potentially important supply-side effects of taxation, as represented by a Laffer curve. A rise in the tax rate initially raises total tax revenue; after some point, however, further increases in the tax rate reduce the incentive to produce taxable income, and so total tax revenue falls. Thus, governments cannot always raise tax revenues by raising tax rates.

Public Expenditure in Canada

LO 5 6

- A large part of public expenditure is for the provision of goods and services. Other types of expenditures, including subsidies, transfer payments to individuals, and intergovernmental transfers are also important.
- Fiscal federalism is the idea that the various fiscal authorities should be coordinated in their spending plans and should have a mechanism for transfers between the various levels of government. Understanding the relationship between the federal government and the various provincial governments is of utmost importance in

understanding many of Canada's most important government spending programs.

- The five pillars of Canadian social policy are:

  1. Education
  2. Health care
  3. Income support programs (welfare and child benefits)
  4. Employment insurance
  5. Retirement benefits (CPP, GIS, OAS, and tax-assisted saving plans)

Evaluating the Role of Government

LO 7

- Government taxation and expenditure has a major effect on the allocation of resources. The government determines how much of society's total output is devoted to education, health care, highways, the armed forces, and so on.
- When evaluating the overall role of government in the economy, we should keep three basic issues in mind:

  1. What is the appropriate mix between public goods and private goods?

  2. Much government activity is directed to providing goods and services that add directly to the welfare of the private sector (health and education, for example).
  3. We should continually reevaluate existing programs; some that were needed in the past may no longer be needed; others may have unintended and undesirable side effects.

K E Y   C O N C E P T S

Tax expenditures
Progressive, proportional, and regressive taxes
The benefit principle and the ability-to-pay principle

Vertical and horizontal equity
Direct and excess burdens of a tax
Disincentive effects of taxation
Transfer payments to individuals

Fiscal federalism
Intergovernmental transfers
Canadian social policy

STUDY EXERCISES

1. Consider an income-tax system that has four tax brackets. The following table shows the tax rate which applies to the income in each tax bracket.

Earned Income	Tax Rate in Bracket
up to $20 000	0%
$20 001–$40 000	15%
$40 001–$80 000	30%
$80 001 and higher	35%

   a. Compute the average income-tax rate at income levels $10 000, $20 000, and each increment of $10 000 up to $120 000.
   b. Compute the marginal income-tax rate for each level of income in part **a**.
   c. On a graph with the tax rates on the vertical axis and income on the horizontal axis, plot the average and marginal tax rates for each level of income.
   d. Is this tax system progressive? Explain.

2. The diagram below shows the market for gasoline in two countries, Midas and Neptune. In Midas, demand is perfectly inelastic; in Neptune, demand is relatively elastic. In both countries, supply is identical and upward sloping. The government in each country imposes an excise tax of $t per litre on the producers of gasoline. This tax shifts the supply curve up by $t.

Midas

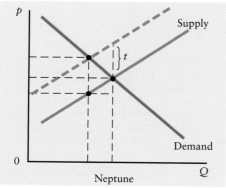

Neptune

   a. In each case, shade the area that is the direct burden of the tax.
   b. In each case, shade the area that is the excess burden of the tax.
   c. In which country does the tax cause the greater allocative inefficiency? Explain.

3. Rank the following taxes according to which has the highest excess burden relative to the direct burden. Start with the highest. Recall that the direct burden of the tax is equal to the revenue that the tax raises.

   a. An excise tax on one brand of breakfast cereal
   b. An excise tax on all breakfast cereals
   c. An excise tax on all food
   d. An excise tax on everything (which is basically what the GST is)

4. Classify each of the following government expenditures as either a transfer payment or a purchase of goods and services. Which ones clearly tend to decrease the inequality of income distribution?

   a. Payments of wages and family living allowances to Canadian peacekeepers overseas
   b. Employment insurance payments to unemployed workers
   c. Payments to provinces for support of highway construction
   d. Pensions of retired Supreme Court justices
   e. Salaries paid to government workers

5. Governments in Canada, at all levels, make considerable transfer payments to individuals and to businesses. This question will show you how significant these transfer payments are. Go to Statistics Canada's website (www.statcan.ca), click on "government" and locate the data on government transfer payments. Then answer the following questions.

   a. For the years 1993–1998, what were the federal transfers for (un)employment insurance benefits? Can you explain why they were falling over those years?
   b. Have total government transfers been growing faster or slower than GDP?
   c. Why did transfers for "family allowance" fall so drastically in 1993? (Hint: Reread the brief section on Child Benefits in the text.)

6. The Negative Income Tax has been proposed as a means of increasing both the efficiency and equity of Canada's tax system (see *Applying Economic Concepts 18-1*). The most basic NIT can be described by two variables, the guaranteed annual income and the marginal tax rate. Suppose the guaranteed annual income is $8000

and the marginal tax rate on *every dollar earned* is 35 percent. With this NIT, after-tax income is given by:

After-tax income = $8000 + (1−0.35) × (Earned Income)

a. On a scale diagram with after-tax income on the vertical axis and earned income on the horizontal axis, draw the NIT relationship between earned income and after-tax income.

b. What is the level of income at which taxes paid on earned income exactly equals the guaranteed annual income?

c. The average tax rate is equal to total *net* taxes paid divided by earned income. Provide an algebraic expression for the average tax rate.

d. On a scale diagram with earned income on the horizontal axis and tax rates on the vertical axis, plot the average and marginal tax rates for the NIT. Is the NIT progressive?

DISCUSSION QUESTIONS

1. In Canada, capitals gains are taxed at three-quarters the rates applicable to other income. Who are the likely beneficiaries of this policy? What are the likely effects on the distribution of income and the allocation of resources? Can you think of both equity and efficiency arguments supporting the special treatment of capital gains?

2. "Taxes on tobacco and alcohol are nearly perfect taxes. They raise lots of revenue and discourage smoking and drinking." In this statement, to what extent are the two effects inconsistent? How is the incidence of an excise tax related to the extent to which it discourages use of the product?

3. Suppose the government spends $1 billion on a new program to provide the poor with housing, better clothing, more food, and better health services.

   a. Argue the case for and against assistance of this kind rather than giving the money to the poor to spend as they think best.

   b. Should federal transfers to the provinces be conditional grants or grants with no strings attached? Is this issue the same as that raised in **a** or is it a different one?

4. Is the tax deduction allowed for RRSPs progressive or regressive (or neither)?

5. Due to the ageing of the population, the Canada Pension Plan is predicted to become insolvent sometime early in this century. One proposal is to increase the contributions made by workers to the CPP fund. Another proposal is to reduce the benefits paid out to seniors. Who stands to lose and benefit from each proposal? Which proposal is likely to receive more political support?

6. It is common to read articles in the newspapers by people who think Canadians pay too much in taxes. One popular concept is "tax freedom day," the day in the year beyond which you get to keep your income rather than pay it to the government as taxes. For example, if the government collects 33 percent of GDP in taxes, then "tax freedom day" is the 122nd day of the year, May 2.

   a. Does everyone in the economy have the same tax freedom day, no matter what their income?

   b. How sensible is the concept of "tax freedom day" in a country where the government provides some goods and services to the people that they would otherwise purchase on their own, such as primary education?

PART SEVEN

An Introduction to Macroeconomics

What is macroeconomics all about? What do we mean when we talk about national income, and what is the difference (if any) between national income and national output? What is unemployment, and is it a problem? Is it possible to eliminate unemployment entirely? What do we mean by inflation, and what causes it? What are interest rates, and how are they related to inflation? Is it just a coincidence that periods of high inflation are also periods of high interest rates? What is the exchange rate, and how is this related to Canada's trade balance with the rest of the world? What determines Canada's rate of productivity growth, and how is this related to overall living standards? These are some of the questions that dominate macroeconomics and that we will examine in the next three chapters.

Chapter 19 is an overview chapter that introduces all of the major issues discussed in Chapters 22 through 36. One of the central themes of this chapter (and of macroeconomics itself) is the distinction between trends and cycles. This reflects a difference between the short run—in which our focus is on the cyclical fluctuations in macroeconomic variables—and the long run—in which our primary focus is on the trends in those same variables.

Chapter 20 explains how Gross Domestic Product (GDP) measures the value of national income, national output and national expenditure. The important distinction between real and nominal national income helps to explain why measured national income can rise even though no more goods are being produced (the answer has something to do with inflation). Finally, we examine some of the things that national income does not measure. Illegal activities, nonmarket activities, and economic "bads" (such as pollution) are just some of the omissions from measures of national income.

Chapter 21 examines the important difference between the short run and the long run in macroeconomics. A central theme of this chapter is that, in response to various shocks or policy changes, the behaviour of the macro economy over a period of just a few months is different from the behaviour over a few years. This makes the study of macroeconomics very complex, but also very interesting.

CHAPTER 19

What Macroeconomics Is All About

🔵 *LEARNING OBJECTIVES*

❶ View most macroeconomic issues as being about either long-run growth or short-run fluctuations, and see that government policy enters both categories.

❷ Understand the meaning and importance of the key macroeconomic variables, including national income, unemployment, inflation, interest rates, exchange rates, and trade flows.

Turn on the evening news or read your local newspaper, and you will likely hear talk of unemployment, inflation, recession, changes in exchange rates, and productivity growth. Almost everyone cares about economic issues. Workers are anxious to avoid the unemployment that comes with recessions and to share in the rising income that is brought about by economic growth. Firms are concerned about how interest rates, recession, and foreign competition affect their profits. Few things are more likely to bring a change of government than bad economic performance.

Macroeconomics is the study of how the economy behaves in broad outline without dwelling on much of its interesting but sometimes confusing detail. Macroeconomics is largely concerned with the behaviour of economic *aggregates*, such as total output, total investment, total exports, and the price level (the average price of all goods and services). These aggregates result from activities in many different markets and from the combined behaviour of different decision makers in households, firms, and governments.

We know perfectly well that an economy producing much wheat and few computers is different from one producing many computers but little wheat. We also know that an economy with cheap wheat and expensive computers is different from one with cheap computers and expensive wheat. Studying aggregates alone may cause us to miss these important differences, but it focuses our attention on some important issues for the economy as a whole.

In return for losing sight of some valuable detail, studying economic aggregates allows us to view the big picture. When aggregate output rises, the output of many commodities and the incomes of many people rise with it. When the price level rises, virtually everyone in the economy is forced to make adjustments. When the unemployment rate rises, many workers suffer reductions in their incomes. Such movements in economic aggregates matter for most individuals because they influence the health of the industries in which they work and the prices of the goods that they purchase. This is why macroeconomic issues get airtime on the evening news, and it is one of the important reasons why we study macroeconomics.

macroeconomics
The study of the determination of economic aggregates, such as total output, total employment, the price level, and the rate of economic growth.

Growth Versus Fluctuations

Most important macroeconomic issues can be divided into two broad categories—long-term economic growth and short-term fluctuations. Broad government policies, such as monetary policy and fiscal policy, typically make an appearance in both discussions.

Economic Growth

Both total output and output per person have risen for many decades in most industrial countries. These long-term trends have meant rising average living standards. Since the early 1970s, however, average living standards have grown less rapidly than during the preceding decades of the twentieth century. Although long-term growth gets less play on the evening news than current economic developments, it has considerably more importance for a society's prospects from decade to decade and generation to generation. For this reason, many macroeconomists devote their research time to answering this question: What caused the slowdown in worldwide growth rates that began in the 1970s?

A second set of questions regarding economic growth involves government policy. Can governments do anything to promote economic growth? Do some government policies, directed to quite different goals, have unintended consequences on the long-term rate of economic growth? What is the connection between the *monetary policy* conducted by the Bank of Canada and the rate of growth of the Canadian economy? Does the adherence to a low-inflation policy have any effects on the growth rate?

The government's *fiscal policy* also enters into the discussion of economic growth. Many economists believe that when governments spend less than they raise in tax revenue—and thus have a budget surplus—the reduced need for borrowing drives down interest rates and stimulates investment by the private sector. Such increases in investment imply a higher stock of physical capital available for future production, and thus an increase in economic growth. Do government budget surpluses increase future growth? Or do budget surpluses have no effect at all on the economy's future ability to produce?

Short-Term Fluctuations

The economy's short-term fluctuations in output and employment are often called *business cycles*. What caused the Great Depression in the 1930s, when almost one-fifth of the Canadian labour force was out of work and massive unemployment plagued all major industrial countries? Why did the Canadian economy begin a significant recession in 1990–91, from which recovery was initially very gradual? What explains why nine years later, the Canadian unemployment rate was lower than it had been in almost thirty years?

Understanding business cycles requires an understanding of monetary policy. Most economists agree that the increase in inflation in the 1970s and early 1980s was related to monetary policy, though they also agree that other events were partly responsible. When the Bank of Canada implemented a policy in the early 1990s designed to reduce inflation, was it merely a coincidence that a significant recession followed? Most economists think not, though they also think that the slowdown in the U.S. economy was an important contributor to Canada's recession.

Government budget deficits and surpluses also enter the discussion of business cycles. Some economists think that, in recessionary years, the government ought to increase spending (and reduce taxes) in an effort to stimulate economic activity. Similarly, they believe that taxes should be raised to slow down a booming economy. Indeed, several government policies, from income taxation to unemployment insurance, are actually designed to mitigate the short-term fluctuations in national income. Other economists believe that the government cannot successfully "fine-tune" the economy by spending and taxing because our knowledge of how the economy works is imperfect and because such policies tend to be imprecise.

Key Macroeconomic Variables

In this chapter, we discuss several important macroeconomic variables, with an emphasis on why and how they matter for our well-being. Here and in Chapter 20 we also explain how the key macroeconomic variables are measured. The remainder of this book is largely about the causes and consequences of changes in each of these variables, the many ways in which they interact, and the effect they have on the well-being of Canadians.

Output and Income

The most comprehensive measure of a nation's overall level of economic activity is the value of its total production of goods and services, called *national product*.

One of the most important ideas in economics is that the production of output generates income.

For the nation as a whole, all of the value that is produced must ultimately belong to someone in the form of an income claim on that value. For example, if a firm produces $100 worth of ice cream, then that $100 must ultimately represent income for the firm's workers, the firm's suppliers of material inputs, or the firm's owners. Thus, the national product is *by definition* equal to the total income claims generated by the production of goods and services. In short, when we study national product, we are also studying national income. Figure 19-1 depicts national income and expenditure as a circular flow. You may recall first encountering the circular-flow diagram in Chapter 1. The concept is the same but now there are more flows to consider because we recognize the role of government, financial markets, and international trade.

There are several related measures of a nation's total output and total income. Their various definitions, and the relationships among them, are discussed in detail in the next chapter. In this chapter, we use the generic term *national income* to refer to both the value of total output and the value of the income claims generated by the production of that output.

Aggregating Total Output

To measure total output, quantities of many different goods are *aggregated*. To construct such totals, we add up the *values* of the different products. We cannot add tons of steel to loaves of bread, but we can add the money value of steel production to the money value of bread production. Hence by multiplying the physical output of a good by its price per unit and then summing this value for each good produced, we can calculate the quantity of total output *measured in dollars*.

This value of total output gives the money value of national output, usually called **nominal national income**. A change in this measure can be caused by a change in ei-

nominal national income Total national income measured in current dollars. Also called current-dollar national income.

FIGURE 19-1   The Circular Flow of Expenditure and Income

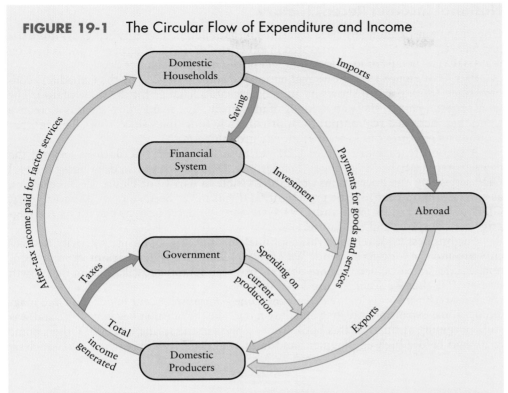

National income is equal to national product. Their flows are shown by the circular flow of income and expenditure. Consider first only the red lines. In this case, the flow would be a simple circle from households to producers and back to households. Now add the blue and green lines. The blue lines represent *injections* to the circular flow (exports, investment, and government purchases) while the green lines represent *withdrawals* from the circular flow (imports, saving, and taxes). Injections and withdrawals complicate the picture but do not change the basic relationship: Domestic production creates a claim on the value of that production. When all of the claims are added up, they must be equal to the value of all of the production.

ther the physical quantities or the prices on which it is based. To determine the extent to which any change is due to quantities or to prices, economists calculate **real national income.** This measures the value of individual outputs not at current prices but at a set of prices that prevailed in some base period.

Nominal national income is often referred to as *current-dollar national income.* Real national income is often called *constant-dollar national income.* Denoted by the symbol *Y,* real national income tells us the value of current output measured at constant prices—the sum of the quantities valued at prices that prevailed in the base period. Since prices are held constant when computing real national income, changes in real national income reflect *only* changes in quantities. Comparing real national incomes of different years therefore provides a measure of the change in real output that has occurred during the intervening period.

Since our interest is primarily the *real* output of goods and services, we shall use the terms national income and national output to refer to *real* national income unless otherwise specified.

real national income
National income measured in constant dollars. It changes only when quantities change.

National Income: Recent History

One of the most commonly used measures of national income is called *gross domestic product (GDP)*. GDP can be measured in either real or nominal terms; we focus here on real GDP. The details of its calculation will be discussed in Chapter 20.

Part (i) of Figure 19-2 shows real national income produced by the Canadian economy since 1960; part (ii) shows its annual percentage change for the same period. The GDP series in part (i) shows two kinds of movement. The major movement is a positive trend that increased real output by approximately four times since 1960. This is what economists refer to as long-term economic growth.

A second feature of the real GDP series is short-term fluctuations around the trend, often described as cyclical fluctuations. Overall growth so dominates the real GDP series that the fluctuations are hardly visible in part (i) of Figure 19-2. However, as can be seen in part (ii), the growth of GDP has never been smooth. In most years, GDP increases, but in 1981 and 1991 GDP actually decreased, as shown by the negative rate of growth in the figure.

The **business cycle** refers to this continual ebb and flow of business activity that occurs around the long-term trend. We observe such cyclical fluctuations in many economic series; in particular, they are obvious from the continual oscillations in the growth rate of GDP that we see in Figure 19-2(ii).

No two business cycles are exactly the same—variations occur in duration and magnitude. Some expansions are long and drawn out, like the one that began in 1992 and was still continuing at the time this book went to press in the spring of 2000. Others come to an end before high employment and industrial capacity are reached. Nonetheless,

business cycle
Fluctuations of national income around its trend value that follow a wavelike pattern.

FIGURE 19-2   Growth and Fluctuations in Real GDP, 1960–1998

(i) Annual real GDP

(ii) Annual rate of growth of real GDP

Real GDP measures the quantity of total output produced by the nation's economy over the period of a year. Real GDP is plotted in part (i). It has risen steadily since 1960, with only a few interruptions. This demonstrates the long-term growth of the Canadian economy.

Short-term fluctuations are obscured by the long-term trend in part (i) but are highlighted in part (ii). The growth rate fluctuates considerably from year to year. The long-term upward trend of real GDP shows up in part (i) because most of the observations in part (ii) are positive.

(*Source:* These data are available on Statistics Canada's website: www.statcan.ca.)

fluctuations are systematic enough that it is useful to identify common factors in each of the four phases. These factors are outlined in *Applying Economic Concepts 19-1.*

Potential Output and the Output Gap

Actual national output represents what the economy *actually* produces. An important related concept is *potential* output, which measures what the economy could produce if all resources—land, labour, and productive capacity—were employed at their normal levels of utilization. This concept is usually referred to as **potential output** (but is sometimes called *full-employment output*).[1] Its symbol, Y^*, distinguishes it from actual output, indicated by Y.

The **output gap** (sometimes called the *GDP gap*) measures the difference between potential output and actual output. The gap is calculated by subtracting potential output from actual output ($Y - Y^*$). The output gap is thus positive when actual output exceeds potential output and it is negative when actual output is less than potential output.

When actual output is less than potential output, the gap measures the market value of goods and services that are not produced because the economy's resources are not fully employed. The goods and services that are not produced when the economy is operating below Y^* are permanently lost to the economy. When the economy is operating below its potential level of output—that is, when Y is less than Y^*—the output gap is called a **recessionary gap.**

In booms, actual output exceeds potential output. Actual output can exceed potential output because potential output is defined for a *normal* rate of utilization of factors of production, and there are many ways in which these normal rates can be exceeded temporarily. Labour may work longer hours than normal; factories may operate an extra shift or delay closing for routine repairs and maintenance. Although these expedients are only temporary, they are effective in the short term. When actual GDP exceeds potential GDP, there is often upward pressure on prices. Thus, when Y exceeds Y^*, we say the output gap is an **inflationary gap.**

When actual output is less than potential output, there is a recessionary gap. When actual output exceeds potential output, there is an inflationary gap.

Figure 19-3 shows potential GDP for the years since 1965. The upward trend reflects the growth in the productive capacity of the Canadian economy over this period. The figure also shows actual GDP (reproduced from Figure 19-2), which has kept approximately in step with potential GDP. The distance between the two, which is the output gap, is plotted in part (ii) of Figure 19-3. Fluctuations in economic activity are apparent from fluctuations in the size of the gap. The loss in production from unemployed resources over any time span is indicated by the overall amount of the gap over that time span. It is shown in part (ii) of the figure by the shaded area between the curve and the zero line, which represents the equality of actual output with potential output.

Why National Income Matters

National income is an important measure of economic performance in both the short run and the long run. Short-run movements in the business cycle receive the most attention in politics and in the press, but most economists agree that long-term growth—as reflected by the growth of *potential GDP*—is in many ways the more important of the two.

---

[1]The words *real* and *actual* have similar meanings in everyday usage. When national income is measured, however, their meanings are different. *Real* national income is distinguished from *nominal* national income; and *actual* national income is distinguished from *potential* national income. The latter both refer to *real* measures of national income.

APPLYING ECONOMIC CONCEPTS 19-1

The Terminology of Business Cycles

The accompanying figure shows a stylized business cycle, with real GDP fluctuating around a steadily rising level of potential GDP—the economy's normal capacity to produce output. We begin our discussion of terminology with a trough.

A *trough* is characterized by unemployed resources and a level of output that is low in relation to the economy's capacity to produce. There is thus a substantial amount of unused productive capacity. Business profits are low; for some individual companies, they are negative. Confidence about economic prospects in the immediate future is lacking, and, as a result, many firms are unwilling to risk making new investments.

The process of *recovery* moves the economy out of a trough. The characteristics of a recovery, or expansion, are

many: Run-down equipment is replaced; employment, income, and consumer spending all begin to rise; and expectations become more favourable. Investments that once seemed risky may be undertaken as firms become more optimistic about future business prospects. Production can be increased with relative ease merely by reemploying the existing unused capacity and unemployed labour.

Eventually the recovery comes to a *peak* at the top of the cycle. At the peak, existing capacity is used to a high degree; labour shortages may develop, particularly in categories of key skills, and shortages of essential raw materials are likely. As shortages develop in more and more markets, a situation of general excess demand develops. Costs rise, but because prices rise also, business remains profitable.

Peaks are eventually followed by *recessions*. A **recession**, or contraction, is a downturn in economic activity. Common usage defines a recession as a fall in real GDP for two successive quarters. As output falls, so do employment and households' incomes. Profits drop, and some firms encounter financial difficulties. Investments that looked profitable with the expectation of continually rising income now appear unprofitable. It may not even be worth replacing capital goods as they wear out because unused capacity is increasing steadily. In historical discussions, a recession that is deep and long-lasting is often called a **depression**.

These terms are nontechnical but descriptive. The entire falling half of the cycle is often called a *slump*, and the entire rising half is often called a *boom*.

---

recession A downturn in the level of economic activity. Often defined precisely as two consecutive quarters in which real GDP falls.

depression A persistent period of very low economic activity with very high unemployment and high excess capacity.

Short-Term Fluctuations.   Recessions are associated with unemployment and lost output. When actual GDP is below potential GDP, economic waste and human suffering result from the failure to use the economy's resources (including its human resources) at their normal intensity of use.

Booms, although associated with high employment and high output, can bring problems of their own. When actual GDP exceeds potential GDP, inflationary pressure usually ensues, causing serious concern for any government that is committed to keeping the inflation rate low.

Long-Term Growth.   The long-run trend in real per capita national income is an important determinant of improvements in a society's overall standard of living. When income per person grows, each generation can expect, on average, to be better off than preceding ones. For example, if real per capita income grows at the relatively modest rate of 1.5

percent per year, the average person's lifetime income will be about *twice* that of his or her grandparents.[2]

In the long run, national income per person can grow for two reasons. One is growth in the amount of output produced per unit of input. It is this growth in *productivity* that has generally eliminated the low living standards that prevailed at the start of the Industrial Revolution two hundred years ago. A second source of growth in per capita income arises from changes in the amount of capital and labour supplied in the economy. If people work more hours, they will produce more output. If there are more machines and factories in operation, more output will be produced. The difference between productivity growth and the growth in the number of inputs is important. When productivity increases, more output is obtained for a given amount of effort. When total inputs increase, more output is obtained by using more resources. Income rises, but people (and other resources) are working harder.

In Canada, much of the growth in per capita income during the past three decades has been due to increases in the amounts of input of labour and capital. A relatively small part of that growth, compared to the trend of the rest of the century, is attributed to growth in productivity. This slowdown in productivity growth has created new interest in the sources of long-term growth, a subject that is one of the major themes in our discussion of macroeconomics.

Finally, it is important to remember that although economic growth makes people better off *on average*, it does not necessarily make *every* individual better off—the benefits of growth do not typically fall evenly on all members of the population. For example, if growth involves significant changes in the structure of the economy, such as a shift away from agriculture and toward manufacturing (as happened in the first part of this century), then these changes will hurt some people for extended periods of time.

Employment, Unemployment, and the Labour Force

National income and employment are closely related. If more is to be produced, either more workers must be used in production, or existing workers must produce more. The first change means a rise in employment;

FIGURE 19-3 Potential GDP and the Output Gap, 1965–1998

(i) Potential and actual GDP

(ii) The GDP gap

Potential and actual GDP both display an upward trend. The output gap measures the difference between an economy's potential output and its actual output; the gap is expressed here as a percentage of potential output. Since 1965, potential and actual GDP have increased by more than three times. The distance between the two is the output gap, which shows clearly the cyclical behaviour. Shaded regions in part (ii) show recessionary gaps.

(*Source:* Data for potential GDP provided by the Bank of Canada.)

---

[2]We discuss several reasons in Chapter 20 why national income is not a perfect measure of well-being. The main reason is that there are many things—like leisure, non-market production, and environmental degradation—that affect our well-being but are not captured in measures of national income.

employment   The number of persons 15 years of age and older who hold jobs.

unemployment   The number of persons 15 years of age and older who are not employed and are actively searching for a job.

labour force   The total number of persons employed in both civilian and military jobs, plus the number of persons who are unemployed.

unemployment rate   Unemployment expressed as a percentage of the labour force, denoted U.

full employment   Employment that is sufficient to produce the economy's potential output; at full employment, all remaining unemployment is frictional and structural.

the second means a rise in output per person employed, which, as we have seen, is a rise in productivity. In the short run—a span of several months—changes in productivity tend to be very small; thus, most changes in output are accomplished by changes in employment. Over the long run, however, changes in both productivity and employment are significant.

Employment denotes the number of adult workers (defined in Canada as workers aged 15 and over) who hold jobs. **Unemployment** denotes the number of adult workers who are not employed but who are actively searching for a job. The **labour force** is the total number of people who are either employed or unemployed. The **unemployment rate** is equal to the number of unemployed people expressed as a fraction of the labour force—it represents the fraction of people wanting jobs who do not currently have one.

$$\text{Unemployment Rate} = \frac{\text{number of people unemployed}}{\text{number of people in the labour force}} \times 100 \text{ percent}$$

The level of unemployment in Canada is estimated from the Labour Force Survey conducted each month by Statistics Canada. Persons who are currently without a job but who say they have searched actively for one during the sample period are recorded as unemployed. The estimated total number of unemployed is then expressed as a percentage of the labour force to obtain the figure for the unemployment rate. *Applying Economic Concepts 19-2* discusses some difficulties in the measurement of unemployment.

Economists make the distinction between frictional, structural, and cyclical unemployment. But this distinction matters little to the individual who has difficulty finding an appropriate job.

frictional unemployment   Unemployment caused by the time that is taken for labour to move from one job to another.

structural unemployment   Unemployment due to a mismatch between characteristics required by available jobs and characteristics possessed by unemployed workers.

Frictional, Structural, and Cyclical Unemployment

When the economy is at potential GDP, economists say there is **full employment**. But it is important to understand that there will still be some unemployment even when the economy is at potential GDP. There are two main reasons why this is so.

First, there is a constant turnover of individuals in given jobs and a constant change in job opportunities. New members enter the workforce; some people quit their jobs; others are fired. It may take some time for these people to find jobs. So at any point in time, there is unemployment due to the normal turnover of labour. Such unemployment is called **frictional unemployment**.

Second, because the economy is constantly changing and adapting, at any moment there will always be some mismatch between the characteristics of the labour force and the characteristics of the available jobs. This is a mismatch between the *structure* of the supplies of labour and the *structure* of the demands for labour. Such unemployment is called **structural unemployment**. The mismatch may occur, for example, because labour does not currently have the skills that are in demand or because labour is not in the part of the country where the demand is located.

Even when the economy is said to be at full employment, some unemployment exists due to natural turnover in the labour market and to mismatch between jobs and workers.

Full employment is said to occur when the only existing unemployment is frictional and structural. At full employment, factors of production are being used at their normal intensity, and the economy is at potential GDP. At less than full employment, other types of unemployment are present as well. One major reason for lapses from full employment lies in the business cycle. During recessions, unemployment rises above its full-

APPLYING ECONOMIC CONCEPTS 19-2
Problems in Measuring Unemployment

Statistics Canada measures unemployment by its monthly Labour Force Survey. What economists want to know is how many people genuinely want a job but are unable to find one. But this is not always what the official measure of unemployment provides.

On the one hand, measured unemployment overstates the amount of "true" unemployment by including some people who are *voluntarily* out of work. For example, Canada's program of Employment Insurance provides protection against genuine hardship caused by job loss, but it also induces some people to stay out of work to collect Employment Insurance benefits for as long as the benefits last. Such people have, in fact, voluntarily withdrawn from the labour force, although to remain eligible for benefits they must make a show of looking for a job. Such people are usually included in the ranks of the unemployed because, for fear of losing their benefits, they tell the person who surveys them that they are actively looking for a job even though they are not really trying very hard to find one.

On the other hand, measured unemployment understates the amount of "true" unemployment by omitting some people who would accept a job if one were available but who did not actively look for one during the week in which the data were collected. For example,

people who have not found jobs after searching for a long time may become discouraged and stop actively looking for work. Such people have withdrawn from the labour force and are not recorded as unemployed. They are, however, unemployed in the sense that they would willingly accept a job if one were available. People in this category are referred to as *discouraged workers*. They have withdrawn from the labour market because they believe that they cannot find a job under current conditions.

In addition, there are part-time unemployed people. If some people are working six hours instead of eight hours per day because there is insufficient demand for the product that they help to make, these workers are suffering 25 percent unemployment even though none of them are reported as unemployed.

The official figures for unemployment are useful, particularly because they tell us the *direction* of changes in unemployment. It is unlikely, for example, that the official unemployment figures will be rising when "true" unemployment is actually falling. For the reasons that we have just discussed, however, they can at times give under- or over-estimates of the total number of persons who would be genuinely willing to work if they were offered a job at the going rate of pay.

---

employment level. This excess amount is called **cyclical unemployment** (or, sometimes, *deficient-demand unemployment*).

The measured unemployment rate when the economy is at full employment (that is, at potential output) is often called the *natural rate of unemployment* or the **NAIRU**, the cumbersome acronym standing for the Non-Accelerating Inflation Rate of Unemployment. Although estimates of this rate are difficult to obtain, they provide a useful benchmark against which to gauge the current performance of the economy, as measured by the actual unemployment rate. Estimates indicate that the NAIRU rose throughout the 1970s, from around 5.5 percent to a high of around 8 percent in the early 1980s, and it has now fallen to below 7 percent. (We will discuss the reasons for these changes in Chapter 30.)

Unemployment: Recent History

Figure 19-4 shows the trends in the labour force, employment, and unemployment since 1960. Despite booms and slumps, employment has grown roughly in line with the growth in the labour force (which itself grew in part because of the increasing participation of women in the labour force, especially in the 1970s and 1980s).

Although the long-term trend dominates the employment data, Figure 19-4 shows that the short-term fluctuations in the unemployment rate have been substantial. The

cyclical unemployment
Unemployment in excess of frictional and structural unemployment. Sometimes called *deficient-demand unemployment*.

NAIRU   Short for *nonaccelerating inflation rate of unemployment*. The rate of unemployment associated with potential national income. Also called the *natural rate of unemployment*.

FIGURE 19-4   Labour Force, Employment, and Unemployment, 1960–1998

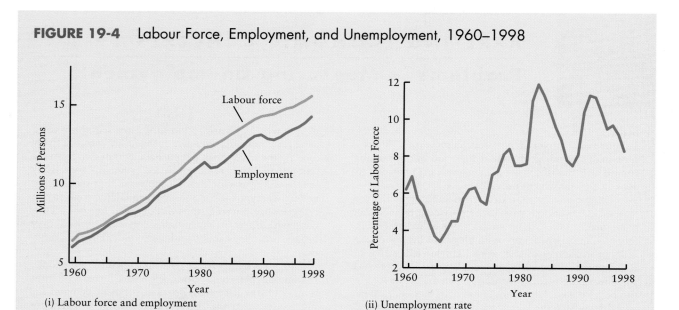

(i) Labour force and employment   (ii) Unemployment rate

The labour force and employment have grown since 1960 with only a few interruptions. The unemployment rate responds to the cyclical behaviour of the economy. The labour force and the level of employment in Canada have both almost tripled since 1960. Booms are associated with a low unemployment rate and slumps with a high unemployment rate.

(*Source:* Current labour-force statistics are available on Statistics Canada's website at www.statcan.ca.)

unemployment rate has been as low as 3.4 percent in 1966 and as high as 12.6 percent in 1982. By 1999, after the economy had been growing steadily for several years, the unemployment rate was approximately 7.5 percent, the lowest it had been in nearly 20 years.

Figure 19-4(ii) reveals an upward trend in the Canadian unemployment rate over the past few decades. For example, the cyclical low-point for unemployment in 1966 was below 4 percent, but by 1989 it was almost 8 percent. In Chapter 30 we will discuss how structural changes in the economy as well as some government labour-market policies may help to explain this upward trend.

Why Unemployment Matters

The social and political significance of the unemployment rate is enormous. The government is blamed when it is high and takes credit when it is low. Few macroeconomic policies are planned without some consideration of how they will affect unemployment. No other summary statistic carries such weight as a source of both formal and informal policy concern.

Unemployment involves economic waste and human suffering. Human effort is the least durable of economic commodities. If a fully employed economy has 16 million people who are willing to work, their services must either be used this year or wasted. When only 14.7 million people are actually employed, one year's potential output of

1.3 million workers is lost forever. In an economy in which there is not enough output to meet everyone's needs, such a waste of potential output is cause for concern.

The loss of income associated with unemployment is clearly harmful to individuals. In some cases, the loss of income pushes people into poverty. But this lost income does not capture the full cost of unemployment. A person's spirit can be broken by a long period of desiring work but being unable to find it. Research has shown that crime, mental illness, and general social unrest tend to be positively associated with long-term unemployment.

In the not-so-distant past, only personal savings, private charity, or help from friends and relatives stood between the unemployed and starvation. Today, welfare and employment insurance have created a safety net, particularly when unemployment is for short periods, as is most often the case in Canada. However, when an economic slump lasts long enough, as in the early 1980s and the early 1990s, some unfortunate people begin to exhaust their employment insurance and so part of that safety net disappears.

Inflation and the Price Level

Most people know what inflation is, even though they might not be able to define it precisely. Inflation means that prices in general are going up—not just the price of gasoline, jeans, or burritos, but the price of almost everything. If you are a typical reader of this book, inflation has not been very noticeable during your lifetime. When your parents were your age, however, high inflation was a major economic problem.

To study inflation, economists use two concepts. The first is the **price level**, which refers to the average level of all prices in the economy and is given by the symbol, P. The second is the rate of **inflation**, which is the rate at which the price level is rising.

To measure the average price level, economists construct a *price index,* which averages the prices of various commodities according to how important they are. The best-known price index in Canada is the **Consumer Price Index (CPI)**, which measures the average cost of the goods and services that are bought by the typical Canadian household. *Applying Economic Concepts 19-3* shows how a price index such as the CPI is constructed.

Price indexes compare the cost of a given bundle of goods and services purchased at different times. The base period used for the CPI in 1999 was 1992, for which the average value of the index is set to 100. Thus, when we read that the CPI for January 1999 had a value of 109.2, we know that a bundle of goods and services that cost $100 in 1992 would cost $109.20 to purchase in January 1999.

The CPI is designed to measure changes in the cost of living for the average household in Canada. Because it is based on consumption for the *average* household, it does not measure accurately the change in the cost of living for *each* household. Rich, poor, young, old, single, married, urban, and rural households typically consume goods in different proportions. An increase in air fares, for example, will raise the cost of living of a frequent traveller but not affect that of a nontravelling household.

The more an individual household's consumption pattern conforms to that of the typical pattern used to create a price index, the better the index will reflect changes in that household's cost of living.

By allowing us to compare the general price level at different times, a price index such as the CPI also allows us to measure the rate of inflation. For example, the value of the CPI in January 1999 was 109.2 and in January 1998 was 108.1 The *rate of inflation* during that one-year period, expressed in percentage terms, is equal to the change in the price level divided by the initial price level, times 100:

price level   The average level of all prices in the economy, usually expressed as an index number.

inflation   A rise in the average level of all prices.

Consumer Price Index (CPI)   An index of the average prices of goods and services commonly bought by households.

To compute the rate of inflation from any point in your lifetime to today, check out the "inflation calculator" at the Bank of Canada's website: www.bank-banque-canada.ca.

APPLYING ECONOMIC CONCEPTS 19-3
How the CPI Is Constructed

Although the details are somewhat more complicated, the basic idea behind the Consumer Price Index is straight-forward, as is illustrated by the following hypothetical example.

Suppose we wish to discover what was happening to the overall cost of living for typical university students. A survey of student behaviour in 1990 shows that the average university student consumed only three goods—pizza, coffee, and photocopying—and spent a total of $200 a month on these items, as shown in Table 1.

TABLE 1   Expenditure Behaviour in 1990

Product	Price	Quantity per Month	Expenditure per Month
Photocopies	$0.10 per sheet	140 sheets	$14.00
Pizza	8.00 per pizza	15 pizzas	120.00
Coffee	0.75 per cup	88 cups	66.00
Total expenditure			$200.00

By 2000, the price of photocopying has fallen to 5 cents per copy, the price of pizza has increased to $8.50, and the price of coffee has increased to 80 cents. What has happened to the cost of living? In order to find out, we calculate the cost of purchasing the 1990 bundle of goods at the prices that prevailed in 2000, as shown in Table 2.

The total expenditure required to purchase the bundle of goods that cost $200.00 in 1990 has risen to $204.90. The increase in required expenditure is $4.90, which is a 2.45 percent increase over the original $200.00.

If we define 1990 as the *base year* for the "student price index" and assign an index value of 100 to the cost of the average student's expenditure in that year, the value of the index in 2000 is 102.45. Thus, goods and services that cost $100.00 in the base year cost $102.45 in 2000, exactly what is implied by Table 2.

The Consumer Price Index, as constructed by Statistics Canada, is built on exactly the same principles as the preceding example. In the case of the CPI, many

TABLE 2   1990 Expenditure Behaviour at 2000 Prices

Product	Price	Quantity per Month	Expenditure per Month
Photocopies	$0.05 per sheet	140 sheets	$7.00
Pizza	8.50 per pizza	15 pizzas	127.50
Coffee	0.80 per cup	88 cups	70.40
Total expenditure			$204.90

thousands of consumers are surveyed, and the prices of thousands of products are monitored, but the basic method is the same:

1. Survey the consumption behaviour of consumers.
2. Calculate the cost of the goods and services purchased by the average consumer in the year in which the original survey was done. Define this as the *base period* of the index.
3. Calculate the cost of purchasing the same bundle of goods and services in other years.
4. Divide the result of step 3 (in each year) by the result of step 2, and multiply by 100. The result is the value of the CPI for each year.

The CPI is not a perfect measure of the cost of living because it does not account for quality improvements or for changes in consumers' expenditure patterns. For example, the use of home computers is much more widespread today than it was even ten years ago, when they would have appropriately had a very small role in the CPI. Changes of this type require the underlying survey of consumer expenditure to be updated from time to time to make sure that the expenditure patterns in the survey approximately match consumers' actual expenditure patterns.

$$\text{Rate of Inflation} = \frac{109.2 - 108.1}{108.1} \times 100 \text{ percent}$$

$$= 1.02 \text{ percent}$$

Practise with Study Guide Chapter 19, Extension Exercise E1.

The inflation rate just computed is an *annual* inflation rate, often called the *year-on-year* inflation rate. When time periods are not exactly one year apart, changes in price levels are usually converted to annual rates, the average year-to-year percentage change in prices over the period measured. For example, in May 1998, the CPI was 108.4 and in February 1998 it was 108.0. During the three months separating February and May, the CPI rose by 0.37 percent. If the CPI continued to grow at 0.37 percent every three months for a whole year, the percentage increase over the year would be 1.49. Thus, we say that over the period from February 1998 to May 1998, the CPI was growing at an *annual rate* of 1.49 percent.[3]

Inflation: Recent History

If you are a typical reader of this textbook (roughly 18–22 years old), inflation has probably not been an important part of your life experience, especially if you have lived in Canada for the past decade or so. Inflation in Canada is currently around 1.5 percent per year, and has been below 2 percent since 1992. But it has not always been so. There was a time—not so long ago—when inflation in Canada was both high and unpredictable from year to year.

Figure 19-5 shows the CPI and the inflation rate (measured by the annual rate of change in the CPI) from 1960 to 1998. What can we learn from this figure? First, we learn that the price level is constantly changing. Second, we learn that the price level has not fallen at all since 1960 (in fact, the last time it fell was in 1953, and even then it fell only briefly). The cumulative effect of this sequence of repeated price increases is quite dramatic: By 1998, the price level was over seven times higher than it was in 1960. In other words, you now pay $7 for what cost $1 in 1960.

Third, we learn that although the long-term upward trend stands out when we look at the price level, the short-term fluctuations stand out when we look at the inflation rate. The sharp year-to-year swings in the inflation rate have sometimes been dramatic. The increase in the inflation rate into double-digit levels in 1974, and again in 1979, were associated with major increases in the world prices of oil and foodstuffs and with loose monetary policy. The declines in inflation that followed were delayed responses to major recessions. Note that even when the inflation rate *falls*, as it did from 1980 to 1982 and from 1990 to 1992, for example, the price level continues to rise as long as inflation remains *positive*.

Why Inflation Matters

Money is the universal yardstick in our economy. This does not mean that we care only about money—it means simply that we measure *economic values* in terms of money, and we use money to conduct our economic affairs. Things as diverse as wages, bank balances, the value of a house, and a university's endowment are all stated in terms of money. We value money, however, not for itself but for what we can purchase with it. The terms **purchasing power of money** and *real value of money* refer to the amount of goods and services that can be purchased with a given amount of money. The purchasing power of

purchasing power of money   The amount of goods and services that can be purchased with a unit of money.

---

[3]Notice that 1.49 is slightly more than 0.37 × 4. The reason for this is that the growth rate of 0.37 percent per quarter is *compounded* when the annual rate is calculated. **[28]**

FIGURE 19-5   The Price Level and the Inflation Rate, 1960–1998

The trend in the price level has been upward over the past half century. The rate of inflation has varied from almost 0 to over 12 percent since 1960.

(*Source*: Data taken from various issues of *Bank of Canada Review* and data provided by Department of Finance.)

money is negatively related to the price level. For example, if the price level doubles, a dollar will buy only half as much, whereas if the price level halves, a dollar will buy twice as much.

Inflation also reduces the real value of anything else whose price is *fixed* in money terms. Thus, the real value of a money wage, a savings account, or the balance that is owed on a student loan is reduced by inflation.

The real effects of inflation depend to a great extent on whether the inflation is *anticipated* or *unanticipated*.

A Fully Anticipated Inflation.   We can imagine an inflation that has no real effects. There are two requirements for this to happen: first, everyone who is making any sort of financial arrangement must know what the inflation rate will be over the life of the contract and, second, *all* financial contracts must be written to incorporate the expected inflation. In this case, the real value of the financial obligations will not change when the price level changes. The real behaviour of the economy would then be exactly the same with and without inflation.

If all financial contracts are written to incorporate a fully anticipated inflation, then such an inflation will have no real effects.

For example, suppose that a firm and its workers agree that wages should go up by 3 percent in real terms. If the inflation rate is expected to be zero, they would agree to a 3 percent increase in money wages. If 5 percent inflation is expected, however, they would agree to an 8 percent increase in money wages. Five percent would be needed to maintain the purchasing power of the money wages that would be paid, and 3 percent would be needed to bring about the desired increase in purchasing power.

If all such adjustments were made, not just to labour contracts but also to life-insurance benefits, pension plans, and income-support payments, the result would be a 5 percent increase in everyone's money incomes and money assets combined with a 5 percent increase in all money prices and all money liabilities. Nothing real would have changed. People's higher money incomes would buy the same amount of goods as before, and the real value of their assets and liabilities would be unchanged.

An Unanticipated Inflation.   At the opposite extreme from a fully anticipated inflation is a completely unanticipated inflation. No one sees it coming; no one is prepared to offset its consequences. The real value of all contracts that are specified in nominal terms will change unexpectedly. Who will gain and who will lose?

An unexpected inflation benefits anyone who has an obligation to pay money and harms anyone who is entitled to receive money.

For example, consider a wage contract that specifies a wage increase of 3 percent agreed to under the assumption that the price level will remain constant. Both employers and employees expect that the purchasing power of wages paid will rise by 3 percent as a result of the contract. Now suppose, however, that the price level unexpectedly rises by 5 percent over the life of the wage contract. The combination of the 5 percent inflation and the 3 percent increase in money wages implies a reduction in the purchasing power of wages of 2 percent. Employers gain because their wage payments represent a smaller part of the value of their output than they had expected. Workers lose because their wages represent a smaller receipt of purchasing power than they had expected.

Employers and workers will be able to adjust to the new price level when they make new contracts, but some people will be locked in to their old nominal contracts for the rest of their lives. The extreme case is suffered by those who live on fixed money incomes. For example, pensions that are provided by the private sector often promise to pay a certain number of dollars per year for life. On retirement, this sum may look adequate, even generous. Twenty years later, however, inflation may have reduced its purchasing power to the poverty level. A family that retired on a fixed money income in 1980 would have found the purchasing power of that income reduced year by year until, in 1999, it would have had only 42 percent of its original value.

Intermediate Cases.   There are several reasons why virtually all real inflations fall somewhere between the two extremes that we have just discussed.

First, the inflation rate is usually variable and seldom foreseen exactly, even though its general course may be anticipated. Thus, the actual rate will sometimes be higher than expected—to the benefit of those who have contracted to pay money. At other times the inflation rate will be lower than expected—to the benefit of those who have contracted to receive money.

Second, even if the inflation rate is accurately anticipated, all adjustments to it cannot occur at the same speed. As a result, inflation redistributes income, and it does so in a haphazard way. People whose money incomes rise more slowly than prices will lose; those whose money incomes rise faster than prices will gain.

Third, even if the inflation rate is anticipated, the full set of institutions that would be needed for everyone to avoid its consequences does not exist. For example, many private pension plans are stated in money terms and employees have little choice but to take the only plan that their employers make available to them. Thus, even when inflation is predicted, some people will wind up living on fixed nominal incomes and will see their real incomes erode over time.

The Interest Rate

If a bank lends you money, it will require you to agree to a schedule for repayment. Furthermore, it will charge you **interest** for the privilege of borrowing the money. If, for example, you borrow $1000 today, repayable in one year's time, you may also be asked to pay $6.67 per month in interest. This makes $80 in interest over the year, which can be expressed as an interest rate of 8 percent per annum.

The **interest rate** is the price that is paid to borrow money for a stated period of time. It is expressed as a percentage amount per year per dollar borrowed. For example, an interest rate of 8 percent per year means that the borrower must pay 8 cents per year for every dollar that is borrowed.

There are many interest rates. A bank will lend money to an industrial customer at a lower rate than it will lend money to you—there is a lower risk of not being repaid. The

interest   The payment for the use of borrowed money.

interest rate   The price paid per dollar borrowed per period of time, expressed either as a proportion (e.g., 0.06) or as a percentage (e.g., 6 percent).

rate charged on a loan that is not to be repaid for a long time will usually differ from the rate on a loan that is to be repaid quickly.

When economists speak of "the" interest rate, they mean a rate that is typical of all the various interest rates in the economy. Dealing with only one interest rate suppresses much interesting detail. However, because interest rates commonly move together, at least for major changes, following the movement of one rate allows us to consider changes in the general level of interest rates. The *prime interest rate,* the rate that banks charge to their best business customers, is an interest rate which attracts much attention because when the prime rate changes, most other rates change in the same direction. Another high-profile interest rate is the *bank rate,* the interest rate that the Bank of Canada (Canada's central bank) charges on short-term loans to commercial banks.

Interest Rates and Inflation

nominal interest rate
The price paid per dollar borrowed per period of time.

How does inflation affect interest rates? To begin developing an answer, imagine that your friend lends you $100 and that the loan is repayable in one year. The amount that you pay her for making this loan, measured in money terms, is the **nominal interest rate.** If you pay her $108 in one year's time, $100 will be repayment of the amount of the loan (which is called the *principal*) and $8 will be payment of the interest. In this case, the nominal interest rate is 8 percent.

How much purchasing power has your friend gained or lost by making this loan? As we have already noted in our discussion of the consequences of inflation, the answer depends on what happens to the price level during the year. Intuitively, the more the price level rises, the worse off your friend will be and the better the transaction will be for you. This result occurs because the more the price level rises, the less valuable are the dollars that you use to repay the loan. The **real interest rate** measures the *real* return on a loan, in terms of purchasing power.

real interest rate
The nominal rate of interest corrected for the change in the purchasing power of money. Equal to the nominal interest rate minus the rate of inflation.

If the price level remains constant over the year, the real rate of interest that your friend earns would also be 8 percent, because she can buy 8 percent more goods and services with the $108 that you repay her than with the $100 that she lent you. However, if the price level rises by 8 percent, the real rate of interest would be zero because the $108 that you repay her buys the same quantity of goods as the $100 that she originally gave up. If she is unlucky enough to lend money at 8 percent in a year in which prices rise by 10 percent, the real rate of interest that she earns is −2 percent. The repayment of $108 will purchase 2 percent fewer goods and services than the original loan of $100.

The burden of borrowing depends on the real, not the nominal, rate of interest.

For example, a nominal interest rate of 8 percent combined with a 2 percent rate of inflation is a much greater real burden on borrowers than a nominal rate of 16 percent combined with a 14 percent rate of inflation.

Figure 19-6 shows the nominal and real interest rate paid on short-term government borrowing since 1960. Both nominal and real interest rates were high and volatile during the early part of the 1980s. During the latter part of the 1980s, nominal rates fell somewhat and became somewhat less variable, though real rates remained relatively high. In the 1990s, both real and nominal interest rates fell and stabilized.

Why Interest Rates Matter

Changes in real interest rates affect the standard of living of savers and borrowers. Many retirees, for example, rely on interest earnings from their stock of accumulated assets to provide much of their household income. In the early 1990s, as real interest rates fell to 2–3 percent (from 5–6 percent a decade earlier), many retirees experienced a significant decline in their real incomes.

In contrast, borrowers are made better off with low real interest rates. This point was dramatically illustrated during the late 1970s when homeowners who had long-term fixed-rate mortgages benefitted tremendously from several years of unanticipated inflation which resulted in negative real interest rates.

Interest rates also matter for the economy as a whole. As we shall see in Chapter 22, real interest rates help to determine the amount of investment. High real interest rates make borrowing costly, and there is less real investment than when interest rates are low. But less investment today implies less productive capacity in the future. Thus, real interest rates, through their effect on investment, affect long-term growth and *future* living standards. Changes in investment also cause swings in the business cycle. A slowdown in investment can trigger a slump; conversely, when investment increases sharply, GDP generally follows. Thus, through their effect on investment, real interest rates also affect employment and output in the short run.

The International Economy

The two important indicators of the Canadian position in the international economy are the *exchange rate*, which measures the external value of the dollar, and the *balance of payments*, which records all transactions between Canada and the rest of the world.

The Exchange Rate

If you are going on a holiday to France, you will need French francs to pay for your purchases. Many of the larger banks, as well as any foreign-exchange office, will make the necessary exchange of currencies for you; they will sell you francs in return for your Canadian dollars. If you get 4 francs for each dollar that you give up, the two currencies are trading at a rate of 1 dollar = 4 francs or, expressed another way, 1 franc = 0.25 dollars.

As our example shows, the exchange rate can be defined either as dollars per franc or francs per dollar. In this book we adopt the convention of defining the **exchange rate** between the Canadian dollar and any foreign currency as the number of Canadian dollars required to purchase one unit of foreign currency. For example, on March 10, 1999, 1 Canadian dollar was worth 3.94 French francs; expressed the other way, 1 French franc was worth 0.254 Canadian dollars. The exchange rate on that day was therefore equal to 0.254, telling us that it took just over 25 Canadian cents to purchase one French franc.

FIGURE 19-6   Real and Nominal Interest Rates, 1960–1998

Inflation over the past four decades has meant that the real interest rate has always been less than the nominal interest rate. The data for the nominal interest rate show the average rate on three-month treasury bills in each year since 1960. The real interest rate is calculated as the nominal interest rate minus the actual rate of inflation over the same period. For the most part, the real interest rate has been below 4 percent for the past four decades. Through much of the 1970s, the real interest rate was negative, indicating that the inflation rate exceeded the nominal interest rate. The 1980s saw real interest rates rise as high as 8 percent. Since then, real rates have declined again to levels that are closer to the long-term historical average.

(*Source: Bank of Canada Review,* Spring 1999.)

exchange rate   The number of units of domestic currency required to purchase one unit of foreign currency.

---

[4]Some economists use a reverse definition of the exchange rate—the number of units of foreign currency that can be purchased by one Canadian dollar. It is up to the student, then, to examine carefully the definition that is being used by a particular writer or speaker. In this book the exchange rate is defined as the number of Canadian dollars required to purchase one unit of foreign currency because this measure emphasizes that foreign currency, like any other good or service, has a price. In this case, the price has a special name—the exchange rate.

The exchange rate is the number of Canadian dollars required to purchase one unit of foreign currency.[4]

The term **foreign exchange** refers to foreign currencies or claims on foreign currencies, such as bank deposits, cheques, and promissory notes, that are payable in foreign money. The **foreign-exchange market** is the market where foreign exchange is traded—at a price expressed by the exchange rate.

Internal Versus External Value of the Dollar

We can view the value of the Canadian dollar in two ways. The **internal value of the dollar** refers to its power to purchase goods in domestic markets. We have already seen that the internal value of the dollar is reflected by the price level—specifically, increases in the price level reduce the internal value of the dollar.

The **external value of the dollar** refers to its power to purchase foreign currencies. This is reflected by the exchange rate. A rise in the exchange rate means that it takes *more* Canadian dollars to purchase one unit of foreign currency—this is a *reduction* in the external value of the dollar and is referred to as a **depreciation** of the Canadian dollar. Conversely, a fall in the exchange rate means that it takes *fewer* Canadian dollars to purchase one unit of foreign currency—this is an *increase* in the external value of the dollar and is referred to as an **appreciation** of the dollar.

A rise in the exchange rate reflects a depreciation of the Canadian dollar; a fall in the exchange rate reflects an appreciation of the Canadian dollar.

Understanding exchange rates, appreciations, depreciations, and changes in the external value of the dollar is difficult. (Many students appear to have difficulties even after studying economics for three years!) But it is important to get these concepts straight in your mind. *Applying Economic Concepts 19-4* presents the basic definitions and interpretations one more time, and uses the more familiar example of the Canadian-U.S. exchange rate.

Figure 19-7 shows two measures of the Canadian exchange rate since 1970. The first is the Canadian-dollar price of one U.S. dollar; the second is an index of the weighted-average Canadian-dollar price of the currencies of a group of major industrial countries, called the G-10. Since the United States is Canada's largest trading partner, the U.S. dollar gets a large weight in this index, and so the two series move closely together.

For the first half of the 1970s, the external value of the Canadian dollar was relatively stable, fluctuating only modestly and showing no clear trend. From 1976 through 1986, however, the Canadian dollar depreciated sharply, by roughly 40 percent over that ten-year period. This depreciation in the Canadian dollar is reflected by a rise in the exchange rate. During this period, therefore, the external value of the Canadian dollar was *falling*. From 1986 through the early 1990s, the Canadian dollar appreciated, shown as a reduction in both measures of the exchange rate. During this period, the external value of the Canadian dollar was *rising*. By 1992, the external value of the Canadian dollar had returned approximately to where it was in 1980. In the several years following 1992, however, the Canadian dollar depreciated again significantly, by over 25 percent (its external value fell from 88 to 65 U.S. cents).

What explains the considerable volatility in Canada's exchange rate? As we will see in later chapters, both domestic policy and external events have important effects on the Canadian exchange rate. For example, most economists believe that the appreciation of the Canadian dollar between 1986 and 1992 was caused in part by the Bank of Canada's efforts to reduce the rate of inflation. The Bank's policy was

foreign exchange Actual foreign currencies or various claims on them, such as bank balances or promises to pay, that are traded on the foreign-exchange market.

foreign-exchange market The market where different national currencies, or claims to these currencies, are traded.

internal value of the dollar The purchasing power of the dollar measured in terms of domestic goods and services.

external value of the dollar The value of the dollar expressed in terms of foreign currencies. The inverse of the exchange rate.

depreciation A fall in the external value of domestic currency in terms of foreign currency; that is, a rise in the exchange rate.

appreciation A rise in the external value of the domestic currency in terms of foreign currencies; a fall in the exchange rate.

International trade is very important to the Canadian economy. Exports and imports of goods and services each represent about 40 percent of Canada's GDP.

APPLYING ECONOMIC CONCEPTS 19-4

The Exchange Rate and the External Value of the Canadian Dollar

To illustrate these important relations, we concentrate on the rates that are most familiar to all of us, those between the Canadian dollar and the U.S. dollar. Recall once again the critical definitions.

The exchange rate is the number of Canadian dollars required to buy one U.S. dollar. The external value of the Canadian dollar is its power to purchase U.S. currency. Thus, a rise in the Canada-U.S. exchange rate is a *reduction* in the external value of the Canadian dollar. A fall in the exchange rate is an *increase* in the external value of the Canadian dollar.

Consider an example. Suppose you are told that the cost of one U.S. dollar is 1.50 Canadian dollars. In this case, the exchange rate is 1.50. But what is the external value of the Canadian dollar? What we know is

$$1 \text{ U.S. dollar} = 1.50 \text{ Canadian dollars}$$

Dividing through by 1.50 tells us that

$$\frac{1 \text{ U.S. dollar}}{1.50} = 1 \text{ Canadian dollar}$$

which, doing the division, is

$$0.667 \text{ U.S. dollar} = 1 \text{ Canadian dollar, or}$$

$$66.7 \text{ U.S. cents} = 1 \text{ Canadian dollar}$$

This shows that the exchange rate and the external value of the currency are the reciprocals of each other. It follows that they move in opposite directions. Thus, when the exchange rate rises, the external value of the Canadian dollar falls—this is called a *depreciation* of the Canadian dollar. Conversely, when the exchange rate falls, the external value of the Canadian dollar rises—this is called an *appreciation* of the Canadian dollar.

It may sound confusing that a fall in the external value of the Canadian dollar is shown by a rise in the exchange rate, while a rise in the external value of the Canadian dollar is shown by a fall in the exchange rate. This, however, is no more confusing than the definition of the *internal* value of the dollar. Recall that when all Canadian prices go up, the internal value of the Canadian dollar goes down (and when all prices fall, the internal value of the Canadian dollar rises).

All you need to remember is that the exchange rate tells us how many Canadian dollars are needed to buy one U.S. dollar, and the higher that number, the less each Canadian dollar is worth.

---

controversial at the time, not least because of the effect it had on the exchange rate and the many export-oriented firms who were harmed by Canada's strong dollar. We examine the link between monetary policy and exchange rates in detail in Chapters 27 and 28.

The depreciation of the Canadian dollar from 1997 to 1999 is thought by most economists to have resulted from a nearly 30 percent decline in the world prices of commodities, many of which are important Canadian exports. The decline in commodity prices was partly caused by a significant recession that started in several Asian economies in the summer of 1997—economies that are large importers of Canadian commodities. Thus, events in faraway lands can have dramatic effects on the Canadian exchange rate. We examine the link between world commodity prices and the Canadian exchange rate in Chapter 36.

The Balance of Payments

To know what is happening to the course of international trade and international capital movements, governments keep an account of the transactions among countries. These accounts are called the **balance-of-payments accounts.** They record all international

Practise with Study Guide Chapter 19, Exercise 5.

balance-of-payments accounts   A summary record of a country's transactions with the rest of the world, including the buying and selling of goods, services, and assets.

FIGURE 19-7   Exchange Rates for the Canadian Dollar, 1970–1998

The exchange rate rose—the Canadian dollar depreciated—steadily from the mid 1970s through the mid 1980s. From 1986 to 1992, the Canadian dollar appreciated; since 1992, the dollar has been depreciating. The black line shows the Canada-U.S. exchange rate, defined as the Canadian-dollar price of one U.S. dollar. The coloured line shows the Canadian dollar exchange rate in terms of ten major industrialized countries. It is expressed as an index, with the 1981 value set equal to 1. Since the United States is Canada's largest trading partner by far, the two exchange rates move closely together.

(*Source: Bank of Canada Review,* Spring 1999.)

payments that are made for the buying and selling of both goods and services, as well as financial assets such as stocks and bonds.

Figure 19-8 shows one part of the balance of payments that is most often at the centre of controversy—the balance of trade.[5] This balance, also called net exports, is the difference between the value of Canadian exports and the value of Canadian imports. As we can see from Figure 19-8, Canadian exports and imports have increased fairly closely in step with each other over the past thirty years. The trade balance has thus had mild fluctuations over the years, but has stayed at or near a roughly balanced position. Also apparent in Figure 19-8 is that Canadian trade flows (both imports and exports) began to grow more quickly after 1990. The increased importance of international trade is largely due to the Canada-U.S. Free Trade Agreement, that began in 1989, and to the North American Free Trade Agreement (which added Mexico), that began in 1993.

In Part 11 of this textbook, we explore in detail the reasons for international trade and the benefits that trade brings. At that time, we will be better able to interpret the data shown in Figure 19-8.

What Lies Ahead

This chapter has provided a quick tour of macroeconomics. The purpose of this tour has been to whet your appetite for the many complex and interesting issues that macroeconomists think about. Having read this chapter, you should have in place a basic understanding of what the central macroeconomic variables are and why they matter.

In the next chapter we discuss the measurement of GDP, and emphasize why, even though GDP is not a perfect measure of our well-being, it is viewed as the best available single measure of the country's level of economic activity. In Chapter 21 we take a brief look at the difference between the short run and the long run in macroeconomics. In particular, we see that changes in productivity and in the economy's amount of labour and capital are the main determinants of long-run changes in GDP. In contrast, short-run changes in GDP are mostly caused by changes in the economy's ability to put a given amount of labour and capital to work—the *factor utilization rate*. This difference between

---

[5]The trade balance that one reads about in the newspapers is often the *merchandise* trade balance, which counts only trade in tangible goods, but excludes trade in services such as engineering or legal services. There is no economic rationale for treating goods differently from services, and in this book unless otherwise specified, when we refer to the balance of trade we mean the balance on both goods and services.

short-run and long-run changes in GDP implies that we must think differently about the economy's short-run and long-run behaviour.

The chapters that follow lay out a short-run model of the macro economy and emphasize the determination of output, employment, and interest rates, all under the assumption that the price level is held constant. We then allow the price level to adjust to excess demand or supply and see the short-run macro model evolve into a long-run model. Once our model has been developed in this way, we will then be in a position to discuss the role of fiscal policy and monetary policy, and how the effects of such policies are generally different in the short run than in the long run.

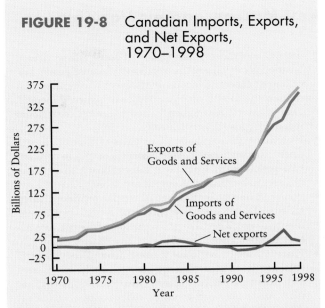

FIGURE 19-8   Canadian Imports, Exports, and Net Exports, 1970–1998

Though imports and exports have increased dramatically over the past 40 years, the trade balance has remained roughly in balance. The nominal values of imports and exports rose steadily over the past few decades, due to price increases and quantity increases. The growth of trade increased sharply after the early 1990s. The trade balance—net exports—is always close to zero.

(*Source: Bank of Canada Review,* Spring 1999; Department of Finance, Economic Reference Tables, July 1994.)

S U M M A R Y

Growth Versus Fluctuations

- Macroeconomics examines the behaviour of such broad aggregates and averages as the price level, national income, potential output, the GDP gap, employment, unemployment, the exchange rate, and the balance of payments.

- The most important macroeconomic issues can be divided into two broad categories—long-term economic growth and short-term fluctuations. Broad government policies, such as monetary policy and fiscal policy, typically make an appearance in both discussions.

Key Macroeconomic Variables

LO 2

- The value of the total production of goods and services in a nation is called its national product. Because production of output generates income in the form of claims on that output, the total is also referred to as national income. One of the most commonly used measures of national income is gross domestic product (GDP).
- Nominal national income evaluates output in current prices. Real national income evaluates output in constant base-period prices. Changes in real national income reflect changes in quantities of output produced.
- Potential output is the level of output produced when factors of production are employed at their normal intensity of use. The GDP gap is the difference between actual and potential output.
- Fluctuations of national income around its potential level are associated with the business cycle. Recoveries pass through peaks and turn into recessions that, in turn, pass through troughs to become recoveries. Although these movements are systematic rather than random, they are by no means predictably regular.
- The unemployment rate is the percentage of the labour force not employed and actively searching for a job. The labour force and employment have both grown steadily for the past half century. The unemployment rate fluctuates considerably from year to year. Unemployment imposes serious costs on the economy in the form of economic waste and human suffering.
- The average price level is measured by a price index, which measures the cost of a set of goods in one year relative to their cost in an (arbitrary) base year. The price level has displayed a continual upward trend since 1960. The inflation rate measures the rate of change of the price level. Although it fluctuates considerably, the inflation rate has been consistently positive.
- The interest rate is the price that is paid to borrow money for a stated period and is expressed as a percentage amount per dollar borrowed. The nominal interest rate is this price expressed in money terms; the real interest rate is this price expressed in terms of goods or purchasing power.
- The exchange rate is the number of Canadian dollars needed to purchase one unit of foreign currency. A rise in the exchange rate is a reduction in the external value of the Canadian dollar. The balance of payments is a record of all international transactions made by Canadian firms, households, and governments.

K E Y   C O N C E P T S

National product and national income
Real and nominal national income
Potential and actual output
The output (or GDP) gap
Employment, unemployment, and the labour force

Full employment
Frictional, structural, and cyclical unemployment
The price level and the rate of inflation
The effects of anticipated and unanticipated inflation

Real and nominal interest rates
The exchange rate
Depreciation and appreciation of the Canadian dollar
The balance of payments

STUDY EXERCISES

1. Consider the macroeconomic data shown below for a hypothetical country's economy.

Year	Real GDP Actual (billions of $)	Real GDP Potential (billions of $)	Output Gap (% of potential)	Unemployment Rate (% of labour force)
1994	768	788	—	11.1
1995	784	796	—	10.2
1996	797	805	—	9.1
1997	811	815	—	8.3
1998	825	825	—	7.6
1999	840	836	—	7.3
2000	853	847	—	7.1
2001	862	858	—	7.3
2002	870	870	—	7.6

   a. Compute the output gap for each year.
   b. Identify the periods in which there is an inflationary output gap, and those periods in which there is a recessionary output gap.
   c. Explain how GDP can exceed potential GDP.
   d. Does real GDP ever fall in the time period shown? What is the relationship between falling GDP and a recessionary gap?
   e. What is the natural rate of unemployment in this economy? What kind of unemployment exists when unemployment is equal to the natural rate?

2. Consider the data shown below for the Canadian Consumer Price Index (CPI), drawn from the *Bank of Canada Review.*

Year	CPI (1992=100)	CPI Inflation (% change from previous year)
1987	81.5	4.35
1988	84.8	4.05
1989	89.0	——
1990	93.3	——
1991	98.5	5.57
1992	100.0	——
1993	101.8	——
1994	102.0	0.20
1995	104.2	2.16
1996	105.9	——
1997	107.6	——
1998	108.9	1.21

   a. Compute the missing data in the table.
   b. Do average prices ever fall in the time period shown? In which year do prices come closest to being stable?
   c. Across which two consecutive years is the rate of inflation closest to being stable?
   d. In a diagram with the price level on the vertical axis and time on the horizontal axis, illustrate the difference between a situation where the price level is stable and a situation where the rate of inflation is stable.

3. The data below show the nominal interest rate and the inflation rate for several developed economies (drawn from *The Economist*, March 13, 1999).

Country	Nominal Interest Rate (on 10-year government bonds)	Inflation Rate (% change in CPI from previous year)	Real Interest Rate
Australia	5.61	1.6	—
Canada	5.25	0.6	—
France	4.13	0.2	—
Germany	4.03	0.2	—
Japan	1.79	0.2	—
Switzerland	2.50	0.3	—
UK	4.71	2.4	—
USA	5.19	1.7	—

   a. Compute the real interest rate for each country, assuming that people expected the inflation rate at the time to persist.
   b. If you were a lender, in which country would you have wanted to lend in March of 1999? Explain.
   c. If you were a borrower, in which country would you have wanted to borrow in March of 1999? Explain.

4. Consider the following data drawn from *The Economist* in March 1999. Recall that the external value of the Canadian dollar is the number of units of some foreign currency needed to purchase one Canadian dollar. The Canadian exchange rate is the number of Canadian dollars needed to purchase one unit of some foreign currency.

Currency	External Value of Cdn Dollar		Cdn Dollar Exchange Rate	
	March 1999	March 1998	March 1999	March 1998
U.S. dollar	—	—	1.520	1.410
Japanese yen	0.789	0.915	—	—
British pound	—	—	2.492	2.311
Swedish krona	5.342	—	—	0.176
Brazilian real	1.441	0.801	—	—
Mexican peso	6.553	—	—	0.162

a. Provide the missing data in the table.
b. Which currencies appreciated relative to the Canadian dollar from March 1998 to March 1999?
c. Which currencies depreciated relative to the Canadian dollar from March 1998 to March 1999?
d. Using the information provided in the table, can you tell whether the Japanese yen depreciated or appreciated *against the U.S. dollar* from March 1998 to March 1999?

DISCUSSION QUESTIONS

1. Explain carefully what has happened to the CPI to justify each of the following newspaper headlines.

   a. "Prices on the rise again after a year of stability"
   b. "Inflation increases for three successive months"
   c. "Finance Minister pleased at moderation in inflation rate"
   d. "Cost-of-living increases devastating pensioners"

2. Explain why during booms it is possible for the unemployment rate to increase even while total employment is rising.

3. Evaluate the following statements about unemployment.

   a. "Unemployment is a personal tragedy and a national waste."

   b. "No one needs to be unemployed these days; just look at the Help Wanted ads in the newspapers and the signs in the stores."
   c. "Unemployment insurance is a boondoggle for the lazy and unnecessary for the industrious."

4. Consider a 10-year period over which output per worker falls, but GDP increases. How can this happen? Do you think this is likely to be good for the economy?

5. When the Canadian dollar depreciates in foreign-exchange markets, many people view this as "good" for the Canadian economy. Who is likely to be harmed by and who is likely to benefit from a depreciation of the Canadian dollar?

CHAPTER 20

The Measurement of National Income

(LO) *LEARNING OBJECTIVES*

1 Recognize the problem of "double counting" and how the concept of value added solves this problem when measuring national income.

2 Understand that the circular flow of income implies three ways of computing national income—total value added, total expenditure, and total income.

3 Explain the basic methods of measuring national income, using either the income approach or the expenditure approach.

4 Understand the difference between real and nominal GDP, and why GDP per worker is a better measure of living standards than just GDP itself.

5 Recognize that many things affecting our well-being are omitted from official measures of GDP.

This chapter provides a detailed look at the measurement of national income. Once we know more precisely what is being measured and how it is measured, we will be ready to build a macroeconomic model to explain the determination of national income. Understanding how national income is measured is an important part of understanding how and why it changes. Indeed, this is a general rule of all economics and all science: Before using any data, it is essential to understand how those data are developed and what they measure.

National Output and Value Added

The central topic of macroeconomics is the overall level of economic activity—aggregate output and the income that is generated by its production. We start by asking what we mean by output.

It may seem strange to ask what we mean by output. Surely the town bakery knows what it produces, and if General Motors or Bombardier do not know their own output, what do they know? If each firm knows the value of its total output, the national income statisticians simply have to add up each separate output value to get the nation's output—or is that really all?

The reason that obtaining a total for the nation's output is not quite that simple is that one firm's output is often another firm's input. The local baker uses flour that is the output of the flour milling company, and the flour milling company, in turn, uses wheat that is the farmer's output. What is true for bread is true for most commodities.

Production occurs in stages: Some firms produce outputs that are used as inputs by other firms, and these other firms, in turn, produce outputs that are used as inputs by yet other firms.

If we merely added up the market values of all outputs of all firms, we would obtain a total greatly in excess of the value of the economy's actual output.

Consider the baker as a simple example. If we added the total value of the output of the wheat farmer, the flour mill, and the baker, we would be counting the value of the wheat three times, the value of the milled flour twice, and the value of the bread once.

The error that would arise in estimating the nation's output by adding all sales of all firms is called **double counting**. "Multiple counting" would actually be a better term because if we added up the values of all sales, the same output would be counted every time that it was sold by one firm to another.

The problem of double counting could in principle be solved by distinguishing between two types of output. **Intermediate goods** are outputs of some firms that are used as inputs by other firms. **Final goods** are products that are not used as inputs by other firms, at least not in the period of time under consideration. The term final demand refers to the purchase of final goods for consumption, for investment (including inventory accumulation), for use by governments, and for export.

If the sales of firms could be easily disaggregated into sales of final goods and sales of intermediate goods, then measuring total output would be straightforward. It would simply equal the value of all *final* goods produced by firms. However, when Stelco sells steel to the Ford Motor Company, it does not care, and usually does not know, whether the steel is for final use (say, construction of a warehouse that will not be sold by Ford) or for use as part of an automobile that will be sold again. Even in our earlier example of bread, a bakery cannot be sure that its sales are for final use, for the bread may be further "processed" by a restaurant prior to its final sale to a customer. In general, it is extremely difficult if not impossible to successfully distinguish final from intermediate goods. The problem of double counting must therefore be resolved in some other manner.

To avoid double counting, statisticians use the important concept of **value added**. Each firm's value added is the value of its output minus the cost of the intermediate goods that it purchases from other firms.

$$\text{Value Added} = \text{Revenue} - \text{Costs of Intermediate Goods}$$

Thus a steel mill's value added is the revenue it earns from selling the steel it produces minus the value of the ore that it buys from the mining company, the value of the electricity and fuel oil that it uses, and the values of all other inputs that it buys from other firms. A bakery's value added is the revenue it earns minus the value of the flour and other inputs that it buys from other firms.

Note that a firm's value added equals the value of its output minus the value of inputs *purchased from other firms*. Earnings by factors of production, such as labour income or profits, are not purchases from other firms, and hence are not subtracted from the value of output when computing value added. Since the total value of output is simply the sum of materials inputs plus earnings by factors of production, value added is exactly equal to the sum of factor incomes.[1]

---

double counting   In national income accounting, adding up the total outputs of all the sectors in the economy so that the value of intermediate goods is counted in the sector that produces them as well as every time they are purchased as an input by another sector.

intermediate goods   All outputs that are used as inputs by other producers in a further stage of production.

final goods   Goods that are not used as inputs by other firms but are produced to be sold for consumption, investment, government, or exports during the period under consideration.

value added   The value of a firm's output minus the value of the inputs that it purchases from other firms.

---

[1]We are ignoring here the role of indirect taxes, such as provincial sales taxes or the Goods and Services Tax (GST). Such taxes are included in the market value of a firm's output, but these taxes are remitted to the government and do not represent a payment to a factor of production.

APPLYING ECONOMIC CONCEPTS 20-1

Value Added Through Stages of Production

Because the output of one firm often becomes the input of other firms, the total value of goods sold by all firms greatly exceeds the value of the output of final products. This general principle is illustrated by a simple example in which Firm R starts from scratch and produces goods (raw materials) valued at $100; the firm's value added is $100. Firm I purchases raw materials valued at $100 and produces semi-manufactured goods that it sells for $130. Its value added is $30, because the value of the goods is increased by $30 as a result of the firm's activities. Firm F purchases the semi-manufactured (intermediate) goods for $130, works them into a finished state, and sells the final products for $180. Firm F's value added is $50. We find the value of the final goods, $180, either by counting only the sales of Firm F or by taking the sum of the values

added by each firm. This value is much smaller than the $410 that we would obtain if we merely added up the market value of the commodities sold by each firm.

For products that go through many stages of production, the product's final value is equal to the total of the values added at all stages of production.

	Transactions at Three Different Stages of Production				
	Firm R	Firm I	Firm F	All Firms	
A. Purchases from other firms	$ 0	$100	$130	$230	Total interfirm sales
B. Purchases of factors of production (wages, rent, interest, profits)	100	30	50	180	Total value added
A + B = value of product	$100	$130	$180	$410	Total value of all sales

Value Added = Income to Factors of Production

Value added is the correct measure of each firm's contribution to total output—the amount of market value that is produced by that firm.

The firm's value added is the *net value* of its output. It is this net value that is the firm's contribution to the nation's total output, representing the firm's own efforts that add to the value of what it takes in as inputs. The concept of value added is further illustrated in *Applying Economic Concepts 20-1*. In this simple example, as in all more complex cases, the value of the nation's total output is obtained by summing all the individual values added.

The sum of all values added in an economy is a measure of the economy's total output.

National Income Accounting: The Basics

The measures of national income and national product that are used in Canada derive from an accounting system called the National Income and Expenditure Accounts (NIEA). The accounts, produced by Statistics Canada, provide us with a framework for analysing the generation of national income. The National Income and Expenditure Accounts are not simply collections of economic data. They have a logical structure, based on the simple yet important idea of the circular flow of income, which you may recall from Chapter 19 (see Figure 19-1). The key point from the circular flow is:

The value of domestic output is equal to the value of the expenditure on that output, and is also equal to the total claims to income that are generated by producing that output.

The circular flow of income suggests three different ways of measuring national income. The first is simply to add up the value of all goods and services produced in the economy. This requires the concept of value added, which we discussed in the previous section. The remaining two approaches correspond to the two halves of the circular flow of income. One approach is to add up the total flow of expenditure on domestic output; the other is to add up the total flow of income claims generated by the flow of domestic production. All three measures yield the same total, which is called **gross domestic product** (GDP). When it is calculated by adding up the total value added in the economy, it is called *GDP by value added*. When it is calculated by adding up total expenditure for each of the main components of final output, the result is called *GDP on the expenditure side*. When it is calculated by adding up all the income claims generated by the act of production, it is called *GDP on the income side*.

The conventions of double-entry bookkeeping require that all value produced must be accounted for by a claim that someone has to that value. Thus the two values calculated from the income and the expenditure sides are identical conceptually and differ in practice only because of errors of measurement. Any discrepancy arising from such errors is then reconciled so that one common total is given as *the* measure of GDP. Both calculations are of interest, however, because each gives a different and useful breakdown. Also, having two independent ways of measuring the same quantity provides a useful check on statistical procedures and on unavoidable errors in measurement.

GDP from the Expenditure Side

GDP for a given year is calculated from the expenditure side by adding up the expenditures needed to purchase the final output produced in that year. Total expenditure on final output is the sum of four broad categories of expenditure: consumption, investment, government, and net exports. In the following chapters, we will discuss in considerable detail the causes and consequences of movements in each of these four expenditure categories. Here we define what they are and how they are measured. Throughout, it is important to remember that these four categories of expenditure are exhaustive—they are *defined* in such a way that all expenditure on final output falls into one of the four categories.

Consumption Expenditure

Consumption expenditure includes expenditure on all goods and services sold to their final users during the year. It includes services, such as haircuts, dental care, and legal advice; nondurable goods, such as fresh vegetables, clothing, cut flowers, and fresh meat; and durable goods, such as cars, television sets, and air conditioners. *Actual* measured consumption expenditure is denoted by the symbol C_a.

Investment Expenditure

Investment expenditure is expenditure on goods not for present consumption, including inventories, capital goods such as factories, machines and warehouses, and residential housing. Such goods are called *investment goods*.

gross domestic product (GDP)
National income as measured by the output approach; equal to the sum of all values added in the economy or, what is the same thing, the values of all final goods produced in the economy.

Practise with Study Guide Chapter 20, Exercise 3.

consumption expenditure
Household expenditure on all goods and services. Represented by the symbol C as one of the four components of aggregate expenditure.

investment expenditure
Expenditure on the production of goods not for present consumption. Represented by the symbol I.

Inventories. Almost all firms hold stocks of their inputs and their own outputs. These stocks are called **inventories.** Inventories of inputs and unfinished materials allow firms to maintain a steady stream of production despite interruptions in the deliveries of inputs bought from other firms. Inventories of outputs allow firms to meet orders despite fluctuations in the rate of production.

The accumulation of inventories counts as current investment because it represents goods produced but not used for current consumption. These goods are included in the national income accounts at market value, which includes the wages and other costs that the firm incurred in producing them and the profit that the firm will make when they are sold. Thus, in the case of inventories of a firm's own output, the expenditure approach measures what will have to be spent to purchase the inventories when they are sold rather than what has so far been spent to produce them.

The drawing down of inventories, often called *decumulation,* counts as disinvestment because it represents a reduction in the stock of finished goods that are available to be sold.

Plant and Equipment. All production uses capital goods, which are manufactured aids to production, such as tools, machines, and factory buildings. The economy's total quantity of capital goods is called the **capital stock.** Creating new capital goods is an act of investment and is called *business fixed investment,* often shortened to **fixed investment.**

Residential Housing. A house or an apartment building is a durable asset that yields its utility over a long period of time. Because such an asset meets the definition of investment that we gave earlier, housing construction—the building of a *new* house—is counted as investment expenditure rather than as consumption expenditure. However, when an individual purchases a house from a builder or from another individual, an existing asset is simply transferred, and the transaction is not part of national income. Only when a new house is built does it appear as residential investment in the national accounts.

Gross and Net Investment. The total investment that occurs in the economy is called gross investment. Gross investment is divided into two parts: replacement investment and net investment. Replacement investment is the amount of investment that just maintains the level of existing capital stock; it is called the *capital consumption allowance* or simply **depreciation.** Gross investment minus replacement investment is net investment. Positive net investment increases the economy's total stock of capital, whereas replacement investment simply keeps the existing stock intact by replacing what has been used up.

All investment goods are part of the nation's total current output, and their production creates income whether the goods produced are a part of net investment or are merely replacement investment. Thus, all of gross investment is included in the calculation of national income. *Actual* total investment expenditure is denoted by the symbol I_a.

Government Purchases

When governments provide goods and services that households want, such as highways and libraries, they are adding to the sum total of valuable output in the economy. With other government activities, the case may not seem so clear. Should expenditures by the federal government to send peacekeepers overseas, or to pay a civil servant to refile papers from a now-defunct department, be regarded as contributions to national income?

National income statisticians do not speculate about such matters. Instead they include all **government purchases** of goods and services as part of national income.

---

inventories Stocks of raw materials, goods in process, and finished goods held by firms to mitigate the effect of short-term fluctuations in production or sales.

capital stock The aggregate quantity of capital goods.

fixed investment Investment in plant and equipment.

depreciation The amount by which the capital stock is depleted through its contribution to current production. Also called *capital consumption allowance.*

government purchases All government expenditure on currently produced goods and services, exclusive of government transfer payments. Represented by the symbol G.

(Government expenditure on investment goods is included as government purchases rather than investment expenditure.) *Actual* government purchases of goods and services is denoted G_a.

Cost Versus Market Value.   Government output is typically valued at cost rather than at market value. In many cases, there is really no choice. What, for example, is the market value of the law courts? No one knows. But, since we do know what it costs the government to provide these services, we value them at their cost of production.

Although valuing at cost is the only possible way to measure many government activities, it does have one curious consequence. If, because of an increase in productivity, one civil servant now does what two used to do, and the displaced worker shifts to the private sector, the government's measured contribution to national income will fall (but the private sector's contribution will rise). Conversely, if two workers now do what one worker used to do, the government's contribution will rise. Both changes could occur even though what the government actually produces has not changed. This is an inevitable but curious consequence of measuring the value of the government's output by the cost of producing it.

Government Purchases Versus Government Expenditure.   Only government *purchases* of currently produced goods and services are included as part of GDP. A great deal of government expenditure does *not* count as part of GDP. For example, when the government makes payments to a retired person through the Canada Pension Plan, it is not purchasing any currently produced goods or services from the retiree. The payment itself does not add to total output. The same is true of payments for unemployment insurance, welfare, and interest on the national debt (which transfers income from taxpayers to holders of government bonds). These are examples of **transfer payments,** which are government expenditures that are not made in return for currently produced goods and services. They are not a part of expenditure on the nation's total output and are therefore not included in GDP. (Of course, the recipients of transfer payments often choose to spend their money on consumption goods. Such expenditure then counts in the same way as any other consumption expenditure.)

transfer payment
A payment to a private person or institution that does not arise out of current productive activity.

imports   The value of all goods and services purchased from firms, households, or governments in other countries.

exports
The value of all goods and services sold to firms, households, and governments in other countries.

Net Exports

The fourth category of aggregate expenditure arises from foreign trade. How do imports and exports influence national income? **Imports** are domestic expenditure on foreign-produced goods and services, whereas **exports** are foreign expenditure on domestically produced goods and services.

Imports.   A country's national income is the total value of final commodities produced in that country. If you buy a car that was made in Japan, only a small part of that value will represent expenditure on Canadian production. Some of it represents payment for the services of the Canadian dealers and for transportation; the rest is expenditure on Japanese products. If you take your next vacation in Italy, much of your expenditure will be on goods and services produced in Italy and thus will contribute to Italian GDP rather than to Canadian GDP.

Similarly, when a Canadian firm makes an investment expenditure on a machine that was made partly with imported raw materials, only part of the expenditure is on Canadian production; the rest is expenditure on foreign production. The same is true for government expenditure on such things as roads and dams; some of the expenditure is for imported materials, and only part of it is for domestically produced goods and services.

Consumption, investment, and government expenditures all have an import content. To arrive at total expenditure *on Canadian products*, we need to subtract from total Canadian expenditure any expenditure on imports, which is given the symbol IM_a.

Exports.   If Canadian firms sell goods to German households, the goods are part of German consumption expenditure but also constitute expenditure on Canadian output. Indeed, all goods and services that are produced in Canada and sold to foreigners must be counted as part of Canadian production and income; they are produced in Canada, and they create incomes for the Canadian residents who produce them. They are not purchased by Canadian residents, however, so they are not included as part of C_a, I_a, or G_a. Therefore, to arrive at the total value of expenditure on *Canadian* output, it is necessary to add in the value of Canadian exports of goods and services. Actual exports are denoted X_a.

It is customary to group actual imports and actual exports together as **net exports.** Net exports are defined as total exports minus total imports ($X_a - IM_a$), which is also denoted NX_a. When the value of Canadian exports exceeds the value of Canadian imports, net exports are positive. When the value of imports exceeds the value of exports, net exports are negative.

net exports   The value of total exports minus the value of total imports. Represented by the symbol NX.

Total Expenditures

Gross domestic product measured from the expenditure side is equal to the sum of the four expenditure categories that we have just discussed. In terms of a simple equation, we have

$$GDP = C_a + I_a + G_a + (X_a - IM_a)$$

GDP, calculated from the expenditure side, is the sum of consumption, investment, government, and net export expenditures.

These data are shown in Table 20-1 for Canada in 1998.

GDP from the Income Side

The production of a nation's output generates income equal to the value of production. Labour must be employed, land must be rented, and capital must be used. The calculation of GDP from the income side involves adding up factor incomes and other claims on the value of output until all of that value is accounted for.

TABLE 20-1   GDP from the Expenditure Side, 1998

Category	Billions of Dollars	Percent of GDP
Consumption	$536.1	59.7
Government purchases	191.8	21.4
Investment	155.8	17.4
Net exports	12.8	1.4
Statistical discrepancy	0.8	0.1
Total	$897.3	100.0

GDP measured from the expenditure side of the national accounts gives the size of the major components of aggregate expenditure. Consumption was by far the largest expenditure category, equal to 60 percent of GDP. In 1998, as in most years for Canada, net exports of goods and services were positive; thus, the other three components of aggregate expenditure added up to slightly less than total GDP.

(*Source:* These data are available at the website for Statistics Canada: www.statcan.ca)

Factor Payments

National income accountants distinguish three main components of factor incomes: wages and salaries, interest, and business profits.

Wages and Salaries.   Wages and salaries are the payment for the services of labour. They include take-home pay, taxes withheld, unemployment-insurance contributions,

For the most recent data on national income, see Statistics Canada's website: www.statcan.ca

pension fund contributions, and other fringe benefits. In total, wages and salaries represent the part of the value of production that is attributable to labour.

Interest.   Interest includes interest that is earned on bank deposits, interest that is earned on loans to firms, and miscellaneous other investment income (but excludes interest income generated from loans to Canadian governments).[2]

dividends Profits paid out to shareholders of a corporation. Sometimes called *distributed profits*.

Business Profits.   Some profits are paid out as **dividends** to owners of firms; the rest are retained for use by firms. The former are called *distributed profits,* and the latter are called *undistributed profits* or *retained earnings*. Both distributed and undistributed profits are included in the calculation of GDP. For accounting purposes, total profits include corporate profits, incomes of unincorporated businesses (mainly small businesses, farmers, partnerships, and professionals), and profits of government business enterprises and crown corporations (such as Canada Post).

Profits and interest together represent the payment for the use of capital—interest for borrowed capital and profits for capital contributed by the owners of firms.

The sum of wages and salaries, interest, and profits is called *net domestic income at factor cost*. It is "net" because it excludes the value of output that is used as replacement investment. It is "domestic income" because it is the income accruing to domestic factors of production. It is "at factor cost" because it represents only that part of the value of final output that accrues to factors in the form of payments due to them for their services. As we will see immediately, some part of the value of final output does not accrue to the factors at all.

Nonfactor Payments

Every time a consumer spends $10 on some item, less than $10 is generated as income for factors of production. This shortfall is due to the presence of indirect taxes and depreciation.

Indirect Taxes and Subsidies.   An important claim on the market value of output arises out of indirect taxes, which are taxes on the production and sale of goods and services. In Canada, the most important indirect taxes are provincial excise and retail sales taxes which differ across provinces, and the federal Goods and Services Tax (GST), which is uniform across all provinces.

For example, if a good's market price of $10.00 includes 50 cents in sales taxes, only $9.50 is available as income to factors of production. Fifty cents worth of market value represents some government's claim on that value. Adding up income claims to determine GDP therefore necessitates including the portion of the total market value of output that is the government's claim exercised through its taxes on goods and services.

It is also necessary to subtract government subsidies on goods and services, since these payments allow factor incomes to *exceed* the market value of output. Suppose that a municipal bus company spends $150 000 producing bus rides and covers its costs by selling $140 000 in fares and obtaining a $10 000 subsidy from the local government. The total income that the company will generate from its production is $150 000, but the total market value of its output is only $140 000, with the difference made up by the subsidy. To get from total income to the market value of its total output, we must subtract the amount of the subsidy.

---

[2]The treatment of interest in the national accounts is a little odd. Interest paid by the government is considered a transfer payment whereas interest paid by private households or firms is treated as expenditure (and its receipt is counted as a factor payment). This is only one example of arbitrary decisions in national income accounting. Others are discussed in *Extensions in Theory 20-1*.

Depreciation.   Another claim on the value of final output is depreciation, or capital consumption allowance. Depreciation is the value of capital that has been used up in the process of producing final output. It is part of gross profits, but because it is needed to compensate for capital used up in the process of production, it is not part of net profits. Hence, depreciation is not income earned by any factor of production. Rather, it is value that must be reinvested just to maintain the existing stock of capital equipment.

Total Income

To measure GDP from the income side, we begin with total payments to the factors of production and add total non-factor payments. That is, GDP equals factor payment plus depreciation plus indirect taxes (net of subsidies).

From the income side, GDP is the sum of factor payments *plus* indirect taxes (net of subsidies) *plus* depreciation.

The various components of the income side of the GDP in the Canadian economy in 1998 are shown in Table 20-2. Note that one of the terms in the table is called *statistical discrepancy*. This is a "fudge factor" to make sure that the independent measures of income and expenditure come to the same total. Statistical discrepancy is a clear indication that national income accounting is not error-free. Although national income and national expenditure are conceptually identical, in practice both are measured with slight error.

Extensions in Theory 20-1 provides a discussion of the way in which arbitrary accounting decisions affect measured GDP, and whether such arbitrariness matters.

TABLE 20-2   GDP from the Income Side, 1998

Category	Billions of Dollars	Percent of GDP
Wages, salaries and supplementary income	$ 471.3	52.5
Interest and miscellaneous investment income	45.8	5.1
Business profits (including net income of farmers and unincorporated businesses)	144.6	16.1
Net Domestic Income at factor cost	661.7	73.7
Capital consumption allowance	116.2	12.9
Indirect taxes less subsidies	120.2	13.5
Statistical discrepancy	–0.8	–0.1
Total	$ 897.3	100.0

GDP measured from the income side of the national accounts gives the size of the major components of the income that is generated by producing the nation's output. The largest category, equal to about 53 percent of income, is compensation to employees, which includes wages and salaries and other benefits.

(*Source:* These data are available at the website for Statistics Canada: www.statcan.ca.)

National Income Accounting: Some Extra Issues

Now that we have examined the basics of national income accounting, we are ready to explore some more detailed issues. We discuss the distinction between GDP and the related concept of gross national product (GNP), the important difference between real and nominal GDP, and some simple measures for productivity.

GDP and GNP

A measure of national output closely related to GDP is **gross national product (GNP)**. The difference between GDP and GNP is the difference between *income produced* and *income received*. GDP measures the total output *produced in Canada* and the total income generated as a result of that production. GNP measures the total amount of income

gross national product (GNP)   The value of total incomes earned by domestically based producers and factors of production.

EXTENSIONS IN THEORY 20-1

Arbitrary Decisions in National Income Accounting

National income accounting practices contain many arbitrary decisions. For example, goods that are finished and held in inventories are valued at market value, thereby anticipating their sale, even though the actual selling price may not be known. In the case of a Ford in a dealer's showroom, this practice may be justified because the *value* of this Ford is perhaps virtually the same as that of an identical Ford that has just been sold to a customer. However, what is the correct market value of a half-finished house or an unfinished novel? Accountants arbitrarily treat goods in process at cost (rather than at market value) if the goods are being made by firms. They ignore completely the value of the unfinished novel. The arbitrary nature of these decisions is inevitable: Because people must arrive at some practical compromise between consistent definitions and measurable magnitudes, any decision will be somewhat arbitrary.

Such arbitrary decisions surely affect the size of measured GDP. But does it matter? The surprising answer,

for many purposes, is no. It is wrong to think that just because a statistical measure is imperfect (as all statistical measures are), it is useless. Simple measures often give estimates to the right order of magnitude, and substantial improvements in sophistication may make only trivial improvements in these estimates.

In 1998, for example, Canadian GDP was measured as $897.3 billion. It is certain that the market value of all production in Canada in that year was neither $100 billion nor $2000 billion, but it might well have been $800 billion or $975 billion had different measures been defined with different arbitrary decisions built in. Similarly, Canadian per capita GDP is about three times the Spanish per capita GDP and is a little less than U.S. per capita GDP. Other measures might differ, but it is unlikely that any measure would reveal the Spanish per capita GDP to be higher than Canada's, or Canada's to be significantly above that of the United States.

---

received by Canadian residents, no matter where that income was generated. How can GDP differ from GNP? GDP differs from GNP for two reasons.

First, some Canadian production creates factor income for foreigners. For example, the profit generated by the Toyota factory in Cambridge, Ontario, is income generated from production in Canada (part of GDP). But some part of this profit is sent outside of Canada to the foreign shareholders of Toyota, and this part of the profit is not part of Canadian GNP. (Note that the wages earned by the Canadian workers in the Cambridge plant count as both GDP and GNP.)

Toyota cars produced in Canada contribute to Canada's GDP. But the portion of profits that returns to foreign shareholders is not part of Canada's GNP.

Second, many Canadian residents earn income as a result of foreign investments and factor services sold abroad. Income accruing to Canadian residents from activities undertaken abroad is part of GNP but is not part of GDP. For example, when Newbridge Networks, a high-tech communications firm based in Ottawa, earns profits from its production plant in Wales, those profits are returned to the Canadian owners of the firm. This payment represents income to Canadians (and thus is part of Canadian GNP) even though the production does not take place in Canada and so is not included in Canadian GDP.

The relative sizes of GDP and GNP depend on the balance between income from Canadian investments abroad and income from foreign investments in Canada. For most of Canada's history, Canada has been a net debtor country. Thus, the value of foreign-based assets owned by Canadian residents has been less than the value of Canadian-based assets owned by foreigners. As a result, the foreign-generated income received by Canadian residents is less than the Canadian-generated income going to foreigners. This makes Canadian GNP less than Canadian GDP. But the difference is small. In most years, GNP is only three or four percent lower than GDP.

Which Measure Is Better?

Given the difference between GDP and GNP, we are naturally led to ask if one measure is better than the other. The answer depends on what we want to measure.

GDP is superior to GNP as a measure of domestic economic activity. GNP is superior to GDP as a measure of the economic well-being of domestic residents.

If you want to know how easy it will be to find a job or whether factories are working double shifts or whether new buildings are going up right and left, look to changes in the GDP. By its definition, it is the GDP that tells us how much is being produced within a nation's borders. To know how much income is available to the residents of a country, however, one should look at the GNP, which counts income earned abroad and subtracts out income produced at home that accrues to residents of other nations. Thus, the GNP is a better measure of the economic well-being of a country's residents.

Disposable Personal Income

Both GDP and GNP are important measures of overall economic activity and of national income. Most important to consumers, however, is **disposable personal income,** the part of national income that is available to households to spend or to save. The easiest way to calculate disposable personal income is to subtract from GNP the parts of the GNP that are not available to households. Hence, we must subtract all taxes (both income and sales taxes), capital consumption allowances, retained earnings, and interest paid to institutions. However, having subtracted taxes, we need to add back in transfer payments made to households. In recent years, disposable income has represented about 65 percent of GDP.

disposable personal income   GNP minus any part of it not actually paid to households minus personal income taxes paid by households plus transfer payments to households.

Real and Nominal GDP

In Chapter 19, we distinguished between real and nominal measures of aggregate output. When we add up money values of outputs, expenditures, or incomes, we end up with what are called *nominal values*. Nominal GDP increased by 28.5 percent between 1992 and 1998. If we want to compare *real* GDP in 1998 to that in 1992, we need to determine how much of that 28.5 percent nominal increase was due to increases in prices and how much was due to increases in quantities produced. Although there are many possible ways of doing this, the underlying principle is always the same: The value of output in each period is computed by using a common set of *base-period prices*. When this is done, economists say that real output is measured in *constant dollars*.

Total GDP valued at current prices is called *nominal national income*. GDP valued at base-period prices is called *real national income*.

Any change in nominal GDP reflects the combined effects of changes in quantities and changes in prices. However, when real income is measured over different periods by using a common set of base-period prices, changes in real income reflect only changes in quantities. Table 20-3 shows real and nominal GDP for selected years in Canada since 1980.

TABLE 20-3 Nominal and Real GDP in Canada: Selected Years Since 1980 (billions of dollars)

Year	Nominal GDP (current prices)	Real GDP (1992 prices)	Implicit GDP Deflator
1980	315.2	535.0	58.9
1985	485.1	612.4	79.2
1990	678.1	705.5	96.1
1992	698.5	698.5	100.0
1995	806.8	767.9	105.1
1998	897.3	840.2	106.8

Nominal GDP tells us about the money value of output; real GDP tells us about change in physical output. Nominal GDP gives the total value of output in any year, valued at the prices of that year. Real GDP gives the total value of output in any year, *valued at prices from some base year,* in this case 1992. The comparison of real and nominal GDP implicitly defines a price index, changes in which reveal changes in the (average) prices of goods produced domestically. Note that in 1992, nominal GDP equals real GDP (measured in 1992 prices) and thus the implicit GDP deflator equals 100.

(*Source: Bank of Canada Review*, Spring 1999.)

implicit GDP deflator An index number derived by dividing GDP, measured in current dollars, by GDP, measured in constant dollars, and multiplying by 100. In effect, a price index, with current-year quantity weights, measuring the average change in price of all the items in the GDP.

The Implicit GDP Deflator

If nominal and real GDP change by different amounts over a given time period, then prices must have changed over that period. Comparing what has happened to nominal and real GDP over the same period implies the existence of a price index measuring the change in prices over that period—"implies" because no price index is used in calculating either real or nominal GDP. However, an index can be inferred by comparing these two values. Such an index is called an *implicit price index* or an *implicit deflator.* It is defined as follows:

$$\text{Implicit GDP Deflator} = \frac{\text{GDP at current prices}}{\text{GDP at base-period prices}} \times 100$$

The **implicit GDP deflator** is the most comprehensive available index of the price level because it includes all the goods and services that are produced by the entire economy. Implicit deflators use the current year's bundle of production to compare the current year's prices with those prevailing in the base period. The GDP deflator was 6.8 percent higher in 1998 than in 1992 (see Table 20-3). Thus, in 1998, it cost 6.8 percent more to produce the goods and services than it would have cost to produce the same goods and services in 1992. *Applying Economic Concepts 20-2* illustrates the calculation of real and nominal GDP and an implicit deflator for a simple hypothetical economy that produces only wheat and steel.

As we said above, a change in nominal national income can be split into a change due to prices and a change due to quantities. For example, from the data in Table 20-3 we see that in 1998, Canadian nominal GDP was 28.5 percent higher than in 1992. This increase was due to a 6.8 percent increase in prices and a 20.3 percent increase in real GDP.[3]

Output and Productivity

The rise in real GDP during this century has had two main causes:

1. an increase in the amounts of land, labour, and capital used in production; and,

2. an increase in the amount of output produced *per unit of input.*

---

[3]For large percentage changes in price and quantity, the nominal percentage change is not exactly equal to the sum of the price and the quantity changes; generally, the relationship is multiplicative. In this case, prices and quantities are respectively 1.068 and 1.203 times their original values. Thus, nominal GDP is $(1.068) \times (1.203) = 1.285$ times its original value, which is an increase of 28.5 percent. For small percentage changes, the sum is a very good approximation of the multiplicative change. If prices grow by 2 percent and quantities by 3 percent, the nominal change is $(1.02) \times (1.03) = 1.0506$, which is very close to 1.05.

APPLYING ECONOMIC CONCEPTS 20-2

Calculating Nominal and Real GDP

To see what is involved in calculating nominal GDP, real GDP, and the implicit GDP deflator, an example may be helpful. Consider a simple hypothetical economy that produces only two commodities, wheat and steel. Table 1 gives the basic data for output and prices in the economy for two years.

TABLE 1   Data for a Hypothetical Economy

	Quantity produced		Prices	
	Wheat (bushels)	Steel (ton)	Wheat ($/bushel)	Steel ($/ton)
Year 1	100	20	10	50
Year 2	110	16	12	55

Table 2 shows nominal GDP, calculated by adding the money values of wheat output and of steel output for each year. In year 1, the value of both wheat and steel production was $1000, so nominal GDP was $2000. In year 2, wheat output rose to $1320, and steel output fell to $880. Since the rise in value of wheat was greater than the fall in value of steel, nominal GDP rose by $200.

TABLE 2   Calculation of Nominal GDP

Year 1: (100 × $10) + (20 × $50) = $2000
Year 2: (110 × $12) + (16 × $55) = $2200

Table 3 shows real GDP, calculated by valuing output in each year *at year 2 prices*; that is, year 2 is used as the base year. In year 2, wheat output rose, but steel output fell. If we use year 2 prices, the value of the fall in steel output between years 1 and 2 exceeded the value of the rise in wheat output, and so real GDP fell.

TABLE 3   Calculation of Real GDP Using Year 2 Prices

Year 1: (100 × $12) + (20 × $55) = $2300
Year 2: (110 × $12) + (16 × $55) = $2200

In Table 4, the ratio of nominal to real GDP is calculated for each year and multiplied by 100. This ratio implicitly measures the change in prices over the period in question and is called the *implicit GDP deflator*. The implicit deflator shows that the price level increased by 15 percent between year 1 and year 2.

TABLE 4   Calculation of the Implicit GDP Deflator

Year 1: (2000/2300) × 100 = 86.96
Year 2: (2200/2200) × 100 = 100.00

Throughout this box we have used year 2 as the base year. But we could just as easily have used year 1. The changes we would have computed in real GDP and the implicit deflator would have been very similar—but not identical—to the ones we did compute using year 2 as the base year. The choice of base year matters because of different *relative* prices in the different years (note that the price of steel relative to the price of wheat is lower in year 2 than in year 1). Put simply, with different relative prices in different years, the various output changes get weighted differently depending on which prices we use, and thus the *aggregate* measure of real GDP changes by different amounts. (If you want to understand this point in more detail, try doing Study Exercise #6 at the end of the chapter.)

But if it matters which year we choose as the base year, how do we choose the "right" base year? As with many other elements of national income accounting, there is some arbitrariness in the choice. There is no "right" year. The important thing is not which year to use—the important thing is to be clear about which year you are using and then, for a given set of comparisons, to be sure that you are consistent in your choice.

In other words, more inputs have been used, and each input has become more productive. Although it is useful to measure total output for some purposes, such as assessing the total size of a particular economy, for other purposes, such as studying changes in overall living standards, it is better to use output per person, which is called **per capita output.**

Per capita GDP measures the average amount of output (and income) per person.

per capita output
GDP divided by total population.

Practise with Study Guide Chapter 20, Extension Exercise 1.

See Chapter 20 of www.pearsoned.ca/lipsey for an interesting discussion of why the computer revolution has not yet appeared in measurements of productivity growth: Jeremy Leonard, "Computers and Productivity in the Information Economy," *World Economic Affairs*.

A different way of assessing overall living standards is to consider measures of *productivity*. For example, GDP divided by the number of *employed* persons tells us the average output per employed worker. This is one measure of *labour productivity*. GDP divided by the total number of hours worked measures output per hour of labour input and provides a second measure of labour productivity.

Is the level of per capita output a better measure of average well-being than the level of productivity? The answer depends on which things determine our well-being. To the extent that the level of per capita income and consumption are the most important determinants of well-being, then per capita GDP is probably the best single measure. But if well-being also depends on the amount of leisure that we have, the level of productivity may be the better measure. Productivity improvements allow more output for an unchanged amount of input. (We can consume more without having to work harder.) In contrast, if productivity is not improving, then per capita output can increase only with an increase in inputs. (In order to consume more, we have to work harder.) In this second case, per capita income and consumption may have increased but we may be worse off overall because of the reduction in leisure.

Omissions from GDP

National income as measured in the National Income and Expenditure Accounts provides an excellent measure of the flow of economic activity in organized markets in a given year. But much economic activity takes place outside of the markets that the national income accountants survey. Although these activities are not typically included in the measure of GDP, they nevertheless use real resources and satisfy real wants and needs.

Illegal Activities

GDP does not measure illegal activities, even though many of them are ordinary business activities that produce goods and services sold in markets and that generate factor incomes. Many forms of illegal gambling, prostitution, and drug trade come into this category. To gain an accurate measure of the total demand for factors of production, of total marketable output, or of total incomes generated, we should include these activities, whether or not we as individuals approve of them. The omission of illegal activities is no trivial matter: The drug trade alone is a multi-billion-dollar business.

Note that some illegal activities do get included in national income measures, although they are generally misclassified by industry. The income is included because people sometimes report their earnings from illicit activities as part of their earnings from legal activities. They do this to avoid the fate of Al Capone, the famous Chicago gangster in the 1920s and 1930s, who, having avoided conviction on many counts, was finally caught for income-tax evasion.

Prostitution and other illegal activities involve genuine market transactions, but they are not included in official measures of national income.

The Underground Economy

A significant omission from GDP is the so-called underground economy. The transactions that occur in the underground economy are perfectly legal in themselves; the only illegality involved is that such transactions are not reported for tax purposes. One example of this is the carpenter who repairs a leak in your roof and takes payment in cash or in kind to avoid taxation. Because such transactions go unreported, they are omitted from GDP.

The growth of the underground economy is facilitated by the rising importance of services in the nation's total output. It is much easier for a carpenter to pass unnoticed by government authorities than it is for a manufacturing establishment. Estimates of the value of income earned in the underground economy run from 2 percent to 15 percent of GDP. In some countries, the figures are even higher. The Italian underground economy, for example, has been estimated at close to 25 percent of that country's GDP.

Home Production

If a homeowner hires a firm to do some landscaping, the value of the landscaping enters into GDP; if the homeowner does the landscaping herself, the value of the landscaping is omitted from GDP because there is no market transaction. Such production of goods and services in the home is called *home production*. Other nonmarket activities include voluntary work such as canvassing for a political party, helping to run a volunteer day-care centre, or leading a scout troop. Both home production and volunteer activities clearly add to economic well-being, and both use economic resources. Yet neither of them is included in official measures of national income.

Compared to developing countries, the nonmarket sector in most advanced industrial economies is relatively small, although much household maintenance, education, and child care are performed at home. The omissions become very misleading when national income measures are used to compare living standards in structurally different economies. Generally, the nonmarket sector of the economy is larger in rural than in urban settings and in less developed than in more developed economies. Be cautious, then, when interpreting data from a country with a very different climate and culture. When you hear that the per capita GDP of Nigeria is about $1200 per year (compared to about $26 000 in Canada), you should not imagine that living in Nigeria is like living in Canada with only $1200.

One extremely important nonmarket activity is leisure itself. If an attorney voluntarily chooses to reduce her time at work from 2400 hours to 2200 hours per year, measured national income will fall by the attorney's wage rate times 200 hours. Yet the value to the attorney of the 200 hours of new leisure which is enjoyed outside of the marketplace must exceed the lost wages (otherwise she would choose to work the extra 200 hours), so total economic welfare must rise rather than fall. Until recently, one of the most important ways in which economic growth benefited people was by permitting increased amounts of leisure. Because the time off is not marketed, its value does not show up in measures of national income.

Economic "Bads"

When an electric power plant sends sulfur dioxide into the atmosphere, leading to acid rain and environmental damage, the value of the electricity sold is included as part of GDP, but the value of the damage done by the acid rain is not deducted. Similarly, the gasoline that we use in our cars is part of national income when it is produced, but the damage done by burning that gasoline is not deducted. To the extent that economic growth brings with it increases in pollution, congestion, and other disamenities of modern living, measurements of national income will overstate the improvement in living standards. Such measures capture the increased output of goods and services, but they fail to account for the increased output of "bads" that generally accompany economic growth.

Do the Omissions Matter?

GDP does a good job of measuring the flow of goods and services through the market sector of the economy. Usually, an increase in GDP implies greater opportunities for employment for households that sell their labour services in the market.

Unless the importance of unmeasured economic activity changes rapidly, *changes* in GDP will probably do a satisfactory job of measuring *changes* in economic opportunities.

See Chapter 20 of www.pearsoned.ca/lipsey for an excellent discussion of the role of per capita income in determining a country's overall "human development": William Watson, "If Canada Is Number One, Why Would Anyone Leave?" *World Economic Affairs*.

However, when the task at hand is measurement of the overall flow of goods and services available to satisfy people's wants, regardless of the source of the goods and services, then the omissions that we have discussed become undesirable and potentially serious. Still, in the relatively short term, changes in GDP will usually be a good measure of the direction, if not the exact magnitude, of changes in economic well-being. *Lessons from History 20-1* provides many examples from the Industrial Revolution to illustrate the point that changes in real GDP do not always capture improvements in living standards.

LESSONS FROM HISTORY 20-1
GDP and Economic Growth

GDP is not a very good indicator of the growth in well-being that accompanies long-term economic growth. The reason is that so many of the major benefits that growth provides are imperfectly measured or not measured at all by GDP. This can be dramatically illustrated by looking at some of the most important changes that accompanied the first Industrial Revolution (1784–1870).

1. In early eighteenth-century Europe, average life expectancy was around 30 years; in France, one in five children were dead by the end of the first year of life, and 50 percent of registered children were dead by age 10. Life expectancy rose dramatically during the Industrial Revolution.

2. Industrialization reduced famine and hunger. Not only did the average food intake rise, its year-to-year variation fell. It is of little consolation to a peasant that the average food consumption is above the subsistence level over the decades if fluctuations in harvests periodically drive it below the subsistence level, thus causing starvation.

3. Technological changes that accompanied the Industrial Revolution virtually eliminated many terrible diseases that had been common until that time, such as plague, tuberculosis, cholera, dysentery, smallpox, and leprosy.

4. The urbanization that accompanied industrialization increased literacy and education and broadened experience. Before then, poverty and a rural, peasant

existence, with little or no communication between the village and the outside world, tended to be associated with superstition and very narrow experience.

5. Privacy became possible when people moved from the peasant dwelling, where the entire family lived, ate, and slept in one room, to multiroom urban sites.

6. The introduction of a market economy greatly increased the mobility of persons among jobs. In the rural societies, there were few options for employment, and customary behaviour—doing what one's parents did—dominated job selection.

7. The Industrial Revolution was based on mass production of goods sold mainly to low- and middle-income people. These changed the quality of consumption. For example, instead of wooden clogs, people adopted leather shoes; instead of rough, homespun cloth, people had factory-made shirts and skirts; instead of mud floors and thatched roofs, people had wooden floors and rain-proof roofs; instead of all living in one room, parents had a room separate from their children. These things may seem trivial to us today, but they changed the way of life of ordinary people.

Throughout the late eighteenth century and all of the nineteenth century, a succession of new products continued to alter the way ordinary people lived until, by the mid-twentieth century, the ordinary working person had a structurally different way of life from his or her counterpart in the mid-eighteenth century. Statistics, however, are the same if a doubling of GDP takes the form of twice as much of the same, or of new things that enhance the quality of life. The effect on living standards is, however, much greater when new commodities replace older ones rather than just more of the same becoming available.

This box draws on material in: J. Blum, *Our Forgotten Past: Seven Centuries of Life on the Land* (London: Thames and Hudson, 1982); F. Braudel, *Structures of Everyday Life, 15th–18th Century* (New York: Harper and Row, 1981); and N. Rosenberg and L. E. Birdzell, Jr., *How the West Grew Rich* (New York: Basic Books, 1986).

S U M M A R Y

National Output and Value Added

(LO)(1)(2)

- Each firm's contribution to total output is equal to its value added, which is the value of the firm's output minus the value of all intermediate goods and services—that is, the outputs of other firms—that it uses. The sum of all the values added produced in an economy is the economy's total output, which is called gross domestic product (GDP).

National Income Accounting: The Basics

(LO)(3)

- From the circular flow of income, there are three ways to compute national income. One is to add up each firm's value added. The second is to add up total expenditure on domestic output. The third is to add up the total income generated by domestic residents. By standard accounting conventions, these three aggregations define the same total.
- From the expenditure side of the national accounts,

$$\text{GDP} = C_a + I_a + G_a + (X_a - IM_a)$$

C_a comprises consumption expenditures of households. I_a is investment in plant and equipment, residential construction, and inventory accumulation. G_a is government purchases of goods and services. $(X_a - IM_a)$ represents net exports of goods and services.
- GDP measured from the income side adds up all claims to the market value of production. Wages, interest, profits, depreciation (or capital consumption allowance), and indirect taxes net of subsidies are the major categories.

National Income Accounting: Some Extra Issues

(LO)(4)(5)

- GDP measures the value of production that is located in Canada, and gross national product (GNP) measures income accruing to Canadian residents. The difference is due to the balance between Canadian claims to incomes that are generated abroad and foreign claims to incomes that are generated in Canada. Throughout Canada's history, GNP has been slightly less than GDP.
- Real measures of national income are calculated to reflect changes in real quantities. Nominal measures of national income are calculated to reflect changes in both prices and quantities. Any change in nominal income can be split into a change in quantities and a change in prices. Appropriate comparisons of nominal and real measures yield implicit deflators.
- Economists frequently use measures of GDP, GDP per capita, and various measures of labour productivity such

as GDP per employed worker or GDP per hour worked. Changes in overall living standards are better reflected by changes in productivity than by changes in GDP per capita.
- GDP and related measures of national income must be interpreted with their limitations in mind. GDP excludes production resulting from activities that are illegal, that take place in the underground economy, or that do not pass through markets. Hence GDP does not measure everything that contributes to (or detracts from) human well-being.
- Notwithstanding its limitations, GDP remains a useful measure of the total economic activity that passes through the nation's markets. Recorded *changes* in GDP will generally do an accurate job of measuring *changes* in economic activity and economic opportunities.

K E Y   C O N C E P T S

Intermediate and final goods
Value added
GDP as the sum of all values added
GDP from the expenditure side

GDP from the income side
GNP versus GDP
Disposable personal income
Implicit GDP deflator

Per capita GDP and labour
  productivity
Omissions from GDP

STUDY EXERCISES

1. In measuring GDP from the expenditure side (GDP = $C_a + I_a + G_a + NX_a$), which of the following expenditures are included, and within which of the four categories?

   a. expenditures on automobiles by consumers
   b. expenditures on automobiles by firms
   c. expenditures on new machinery by Canadian-owned forest companies in Canada
   d. expenditures on new machinery by Canadian-owned forest companies in the United States
   e. expenditures on new machinery by U.S.-owned forest companies in Canada
   f. reductions in business inventories
   g. purchases of second-hand cars and trucks
   h. the hiring of economic consultants by the Manitoba government
   i. the purchase of Canadian-produced software by a firm in Japan

2. The list below provides some national income figures for the country of Econoland. All figures are in millions of dollars.

Wages and salaries	5000
Interest income	200
Personal consumption	3900
Personal saving	1100
Personal income taxes	200
Business profits	465
Indirect taxes	175
Subsidies	30
Government purchases	1000
Exports	350
Imports	390
Net private investment	950
Depreciation	150

   a. Using the expenditure approach, what is the value of GDP for Econoland?
   b. Using the income approach, what is the value of GDP?
   c. What is the value of net domestic income at factor cost?

3. The table below shows data for real and nominal GDP for a hypothetical economy over several years.

Year	Nominal GDP (billions of $)	Real GDP (billions of 1996 $)	Implicit GDP Deflator
1994	775.3	798.4	—-
1995	814.1	838.6	—
1996	862.9	862.9	—
1997	901.5	882.5	—
1998	951.3	920.6	—
1999	998.8	950.5	—

   a. Compute the implicit GDP deflator for each year.
   b. Compute the total percentage change in nominal GDP from 1994 to 1999. How much of this change was due to increases in prices and how much was due to changes in quantities?

4. Would inflation, as measured by the rate of change in the Implicit GDP Deflator, ever be different from inflation as measured by the rate of change in the Consumer Price Index? Would it ever be the same? Explain.

5. For each of the following events, describe the likely effect on real GDP.

   a. The Quebec ice storm of 1998 increases the demand for building materials to repair damage to homes.
   b. The Quebec ice storm of 1998 damages many factories.
   c. The building of a baseball stadium in Montreal increases the demand for *Expos* tickets by Montrealers.
   d. The building of a baseball stadium in Montreal increases the demand for *Expos* tickets by residents of Vermont and New Hampshire.

6. This is a challenging question to give you practice in computing real GDP and implicit GDP deflators. Consider the following data for a hypothetical economy that produces two goods, milk and honey.

	Quantity Produced		Prices	
	Milk (litres)	Honey (kg)	Milk ($/litre)	Honey ($/kg)
Year 1	100	40	2	6
Year 2	120	25	3	6

   a. Compute nominal GDP for each year in this economy.

b. Using year 1 as the base year, compute real GDP for each year. What is the percentage change in real GDP from year 1 to year 2?

c. Using year 1 as the base year, compute the implicit price deflator for each year. What is the percentage change in real GDP from year 1 to year 2?

d. Now compute the implicit GDP deflator for each year, using year 1 as the base year.

e. Now compute the implicit GDP deflator for each year, using year 2 as the base year.

f. Explain why the measures of real GDP growth (and growth in the implicit deflator) depend on the choice of base year.

DISCUSSION QUESTIONS

1. Residents of some Canadian cities have recently become concerned about the growing proportion of their local real estate that is being bought up by foreign residents. What is the effect of this transfer of ownership on Canadian GDP and GNP?

2. What would be the effect of the following events on the measured value of Canada's real GDP? Speculate on the effects of each event on the true well-being of Canadians.

   a. destruction of thousands of homes by flood water
   b. destruction of hundreds of businesses by an ice storm
   c. complete cessation of all imports from Europe
   d. an increase in the amount of acid rain that falls
   e. an increase in the amount of spending on devices that reduce pollution at a major hydroelectricity plant
   f. reduction in the standard work week from 37 hours to 30 hours
   g. hiring of all welfare recipients as government employees
   h. outbreak of hostilities in the Middle East in which Canadian troops became involved as peacekeepers

3. A recent United Nations study concluded that Canada is the best country in which to live—that Canada has the best "quality of life." In view of the fact that Canada does not have the highest per capita real GDP in the world, explain how it can be ranked as the "best."

4. One way of estimating the size of the underground economy is to see the amount of cash Canadians are carrying relative to the total value of GDP. Why would a rapid rise in the ratio of cash held by the public to GDP indicate a rise in the underground economy? Can you offer an explanation for why this ratio has risen steadily since the introduction of the GST in 1991?

5. A company's wages and salaries are part of its value added. Suppose, however, that the cleaning and machinery maintenance that its own employees used to do are now contracted out to specialist firms who come in to do the same work more cheaply. What happens to the company's value added when a company follows this recent trend of "contracting out"? What happens to value added in the economy as a whole?

CHAPTER 21

Short-Run Versus Long-Run Macroeconomics

LEARNING OBJECTIVES

1 Recognize why economists think differently about short-run and long-run changes in macroeconomic variables.

2 Explain why any change in GDP can be decomposed into changes in: the amount of factors, the employment of factors, and the productivity of factors.

3 Realize that short-run changes in GDP are mostly caused by changes in factor utilization, whereas long-run changes in GDP are mostly caused by changes in factor supplies and productivity.

4 Recognize that fiscal and monetary policy each have different effects in the short run than in the long run.

We began our introduction to macroeconomics in Chapter 19 by emphasizing that most macroeconomic issues can be divided into two broad categories—long-run trends and short-run fluctuations. But what do we mean by the "short run" and "long run," and why is the distinction so important? These are the two questions we examine in this chapter. We will not go into a lot of theoretical or empirical detail—the necessary details will be presented in the following chapters. The purpose of this chapter is to introduce one very important idea: in response to a shock or a change in government policy, the economy behaves differently over several months than it does over several years.

This distinction between short-run and long-run behaviour makes the study of macroeconomics more challenging but it also makes it more interesting. The difference is often not fully appreciated by newspaper writers and TV news reporters. This chapter presents a brief introduction to this important distinction.

Practise with Study Guide Chapter 21, Exercise 2.

Two Examples

We begin by giving two examples of the difference between short-run and long-run behaviour.

Inflation and Interest Rates in Canada

In April of 1995, the Governor of the Bank of Canada, Gordon Thiessen, was interviewed by Peter Gzowski on CBC Radio. Thiessen was asked about the Bank's policy of reducing inflation, from about 6 percent a few years earlier, and maintaining it since then between 1 percent and 3 percent annually. Thiessen argued that the high nominal interest rates of the past were caused mostly by high inflation. The main reason for this connection between inflation and nominal interest rates is that inflation erodes the value of money. Lenders need to be compensated for the inflation-induced fall in the real value of their money between the time they lend it and the time that they are repaid. This can only be done by charging a nominal interest rate high enough to cover the reduction in value. Thus, higher inflation pushes up interest rates; lower inflation pushes them down. Thiessen also argued that in order to reduce inflation the Bank must reduce the growth rate of the money supply. This action, he admitted, tends to push up interest rates. Apparently puzzled, Peter Gzowski then asked the crucial question: how is it possible that a policy which raises interest rates can be a necessary part of reducing both inflation and interest rates?

The key to answering Gzowski's question is to understand the different short-run and long-run effects of monetary policy. In the short run, a policy by the Bank of Canada to reduce the growth rate of money will make credit more scarce (as we will see in detail in Chapter 27). This greater scarcity of credit causes both nominal and real interest rates to rise. Firms will reduce their investment in new factories, machines, and warehouses, and households will purchase fewer big-ticket items, such as cars, ski vacations, and furniture. Such reductions in expenditure will lead to a reduction in national output because firms faced with less demand for their goods have less need to produce output. But as firms scale back their production, workers get laid off and the unemployment rate increases—the economy will be in recession. Indeed, when we examine the detailed workings of monetary policy in later chapters, we will see that a monetary policy designed to reduce inflation is effective precisely because *it creates a recession.*

So much for the short-run effects of the Bank's policy. Interest rates rise and the economy slows down. But how does this reduce the inflation rate? Over a longer period of time, perhaps several years, the excess supply of labour that is a key part of the unemployment and recession puts downward pressure on wages. In other words, wages start to increase at a slower rate than before, and maybe even begin to fall. Wages, however, are one of the most important components of production costs. Thus, as wage growth declines the pressure on prices to rise also declines. That is, the rate of inflation falls. As inflation falls, and the rate of erosion of money's value falls with it, so too will nominal interest rates fall. Thus, as Gordon Thiessen said in the interview, "the best way to get low interest rates is to get low inflation."

The details of monetary policy will be discussed in Chapters 27 and 28, and this argument will be repeated in considerable detail. At that time, we will more clearly see the difference between the short-run and long-run effects of monetary policy. Economists have a special term to reflect this difference. In the long run, economists say that *money is neutral*—meaning that changes in the money supply have no long-run effect on *real* variables such as GDP, employment, and investment but do have an effect on *nominal* variables such as the price level or the rate of inflation. In the short run, however, economists say that *money is not neutral* because changes in the money supply affect real variables. Understanding this difference is crucial to understanding most debates about monetary policy.

Saving and Growth in Japan

By early in 1999, the Japanese economy had been in recession for over a year—that is, real GDP had been falling for more than a year. Moreover, Japan had experienced very low rates of employment growth and GDP growth over the previous six years. Japan's economy was stagnant. Many economists argued that the solution to Japan's economic malaise was for its firms and consumers to spend more. The problem with Japan, they argued, was simply that its firms and consumers saved "too much." On the other hand, many of these same economists acknowledged that Japan's remarkable economic success in the forty years following the Second World War—high growth rates of real GDP and low unemployment—was largely due to its high saving rate. But if "too much" saving is an important reason for Japan's economic slump during the 1990s, how can high saving be the reason for Japan's economic success over four decades? How can both these views be correct?

Once again, the key to understanding this apparent contradiction is to recognize that the short-run effect of saving is different from its long-run effect. In the short run, an increase in firms' and households' desire to save, perhaps caused by some uncertainty about future economic events, implies a reduction in expenditure. Firms spend less on investment goods; households spend less on all sorts of consumer goods. This reduction in expenditure leads to a reduction in output as firms decide to reduce their production rather than stockpile unneeded inventories. Increased saving in the short run, therefore, can be one reason why an economy such as Japan's enters an economic slump.

The high private saving rate in Japan is one reason that the Japanese economic recovery in the late 1990s was so slow.

But if an increase in firms' and households' saving can cause a recession, how can a high saving rate also explain Japan's many years of healthy economic growth? The answer is that in the long run, over periods of several years, greater saving leads to a larger pool of funds. This larger pool of available funds drives down the price of credit—the interest rate—and makes firms' investment projects more profitable. More investment in factories, machines, and warehouses leads to a higher level of potential output, and it is to this higher level of potential output that the economy converges in the long run. This long-run relationship between saving, investment, and growth explains the striking correlation that we will see in Chapter 32—countries with high long-run investment rates tend to be countries with high rates of long-run per capita GDP growth.

When we examine the short-run effects of saving in Chapter 22 and 23, and the long-run effects of saving in Chapter 32, we will note the different role that saving plays over a period of several months as compared to a period of many years. Economists have special terminology to describe this difference. Economists say that national income in the short run is *demand determined*, meaning that increases in demand will lead to increases in output. Thus, an increase in the desire to save, which is a reduction in the desire to spend, leads to less total spending and a reduction in national income. In the long run, however, economists say that national income is *supply determined*, meaning that long-run increases in output will only be possible if the supply of output increases. Such an increase in supply requires either more factors of production (like labour and capital) or greater productivity. As we will see shortly (and in detail in Chapter 32), both increases in productivity and in the amount of productive factors play an important part in explaining a country's long-run economic growth.

A Need to Think Differently

The two examples above suggest that a complete understanding of macroeconomics requires an understanding of both the short run and the long run. Such an understanding, in turn, requires us to think differently about short-run and long-run behaviour. It is one thing to say that macroeconomic variables behave differently over the short run than over the long run; it is quite another to understand *why* this is the case. A complete understanding of the various reasons will only develop gradually as you progress through the several chapters of this book. In the next section, we will introduce a simple equation to account for changes in GDP, and we will use this equation to separate the sources of short-run and long-run changes.

So far, we have been vague about the meaning of the short run and the long run. Can't we remove the mystery and say precisely what we mean by these terms? The answer is partly yes and partly no. We can be precise about *what* we mean by the short run and long run, but we can't be precise about *how much time* is involved in each. The short run is a time period over which changes in economic conditions tend to cause changes in output and employment, with relatively small changes in prices or wages. In contrast, the long run is a time period over which wage and price adjustment takes place—a process set in motion by the short-run changes in output and employment. The two "runs" are therefore not completely separate; the short run evolves into the long run with the passage of time and the adjustment of wages and prices.

Defining the precise time spans involved is much more difficult. The short run is a span of time over which wages and prices do not significantly adjust to changes in economic events. Over the long run, full wage and price adjustment takes place. But how long does the short run last? In other words, how quickly do wages and prices respond to changes in economic events? The answer depends on the context. In Chapter 25, for example, we will see that wages and prices usually fall more slowly during recessions than they increase during booms. Also, wages and prices tend to rise faster in bigger booms than in smaller ones.

For the remainder of this chapter, it is helpful to think of the short run as a span of time that lasts up to many months, maybe even three or four years. In contrast, think of the long run as anything beyond that. This is not meant to be exact—it is only a rule of thumb to help set the context for our distinction between short-run fluctuations and long-run trends.

Accounting for Changes in GDP

The simplest illustration of short-run versus long-run changes in economic activity is the behaviour of real GDP over time, as shown in Figure 21-1. The figure shows the path of Canadian real GDP and potential GDP, beginning from 1970. Actual GDP is measured by Statistics Canada. Potential GDP, as you may recall from Chapter 19, is the level of output that the economy produces when all factors of production are being utilized at their "normal" rates. But Statistics Canada can't tell us the value of potential GDP because it is not an observed variable—it must be estimated. The value of potential GDP is estimated by combining three pieces of information: the amounts of available factors of production (like the labour force and the capital stock); an estimate of these factors' "normal" rates of utilization; and an estimate of the factors' productivity.

Figure 21-1 shows two different types of changes in GDP. First, there are those changes that involve departures of actual GDP from potential GDP. For example, notice that actual GDP is equal to potential GDP at point B in 1981. As the Canadian economy entered a major recession, actual GDP then dropped below potential GDP to point C in 1982. An economic recovery then took place, taking actual GDP back to potential GDP at point D in 1986. Such changes in GDP are what economists call short-run changes in GDP—they involve primarily the opening and then closing of an output gap. In this case, the output gap between 1981 and 1986 was a recessionary output gap.

The second type of change in GDP involves changes in potential GDP, with little or no change in the output gap. For example, the change in actual GDP from point A in

FIGURE 21-1 Actual and Potential GDP in Canada, 1970–1998

Long-run changes in GDP are reflected by changes in the level of potential GDP. Short-run changes in GDP are shown mostly by changes in the output gap.

1976 to point E in 1990 represents entirely a change in potential GDP. We know this because the output gap in both years is zero (that is, in both 1976 and 1990 GDP is equal to potential GDP). Such changes in GDP are what economists call long-run changes in GDP— they involve a change in potential GDP, with little or no change in the output gap.

When studying long-run trends in GDP, economists focus on the change in potential output. When studying short-run fluctuations, economists focus on the change in the output gap.

Figure 21-1 may make us wonder whether short-run changes in GDP have a different cause than long-run changes. After all, the discussion in the previous section suggested that output is *demand determined* in the short run but *supply determined* in the long run. Aren't the determinants of supply different from the determinants of demand? To explore this issue, we turn to a very simple accounting framework that applies to *all* changes in GDP.

GDP Accounting: The Basic Principle

Suppose we want to *account for* changes in GDP. By this we simply mean breaking down any change in GDP into its component parts. By understanding how each component changes, we may then gain some insights into how short-run changes differ from long-run changes.

To break up GDP into the parts we want to study, we do the following obvious but useful things. First, we write

$$GDP = GDP$$

This is obviously true! Next, we multiply the right-hand side of the equation by F/F, where F is the economy's total available stock of factors. This gives

$$GDP = F \times (GDP/F)$$

Next, we multiply the right-hand side by F_E/F_E, where F_E is the number of the economy's factors that are employed. This gives

$$GDP = F \times (F_E/F) \times (GDP/F_E) \qquad (21\text{-}1)$$

It may seem like we have done nothing useful since we have simply twice multiplied the right-hand side of an obviously true equation by one. But, in fact, Equation 21-1 is very useful when thinking about the different sources of change in GDP.

First, however, note that Equation 21-1 is written as if we could add together units of labour and land and capital to get a meaningful number for the economy's "available factors." But this is not actually possible since different factors are measured in different units. For example, we can't add together six workers and five machines to get a total of 11 factors. In the next section, we will focus on a single factor to avoid this problem. For now, however, our point is simplified by thinking about the economy's total available factors, F, and the number of those factors that are employed, F_E.

To make the discussion less cumbersome, let's name the three components of Equation 21-1. Instead of the term "available factors" let's call F the economy's *factor supply*. The term F_E/F is the *factor utilization rate* because it is the fraction of the total factors that are employed or utilized. Finally, the term GDP/F_E is the economy's *productivity* because it is a measure of output per unit of input employed.

Note that Equation 21-1 does nothing more than separate any change in GDP into a change in one or more of the three components, F, F_E/F, or GDP/F_E. For example, Canadian GDP increased dramatically in the fifty years between 1947 and 1997. Also, Canadian GDP increased by a few percentage points from 1997 to 1999. In both cases, the increase in GDP was only possible because one of three things, and possibly more than one, happened—either the factor supply (F) increased, the factor utilization rate (F_E/F) increased, or the level of productivity (GDP/F_E) increased.

Any change in GDP must be the result of a change in factor supply, a change in factor utilization, or a change in productivity.

The value of this accounting exercise becomes clear when we recognize that two of these components, factor supply and productivity, typically change most over long periods of time whereas the third component, factor utilization, changes mostly only over shorter periods. We discuss each component in turn.

The Long Run: Factor Supply

There are two main factors of production—labour and capital—that make up the economy's factor supply.

Labour.   The economy's supply of labour can increase for two main reasons. First, population can increase. An increase in population can be caused, in turn, either by greater immigration, an increase in birth rates, or a decrease in the mortality rate. The second way to increase the economy's supply of labour is to increase the fraction of the population that chooses to seek employment. This fraction is called the *labour-force participation rate*. In Canada, the labour-force participation rate is currently about 66 percent. It has increased steadily from the 1960s, due mostly to the increase in the participation rate of married women and the coming-of-age of the baby-boom generation.

No matter how the economy's supply of labour increases, the important point for our purposes is that such changes are mostly *long-run changes*. Population growth, through whatever means, is a very gradual process. Changes in labour-force participation also tend to be gradual. As a result, the economy's supply of labour does not usually change dramatically from year to year. Over a period of many years, however, the increase in the supply of labour can be significant.

Capital.   The economy's supply of physical capital—machines, factories, and warehouses—increases for one reason. Firms that choose to purchase or build such investment goods today are accumulating physical capital that will be used to produce output in the future. Thus, today's flow of investment expenditure adds to the economy's stock of physical capital.

As is the case for labour, the economy's stock of physical capital changes only very gradually. This is not to be confused with the very dramatic swings in investment that are often observed over the course of the business cycle. The difference is that investment is the *flow* that contributes to the *stock* of capital. But the economy's capital stock is so large compared to the annual flow of investment expenditure that even dramatic swings in the annual level of investment generate only small changes in the stock of capital.

Changes in the economy's supply of labour and capital occur only gradually. As a result, changes in factor supply are important for explaining long-run changes in output, but relatively unimportant for explaining short-run changes.

The Long Run: Productivity

The economy's level of productivity is a measure of the amount of output that is produced with a given level of input. In practice, there are several possible measures of productivity, each one measuring something slightly different. Although there is more than one measure of productivity, Equation 21-1 uses the concept of output per employed factor, GDP/F_E. An increase in productivity is called *productivity growth*. As we discussed in the previous two chapters, rising productivity—productivity growth—is an important source of rising living standards.

The economy's level of productivity changes only slowly over time. For example, a typical rate of productivity growth in Canada over the past few decades is 1 percent per year, and often less. Such low growth rates do not lead to significant changes in GDP or living standards over short periods of time, but can generate huge improvements in living conditions over many years. For example, you might not notice a two percent increase in your productivity from one year to the next, but you would surely notice the doubling that this annual growth rate would produce if it were sustained over 35 years.

The economy's level of productivity changes only gradually. As a result, productivity growth is very important for explaining long-run changes in output, but less important for explaining short-run changes.

The Short Run: Factor Utilization

The factor utilization rate is the last remaining component from our equation. Recall that it is simply the fraction of the total supply of factors that is employed. An immediate question comes to mind: Why would firms ever use fewer factors than are available to them? The answer has to do with how firms respond to changes in the demand for their product. When a firm's sales start dropping off, it must make a choice. It can continue producing at the current rate and let its inventories build up. Or it can reduce its rate of production. For a firm that is interested in maximizing profits, there is a limit to the amount of costly inventories it will be prepared to accumulate. Eventually, a reduction in demand for its product leads the firm to reduce its output and, in turn, reduce its employment of factors. Workers are laid off and equipment and other physical capital is used less intensively.

Similarly, a firm that is faced with a sudden increase in demand for its product has two alternatives. It can continue with its previous rate of production and satisfy the increased demand by letting its inventories run down. Or it can increase its rate of production by hiring more factors. Since profit-maximizing firms do not want to miss an opportunity to make a profitable sale, as would happen if the stockpile of inventories gets fully depleted, eventually the increase in demand leads them to increase production and hire more factors. Extra workers are hired, existing workers work overtime, and machines and other physical capital are used more intensively.

But these responses by firms to changes in demand are only the firms' short-run responses. A low factor utilization rate describes *excess supply* in the factor markets. Such a situation of excess supply typically causes downward pressure on factor prices. This reduction of factor prices, in turn, puts downward pressure on product prices. Similarly, in the case of the increase in demand, the situation of a high factor utilization rate describes *excess demand* in factor markets. Such excess demand causes upward pressure on factor prices. This, in turn, puts upward pressure on product prices.

The factor utilization rate fluctuates in response to changes in the demand for firms' output. Over time, however, excess supply or excess demand for factors causes an adjustment in factor prices that brings the factor utilization rate back to its "normal" level.

What do we mean by a "normal" factor utilization rate? In Chapter 19 we briefly discussed the idea of the *natural rate of unemployment*. This "natural" or "normal" rate of unemployment is the rate of unemployment against which we compare the actual unemployment rate to judge whether the labour market has excess supply or excess demand. That is, if unemployment is above the natural rate, there is an excess supply of labour; if unemployment is below the natural rate, there is an excess demand for labour. For physical capital, the utilization rate is called the *capacity utilization rate* because the amount of physical capital largely determines the productive *capacity* of a given plant or factory. As with labour, so too is there a "natural" or "normal" capacity utilization rate.

The statement that factor utilization rates eventually return to their "normal" level simply means that factor prices adjust in the long run to eliminate excess demands or excess supplies. This adjustment process will be an important topic of discussion in Chapters 24 and 25. An important implication of such long-run adjustment in factor prices is that changes in the factor utilization rate, though important for explaining short-run changes in GDP, are not an important determinant of long-run changes in GDP.

Changes in the factor utilization rate are important for explaining short-run changes in GDP. But, because factor prices adjust in the long run, the factor utilization rate returns to its "normal" level and, hence, is not important for explaining long-run changes in GDP.

GDP Accounting: An Application

We made some strong statements in the previous section regarding short-run versus long-run changes in various economic variables. Are these statements supported by the evidence? In this section, we apply the accounting concept contained in Equation 21-1 to Canadian GDP data to illustrate the basic arguments. Unfortunately, we cannot use *exactly* the same equation because, as we noted then, it is not possible to add units of labour together with units of physical capital. But, using exactly the same intuition as earlier, we can express the GDP accounting equation in terms of a single factor of production—labour. Letting L be the labour force and E be the level of employment, the new equation is:[1]

$$\text{GDP} = L \times (E/L) \times (\text{GDP}/E) \qquad (21\text{-}2)$$

The basic interpretation of Equation 21-2 is the same as for Equation 21-1, except now the discussion relates only to labour. The labour force (L) is the supply of labour. The employment rate (E/L) is the fraction of the labour force actually employed (which is equal

---

[1]We get this equation by beginning with GDP = GDP. We then multiply the right-hand side by E/E and then by L/L.

FIGURE 21-2   Three Sources of Changes in GDP

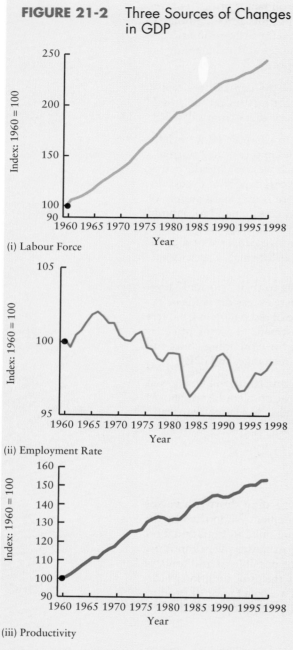

(i) Labour Force

(ii) Employment Rate

(iii) Productivity

The sources of long-run changes in GDP differ from the sources of short-run changes in GDP. Panel (i) shows the upward trend in the Canadian labour force. Panel (iii) shows the upward tend in productivity, measured as GDP per worker. Both show substantial growth over the long run, but relatively small short-run fluctuations. Panel (ii) shows the employment rate, the fraction of the labour force that is employed. It shows almost no long-run trend but considerable short-run fluctuations.

to one minus the unemployment rate). And the measure of productivity—in this case, labour productivity—is GDP/E.

Figure 21-2 shows the behaviour of these three components for Canada beginning in 1960. Each variable is expressed as an index number, with the value in 1960 set equal to 100. Expressing each variable in this way makes it easy to see each variable's percentage change over the four decades. The first panel in the figure shows the growth of the Canadian labour force. From 1960 to1998, the index number increased from 100 to 245, an increase of 145 percent. It is clear from the graph that any short-run fluctuations in the Canadian labour force are dwarfed in importance by the long-run upward trend.

Now look at the third panel, showing the growth of Canadian labour productivity. The level of GDP per person employed, expressed as an index number, increases from 100 in 1960 to 169 in 1998, an increase of 69 percent. Like the labour force, the level of labour productivity has its short-run fluctuations, but it is clear that the overriding change—the upward trend— takes place over many years.

Finally, consider the middle panel, showing the Canadian employment rate—the utilization rate of labour. Compared to the other two variables graphed in Figure 21-2, the employment rate shows much more short-run volatility and much less long-run change. The employment rate (expressed as an index number) falls slightly from 100 in 1960 to 98 in 1998, a long-run decrease of only 2 percent. There is very little change over the long run, but considerable changes are occurring over shorter periods of time.

Summing Up

To summarize, we can account for *any* change in GDP by changes in factor supply, the factor utilization rate, and productivity. But these three components typically contribute to GDP changes over different spans of time. In particular, factor supply and productivity typically change very slowly over time and hence are important for explaining long-run changes in GDP, but are not usually helpful in explaining short-run changes in GDP. In contrast, the factor utilization rate typically changes substantially over short periods of time but returns to its normal level over several years. Thus, changes in the factor utilization rate are important for explaining short-run changes in GDP but are not of central importance for explaining long-run changes.

Policy Implications

Because of this important difference between the source of short-run and long-run changes in GDP, economists think differently about short-run and long-run macroeconomic relationships. When thinking about short-run fluctuations, economists focus on understanding why actual GDP deviates from potential GDP. As we said above, such deviations are usually explained by changes in the demand for output. Thus, in understanding short-run fluctuations, economists focus on the *demand side* of the economy.

When thinking about long-run changes in GDP, however, economists focus on understanding why potential GDP changes over time. As we said above, such long-run growth has its source in the growth of factor supplies and productivity. Thus, in understanding long-run growth, economists focus on the *supply side* of the economy.

When studying short-run fluctuations, economists ignore changes in potential output and focus instead on the deviations of actual output from potential. When studying long-run changes, economists ignore such deviations and focus instead on changes in potential output.

Much of what we discuss in the chapters ahead will be explaining the details of this distinction between the short run and the long run. We will do so through the use of a formal macroeconomic model. Before we go on to build this model, however, it is useful to make one final point about what this distinction implies for the effects of macroeconomic policy. As we discussed in the examples at the beginning of this chapter, the long-run and short-run effects of policy are different.

We have discussed in this chapter how changes in demand may cause actual GDP to depart from potential GDP. For example, firms may feel optimistic about the future and increase their investment expenditure, thereby increasing the overall level of demand. Or the government may increase its purchases of goods and services, thus adding to demand. Or foreigners may decide to increase their demand for Canadian goods, thus adding to the overall demand for goods produced by Canadian firms. All of these changes would increase the overall level of demand in the economy and, in the short run, would lead actual GDP to rise above potential GDP. Conversely, any decrease in the demand for goods would, in the short run, cause actual GDP to fall below potential GDP.

We have also mentioned that the economy has an adjustment mechanism that returns the factor utilization rate to its "normal" level in the long run. In particular, when actual GDP is above potential GDP, there is an excess demand for factors. This causes factor prices to rise and thereby eliminates the excess demand, bringing actual GDP back to potential. Conversely, when actual GDP is less than potential GDP, there is an excess supply of factors. This causes factor prices to fall and eliminates the excess supply, thereby bringing actual GDP back to potential.

This adjustment process that brings the economy back to the level of potential output in the long run implies a stark result regarding the effects of macroeconomic policy:

Fiscal and monetary policies affect the short-run level of GDP because they alter the level of demand. But unless they are able to affect the level of *potential* output, they will have no long-run effect on GDP.

The consensus among economists is that monetary policy does *not* affect the level of potential output and thus does not have a long-run effect on GDP. As we will see in later chapters, monetary policy *does* affect the level of demand in the short run by changing interest rates and affecting firms' investment expenditures. But most economists believe, on the basis of both theory and considerable empirical evidence, that changes in monetary policy are *neutral* in the long run—that is, that monetary policy has long-run effects only on *nominal* variables such as nominal wages, the price level, and the rate of inflation.

There is also a broad consensus among economists that fiscal policy—in particular, a change in the level of government spending—*probably does* affect the level of potential output, but that it is *opposite* to its short-run effect on actual GDP. In the chapters ahead, we will see that when the government decides to increase its level of spending on goods and services, it will add to the overall level of demand. This stimulus to demand will, in the short run, lead to an increase in actual GDP. And in the long run, the adjustment process that we have discussed will bring the level of actual GDP back to potential GDP. In this case, however, the long-run effect of the higher level of government spending will actually be to *reduce* the level of potential GDP. The explanation is fairly involved and we will see it in detail later. But the basic story is that the higher government spending will push up interest rates and "crowd out" private spending, especially private investment. And less private investment in equipment and factories means less physical capital in the future and thus a lower level of potential output.

Looking Ahead

The discussion in this chapter has been centred around one topic—the difference between the short run and the long run in macroeconomics. We have shown that short-run movements in GDP are mostly accounted for by changes in the factor utilization rate, whereas long-run changes in GDP are mostly accounted for by changes in factor supplies and productivity. This difference forces economists to think differently about macroeconomic relationships that exist over a few months as compared to those that exist over several years.

In the next two chapters, we will explore the workings of a simple short-run model of the economy. In this model, we will see the emphasis on the demand side and understand why increases in demand usually lead to increases in actual GDP. In the following two chapters, we will discuss the adjustment process that takes the economy from the short run to the long run, so that actual GDP returns to potential GDP. With this basic macro model in place, we will then be ready to explore many interesting macroeconomic issues, such as inflation, unemployment, and government debt. A particularly important macroeconomic issue is the study of long-run economic growth, which we explore in Chapter 32.

As you learn about the formal macroeconomic model that we develop in the next few chapters, try not to lose sight of the central message in this chapter: understanding both short-run fluctuations and long-run trends is central to a complete understanding of macroeconomics and macroeconomic policy.

S U M M A R Y

Two Examples

- Macroeconomic variables behave differently over the short run than over the long run. One example: a monetary policy designed to reduce inflation and nominal interest rates in the long run requires an *increase* in interest rates in the short run. Another example: an increase in households' or firms' saving rates will reduce the level of output in the short run, but it will increase output in the long run.

- In the short run, there is some adjustment of output and employment, but little adjustment of wages and prices.

In the long run, full adjustment of wages and prices takes place.

Accounting for Changes in GDP

- All changes in GDP can be accounted for by changes in one or more of the following three variables:
  - supply of factors
  - factor utilization rates
  - factor productivity
- Long-run changes in GDP are caused mostly by changes in factor supplies and factor productivity; the utilization

rate of factors does not change significantly over the long run.
- Short-run changes in GDP are caused mostly by changes in the factor utilization rate; factor supplies and productivity have relatively minor short-run fluctuations.

Policy Implications

- When studying short-run fluctuations, economists focus on changes in the output gap and ignore changes in potential output. When studying long-run fluctuations, economists focus on changes in potential output and ignore changes in the output gap.

- Fiscal and monetary policies affect GDP in the short run because they affect the level of demand. Unless they are able to affect the level of *potential* output, they will have no long-run effect on GDP.

K E Y   C O N C E P T S

Short-run fluctuations
Long-run trends

Changes in the output gap versus changes in potential output
Accounting for changes in GDP

Factor supplies
Factor utilization rates
Productivity

S T U D Y   E X E R C I S E S

1. Consider the data below for a hypothetical country.

Year	Real GDP (billions of real dollars)	Labour Force (millions of people)	Employment (millions of people)
1950	100	1.5	1.4
1955	130	1.6	1.45
1960	175	1.75	1.55
1965	210	1.95	1.65
1970	230	2.15	1.85
1975	265	2.40	2.0
1980	300	2.70	2.2
1985	340	3.0	2.8
1990	375	3.3	3.05

a. Using the definitions in the chapter, compute the employment rate and the level of productivity (measured as GDP per worker) for each year.

b. For each 5-year period, compute the percentage change in the labour force, the employment rate, and the level of productivity. Compute the same three things over the entire 40-year period.

c. Compute the percentage change in real GDP over each 5-year period. Do it also for the entire 40-year period.

d. Based on Equation 21-1, it can be shown that the percentage change in real GDP is approximately equal to the percentage change in the labour force *plus* the percentage change in the employment rate *plus* the percentage change in the level of productivity. Compare the sum of your answers from part **b.** with your answers from part **c.** Are they close?

e. For each 5-year period, what fraction of the percentage change in GDP is accounted for by the change in the employment rate?

f. Over the entire 40-year period, what fraction of the percentage change in GDP is accounted for by the change in the employment rate?

2. Go to Statistics Canada's website (*www.statcan.ca*) and look for data on capacity utilization rates in Canadian industries. The capacity utilization rate is, roughly, the fraction of the capital stock that is utilized or employed. How has this variable changed over the past several decades? Contrast the short-run versus the long-run movements.

DISCUSSION QUESTIONS

1. Figure 21-1 shows the path of actual GDP as well as the path of potential GDP. The chapter mentioned that the economy has an adjustment mechanism that brings actual GDP back to potential.

   a. Describe this adjustment process, and how it relates to the concept of market-clearing.

   b. If, following the implementation of some policy, actual GDP eventually returns to potential GDP, does this mean that policy can have no long-run effect on GDP? Contrast the long-run effects of monetary and fiscal policy.

PART EIGHT

National Income and Fiscal Policy

What determines the level of national income? Why, in the midst of a recession, does the government sometimes attempt to increase national income by spending a few billion dollars? During other recessions our elected leaders implore us to "go out and spend." Can such increased spending end a recession? At other times, when the economy has been growing quickly for several years, the government may be worried that any further spending will add to inflationary pressures. What then determines when an increase in spending leads to an increase in national income and when it leads to inflation? These are the sorts of questions you will be able to answer after reading the next four chapters.

Chapter 22 examines the determination of national income under the assumption that the price level is held constant. It introduces the simplest possible model of the macro economy to explain how equilibrium national income is determined. The key to understanding this model involves understanding the essential distinction between desired expenditure and actual expenditure. One of the key aspects of this model is the multiplier, which explains why a $1 billion increase in desired expenditure will end up increasing equilibrium national income by more than $1 billion.

Chapter 23 extends this simple model by adding a government sector and international trade. This is your introduction to fiscal policy; it is also the first time we see the relationship between the exchange rate and a country's exports and imports. Surprisingly, this more complicated model works in exactly the same way as the simple one but it allows us to consider a more realistic setting.

Chapter 24 removes the assumption of the fixed price level. We make the distinction between the demand side and the supply side of the economy and examine the important concepts of aggregate demand and aggregate supply. We then examine what is called macroeconomic equilibrium—the simultaneous determination of the equilibrium level of national income and the equilibrium price level.

Finally, Chapter 25 examines the behaviour of the economy in the long run—when the price level is free to adjust to excess demand or excess supply in the economy as a whole. We discuss the concepts of potential output, the output gap, and the Phillips Curve. The chapter ends with a detailed discussion of fiscal policy in the short run and in the long run. (Many of these issues will resurface in Chapter 31 when we examine government debt and deficits.)

CHAPTER 22

The Simplest Short-Run Macro Model

LO LEARNING OBJECTIVES

1 Understand the difference between desired expenditure and actual expenditure.

2 Explain the determinants of desired consumption and desired investment expenditures.

3 Understand the meaning of equilibrium national income.

4 Recognize the difference between movements along and shifts of the aggregate expenditure function.

5 Explain how a change in desired expenditure affects equilibrium income, and how this change is reflected by the multiplier.

In Chapters 19 and 20, we encountered a number of important macroeconomic variables. We considered how they are measured and how they have behaved over the past several decades. We now turn to a more detailed study of what *causes* these variables to behave as they do. In particular, we study the forces that determine real national income and the price level.

Real national income and the price level are determined simultaneously. It is, however, easier to study them one at a time. So, in this chapter and the next, we simplify matters by seeing how real national income is determined *under the assumption that the price level is constant*. The simplified analysis will be an important first step toward understanding how prices and incomes are determined together, which is the subject of Chapters 24 and 25.

Our ability to explain the behaviour of real national income depends on our understanding of what determines the amount that households and firms spend. So, we begin with an examination of the expenditure decisions of households and firms.

Desired Expenditure

In Chapter 20, we discussed how national income statisticians divide *actual* GDP into its expenditure components: consumption, investment, government purchases, and net exports.

In this chapter and the next, we are concerned with a different concept. It is variously called *desired* or *planned* expenditure. Of course, all people would like to spend virtually unlimited amounts, if only they had the resources. Desired expenditure does not refer, however, to what people would like to do under imaginary circumstances; it refers to what people would like to spend out of the resources that are at their command. Recall from Chapter 20 that the *actual* values of the various categories of expenditure are indicated by C_a, I_a, G_a, and $(X_a - IM_a)$. Economists use the same letters without the subscript "a" to indicate the *desired* expenditure in the same categories: *C, I, G,* and $(X - IM)$.

Everyone makes expenditure decisions. Fortunately, it is unnecessary for our purposes to look at each of the millions of such individual decisions. Instead, it is sufficient to consider four main groups of decision makers: domestic households, firms, governments, and foreign purchasers of domestically produced commodities. The *actual* purchases made by these four groups account for the four main categories of expenditure that we studied in Chapter 20: consumption, investment, government purchases, and net exports. The sum of their *desired* expenditures on domestically produced output is called desired aggregate expenditure, or more simply **aggregate expenditure (AE)**:

$$AE = C + I + G + (X - IM)$$

Desired expenditure need not equal actual expenditure, either in total or in any individual category. For example, firms might not plan to invest in inventory accumulation this year but might do so unintentionally if sales are unexpectedly low—the unsold goods that pile up on their shelves are undesired inventory accumulation. In this case, actual investment expenditure, I_a, will exceed desired investment expenditure, *I*.

National income accounts measure *actual* expenditures in each of the four expenditure categories. National income theory deals with *desired* expenditures in each of these four categories.

You are probably wondering why the distinction between desired and actual expenditure is so important. The answer will become clear in the next section where we discuss the concept of *equilibrium* national income, which involves the relationship between desired and actual expenditure. For now, however, the remainder of this section examines more fully the various components of desired expenditure.

Autonomous Versus Induced Expenditure.   In what follows, it will be useful to distinguish between *autonomous* and *induced* expenditure. Components of aggregate expenditure that do *not* depend on national income are called **autonomous expenditures**. Autonomous expenditures can and do change, but such changes do not occur systematically in response to changes in national income. Components of aggregate expenditure that *do* change in response to changes in national income are called **induced expenditures**. As we will see, the induced response of desired aggregate expenditure to a change in national income plays a key role in the determination of equilibrium national income.

Important Simplifications.   Our goal in this chapter is to develop the simplest possible model of national-income determination. To do so, we focus on only two of the four components of desired aggregate expenditure—consumption and investment. Consumption is by far the largest component of aggregate expenditure; it also provides the most important link between desired aggregate expenditure and real national income. Investment is output that is used to add to the stock of physical capital rather than for current consumption purposes. It is much smaller than consumption but also

aggregate expenditure (AE) function   The function that relates desired aggregate expenditure to actual national income.

autonomous expenditure   Elements of expenditure that do not vary systematically with national income.

induced expenditure   Any component of expenditure that is systematically related to national income.

much more volatile; understanding investment is therefore important for understanding fluctuations in real national income.

closed economy An economy that has no foreign trade.

We begin by considering a **closed economy**—that is, one that does not trade with other countries. We also suppose that there is no government and that the price level is constant. These assumptions are clearly extreme, but they serve a vital purpose. As we will see in this chapter, the presence of government and foreign trade is *not* essential to understanding the basic principles of national-income determination. By simplifying the model as much as possible, we are better able to understand the structure of this simple model.

In following chapters we will complicate our simple macro model by adding a government and international trade and then by removing the assumption of a fixed price level. The result will be a much more complete model of the macro economy. For now, however, we begin the discussion of our simplest model by considering the two crucial components of desired aggregate expenditure—consumption and investment.

Desired Consumption Expenditure

saving All disposable income that is not spent on consumption.

Households can do one of two things with their disposable income: spend it on consumption or save it. **Saving** is all disposable income that is not spent on consumption.

By definition, there are only two possible uses of disposable income—consumption and saving. When the household decides how much to put to one use, it has automatically decided how much to put to the other use.

What determines the division between the amount that households decide to consume and the amount they decide to save? The factors that influence this decision are summarized in the *consumption function* and the *saving function*.

The Consumption Function

consumption function The relationship between desired consumption expenditure and all the variables that determine it; in the simplest case, the relationship between consumption expenditure and disposable income.

The **consumption function** relates the total desired consumption expenditure of all households to the factors that determine it. It is, as we shall see, one of the central relationships in macroeconomics.

The consumption behaviour of households depends on the income that they actually have to spend, which is called their *disposable income*. Under the simplifying assumptions that we have made in this chapter, however, there are no taxes, and so all income that is generated is received by households. Therefore, disposable income, which we denote by Y_D, is equal to national income, Y.

It is not surprising that a household's expenditure is related to the amount of income that it has at its disposal. However, there is more than one way this relationship can work. To see what is involved, let's consider two quite different households.

The first household is short-sighted and spends everything it receives and puts nothing aside for a rainy day. When some overtime work results in a large paycheque, the members of the household go out and spend it. When it is hard to find work, the household's paycheque is small and its members reduce their expenditures. This household's monthly expenditure is therefore exactly equal to its current disposable income.

The second household is forward-looking. Its members think about the future as much as the present and make plans that stretch over their lifetimes. They put money aside for retirement and for the occasional rainy day when disposable income may fall temporarily. An unexpected windfall of income will be saved. An unexpected shortfall of income will be cushioned by spending some of the accumulated savings that were put aside for just such a rainy day. In short, this household's current expenditure will be closely related to its expected *lifetime income*. Fluctuations in its *current income* will have little effect on its current consumption expenditure. Economists refer to this behaviour as *consumption smoothing*.

Figure 22-1 shows the difference between our two sample households, short-sighted and forward-looking, and how their respective consumption expenditure is related to their current disposable income.

John Maynard Keynes (1883–1946), the famous English economist who developed much of the basic theory of macroeconomics—and gave his name to Keynesian economics—inhabited his theory with households whose current consumption expenditure depended mostly on their current income. But these households are not as extreme as the short-sighted households we discussed above. Keynes did not assume that households *never* saved. He simply assumed that their current level of expenditure and saving depended on their *current* level of income. To this day, a consumption function based on this assumption is called a *Keynesian consumption function*.

During the 1950s, two U.S. economists, Franco Modigliani and Milton Friedman, both of whom were subsequently awarded Nobel Prizes in economics, analysed the behaviour of forward-looking households. Their theories, which Modigliani called the *life-cycle theory* and Friedman called the *permanent-income theory*, explain some observed consumer behaviour that cannot be explained by the Keynesian consumption function.

The differences between the theories of Keynes, on the one hand, and Friedman and Modigliani, on the other, are not as great as it might seem at first sight. To see why this is so, let us return to our two imaginary households.

Even the extremely short-sighted household may be able to do some consumption smoothing in the face of income fluctuations. Most households have some money in the bank and some ability to borrow, even if it is just from friends and relatives. As a result, every change in income need not be matched by a proportional change in consumption expenditures.

In contrast, although the forward-looking household wants to smooth its pattern of consumption completely, it may not have the borrowing capacity to do so. Its bank may not be willing to lend money for consumption when the security consists of nothing more than the *expectation* that the household's income will be much higher in later years. As a result, the household's consumption expenditure might fluctuate with its current income more than it would wish.

The foregoing discussion suggests that the consumption expenditure of both types of households will fluctuate to some extent with their current disposable incomes and to some extent with their expectations of future disposable income.

Practise with Study Guide Chapter 22, Exercise 1.

FIGURE 22-1   Consumption and Disposable Income for Short-Sighted and Forward-Looking Households

How consumption relates to current disposable income depends on whether the household is short-sighted or forward-looking. Disposable income, Y_D, is shown to fluctuate over time. If the household is short-sighted, it doesn't think about the future and thus spends all of its income each year. Its consumption rises and falls with its income, so its path of consumption, C_{SS}, is the same as the path of Y_D. A forward-looking household plans for the future and wants to smooth its consumption as much as possible. Its path of consumption is given by C_{FL}. When Y_D exceeds C_{FL}, the forward-looking household is saving; when Y_D is less than C_{FL}, the household is spending from its accumulated savings. If the economy is made up of both types of households, the *average* household will have a pattern of consumption that is smoother than C_{SS} but not as smooth as C_{FL}—a path like C^*. Aggregate consumption will rise when aggregate disposable income rises; consumption will fall when disposable income falls.

Moreover, in any economy there will be households of both types, both spendthrifts and planners, and aggregate consumption will be determined by a mix of the two types. The consumption behaviour for the *average* household in such an economy is shown in Figure 22-1 as the path C^*. Consumption fluctuates in response to changes in disposable income, rising when income rises and falling when income falls.

The consumption function describes the relationship between consumption and the variables that influence it; in the simplest theory, consumption is determined primarily by current disposable income.

When a household's income is zero, it will still consume some minimal amount (via begging, borrowing, or drawing down savings). This level of consumption expenditure is *autonomous* because it persists even when there is no income. The higher a household's income, the more it will want to consume. This part of consumption is *induced*; that is, it varies with disposable income.

Consider the schedule relating disposable income to desired consumption expenditure for a hypothetical economy that appears in the first two columns of the table in Figure 22-2. In this example, autonomous consumption expenditure is $30 billion, whereas induced consumption expenditure is 80 percent of disposable income (for every $1 increase in disposable income, there is an 80 cent increase in consumption). The equation for this simple consumption function is $C = a + b Y_D$ where a is equal to $30 billion and b is equal to 0.8. In what follows, we use this hypothetical example to illustrate the various properties of the consumption function.

Average and Marginal Propensities to Consume.
To discuss the consumption function concisely, economists use two technical expressions.

average propensity to consume (APC)
The level of consumption divided by the level of disposable income.

The **average propensity to consume** *(APC)* is total consumption expenditure divided by total disposable income:

$$APC = C/Y_D$$

The fourth column of the table in Figure 22-2 shows the *APC* calculated from the data in the table. Note that *APC* falls as disposable income rises.

marginal propensity to consume (MPC)
The change in consumption divided by the change in disposable income that brought it about.

The **marginal propensity to consume** *(MPC)* relates the *change* in desired consumption to the *change* in disposable income that brought it about. *MPC* is the change in desired consumption divided by the change in disposable income:

$$MPC = \Delta C/\Delta Y_D,$$

where the Greek letter Δ, delta, means "a change in." The last column of the table in Figure 22-2 shows the *MPC* that corresponds to the data in the table. Note that by construction in this example, the *MPC* is constant. [29]

The Slope of the Consumption Function.
Part (i) of Figure 22-2 shows a graph of the consumption function. The consumption function has a slope of $\Delta C/\Delta Y_D$, which is, by definition, the marginal propensity to consume. The positive slope of the consumption function shows that the *MPC* is positive; increases in income lead to increases in consumption expenditure.

The 45° Line.
Figure 22-2(i) contains a line that is constructed by connecting all points where desired consumption (measured on the vertical axis) equals disposable income (measured on the horizontal axis). Because both axes are given in the same units,

this line has a positive slope equal to one; that is, it forms an angle of 45° with the axes. The line is therefore called the *45° line*.

The 45° line is a useful reference line. In part (i) of Figure 22-2, the consumption function cuts the 45° line at the break-even level of income—in this example, at $150 billion. The 45° line is also useful because its slope, which is equal to one, is greater than the slope of the consumption function, which is equal to the marginal propensity to consume. This is simply a graphic reminder that the *MPC* is less than one, and that the higher is the *MPC*, the steeper is the consumption function.

Disposable income can either be saved or spent on consumption goods. Bank deposits are one important form of saving.

FIGURE 22-2   The Consumption and Saving Functions

Disposable Income (Y_D)	Desired Consumption (C)	Desired Saving (S)	$APC = C/Y_D$	ΔY_D	ΔC	$MPC = \Delta C/\Delta Y_D$
0	30	−30	—			
				30	24	0.8
30	54	−24	1.800			
				90	72	0.8
120	126	−6	1.050			
				30	24	0.8
150	150	0	1.000			
				150	120	0.8
300	270	30	0.900			
				150	120	0.8
450	390	60	0.867			
				75	60	0.8
525	450	75	0.857			
				75	60	0.8
600	510	90	0.850			

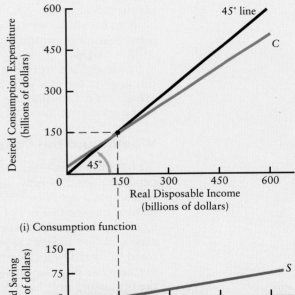

(i) Consumption function

(ii) Saving function

Both consumption and saving rise as disposable income rises. Line C in part (i) of the figure relates desired consumption expenditure to disposable income by plotting the data from the second column of the accompanying table. The consumption function cuts the 45° line at the break-even level of disposable income. Note that the level of autonomous consumption is $30 billion. The slope of the consumption function is equal to the marginal propensity to consume, which is shown in the table to be 0.8.

The relationship between desired saving and disposable income is shown in part (ii) by line S, which plots the data from the third column of the table. The vertical distance between C and the 45° line in part (i) is by definition the height of S in part (ii); that is, any given level of disposable income must be either consumed or saved. Note that the level of autonomous saving is −$30 billion.

The Saving Function

Households decide how much to consume and how much to save. As we have said, this is only a single decision—how to divide disposable income between consumption and saving. It follows that once we know the dependence of consumption on disposable income, we automatically know the dependence of saving on disposable income.

There are two saving concepts that are exactly parallel to the consumption concepts of *APC* and *MPC*. The **average propensity to save** *(APS)* is the proportion of disposable income that households want to save, computed by dividing total desired saving by total disposable income:

$$APS = S/Y_D$$

The **marginal propensity to save** *(MPS)* relates the change in desired saving to the change in disposable income that brought it about:

$$MPS = \Delta S/\Delta Y_D$$

There is a simple relationship between the saving and the consumption propensities. *APC* and *APS* must sum to one, and so must *MPC* and *MPS*. Because all disposable income is either spent or saved, it follows that the fractions of income consumed and saved must account for all income (*APC* + *APS* = 1). It also follows that the fractions of any *increment* to income consumed and saved must account for all of that increment (*MPC* + *MPS* = 1). [30]

Calculations from the table in Figure 22-2 will allow you to confirm these relationships in the case of the example given. Figure 22-2(ii) shows the saving function. Where desired consumption equals disposable income, desired saving is zero. The slope of the saving function, $\Delta S/\Delta Y_D$, is equal to the *MPS*.

Wealth and the Consumption Function

We have been analysing the Keynesian consumption function—where consumption expenditure depends only on current disposable income. But this extreme depiction of consumption behaviour can easily be combined with the more recent life-cycle and permanent-income theories of consumption. According to these theories, households save to accumulate wealth that they can use during their retirement or during periods of unexpectedly low income. Suppose that there is an unexpected rise in aggregate wealth. This could be caused by an increase in the values of the shares that households own in the stock market. The increase in wealth means that less current income needs to be saved for the future and thus households will spend a larger fraction of income on current consumption. Hence, the consumption function will be shifted upward and the saving function downward, as shown in Figure 22-3. Conversely, a fall in wealth increases the incentive to save in order to restore wealth. This change shifts the consumption function downward and the saving function upward.

Practise with Study Guide Chapter 22, Exercise 3.

Consumption and Disposable Income in Canada

We have devoted considerable time and space to discussing the consumption function, as this relationship between desired consumption and disposable income is of central importance in the determination of national income. It is worthwhile, therefore, to take a brief look at actual data to see if such a relationship exists in Canada.

Figure 22-4 plots real per capita consumption expenditure against real per capita disposable income for Canada from 1977 to 1998. The straight line drawn through the data points is the straight line that shows the single "best fit" in the relationship between consumption and disposable income. Notice also the two clusters of points above and below the line of best fit. The cluster below the line corresponds to the significant recession in the early 1990s, when households increased their saving and reduced their consumption. The cluster above the line corresponds to the boom in the late 1990s when households did the opposite.

Keep in mind that when we simply plot the data and draw the line of best fit as in Figure 22-4, we are not accounting for changes in those variables that could *shift* the consumption function. Failure to account for such changes means that the true marginal propensity to consume is not necessarily well represented by the slope of the best-fit line. A precise estimate of the marginal propensity to consume therefore requires more complicated statistical techniques. (You will learn about the appropriate estimation methods if you go on to study econometrics.) For now, however, Figure 22-4 does give us a very rough estimate of the consumption function. It suggests that the theoretical consumption function we have been discussing is indeed broadly supported by a first glance at the Canadian data.

Desired Investment Expenditure

Investment expenditure is the most volatile component of GDP, and changes in investment expenditure are strongly associated with economic fluctuations. For example, as shown by the top line in Figure 22-5, total investment in Canada fell from over 18 percent of GDP in 1989, the peak of the business cycle, to 14.5 percent of GDP in 1993, the trough of the business cycle. Then, as GDP recovered from 1993 to 1999, investment increased back up toward its previous peak.

What explains such fluctuations in investment? Here we examine three important determinants of aggregate investment expenditure—the real interest rate, changes in sales, and business confidence.

Investment and the Real Interest Rate

The real interest rate represents the real cost of borrowing money for investment purposes. A rise in the real interest rate therefore reduces the amount of desired investment expenditure. This relationship is most easily seen if we separate investment into three components: inventories, residential construction, and plant and equipment.

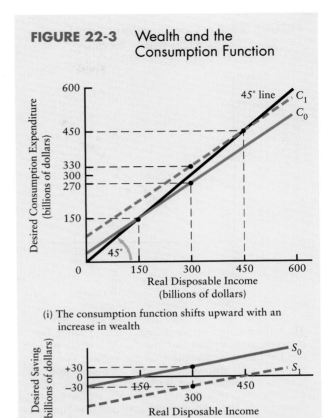

FIGURE 22-3   Wealth and the Consumption Function

(i) The consumption function shifts upward with an increase in wealth

(ii) The saving function shifts downward with an increase in wealth

Changes in wealth shift the consumption function. In part (i), line C_0 reproduces the consumption function from Figure 22-2(i). An increase in wealth raises desired consumption at each level of disposable income, thus shifting the consumption function up to C_1. In the figure, the consumption function shifts up by $60 billion, so with disposable income of $300 billion, for example, desired consumption rises from $270 billion to $330 billion.

The saving function in part (ii) shifts down by $60 billion, from S_0 to S_1. Thus, for example, at a disposable income of $300 billion, desired saving falls from $30 billion to −$30 billion.

Inventories.   Changes in inventories represent only a small percentage of private investment in a typical year. As shown by the bottom line in Figure 22-5, inventory investment has always been between −2 percent and 2 percent of GDP over the past 20 years. But the average size of such changes is not an adequate measure of their importance. Since they

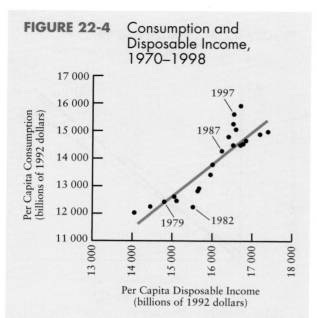

FIGURE 22-4   Consumption and Disposable Income, 1970–1998

The Canadian data suggest a clear, positive relationship between consumption and income. The figure plots real per capita consumption on the vertical axis and real per capita disposable income on the horizontal axis. Each point corresponds to the data from one year. The straight line is the line which shows the single "best fit" in the relationship between consumption and income.

(*Source:* Data prior to 1992 are from Department of Finance, *Economic Reference Tables*, August 1995. Data after 1992 are from CANSIM; D28390, D28391.)

are one of the more volatile elements of total investment, they have an important influence on fluctuations in investment expenditure.

When a firm ties up funds in inventories, those same funds cannot be used elsewhere to earn income. As an alternative to holding inventories, the firm could lend the money out at the going rate of interest. Hence, the higher the real rate of interest, the higher the opportunity cost of holding an inventory of a given size; the higher the opportunity cost, the smaller the inventories that will be desired.

Residential Construction.   Expenditure on residential housing is also volatile. Most houses are purchased with money that is borrowed by means of mortgages. Interest on the borrowed money typically accounts for over one-half of the purchaser's annual mortgage payments; the remainder is repayment of the original loan, called the *principal*. Because interest payments are such a large part of mortgage payments, variations in interest rates exert a substantial effect on the demand for housing.

Plant and Equipment.   Investment in plant and equipment is the largest component of domestic investment. Over one-half is financed by firms' retained earnings (profits that are not paid out to shareholders). Current profits are thus an important determinant of investment.

The rate of interest is also a major determinant of investment in plant and equipment. When interest rates are high, it is expensive for firms to borrow funds that can be used for fixed investment. At the same time, firms with cash on hand can earn high returns on interest-earning assets, again making investment in plant and equipment a less attractive alternative. Thus, high real interest rates lead to reduced investment in plant and equipment, and low real interest rates increase such investment.

The real interest rate reflects the opportunity cost associated with investment, whether it is investment in inventories, residential construction, or plant and equipment. The higher the real interest rate, the higher the opportunity cost of investment, and thus the lower the amount of desired investment.

Figure 22-5 shows these three components of investment over the past 20 years. Inventory investment is clearly the smallest of the three but in relative terms is the most volatile. Note that the three components move broadly together. They all fell in the 1981–82 recession, and again in the 1990–91 recession.

The largest part of investment by firms is the building of new plants and equipment, such as this expansion of a pulp mill in British Columbia.

Investment and Changes in Sales

Studies show that the stock of inventories tends to rise as production and sales rise. Because the size of inventories is related to the level of sales, the *change* in inventories (which is part of current investment) is related to the *change* in the level of sales.

Suppose a firm wants to hold inventories equal to 10 percent of its sales. If sales are $100 000, it will wish to hold inventories of $10 000. If sales increase to $110 000, it will want to hold inventories of $11 000. Over the period during which its stock of inventories is being increased, there will be a total of $1000 of new inventory investment.

The higher the level of production and sales, the larger the desired stock of inventories. Changes in the rate of production and sales therefore cause temporary bouts of investment (or disinvestment) in inventories.

Changes in sales have similar effects on investment in plant and equipment. For example, if there is a general increase in consumers' demand for products that is expected to persist and that cannot be met by existing capacity, investment in new plant and equipment will be needed. Once the new plants have been built and put into operation, however, the rate of new investment will fall.

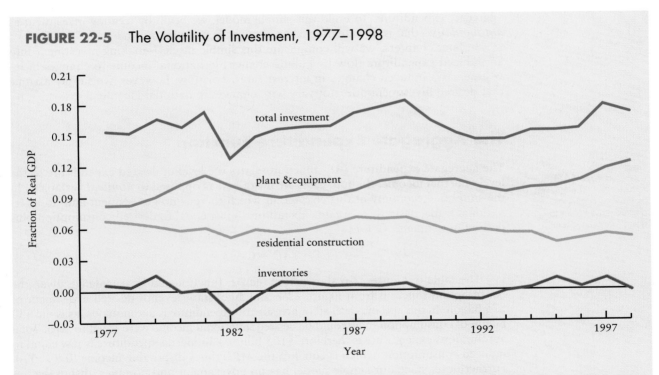

FIGURE 22-5   The Volatility of Investment, 1977–1998

Total investment as a share of GDP fluctuates considerably. In percentage terms, changes in inventories are the most volatile component of investment.

(*Source: Bank of Canada Review,* Winter 1998–99.)

Investment and Business Confidence

Investment takes time. When a firm invests, it increases its future capacity to produce output. If it can sell the new output profitably, the investment will prove to be a good one. If the new output does not generate profits, the investment will have been a bad one. When it undertakes an investment, the firm does not know if it will turn out well or badly—it is betting on a favourable future that cannot be known with certainty.

When firms expect good times ahead, they will want to invest now so that they have a larger productive capacity in the future ready to satisfy the greater demand. When they expect bad times ahead, they will not invest because they expect no payoff from doing so.

Investment depends in part on firms' forecasts of the future state of the economy.

The Conference Board of Canada publishes regular surveys of business and consumer confidence. Visit their website: www.conferenceboard.ca.

Investment as Autonomous Expenditure

We have seen that investment is influenced by many things, and a complete discussion of the determination of national income is not possible without including all of these factors.

For the moment, however, our goal is to build the *simplest* model of the aggregate economy in which we can examine the interaction of actual national income and desired aggregate expenditure. To build this simple model, we begin by treating investment as *autonomous*—that is, it is unaffected by changes in national income.

In later chapters, we will complicate this simple model—making investment into an induced expenditure flow by linking changes in national income to changes in investment via induced changes in interest rates. For now, however, we simply assume that desired investment does not vary with changes in national income.

The Aggregate Expenditure Function

aggregate expenditure (AE) function   The function that relates aggregate desired expenditure to actual national income.

The **aggregate expenditure (AE) function** relates the level of desired expenditure to the level of actual income. (In both cases we mean *real* as opposed to *nominal* variables.) In the simplified economy of this chapter, in which there is no government and no international trade, desired aggregate expenditure is just equal to desired consumption plus desired investment, $C + I$.

$$AE = C + I$$

The table in Figure 22-6 shows how the AE function can be calculated, given the consumption function from Figure 22-2 and a constant level of desired investment of $75 billion. In this specific case, all of investment expenditure is autonomous, as is the $30 billion of consumption that would be desired if national income were equal to zero. Total autonomous expenditure is therefore $105 billion—induced expenditure is just equal to induced consumption, which is equal to the MPC times disposable income ($0.8 \times Y_D$). Furthermore, since our simple model has no government and no taxes, disposable income, Y_D, is equal to national income, Y. Hence, desired aggregate expenditure can be written as:

$$AE = \$105 \text{ billion} + 0.8 \times Y$$

The Propensity to Spend Out of National Income

The fraction of any increment to national income that people spend on purchasing domestic output is called the economy's **marginal propensity to spend**. The marginal propensity to spend is measured by the change in desired aggregate expenditure divided by the change in national income, or $\Delta AE/\Delta Y$, the slope of the aggregate expenditure function. In this book, the marginal propensity to spend is denoted by the symbol z, which is a number greater than zero and less than one.

For the example given in Figure 22-6, the marginal propensity to spend is 0.8. If national income increases by a dollar, 80 cents will go into increased expenditure; 20 cents will go into increased saving and will not be spent.

The marginal propensity to spend should not be confused with the marginal propensity to consume.

The marginal propensity to spend is the amount of extra total expenditure induced when national income rises by $1, whereas the marginal propensity to consume is the amount of extra consumption expenditure induced when households' disposable income rises by $1.

In the simple model of this chapter, the marginal propensity to spend is equal to the marginal propensity to consume. In later chapters, however, when we add government and international trade to the model, the marginal propensity to spend differs from the marginal propensity to consume. Both here and in later chapters, it is the more general measure—the marginal propensity to spend—that is important for determining equilibrium national income.

> **marginal propensity to spend (MPS)**   The change in total desired spending on domestic output divided by the change in national income that brought it about.

FIGURE 22-6   The Aggregate Expenditure Function

National Income (Y)	Desired Consumption Expenditure (C = 30 + 0.8 × Y)	Desired Investment Expenditure (I = 75)	Desired Aggregate Expenditure (AE = C + I)
30	54	75	129
120	126	75	201
150	150	75	225
300	270	75	345
450	390	75	465
525	450	75	525
600	510	75	585
900	750	75	825

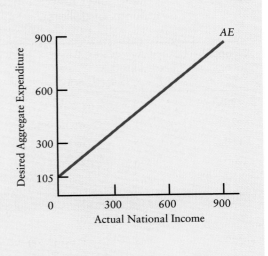

The aggregate expenditure function relates total desired expenditure to actual national income. The curve *AE* in the figure plots the data from the first and last columns of the accompanying table. Its intercept, which in this case is $105 billion, shows the sum of autonomous consumption and autonomous investment. Its slope is equal to the marginal propensity to spend (which in this simple economy is just the marginal propensity to consume).

Equilibrium National Income

We are now ready to see what determines the *equilibrium* level of national income. When something is in equilibrium, there is no tendency for it to change. Any conditions that are required for something to be in equilibrium are called its *equilibrium conditions*. We will see that the distinction between desired and actual expenditure is central to the equilibrium conditions for national income.

Desired Expenditure and Actual Output

Table 22-1 illustrates the determination of equilibrium national income for our simple hypothetical economy. Suppose that firms are producing a final output of $300 billion, and thus national income is $300 billion. According to the table, at this level of income, aggregate desired expenditure is $345 billion. If firms persist in producing a current output of only $300 billion in the face of an aggregate desired expenditure of $345 billion, one of two things will happen.

One possibility is that households and firms will be unable to spend the extra $45 billion that they would like to spend, so lines or waiting lists of unsatisfied customers will appear. These shortages will send a signal to firms that they can increase their sales if they increase their production. When the firms increase production, national income rises. Of course, the individual firms are interested only in their own sales and profits, but their individual actions have as their inevitable consequence an increase in GDP.

A more realistic possibility is that all spenders will spend everything that they wanted to spend. In this case, however, expenditure will exceed current output, which can happen only if some sales come from the producers' accumulated inventories. In our example, the fulfillment of plans to purchase $345 billion worth of commodities in the face of a current output of only $300 billion will reduce inventories by $45 billion. As long as inventories last, more goods can be sold than are currently being produced.

Eventually, however, inventories will run out. But before this happens, firms will increase their outputs as they see their inventories being depleted. Extra sales can then be made without a further depletion of inventories. Once again, the consequence of each individual firm's behaviour is an increase in national income. Thus, the final response to an excess of aggregate desired expenditure over actual output is a rise in national income.

For any level of national income at which aggregate desired expenditure exceeds actual income, there will be pressure for national income to rise.

TABLE 22-1   Equilibrium National Income (billions of dollars)

National Income (Y)	Desired Aggregate Expenditure (AE = C + I)	Effect
30	129	Pressure
120	201	on income
150	225	to rise
300	345	↓
450	465	↓
525	525	Equilibrium income
600	585	↑
900	825	Pressure on income to fall

National income is in equilibrium when aggregate desired expenditure equals actual national income. The data are from Figure 22-6.

Next consider the $900 billion level of national income in Table 22-1. At this level, desired expenditure on domestically produced goods is only $825 billion. If firms persist in producing $900 billion worth of goods, $75 billion worth must remain unsold. Therefore, inventories must rise. However, firms will not allow inventories of unsold goods to rise indefinitely; sooner or later, they will reduce the level of output to the level of sales. When they do, national income will fall.

For any level of income at which aggregate desired expenditure is less than actual output, there will be pressure for national income to fall.

Finally, look at the national income level of $525 billion in Table 22-1. At this level, and only at this level, aggregate desired expenditure is equal to actual national income. Purchasers can fulfill their spending plans without causing inventories to change. There is no incentive for firms to alter output. Because everyone wishes to purchase an amount equal to what is being produced, output and income will remain steady; they are in equilibrium.

The equilibrium level of national income occurs where aggregate desired expenditure equals actual national income.

Desired Saving and Desired Investment

We have just seen that equilibrium national income occurs where desired aggregate expenditure equals actual national income. The same equilibrium can also be described as the level of national income where *desired saving equals desired investment.*

The saving-investment formulation of the model is useful because it adds perspective on how equilibrium national income is determined. Later in this book, the saving-investment formulation will illuminate a key issue in economic policy—the influence of macroeconomic policy on long-run economic growth. Since investment adds to an economy's stock of productive resources, investment is often the only way for new and better technologies to be introduced to the workplace. In the long run, the level of a country's saving, through its effect on investment, can exert an important influence on economic growth. We are not yet ready to explore this important point, but when we are, the saving-investment balance will be an important part of the story. For now, our goal is to show that the equilibrium level of national income can be examined in terms of desired saving and desired investment.

Table 22-2 repeats data from Table 22-1, with three columns added: desired consumption, desired saving (which is disposable income minus desired consumption), and investment. Careful examination of this table reveals an important point: *The difference between desired investment and desired saving is exactly equal to the difference between desired aggregate expenditure and actual national income.*

This equality is no accident, but rather comes straight from the definition of desired aggregate expenditure. To see this, suppose the difference between desired saving and desired investment is equal to some number, W. Thus,

$$S - I = W$$

Now, recall that we use Y to denote actual national income, and that desired saving is just equal to actual national income minus desired consumption, $S = Y - C$. We can therefore rewrite the equation above to get

$$Y - C - I = W$$

TABLE 22-2 The Saving-Investment Balance

National Income (Y)	Desired Aggregate Expenditure (AE = C + I)	Desired Consumption (C = 30 + 0.8 × Y)	Desired Saving (S = Y − C)	Desired Investment (I)
30	129	54	−24	75
120	201	126	−6	75
300	345	270	30	75
525	525	450	75	75
600	585	510	90	75
900	825	750	150	75

National income is in equilibrium where desired saving is equal to desired investment. The data for Y, AE, and I are from Figure 22-2. At every level of national income, the difference between national income and desired aggregate expenditure is exactly equal to the difference between desired saving and desired investment.

But since desired aggregate expenditure is just the sum of desired consumption and desired investment, $AE = C + I$, we can rewrite the equation again to get

$$Y - (C + I) = W$$
$$\Rightarrow Y - AE = W$$

Thus, the difference between desired saving and desired investment is always equal to the difference between actual national income and desired aggregate expenditure.

In the simple model of this chapter, with no government and no international trade, the difference between desired saving and desired investment is exactly the same as the difference between actual national income and desired aggregate expenditure. Thus, the economy is in equilibrium when desired investment equals desired saving.

Practise with Study Guide Chapter 22, Exercise 5.

Equilibrium Illustrated

Figure 22-7 shows the determination of the equilibrium level of national income. The line labeled *AE* graphs the specific aggregate expenditure function that we have been working with throughout this chapter. The 45° line (*AE = Y*) graphs the equilibrium condition that aggregate desired expenditure equals actual national income. Anywhere along the 45° line, the value of desired aggregate expenditure, which is measured on the vertical axis, is equal to the value of actual national income, which is measured on the horizontal axis.[1]

Graphically, equilibrium occurs at the level of income at which the *AE* line intersects the 45° line. This is the level of income where desired expenditure is just equal to actual national income and hence is just sufficient to purchase total final output.

---

[1]Because it turns up in many different guises, the 45° line can cause a bit of confusion until one gets used to it. The main thing to remember is that it can be used whenever the variables plotted on the two axes are measured in the same units, such as dollars, and are plotted on the same scale. In that case, equal distances on the two axes measure the same amounts.

The equilibrium is also illustrated in part (ii) of the figure, but in terms of the saving-investment balance. The line labeled S is equal to desired saving. The line labeled I is desired investment.

Notice that the vertical distance between S and I is exactly equal to the distance between the 45° line and AE. When desired investment exceeds desired saving, desired aggregate expenditure exceeds actual national income by the same amount. When desired investment is less than desired saving, desired aggregate expenditure is less than actual national income by the same amount.

Now that we have explained the meaning of equilibrium national income, we will go on to examine the various forces that can *change* this equilibrium. We will then be well on our way to understanding some of the sources of short-run fluctuations in national income.

Changes in Equilibrium National Income

Because the AE function plays a central role in determining equilibrium national income, you should not be surprised to hear that shifts in the AE function are central to explaining why national income changes. To understand this influence, we must recall an important distinction we first encountered in Chapter 3—the distinction between *shifts of* a curve and *movements along* a curve.

Suppose that desired aggregate expenditure rises. This may be a response to a change in national income, or it may be the result of an increased desire to spend *at each level* of national income. A change in national income causes a *movement along* the AE function. An increased desire to spend at each level of national income causes a *shift of* the AE function. Figure 22-8 illustrates this important distinction.

FIGURE 22-7 Equilibrium National Income

(i) Income and expenditure

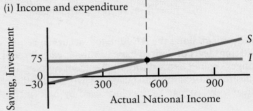

(ii) Saving and investment

Equilibrium national income is that level of national income where desired aggregate expenditure equals actual national income. If actual national income is below Y_0 in panel (i), desired aggregate expenditure will exceed national income, and output will rise. This is shown by the arrow to the left of Y_0. If national income is above Y_0, desired aggregate expenditure will be less than national income, and production will fall. This is shown by the arrow to the right of Y_0. Only when national income is equal to Y_0 will the economy be in equilibrium.

Panel (ii) shows desired saving and desired investment on the same scale as panel (i). Equilibrium national income occurs where desired saving equals desired investment. The vertical distance between saving and investment is exactly the same as the vertical distance in part (i) between AE and the 45° line.

Shifts of the *AE* Function

The AE function shifts when one of its components shifts—that is, when there is a shift in the consumption function or in desired investment expenditure.

Upward Shifts in the *AE* Function

What will happen if households experience an increase in wealth and thus increase their desired levels of consumption spending at each level of disposable income? What

FIGURE 22-8   Movements Along and Shifts of the *AE* Function

(i) A movement along the *AE* function

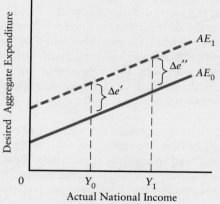

(ii) A shift of the *AE* function

A movement along the *AE* function occurs in response to a change in national income; a shift of the *AE* function indicates a different level of desired expenditure at each level of national income. In part (i), a change in income of ΔY, from Y_0 to Y_1, changes desired expenditure by Δe, from e_0 to e_1. In part (ii), a shift in the *AE* function from AE_0 to AE_1 raises the amount of desired expenditure associated with each level of national income. At Y_0, for example, desired aggregate expenditure is increased by $\Delta e'$; at Y_1, it is increased by $\Delta e''$. (If the *AE* function shifts in a parallel manner, then $\Delta e' = \Delta e''$.)

will happen if the expectation of higher future sales causes domestic auto makers to increase their planned investment?

Because any such increase in autonomous expenditure shifts the entire *AE* function upward, the same analysis applies to each of the changes mentioned. Two types of shift in *AE* can occur. First, if the same addition to expenditure occurs at all levels of income, the *AE* function shifts parallel to itself, as shown in part (i) of Figure 22-9. Second, if there is a change in the marginal propensity to spend, the slope of the *AE* function changes, as shown in part (ii) of Figure 22-9.

Figure 22-9 shows that an upward shift in the *AE* function increases equilibrium national income. After the shift in the *AE* curve, income is no longer in equilibrium at its original level because at that level desired expenditure exceeds actual national income. Given this excess demand, firms' inventories are being depleted and firms then respond by increasing production. Equilibrium national income rises to the higher level indicated by the intersection of the new *AE* curve with the 45° line.

Downward Shifts in the Saving Function.   We saw earlier that, in equilibrium, desired aggregate expenditure is equal to actual national income, and desired saving is equal to desired investment. When the *AE* function shifts and equilibrium income changes, this equality must still hold true at the new equilibrium.

Consider the case of a shift in the *AE* function that is caused by a shift in the consumption function. As we discussed earlier (see Figure 22-2), when the consumption function shifts, the saving function shifts as well, and by an equal and opposite amount. This is true because consumption and saving always adds up to disposable income.

FIGURE 22-9   Shifts in the Aggregate Expenditure Function

(i) A parallel shift in *AE*

(ii) A change in the slope of *AE*

Upward shifts in the *AE* function increase equilibrium income; downward shifts decrease equilibrium income. In parts (i) and (ii), the *AE* function is initially AE_0 with equilibrium national income equal to Y_0.

In part (i), a parallel upward shift in the *AE* curve from AE_0 to AE_1 reflects an increase in desired expenditure at each level of national income. For example, at Y_0, desired expenditure rises from e_0 to e_1' and therefore exceeds national income. Equilibrium is reached at E_1, where income is Y_1. The increase in desired expenditure from e_1' to e_1, represented by a movement along AE_1, is an induced response to the increase in income from Y_0 to Y_1.

In part (ii), a nonparallel upward shift in the *AE* curve from AE_0 to AE_2 reflects an increase in the marginal propensity to spend. This leads to an increase in equilibrium national income. Equilibrium is reached at E_2, where national income is equal to Y_2.

Hence, if the consumption function shifts up by some amount at every level of income, the saving function *must* shift down by exactly the same amount.

Figure 22-10 shows a downward shift in the saving function (corresponding to an upward shift in the consumption function). Equilibrium national income occurs where desired saving equals desired investment. With desired investment fixed, a downward shift in the saving function leads to an *increase* in equilibrium national income. This is just as it should be—a downward shift in the saving function implies an upward shift in the consumption and *AE* functions.

Downward Shifts in the *AE* Function

What happens to national income if there is a decrease in the amount of consumption or investment expenditure desired at each level of income? These changes shift the *AE* function downward. A constant reduction in desired expenditure at all levels of income shifts *AE* parallel to itself. A fall in the marginal propensity to spend out of national income reduces the slope of the *AE* function. When we use the saving-investment relation, we must note that a downward shift in the consumption function implies an upward shift in the saving function, reducing the equilibrium level of income.

The Results Restated

We have derived two important general propositions from our simple model of national income determination.

1. A rise in the amount of desired aggregate expenditure associated with each level of national income will increase equilibrium national income.

2. A fall in the amount of desired aggregate expenditure associated with each level of national income will reduce equilibrium national income.

The Multiplier

We have learned how to predict the direction of the changes in national income that occur in response to various shifts in the *AE* function. We would like also to predict the *magnitude* of these changes.

Economists need to know the *size* of the effects of changes in expenditures. During a recession, the government sometimes takes measures to stimulate the economy. If these measures have a larger effect than estimated, demand may rise too much, and full employment may be reached while demand is still rising. As we will see in Chapters 24 and 25, this outcome will have an inflationary effect on the economy. On the other hand, if the government overestimates the impact of its measures, the recession will persist longer than necessary. In this case, there is a danger that the policy will be discredited as ineffective, even though the correct diagnosis is that too little of the right thing was done.

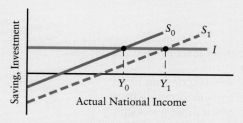

FIGURE 22-10 Shifts in Desired Saving

A downward shift in the saving function increases equilibrium national income. If the consumption function shifts up, the saving function must shift down by an equal amount, indicating a reduction in desired saving at every level of national income. Since equilibrium occurs where desired saving equals desired investment, the new equilibrium occurs at a higher national income—the economy moves from Y_0 to Y_1. The saving function has indeed shifted down, but the increase in equilibrium income has caused a movement *along* the new S_1 function and restored the level of saving to its previous level.

Defining the Multiplier

A measure of the magnitude of changes in national income is provided by the *multiplier*. We have just seen that a shift in the *AE* curve will cause a change in equilibrium national income. Such a shift could be caused by a change in any autonomous component of aggregate expenditure. An increase in desired aggregate expenditure increases equilibrium national income by a *multiple* of the initial increase in autonomous expenditure. That is, the increase in national income is *larger than* the initial increase in desired expenditure.

The multiplier is the change in equilibrium national income divided by the change in autonomous expenditure that brought it about. In the simple macro model, the multiplier is greater than one.

To see why the multiplier is greater than one, consider a simple example. Imagine what would happen to national income if Kimberley-Clark decided to spend $500 million per year on new paper mills. Initially, the construction of the paper mills would create $500 million worth of new national income and a corresponding amount of income for households and firms on which the initial $500 million is spent. But this is not the end of the story. The increase in national income of $500 million would cause an increase in disposable income, which would cause an induced rise in consumption expenditure.

Electricians, masons, and carpenters—who gain new income directly from the building of the paper mills—would spend some of it on food, clothing, entertainment, cars, TVs, and other commodities. When output expands to meet this demand, new incomes would be created for workers and firms in these industries. When they, in turn, spend their newly earned incomes, output would rise further. More income would be created, and more expenditure would be induced. Indeed, at this stage, we might wonder whether the increases in income would ever come to an end. To deal with this concern, we need to consider the multiplier in somewhat more precise terms.

Suppose we let autonomous expenditure be denoted by A. Now consider an increase in autonomous expenditure of ΔA, which in our example above was $500 million per year. Remember that ΔA stands for *any* increase in autonomous expenditure; this could be an increase in investment or in the autonomous component of consumption. The new autonomous expenditure shifts the AE function upward by that amount. National income is no longer in equilibrium at its original level because desired aggregate expenditure now exceeds actual income. Equilibrium is restored by a *movement along* the new AE curve.

The **simple multiplier** measures the change in equilibrium national income that occurs in response to a change in autonomous expenditure *at a constant price level*. We refer to it as "simple" because we have simplified the situation by assuming that the price level is fixed (an assumption we will remove following Chapter 23). Figure 22-11 illustrates the simple multiplier and makes clear that it is greater than one. *Applying Economic Concepts 22-1* provides a numerical example.

The Size of the Simple Multiplier

The size of the simple multiplier depends on the slope of the AE function—that is, on the marginal propensity to spend, z.

As shown in Figure 22-12, a high marginal propensity to spend means a steep AE curve. The expenditure induced by any initial increase in income is large, with the result that the final rise in income is correspondingly large. By contrast, a low marginal propensity to spend means a relatively flat AE curve. The expenditure induced by the initial increase in income is small, and the final rise in income is not much larger than the initial rise in autonomous expenditure that brought it about.

FIGURE 22-11 The Simple Multiplier

An increase in the autonomous component of desired aggregate expenditure increases equilibrium national income by a multiple of the initial increase. The initial equilibrium is at E_0, where AE_0 intersects the 45° line. At this point, desired expenditure, e_0, is equal to national income, Y_0. An increase in autonomous expenditure of ΔA then shifts the AE function upward to AE_1.

Equilibrium occurs when income rises to Y_1. Here desired expenditure, e_1, equals national income, Y_1. The increase in desired expenditure from e_1' to e_1 represents the induced increase in expenditure. It is the amount by which the overall increase in national income, ΔY, exceeds the initial increase in autonomous expenditure, ΔA. Because ΔY is greater than ΔA, the simple multiplier is greater than one ($\Delta Y / \Delta A > 1$).

APPLYING ECONOMIC CONCEPTS 22-1

The Multiplier: A Numerical Example

Consider an economy that has a marginal propensity to spend out of national income of 0.80. Suppose an increase in business confidence leads many firms to increase their spending on new buildings and factories. Specifically, suppose desired investment increases by $1 billion per year. National income initially rises by $1 billion, but that is not the end of it. The factors of production that received the first $1 billion spend $800 million. This second round of spending generates $800 million of new income. This new income, in turn, induces $640 million of third-round spending, and so it continues, with each successive round of new income generating 80 percent as much in new expenditure. Each additional round of expenditure creates new income and yet another round of expenditure.

The table carries the process through 10 rounds. Students with sufficient patience (and no faith in mathematics) may compute as many rounds in the process as they wish; they will find that the sum of the rounds of expenditures approaches a limit of $5 billion, which is five times the initial increase in expenditure. [31]

The graph of the cumulative expenditure increases shows how quickly this limit is approached. The multiplier is 5, given that the marginal propensity to spend is 0.8. Had the marginal propensity to spend been lower, say, 0.667, the process would have been similar, but it would have approached a limit of three instead of five times the initial increase in expenditure.

Round of spending	Increase in Expenditure (millions of dollars)	Cumulative Total (millions of dollars)
1 (initial increase)	1000.0	1000.0
2	800.0	1800.0
3	640.0	2440.0
4	512.0	2952.0
5	409.6	3361.6
6	327.7	3689.3
7	262.1	3951.4
8	209.7	4161.1
9	167.8	4328.9
10	134.2	4463.1
11 to 20 combined	479.3	4942.4
All others	57.6	5000.0

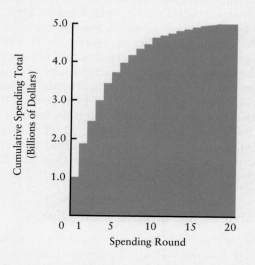

The larger the marginal propensity to spend, the steeper the *AE* function and thus the larger the simple multiplier.

We can derive the precise value of the simple multiplier by using elementary algebra. (The formal derivation is given in *Extensions in Theory 22-1*.) The result is that the simple multiplier, which is called *K*, is

$$\text{Simple Multiplier} = K = \frac{\Delta Y}{\Delta A} = \frac{1}{1 - z}$$

FIGURE 22-12 The Size of the Simple Multiplier

(i) Flat *AE*, multiplier equal to one

(ii) Intermediate case

(iii) Steep *AE*, multiplier large

The larger the marginal propensity to spend out of national income (z), the steeper is the AE curve and the larger is the multiplier. In each part of the figure, the initial AE function is AE_0, equilibrium is at E_0, with income Y_0. The AE curve then shifts upward to AE_1 as a result of an increase in autonomous expenditure of ΔA. ΔA is the same in each part. The new equilibrium in each case is at E_1.

In part (i), the AE function is horizontal, indicating a marginal propensity to spend of zero ($z = 0$). The change in equilibrium income ΔY is only the increase in autonomous expenditure because there is no induced expenditure by the people who receive the initial increase in income. The simple multiplier is then equal to one, its minimum possible value.

In part (ii), the AE curve slopes upward but is still relatively flat (z is low). The increase in equilibrium national income to Y_2 is only slightly greater than the increase in autonomous expenditure that brought it about.

In part (iii), the AE function is quite steep (z is high). Now the increase in equilibrium income to Y_3 is much larger than the increase in autonomous expenditure that brought it about. The simple multiplier is quite large.

Recall that z is the marginal propensity to spend out of national income and is between zero and one. The *smallest* simple multiplier occurs when z equals zero. In this case, $(1 - z)$ equals one and so the multiplier equals one. On the other hand, if z is very close to one, $(1 - z)$ is close to zero and so the multiplier becomes very large. The relationship between z, the slope of the AE function, and the size of the multiplier is shown in Figure 22-12.

To estimate the size of the multiplier in an actual economy, we need to estimate the value of the marginal propensity to spend out of national income in that economy. Evidence suggests that the Canadian value is much smaller than the 0.8 that we used in our example, in large part because there are a number of withdrawals from the circular flow of income that we have not yet included in our model of the economy. In addition to saving, which we have discussed, these withdrawals include income taxes and import expenditures. For the current Canadian economy these adjustments lead to a realistic estimate of around 0.3 for z. Hence, the simple multiplier in Canada is approximately $K = 1/(1 - 0.3) = 1/0.7 = 1.43$. The simple multiplier is closer to 1.5 than to 5, as in the example.

The simple multiplier is a useful starting point for understanding the effects of changes in autonomous expenditures on equilibrium national income; however, as we shall see in subsequent chapters, many complications that make the story more complex will arise.

EXTENSIONS IN THEORY 22-1

Deriving The Simple Multiplier

Basic algebra is all that is needed to derive the exact expression for the multiplier. Readers who feel at home with algebra may want to follow this derivation. Others can skip it and rely on the graphical and numerical arguments that have been given in the text.

First, we derive the equation for the AE curve. Desired aggregate expenditure can be decomposed into autonomous expenditure and induced expenditure. In the simple model of this chapter, autonomous expenditure is just equal to investment plus autonomous consumption. Induced expenditure is just equal to induced consumption.

Hence, we can write

$$AE = zY + A \qquad [1]$$

where A is autonomous expenditure and zY is induced expenditure, z being the marginal propensity to spend out of national income. In the simple model of this chapter, with no government and no international trade, z is equal to the marginal propensity to consume.

Now we write the equation of the 45° line,

$$AE = Y \qquad [2]$$

which states the equilibrium condition that desired aggregate expenditure equals actual national income. Equations 1 and 2 are two equations with two unknowns,

AE and Y. To solve them, we substitute Equation 1 into Equation 2 to obtain

$$Y = zY + A \qquad [3]$$

Equation 3 can be easily solved to get Y expressed in terms of A and z. The solution is

$$Y = \frac{A}{1 - z} \qquad [4]$$

Equation 4 tells us the equilibrium value of Y in terms of autonomous expenditures and the marginal propensity to spend out of national income. Now consider a \$1 increase in A. The expression $Y = A/(1 - z)$ tells us that if A changes by one dollar, the change in Y will be $1/(1 - z)$ dollars. Generally, for a change in autonomous spending of ΔA, the change in Y will be

$$\Delta Y = \frac{\Delta A}{1 - z} \qquad [5]$$

Dividing through by ΔA gives the value of the multiplier, which is designated by K:

$$K = \frac{\Delta Y}{\Delta A} = \frac{1}{1 - z} \qquad [6]$$

S U M M A R Y

Desired Expenditure

- Desired aggregate expenditure is equal to desired consumption plus desired investment plus desired government purchases plus desired net exports. It is the amount that economic agents want to spend on purchasing the national product. In this chapter, we consider only consumption and investment.

- The relationship between disposable income and consumption is called the consumption function. The constant term in the consumption function is autonomous expenditure. The part of consumption that responds to income is called induced expenditure.

- A change in disposable income leads to a change in desired consumption and desired saving. The responsiveness of these changes is measured by the marginal propensity to consume (*MPC*) and the marginal propensity to save (*MPS*), both of which are positive, and which sum to one, indicating that all disposable income is either consumed or saved.

- A change in wealth tends to cause an increase in the portion of disposable income that is consumed. The consumption function shifts up.
- Investment depends, among other things, on real interest rates, changes in sales, and business confidence. In our simplest model of the economy, investment is treated as an autonomous expenditure.

Equilibrium National Income

- Equilibrium national income is defined as that level of national income where desired aggregate expenditure equals actual national income. At incomes above equilibrium, desired expenditure falls short of national income. In this case, inventories accumulate and output will sooner or later fall. At incomes below equilibrium, desired expenditure exceeds national income. In this case, inventories are depleted and output will sooner or later rise.
- In a closed economy with no government, an alternative definition of equilibrium national income is that level of

national income where desired saving equals desired investment.
- Equilibrium national income is represented graphically by the point at which the aggregate expenditure curve cuts the 45° line—that is, where desired aggregate expenditure equals national income. This is the same level of income at which the saving function intersects the investment function.

Changes in Equilibrium National Income

- Equilibrium national income is increased by a rise in either autonomous consumption or autonomous investment expenditure. Equilibrium national income is reduced by a fall in these desired expenditures.
- The magnitude of the effect on national income of shifts in autonomous expenditure is given by the multiplier. It is defined as $K = \Delta Y/\Delta A$, where ΔA is the change in autonomous expenditure.

- The simple multiplier is the multiplier when the price level is constant. It is equal to $1/(1 - z)$, where z is the marginal propensity to spend out of national income. The larger is z, the larger is the multiplier. It is a basic prediction of national income theory that the simple multiplier, relating an increase in spending on domestic output to the resulting increase in national income, is greater than one.

K E Y   C O N C E P T S

Desired versus actual expenditure
The consumption function
Average and marginal propensities to consume
Average and marginal propensities to save

The aggregate expenditure *(AE)* function
Marginal propensity to spend
Equilibrium national income
Shifts of and movements along *AE* curves

Effect on national income of shifts in the *AE* curve
The simple multiplier
The size of the multiplier and slope of the *AE* curve

STUDY EXERCISES

1. Consider the following table for a household's consumption expenditures and disposable income. All values are expressed in real 1992 dollars.

Disposable Income (Y_D)	Desired Consumption (C)	$APC = C/Y_D$	$MPC = \Delta C/\Delta Y_D$
0	150	—	
100	225	—	—
200	300	—	—
300	375	—	—
400	450	—	—
500	525	—	—
600	600	—	—
700	675	—	—
800	750	—	—

a. Compute the average propensity to consume for each level of income and fill in the table.
b. Compute the marginal propensity to consume for each successive change in income and fill in the table.
c. Plot the consumption function on a scale diagram. What is its slope?

2. This question relates to desired saving, and is based on the table from Question 1.

a. Compute desired saving at each level of disposable income. Plot the saving function on a scale diagram. What is its slope?
b. Show that the average propensity to save plus the average propensity to consume must equal one.

3. In the chapter we explained at length the difference between *desired* expenditures and *actual* expenditures.

a. Is national income accounting based on desired or actual expenditures? Explain.
b. Suppose there were a sudden decrease in consumer expenditure. Explain why this would lead to an equally sudden increase in *actual* investment. Which type of investment would rise?
c. Illustrate the event from part b in a 45° line diagram. Illustrate the increase in actual investment.

4. Consider the following diagram of the AE function and the 45° line.

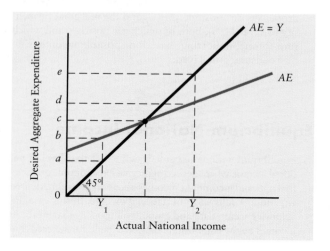

a. Suppose the level of actual national income is Y_1. What is the level of desired aggregate expenditure? Is it greater or less than actual output? Are inventories being depleted or accumulated?
b. If actual income is Y_1, explain the process by which national income changes toward equilibrium.
c. Suppose the level of actual national income is Y_2. What is the level of desired aggregate expenditure? Is it greater or less than actual output? Are inventories being depleted or accumulated?
d. If actual income is Y_2, explain the process by which national income changes toward equilibrium.

5. Suppose that you are given the following information for an economy without government spending, exports, or imports. C is desired consumption, I is desired investment, and Y is income. C and I are given by:

$$C = 1400 + 0.8Y$$
$$I = 400$$

a. What is the equation for the aggregate expenditure (AE) function?
b. Applying the equilibrium condition that $Y = AE$, determine the level of equilibrium national income.
c. Using your answer from part b, determine the values of consumption, saving and investment when the economy is in equilibrium.

6. Consider an economy characterized by the following equations:

$$C = 500 + 0.75Y$$
$$I = 150$$

   where C is desired consumption, I is desired investment, and Y is national income.

   a. Draw the aggregate expenditure function on a scale diagram along with the 45° line. What is the equilibrium level of national income?
   b. The marginal propensity to spend in this economy is 0.75. What is the value of the multiplier?

   c. Using your answer from part **b**, what would be the change in equilibrium national income if desired investment increased to 250? Can you show this in your diagram?

7. The "Paradox of Thrift" is a famous idea in macroeconomics—one that we will discuss in later chapters. The basic idea is that if every household in the economy tries to increase its level of desired saving, the level of national income will fall and they will end up saving no more than they were initially. Use the model and diagrams of this chapter to show how an (autonomous) increase in desired saving would reduce equilibrium income and lead to no change in aggregate saving.

DISCUSSION QUESTIONS

1. Relate the following newspaper headlines to shifts in the C, S, I, and AE functions and to changes in equilibrium national income.

   a. "Revival of consumer confidence leads to increased spending."
   b. "High mortgage rates discourage new house purchases."
   c. "Concern over future leads to a reduction in inventories."
   d. "Accelerated depreciation allowances in the new federal budget sets off boom on equipment purchases."
   e. "Consumers spend as stock market soars."

2. Why might an individual's marginal propensity to consume be higher in the long run than in the short run? Why might it be lower? Is it possible for an individual's average propensity to consume to be greater than one in the short run? In the long run? Can a country's average propensity to consume be greater than one in the short run? In the long run?

3. Explain why a sudden, unexpected fall in consumer expenditure would initially cause an increase in actual investment expenditure by firms.

4. In the simple model of this chapter, aggregate investment was assumed to be autonomous. The simple multiplier was $K = 1/(1 - z)$, where z was the marginal propensity to spend. With autonomous investment, the marginal propensity to spend is simply the marginal propensity to consume. Now suppose that investment is *not* completely autonomous. That is, suppose that $I = \bar{I} + mY$, where $\bar{I}$ is autonomous investment and m is the "marginal propensity to invest" $(m > 0)$. Explain how this modification to the simple model changes the simple multiplier.

CHAPTER 23

Adding Government and Trade to the Simple Macro Model

LEARNING OBJECTIVES

1 Understand how the government budget surplus is related to national income.

2 Understand how net exports are related to national income.

3 Recognize the difference between the marginal propensity to consume and the marginal propensity to spend.

4 Explain why net exports lead the economy to accumulate assets.

5 Understand why the presence of government and foreign trade reduces the value of the simple multiplier.

6 Explain how government can use its fiscal policy to influence the level of national income.

7 Recognize that the simple income-expenditure model of national income determination is based on the assumption of a given price level.

In Chapter 22, we developed a simplified model of national income determination in a closed economy with fixed prices. In this chapter, we add a government and a foreign sector to our simple model. In Chapters 24 and 25, we will expand the model further to explain the determination of the price level.

Adding government to the model allows us to study *fiscal policy*, the government's use of its taxing and spending powers to affect the level of national income. Adding foreign trade allows us to examine how external events—such as the 1997–98 Asian financial and economic crisis—affect the Canadian economy. Fortunately, the key elements of last chapter's theory of income determination are unchanged even after government and the foreign sector are incorporated.

Introducing Government

fiscal policy The use of the government's tax and spending policies in an effort to influence the behaviour of GDP.

A government's **fiscal policy** is defined by its plans for taxes and spending. These influence the size of national income in both the short and the long run. Our discussion of fiscal policy begins in this chapter; we go into more detail in Chapter 25 and again in Chapter 31.

Government Spending

In Chapter 20, we distinguished between government *purchases of goods and services* and government *transfer payments*. The distinction bears repeating here. Government purchases are part of GDP. When the government hires a bureaucrat, buys a paper clip, or purchases fuel for the armed forces, it is adding directly to the demands for the economy's current output of goods and services. Hence, desired government purchases, G, are part of aggregate desired expenditure.

The other part of government spending, transfer payments, also affects desired aggregate expenditure, but only indirectly. Consider welfare or unemployment-insurance payments, for example. These government expenditures place no demand on the nation's production of goods and services. However, when recipients spend some of these payments on consumption, their expenditure is part of aggregate expenditure. Thus, government transfer payments do affect aggregate expenditure but only through the effect that these payments have on *disposable* income. An increase in transfer payments increases disposable income, and an increase in disposable income increases households' desired consumption expenditure.

Tax Revenues

Taxes reduce households' disposable income relative to national income. In contrast, transfer payments raise disposable income relative to national income. For the purpose of calculating the effect of government policy on desired consumption expenditure, it is the net effect of the two that matters.

Net taxes are defined as total tax revenue received by the government minus total transfer payments made by the government, and it is denoted as T. (For convenience, the term "taxes" means "net taxes" unless explicitly stated otherwise.) Because transfer payments are smaller than total tax revenues, net tax revenues are positive. This makes disposable personal income substantially less than national income. (It was about 67 percent of GDP in 1998.)

net taxes   Total tax revenue minus transfer payments, denoted T.

The Budget Balance

The *budget balance* is the difference between total government revenue and total government expenditure; equivalently, it equals net tax revenue minus government purchases, $T - G$. When revenues exceed expenditures, the government is said to be running a **budget surplus**. When expenditures exceed revenues, the government is said to be running a **budget deficit**.[1] When the two amounts are equal, the government has a *balanced budget*.

In the simple model of Chapter 22, all saving was private since we had no government in the model. But now we must make a distinction between *private saving* and *public saving*.

Private saving is the difference between disposable income and consumption expenditure, or the amount that households choose to save. **Public saving** is the difference between the government's tax revenues (its income) and its expenditures (its consumption). Public saving is therefore equal to the budget surplus, $T - G$.

budget surplus   Any excess of current revenue over current expenditure.

budget deficit   Any shortfall of current revenue below current expenditure.

private saving   Saving on the part of households—the part of disposable income that is not spent on current consumption.

public saving   Saving on the part of governments equal to the government budget surplus.

---

[1]When the government runs a budget deficit, it must borrow the excess of spending over revenues. It does this by issuing and selling *government bonds*. When the government runs a surplus, it uses the excess revenue to purchase outstanding government bonds. The stock of outstanding bonds is termed the *national debt*. Deficits and the national debt are the principal topics of Chapter 31.

When government runs a budget surplus, public saving is positive; when government runs a budget deficit, public saving is negative.

The Public Saving Function

The federal Department of Finance designs and implements Canada's fiscal policy. See their website: www.fin.gc.ca.

In this chapter, government purchases of goods and services are treated as autonomous—that is, the level of government purchases *(G)* does not depend on the level of national income. We also treat *tax rates* as autonomous. This, however, implies that *tax revenues* are induced. As national income rises, a tax system with given tax rates will yield more revenue. For example, when income rises, people will pay more income tax in total even though the tax *rates* are unchanged.

Figure 23-1 illustrates these assumptions with a specific example using hypothetical data. It shows public saving when government purchases *(G)* are constant at $51 billion and net taxes are equal to 10 percent of national income. Notice that public saving (which is exactly equal to the government budget surplus) increases with national income. This relationship occurs because net tax revenues rise with income but, by assumption, government purchases do not. The slope of the public saving function (which can also be called the *budget surplus function*) is just equal to the income-tax rate. The position of the budget surplus function is determined by fiscal policy, as we discuss later in this chapter.

Practise with Study Guide Chapter 23, Exercise 3.

Provincial and Municipal Governments

Most of our discussion of government spending and taxing is focused on the federal government, which generally has more discretion over its fiscal policy than do provincial and municipal governments. However, it is important to remember that the Canadian provincial and municipal governments account for *more* purchases of goods and services than does the federal government. The federal government raises about the same amount of tax revenue as do the provincial and municipal governments combined, but spends much more of its revenues on transfer payments.

FIGURE 23-1   The Public Saving (Budget Surplus) Function

National Income (Y)	Government Purchases (G)	Net Taxes (T = 0.1 × Y)	Public Saving (T − G)
150	51	15	−36
300	51	30	−21
525	51	52.5	1.5
600	51	60	9
900	51	90	39

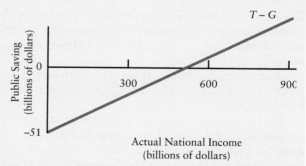

Public saving, which is just equal to the budget surplus, is negative at low levels of national income but rises with national income. The slope of the public saving function is equal to the income-tax rate, 0.1. As national income rises, public saving rises by the income-tax rate times the change in national income. Thus, when national income rises by $300 billion, public saving rises by $30 billion.

When measuring the overall contribution of government to desired aggregate expenditure and to public saving, all levels of government must be included.

As we proceed through this chapter discussing the role of government in the determination of national income, think of "the government" as the combination of all levels of government—federal, provincial, and municipal.

Introducing Foreign Trade

Of all the goods and services produced in Canada in a given year, roughly 40 percent are exported. A similar value of goods and services is imported into Canada every year. Thus, while *net* exports may not contribute much to Canada's GDP (1.4 percent in 1998), trade is tremendously important to Canada's economy.

Canada imports all kinds of goods and services, from French wine and Peruvian anchovies to Swiss financial and American architectural services. Canada also exports a variety of goods and services, including timber, nickel, automobiles, engineering services, computer software, and commuter jets. U.S.-Canadian trade is the largest two-way flow of trade between any two countries in the world today.

The Net Export Function

Exports depend on spending decisions made by foreign households and firms that purchase Canadian goods and services. Typically, exports will not change as a result of changes in Canadian national income. We therefore treat exports as autonomous expenditure.

Imports, however, depend on the spending decisions of Canadian households and firms. Almost all consumption goods have an import content. Canadian-made cars, for example, use large quantities of imported components in their manufacture. Canadian-made clothes most often use imported textiles, such as cotton or wool. And most restaurant meals contain some imported fruits, vegetables, or meats. Hence, as consumption rises, imports will also increase. Because consumption rises with national income, we also get a positive relationship between imports and national income. The **marginal propensity to import** (denoted m) is the change in imports that comes about from a $1 change in national income.

marginal propensity to import   The change in import divided by the change in real GDP that brought it about. Denoted by m.

There is a positive relationship between desired imports and national income. Since exports are autonomous with respect to national income, desired net exports (exports minus imports) are negatively related to national income.

This negative relationship between net exports and national income is called the *net export function*. Data for a hypothetical economy with autonomous exports and with imports that are 10 percent of national income are illustrated in Figure 23-2. In this example, exports form the autonomous component and imports the induced component of the desired net export function.

Shifts in the Net Export Function

The net export function relates net exports $(X - IM)$, which we also denote NX, to national income. It is drawn under the assumption that everything affecting net exports, except domestic national income, remains constant. The major factors that must be held

FIGURE 23-2   The Net Export Function

National Income (Y)	Exports (X)	Imports (IM = 0.1 × Y)	Net Exports
0	72	0	72
300	72	30	42
600	72	60	12
720	72	72	0
900	72	90	−18

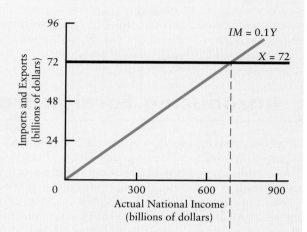

(i) Export and import functions

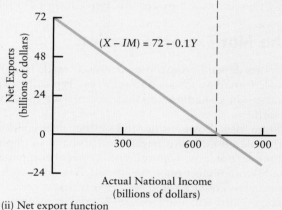

(ii) Net export function

Net exports, defined as the difference between exports and imports, fall as income rises. The data are hypothetical. They assume that exports are constant and that imports are 10 percent of national income. In part (i), exports are constant at $72 billion while imports rise with national income. Therefore, net exports, shown in part (ii), decline with national income. The slope of the import function in part (i) is equal to the marginal propensity to import. The slope of the net export function in part (ii) is the negative of the marginal propensity to import.

constant are foreign national income, domestic and foreign prices, and the exchange rate. A change in any of these factors will affect the amount of net exports that will occur at each level of Canadian national income and hence will shift the net export function.

Notice that anything affecting Canadian exports will shift the net export function parallel to itself, upward if exports increase and downward if exports decrease. Also notice that anything affecting the *proportion of income* that Canadian consumers wish to spend on imports will change the *slope* of the net export function.

Foreign Income

An increase in foreign income, other things being equal, will lead to an increase in the quantity of Canadian goods demanded by foreign countries—that is, to an increase in Canadian exports. This change causes the net export function to shift upward, parallel to its original position. A fall in foreign income leads to a reduction in Canadian exports and thus to a parallel downward shift in the net export function.

Relative International Prices

Any change in the prices of Canadian goods relative to those of foreign goods will cause both imports and exports to change. These changes will shift the net export function.

Consider what happens with a rise in Canadian prices relative to those in foreign countries. The increase in Canadian prices means that foreigners now see Canadian goods as more expensive relative both to goods produced in their own country and to goods imported from countries other than Canada. As a result, the value of Canadian exports will fall.[2] The X curve shifts down in Figure 23-3. Similarly, Canadians will see imports from foreign countries become cheaper relative to the prices of Canadian-made goods. As a result, they will shift their expenditures toward foreign goods and away from Canadian goods. That is, Canadians will spend a higher fraction of national income on imports—the IM curve in Figure 23-3 will rotate up. The combination of these two effects is that the net export function shifts downward and changes its slope.

Now consider the opposite case of a fall in Canadian prices relative to prices of foreign-made goods. The decline in Canadian prices means that Canadian exports now look cheaper in foreign markets relative both to foreign goods and to goods imported from countries other than Canada. As a result, Canadian exports rise. Similarly, the same change in relative prices causes Canadian imports to fall. Thus, the net export function shifts upward and changes its slope.

A rise in Canadian prices relative to those in other countries reduces Canadian net exports at any level of national income. A fall in Canadian prices increases net exports at any level of national income.

The most important cause of a change in international relative prices is a change in the exchange rate. A fall in the external value of the Canadian dollar (a *depreciation* of the Canadian dollar) means that foreigners must pay less of their money to buy one Canadian dollar, and Canadian residents must pay more Canadian dollars to buy a unit of any foreign currency. As a result, the price of foreign goods in terms of Canadian dollars rises, and the price of Canadian goods in terms of foreign currency falls. This reduction in the relative price of Canadian goods will cause a shift in expenditure away from foreign goods and toward Canadian goods. Canadian residents will im-

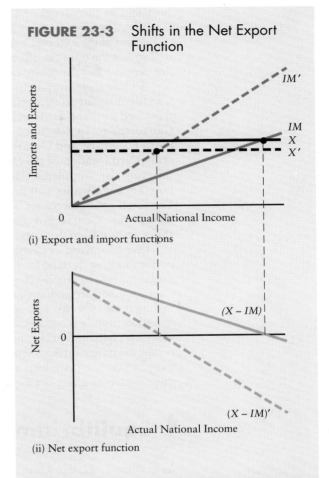

FIGURE 23-3   Shifts in the Net Export Function

(i) Export and import functions

(ii) Net export function

Changes in relative international prices shift the NX function. A rise in Canadian prices relative to foreign prices, or a rise in the external value of the Canadian dollar, lowers exports from X to X' and raises the import function from IM to IM'. This shifts the net export function downward from $(X - IM)$ to $(X - IM)'$. A fall in Canadian prices has the opposite effect.

For lots of interesting information on Canada's international trade, go to the website for the Department of Foreign Affairs and International Trade: www.dfait-maeci.gc.ca.

---

[2]The rise in Canadian prices clearly leads to a reduction in the demand for Canadian goods by foreigners. But in order for the *value* of Canadian exports to fall, the price elasticity of demand for Canadian exports must exceed one (so that the quantity reduction dominates the price increase). We make this assumption, which is generally believed to be true, throughout this book.

port less at each level of Canadian national income, and foreigners will buy more Canadian exports. The net export function thus shifts upward.

A rise in the external value of the Canadian dollar (an *appreciation* of the Canadian dollar) has the opposite effect: It causes a fall in exports and a rise in imports, shifting the net export function downward.

An example may help to clarify the argument. Suppose something causes the Canadian dollar to depreciate relative to the euro (the common currency recently introduced into the European Union). The depreciation of the Canadian dollar leads Canadians to switch away from French wines and German cars, purchasing instead more B.C. wine and Ontario-made cars. This reduction in imports is reflected by the downward rotation of the *IM* curve. The depreciation of the Canadian dollar relative to the euro also stimulates Canadian exports. Quebec furniture and Maritime vacations now appear cheaper to Europeans than previously, and so their expenditure on such Canadian goods increases. This increase in Canadian exports is reflected by the upward shift in the *X* curve in Figure 23-3. The overall effect is that the net export function shifts up and becomes flatter.

One final word of caution regarding prices, exchange rates, and net exports. It is important to keep in mind that the simple model in this chapter *takes the price level and the exchange rate as given*—they are exogenous variables in this chapter. But, in the actual economy they are endogenous variables. We discuss the determination of the price level in Chapters 24 and 25 (where we still take the exchange rate as given) and the determination of the exchange rate in Chapter 36. In a more complete model of the economy, in which prices and exchange rates are determined endogenously, the relationship among prices, exchange rates, and net exports is more complicated. For now, however, we continue to take the price level and exchange rate as given, and we consider how changes in these variables affect net exports and equilibrium national income.

Equilibrium National Income

As in Chapter 22, equilibrium national income is the level of income where desired aggregate expenditure equals actual national income. The addition of government and net exports changes the calculations that we must make but does not alter the basic principles that are involved.

Desired Consumption and National Income

When there are taxes, disposal income (Y_D) is less than national income (Y). The relationship between consumption and national income involves both the relationship between consumption and disposable income and the relationship, via taxes, between disposable income and national income.

Continuing the example from Figure 23-1, suppose that disposable income is always 90 percent of national income—that is, net taxes (T) is given by the function $T = (0.1)Y$. Thus, whatever the relationship between C and Y_D, we can always substitute $(0.9)Y$ for Y_D. Hence, if changes in consumption were always 80 percent of changes in Y_D—that is, an *MPC* out of disposable income equal to 0.8—changes in consumption would always be 72 percent (80 percent of 90 percent) of changes in Y.

To see that this is true, let's use a little simple algebra. The consumption function is given by

$$C = 30 + (0.8)Y_D$$

and disposable income given by

$$Y_D = (0.9)Y$$

Substituting the second equation into the first gives:

$$C = 30 + (0.8)(0.9)Y$$

Therefore,

$$C = 30 + (0.72)Y$$

Thus, we can express desired consumption as a function of Y_D or as a *different* function of Y. In this example, 0.72 is equal to the *MPC* times $(1 - t)$, where t is the income-tax rate. So, whereas 0.8 is the marginal propensity to consume out of *disposable* income, 0.72 is the marginal propensity to consume out of *national* income.

In the presence of income taxes, the marginal propensity to consume out of national income is less than the marginal propensity to consume out of disposable income.

The *AE* Function

In order to determine equilibrium national income, we must define the desired aggregate expenditure *(AE)* function. In Chapter 22, it had only consumption and investment. Now we must include government purchases and net exports to get:

$$AE = C + I + G + NX$$

Figure 23-4 illustrates the aggregate expenditure function and shows how it is constructed from its various components.

The Marginal Propensity to Spend

As in Chapter 22, the slope of the *AE* function is the *marginal propensity to spend* out of national income (z). With the addition of net taxes and net exports, however, the marginal propensity to spend is no longer simply equal to the marginal propensity to consume.
    Suppose that the economy produces $1 of extra national income and that the response to this is governed by the relationships in Figure 23-4. Because 10 cents is collected by the government as net taxes, 90 cents becomes disposable income, and 80 percent of this amount (72 cents) is spent on consumption. However, 10 cents of all expenditure goes to imports, so expenditure on domestic goods, that is, aggregate expenditure, rises by only 62 cents $(72 - 10)$. Hence, z, the marginal propensity to spend, is 0.62. What is not spent on domestic output includes the 10 cents in taxes, the 18 cents of disposable income that is saved, and the 10 cents of import expenditure, for a total of 38 cents.

Equilibrium National Income

The *AE* function can be used directly to determine equilibrium national income. In Figure 23-5, the *AE* function from Figure 23-4 is drawn again, together with the 45° line. As was the case in Chapter 22, the 45° line is the *equilibrium condition* that actual national income equals desired aggregate expenditure. The equilibrium level of national income is $600 billion. When national income is equal to $600 billion, it is also equal to desired aggregate expenditure.

FIGURE 23-4   The Aggregate Expenditure Function

The aggregate expenditure function is the sum of desired consumption, investment, government purchases, and net export expenditures. The autonomous components of desired aggregate expenditure are desired investment, desired government purchases, desired export expenditures, and the constant term in desired consumption expenditure. These sum to $228 billion in the given example and this sum is the vertical intercept of the AE curve. The induced components are the second terms in desired consumption expenditure (0.72 Y) and desired imports ($-0.1 Y$).

The response of consumption to a change in national income is 0.72, calculated as the product of the marginal propensity to consume (0.8) times the fraction of national income that becomes disposable income (0.9). The response of desired aggregate expenditure to a change in national income, $\Delta AE / \Delta Y$, is 0.62. For example, as national income rises from $300 billion to $600 billion, desired aggregate expenditure increases from $414 billion to $600 billion. The slope of the AE curve, $\Delta AE / \Delta Y$, is therefore equal to 186/300 = 0.62.

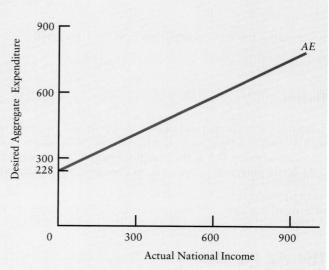

National Income (Y)	Desired Consumption Expenditure $(C = 30 + 0.72\ Y)$	Desired Investment Expenditure $(I = 75)$	Desired Government Expenditure $(G = 51)$	Desired Net Export Expenditure $(X - IM = 72 - 0.1\ Y)$	Desired Aggregate Expenditure $(AE = C + I + G + X - IM)$
0	30	75	51	72	228
150	138	75	51	57	321
300	246	75	51	42	414
600	462	75	51	12	600
900	678	75	51	−18	786

Suppose that national income is less than its equilibrium amount. The forces leading back to equilibrium are exactly the same as those described in Chapter 22. When households, firms, foreign demanders, and governments try to spend at their desired amounts, they will try to purchase more goods and services than the economy is currently producing. Hence, some of the desired expenditure must either be frustrated or take the form of purchases of inventories of goods that were produced in the past. As firms see their inventories being depleted, they will increase production, thereby increasing the level of national income.

The opposite sequence of events occurs when national income is greater than the level of desired aggregate expenditure. Now the total of desired household consumption, business investment, government purchases, and net foreign demand on the economy's production is less than national output. Firms will notice that they are unable to sell all of their output. Their inventories will be rising, and sooner or later they will seek to reduce the level of output until it equals the level of sales. When they do, national income will fall.

Finally, when national income is equal to desired aggregate expenditure ($600 billion in Figure 23-5), there is no pressure for output to change. Desired consumption, investment, government purchases, and net exports just add up to national product. Firms are producing exactly the quantity of goods and services that purchasers want to use, given the level of income.

The Saving-Investment Approach

In the closed-economy model of Chapter 22, we saw an alternative way of stating the equilibrium condition for national income: At the equilibrium level of income, desired saving equals desired investment. Adding government and international trade changes the precise form that this condition takes, but not the central underlying principle. Now, instead of describing equilibrium as desired saving equals desired investment, equilibrium will be characterized by desired *national* saving equal to desired *national asset formation*. We define these new terms in turn.

Practise with Study Guide Chapter 23, Exercise 7.

National Saving

National saving is the sum of private and public saving, $S + (T - G)$. Private saving (S) is the part of disposable income that is not used for current consumption. Public saving ($T - G$) is the part of government revenue that is not spent by governments. Between them, households and governments account for all claims to national income. Thus, the sum of what households and governments save accounts for all national saving.

national saving
The sum of public saving and private saving; all national income that is not spent on government purchases or private consumption.

The national saving function is illustrated in Figure 23-6. The slope of this function is the sum of the slopes of its two parts, private saving and public saving. In the example that we have been using throughout this chapter, the income-tax rate, t, is 0.1. Thus, when national income rises by $1, public saving ($T - G$) rises by 10 cents. (Recall that G is assumed to be autonomous and so does not change when national income changes.) The remaining 90 cents is added to disposable income. From this 90-cent increase in disposable income, private saving is increased by the marginal propensity to save (MPS), which is equal to 0.2 in our example. The total increase in saving per marginal dollar of national income is therefore $t + MPS(1 - t)$, or $0.1 + (0.2)(0.9) = 0.28$. This is the slope of the national saving function.

National Asset Formation

In Chapter 22, all of national output was either consumption or investment goods. In addition, all income that was received by households was either consumed or saved. So the saving of households was the counterpart of the economy's investment. In the closed economy of Chapter 22—and indeed in any closed economy—the only way to accumulate assets for future use is to devote some part of national product to investment, and that investment must be financed by saving. In an open economy, however, it is possible to accumulate assets in a different form—as net claims on foreigners. Net exports are central to determining the rate at which a country acquires such claims on foreigners.

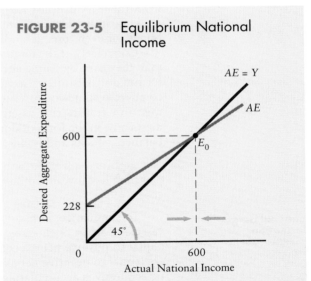

FIGURE 23-5   Equilibrium National Income

Equilibrium national income occurs at E_0, where the *AE* function intersects the 45° line. The *AE* line is taken from Figure 23-4; autonomous expenditure is $228 billion and the slope of *AE* is 0.62. If actual national income is below $600 billion, desired aggregate expenditure will exceed national income, and output will rise. If actual national income is above $600 billion, desired aggregate expenditure will be less than national income, and output will fall. Only when actual national income is $600 billion will desired aggregate expenditure equal actual national income.

Investment and net exports thus have a great deal in common: They are the two ways that current output can be used to accumulate assets. Investment, by definition, is production that will yield services in the future rather than in the present. Clearly, an economy that invests is adding to its assets.

To demonstrate that net exports also lead to asset accumulation, we must go through a number of steps. First, we note that net exports are the difference between what an economy produces and what it uses for consumption, investment, and government. An economy whose net exports are positive is producing more than it is using, with the difference sold abroad. Similarly, an economy that has negative net exports is using more than it is producing, with the difference purchased from abroad.

What happens when a country produces more or less than it uses? Here, the analogy to an individual is instructive. Suppose that you spend more than you earn and that you borrow money to cover the difference. You consequently go into debt. Now suppose that you earn more than you spend. As a result, you acquire assets (or reduce your debts). When you earn more than you spend and do nothing with the balance, you end up holding cash. If you put the money into a bank, you have a bank balance; if you buy stocks or bonds with money, you hold the stocks or bonds. Spending more than you earn reduces your net asset position, and earning more than you spend increases your net asset position.

This simple idea can be extended to the national level because a nation's balances between expenditure and income are simply the total of what individual citizens do. If a nation's firms, households, and governments sell more to other countries than they buy from them (X exceeds IM), that nation must accumulate foreign assets. These assets could be in the form of foreign currency, balances in foreign banks, foreign stocks and bonds, or even foreign lands and factories.

Conversely, if the nation's firms, households, and governments spend more abroad than they earn by selling abroad (IM exceeds X), the nation must incur foreign liabilities (or run down its foreign assets.) To finance the excess of imports over exports, funds must come from somewhere. Since they are not earned by selling current output, they must be raised by transferring assets to foreigners. As a result, a new liability is generated domestically, in the form of domestic assets held by foreigners. Again, these could be bank balances, stocks and bonds, or titles to factories and farms.

Net exports result in the accumulation of assets for the exporting country. Hence, net exports are like investment in the sense that they generate future income for the exporting country.

national asset formation The sum of investment and net exports. The extent to which the domestic economy is accumulating assets.

To summarize, in a closed economy, **national asset formation** is just equal to investment. In an open economy, however, we must add net assets accumulated abroad (equal to positive net exports) or subtract net domestic assets accumulated by foreigners (equal to negative net exports) in order to calculate the extent to which the domestic economy is accumulating assets worldwide.

Figure 23-6 shows the national asset formation function, $I + (X - IM)$. Recall that I and X are both autonomous whereas IM rises as national income rises. The result is a negative relationship between national income and national asset formation.

Equilibrium

Figure 23-6 shows both the national saving function and the national asset formation function. With the two relationships together, we can determine the equilibrium level of national income.

When desired national saving is equal to desired national asset formation, national income is at its equilibrium level.

FIGURE 23-6 National Saving and National Asset Formation

The economy is in equilibrium when desired national saving, $(S + T - G)$, equals desired national asset formation, $(I + X - IM)$. The figure graphs the function from the second and third columns of the accompanying table; equilibrium national income is equal to \$600 billion. When national income is less than \$600 billion, desired national asset formation exceeds desired national saving and desired aggregate expenditure exceeds national income. Firms will respond to the imbalance by producing more, moving the economy toward equilibrium. When national income is above \$600 billion, desired national asset formation is less than desired national saving, and desired aggregate expenditure is less than national income. Firms will reduce output to avoid accumulating excess inventories, and the economy will move toward equilibrium.

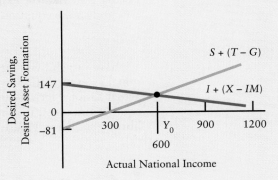

National Income (Y)	Desired National Saving (S + T − G)	Desired National Asset Formation (I + X − IM)	Saving Minus Asset Formation (S + T − G) − (I + X − IM)
0	−81	147	−228
300	3	117	−114
600	87	87	0
900	171	57	114
1200	255	27	228

To see why equilibrium occurs when desired national saving equals desired national asset formation, it is crucial to recognize that the vertical distance between the two curves in Figure 23-6 is exactly the same as the distance between the AE curve and the 45° line in Figure 23-4. Indeed, by picking any level of national income and comparing the tables in these two figures you will see that the difference between actual national income and desired aggregate expenditure is *always* equal to the difference between desired national saving and desired national asset formation.

Let's use a little algebra to see why this must be the case. Suppose the difference between desired national saving, $(S + T - G)$, and desired national asset formation, $(I + X - IM)$, is equal to some number which we call W. In symbols, this is

$$(S + T - G) - (I + X - IM) = W$$

Now, recall that disposable income is equal to actual income minus taxes, $Y - T$. Further, note that all of disposable income must be used up by consumption and saving. That is,

$$Y - T = C + S$$

which implies

$$S = Y - T - C$$

Now, this last equation can be substituted into our first equation above and, after a little rearranging of terms, we get

$$Y - (C + G + I + (X - IM))= W$$

Finally, note that the expression in parentheses is simply desired aggregate expenditure, AE, and so the equation can be rewritten to be

$$Y - AE = W$$

We have just shown that the difference between desired national saving and desired national asset formation, which we called W, is exactly the same as the difference between actual national income and desired aggregate expenditure. It immediately follows that the equilibrium illustrated in Figure 23-6 is just another way of looking at the same equilibrium shown in Figure 23-5.

Changes in Equilibrium National Income

Changes in any of the components of desired aggregate expenditure will cause changes in equilibrium national income. In Chapter 22, we investigated the consequences of shifts in the consumption function and in the investment function. Here we take a first look at fiscal policy—the effects of government spending and taxes. We also consider shifts in the net export function. First, we explain why the simple multiplier is reduced by the presence of taxes and imports.

The Multiplier with Taxes and Imports

In Chapter 22, we saw that the *simple multiplier,* the amount by which equilibrium national income changes when autonomous expenditure changes by one dollar, was equal to $1/(1 - z)$, where z is the marginal propensity to spend out of national income. In the simple model of Chapter 22, with no government and no international trade, z is simply the marginal propensity to consume out of disposable income. But in the more complex model of this chapter, in which we have added government and net exports, the marginal propensity to spend out of national income is slightly more complicated. The central point here is as follows:

The presence of imports and income taxes reduces the marginal propensity to spend out of national income and thus reduces the value of the simple multiplier.

To see this, note that in Chapter 22 the marginal propensity to spend was equal to 0.8 and the multiplier was therefore equal to 5. In the example that we have developed in this chapter, with a marginal propensity to import of 0.1 and an income-tax rate of 0.1, the marginal propensity to spend is 0.62. Ten percent of a $1 increase in national income goes to taxes, leaving 90 cents of disposable income. With a marginal propensity to consume of 0.8, 72 cents is spent. Of this, 10 cents is spent on imports, leaving a total of 62 cents to be spent on domestically produced goods. Hence, the simple multiplier is $1/(1 - 0.62) = 2.63$.

Dealing with the numbers in a specific example is sometimes confusing, and it is useful to think more generally about why the presence of imports and income taxes reduces the value of the simple multiplier. With taxes and imports both increasing in response to an increase in national income, every increase in national income generates more leakages from the flow of expenditure than would be the case in the simpler world with no taxes and no imports. Thus, as national income increases, there is less induced expenditure *on domestically produced goods* and therefore the overall change in equilibrium national income is lower.

The higher is the marginal propensity to import, the lower is the simple multiplier. The higher is the income-tax rate, the lower is the simple multiplier.

We have explained why z, the marginal propensity to spend out of national income, is smaller in the presence of government and foreign trade than it is in the simple model of Chapter 22. As a result, the multiplier is also smaller. But what is z precisely equal to? In the model we have been developing in this chapter, z is given by

$$z = MPC(1-t) - m$$

where MPC is the marginal propensity to consume out of disposable income, t is the income-tax rate, and m is the marginal propensity to import. From this formula for z, it is clear that the higher is the tax rate, the lower is z (and thus the lower is the multiplier). It is also clear that the higher is the marginal propensity to import, the lower is z (and thus the lower is the multiplier).

Net Exports

Earlier in this chapter, we discussed the determinants of net exports and of shifts in the net export function. As with the other elements of desired aggregate expenditure, if the net export function shifts upward, equilibrium national income will rise; if the net export function shifts downward, equilibrium national income will fall.

Generally, exports themselves are autonomous with respect to domestic national income. Foreign demand for Canadian goods and services depends on foreign income, on foreign and Canadian prices, and on the exchange rate, but it does not depend on Canadian income. Export demand could also change because of a change in tastes. Suppose that foreign consumers develop a taste for Canadian-made furniture and desire to consume $1 billion more per year of these goods than they had in the past. The net export function (and the aggregate expenditure function) will shift up by $1 billion, and equilibrium national income will increase by $1 billion times the multiplier.

Fiscal Policy

Fiscal policy involves the use of government spending and tax policies to influence total desired expenditure so as to change the equilibrium level of national income. Because government purchases increase desired aggregate expenditure and taxation decreases it, the *directions* of the required changes in spending and taxation are generally easy to determine once we know the direction in which the government wishes to change national income. But the *timing, magnitude,* and *mixture* of the changes are more difficult issues.

Any policy that attempts to stabilize national income at or near any particular level (usually potential national income) is called **stabilization policy**. Here we introduce the idea of stabilization through fiscal policy. In Chapters 25 and 31, we return to discuss some of its complications after we have developed the required theory.

The basic idea of stabilization policy follows from what we have already learned. A reduction in tax rates or an increase in government purchases shifts the *AE* curve upward, causing an increase in equilibrium national income. An increase in tax rates or a decrease

stabilization policy
Any policy designed to reduce the economy's cyclical fluctuations and thereby to stabilize national income.

Changes in government purchases and tax rates can have significant effects on desired aggregate expenditure and thus on equilibrium national income.

in government purchases shifts the *AE* curve downward, causing a decrease in equilibrium income.

If the government has some target level of national income, it can use its taxes and expenditures in an attempt to push the economy toward that target. First, suppose that national income is well below the level of potential national income. In this case, the government would like to increase national income. The appropriate fiscal tools are to raise expenditures or to lower tax rates (or both). Second, suppose that the economy is "overheated," meaning that national income is above potential. What can the government do? The fiscal tools at its command are to reduce government expenditure and to raise tax rates, both of which have a depressing effect on national income.

Changes in Government Purchases

Suppose the government decides to reduce its purchases of all consulting services, saving $100 million per year in spending. Planned government purchases (*G*) would fall by $100 million at every level of income, shifting *AE* downward by the same amount. How much would equilibrium income change? This amount can be calculated by using the multiplier. Government purchases are part of autonomous expenditure, so a *change* in government purchases of Δ*G* will lead to a *change* in equilibrium national income equal to the multiplier times Δ*G*. In this example, equilibrium income will fall by $100 million times the multiplier.

Increases in government purchases would have the opposite effect. If the government were to spend $1 billion on new highways, equilibrium national income would rise by $1 billion times the multiplier.

Changes in Tax Rates

If tax rates change, the relationship between disposable income and national income changes. As a result, the relationship between desired consumption and national income also changes. For any given level of national income, there will be a different level of disposable income and hence a different level of consumption. Consequently, a change in tax rates will also cause a change in *z*, the marginal propensity to spend out of national income.

Consider first a decrease in tax rates. If the government decreases its rate of income tax so that it collects 5 cents less out of every dollar of national income, disposable income rises in relation to national income. Hence, consumption also rises at every level of national income. This increase in consumption results in a (nonparallel) upward shift of the *AE* curve, that is, an increase in the slope of the curve, as shown in Figure 23-7. The result of this shift will be a rise in equilibrium national income.

A rise in tax rates has the opposite effect. A rise in tax rates causes a decrease in disposable income, and hence consumption expenditure, at each level of national income. This results in a (nonparallel) downward shift of the *AE* curve and decreases the level of equilibrium national income.

Balanced Budget Changes

Another policy available to the government is to make a *balanced budget change* by altering spending and taxes equally. For example, suppose the government increases tax rates enough to raise an extra $1 billion in tax revenues that it then uses to purchase goods and services. Aggregate expenditure would remain unchanged if, and only if, the $1 billion that the government takes from the private sector in higher taxes would otherwise have been entirely spent by that sector. If so, the government's policy would reduce private expenditure by $1 billion and raise its own spending by $1 billion. Aggregate expenditure, and hence national income, would remain unchanged.

But this is not the usual case. When an extra $1 billion in taxes is taken away from households, spending on domestically produced goods falls by *less than* $1 billion. If the marginal propensity to consume out of disposable income is, say, 0.8, consumption expenditure will fall by only $800 million. If the government spends the entire $1 billion on domestically produced goods, aggregate expenditure will increase by $200 million. In this case, the balanced budget increase in government expenditure has an expansionary effect because it shifts the *AE* function upward.

In the simple model of national income determination, a balanced budget increase in government expenditure will have a mild expansionary effect on national income, and a balanced budget decrease will have a mild contractionary effect.

The **balanced budget multiplier** measures these effects. It is the change in income divided by the balanced budget change in government expenditure that brought it about. If the extra $1 billion of spending and taxes causes national income to rise by $800 million, the balanced budget multiplier is 0.8; if income rises by only $200 million, it is 0.2.

Now compare the sizes of the multipliers for a balanced budget and a deficit-financed increase in government spending. (When expenditure is increased with no corresponding increase in tax rates, we say it is deficit financed.) With a deficit-financed increase in expenditure, there is no increase in taxes and hence no resulting decrease in consumption expenditure to offset the increase in government expenditure. With a balanced budget increase in expenditure, however, the offsetting increase in tax rates and decrease in consumption do occur. Consequently, the balanced budget multiplier is smaller than the simple multiplier.

FIGURE 23-7 The Effect of Changing the Tax Rate

Changing the tax rate changes equilibrium income by shifting (and changing the slope of) the *AE* curve. A reduction in tax rates rotates the *AE* curve from AE_0 to AE_1. The new curve has a steeper slope because the lower tax rate withdraws a smaller amount of national income from the desired consumption flow. Equilibrium income rises from Y_0 to Y_1 because, at every level of national income, desired consumption, and, hence, desired aggregate expenditure is higher.

balanced budget multiplier The change in equilibrium national income divided by the tax-financed change in government expenditure that brought it about.

Limitations of the Income-Expenditure Approach

In this and the preceding chapter, we have discussed the determination of the four categories of aggregate expenditure and have seen how they simultaneously determine equilibrium national income. The basic approach is the same no matter how many categories are considered. An algebraic exposition of the model is presented in the appendix to this chapter.

The simple income-expenditure model that we have developed is based on three central concepts.

Equilibrium National Income.   The equilibrium level of national income is that level where *desired* aggregate expenditure equals *actual* national income. If actual national income exceeds desired expenditure, then the unintended accumulation of inventories eventually leads firms to reduce production—national income falls. If actual national income is less than desired expenditure, then the unintended running-down of inventories eventually leads firms to increase production—national income rises.

The Multiplier.   The multiplier measures the change in equilibrium national income that results from a change in the *autonomous* part of desired aggregate expenditure. The multiplier is equal to $1/(1 - z)$, where z is the marginal propensity to spend out of national income. In the model of Chapter 22, in which there is no government and no international trade, z is simply the marginal propensity to consume out of disposable income. The addition to the model of government and net exports reduces the value of z, and thus reduces the value of the simple multiplier.

Demand-Determined Output.   The income-expenditure model that we have examined is constructed *for a given price level*—that is, the price level is assumed to be constant. This assumption of a given price level is related to another assumption that we have been (implicitly) making. We have implicitly assumed that firms are able and willing to produce any amount that is demanded without requiring any change in prices. When this is true, national income depends only on how much is demanded—that is, national income is *demand determined*. Things get more complicated if firms are either unable or unwilling to produce enough to meet all demands without requiring a change in prices. We deal with this possibility in Chapter 24 when we consider *supply-side* influences on national income.

There are two situations in which we might expect national income to be demand determined. First, when there are unemployed resources and firms have excess capacity, firms will be prepared to provide whatever is demanded from them at unchanged prices. In contrast, if the economy's resources are fully employed and firms have no excess capacity, increases in output may only be possible with higher unit costs, and these cost increases may lead to price increases.

The second situation is where firms are *price setters*. Readers who have studied some microeconomics will recognize this term. It means that the firm has the ability to influence the price of its product, either because it is large relative to the market or, more usually, because it sells a product that is *differentiated* to some extent from the products of its competitors. Firms that are price setters often respond to changes in demand by altering their production and sales, at least initially, rather than by adjusting their prices. Only after some time has passed, and the change in demand has persisted, do such firms adjust their prices. This type of behaviour corresponds well to our short-run macro model in which changes in demand lead to changes in output (for a given price level).

The simple income-expenditure model of national income determination assumes a constant price level. In this model, national income is demand determined.

In the following chapters, we augment the income-expenditure model by making the price level endogenous to the model. We do this by considering the *supply side* of the economy—that is, those things that influence firms' abilities to produce output, such as technology and factor prices. When we consider the demand side and the supply side of the economy simultaneously, we will see that changes in desired aggregate expenditure usually cause both prices and real national income to change. This is why the simple multiplier, derived under the assumption that prices do not change, is too simple.

Nonetheless, there are three ways in which the simple income-expenditure models of Chapters 22 and 23 remain useful, even when the price level does change. First, the simple multiplier will continue to be a valuable starting place in calculating actual changes in national income in response to changes in autonomous expenditure. Second, no matter what the price level may be, the components of desired aggregate expenditure add up to actual national income *in equilibrium*. Third, no matter what the price level may be, equilibrium requires that desired national saving be equal to desired national asset formation. This last point will be especially important when we consider the determinants of national income and prices in the long run.

S U M M A R Y

Introducing Government   LO ❶

- Government purchases, G, is part of autonomous aggregate expenditure. Taxes minus transfer payments are called net taxes and affect aggregate expenditure indirectly. Taxes reduce disposable income, whereas transfers increase disposable income.

- The budget balance is defined as net tax revenues minus government purchases, $(T - G)$. When $(T - G)$ is positive, there is a budget surplus; when $(T - G)$ is negative, there is a budget deficit.
- When there is a budget surplus, there is positive public saving.

Introducing Foreign Trade   LO ❷

- Exports are foreign purchases of Canadian goods, and thus do not depend on Canadian national income. Desired imports increase as national income increases. Hence, net exports decrease as national income increases.
- Changes in international relative prices lead to shifts in the net export function. A rise in the exchange rate (a de-

preciation of the Canadian dollar) implies that Canadian goods are now cheaper relative to foreign goods. This leads to a rise in exports and a fall in imports, shifting the net export function up. A fall in the exchange rate (an appreciation of the Canadian dollar) has the opposite effect.

Equilibrium National Income   LO ❸ ❹

- As in Chapter 22, national income is in equilibrium when desired aggregate expenditure equals actual national income. The equilibrium condition is

$$Y = AE, \quad \text{where } AE = C + I + G + (X - IM)$$

- The sum of investment and net exports is called *national asset formation* because investment and net exports rep-

resent the two ways in which national income that is not used in the current year can be used to generate future national income. At the equilibrium level of national income, desired national saving is equal to desired national asset formation:

$$S + (T - G) = I + (X - IM)$$

Changes in Equilibrium National Income

- The presence of taxes and net exports reduces the value of the simple multiplier. With taxes and imports both increasing in response to an increase in national income, every increase in national income generates more leakages from the flow of expenditure.
- An increase in government purchases shifts up the *AE* function and thus increases the equilibrium level of national income. A decrease in the income-tax rate makes

the *AE* function rotate upward and increases the equilibrium level of national income.
- An increase in exports can be caused by either an increase in foreign demand for Canadian goods, a fall in the Canadian price level, or a depreciation of the Canadian dollar. An increase in exports shifts the *AE* function up and increases the equilibrium level of national income.

Limitations of the Income-Expenditure Approach

- The simple income-expenditure model of national income determination is constructed for a given price level. That prices are assumed not to change in response to an increase in desired expenditure reflects a related assumption that output is demand determined. This implies that national income is demand determined.

- Output would be demand determined in two situations. One is where there are unemployed resources; the other is where firms are price setters.
- In later chapters when we consider the demand side and the supply side of the economy simultaneously, we will see that changes in desired aggregate expenditure usually cause both prices and real national income to change.

KEY CONCEPTS

Taxes, transfers, and net taxes
The budget balance
The public saving (budget surplus) function
The net export function

National saving
National asset formation
Calculation of the simple multiplier in an open economy with government

Fiscal policy and equilibrium income
The balanced budget multiplier

STUDY EXERCISES

1. Consider the following table showing national income and government tax revenues in billions of dollars. Assume that the level of government purchases is $155 billion.

National Income (*Y*)	Net Tax Revenues (*T*)	Public Saving (*T* – *G*)
100	45	—
200	70	—
300	95	—
400	120	—
500	145	—
600	170	—
700	195	—
800	220	—

a. Compute the level of public saving (the government budget surplus) for each level of national income and fill in the table.
b. Plot the public saving function on a scale diagram. Explain the economics of why it is upward sloping.
c. What is the tax rate? Explain.
d. Suppose the government decides to increase the level of its purchases of goods and services by $15 billion. Show in your diagram what happens to the public saving function.

2. Consider the following table showing national income and imports in billions of dollars. Assume that the level of exports is $300 billion.

National Income (Y)	Imports (IM)	Net Exports ($X - IM$)
100	85	—
200	120	—
300	155	—
400	180	—
500	215	—
600	250	—
700	285	—
800	320	—

a. Compute the level of net exports for each level of national income and fill in the table.
b. Plot the net export function on a scale diagram. Explain the economics of why it is downward sloping.
c. What is the marginal propensity to import? Explain.
d. Suppose one of Canada's major trading partners experiences a significant recession. Explain how this will affect the net export function. Show the effect in your diagram.

3. Each of the following headlines describes an event that will have an effect on desired aggregate expenditure. What will be the effect on equilibrium national income? In each case, describe how the event would be illustrated in the 45° line diagram.

a. "Minister takes an axe to the Armed Forces."
b. "Russia agrees to buy more Canadian wheat."
c. "High-tech firms to cut capital outlays."
d. "Finance Minister pledges to cut income-tax rates."
e. "U.S. imposes import restrictions on Canadian lumber."
f. "Asian slump means smaller market for B.C. lumber."
g. "Weak dollar spurs exports from Ontario manufacturers."

4. The following table shows alternative hypothetical economies and the relevant values for the marginal propensity to consume out of disposable income (MPC), the income-tax rate (t), and the marginal propensity to import, m.

Economy	MPC	t	m	z	Multiplier $K = 1/(1 - z)$
Economy A	0.75	0.2	0.15	—	—
Economy B	0.75	0.2	0.30	—	—
Economy C	0.75	0.4	0.30	—	—
Economy D	0.90	0.4	0.30	—	—

a. Recall that z, the marginal propensity to spend out of national income, is given by the simple expression $z = MPC(1 - t) - m$. Using this expression, compute z for each of the economies and fill in the table.
b. Compare Economies A and B (they differ only by the value of m). Which one has the larger multiplier? Explain the economics of why the size of the multiplier depends on m.
c. Compare Economies B and C (they differ only by the value of t). Which one has the larger multiplier? Explain the economics of why the size of the multiplier depends on t.
d. Compare Economies C and D (they differ only by the value of MPC). Which one has the larger multiplier? Explain the economics of why the size of the multiplier depends on MPC.

5. Consider the diagram below showing the national saving function and the national asset formation function.

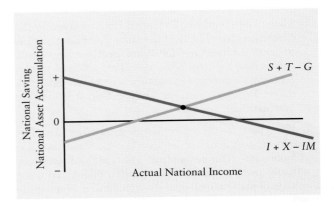

a. Explain why the national asset formation function is downward sloping. What determines its slope?
b. Explain why the national saving function is upward sloping. What determines its slope?
c. Suppose the government decided to increase its level of purchases. How would this policy change be illustrated in the diagram? What would happen to national income?
d. Suppose domestic firms decided to increase their desired investment. How would this change be illustrated in the diagram? What would happen to national income?
e. Suppose that the Canadian government reduced income-tax rates. How would this change be illustrated in the diagram? What would happen to national income?

6. This question requires you to solve a macro model algebraically. Reading the appendix to Chapter 23 will help you to answer this question. But, just in case, we lead you through it step by step. The equations for the model are as follows:

i) $C = a + bY_D$ Consumption
ii) $I = I_0$ Investment (autonomous)
iii) $G = G_0$ Government purchases
(autonomous)
iv) $T = T_0 + tY$ Tax revenue
v) $X = X_0$ Exports (autonomous)
vi) $IM = mY$ Imports

a. Step 1: Substituting the tax function into the consumption function, derive the relationship between desired consumption and national income.

b. Step 2: Sum the four components of desired aggregate expenditure (C, I, G, NX). This is the aggregate expenditure (AE) function.

c. Step 3: Now recall the equilibrium condition, $Y = AE$. Form the equation $Y = AE$, where AE is your expression for the AE function from part **b**.

d. Step 4: Now collect terms and solve for Y. This is the equilibrium value of national income.

e. Step 5: Suppose the level of autonomous expenditure, which we could call A, rises by ΔA. What is the effect on the level of equilibrium national income?

DISCUSSION QUESTIONS

1. The countries of the European Union agreed in the Maastricht Treaty of 1991 to reduce their budget deficits to below 3 percent of GDP. What fiscal measures would reduce their deficits? Why might a reduction of 10 percent in government expenditure accomplish much less than a 10 percent decrease in the deficit, at least in the first instance?

2. It is typical for the federal government's forecasts of its own budget deficit to be less than the forecasts made by private-sector economists. Much of the discrepancy seems to be accounted for by assumptions about the state of the economy over the coming year. How do assumptions about the economy affect estimates of the budget deficit?

3. Classify each of the following government activities as either government purchases or transfers.

   a. Welfare payments for the poor
   b. Payments to teachers in public schools
   c. Payments to teachers at military colleges
   d. Payments on account of hospital and medical care
   e. Public Health Service vaccination programs

4. The trade deficit that the United States has with Japan has received much attention over the last 20 years. Given an economy in equilibrium, what is the relationship between saving and investment if the government budget remains balanced but there exists a trade deficit? What additional role must foreigners play in this situation? Can you explain why this situation is viewed by many Americans as troublesome? Do you agree with them?

5. In Chapter 20 we examined how national income was *measured*. Using the expenditure approach, we showed that GDP is always equal to the sum of consumption, investment, government purchases, and net exports. In Chapters 22 and 23 we examined the *determination* of national income. We showed that equilibrium national income occurs when actual national income equals the sum of desired consumption, investment, government purchases, and net exports. Does this mean that national income is always at its equilibrium level? Explain the important difference between "actual" and "desired" expenditures.

An Algebraic Exposition of the Income-Expenditure Model

We start with the definition of desired aggregate expenditure:

$$AE = C + I + G + (X - IM) \qquad [1]$$

For each component of AE, we write down a behavioural function.

$$C = a + bY_D \quad \textit{(consumption function)} \qquad [2]$$

$$I = I_0 \quad \textit{(autonomous investment)} \qquad [3]$$

$$G = G_0 \quad \textit{(autonomous government purchases)} \quad [4]$$

$$X = X_0 \quad \textit{(autonomous exports)} \qquad [5]$$

$$IM = mY \quad \textit{(imports)} \qquad [6]$$

where a is autonomous consumption spending, b is the marginal propensity to consume, and m is the marginal propensity to import. Obviously, the "behavioural" functions for investment, government purchases, and exports are very simple: These are all assumed to be independent of the level of national income.

Before deriving aggregate expenditure, we need to determine the relationship between national income (Y) and disposable income (Y_D), because it is Y_D that determines desired consumption expenditure. Y_D is defined as income after net taxes. In Chapter 23 we examined a very simple linear income tax of the form $T = tY$. More generally, we might imagine autonomous net taxes T_0 and induced net taxes tY, so that the tax function is given by:

$$T = T_0 + tY \qquad [7]$$

Taxes must be subtracted from national income to obtain disposable income:

$$Y_D = Y - T_0 - tY = Y(1 - t) - T_0 \qquad [8]$$

Substituting Equation 8 into the consumption function allows us to write consumption as a function of national income.

$$C = a - bT_0 + b(1 - t)Y \qquad [9]$$

Notice that autonomous consumption now has two parts, a and $-bT_0$, where the latter term is the effect of autonomous taxes on consumption.

Now we can add up all of the components of desired aggregate expenditure, substituting Equations 3, 4, 5, 6, and 9 into Equation 1:

$$AE = a - bT_0 + b(1 - t)Y + I_0 + G_0 + X_0 - mY \qquad [10]$$

Equation 10 is the AE function which shows desired aggregate expenditure as a function of actual national income.

In equilibrium, desired aggregate expenditure must equal actual national income:

$$AE = Y \qquad [11]$$

Equation 11 is the equilibrium condition for the income-expenditure model. It is the equation of the 45° line in the figures in this chapter.

To solve for the equilibrium level of national income, we want to solve for the level of Y that satisfies both equations 10 and 11. That is, solve for the level of Y which is determined by the intersection of the AE curve and the 45° line. Substitute equation 11 into 10:

$$Y = a - bT_0 + b(1 - t)Y + I_0 + G_0 + X_0 - mY \qquad [12]$$

Group all the terms in Y on the right-hand side, and subtract them from both sides:

$$Y = Y[b(1 - t) - m] + a - bT_0 + I_0 + G_0 + X_0 \qquad [13]$$

$$Y - Y[b(1 - t) - m] = a - bT_0 + I_0 + G_0 + X_0 \qquad [14]$$

Notice that $[b(1 - t) - m]$ is exactly the marginal propensity to spend out of national income, defined earlier as z. When national income goes up by one dollar, only $1 - t$ dollars go into disposable income, and only b of that gets spent on consumption. Additionally, m gets spent on imports, which are not expenditure on domestic national income. Hence $[b(1 - t) - m]$ gets spent on domestic output.

Substituting z for $[b(1 - t) - m]$ and solving Equation 14 for equilibrium Y yields

$$Y = \frac{a - bT_0 + I_0 + G_0 + X_0}{1 - z} \qquad [15]$$

555

Notice that the numerator of Equation 15 is total autonomous expenditure, which we call A. Hence, Equation 15 can be rewritten as

$$Y = \frac{A}{1 - z} \quad [16]$$

Notice also that if autonomous expenditure rises by some amount ΔA, Y will rise by $\Delta A/(1 - z)$. So, the simple multiplier is $1/(1 - z)$.

The Algebra Illustrated

The numerical example that was carried through Chapters 22 and 23 can be used to illustrate the preceding exposition. In that example, the behavioural equations are:

$$C = 30 + 0.8Y_D \quad [17]$$
$$I = 75 \quad [18]$$
$$G = 51 \quad [19]$$
$$X - IM = 72 - 0.1Y \quad [20]$$
$$T = 0.1Y \quad [21]$$

T_0 is 0, so, from Equation 8, disposable income is given by $Y(1 - t) = 0.9Y$. Substituting this into

Equation 17 yields

$$C = 30 + 0.72Y$$

as in Equation 9.

Now, recalling that in equilibrium $AE = Y$, we add up all of the components of AE and set the sum equal to Y, as in Equation 12:

$$Y = 30 + 0.72Y + 75 + 51 + 72 - 0.1Y \quad [22]$$

Collecting terms yields

$$Y = 228 + 0.62Y$$

Subtracting $0.62Y$ from both sides gives

$$0.38Y = 228$$

and dividing through by 0.38, we have

$$Y = \frac{228}{0.38} = 600$$

This can also be derived by using Equation 16. Autonomous expenditure is 228, and z, the marginal propensity to spend out of national income, is 0.62. Thus, from Equation 16, equilibrium income is $228/(1 - 0.62) = 600$, which is exactly the equilibrium we obtained in Figure 23-4.

CHAPTER 24

Output and Prices in the Short Run

LEARNING OBJECTIVES

① Understand why an exogenous change in the price level shifts the *AE* curve and changes the equilibrium level of real GDP.

② Explain the meaning of the *AD* curve, and which factors lead it to shift.

③ Explain the meaning of the *SRAS* curve and why changes in technology or factor prices cause it to shift.

④ Understand the concept of macroeconomic equilibrium.

⑤ Explain the effects of aggregate demand and aggregate supply shocks on real GDP and the price level.

In Chapters 22 and 23, we developed a model of national income determination in an economy with a constant price level. Of course, in any real economy, prices are changing more or less all the time. On the supply side of the economy, the prices of imported raw materials used by firms change frequently and sometimes dramatically, as when oil prices soared during 1973–1974 and 1979–1980 in response to the actions of the OPEC oil cartel. On the demand side of the economy, a major downturn in the economies of Japan and Southeast Asia, as happened in 1997 and 1998, reduced the demand for Canadian exports. This slowed a rapidly growing Canadian economy and helped to contain inflationary pressures.

Virtually all shocks to the economy affect *both* real national income and the price level. To understand why this happens, we need to drop the assumption that the price level is constant.

We make the transition to a variable price level in three steps. First, we study the consequences for national income of *exogenous* changes in the price level—changes that happen for reasons that are not explained by our model of the economy. We ask how changes in the price level affect desired aggregate expenditure. That is, we examine the *demand side* of the economy. Second, we examine the *supply side* by exploring the relationship between the price level, the prices of factor inputs, and the level of output firms would like to supply. Finally, we examine the concept of *macroeconomic equilibrium* that combines both the demand and supply sides to simultaneously determine the price level and real national income.

The Demand Side of the Economy

What happens to equilibrium GDP when the price level changes for some exogenous reason, such as a rise in the price of imported raw materials? To find out, we need to understand how the change affects desired aggregate expenditure.

Shifts in the *AE* Curve

We need to establish one key result: A change in the price level shifts the *AE* curve—downward when the price level rises and upward when the price level falls. Part of the explanation lies with how the change in the price level affects desired consumption expenditure and desired net exports.

In later chapters, we will discuss why changes in the price level also have an effect on investment, through changes in the interest rate. To fully understand why this happens, however, we need to know about the demand and supply of money. This discussion must await our treatment of money and banking in Chapters 26 and 27; for now we focus only on the effects of a change in the price level on consumption and net exports.

Changes in Consumption

One link between a change in the price level and changes in desired consumption expenditure is provided by wealth. We first consider the link between the price level and wealth, and then the link between wealth and consumption.

Much of the private sector's total wealth is held in the form of assets with a fixed nominal value. The most obvious example is money itself. We will discuss money in considerable detail in Chapters 26 and 27, but for now just note that most individuals and businesses hold money in their wallets, in their cash registers, or in their chequing accounts. What this money can buy—its real value—depends on the price level. The higher price level, the less a given amount of money can purchase. For this reason, a rise in the domestic price level lowers the real value of money holdings. Similarly, a reduction in the price level raises the real value of money holdings.

Changes in the price level cause changes in the real value of cash held by the private sector. This leads to changes in the amount of desired consumption expenditure.

A rise in the price level lowers the real value of money held by the private sector. A fall in the price level raises the real value of money held by the private sector.

Other examples of assets that have fixed nominal values include government and corporate bonds. The bondholder has lent money to the issuer of the bond and receives a repayment from the issuer when the bond matures. What happens when there is a change in the price level in the intervening period? A rise in the price level means that the repayment to the bondholder is lower in real value. This is a decline in wealth for the bondholder. However, the issuer of the bond, having made a repayment of lower real value because of the increase in the price level, has experienced an increase in wealth. In dollar terms, the bondholder's reduction in wealth is exactly offset by the issuer's increase in wealth.

Changes in the price level change the wealth of bondholders and bond issuers, but because the changes offset each other there is no change in aggregate wealth.

What happens when the issuer of the bond is the government? It is still true that a rise in the price level leads to no change in aggregate wealth—the reduction in the bondholder's wealth being exactly offset by an increase in the government's (that is, taxpayers') wealth. But the key question here is whether the private sector *recognizes* such changes in the government's (taxpayers') wealth. This issue is hotly debated among economists. Many economists argue that when individuals hold *government* bonds, they think they are made less wealthy by an increase in the price level, even though, in principle, they have some claim—as taxpayers—on the associated increase in the government's wealth. Other economists argue that the private sector takes full account of the changes in the government's wealth when computing their own wealth because any increase in the government's wealth must ultimately accrue to the private sector in the form of lower future taxes. In this case, holders of government bonds would feel no wealthier (or less wealthy) after a change in the price level. This contentious issue of "Ricardian Equivalence" is discussed in Chapter 31 when we examine the effects of government budget deficits. For now, we simply note that a rise in the price level reduces the private sector's perception of its wealth, at least for one reason (the reduced value of money holdings) and possibly for a second reason (the reduced value of government bonds).

The second link in the chain running from changes in the price level to changes in desired consumption is provided by the relationship between wealth and consumption that we stressed in Chapter 22. In that discussion we noted that forward-looking consumers save partly to accumulate assets for future use. A change in wealth will then change households' consumption and saving behaviour. In particular, when households suffer a decrease in their wealth, they will increase their saving so as to restore their wealth to their desired level. An increase in desired saving, of course, implies a reduction in desired consumption. Conversely, when households get an increase in their wealth, they will reduce their saving and consume more, causing an upward shift in the consumption function.

A rise in the domestic price level lowers private-sector wealth; this leads to a fall in desired consumption, and thus a downward shift in the *AE* curve. A fall in the domestic price level leads to a rise in wealth and desired consumption and thus to an upward shift in the *AE* curve.

Changes in Net Exports

When the domestic price level rises, Canadian goods become more expensive relative to foreign goods. As we saw in Chapter 23, this change in relative prices causes Canadian consumers to reduce their purchases of Canadian-made goods, which have now become relatively more expensive, and to increase their purchases of foreign goods, which have now become relatively less expensive. At the same time, consumers in other countries reduce their purchases of the now relatively more expensive Canadian-made goods. We saw in Chapter 23 that these changes cause a downward shift in the net export function.

A rise in the domestic price level shifts the net export function downward, which causes a downward shift in the *AE* curve. A fall in the domestic price level shifts the net export function and hence the *AE* curve upward.

Changes in Equilibrium GDP

Because it causes downward shifts in both the net export function and the consumption function, an exogenous rise in the price level causes a downward shift in the *AE* curve, as shown in Figure 24-1. When the *AE* curve shifts downward, the equilibrium level of real GDP falls.

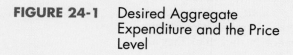

FIGURE 24-1   Desired Aggregate Expenditure and the Price Level

An exogenous change in the price level causes the *AE* curve to shift and thus causes equilibrium GDP to change. At the initial price level, the *AE* curve is given by the solid line AE_0, and hence equilibrium GDP is Y_0. An increase in the price level reduces desired aggregate expenditure and thus causes the *AE* curve to shift downward to the dashed line, AE_1. As a result, equilibrium GDP falls to Y_1.

aggregate demand (AD) curve   A curve showing combinations of real GDP and the price level that make desired aggregate expenditure equal to national income.

Practise with Study Guide Chapter 24, Exercises 1 and 2.

Now suppose that there is a fall in the price level. Canadian goods become relatively cheaper internationally, so net exports rise. Also, the purchasing power of assets denominated in money terms is increased, so households spend more. The resulting increase in desired expenditure on Canadian goods causes the *AE* curve to shift upward. The equilibrium level of real GDP therefore rises.

In Chapters 22 and 23 the horizontal axis was labeled "Actual National Income." Notice in Figure 24-1, however, that we have labelled the horizontal axis "Real GDP." We use GDP rather than *national income* but the two are clearly the same. It is still *actual,* as opposed to *desired,* but we leave that off, also for simplicity. Finally, we add *real* because from this chapter onward the price level will be determined endogenously and thus it is necessary to distinguish changes in nominal GDP from changes in real GDP.

The Aggregate Demand Curve

We now know from the behaviour underlying the *AE* function that the price level and real equilibrium GDP are negatively related to each other. This negative relationship can be shown in an important new concept, the *aggregate demand curve.*

Recall that the *AE* curve relates real GDP to desired aggregate expenditure for a given price level, plotting real GDP on the horizontal axis. The **aggregate demand (AD) curve** relates equilibrium real GDP to the price level, again plotting GDP on the horizontal axis. Because the horizontal axes of both the *AE* and *AD* curves measure real GDP, the two curves can be placed one above the other so that the level of GDP on each can be compared directly. This is shown in Figure 24-2.

Now let us see how the *AD* curve is derived. Given a value of the price level, equilibrium GDP is determined in part (i) of Figure 24-2 at the point where the *AE* curve crosses the 45° line. In part (ii) of Figure 24-2, the combination of the equilibrium level of GDP and the corresponding value of the price level is plotted, giving one point on the *AD* curve.

As we have seen, the *AE* curve shifts when the price level changes. The new position of the *AE* curve gives rise to a new equilibrium level of GDP that is associated with the new price level. This determines a second point on the *AD* curve, as shown in part (ii) of Figure 24-2. By joining these points, we trace out the *AD* curve.

For any given price level, the *AD* curve shows the level of real GDP for which desired aggregate expenditure equals actual GDP.

Note that because the *AD* curve relates equilibrium GDP to the price level, changes in the price level that cause *shifts in* the *AE* curve cause *movements along* the *AD* curve. A movement along the *AD* curve thus traces out the response of equilibrium GDP to a change in the price level.

The Slope of the *AD* Curve

Figure 24-2 provides us with sufficient information to establish that the *AD* curve is negatively sloped.

1. A rise in the price level causes the *AE* curve to shift downward and hence leads to a movement upward and to the left along the *AD* curve, reflecting a fall in the equilibrium level of GDP.

2. A fall in the price level causes the *AE* curve to shift upward and hence leads to a movement downward and to the right along the *AD* curve, reflecting a rise in the equilibrium level of GDP.

In Chapter 3, we saw that demand curves for individual goods such as coffee, CD players, and automobiles are downward sloping. However, the reasons for the negative slope of the *AD* curve are different from the reasons for the negative slope of individual demand curves used in microeconomics. Why is this the case?

An individual demand curve describes a situation in which the price of one commodity changes *while the prices of all other commodities and consumers' money incomes are constant.* Such an individual demand curve is downward sloping for two reasons. First, as the price of the commodity rises, the purchasing power of each consumer's money income will fall, and this fall in real income will lead to fewer units of the good being purchased. Second, as the price of the commodity rises, consumers buy less of that commodity and more of the now relatively cheaper substitutes.

The first reason has no application to the *AD* curve, which relates the total demand for all output to the *price level* rather than to any particular (relative) price. All prices and total output are changing as we move along the *AD* curve. Because the value of output determines income, consumers' money incomes will also be changing along this curve.

The second reason does apply to the aggregate demand curve, but only in a limited way. A rise in the price level entails a rise in *all* domestic commodity prices. Hence, there is no incentive to substitute among domestic commodities whose prices do not change relative to each other. However, it does give rise, as we saw earlier in this chapter, to some substitution between domestic and foreign products. Domestic goods rise in price relative to imported goods, and the switch in expenditure will reduce desired aggregate expenditure on domestic output and hence will reduce equilibrium national income.

FIGURE 24-2 Derivation of the *AD* Curve

Equilibrium GDP is determined by the *AE* curve for each given price level; the level of equilibrium GDP and its associated price level are then plotted to yield a point on the *AD* curve. When the price level is P_0, the *AE* curve is AE_0, and hence equilibrium GDP is Y_0, as shown in part (i). Plotting Y_0 against P_0 yields the point E_0 on the *AD* curve in part (ii).

An increase in the price level to P_1 causes the *AE* curve to shift downward to AE_1 and causes equilibrium GDP to fall to Y_1. Plotting this new level of GDP against the higher price level yields a second point, E_1, on the *AD* curve. A further increase in the price level to P_2 causes the *AE* curve to shift downward to AE_2, and thus causes equilibrium GDP to fall to Y_2. Plotting P_2 and Y_2 yields a third point, E_2, on the *AD* curve.

Thus, a change in the price level causes a shift in the *AE* curve but a movement along the *AD* curve.

aggregate demand shock Any event that causes a shift in the aggregate demand curve.

Shifts in the *AD* Curve

Figure 24-3 shows a shift in the *AD* curve. Because the *AD* curve plots equilibrium GDP as a function of the price level, anything that alters equilibrium GDP *at a given price level* must shift the *AD* curve. In other words, any change—other than a change in the price level—that causes the *AE* curve to shift will also cause the *AD* curve to shift. Such a shift is called an **aggregate demand shock**.

For example, in the late 1990s, the U.S. economy was growing quickly. The U.S. economic boom led to an increase in America's demand for Canadian products, which caused an upward shift in Canada's net export function. This event, taken by itself, would shift Canada's *AE* function upward and thus would shift Canada's *AD* curve to the right. Working in the opposite direction, however, the economies of Japan and Southeast Asia experienced a significant recession in 1997 and 1998. The economic slump in these countries led to reduced demands for Canadian goods, especially raw materials. This event, taken by itself, would shift Canada's *NX* and *AE* functions down, thus shifting Canada's *AD* curve to the left.

For a given price level, a rise in the amount of desired aggregate expenditure associated with each level of national income shifts the *AE* curve upward and the *AD* curve to the right. A fall in desired aggregate expenditure shifts the *AE* curve downward and the *AD* curve to the left.

Remember the following important point. In order to shift the *AD* curve, the change in desired expenditure must be caused by something other than a change in the domestic price level. As we saw earlier in this chapter, a change in aggregate expenditure caused by a change in the domestic price level leads to a movement along (not a shift of) the *AD* curve.

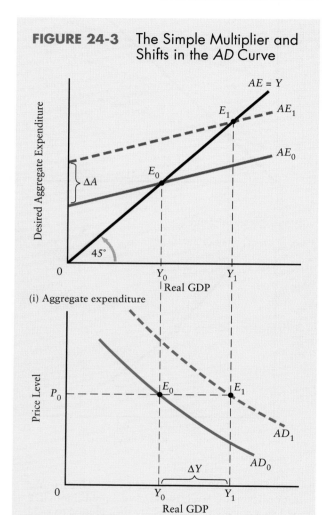

FIGURE 24-3   The Simple Multiplier and Shifts in the *AD* Curve

(i) Aggregate expenditure

(ii) Aggregate demand

A change in autonomous expenditure changes equilibrium GDP for any given price level. The simple multiplier measures the resulting horizontal shift in the *AD* curve. The original *AE* curve is AE_0 in part (i). Equilibrium is at E_0, with GDP of Y_0 at price level P_0. This yields point E_0 on the curve AD_0 in part (ii).

The *AE* curve in part (i) then shifts upward from AE_0 to AE_1, due to an increase in autonomous expenditure of ΔA. Equilibrium GDP now rises to Y_1, with the price level still constant at P_0. Thus, the *AD* curve in part (ii) shifts to the right to point E_1, indicating the higher equilibrium GDP of Y_1 associated with the same price level P_0. The magnitude of the shift, ΔY, is equal to the simple multiplier times ΔA.

The Simple Multiplier and the *AD* Curve

We saw in Chapters 22 and 23 that the simple multiplier measures the magnitude of the change in equilibrium national income in response to a change in autonomous expenditure *when the price level is held constant*. It follows that this multiplier gives the magnitude of the *horizontal shift* in the *AD* curve in response to a change in autonomous expenditure, as illustrated in Figure 24-3.

The simple multiplier measures the horizontal shift in the *AD* curve in response to a change in autonomous expenditure.

If the price level remains constant and firms are willing to supply everything that is demanded at that price level, the simple multiplier will also show the change in equilibrium income that will occur in response to a change in autonomous expenditure. This mention of firms' willingness to supply output brings us to a discussion of the *supply side* of the economy.

The Supply Side of the Economy

So far, we have explained how the equilibrium level of GDP is determined *when the price level is taken as given* and how that equilibrium changes as the price level is changed exogenously. We are now ready to take the important next step: adding an *explanation* for the behaviour of the price level. To do this, we need to take account of the supply decisions of firms.

The Aggregate Supply Curve

Aggregate supply refers to the total output of goods and services that firms would like to produce. An *aggregate supply curve* relates aggregate supply to the price level. It is necessary to define two types of such curves. The **short-run aggregate supply (SRAS) curve** relates the price level to the quantity of output that firms would like to produce and sell *on the assumption that technology and the prices of all factors of production remain constant.* The **long-run aggregate supply (LRAS) curve,** which we discuss in detail in the next chapter, also assumes that technology is constant. It relates the price level to the level of output firms would like to sell after factor prices have adjusted to any excess demands or supplies. For the remainder of this chapter, we confine our attention to the *SRAS* curve.

The short-run aggregate supply curve (*SRAS*) is drawn with the assumption that technology and factor prices are held constant.

The Slope of the *SRAS* Curve

To study the slope of the *SRAS* curve, we need to see how costs are related to output and then how prices are related to output.

Costs and Output.   Suppose that firms wish to increase their output above current levels. What will this do to their costs per unit of output—usually called their **unit costs?** The short-run aggregate supply curve is drawn on the assumption that technology and the prices of all factors of production remain constant. This does not, however, mean that unit costs will be constant. As output increases, less efficient standby plants may have to be used, and less efficient workers may have to be hired, while existing workers may have to be paid overtime rates for additional work. For these and other similar reasons, unit costs will tend to rise as output rises, even when technology and input prices are constant. (Readers who have studied microeconomics will recognize the *law of diminishing returns* as one reason why costs rise in the short run as firms squeeze more output out of a fixed quantity of capital equipment.)

Prices and Output.   To consider the relationship between price and output, we need to consider firms that sell in two distinct types of markets: those in which firms are *price takers* and those in which firms are *price setters*.

short-run aggregate supply (*SRAS*) curve
A curve showing the relation between the price level and the quantity of aggregate output supplied on the assumption that technology and all factor prices are held constant.

long-run aggregate supply (*LRAS*) curve
A curve showing the relationship between the price level and the quantity of aggregate output supplied when all markets have fully adjusted to the existing price level; a vertical line at $Y = Y^*$.

unit cost   Cost per unit of output, equal to total cost divided by total output.

FIGURE 24-4   The Short-Run Aggregate Supply Curve

The *SRAS* curve is positively sloped, indicating that firms will provide more aggregate output only at a higher price level. The *SRAS* curve is drawn for a given level of technology and factor prices. Any change in technology or factor prices will shift the *SRAS* curve.

A shift up and to the left reflects a decrease in supply; a shift down and to the right reflects an increase in supply. Starting from (P_0, Y_1) on $SRAS_0$, suppose that there is an increase in input prices. At price level P_0, only Y_0 would be produced. Alternatively, to get output Y_1 would require a rise to price level P_1. The new supply curve is $SRAS_1$, which may be viewed as being above and to the left of $SRAS_0$. An increase in supply, caused by a decrease in input prices or an improvement in technology, would shift the *SRAS* curve downward and to the right, from $SRAS_1$ to $SRAS_0$.

Some industries, especially those that produce raw materials, contain many individual firms. In these cases, each one is too small to influence the market price, which is set by the overall forces of demand and supply. Each firm must accept whatever price is set by the market. Such firms are said to be *price takers*. When the market price changes, these firms will react by altering their level of production.

Because their unit costs rise with output, price-taking firms will produce more only if price increases and will produce less if price falls.

Many other industries, including most of those that produce manufactured products, contain few enough firms that each can influence the market price of its product. Most such firms sell products that differ from one another, although all are similar enough to be thought of as a single product produced by one industry. For example, no two kinds of automobiles are the same, but all automobiles are sufficiently alike that we have no trouble talking about the automobile industry and its product, automobiles. In such cases, each firm must quote a price at which it is prepared to sell each of its products; that is, the firm is a *price setter*. If the demand for the output of price-setting firms increases sufficiently to take their outputs into the range in which their unit costs rise, these firms will not increase their outputs unless they can pass at least some of these extra costs on through higher prices. When demand falls, they will reduce output, and competition among them will tend to cause a reduction in prices whenever their unit costs fall.

Price-setting firms will increase their prices when they expand output into the range in which unit costs are rising.

This is the basic behaviour of firms in response to the changes in demand and prices when technology and factor prices are constant, and it explains the slope of the *SRAS* curve, such as the one shown in Figure 24-4.

The actions of both price-taking and price-setting firms cause the price level and the supply of output to be positively related—the short-run aggregate supply (*SRAS*) curve is upward sloping.

The Increasing Slope of the *SRAS* Curve

In Figure 24-4 we see that the *SRAS* curve not only slopes up but also gets steeper as real GDP increases. That is, at low levels of GDP the *SRAS* curve is relatively flat, but as GDP rises the *SRAS* curve gets progressively steeper. What explains this shape?

When output is low (below potential output), firms typically have excess capacity—some plant and equipment are idle. When firms have excess capacity, only a small increase in the price of their output may be needed to induce them to expand production. Once output is pushed above normal capacity, however, unit costs tend to rise quite rapidly. Many higher-cost expedients may have to be adopted—such as standby capacity, overtime, and extra shifts. These higher-cost methods will not be used unless the selling price of the output has risen enough to cover them. The more output is expanded beyond normal capacity, the more that unit costs rise and hence the larger is the rise in price that is necessary to induce firms to increase output. This increasing slope of the *SRAS* curve is sometimes called the *first asymmetry* in the behaviour of aggregate supply. (The second, *sticky wages*, will be discussed in the next chapter.)

As we will see later in this chapter, the shape of the *SRAS* curve is crucial for determining how the effect of an aggregate demand shock is divided between a change in the price level and a change in real GDP.

Shifts in the *SRAS* Curve

Shifts in the *SRAS* curve, which are shown in Figure 24-4, are called **aggregate supply shocks.** Two sources of aggregate supply shocks are of particular importance: changes in the price of inputs and changes in productivity.

aggregate supply shock   Any event that causes a shift in the aggregate supply curve.

Changes in Input Prices.

Factor prices are held constant along the *SRAS* curve, and when they change, the curve shifts. If factor prices rise, firms will find the profitability of their current production reduced. For any given level of output to be produced, an increase in the price level will be required. If prices do not rise, firms will react by decreasing production. For the economy as a whole, there will be less output supplied at each price level than before the increase in factor prices. Or, to put it another way, there will be a higher price level for each level of output than before the increase in factor prices. Thus, if factor prices rise, the *SRAS* curve shifts upward (or to the left). This is a decrease in aggregate supply.

Similarly, a fall in factor prices causes the *SRAS* curve to shift downward (or to the right). There will be more output supplied at each price level. Or, to put it differently, the same amount of output will be supplied at a lower price level. This is an increase in aggregate supply. A dramatic example of such a reduction in factor prices occurred in 1997 and 1998 when the world prices of raw materials fell by an average of 30 percent. In the many countries that use raw materials as inputs in manufacturing, the *SRAS* curve shifted to the right.

Changes in the prices of raw materials—such as the lumber shown here—lead to changes in firms' production costs. Such changes cause shifts in the SRAS curve.

Changes in Productivity.

If labour productivity rises—that is, each worker can produce more—the unit costs of production will fall (for given wages). Lower costs typically lead to lower prices. Competing firms cut prices in attempts to raise their market shares, and the net result of such competition is that the fall in production costs is accompanied by a fall in prices. That the same output is sold at a lower price causes a shift in the *SRAS* curve downward and to the right. This shift is an increase in aggregate supply, as illustrated in Figure 24-4.

A change in either factor prices or productivity will shift the *SRAS* curve because any given output will be supplied at a different price level than previously. An increase in factor prices

FIGURE 24-5 Macroeconomic Equilibrium

Macroeconomic equilibrium occurs at the intersection of the *AD* and *SRAS* curves and determines the equilibrium values for real GDP and the price level. Given the *AD* and *SRAS* curves in the figure, macroeconomic equilibrium occurs at E_0.

If the price level were equal to P_1, the desired output of firms would be Y_1. However, at P_1, the level of output that is consistent with expenditure decisions would be Y_2. Hence, when the price level is less than P_0, the desired output of firms will be less than the level of real GDP that is consistent with expenditure decisions. This causes upward pressure on the price level.

Similarly, for any price level above P_0, the desired output of firms exceeds the level of output that is consistent with expenditure decisions. This causes downward pressure on the price level.

The only price level where the supply decisions of firms are consistent with desired expenditure is at macroeconomic equilibrium. At P_0, firms wish to produce Y_0. When they do so, they generate a real GDP of Y_0; when real GDP is Y_0, decision makers wish to spend exactly Y_0, thereby purchasing the nation's output. Hence, all decisions are consistent with each other.

or a decrease in productivity shifts the *SRAS* curve to the left; an increase in productivity or a decrease in factor prices shifts it to the right.

Macroeconomic Equilibrium

We have now reached our objective: We are ready to see how both real GDP and the price level are simultaneously determined by the interaction of aggregate demand and aggregate supply.

The equilibrium values of real GDP and the price level occur at the intersection of the *AD* and *SRAS* curves, as shown by the pair Y_0 and P_0 that arise at point E_0 in Figure 24-5. The combination of real GDP and price level that is on both the *AD* and *SRAS* curves is called a *macroeconomic equilibrium*.

To see why the point (Y_0, P_0) is the only macroeconomic equilibrium, first consider what Figure 24-5 shows would happen if the price level were below P_0. At this lower price level, the desired output of firms, as given by the *SRAS* curve, is less than desired aggregate expenditure. The excess desired aggregate expenditure will cause prices to be bid up. Similarly, the figure shows that when the price level is above P_0, the behaviour underlying the *SRAS* and *AD* curves is not consistent. In this case, producers will wish to supply more than the amount that is demanded at that price level. This excess of output supplied over desired aggregate expenditure will cause prices to fall.

Only at the combination of real GDP and price level given by the intersection of the *SRAS* and *AD* curves are demand behaviour and supply behaviour consistent.

Macroeconomic equilibrium thus requires that two conditions be satisfied. The first is familiar to us because it comes from Chapters 22 and 23. At the prevailing price level, desired aggregate expenditure must be equal to actual GDP—that is, households are just willing to buy all that is produced. The *AD* curve is constructed in such a way that this condition holds everywhere along it. The second requirement for equilibrium is introduced by consideration of aggregate supply. At the prevailing price level, firms must wish to produce the prevailing level of GDP, no more and no less. This condition is fulfilled everywhere along the *SRAS* curve. Only where the two curves intersect are both conditions fulfilled simultaneously.

Changes in the Macroeconomic Equilibrium

The aggregate demand and aggregate supply curves can now be used to understand how various shocks to the economy change both real GDP and the price level.

As indicated earlier, a shift in the *AD* curve is called an aggregate demand shock. A rightward shift in the *AD* curve is an increase in aggregate demand; it means that at all price levels, expenditure decisions will now be consistent with a higher level of real GDP. This is called an *expansionary shock*. Similarly, a leftward shift in the *AD* curve is a decrease in aggregate demand—that is, at all price levels, expenditure decisions will now be consistent with a lower level of real GDP. This is called a *contractionary shock*.

Also as indicated earlier, a shift in the *SRAS* curve is called an aggregate supply shock. A rightward shift in the *SRAS* curve is an increase in aggregate supply; at any given price level, more real GDP will be supplied. A leftward shift in the *SRAS* curve is a decrease in aggregate supply; at any given price level, less real GDP will be supplied.

What happens to real GDP and to the price level when either the *AD* or *SRAS* curve shifts?

A shift in either the *AD* or the *SRAS* curve leads to changes in the equilibrium values of the price level and real GDP.

Let's now examine such shocks in a little more detail.

Aggregate Demand Shocks

Figure 24-6 shows the effects of an increase in aggregate demand. This increase could have occurred because of, say, increased investment or government purchases, an increase in foreigners' demand for Canadian goods, or an increase in household consumption resulting from a reduction in personal income taxes. Whatever the cause, the increase in aggregate demand means that more domestic output is demanded at any given price level. As is shown in the figure, following an increase in aggregate demand, both the price level and real GDP rise. Conversely, a decrease in demand causes both the price level and real GDP to fall.

Aggregate demand shocks cause the price level and real GDP to change in the same direction; both rise with an increase in aggregate demand, and both fall with a decrease in aggregate demand.

The Multiplier When the Price Level Varies

We saw earlier in this chapter that the simple multiplier (which we examined in detail in Chapters 22

FIGURE 24-6   Aggregate Demand Shocks

Shifts in aggregate demand cause the price level and real GDP to move in the same direction. An increase in aggregate demand shifts the *AD* curve to the right, from AD_0 to AD_1. Macroeconomic equilibrium moves from E_0 to E_1. The price level rises from P_0 to P_1, and real GDP rises from Y_0 to Y_1, reflecting a movement along the *SRAS* curve.

FIGURE 24-7   The Multiplier When the Price Level Varies

(i) Aggregate expenditure

(ii) Aggregate demand and supply

An increase in autonomous expenditure causes the AE curve to shift upward, but the rise in the price level causes it to shift part of the way down again. Hence, the multiplier is smaller than when the price level is constant. Originally, equilibrium is at point E_0 in both part (i) and part (ii). Desired aggregate expenditure then shifts by ΔA to AE_1', shifting the AD curve to AD_1. These shifts are shown by arrow 1 in both parts. But the adjustment is not yet complete.

The shift in the AD curve raises the price level to P_1 because the $SRAS$ curve is positively sloped. The rise in the price level shifts the AE curve down to AE_1, as shown by arrow 2 in part (i). This is shown as a *movement along* the new AD curve, as indicated by arrow 2 in part (ii). The new equilibrium is thus at E_1. The amount Y_0Y_1 is ΔY, the actual increase in real GDP. The multiplier, adjusted for the effect of the price increase, is the ratio $\Delta Y/\Delta A$ in part (i).

and 23) gives the extent of the horizontal shift in the AD curve in response to a change in autonomous expenditure. If the price level remains constant and firms are willing to supply all that is demanded at the existing price level (as would be the case with a horizontal $SRAS$ curve), the simple multiplier gives the increase in equilibrium national income.

But what happens in the more usual case in which the $SRAS$ curve slopes upward? As can be seen in Figure 24-6, when the $SRAS$ curve is positively sloped, the change in real GDP caused by a change in autonomous expenditure is no longer equal to the size of the horizontal shift in the AD curve. Part of the expansionary impact of an increase in demand is dissipated by a rise in the price level, and only part is transmitted to a rise in real GDP. Of course, an increase in output does occur; thus, a multiplier may still be calculated, but its value is not the same as that of the *simple* multiplier.

When the $SRAS$ curve is upward sloping, the multiplier is smaller than the simple multiplier.

Why is the multiplier smaller when the $SRAS$ curve is positively sloped? The answer lies in the behaviour that is summarized by the AE curve. To understand this, it is useful to think of the final change in real GDP as occurring in two stages, as shown in Figure 24-7.

First, with prices remaining constant, an increase in autonomous expenditure shifts the AE curve upward (from AE_0 to AE_1') and therefore shifts the AD curve to the right. This increase in autonomous expenditure is shown by a shift upward of the AE curve in part (i) of the figure and a shift to the right of the AD curve in part (ii). The horizontal shift in the AD curve is measured by the simple multiplier, but this cannot be the final equilibrium position because firms are unwilling to produce enough to satisfy the extra demand at the existing price level. The final equilibrium must be a point on the $SRAS$ curve.

Second, we take account of the rise in the price level that occurs because of the positive slope of the $SRAS$ curve. As we saw earlier in this chapter, a rise in the price level, via its effect on net exports and on wealth, leads to a downward shift in the AE curve (from AE_1' to AE_1). This second shift of the AE curve partly counteracts the initial rise in real GDP and so reduces the size of the multiplier. The second stage shows up as a downward shift of the AE curve in part (i) of Figure 24-7 and a movement upward and to the left along the new AD curve in part (ii).

The Importance of the Shape of the *SRAS* Curve

We have now seen that the shape of the *SRAS* curve has important implications for how the effects of an aggregate demand shock are divided between changes in real GDP and changes in the price level. Figure 24-8 highlights the price level and GDP effects of aggregate demand shocks by considering *AD* shocks in the presence of an *SRAS* curve that exhibits three distinct ranges.

Over the *flat* range, from 0 to Y_0, any change in aggregate demand leads to no change in prices and, as seen earlier, a response of output equal to that predicted by the simple multiplier.

Over the *intermediate* range, along which the *SRAS* curve is positively sloped, a shift in the *AD* curve gives rise to appreciable changes in both real GDP and the price level. Because of the increase in the price level, the multiplier in this case is positive, but smaller than the simple multiplier.

Over the *steep* range, very little more can be produced, however large the increase in demand. This range deals with an economy near its capacity constraints. Any change in aggregate demand leads to a sharp change in the price level and to little or no change in real GDP. The multiplier in this case is nearly zero.

The effect of any given shift in aggregate demand will be divided between a change in real output and a change in the price level, depending on the conditions of aggregate supply. The steeper the *SRAS* curve, the greater the price effect and the smaller the output effect.

Extensions in Theory 24-1 deals with the special case of a horizontal *SRAS* curve—sometimes called a *Keynesian SRAS* curve. In that case, the aggregate supply curve determines the price level by itself, and the *AD* curve then determines real GDP by itself.

Reconciliation with Previous Analysis

One of the central points of this chapter is that aggregate demand shocks typically lead to changes in *both* the price level and the level of real GDP. Furthermore, with a steep enough *SRAS* curve, such aggregate demand shocks will result in no change in real GDP, but only a change in the price level. How do we reconcile this possibility with the analysis of Chapters 22 and 23, where shifts in *AE* *always* change real GDP? The answer is that each *AE* curve is drawn on the assumption that there is a constant price level. An upward shift in the *AE* curve shifts the *AD* curve to the right. However, a steep *SRAS* curve means that the price level rises significantly, and this rise shifts the *AE* curve back down, offsetting some of its initial rise.

We can see this interaction most easily if we study the extreme case, shown in Figure 24-9, in which the *SRAS* curve is vertical. An increase in autonomous expenditure shifts the *AE* curve upward, thus raising the amount demanded. However, a vertical *SRAS* curve means that

Practise with Study Guide Chapter 24, Exercise 4.

FIGURE 24-8   The Effects of Increases in Aggregate Demand

The effect of increases in aggregate demand is divided between increases in real GDP and increases in prices, depending on the slope of the *SRAS* curve. Because of the increasing slope of the *SRAS* curve, increases in aggregate demand up to AD_0 have virtually no impact on the price level. Successive further increases bring larger price increases and relatively smaller output increases. By the time aggregate demand is at AD_4 or AD_5, virtually all of the effect is on the price level.

EXTENSIONS IN THEORY 24-1

The Keynesian *SRAS* Curve

In this box, we consider an extreme version of the *SRAS* curve that is horizontal over some range of real GDP. It is called the *Keynesian short-run aggregate supply curve,* after John Maynard Keynes (1883–1946), who in his famous book *The General Theory of Employment, Interest and Money* (1936) pioneered the study of the behaviour of economies under conditions of high unemployment. Despite its name, this curve does not describe Keynes' own views on the behaviour of the price level. It is instead the version of aggregate supply used by many of Keynes' followers in their early attempts to express Keynes' work in a formal model—something Keynes himself did not do.

The behaviour that gives rise to the Keynesian *SRAS* curve can be described as follows. When real GDP is below potential GDP, individual firms are operating with excess capacity. They then respond to demand variations by altering output while keeping prices constant. In other words, they will supply whatever they can sell at their existing prices as long as they are producing below their normal capacity.*

Under these circumstances, the economy has a horizontal *SRAS* curve, indicating that any output up to potential output will be supplied at the going price level. The amount that is actually produced is then de-

termined by the position of the *AD* curve, as shown in the figure. Thus, real GDP is said to be *demand determined.* If demand rises enough so that firms are trying to squeeze more than normal output out of their plants, their costs will rise, and so will their prices. Hence, the horizontal Keynesian *SRAS* curve applies only to levels of GDP below potential GDP.

This special case of a horizontal *SRAS* curve corresponds to the macro model that we developed in Chapters 22 and 23. Recall in that simple model that we assumed a constant price level. In other words, if the *SRAS* curve is horizontal, our macro model in this chapter is *exactly the same* as the simple version in Chapters 22 and 23. In this case, a change in autonomous expenditure, ΔA, will lead to increases in equilibrium GDP equal to ΔA times the simple multiplier. (In Figure 24-3 this is exactly the distance of the horizontal shift in the *AD* curve in response to any given ΔA.)

---

*There is considerable evidence that many firms do behave like this in the short run. One possible explanation for this is that changing prices frequently is too costly, so firms set the best possible (profit-maximizing) prices when output is at normal capacity and then do not change prices in the face of short-term fluctuations in demand.

Practise with Study Guide Chapter 24, Exercise 6.

output cannot be expanded to satisfy the increased demand. Instead, the extra demand merely forces prices up, and as prices rise, the *AE* curve shifts down again. The rise in prices continues until the *AE* curve is back to where it started. Thus, the rise in prices offsets the expansionary effect of the original shift and consequently leaves both real aggregate expenditure and equilibrium real GDP unchanged.

A vertical *SRAS* curve, however, is quite unrealistic. Most economists agree that the *SRAS* curve is shaped something like the one shown in Figure 24-8—that is, relatively flat for low levels of GDP and becoming steeper as GDP rises. This shape suggests that if GDP is below potential GDP, shifts in aggregate demand primarily affect output; whereas if GDP is above potential GDP, shifts in aggregate demand primarily affect the price level.

Of course, as we have noted already, treating technology and factor prices as constant is appropriate only when the time period under consideration is short. Hence, the *SRAS* curve is used only to analyse the economy in the short run. In the next chapter, we will see what happens in the long run when factor prices respond to changes in real GDP and the price level. First, however, our analysis of the short run needs to be rounded out with a discussion of aggregate supply shocks.

Aggregate Supply Shocks

A decrease in aggregate supply, shown by a shift to the left in the *SRAS* curve, means that less real output will be supplied at any given price level. An increase in aggregate supply, shown by a shift to the right in the *SRAS* curve, means that more real output will be supplied at any given price level.

Figure 24-10 illustrates the effects on the price level and real GDP of a decrease in aggregate supply. This decrease could have occurred because of, say, an increase in the world price of important inputs, such as oil, copper or iron ore. As can be seen from the figure, following the decrease in aggregate supply, the price level rises and real GDP falls. This combination of events is called *stagflation,* a term derived by combining *stagnation* (sometimes used to mean less than full employment) and *inflation.* Conversely, an increase in aggregate supply leads to an increase in real GDP and a decrease in the price level.

Aggregate supply shocks cause the price level and real GDP to change in opposite directions. With an increase in supply, the price level falls and GDP rises; with a decrease in supply, the price level rises and GDP falls.

Oil prices have provided two major examples of negative aggregate supply shocks in recent decades. The economy is especially responsive to changes in the price for oil because, in addition to being used to produce energy, oil is an input into plastics and many other materials that are widely used in manufacturing. Massive increases in oil prices occurred during 1973–1974 and 1979–1980, caused by the successful efforts of the OPEC countries to form a cartel and restrict the output of oil. These increases in the price of oil caused leftward shifts in the *SRAS* curve in most countries. Real GDP fell while the price level rose—stagflation. (In subsequent years the price of oil fell, shifting the *SRAS* curve back to the right, but the declines were more gradual and thus less dramatic than the initial increases.)

FIGURE 24-9 Demand Shocks When the *SRAS* Curve Is Vertical

(i) Aggregate expenditure

(ii) Aggregate demand and supply

In the extreme case where the *SRAS* curve is vertical, the effect of an increase in autonomous expenditure is solely to increase price level. An increase in autonomous expenditure shifts the *AE* curve upward from AE_0 to AE_1, as shown by arrow 1 in part (i). Given the initial price level P_0, equilibrium would shift from E_0 to E_1' and real GDP would rise from Y_0 to Y_1'. However, the price level does not remain constant. This is shown by the *SRAS* curve in part (ii). Instead, the price level rises to P_1. This causes the *AE* curve to shift back down all the way to AE_0, as shown by arrow 2 in part (i), and equilibrium GDP stays at Y_0. In part (ii), the new equilibrium is at E_1 with GDP at Y_0 and the price level at P_1.

For information on OPEC, see its website: www.opec.org.

FIGURE 24-10 Aggregate Supply Shocks

(i) Aggregate expenditure

(ii) Aggregate demand and supply

Aggregate supply shocks cause the price level and real GDP to move in opposite directions. The original equilibrium is at E_0, with GDP of Y_0 appearing in both parts of the figure. The price level is P_0 in part (ii), and at that price level, the desired aggregate expenditure curve is AE_0 in part (i).

A negative aggregate supply shock now shifts the $SRAS$ curve in part (ii) to $SRAS_1$. At the original price level of P_0, firms are now only willing to supply Y_1'. The fall in supply, with no corresponding fall in demand, causes a shortage that leads to a rise in the price level. The new equilibrium is reached at E_1, where the AD curve intersects $SRAS_1$. At the new and higher equilibrium price level of P_1, the AE curve has fallen to AE_1, as shown in part (i).

Commodity prices have provided an important recent example of a positive aggregate supply shock. The Southeast Asian countries of Indonesia, Malaysia, Thailand, and South Korea are all significant users of raw materials. When their economies plunged into a major recession in 1997 and 1998, the world demand for raw materials fell, and the prices of such goods fell as a result. From the summer of 1997 to the end of 1998, the average price of raw materials fell by approximately 30 percent.

Though this was clearly bad economic times for much of Southeast Asia, the reduction in raw materials prices was a *positive* aggregate supply shock for countries that used raw materials as inputs for production. In countries like Canada, the United States, and most of western Europe, the $SRAS$ curves shifted to the right. The effect was to increase real GDP and reduce the price level.[1]

A Word of Warning

We have discussed the effects of aggregate demand and aggregate supply shocks on the economy's price level and real GDP. Students are sometimes puzzled, however, because some events would appear to be *both* demand and supply shocks. How do we analyse such complicated shocks? For example, when OPEC restricted the supply of oil and thus drove up the world price of oil, this was clearly a negative supply shock. After all, oil is a very important input to production for so many firms and so many industries. But for Canada, which produces and exports oil, doesn't the increase in the world price of oil also imply an increase in export revenue? And doesn't this imply a *positive* aggregate demand shock?

The answer to both questions is yes. The OPEC oil shock was indeed a negative aggregate supply shock to any country that uses oil as an input (which means most countries). But for those countries that also produce and export oil—like Canada—the OPEC oil shock was also a positive aggregate demand shock. The rise in the price of oil generated an increase in income to Canadian oil producers—it is no surprise that Alberta's economy was booming throughout the 1970s.

For such countries, a complete analysis of the OPEC oil shocks involves both a leftward shift of the $SRAS$ curve and a rightward shift of the AD curve. In

---

[1]Actually, it is more correct to say that the shock reduced the price level *compared to what it otherwise would have been*. Due to ongoing inflation, the causes of which we will discuss in Chapters 28 and 29, the price level in Canada rarely falls. But we have been assuming throughout this chapter that there is no ongoing inflation, and in that setting a positive $SRAS$ shock like the one described in the text would indeed cause the price level to fall.

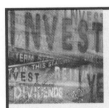

APPLYING ECONOMIC CONCEPTS 24-1

The Asian Crisis and the Canadian Economy

In the summer of 1997, the currencies of several countries in Southeast Asia plummeted (relative to the U.S. and Canadian dollars) as their central banks were no longer able to "peg" their exchange rates. We will discuss how such pegged exchange rates operate in Chapter 36. For now, the important point is that, for various reasons, banks, firms, and households in these countries had accumulated a large stock of debt denominated in foreign currencies, especially U.S. dollars. The sudden depreciations of their currencies—in some cases by 70 percent in just a few days—led to dramatic increases in the amount of domestic income required to pay the interest on this debt. Manufacturing firms and financial institutions went bankrupt, workers were laid off, and economic output fell sharply. By late in 1997, the economies of Malaysia, Indonesia, Thailand, South Korea, and the Philippines were suffering major recessions.

How did this Asian crisis affect Canada? It had offsetting positive and negative effects on the level of economic activity in Canada. The events in Asia generated both a *negative* aggregate demand shock and a *positive* aggregate supply shock for Canada.

To understand the demand side of the story, we must recognize that these Asian economies are important users of raw materials. When their level of economic activity declined sharply, so, too, did their demand for raw materials. Indeed, average raw materials prices fell by roughly 30 percent between the summer of 1997 and the end of 1998. But raw materials are an important export for Canada. The decline in the world's demand for raw materials implied a reduction in demand for Canadian goods. As a result, Canadian producers of copper, pork, newsprint, lumber, and iron ore suffered significantly. In terms of the simple diagram we have been using in this chapter, the demand part of the Asian crisis is represented as a leftward shift of the Canadian *AD* curve.

But the story does not end there. Also important to Canada is the fact that many Canadian manufacturing firms use those same raw materials as inputs for their production of car parts, pre-fabricated houses and trailers, electrical equipment, and so on. A dramatic reduction in the prices of raw materials implies a reduction in costs for manufacturing firms. This is a positive aggregate supply shock, and is illustrated by a rightward shift of the Canadian *SRAS* curve.

What is the overall effect on the Canadian economy? The effect of each shock taken separately is to reduce the price level—so the overall effect is unambiguously a lower price level.* In contrast, the effect on real GDP would ap-

pear to be ambiguous since the *AD* shock reduces GDP whereas the *SRAS* curve increases it. But this is not quite right. Since Canada is a net exporter of raw materials (it exports more raw materials than it imports), it must experience a decrease in national income when these prices fall. In other words, the net effect of the negative demand shock and the positive supply shock is to reduce Canadian GDP. The figure is therefore drawn with the *AD* shock being larger than the *SRAS* shock and so the new equilibrium level of GDP, Y_0, is lower than in the initial equilibrium, Y_1.

In contrast, the appropriate diagram for the United States would show a similar rightward *SRAS* shift (because raw materials are equally important for production in the United States) but a smaller leftward *AD* shift (because as a share of its economy, the United States is a much smaller producer of raw materials than is Canada). Since the United States is a net importer of raw materials, its level of income must be *increased* when the prices of raw materials decline. In other words, the net effect of the negative demand shock and the positive supply shock is to increase U.S. GDP. Thus, the overall effect of the Asian crisis on the U.S. economy is different from its effect on the Canadian economy.

By the time this book went to press, in the fall of 1999, the Asian economies were on the road to economic recovery and the world prices of raw materials had begun to increase. Thus, the shifts of the *AD* and *SRAS* curves shown in the figure began to reverse themselves.

*Recall footnote 1 on page 572. We are assuming in this analysis that there is no ongoing inflation, so a positive *SRAS* shock or a negative *AD* shock reduces the price level. A more accurate description for the Canadian economy in 1998, with some ongoing inflation, is that the price level fell below what it otherwise would have been. This appears as a reduction in the rate of inflation.

For interesting information on the Asian crisis, see Nouriel Roubini's website: www.stern.nyu.edu/~nroubini.

this case, the equilibrium price level clearly rises. The overall effect on real GDP, however, then depends on the relative importance of the supply and demand effects. For example, the United States and Canada both use oil as an important input to production, and so the *SRAS* shifts were similar in the two countries. As a share of its economy, however, the United States produces much less oil than does Canada, and so the rightward *AD* shift in Canada was larger than in the United States. The overall effect was that the United States suffered a larger reduction in real GDP than did Canada as a result of the OPEC oil shock.

The important message here is a simple one:

Many economic events—especially changes in the world prices of raw materials—cause both aggregate demand and aggregate supply shocks. The overall effect on the economy depends on the relative importance of the two separate effects.

Applying Economic Concepts 24-1 discusses the effect of the 1997–98 Asian economic crisis on the Canadian economy. The Asian crisis represented both a negative demand shock and a positive supply shock to Canada.

SUMMARY

The Demand Side of the Economy

- The *AE* curve shows desired aggregate expenditure for each level of GDP at a particular price level. Its intersection with the 45° line determines equilibrium GDP for that price level. Equilibrium GDP thus occurs where desired aggregate expenditure equals actual GDP. A change in the price level changes household wealth and thus causes a shift in the *AE* curve: upward when the price level falls and downward when the price level rises. This leads to a new equilibrium level of real GDP.
- The *AD* curve plots the equilibrium level of GDP that corresponds to each possible price level. A change in equi-

librium GDP following a change in the price level is shown by a movement along the *AD* curve.
- A rise in the price level lowers exports and lowers consumers' spending (because it decreases consumers' wealth). Both of these changes reduce equilibrium GDP and cause the *AD* curve to have a negative slope.
- The *AD* curve shifts horizontally when any element of autonomous expenditure changes, and the simple multiplier measures the magnitude of the shift.

The Supply Side of the Economy

- The short-run aggregate supply *(SRAS)* curve, drawn for given technology and factor prices, is positively sloped because unit costs rise with increasing output and because rising product prices make it profitable to increase output.

- An increase in productivity or a decrease in factor prices shifts the *SRAS* curve to the right. This is an increase in aggregate supply. A decrease in productivity or an increase in factor prices shifts the *SRAS* curve to the left. This is a decrease in aggregate supply.

Macroeconomic Equilibrium

LO 4 5

- Macroeconomic equilibrium refers to equilibrium values of real GDP and the price level, as determined by the intersection of the *AD* and *SRAS* curves. Shifts in the *AD* and *SRAS* curves, called aggregate demand shocks and aggregate supply shocks, change the equilibrium values of real GDP and the price level.
- When the *SRAS* curve is upward sloping, an aggregate demand shock causes the price level and real GDP to move in the same direction. The division of the effects between a change in real GDP and a change in the price level depends on the shape of the *SRAS* curve. When the *SRAS* curve is flat, shifts in the *AD* curve primarily affect real GDP. When the *SRAS* curve is steep, shifts in the *AD* curve primarily affect the price level.

- An aggregate supply shock moves equilibrium GDP along the *AD* curve, causing the price level and real GDP to move in opposite directions. A leftward shift in the *SRAS* curve causes stagflation—rising prices and falling real GDP. A rightward shift causes an increase in real GDP and a fall in the price level.
- Some events are both aggregate supply and aggregate demand shocks. Changes in the world prices of raw materials, for example, shift the *SRAS* curve. If the country (like Canada) is also a producer of such raw materials, there will also be a shift in the *AD* curve. The overall effect then depends on the relative sizes of the separate effects.

K E Y   C O N C E P T S

Effects of an exogenous change in the price level
Relationship between the *AE* and *AD* curves

Negative slope of the *AD* curve
Positive slope of the *SRAS* curve
Macroeconomic equilibrium
Aggregate demand shocks

The multiplier when the price level varies
Aggregate supply shocks

S T U D Y   E X E R C I S E S

1. Consider the effects of an exogenous increase in the domestic price level. For each of the assets listed, explain how the change in the price level would affect the wealth of the asset holder. Then explain the effect on *aggregate* (private sector) wealth.

   a. Cash holdings
   b. Deposits in a bank account
   c. A household mortgage
   d. A corporate bond that promises to pay the bondholder $10 000 on January 1, 2006
   e. A government Treasury bill that promises to pay the holder $10 000 on January 1, 2006

2. Consider the following simplified *AE* function:

   $$AE = 350 + 0.8Y + 0.1(M/P)$$

   where *AE* is desired aggregate expenditure, *Y* is real GDP, *M* is the private sector's *nominal wealth*, and *P* is the price level. Suppose that *M* is constant and equal to 6000.

   a. Explain why the expression for *AE* above makes sense. Why do *M* and *P* enter the *AE* function?
   b. Fill in the table below:

P	M/P	AE
1	—	—
2	—	—
3	—	—
4	—	—
5	—	—
6	—	—

   c. Plot each of the *AE* functions—one for each price level—on the same scale 45° line diagram.
   d. Compute the level of equilibrium national income for each of the values of *P*.
   e. Plot the pairs of price level and equilibrium national income on a scale diagram with *P* on the vertical axis and *Y* on the horizontal axis.

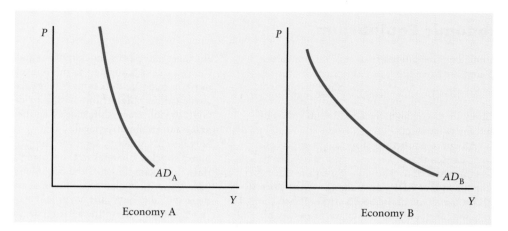

Economy A   Economy B

3. Consider the diagrams above showing the *AD* curves in two economies. Economy A is Autarkland—it does not trade with the rest of the world (*autarky* is a situation in which a country does not trade with other countries). Economy B is Openland—it exports to and imports from the rest of the world.

   a. Explain why an increase in the domestic price level (for a given exchange rate) reduces net exports in Openland. How would you illustrate this with the *AE* curve in the 45° line diagram?
   b. Explain why the *AD* curve is steeper in Autarkland than in Openland.
   c. If there are never any net exports in Autarkland, why isn't the *AD* curve vertical? Explain what other aspect of the economy generates a downward-sloping *AD* curve.

4. The economy of Neverland has the following *AD* and *SRAS* schedules. Denote Y_{AD} as the level of real GDP along the *AD* curve; let Y_{SRAS} be the level of real GDP along the *SRAS* curve. GDP is shown in billions of 1992 dollars.

Price Level	Y_{AD}	Y_{SRAS}
90	1100	750
100	1000	825
110	900	900
120	800	975
130	700	1050
140	600	1125

   a. Plot the *AD* and *SRAS* curves on a scale diagram.
   b. What is the price level and level of real GDP in Neverland's macroeconomic equilibrium?
   c. Suppose the level of potential output in Neverland is $950 billion. Is the current equilibrium level of real GDP greater than or less than potential?

5. Each of the following events is either a *cause* or a *consequence* of a shift in the *AD* or *SRAS* curve. Identify which it is and, if it is a cause, describe the effect on equilibrium real GDP and the price level.

   a. OPEC's actions significantly increased the world price of oil in 1979–80.
   b. During 1996–99, Canadian real GDP was growing at a healthy pace but inflation showed no signs of rising.
   c. World commodity prices declined sharply in 1997–98. Many of these commodities are both produced in Canada and are used as important inputs for Canadian firms.
   d. The end of the Cold War led to large declines in defence spending in many countries (including Canada).
   e. Canadian exports increased in response to a falling external value of the Canadian dollar in the mid 1990s.
   f. Several provinces lowered their personal income-tax rates in the late 1990s.
   g. The federal government reduced its level of government purchases (G) in the late 1990s.

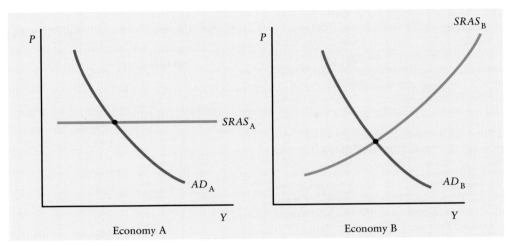

Economy A   Economy B

6. The diagrams above show the *AD* and *SRAS* curves in two different economies.

   a. Explain what aspect of firms' behaviour might give rise to the horizontal *SRAS* curve in Economy A.

   b. Explain what aspect of firms' behaviour gives rise to the upward-sloping *SRAS* curve in Economy B.

   c. In which economy is output demand determined? Explain.

   d. Consider the effects of an increase in autonomous expenditure. Which economy has the larger multiplier? Explain your reasoning.

7. This is a challenging question and involves algebraically solving the system of two equations given by the *AD* and *SRAS* curves. The equations for the curves are given by:

   AD: $Y_{AD} = 710 - 30P + 5G$

   SRAS: $Y_{SRAS} = 10 + 5P - 2P_{OIL}$

where Y is real GDP, P is the price level, G is the level of government purchases, and P_{OIL} is the world price of oil.

   a. Explain the various terms in the *AD* curve. What is the value of the simple multiplier? (Hint: the simple multiplier is the change in equilibrium real GDP when some autonomous component of expenditure, like G, changes by $1.)

   b. Explain the various terms in the *SRAS* curve. Explain why the price of oil enters negatively.

   c. Solve for the equilibrium value of real GDP and the price level.

   d. Using your solution to part **c**, what is the effect of a change in G on equilibrium Y and P?

   e. Using your solution to part **c**, what is the effect of a change in P_{OIL} on equilibrium Y and P?

DISCUSSION QUESTIONS

1. In 1979 and 1980, the British government greatly reduced income taxes but restored the lost government revenue by raising excise and sales taxes. These actions led to a sharp increase in the price level and a fall in output. Explain these events in terms of shifts in the aggregate demand or aggregate supply curves (or both).

2. This chapter discussed the meaning of aggregate demand and aggregate supply shocks, and several examples were given of each. But some shocks can be both demand-side shocks and supply-side shocks. Consider the prices of many commodities, such as lumber, newsprint, oil, copper, grains, and iron ore. The prices

of such commodities are determined in world markets, and are subject to significant fluctuations from year to year. For example, in 1997–98, there was a significant decline in the prices of many such commodities. Explain how such a decline in commodity prices can lead to both a decline in Canadian aggregate demand and an increase in Canadian aggregate supply. How would you determine the net effect on real GDP and the price level?

3. Show the effects on the price level and real GDP of a major union wage settlement that significantly increases wages. Is this a supply shock, a demand shock, or both?

4. Following are the combinations of output and price level given by real GDP and the CPI, respectively, for some recent years. Treat each pair as if it is the intersection of an *AD* and an *SRAS* curve. Plot these data. Then think about the possible shifts in the *AD* or *SRAS* curves that could have caused them. Is it possible to know what the underlying shifts are? Why or why not?

Year	CPI (1992 = 100)	GDP (billions of 1992 dollars)
1990	93.3	709.9
1991	98.5	697.3
1992	100.0	702.6
1993	101.8	718.2
1994	102.0	751.1
1995	104.2	767.9
1996	105.9	777.2
1997	107.6	806.7
1998	108.9	830.7

CHAPTER 25

Output and Prices in the Long Run

This chapter examines how the economy's *long-run* values of real GDP and the price level are determined. In the previous chapter, we introduced the short-run aggregate supply (*SRAS*) curve to represent the supply side of the economy—that is, firms' willingness to supply output at various price levels. Central to our discussion of the *SRAS* curve was the assumption that all factor prices were constant. It is now time to relax the assumption of constant factor prices and examine how factor prices are influenced by the state of the economy. The flexibility of wages and other factor prices is the fundamental difference between the short run and long run in macroeconomics.

Every worker knows that the best time to ask for a raise is during a boom, and that it is difficult to get significant wage increases during a recession. Every businessperson knows that the cost of many materials tends to rise rapidly during business expansions and to fall—often dramatically—during recessions. In short, factor prices change with economic conditions, and we need to allow for these effects. To do this, we need to see what happens in a longer-term setting, when changes in real GDP induce changes in factor prices.

Before we proceed, however, there is one important point that must be made. In Chapter 24 the *SRAS* curve was drawn under the assumption of given factor prices *and* a given state of technology. In this chapter we will examine in detail how factor prices change, but throughout the chapter we will maintain the assumption that technology (and thus productivity) is constant. This allows us to focus more clearly on the process of factor-price adjustment. In Chapter 32, where we explore the details of long-run economic growth, technological change will take centre stage. But, for now, technology is held constant.

Induced Changes in Factor Prices

We must begin by reconsidering two key concepts that we first encountered in Chapter 19—potential output and the output gap.

Potential Output and the Output Gap

Recall from our discussion in Chapter 19 that *potential output* is the total output that can be produced when all productive resources—labour and capital equipment, in particular—are being used at their *normal rates of utilization*. When a nation's actual GDP diverges from its potential GDP, the difference is called the output gap (or GDP gap).

Although growth in potential output has powerful effects from one decade to the next, its change from one *year* to the next is small enough to be ignored when studying the year-to-year behaviour of real GDP and the price level. In this chapter, therefore, we view variations in the output gap as determined solely by variations in *actual* GDP around a constant level of *potential* GDP.

Figure 25-1 shows real GDP being determined by the intersection of the *AD* and *SRAS* curves. Potential output is constant, and it is shown by identical vertical lines in the two parts of the figure. In part (i), the *AD* and *SRAS* curves intersect to produce an equilibrium real GDP less than potential output. The result, as we saw in Chapter 19, is called a *recessionary output gap* because recessions are often characterized as having

FIGURE 25-1   The Output Gap

(i) A recessionary output gap   (ii) An inflationary output gap

The output gap is the difference between potential output, Y^*, and actual GDP, Y. Potential output is shown by the vertical line at Y^*. A recessionary gap, shown in panel (i), occurs when potential output is greater than real GDP. An inflationary gap, shown in panel (ii), occurs when real GDP is greater than potential output.

GDP below potential output. In part (ii), the *AD* and *SRAS* curves intersect to produce an equilibrium real GDP above potential output, resulting in what is called an *inflationary output gap*. The way in which an inflationary output gap puts upward pressure on prices will become clear in the ensuing discussion.

Factor Prices and the Output Gap

The output gap provides a convenient measure of the pressure on factor prices to change. When real GDP is above potential output, demand for factors will also be high. When real GDP is below potential output, demand for factors will be correspondingly low. This relationship holds for all factors of production, including labour, land, raw materials, and capital equipment. The discussion that follows is simplified, however, by focusing on one key factor, labour, and on its price, the wage rate.

When there is an inflationary gap, actual GDP exceeds potential GDP, and the demand for labour services will be relatively high. When there is a recessionary gap, actual GDP is below potential GDP, and the demand for labour services will be relatively low.

These two situations have implications for wages. In the previous chapter we referred to average costs per unit of output as *unit costs;* to focus on labour costs, we now use average wage costs per unit of output, which we refer to as *unit labour costs*.

Before we examine the effects of output gaps on wages and unit labour costs, it is worth noting that even in the absence of an output gap, the presence of ongoing inflation would influence the normal pattern of wage changes. Wage contracts often allow for changes in the price level that are expected to occur during the life of the contract. For the discussion in this chapter we make the simplifying assumption that the price level is expected to be constant; hence changes in money wages are also expected to be changes in real wages. We will discuss the distinction between changes in money wages and real wages and the important role played by expectations of price level changes in Chapter 29 when we examine the process of inflation.

Output Above Potential

Sometimes the *AD* and *SRAS* curves intersect where actual output exceeds potential, as illustrated in part (ii) of Figure 25-1. Because firms are producing beyond their normal capacity output, there is an unusually large demand for all factor inputs, including labour. Labour shortages will emerge in some industries and among many groups of workers. Firms will try to bid workers away from other firms in order to maintain the high levels of output and sales made possible by the boom conditions.

As a result of these tight labour-market conditions, workers will find that they have considerable bargaining power with their employers, and they will put upward pressure on wages. Firms, recognizing that demand for their goods is strong, will be anxious to maintain a high level of output. To prevent their workers from either striking or quitting and moving to other employers, firms will be willing to accede to some of these upward pressures.

The boom that is associated with an inflationary gap generates a set of conditions—high profits for firms and unusually large demand for labour—that causes wages and thus unit labour costs to rise.

When output is above potential, the excess demand for labour tends to push up wages.

As unit labour costs increase in response to the inflationary gap, firms reduce the quantity of output supplied for any given price level—the *SRAS* curve shifts up and to the left. This shift has the effect of reducing equilibrium real GDP and raising the price level. Real GDP moves back toward potential and the inflationary gap begins to close.

Output Below Potential

Sometimes the *AD* and *SRAS* curves intersect where actual output is less than potential, as illustrated in part (i) of Figure 25-1. Because firms are producing below their normal-capacity output, there is an unusually low demand for all factor inputs, including labour. There will be labour surpluses in some industries and among some groups of workers. Firms will have below-normal sales and not only will resist upward pressures on wages but will seek reductions in wages.

The slump that is associated with a recessionary gap generates a set of conditions—low profits for firms and low demand for labour—that causes wages, and thus unit labour costs, to fall.

As unit labour costs fall in response to the recessionary gap, firms increase the quantity of output supplied for any given price level—the *SRAS* curve shifts down and to the right. This shift has the effect of increasing equilibrium real GDP and reducing the price level. Real GDP moves back toward potential and the recessionary gap begins to close.

Adjustment Asymmetry

At this stage, we encounter an important asymmetry in the economy's aggregate supply behaviour. Boom conditions (an inflationary gap), along with labour shortages, cause wages and unit labour costs to rise. The experience of many developed economies, however, suggests that the downward pressures on wages during slumps (recessionary gaps) often do not operate as quickly as the upward pressures during booms. Even when wages fall, they tend to fall more slowly than they would rise in an equally sized inflationary gap. This *wage stickiness* implies that the rightward shift in the *SRAS* curve and the downward pressure on the price level are correspondingly slight.[1]

Both upward and downward adjustments to wages and unit labour costs do occur, but there are differences in the speed at which they typically operate. Booms can cause wages to rise very rapidly; recessions usually cause wages to fall only slowly.[2]

The Phillips Curve

We saw in Chapter 19 that when real GDP is equal to potential GDP, the unemployment rate is equal to the *nonaccelerating inflation rate of unemployment*, or NAIRU. This cumbersome acronym will be explained in detail in Chapter 29; economists often use the easier term, the *natural rate of unemployment*. We use U^* to designate the NAIRU (or the natural rate of unemployment).

---

[1]This is the second asymmetry in aggregate supply that we have encountered. The first involves the changing slope of the *SRAS* curve, discussed in Chapter 24.

[2]Though unit labour costs do tend to fall during recessionary gaps, nominal wages rarely fall. The reason is that productivity tends to increase continually, thus allowing wages to rise, even though more slowly than productivity. But such changes in productivity shift the *LRAS* curve to the right and complicate our analysis. In this chapter we hold productivity and thus the *LRAS* curve constant. We then talk of how nominal wages—and thus unit labour costs—respond to output gaps.

U^* is not zero. Instead, even when output is equal to potential, there may be significant *frictional* and *structural* unemployment. A detailed discussion of U^* and its determinants must await Chapter 30, but for now we simply note the relationship between output gaps and the gap between the unemployment rate and U^*. Our previous discussion emphasized that when real GDP exceeds potential, the excess demand for labour pushes wages up. In these situations, the unemployment rate is less than U^*. That discussion also emphasized that when real GDP is less than potential, the excess supply of labour puts downward pressure on wages. In these situations, the unemployment rate exceeds U^*.

This relationship between U^*, the actual unemployment rate, and the rate of change of wages is illustrated by one of the most famous curves in macroeconomics—the *Phillips curve. Extensions in Theory 25-1* discusses the Phillips curve and how it relates to the short-run aggregate supply curve. The key point is that the Phillips curve describes the adjustment process we have been discussing. A *movement along* the Phillips curve leads to a change in the rate at which the *SRAS* curve is shifting.

In Chapter 29 we will discuss the Phillips curve in more detail when we discuss the relationship between inflation and unemployment.

Inflationary and Recessionary Gaps

Now it should be clear why the output gaps are named as they are. When real GDP exceeds potential GDP, there will normally be rising unit costs, and the *SRAS* curve will be shifting upward. This will in turn push the price level up. Indeed, the most obvious event accompanying these conditions is likely to be significant inflation. The larger the excess of real GDP over potential GDP, the greater the inflationary pressure. The term *inflationary gap* emphasizes this salient feature when output exceeds potential output.

When actual output is less than potential output, as we have seen, there will be unemployment of labour and other productive resources. Unit labour costs will fall only slowly, leading to a slow downward shift in the *SRAS* curve. Hence, the price level will be falling only slowly, so that *unemployment* will be the output gap's most obvious result. The term *recessionary gap* emphasizes this salient feature that high rates of unemployment occur when actual output falls short of potential output.

The induced effects of output gaps on unit labour costs and the consequent shifts in the *SRAS* curve play an important role in our analysis of the long-run consequences of aggregate demand and aggregate supply shocks, to which we now turn.

Demand and Supply Shocks

We can now extend our study to cover the longer-run consequences of aggregate demand and aggregate supply shocks, incorporating changes in factor prices. We need to examine the effects of expansionary and contractionary shocks separately because the behaviour of unit costs is not symmetrical for the two cases. Let's begin with demand shocks.

Expansionary *AD* Shocks

Suppose the economy starts with a stable price level and that real GDP equals potential GDP as shown by the initial equilibrium in part (i) of Figure 25-2. Now suppose that this

EXTENSIONS IN THEORY 25-1

The Phillips Curve and the Shifting *SRAS* Curve

In the early 1950s, Professor A. W. Phillips of the London School of Economics was conducting pioneering research on macroeconomic policy. In his early models, he related the rate of inflation to the difference between actual and potential output. Later he investigated the empirical underpinnings of this equation by studying the relationship between the rate of increase of wages and the level of unemployment. He studied these variables because unemployment data were available as far back as the mid-nineteenth century, whereas very little data on output gaps were available when he did his empirical work. In 1958, he reported that a stable relationship had existed between these two variables for 100 years in the United Kingdom. This relationship came to be known as the Phillips curve. The **Phillips curve** provided an explanation, rooted in empirical observation, of the speed with which wage changes shifted the *SRAS* curve by changing unit labour costs.

The original Phillips curve related wage changes to the level of unemployment. But we can express the same information in a slightly different way. Note that unemployment and output gaps are negatively related—a recessionary gap is associated with high unemployment, and an inflationary gap is associated with low unemployment. We can therefore create another Phillips curve which plots wage changes against output (rather than against unemployment). Both figures show the same information.

Inflationary gaps (when $Y>Y^*$ and $U<U^*$) are associated with *increases* in wages. Recessionary gaps (when $Y<Y^*$ and

$U>U^*$) are associated with *decreases* in wages.* Thus, a Phillips curve that plots wage changes against real GDP is upward sloping whereas a Phillips curve that plots wage changes against the unemployment rate is downward sloping. Both versions of the Phillips curve are shown in the accompanying figure.

When output is at potential, firms are at their capacity level of output and all factors are being used at their normal rates of utilization. There is neither upward nor downward pressure on wages (or other factor prices) because there is neither an excess demand nor an excess supply of labour. Hence, the Phillips curve cuts the horizontal axis at Y^* (and at U^*). This is how Phillips drew his original curve.

The Phillips curve is *not* the same as the *SRAS* curve. The *SRAS* curve has the *price level* on the vertical axis whereas the Phillip curve has the *rate of change of wages* on the vertical axis. How are the two curves related? The economy's location on the Phillips curve indicates how the *SRAS* curve is shifting as a result of the existing output gap.

For example, suppose a positive aggregate demand (or supply) shock causes real GDP to increase to Y_1 and thus

---

*Recall that we are assuming productivity to be constant so that changes in wages imply changes in unit labour costs. When productivity is growing, however, recessionary output gaps cause unit labour costs to fall. This only requires wages to be growing more slowly than productivity, not to be actually falling.

Phillips curve
Originally, a relationship between the unemployment rate and the rate of change of money wages. Now often drawn as a relationship between actual GDP and the rate of price inflation.

situation is disturbed by an increase in autonomous expenditure, perhaps caused by an upturn in business confidence and a resulting boom in investment spending. Figure 25-2(i) shows the effects of this aggregate demand shock in raising both the price level and real GDP. The *AD* curve shifts from AD_0 to AD_1, and real GDP rises above potential GDP. An inflationary gap opens up.

We have seen that an inflationary gap leads to increases in wages, which cause unit costs to rise. The *SRAS* curve shifts to the left as firms respond to the higher input costs by increasing their output prices. As seen in part (ii) of the figure, the upward shift of the *SRAS* curve causes a further rise in the price level, but this time the price rise is associated with a *fall* in output.

The cost increases (and the consequent upward shifts of the *SRAS* curve) continue until the inflationary gap has been removed—that is, until in part (ii) real GDP returns to Y^*. Only then is there no excess demand for labour, and only then do wages and unit costs, and hence the *SRAS* curve, stabilize.

produces an inflationary gap. The excess demand for labour puts upward pressure on wages and the economy moves along the Phillips curve to point A, where wages begin rising. The increase in wages, as we have seen both in this chapter and the previous one, increases unit costs and causes the SRAS curve to shift up and to the left. Thus, each point on the Phillips curve determines the rate at which the SRAS curve is shifting. To complete the example, note that as the SRAS curve shifts to the left, the level of GDP will fall and the inflationary gap will begin to close. The economy thus moves back along the Phillips curve to where it started.

Note that the convex shape of the Phillips curve is not accidental—it reflects the adjustment asymmetry we mentioned in the text. The convexity of the Phillips curve im-plies that an inflationary gap of a given amount will lead to faster wage increases than an equally sized recessionary gap will lead to wage reductions. In other words, an inflationary gap will cause the SRAS curve to shift up more quickly than a recessionary gap will cause the SRAS curve to shift down.

Finally, you might be wondering what would happen if the Phillips curve were to shift. And what would cause such a shift? As we will see in Chapter 29 when we discuss the phenomenon of sustained inflation, an important cause of shifts of the Phillips curve is changes in firms' and households' *expectations* of future inflation. For now, the best way to think of the Phillips curve is as an easy graphical way of describing the process of wage adjustment in response to output gaps.

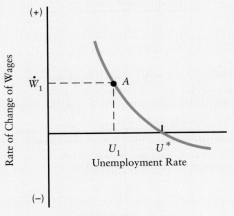

(i) Wage changes and unemployment

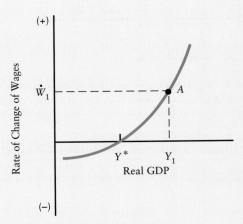

(ii) Wage changes and output

The ability to get more output from the economy than its underlying potential output is only a short-term possibility. When real GDP is greater than Y^*, inflationary forces are set in motion that bring GDP back to Y^*.

An adjustment mechanism eventually eliminates any boom caused by a demand shock by returning real GDP to its potential level.

Practise with Study Guide Chapter 25, Exercise 2.

Contractionary *AD* Shocks

Suppose again that the economy starts with stable prices and real GDP equal to potential, as shown in part (i) of Figure 25-3. Now assume that there is a *decline* in aggregate demand. This negative aggregate demand shock might be a reduction in investment expenditure, or perhaps a decline in the world demand for Canadian lumber or computer software.

FIGURE 25-2   The Long-Run Effect of a Positive Aggregate Demand Shock

(i) Autonomous increase in aggregate demand   (ii) Induced shift in aggregate supply

A rightward shift of the *AD* curve first raises prices and output along the *SRAS* curve. It then induces a shift of the *SRAS* curve that further raises prices but lowers output along the new *AD* curve. In part (i), the economy is in equilibrium at E_0, at its level of potential output, Y^*, and price level P_0. The *AD* curve then shifts from AD_0 to AD_1. This moves equilibrium to E_1, with income Y_1 and price level P_1, and opens up an inflationary gap.

In part (ii), the inflationary gap results in an increase in wages and other input costs, shifting the *SRAS* curve leftward. As this happens, output falls and the price level rises along AD_1. Eventually, when the *SRAS* curve has shifted to $SRAS_1$, output is back to Y^* and the inflationary gap has been eliminated. However, the price level has risen to P_2. The long-run result of the aggregate demand shock is therefore a higher price level with no change in real GDP.

The first effects of the decline are a fall in output and some downward adjustment of prices, as shown in part (i) of the figure. As real GDP falls below potential, a recessionary gap is created, and unemployment rises. At this point we must analyse two separate cases. The first is where wages fall quickly in response to the excess supply of labour. The second is where wages fall only slowly.

Flexible Wages

Suppose wages (and other factor prices) fall quickly in response to the recessionary gap. The *SRAS* curve would therefore shift quickly to the right as the lower wages lead to reduced unit costs.

As shown in part (ii) of Figure 25-3, the economy would move along the new *AD* curve, with falling prices and rising output, until real GDP was quickly restored to potential, Y^*. We conclude that if wages were to fall rapidly whenever there was unemployment, the resulting shift in the *SRAS* curve would quickly restore full employment.

Flexible wages that fall rapidly during periods of unemployment provide an automatic adjustment mechanism that pushes the economy back toward potential output.

Sticky Wages

Boom conditions, along with labour shortages, do cause wages to rise, shifting the *SRAS* curve upward. In general, the bigger the inflationary gap, the faster wages will rise and

FIGURE 25-3   The Long-Run Effect of a Negative Aggregate Demand Shock

A leftward shift of the *AD* curve first lowers the price level and GDP along the *SRAS* curve and then induces a (slow) shift of the *SRAS* curve that further lowers prices but raises output along the new *AD* curve. In part (i), the economy is in equilibrium at E_0, at its level of potential output, Y^*, and price level P_0. The *AD* curve then shifts to AD_1, moving equilibrium to E_1, with income Y_1 and price level P_1, and opens up a recessionary gap.

Part (ii) shows the adjustment back to potential output that occurs from the supply side of the economy. The fall in wages shifts the *SRAS* curve to the right. Real GDP rises, and the price level falls further along the new *AD* curve. Eventually, the *SRAS* curve reaches $SRAS_1$, with equilibrium at E_2. The price level stabilizes at P_2 when real GDP returns to Y^*, closing the recessionary gap.

the more quickly the *SRAS* curve will shift upward. However, as we noted earlier when we encountered the second asymmetry of aggregate supply, the experience of many economies suggests that wages typically do not fall rapidly in response to even large recessionary gaps. It is sometimes said that wages are "sticky" in the downward direction. This does not mean that wages never fall, only that they tend to fall more slowly in a recessionary gap than they rise in an equally sized inflationary gap. When wages are sticky, the analysis is the same as when wages are flexible, and thus Figure 25-3 tells the right story. The only difference is that the *SRAS* curve shifts more slowly when wages are sticky and thus the recessionary gap remains open for longer. An important implication of sticky wages is that high unemployment may not be quickly eliminated.

If wages are downwardly sticky, the economy's adjustment mechanism is sluggish and thus recessionary gaps tend to persist.

The weakness of the adjustment mechanism does not mean that slumps must always be prolonged. Rather, this weakness means that speedy recovery back to potential output must be generated mainly from the demand side. If wages are downwardly sticky and the economy is to avoid a persistent recessionary gap, a quick recovery requires a rightward shift of the *AD* curve. The possibility that government *stabilization policy* might accomplish such a rightward shift in the *AD* curve is an important and contentious issue in macroeconomics, one that we will return to often throughout the remainder of this book.

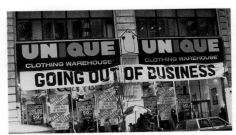

The slow adjustment of wages and prices when output is below potential means that the recessionary effects of negative shocks sometimes persist for long periods.

The difference in the speed of adjustment of wages (and other factor prices) is the important asymmetry in the behaviour of aggregate supply that we noted earlier in this chapter. This asymmetry helps to explain two key facts about the Canadian economy. First, unemployment can persist for quite long periods without causing decreases in wages and prices of sufficient magnitude to remove the unemployment. Second, booms, along with labour shortages and production beyond normal capacity, do not persist for long periods without causing increases in wages and the price level.

Aggregate Supply Shocks

We have discussed the long-run effects of aggregate demand shocks, and the economy's automatic adjustment mechanism that returns real GDP to its potential level, Y^*. The same adjustment process operates following an aggregate supply shock.

Consider an economy that has a stable price level and real GDP at its potential level, as illustrated by point E_0 in part (i) of Figure 25-4. Suppose there is an increase in the world price of an important input, such as oil. As we have mentioned several times in this book, the OPEC oil shocks of 1973–74 and 1979–80 involved enormous increases in the price of oil and, to date, are surely the best examples that economists have of large negative aggregate supply shocks.

An increase in the price of oil increases unit costs for firms and causes the $SRAS$ curve to shift to the left. Real GDP falls and the price level increases—this is *stagflation*.

FIGURE 25-4   The Long-Run Effect of a Negative Aggregate Supply Shock

(i) An increase in the price of oil   (ii) Induced shift in $SRAS$

A leftward shift of the $SRAS$ curve caused by an increase in input prices causes real GDP to fall and the price level to rise. The economy's adjustment mechanism then reverses the $SRAS$ shift and returns the economy to its starting point.

The economy begins at point E_0 in part (i). The increase in the price of oil increases unit costs and causes the $SRAS$ curve to shift up to $SRAS_1$. Real GDP falls to Y_1 and the price level rises to P_1. A recessionary gap is created.

In part (ii), the excess supply of labour associated with the recessionary gap causes wages to fall, possibly slowly. As wages fall, unit costs fall and so the $SRAS$ curve shifts back down to $SRAS_0$. The economy is finally in long-run equilibrium at Y^* and P_0, its starting point.

The short-run equilibrium is at point E_1 in Figure 25-4. With the opening of a recessionary gap, the economy's adjustment mechanism comes into play, though sticky wages reduce the speed of this adjustment.

The recessionary gap caused by the negative supply shock causes firms to shut down and workers to be laid off. The excess supply of labour (and other factors) eventually pushes wages down and begins to reverse the initial increase in unit costs caused by the increase in the price of oil. This adjustment is shown in part (ii) of the figure. As wages fall, the SRAS curve shifts back toward its starting point, and real GDP rises back toward its potential level, Y^*. Eventually, the economy returns to its initial point, E_0.

We leave it to the reader to analyse the long-run effects of a positive aggregate supply shock, such as the dramatic reduction in the world price of raw materials that occurred in 1997 and 1998. The logic of the analysis is exactly the same as illustrated in Figure 25-4, except that the initial shift in the SRAS curve is to the right, creating an inflationary gap.

Exogenous changes in input prices cause the SRAS curve to shift, creating an output gap. The adjustment mechanism then reverses the initial SRAS shift and brings the economy back to potential output and the initial price level.

Economic Shocks and Business Cycles

Aggregate demand and aggregate supply shocks are a major source of fluctuations in real GDP around potential. As we have seen, a positive demand shock, such as increase in desired investment, will lead to an increase in output and prices. This will be followed by a fall in output and a further increase in prices as the adjustment mechanism restores the economy to long-run equilibrium. Depending on the nature and magnitude of the shock, the adjustment will take many months, maybe even a year or two.

Similarly, a positive supply shock, such as a reduction in the world price of an important input, will cause real GDP to rise and the price level to fall. As the adjustment mechanism comes into play, real GDP will fall back to potential and the price level will rise back to its initial level. As with a demand shock, the full adjustment may take many months.

No matter what the cause of the expansionary shock, the economy will not respond instantaneously. In many industries, it takes weeks or months or even longer to bring new or mothballed capacity into production and to hire and train new workers. Because of these lags in the economy's response, changes in output are spread out over a substantial period of time. An increase in demand or supply may lead to a gradual increase in output that lasts several months. Then, as output does change, the adjustment mechanism comes into play, eventually returning real GDP to its potential level.

Thus, a positive shock—demand or supply—initially leads to an increase in output and then, as the adjustment mechanism begins to operate, is followed by a reduction in output back to potential. Conversely, a negative demand or supply shock initially leads to a reduction in output and then, as the (slower) adjustment mechanism comes into play, is eventually followed by an increase in output back to potential. In both cases, the impact effect of the shock is reversed by the economy's adjustment mechanism. Shocks, therefore, generate *cyclical* movements in real GDP. Such shocks are the fundamental cause of *business cycles*.

Both aggregate demand and aggregate supply are subject to continual random shocks. The economy's adjustment mechanism can convert these shocks into cyclical fluctuations in real GDP.

The Long-Run Aggregate Supply Curve

long-run aggregate supply (LRAS) curve
A curve showing the relationship between the price level and the quantity of aggregate output supplied when all markets have fully adjusted to the existing price level; a vertical line at $Y = Y^*$.

The economy's adjustment mechanism leads us to an important concept: the **long-run aggregate supply (LRAS) curve.** This curve relates the price level to real GDP after wage rates and all other input costs have been fully adjusted to eliminate any unemployment or overall labour shortages. (Recall that we are holding technology, and thus productivity, constant.)

Once all the adjustments have occurred, any excess demand or excess supply of labour will have been eliminated. In other words, full employment will prevail, and output will be at its potential level, Y^*. The value of Y^* depends on real variables such as factor supplies and technology, but is independent of nominal variables like the price level. It follows that the LRAS curve is vertical at Y^*, as shown in Figure 25-5. The LRAS curve is sometimes called the *Classical aggregate supply curve* because the Classical economists were mainly concerned with the behaviour of the economy in long-run equilibrium.[3]

The economy's long-run aggregate supply (LRAS) curve is vertical at the level of potential output, Y^*.

Notice that the vertical LRAS curve does not represent the same thing as the vertical portion of the SRAS curve (see Figure 24-8). Over the vertical range of the SRAS curve, the economy is at its utmost limit of productive capacity, when no more output can be squeezed out under any circumstances. In contrast, the vertical shape of the LRAS curve is due to the workings of an adjustment mechanism that brings the economy back to its potential output, even though output may differ from potential for considerable periods of time. It is called the long-run aggregate supply curve because it describes what happens as a result of adjustments that occur over an extended period of time.

Long-Run Equilibrium

Figure 25-5 shows the equilibrium output and the price level as they are determined by the intersection of the AD curve and the vertical LRAS curve. Because the LRAS curve is vertical, shifts in the AD curve change the price level but not the level of equilibrium output, as shown in part (i). By contrast, a shift in the LRAS curve changes both output and the price level, as shown in part (ii). For example, a rightward shift of the LRAS curve increases real GDP and leads to a fall in the price level.

In the long run, total output is determined solely by conditions of aggregate supply, and the role of aggregate demand is only to determine the price level.

Consider the effect of an increase in government purchases in a situation where the economy begins in long-run equilibrium. In part (i) of Figure 25-5 it is clear that the long-run effect of an increase in government purchases is to increase the price level but to leave the level of real GDP unchanged at Y_0^*. What the figure does not show, how-

---

[3]The Classical school of economic thought began with Adam Smith (1723–1790) and was developed through the work of David Ricardo (1772–1823), Thomas Malthus (1766–1834) and John Stuart Mill (1806–1873). These economists emphasized the long-run behaviour of the economy. Beginning in the middle of the nineteenth century, Neoclassical economists devoted much time and effort to studying short-term fluctuations. *The General Theory of Employment, Interest and Money* (1936), written by John Maynard Keynes (1883–1946), was in a long tradition of the study of short-term fluctuations. Where Keynes differed from the Neoclassical economists was in approaching the issues from a macroeconomic perspective that emphasized fluctuations in real expenditure flows. Each of the economists mentioned in this footnote, along with several others, are discussed in more detail in the timeline at the back of the book.

ever, is that while the *level* of GDP may be unchanged, the *composition* of GDP has changed.

To see how the composition of GDP is affected by the increase in G, consider what happens as the price level rises from P_0 to P_1 in part (i) of the figure. For a given stock of nominal assets (money and bonds), the rise in the price level reduces the wealth of the private sector and thus reduces household consumption. In addition, for a given exchange rate, the rise in the domestic price level makes Canadian goods more expensive relative to foreign goods, and thus reduces Canada's net exports. (You will recall that these are the two reasons why the AD curve is downward sloping, as we discussed at the beginning of Chapter 24.) Thus, the increase in government purchases, by creating an inflationary gap and forcing up the price level, has "crowded out" some elements of private expenditure—in this case, consumption and net exports.

So, while real GDP is the same at points E_0 and E_1 in part (i) of Figure 25-5, the composition of the GDP is different. Specifically, G is higher at E_1 than it is at E_0; C and NX are lower at E_1 than at E_0.

Why do we care about the composition of GDP? Recall from Chapter 23 that net exports and investment are similar in the sense that they both imply *asset accumulation* for the domestic economy. Thus, other things equal, the more of GDP that is used for asset accumulation, the higher national income will be in the future. Thus, "crowding out" is potentially important if it hinders the economy's prospects for long-run growth. In later chapters we will examine a type of crowding out (of investment) that reduces the economy's long-run growth. In order to do that, however, we must learn some details about money and interest rates, which we examine in Chapters 26 and 27. Until then, our discussion about the composition of GDP is summarized as follows:

The vertical $LRAS$ curve shows that given full adjustment of input prices, potential output is compatible with any price level, although its composition among consumption, investment, government, and net exports may vary at different price levels.

FIGURE 25-5 Long-Run Equilibrium and Aggregate Supply

(i) A rise in aggregate demand

(ii) A rise in long-run aggregate supply

Because the $LRAS$ curve is vertical, aggregate supply determines the long-run equilibrium value of real GDP at Y^*. Given Y^*, aggregate demand determines the long-run equilibrium value of the price level. In both parts of the figure, the initial long-run equilibrium is at E_0, so the price level is P_0 and real GDP is Y_0^*.

In part (i), a shift in the AD curve from AD_0 to AD_1 moves the long-run equilibrium from E_0 to E_1. This raises the price level from P_0 to P_1 but leaves real GDP unchanged at Y_0^* in the long run.

In part (ii), a shift in the $LRAS$ curve from $LRAS_0$ to $LRAS_1$ moves the long-run equilibrium from E_0 to E_2. This raises real GDP income from Y_0^* to Y_1^* and lowers the price level from P_0 to P_2.

National Income in the Short and Long Run

In Chapter 21 we discussed the difference between short-run and long-run macroeconomics. Without developing any formal theory at that time, we described how output is affected by changes in demand in the short run, whereas changes in supply are the crucial factor determining output in the long run. Now, after developing some formal macroeconomic theory, we have come full circle. We now have the theoretical tools to *understand* this important distinction between the short run and the long run.

1. In the short run, the economy is in equilibrium at the level of real GDP and prices where the *SRAS* curve intersects the *AD* curve.

2. In the long run, the economy is in equilibrium at potential output, the position of the vertical *LRAS* curve. The price level is determined where the *AD* curve intersects the *LRAS* curve.

The position of the *LRAS* curve is at Y^*, which is determined by past economic growth. Since in the long run output equals Y^*, it follows that economic growth explains long-run movements in output. In contrast, deviations of actual output from potential output—output gaps—are short-run phenomena and are generally associated with *business cycles*. Changes in total real output may therefore take place either because of long-term growth or because of business cycles.

This suggests a need to distinguish three ways in which Y can increase. The first two relate to short-run changes in Y; the third is a long-run change in Y. These are illustrated in Figure 25-6. In each case, the economy begins with real GDP equal to Y^*.

Aggregate Demand Shocks.   As shown in part (i) of Figure 25-6, an increase in aggregate demand will yield a one-time increase in real GDP. The demand shock

FIGURE 25-6   Three Ways that Real GDP Can Increase

(i) An increase in aggregate demand

(ii) An increase in aggregate supply

(iii) Increases in long-run aggregate supply

Real GDP will increase in response to an increase in aggregate demand or an increase in aggregate supply. The increase will be permanent only if the *LRAS* curve shifts. In the cases shown in parts (i) and (ii), any increase in GDP beyond potential is temporary because the inflationary gap will cause wages and other factor prices to rise; this will cause the *SRAS* curve to shift upward and hence cause real GDP to converge to Y^*.

In part (iii), the *LRAS* curve shifts to the right, causing potential output to increase. Whether or not actual GDP increases immediately depends on what happens to the *AD* and *SRAS* curves. Because, in the absence of other shocks, actual output eventually converges to potential output, a rightward shift in the *LRAS* curve eventually leads to an increase in actual output. If the shift in the *LRAS* curve is recurring, real GDP will grow continually.

pushes Y beyond Y^* (a shift from AD_1 to AD_2). The inflationary gap will cause wages and other costs to rise, shifting the $SRAS$ curve to the left. This drives Y back toward potential so that the only lasting effect is on the price level.

Aggregate Supply Shocks.   Increases in aggregate supply will also lead to a temporary increase in real GDP. Part (ii) of Figure 25-6 shows the effects of an increase in aggregate supply caused, for example, by the reduction of input prices. This will shift the $SRAS$ curve to the right but will have no effect on the $LRAS$ curve and hence on potential output. The shock will thus cause Y to rise above Y^*, but the increase will eventually be reversed by the economy's adjustment mechanism.

Increases in Long-Run Aggregate Supply.   Part (iii) of Figure 25-6 shows the effects of shocks that shift the $LRAS$ curve. There are several possible explanations for such a shift. For example, a once-and-for-all change in a labour-market policy that reduces the level of structural unemployment will lead to a one-time rightward shift in the $LRAS$ curve. Another example might be a one-time improvement in the education system that makes workers more productive, shifting the $LRAS$ curve to the right. More important, however, are the ongoing changes such as population growth, capital accumulation, or improvements in productivity—these all cause a continual rightward shift in the $LRAS$ curve, giving rise to a continual increase in the level of potential output.

Unlike the case of AD or $SRAS$ shocks, the changes in real GDP in part (iii) of Figure 25-6 are permanent effects—no natural adjustment mechanism will bring real GDP back to its previous level of potential. Indeed, GDP is equal to potential GDP, but potential GDP has increased.

In the long run, only changes to the level of Y^* can change the level of real GDP.

In Chapter 32 we will study changes in potential output over long periods of time. To complete this chapter, however, we return briefly to a topic that we first discussed in Chapter 23—fiscal policy. Now that we understand the distinction between the short run and the long run, we are ready to discuss some details about the effects of government spending and taxation.

Fiscal Policy and the Business Cycle

In Chapter 23, we briefly considered the basic concepts of fiscal stabilization policy. In principle, this policy can be used in attempts to stabilize real GDP at or near some desired level (usually potential output). In the remainder of this chapter, we look into taxing and spending as tools of fiscal stabilization policy. We will return to the subject in more detail in Chapter 31, after we have discussed money and the banking system.

So far in this chapter we have discussed shocks and economic fluctuations but have not looked at any actual data. If significant fluctuations don't really exist, there is not much point in thinking about fiscal stabilization policy, for there would be no fluctuations to stabilize. A quick look at Figure 25-7, however, should assure you that economic fluctuations are the rule rather than the exception. There is no single "correct" way to measure fluctuations in the level of economic activity because different macroeconomic variables fluctuate in different degrees. But many of them travel broadly together. Figure 25-7 shows that the changes in three key variables—real GDP, the number of housing starts, and firms' capacity utilization rate—are considerable on a year-to-year basis. The government could use its fiscal policy tools—expenditure and taxation—to try to smooth these fluctuations.

FIGURE 25-7   Fluctuations in Economic Activity, 1970–1998

Fluctuations follow similar, but not identical, paths for various measures of economic activity. Fluctuations are easily seen in these three series—the annual percentage changes in real GDP, annual housing starts, and the capacity utilization rate.

(*Source:* Department of Finance, *Economic Reference Tables,* August 1995, and *Bank of Canada Review,* Winter 1998–99.)

Because government expenditure increases aggregate demand and taxation decreases it, the *direction* of the required changes in spending and taxation is generally easy to determine once we know the direction of the desired change in real GDP. However, the *timing, magnitude,* and *mixture* of the changes are more difficult issues.

There is no doubt that the government can exert a major influence on real GDP. Prime examples are the massive increases in military spending during major wars. Canadian federal expenditure during World War II rose from 12.2 percent of GDP in 1939 to 41.8 percent in 1944. At the same time, the unemployment rate fell from 11.4 percent to 1.4 percent. Economists agree that the increase in government spending helped to bring about the rise in output and the associated fall in unemployment.

In the heyday of fiscal policy, from about 1945 to about 1970, many economists were convinced that the economy could be stabilized adequately just by varying the size of the government's taxes and expenditures. That day is past. Today, most economists are aware of the many limitations of fiscal policy.

The Basic Theory of Fiscal Stabilization

A reduction in tax rates or an increase in government purchases will shift the *AD* curve to the right, causing an increase in real GDP. An increase in tax rates or a cut in government expenditure will shift the *AD* curve to the left, causing a decrease in real GDP.

FIGURE 25-8   The Closing of a Recessionary Gap

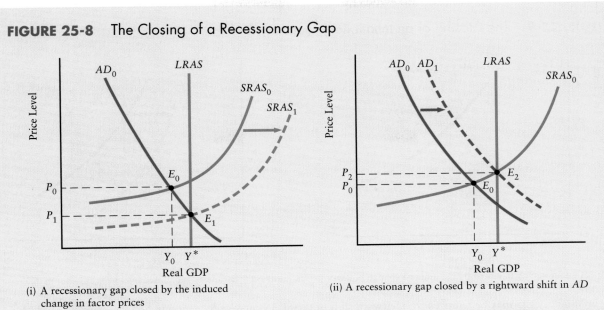

(i) A recessionary gap closed by the induced change in factor prices

(ii) A recessionary gap closed by a rightward shift in *AD*

A recessionary gap may be closed by a (slow) rightward shift of the *SRAS* curve or an increase in aggregate demand. Initially, equilibrium is at E_0, with real GDP at Y_0 and the price level at P_0. There is a recessionary gap.

As shown in part (i), the gap might be removed by a shift in the *SRAS* curve to $SRAS_1$, as will eventually happen when wages and other factor prices fall in response to excess supply. The shift in the *SRAS* curve causes a movement down and to the right along AD_0 to a new equilibrium at E_1, achieving potential output Y^* and lowering the price level to P_1.

As shown in part (ii), the gap might also be removed by a shift of the *AD* curve to AD_1, caused by an expansionary fiscal policy or a recovery of private-sector spending. The shift in the *AD* curve causes a movement up and to the right along $SRAS_0$. This movement shifts the equilibrium to E_2, raising output to Y^* and the price level to P_2.

How Fiscal Stabilization Works

A more detailed look at how fiscal stabilization works will help to show some of the complications that arise when implementing fiscal policy.

A Recessionary Gap.   The closing of a recessionary gap is illustrated in Figure 25-8. There are two ways the gap can be closed. First, the recessionary gap may eventually drive wages and other factor prices down enough to shift the *SRAS* curve to the right and thereby reinstate potential output. The evidence, however, is that this process takes a substantial period of time.

Second, the *AD* curve could shift to the right, restoring the economy to potential output. The government can cause such a shift by using expansionary fiscal policy (or, as we shall see in Chapter 27, expansionary monetary policy). The advantage of using fiscal policy rather than allowing the economy's natural adjustment mechanism to operate is that it may substantially shorten what would otherwise be a long recession. One disadvantage is that the use of fiscal policy may stimulate the economy just before private-sector spending recovers on its own. As a result, the economy may overshoot its potential output, and an inflationary gap may open up. In this case, fiscal policy that is intended to promote economic stability can actually cause instability.

FIGURE 25-9   The Closing of an Inflationary Gap

(i) An inflationary gap closed by the induced change in factor prices

(ii) An inflationary gap closed by a leftward shift in AD

An inflationary gap may be removed by a leftward shift of the $SRAS$ curve, a reduction in private-sector demand, or a policy-induced reduction in aggregate demand. Initially, equilibrium is at E_0, with real GDP at Y_0 and the price level at P_0. There is an inflationary gap.

As shown in part (i), the gap might be removed by a shift in the $SRAS$ curve to $SRAS_1$, as will eventually happen when wages and other factor prices rise in response to the excess demand. The shift in the $SRAS$ curve causes a movement up and to the left along AD_0. This movement establishes a new equilibrium at E_1, reducing output to its potential level Y^* and raising the price level to P_1.

As shown in part (ii), the gap might also be removed by a shift in the AD curve to AD_1 caused by, for example, a contractionary fiscal policy. The shift in the AD curve causes a movement down and to the left along $SRAS_0$. This movement shifts the equilibrium to E_2, lowering income to Y^* and the price level to P_2.

An Inflationary Gap.   Figure 25-9 shows how an inflationary gap can be closed. First, wages and other factor prices may be pushed upward by the excess demand. The $SRAS$ curve will therefore shift to the left, eventually closing the gap, reducing output back to Y^*. Second, the AD curve can shift to the left, restoring equilibrium output at Y^*. The government, by raising taxes or cutting spending, can induce such a shift, reducing aggregate demand sufficiently to close the inflationary gap. The advantage of this approach is that it avoids the inflationary increase in prices that accompanies the first method. One disadvantage is that if private-sector expenditures fall because of natural causes, real GDP may be pushed below potential, thus opening up a recessionary gap.

This discussion leads to a key proposition:

When the economy's adjustment mechanism is slow to operate, or produces undesirable side effects such as rising prices, there is a potential stabilization role for fiscal policy.

The Paradox of Thrift

The theory of national income determination predicts that an increase in national saving (either an increase in private-sector saving or an increase in the government's budget surplus) will shift the AD curve to the left and hence *reduce* the equilibrium level of real GDP in the short run. The contrary case, a decrease in saving and increase in expenditure, shifts the AD curve to the right and hence increases real GDP in the short run. Thus, frugality on the part of individuals, which may seem to be prudent behaviour for each individual taken separately, ends up reducing short-run real GDP. This prediction is known as the *paradox of thrift*—the paradox being that what may be good for any individual when viewed in isolation ends up being undesirable for the economy as a whole.

The policy implication of this prediction is that a major and persistent recession can be battled by encouraging governments, firms, and households to spend more, *not* to save more. In times of unemployment and recession, frugality will only make things worse. This prediction goes directly against the idea that we should tighten our belts when times are tough. The notion that it is not only possible but even *desirable* to spend one's way out of a recession touches a sensitive point with people raised on the belief that success is based on hard work and frugality, not on prodigality; as a result, the idea often arouses great hostility.

As is discussed in *Lessons from History 25-1*, the implications of the paradox of thrift were not generally understood during the Great Depression of the 1930s. Most governments, faced with depression-induced reductions in tax revenues, reduced their expenditures to balance their budgets. As a result, many economists argue that the fiscal policies at the time actually made things worse. When Milton Friedman (many years later) said, "We are all Keynesians now," he was referring to the general acceptance of the view that the government's budget is much more than just the revenue and expenditure statement of a very large organization. Whether we like it or not, the sheer size of the government's budget inevitably makes it a powerful tool for influencing the economy.

The paradox of thrift concentrates on shifts in aggregate demand that have been caused by changes in saving (and hence spending) behaviour. That is why it applies only in the short run, when the *AD* curve plays an important role in the determination of real GDP.

In the long run, however, the paradox of thrift does not apply. Remember that in the long run, aggregate demand is *not* the determinant of real GDP—only the position of the *LRAS* curve determines long-run real GDP. In the long run, the more people and governments save, the larger is the supply of funds available for investment. And the more that people invest, the greater is the growth of potential output, shifting the *LRAS* curve to the right.

The paradox of thrift—the idea that an increase in saving reduces the level of real GDP—is only true in the short run when the level of aggregate demand is relevant for determining real GDP. In the long run, a larger amount of saving increases investment and thus increases the level of potential output.

At this point it would be useful to re-read the brief discussion at the beginning of Chapter 21 regarding Japan's economic malaise during the late 1990s. There we posed a puzzling question: If Japan's high saving rate is partly responsible for its economic stagnation during the 1990s, how can its high saving rate also be responsible for its remarkable growth from the 1950s to the 1990s? As we said in Chapter 21, many economists believe that both statements are true. The solution to this apparent contradiction is to recognize that the paradox of thrift is an important short-run phenomenon but does not apply in the long run. In other words, a high rate of saving may well reduce real GDP in the short run, but after the economy's adjustment mechanism operates (which may take some time), the higher saving will eventually increase investment and long-run growth.

Automatic Stabilizers

In Chapter 23, we considered the *budget surplus function* (the function showing how the government's budget surplus changes as national income changes). The *discretionary* fiscal policy that we have been discussing in this chapter involves *shifts* in the budget surplus function. Expansionary policies, whether they involve increases in government purchases

LESSONS FROM HISTORY 25-1

Fiscal Policy in the Great Depression

The Great Depression, which is usually dated as beginning with the massive stock-market crash on October 29, 1929, was by far the most dramatic economic event this century. As the accompanying figure shows, Canadian real GDP plummeted by almost 30 percent from its peak in 1929 to its low point in 1933. The price level actually *fell* beginning in 1930 and declined by about 20 percent over the next five years. The unemployment rate increased from 3 percent in 1929 to an unparalleled 19.3 percent four years later. To put these numbers in perspective, by today's standards a very serious recession (like the most recent one in 1991–92) sees real GDP fall by 2 percent, the unemployment rate rise to 11 percent, and prices continue rising but perhaps at a slower rate. The economic events of the 1930s certainly deserve to be called the Great Depression!

As we will see in this box, however, the Great Depression was not just a catastrophic event that happened exogenously—its depth and duration were made worse by some fundamental mistakes in policy.

Failure to understand the implication of the paradox of thrift led many countries to adopt disastrous policies during the Great Depression. In addition, failure to understand the role of built-in stabilizers has led many observers to conclude, erroneously, that fiscal expansion was tried in the Great

Depression but failed. Let us see how these two misperceptions are related.

The Paradox of Thrift in Action

In 1932, Canadian Prime Minister R. B. Bennett said, "We are now faced with the real crisis in the history of Canada. To maintain our credit we must practice the most rigid economy and not spend a single cent." His government that year brought down a budget based on the principle of trying to balance revenues and expenditures, and it included *increases* in tax rates.

In the same year, Franklin Roosevelt was elected U.S. president on a platform of fighting the Great Depression with government policies. In his inaugural address he urged, "Our great primary task is to put people to work. . . . [This task] can be helped by insistence that the federal, state, and local governments act forthwith on the demand that their costs be drastically reduced. . . . "

Across the Atlantic, King George V told the British House of Commons in 1931, "The present condition of the national finances, in the opinion of His Majesty's ministers, calls for the imposition of additional taxation and for the effecting of economies in public expenditure."

For information on the Federal Department of Finance, the ministry in charge of fiscal policy, see: www.fin.gc.ca.

procyclical   Moving in the same direction as the business cycle—up in booms and down in slumps.

or decreases in net taxes, reduce the budget surplus (increase the deficit) at every level of real GDP, shifting the *AD* curve to the right. Contractionary policies increase the surplus (reduce the deficit) at every level of real GDP, shifting the *AD* curve to the left.

Even when the government does not attempt to stabilize the economy via discretionary fiscal policy, the upward slope of the budget surplus function means that there are fiscal effects that cause the budget to act as an "automatic stabilizer" for the economy.

The budget surplus increases as real GDP increases because tax revenues rise and some transfer payments, especially unemployment insurance, fall. Thus, net taxes move in the same direction as real GDP. (Unless there are changes in policy, government purchases are generally unaffected by cyclical movements in the economy.) With **procyclical** net tax revenues, disposable income moves in the same direction as real GDP but does not move by as much. The government keeps a share of the increased real GDP when it rises. When real GDP falls, the fall in taxes and the rise in transfers make disposable income fall by less.

In Chapter 23, for example, we assumed that the net income tax rate was 10 percent of national income. This assumption implies that a 1 dollar rise in national income would increase disposable income by only 90 cents, dampening the multiplier effect of into depression. The various governments did not advocate programs of massive deficit-financed spending to shift the *AD* curve to the right. Instead, they hoped that a small amount of government spending in addition to numerous policies designed to stabilize prices and to restore confidence would lead to a recovery of private investment expenditure that would substantially shift the *AD* curve. To have expected a massive revival of private investment expenditure as a result of the puny increase in aggregate demand that was instituted by the federal government now seems hopelessly naive.

When we judge these policies from the viewpoint of modern theory, their failure is no mystery. Indeed, Professor E. Cary Brown of MIT, after a careful study, concluded, "Fiscal policy seems to have been an unsuccessful recovery device in the thirties—not because it did not work, but because it was not tried." Once the massive, war-geared expenditure of the 1940s began, output responded sharply and unemployment all but evaporated, as seen clearly in the figure.

The performance of the Canadian and U.S. economies from 1930 to 1945 is well explained by the theory of national income determination that we have developed in the last few chapters. It is clear that the governments did not effectively use fiscal policy to stabilize their economies. War brought the Depression to an end because war demands made acceptable a level of government expenditure sufficient to remove the recessionary gap. Had the Canadian and American administrations been able to do the same, it might have ended the waste of the Great Depression many years sooner.

As the paradox of thrift predicts, these policies tended to worsen, rather than cure, the Depression.

Interpreting the Deficit in the 1930s

Government deficits did increase in the 1930s, but they were not the result of a program of deficit-financed public expenditure. Rather, they were the result of the fall in tax revenues, brought about by the fall in real GDP as the economy sank

---

any change in autonomous expenditure. Generally, the wedge that income taxes place between national income and disposable income reduces the marginal propensity to spend out of national income, thereby reducing the size of the multiplier. The effect is to stabilize the economy, reducing the fluctuations in national income that are caused by changes in autonomous expenditure. Because no policies need to be changed to achieve this result, these properties of the government budget that cause the multiplier to be reduced are called **automatic fiscal stabilizers.**

Limitations of Discretionary Fiscal Policy

According to the foregoing discussion, returning the economy to potential output would simply be a matter of cutting taxes and raising government spending, in some combination. Why do so many economists believe that such policies would be "as likely to harm as help"? Part of the answer is that the execution of discretionary fiscal policy is anything but simple.

Lags.   To change fiscal policy requires making changes in taxes and government expenditures. The changes must be agreed on by the cabinet and passed by parliament.

automatic fiscal stabilizers   Elements of the tax and transfer systems that automatically lessen the magnitude of the fluctuations in national income caused by changes in autonomous expenditures.

The political stakes in such changes are generally very large; taxes and spending are called "bread-and-butter issues" precisely because they affect the economic well-being of almost everyone. Thus, even if economists agreed that the economy would be helped by, say, a tax cut, politicians would likely spend a good deal of time debating *whose* taxes should be cut and by *how much*. The delay between the initial recognition of a recessionary or inflationary gap and the enactment of legislation to change fiscal policy is called a **decision lag.**

Once policy changes are agreed on, there is still an **execution lag,** adding time between the enactment and the implementation of the change. Furthermore, once policies are in place, it will usually take still more time for their economic consequences to be felt. Because of these lags, it is quite possible that by the time a given policy decision has any impact on the economy, circumstances will have changed such that the policy is no longer appropriate.

decision lag   The period of time between perceiving some problem and reaching a decision on what to do about it.

execution lag   The time that it takes to put policies in place after a decision has been made.

Temporary Versus Permanent Policy Changes.   To make matters even more frustrating, tax measures that are known to be temporary are generally less effective than measures that are expected to be permanent. If households know that a given tax cut will last only a year, they may recognize that the effect on their long-run consumption possibilities is small and may adjust their short-run consumption relatively little. Thus, the more closely household consumption expenditure is related to lifetime income rather than to current income, the smaller will be the effects on current consumption of tax changes that are known to be of short duration. Or, to use the language that we used when introducing the consumption function in Chapter 22, the more forward-looking are households, the smaller will be the effects of temporary changes in taxes.

The Role of Discretionary Fiscal Policy.   All of these difficulties suggest that attempts to use discretionary fiscal policy to "fine tune" the economy are fraught with difficulties. **Fine tuning** refers to the use of fiscal (and monetary) policy to offset virtually all fluctuations in private-sector spending so as to hold real GDP at or near its potential level at all times. However, neither economic nor political science has yet advanced far enough to allow policymakers to undo the consequences of every aggregate demand or supply shock. Nevertheless, many economists still argue that when a recessionary gap is large enough and persists for long enough, *gross tuning* may be appropriate. **Gross tuning** refers to the occasional use of fiscal and monetary policy to remove large and persistent output gaps. Other economists believe that fiscal policy should not be used for economic stabilization under any circumstances. Rather, they would argue, tax and spending behaviour should be the outcome of public choices regarding the long-term size and financing of the public sector and should not be altered for short-term considerations. We return to these debates in Chapter 31.

fine tuning   The attempt to maintain national income at its full-employment level by means of frequent changes in fiscal or monetary policy.

gross tuning   The use of macroeconomic policy to stabilize the economy such that large deviations from full employment do not persist for extended periods of time.

Fiscal Policy and Growth

The desirability of using fiscal policy to stabilize the economy depends a great deal on the speed with which the economy's own adjustment mechanism returns the economy to potential output. If the adjustment mechanism works very quickly, there is little value to discretionary fiscal policy. If the adjustment mechanism works slowly, however, there may well be a role for fiscal policies that can be used to shift aggregate demand.

Fiscal stabilization policy will generally have consequences for economic growth—for the rightward shifting of the *LRAS* curve over time. In an economy at or near potential output, the more expansive is its fiscal policy, the lower will be national saving and national asset formation and, consequently, the lower will be future economic growth. Of course, if the economy would otherwise stay in recession for a period of years, the gain in output in the near term may outweigh the longer-term consequences of a smaller stock of productive assets. After all—and this was part of Keynes' message—the state of the world at potential output is not very interesting to members of a society who are a long way from it.

Stability, growth, and the effect of economic policy on both are among the key subjects of this book. With the tools that we have developed so far, we can begin to see how they fit together. Once we add a better understanding of money and monetary policy, presented in the next three chapters, we will be able to complete the story.

S U M M A R Y

Induced Changes in Factor Prices

LO 1

- Potential output is treated as given and is represented by a vertical line at Y^*. The output gap is equal to the horizontal distance between Y^* and the actual level of real GDP, Y, as determined by the intersection of the AD and $SRAS$ curves.
- An inflationary gap means that Y is greater than Y^*, and hence there is excess demand in the labour market. As a

result, wages rise causing unit costs to rise. The $SRAS$ curve shifts leftward, and the price level rises.
- A recessionary gap means that Y is less than Y^*, and hence there is excess supply in the labour market. Although there is some resulting tendency for wages to fall, the strength of this force is typically weaker than is the case with an inflationary gap. Because unit costs will fall only slowly, the output gap will persist for some time.

Demand and Supply Shocks

LO 2 3

- Beginning from a position of potential output, an expansionary demand shock creates an inflationary gap, causing wages to rise. Unit costs rise, shifting the $SRAS$ curve to the left and bringing output back to its potential level.
- Beginning from a position of potential output, a contractionary demand shock creates a recessionary gap. Because factor prices tend to be sticky downwards, the automatic adjustment process tends to be slow, and a recessionary gap tends to persist for some time.
- Aggregate supply shocks, such as those caused by changes in the price of inputs, lead the $SRAS$ curve to shift, changing real GDP and the price level. But the economy's ad-

justment mechanism reverses the shift in $SRAS$, bringing the economy back to its initial level of output and prices.
- Demand and supply shocks are important sources of business cycles. As a shock works its way through the economy and the adjustment mechanism comes into play, real GDP will often exhibit a cyclical pattern.
- The long-run aggregate supply ($LRAS$) curve relates the price level and real GDP after all wages and other input prices have been adjusted fully to long-run equilibrium. The $LRAS$ curve is vertical at the level of potential output, Y^*.

National Income in the Short and Long Run

LO 4

- In the short run, macroeconomic equilibrium is determined by the intersection of the AD and $SRAS$ curves. In the long run, the economy is in equilibrium when real GDP is equal to potential output—the economy is therefore on the $LRAS$ curve. In the long run, the price level is

determined by the intersection of the AD and $LRAS$ curves.
- Shocks to the AD or $SRAS$ curves can change real GDP in the short run. Only shifts in the $LRAS$ curve can change output in the long run.

Fiscal Policy and the Business Cycle

- In principle, fiscal policy can be used to stabilize output at or near potential output. To remove a recessionary gap, governments can shift *AD* to the right by cutting taxes and increasing spending. To remove an inflationary gap, governments can pursue the opposite policies.
- In the short run, increases in desired saving on the part of firms, households, and governments leads to further reductions in real GDP. This phenomenon is often called the paradox of thrift. In the long run, the paradox of thrift does not apply, and increased saving will lead to increased asset accumulation and economic growth.
- Because government tax and transfer programs tend to reduce the size of the multiplier, they act as automatic stabilizers. When real GDP changes, disposable income changes by less because of taxes and transfers.

- Discretionary fiscal policy is subject to decision lags and execution lags that limit its ability to take effect quickly. Some economists argue that these limitations are so severe that discretionary fiscal policy should never be used for stabilization because it will end up increasing instability. Others argue that the automatic adjustment mechanism works so slowly that discretionary fiscal policy can play a useful role in stabilizing the economy.
- Fiscal policy has very different effects in the short and long run. The same fiscal policies (reduced taxes and increased spending) that stimulate the economy in the short run will, if pursued when the economy is at potential output, reduce national saving, asset formation, and economic growth in the long run.

KEY CONCEPTS

The output gap and factor prices
Wages and unit labour costs
Inflationary and recessionary gaps
Asymmetry of wage adjustment: flexible and sticky wages

Long-run effects of *AD* and *SRAS* shocks
The long-run aggregate supply (*LRAS*) curve
Fiscal stabilization policy

Decision lags and execution lags
Automatic stabilizers
Fine tuning and gross tuning

STUDY EXERCISES

1. The following diagram shows two economies, A and B. Both are in short-run equilibrium at point *E*, where the *AD* and *SRAS* curves intersect.

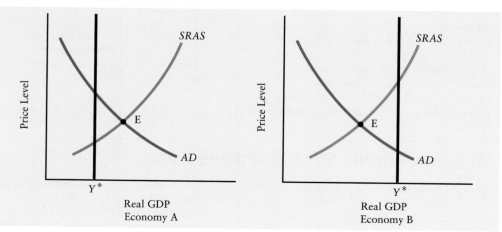

a. Explain why in Economy A wages and other factor prices will begin to rise, and why this will increase unit costs.

b. Following your answer in part a, show the effect on the SRAS curve. Explain what happens to real GDP and the price level.

c. Explain why in Economy B wages and other factor prices will begin to fall, and why this will decrease unit costs.

d. Following your answer in part c, show the effect on the SRAS curve. Explain what happens to real GDP and the price level.

2. The table shows several possible situations for the economy in terms of output gaps and the rate of change of wages. Real GDP is measured in billions of dollars. Assume that potential output is $800 billion.

Situation	Real GDP	Output Gap	Rate of Wage Change	Shift of SRAS Curve (+/0/−)
A	775	—	−2.0 %	—
B	785	—	−1.2 %	—
C	795	—	−0.2 %	—
D	800	—	0.0 %	—
E	805	—	1.0 %	—
F	815	—	2.4 %	—
G	825	—	4.0 %	—
H	835	—	5.8 %	—

a. Compute the output gap $(Y−Y^*)$ for each situation and fill in the table.

b. Explain why wages rise when output is greater than potential but fall when output is less than potential.

c. For each situation, explain whether the economy's SRAS curve is shifting up, shifting down, or is stationary. Fill in the table.

d. Plot the Phillips curve on a scale diagram for this economy. (See *Extensions in Theory 25-1* for a review of the Phillips curve.)

3. Consider an economy that is in equilibrium with output equal to Y^*. There is then a sudden and significant reduction in the world's demand for this country's goods.

a. Illustrate the initial equilibrium in a diagram.

b. What kind of shock occurred—aggregate demand or aggregate supply? Show the effects of the shock in your diagram.

c. Explain the process by which the economy will adjust back toward Y^* in the long run. Show this in your diagram.

d. Explain why policymakers may want to use a fiscal expansion to restore output back to Y^* rather than wait for the process you described in part c. What

role does downward wage stickiness play in the policymakers' thinking?

4. Consider an economy that is in equilibrium with output equal to Y^*. There is then a sudden and significant reduction in the world price of an important raw material, such as iron ore.

a. Illustrate the initial equilibrium in a diagram.

b. What kind of shock occurred—aggregate demand or aggregate supply? Show the effects of the shock in your diagram.

c. Explain the process by which the economy will adjust back toward Y^* in the long run. Show this in your diagram.

5. We explained in the chapter how shocks—demand or supply—tend to lead to cyclical fluctuations in real GDP and the price level. The following diagram shows the time paths of real GDP and the price level for an economy that begins at $Y=Y^*$ and is then subjected to a shock that shifts the AD curve to the right. We define t^* as the time the shock hits the economy; we define t^{**} to be the time when the economy has adjusted fully and is back in long-run equilibrium.

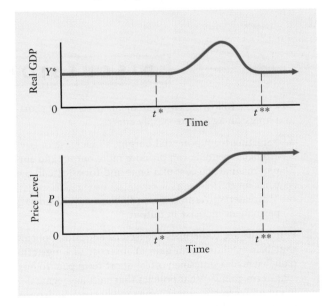

a. Draw the same types of diagrams for a negative AD shock. How does t^{**} for this shock compare to t^{**} for the positive AD shock?

b. Draw the same types of diagrams for a positive SRAS shock. How does t^{**} for this shock compare to t^{**} for the positive AD shock?

c. Draw the same types of diagrams for a negative SRAS shock. How does t^{**} for this shock compare to t^{**} for the positive SRAS and AD shock?

6. In our discussion of fiscal stabilization policy, we explained how income taxes and transfers affected the size of the multiplier. The accompanying diagrams show the initial equilibrium of two hypothetical economies that are each about to experience a $10 billion increase in autonomous net exports. Economy A has high (net) tax rates whereas Economy B has low (net) tax rates. Both economies have the same *SRAS* curve.

Economy B

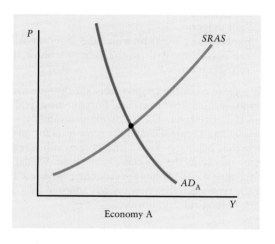

Economy A

a. Explain why Economy A is shown to have a steeper *AD* curve than Economy B.
b. Explain which economy has the larger multiplier, and why.
c. Illustrate the shifts in the *AD* curves that result from the increases in net exports. (Hint: you may want to review at this point the relationship between the *AD* curve and the *AE* curve, which we discussed in Chapter 24.)

DISCUSSION QUESTIONS

1. Discuss the following two statements in terms of short- and long-run aggregate supply curves.

   a. "Starting from potential output, an increase in government spending can produce more output and employment at the cost of a once-and-for-all rise in the price level."
   b. "Increased government spending can never lead to a permanent increase in output."

2. Politicians are sometimes accused of adopting policies that bring "short-term gain at the cost of long-term pain," whereas statesmen offer "short-term pain to buy long-term gain." What policies that shift aggregate demand or aggregate supply curves might come under one or the other of these descriptions?

3. If downward flexibility of money wages would allow the automatic adjustment mechanism to eliminate recessionary gaps quickly, why do workers usually resist wage cuts during times of economic slump?

4. Which of the following would be built-in stabilizers?

   a. Employment insurance payments
   b. Cost-of-living escalators in government contracts and pensions
   c. Income taxes
   d. Free university tuition for unemployed workers after six months of unemployment, provided that they are under 30 years old and have had five or more years of full-time work experience since high school

5. During 1998 and 1999, the Canadian economy was experiencing a sufficiently high rate of growth of real GDP that many economists predicted an increase in inflation. Yet inflation, if anything, declined slightly. At the same time, world commodity prices continued their decline that began in mid 1997. Explain the behaviour of the Canadian economy—high growth and falling inflation—in terms of aggregate demand and aggregate supply curves. What role, if any, is played by the falling commodity prices? What role is played by the U.S. economy, which at this point was experiencing very strong growth?

PART NINE

Money, Banking, and Monetary Policy

What is money, and where does it come from? Is the amount of money in the Canadian economy equal only to the actual value of bills and coins in circulation, or do accounts at commercial banks matter? If bank accounts matter, does this mean commercial banks can create money? Does the Bank of Canada control interest rates or are these rates determined by market forces? How does the Bank's monetary policy affect real GDP and employment? These are the sorts of questions you will be able to answer after reading the next three chapters.

Chapter 26 traces the development of money, from the use of barter in ancient economies to deposit money that is so important today. We will examine the Canadian banking system, from the commercial banks to the Bank of Canada, Canada's central bank. The idea of money creation will then be examined, and we will see that commercial banks do indeed create money. Finally, we will discuss several formal measures of the Canadian money supply.

Chapter 27 begins with a discussion of the demand for money. Here we see the various reasons why households and firms hold money, and why the level of interest rates is so important in these decisions. We then examine the concept of monetary equilibrium, and it is here that we consider the Bank of Canada's role in determining interest rates. We also see how changes in the Bank of Canada's policy can affect interest rates, aggregate expenditure, and eventually real GDP and the price level.

In Chapter 28 we focus on monetary policy. We will explore some of the details of how the Bank of Canada's actions influence the commercial banking system. The Bank's policy variables, policy instruments, and policy targets will all be discussed, and it is here that we discuss the lags and uncertainty that make the conduct of monetary policy so difficult. We then give a brief review of the past three decades of monetary policy in Canada. This discussion will help to put together the lessons learned throughout this part of the book.

CHAPTER 26

The Nature of Money

(LO) LEARNING OBJECTIVES

1 Understand the Classical dichotomy and how this relates to the neutrality of money.

2 Explain the various functions of money.

3 Understand the historical origins of money.

4 Recognize that modern banking systems comprise both privately owned commercial banks and government-owned central banks.

5 Explain how commercial banks create money through the process of taking deposits and making loans.

6 Know what is included in various measures of the money supply.

In the next three chapters, we examine the significance of money in market economies. The role of money may seem obvious—money is what people use to buy things. Yet as we shall see, increasing the amount of money circulating in Canada would not make the average Canadian better off in the long run. Although money allows those who have it to buy someone else's output, the total amount of goods and services available for everyone to buy depends on the total output produced, not on the total amount of money that people possess. In short, an increase in the quantity of money will not increase the level of potential real GDP, Y^*. Still, without money, modern economies could not function, and most economists would agree that the quantity of money, although it cannot affect Y^*, can and does affect short-run movements in national income.

Two Perspectives on Money

Theories on the role of money in a market economy have been evolving for several centuries.

The Classical View

In the eighteenth and nineteenth centuries, economists articulated the independence of Y^* from monetary factors in terms of an economic theory that distinguished sharply between the "real sector" of the economy and the "monetary sector" of the economy. This approach led to a view that is now referred to as the *Classical dichotomy*.

According to the **Classical dichotomy**, the allocation of resources, and hence the determination of real GDP, is determined only by the real sector of the economy. It is *relative prices* that matter for this process. Early economists argued that the price level is determined in the monetary sector of the economy. If the quantity of money were doubled, other things being equal, the prices of all commodities and money income would also double. Relative prices would remain unchanged, and the real sector of the economy would be unaffected.

According to the Classical economists, the allocation of resources—and the determination of real GDP—depends only on relative prices. An increase in the money supply leads to a proportionate increase in all money prices, with no change in the allocation of resources or the level of real GDP.

The doctrine that the quantity of money influences the level of money prices but has no effect on the real part of the economy is called the **neutrality of money**. Because early economists believed that the most important questions—How much does the economy produce? What share of it does each group in society get?—were answered in the real sector, they spoke of money as a "veil" behind which occurred the real events that affected material well-being.

The Modern View

Most modern economists still accept the neutrality of money in the long run when all the forces causing change have fully worked themselves out. However, they do not accept the neutrality of money when the economy is adjusting to the various forces that cause it to change—that is, when the economy is not in a state of long-run equilibrium. Consequently, they reject the Classical dichotomy as a description of the economy in the short run.

The view that the neutrality of money holds in the long run leads modern economists to stress the strong link between changes in the money supply and changes in the price level, at least over long periods of time. Figure 26-1 shows a scatter-plot of inflation and money growth for 82 countries over the four decades following the Second World War. Each point in the figure represents the rates of inflation and money supply growth for one country averaged over the forty-year period. The vertical axis measures each country's average annual inflation rate—that is, the average annual rate of increase of the price level. The horizontal axis measures each country's average annual rate of growth of the money supply (which we will define precisely later in the chapter). As is clear in the figure, there is a positive relationship between money supply growth and inflation, as reflected by the tight bunching of points around the upward-sloping line, the "line of best fit" between money supply growth and inflation. The slope of the line of best fit is 0.97, indicating that two countries that differ in their money growth rates by 10 percent will, on average, differ in their inflation rates by 9.7 percent.

Classical dichotomy
The view that national income is determined only by the real sector of the economy and that changes in the money supply lead only to changes in the price level.

neutrality of money
The doctrine that the money supply affects only the absolute level of prices and has no effect on relative prices, the allocation of resources, or the distribution of income.

To see how much Canada's price level has increased from anytime in the past fifty years to today, see the Bank of Canada's "inflation calculator" at: www.bank-banque-canada.ca.

FIGURE 26-1   Inflation and Money Growth Across Many Countries

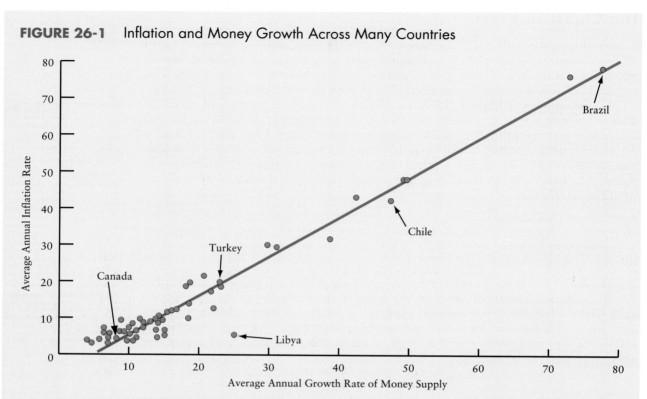

Countries with higher inflation rates tend also to be countries with higher rates of growth of the money supply. This figure plots long-run data for many countries. Each point shows the average annual inflation rate and the average annual growth rate of the money supply for a specific country over the post World War II period (the precise years vary slightly across countries). For all countries, the inflation data refer to the rate of change of the consumer price index; the money supply data refer to the growth rate of currency. The positive relationship between inflation and money supply growth (with a slope of the best-fit line very close to one) is consistent with the proposition of long-run money neutrality.

(*Source:* The data are from the International Monetary Fund's *International Financial Statistics,* as compiled by R.J. Barro and R.F. Lucas.)

Most modern economists believe that money is neutral in the long run. Long-run neutrality implies that, in the absence of other shocks to the economy, changes in money and changes in the price level are closely linked over long periods of time.

The Nature of Money

What exactly is money? In this section, we describe the functions of money and briefly outline its history.

What Is Money?

money   A medium of exchange that can also serve as a store of value and a unit of account.

medium of exchange Anything that is generally acceptable in return for goods and services sold.

In economics, **money** has usually been defined as any generally accepted medium of exchange. A **medium of exchange** is anything that will be widely accepted in a society in exchange for goods and services. Although its medium-of-exchange role is perhaps its most important one, money also acts as a *store of value* and as a *unit of account*. Different kinds of money vary in the degree of efficiency with which they fulfill these functions. As we shall see, the *money supply* is measured by using different definitions for different purposes.

Money as a Medium of Exchange

If there were no money, goods would have to be exchanged by barter. **Barter** is the system whereby goods and services are exchanged directly with each other. The major difficulty with barter is that each transaction requires a *double coincidence of wants*: anyone who specialized in producing one commodity would have to spend a great deal of time searching for satisfactory transactions. For example, the barber who needs his sink repaired would have to find a plumber who wants a haircut. In a world of many different goods and many different people, the effort required to make transactions would be extreme.

barter   A system in which goods and services are traded directly for other goods and services.

The use of money as a medium of exchange solves this problem. People can sell their output for money and then use the money to buy what they wish from others.

The double coincidence of wants is unnecessary when a medium of exchange is used.

By facilitating transactions, money makes possible the benefits of specialization and the division of labour, which in turn contribute to the efficiency of the economic system. It is not without justification that money has been called one of the great inventions contributing to human freedom and well-being.

To serve as an efficient medium of exchange, money must have a number of characteristics. It must be readily acceptable. It must have a high value relative to its weight (otherwise it would be a nuisance to carry around). It must be divisible, because money that comes only in large denominations is useless for transactions having only a small value. Finally, it must be difficult, if not impossible, to counterfeit.

Money as a Store of Value

Money is a convenient way to store purchasing power; goods may be sold today for money and the money may then be stored until it is needed for some future purchase. To be a satisfactory store of value, however, money must have a relatively stable value. A rise in the price level is also a decrease in the purchasing power of money. When the price level is stable, the purchasing power of a given sum of money is also stable; when the price level is highly variable, so is the purchasing power of money, and the usefulness of money as a store of value is undermined.

Between the early 1970s and the early 1990s, inflation in Canada was high enough and sufficiently variable to diminish money's usefulness as a store of value. Since 1992, inflation has been both low and relatively stable, thus increasing money's role as a store of value. Even Canada's high-inflation experience, however, is very modest compared to that in some other countries, such as Chile in the mid 1970s, Bolivia in the mid 1980s, and Romania and Brazil in the early 1990s. Perhaps the most infamous experience of *hyperinflation* comes from Germany in the early 1920s. This case is discussed in *Lessons from History 26-1*.

Money as a Unit of Account

Money may also be used purely for accounting purposes without having a physical existence of its own. For instance, a government store in a truly communist society might say that everyone had so many "dollars" to use each month. Goods could then be assigned prices and each consumer's purchases recorded, the consumer being allowed to buy until the allocated supply of dollars was exhausted. These dollars need have no existence other

LESSONS FROM HISTORY 26-1

Hyperinflation

Hyperinflation is generally defined as inflation that exceeds 50 percent per month. At this rate of inflation a chocolate bar that costs $1 on January 1 would cost $129.74 by December 31 of the same year. When prices are rising at such rapid rates, is it possible for money to maintain its usefulness as a medium of exchange or as a store of value? There are several examples from history that have allowed economists to study the role of money during hyperinflation. This historical record is not entirely reassuring. In a number of instances, prices rose at an ever-accelerating rate until a nation's money ceased to be a satisfactory store of value, even for the short period between receipt and expenditure, and hence ceased also to be useful as a medium of exchange.

The most spectacular example of hyperinflation is the experience of Germany in the period after World War I. The index shows that a good purchased for one 100-mark note in July 1923 would cost *10 million* 100-mark notes only four months later! Although Germany had experienced substantial inflation during World War I, averaging more than 30 percent per year, the immediate postwar years of 1920 and 1921 gave no sign of explosive inflation. Indeed, prices were relatively stable until 1922 and 1923 when they exploded. On November 15, 1923, the German mark was officially repudiated, its value wholly destroyed. How could such a dramatic increase in prices happen?

When inflation becomes so rapid that people lose confidence in the purchasing power of their currency, they rush to spend it. People who have goods become increasingly reluctant to accept the rapidly depreciating money in exchange. The rush to spend money accelerates the increase in prices until people finally become unwilling to accept money on any terms. What was once money ceases to be money. The price system can then be restored only by repudiation of the old monetary unit and its replacement by a new unit.

About a dozen hyperinflations in world history have been documented, among them the collapse of the continental during the American Revolution in 1776, the ruble during the Russian Revolution in 1917, the drachma during and after the German occupation of Greece in World War II, the pengö in Hungary in 1945 and 1946, the Chinese national currency from 1946 to 1948, and the Bolivian peso in 1984 and 1985. Every one of these hyperinflations was accompanied by great increases in the money supply; new money was printed to give governments purchasing power that they could not or would not obtain by taxation. Further, every one occurred in the midst of a major political upheaval in which grave doubts existed about the stability and the future of the government itself.

Is hyperinflation likely in the absence of civil war, revolution, or collapse of the government? Most economists think not. Further, it is clear that high inflation rates over a period of time do not mean the inevitable or even likely onset of hyperinflation, however serious the distributive and social effects of such rates may be.

During hyperinflation money loses its value so quickly that people cease to accept it as a means of payment. At that point, money may as well be used for wallpaper.

Date	German Wholesale Price Index (1913 = 1)
January 1913	1
January 1920	13
January 1921	14
January 1922	37
July 1922	101
January 1923	2 785
July 1923	74 800
August 1923	944 000
September 1923	23 900 000
October 1923	7 096 000 000
November 1923	750 000 000 000

than as entries in the store's books, yet they would serve as a perfectly satisfactory unit of account.

Whether they could also serve as a medium of exchange between individuals depends on whether the store would agree to transfer dollar credits from one customer to another at the customer's request. Canadian banks transfer dollars credited to deposits in this way each time you make a purchase with your ATM card. Thus, a bank deposit can serve as both a unit of account and a medium of exchange. Notice that the use of *dollars* in this context suggests a further sense in which money is a unit of account. People think about values in terms of the monetary unit with which they are familiar.

The Origins of Money

The origins of money go far back in antiquity. Most primitive tribes are known to have made some use of it.

Metallic Money

All sorts of commodities have been used as money at one time or another, but gold and silver proved to have great advantages. They were precious because their supplies were relatively limited, and they were in constant demand by the wealthy for ornament and decoration. Hence, these metals tended to have high and stable prices. Further, they were easily recognized, they were divisible into extremely small units, and they did not easily wear out. Thus, precious metals came to circulate as money and to be used in many transactions.

Before the invention of coins, it was necessary to carry the metals in bulk. When a purchase was made, the requisite quantity of the metal was carefully weighed on a scale. The invention of coinage eliminated the need to weigh the metal at each transaction, but it created an important role for an authority, usually a monarch, who made the coins and affixed his or her seal, guaranteeing the amount of precious metal that the coin contained. This was clearly a great convenience, as long as traders knew that they could accept the coin at its "face value." The face value was nothing more than a statement that a certain weight of metal was contained therein.

However, coins often could not be taken at their face value. The practice of clipping a thin slice off the edge of the coin and keeping the valuable metal became common. This, of course, served to undermine the acceptability of coins, even if they were stamped. To get around this problem, the idea arose of minting the coins with a rough edge. The absence of the rough edge would immediately indicate that the coin had been clipped. This practice, called *milling*, survives on Canadian dimes, quarters, and "twoonies" as an interesting anachronism to remind us that there were days when the market value of the metal in the coin was equal to the face value of the coin.

Not to be outdone by the cunning of their subjects, some rulers were quick to seize the chance of getting something for nothing. The power to mint placed rulers in a position to work a very profitable fraud. They often used some suitable occasion—a marriage, an anniversary, an alliance—to remint the coinage. Subjects would be ordered to bring their coins in to the mint to be melted down and coined afresh with a new stamp. Between the melting down and the recoining, however, the rulers had only to toss some further inexpensive base metal in with the molten gold. This *debasing* of the coinage allowed the ruler to earn a handsome profit by minting more new coins than the number of old ones collected, and putting the extras in the royal vault.

The result of debasement was inflation. The subjects had the same number of coins as before and hence could demand the same quantity of goods. When rulers paid their bills, however, the recipients of the extra coins could be expected to spend them. This caused a net increase in demand, which in turn bid up prices. Thus, debasing of the coinage was a common cause of increases in prices.

Gresham's law   The theory that "bad," or debased, money drives "good," or undebased, money out of circulation.

Gresham's Law.   The early experience of currency debasement led to the observation known as **Gresham's law,** after Sir Thomas Gresham (1519–1579), an adviser to the Elizabethan court, who coined the phrase "bad money drives out good."

When Queen Elizabeth I came to the throne of England in the middle of the sixteenth century, the coinage had been severely debased. Seeking to help trade, Elizabeth minted new coins that contained their full face value in gold. However, as fast as she fed these new coins into circulation, they disappeared. Why?

Suppose that you possessed one of these new coins and one of the old ones, each with the same face value, and had to make a purchase. What would you do? You would use the debased coin to make the purchase and keep the undebased one; you part with less gold that way. Suppose that you wanted to obtain a certain amount of gold bullion by melting down the gold coins (as was frequently done). Which coins would you use? You would use new, undebased coins because you would part with less face value that way (it would take more of the debased coins than the new coins to get a given amount of gold bullion). The debased coins (bad money) would thus remain in circulation, and the undebased coins (good money) would disappear—the "bad" money would drive out the "good" money.

Gresham's law predicts that when two types of money are used side by side, the one with the greater intrinsic value will be driven out of circulation.

Gresham's insights have proved helpful in explaining the experience of a number of modern high-inflation economies. For example, in the 1970s, inflation in Chile raised the value of the metallic content in coins above their face value. Coins quickly disappeared from circulation as private citizens sold them to entrepreneurs who melted them down for their metal. Only paper currency remained in circulation and was used even for tiny transactions such as purchasing a pack of matches. Gresham's law is one reason why modern coins, unlike their historical counterparts, are merely tokens that contain a metallic value that is only a small fraction of their face value.

Paper Money

The next important step in the history of money was the evolution of paper currency. Artisans who worked with gold required secure safes, and the public began to deposit gold with such goldsmiths for safekeeping. Goldsmiths would give their depositors receipts promising to hand over the gold on demand. When a depositor wished to make a large purchase, he could go to his goldsmith, reclaim some of his gold, and hand it over to the seller of the goods. If the seller had no immediate need for the gold, he would carry it back to the goldsmith for safekeeping.

If people knew the goldsmith to be reliable, there was no need to go through the cumbersome and risky business of physically transferring the gold. The buyer needed only to transfer the goldsmith's receipt to the seller, who would accept it as long as he was confident that the goldsmith would pay over the gold whenever it was needed. If the seller wished to buy a good from a third party, who also knew the goldsmith to be reliable, this transaction could also be effected by passing the goldsmith's receipt from the buyer to the seller. This transferring of paper receipts rather than gold was essentially the invention of paper money.

When it first came into being, paper money represented a promise to pay so much gold on demand. In this case, the promise was made first by goldsmiths and later by banks. Such paper money was *backed* by precious metal and was *convertible on demand* into this metal. In the nineteenth century, private banks commonly issued paper money, called **bank notes,** nominally convertible into gold. As with the goldsmiths, each bank issued its own notes, and these notes were convertible into gold at the issuing

bank notes   Paper money issued by commercial banks.

bank. Thus, in the nineteenth century, bank notes from many different banks circulated side by side, each of them being backed by gold at the bank that issued them.

Fractionally Backed Paper Money.   Early on, many goldsmiths and banks discovered that it was not necessary to keep one ounce of gold in the vaults for every claim to one ounce circulating as paper money. This is because at any one time, some of the bank's customers would be withdrawing gold, others would be depositing it, and most would be trading in the bank's paper notes without any need or desire to convert them into gold. As a result, the bank was able to issue more money redeemable in gold than the amount of gold that it held in its vaults. This was good business because the money could be invested profitably in interest-earning loans to households and firms. To this day, banks have many more claims outstanding against them than they actually have in reserves available to pay those claims. We say that the currency issued in such a situation is *fractionally backed* by the reserves.

The major problem with a fractionally backed convertible currency was maintaining its convertibility into the precious metal behind it. The imprudent bank that issued too much paper money would find itself unable to redeem its currency in gold when the demand for gold was even slightly higher than usual. It would then have to suspend payments, and all holders of its notes would suddenly find that the notes were worthless. The prudent bank that kept a reasonable relationship between its note issues and its gold reserves would find that it could meet a normal range of demand for gold without any trouble.

If, for whatever reason, the public lost confidence in the banks and demanded redemption of its currency *en masse,* the banks would be unable to honour their pledges. The history of nineteenth- and early-twentieth-century banking on both sides of the Atlantic is full of examples of banks that were ruined by "panics," or sudden runs on their gold reserves. When these happened, the banks' depositors and the holders of their notes would find themselves with worthless pieces of paper.

Fiat Money

As time went on, currency (notes and coins) issued by private banks became less common, and central banks took control of the currency. In time, *only* central banks were permitted to issue currency. Originally, the central banks issued currency that was fully convertible into gold. In those days, gold would be brought to the central bank, which would issue currency in the form of "gold certificates" that asserted that the gold was available on demand. The gold supply thus set some upper limit on the amount of currency. This practice of backing the currency with gold is known as a **gold standard.**

However, central banks, like private banks before them, could issue more currency than they had in gold because in normal times only a small fraction of the outstanding currency was presented for payment at any one time. Thus, even though the need to maintain convertibility into gold put an upper limit on note issuance, central banks had substantial discretionary control over the quantity of currency outstanding.

During the period between the World Wars (1919–1939), almost all of the countries of the world abandoned the gold standard; their currencies were thus no longer convertible into gold. Money that is not convertible by law into anything valuable derives its value from its acceptability in exchange. Such **fiat money** is widely acceptable because it is declared by government order, or *fiat,* to be legal tender. **Legal tender** is anything that by law must be accepted when offered either for the purchase of goods or services or to discharge a debt.

Today, a few countries preserve the fiction that their currency is backed by gold, but no country allows its currency to be converted into gold on demand. Gold backing for Canadian currency was eliminated in 1940, although note issues continued to carry

gold standard
A currency standard whereby a country's currency is convertible into gold at a fixed rate of exchange.

fiat money   Paper money or coinage that is neither backed by nor convertible into anything else but is decreed by the government to be accepted as legal tender.

legal tender
Anything that by law must be accepted for the purchase of goods and services or in discharge of a debt.

the traditional statement "will pay to the bearer on demand" until 1954. Today's Bank of Canada notes simply say, "This note is legal tender." It is, in other words, fiat money pure and simple.

If fiat money is acceptable, it is a medium of exchange. If its purchasing power remains stable, it is a satisfactory store of value. If both of these things are true, it serves as a satisfactory unit of account. Today, almost all currency is fiat money.

Many people are disturbed to learn that present-day paper money is neither backed by nor convertible into anything more valuable—that it consists of nothing but pieces of paper whose value derives from common acceptance and from confidence that it will continue to be accepted in the future. Many people believe that their money should be more "substantial" than this. Yet money is, in fact, nothing more than pieces of paper.

Modern Money: Deposit Money

Early in the twentieth century, private banks lost the authority to issue bank notes, and this authority was reserved for central banks (which we discuss shortly). Yet, as we shall see, they did not lose the power to create *deposit money*. (A number of terms that will be encountered as we discuss modern money and the institutions related to it are discussed in *Applying Economic Concepts 26-1*.)

Today's bank customers frequently deposit coins and paper money with the banks for safekeeping, just as in former times they deposited gold. Such a deposit is recorded as a credit to the customer's account. A customer who wishes to pay a debt may come to the bank and claim the money in dollars and then pay the money to other persons who may themselves redeposit the money in a bank.

As with gold transfers, this is a tedious procedure. It is more convenient to have the bank transfer claims to money on deposit. As soon as cheques, which are written instructions to the bank to make a transfer, became widely accepted in payment for commodities and debts, bank deposits became a form of money called *deposit money*. **Deposit money** is defined as money held by the public in the form of deposits in commercial banks that can be withdrawn on demand. Such deposits are called *demand deposits;* the most important of which are chequing accounts. Cheques, unlike bank notes, do not circulate freely from hand to hand; hence cheques themselves are not currency. However, a balance in a demand deposit *is* money; the cheque transfers money from one person to another. Because cheques are easily drawn and deposited and are relatively safe from theft, they are widely used. In recent years, the development of debit cards has taken the place of cheques for many transactions. The use of a debit card instantly (electronically) transfers funds from the bank account of the purchaser to the bank account of the seller—it thus has the same effect as a cheque, only faster.

Thus, when commercial banks lost the right to issue notes of their own, the form of bank money changed, but the substance did not. Today, banks have money in their vaults (or on deposit with the central banks), just as they always did. Once it was gold; today it is the legal tender of the times—fiat money. It is true today, just as in the past, that most of the bank's customers are content to pay their bills by passing among themselves the bank's promises to pay money on demand. Only a small proportion of the transactions made by the bank's customers are made in cash.

Bank deposits are money. Today, just as in the past, banks create money by issuing more promises to pay (deposits) than they have cash reserves available to pay out.

deposit money
Money held by the public in the form of demand deposits with commercial banks.

APPLYING ECONOMIC CONCEPTS 26-1

A Guide to Financial Assets

Throughout this and subsequent chapters, we will encounter many different types of financial assets, or *securities*. It is important to understand the meaning of some of the more commonly used terms.

Equity refers to assets such as stocks or shares that represent evidence of partial ownership of a firm and hence provide a claim on the earnings of that firm; the return on equity depends on the performance of the firm. Equity is also often called *capital*; unless the context makes it clear, care must be taken to distinguish between use of the term capital to refer to the actual plant, equipment, and machinery that constitute a firm's physical assets and use of the term to refer to the financial assets that represent a claim on the firm's earnings.

Debt refers to assets issued by firms and governments that promise to pay a specified rate of interest over a specified period of time. Unless the firm in question goes bankrupt and cannot meet its obligations, the return on debt does not depend on the earnings of the firm—the interest must be paid whether the firm is profitable or not and thus represents a prior claim on the firm's earnings before any payment to equity holders is made.

Most debt instruments, often called *bonds*, promise to pay a stated sum of money as interest each year and to repay the principal (often called the *face value* or the *redemption value*) of the bond at some future maturity date, often many years distant. The time until the maturity date is called the *term to maturity*, or simply the *term*, of the bond. Some bonds, called *perpetuities*, pay interest forever and never repay the principal.

Very-short-term bonds that promise a single payment (combining interest and principal) are called *money-market instruments* and include *treasury bills* (short-term government bonds), certificates of deposit (CDs), banker's acceptances, and commercial paper. The price paid for one of these instruments is less than the amount that the instrument pays on maturity, and the difference is called the *discount*. For example, the government issues three- and six-month treasury bills each week that are priced on a discount basis. The difference between the purchase price and the payment on maturity represents the interest on the bill.

The ownership of most financial assets is transferable, and hence they can be bought and sold in financial markets. As with anything else that is bought and sold, the price of financial assets fluctuates in response to shifts in supply and demand. In the next chapter we will look more carefully at the determination of the price of financial assets.

One important characteristic of financial assets is their *riskiness,* which refers to the possibility that the future payments will not be made in full or at all. Typically, investors are thought to be risk-averse—that is, the riskier an asset is, the higher is the yield it will have to offer to induce investors to buy it.

Another important characteristic of financial assets is their *liquidity,* which refers to their usefulness as a ready means of payment. Money can always be used as a means of payment and hence is a perfectly liquid asset. Since other financial assets can be sold in the market and hence are convertible into cash, they appear to be just as liquid as money. However, the markets for some assets are such that they cannot always be instantly sold, or at least not at anything other than a "bargain-basement" price; to receive the price that is justified by the asset's risk and return, some time and expense must be incurred.

The Canadian Banking System

Many types of institutions make up a modern banking system such as exists in Canada today. The **central bank** is the government-owned and government-operated institution that serves to control the banking system. Through it, the government's monetary policy is conducted. In Canada, the central bank is the Bank of Canada, often called just the Bank.

central bank   A bank that acts as banker to the commercial banking system and often to the government as well. Usually a government-owned institution that controls the banking system and is the sole money-issuing authority.

Financial intermediaries are privately owned institutions that serve the general public. They are called *intermediaries* because they stand between savers, from whom they accept deposits, and investors, to whom they make loans. For many years, government regulations created a sharp distinction among the various types of financial intermediaries by limiting the types of transactions that each could engage in. The past two decades have seen a sweeping deregulation of the financial system so that many of these traditional distinctions no longer apply. In this book, we use the term *commercial banks* to extend to all financial intermediaries that create deposit money, including chartered banks, trust companies and credit unions.

The Bank of Canada

All advanced free-market economies have, in addition to commercial banks, a central bank. Many of the world's early central banks were private, profit-making institutions that provided services to ordinary banks. Their importance, however, caused them to develop close ties with government. Central banks soon became instruments of the government, though not all of them were publicly owned. The Bank of England (the "Old Lady of Threadneedle Street"), one of the world's oldest and most famous central banks, began to operate as the central bank of England in the seventeenth century, but it was not formally taken over by the government until 1947.

The similarities in the functions performed and the tools used by the world's central banks are much more important than the differences in their organization. Although our attention is given to the operations of the Bank of Canada, its basic functions are similar to those of the Bank of England, the Federal Reserve System in the United States, or the new European Central Bank.

Organization of the Bank of Canada

The Bank of Canada commenced operations on March 11, 1935. It is a publicly owned corporation; all profits accruing from its operations are remitted to the Government of Canada. The responsibility for the Bank's affairs rests with a board of directors composed of the governor, the senior deputy governor, the deputy minister of finance, and 12 directors. The governor is appointed by the directors, with the approval of the federal cabinet, for a seven-year term. Since the Bank's inception, there have been six governors:

- Graham Towers (1935–54)
- James Coyne (1955–61)
- Louis Rasminsky (1961–73)
- Gerald Bouey (1973–87)
- John Crow (1987–94)
- Gordon Thiessen (1994–)

The organization of the Bank of Canada is designed to keep the operation of monetary policy free from day-to-day political influence. The Bank is not responsible to Parliament for its day-to-day behaviour in the way that the Department of Finance is for the operation of fiscal policy. In this sense, the Bank of Canada has considerable autonomy in the way it carries out monetary policy. Despite this considerable autonomy, however, the Bank of Canada is not completely independent. The *ultimate* responsibility for the Bank's actions rest with the government, since it is the government which must answer to Parliament. This system is known as "joint responsibility," and it dates back to 1967.

Under the system of joint responsibility, the governor of the Bank and the minister of finance consult regularly. In the case of fundamental disagreement over policy, the minister of finance has the option of issuing an explicit *directive* to the governor. In such a case (which has not happened since the inception of joint responsibility), the governor would simply carry out the minister's directive (or resign), and the responsibility for monetary policy would rest with the government. In the absence of such a directive, however, responsibility for monetary policy rests with the governor of the Bank.

The system of joint responsibility keeps the conduct of monetary policy free from day-to-day political influence while ensuring that the government retains ultimate responsibility for monetary policy.[1]

For information on the Bank of Canada, see its website: www.bank-banque-canada.ca.

Basic Functions of the Bank

A central bank serves four main functions: as a banker for private banks, as a bank for the government, as the regulator of the nation's money supply, and as a supporter of financial markets. The first three functions are reflected in Table 26-1, which shows the balance sheet of the Bank of Canada.

Banker to the Chartered Banks.   The central bank accepts deposits from the chartered banks and will, on order, transfer them to the account of another bank. In this way, the central bank provides the chartered banks with the equivalent of a chequing account and with a means of settling debts to other banks. The deposits of the chartered banks with the Bank of Canada—also called *reserves*—appear in Table 26-1. In

TABLE 26-1   Assets and Liabilities of the Bank of Canada, March 1999 (millions of dollars)

Assets		Liabilities	
Government of Canada securities	30 042	Notes in circulation	30 882
Advances to banks	737	Government of Canada deposits	12
Foreign-currency assets	323	Deposits of banks (reserves)	1 115
Other assets	1 696	Foreign-currency liabilities	159
		Other liabilities and capital	630
Total	32 798	Total	32 798

The balance sheet of the Bank of Canada shows that it serves as banker to the commercial banks and to the Government of Canada and as issuer of our currency; it also suggests the Bank's role as regulator of money markets and the money supply. The principal liabilities of the Bank are the basis of the money supply. Bank of Canada notes are currency, and the deposits of the commercial banks give them the reserves they need to create deposit money. The Bank's holdings of Government of Canada securities arise from its operations designed to regulate the money supply and financial markets.

(*Source: Bank of Canada Review*, Spring 1999)

[1]This system was motivated by the "Coyne Affair" in 1961. James Coyne, then governor of the Bank of Canada, disagreed with the minister of finance over the conduct of monetary policy and was eventually forced to resign. Louis Rasminsky then accepted the position as governor of the Bank on the condition that the Bank of Canada Act be modified to incorporate the idea of joint responsibility. The Bank of Canada Act was so amended in 1967. For a discussion of the early history of the Bank of Canada, see George Watts, *The Bank of Canada: Origins and Early History* (Carleton University Press, 1993).

March 1999 the banks had $1.11 billion on reserve at the Bank of Canada. Notice that the cash reserves of the chartered banks deposited with the central bank are liabilities of the central bank, because it promises to pay them on demand.

Historically, one of the earliest services provided by central banks was that of "lender of last resort" to the banking system. Central banks would lend money to private banks that had sound investments (such as government securities) but were in urgent need of cash. If such banks could not obtain ready cash, they might be forced into insolvency, because they could not meet the demands of their depositors, in spite of their being basically sound. Today's central banks continue to be lenders of last resort.

Banker to the Federal Government. Governments, too, need to hold their funds in an account into which they can make deposits and on which they can write cheques. The government of Canada keeps some of its chequing deposits at the Bank of Canada, replenishing them from much larger accounts kept at the chartered banks. In March 1999 the federal government had only $12 million in deposits at the Bank of Canada.

When the government requires more money than it collects in taxes, it needs to borrow, and it does so by issuing government securities (short-term treasury bills or longer-term bonds). Most are sold directly to the public, but occasionally the government raises funds by selling securities to the central bank which "buys" them by crediting the government's account with a deposit for the amount of the purchase. In March 1999, the Bank of Canada held $30 billion in government of Canada securities. These securities are an asset for the Bank of Canada but a liability for the government. (It is largely by earning interest on these securities that the Bank of Canada earns a profit every year—a profit that is eventually remitted to the government.)

We will see in Chapter 28 that the Bank's holdings of government securities and its control over the location of government deposits (switching them between the central bank and the commercial banks) are the primary tools for the conduct of monetary policy.

Regulator of the Money Supply. One of the most important functions of a central bank is to regulate the *money supply*. Though we have not yet defined the money supply precisely—and there are several different definitions of the money supply that we will encounter—we will see that most measures of the money supply include currency plus deposits held at commercial banks. From Table 26-1, it is clear that the overwhelming proportion of a central bank's liabilities (its promises to pay) are either currency (notes and coins) or the reserves of the chartered banks. These reserves, in turn, underlie the deposits of households and firms—in exactly the same way that the nineteenth century goldsmith's holdings of gold underlay its issue of notes.

Thus, by changing its liabilities (currency plus reserves), the Bank of Canada can change the money supply. The Bank of Canada can change the levels of its assets and liabilities in many ways and, as its liabilities rise and fall, so does the money supply. In Chapter 28, we will explore in detail how this happens and how the Bank uses this ability to conduct monetary policy.

Regulator and Supporter of Money Markets. Central banks usually assume a major responsibility to support the country's financial system and to prevent serious disruption by wide-scale panic and resulting bank failures.

Various institutions—including chartered banks, credit unions, and trust companies—are in the business of borrowing on a short-term basis and lending on a long-term basis. Large, unanticipated increases in interest rates tend to squeeze these institutions. The average rate they earn on their investments rises only slowly as old contracts mature and new ones are made, but they must either pay higher rates to hold on to their deposits or accept wide-scale withdrawals that could easily bring about insolvency. To prevent such financial disasters, central banks often buy and sell government bonds either to slow the rate of change in interest rates or to narrow the range over which the rates are allowed to fluctuate.

Conflicts Among Functions.   The several functions of the Bank of Canada are not always compatible. For example, we will see in Chapter 27 that a policy designed to reduce the rate of inflation requires the Bank to raise short-term interest rates. The resulting squeeze makes life uncomfortable for banks and other financial institutions and makes borrowing expensive for the government. If the Bank of Canada acts to ease those problems, say, by lending money to chartered banks, it is relaxing its anti-inflationary policy. The Bank must strive to balance conflicting objectives. We discuss a number of aspects of this conflict in Chapter 28.

Commercial Banks in Canada

All Canadian banks owned in the private sector are referred to as **commercial banks.** The Canadian banking system is controlled by the provisions of the Bank Act, first passed in 1935 and revised several times since. Under the Bank Act, charters can be granted to financial institutions to operate as banks and, until 1980, there were only a few chartered banks, most of which were very large and each of which operated under identical regulatory provisions.

The 1980 revisions to the Bank Act allowed foreign banks to commence operations in Canada, although it severely limited the scale and scope of their activity. Subsequent revisions have removed some of these restrictions and made it easier to obtain new banking charters, but the revisions have maintained the distinction between these newer institutions and banks operating under what are essentially the pre-1980 provisions of the Bank Act. The original provisions, in slightly modified form, are now known as Schedule A of the Bank Act; the foreign banks and the new, smaller domestic banks operate under Schedules B and C. The term *chartered banks* is usually reserved for the Schedule A banks.

The chartered banks have common attributes: they hold deposits for their customers; they permit certain deposits to be transferred by cheque from an individual account to other accounts held in any bank branch in the country; they make loans to households and firms; they invest in government securities.

Banks are not the only financial institutions in the country. Many other privately owned, profit-seeking institutions, such as trust companies and credit unions, accept savings deposits and grant loans for specific purposes. Finance companies make loans to households for practically any purpose—sometimes at very high interest rates. Department stores and credit-card companies will extend credit so that purchases can be made on a buy-now, pay-later basis.

The chartered banks are subject to federal regulations and until recently were required to hold reserves with the Bank of Canada against their deposit liabilities. Other institutions do not face reserve requirements, but most are subject to various federal and provincial regulations concerning ownership and control and the types of financial activities they are allowed to engage in. Thus, there are differences among all types of financial institutions, not just between banks and others.

The Canadian chartered banks have historically been such a stable and dominant group that the terms *chartered banks* and *banking system* have been considered virtually synonymous. However, events over the past 15 years have broken this identification. Especially important have been sweeping changes in the structure and functioning of international financial markets; some of these developments are discussed further in *Applying Economic Concepts 26-2.*

commercial bank
A privately owned, profit-seeking institution that provides a variety of financial services, such as accepting deposits from customers and making loans and other investments.

For information and history of Canada's largest chartered bank, see the Royal Bank's website: www.royal-bank.com. Go to "corporate information" and then "history."

APPLYING ECONOMIC CONCEPTS 26-2

The Globalization of Financial Markets

Technological innovations in communication over the past two decades have led to a globalization of the financial service industry. Computers, satellite communication systems, reliable telephones with direct worldwide dialing, fax machines, and the widespread use of the Internet have put people in instantaneous contact anywhere in the world.

As a result of these new technologies, borrowers and lenders can learn about market conditions and then move their funds instantly in search of the best loan rates. Large firms need transaction balances only while banks in their area are open. Once banks close for the day in each centre, the firms will not need these balances until tomorrow's reopening; hence the funds can be moved to another market, where they are used until it closes. They are then moved to yet another market. Funds are thus free to move from London to New York to Tokyo and back to London on a daily rotation. This is a degree of global sophistication that was inconceivable before the advent of the computer, when international communication was much slower and costlier than it now is. To facilitate the movement in and out of various national currencies, increasing amounts of bank deposits are denominated in foreign rather than domestic currencies.

One of the first developments in this movement toward globalization was the growth of the foreign-currency markets in Europe in the 1960s. Initially, the main currency involved was the U.S. dollar, which is why *Eurodollar* markets were the first to develop. Today, the *Eurobond* market is an international market where bonds of various types, denominated in various national currencies, are issued and sold to customers located throughout the world. The customers are mainly public corporations, international organizations, and multinational enterprises. The *Eurocurrency* market is a market for short-term bank deposits and bank loans denominated in various currencies.

The increasing sophistication of information transfer has led to a breakdown of the high degree of specialization that characterized financial markets in earlier decades. When information was difficult to obtain and analyse, an efficient division of labour called for a host of specialist institutions, each with expertise in a narrow range of transactions. As a result of the new developments in communication technology, economies of large scale led to the

integration of various financial operations within one firm. For example, in Canada and many other countries, banks will sell you securities (in mutual funds) and, similarly, the mutual-fund companies will now sell you banking services. As the scale of such integrated firms increases, these firms find it easier to extend their operations geographically as well as functionally.

The forces of globalization and Canadian banks' perceived need to achieve larger scale in order to compete successfully against larger foreign-based banks led the four largest Canadian chartered banks to attempt to merge in 1998 (Royal Bank with Bank of Montreal, and CIBC with Toronto Dominion). The proposed mergers, however, were prevented by the Canadian government on the grounds that they would unduly lessen competition in the Canadian banking industry. Many critics argue that globalization has made the eventual consolidation of Canadian banks all but inevitable. Globalization, they argue, means that governments that are slow to relax their regulations will see their country's financial firms lose ground to fierce international competitors.

Whether Canadian banks will merge, and to what extent the Canadian financial-services industry will be opened-up to further international competition, is yet to be determined. But it is clear that the globalization of financial markets is real and is showing no signs of slowing down.

Dramatic reductions in communications costs over the past few decades have meant that financial markets in one country are closely linked to those in the rest of the world.

Interbank Activities

Commercial banks have a number of interbank cooperative relationships. For example, banks often share loans. Even the biggest bank cannot meet all the credit needs of a giant corporation, and often a group of banks will offer a "pool loan," agreeing on common terms and dividing the loan up into manageable segments.

Another form of interbank cooperation is the bank credit card. Visa and MasterCard are the two most widely used credit cards, and each is operated by a group of banks.

Probably the most important form of interbank cooperation is cheque clearing and collection. Bank deposits are an effective medium of exchange only because banks accept each other's cheques. If a depositor in the Bank of Montreal writes a cheque to someone who deposits it in the Toronto Dominion Bank, the Bank of Montreal now owes money to the Toronto Dominion Bank. This creates a need for the banks to present cheques to each other for payment. The same is true for transactions made with bank ATM cards.

Millions of such transactions take place in the course of a day, and they result in an enormous sorting and bookkeeping job. Multibank systems make use of a **clearing house** where interbank debts are settled. At the end of the day, all the cheques drawn by the Bank of Montreal's customers and deposited in the Toronto Dominion Bank are totalled and set against the total of all the cheques drawn by the Toronto Dominion's customers and deposited in the Bank of Montreal. It is necessary only to settle the difference between the two sums. The actual cheques are passed through the clearing house back to the bank on which they were drawn. Both banks are then able to adjust the individual accounts by a set of book entries. A flow of cash between banks is necessary only when there is a net transfer of cash from the customers of one bank to those of another. This flow of cash is accompanied by a daily transfer of deposits held by the chartered banks with the Bank of Canada.

See Chapter 26 of www.pearsoned.ca/lipsey for an interview with the Royal Bank's Chairman on the need for bank mergers: "A Case for Bank Mergers," *World Economic Affairs.*

clearing house   An institution where interbank indebtedness, arising from the transfer of cheques between banks, is computed and offset and net amounts owing are calculated.

Banks as Profit Seekers

Banks are private firms that seek to make profits in the same sense as firms making neckties or bicycles. A chartered bank provides a variety of services to its customers: a safe place to store money, the convenience of demand deposits that can be transferred by personal cheque or a debit card, a safe and convenient place to earn a modest but guaranteed return on savings, and often financial advice and estate-management services.

Table 26-2 is the combined balance sheet of the chartered banks in Canada. The bulk of a bank's liabilities are deposits owed to its depositors. The principal assets of a bank are

TABLE 26-2   Consolidated Balance Sheet of the Canadian Chartered Banks, February 1999 (millions of dollars)

Assets		Liabilities	
Reserves (including deposits with Bank of Canada)	3 865	Demand deposits	56 310
Government of Canada securities	74 673	Savings deposits	292 499
Mortgage and nonmortgage loans	536 439	Time deposits	131 165
Canadian securities (corporate and provincial		Government of Canada deposits	5 976
and municipal governments)	66 462	Foreign-currency liabilities	636 120
Foreign-currency assets	612 931	Shareholders' equity	61 238
Other assets	95 141	Other liabilities	206 203
Total	1 389 511	Total	1 389 511

Reserves are only a tiny fraction of deposit liabilities. If all the commercial banks' customers who held demand deposits tried to withdraw them in cash, the banks could not meet this demand without liquidating about $52 billion of other assets. This would be impossible without assistance from the Bank of Canada.

(*Source: Bank of Canada Review*, Spring 1999.)

the *securities* it owns (including government bonds), which pay interest or dividends, and the interest-earning *loans* it makes to individuals and to businesses. A bank loan is a liability to the borrower (who must pay it back) but an asset to the bank.

Banks attract deposits by paying interest to depositors and by providing them with services such as clearing cheques, automatic-teller machines, debit cards, and the provision of regular monthly statements. Banks earn profits by lending and investing money deposited with them for more than they pay their depositors in terms of interest and other services provided.

Competition for Deposits

Competition for deposits is active among banks and between banks and other financial institutions. Financial deregulation, which removed restrictions on the activities of various financial institutions, has contributed to this competition. Interest paid on deposits, special high-interest certificates of deposit (CDs), advertising, personal solicitation of accounts, giveaway programs for new deposits to existing accounts, and improved services are all forms of competition for funds. Among the special services are payroll-accounting and pension-accounting schemes for corporate customers. Banks also establish locked deposit-boxes in which retail customers of large companies send their payments, with the bank then crediting them to the company's account. All of these services are costly to the bank, but they serve as inducements for customers to make deposits.

Reserves

All bankers would as a matter of convenience and prudence keep sufficient cash on hand to be able to meet depositors' day-to-day requirements for cash. However, just as the goldsmiths of long ago discovered that only a fraction of the gold they held was ever withdrawn at any given time and, just as banks of long ago discovered that only a small fraction of convertible bank notes was actually converted, so too do modern bankers know that only a small fraction of their deposits will be withdrawn in cash at any one time.

The reserves needed to assure that depositors can withdraw their deposits on demand will be quite small in normal times.

In abnormal times, however, nothing short of 100 percent would do the job if the commercial banking system had to stand alone. When a few bank failures cause a general loss of confidence in banks' ability to redeem their deposits, the results can be devastating. Until relatively recently, such an event—or even the rumour of it—could lead to a "run" on banks as depositors rushed to withdraw their money. Faced with such a panic, banks would have to close until they had borrowed enough funds or sold enough assets to meet the demand or until the demand subsided. However, banks could not instantly turn their loans into cash because the borrowers would have the money tied up in such things as real estate or business enterprises. Neither could the banks obtain cash by selling their securities to the public because payments would be made by cheques, which would not provide cash to pay off depositors.

The difficulty of providing sufficient reserves to meet abnormal situations is alleviated by the central bank. Because it controls the supply of bank reserves, the central bank can provide all the reserves that are needed to meet any abnormal situation. It can do this in two ways. First, it can lend reserves directly to commercial banks on the security of assets that are sound but not easy to liquidate quickly, such as interest-earning residential or commercial mortgages. Second, it can enter the open market and buy all the securities that commercial banks need to sell. Once the public finds that deposits can be turned into cash, any panic will usually subside and any further drain of cash out of banks will cease.

The possibility of panic withdrawals is also greatly diminished by the provision of deposit insurance, provided in Canada by the Canada Deposit Insurance Corporation (CDIC), a crown corporation. The CDIC guarantees that depositors will get their money back even if a bank fails completely. Most depositors will not withdraw their money as long as they are certain they can get it when they need it. Although deposit insurance confers a number of benefits on the operation of the financial system, it has also been subject to considerable criticism in recent years. This is explored in more detail in *Applying Economic Concepts 26-3*.

Target Reserves

We have seen that commercial banks hold reserves in order to meet temporary cash drains that arise when a bank's payments exceed its receipts. Receipts occur when the bank's customers deposit either cash or cheques drawn on other banks; payments are required either when cheques drawn by the bank's customers are deposited in other banks or when customers make cash withdrawals. A bank with no access to reserves will be unable to meet even a temporary cash drain and will be forced to suspend payments. This is something that banks must avoid at almost any cost, so that banking panics can be avoided.

A bank's **reserve ratio** is the fraction of its deposit liabilities that it *actually* holds as reserves, either as cash or as deposits with the central bank. A bank's **target reserve ratio** is the fraction of its deposits it *wishes* to hold as reserves.

In the past, legislation contained in the Bank Act required the chartered banks to hold reserves. These requirements were thought necessary to ensure the stability of the banking system. The reserves that the Bank Act required the banks to hold were called *required reserves*. Starting in the early 1980s, however, Canadian banks argued that the legal requirement to hold some of their assets as non-interest-bearing reserves placed them at a disadvantage relative to their competitors that were not subject to such requirements. The competitors included both foreign commercial banks and Canadian nonbank financial institutions, such as trust companies and credit unions. Globalization of financial markets had brought domestic financial institutions into direct competition with foreign ones, and continuing deregulation of financial markets had enhanced the competition between banks and nonbank financial institutions. After much deliberation, the government responded to these complaints by phasing out all legal reserve requirements early in the 1990s.

Despite the fact that Canadian banks are no longer legally required to hold reserves against their deposits, the banks' actual reserve ratio is greater than zero. Commercial banks hold some reserves for the simple reason that it is quite costly for them to borrow funds from the Bank of Canada to make up for any shortfall they may have. (Commercial banks pay the bank rate on any overdrafts from the Bank of Canada.)

Look again at Table 26-2. Notice that the banking system's cash reserves of just under $4 billion are less than one-half of 1 percent of its total liabilities of almost $1.4 trillion. If the holders of even 5 percent of its deposits demanded cash, the banks would be unable to meet the demand without outside help. Reserves can be as low as they are because the banks know that the Bank of Canada will help them out in time of temporary need. The Canadian banking system is thus a **fractional-reserve system,** with commercial banks holding reserves—either as cash or as deposits at the Bank of Canada—of much less than 100 percent of their deposits.

reserve ratio The fraction of its deposits that a commercial bank holds as reserves in the form of cash or deposits with a central bank.

target reserve ratio The fraction of its deposits that a commercial bank wants to hold as reserves.

fractional-reserve system A banking system in which commercial banks keep only a fraction of their deposits in cash or on deposit with the central bank.

APPLYING ECONOMIC CONCEPTS 26-3

Deposit Insurance and the Financial System

Deposit insurance, provided in Canada by the government-owned Canada Deposit Insurance Corporation (CDIC), assures depositors that their funds are secure whatever the fate of their deposit institution. This is a great boon for depositors, but experience has shown that it is a double-edged sword.

The obvious benefit of deposit insurance is that it provides security to depositors. This greater security makes it less likely that a bank panic will start, thereby increasing the stability of the financial system.

On the other hand, deposit insurance creates an incentive for banks to pursue riskier investments than they would if depositors had to worry about losing their deposits should the institution fail. Because of deposit insurance, depositors have no reason to select banks according to the riskiness of their investments. They are free instead to select the bank that pays the highest interest without worrying about the associated risk.

Deposit insurance is thus an example of an important class of government institutions that create situations whereby "heads the private investor wins, tails the taxpayer loses." Financial institutions take in depositors' insured funds; if the owners place them in risky ventures that pay off, the owners get the profits; if the owners place the funds in ventures that fail often enough to bring down the whole institution, the taxpayers must meet the bill by repaying those who provided the capital (the depositors). Canadian financial institutions have occasionally failed, including two western banks in the mid 1980s. When those institutions went under, depositors were repaid by the CDIC. Although the legal ceiling on deposit insurance was $60 000, deposits in excess of that amount were also repaid, using taxpayer money. This created the precedent that ceilings on deposit insurance were not to

be taken seriously. Any amount would be likely to be repaid. Hence, no investor need worry about the financial probity of the investments made by the institutions in which his or her money was deposited.

Two types of reforms are possible. One type would keep deposit insurance and provide the necessary accompanying regulations. The implications of deposit insurance for the investment behaviour of financial intermediaries suggest that if deposit insurance is to be maintained, other regulations concerning capital requirements and investment standards need to be applied. In addition, the deposit insurance system might be reformed in order to relate the cost of insurance for a particular institution to the risks implied by that institution's asset position.

The other type of reform would take deregulation to its logical conclusion of ending deposit insurance. Many economists believe that if deregulation of financial institutions is regarded as desirable, it should be accompanied by a removal of deposit insurance, so that the people who use the funds will be accountable to those who provide them.

The Canada Deposit Insurance Corporation guarantees depositors that their deposits (up to a limit) are secure no matter what happens to the financial institution accepting their deposit.

In Chapter 28 we will study how the Bank of Canada can influence the money supply under a zero required reserve system after we have examined how the money supply is itself determined. Our analysis of the money supply process is based on the following behaviour of the commercial banks:

Commercial banks strive to maintain some target ratio of reserves to deposits. In the past, this target ratio was legally imposed; today, it is determined by the banks themselves.

excess reserves
Reserves held by a commercial bank in excess of its target reserves.

Any reserves in excess of target reserves are called **excess reserves**. All that matters for what follows is that there is some target reserve ratio, no matter how small.

Money Creation by the Banking System

We noted before that the *money supply* refers to both currency and deposits at commercial banks. The fractional-reserve system provides the leverage that permits commercial banks to create new deposits, and thus to create new money. The process is important, so it is worth examining in some detail.

Some Simplifying Assumptions

To focus on the essential aspects of how banks create money, suppose that banks can invest in only one kind of asset—loans—and that there is only one kind of deposit—a demand deposit.

Two other assumptions are provisional. When we have developed the basic ideas concerning the banks' creation of money, these assumptions will be relaxed.

1. *Fixed reserve ratio*. We assume that all banks have the same target reserve ratio which does not change. In our numerical illustration, we will assume that the target reserve ratio is 20 percent (0.20); that is, for every $5 of deposits the banks wish to hold $1 in cash reserves, investing the rest in new loans.

2. *No cash drain from the banking system*. We also assume that the public holds a fixed amount of currency in circulation. Thus any transfers of funds between individuals will not cause changes in the total amount of currency available for the banks to hold as reserves.

The Creation of Deposit Money

A hypothetical balance sheet, showing assets and liabilities, is shown for the Toronto Dominion (TD) Bank in Table 26-3. TD has assets of $200 of reserves, held partly as cash on hand and partly as deposits with the central bank, and $900 of loans outstanding to its customers. Its liabilities are $100 to investors who contributed capital to start the bank and $1000 to current depositors. The bank's ratio of reserves to deposits is 0.20 (200/1000), exactly equal to its target reserve ratio.

TABLE 26-3 The Initial Balance Sheet of the Toronto Dominion (TD) Bank

Assets ($)		Liabilities ($)	
Cash and other reserves	200	Deposits	1000
Loans	900	Capital	100
	1100		1100

The TD Bank has a reserve of 20 percent of its deposit liabilities. The commercial bank earns money by finding profitable investments for much of the money deposited with it. In this balance sheet, loans are its earning assets.

New Deposits

In what follows, we are interested in knowing how the commercial banking system can "create money" when confronted with a new deposit. But what do we mean by a new deposit? By "new," we mean a deposit of cash that is new to the *commercial banking system*. There are three examples. First, an individual might immigrate to Canada and bring cash with them. When that cash is deposited into a commercial bank, it constitutes a new deposit to the (Canadian) banking system. A second example is an individual that had some cash stashed under his bed (or in a safe-deposit box) and who has now decided to deposit it into an account at a commercial bank. The final example is the most interesting, but is also the most complicated. If the Bank of Canada were to purchase a government security from an individual or from a firm, it would purchase that asset with a cheque drawn on the Bank of Canada. When the individual or firm deposits the cheque with their commercial bank, it would be a new deposit to the commercial banking system.

The important point to keep in mind here is that the *source* of the new deposit is irrelevant to the process of money creation by the commercial banks. In the discussion that follows, we use the example of the Bank of Canada buying government securities from firms or households as a way of generating a new deposit. But this is not central. We use this example because, as we shall see in Chapter 28, this is one way that the Bank of Canada conducts its monetary policy. But the general process of money creation that we are about to describe applies to *any* new deposit.

A Single New Deposit

Suppose that the Bank of Canada buys $100 worth of securities on the open market. It issues a cheque to the seller, and that individual or firm opens an account with TD and deposits the $100 cheque. This is a wholly new deposit for the commercial bank, and it results in a revised balance sheet (Table 26-4). As a result of the new deposit, TD's cash assets and deposit liabilities have both increased by $100. More important, TD's ratio of reserves to deposits has increased from 0.20 to 0.27 (300/1100). The bank now has $80 in excess reserves; with $1100 in deposits, its target reserves are only $220.

TD can now lend the $80 in excess reserves that it is holding. Table 26-5 shows the position after this has been done and after the proceeds of the loan have been withdrawn to be deposited to the account of a customer of another bank. TD once again has a 20 percent reserve ratio.

So far, of the $100 initial deposit at TD, $20 is held by TD as reserves against the deposit and $80 has been lent out in the system. As a result, other banks have received new deposits of $80 stemming from the loans made by TD; persons receiving payment from those who borrowed the $80 from TD will have deposited those payments in their own banks. Note that even though the *banking system* suffers no cash drain, TD does suffer a cash drain because most of the $80 goes to other banks and is not redeposited at TD.

The banks that receive deposits from the proceeds of TD's loan are called second-round banks, third-round banks, and so on. In this case, the second-round banks receive new deposits of $80, and when the cheques clear, they have new reserves of $80. Because they desire to hold only $16 in additional reserves to support the new deposits, they have $64 of excess reserves. They now increase their loans by $64. After this money has been spent by the borrowers and has

TABLE 26-4   TD's Balance Sheet Immediately After a New Deposit of $100

Assets ($)		Liabilities ($)	
Cash and other reserves	300	Deposits	1100
Loans	900	Capital	100
	1200		1200

The deposit raises liabilities and assets by the same amount. Because both cash and deposits rise by $100, the bank's actual reserve ratio, formerly 0.20, increases to 0.27. The bank has excess reserves.

TABLE 26-5   TD's Balance Sheet After Making a New Loan of $80

Assets ($)		Liabilities ($)	
Cash and other reserves	220	Deposits	1100
Loans	980	Capital	100
	1200		1200

TD lends its surplus cash and suffers a cash drain. The bank keeps $20 as a reserve against the initial new deposit of $100. It lends $80 to a customer, who writes a cheque to someone who deals with another bank. When the cheque is cleared, TD suffers an $80 cash drain. Comparing Tables 26-3 and 26-5 shows that the bank has increased its deposit liabilities by the $100 initially deposited and has increased its assets by $20 of cash reserves and $80 of new loans. It has also restored its target reserve ratio of 0.20.

been deposited in other, third-round banks, the balance sheets of the second-round banks will have changed, as in Table 26-6.

The third-round banks now find themselves with $64 of new deposits. Against these they want to hold only $12.80 as reserves, so they have excess reserves of $51.20 that they can immediately lend out. Thus, there begins a long sequence of new deposits, new loans, new deposits, and new loans. These stages are shown in Table 26-7.

The banking system has created new deposits and thus new money, although each banker can honestly say, "All I did was invest my excess reserves. I can do no more than manage wisely the money that I receive." At the end of the process depicted in Table 26-7, the change in the combined balance sheets of the entire banking system is shown in Table 26-8.

If v is the target reserve ratio, the ultimate effect on the deposits of the banking system of a new deposit will be $1/v$ times the new deposit. [32]

In our example in which there was an initial new deposit of $100, this $100 was also the amount by which reserves increased in the banking system as a whole. This is because the entire amount of new cash eventually ends up in reserves held against a much larger volume of new deposits. Identifying a new deposit as the change in reserves in the banking system permits us to state our central result slightly differently.

With no cash drain from the banking system, a banking system with a target reserve ratio of v can change its deposits by $1/v$ times any change in reserves.

Recalling that the Greek letter delta, Δ, means "the change in," we can express this result in a simple equation. We have

$$\Delta \text{ Deposits} = \frac{\Delta \text{ Reserves}}{v}$$

The "multiple expansion of deposits" that we have just described applies in reverse to a withdrawal of funds. Deposits of the banking system will fall by $1/v$ times the amount withdrawn from the banking system.

Excess Reserves and Cash Drains

The two simplifying assumptions that were made earlier can now be relaxed.

TABLE 26-6 Changes in the Balance Sheets of Second-Round Banks

Assets ($)		Liabilities ($)	
Cash and other reserves	+16	Deposits	+80
Loans	+64		
	+80		+80

Second-round banks receive cash deposits and expand loans. The second-round banks gain new deposits of $80 as a result of the loan granted by TD. These banks keep 20 percent of the cash that they acquire as their reserve against the new deposit, and they can make new loans using the other 80 percent.

TABLE 26-7 The Sequence of Loans and Deposits After a Single New Deposit of $100

Bank	New Deposits	New Loans	Addition to Reserves
TD	100.00	80.00	20.00
2nd-round bank	80.00	64.00	16.00
3rd-round bank	64.00	51.20	12.80
4th-round bank	51.20	40.96	10.24
5th-round bank	40.96	32.77	8.19
6th-round bank	32.77	26.22	6.55
7th-round bank	26.22	20.98	5.24
8th-round bank	20.98	16.78	4.20
9th-round bank	16.78	13.42	3.36
10th-round bank	13.42	10.74	2.68
Total for first 10 rounds	446.33	357.07	89.26
All remaining rounds	53.67	42.93	10.74
Total for banking system	500.00	400.00	100.00

The banking system as a whole can create deposit money whenever it receives new deposits. The table shows the process of the creation of deposit money on the assumptions that all the loans made by one set of banks end up as deposits in another set of banks (the next-round banks), that the target reserve ratio (v) is 0.20, and that banks always lend out any excess reserves. Although each bank suffers a cash drain whenever it grants a new loan, the system as a whole does not, and in a series of steps it increases deposit money by $1/v$, which, in this example, is five times the amount of any increase in reserves that it obtains.

Practise with Study Guide Chapter 26, Exercise 4.

Excess Reserves

If banks do not choose to invest their excess reserves, the multiple expansion that we discussed will not occur. Go back to Table 26-4. If TD had been content to hold 27 percent in reserves, it might well have done nothing more. Other things being equal, banks will choose to invest their excess reserves because of the profit motive, but there may be times when they believe that the risk is too great. It is one thing to be offered a good rate of interest on a loan, but if the borrower defaults on the payment of interest and principal, the bank will be the loser. Similarly, if the bank expects interest rates to rise in the future, it may hold off making loans now so that it will have reserves available to make more profitable loans after the interest rate has risen.

Deposit creation does not happen automatically; it depends on the decisions of bankers. If banks do not choose to use their excess reserves to expand their investments, there will not be an expansion of deposits.

Recall that we have said that the money supply includes both currency and bank deposits. What we have just seen is that the behaviour of commercial banks is central to the process of deposit creation. It follows that the money supply is thus at least partly determined by the commercial banks—in response, for example, to changes in national income, interest rates, and expectations of future business conditions.

Cash Drain

Practise with Study Guide Chapter 26, Exercise 6.

Suppose that firms and households find it convenient to keep a fixed *fraction* of their money holdings in cash (say, 5 percent) instead of a fixed *number* of dollars. In that case, an extra $100 that gets injected into the banking system will not all stay in the banking system—only $95 will remain on deposit, and the rest will be added to currency in circulation. In such a situation, any multiple expansion of bank deposits will be accompanied by a cash drain to the public. This cash drain will reduce the maximum expansion below what it was when the public was content to hold all its new money as bank deposits.

In the case of a cash drain, the relationship between the eventual change in deposits and an injection of cash into the banking system is slightly more complicated. If $X is injected into the system then ultimately reserves will increase by $X. But if c is the ratio of cash to deposits that people want to maintain, the final change in deposits will be given by: [33]

$$\Delta \text{Deposits} = \frac{\Delta \text{Reserves}}{c + v}$$

For example, suppose the Bank of Canada were to enter the open market and purchase $1000 of government securities. As the previous bondholders deposit their $1000 into their bank accounts, there is an injection of $1000 into the banking system. If commercial banks' target reserve ratio was 10 percent and there was *no* cash drain, the eventual expansion of deposits would be $10 000 ($\Delta$Deposits = $1000/0.10). But if there were also a cash drain of 10 percent, the eventual expansion of deposits would only be $5000 ($\Delta$Deposits = $1000/(0.10 + 0.10)).

Assets ($)		Liabilities ($)	
Cash and other reserves	+100	Deposits	+500
Loans	+400		
	+500		+500

TABLE 26-8   Change in the Combined Balance Sheets of All the Banks in the System Following the Multiple Expansion of Deposits

The reserve ratio is returned to 0.20. The entire initial deposit of $100 ends up as reserves of the banking system. Therefore, deposits rise by (1/0.2) times the initial deposit—that is, by $500.

The Money Supply

Several times in this chapter we have mentioned the *money supply* without ever defining it precisely. But now that you are familiar with the balance sheets of the Bank of Canada and the commercial banking system, and are comfortable with the idea of deposit creation by the commercial banks, we are ready to be more precise about what we mean by the money supply.

The total stock of money in the economy at any moment is called the **money supply** or the *supply of money*. Economists use several alternative definitions for the money supply, most of which are regularly reported in the *Bank of Canada Review*—a quarterly publication of the Bank of Canada. Each definition of the money supply includes the amount of currency in circulation *plus* some types of deposit liabilities of the financial institutions. The different definitions vary only by which deposit liabilities are included. We begin by looking at the different kinds of deposits.

money supply The total quantity of money in an economy at a point in time. Also called the *supply of money*.

Kinds of Deposits

Over the past 20 years or so, banks have evolved a bewildering array of different types of deposits. From our point of view, the most important distinction is between deposits that can be transferred by cheque, called "chequable," and those that cannot, called "nonchequable." Chequable deposits are media of exchange; nonchequable ones are not.

Until recently, the distinction lay between *demand deposits*, which earned little or no interest but were chequable, and *savings deposits*, which earned a higher interest return but were nonchequable.

Today, however, it is so easy to transfer funds from accounts that are technically nonchequable to other accounts that are chequable that the distinction becomes quite blurred. The deposit that is genuinely tied up for a period of time now takes the form of a **term deposit**, which has a specified withdrawal date, a minimum of 30 days into the future, and which pays a much reduced interest rate in the event of early withdrawal. Term and other nonchequable deposits pay significantly higher interest rates than do chequable deposits.

term deposit An interest-earning bank deposit, legally subject to notice before withdrawal (in practice, the notice requirement is not normally enforced).

Nonbank financial institutions such as brokerage firms now offer *money market mutual funds* and *money market deposit accounts*. These accounts earn high interest and are chequable, although some are subject to minimum withdrawal restrictions and others to prior notice of withdrawal.

The long-standing distinction between money and other highly liquid assets used to be that, narrowly defined, money was a medium of exchange that did not earn interest, whereas other liquid assets earned interest but were not media of exchange. Today, this distinction has almost completely broken down.

Definitions of the Money Supply

Different definitions of the money supply include different types of deposits. The narrowly defined money supply, called **M1**, includes currency and deposits that are themselves usable as media of exchange (such as chequable deposits). A broader definition, **M2**,

M1 Currency plus demand deposits plus other chequable deposits.

M2 M1 plus saving deposits at the chartered banks.

M2+   M2 plus deposits held at institutions that are *not* chartered banks.

includes M1 plus savings accounts at the chartered banks. A still broader measure, **M2+**, includes M2 plus the deposits held at the financial institutions that are *not* chartered banks, such as trust companies and credit unions.

M1 concentrates on the medium-of-exchange function of money. M2 and M2+ contain assets that serve the temporary store-of-value function and are in practice quickly convertible into a medium of exchange. Table 26-9 shows the principal elements in these definitions of the money supply. The details of the differences are not important at this stage; what matters is that, broadly defined, money comprises a spectrum of closely related financial assets that their holders regard as highly substitutable for each other.

TABLE 26-9   Three Measures of the Money Supply in Canada, January 1999 (millions of dollars)

Currency	30 016
+ Demand deposits	52 490
= M1	82 506
+ Personal saving deposits and nonpersonal notice deposits	325 791
= M2	408 297
+ Deposits at trust and mortgage loan companies, credit unions, and caisses populaires	144 702
+ Money market mutual funds and deposits at other institutions	85 694
= M2+	638 693

The three widely used measures of the money supply are M1, M2, and M2+. The narrowest definition, M1, concentrates on what can be used directly as media of exchange, and thus includes only currency and demand deposits. The broader definitions then add in deposits that serve the store-of-value function but can be readily converted to a medium of exchange. M2 is thus M1 plus saving deposits. M2+ is M2 plus deposits at the nonbank financial institutions.

(*Source: Bank of Canada Review,* Spring 1999.)

Near Money and Money Substitutes

Over the past two centuries, what has been accepted by the public as money has expanded from gold and silver coins to include bank notes and bank deposits subject to transfer by cheque. Until recently, most economists would have agreed that money stopped at that point. No such agreement exists today.

The problem of deciding what constitutes money arises because some assets may provide relatively poor ways to meet the store-of-value function whereas others may perform poorly as media of exchange. For example, during times of high inflation, currency may serve well as a medium of exchange but poorly as a store of value (because the rising price level erodes the purchasing power of cash). In contrast, heavy gold bars may serve well as a store of value but poorly as a medium of exchange (because they are both heavy and difficult to divide into small units).

If we concentrate only on the medium-of-exchange function of money, money certainly consists of the assets included in M1, and most economists would argue that it extends to those included in M2 and M2+. Some of these assets that are effective media of exchange, however, are poor stores of value because they earn little or no interest. Assets that earn higher interest—like term deposits—will do a better job of meeting the store-of-value function than will currency or demand deposits. At the same time, however, these other assets are less capable of fulfilling the medium-of-exchange function.

Assets that fulfill adequately the store-of-value function and are readily converted into a medium of exchange but are not themselves a medium of exchange are sometimes called **near money**. Term deposits are a characteristic form of near money. When you have such a term deposit, you know exactly how much purchasing power you hold (at current prices), and, given modern banking practices, you can turn your deposit into a medium of exchange—cash or a chequing deposit—at a moment's notice (though you may pay a penalty in the form of reduced interest if you withdraw the funds before the end of the specified term).

near money   Liquid assets that are easily convertible into money without risk of significant loss of value and can be used as short-term stores of purchasing power but are not themselves media of exchange.

Why then does everybody not keep his or her money in such deposits instead of in demand deposits or currency? The answer is that the inconvenience of continually shifting money back and forth may outweigh the interest that can be earned. One week's interest on $100 (at 10 percent per year) is only about 20 cents, not enough to cover bus fare to the trust company, the cost of mailing a letter, or the time lining up at an automatic teller machine. For money that will be needed soon, it would hardly pay to shift it to a term deposit.

In general, whether it pays to convert cash or chequable deposits into higher interest-earning term deposits for a given period will depend on the inconvenience and other transactions costs of shifting funds and on the amount of interest that can be earned.

Things that serve as temporary media of exchange but are not a store of value are sometimes called **money substitutes**. Credit cards are a prime example. With a credit card, many transactions can be made without either cash or a cheque. The evidence of credit, the credit slip you sign and hand over to the store, is not money, because it cannot be used to make other transactions. The credit card serves the short-run function of a medium of exchange by allowing you to make purchases, even though you have no cash or bank deposit currently in your possession. But this is only temporary; money remains the final medium of exchange for these transactions when the credit account is settled.

money substitute
Something that serves as a temporary medium of exchange but is not a store of value.

Choosing a Measure

Since the eighteenth century, economists have known that the amount of money in circulation is an important economic variable. As theories became more carefully specified in the nineteenth and early twentieth centuries, they included a variable called the "money supply." But for theories to be useful (and especially for the predictions to be testable), we must be able to identify real-world counterparts of these theoretical variables.

The specifics of the definition of money have changed and will continue to change over time. New monetary assets are continually being developed to serve some, if not all, of the functions of money, and they are more or less readily convertible into money. There is no single, timeless definition of money and what is only near money or a money substitute. Indeed, as we have seen, the Bank of Canada uses several definitions of money, and these definitions change from year to year.

The Role of the Bank of Canada

In this chapter, we have seen that the commercial banking system, when confronted with a new deposit, can create a multiple expansion of bank deposits. This shows how the reserves of the banking system are systematically related to the money supply. We have also seen a glimpse of how the Bank of Canada can affect the reserves of the banking system—we will see in Chapter 28 that the Bank of Canada has almost complete control over these reserves. Thus, the Bank of Canada controls reserves, and the commercial banking system turns those reserves into bank deposits.

This is the basis for the view taken throughout the remainder of this book that the Bank of Canada controls the money supply. In the next two chapters, we examine how the Bank uses this power to conduct monetary policy, and how monetary policy affects interest rates, real GDP, and the price level.

S U M M A R Y

Two Perspectives on Money

- Early economists regarded the economy as being divided into a real sector and a monetary sector. The real sector is concerned with production, allocation of resources, and distribution of income, determined by relative prices. The level of prices at which all transactions take place is determined by the monetary sector—that is, by the demand for and supply of money. With the demand for money being constant, an increase in the money supply would cause all equilibrium money prices to increase, but relative prices, and hence everything in the real sector, would be left unaffected.

- Today, most economists do not hold the view that changes in the money supply will only affect the price level, except as a description of the economy in long-run equilibrium. Most economists believe that changes in the supply of money have important short-run effects on real GDP, employment, and unemployment.

The Nature of Money

- A number of functions of money may be distinguished. Generally, money acts as a medium of exchange, a store of value, and a unit of account.

- Money arose because of the inconvenience of barter, and it developed in stages: from precious metal to metal coinage, to paper money convertible to precious metals, to token coinage and paper money fractionally backed by precious metals, to fiat money, and to deposit money. Societies have shown great sophistication in developing monetary instruments to meet their needs.

The Canadian Banking System

- The banking system in Canada consists of two main elements: the Bank of Canada (which is the central bank) and the commercial banks. The Bank of Canada is a publicly owned corporation that is responsible for the day-to-day conduct of monetary policy. Though the Bank has considerable autonomy in its policy decisions, ultimate responsibility for monetary policy resides with the government.

- Commercial banks are profit-seeking institutions that allow their customers to transfer demand deposits from one bank to another by means of cheques or debit cards. They create money as a by-product of their commercial operations by making or liquidating loans and various other investments.

Money Creation by the Banking System

- Because most customers are content to pay by cheque or debit card rather than with cash, banks need only small reserves to back their deposit liabilities. It is this *fractional-reserve* aspect of the banking system that enables commercial banks to create deposit money.

- When the banking system receives a new cash deposit, it can create new deposits to some multiple of this amount. The amount of new deposits created depends on the banks' target reserve ratio, the amount of cash drain to the public, and whether the banks choose to hold excess reserves.

The Money Supply

- The money supply—the stock of money in an economy at a specific moment—can be defined in various ways. M1, the narrowest definition, includes currency and chequable deposits. M2 includes M1 plus savings deposits and smaller term deposits. M2+ includes M2 plus deposits at non-bank financial institutions and money-market mutual funds.

- Near money includes interest-earning assets that are convertible into money on a dollar-for-dollar basis but that are not currently included in the definition of money. Money substitutes are things such as credit cards that temporarily serve as a medium of exchange but are not money.

KEY CONCEPTS

The real and monetary sectors of the economy
Medium of exchange, store of value, and unit of account
Fully backed, fractionally backed, and fiat money

The banking system and the Bank of Canada
Target reserve ratio and excess reserves
The creation of deposit money

Demand and term deposits
The money supply
Near money and money substitutes

STUDY EXERCISES

1. Which of the following items can be considered money in the Canadian economy? Explain your answers by discussing the three functions of money—medium of exchange, store of value, and unit of account.

   a. A $100 Bank of Canada note
   b. A Visa credit card
   c. A well-known painting by Robert Bateman
   d. An interest-earning savings account
   e. A U.S. Treasury bill payable in three months
   f. A share of Nortel stock

2. The table below shows the balance sheet for the Regal Bank, a hypothetical commercial bank. Assume that the Regal Bank has achieved its target reserve ratio.

   Balance Sheet: Regal Bank

Assets		Liabilities	
Reserves	$ 200	Deposits	$4000
Loans	$4200	Capital	$ 400

   a. What is the Regal Bank's target reserve ratio?
   b. What is the value of the owners' investment in the bank?
   c. Suppose that someone makes a new deposit to the Regal Bank of $100. Draw a new balance sheet showing the *immediate* effect of the new deposit. What is the Regal Bank's new reserve ratio?

3. Consider a new deposit to the Canadian banking system of $1000. Suppose that all commercial banks have a target reserve ratio of 10 percent and there is no cash drain. The following table shows how deposits, reserves, and loans change as the new deposit permits the banks to "create" money.

Round	ΔDeposits	ΔReserves	ΔLoans
First	$1000	$100	$900
Second	—	—	—
Third	—	—	—
Fourth	—	—	—
Fifth	—	—	—

a. The first round has been completed in the table. Now, recalling that the new loans in the first round become the new deposits in the second round, complete the second round in the table.

b. Using the same approach, complete the entire table.

c. You have now completed the first five rounds of the deposit-creation process. What is the total change in deposits *so far* as a result of the single new deposit of $1000?

d. This deposit-creation process will go on forever, but it will have a *finite* sum. In the text, we showed that the eventual total change in deposits is equal to $1/v$ times the new deposit, where v is the target reserve ratio. What is the eventual total change in deposits in this case?

e. What is the eventual total change in reserves? What is the eventual change in loans?

4. Consider a new deposit of $5000 to the Canadian banking system. Suppose that all commercial banks have a target reserve ratio of 8 percent and that there is no cash drain.

a. Using a table like that shown in the previous question, show the change in deposits, reserves, and loans for the first three "rounds" of activity.

b. Compute the eventual total change in deposits, reserves, and loans.

5. Consider an individual who immigrates to Canada and deposits $3000 into the Canadian banking system. Suppose that all commercial banks have a target reserve ratio of 10 percent and that individuals choose to hold cash equal to 10 percent of their bank deposits.

a. In the text, we showed that the eventual total change in deposits is equal to $1/(v+c)$ times the new deposit, where v is the target reserve ratio and c is the ratio of cash to deposits. What is the eventual total change in deposits in this case?

b. What is the eventual total change in reserves?

c. What is the eventual total change in loans?

6. Consider an individual who moves from Europe to Canada and brings with him his life savings of $40 000, which he deposits in a Canadian bank. For each of the cases below, compute the overall change in deposits and reserves in the Canadian banking system as a result of this new deposit.

a. 10 percent target reserve ratio; no cash drain; no excess reserves

b. 10 percent target reserve ratio; 5 percent cash drain; no excess reserves

c. 10 percent target reserve ratio; 5 percent cash drain; 5 percent excess reserves

DISCUSSION QUESTIONS

1. A Canadian who receives a U.S. coin has the option of spending it at face value or taking it to the bank and converting it to Canadian money at the going rate of exchange. When the rate of exchange was near par (in the early 1970s), so that $1 Canadian was within 3 cents of $1 U.S., U.S. and Canadian coins circulated side by side, exchanged at face value. Use Gresham's law to predict which coinage disappeared from circulation in Canada when the Canadian dollar fell to 67cents U.S. Why did a 3-cent differential not produce this result?

2. During hyperinflations in several foreign countries after World War II, American cigarettes were sometimes used in place of money. What made them suitable?

3. Suppose that on January 1, 1999, a household had $100 000, which it wished to hold for use one year later. Calculate, using resources available, which of the following would have been the best store of value over that period. Will the best store of value over that period necessarily be the best over the next 24 months?

a. The (Canadian) dollar

b. Stocks whose prices moved with the Toronto Stock Exchange (TSE) 300

c. An Ontario Hydro 9.0 percent bond coming due in June 2002

d. Gold

4. If all depositors tried to turn their deposits into cash at once, they would find that there are not sufficient reserves in the system to allow all of them to do this at the same time. Why then do we not still have panicky runs on the banks? Would it be better for the Bank of Canada to impose a 100 percent reserve requirement? What effect would such a reserve requirement have on the banking system's ability to create money? Would it preclude any possibility of a panic?

5. Compared to a few years ago, credit and bank cards are used extensively today to facilitate purchase of goods and services all over the world. Does this distort the true measure of money in the economy? Should credit and bank cards be incorporated in the definitions of M1 or M2?

CHAPTER 27

Money, Output, and Prices

LO LEARNING OBJECTIVES

1. Explain how the present value of an asset is related to the market interest rate.

2. Know the three motives for holding money.

3. Understand how changes in the demand for money or the supply of money influence the interest rate.

4. Explain the transmission mechanism of monetary policy.

5. Distinguish between the short-run and long-run effects of changes in the money supply.

In Chapter 26, we saw how commercial banks lend their excess reserves to create bank deposits. The banking system transforms a given amount of reserves into the nation's money supply. We then concluded that chapter by saying that because the Bank of Canada can control the reserves in the banking system, the Bank of Canada effectively controls Canada's money supply. What we have not yet discussed, however, is how the Bank of Canada controls the reserves of the banking system. We leave that discussion until the next chapter when we discuss the details of monetary policy. For now, just think of the supply of money as being determined by the Bank of Canada.

In this chapter, we focus on how money affects the economy. Understanding the role of money, however, requires an understanding of the interaction of money supply and money demand. To examine the nature of money demand, we begin by examining how households decide to divide their total holdings of assets between money and interest-earning assets (which here are called "bonds"). Once that is done, we put money supply and money demand together to examine *monetary equilibrium*. Only then can we ask how changes in the supply of money or in the demand for money affect the economy—interest rates, real GDP, and the price level. We begin with a discussion of financial assets and interest rates.

Understanding Financial Assets

At any moment, households have a stock of wealth that they hold in many forms. Some of it is money in the bank or in the wallet, some may be in treasury bills and bonds, and some may be in stocks and shares.

Economists often simplify the analysis of financial assets by considering only two types of assets—money and bonds.

To simplify our discussion, we will group wealth into just two categories, which we call "money" and "bonds." By money we mean all assets that serve as a medium of exchange—that is, paper money, coins, and deposits on which cheques can be drawn. By bonds we mean all other forms of wealth; this includes interest-earning financial assets and claims on real capital (equity). This simplification can take us quite a long way because it serves to emphasize the important distinction between interest-earning and non-interest-earning assets. For some issues, however, it is necessary to treat debt and equity as distinct assets, in which case at least three categories—money, bonds, and stocks—are used. For our purposes, however, we continue with the simple division of wealth into either "money" or "bonds."

Present Value and the Interest Rate

present value (PV)
The value now of one or more payments or receipts made in the future; often referred to as *discounted present value*.

Recall from Chapter 26 that a bond is a financial asset that promises to make one or more specified payments at specified dates in the future. The **present value** *(PV)* of any asset refers to the value now of the future payments that the asset offers. Present value depends on the interest rate because when we calculate present value, the interest rate is used to *discount* the future payments. We can see this relationship between the interest rate and present value by considering two extreme examples.

A Single Payment One Year Hence

We start with the simplest case. How much would you be prepared to pay *now* to purchase a bond that will return a single payment of $100 in one year's time?

Suppose that the interest rate is 5 percent. Now ask how much you would have to lend out at that interest rate today in order to have $100 a year from now. If we use *PV* to stand for this unknown amount, we can write $PV \times (1.05) = \$100$. Thus, $PV = \$100/1.05 = \$95.24$.[1] This tells us that the present value of a $100 receivable in one year's time is $95.24; if you lend out $95.24 for one year at 5 percent interest you will get back the $95.24 plus $4.76 in interest, which makes $100.

What if the interest rate had been 7 percent? At that interest rate, the present value of the $100 receivable in one year's time would be $100/1.07 = $93.46, which is less than the present value when the interest rate was 5 percent.

A Perpetuity

Now consider another extreme case—a *perpetuity* that promises to pay $100 per year to its holder *forever*. The present value of the perpetuity depends on how much $100 per year is worth, and this again depends on the interest rate.

A bond that will produce a stream of income of $100 per year forever is worth $1000 at 10 percent interest because if you invest $1000 at 10 percent per year that investment will yield $100 interest per year forever. However, the same bond is worth

---

[1]Notice that in this type of formula, the interest rate is expressed as a decimal fraction where, for example, 5 percent is expressed as 0.05, so $1 + i$ equals 1.05.

$2000 when the interest rate is 5 percent per year because you must invest $2000 at 5 percent per year to get $100 interest per year.

A General Statement

Most bonds are not as simple as in these two extreme examples because they have several payments over many years and are then redeemable for cash. But the same basic relationship between interest rates and the present value of the asset applies.

The present value of any asset that yields a given stream of payments over time is negatively related to the interest rate.

Further details on the calculation of present value are given in *Extensions in Theory 27-1.*

Practise with Study Guide Chapter 27, Exercise 1.

Present Value and Market Price

Present value is important because it establishes the market price for an asset.

The present value of an asset is also the amount that someone would be willing to pay now to own the future stream of payments delivered by the asset.

To understand this concept, let us return to our example of a bond that promises to pay $100 one year from now. When the interest rate is 5 percent, the present value is $95.24. To see why this is the maximum that anyone would pay for this bond, suppose that some sellers offer to sell the bond at some other price, say, $98. If, instead of paying this amount for the bond, a potential buyer lends its $98 out at 5 percent interest, it would have at the end of one year more than the $100 that the bond will produce. (At 5 percent interest, $98 yields $4.90 in interest, which when added to the principal makes $102.90.) Clearly, no well-informed individual would pay $98—or, by the same reasoning, any sum in excess of $95.24—for the bond.

Now suppose that the bond is offered for sale at a price less than $95.24, say, $90. A potential buyer could borrow $90 to buy the bond and would pay $4.50 in interest on the loan. At the end of the year, the bond yields $100. When this is used to repay the $90 loan and the $4.50 in interest, $5.50 is left as profit. Clearly, it would be worthwhile for someone to buy the bond at the price of $90 or, by the same argument, at any price less than $95.24.

This discussion should make clear that the present value of an asset determines its market price. If the market price of any asset is greater than the present value of its income stream, no one will want to buy it, and this excess supply will push down the market price. If the market value is below its present value, there will be a rush to buy it, and this excess demand will push up the market price.

The equilibrium market price of any asset will be the present value of the income stream that it produces.

The Interest Rate and Market Price

The foregoing discussion leads us to two important propositions, both of which stress the negative relationship between interest rates and asset prices:

1. If the interest rate falls, the present value of an asset with a given income stream will rise.

EXTENSIONS IN THEORY 27-1

Calculating Present Value

An asset held now will generate a stream of returns in the future. What that stream of future income is worth now is called the asset's *present value (PV)*. This box provides some details concerning the calculation of present value that will prove helpful for understanding the material in the text.

The Present Value of a Single Future Payment

The numerical examples given in the text are easy to generalize. In calculating the present value of a payment one year hence, we divided the sum that is receivable in the future by 1 plus the rate of interest. In general, the present value of R dollars one year hence at an interest rate of i per year is

$$PV = \frac{R}{(1 + i)}$$

What happens to our calculation if the bond still offers a single future payment but the payment is receivable at a date later than one year from now? For example, what is the present value of $100 to be received *two* years hence if the interest rate is 5 percent? This is $100/(1.05 \times 1.05) = $90.70. We can check this answer by seeing what would happen if $90.70 were lent out for two years. In the first year the loan would earn interest of $0.05 \times $90.70 = $4.54, and hence after one year, the lender would receive $95.24. In the second year the interest would be earned on this entire amount; interest earned in the second year would thus equal $0.05 \times $95.24 = $4.76. Therefore, in two years the lender would have $100. (Payment of interest in the second year on the interest income earned in the first year is called *compound interest.*)

In general, the present value of R dollars received t years in the future at an interest rate of i percent is

$$PV = \frac{R}{(1 + i)^t}$$

This formula simply discounts the sum R by the interest rate i repeatedly—once for each of the t periods that pass until the sum becomes available. If we look at the for-

mula, we see that the higher is i or t, the higher is the whole term $(1 + i)^t$. This term, however, appears in the denominator, indicating that PV is *negatively* related to both i and t. (Try manipulating the formula yourself with different numbers to see that this is the case.)

The Present Value of a Sequence of Payments

Suppose now that we wish to calculate the present value of a bond that promises a sequence of payments for a given number of periods. Let R_1, R_2, R_3, and so on represent the payment promised after period 1, period 2, period 3, and so on, and let the last period for which a payment is promised be period T.

If we also suppose that the interest rate remains constant at i percent, the present value of this bond can be written as follows:

$$PV = \frac{R_1}{1 + i} + \frac{R_2}{(1 + i)^2} + \frac{R_3}{(1 + i)^3} + \ldots + \frac{R_T}{(1 + i)^T}$$

The Present Value of a Perpetual Stream of Payments

Now consider the value that a buyer would place on a perpetuity for R dollars—that is, on a bond that produces a stream of payments of R per year *forever*. To find the present value of R payable every year in the future, we ask how much money would have to be invested now at an interest rate of i per year to obtain R every year in the future. This present value is simply $i \times PV = R$, where PV is the sum required. In other words,

$$PV = \frac{R}{i}$$

Here, as before, PV is related to the rate of interest: The higher the interest rate, the less the present value of any particular stream of future receipts, and hence the lower the price that anyone would be prepared to pay to purchase the bond.

2. A rise in the market price of an asset with a given income stream is equivalent to a decrease in the rate of return earned by the asset.

The first proposition is illustrated by the following example. When the interest rate is 8 percent, you would have to pay $92.59 now for a bond promising to pay you $100 one year from now ($92.59 × 1.08 = $100). When the interest rate is 12 percent, you would have to pay $89.29 for the same bond ($89.29 × 1.12 = $100). Thus, the higher the interest rate, the lower the present value of the asset.

The second proposition is illustrated as follows. If you buy for $89.29 a bond that promises to pay $100 one year from now, then your asset will earn a 12 percent rate of return. But if you must pay $92.59 for the same bond, the rate of return will be only 8 percent. Thus, the higher asset price implies a lower rate of return.

Stocks and Bonds

We have been discussing the relationship between interest rates and the present value of an asset that generates a stream of returns in the future. Bonds generate a stream of interest payments whereas stocks generate a stream of dividend payments. As we said at the beginning of this section, however, for understanding the demand for money it is helpful to lump together all such assets and call them "bonds." This does not imply that stocks and the stock market are not important, however.

For the remainder of this chapter we focus on the distinction between bonds and money. In the next chapter, where we discuss the details of monetary policy, we discuss the stock market more completely.

The Demand for Money

The amount of money balances that everyone in the economy wishes to hold is called the **demand for money.** Because households are choosing how to divide their given stock of wealth between money and bonds, it follows that if we know the demand for money, we also know the demand for bonds. For a given amount of wealth, if people wish to hold $1 billion more money, they must also wish to hold $1 billion less of bonds.

When economists say that in February 1999 the quantity of money demanded was $410 billion, they mean that on that date the public wished to hold money balances that totaled $410 billion. But why do firms and households wish to hold money balances at all? There is a cost to holding any money balance because the money could have been used to purchase bonds, which earn higher interest than money.

The opportunity cost of holding any money balance is the interest that could have been earned if the money had been used instead to purchase bonds.

The opportunity cost of holding money is equal to the *nominal* rate of interest. Recall from Chapter 19 the distinction between real and nominal interest rates caused by the presence of inflation. However, because in this chapter we make the simplifying assumption that there is no ongoing inflation, the nominal and real rates of interest are the same.

demand for money
The total amount of money balances that the public wishes to hold for all purposes.

Households and firms will only choose to hold money if it provides services that are valued at least as highly as the opportunity cost of holding it. Three important services that are provided by money balances give rise to three motives for holding money: the *transactions, precautionary,* and *speculative* motives.

The Transactions Motive

Most transactions require money. Money passes from households to firms to pay for the goods and services produced by firms; money passes from firms to households to pay for the factor services supplied by households to firms. Money balances that are held to finance such flows are called **transactions balances.**

transactions balances Money balances held to finance payments because payments and receipts are not perfectly synchronized.

In an imaginary world in which the receipts and disbursements of households and firms were perfectly synchronized, it would be unnecessary to hold transactions balances. If every time a household spent $10 it received $10 as partial payment of its income, no transactions balances would be needed. In the real world, however, receipts and disbursements are not perfectly synchronized.

Consider the balances that are held by firms because of wage payments. Suppose, for purposes of illustration, that firms pay wages every Friday and that households spend all their wages on the purchase of goods and services, with the expenditure spread out evenly over the week. On Friday morning, firms must therefore hold balances equal to the weekly wage bill; on Friday afternoon, households will hold these balances.

Over the week, households' balances will be drawn down as a result of purchasing goods and services. Over the same period, the balances held by firms will build up as a result of selling goods and services until, on the following Friday morning, firms will again have amassed balances equal to the wage bill that must be met that day.

People hold money in order to make transactions. As income rises, the volume of transactions also rises, and so people typically decide to hold more money.

What determines the size of the transactions balances to be held? It is clear that in our example total transactions balances vary with the value of the wage bill. If the wage bill increases for any reason, the transactions balances held by firms and households for this purpose will also increase. As it is with wages, so it is with all other transactions: The size of the balances held is positively related to the value of the transactions.

It is not surprising then that the value of transactions is, in turn, positively related to national income. A greater value of output and income, after all, leads to greater spending by households and firms in the economy. Thus, a rise in national income leads to a rise in the total value of transactions and hence to an associated rise in the demand for transactions balances.

The larger the value of national income, the more transactions are made and thus the larger will be the value of transactions balances.

The Precautionary Motive

precautionary balances Money balances held for protection against the uncertainty of the timing of cash flows.

Many goods and services are sold on credit. The seller can never be certain when payment will be made, and the buyer can never be certain of the day of delivery and hence when payment will fall due. As a precaution against cash crises, when receipts are abnormally low or disbursements are abnormally high, firms and households carry money balances. **Precautionary balances** provide a cushion against uncertainty about the timing of cash words, it continues until everyone is content to hold the existing supply of money and bonds, as at point E in Figure 27-2.

Monetary equilibrium occurs when the rate of interest is such that the quantity of money demanded equals the quantity of money supplied.

The determination of the interest rate depicted in Figure 27-2 is often called the *liquidity preference theory of interest*. This name reflects the fact that a demand to hold money (rather than bonds) is a demand for the more liquid of the two assets—a preference for liquidity.

The Transmission Mechanism

The mechanism by which changes in the demand for and supply of money affect aggregate demand is called the **transmission mechanism.** It operates in three stages: The first is the link between monetary equilibrium and the interest rate, the second is the link between the interest rate and investment expenditure, and the third is the link between investment expenditure and aggregate demand.

Changes in the Interest Rate.   The interest rate will change if the equilibrium depicted in Figure 27-2 is disturbed by a change in either the supply of money or the demand for money. For example, as shown in Figure 27-3(i), an increase in the supply of money, with an unchanged liquidity preference function, creates an excess supply of

transmission mechanism   The channels by which a change in the demand or supply of money leads to a shift of the aggregate demand curve.

FIGURE 27-3   Changes in the Monetary Equilibrium

(i) A change in the supply of money

(ii) A change in the demand for money

Shifts in the supply of money or in the demand for money cause the equilibrium interest rate to change. In both parts of the figure, the money supply is shown by the vertical curve M_{S0}, and the demand for money is shown by the negatively sloped curve LP_0. The initial monetary equilibrium is at E_0, with corresponding interest rate i_0. In part (i), an increase in the money supply causes the money supply curve to shift to the right, from M_{S0} to M_{S1}. The new equilibrium is at E_1, where the interest rate is i_1. In part (ii), an increase in the demand for money causes the LP curve to shift to the right from LP_0 to LP_1. The new monetary equilibrium occurs at E_2, and the new equilibrium interest rate is i_2.

FIGURE 27-4   The Effects of Changes in the Money Supply on Investment Expenditure

Increases in the money supply reduce the interest rate and increase desired investment expenditure. Equilibrium in the money market, in panel (i), is at E_0, with a quantity of money of M_0 and an interest rate of i_0. The corresponding level of investment expenditure is I_0 (point A) in panel (ii). The Bank of Canada then increases the money supply to M_1. This reduces the interest rate to i_1 and increases investment expenditure by ΔI to I_1 (point B).

money at the original interest rate. As we have seen, an excess supply of money leads firms and households to attempt to buy bonds, thus driving up the price of bonds and pushing down the interest rate.

As shown in Figure 27-3(ii), an increase in the demand for money, with an unchanged supply of money, creates an excess demand for money at the original interest rate. Firms and households try to acquire more money by selling their holdings of bonds. This drives down the price of bonds and pushes up the interest rate.

Changes in either the demand for or the supply of money cause changes in the interest rate.

Changes in Desired Investment.   The second link in the transmission mechanism relates interest rates to desired investment expenditure. We saw in Chapter 22 that investment, which includes expenditure on inventory accumulation, residential construction, and business fixed investment, responds to changes in the real rate of interest. Other things being equal, a decrease in the real rate of interest makes borrowing cheaper and generates new investment expenditure. This negative relationship between desired investment and the interest rate is labelled I^D in Figure 27-4.

The first two links in the transmission mechanism are shown in Figure 27-4.[2] We concentrate for the moment on changes in the money supply, although, as we have seen already, the process can also be set in motion by changes in the demand for money. In part (i), we see that a change in the money supply causes the rate of interest to change in the

---

[2]In part (i) of Figure 27-4, it is the nominal interest rate that affects money demand. In part (ii), however, it is the real interest rate that influences desired investment expenditure. It is therefore worth emphasizing that we are continuing with the assumption that there is no inflation and so the nominal and real interest rates are the same. This allows us to use the same vertical axis in the two parts of the figure.

opposite direction. In part (ii), we see that a change in the interest rate causes the level of desired investment expenditure to change in the opposite direction.

An increase in the money supply leads to a fall in the interest rate and an increase in investment expenditure. A decrease in the money supply leads to a rise in the interest rate and a decrease in investment expenditure.

Changes in Aggregate Demand.   Now that we see how monetary disturbances lead to changes in desired aggregate expenditure, we are back on familiar ground. In Chapter 24, we saw that a shift in the aggregate expenditure curve (caused by something *other than* a change in the price level) leads to a shift in the *AD* curve. This situation is shown again in Figure 27-5.

A change in the money supply, by causing a change in desired investment expenditure and hence a shift in the *AE* curve, causes the *AD* curve to shift. An increase in the money supply causes an increase in desired investment expenditure and therefore a rightward shift of the *AD* curve. A decrease in the money supply causes a decrease in desired investment expenditure and therefore a leftward shift of the *AD* curve.

The entire transmission mechanism is illustrated in Figure 27-6 for the case of an expansionary monetary shock. An increase in money supply or a decrease in money demand tends to reduce interest rates and increase aggregate demand.

An Open-Economy Modification

So far, the emphasis in our discussion of the transmission mechanism has been on the effect that a change in the interest rate has on desired investment. In an open economy, however, where financial capital flows easily across borders, the transmission mechanism is a little more complex.

Financial capital is very mobile across international boundaries. Bondholders, either in Canada or abroad, are able to substitute between Canadian bonds, U.S. bonds, German bonds or bonds from almost any country you can think of. Bonds from different countries are generally not *perfect* substitutes for each other because of varying amounts of political and economic instability. But bonds from similar countries—Canada and the United States, for example—are often viewed as very close substitutes.

The ability of bondholders to easily substitute between bonds from different countries implies that monetary disturbances will generally lead to capital flows, which in turn will cause changes in exchange rates and changes in exports and imports.

FIGURE 27-5   The Effects of Changes in the Money Supply on Aggregate Demand

(i) A shift in aggregate expenditure

(ii) A shift in aggregate demand

Changes in the money supply cause shifts in the aggregate expenditure and aggregate demand functions. In Figure 27-4, an increase in the money supply increased desired investment expenditure by ΔI. In part (i) of this figure, the aggregate expenditure function shifts up by ΔI (which is the same as ΔI in Figure 27-4), from AE_0 to AE_1. At the fixed price level P_0, equilibrium GDP rises from Y_0 to Y_1, as shown by the horizontal shift in the aggregate demand curve from AD_0 to AD_1 in part (ii).

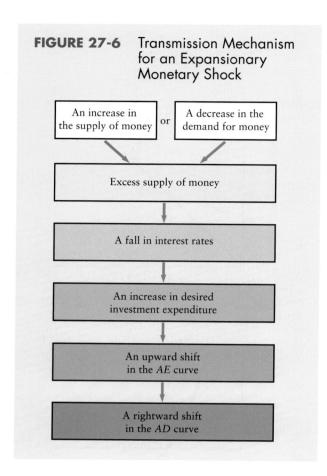

FIGURE 27-6 Transmission Mechanism for an Expansionary Monetary Shock

An increase in the supply of money *or* A decrease in the demand for money

Excess supply of money

A fall in interest rates

An increase in desired investment expenditure

An upward shift in the *AE* curve

A rightward shift in the *AD* curve

Practise with Study Guide Chapter 27, Exercise 5.

In an open-economy with capital mobility, monetary disturbances lead to capital flows, exchange rate changes and changes in net exports.

The Open-Economy Transmission Mechanism

To understand how capital mobility adds this second channel to the transmission mechanism, consider an example. Suppose the Bank of Canada decides to increase the money supply. As shown in Figure 27-4, the increase in money supply reduces the interest rate and increases desired investment expenditure. This is the first channel of the transmission mechanism. But the story does not end there.

The reduction in Canadian interest rates also makes Canadian bonds less attractive relative to foreign bonds. Canadian and foreign investors alike will sell some of their Canadian bonds and buy more of the high-return foreign bonds. But in order to buy foreign bonds, it is necessary first to exchange Canadian dollars for foreign currency. The increase in the demand for foreign currency causes the Canadian dollar to depreciate relative to other currencies.

An increase in the Canadian money supply reduces Canadian interest rates and leads to a capital outflow. This causes the Canadian dollar to depreciate.

As the Canadian dollar depreciates, however, Canadian goods and services become less expensive relative to those from other countries. This change in international relative prices causes households and firms—both in Canada and abroad—to substitute away from foreign goods and toward Canadian goods. Imports fall and exports rise.

So the overall effect of the increase in the Canadian money supply is not just a fall in interest rates and an increase in investment. Because of the international mobility of financial capital, the low Canadian interest rates also lead to a capital outflow, a depreciation of the Canadian dollar, and an increase in Canadian net exports. This increase in net exports, of course, *strengthens* the positive effect on aggregate demand already coming from the increase in desired investment.

This complete open-economy transmission mechanism is shown in Figure 27-7. This figure is based on Figure 27-6, but simply adds the second channel of the transmission mechanism that works through capital mobility, exchange rates and net exports.

In an open economy with capital mobility, an increase in the money supply results in an increase in aggregate demand for two reasons. First, there is a reduction in interest rates that causes an increase in investment. Second, the lower interest rate causes a capital outflow, a currency depreciation, and a rise in net exports.

Our example has been that of a monetary expansion. A monetary contraction would have the opposite effect, but the logic of the mechanism is the same. A reduction in the

Canadian money supply would raise Canadian interest rates and reduce desired investment expenditure. The higher Canadian interest rates would attract foreign financial capital as bondholders sell low-return foreign bonds and purchase high-return Canadian bonds. This action would increase the demand for Canadian dollars in the foreign-exchange market and thus appreciate the Canadian dollar. Finally, the appreciation of the Canadian dollar would increase Canadians' imports of foreign goods and reduce Canadian exports to other countries. Canadian net exports would fall.

The Slope of the *AD* Curve

We can now use the transmission mechanism to add to the explanation (given in Chapter 24) of the negative slope of the *AD* curve. In Chapter 24, we mentioned two reasons for the negative slope of the *AD* curve: the change in wealth, and the substitution between domestic for foreign goods, both of which occur when the price levels changes. A third effect operates through interest rates. And we are now in a position to understand this third effect.

The essential feature of this third effect is that a rise in the price level raises the money value of transactions. This leads to an increased demand for money, which brings the transmission mechanism into play. People try to sell bonds to add to their money balances; but, collectively, all they succeed in doing is forcing up the interest rate. The rise in the interest rate then reduces desired investment expenditure and so reduces equilibrium national income.

This effect is important because, empirically, the interest rate is the most important link between monetary factors and real expenditure flows. This reason for the negative slope of the *AD* curve is discussed in more detail in the appendix to this chapter.

FIGURE 27-7   The Open-Economy Transmission Mechanism for an Expansionary Monetary Shock

The Strength of Monetary Forces

In the previous section we saw that a change in the money supply leads to a change in interest rates. The change in interest rates, in turn, leads to changes in investment and (through capital flows and changes in the exchange rate) net exports. Thus, a change in the money supply leads to a change in desired aggregate expenditure and therefore to a shift in the *AD* curve.

What will be the effect on real GDP and the price level of the change in the money supply? Because a change in the money supply leads to a shift in the *AD* curve, we know from our analysis in Chapter 25 that the short-run effects will differ from the long-run effects.

FIGURE 27-8   The Long-Run Neutrality of Money

An increase in the money supply leads to a rightward shift in the *AD* curve, but because it has no effect on potential income, in the long run it has no effect on real GDP and results only in a change in the price level. The economy is initially in equilibrium at E_0, with price level of P_0 and real GDP of Y^*. An increase in the money supply causes the *AD* curve to shift rightward from AD_0 to AD_1. Real GDP rises to Y_1, and the price level rises to P_1. The inflationary gap of Y^*Y_1 sets the adjustment mechanism in action, driving up wages and causing the *SRAS* curve to shift up and to the left. The process comes to a halt when real GDP has returned to its potential level, Y^*, thus eliminating the inflationary gap, and the price level has increased to P_2. In the long run, the monetary expansion has no effect on any real variables—money is *neutral*.

Long-Run Effects on Real GDP

We saw in Chapter 25 that any shock—either to aggregate demand or aggregate supply—that creates an output gap sets in place an adjustment mechanism that will eventually close that gap and return real GDP to its potential level, Y^*. The operation of this adjustment mechanism following an increase in the money supply is illustrated in Figure 27-8.

Although a change in the money supply causes the *AD* curve to shift, it has no effect on the level of real GDP in the long run.

Figure 27-8 shows that the only long-run effect of a shift in the *AD* curve following a change in the money supply is a change in the price level. This result is often referred to as the *neutrality of money*, as discussed at the beginning of Chapter 26.

Short-Run Effects on Real GDP

We now focus on the effects of a change in the money supply on the short-run equilibrium level of real GDP. As we will see, there are several factors that determine the short-run strength of monetary changes.

The Role of Aggregate Demand

The size of the shift in the *AD* curve in response to an increase in the money supply depends on the amount of investment expenditure that is stimulated. This in turn depends on the strength of the two key linkages that make up the transmission mechanism.

The first consideration is how much interest rates fall in response to an increase in the money supply. Interest rates must fall to induce households and firms to hold the increased amount of money. The more interest sensitive the demand for money is (the flatter is the *LP* curve), the less interest rates must fall.

The second consideration is how much investment expenditure increases in response to the fall in interest rates. Desired investment expenditure increases in response to a fall in the interest rate. The more interest sensitive desired investment expenditure is (the flatter is the I^D curve), the greater the response will be.

It follows that the size of the shift of the *AD* curve in response to a change in the money supply depends on the shapes of the *LP* and I^D curves. The influence of the shapes of the two curves is shown in Figure 27-9 and can be summarized as follows:

1. The steeper (less interest-sensitive) the *LP* curve, the greater the effect on interest rates of a given change in the money supply.

2. The flatter (more interest-sensitive) the I^D curve, the greater the effect on investment expenditure a change in the interest rate will have and hence the larger will be the shift in the *AD* curve.

The combination that produces the largest shift in the *AD* curve for a given change in the money supply is a steep *LP* curve and a flat *I*^{D} curve. This combination is illustrated in Figure 27-9(i). It accords with the view that monetary policy is relatively effective as a means of influencing real GDP in the short run. The combination that produces the smallest shift in the *AD* curve is a flat *LP* curve and a steep *I*^{D} curve. This combination is illustrated in Figure 27-9(ii). It accords with the view that monetary policy is relatively ineffective in the short run.

FIGURE 27-9   Two Views on the Strength of Monetary Changes

(i) Changes in the money supply effective

(ii) Changes in the money supply ineffective

The strength of the effect of a change in the money supply on investment and hence on aggregate demand depends on the interest elasticity of both the demand for money and desired investment expenditure. Initially, in parts (i) and (ii), the money supply is M_{S0}, and the economy has an interest rate of i_0 and investment expenditure of I_0. The central bank then expands the money supply from M_{S0} to M_{S1}. The rate of interest thus falls from i_0 to i_1, as shown in each of the left panels. This causes an increase in investment expenditure of ΔI, from I_0 to I_1, as shown in each of the right panels.

In part (i), the demand for money is highly interest-inelastic, so the increase in the money supply leads to a large fall in the interest rate. Further, desired investment expenditure is highly interest-elastic, so the large fall in interest rates also leads to a large increase in investment expenditure. Hence, in this case, the change in the money supply will be very effective in stimulating aggregate demand.

In part (ii), the demand for money is more interest-elastic, so the increase in the money supply leads to only a small fall in the interest rate. Further, desired investment expenditure is interest-inelastic, so the small fall in interest rates leads to only a small increase in investment expenditure. Hence, in this case, the change in the money supply will be less effective in stimulating aggregate demand.

The effectiveness of monetary policy in inducing short-run changes in real GDP depends on the slopes of the *LP* and *I*^{D} curves. The steeper is the *LP* curve, and the flatter is the *I*^{D} curve, the more effective is monetary policy.

Figure 27-9 characterizes a famous debate among economists during the 1950s and early 1960s. Some economists, following the ideas of John Maynard Keynes, argued that changes in the money supply led to relatively small changes in interest rates and that investment was relatively insensitive to changes in the interest rate. These economists, who called themselves *Keynesians*, concluded that monetary policy was not a very effective method of stimulating aggregate demand—they therefore emphasized the value of using fiscal policy (as Keynes himself had argued during the Great Depression). Another group of economists, led by Milton Friedman, who then was at the University of Chicago, argued that changes in the money supply caused sharp changes in interest rates which, in turn, led to significant changes in investment expenditure. These economists called themselves *Monetarists* and concluded that monetary policy was a very effective tool for stimulating aggregate demand.[3]

Several decades later, however, this debate between Keynesians and Monetarists is all but over. A great deal of empirical research devoted to uncovering the relationship between interest rates and money demand suggests that money demand is relatively insensitive to changes in the interest rate. That is, the *LP* curve is quite steep and, as a result, changes in the money supply cause relatively large changes in interest rates (as argued by the Monetarists). The evidence is much less clear, however, on the slope of the *I*^{D} curve. Though the evidence confirms that *I*^{D} is clearly downward sloping, there is no consensus on whether the curve is steep or flat. Part of the problem facing researchers is that an important determinant of investment is not observable. Firms' expectations about the future have a significant effect on their investment decisions but this variable is not easily measured by researchers. The unobservability of this variable makes it very difficult to precisely estimate the relationship between interest rates and investment.

The Role of Aggregate Supply

As we saw in Chapters 24 and 25, the response of real GDP and the price level to any given shift in the *AD* curve depends on the slope of the *SRAS* curve.

As you will recall from Chapter 24, the steeper the *SRAS* curve, the larger the change in the price level and the smaller the change in real GDP following a given shift in the *AD* curve. Many economists think that when the level of real GDP is near or above its potential level, the *SRAS* curve is very steep.

When the economy is operating near or above its potential level of output, increases in aggregate demand (including those caused by increases in the money supply) will lead to small increases in real GDP but will have a substantial effect on the price level.

What Lies Ahead

In this and the previous chapter we incorporated money into our macro model. You now know what money is and how it is created by the banking system. You also know how the money market determines the interest rate. Finally, you have seen in general

---

[3]Monetarists argued that monetary policy was very effective for stimulating aggregate demand but they *did not* advocate an "activist" monetary policy. One of their concerns was that an activist monetary policy would destabilize the economy. We address these issues in Chapter 28.

terms how monetary disturbances—changes in the demand or supply for money—affect real GDP and the price level.

What we have not yet discussed is how the Bank of Canada influences the money supply and what factors it must consider when doing so. What are the Bank's objectives? How does it achieve these objectives? With the basics of money now in place, we are ready to discuss the details of monetary policy. We do so in the next chapter.

S U M M A R Y

Understanding Financial Assets

- For simplicity, we divide all forms of wealth into "money," which is a medium of exchange, and "bonds," which earn a higher interest return than money and can be turned into money by being sold at a price that is determined on the open market.

- The price of bonds varies negatively with the rate of interest—a rise in the interest rate lowers the prices of all bonds.

The Demand for Money

- The opportunity cost of holding money (rather than bonds) is the interest earnings that are forgone—the interest that would have been earned had bonds been held instead of money.
- Despite the opportunity cost of holding money, households and firms hold money for three reasons—the transactions, precautionary, and speculative motives. Taken together, they have the effect of making the real demand

for money vary positively with real GDP, and negatively with the nominal interest rate.
- The real demand for money is independent of the price level. The nominal demand for money varies in direct proportion with the price level.
- The liquidity preference *(LP)* function is the relationship between money demand and the nominal interest rate (holding real income and the price level constant).

Monetary Forces and National Income

- The interest rate is determined by the interaction of the demand for money and the supply of money. An excess demand for money balances leads people to sell bonds. This pushes the price of bonds down and the interest rate up. An excess supply of money balances leads people to buy bonds. This pushes the price of bonds up and the rate of interest down. Monetary equilibrium is established when people are willing to hold the fixed stock of money (and therefore bonds) at the current rate of interest.

- A change in the (real) interest rate causes desired investment to change along the investment demand *(I^D)* curve. This shifts the *AE* function and causes equilibrium GDP to change. The *AD* curve also shifts.
- The link between money and aggregate demand is known as the transmission mechanism. A decrease in the supply of money raises interest rates, reduces desired investment expenditure, and thus reduces aggregate demand. An increase in the supply of money reduces interest rates, in-

creases desired investment expenditure, and thus increases aggregate demand.

- In an open economy with capital mobility there is a second part to the transmission mechanism. An increase in the money supply reduces interest rates and makes domestic bonds less attractive than foreign bonds. The capital outflow causes a depreciation of the Canadian dollar that stimulates net exports, and thus increases aggregate demand. A decrease in the money supply raises interest rates, causes a capital inflow, appreciates the currency and reduces net exports.

- The negatively sloped *AD* curve indicates that the higher the price level, the lower the equilibrium national income. The explanation lies in part with the effect of money on the adjustment mechanism: Other things being equal, the higher the price level, the higher the demand for money and the rate of interest; the lower the aggregate expenditure function, the lower the equilibrium income.

The Strength of Monetary Forces

LO 5

- Changes in the money supply affect real GDP via shifts in the *AD* curve. But such changes do not affect potential output. Hence, changes in the money supply can affect output in the short run but not in the long run.

- The steeper the *LP* curve and the flatter the I^D curve, the greater the effect on aggregate demand of a given change in the money supply. The steeper the *SRAS* curve, the smaller the transitory effect on real GDP of a given shift in the *AD* curve.

KEY CONCEPTS

Interest rates and bond prices
The transactions, precautionary, and
  speculative motives for holding money
The liquidity preference *(LP)* function

Monetary equilibrium
The transmission mechanism
The investment demand *(I^D)* curve

Money and the adjustment mechanism
The strength of monetary forces

STUDY EXERCISES

1. The following table shows the stream of income produced by several different assets. In each case, P_1, P_2, and P_3 are the payments made by the asset in years 1, 2 and 3.

Asset	(*i*)	P_1	P_2	P_3	Present Value
Treasury Bill	8%	$1000	$0	$0	—
Bond	7%	$0	$0	$5000	—
Bond	9%	$200	$200	$200	—
Stock	10%	$50	$40	$60	—

  a. For each asset, compute the asset's present value. (Note that the market interest rate, *i*, is not the same in each situation.)
  b. Explain why the market price for each asset is likely to be the asset's present value.

2. What motives for holding money—transactions, precautionary, or speculative—do you think explain the following holdings? Explain.

  a. Currency in the cash register of the local grocery store at the start of each working day.
  b. Money to meet Stelco's bi-weekly payroll deposited in the local bank.
  c. A household tries to keep a "buffer" of $1000 in their saving account.
  d. An investor sells bonds for cash, which he then deposits in a low-return bank account.
  e. You carry $20 in your pocket even though you have no planned expenditures.

3. The diagram opposite shows the demand for money and the supply of money.

   a. Explain why the *LP* function is downward sloping.
   b. Suppose the interest rate is at i_A. Explain how firms and households attempt to satisfy their excess demand for money. What is the effect of their actions?
   c. Suppose the interest rate is at i_B. Explain how firms and households attempt to dispose of their excess supply of money. What is the effect of their actions?
   d. Now suppose there is an increase in the transactions demand for money (perhaps because of growth in real GDP). Beginning at i^*, explain what happens in the money market. How is this shown in the diagram?

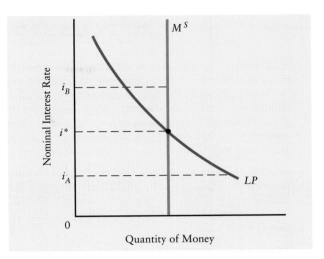

4. The following diagrams show the determination of monetary equilibrium and the demand for investment. The economy begins with money supply M_{S0}, liquidity preference curve *LP*, and investment demand I^D. The interest rate is i_0 and investment is I_0.

   a. Beginning at the initial equilibrium, suppose the Bank of Canada increases the money supply. What happens in the money market and what happens to desired investment expenditure?

   b. Beginning in the initial equilibrium, suppose there is a reduction in the demand for money (caused, perhaps, by bonds becoming more attractive to firms and households). What happens in the money market and what happens to desired investment expenditure?
   c. Explain why an increase in money supply can have the same effects as a reduction in money demand.

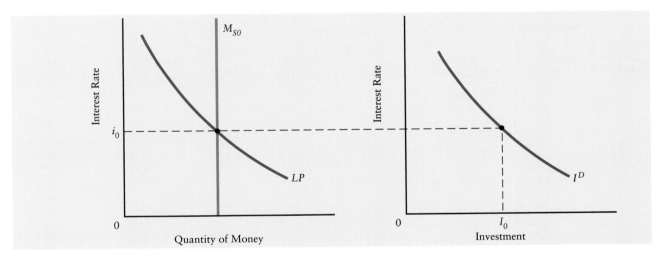

5. In the text we discussed why, in an open economy with international capital mobility, there is a second part to the monetary transmission mechanism. (It may be useful to review Figure 27-7 when answering this question.)

   a. Explain why an increase in Canada's money supply makes Canadian bonds less attractive relative to foreign bonds.
   b. Explain why Canada's bonds being less attractive leads to a depreciation of the Canadian dollar.
   c. Why would such a depreciation of the Canadian dollar lead to an increase in Canada's net exports?

   d. Now suppose that the Bank of Canada does not change its policy at all, but the Federal Reserve (the U.S. central bank) increases the U.S. money supply. What is the likely effect on Canada? Explain.

6. In the text we discussed the debate between Keynesians and Monetarists regarding the effectiveness of monetary policy in changing real GDP (see Figure 27-9 to review). Using the same sort of diagram, discuss two conditions in which a change in the money supply would have *no* effect on real GDP.

DISCUSSION QUESTIONS

1. Historically, construction of new houses has been one of the most interest-sensitive categories of aggregate expenditure. Recently, the financial press have carried a number of stories suggesting that because of financial deregulation and innovations in housing finance, this interest sensitivity has apparently decreased. If this is true, what are the implications for monetary policy?

2. Suppose that you alone know that the Bank of Canada is going to engage in policies that will decrease the money supply sharply, starting next month. How might you make speculative profits by purchases or sales of bonds now?

3. In recent years, central bankers in Canada and elsewhere (especially the United States) have expressed concern about the dramatic increases in stock-market values. In December 1996, U.S. Federal Reserve Chairman, Alan Greenspan, alarmed the markets by referring to investors' "irrational exuberance."

   a. Explain why central bankers might be concerned about "excessive" increases in stock-market values.
   b. Explain how a policy-induced increase in interest rates would affect the stock market.

   c. Suppose prices in the stock market fell sharply for reasons unrelated to domestic interest rates. What would be the likely effect on aggregate demand?

4. In 1997–98, there was a significant recession in the Southeast Asian economies of Malaysia, Indonesia, Thailand, and South Korea.

   a. Explain the likely effects of these events on the demand for Canadian exports. What would be the effect on Canadian aggregate demand?
   b. Suppose the Bank of Canada viewed its monetary policy as being appropriate (for keeping output close to potential) before this "Asian Crisis" occurred. What would you then predict to be the bank's response to the crisis?

5. In the text we discussed how capital mobility in an open economy added a second part to the transmission mechanism. In this setting, discuss why changes in the Federal Reserve's policy in the United States are carefully watched—and often matched—by the Bank of Canada.

Interest Rates and the Slope of the *AD* Curve

The *AD* curve relates the price level to the equilibrium level of real GDP. Its negative slope means that the higher the price level, the lower the equilibrium GDP. In Chapter 24 we explained the slope of the aggregate demand curve by arguing that a change in the price level changed the wealth of firms and households (by changing the real value of money and bond holdings). We also argued that a change in the price level changed the prices of Canadian goods relative to foreign goods, and so affected net exports. What we *did not say* in Chapter 24, however, is that a third reason for a negatively sloped *AD* curve is due to the changes in the interest rate that are caused by the change in the price level. We omitted this argument then for the simple reason that we had not yet introduced the concepts of money demand, money supply, and the determination of interest rates. But we now have the tools in hand to do this.

Let us look at the monetary transmission mechanism in detail. Although the argument contains nothing new, it does require that you follow carefully through several steps.

We start with an initial equilibrium position, corresponding to a given price level P_0, shown by the 0 subscripts in the two figures. Figure 27A-1 shows the determination of the interest rate by the conditions of monetary equilibrium in part (i); that in turn determines the level of desired investment spending by the investment demand curve in part (ii). Figure 27A-2 shows the *AE* curve, drawn for that level of investment spending, and the determination of equilibrium real GDP in part (i); that level of real GDP is then plotted against the price level to give point *A* on the *AD* curve in part (ii).

A rise in the price level raises the money value of transactions and increases the quantity of nominal money demanded at each possible value of the interest rate. As a result, the *LP* function shifts upward, raising the equilibrium interest rate and reducing the level of desired investment expenditure. The reduction in investment spending in turn causes the *AE* curve to shift downward, leading to a reduction in the equilibrium level of national income.

The negative relationship between the price level and equilibrium real GDP shown by the *AD* curve

FIGURE 27A-1 Changes in the Price Level: Interest Rates and Investment

(i) Monetary equilibrium   (ii) Investment demand

Changes in the price level influence the demand for money and hence cause the level of interest rates and desired investment spending to change. In part (i), the money supply is fixed at M_0. Initially, money demand is given by LP_0, equilibrium is at E_0, and the interest rate is i_0. Given that interest rate, desired investment spending is I_0, as shown in part (ii) by the I^D curve.

An increase in the price level causes an increase in the demand for money, and hence the *LP* curve shifts upward to LP_1. Monetary equilibrium is at E_1, the interest rate rises to i_1, and desired investment spending falls by ΔI_1 to I_1. A further increase in the price level causes a further increase in the demand for money, to LP_2. Monetary equilibrium is at E_2, the interest rate rises to i_2, and desired investment spending falls by ΔI_2 to I_2.

occurs because, other things being equal, a rise in the price level raises the quantity of money demanded. This increase in money demand pushes up the interest rate, which then reduces investment and equilibrium GDP. Note the qualification "other things being equal." It is important for this process that the nominal money *supply* remain constant. The adjustment mechanism operates because the demand for money increases when the price level rises whereas the money supply remains constant. The attempt to add to money balances by selling bonds is what drives the interest rate up and reduces desired expenditure, thereby reducing equilibrium GDP. (This argument is conducted in terms of the nominal supply of and demand for money. Arguing in terms of the real demand and supply of money leads to identical results. [34])

FIGURE 27A-2 Changes in the Price Level: Aggregate Expenditure and Real GDP

(i) Aggregate expenditure

(ii) Aggregate demand

Changes in the price level lead to changes in desired aggregate expenditure and hence in the equilibrium level of real GDP. Equilibrium GDP is determined in part (i). At a given initial price level—hence with an initial level of desired investment spending of I_0 from Figure 27A-1—desired aggregate expenditure is shown by AE_0. Equilibrium is at E_0, and equilibrium real GDP is Y_0. In part (ii), Y_0 is plotted against P_0 to give point A on the AD curve.

An increase in the price level causes a decrease of ΔI_1 in the level of desired investment spending, as determined in Figure 27A-1 and shown in part (i) here. Thus, the AE curve shifts down to AE_1. Equilibrium is at E_1, and equilibrium real GDP falls to Y_1. In part (ii), the higher price level P_1 is plotted against the lower equilibrium level of income Y_1 as point B on the AD curve.

CHAPTER 28

Monetary Policy in Canada

LEARNING OBJECTIVES

1 Explain the two methods by which the Bank of Canada changes the money supply.

2 Understand the difference between the Bank's policy variables and its policy instruments.

3 Recognize why the Bank of Canada cannot target the money supply and the interest rate independently.

4 Explain why monetary policy affects real GDP and the price level only after long lags.

5 Have a basic understanding of the main challenges that the Bank of Canada has faced over the past two decades.

In the previous two chapters, we saw how money supply and money demand interact to determine interest rates. Further, we saw how monetary disturbances—changes in either the demand for money or the supply of money—affect interest rates, desired aggregate expenditure and, thus, the level of real GDP.

We also saw how commercial banks, through the process of making loans and new deposits, are able to affect the money supply. But there is still one important piece missing from our analysis. Though we discussed some of the functions of the Bank of Canada in Chapter 26, we have not yet examined how the Bank of Canada influences the level of reserves in the commercial banking system. And it is these reserves that form the basis of commercial-bank lending. Until we have examined the operations of the Bank of Canada in more detail, we do not have a full picture of the determinants of the money supply.

In this chapter, we examine the Bank of Canada's monetary policy—how it sets the level of reserves in the banking system to affect interest rates, the exchange rate, real GDP and, eventually, the price level.

The Bank of Canada and the Money Supply

Deposit money is by far the most important part of the money supply. It accounts for about 65 percent of M1, the narrowest definition of money, and for about 90 percent of

M2, the broader measure. As we have seen, the ability of banks to create such deposit money depends on their target level of reserves. These reserves, in turn, are determined by the Bank of Canada. Thus, the ability of the central bank to affect the money supply is critically related to its ability to determine the reserves of the commercial banking system.

In the following sections, we discuss two ways in which the Bank of Canada alters the reserves of the banking system and hence influences the money supply. In Chapter 26, we identified the *target reserve ratio* of the commercial banks as the ratio of reserves they wished to hold relative to their deposit liabilities. At this stage of our discussion of the money supply, we suppose that the target reserve ratio is constant.

Open-Market Operations

open-market operations The purchase and sale of government securities on the open market by the central bank.

One tool that the Bank of Canada can use for influencing the supply of money is the purchase or sale of government securities on the open market. These actions are known as **open-market operations.** Just as there are stock markets, there are active and well-organized markets for government securities. Anyone, including you, the Toronto Dominion Bank, Ford Motor Company, or the Bank of Canada can enter this market to buy or sell negotiable government securities at whatever price the market establishes. But there is an important difference between the purchase and sale of government securities *among members of the private sector* and *between the central bank and the private sector.* As we shall see, whenever the Bank of Canada is involved in either the purchase or the sale of government securities, the reserves of the entire banking system are altered, and this change affects the money supply.

At the start of 1999, the Bank of Canada held about $30 billion in government securities. In a typical year, the Bank of Canada may make a *net* addition of $1–2 billion to these holdings. During the year, however, its *gross* purchases and sales of government securities on the open market amount to many times this amount. What is the effect of these open-market purchases and sales?

TABLE 28-1 Initial Balance Sheet Changes Caused by an Open-Market Purchase from a Household

Private households	
Assets	Liabilities
Bonds −100 000	No change
Deposits +100 000	

Commercial banks	
Assets	Liabilities
Reserves +100,000	Demand deposits +100 000

Bank of Canada	
Assets	Liabilities
Bonds +100 000	Commercial bank deposits +100 000

An open-market purchase by the Bank of Canada from the private sector increases commercial bank reserves and thus, through an expansion of bank lending, increases the money supply. When the Bank of Canada buys a $100 000 bond from a household, the household gains money and gives up a bond. The commercial banks gain a new deposit of $100 000 and thus new reserves of $100 000. Commercial banks can now engage in a multiple expansion of deposit money, as analysed in Chapter 26.

Open-Market Purchases

When the Bank of Canada buys a treasury bill or a bond from a household or a firm, it pays for the bond with a cheque drawn on itself and payable to the seller. The seller deposits this cheque in a commercial bank, which then presents the cheque to the Bank of Canada for payment. The Bank of Canada then makes a book entry, increasing the deposit of the commercial bank at the central bank, and thus adds to the commercial bank's reserves.

Table 28-1 shows the changes in the balance sheets of the several parties involved in a Bank of Canada purchase of $100 000 in government securities from a household. At the end of these transactions, the central bank has acquired a new asset in the form of a security and a new liability in the form of a deposit by the commercial bank. The seller has reduced its security holdings and increased its deposits. The commercial bank has increased its deposit liabilities and its reserves by the amount of the transaction. When the Bank of Canada buys securities on the open market, the entire banking system gains new reserves.

Given a constant target reserve ratio, after the transactions shown in Table 28-1 are completed, the commercial banks have excess reserves—that is, reserves over and above those needed to maintain their target reserve ratio. To see this, simply note that deposits and reserves have increased by the same amount ($100 000 in this case). As long as the target reserve ratio is less than 100 percent (and it would typically be only a tiny fraction of that), there are now excess reserves. Thus, the commercial banks are in a position to expand their loans and deposits.

When the central bank buys securities on the open market, the reserves of the commercial banks are increased. These banks can then expand deposits, thereby increasing the money supply.

Open-Market Sales

When the Bank of Canada sells a security to a household or firm, it receives in return the buyer's cheque drawn against a deposit in a commercial bank. The Bank of Canada presents the cheque to the commercial bank for payment. Payment is made by a book entry that reduces the commercial bank's deposit at the central bank, and hence reduces its reserves.

The changes in this case are the opposite of those shown in Table 28-1. The central bank has reduced its assets by the value of the security it sold and reduced its deposit liabilities to the banks. The household or firm has increased its holdings of securities and reduced its deposit with a commercial bank. The commercial bank has reduced its deposit liability to the household or firm and reduced its reserves (on deposit with the central bank) by the same amount. In each case, the asset change is balanced by a liability change.

Given a constant target reserve ratio, the commercial bank finds that by suffering an equal reduction in its reserves and its deposit liabilities, its actual ratio of reserves to deposits falls below its target ratio. Banks will then take steps to restore their reserve ratios. The necessary reduction in deposits can be accomplished by not granting new loans when old ones are repaid or by selling (liquidating) existing investments.

When the central bank sells securities on the open market, the reserves of the commercial banks are decreased. These banks must in turn contract deposits, thereby decreasing the money supply.

Although the process just described reflects the mechanics of an open-market sale by the Bank of Canada, it does not fully capture some of the subtleties involved in the Bank's selling of securities. For example, how is the Bank sure that it can always find a willing buyer? Or every time the Bank successfully sells government securities and thus decreases the reserves of the banking system, is this necessarily a "contractionary" monetary policy? These issues are examined in *Extensions in Theory 28-1*.

Shifting Government Deposits

In addition to open-market operations, the Bank of Canada has a second general method for changing the level of reserves in the banking system. As the government's *fiscal agent,* the Bank of Canada manages a large amount of government funds. It maintains

Changes money supply

EXTENSIONS IN THEORY 28-1

Open-Market Sales and "Contractionary" Monetary Policy

This box looks at two additional issues that arise whenever the Bank of Canada conducts an open-market sale of government securities (which reduces the reserves of the banking system and is thus called a *contractionary monetary policy*).

Can the Bank of Canada Always Find a Buyer?

One way in which the Bank pursues a contractionary monetary policy is to sell government securities, thus reducing the reserves available to the banking system. What if the public does not wish to buy the securities that the Bank wants to sell? Can the Bank force them to do so?

The answer is that there is always a price at which the public will buy. The Bank must be prepared in its open-market operations to lower the price of securities as far as necessary in order to sell them. This fall in price is, as we have seen, the same thing as an increase in the interest rate. If the Bank wishes to pursue a contractionary policy by selling government securities, it will have to accept that interest rates must rise.

Do Reserves Actually Fall?

In every year since 1950, real GDP growth and inflation have ensured that nominal national income has risen. As a result, the demand for money has grown. In every year in the period, the nominal money supply has grown, reflecting the Bank's decision to supply additional reserves to the banking system to meet the growing demand for money. Does this mean that the Bank has never followed a contractionary monetary policy?

The answer is no. When real income growth and inflation result in a continually growing nominal national income, the stance of monetary policy depends upon the rate at which the money supply is allowed to grow *relative to the rate of growth of the demand for money*. A contractionary monetary policy occurs when the growth in the money supply is held below the rate of growth in the demand for money; it does not require a fall in the absolute size of the money supply.

For example, if the nominal demand for money is growing at 4 percent per year, the Bank of Canada can follow a contractionary policy if it limits the rate of growth of the money supply to 2 percent. This would create an excess demand for money, causing interest rates to rise. The higher interest rates, in turn, would feed through the transmission mechanism to slow the growth in spending and, hence, slow the growth in real GDP.

government accounts on its own books, into which funds are deposited and from which funds are withdrawn. In addition, it manages some government accounts with the chartered banks. Alterations in the amount held in these accounts will affect the reserves of the chartered banks. The process of shifting government accounts from the Bank of Canada to the chartered banks (or in the other direction) is referred to as *cash management*.

Cash management—the shifting of government deposits between the Bank of Canada and the chartered banks—is a major tool used by the Bank of Canada in its day-to-day operations.

Suppose, for example, that the Bank of Canada transfers $100 000 from the government's account at the Bank to the government's account with a chartered bank. The transactions involved are illustrated in Table 28-2. From the government's view, nothing substantial has changed, since its deposits with one financial institution will have fallen, but its deposits with another have risen by the same amount. However, the chartered bank in question will find that its deposit liabilities and reserves will each have increased by $100 000, and hence its ratio of reserves to deposits will have risen. With an unchanged target reserve ratio, the bank will have excess reserves. As with the situation following a Bank of Canada purchase of government securities on the open market, the chartered bank will wish to loan out some of its excess reserves, thus setting in motion an expansion of deposits.

A transfer of government deposits from the chartered banks to the Bank of Canada has the opposite effect. The reserves and deposit liabilities of the banking system fall by the same amount, thus driving the actual reserve ratio below the target reserve ratio. Banks will now have insufficient reserves and will begin to call in existing loans and stop making new ones, setting in motion a process of deposit contraction.

When government deposits are transferred between the Bank of Canada and the chartered banks, the reserves of the chartered banks are changed. Such changes in reserves, through the expansion or contraction of lending, lead to changes in the money supply.

Effects on the Money Supply

Recall from Table 26-2 that the Bank of Canada holds government securities among its assets and government deposits among its liabilities. Either through open-market operations or switching these government deposits, the Bank can significantly change the reserves of the commercial banks.

Open-market operations and control of government deposits give the Bank of Canada potent tools for affecting the size of commercial-bank reserves and thus for affecting the money supply.

TABLE 28-2 Initial Balance Sheet Changes Caused by a Transfer of Government Deposits from the Bank of Canada to a Commercial Bank

Commercial bank		
Assets	Liabilities	
Reserves +100 000	Government deposits	+100 000

Bank of Canada		
Assets	Liabilities	
No change	Government deposits	−100 000
	Commercial bank deposits	+100 000

A transfer of government deposits from the Bank of Canada to a commercial bank increases bank reserves and, thus, through an expansion of bank lending, increases the money supply. When the Bank of Canada transfers $100 000 of government deposits to a commercial bank, the commercial bank's account with the Bank of Canada is credited with a deposit of $100 000. The commercial bank's increase in its deposit liabilities to the government is balanced by the increase in its reserves on deposit with the Bank of Canada. Since its deposits and its reserves have increased by the same amount, it has excess reserves and the potential is created for multiple expansion of deposit money as analysed in Chapter 26.

Though the details of an open-market operation differ from the details of switching government deposits, both actions have the same basic result: They change the reserves of the banking system, and this change in reserves then gets transformed, through commercial-bank lending, into changes in the money supply. In the remainder of this chapter, we focus on the Bank's control of reserves, ignoring the precise way in which these reserves are altered.

Practise with Study Guide Chapter 28, Exercise 1.

Monetary Policy with Zero Required Reserves

In many countries, commercial banks are *required* to hold some fraction of their deposit liabilities in reserves, either in their own vaults or as deposits at the central bank. In the past, Canadian banks faced such requirements as well, but these were eliminated in the early 1990s.

As we observed in Chapter 26, even without legal requirements to hold reserves, banks would still choose to hold quite large reserves if they did not have a central bank to fall back on, for the simple reason that there is considerable uncertainty over how many customers will enter the bank on any given day wanting the value of their deposits in cash. Today, however, in the absence of reserve requirements, the commercial banks know that as long as their balance sheets show them to be solvent, the Bank of Canada will provide them, on a temporary basis, with whatever liquidity they require.

Borrowing from the central bank is not free, however. When commercial banks borrow from the Bank of Canada, they are charged interest on their loan—the interest rate they are charged is called the **bank rate**. The bank rate changes quite frequently and draws considerable public attention when it does. See *Applying Economic Concepts 28-1* for some detailed information about how the bank rate is determined.

bank rate The rate of interest at which the Bank of Canada makes loans to commercial banks.

The current Canadian policy of "zero required reserves" is really a policy that requires the banks to have zero (or positive) reserves on *average* over a four-week averaging period. Thus, if a commercial bank has a negative balance of $10 million for one day they are required to balance that shortfall with positive reserves of $10 million on some other day during the four-week averaging period. The $10 million negative balance is financed by a loan from the Bank of Canada, which charges an interest rate equal to the bank rate. The $10 million positive balance is effectively a loan from the commercial bank to the Bank of Canada on which the Bank pays half a percentage point below the bank rate.

Since commercial banks pay a higher interest rate on negative balances than they earn on positive balances, they have an incentive to avoid negative balances. In addition, since the rate they earn on positive balances is typically less than what they could earn in the market, they also have an incentive to avoid positive balances.

Commercial banks have an incentive to maintain zero balances at the Bank of Canada.

Monetary policy now works in the same way as described in the earlier sections. When the Bank of Canada buys government securities in the open market, the commercial banks find themselves with excess reserves. They will expand their loans until the excess reserves drain away. When the Bank sells government securities, the commercial banks find themselves short of reserves and hence suffer increased risk of being forced to borrow reserves from the Bank. They will cut down on their loans in an attempt to restore their reserves.

A Review of the Transmission Mechanism

We have now seen how the Bank of Canada can alter the money supply: The Bank of Canada, through its open-market operations or the switching of government deposits, changes the reserves of the banking system. The commercial banks, facing a different level of reserves, then alter their loans and deposits to change the money supply. Before turning to a more detailed discussion of the policy choices faced by the Bank, we briefly review the analysis in Chapter 27 of the effects of changes in the money supply on the economy—this is a review of the *transmission mechanism*.

Suppose the Bank of Canada increases the reserves of the banking system (either through an open-market purchase or by switching government deposits toward the chartered banks). This action leads to an increase in the money supply and thus a fall in interest rates. This reduction in interest rates has two effects. First, lower interest rates lead to an increase in desired investment. Second, lower interest rates lead to a capital outflow as Canadian bonds become less attractive relative to foreign ones, and this capital

APPLYING ECONOMIC CONCEPTS 28-1

Monetary Policy and the Bank Rate

When commercial banks find it necessary to borrow funds temporarily from the Bank of Canada—such as when their reserves at the Bank are negative (overdrawn)—they are charged an interest rate on their loan. The bank rate is the interest rate at which the Bank of Canada makes loans to the commercial banks.

Commercial banks in need of temporary financing are not forced to borrow from the Bank of Canada, however. They can also borrow from each other or from investment dealers. The interest rate for these loans, which are often overnight (or just a few days), is called the **overnight rate.**

A higher bank rate (or a higher overnight rate) induces the commercial banks to hold more reserves in view of the higher cost of borrowing they would have to incur if they should suffer a loss of cash and are forced to seek a loan either from the Bank or from the overnight market. Thus, other things equal, an increase in the bank rate increases the target reserve ratio of the commercial banks and thus reduces the amount by which a given level of reserves in the banking system can be expanded into bank deposits.

The bank rate is set at the upper end of a range that the Bank of Canada announces as its *desired* range for the overnight rate. By moving this range (which is one-half of a percentage point wide) up or down, the Bank sig-

nals to the financial markets where it thinks the overnight rate needs to be in order to accomplish its policy goals. Since commercial banks can borrow from the Bank of Canada at the bank rate (the upper end of the range), they won't be prepared to pay a higher rate to other lenders in the overnight market. Conversely, since commercial banks can lend money to the Bank of Canada (by keeping positive balances there) and earn an interest rate given by the lower end of the desired range, they won't be prepared to lend money for a lower rate to other borrowers in the overnight market. Thus, by announcing this desired range, the Bank of Canada is able to control the range of the overnight rate.

If the overnight rate does not move quickly into the Bank's desired range, the Bank takes action to change the overnight rate. It does this by changing the reserves in the banking system. An increase in reserves (through either an open-market purchase or a switch of government deposits toward the commercial banks) puts commercial banks in the position of having excess reserves. As they try to lend these funds on the overnight market, the overnight rate falls. A decrease in reserves (through either an open-market sale or a switch of government deposits away from the commercial banks) puts commercial banks in the position of having deficient reserves. As they try to borrow funds in the overnight market, the overnight rate rises.

---

outflow depreciates the Canadian dollar and stimulates net exports. As a result of both the higher investment and the higher net exports, there is an increase in aggregate demand. The *AD* curve shifts to the right, and the equilibrium level of real GDP rises.

The opposite occurs when the Bank of Canada reduces the reserves of the banking system (through an open-market sale or switching government deposits away from the chartered banks). As reserves fall, the commercial banks reduce their loans and the money supply falls, thus raising interest rates. The higher interest rates have two effects. First, desired investment falls. Second, capital flows into Canada in pursuit of high-return Canadian bonds, causing an appreciation of the Canadian dollar and thus reducing net exports. The lower investment and lower net exports implies a reduction in aggregate demand. The *AD* curve shifts to the left, and the equilibrium level of real GDP falls.

Thus, monetary policy works through the transmission mechanism to shift the *AD* curve and thus to change equilibrium GDP. An *expansionary* monetary policy is one that

overnight rate   The interest rate that commercial banks charge each other for very-short-term loans.

See the Bank of Canada's website for information about Canada's monetary policy: www.bank-banque-canada.ca.

shifts the *AD* curve to the right and increases real GDP; a *contractionary* monetary policy is one that shifts the *AD* curve to the left and reduces real GDP.

Policy Variables and Policy Instruments

policy variables   The variables that the government seeks to influence, such as real GDP and the price level.

The Bank conducts monetary policy to influence real GDP and the price level. These ultimate objectives of the Bank's policy are called **policy variables.** The variables that it *directly* controls to achieve these objectives are called its **policy instruments.** The Bank also has **intermediate targets,** which are neither the ultimate objective of policy nor variables under the direct control of the Bank. Intermediate targets nevertheless play a key role in the execution of monetary policy; their importance lies in their close relationship to policy variables.

policy instruments
The variables that the government can control directly to achieve its policy objectives.

Policy Variables

intermediate targets
Variables that the government cannot control directly and does not seek to control ultimately, yet that have an important influence on policy variables.

The Bank of Canada's twin policy variables are real GDP and the price level. Recall from Chapter 27 that monetary policy operates by influencing aggregate demand; the resulting link between the Bank's monetary actions and the determination of the price level and real GDP is summarized in Figure 28-1.

Short Run: Nominal GDP

We also saw in Chapter 27 that the short-run effects of a shift in the *AD* curve are divided between the price level and real output in a manner determined by the slope of the *SRAS*

FIGURE 28-1   Monetary Policy and Macroeconomic Equilibrium

Monetary policy influences aggregate demand through the transmission mechanism; macroeconomic equilibrium then determines the price level and the level of real output. Monetary equilibrium requires that the interest rate be such that money supply equal the quantity of money demanded. Changes in the money market give rise to changes in the interest rate and hence, via the transmission mechanism, to changes in desired aggregate expenditure (net exports and investment). Aggregate demand and short-run aggregate supply then determine the price level and the level of real GDP.

curve. However, the Bank has no control over this slope. Thus, although the Bank cares about the separate reactions of the price level and of real output, there is little that it can do in the short run to control them independently.

Monetary policy is therefore not capable of pushing the price level (P) and real GDP (Y) toward independently determined targets simultaneously. For this reason, central banks often focus on nominal GDP (PY) as the target for monetary policy in the short run.

Long Run: The Price Level

We have seen that in the long run, when the level of wages is fully adjusted to the price level, the *LRAS* curve is vertical. The vertical *LRAS* curve implies that the only long-run impact of monetary policy will be on the price level. The absence of any long-run impact of monetary policy on real output, as we discussed in Chapter 26, is referred to as the *neutrality* of money. The long-run neutrality of money has led many central banks to focus on the price level (or its rate of change, the rate of inflation) as the long-run target for monetary policy. For example, the central banks in Sweden, Canada, and New Zealand have all adopted formal inflation targets in recent years.

Policy Instruments

Having selected its policy variables and formulated targets for their behaviour, the Bank of Canada must decide how to achieve these targets. Because the Bank can control neither real output nor the price level directly, it must employ its *policy instruments*, which it does control directly, to influence aggregate demand in the desired manner.

The Bank of Canada's policy instrument is the level of reserves in the banking system. It can adjust reserves either through open-market operations or by the switching of government deposits.

The reserves of the banking system, together with the currency in circulation, make up the Bank of Canada's liabilities (see Tables 26-1 and 26-2). Commercial bank reserves are held on deposit with the Bank of Canada and are the Bank's liability because they can be redeemed on demand. The Bank's monetary liabilities, as we saw in Chapter 26, form the *base* on which commercial banks can expand and create deposits. For this reason, the Bank's liabilities are often referred to as the *monetary base*. Therefore, economists say that the Bank's policy instrument is the monetary base. It is this monetary base that the Bank is changing when it conducts open-market operations or when it switches government deposits.

Intermediate Targets

Major changes in the direction of monetary policy are made only infrequently. Decisions regarding the implementation of policy must, however, be made almost daily. Given the values that the Bank of Canada wishes its policy variables to take on, and given the current state of the economy, are increases or decreases in the monetary base called for? How big an increase, or how big a decrease? Such questions must be answered continually in the Bank's day-to-day operations.

Daily information about the policy variables, however, is rarely available. Inflation and unemployment rates are available only on a monthly basis and with a considerable lag. National income figures are available even less frequently; they appear on a quarterly basis. Thus, the policy makers do not know exactly what is happening to the policy variables when they make their daily decisions regarding the Bank's policy instruments.

How, then, does the Bank of Canada make decisions? Central banks have typically used *intermediate targets* to guide them when implementing monetary policy in the very short run. To serve as an intermediate target, a variable must satisfy two criteria. First, information about it must be available on a frequent basis, daily if possible. Second, its movements must be closely correlated with those of the policy variable, so that changes in it can reasonably be expected to indicate that the policy variable is also changing (or will do so in the near future).

Consistency of Intermediate Targets

The two most commonly used intermediate targets have been the money supply and the interest rate. However, these two variables are not independent of each other; recall that the liquidity preference function relates the quantity of money demanded to the rate of interest. This relationship and its implications for the Bank's choice of intermediate targets are reviewed in Figure 28-2.

The Bank of Canada cannot use its control of the monetary base to influence both the interest rate and the money supply independently.

FIGURE 28-2   Alternative Intermediate Targets

For a given liquidity preference function, the Bank of Canada cannot choose independent targets for the money supply and the interest rate. If the Bank chooses a target of M_{S0} for the money supply, it must accept the interest rate of i_0. If it then decides to increase the money supply to M_{S1}, it must accept the lower interest rate of i_1.

If the Bank chooses a target of i_0 for the interest rate, it must accept the money supply of M_{S0}. If it then decides to reduce the interest rate to i_1, it must accept the higher money supply of M_{S1}.

Because the money supply and interest rates are closely related (along the *LP* function), it might appear not to matter whether the Bank chooses to target the interest rate or instead chooses to target the money supply. For example, if the Bank wishes to remove an inflationary gap by reducing aggregate demand, it will sell government securities and thus drive their prices down and interest rates up. These open-market sales will also reduce the monetary base and thus contract the money supply. It is largely immaterial whether the Bank seeks to force interest rates up or to contract the money supply; doing one accomplishes the other. Similarly, driving interest rates down by means of open-market purchases of government securities will tend to expand the money supply as the public gains money in return for the securities that it sells to the Bank.

But the world is not quite as simple as we have just described. Whether the Bank uses interest rates or the money supply as an intermediate target can actually matter in some situations. Let's see why this is the case.

Choice of Intermediate Targets

Prior to the early 1970s, the Bank of Canada primarily used the interest rate as its intermediate target. Many economists, especially Monetarists, criticized this choice. They pointed out that since interest rates tended to vary directly with the business cycle, rising on the upswing and falling on the downswing, it was difficult for the central bank to determine the impact of its monetary policy by observing the interest rate alone. They cited historical examples in which central banks wished to restrain a boom and were convinced that they were doing so because interest rates were rising sharply, only to later determine that it was the boom itself that was driving up the demand for money and thus driving up interest rates.

This experience with focusing on interest rates led to changes in intermediate targets.

In the 1970s, the Bank of Canada began to focus on the money supply as its intermediate target.

At the outset, the measure that was used for this purpose was the narrowly defined money supply, M1. However, it soon became clear that problems also arose when the Bank focused exclusively on M1 as its intermediate target.

To understand the problems associated with focusing on a single measure of the money supply, note that changes in the money supply are reliable indicators of the direction of monetary policy *only if the demand for money is stable.* However, the demand for money can be unstable for two reasons. First, we have just seen that money demand tends to rise in booms and fall in slumps, as fluctuations in real GDP lead to similar changes in the transactions demand for money. Second, the demand for *any particular monetary aggregate* can change quite substantially as firms and households *substitute* one type of financial asset for another. For example, households might reduce their deposits in chequing accounts and increase their deposits in saving accounts. This would be a reduction in M1 but, because M2 includes both chequing and saving deposits, there would be no change in M2. But if the Bank is only monitoring M1, then this reduction in the money supply (as defined by M1) suggests that monetary policy is becoming tighter. In fact, however, all that is happening is a substitution of one type of asset for another. The Bank's response to the problems caused by the instability of money demand was again to change its intermediate targets.

In the early 1980s, dissatisfaction with M1 as an intermediate target led the Bank of Canada to monitor several monetary aggregates rather than just one.

Even the monitoring of several different monetary aggregates, however, does not solve the problem of the instability of money demand. There are times when the current state of monetary policy needs to be gauged by measures other than money supply magnitudes, and interest rates can provide valuable additional information.

For example, during the last half of the 1970s, slow growth in all measures of the money supply suggested (to those who were monitoring only the money supply) that monetary policy was fairly tight. However, decreases in the demand for money that were not fully recognized at the time meant that the money supply was growing quite rapidly *relative to demand,* and hence monetary policy was much more expansionary than was thought at the time. More attention to interest rates would have given an important signal of this, because throughout this period interest rates were quite low. Figure 28-3 illustrates the general lesson.

Changes in the demand for money imply that the stance of monetary policy cannot be judged only by looking at measures of the money supply. In such cases, interest rates provide additional information about monetary policy.

Practise with Study Guide Chapter 28, Exercise 3.

The Role of the Exchange Rate

As we have seen, the transmission mechanism of monetary policy in an open economy involves changes in both the interest rate and the exchange rate. So you should not be surprised to learn that the Bank of Canada pays close attention to movements in the exchange rate.

As with interest rates, however, care must be taken in drawing inferences about monetary policy from changes in the exchange rate. Care must be taken because the exchange rate can change for different reasons, which have different implications for

FIGURE 28-3   Intermediate Targets When the Demand for Money Shifts

Shifts in the liquidity preference function change the relationship between the money supply and the interest rate. The demand for money is initially given by the LP function, LP_0. It then shifts to the left to the dashed LP function, LP_1—this is a reduction in the demand for money.

Suppose that, following the shift in the LP function, the money supply falls from M_{S0} to M_{S1} and so the interest rate falls from i_0 to i_1. If the Bank were to focus on the fall in the money supply (and did not recognize the reduction in money demand), it would conclude that monetary policy had tightened. But if it focused on the fall in the interest rate (and did not recognize the reduction in money demand), it would conclude that monetary policy had loosened.

Since the combination of demand and supply shifts led to a reduction in the interest rate, the truth is that money supply fell by less than money demand. From the discussion in *Extensions in Theory 28-1*, this reduction in money supply would *not* be viewed as a contractionary monetary policy. Indeed, given the reduction in money demand, the *smaller* reduction in money supply would be viewed as an *expansionary* monetary policy.

the desired direction of monetary policy. Here are two examples to illustrate this point. In both cases, suppose that we begin in a situation where real GDP is equal to its potential level.

First, suppose that Canada's trading partners are booming and thus demanding more Canadian exports. Foreigners' heightened demand for Canadian goods creates an increase in demand for the Canadian dollar in foreign-exchange markets. The Canadian dollar therefore appreciates. But the increase in demand for Canadian goods also adds directly to Canadian aggregate demand. If this shock persists, it will therefore add to domestic inflationary pressures. In this case, if the Bank notes the appreciation of the dollar (and correctly determines its cause), it can take early action to offset the positive demand shock by tightening monetary policy.

A second example involves an increase in demand for Canadian *assets* rather than Canadian goods, and has quite different implications from the first example. Suppose that investors, because of events happening elsewhere in the world, decide to liquidate some of their foreign assets and purchase more Canadian assets instead. In this case, the increase in demand for Canadian assets leads to an increase in demand for the Canadian dollar in foreign-exchange markets. This causes an appreciation of the Canadian dollar. As the dollar appreciates, however, Canadian exports become more expensive to foreigners. There will be a reduction in Canadian net exports and thus a reduction in Canadian aggregate demand. If this shock persists, it will reduce inflationary pressure in Canada. In this case, if the Bank notes the appreciation of the dollar (and correctly determines its cause), it can take early action to offset the negative demand shock by loosening monetary policy.

Notice in both examples that the Canadian dollar appreciated as a result of the external shock, but the causes of the appreciation were different. In the first case, there was a positive demand shock to net exports, which then caused the appreciation, which in turn dampened the initial increase in net exports. But the overall effect on the demand for Canadian goods was positive. In the second case, there was a positive shock to the asset market, which then caused the appreciation, which in turn reduced the demand for net exports. The overall effect on the demand for Canadian goods was negative. Thus, in the first case, the appropriate monetary policy was contractionary, whereas in the second case the appropriate monetary policy was expansionary.

Changes in the exchange rate can signal the need for changes in the stance of monetary policy. But care must be taken to identify the cause of the exchange-rate change.

Since the early 1990s, the Bank of Canada has formalized the role of the exchange rate by constructing what it calls the Monetary Conditions Index (MCI). The MCI is a weighted average of the interest rate and the exchange rate. *Applying Economic Concepts 28-2* discusses how the Bank uses the MCI as an intermediate target.

APPLYING ECONOMIC CONCEPTS 28-2

The Monetary Conditions Index as an Intermediate Target

Because monetary policy in an open economy works through changes in both the interest rate and the exchange rate, the Bank of Canada closely monitors what it calls the *Monetary Conditions Index* (*MCI*). The MCI is an index that reflects changes in short-term interest rates (typically the 90-day rate on corporate bonds) and the exchange rate. The Bank uses its policy instrument—changes in bank reserves—to alter the MCI so that it is consistent with the Bank's longer-term inflation goals. In this box, we explain the MCI and how the Bank uses it to conduct its monetary policy.

The Monetary Conditions Index

Suppose we let i be the current interest rate and e be the current exchange rate. Recall from Chapter 19 that e is defined as the number of Canadian dollars required to purchase one unit of foreign currency, so an increase in e is a depreciation of the Canadian dollar. Further, let i_B and e_B be the values taken by i and e in some base year (the Bank currently uses 1987 as the base year). The MCI is then defined to be

$$MCI = (i - i_B) - \theta (e - e_B)$$

where θ is a positive parameter estimated by the Bank's economists to be about 1/3. (We discuss θ in a moment.)

To see how the MCI is influenced by monetary policy, consider what would happen if the Bank engineered a monetary contraction. The Bank reduces reserves to the banking system and this reduces the money supply. For given money demand, the reduction in money supply pushes up interest rates. But that is not the end of the story in an open economy. The high interest rates on Canadian bonds then attract foreign purchasers, who must buy Canadian dollars in order to purchase these high-yield bonds. The increase in demand for the Canadian dollar leads to an appreciation of the Canadian dollar, which is a fall in e. Thus, as a result of the reduction in the money supply, i has increased and e has fallen. On both counts, the MCI increases. By similar reasoning, a monetary expansion reduces i, raises e, and thus lowers the MCI.

Following this logic, the Bank refers to an increase in the MCI as a tightening of *monetary conditions*; a reduction in the MCI is referred to as a loosening of monetary conditions.

How the Bank Uses the MCI

As we will see later in this chapter, the Bank of Canada in 1991 announced formal *inflation-control targets*. Suppose that the Bank's target is to keep inflation between 1 and 3 percent (this is indeed the Bank's current goal). Given this long-term inflation target, how is the MCI used as an intermediate target?

The economists at the Bank use complex statistical methods to estimate the relationship between their policy instrument—changes in reserves—and real GDP and inflation. Since monetary policy works by changing i and e, and thus the MCI, they need to know the relationship between the MCI and real GDP. This is where θ comes in. The estimate of θ of 1/3 reflects the empirical finding by the Bank's economists that a 3 percent change in e has roughly the same impact on real GDP as a 1 percentage point change in i. The Bank must also make predictions of what events are likely to occur in the world economy that will affect the level of economic activity in Canada.

Given all this information, the Bank must arrive at an estimate of the level of the *current* MCI that is consistent with its inflation target *6–8 quarters in the future*. Given this desired level of the MCI, the Bank then uses its policy instrument (changes in reserves) to alter the MCI so that it is consistent with the desired level.

After the Bank has adjusted its policy instruments to get the MCI to its desired level, it must continue to monitor the economy, both within Canada and in the rest of the world. As new information becomes available, and as unforeseen events occur, the Bank revises its estimate of where the current MCI ought to be in order to reach the inflation target 6 to 8 quarters in the future.

This box draws on the discussion in Charles Freedman, "The Role of Monetary Conditions and the Monetary Conditions Index in the Conduct of Policy," *Bank of Canada Review*, Autumn 1995.

Lags in the Conduct of Monetary Policy

In Chapter 27 we encountered one difference between two groups of macroeconomists involved in a debate that was prominent in the 1950s and 1960s. *Monetarists* argued that monetary policy was potentially very powerful in the sense that a given change in the money supply would lead to a substantial change in aggregate demand, whereas *Keynesians* were associated with the view that monetary policy was much less powerful.

This debate had some of its roots in differing interpretations of the causes of the Great Depression, especially as it occurred in the United States amid a large number of commercial-bank failures. Now that you better understand the role of central banks and commercial banks in the determination of the money supply, you can better understand this debate. One interesting part of the debate is why Canada and the United Kingdom had collapses in economic activity similar in magnitude to that in the United States even though they did not suffer the same banking crisis. *Lessons from History 28-1* provides a brief summary of this interesting debate.

The debate between the Monetarists and the Keynesians, however, involved more than just the *size* of the effect of a change in the money supply on national income; it also focused on the question of whether active use of monetary policy in an attempt to stabilize output and the price level was likely to be successful, or whether it would instead lead to an increase in fluctuations in those variables. This debate is as important today as it was then, and at its centre is the role of *lags*.

Execution Lags

Experience has shown that lags in the operation of policy can actually cause stabilization policy to be destabilizing. In Chapter 25, we discussed how decision and implementation lags might limit the extent to which active use of fiscal policy can be relied upon to stabilize the economy. Although both of these sources of lags are much less relevant for monetary policy, the full effects of monetary policy nevertheless occur only after quite long time lags. *Execution lags,* lags that occur after the decision has been made to implement the policy, can have important implications for the conduct of monetary policy.

There are three reasons why a change in monetary policy does not affect the economy instantly.

Deposit Creation Takes Time

Open-market operations or the switching of government deposits affect the reserves of the banks. This process takes place more or less instantly. But the full increase in the money supply occurs only when the commercial banks have granted enough new loans and made enough investments to expand the money supply by the full amount that is possible by existing reserve ratios. This process can take quite a long time.

Changes in Expenditure Take Time

A change in the money supply leads to a change in the interest rate. This, in turn, affects interest-sensitive expenditures. But it takes time for new investment plans to be drawn up, approved, and put into effect. It may take a year or more before the full increase in investment expenditure occurs in response to a fall in interest rates. In an open economy like Canada's, the change in the interest rate also leads to capital flows and a change in the exchange rate. These changes occur very quickly. But the effect on net exports takes more time while purchasers of internationally traded goods and services switch to lower-cost suppliers.

The Multiplier Process Takes Time

Changes in investment and net export expenditures brought about by a change in monetary policy set off the multiplier process that increases national income. This process, too, takes some time to work out.

Furthermore, although the end result is fairly predictable, the speed with which the entire expansionary or contractionary process works itself out can vary in ways that are hard to predict. Thus, though the effects of monetary policy might be reasonably straightforward to predict, the timing of those effects is difficult to predict.

Monetary policy is capable of exerting expansionary and contractionary forces on the economy, but it operates with a time lag that is long and variable.

Economists at the Bank of Canada estimate that it takes between 9 and 12 months for a change in monetary policy to have an effect on real GDP, and a further 9 to 12 months for the policy to have an effect on the price level.

Destabilizing Policy?

To see the significance of execution lags for the conduct of monetary policy, consider a simple example. To begin, suppose that the lag is known to be exactly 18 months. If on January 1, the Bank of Canada determines that the economy needs a stimulus, it can increase the reserves of the banking system within the day and the money supply can then begin to increase. By the end of that month a significant increase may be registered.

However, because the full effects of this policy take time to work out, the policy may prove to be destabilizing. By October, a substantial inflationary gap may have developed because of cyclical forces unrelated to the Bank's monetary policy. However, since the effects of the monetary expansion that was initiated nine months earlier are just beginning to be felt, an expansionary monetary stimulus is adding to the existing inflationary gap.

If the Bank now applies the monetary brakes by contracting the money supply, the full effects of this move will not be felt for another 18 months. By that time, a contraction may have already set in because of the natural cyclical forces of the economy. Thus, the delayed effects of the monetary policy may turn a minor downturn into a major recession.

The long execution lag of monetary policy makes monetary fine-tuning difficult; the policy may have a destabilizing effect.

We supposed in this example that the execution lag was known with certainty to be 18 months. In this case, it could be built into the Bank's calculations. But the fact that the lag is actually highly variable makes this nearly impossible. Of course, when a persistent gap has existed and is predicted to continue for a long time, monetary policy may be stabilizing even when its effects occur after a long time lag.

Political Difficulties

Long execution lags in the workings of monetary policy also imply political difficulties for the central bank.

LESSONS FROM HISTORY 28-1

Two Views on the Role of Money in the Great Depression

In most peoples' minds, the Great Depression began with the stock market crash of October 1929. In the United States, Canada, and Europe, the decline in economic activity over the next four years was massive. From 1929 to 1933, real output fell by roughly 25 percent, one quarter of the labour force was unemployed by 1933, the price level fell by over 25 percent, and businesses failed on a massive scale. In the six decades that have followed, no recession has come close to the Great Depression in terms of reduced economic activity, business failures, or unemployment.

The Great Depression has naturally attracted the attention of economists and, especially in the United States, these few years of experience have served as a kind of "retrospective laboratory" in which they have tried to test their theories.

_____

For a discussion of these two views, and some attempts to discriminate between them, see Peter Temin, *Did Monetary Forces Cause the Great Depression?* (New York: Norton, 1976). For the classic statement of the Monetarist view, see Milton Friedman and Anna Schwartz, *A Monetary History of the United States 1867–1960* (Princeton: Princeton University Press, 1963).

The Basic Facts

The stock market crash of 1929, and other factors associated with a moderate downswing in business activity during the late 1920s, caused the U.S. public (firms and households) to wish to hold more cash and fewer demand deposits. The banking system, however, could not meet this increased demand for liquidity without help from the Federal Reserve System (the U.S. central bank). As we saw in Chapter 26, because of the fractional-reserve banking system, commercial banks are never able to satisfy from their own reserves a large and sudden demand for cash—their reserves are always only a small fraction of total deposits.

The Federal Reserve had been set up to provide just such emergency assistance to commercial banks that were basically sound but were unable to meet sudden demands by depositors to withdraw cash. However, the Fed refused to extend the necessary help, and successive waves of bank failures followed as a direct result. During each wave, hundreds of banks failed, ruining many depositors and thereby worsening an already severe depression. In the second half of 1931, almost 2000 U.S. banks were forced to suspend operations. One consequence of these failures was a sharp drop in the money supply; by 1933, M2 was 33 percent lower than it had been in 1929.

Figure 28-4 shows a situation in which the current inflation rate is at the bottom of the Bank's 1–3 percent target band, but the expectation of future events suggests that inflation will be rising sharply. This situation was faced by the Bank of Canada in the spring of 1997. At that time, the Canadian economy was experiencing healthy growth. But a fast-growing U.S. economy, through its growing demand for Canadian exports, was expected to increase Canadian growth sharply, which would then increase inflationary pressures.

What is the political problem? Remember that because of the time lags involved, any policy change that occurs today has no effect on real GDP for roughly 9 months and the full effect on the price level does not occur for 18–24 months. If the economy is at point A in Figure 28-4, and inflation is expected to rise in the near future, then monetary policy must be changed *now* in order to counteract this future inflation. But this is politically difficult because the *current* inflation rate is low. The Bank finds itself in the awkward position of advocating a tightening of monetary policy, in order to fight the expectation of future inflation, at a time when the *current* inflation rate suggests no need for tightening. But if the goal is to keep inflation within the target range, such *preemptive* monetary policy is necessary because of the unavoidable time lags.

Competing Explanations

To Monetarists, these facts seem decisive: To them, the fall in the money supply was clearly the major cause of the fall in output and employment that occurred during the Great Depression. Monetarists see the Great Depression as perhaps the single best piece of evidence of the strength of monetary forces, and the single best lesson of the importance of monetary policy. In their view, the increased cash drain that led to the massive monetary contraction could have been prevented had the Federal Reserve quickly increased the level of reserves in the commercial banking system. In this case, the rise in the monetary base would have offset the increase in the cash drain, so that the money supply (currency plus bank deposits) could be maintained.

Keynesians argue that the fundamental cause of the Great Depression was a reduction in autonomous expenditure. They cite a large decline in housing construction (in response to a glut of housing) and a reduction in consumption driven largely by pessimism caused by the stock market crash. Although Keynesians accept the argument that the Fed's behaviour was perverse, and exacerbated an already bad situation, they do not attribute a pivotal role to the Fed or to the money supply. Indeed, they see the fall in the money supply as a *result* of the decline in economic activity (through a reduced demand for loans and thus reduced bank lending) rather than as its cause.

Lessons from Canada's Experience

Canada has been used as a "control" in this retrospective laboratory, for the simple reason that Canada had broadly the same magnitude of economic collapse as did the United States, but *did not* have the same magnitude of bank failures. Unfortunately, Canada's experience is not able to resolve the disagreement—both sides of the debate offer explanations of the Canadian experience consistent with their central arguments.

Keynesians look to Canada's experience to support their view that money was not central to the cause of the economic collapse in the United States. They point out that in Canada, where the central bank came to the aid of the banking system, bank failures were much less common during the Great Depression, and as a consequence, the money supply did not shrink drastically as it did in the United States. Thus, their argument is that since Canada did not escape the Great Depression, but it *did* escape the collapse in the money supply, then money must not have been the central cause of the U.S. economic collapse.

Monetarists accept the point that Canada did not have a massive reduction in the money supply, but they argue that the economic contraction in the United States (which *was* caused by the collapse in the money supply) spilled over into Canada, largely through a dramatic reduction in demand for Canadian goods. This spillover implies a large decline in autonomous export expenditure for Canada, and thus a decline in Canadian national income. Thus, Monetarists essentially argue that money in the United States was an important contributor to the economic decline in Canada.

Time lags in monetary policy require that decisions regarding a loosening or tightening of monetary conditions be forward-looking. This often creates political difficulties for the central bank.

A Monetary Rule?

Monetarists have criticized the Bank for fine-tuning, and the poor record of monetary policy as a short-run stabilizer, especially in the late 1970s and early 1980s, has lent force to their criticisms. Monetarists in Canada have argued that:

- monetary policy is a potent force of expansionary and contractionary pressures;
- monetary policy works with long and variable lags;
- the Bank has been prone to sharp reversals of its policy stance.

Given these three premises, Monetarists have concluded that monetary policy has sometimes had a destabilizing effect on the economy, the policy itself accentuating rather than dampening the economy's natural cyclical swings.

FIGURE 28-4   Political Difficulties of Forward-Looking Monetary Policy

Since monetary policy works only with a considerable time lag, central-bank actions to keep inflation within its target range must be taken in advance of expected future events. Suppose the economy is currently at point *A* with inflation at the lower bound of the target range. If events in the near future are expected to cause inflation to rise sharply, then monetary policy must be tightened immediately to keep inflation within the desired range. The central bank then faces the politically awkward situation of tightening policy at a time when *current* inflation is low.

Monetarists argue from this position that the stability of the economy would be much improved if the Bank *stopped trying to stabilize it*. What then should the Bank do? Because growth of population and of productivity leads to a rising level of real output, Monetarists think the Bank ought to expand the money supply year in and year out at a constant rate that is equal to the long-run rate of growth of real GDP. When the growth rate shows signs of long-term change, the Bank can adjust its rate of monetary expansion. It should not, however, alter this rate with a view to stabilizing the economy against short-term fluctuations.

Many other economists disagree with the Monetarists' position against fine tuning. They argue that an appropriate monetary policy of fine tuning can, *in principle*, reduce cyclical fluctuations below what they would be under a constant-rate rule. Monetarists respond, however, by arguing that whatever may be true of the *best conceivable* monetary policy, the Bank's *actual* policy over the past many years has made cyclical fluctuations larger than they would have been under a constant-rate rule. They argue that attempts to use monetary policy to fine-tune the economy inevitably are fraught with dangers.

There is another argument against a constant-rate rule, however. Experience has shown that the demand for money sometimes can shift quite substantially. A stable money supply rule in the face of demand instability guarantees monetary shocks, rather than monetary stability (recall Figure 28-3). Such demand instability undermines confidence in the appropriateness of a monetary rule. The daunting challenge that faces central banks in this situation is to offset such shifts in the demand for money while not overreacting and thereby destabilizing the economy.

20 Years of Canadian Monetary Policy

This section describes a few key episodes in recent Canadian monetary history. This is not done to teach history for its own sake, but because the lessons of past experience and past policy mistakes, interpreted through the filter of economic theory, provide our best hope for improving our policy performance in the future.

By 1980, partly as a result of the two OPEC oil shocks, in 1974 and 1979–80, inflation in Canada was over 12 percent. The Bank of Canada (and also the U.S Federal Reserve) embarked on a strict policy of monetary restraint aimed at fighting inflation. Interest rates rose sharply, as shown in Figure 28-5. The result of this aggressive disinflation policy was, in both countries, the most serious recession since the 1930s.

These high interest rates, and the recession they wrought, were more severe than might have been expected from the relatively moderate slowdown in the rate of growth of the money supply induced by the central banks.

FIGURE 28-5 Short-Term Interest Rates, Canada and the United States, 1979–1999

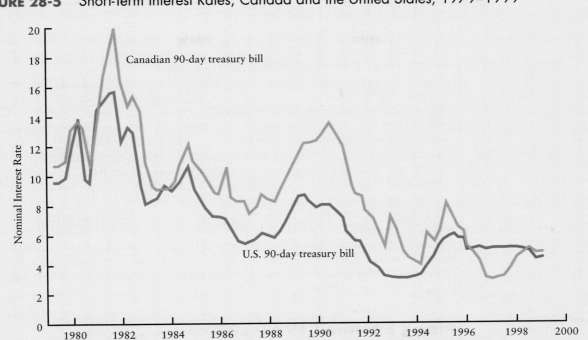

Canadian nominal interest rates have been highly variable over the period shown. They increased with the rising inflation from 1980 to mid 1981. They then fell as inflation fell through most of the 1980s. Starting in 1988, the rates rose steadily under the impact of the Bank of Canada's anti-inflation policy, eventually reaching a level five percentage points above U.S. rates by the end of 1990. As the inflation rate tumbled in mid 1992, interest rates, which began to decline in 1990, by 1993 reached levels lower than they had been seen since the 1960s. These low interest rates continued (with some ups and downs) through to the middle of 1996 when Canadian rates fell below U.S. rates. Throughout 1996 and 1997, Canadian rates remained below U.S. rates. By mid 1998, however, Canadian interest rates rose slightly above those in the United States.

(*Source: Bank of Canada Review,* various issues; and *Economic Report of the President,* various issues.)

An unanticipated surge in the demand for money led to a much tighter monetary policy than the Bank had intended.

In other words, this unplanned tight monetary policy did not occur because money supply fell more than intended, but because money demand increased sharply. With the dramatic fall in inflation and the serious recession, the Bank eased monetary policy in the second half of 1982.

Economic Recovery: 1983–1987

In early 1983, a sustained recovery began, and by mid 1987, real GDP had moved back toward potential. Much of the growth was centred in the export-oriented manufacturing industries in Ontario and Quebec. The first four years of the recovery saw cumulative output growth of 15.7 percent.

The main challenge for monetary policy in this period was to create sufficient liquidity to accommodate the recovery without triggering a return to the high inflation rates that prevailed at the start of the decade.

In other words, the Bank of Canada had to increase the money supply to *accommodate* the recovery-induced increase in money demand *without* increasing the money supply so much that it refueled inflationary pressures.

In spite of much debate and uncertainty, the Bank handled this "reentry" problem quite well. The Bank allowed a short but rapid burst of growth in the nominal money supply, thus generating the desired increase in real money balances. Once the new level of real balances was achieved, money growth was cut back to a rate consistent with low inflation, allowing for the underlying rate of growth in real income. The trick with this policy was that to avoid triggering expectations of renewed inflation, the Bank had to generate a one-shot increase in the *level* of the money supply without creating the impression that it was raising the long-term *rate of growth* of the money supply.

In late 1983 and early 1984, when growth in monetary aggregates first started to surge, many voiced the fear that the Bank was being overly expansionary and was risking a return to higher inflation. As the reentry problem came to be more widely understood and as inflationary pressures failed to reemerge, these criticisms subsided, and the consensus appeared to be that the Bank had done a commendable job of handling the reentry problem.

Rising Inflation: 1987–1990

By mid 1987, many observers began to worry that Canadian policy makers were too complacent in accepting the 4 percent range that Canadian inflation had settled into. Further, there was concern that inflationary pressures were starting to build—monetary aggregates were growing quickly, real output growth was strong, unemployment was falling, and an inflationary gap was opening.

In 1987, many economists argued that if monetary policy was not tightened, Canada would experience gradually increasing inflation until once again a severe monetary restriction would be necessary.

Inflation slowly crept upward. A monetary restriction designed to reduce inflation would obviously impose costs in the form of lower output and higher unemployment. Was the Bank prepared to inflict such costs, especially given that Canada had emerged from a deep recession only five years earlier?

Disinflation: 1990–92

In January 1988, Bank of Canada Governor John Crow announced that monetary policy would henceforth be guided less by short-term stabilization issues and more by the goal of long-term "price stability." Specifically, he said that "monetary policy should be conducted so as to achieve a pace of monetary expansion that promotes stability in the value of money. This means pursuing a policy aimed at achieving and maintaining stable prices."[1]

---

[1]John W. Crow, "The Work of Canadian Monetary Policy," speech given at the University of Alberta, January 18, 1988; reprinted in *Bank of Canada Review,* February 1988.

This explicit adoption of price stability as the Bank's only target set off a heated debate about the appropriate stance for monetary policy. The debate was fueled by Crow's decision to give a high profile to his policy by repeatedly articulating and defending it in speeches and public appearances. Some critics said that price stability was unobtainable. Others said the costs of reaching it would be too large in terms of several years of recessionary gaps. Supporters said that the long-term gains from having a stable price level would exceed the costs of getting there.

Despite the Bank's explicit policy of "price stability," the actual inflation rate increased slightly in the years immediately following John Crow's policy announcement, from about 4 percent in 1987 to just over 5 percent in 1990.

John Crow was the governor of the Bank of Canada from 1987 to 1994. In 1988 he announced that "price stability" would thenceforth be the Bank of Canada's objective.

The controversy reached new heights when in 1990 the country (and much of the world) entered a sustained recession. Maintaining the policy of tight money with high interest rates seemed perverse to many when the economy was already suffering from too little aggregate demand to sustain potential output.

Furthermore, the high Canadian interest rates attracted foreign funds. Foreigners who wished to buy Canadian bonds needed Canadian dollars, and their demands led to an appreciation of the Canadian dollar. This increased the price of Canadian exports while reducing the price of Canadian imports, putting Canadian export and import-competing industries at a competitive disadvantage, and further increasing the unemployment that had been generated by the worldwide recession.

In spite of heavy political pressure to lower interest rates, and of criticism from many economists who might have supported a move toward price stability in less depressed times, the Bank stood by its tight monetary policy. Indeed, in 1991, it formally announced *inflation-control targets* for the next several years. Beginning in 1992, inflation was to lie within the 3–5 percent range, with the range falling to 2–4 percent by 1993 and to 1–3 percent by the end of 1995.

The result of this commitment to tight money was an unprecedented differential between Canadian and U.S. interest rates (see Figure 28-5), and a high value of the Canadian dollar, which temporarily hurt the international competitiveness of Canadian goods.

As a result of the tight monetary policy of the Bank, the inflation rate fell sharply, from about 5 percent in 1990 to less than 2 percent in 1992. For 1993 and 1994, inflation hovered around 2 percent. Furthermore, short-term nominal interest rates fell from a high of 12 percent in 1990 to about 6 percent by the end of 1993. Recall that the nominal interest rate is equal to the real interest rate plus the rate of inflation. So this decline in nominal interest rates was the eventual result of the tight money policy that reduced inflation. The differential between Canadian and U.S. rates also fell and the Canadian dollar depreciated. Figure 28-5 tells the story in detail.

Price-Stability: 1992–?

Clearly, the Bank had succeeded in coming close to its target of price stability. Controversy continued, however, on two issues. First, was the result worth the price of a deeper, possibly more prolonged recession than might have occurred if the Bank had been willing to accept 3–4 percent inflation? Second, would the low inflation rate be sustainable once the recovery took the economy back toward potential income? If the inflation rate were to rise to 4 percent during the post-1993 recovery, then the verdict might well be that the cost of temporarily reducing the rate to below 2 percent was not worth the transitory gains.

The debate over the Bank's disinflation policy became centred on Governor John Crow, especially during the federal election campaign of 1993. Some called for the non-renewal of Crow's term as Governor (which would end in 1994), and his replacement with someone more concerned with the costs of disinflation. Others argued that the Bank's policy of "price stability" under Crow's stewardship was the right policy for the times, and that the long-run benefits of low inflation would be worth the costs required to achieve it.[2]

In 1994, the minister of finance appointed Gordon Thiessen, the former deputy governor of the Bank, to be the new governor. With some irony, the minister of finance, whose party had been severe critics of Crow's policy while they were in opposition, affirmed the previous monetary policy of the Bank and urged the new governor to maintain the hard-won low inflation rate. The new governor also affirmed the policy of price stability, and extended the formal inflation target of 1 to 3 percent.

For the next five years, the rate of inflation continued to hover between 1 and 2 percent. The main challenge for the Bank in the next few years was to keep inflation low while at the same time encouraging the economy to progress through what was viewed as a fragile economic recovery. Excessive stimulation of the economy would lead to the rise of inflation which would sacrifice the hard-won gains achieved only a few years earlier. On the other hand, insufficient stimulation would itself be an obstacle to economic recovery. By 2000, real GDP in Canada was close to its potential level and inflation was just below 2 percent.

Gordon Thiessen became the governor of the Bank of Canada in 1994 after inflation had hovered around 2 percent for about two years.

Concerns in the Late 1990s

During the late 1990s, three issues complicated the conduct of Canadian monetary policy. One was the "Asian Crisis" of 1997–98. The second was the remarkable growth in the Canadian and U.S. stock markets. The third was the possibility that inflation had become *too low*.

The Asian Crisis

Beginning in the summer of 1997, the economies of Thailand, Malaysia, Indonesia, and South Korea fell into serious recessions.[3] Since these countries are major importers of raw materials, their recessions led to a large decline in the world's demand for raw materials. As a result, the world price of raw materials fell by an average of about 30 percent in the subsequent year. Since Canada is a major producer and exporter of raw materials, this decline in the demand for raw materials was a negative aggregate demand shock for Canada. The decline in Canada's net exports led to a leftward shift in Canada's *AD* curve.

Working in the opposite direction, however, was the expansionary supply-side effect of lower raw materials prices for the many Canadian manufacturing firms that use raw

---

[2]For a very readable account of Canadian monetary policy from 1988 to 1993, see William Robson and David Laidler, *The Great Canadian Disinflation* (Toronto: C. D. Howe Institute, 1993).

[3]An important part of the cause of these recessions was the sudden collapse of their currencies, which were previously pegged in value to the U.S. dollar. We examine fixed and flexible exchange rates in detail in Chapter 36.

materials as inputs. Remember from Chapter 24 that reductions in input prices shift the *SRAS* curve to the right and increase real GDP—a positive supply shock.

This positive supply shock was especially important for the United States, a major importer and user of raw materials. The impact of the Asian Crisis on the U.S. economy produced a third effect on Canada as the quickly growing U.S. economy increased its demand for Canadian goods and services.

The Asian Crisis therefore produced a complicated combination of forces on the Canadian economy, including

- a negative *AD* effect from the reduction in demand (and thus the prices) for Canadian exports
- a positive *SRAS* effect from the lower-price inputs for Canadian manufacturing firms
- a positive *AD* effect from the increase in U.S. demand for Canadian goods (caused, in turn, by the positive *SRAS* effect in the United States)

In the spring of 1997, before the Asian Crisis had begun, the Canadian economy was growing and steadily closing a recessionary gap. The combination of forces created by the Asian Crisis presented problems for the Bank of Canada and for the appropriate direction for monetary policy. Especially difficult was judging the relative strengths of the three separate effects. As it turned out, Canada's recessionary gap continued to shrink as the economy grew steadily. By 1999, the Asian economies were on their way to a healthy recovery.

See Chapter 28 of www.pearsoned.ca/lipsey for an interesting discussion of how monetary policy responded to the Asian crisis: Stephen Poloz, "How Will Central Banks Cope with a Non-Inflationary World?" *World Economic Affairs.*

The Stock Market

A rising stock market can cause problems for the conduct of monetary policy. From 1994 through 1999, U.S. and Canadian stocks enjoyed unprecedented bull markets. The Dow Jones Industrial Average (an index of U.S. stock prices) increased from about 3500 in mid 1994 to about 11 000 in late 1999, an average annual increase of 26 percent. The Toronto Stock Exchange (TSE) 300 Index increased from roughly 4000 to 8000 over the same period, an average annual increase of 14 percent.

The concern for the Bank of Canada during this time was that the increase in wealth generated by these stock-market gains would stimulate consumption expenditures in what was already a steadily growing economy, thus increasing inflationary pressures. A second concern by 1998–99 was that the stock market had reached such heights that, in the views of many commentators, a "crash" (or a "correction" when it is less dramatic) was imminent. The concern was that a large stock market crash would reduce household wealth significantly and thus cause a major and sudden reduction in aggregate demand.

The appendix to this chapter contains a brief discussion of the stock market and how it is related to macroeconomic developments.

Is Inflation Too Low?

The third problem faced by the Bank during the late 1990s was, ironically, caused by its success in reducing inflation and maintaining it at a low level. Some economists argued that Canadian inflation had reached *too low* a level, and that the cost of having such low inflation was that Canadian unemployment was higher than would otherwise be the case. Indeed, these economists used the comparison between Canada and the United States as evidence. They noted that Canada's significantly higher unemployment rate and slightly lower inflation rate suggested that there may indeed be costs associated with pushing inflation too low.

Central to their argument is the importance of *downward nominal wage rigidity*— the inability of wages to fall, in dollar terms, in response to a reduction in demand. In

Chapter 24 we discussed this idea but referred to it as *sticky wages*—the idea that wages rise faster in response to excess demand than they fall in response to excess supply. These economists argued that when nominal wages are sticky downward, and inflation is very low, the invariable result is higher *permanent* unemployment. This argument was first put forward by James Tobin, the 1981 Nobel Laureate from Yale University. The argument was made recently in Canada by Pierre Fortin from the Université du Québec à Montréal.

Other economists, including many at the Bank of Canada, agreed that nominal wages may be temporarily sticky downward as the economy adjusts to an environment of very low inflation. But as firms and workers get used to a low-inflation environment, wages will become as flexible downward as they are upward. These economists do not believe, therefore, that there will be a long-run effect from low inflation on Canada's unemployment rate.

This is a contentious issue, both on theoretical and empirical grounds, and the debate is not yet settled. We address it in more detail in the next chapter when we examine inflation—its causes, costs, and cures.

S U M M A R Y

The Bank of Canada and the Money Supply   LO ①

- The major tool the Bank of Canada uses to control the supply of money is control of reserves of the commercial banking system through open-market operations and by switching government deposits between itself and the chartered banks. Purchases of bonds on the open market or switching government deposits toward the chartered banks increases the reserves of the banking system.

- Sales on the open market or withdrawing government deposits away from the chartered banks reduces bank reserves.
- The Bank of Canada now operates a system of zero required reserves, which means that each commercial bank's reserves must average to zero (or a positive amount) over a four-week averaging period.

Policy Variables and Policy Instruments   LO ② ③

- The Bank's policy variables are real GDP and the rate of inflation. To influence these, the Bank works through policy instruments that it can control and that will in turn influence its policy variables. Intermediate targets are used to guide decisions about policy instruments.
- Because changes in reserves have an effect on both the interest rate and the exchange rate, the Bank uses a combination of the two—the Monetary Conditions Index—as an intermediate target.

- To reduce real GDP, the Bank reduces bank reserves. This drives up the interest rate and causes an appreciation of the Canadian dollar, reducing investment and net exports and shifting the *AD* curve to the left. To increase real GDP, the Bank increases reserves, driving down the interest rate and causing a depreciation of the Canadian dollar, shifting the *AD* curve to the right.

Lags in the Conduct of Monetary Policy

- Though the Bank can change the reserves of the banking system more or less instantly, it takes time for this change in reserves to be transformed into a change in bank deposits and thus a change in the money supply.
- Once interest rates change in response to a change in the money supply, it takes time for firms and households to change their expenditure. Even once those new plans are carried out, it takes time for the multiplier process to work its way through the economy, eventually increasing equilibrium national income.
- Not only is there a significant lag from when bank reserves are changed to when national income changes, but this time lag is itself uncertain. Monetary policy is thus said to work with "long and variable lags."

- The existence of such long and variable lags have led some economists to argue that the Bank of Canada should not use monetary policy in an attempt to stabilize national income. They argue that attempts to stabilize will in fact be destabilizing, and advocate the use of a monetary rule whereby bank reserves are increased at a constant rate.
- Others argue that such a monetary rule would be undesirable, especially since experience shows that the demand for money is unstable. They argue that the Bank of Canada could *in principle* reduce fluctuations in national income by responding to sudden changes in money demand.

20 Years of Canadian Monetary Policy

- In the early 1980s, the Bank of Canada embarked on a policy of tight money to reduce inflation. This policy contributed to the severity of the recession.
- A sustained economic recovery occurred from 1983 to 1987. The main challenge for monetary policy during this time was to create sufficient liquidity to accommodate the recovery without triggering a return to the high inflation rates that prevailed at the start of the decade.
- In 1988, when inflation was between 4 and 5 percent, the Bank of Canada announced that monetary policy would no longer be guided by short-term stabilization and instead would be guided by the long-term goal of "price stability." By 1992, the Bank's tight money policy had reduced inflation to below 2 percent.
- Controversy concerned two issues. First, was the cost in terms of lost output, heavy unemployment and a temporary reduction in international competitiveness worth the benefit in terms of long-term stable currency? Second, could the low inflation rate be sustained?
- This controversy was partly responsible for the 1994 change in the Bank of Canada's Governor, from John Crow to Gordon Thiessen. Despite this administrative change, the stated policy of price stability continued. By 1999, the rate of inflation had been hovering between 1 and 2 percent for about seven years.
- In the late 1990s, the central challenges faced by the Bank included (1) how to respond to the Asian Crisis, (2) how to respond to the rising stock market, and (3) whether very low inflation might involve permanent costs in the form of higher unemployment.

K E Y   C O N C E P T S

Open-market operations
Shifting government deposits
The bank rate

Policy variables
Policy instruments
Intermediate targets
The Monetary Conditions Index
   (MCI)

Variability of monetary policy
Monetary rules
Lags in the effect of monetary policy
Shifts in the demand for money

STUDY EXERCISES

1. Suppose the Bank of Canada enters the open market and sells $100 000 of government securities to a wealthy Canadian household. The three balance sheets below are for the *changes* in assets and liabilities for the household, commercial banks, and the Bank of Canada.

Household		Commercial Banks		Bank of Canada	
Assets	Liabilities	Assets	Liabilities	Assets	Liabilities
Bonds —		Reserves —	Deposits —	Bonds —	Commercial bank deposits —
Deposits —					

a. How do the household's assets and liabilities change as a result of the open-market sale? Fill in the left-hand table.
b. If the household pays for the government securities with a cheque drawn on its account at a commercial bank, what are the immediate effects on assets and liabilities for the commercial banks? Fill in the middle table.
c. What are the changes for the Bank of Canada? Fill in the right-hand table.
d. Explain how this open-market sale will affect the total money supply.

2. Suppose the Bank of Canada transfers $100 000 of government deposits from the government's account at the Bank of Canada to the government's account in a commercial bank. The two balance sheets below are for the *changes* in assets and liabilities for commercial banks and the Bank of Canada.

Commercial Banks		Bank of Canada	
Assets	Liabilities	Assets	Liabilities
Reserves —	Deposits —	Bonds —	Commercial bank deposits —
			Government deposits —

a. What are the immediate effects on assets and liabilities for the commercial banks? Fill in the left-hand table.
b. What are the changes for the Bank of Canada? Fill in the right-hand table.

c. Explain how this transfer of government deposits will affect the total money supply.

3. In the text we stated that the Bank of Canada's long-run policy variable is the price level (or its growth rate, the rate of inflation).

a. How is this choice of a long-run policy variable related to the idea of long-run money neutrality?
b. If money were not neutral in the long run, do you think the Bank might choose a different long-run policy variable? Explain.

4. The diagram below shows the demand for money (the LP function) and the supply of money.

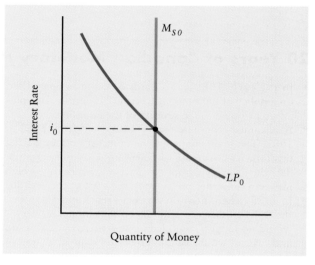

a. Explain (and show in the diagram) why the Bank of Canada cannot have independent targets for the money supply and the interest rate.
b. Suppose the Bank leaves the money supply unchanged but that the demand for money increases. Show this in the diagram. What happens to interest rates? What happens to investment?
c. In the situation of part b, explain why monetary policy has been contractionary even though the Bank did not change the money supply.

5. Milton Friedman for many years was a professor of economics at the University of Chicago, and was the most influential Monetarist of his generation. He is known for accusing the Federal Reserve (the U.S. central bank) of following "an unstable monetary policy," arguing that although the Fed "has given lip service to controlling the quantity of money…it has given its heart to controlling interest rates."

a. Explain why, if the *LP* function were approximately stable, targeting the quantity of money would produce a "stable" monetary policy. Show this in a diagram.

b. Explain why, if the *LP* function moves suddenly and in unpredictable ways, targeting the quantity of money produces an "unstable" monetary policy. Show this in a diagram.

c. What has the Canadian experience suggested about the relative likelihood of the conditions in part **a** as opposed to those in part **b**?

6. Suppose it is mid 1999 and the stock market has been growing rapidly for the past four years. Some economists argue that the stock market has become "overvalued" and thus a "crash" is imminent.

a. How does a rising stock market affect aggregate demand? Show this in an *AD/SRAS* diagram.

b. For a central bank that is trying to keep real GDP close to potential, explain what challenges are posed by a rapidly rising stock market.

c. Suppose the stock market "crashes," falling suddenly by 30 percent. How does this affect aggregate demand? Show this in an *AD/SRAS* diagram.

d. Consider the policy dilemma faced by the central bank when prices in the stock market are very high and are continuing to rising rapidly. What are the implications of tightening monetary policy in such a situation? What are the implications of leaving monetary policy unchanged?

DISCUSSION QUESTIONS

1. Describe the chief tools of monetary policy available to the Bank of Canada, and indicate whether—and if so, how—they might be used for the following purposes:

   a. To create a mild tightening of bank credit
   b. To signal that the Bank of Canada favours a sharp curtailment of bank lending
   c. To permit an expansion of bank credit with existing reserves
   d. To supply banks and the public with a temporary increase of currency for Christmas shopping

2. It is often said that an expansionary monetary policy is like "pushing on a string." What is meant by this statement? How does this contrast with a contractionary monetary policy?

3. In 1988, the Bank of Canada announced that it was committed to achieving "price stability," but it did not commit itself to a particular target growth rate for any monetary aggregate that would be consistent with achieving its price stability target. Why do you think it failed to make such a commitment?

4. In 1993, with 11 percent unemployment, a slow recovery just underway and inflation in the 1 to 2 percent range, the Bank permitted a rapid expansion of M1. Was this inflationary? Why might the Bank have adopted this policy? What is meant by the "reentry" problem?

5. The term "moral suasion" is generally used to describe attempts by central banks to enlist the cooperation of private financial institutions in the pursuit of some objective of monetary policy. In a country such as Canada, where there are only a few banks, the central bank can easily communicate its view to the chartered banks. Using the balance sheets of the Bank of Canada and the commercial banking system, explain how an attempt by the Bank of Canada to persuade commercial banks to increase their lending would affect bank reserves and total bank deposits. How is this question related to Question 2?

6. Suppose the Canadian economy has real GDP equal to potential and that nothing significant is expected to change in the near future. Then the Canadian dollar suddenly depreciates—apparently permanently—by 5 percent against the U.S. dollar. Explain why the appropriate response of monetary policy depends on the *cause* of the depreciation. In particular, make a distinction between:

   a. a depreciation caused by a reduction in demand for Canadian exports of raw materials; and
   b. a depreciation caused by a reduction in demand for Canadian bonds that are now perceived as less attractive than U.S. bonds.

The Stock Market

An organized market in which stocks or bonds are bought and sold is called a *securities market*. Securities markets that deal in shares, or equities, are known as *stock markets*. Two of the best known stock markets are the Toronto Stock Exchange and New York Stock Exchange. The trading of *existing* shares on the stock market indicates that ownership is being transferred; it does not indicate that companies are raising new money from the public, although firms also do raise funds by issuing new shares.

The Function of Stock Markets

When a household buys shares—either existing or newly issued—it becomes one of the firm's owners. If, at some future date, the household wishes to cease being a shareholder in the firm, the household can simply sell the shares. It can do so only by persuading someone else to buy its shares in the company.

Stock markets are important because they allow people to put their savings into assets that may earn a good rate of return and are, in general, very liquid.

For example, if I want to invest in a particular stock that I think will earn a high return, I may do so, even though I know that I will want my money back after only a year. And I can be confident that I will be able to sell the stock a year from now. Nevertheless, although stock markets provide for the quick sale of stocks, they do not guarantee the price at which stocks can be sold. The price at any time is the one that equates the demand and supply for the particular stock, and rapid fluctuations in stock prices are common.

Prices on the Stock Market

Stock market values sometimes display cumulative upward movements, or *bull markets*. They also sometimes display cumulative downward movements, or *bear markets*. The Great Depression of the 1930s was preceded by the stock market crash of 1929, which caused what is still the largest percentage loss of stock values ever to be suffered by investors worldwide.

Figure 28A-1 shows the path of the Toronto Stock Exchange 300 Index since 1980. Notice the signifi-

FIGURE 28A-1 The TSE 300 Index, 1980–1999

The Toronto Stock Exchange 300 Index has increased at an annual average rate of 6.5 percent over the past 20 years. There is clearly an upward long-run trend to the price of shares in the TSE 300 Index. But the sharp reduction during the 1981–82 recession is clear, as are the sudden "crashes" of October 1987 and July 1998. Note that the vertical scale is logarithmic. This means that equal distances on the scale represent *proportional* changes.

(*Source: The International Bank Credit Analyst,* June 1999) cant decline from 1981 to 1982 during a recession, and also the sharp "crashes" in October 1987 and July 1998. The long-term trend, however, is clearly positive. Over the past twenty years, prices on the TSE 300 have increased at an average annual rate of roughly 6.5 percent.

There is clearly some association between fluctuations in the stock market and those in the economy, but is there a causal connection? Do stock market fluctuations cause business cycle fluctuations, or is it the other way around?

Causes of Stock Market Swings

Before we can answer these questions, we need to know a little about how stock markets function. In particular, what causes stock market prices to fluctuate?

When investors buy a company's stocks, they are buying rights to share in the stream of dividends to be paid out by that company. They are also buying an asset that they can sell in the future for a gain or a loss.

The value of a stock thus depends on two factors: first, what people expect the stream of future dividend payments to be, and, second, what price people expect to receive when the stock is sold. (If the price rises, the owner earns a *capital gain*: if the price falls, the owner suffers a *capital loss*.) Both influences make dealing in stocks an inherently risky operation. Will the company be profitable in future years, and thus be more likely to pay high dividends? Will the price of the stock rise so that current shareholders will earn a capital gain if they sell their shares?

The Influence of Present and Future Business Conditions

Many influences affect stock market prices, including the state of the business cycle and the stance of government policies.

Cyclical Forces.   If investors expect a firm's earnings to increase, the firm will become more valuable and the price of its stock will rise. Such influences cause stock prices to move with the business cycle, being high when current profits are high and low when current profits are low. These influences also cause stock prices to vary with a host of factors that influence expectations of future profits. A poor crop, destruc-

tion of trees by acid rain, an announcement of new defence spending, a change in the exchange rate, and a change in the governing political party can all affect profit expectations and hence stock prices.

Policy Factors.   Changes in monetary policy affect the economy by first changing interest rates. Such changes, or just the expectation of them, will have effects on stock prices. For example, suppose that the threat of future inflation leads the Bank of Canada to tighten monetary policy sharply, thus raising interest rates. Shareholders will now want to sell their shares for two reasons. First, higher interest rates imply that any given stream of future dividends now has a lower present value (see Chapter 27). Second, higher interest rates will reduce the flow of profits (and dividends) from firms as the economy slows down (which is exactly the intention of the monetary tightening). For both reasons, stocks will be a less attractive investment relative to the alternatives (mainly bonds), and so holders of stocks will decide to sell. Everyone cannot do this, however, because only so many stocks are available to be held at any given time. As all investors try to sell their stocks, prices fall. The fall will stop only when the expected rate of return to investment in stocks, based on their lower purchase price, makes stocks as attractive as alternative investments. Then investors will no longer try to shift out of stocks *en masse*.

Speculative Booms

In addition to responding to a host of factors that reasonably can be expected to influence the earnings of companies, stock prices often develop an upward or downward movement of their own, propelled by little more than speculation that feeds on itself.

In major stock market booms, people begin to expect rising stock prices and hurry to buy while stocks are cheap. This action bids up the prices of shares and creates the capital gains that justify the original expectations. Such a situation is an example of *self-realizing expectations*. Investors get rich on paper, in the sense that the market value of their holdings rises. Money making now looks easy to others, who also rush in to buy stocks, and new purchases push prices up still further. At this stage attention to the firm's actual profits all but ceases. If a stock can yield, say, a 50 percent capital gain in one year, it does not matter much if dividends rise or fall slightly. Everyone is "making money," so more people become attracted to the get-rich-quick opportunities. Their attempts to buy push prices up even further.

Eventually, something breaks the period of unrestrained optimism. Some investors may begin to worry about the very high prices of stocks in relation not only to current dividends but also to possible future dividends, even when generous allowances for growth are made. Or it may be that the prices of stocks become depressed slightly when a sufficiently large number of persons try to sell out in order to realize their capital gains. As they offer their stocks on the market, they cannot find purchasers without some fall in prices. Even a modest price fall may be sufficient to persuade others that it is time to sell. However, every share that is sold must be bought by someone. A wave of sellers may not find new buyers at existing prices, causing prices to fall. Panic selling may now occur.

This is a very simple and stylized description of a speculative cycle, yet it describes the basic elements of market booms and busts that many believe have recurred throughout stock market history. In the United States, it happened in the Jay Cooke panic of 1873 and in the Grover Cleveland panic of 1893.[1] The biggest boom of all began in the mid 1920s and ended on Black Tuesday, October 29, 1929. The collapse was dramatic, with U.S. stocks losing about 50 percent of their value in about two months. Nor did it stop there. For four years stock prices continued to decline, until the average value of stock on the New York Stock Exchange had fallen from its 1929 high of $89.10 per share to $17.35 per share by late 1933.

Speculative behaviour means that stock market prices do not always just reflect the fundamentals that underlie the expected profitability of companies; in this sense, the stock market is sometimes said to be overvalued or undervalued. However, the extent of the over- or undervaluation is difficult to determine, and hence it is hard to predict when, and by how much, prices will "correct." For example, consider the long upswing that increased prices on the TSE by 75 percent between January 1995 and the summer of 1999 (the bull market in the United States was even more dramatic). During this period, the Canadian economy was experiencing a healthy recovery, and the rising stock prices no doubt reflected the resulting favourable profit outlook of companies. However, many doubted that the full increase was justified by underlying business opportunities and hence felt that there may have been a speculative component to the rise in stock values. These people argued (and were still arguing when this book went to press in the fall of 1999) that a "correction" was long overdue.

Stock Market Swings: Cause or Effect of Business Cycles?

Stock markets tend often to lead, and sometimes to follow, booms and slumps in business activity. In both cases the causes usually run from real business conditions, whether actual or anticipated, to stock market prices. This is the dominant theme: the stock market as a reflector.

Stock market fluctuations are usually a consequence, rather than a cause, of the business cycle.

For example, an economy that is growing steadily over a number of years will generally have rising profits. The increase in profits will cause stock market prices to rise. Conversely, an economy that enters a recession with high unemployment and bankruptcies will naturally have low profits. These low profits will cause stock market prices to fall.

Though we have said that stock market movements are *usually* the consequence of the business cycle, it is *sometimes* true that the stock market is the cause of the business cycle. The value of the stock market influences the wealth of households, which ultimately own the market, either directly or through their pension funds. (The direct holding of stocks by households has become much more common in the past decade with the widespread availability of mutual funds.) And, as we saw in Chapter 22, changes in household wealth lead to changes in desired consumption spending. Thus, as prices rise in the stock market, the increase in household wealth will generally lead to increases in aggregate demand. This will naturally have an effect on real GDP and the price level. In addition, firms use the stock market to issue new shares in order to finance investment spending. When stock market prices are high, they find this a very attractive way to raise new money and thus may choose to undertake new investments, thereby adding to aggregate demand.

For these reasons, many people believed that the dramatic fall in stock value in the October 1987 crash would cause households to curtail their consumption spending in response to their perceived fall in wealth. On this basis many forecasters predicted that the stock market crash would lead to a serious downturn in economy. After the event, such gloom-and-doom forecasts turned out to be inaccurate; apparently, people

---

[1]For a wonderful discussion of the history of speculative booms (and their aftermath), see John Kenneth Galbraith, *A Short History of Financial Euphoria*, 1990, Viking Press.

did not perceive the fall in the stock market as an indication that their *permanent* incomes or wealth had fallen dramatically, and hence they did not reduce their consumption spending.

Investment Marketplaces or Gambling Casinos?

Stock markets fulfill many important functions. It is doubtful that the great aggregations of capital that are needed to finance modern firms could be raised under a private-ownership system without them. There is no doubt, however, that they also provide an unfortunate attraction for many naive investors, whose get-rich-quick dreams are more often than not destroyed by the fall in prices that follows the occasional speculative booms that they help to create.

To some extent public policy has sought to curb the excesses of stock market speculation through supervision of security issues. Public policy seeks, among other things, to prevent both fraudulent or misleading information and trading by "insiders" (those in a company who have confidential information).

All in all, the stock market is both a real marketplace and a place to gamble. As in all gambling situations, players who are less well informed and less clever than the average player tend to be losers in the long term.

For information on the Toronto Stock Exchange, see its website: www.tse.com.

PART TEN

Macroeconomic Problems and Policies

What causes sustained inflation and how can it be reduced? What is the "natural" rate of unemployment, and how is it affected by labour-market policies such as unemployment insurance? Do government budget deficits raise interest rates, or do they have little or no effect on key macroeconomic variables? Can the market be left to its own to provide long-run economic growth, or are government policies to encourage growth necessary? What explains the different rates of economic growth in developed versus developing countries? These are the sorts of questions you will be able to answer after reading the next five chapters.

This part of the book contains five chapters on key macroeconomic issues. The chapters may be read in any order and each one may be read independently of the others. Chapter 29 discusses the causes of inflation. We will see the important distinction between cyclical inflation and sustained inflation. We examine the Bank of Canada's role in maintaining a sustained inflation, as well as its role in ending one.

In Chapter 30 we discuss unemployment. Two different theories of cyclical unemployment are considered—New Classical and New Keynesian. We then discuss the natural rate of unemployment—often called the Nonaccelerating Inflation Rate of Unemployment (NAIRU). We examine what determines the NAIRU and why several labour-market policies have the unintended consequence of increasing the NAIRU.

Chapter 31 returns us to the issues of fiscal policy, examining in detail government deficits, surpluses, and government debt. We will see how to judge the stance of fiscal policy, as well as the important connection between government deficits and national saving. We will consider under which conditions government deficits raise interest rates, and what happens as a result.

Chapters 32 and 33 examine economic growth. Chapter 32 emphasizes the theory of economic growth, discussing some established theories based on capital accumulation as well as some more recent theories based on endogenous technical change. Chapter 33 then examines the issue of economic growth in the developing economies and examines why some countries have had such slow rates of growth. We then discuss some of the recent views about which policies these countries might implement to improve their growth rates.

CHAPTER 29

Inflation

🔵 LEARNING OBJECTIVES

1 Explain how wage changes are driven by both excess demand and inflationary expectations.

2 Show how constant inflation can be incorporated into the basic macroeconomic model.

3 Understand the effects of aggregate demand and supply shocks on inflation and real GDP.

4 Explain how the Bank of Canada may validate demand and supply shocks.

5 Explain the three phases of a disinflation.

6 Understand how the cost of disinflation can be measured by the sacrifice ratio.

7 Have a general understanding of Canadian inflation policy over the past two decades.

inflation A rise in the average level of all prices. Often expressed as the annual percentage change in the Consumer Price Index.

If you are a typical reader of this book, you were born in the late 1970s or early 1980s. By the time you were old enough to notice some economic developments going on around you, it was the early 1990s. By that time, the rate of inflation in Canada was less than 5 percent per year. Thus, unless you are older than the typical student taking a course in introductory economics, or you have come to Canada recently from a high-inflation country, inflation has not been a significant phenomenon in your life. But it is not so long ago that inflation was considered to be a serious problem in Canada (and many other countries as well).

Recall from Chapter 19 that **inflation** is a rise in the average level of prices—that is, a rise in the price level. If you look again at Figure 19-5 in Chapter 19, you will see that inflation was relatively low throughout the 1960s. Starting in the late 1960s, the inflation rate slowly rose, reaching the double-digit range by the mid 1970s. It fell only slightly during the late 1970s, despite a concerted anti-inflationary policy, and rose again to the double-digit level in 1980. It remained quite high during the recession of 1981–1982, fell dramatically to 4 percent in 1983, and remained near that figure through 1987. Although this was an improvement over the double-digit inflation rates experienced earlier, 4 percent was, historically, a high inflation rate to be experienced at the end of a serious recession.

During the latter half of 1988, after several years of a vigorous economic recovery, the inflation rate crept up to over 5 percent, where it stayed through 1989 and the early part of 1990. The Bank of Canada's attempt to reduce inflation—first back to the 4 percent level and then down to below 2 percent—caused renewed controversy about the methods, the costs, and the benefits of fighting inflation. By mid 1999, inflation was between 1 and 2 percent and had been there for about 7 years. In recent years some economists have begun questioning whether inflation at such low levels is actually *bad* for the economy.

We now turn to the subject of inflation in detail. What causes inflation? What are the costs of reducing it? Can inflation be prevented from rising into the double-digit range again? Can inflation ever be too low?

To compute the total inflation from the day of your birth to today, check out the "inflation calculator" at the Bank of Canada's website: www.bank-banque-canada.ca.

Adding Inflation to the Model

In the previous several chapters we examined the effects of shocks to aggregate demand and aggregate supply. Such shocks influenced the values of both real GDP and the price level. Following these shocks, the economy's adjustment mechanism always brought the economy back to the potential level of real GDP with a stable price level. In other words, any inflation that we have so far seen in our macroeconomic model was temporary—it only existed while the economy was adjusting to its long-run equilibrium.

In this chapter we want to understand how a *sustained* inflation can exist, and how we modify our model to account for its presence. After all, even though inflation in Canada is very low, it still appears to be sustained at a rate of between 1 and 2 percent per year.

As we will soon see, the key to understanding sustained inflation is to understand the role of *inflation expectations*. When combined with excess demand or excess supply, as reflected by the economy's output gap, such expectations give us a more complete understanding of why wages (and therefore prices) change. Let's begin our analysis by examining in more detail why wages change.

Why Wages Change

In Chapter 25, increases in wages led to increases in unit costs because we maintained the assumption that technology (and thus productivity) was held constant. We continue with that assumption in this chapter. Thus, as wages and other factor prices rise, unit costs increase and the *SRAS* curve shifts up. Conversely, when wages and other factor prices fall, unit costs fall and the *SRAS* curve shifts down.

But what are the forces that cause wages (and, similarly, other factor prices) to change? Two of the main forces are the demand for labour and expectations of future inflation.[1] Much of what we discuss in the case of labour demand was first seen in Chapter 25, but the points are important enough to bear repeating.

Labour Demand and the NAIRU

In Chapter 25, we encountered three propositions about how changes in money wages were influenced by the relationship between aggregate demand and aggregate supply:

---

[1]Wages may be affected by other forces that are associated with neither excess demand nor expectations of inflation, such as government guidelines, union power, and employers' optimism. Because there are many such forces that tend to act independently of one another, they may be regarded as random shocks and must be analysed as separate causes for shifts in the *SRAS* curve.

1. The excess demand for labour that is associated with an inflationary gap puts upward pressure on money wages.

2. The excess supply of labour associated with a recessionary gap puts downward pressure on money wages.

3. The absence of either an inflationary or a recessionary gap means that demand forces do not exert any pressure on money wages.[2]

When real GDP is equal to its potential level (Y^*), the unemployment rate is said to be equal to the NAIRU, which stands for the *nonaccelerating inflation rate of unemployment*. The use of this particular name will be explained later in this chapter. Another name sometimes used in place of NAIRU is the *natural rate of unemployment*, but NAIRU is now the more common usage. It is designated here by the symbol U^*.

The NAIRU is not zero. Instead, even when output equals potential output, there may be a substantial amount of *frictional* and *structural* unemployment caused, for example, by the movement of people between jobs or between regions. When real output exceeds potential output ($Y > Y^*$), the unemployment rate will be less than the NAIRU ($U < U^*$). When real output is less than potential output ($Y < Y^*$), the unemployment rate will exceed the NAIRU ($U > U^*$).

We have seen that wages and unit costs react to various pressures of demand. These demand pressures can be stated either in terms of the relationship between actual and potential output or in terms of the relationship between the actual unemployment rate and the NAIRU. When $Y > Y^*$ (or $U < U^*$), there is an inflationary gap characterized by excess demand for labour. Wages and unit costs tend to rise. Conversely, when $Y < Y^*$ (or $U > U^*$), there is a recessionary gap characterized by excess supply of labour. Wages and unit costs tend to fall.

This relationship between the excess demand or supply of labour and the rate of change of money wages is represented by the Phillips Curve, which we first discussed in Chapter 25.

Expected Inflation

A second force that can influence wages is *expectations* of future inflation. Suppose that both employers and employees expect 4 percent inflation next year. Workers will start negotiations from a base of a 4 percent increase in money wages, which would hold their *real wages* constant. Firms will also be inclined to begin bargaining by conceding at least a 4 percent increase in money wages because they expect that the prices at which they sell their products will rise by 4 percent. Starting from that base, workers may attempt to obtain some desired increase in their real wages. At this point, such factors as profits and bargaining power become important.

The expectation of some specific inflation rate creates pressure for wages to rise by that rate and hence for unit costs to rise at that rate.

The key point is that money wages can be rising even if no inflationary gap is present. As long as people *expect* prices to rise, their behaviour will put upward pressure on money wages, causing unit costs to rise, thus shifting the *SRAS* curve upward.

---

[2]As in Chapter 25, we are holding productivity constant in our analysis in this chapter. Otherwise, output gaps would cause changes in wages *relative to productivity*.

The Formation of Expectations

The way people form their expectations about future inflation may have an important effect on that inflation. Generally, we can distinguish two main patterns: One is to look backward at past experience; the other is to look at current circumstances for a clue as to what may happen in the near future.

The first type of expectations are called *backward-looking*. People look at the past in order to predict what will happen in the future. The simplest possible form of such expectations is to expect the past to be repeated in the future. According to this view, if inflation has been 5 percent over the past year, people will expect it to be 5 percent next year. This expectation, however, is quite naive. Everyone knows that the inflation rate does change, and therefore the past cannot be a perfectly accurate guide to the future.

A less naive version has people revise their expectations in light of the mistakes that they made in estimating inflation in the past. For example, if you thought that this year's inflation rate was going to be 5 percent but it turned out to be only 3 percent, you might revise your estimate of next year's rate down somewhat from 5 percent.

Backward-looking expectations tend to change slowly because some time must pass before a change in the actual rate of inflation provides enough past experience to cause expectations to adjust.

The second main type of expectations are those that look to current conditions to estimate what is likely to happen in the future. One version of this type assumes that people look to the government's current macroeconomic policy to form their expectations of future inflation. They are assumed to understand how the economy works, and they form their expectations by predicting the outcome of the policies now being followed. In an obvious sense, such expectations are *forward-looking*.

A strong version of forward-looking expectations is called **rational expectations.** Rational expectations are not necessarily always correct; rather, the *rational expectations hypothesis* assumes that people make the best possible use of all the available information. One implication is that they will not continue to make persistent, systematic errors when forming their expectations. Thus, if the economic system about which they are forming expectations remains stable, their expectations will be correct *on average*. Sometimes next year's inflation rate will turn out to be above what people expected it to be; at other times, it will turn out to be below what people expected it to be. On average over many years, however, the actual rate will not, according to the rational expectations theory, be consistently under- or overestimated.

Forward-looking expectations can adjust quickly to changes in events. Instead of being based on past inflation rates, expected inflation is based on expected economic conditions and government policies.

The importance of rational expectations in the study of macroeconomics is reflected by the fact that the economist most closely associated with the development of the idea, Robert E. Lucas Jr. of the University of Chicago, was awarded the Nobel Prize in 1995 for his work in this area.

Assuming that expectations are solely backward-looking seems overly naive. People do look ahead and assess future possibilities rather than just blindly reacting to what has gone before. Yet the assumption of "fully rational" forward-looking expectations requires workers and firms to have a degree of understanding of the economy that few economists would claim to have.

Of course, people will not make the same error of consistently underpredicting (or overpredicting) the inflation rate for decades, but evidence suggests that they can do so

Practise with Study Guide Chapter 29, Exercise 2.

rational expectations
The theory that people understand how the economy works and learn quickly from their mistakes so that even though random errors may be made, systematic and persistent errors are not.

for substantial periods, especially when they do not fully understand the causes of current inflation. Every past period of inflation has led to intense debate among economists about its causes, cures, and probable future course. If professional economists are uncertain, it would be surprising if wage and price setters made correct predictions on average over any short period of time.

The actual process of wage setting probably combines forward-looking behaviour with expectations based on the experience of the recent past. Depending on the circumstances, expectations will sometimes tend to rely more on past experience and at other times more on present events whose effects are expected to influence the future.

Overall Effect

We can now think of changes in money wages as resulting from two different forces:

$$\text{Change in Money Wages} = \text{Excess-Demand Effect} + \text{Expectational Effect}$$

It is important to realize that what happens to wages is the *net* effect of the two forces. Consider two examples.

First, suppose that both labour and management expect 3 percent inflation next year and are therefore willing to allow money wages to increase by 3 percent. Doing so would leave *real* wages unchanged. Suppose as well that there is a significant inflationary gap with an associated labour shortage. The demand pressure causes wages to rise by an additional 2 percentage points. The final outcome is that wages rise by 5 percent, the net effect of a 3 percent increase due to expected inflation and a 2 percent increase due to demand forces.

For the second example, assume again that expected inflation is 3 percent, but that this time there is a recessionary gap. The associated heavy unemployment exerts downward pressure on wage bargains. Hence, the demand effect now works to dampen wage increases, say, to the extent of 2 percentage points. Wages therefore rise by 1 percent, the net effect of a 3 percent increase due to expected inflation and a 2 percent decrease due to demand forces.

From Wages to Prices

We saw in Chapter 24 and 25 that shifts in the *SRAS* curve depend on what happens to factor prices. We have just seen that inflationary gaps and expectations of future inflation put pressure on wages to rise and hence cause the *SRAS* curve to shift upward. Recessionary gaps and expectations of future deflation put pressure on wages to fall and hence cause the *SRAS* curve to shift downward.

The net effect of the two forces acting on wages—excess demand and inflation expectations—determines what happens to the *SRAS* curve.

If the net effect of the demand and expectational forces is to raise wages, then the *SRAS* curve will shift up. This shift will cause the price level to rise—that is, the forces pushing up wages will be *inflationary*. On the other hand, if the net effect of the demand and expectational forces is to reduce wages, then the *SRAS* curve will shift down—the forces reducing wages will be *deflationary*.

This link between wages and prices implies that our previous decomposition of wage changes into separate forces also holds for inflation. But because the *SRAS* curve can also shift for reasons unrelated to changes in wages, we must complicate the story slightly. Specifically, we must consider the effect of non-wage supply shocks on the *SRAS* curve and thus on the price level. The best example of a non-wage supply shock is a change in the prices of raw materials. We can then decompose actual inflation into its three component parts:

$$\begin{array}{c}\text{Actual}\\\text{Inflation}\end{array} = \begin{array}{c}\text{Excess-Demand}\\\text{Inflation}\end{array} + \begin{array}{c}\text{Expected}\\\text{Inflation}\end{array} + \begin{array}{c}\text{Supply-Shock}\\\text{Inflation}\end{array}$$

For example, consider an economy that begins with real GDP equal to potential GDP and expectations of inflation are zero. In this case, the first two terms on the right-hand side are zero. But if an adverse supply shock occurs, such as a significant increase in the price of imported raw materials, then the *SRAS* curve shifts up and the price level rises. Actual inflation will be positive. As we will see later in the chapter, such supply shocks are not uncommon, and they generate problems for the conduct of monetary policy.

Having discussed the component parts of the inflation process, we are now in a position to see how sustained inflation can be included in our macroeconomic model.

Constant Inflation

We now know what forces cause wages to change, and how the change in wages leads to changes in the price level. So what would a constant inflation of, say, 5 percent per year look like in our macroeconomic model? To answer this question we need to consider two things. First, we must distinguish between the excess demand and expectational components of inflation. Second, we must consider the way people form their expectations of inflation. In what follows, we simplify the setting by assuming that no supply shocks occur (we address them later in the chapter).

Actual and Expected Inflation

Suppose the inflation rate is 5 percent per year and has been 5 percent for several years. This is what we mean by a *constant* inflation. In such a setting, people with backward-looking expectations about inflation will expect the actual level to continue into the future. Furthermore, in the absence of any announcements that the central bank will be attempting to alter the rate of inflation, people with forward-looking expectations will expect the actual inflation rate to continue. Thus, for the economy as a whole, the expected rate of inflation will equal the actual rate of inflation.

The Conference Board of Canada conducts a regular survey about people's expectations about inflation. See their website at: www.conferenceboard.ca.

If inflation and monetary policy have been constant for several years, the expected rate of inflation will equal the actual rate of inflation.

In the absence of temporary supply shocks, the equality of actual and expected inflation implies something about the amount of demand inflation. Since actual inflation equals excess-demand inflation plus expected inflation, it immediately follows that actual and expected inflation can only be equal if there is *no* excess-demand inflation. This, in turn, implies that there is no inflationary (or recessionary) gap—real GDP must equal its potential level, Y^*.

If expected inflation equals actual inflation, real GDP must be equal to potential GDP.

Expectational Inflation

But if there is no excess demand, what is causing the inflation? The answer is that peoples' *expectations* are causing inflation. Figure 29-1 shows a constant inflation that is purely

FIGURE 29-1   Constant Expectational Inflation

A constant expectational inflation is only possible when $Y=Y^*$. Expectations of a constant rate of inflation cause wages and thus the $SRAS$ curve to shift upward at a uniform rate from $SRAS_0$ to $SRAS_1$ to $SRAS_2$. Monetary validation is causing the AD curve to shift upward at the same time from AD_0 to AD_1 to AD_2. As a result, real GDP remains at Y^*. The constant inflation rate takes the price level from P_0 to P_1 to P_2. Wage costs are rising due to expectations of inflation, and these expectations are being fulfilled.

expectational. But as we will now see, in order for a purely expectational inflation to continue, the central bank must be *validating* the expectations by constantly increasing the money supply. Let's see how this works.

Suppose that both workers and employers expect 4 percent inflation over the coming years and that employers are therefore prepared to increase wages by 4 percent per year. As wages rise by 4 percent, the $SRAS$ curve shifts up by that amount. But, in order for 4 percent to be the *actual* rate of inflation, the intersection of the $SRAS$ and AD curves must be shifting up at the rate of 4 percent. This requires the AD curve to be shifting up at the same 4 percent rate—this AD shift is caused by the growth of the money supply. So in this case there is no excess-demand inflation ($Y=Y^*$), and actual and expected inflation are equal. When the central bank increases the money supply at such a rate that the expectations of inflation end up being correct, it is said to be *validating* the expectations.

Constant inflation with $Y=Y^*$ occurs when the rate of monetary growth, the rate of wage increase, and the expected rate of inflation are all consistent with the actual inflation rate.

The key point about constant, purely expectational inflation is that there is no excess-demand effect operating on wages. Wages rise at the expected rate of inflation. The labour shortages that accompany an inflationary gap are absent, as are the labour surpluses that accompany a recessionary gap.

Shocks and Policy Responses

We have now seen how our macroeconomic model can incorporate a constant rate of inflation. Analysing constant inflation is very useful because it helps us understand some details about our macroeconomic model. But it is a special case because, as we saw above, there was no inflationary (or recessionary) gap putting pressure on inflation. We now want to go on and understand some more complicated situations where an aggregate demand or supply shock creates an output gap, and this gap, in turn, creates inflationary pressures. In this case, we will see how inflationary gaps and expectations both are important for understanding inflation.

Demand Shocks

demand inflation
Inflation arising from excess aggregate demand, that is, when actual GDP exceeds potential GDP.

Inflation that is caused by a rightward shift in the AD curve is called **demand inflation**. The shift in the AD curve could have been caused by a reduction in taxes, by an increase in such autonomous expenditure items as investment, government, and net exports, or by an increase in the money supply.

Major demand-shock inflations occurred in Canada during and after World Wars I and II. In these cases, large increases in government expenditure without fully offsetting increases in taxes led to general excess demand. More generally, demand inflation sometimes occurs at the end of a strong upswing, as rising output causes excess demand to develop simultaneously in the markets for labour, intermediate goods, and final output.

To begin our study of demand inflation, suppose that an initial long-run equilibrium is disturbed by a rightward shift in the AD curve. This shift causes the price level and output to rise. It is important next to distinguish between the case in which the Bank of Canada validates the demand shock and the case in which it does not.

No Monetary Validation

Because the initial rise in AD takes output above potential, an inflationary gap opens up. The pressure of excess demand soon causes wages to rise, shifting the $SRAS$ curve upward and to the left. As long as the Bank of Canada holds the money supply constant, the rise in the price level moves the economy upward and to the left along the new AD curve, reducing the inflationary gap. Eventually, the gap is eliminated, and equilibrium is established at a higher but stable price level, with output at its potential level. In this case, the initial period of inflation is followed by further inflation that lasts only until the new equilibrium is reached.

The case of a non-validated demand shock was examined in detail in Chapter 25. It is shown again in Figure 29-2.

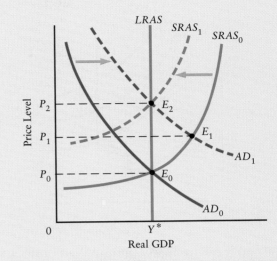

FIGURE 29-2   A Demand Shock with No Validation

A demand shock that is not validated produces temporary inflation, but the economy's adjustment process eventually restores potential GDP and stable prices. The initial long-run equilibrium is at P_0 and Y^*. A positive demand shock shifts AD_0 to AD_1, generating an inflationary gap. The excess demand puts upward pressure on wages, thus shifting $SRAS_0$ to $SRAS_1$. There is inflation as the economy moves from E_0 to E_1 to E_2, but at E_2 the price level is stable.

Monetary Validation

Suppose that after the demand shock has created an inflationary gap, the Bank of Canada increases the money supply whenever output starts to fall. This case takes us beyond our discussions in earlier chapters. It is analysed in Figure 29-3.

Two forces are now brought into play. Spurred by the inflationary gap, the increase in wages causes the $SRAS$ curve to shift upward and to the left. Fueled by the expansionary monetary policy, however, the AD curve shifts to the right. As a result of both of these shifts, the price level rises, but real GDP need not fall. Indeed, if the shift in the AD curve *exactly* offsets the shift in the $SRAS$ curve, real GDP and the inflationary gap will remain constant.

Continued validation of a demand shock turns what would have been transitory inflation into sustained inflation fueled by monetary expansion.

Supply Shocks

Any rise in the price level originating from increases in costs that are *not caused by excess demand* in the markets for factors of production is called **supply inflation**.

supply inflation
A rise in the price level originating from increases in costs that are not caused by excess demand in the domestic markets for factors of production.

FIGURE 29-3   A Demand Shock with Validation

Monetary validation of a positive demand shock causes the AD curve to shift further to the right, off-setting the leftward shift in the SRAS curve and thereby leaving an inflationary gap despite the ever-rising price level. An initial demand shock shifts equilibrium from E_0 to E_1, taking output to Y_1 and the price level to P_1. The resulting inflationary gap then causes the SRAS curve to shift to the left. This time, however, the Bank of Canada validates the demand shock by increasing the money supply. As the money supply is increased, the AD curve shifts to the right. By the time the aggregate supply curve has reached $SRAS_1$, the aggregate demand curve has reached AD_2. Now instead of being at E_2', equilibrium is at E_2. Output remains constant at Y_1 leaving the inflationary gap constant while the price level rises to P_2.

The persistent inflationary gap continues to push the SRAS curve to the left, while the continued monetary validation continues to push the AD curve to the right. As long as this monetary validation continues, the economy moves along the vertical path of arrow 2.

An example of a supply shock is a rise in the costs of imported raw materials. Another is a rise in domestic wage costs per unit of output. The rise in wage costs may occur, as we saw earlier, because of generally held expectations of future inflation. If both employers and employees expect inflation, money wages are likely to rise in anticipation of that inflation. These shocks cause the SRAS curve to shift upward.[3] Though negative supply shocks are quite common (occurring, for example, every time the prices of raw materials increase), the most significant examples occurred in 1974 and 1979–80 when OPEC restricted the supply of oil and sharply increased world oil prices. We discuss the 1974 OPEC oil shock shortly.

The initial effects of any negative supply shock are that the equilibrium price level rises while equilibrium output falls. The rise in the price level shows up as a temporary burst of inflation. These effects were first discussed in Chapter 24. Although we now wish to go beyond that earlier discussion, we will begin by repeating it in Figure 29-4, which compares the original equilibrium with the equilibrium after the supply shock.

As with the case of a demand shock, what happens next depends on how the Bank of Canada reacts. If the Bank responds by increasing the money supply, it validates the supply shock; if it holds the money supply constant, the shock is not validated.

No Monetary Validation

The leftward shift in the SRAS curve in Figure 29-4 causes the price level to rise and pushes output below its potential level, opening up a recessionary gap. Pressure mounts for money wages and other factor prices to fall. As wages and other factor prices fall, unit costs will fall. Consequently, the SRAS curve shifts rightward, increasing equilibrium output while reducing the price level. The SRAS curve will continue to shift, stopping only when real GDP is returned to its potential level and the price level is returned to its initial value of P_0. Thus, the period of inflation accompanying the original supply shock is eventually followed by a period of *deflation* (negative inflation) that continues until the initial long-run equilibrium is reestablished.

A major concern in this case is the speed of the adjustment, which in earlier chapters was referred to as the second asymmetry of aggregate supply. If wages do not fall rapidly in the face of excess supply in the labour market, the adjustment back to potential output can take a very long time. For example, suppose that the original shock raised costs

---

[3]Such changes in factor prices shift the SRAS curve but do not affect the LRAS curve. We discuss changes in the LRAS curve in Chapter 32 when we examine the process of technological change and long-term economic growth.

by 6 percent. To reverse this shock, unit costs must fall by 6 percent. If money wages fell by only 2 percent per year it would take three years to complete the adjustment.[4]

Whenever factor prices fall only slowly in the face of excess supply, the recovery to potential output after a nonvalidated negative supply shock will take a long time.

Concern that such a lengthy adjustment will occur is the motive that often lies behind the strong pressure on the Bank of Canada to validate negative supply shocks.

Monetary Validation

Now let us see what happens if the money supply is changed in response to a negative supply shock. Suppose that the central bank decides to validate the supply shock because it believes that factor prices fall only slowly. The monetary validation shifts the AD curve to the right and causes both the price level and output to *rise*. As the recessionary gap is eliminated, the price level rises further, rather than falling back to its original value as it did when the supply shock was not validated. These effects are also illustrated in Figure 29-4.

Monetary validation of a negative supply shock causes the initial rise in the price level to be followed by a further rise, resulting in a higher price level than would occur if the recessionary gap were relied on to reduce factor prices.

The most dramatic example of a supply-shock inflation came in the wake of the first OPEC oil-price shock. In 1974, the countries who were members of the Organization of Petroleum Exporting Countries (OPEC) agreed to restrict output. Their action caused a dramatic increase in the prices of petroleum and many petroleum-related products such as fertilizer and chemicals. The resulting increase in industrial costs shifted SRAS curves upward in all industrial countries. At this time, the Bank of Canada validated the supply shock with large increases in the money supply, whereas the Fed (the U.S. central bank) did not. As the theory predicts, Canada experienced a large increase in its price level but almost no recession, and the United States experienced a much smaller increase in its price level but a severe recession.

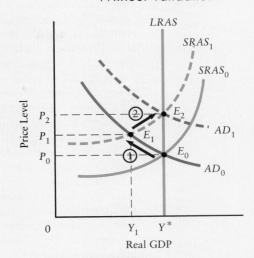

FIGURE 29-4   A Supply Shock With and Without Validation

Adverse supply shocks initially raise prices while lowering output. An adverse supply shock causes the SRAS curve to shift leftward from $SRAS_0$ to $SRAS_1$, as shown by arrow 1. Equilibrium is established at E_1. If there is no monetary validation, the reduction in factor prices makes the SRAS curve shift slowly back to the right, to $SRAS_0$. If there is monetary validation, the AD curve shifts from AD_0 to AD_1, as shown by arrow 2. This reestablishes equilibrium at E_2 with output equal to potential output but with a higher price level, P_2.

A contract settlement that raises wages for a large number of workers will increase firms' costs and shift the SRAS curve upward and to the left.

---

[4]Nominal wages rarely fall because there is ongoing productivity growth that offsets the effect on wages of excess supply. But in this chapter we are holding productivity constant so that we can focus on the causes and consequences of inflation. Productivity growth is addressed in Chapter 32.

For information on OPEC, see their website: www.opec.org.

Is Monetary Validation of Supply Shocks Desirable?

Suppose the central bank validates a negative supply shock and thus prevents what could otherwise be a protracted recession. Expressed in this way, monetary validation sounds like a good policy. Unfortunately, however, there is also a possible cost associated with this policy. The effect of the monetary validation is to extend the period of inflation. If this inflation leads firms and workers to expect *further* inflation, then point E_2 in Figure 29-4 will not be the end of the story. As expectations for further inflation develop, the *SRAS* curve will continue to shift upward. But if the central bank continues its policy of validation, then the *AD* curve will also continue to shift upward. It may not take long before the economy is in a *wage-price spiral*.

Once started, a wage-price spiral can be halted only if the Bank of Canada stops validating the supply shocks that are causing the inflation. But the longer it waits to do so, the more firmly held will be the *expectations* that it will continue its policy of validating the shocks. These entrenched expectations may cause wages to continue rising even after validation has ceased. Because employers expect prices to rise, they go on granting wage increases. If expectations are entrenched firmly enough, the wage push can continue for quite some time, in spite of the downward pressure caused by the rising unemployment associated with the growing recessionary gap.

Because of this possibility, many economists argue that the wage-price spiral should not be allowed to begin. One way to ensure that it does not begin is to refuse to validate any supply shock whatsoever.

To some economists, caution dictates that no supply shock should ever be validated, lest a wage-price spiral be created. Other economists are willing to risk validation in order to avoid the significant, though transitory, recessions that otherwise accompany them.

Accelerating Inflation

Consider a situation where a demand or supply shock increases real GDP above Y^*. Furthermore, suppose the central bank tries to maintain real GDP at this higher level. Can the central bank achieve this objective? If so, what is the effect on inflation?

acceleration hypothesis The hypothesis that when real GDP is held above potential, the persistent inflationary gap will cause inflation to accelerate.

What happens to the rate of inflation is predicted by the **acceleration hypothesis**, which holds that when the central bank engages in whatever rate of monetary expansion is needed to hold the inflationary gap constant, the actual inflation rate will *accelerate*. The Bank of Canada may start by validating 3 percent inflation, but soon 3 percent will become 4 percent and, if the Bank insists on validating 4 percent, the rate will become 5 percent, and so on without limit, until the Bank finally stops its validation.

There are several steps in the reasoning behind this hypothesis. The first concerns the development of inflationary expectations.

Expectational Effects

Recall our earlier discussion in this chapter about how actual inflation can be decomposed into its component parts of excess demand, expectations, and non-wage supply shocks. It is worth restating:

$$\begin{array}{ccccccc} \text{Actual} \\ \text{Inflation} \end{array} = \begin{array}{c} \text{Excess-Demand} \\ \text{Inflation} \end{array} + \begin{array}{c} \text{Expected} \\ \text{Inflation} \end{array} + \begin{array}{c} \text{Supply-Shock} \\ \text{Inflation} \end{array}$$

To illustrate the importance of expectations in accelerating inflation, suppose that the inflationary gap creates sufficient excess demand to push up wages by 2 percent per year. As a result, the *SRAS* curve will also tend to be rising at 2 percent per year.

When inflation has persisted for some time, however, people may come to expect that the inflation will continue. The expectation of 2 percent inflation will tend to push up wages by that amount *in addition to* the demand pressure. As the demand effect on wages is augmented by the expectational effect, the *SRAS* curve will begin to shift upward more rapidly. When expectations are for a 2 percent inflation and demand pressure is also pushing wages up by 2 percent, the overall effect will be a 4 percent increase in wages. Sooner or later, however, 4 percent inflation will come to be expected, and the expectational effect will rise to 4 percent. This new expectational component of 4 percent, when added to the demand component, will create an inflation rate of 6 percent. And so this cycle will go on. As long as there is a demand effect arising from an inflationary gap and as long as actual inflation is equal to the demand effect plus the expectational effect, the inflation rate cannot stay constant because expectations will always be revised upward toward the actual inflation rate.

More Rapid Monetary Validation Required

The second step in the argument is that if the Bank of Canada still wishes to hold the level of output constant, it must increase the rate at which the money supply is growing. This action is necessary because to hold real GDP constant, the *AD* curve must be shifted at an increasingly rapid pace to offset the increasingly rapid shifts in the *SRAS* curve, which are driven by the continually rising rate of expected inflation.

An Increasing Rate of Inflation

The third step in the argument is that the rate of inflation must now be increasing because of the increasingly rapid upward shifts in both the *AD* and *SRAS* curves. The rise in the actual inflation rate will in turn cause an increase in the expected inflation rate. This will then cause the actual inflation rate to increase, which will in turn increase the expected inflation rate, and so on. The net result is a *continually increasing rate of inflation*. Now we see the reason for the name NAIRU. At any level of unemployment less than the NAIRU, real GDP is above Y^*, and the inflation rate tends to accelerate. Thus, the NAIRU is the lowest level of unemployment consistent with a *nonaccelerating* rate of inflation.

According to the acceleration hypothesis, as long as an inflationary gap persists, expectations of inflation will be rising, which will lead to increases in the actual rate of inflation.

The tendency for inflation to accelerate is discussed further in *Extensions in Theory 29-1*, which examines how expected inflation affects the position of the Phillips curve.

Inflation as a Monetary Phenomenon

A long-standing debate among economists concerns the extent to which inflation is a monetary phenomenon. Does it have purely monetary causes—changes in the demand or the supply of money? Does it have purely monetary consequences—only the price level is affected? One slogan that states an extreme position on this issue was popularized

EXTENSIONS IN THEORY 29-1

The Phillips Curve and Accelerating Inflation

As we first saw in Chapter 25, the Phillips curve describes the relationship between unemployment (or output) and the rate of change of wages. The Phillips curve was born in 1958 when Professor A.W. Phillips from the London School of Economics noted a relationship between unemployment and the rate of change of wages over a period of 100 years in the United Kingdom. Phillips was interested in studying the short-run behaviour of an economy subjected to cyclical fluctuations. In the years following Phillips's study, however, some economists treated the Phillips curve as estab-

(i) Wage changes and unemployment

(ii) Wage changes and output

many years ago by Milton Friedman: "Inflation is *everywhere* and *always* a monetary phenomenon." To consider these issues, let us summarize what we have learned already. First, look at the *causes* of inflation:

- *Cause 1:* On the demand side, anything that shifts the AD curve to the right will cause the price level to rise.
- *Cause 2:* On the supply side, anything that increases factor prices will shift the SRAS curve to the left and cause the price level to rise.
- *Cause 3:* Unless continual monetary expansion occurs, the increases in the price level must eventually come to a halt.

The first two points provide the sense in which, in regard to causes, a temporary burst of inflation need not be a monetary phenomenon. It need not have monetary causes, and it need not be accompanied by monetary expansion. The third point provides the sense in which *sustained* inflation *must* be a monetary phenomenon. If a rise in prices is to continue indefinitely, it *must* be accompanied by continuing increases in the money supply. This is true regardless of the cause that set the inflation in motion.

Now, let us summarize the *consequences* of inflation, assuming that real GDP was initially at its potential level.

lishing a long-term tradeoff between inflation and unemployment.

Suppose the government stabilizes output at Y_1 (and hence the unemployment rate at U_1), as shown in the accompanying figures. To do this, it must validate the ensuing wage inflation, which is indicated by $\dot{W}_1$ in the figure. The government thus seems to be able to choose among particular combinations of inflation and unemployment, in which lower levels of unemployment are attained at the cost of higher rates of inflation.

In the 1960s, Phillips curves were fitted to the data for many countries, and governments made decisions about where they wished to be on the tradeoff between inflation and unemployment. Then, in the late 1960s, in country after country, the rate of wage and price inflation associated with any given level of unemployment began to rise. Instead of being stable, the Phillips curves began to shift upward. The explanation lay primarily in a shifting relationship between the pressure of demand and wage increases due to inflationary expectations, as we discussed in the text.

It was gradually understood that the original Phillips curve concerned only the influence of demand and left out inflationary expectations. This omission proved important and unfortunate. An increase in expected inflation shows up as an upward shift in the original Phillips curve that was drawn in Chapter 25. The importance of expectations can be shown by drawing what is called an **expectations-augmented Phillips curve**, as seen here. The heights of the Phillips curves above the axis at Y^* and at U^* show the expected inflation rate. These distances represent the amount that wages will rise when neither excess demand nor excess supply pressures are being felt in labour markets. The actual wage increase is shown by the augmented (dashed) curve, with the increase in wages exceeding expected inflation whenever $Y > Y^*$ ($U < U^*$) and falling short of expected inflation whenever $Y < Y^*$ ($U > U^*$).

Now we can see what was wrong with the idea of a stable inflation-unemployment tradeoff. Targeting a particular output Y_1 or unemployment U_1 in the figures is fine only if no inflation is expected. But getting to Y_1 or U_1 itself requires some inflation ($\dot{W}_1$). And once this rate of inflation comes to be expected, people will demand that much just to hold their own. The Phillips curve will shift upward to the position shown in the figures. Now there is inflation $\dot{W}_2$ because of the combined effects of expectations and excess demand. However, this higher rate is above the expected rate ($\dot{W}_1$). Once this higher rate comes to be expected, the Phillips curve will shift upward once again.

As a result of the combination of excess-demand inflation and expectational inflation, the inflation rate associated with any given positive output gap ($Y > Y^*$ or $U < U^*$) rises over time. This is the phenomenon of accelerating inflation that we discussed in the text.

The shifts in the Phillips curve are such that most economists agree that in the long run, when inflationary expectations have fully adjusted to actual inflation, there is no tradeoff between inflation and unemployment. That is, they believe that the long-run Phillips curve is a vertical line at the NAIRU.

expectations-augmented Phillips curve The relationship between unemployment and the rate of increase of money wages that arises when the demand and expectations components of inflation are combined.

- *Consequence 1:* In the short run, demand-shock inflation tends to be accompanied by an *increase* in real GDP above its potential level.
- *Consequence 2:* In the short run, supply-shock inflation tends to be accompanied by a *decrease* in real GDP below its potential level.
- *Consequence 3:* When all costs and prices are adjusted *fully* (so that the relevant aggregate supply curve is the *LRAS* curve), shifts in either the *AD* or *SRAS* curve leave real GDP unchanged and affect only the price level.

The first two points provide a sense in which, in terms of consequences, inflation is not, in the short run, a purely monetary phenomenon. The third point provides the sense in which inflation is a purely monetary phenomenon from the point of view of long-run equilibrium.

There is still plenty of room for debate, however, on how long the short run will last. Most economists believe that the short run can be long enough for inflation to have major real effects.

We have now reached three important conclusions:

- *Conclusion 1:* Without monetary validation, demand shocks cause temporary bursts of inflation that are accompanied by inflationary gaps. The gaps are removed as rising factor prices push the *SRAS* curve to the left, returning real GDP to its potential level, but at a higher price level.

- *Conclusion 2:* Without monetary validation, negative supply shocks cause temporary bursts of inflation that are accompanied by recessionary gaps. The gaps are removed as factor prices fall, restoring real GDP to its potential and the price level to its initial level.
- *Conclusion 3:* Only with continuing monetary validation can inflation initiated by either supply or demand shocks continue indefinitely.

Reducing Inflation

Suppose an economy has had a sustained rate of inflation for several years. What must the central bank do to reduce the rate of inflation? What are the costs involved in doing so?

The Process of Disinflation

disinflation The process of reducing the rate of inflation.

Disinflation means a reduction in the rate of inflation. In recent years, Canada has had two notable periods of disinflation—in 1981–82 when inflation fell from 12 percent to 4 percent, and in 1990–92 when inflation fell from 5 percent to just over 1 percent.

Reducing the rate of inflation takes time and involves major costs. The process begins when the Bank of Canada stops validating the ongoing inflation. It does this by lowering the rate of growth of the money supply below the rate of growth of money demand, thus creating an excess demand for money. This action forces up interest rates and lowers real aggregate demand, reducing any existing inflationary gap. We will soon see that it is usually necessary for the Bank to go further, creating a substantial recessionary gap that persists until the inflation is eliminated.

The process involves many costs. The recessionary gap hurts all who suffer in recessions, including the unemployed workers and the owners of firms who lose profits and risk bankruptcy. Unemployed resources mean lower output than would otherwise be produced. The temporary rise in interest rates hurts borrowers, including people with mortgages and firms with large loans. Among these groups who are most exposed and may lose their wealth are young households with large mortgages and small firms that have taken on large debts to finance expansions.

Disinflation is thus a classic case of a policy that brings short-term pain for long-term gain. Inevitably, the question arises: Are the future benefits worth the immediate costs?

Reducing sustained inflation quickly incurs high costs for a short period of time; reducing it slowly incurs lower costs but for a longer period of time.

The process of reducing sustained inflation can be divided into three phases. In the first phase, the monetary validation is stopped and the inflationary gap is eliminated. In the second phase, the economy still suffers from declining output and rising prices—stagflation. In the final phase, the economy experiences both increasing output and increasing prices, but the inflation then comes to an end. We now examine these three phases in detail.

Practise with Study Guide Chapter 29, Exercise 3.

The starting point for our analysis is an economy with an inflationary gap ($Y > Y^*$) and rising inflation.[5]

---

[5]In the simpler case where the economy begins with $Y = Y^*$ and constant inflation, only the second and third phases are relevant.

Phase 1: Removing Monetary Validation

The first phase consists of slowing the rate of monetary expansion, thereby slowing the rate at which the *AD* curve is shifting upward. The simplest case is when the Bank of Canada adopts a "cold-turkey approach" in which the rate of monetary expansion is cut to zero so that the upward shift in the *AD* curve is halted abruptly. This halt implies a large and rapid increase in both nominal and real interest rates.

At this point, a controversy often breaks out—as it did in the early 1980s and early 1990s—over the effects that the increase in interest rates has on inflation. One group will point out that the rise in the interest rate increases business costs and that passing on the extra costs through higher prices adds to inflation. They will condemn the Bank's tight monetary policy as inflationary. A second group will argue that the rising interest rate signifies a slowdown in the rate of monetary expansion, without which inflation cannot be curbed.

The first group is correct in pointing out that the rise in interest rates may cause a one-time increase in the price level. The rise in interest costs may shift the *SRAS* curve upward, just as a rise in wage costs does. This rise in interest costs, however, has only a *one-time effect* on the price level. The first group is wrong, therefore, in asserting that the Bank's policy of driving up interest rates is contributing to a long-term increase in the rate of inflation.

The second group is correct in saying that the rise in the interest rate is a necessary part of an anti-inflationary policy. As long as the price level continues to rise, the rise in the interest rate reduces desired aggregate expenditure, thus reducing equilibrium real GDP by moving leftward along a fixed *AD* curve.

Now suppose that the Bank resists the pleas to hold down interest rates. It continues with its no-validation policy. The *AD* curve stops shifting, but under the combined influence of the present inflationary gap and expectations of continued inflation, wages continue to rise. Hence, the *SRAS* curve continues to shift upward. Eventually, the inflationary gap will be removed, as shown in part (i) of Figure 29-5.

If demand were the only influence on wages, the story would be ended. At $Y = Y^*$, there would be no upward demand pressure on wages and other factor prices. The *SRAS* curve would be stabilized, and the economy would remain at full employment with a stable price level.

Phase 2: Stagflation

Governments around the world have often wished that things were really so simple. However, wages depend not only on current excess demand but also on inflation expectations. Once inflation expectations have been established, it is not always easy to get people to revise them downward, even in the face of announced changes in monetary policies. Hence, the *SRAS* curve continues to shift upward, causing the price level to continue to rise and output to fall. This is phase 2, shown in part (ii) of Figure 29-5.

Expectations can cause inflation to persist even after its original causes have been removed. What was initially a demand and expectational inflation due to an inflationary gap becomes a pure expectational inflation.

The ease with which the Bank of Canada can end such an inflation depends on how easy it is to change these expectations of continued inflation. This change is more difficult to the extent that expectations are backward-looking and easier to the extent that expectations are forward-looking.

To the extent that people look mainly to past inflation rates to determine their expectations of the future, they will be slow to change their expectations. As the actual inflation rate falls below the expected rate, a long time will be required for the downward

FIGURE 29-5   Eliminating a Sustained Inflation

(i) Phase 1: Removing the inflationary gap

(ii) Phase 2: Stagflation

(iii) Phase 3: Recovery

(i) Phase 1: The elimination of a sustained inflation begins with a demand contraction to remove the inflationary gap. The initial position is one where fully validated inflation is taking the economy along the path shown by arrow 1. When the curves reach $SRAS_1$ and AD_1, the Bank stops expanding the money supply, thus stabilizing aggregate demand at AD_1. Wages continue to rise, taking the $SRAS$ curve leftward. The economy moves along arrow 2, with output falling and the price level rising. When aggregate supply reaches $SRAS_2$, the inflationary gap is removed, income is Y^*, and the price level is P_2.

(ii) Phase 2: Expectations and wage momentum lead to stagflation, with falling output and continuing inflation. The economy moves along the path shown by arrow 3. The driving force is now the $SRAS$ curve, which continues to shift because inflation expectations cause wages to continue rising. The recessionary gap grows as output falls. Inflation continues, but at a diminishing rate. If wages stop rising when output has reached Y_3 and the price level has reached P_3, the stagflation phase is over, with equilibrium at E_3.

(iii) Phase 3: After expectations are reversed, recovery takes output to Y^*, and the price level is stabilized. There are two possible scenarios for recovery. In the first, the recessionary gap causes wages to fall (slowly), taking the $SRAS$ curve back to $SRAS_2$ (slowly), as shown by arrow 4. The economy retraces the path originally followed in part (ii) back to E_2. In the second scenario, the Bank increases the money supply sufficiently to shift the AD curve to AD_2. The economy then moves along the path shown by arrow 5. This restores output to potential at the cost of further temporary inflation that takes the price level to P_4. Potential output and a stable price level are now achieved.

adjustment to take place. The longer a given rate has persisted, the more firmly will people expect that rate to persist.

To the extent that expectations are forward-looking, people will take notice of the Bank's changed behaviour and revise their expectations of future inflation downward in the light of the new monetary policy. If people fully understand the Bank's policies as soon as they are implemented, if they have full confidence that the Bank will stick to its policies, if they know exactly how much time will be required for the Bank's policies to have effect, and if they adjust their expectations exactly in line with this knowledge, there is little need for any recessionary gap to develop. Once the inflationary gap has been removed, expectations will immediately be revised downward, so there will then be no pressure on wages to rise because of either demand or expectational forces. In Figure 29-5, Y would not fall below Y^* because the $SRAS$ curve would stop shifting upward at $SRAS_2$. The inflation would be eliminated at almost no cost.

How long inflation persists after the inflationary gap has been removed depends on how quickly expectations of continued inflation are revised downward.

When the $SRAS$ curve does continue to shift upward, causing Y to fall below Y^*, the emerging recessionary gap has two effects. First, unemployment is rising; hence the demand influence on wages becomes negative. Second, as the recession deepens and monetary restraint continues, people revise their expectations of inflation downward. When they have no further expectations of inflation, there are no further increases in wages, and the $SRAS$ curve stops shifting. The stagflation phase is over. Inflation has come to a halt, but a large recessionary gap now exists.

Phase 3: Recovery

The final phase is the return to potential output. When the economy comes to rest at the end of the stagflation, the situation is exactly the same as when the economy is hit by a negative supply shock. The move back to potential output can be accomplished in either of two ways. First, the recessionary gap can be relied on to reduce factor prices, thereby shifting the $SRAS$ curve downward, reducing prices but increasing real GDP. Second, the money supply can be increased to shift the AD curve upward, increasing both prices and real GDP. These two possibilities are illustrated in part (iii) of Figure 29-5.

Some economists worry about relying on the $SRAS$ curve to shift downward to return the economy to potential output. Their concern is primarily that it will take too long for prices and wages to fall sufficiently to shift the $SRAS$ curve—though output will eventually return to potential, the long adjustment period will be characterized by high unemployment. These economists have a preference for a monetary expansion to get output back to potential.

Other economists worry about a temporary burst of monetary expansion because they fear that expectations of inflation may be rekindled when the Bank increases the money supply. And, if inflationary expectations *are* revived, the Bank will then be faced with a tough decision—either it must let another recession develop to break these new inflation expectations, or it must validate the inflation to reduce unemployment. In the latter case, the Bank is back where it started, with validated inflation on its hands—and diminished credibility.

The Cost of Disinflation

The foregoing discussion of the process of disinflation makes the cost of disinflation pretty clear:

The cost of disinflation is the cost of the recession that is generated in the process.

As we said earlier, the size and duration of the recession depends to a large extent on how quickly inflation expectations are revised downward. If expectations are backward looking and thus slow to adjust to the changes in policy, the recession will be deep and protracted. Conversely, if expectations are forward looking and quick to adjust to changes in policy, the recession may be mild and of short duration.

The main cost of disinflation is the reduction in economic activity that is a necessary part of the process. Increases in unemployment and plant closures are typical.

But *how costly* is the process of disinflation? Economists have derived a simple measure of the costs of disinflation based on the depth and length of the recession and on the amount of disinflation. This measure is called the **sacrifice ratio**, and is defined to be the cumulative loss of real GDP due to a given disinflation (expressed as a percentage of potential GDP) divided by the number of percentage points by which inflation has fallen. For example, the 1990–92 disinflation in Canada reduced inflation by roughly four percentage points. Suppose that the cumulative loss of real GDP due to that disinflation was equal to $80 billion and that potential GDP at the time was equal to $800 billion. The cumulative loss of output would then be 10 percent of potential output. The sacrifice ratio would therefore have been 10/4 = 2.5. The interpretation of this number is that it "costs" 2.5 percent of real GDP for each percentage point of inflation that is reduced.

The numbers in the above example are hypothetical, but typical estimates of the sacrifice ratio for many developed countries range between 2 and 4. Figure 29-6 illustrates the time paths of real GDP and inflation following a disinflation and shows how to compute the sacrifice ratio. Note an important assumption that is implicit whenever measuring the sacrifice ratio in this way. The assumption is that all changes in the path of real GDP are *caused by* the disinflation.

FIGURE 29-6   The Cost of Disinflation: The Sacrifice Ratio

The sacrifice ratio is larger the deeper the recession and the longer it takes real GDP to return to potential. In this example, the economy begins with $Y = Y^*$ and inflation of 6 percent. At t^*, the disinflation begins. A recessionary gap opens up and inflation falls only slowly. By t^{**}, real GDP has returned to Y^* and inflation has been reduced by 4 percentage points. In this figure, the cumulative loss of real GDP is 10 percent of Y^* and inflation has fallen by 4 percentage points. The sacrifice ratio is therefore 10/4 = 2.5.

Inflation in Canada

In this chapter's final section, we continue the discussion of Canadian inflation policy that we began in Chapter 28. We begin our study with the inflation of the 1970s. See Figure 29-7 for the time path of the annual inflation rate in Canada over the past three decades. In the discussion that follows, it will be useful to refer back to this figure frequently.

The early 1970s witnessed quite expansionary fiscal and monetary policies. The money supply was expanded rapidly, and an inflationary gap opened up as real GDP exceeded its potential level. As a result, inflation began to rise. Expansion continued until early 1974, and inflation rose throughout that period. Then a worldwide recession began, and Canada did not escape its effects. As a recessionary gap began to open up, the normal expectation was that inflation would diminish. Just then, however, the first OPEC shock hit. The prices of oil and other petroleum products soared. This negative supply shock reduced the growth of real GDP and sent inflation into the double-digit range. The result was stagflation.

The Rise of Inflation: 1975–1980

Rather than viewing the stagflation as the result of rising oil prices, Canadian policy makers interpreted the stagflation as accelerating wage-push inflation in a

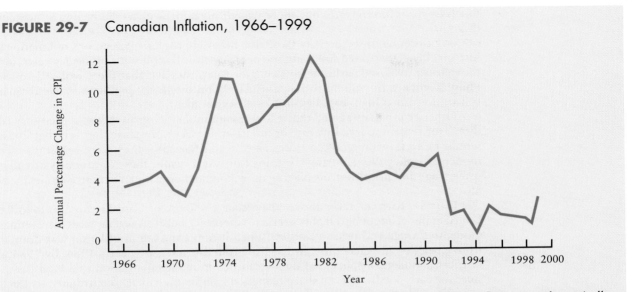

FIGURE 29-7   Canadian Inflation, 1966–1999

Canada's recent experience with inflation is varied. From about 4 percent in the late 1960s, inflation rose dramatically to a high of over 12 percent in 1980–1981. It then fell to about 4 percent by 1984. It hovered between 4 and 5 percent for the next few years, eventually creeping up to 6 percent in 1990. It then fell to about 2 percent by 1992 and then hovered between 1 and 2 percent for the next seven years. By the end of 1999, with a fast-growing economy, the inflation rate had risen above 2 percent. Inflation in this figure is measured as the annual percentage change in the Consumer Price Index (all items).

(*Source: Bank of Canada Review,* various issues.)

time of world recession. Having failed in an attempt to secure the agreement of organized labour in a voluntary policy of reducing wage demands, the government decided to impose **wage and price controls.** An Anti-Inflation Board was set up and given power to control wages and prices for 3 years. At roughly the same time, the Bank of Canada adopted the policy of "monetary gradualism" by announcing its intention to gradually reduce the rate of growth of the money supply.

Whether by accident or by design, the two policies made a coherent package. The monetary policy was meant to reduce the speed with which the *AD* curve was shifting upward. Wage-and-price controls were meant to reduce the speed with which the *SRAS* curve was shifting upward. If the upward rush of the two curves could be slowed at the same rate, the inflation rate could be reduced without having to endure the stagflation phase (phase 2 in Figure 29-5), which occurs when the *AD* curve rises more slowly than the *SRAS* curve.

At first, all seemed to go well. The inflation rate fell in successive years starting in 1975. Then in 1979 and in 1980, a new setback appeared in the form of a substantial supply shock. The cause was another large increase in the world price of oil, due to a second round of OPEC output restrictions. As a result, the 1980 inflation rate became once again as high as it had been just before wage and price controls were introduced.

wage and price controls   Direct government intervention into wage and price formation with legal power to enforce the government's decisions on wages and prices.

The Fall of Inflation: 1981–1984

By the beginning of the 1980s, rapid inflation seemed firmly entrenched, and a major controversy arose over how to reduce it. Most people agreed on the goal of returning to a much lower inflation rate, but there was disagreement as to the means of achieving that goal.

Some economist—especially those that believed peoples' expectations of inflation adjust quickly—advocated breaking the entrenched inflation with monetary restraint in the manner analysed earlier in this chapter. Since they felt that there would be a short Phase 2, they were willing to rely exclusively on monetary policy to bring about the transition from a high- to a low-inflation environment.

Other economists agreed that a low rate of monetary growth was a necessary condition for returning to a low rate of inflation. However, because they felt that Phase 2 would be long—some talked in terms of 5 to 10 years—they were reluctant to use monetary policy *alone* during the transition. As a result, these economists advocated using wage and price controls once again in conjunction with a restrictive monetary policy.

In 1981, with inflation above 12 percent, the Bank of Canada chose to follow the United States in adopting a highly restrictive monetary policy. A serious recession eventually moderated wage and price increases. When it came, the fall in inflation was dramatic: from a peak of 12 percent in mid 1981 to around 4 percent by early 1984. By 1984, the restrictive monetary policy had thus succeeded in reducing inflation to a level not seen since the early 1960s. But the sharp reduction in inflation had also contributed to a major recession with all its attendant costs, including unemployment, lost output, business bankruptcies, and foreclosed mortgages.

The results came out somewhere between the extremes that had been predicted. Thus, as so often happens with great debates, neither the extreme pessimists nor the extreme optimists were right—the truth lay somewhere in between. Whatever the reasons, during the early 1980s, inflation fell faster than many economists had expected, but the slump was deeper and more prolonged than many others had expected.

Recovery: 1985–1990

For several years following 1984, the Canadian inflation rate stabilized at around 4 percent, and it was a time of low inflation in the world as a whole. There was no reason for the inflation rate to rise, since there was no inflationary gap in the Canadian economy. Indeed, since there was actually a *recessionary gap* during this period, the actual inflation seemed to be purely expectational: People expected a 4 percent inflation rate, and the Bank validated that inflation rate through a continued monetary expansion. Thus, inflation persisted at a rate of about 4 percent.

Since there was a recessionary gap during this period, why did inflation not fall further? The answer here seems to be that the weak demand forces that work toward deceleration when there is excess supply were swamped by the forces of expectational inflation and random shocks.

By 1988, a long period of expansion was bringing Canadian real GDP close to its potential level. The inflation rate began to creep upward, exceeding 5 percent in 1989 and reaching 6 percent for a few months in 1990.

As we discussed in Chapter 28, the Bank of Canada in 1988, under the leadership of Governor John Crow, announced that monetary policy would no longer be guided by short-term stabilization issues and instead would be guided by the long-term goal of price stability. This important shift in policy indicated that henceforth the Bank of Canada would be prepared to fight inflation while more-or-less ignoring the short-term pain that such battles would produce.

Disinflation: 1991–1992

In 1989 the Bank of Canada reacted by adopting a restrictive monetary policy. Interest rates were driven up and, as discussed in Chapter 28, the Canadian dollar appreciated, putting tradable-goods producers under heavy competitive pressure. The country's economic expansion proved remarkably resilient. The inflationary gap and the high inflation rate persisted for over a year, in spite of very high interest rates and a strong Canadian dollar. Finally, by the middle of 1990, the inflation rate began to fall. By autumn, it had returned to the 4 percent plateau from which it had accelerated two years earlier. The Bank, however, persisted in its tight policy.

By late 1990, the economy was clearly into a recession and many who supported the Bank's long-term policy of price stability nonetheless called for a little fine tuning to offset some of the short-term pain associated with monetary restraint. They felt that the Bank could mitigate the recession by easing up on its tight monetary policy, returning to it once the next recovery had begun. The Bank responded by reiterating the importance of driving the inflation rate close to zero over a period of a few years.

As a way of formalizing the Bank's shift in policy away from short-term stabilization and toward long-term price stability, the Bank of Canada and the federal Department of Finance announced in 1991 a series of *inflation-control targets*. Beginning in 1992, the Bank would aim at having the rate of inflation in the 3–5 percent range. The target range declined gradually so that by the end of 1995 it was 1 to 3 percent.

This policy sparked enormous controversy. Some critics felt that the costs of reducing the inflation rate below 4 percent, as reflected by the sacrifice ratio, would be excessive. They preferred to have the economy adjust to that rate rather than undergo the costs of reducing the rate to 2 percent, let alone to zero. Other critics, while accepting price stability as the ultimate goal, argued that the policy should not be pursued when the economy was already in the midst of a serious recession.

Supporters pointed out that 4 percent inflation was a high inflation rate by historical standards. They argued that price stability was the best long-run goal. To the critics who said, "yes, but not now," the supporters replied that reducing a sustained inflation is always costly, and there will always be strong arguments for not incurring these costs at present. They felt that the commitment to price stability must be honoured and the costs accepted, since the longer that attempt was postponed, the more entrenched would inflation expectations become and, thus, the greater would be the costs of finally reducing inflation.

In the event, the Bank stuck to its policy. The recession was indeed severe. Canadian interest rates stayed well above U.S. rates, and the Canadian dollar remained high on foreign-exchange markets. However, the inflation rate responded as theory predicts and, by the end of 1992, the Bank was able to declare victory against inflation. Inflation was well below 2 percent.

Recovery and Low Inflation: 1993–?

The subsequent economic recovery was considered to be a fragile one, at least for 1991 and 1992. Many people blamed the Bank for the deep recession that Canada suffered, and much of the disagreement over the Bank's policy became focused on the Governor, John Crow. In 1994, the minister of finance in the newly elected Liberal government appointed Gordon Thiessen as the new governor of the Bank of Canada. At the same time, both the finance minister and Mr. Thiessen affirmed the recent monetary policy of the Bank and announced that the formal inflation targets of 1 to 3 percent would continue. So, political considerations dictated a change in the governor while economic considerations dictated no change in monetary policy.

By 1995, economic growth had picked up considerably, even though the unemployment rate seemed to decline only slowly. The Bank's main challenge during this period of recovery was to provide enough growth in the money supply to allow a healthy recovery while at the same time not expanding so much that inflationary pressures would build. From 1995 to 1999, the rate of inflation was mostly within the established 1 to 3 percent target range, though in 1998 it temporarily dropped below the bottom of the range. By early 2000, real GDP was very close to potential GDP, the economy was growing quickly, and inflationary pressures began to build. The bank began to tighten monetary policy in an effort to keep inflation from rising.

Two Current Debates

The Bank of Canada's success in achieving and maintaining low inflation has led to two interesting debates regarding low inflation. You may recognize both debates from the business pages of Canada's newspapers. Both can be posed as questions. Is inflation dead? Is inflation too low?

The Death of Inflation?

See Chapter 29 of www.pearsoned.ca/lipsey for an excellent debate on the death of inflation: John Crow, "The Death of Inflation and Other Metaphors," and Roger Bootle, "The Death of Inflation," *World Economic Affairs.*

With inflation falling rapidly in many countries in the last few years, and with the apparent success in maintaining inflation at very low levels, some economists and policy makers have started asking an inevitable question: Is inflation dead?

Many arguments have been made in defence of the view that inflation is no longer a threat, and they all involve the greater competition that comes from globalization. As we have noted earlier in this book, globalization—the sharp reductions in the cost of transportation and communication in the past two decades—presents domestic firms and workers with greater competition than they would otherwise have. If firms can easily ship their products to various countries quickly and efficiently, then domestic firms face greater competition from abroad. Similarly, if firms can easily relocate their factories to produce in lower-cost countries, then domestic workers face greater competition from abroad. As a result, domestic firms are less likely to raise prices and domestic workers are less likely to push for wage increases. In short, globalization increases the competitive pressures in the economy, thus reducing the economy's inflationary forces.

Most economists, however, reject this view that the ongoing process of globalization spells an end to inflation. While recognizing that competitive forces may well be enhanced by globalization, most economists argue that such increases in competition will have one-time effects on wages and prices, but will not influence the long-run rate of inflation. (In their view, the increase in competition is best thought of as a one-time shift in the *LRAS* curve to the right.) Central to this argument, as we have seen in this chapter, is the view that *sustained* inflation is indeed a monetary phenomenon—that is, sustained inflation is only possible when there is continual growth in the money supply. Thus, though individual demand and supply shocks may affect inflation temporarily, the long-run rate of inflation is ultimately determined by monetary policy.

In this view, inflation is dead only if central banks maintain their current commitment to keeping inflation at very low levels. Any future negative supply shock, followed by monetary validation, could easily tip any individual country—or group of countries—back into an inflationary wage-price spiral.

Since sustained inflation is ultimately determined by monetary policy, inflation will only remain low if central banks maintain their commitment to low inflation.

Costs of Very Low Inflation?

Canada's inflation rate fell very quickly from 5 percent in 1991 to below 2 percent in 1992. It then remained between 1 and 2 percent for the next seven years. The U.S. Federal Reserve was not as aggressive in their drive to reduce inflation; inflation in the United States did not decline as much or as sharply as in Canada. Interestingly, the Canadian and U.S. economies appeared to perform differently throughout the 1990s. Especially apparent was the difference in unemployment rates between the two countries. From 1985 to 1990, when both economies were growing steadily, the Canadian unemployment rate was just over 2 percentage points higher than the U.S. rate. Beginning in 1991, however, as Canada's sharp disinflation began, the gap increased to 4 percentage points.

Some economists point to the widening gap in unemployment rates as evidence that there are costs associated with very low inflation.[6] These economists argue not only that the process of disinflation involves *temporary* costs in terms of reduced output and higher unemployment, but more controversially that there are *permanent* costs associated with maintaining inflation at very low levels.

That very low inflation may permanently raise unemployment is an argument originally put forward in 1972 by James Tobin, an economist from Yale University who was awarded the Nobel Prize in economics in 1981. In Canada, the argument was made recently by Pierre Fortin of the Université du Québec à Montréal. Central to Tobin's and Fortin's arguments is the importance of downward rigidity in nominal wages—a more extreme version of what we called *wage stickiness* in Chapter 25. Specifically, these economists believe that nominal wages will rise in the presence of excess demand but they will not fall in the presence of excess supply. Why does this wage rigidity lead to higher unemployment when inflation is very low but not when inflation is higher?

Their argument is rather involved, and to understand it we need to proceed carefully. The argument is summarized by the following four points:

- First, the various sectors within the economy are continually being subjected to demand shocks. At any given time, some sectors are expanding while others are contracting. These demand shocks lead to changes in the demand for labour in the various sectors and thus necessitate changes in real wages, rising in expanding sectors and falling in contracting sectors.
- Second, if nominal wages cannot fall because of wage rigidity, then the only way *real* wages can fall is if the price level rises.
- Third, inflation at moderate levels (3–5 percent) is high enough to bring about the necessary drop in real wages in most of the contracting sectors. This is because the pattern of demand shocks across sectors is such that even the sectors with the sharpest contractions require real-wage declines of only 5 percent.
- Finally (and this is the key point), if inflation is very low (1–2 percent), the contracting sectors *cannot* achieve the necessary reduction in real wages through inflation. Firms will instead choose to lay off their workers. Thus, when inflation is very low, the layoffs in the contracting sectors will outnumber the newly hired workers in the expanding sectors. The result is *permanently* higher unemployment.

---

[6]In Chapter 30 we discuss some other explanations for why Canada's unemployment rate is higher than the U.S. rate.

This view is not shared by all economists. The main point of contention is the cause and extent of the downward rigidity in nominal wages. Many economists believe that while nominal wages may be very slow to fall in response to excess supply, this wage stickiness is largely a result of workers' having lived in an inflationary environment for many years. In such an environment, if prices have been rising at 5, 8, or 10 percent annually, it is easy to understand why workers are reluctant to accept an actual decline in their nominal wages. But as low inflation becomes a more permanent part of the economic environment, workers will naturally come to view occasional reductions in nominal wages as one of the unpleasant but inevitable aspects of economic life. If this is true, then the downward rigidity of nominal wages will eventually disappear as Canada's experience with low inflation continues. In this case, real GDP will eventually return to Y^*, unemployment will eventually return to U^*, and low inflation will not involve permanent costs.

This debate is currently unsettled. Much theoretical and empirical research is directed at determining the extent of nominal wage rigidity and how it is related to the overall inflation rate, but it will probably take several years before a consensus emerges on just how important this potential cost of low inflation really is.[7]

Conclusion

Throughout the history of economics, inflation has been recognized as a harmful phenomenon. This view was given renewed strength as a result of the worldwide experiences of high inflation rates since the early 1970s. The resolve is there, at least in advanced industrial countries, to prevent another outbreak of rapid inflation and, should one occur for reasons of unavoidable supply-side shocks, to prevent it from continuing long enough to become firmly entrenched in people's expectations.

It is clear from experience that reducing the inflation rate by any significant amount usually has costs in terms of reduced output and increased unemployment. It is also clear from past policy debates that every time the Bank undertakes to do this, controversy will break out, whatever the current inflation rate. One side will argue that any reduction in the inflation rate is too costly and the other side will argue that these consequences must be accepted as the price of keeping some control over the inflation rate. Otherwise, the rate would slowly ratchet up under the impacts of supply- and demand-side shocks that the Bank was never allowed to counter because of fear of the short-run costs of doing so.

---

[7]The resurrection of Tobin's ideas is found in G. Akerlof, W. Dickens, and G. Perry, "The Macroeconomics of Low Inflation", *Brookings Papers on Economic Activity*, 1996. The argument for Canada was made by Pierre Fortin in "The Great Canadian Slump," *Canadian Journal of Economics*, 1997. For an assessment of the general argument, see Seamus Hogan, "What Does Downward Nominal-Wage Rigidity Imply for Monetary Policy?" *Canadian Public Policy*, 1998.

S U M M A R Y

Adding Inflation to the Model

- Sustained price inflation will be accompanied by closely related growth in wages and other factor prices such that the *SRAS* curve is shifting upward. Factors that influence shifts in the *SRAS* curve can be divided into two main components: demand and expectations. Random supply-side shocks will also exert an influence.
- The influence of demand can be expressed in terms of inflationary and recessionary gaps, which relate real output to potential output, or in terms of the difference between the actual rate of unemployment and the NAIRU.
- Expectations of inflation tend to cause wage increases equal to the expected price-level increases. Expectations

can be backward-looking, forward-looking, or some combination of the two.
- With a constant rate of inflation, expected inflation will eventually come to equal actual inflation. This implies that there is no demand pressure on inflation—that is, real GDP equals its potential level.
- Constant inflation of X percent per year is shown graphically in the macroeconomic model by the *AD* and *SRAS* curves shifting up by X percent per year, keeping real GDP equal to Y^*.

Shocks and Policy Responses

- The initial effects of positive demand shocks are a rise in the price level and a rise in real GDP. If the inflation is unvalidated, output returns to its potential level while the price level rises further (as the *SRAS* curve shifts upward). Monetary validation allows demand inflation to proceed without reducing the inflationary gap (*AD* curve continues to shift upward).
- The initial effects of negative supply shocks are a rise in the price level and a fall in real GDP. If inflation is unvalidated, output will slowly return to its potential level as the price level slowly falls to its preshock level (*SRAS* curve

slowly shifts down). Monetary validation allows supply inflation to continue in spite of a persistent recessionary gap (*AD* curve shifts up with monetary validation).
- If the Bank of Canada tries to keep real GDP constant at some level above Y^*, the actual inflation rate will accelerate. Constant inflation is only possible when there are no demand pressures on inflation—that is, when $Y = Y^*$.
- Aggregate demand and supply shocks have temporary effects on inflation. But *sustained* inflation is a monetary phenomenon.

Reducing Inflation

- The process of ending a sustained inflation can be divided into three phases. Phase 1 consists of ending monetary validation and allowing the upward shift in the *SRAS* curve to remove any inflationary gap that does exist. In Phase 2, a recessionary gap develops as expectations of further inflation cause the *SRAS* curve to continue to shift upward even after the inflationary gap is removed. In Phase 3, the economy returns to poten-

tial output, sometimes aided by a one-time monetary expansion that raises the *AD* curve to the level consistent with potential output at the present price level.
- The cost of disinflation is the recession that is created in the process. The sacrifice ratio is a measure of this cost and is calculated as the cumulative loss in real GDP (expressed as a percentage of Y^*) divided by the reduction in inflation.

Inflation in Canada

- In the early 1980s, inflation peaked at around 13 percent. The Bank of Canada followed the United States in pursuing a tight-money policy. In Canada, inflation fell to around 4 percent by 1984, but the recession Canada experienced in the early 1980s was severe. During the next four years amidst a healthy economic recovery, inflation hovered between 4 and 5 percent, then toward the end of the recovery it crept up until reaching over 5 percent in 1989.
- In 1988, the Bank of Canada announced an important shift in policy. Henceforth, monetary policy would no longer be guided by short-term stabilization issues and instead would be guided by the long-term goal of price stability. As a means of formalizing this shift in policy, the Bank and the federal department of finance announced a series of inflation-control targets, beginning in the 3–5 percent range for 1992 and falling to the 1–3 percent range by the end of 1995. The 1–3 percent range has been extended beyond 2002.
- Despite controversy, the Bank stuck to its policy and lowered inflation to below 2 percent by 1992. For the next seven years, inflation hovered between 1 and 2 percent.
- The persistence of low inflation has led to two current debates. First, is inflation no longer a threat? Second, are there costs associated with maintaining inflation at very low levels?

KEY CONCEPTS

Temporary and sustained inflation
The NAIRU
Rational expectations
Expectational, demand, and supply
  pressures on inflation

Monetary validation of demand and
  supply shocks
Expectations-augmented Phillips curve
Accelerating inflation
Ending sustained inflation

Sacrifice ratio
Inflation in the 1980s and 1990s
Inflation-control targets

STUDY EXERCISES

1. The table below shows several macroeconomic situations, each with a given amount of excess demand (or supply) for labour and a level of inflation expectations. Both are expressed in percent per year. For example, in Case A excess demand for labour is pushing wages up by 4 percent per year, and expected inflation is pushing wages up by 3 percent per year.

Case	Demand	Inflation Expectations	Total Wage Change	SRAS Shift
A	+4	+3	—-	—-
B	+4	0	—-	—-
C	0	+3	—-	—-
D	−3	0	—-	—-
E	−3	+4	—-	—-

a. For each case, identify whether there is an inflationary or a recessionary output gap.
b. For each case, what is the total effect on nominal wages? Fill in the third column.
c. For each case, in which direction is the *SRAS* curve shifting (up or down)? Fill in the last column.

2. This exercise requires you to compute inflationary expectations based on a simple formula, and it will help you to understand why backward-looking expectations adjust slowly to changes in economic events. Suppose that the *actual* inflation rate in year t is denoted Π_t. *Expected* inflation for year $t+1$ is denoted Π^e_{t+1}. Now, suppose that workers and firms form their expectations according to:

$$\Pi^e_{t+1} = \theta \Pi^T + (1-\theta)\Pi_t$$

where Π^T is the central bank's announced *inflation target*. This simple equation says that people's expectations for inflation at $t+1$ are a weighted average of last year's inflation rate and the central bank's currently announced target. We will use this equation to see how the size of θ determines the extent to which expectations are backward looking. Consider the table below, which shows the data for a reduction in inflation from 10 percent to 2 percent.

Year (t)	Π_t	Π^T	Π^e_{t+1}
1	10	2	—
2	9	2	—
3	6	2	—
4	3	2	—
5	2	2	—
6	2	2	—
7	2	2	—
8	2	2	—

a. Assume that θ is equal to 0.1. Compute expected inflation for each year and fill in the table.
b. On a scale diagram, plot the time path of actual inflation, expected inflation, and the inflation target.
c. Now assume that θ equals 0.9. Repeat parts **a** and **b**.
d. Which value of θ corresponds to more backward-looking expectations? Explain.
e. Given the different speed of adjustment of inflationary expectations, predict which disinflation is more costly in terms of lost output—the one with $\theta=0.1$ or with $\theta=0.9$. Explain.

3. The diagram below shows an *AD/SRAS* diagram. The economy is in long-run equilibrium with real GDP equal to Y^* and the price level is stable at P_0.

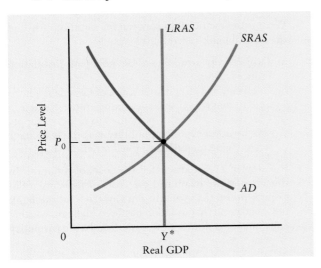

a. Suppose the central bank announces that it will make a one-time increase in the money supply and this will shift the *AD* curve up by 5 percent. Show the likely effect of this announcement on the *SRAS* curve.
b. Why does the shift of the *SRAS* curve in part **a** depend on whether workers and firms believe the central bank's announcement?
c. In a new *AD/SRAS* diagram, show how a sustained and constant inflation of 5 percent is represented.
d. Explain why a constant inflation is only possible when real GDP is equal to Y^*.

4. The diagram below shows an *AD/SRAS* diagram. Suppose the economy is hit by some positive aggregate demand shock—say an increase in the demand for Canada's exports. This increases real GDP to Y_1.

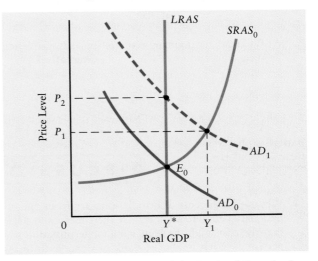

a. Explain what happens if the Bank of Canada does not react to the shock. Show this in the diagram.
b. Now suppose that the Bank decides to maintain real GDP at Y_1—that is, it decides to validate the shock. Explain how this is possible, and show it in a diagram
c. What is the effect on inflation from the policy in part **b**? Is inflation constant or is it rising? Explain.

5. The diagram on the next page shows an *AD/SRAS* diagram. Suppose the economy is hit by some negative aggregate supply shock—say an increase in wages driven by a major union settlement. This reduces real GDP to Y_1.

a. Explain what happens if the Bank of Canada does not react to the shock. Show this in the diagram.
b. Now suppose that the Bank decides to offset the shock's effect on real GDP—that is, it validates the shock. Explain how this is possible, and show it in a diagram.

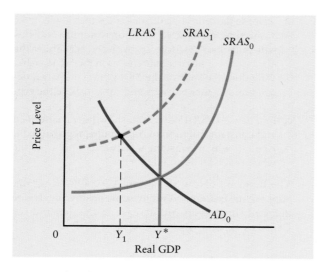

c. What danger do many economists see in validating such supply shocks? What is the alternative?

6. The table below shows some data on various disinflations. In each case, assume that potential GDP is equal to $900 billion.

Case	Inflation Reduction	Cumulative GDP Loss	Sacrifice Ratio
A	5 percentage points	$100 billion	—
B	2	30	—
C	6	60	—
D	8	80	—

a. In each case, compute the sacrifice ratio.
b. Explain why the sacrifice ratio can be expected to be smaller when expectations are more forward looking.
c. Explain why the sacrifice ratio can be expected to be smaller when central-bank announcements are more credible.

DISCUSSION QUESTIONS

1. Why might the cost of disinflation vary from one inflationary period to another? Are there reasons to think that the cost might be higher the longer inflation has persisted? What might the Bank of Canada do to reduce the cost?

2. What sources of inflation are suggested by each of the following quotations?

   a. A newspaper editorial in Manchester, England: "If American unions were as strong as those in Britain, America's inflationary experience would have been as disastrous as Britain's."
   b. An article in The Economist: "Oil price collapse will reduce inflation."
   c. A Canadian newspaper article in October 1990: "The combination of the Kuwaiti crisis and an emerging recession is a sure recipe for worldwide stagflation."
   d. A newspaper headline in May 1999: "Bank's fast growth of M1 will spur inflation."

3. Discuss the apparent conflict between the following views. Can you suggest how they might be reconciled using aggregate demand and aggregate supply analysis?

   a. "A rise in interest rates is deflationary, because ending entrenched inflation with a tight monetary policy usually requires that interest rates rise steeply."
   b. "A rise in interest rates is inflationary, because interest is a major business cost and, as with other costs, a rise in interest will be passed on by firms in the form of higher prices."

4. What is the relationship between the sacrifice ratio and the central bank's credibility?

   a. Explain why a more credible policy of disinflation reduces the costs of disinflation.
   b. Explain how you think the Bank of Canada might be able to make its disinflation policy more credible.
   c. Can the Bank's policy responses to negative supply shocks influence the credibility it is likely to have when trying to end a sustained inflation? Explain.

5. In Chapter 21, we discussed the costs of inflation. In this chapter, we examined the costs of reducing inflation. Suppose that you are the Governor of the Bank of Canada and that inflation has been high and roughly constant for a number of years. You have two policy

choices: you can continue to validate the ongoing inflation; or you can attempt to eliminate the sustained inflation. Outline the issues involved when making this choice. List and explain the costs of ongoing inflation, and also the costs of a potential disinflation. Explain how you make your policy decision.

6. In January 1991, the federal government introduced the Goods and Services Tax (GST). If you were to suppose that the GST was a *new* tax (in fact, it replaced an existing tax), what would be the effect on the *SRAS* curve? Is the introduction of the GST (or an increase in its rate) inflationary? Does it increase inflation permanently?

7. In the summer of 1999 at a time when U.S. GDP was slightly above potential, a story in *The Globe and Mail* reported that the release of strong employment-growth data for the United States led to a plunge in prices on the U.S. stock market.

a. Explain why high employment growth would lead people to expect the U.S. central bank to tighten its monetary policy.
b. Explain why higher U.S. interest rates would lead to lower prices of U.S. stocks.
c. How would you expect this announcement to affect Canada? (At the time, there was still a small recessionary gap in Canada.)

CHAPTER 30

Unemployment

LO LEARNING OBJECTIVES

❶ Understand how employment and unemployment change over the short and long runs.

❷ Explain the difference between the New Classical and New Keynesian views of cyclical unemployment.

❸ Understand the causes of frictional and structural unemployment.

❹ Explain the various forces that cause the NAIRU to change.

❺ Understand how various policies might be used to reduce unemployment.

When the level of economic activity changes, so do the levels of employment and unemployment. Figure 19-5 in Chapter 19 shows the course of unemployment in Canada over the past few decades. It is clear from that figure that the unemployment rate follows a cyclical path, rising during recessions and falling during expansions. In addition, the unemployment rate appears to have experienced a long-term increase. What are the sources of these cyclical fluctuations? What are the sources of this long-term increase?

In macroeconomics, economists distinguish between the NAIRU, which you will recall is the unemployment that occurs when real GDP is equal to its potential (Y^*), and *cyclical* unemployment, which is the unemployment associated with fluctuations of real GDP around its potential. We will see in this chapter that short-run fluctuations in unemployment are mainly changes in cyclical unemployment. In contrast, the long-term upward trend in unemployment is due to gradual increases in the NAIRU. Before examining these types of unemployment in detail, we briefly review the Canadian experience with employment and unemployment.

Employment and Unemployment

Considered over the long term, the most striking features revealed by Figure 19-5(i) are trend increases in both total employment and the total labour force. Over the decades, the pace of creation of new jobs has been roughly equal to the growth in the number of potential workers. Less obvious in Figure 19-5(i), but more clear in Figure 19-5(ii), are the substantial year-to-year fluctuations in the unemployment rate.

Over the span of many years, increases in the labour force are more-or-less matched by increases in employment. But from year to year the unemployment rate fluctuates because changes in the labour force are not exactly matched by changes in employment.

Changes in Employment

The level of employment in Canada has increased dramatically over the past few decades. In 1959, there were approximately 5 million Canadians employed. By 1999, total employment was just under 15 million. The actual level of employment, of course, is determined both by the demand for labour and by the supply of labour. How have the two "sides" of the Canadian labour market been changing?

On the supply side, the labour force has expanded virtually every year since the end of World War II. The causes have included a rising population, which boosts entry into the labour force of people born 15 to 25 years previously; increased labour force participation by various groups, especially women; and net immigration of working-age persons.

On the demand side, many existing jobs are eliminated every year, and many new jobs are created. Economic growth causes some sectors of the economy to decline and others to expand. Jobs are lost in the sectors that are contracting and created in sectors that are expanding. Furthermore, even in stable industries, many firms disappear and many new ones are set up. The net increase in employment is the difference between all the jobs that are lost and all those that are created.

In most years, enough new jobs have been created both to replace old jobs that have been eliminated and to provide jobs for the increased numbers of people in the labour force. The result has been a net increase in employment in almost all years.

Changes in Unemployment

In the early 1980s, worldwide unemployment rose to high levels. The unemployment rate remained high in many advanced industrial countries and only began to come down, and even then very slowly, during the latter half of the decade. Canadian experience reflected these international developments rather closely. From a high of 11.9 percent in 1983, the Canadian unemployment rate fell to 7.5 percent in 1989, a point that many economists at the time thought was close to the Canadian NAIRU.

With the onset of another recession in the early 1990s, the unemployment rate then rose through 1990 and 1991, reaching 11.3 percent by 1992. During the next few years, the unemployment rate fell only slowly as the Canadian recovery was weak; by early 1994 the unemployment rate was still above 10 percent. But the speed of the Canadian recovery quickened and unemployment began to drop. By early 2000, after five years of healthy economic recovery, the unemployment rate was 6.8 percent, the lowest it had been in more than twenty years.

During periods of rapid economic growth, the unemployment rate usually falls. During recessions or periods of slow growth, the unemployment rate usually rises.

Flows in the Labour Market

We know that many existing jobs are eliminated every year, as industries contract and firms either shrink or close down altogether. Similarly, new jobs are continually being created, as other industries expand and new firms are born. The focus on the labour market, however, tends to be on the overall level of employment and unemployment rather than on the amount of *job creation* and *job destruction*. This focus can often lead us to the conclusion that few changes are occurring in the labour market when in fact the truth is exactly the opposite.

For example, the Canadian unemployment rate was roughly constant at 9.5 percent from 1995 to 1996. Does this mean that no jobs were created during the year? Or that the Canadian labour market was stagnant during this period? No. In fact, workers were finding jobs at the rate of roughly 400 000 *per month*. At the same time, however, other workers were leaving jobs or entering the labour force at roughly the same rate. This tremendous number of flows *out of unemployment* was being approximately matched by the number of flows *into unemployment*. The net result was that total unemployment changed only slightly.

The level of activity in the labour market is better reflected by the flows into and out of unemployment than by the overall unemployment rate.

By looking at the *gross flows* in the labour market, we are able to see economic activity that is hidden when we just look at the overall level of employment and unemployment (which is determined by *net* flows). Indeed, these gross flows are typically so large that they dwarf the net flows. See *Applying Economic Concepts 30-1* for more discussion of the gross flows in the Canadian labour market, and how these gross-flows data can be used to compute the average length of unemployment spells.

Consequences of Unemployment

Economists view unemployment as a social "bad" just as they view output as a social "good." But this does not mean that *all* unemployment is bad, just as we know that all output—such as noise or air pollution—is not good. Indeed, we will see later in this chapter that some unemployment is socially desirable as it reflects the necessary time spent searching to make appropriate matches between firms and workers.

We examine two costs of unemployment. The first is reflected by the loss in output. The second is the harm done to the individuals who are unemployed.

Lost Output

Every person counted as unemployed is willing and able to work but unable to find a job. Hence, the unemployed are valuable resources whose contribution to producing output is wasted. The output counterpart of unemployment is the recessionary gap—output that is not produced. In a world of scarcity with many unsatisfied wants, this loss represents a serious waste of resources.

Personal Costs

For the typical worker in Canada, being unemployed is no longer the disaster that it once was. Most spells of unemployment are short (see *Applying Economic Concepts 30-1* for a simple estimate of the average duration of unemployment spells) and many workers experiencing temporary unemployment have access to the unemployment insurance program. But this does not mean there are no problems associated with unemployment. The effects of long-term unemployment, in terms of the disillusioned who have given up trying to make it within the system and who contribute to social unrest,

For data on current employment and unemployment in Canada, see Statistics Canada's website: www.statcan.ca. Click on "Canadian Statistics" and then on "Labour."

Practise with Study Guide Chapter 30, Multiple-Choice Questions 1–7.

should be a matter of serious concern to the "haves" as well as the "have-nots." The loss of self-esteem and the dislocation of families that often result from situations of prolonged unemployment are genuine tragedies.

The general case for concern about high unemployment has been eloquently put by Princeton economist Alan Blinder:

> *A high-pressure economy provides opportunities, facilitates structural change, encourages inventiveness and innovation, and opens doors for society's underdogs. . . . All these promote the social cohesion and economic progress that make democratic mixed capitalism such a wonderful system when it works well. A low-pressure economy slams the doors shut, breeds a bunker mentality that resists change, stifles productivity growth, and fosters both inequality and mean-spirited public policy. All this makes reducing high unemployment a political, economic, and moral challenge of the highest order.*[1]

Cyclical Unemployment

As we saw in Chapter 19, economists classify unemployment into three types—cyclical, frictional and structural. The last two together make up the NAIRU, which is the level of unemployment that exists when real GDP equals potential GDP. Thus we can really divide unemployment into two broad groups. We examine frictional and structural unemployment in the next section when we study the NAIRU. **Cyclical unemployment** is the difference between the actual level of unemployment and the amount that exists when real GDP is at its potential level.

When real GDP is at its potential level, there is no cyclical unemployment—all unemployment then is either frictional or structural.

People who are cyclically unemployed are normally presumed to be suffering **involuntary unemployment** in that they are willing to work at the going wage rate but are unable to find appropriate jobs. The persistence of cyclical unemployment poses a challenge to economic theory.

Why Does Cyclical Unemployment Exist?

To see what is involved in this challenge, suppose that the fluctuations in aggregate demand cause real output to fluctuate around its potential level. This fluctuation will cause the demand for labour in each of the economy's labour markets to fluctuate as well, rising in booms and falling in slumps. If all of the labour markets had fully flexible wage rates, wages would fluctuate to keep quantity demanded in each individual market equal to quantity supplied in that market. We would observe cyclical fluctuations in employment and in the wage rate but no changes in unemployment. This behaviour is illustrated in Figure 30-1.

With perfectly flexible wages, employment and real wages would be procyclical (rising in booms and falling in slumps) but there would be no involuntary unemployment.

cyclical unemployment
Unemployment in excess of frictional and structural unemployment; it is due to a shortfall of real GDP below potential GDP.

involuntary unemployment
Unemployment due to the inability of qualified persons who are seeking work to find jobs at the going wage rate.

---

[1]A. S. Blinder, "The Challenge of High Unemployment," *American Economic Review* 78 (1988), 2:1.

APPLYING ECONOMIC CONCEPTS 30-1

Stocks and Flows in the Canadian Labour Market

In most reports about changes in unemployment, both in Canada and abroad, emphasis is typically on the changes in the *stock* of unemployment—that is, on the number of people who are unemployed at a particular point in time. But as we said in the text, the focus on the stock of unemployment can often hide much activity in the labour market—activity that is revealed by looking at *gross flows* in the labour market.

What Are Labour-Market Flows?

In the accompanying figure, three series of data are shown for Canada from 1976 to 1992—a period that includes the major recessions of 1981 and 1991. The top line is the stock of unemployment—the actual *number* of people unemployed at a specific point in time (it is not the unemployment *rate*). During the severe recession of the early 1980s, unemployment peaked at approximately 1.6 million people, and then fell during the recovery until 1989. With the onset of the next recession in 1990–1991, unemployment rose again, exceeding 1.5 million in early 1992.

The two lower lines in the figure show *gross flows* in the labour market. The orange line shows the *monthly* flow into unemployment. This flow into unemployment represents either:

- workers losing their jobs through layoffs or plant closure; or
- workers quitting their jobs to search for a different job; or
- new entrants to the labour force searching for a job.

Note that the monthly flow into unemployment varies between 300 000 and 500 000 *per month* and also tends to rise and fall together with the overall stock of unemployment.

The green line shows the monthly flow out of unemployment. This outflow represents either:

- unemployed individuals finding new jobs; or
- unemployed individuals becoming discouraged and leaving the labour force.

Note that the monthly flow out of unemployment is roughly the same size as the monthly inflow (300 000–500 000 per month).

What is the connection between the flows and the stocks in the labour market? Whenever the flows into unemployment exceed the flows out of unemployment, the stock of unemployment rises. Conversely, whenever the flows out of unemployment exceed the flows into unemployment, the stock of unemployment falls.

Using Flows Data

There are two reasons why looking at flows can be very useful when we think about the labour market. First, they show the tremendous amount of activity in the labour market even though the stock of unemployment may not be changing. For example, throughout the year 1983 the stock of unemployment in Canada was roughly constant at 1.4 million persons. But during those 12 months, roughly 500 000 persons *per month* either became

---

New Classical economics An approach to explaining macroeconomic fluctuations in which fluctuations in economic activity are explained by shocks to technology and tastes rather than to markets that fail to clear.

The hypothetical situation that we have just described is not what we actually observe. Instead, we see cyclical fluctuations not only in employment but also in unemployment. Furthermore, the changes in wage rates that do occur are insufficient to equate demand and supply, as is shown in Figure 30-2. Unemployment exceeds the NAIRU in slumps and is below it in booms. Although wages do tend to vary over the cycle, the fluctuations are not sufficient to remove all cyclical variations in unemployment. Why is this so?

Two types of explanation have been advanced in recent years. The line of explanation that we consider first is associated with what is called **New Classical economics.** The explanation assumes that labour markets are always in equilibrium in the sense that quantity demanded is continually equated with quantity supplied.

unemployed or ceased being unemployed. This number reflects the massive amount of regular turnover that exists in the Canadian labour market—turnover that is the essence of what economists call *frictional unemployment.*

The second reason why looking at flows is useful is that the relationship between the flows and the stock can tell us something about the amount of time the average unemployed person spends unemployed. If U_s is the stock of unemployment, and U_o is the monthly outflow from unemployment, then one simple estimate of the average duration of an unemployment spell is

To see this, consider the situation in 1989, at the peak of the business cycle. At that time, the stock of unemployment was approximately 1 million people and the outflow from unemployment was at a rate of approximately 400 000 persons per month. Thus, the average unemployed person in 1989 could expect to leave unemployment in about 2½ months (1 000 000 people/400 000 people per month = 2.5 months). In contrast, by early 1992, at the depth of the subsequent recession, the expected duration of an unemployment spell was over 3½ months (1 600 000/450 000 = 3.6).

$$\text{Average duration of unemployment spell} = \frac{U_s}{U_o}$$

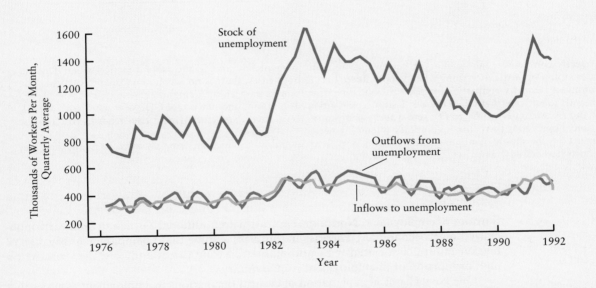

New Classical Theories[2]

Two major characteristics of New Classical theories are that agents continuously optimize and markets continuously clear; hence there can be no involuntary unemployment. These theories then seek to explain employment as the outcome of voluntary decisions made by individuals who are choosing to do what they do, including spending some

[2]The source of the label "New Classical" is that many of the arguments put forward by this group of economists are essentially more detailed and precise versions of arguments that would have been very familiar to the Classical economists, from Adam Smith and David Ricardo to Alfred Marshall.

FIGURE 30-1   Employment and Wages in a Competitive Labour Market

(i) Demand shifts

(ii) Supply shifts

In a perfectly competitive labour market, real wages and employment fluctuate in the same direction when demand fluctuates and in opposite directions when supply fluctuates; in both cases, there is no involuntary unemployment. The figure shows a perfectly competitive market for one type of labour. In part (i), the demand curves D_1, D_2, and D_0 are the demands for this market when there is a slump, when there is a boom, and when real GDP is at its potential level. As demand rises from D_1 to D_0 to D_2, real wages rise from w_1 to w_0 to w_2, and employment rises from L_1 to L_0 to L_2. At no time, however, is there any involuntary unemployment.

In part (ii), the supply of labour fluctuates from S_1 to S_0 to S_2, and wages fluctuate from w_1 to w_0 to w_2. In this case, wages fall when employment rises, and vice versa, but again there is no involuntary unemployment.

time out of employment. Notice the contrast with traditional Keynesian (and early monetarist) macroeconomics. Theories in this class assume that unemployment is a sign of market failure, associated with non-market-clearing prices and/or wages, and that a high proportion of unemployment is involuntary.

One New Classical explanation of cyclical fluctuations in employment assumes that they are caused by fluctuations in the willingness of people to supply their labour, as shown in part (ii) of Figure 30-1. If the supply curves of labour fluctuate cyclically (supply increases during booms and falls during slumps) there will be cyclical variations in employment. This explanation of cyclical behaviour in the labour market has two problems. First, the wage will tend to rise in slumps and fall in booms, which is not what we observe. Second, there will still be no systematic cyclical *unemployment* because labour markets always clear, leaving everyone who wishes to work actually working. Supply-induced fluctuations in employment form part of the basis of what is called real business cycle (RBC) theory, which is discussed in *Extensions in Theory 30-1*.

A second line of explanation lies in errors on the part of workers and employers in predicting the course of the price level over the business cycle. To see the argument, start by supposing that all of the economy's markets are in equilibrium, that there is full employment, that prices are stable, and that the actual and expected rates of inflation are zero. Now suppose the government increases the money supply by 5 percent. Through the transmission mechanism that we studied in Chapter 27, the increase in the money supply leads to an increase in desired aggregate expenditure. For simplicity, suppose there is an increase

EXTENSIONS IN THEORY 30-1

Real Business Cycle Theory

Real business cycle (RBC) theory attempts to explain cyclical fluctuations in the context of models in which wages and prices adjust very quickly to shocks. These models contrast sharply with the models we have discussed in this book in which fluctuations in output arise largely because wages and prices adjust gradually to shocks. In such models, if wages and prices were able to adjust instantly to all shocks, then output would always be equal to potential output—there would never be inflationary or recessionary gaps. The extreme flexibility of wages and prices is therefore a distinguishing feature of RBC models.

Key Propositions and Criticisms

The view of the business cycle found in RBC models is that short-run fluctuations in real GDP are caused by fluctuations in the vertical *LRAS* curve. In this view, unemployment is always equal to the NAIRU, and it is the NAIRU itself that fluctuates. Thus, the explanation of cyclical fluctuations that arises in RBC models is based on the role of supply shocks originating from sources such as oil price changes, technical progress, and changes in tastes.

The RBC approach is controversial. The major claims in its favour include:

1. It has been able to explain the recent behaviour of the economy quite well statistically, while downplaying the role for aggregate demand fluctuations in the business cycle.

2. It suggests that an integrated approach to understanding cycles and growth may be appropriate, as both reflect forces that affect the *LRAS* curve. The distinction it makes is that some shocks are temporary (and hence have cyclical effects) whereas others are permanent (and therefore affect the economy's long-term growth).

3. It provides valuable insights into how shocks, regardless of their origin, spread over time to the different sectors of the economy. By abstracting from monetary issues, it is possible to address more details concerning technology and household choice involving intertemporal tradeoffs between consumption, labour supply, and leisure.

Critics of the RBC approach focus on some implausible results and express concern about its assumptions of individuals' behaviour. More important, they are sceptical about a model in which monetary issues are completely ignored. For example, they point out that RBC models are unable to provide insights into the short-term correlation between money and output that is at the heart of the traditional macro model and for which a considerable amount of empirical evidence exists, in Canada as well as many other countries. Furthermore, RBC models are unable to provide insights into empirical regularities involving nominal variables, such as prices that apparently vary less than quantities and nominal prices that vary procyclically.

Policy Implications

Because the RBC approach gives no role to aggregate demand in influencing business cycles, it provides no role for stabilization operating through monetary and fiscal policies. Indeed, the models predict that the use of such demand-management policies can be *harmful*.

The basis for this prediction is the proposition in RBC models that cycles represent *efficient* responses to the shocks that are hitting the economy. Policymakers may mistakenly interpret cyclical fluctuations as deviations from potential output caused by shifts in either the *AD* or *SRAS* curves. The policymakers may try to stabilize output and thereby distort the maximizing decisions made by households and firms. This distortion will in turn cause the responses to the real shocks (as opposed to nominal, monetary shocks) to be inefficient.

Although a small minority of economists espouse RBC models as complete or even reasonable descriptions of the business cycle, and hence only a minority take seriously the strict implications for policy, many accept the view that real supply-side disturbances can play an important role in business cycles. Moreover, since the RBC approach emphasizes the importance of markets always clearing in response to changes in technology or other shocks, many economists that view RBC models as a poor description of the economy in the short run believe that many of the insights from the RBC approach are invaluable when thinking about the behaviour of the economy in the long run.

in desired expenditure on *all* goods; the demand for each good shifts to the right, and all prices, being competitively determined, rise. Individual decision makers see their selling prices go up and mistakenly interpret the increase as a rise in their own relative price. The reason is that they expect the overall inflation rate to be zero. Firms will produce more, and workers will work more since both groups think they are getting an increased *relative* price for what they sell. Thus, total output and employment rise.

When both groups eventually realize that their own relative prices are in fact unchanged, output and employment fall back to their initial levels. The extra output and employment occur only while people are being fooled. When they realize that *all* prices have increased by 5 percent, they revert to their initial behaviour. The only difference is that now the price level is 5 percent higher, leaving relative prices unchanged.

In both variants of the New Classical approach to explaining employment fluctuations, the labour markets are clearing. In the case of a reduction in the supply of workers (see part (ii) of Figure 30-1), employment falls because workers decide that they no longer want to work. In the case of workers' mistakenly viewing a change in the price level as a change in relative prices, employment falls because workers decide not to work when they think their real wage is low. In both cases, there is no involuntary unemployment.

New Classical explanations assume that labour markets clear, and then they look for reasons why employment fluctuates. They imply, therefore, that people who are not working have voluntarily withdrawn from the labour market for one reason or another; there is no involuntary unemployment.

New Keynesian Theories[3]

Many economists find the New Classical explanations implausible. They believe that people correctly read market signals but react in ways that do not cause markets to clear at all times. These economists—who refer to themselves as New Keynesians—believe that many people who are recorded as unemployed are involuntarily unemployed in the sense that *they would accept an offer of work in jobs for which they are trained, at the going wage rate, if such an offer were made.* These economists concentrate their efforts on explaining why wages do not quickly adjust to eliminate involuntary unemployment. If wages do not respond quickly to shifts in supply and demand in the labour market, quantity supplied and quantity demanded may *not* be equated for extended periods of time. Labour markets will then display unemployment during recessions and excess demand during booms, as shown for a typical labour market in Figure 30-2.

New Keynesian theories start with the everyday observation that wages do not change every time demand or supply shifts. When unemployed workers are looking for jobs, they do not knock on employers' doors and offer to work at lower wages than are being paid to current workers; instead, they answer want ads and hope to get the jobs offered but are often disappointed. Nor do employers, seeing an excess of applicants for the few jobs that are available, go to the current workers and reduce their wages until there is no one who is looking for a job; instead, they pick and choose until they fill their needs and then hang a sign saying "No Help Wanted."

---

[3]The source of the label "New Keynesian" is that many of the arguments put forward by these economists are closely related to the ideas put forward by John Maynard Keynes in *The General Theory of Employment, Interest and Money* (1936).

Long-Term Employment Relationships

One set of theories explains the familiar observations made in the preceding paragraph as results of the advantages to both workers and employers of relatively long-term and stable employment relationships. Workers want job security in the face of fluctuating demand. Employers want workers who understand the firm's organization, production, and marketing plans. Under these circumstances, both parties care about things in addition to the wage rate, and wages become somewhat insensitive to fluctuations in current economic conditions. Wages are, in effect, regular payments to workers over an extended employment relationship rather than a device for fine-tuning the current supplies and demands for labour. Given this situation, the tendency is for employers to "smooth" the income of employees by paying a steady money wage and letting profits and employment fluctuate to absorb the effects of temporary increases and decreases in demand for the firm's product.

A number of labour-market institutions work to achieve these results. For example, many long-term contracts provide for a schedule of money wages over a period of several years. Similarly, fringe benefits, such as pensions and health care, tend to bind workers to particular employers. Another example is pay that rises with years of service. This helps to bind the employee to the company, whereas seniority rules for layoffs bind the employer to the long-term worker.

In labour markets in which long-term relationships are important (as is the case in many labour markets), the wage rate does not fluctuate to continuously clear the market.

Because wages are thus insulated from short-term fluctuations in demand, any market clearing that occurs does so through fluctuations in the volume of employment rather than in wages. Of course, wages must respond to permanent shifts in market conditions—for example, the permanent and unexpected decline in the demand for the output of a particular industry.

Long-term employment relationships are important in the Canadian economy. According to a recent Statistics Canada survey of full-time workers, the average time spent with the same employer—what is referred to as *job tenure*—is just under nine years. Further, over half of them have been with their employer for six years or longer.

Menu Costs and Wage Contracts

A typical large manufacturing firm sells hundreds of differentiated products and employs hundreds of different types of labour. Changing prices and wages in response to every minor fluctuation in demand is a costly and time-consuming activity. Many firms therefore

FIGURE 30-2   Unemployment with Sticky Wages

When the wage rate does not change enough to equate quantity demanded with quantity supplied, there will be unemployment in slumps and labour shortages in booms. When demand is at its normal level D_0, the market is cleared with wage rate w_0, employment is L_0, and there is no unemployment. In a recession, demand falls to D_1, but the wage only falls to w'_1. As a result, L_1 of labour is demanded and L'_1 is supplied. Employment is determined by the quantity demanded at L_1. The remainder of the supply for which there is no demand, $L_1L'_1$, is unemployed. In a boom, demand rises to D_2, but the wage rate rises only to w'_2. As a result, the quantity demanded is L'_2, whereas only L_2 is supplied. Employment rises to L_2, which is the amount supplied. The rest of the demand cannot be satisfied, making excess demand for labour of $L_2L'_2$.

find it optimal to keep their price lists (*menus*) constant for significant periods of time. Since manufacturing firms are often operating in imperfectly competitive markets, they have some discretion over price. Hence, firms often react to small changes in demand by holding prices constant and responding with changes in output and employment. If many firms behave this way, output and employment will respond to changes in aggregate demand.

The Canadian evidence is consistent with the existence of sluggish price adjustment by firms, especially those in manufacturing industries. This, of course, is where Keynesian economics came in with an assumption of price stickiness. The New Keynesian literature attempts to model such sticky prices as resulting from firms' optimal response to adjustment costs.

Money wages tend to be inflexible in the short term because wage rates are generally set only occasionally. Wages are often set on an annual basis; in some unionized contracts wages are set for up to three years. Such inflexibility of wages implies that changes in aggregate demand and supply will tend to cause changes in unemployment.

Efficiency Wages

The idea of *efficiency wages* forms the core of another strand of New Keynesian thinking about why wages do not readily fall in response to excess supply in labour markets. For any of a number of reasons, employers may find that they get more output per dollar of wages paid—that is, a more *efficient* workforce—when they pay labour somewhat more than the minimum amount that would induce workers to work for them.

Suppose it is costly for employers to monitor workers' performance on the job, so that some workers will be able to shirk duties with a low probability of being caught. Given prevailing labour-market institutions, it is generally impossible for employers to levy fines on employees for shirking on the job since the employees could just leave their jobs rather than pay the fines. So firms may instead choose to pay a wage premium— an efficiency wage—to the workers, in excess of the wage that the workers will get elsewhere in the labour market. With such a wage premium, workers will be reluctant to shirk because, if they get caught and laid off, they will then lose this wage premium.

Efficiency-wage theory predicts that firms may find it profitable to pay high enough wages so that working is a clearly superior alternative to being laid off.

Several economists have observed that workers who believe that they are well treated work harder than those who believe that they are treated badly. This gives a reason for paying an efficiency wage—provided that the increased output from treating workers well covers the increased cost of doing so.

Union Bargaining

The final New Keynesian theory to be considered assumes that those already employed ("insiders") have more say in wage bargaining than those currently not employed ("outsiders"). Employed workers are often represented by a union which negotiates the wage rate with firms. The union will generally represent the interests of the insiders but will not necessarily reflect the interests of the outsiders. Insiders will naturally wish to bid up wages even though to do so will harm the employment prospects of the outsiders. Hence this theory generates an outcome to the bargaining process between firms and unions in which the wage is set higher than the market-clearing level, just as with efficiency wages. The consequence is involuntary unemployment.

In addition to explaining the existence of involuntary unemployment, this theory adds one important insight regarding international differences in unemployment. In some countries unions bargain at the level of the firm; in others they bargain at the level of the whole industry or the whole economy. Where bargaining is decentralized, as in Canada and the United States, the union can push for higher wages for the insiders without worrying about the effects on outsiders or on the rest of the economy. However, where bargaining is centralized, as in much of western Europe, the effects on the rest of the economy become internalized into the bargaining process, because union negotiators are bargaining on behalf of all workers (and all potential workers), rather than just the current group of insiders.

This theory leads to the following predictions. Decentralized bargaining with strong unions will lead to higher than market-clearing wages, and higher unemployment as the outsiders are excluded from jobs. In contrast, centralized bargaining will produce an outcome closer to the market-clearing outcome (because outsider concerns are voiced), so unemployment will be low. In situations where unionization is low or unions are weak, the outcome will be close to the market-clearing outcome. This analysis may explain why unemployment is relatively high in EU countries (where unions are strong and bargaining is decentralized), lower in Scandinavia (where unions are also strong but bargaining is centralized), and even lower in Canada and the United States (where unions are relatively weak and the extent of unionization is much lower).

The basic message of New Keynesian theories of unemployment is that labour markets cannot be relied upon to eliminate involuntary unemployment by equating labour demand and labour supply.

New Keynesian theories have concentrated on explaining why wages do not fluctuate to quickly clear labour markets. They therefore help to explain the existence of involuntary unemployment in the face of fluctuations in aggregate demand. These demand fluctuations are, however, still a necessary part of the explanation of cyclical fluctuations. They leave the emphasis on counter-cyclical monetary or fiscal policies whenever the automatic adjustment mechanism does not work fast enough.

Convergence of Theories?

We have examined two classes of theories of cyclical unemployment. In the New Classical theories, wages and prices adjust instantly to clear markets and so real GDP is always equal to potential GDP. Unemployment fluctuates, but it is always equal to the NAIRU, U^*. Using the terminology we introduced earlier, there is no *cyclical* unemployment in New Classical models because there is never a difference between U^* and the actual unemployment rate, U.

In contrast, New Keynesian models emphasize the gradual adjustment of wages and prices and thus the existence of periods in which real GDP is either above or below potential GDP. In these models, unemployment fluctuates around the value of U^*—that is, there is a clear distinction between the actual unemployment rate, U, and the NAIRU, U^*.

Note, however, that the sharp contrast between New Classical and New Keynesian models applies only to the short-run behaviour of the economy. It is in the short run that the extent of wage and price flexibility distinguishes these two classes of models. In the long run, however, even the staunchest New Keynesians accept the proposition that wages and prices adjust to eliminate output gaps and thus return real GDP to its potential level and the unemployment rate to the NAIRU.

Both New Classical and New Keynesians agree that in the long run wage and price flexibility brings the unemployment rate back to U^*.

Let's restate the difference between New Keynesian and New Classical models another way. In New Keynesian models there is a meaningful difference between the short

The quick adjustment of wages to excess demands and supplies is not a characteristic of labour markets in which employees and firms have long-term relationships, such as in the health-care sector.

run and the long run that is determined by the degree of wage and price flexibility. In New Classical models, however, wages and prices adjust instantly, so there is no similar distinction between the short run and the long run. But, since *both* classes of models agree that wages and prices are flexible in the long run, they have the same predictions regarding the long-run effects of policy.

For example, New Keynesians argue that a monetary expansion will raise real GDP above Y^* and reduce U below the NAIRU. In the long run, however, output will return to Y^*, U will return to U^* and the only long-run effect of the monetary expansion will be a higher price level. New Classical economists agree on this predicted long-run effect, but they argue that the short-run real effects on output and unemployment will either be absent or of much shorter duration since wages and prices adjust very quickly.

New Keynesians and New Classical economists agree that the actual unemployment rate is equal to the NAIRU in the long run. Our next job is to understand why the NAIRU changes. We turn to this topic now.

The NAIRU

The NAIRU is composed of frictional and structural unemployment. Our interest is in why the NAIRU changes over time and in the extent that economic policy can affect the NAIRU.

Frictional Unemployment

frictional unemployment Unemployment caused by the time that is taken for labour to move from one job to another.

search unemployment Unemployment caused by people continuing to search for a good job rather than accepting the first job they are offered after they become unemployed.

As we saw in Chapter 19, **frictional unemployment** results from the normal turnover of labour. An important source of frictional unemployment is young people who enter the labour force and look for jobs. Another source is people who leave their jobs. Some may quit because they are dissatisfied with the type of work or their working conditions; others may be fired. Whatever the reason, they must search for new jobs, which takes time. Persons who are unemployed while searching for jobs are said to be frictionally unemployed or in **search unemployment**.

The normal turnover of labour causes frictional unemployment to persist, even if the economy is at potential output.

How "voluntary" is frictional unemployment? Some of it is clearly voluntary. For example, a worker may know of an available job but may not accept it so she can search for a better one. An extreme New Classical view regards *all* frictional unemployment as voluntary. Critics of that view argue that many frictionally unemployed workers are involuntarily unemployed because they lost their jobs through no fault of their own (e.g., their factories may have closed down) and have not yet located specific jobs that they know to be available *somewhere* for which they believe they are qualified.

Extensions in Theory 30-2, which discusses search unemployment in more detail, shows that the distinction between voluntary and involuntary unemployment is not always as clear as it might at first seem.

EXTENSIONS IN THEORY 30-2

Voluntary Versus Involuntary Unemployment

Frictional unemployment is *involuntary* if the job seeker has not yet found a job for which his or her training and experience are suitable. Frictional unemployment is *voluntary* if the unemployed person is aware of available jobs for which he or she is suited but is searching for better options. But how should we classify an unemployed person who refuses to accept a job at a lower skill level than the one for which she is qualified? What if she turns down a job for which she is trained because she hopes to get a higher wage offer for a similar job from another employer?

In one sense, people in search unemployment are voluntarily unemployed because they could almost always find some job; in another sense, they are involuntarily unemployed because they have not yet succeeded in finding the job for which they feel they are suited at a rate of pay that they believe is attainable.

Workers do not have perfect knowledge of all available jobs and rates of pay, and they may be able to gain information only by searching the market. Facing this uncertainty, they may find it sensible to refuse a first job offer, for the offer may prove to be a poor one in light of further market information. But too much search—for example, holding off while being supported by others in the hope of finding a job better than a job for which one is really suited—is an economic waste. Thus, search unemployment is a gray area: Some of it is useful, and some of it is wasteful.

It is socially desirable for there to be sufficient search unemployment to give unemployed people time to find an available job that makes the best use of their skills. How long it pays for people to remain in search unemployment depends on the economic costs of being unemployed. By lowering the costs of being unemployed, unemployment insurance tends to increase the amount of search unemployment. This may or may not increase economic efficiency, depending on whether or not it induces people to search beyond the point at which they acquire new and valuable information about the labour market.

Structural Unemployment

Structural adjustments in the economy can cause unemployment. When the pattern of demand for goods changes, the pattern of the demand for labour changes. Until labour adjusts fully, structural unemployment develops. **Structural unemployment** is caused by a mismatch between the structure of the labour force—in terms of skills, occupations, industries, or geographical locations—and the structure of the demand for labour.

structural unemployment Unemployment due to a mismatch between characteristics required by available jobs and characteristics possessed by the unemployed labour.

Natural Causes

Changes that accompany economic growth shift the structure of the demand for labour. Demand rises in such expanding areas as British Columbia's lower mainland or Ontario's Ottawa valley and falls in declining areas such as Newfoundland and parts of Quebec. Demand rises for workers with certain skills, such as computer programming and electronics engineering, and falls for workers with other skills, such as stenography, assembly line work, and middle management. To meet changing demands, the structure of the labour force must change. Some existing workers can retrain and some new entrants can acquire fresh skills, but the transition is often difficult, especially for already experienced workers whose skills become economically obsolete.

Increases in international competition can also cause structural unemployment. As the geographical distribution of world production changes, so does the composition of production and of labour demand in any one country. Labour adapts to such shifts by changing jobs, skills, and locations, but until the transition is complete, structural unemployment exists.

Structural unemployment will increase if there is either an increase in the pace at which the structure of the demand for labour is changing or a decrease in the pace at which labour is adapting to these changes.

Policy Causes

Government policies can influence the speed with which labour markets adapt to changes. Some countries, including Canada, have adopted policies that *discourage* movement among regions, industries, and occupations. These policies (which may be desirable for other reasons) tend to *raise* structural unemployment rather than lower it.

Policies that discourage firms from replacing labour with machines may protect employment over the short term. However, if such policies lead to the decline of an industry because it cannot compete effectively with innovative foreign competitors, more serious structural unemployment can result in the long run.

Minimum-wage laws can cause structural unemployment by pricing low-skilled labour out of the market. As was explained in Chapter 14, minimum-wage laws have two effects when they are imposed on competitive markets: They reduce employment of the unskilled, and they raise the wages of the unskilled who retain their jobs.

Unemployment insurance also contributes to structural unemployment, for at least two reasons.[4] First, the Canadian UI system ties workers' benefits to the regional unemployment rate in such a way that unemployed workers can collect UI benefits for more weeks in regions where unemployment is high than where it is low. The UI system therefore encourages unemployed workers to remain in high-unemployment regions rather than encouraging them to move to regions where employment prospects are more favourable.

Second, workers are only eligible for unemployment insurance if they have worked for a given number of weeks in the previous year—this is known as the *entrance requirement*. In some cases, however, these entrance requirements are very low and thus seasonal workers are encouraged to work for a few months and then collect unemployment insurance and wait for the next season, rather than finding other jobs during the off season.

The Frictional-Structural Distinction

For information on Canada's Employment Insurance program, see the website for Human Resources Development Canada: www.hrdc-drhc.gc.ca.

As with many distinctions, the one between frictional and structural unemployment is not precise. In a sense, structural unemployment is really long-term frictional unemployment. Consider, for example, what would happen if there was an increase in world demand for Canadian-made car parts but at the same time a decline in world demand for Canadian-assembled cars. This change would require labour to move from one sector (the car-assembly sector) to another (the car-parts manufacturing sector). If the reallocation were to occur quickly, we call the unemployment *frictional*; if the reallocation were to occur slowly, we call the unemployment *structural*.

---

[4]Canada's unemployment-insurance program was renamed Employment Insurance (EI) in 1996. Unemployment insurance is a more general term, however, and so we continue to use it here.

The major characteristic of both frictional and structural unemployment is that there are as many unfilled vacancies as there are unemployed persons.

In the case of pure frictional unemployment, the job vacancy and the searcher are matched—the only problem is that the searcher has not yet located the vacancy. In the case of structural unemployment, the job vacancy and the searcher are mismatched in one or more relevant characteristics, such as occupation, industry, location, or skill requirements.

In practice, structural and frictional unemployment cannot be separated. But the two of them, taken together, *can* be separated from cyclical unemployment. Specifically, when real GDP is at its potential level, the *only* unemployment (by definition) is the NAIRU, which comprises frictional and structural unemployment. For example, most economists agree that real GDP in Canada was approximately equal to potential GDP in late 1999. At that time, the unemployment rate was about 7 percent, and thus the NAIRU was approximately 7 percent. In contrast, seven years earlier in 1992, the unemployment rate was 11.5 percent. To the extent that the underlying frictions and structural change in the economy were unchanged between 1992 and 1999, we can conclude that in 1992, 4.5 percentage points of the actual unemployment rate were due to cyclical factors and the rest was due to frictional and structural factors.

Why Does the NAIRU Change?

We know that structural unemployment can increase because the pace of change accelerates or the pace of adjustment to change slows down. An increase in the rate of growth, for example, usually speeds up the rate at which the structure of the demand for labour is changing. The adaptation of labour to the changing structure of demand may be slowed by such diverse factors as a decline in education and new regulations that make it harder for workers in a given occupation to take new jobs in other areas or occupations. Any of these changes will cause the NAIRU to rise. Changes in the opposite direction will cause the NAIRU to fall.

Demographic Shifts

Because people usually try several jobs before settling into one for a longer period of time, young or inexperienced workers have higher unemployment rates than experienced workers. The proportion of inexperienced workers in the labour force rose significantly as the baby boom generation of the 1950s entered the labour force in the 1970s and 1980s. Because birthrates were low in the 1960s, some demographically induced fall in this type of unemployment has been occurring over the past decade.

During the 1960s and 1970s women tended to have higher unemployment rates than men. Since this was true at all points of the business cycle, the higher unemployment was higher frictional and structural unemployment. Thus, when female labour-force participation rates increased dramatically in the 1960s and 1970s, the NAIRU naturally increased. In recent years, however, female unemployment rates have dropped below the rates for men, and so continued increases in female participation will, if anything, tend to decrease the NAIRU.

Greater labour-force participation by groups with high unemployment rates increases the level of NAIRU.

Young workers have higher unemployment rates than do older workers. As the share of younger workers in the labour force increases, so will the economy's NAIRU.

See Figure 30-3 for Canadian unemployment rates for various demographic groups in 1999. Notice especially the significantly higher

FIGURE 30-3   Unemployment Rates by Demographic Groups, 1999

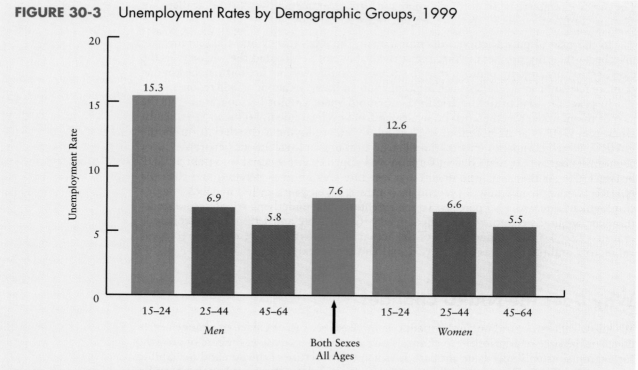

Unemployment is unevenly spread among different groups in the labour force. In 1999, when the overall unemployment rate was 7.6 percent, the unemployment rates for youths (of both sexes) was considerably higher.

(*Source:* These data are available on Statistics Canada's website: www.statcan.ca)

unemployment rates for youth of both sexes. These data form the basis for the often-heard view that while overall unemployment may be at acceptable levels, youth unemployment may be a serious problem.

Hysteresis

Some models of unemployment show that the size of the NAIRU can be influenced by the size of the actual current rate of unemployment. Such models get their name from the Greek word *hysteresis,* meaning "lagged effect."

One mechanism that can lead to hysteresis arises from the importance of experience and on-the-job training. Suppose that a recession causes a significant group of new entrants to the labour force to encounter unusual difficulty obtaining their first jobs. As a result, this unlucky group will be slow to acquire the important skills that workers generally learn in their first jobs. When demand increases again, this group of workers will be at a disadvantage relative to workers with normal histories of experience, and the unlucky group may have unemployment rates that will be higher than average. Hence, the NAIRU will be higher than it would have been had there been no recession.

Another force that can cause such effects is emphasized by commentators in western Europe, which has a more heavily unionized labour force than does either Canada or the United States. In times of high unemployment, people who are currently employed ("insiders") may use their bargaining power to ensure that their own status is maintained and prevent new entrants to the labour force ("outsiders") from competing effectively. In an *insider-outsider* model of this type, a period of prolonged, high unemployment—whatever its initial cause—will tend to become "locked in." If outsiders are denied access to the labour market, their unemployment will fail to exert downward pressure on wages, and the NAIRU will tend to rise.

Increasing Structural Change

The amount of resources being moved between industries and regions increased in the mid 1970s and appears to be carrying on through the 1980s and 1990s. In part, this is the result of the increasing integration of the Canadian economy with the rest of the world and the globalization of world markets. Most economists would argue that this integration has been beneficial overall, for reasons we discuss in Chapters 34 and 35. One less fortunate consequence, however, is that Canadian labour markets are increasingly affected by changes in demand and supply conditions anywhere in the world—changes that require adjustments throughout the world's trading nations. Although evidence is difficult to obtain, some observers argue that the increasing pace and the changing nature of technological change since the mid 1970s has contributed to an increase in the level of structural unemployment.

Policy and Labour-Market Flexibility

We mentioned briefly above how policies can affect structural unemployment and thus affect the NAIRU. It is worthwhile emphasizing again the important role that government policy can have on the NAIRU.

Our discussion in the previous several pages suggests that one important cause of unemployment is *inflexibility* in the labour market. If wages are inflexible, then shocks to labour demand or supply can cause unemployment. If workers are unable or unwilling to move between regions or between industries, then changes in the structure of the economy can cause unemployment. If it is costly for firms to hire workers, then firms will find other ways of increasing output (such as switching to more capital-intensive methods of production). In general, since the economy is always being buffetted by shocks of one sort or another, the more inflexibility there is in the labour market, the higher unemployment will be.

This relationship suggests a general point about the effect of government policy on the NAIRU:

Any government policy that reduces labour-market flexibility is likely to increase the NAIRU.

Consider two examples.

The first example is unemployment insurance (UI). UI provides income support to eligible unemployed workers and thus reduces the costs to the worker of being unemployed. This income support will typically lead the worker to search longer for a new job and thus increase the unemployment rate. This longer search may be desirable since by reducing the cost of unemployment the worker is able to conduct a thorough search for a job that is an appropriate match for his or her specific skills. On the other hand, if the UI system is so generous that workers have little incentive to accept reasonable jobs—instead holding out for the "perfect" job—then the increase in unemployment generated by the UI system will be undesirable.

In general, however, the basic message should be clear. The more generous is the unemployment insurance system, the less motivated unemployed workers will be to quickly accept a new job. This reduction in labour-market flexibility will increase the NAIRU.

The second example concerns policies designed to increase job security for workers. In most western European countries, firms that lay off workers are required either to give

See Chapter 30 of www.pearsoned.ca/lipsey for a debate on the effects of mandated job security: Seamus Hogan, "Should Governments Mandate Job Security?" and Marc Van Audenrode, "A Partial Defence of Job Security Provisions," *World Economic Affairs*.

See Chapter 30 of www.pearsoned.ca/lipsey for a discussion of the likely effects of France's recent policy of shortening the length of the work week: Jan Olters, "Some Doubts About France's 35-Hour Week," *World Economic Affairs*.

several months notice before doing so or, in lieu of such notice, are required to make severance payments equal to several months worth of pay. In Italy, for example, a worker who has been with the firm for ten years is guaranteed either 20 months notice before termination or a severance payment equal to 20 months worth of pay.

Such job-security provisions reduce the flexibility of firms. But this inflexibility on the part of the firms is passed on to workers. Any policy that forces the firm to incur large costs for laying off workers is likely to lead the same firm to be very hesitant about hiring workers in the first place. Given this reduction in labour-market flexibility, such policies are likely to increase the NAIRU.

Such mandated job security is relatively rare in Canada and the United States. Its rarity contributes to the general belief among economists that North American labour markets are much more flexible than those in Europe. Many economists see this as the most important explanation for why unemployment rates in Canada and the United States are significantly below the unemployment rates in Europe, and have been for the past two decades.

Reducing Unemployment

As the Canadian economy grew steadily from 1993 to 1999, the unemployment rate dropped from 11.3 percent to 7 percent. Unemployment in the United States declined by a similar amount, as the U.S. economy was also experiencing steady economic growth. In both cases, most economists viewed the decline in unemployment as a desirable reduction in *cyclical* unemployment.

Despite the reduction in Canada's unemployment rate in the late 1990s, however, many economists have been puzzled at the growing unemployment *gap* between Canada and the United States. Beginning in the early 1980s, the Canadian unemployment rate has increased relative to the U.S. rate. By the late 1990s, the gap was approximately four percentage points. What is the cause of the gap? *Applying Economic Concepts 30-2* examines this issue and concludes that an important part of the answer lies in how the unemployed are counted in the two countries.

In the remainder of this chapter we briefly examine what can be done to reduce unemployment. Other things being equal, all governments would like to reduce unemployment. The questions are "Can it be done?" and "If so, at what cost?"

Practise with Study Guide Chapter 30, Exercise 2.

Cyclical Unemployment

We do not need to say much more about cyclical unemployment because its control is the subject of stabilization policy, which we have studied in several earlier chapters. A major recession that occurs because of natural causes can be countered by monetary and fiscal policies to reduce cyclical unemployment.

There is room for debate, however, about *how much* the government can and should do in this respect. Advocates of stabilization policy call for expansionary fiscal and monetary policies to reduce such gaps, at least when they last for sustained periods of time. Advocates of a hands-off approach say that normal market adjustments can be relied on to remove such gaps and that government policy, no matter how well intentioned, will only make things worse. They call for setting simple rules for monetary and fiscal policy that would make discretionary stabilization policy impossible. This matter was discussed in detail at the end of Chapter 25.

Whatever may be argued in principle, however, policymakers have not yet agreed to abandon such stabilization measures in practice.

Frictional Unemployment

The turnover that causes frictional unemployment is an inevitable part of the functioning of the economy. Some frictional unemployment is a natural part of the learning process for young workers. New entrants to the labour force (many of whom are young) have to try several jobs to see which is most suitable, and this leads to a high turnover rate among the young and hence high frictional unemployment.

To the extent that frictional unemployment is caused by ignorance regarding where the appropriate jobs are, increasing the knowledge of workers about market opportunities may help. But such measures have a cost, and that cost has to be balanced against the benefits.

Unemployment insurance is one method of helping people cope with unemployment. It has reduced significantly the human costs of the bouts with unemployment that are inevitable in a changing society. Nothing, however, is without cost. Although unemployment insurance alleviates the suffering caused by some kinds of unemployment, it also contributes to search unemployment, as we have already observed.

Supporters of unemployment insurance emphasize its benefits. Critics emphasize its costs. As with any policy, a rational assessment of the value of unemployment insurance requires a balancing of its undoubted benefits against its undoubted costs. Many Canadians believe that when this calculation is made, the benefits greatly exceed the costs, although many also recognize the scope for reform of certain aspects of the program.

Many provisions have been added over the years to the unemployment insurance scheme to focus it more on people in general need and to reduce its effect of raising the unemployment rate. For example, workers must be actively seeking employment in order to be eligible for UI. Also, workers who voluntarily quit their jobs (without cause) are not eligible to collect UI. Finally, a system of *experience rating* has recently been proposed to distribute the costs more in proportion to the benefits. In the absence of experience rating all firms pay the same UI tax; this implicitly subsidizes those firms who create the most unemployment and taxes most heavily those firms who create the least unemployment. Under experience rating, firms with histories of sizable layoffs pay more than those with better layoff records.

Structural Unemployment

The reallocation of labour among occupations, industries, skill categories, and regions that gives rise to structural unemployment is an inevitable part of a market economy. There are two basic approaches to reducing structural unemployment: Try to arrest the changes that the economy experiences or accept the changes and try to speed up the adjustments. Throughout history, labour and management have advocated both approaches and governments have tried them both.

Ever since the beginning of the Industrial Revolution, workers have resisted the introduction of new techniques that replace the older techniques at which they were skilled. Such resistance is understandable. New techniques often destroy the value of the knowledge and experience of workers skilled in the displaced techniques. Older workers may not even get a chance to start over with the new technique. Employers may prefer to hire younger persons who will learn the new skills faster than older workers who are set in their ways of thinking. But, from society's point of view, new techniques are beneficial because they are a major source of economic growth. From the point of view of the workers they displace, new techniques can be an unmitigated disaster.

Over the long term, policies that subsidize employment in declining industries run into increasing difficulties. Agreements to hire unneeded workers raise costs and can hasten the decline of an industry threatened by competitive products. An industry that

APPLYING ECONOMIC CONCEPTS 30-2
The Canada–U.S. Unemployment Gap

In recent years economists have been examining why the gap between the Canadian and U.S. unemployment rates has been growing. As the accompanying figure shows, the last year in which the two countries had the same unemployment rate was 1981. Since then the Canadian unemployment rate has exceeded the U.S. rate by an average of two percentage points in the 1980s and by four percentage points in the 1990s. What is the cause of this gap? Does the gap reflect a more poorly functioning Canadian economy?

Craig Riddell from the University of British Columbia and David Card from the University of California at Berkeley have shown that an important part of the explanation lies in the difference between *unemployment* and *non-participation* in the labour force. In short, a randomly selected individual in each country who is not working is more likely to be considered unemployed in Canada but out of the labour force in the United States. This difference naturally increases the Canadian unemployment rate relative to that in the United States. Let's look at this in more detail.

Decomposing the Unemployment Rate

It is helpful to first define some terms. We will use the following symbols to represent the important labour-market variables:

U = number of persons who are unemployed
LF = number of persons in the labour force
POP = number of persons in the working-age population
N = number of persons in the working-age population who are *not* working

Recall that the unemployment rate is simply the fraction of the labour force that is unemployed, U/LF. We can write this differently as

$$U/LF = (U/N) \times (N/POP) \times (POP/LF)$$

It should be clear that this equation always holds since we could cancel the Ns and the POPs to simply get U/LF = U/LF. But this longer equation allows us to see that any change in the unemployment rate *must be* due to a change in one (or more) of these three separate variables. What are these three variables?

An individual can be non-employed either by being out of the labour force or by being in the labour force but unemployed. The ratio U/N is simply the fraction of the total non-working persons who are classified as unemployed. Clearly, a rise in U/N, other things equal, raises the unemployment rate. The second variable, N/POP, is the fraction of the working-age population that is *not* working. This is one minus the country's *employment rate*. A reduction in the employment rate, other things equal, means a rise in N/POP and thus an increase in the unemployment rate. The third variable, POP/LF, is simply the inverse of the labour-force participation rate. A fall in the participation rate, other things equal, means a rise in POP/LF and thus an increase in the unemployment rate.

Growing Labour-Force Attachment in Canada

Card and Riddell argue that the U/N ratio is the key variable for explaining the Canada-U.S. unemployment gap. They refer to U/N as a measure of *labour-force attachment*—since the non-working individuals who are classified as unemployed are "attached" to the labour force.

Card and Riddell find that between 1981 and 1998, fully two-thirds of the Canada-U.S. unemployment gap is explained by an increase in the Canadian U/N ratio relative to that in the United States. One quarter of the gap is accounted for by a lower employment rate (higher N/POP) and less than

is declining because of economic change becomes an increasingly large burden on the public purse as economic forces become less and less favourable to its success. Sooner or later, public support is withdrawn, followed by a precipitous decline.

As we assess these remedies for structural unemployment, it is important to realize that although they are not viable in the long run for the entire economy, they may be the best alternatives for the affected workers during their lifetimes.

There is often a genuine conflict between the private interest of workers threatened by structural unemployment, whose interests lie in preserving existing jobs, and the social interest served by reallocating resources to where they are most valuable.

10 percent of the gap is explained by lower labour-force participation (higher POP/LF).

To put it differently, the principal cause of the rising Canada-U.S. unemployment gap appears to be a change in the way that non-employed Canadians spend their time relative to their U.S. counterparts. When not working, Canadians in the past two decades have become more likely to continue searching for jobs, and thus to be officially counted among the unemployed. In contrast, non-working Americans have become relatively more likely to be counted among the non-participants.

Causes of the Greater Attachment

Two main reasons are offered for why Canadians appear to have a greater attachment to the labour force. First, there are slight but significant differences in how the unemployed are classified in the two countries. In order to be considered unemployed in the United States, individuals must be "actively" searching for work. In contrast, Canadians must only be "passively" looking for work. So, for example, an individual who *only* reads the help-

wanted ads in the newspaper would be classified as unemployed in Canada but as out of the labour force in the United States. This difference alone, although it sounds like a minor point, appears to explain one quarter of the unemployment gap.

Card and Riddell suggest that the greater generosity and availability of the Canadian unemployment-insurance system is also very important for explaining why Canadians have a greater attachment to the labour force. The greater generosity obviously improves the insurance value of the program for those workers who may lose their jobs. But by reducing the costs associated with being unemployed, it also results in longer job search and higher measured unemployment (for a given level of employment).

Is It a Problem?

In order to know whether a rise in unemployment is undesirable, we must know why the increase occurred. To the extent that the higher Canadian unemployment rate is due to poorer employment growth in Canada, this may represent a problem. Some economists argue that tight fiscal and monetary policies, especially in the 1990s, are largely responsible for the rise in the N/POP ratio in Canada relative to that in the United States.

But the findings by Card and Riddell are that the clear majority of the unemployment gap is due to a rise in labour-force attachment (U/N) in Canada. Is this a problem? As Riddell says, "The implications for individuals' welfare of a rise in unemployment that is not associated with a decline in employment are much less obvious." The greater labour-force attachment arising from the different classification of similar workers is obviously not a problem for individual well-being. However, the greater labour-force attachment arising from a more generous UI system may be a problem. As we said earlier in this chapter, an overly generous UI system may encourage unemployed workers to search *too much*, holding out for the "perfect" job match rather than accepting a merely "good" job offer.

This box is based on Craig Riddell, "Canadian Labour-Market Performance in International Perspective," *Canadian Journal of Economics*, November 1999.

A second general approach to dealing with structural change is to accept the decline of specific industries and the loss of specific jobs that go with them and to try to reduce the cost of adjustment for the workers affected. A number of policies have been introduced in Canada to ease the adjustment to changing economic conditions.

One such policy is publicly subsidized education and retraining schemes. The public involvement is motivated largely by imperfections in capital markets that make it difficult for workers to borrow funds for education, training or retraining. A major component of labour-market policies is a system of loans and subsidies for higher education.

Another policy is motivated by the difficulty in obtaining good information about current and future job prospects. In recent years, the development of the Internet has

To learn more about the National Job Bank or the Electronic Labour Exchange, see HRDC's website: www.hrdc-drhc-gc.ca.

greatly improved the flow of this type of information. Human Resources Development Canada (HRDC), for example, operates two Internet-based services to speed up and improve the quality of matches between firms and workers. The HRDC National Job Bank allows workers to search various regions of the country for jobs of specific types. The Electronic Labour Exchange allows firms (or workers) to specify certain characteristics and skills and then match these characteristics with workers (or firms) on the "other side" of the labour market.

Policies to increase retraining and to improve the flow of labour-market information will tend to reduce the amount of structural unemployment.

Conclusion

Over the years, unemployment has been regarded in many different ways. Harsh critics see it as proof that the market system is badly flawed. Reformers regard it as a necessary evil of the market system and a suitable object for government policy to reduce its incidence and its harmful effects. Others see it as overblown in importance and believe that it does not reflect any real inability of workers to obtain jobs if they really want to work.

Most government policy has followed a middle route. Fiscal and monetary policies have sought to reduce at least the most persistent of recessionary gaps, and a host of labour-market policies have sought to reduce the incidence of frictional and structural unemployment. Such social policies as unemployment insurance have sought to reduce the sting of unemployment for the many who were thought to suffer from it for reasons beyond their control.

As global economic competition becomes more and more severe and as new knowledge-driven methods of production spread, the ability to adjust to economic change will become increasingly important. Countries that succeed in the global marketplace, while also managing to maintain humane social welfare systems, will be those that best learn how to cooperate with change. This will mean avoiding economic policies that inhibit change while adopting social policies that reduce the human cost of adjusting to change. This is an enormous challenge for future Canadian economic and social policies.

S U M M A R Y

Employment and Unemployment

- Canadian employment and the Canadian labour force have increased along a strong upward trend throughout all of this century. The unemployment rate has fluctuated significantly; over the past forty years it has also shown an upward trend.
- Looking only at the level of employment or unemployment misses a tremendous amount of activity in the labour market as individuals flow from unemployment to employment or from employment to unemployment. In

recent years in Canada, approximately 400 000 people *per month* flow between employment and unemployment. This level of gross flows reflects the turnover which is a normal part of any labour market.

- It is useful to distinguish among several types of unemployment: cyclical unemployment, which is associated with output gaps; frictional unemployment, which is caused by the length of time it takes to find a first job and to move from job to job as a result of normal labour turnover; and structural unemployment, which is caused by the need to reallocate resources among occupations, regions, and industries as the structure of demand and supply changes.

- Together, frictional unemployment and structural unemployment make up the NAIRU, which is then expressed as a percentage of the total labour force. The actual unemployment rate is equal to the NAIRU when real output is equal to potential output.

Cyclical Unemployment

- There is a long-standing debate among economists regarding the causes of cyclical unemployment.
- New Classical theories look to explanations that allow the labour market to be cleared continuously by perfectly flexible wages and prices. Such theories can explain cyclical variations in employment but do not predict the existence of involuntary unemployment.
- New Keynesian theories have focused on the long-term nature of employer-worker relationships in which wages tend to respond only a little, and employment tends to

respond a lot, to changes in the demand and supply of labour. More recent New Keynesian theories have examined the possibility that it may be efficient for employers to pay wages that are above the level that would clear the labour market (efficiency wages).

- This debate only applies to the short-run behaviour of the economy. Both classes of models, for example, predict that in the long run, monetary expansions or contractions affect only the price level, and do not affect output, employment, or unemployment.

The NAIRU

- The NAIRU will always be positive because it takes time for labour to move between jobs both in normal turnover (frictional unemployment) and in response to changes in the structure of the demand for labour (structural unemployment).
- Because different workers have different sets of skills and because different firms require workers with different sets of skills, some unemployment—resulting from workers searching for appropriate job matches with employers—is socially desirable.

- Anything that increases the rate of turnover in the labour market, or the pace of structural change in the economy, will likely increase the NAIRU.
- Unemployment insurance also increases the NAIRU by encouraging workers to continue searching for an appropriate job. Policies that mandate job security increase the costs to firms of laying off workers. This makes them reluctant to hire workers in the first place and thus increases the NAIRU.

Reducing Unemployment

- Cyclical unemployment can be reduced by using monetary or fiscal policies to close recessionary gaps. Frictional and structural unemployment can be reduced by making it easier to move between jobs and by raising the cost of

staying unemployed (e.g., by reducing unemployment insurance benefits).

- In a growing, changing economy populated by people who wish to change jobs for many reasons, it is neither possible nor desirable to reduce unemployment to zero.

KEY CONCEPTS

Gross flows in the labour market
Cyclical, frictional, and structural unemployment
New Classical and New Keynesian theories of unemployment

Long-term employment relationships
Efficiency wages
Hysteresis
The components of the NAIRU

Determinants of the size of the NAIRU
Policies to reduce the NAIRU
Labour-market flexibility

STUDY EXERCISES

1. The following table shows the pattern of real GDP, potential GDP, and the unemployment rate for several years in Cycleland.

Year	Real GDP (billions of dollars)	Potential GDP (billions of dollars)	Unemployment Rate (%)
1991	790	740	6.3
1992	800	760	6.5
1993	780	780	6.8
1994	750	800	8.2
1995	765	810	8.4
1996	790	830	8.4
1997	815	850	8.0
1998	845	870	7.5
1999	875	890	7.2
2000	900	900	7.0
2001	930	920	6.8

   a. On a scale diagram, draw the path of real GDP and potential GDP (with time on the horizontal axis).
   b. On a separate diagram (below the first one) show the path of the unemployment rate.
   c. For which years is it possible to determine the value of NAIRU?
   d. Does the NAIRU change over the ten-year period? Provide one reason (based on the text) that NAIRU could increase.

2. The diagram below shows a simple AD/SRAS diagram. The economy begins at E_0 with real GDP equal to potential GDP.

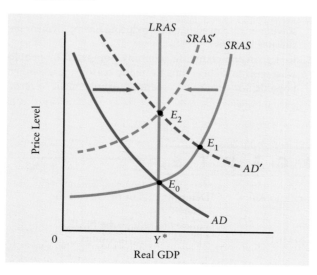

   a. At E_0, the unemployment rate is 8%. What type of unemployment is this?
   b. A positive aggregate demand shock now shifts the AD curve to AD'. At E_1 the unemployment rate is only 6.5% Is there cyclical unemployment at E_1?
   c. Describe the economy's adjustment process to E_2.
   d. What is the unemployment rate at E_2?

3. The diagram below shows a simple AD/SRAS diagram. The economy begins at E_0 with real GDP equal to potential GDP.

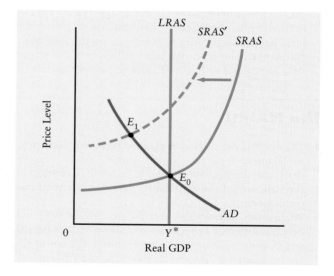

   a. At E_0, the unemployment rate is 6%. What type of unemployment is this?
   b. A negative aggregate supply shock now shifts the SRAS curve to SRAS'. At E_1 the unemployment rate is 7.5% Is there cyclical unemployment at E_1? How much?
   c. If monetary and fiscal policy do not react to the shock, describe the economy's adjustment process to its long-run equilibrium.
   d. What is the unemployment rate at the economy's long-run equilibrium? Explain.

4. The diagram on the next page shows a perfectly competitive labour market. The initial equilibrium is with wage w^* and employment L^*.

   a. Suppose the demand for labour decreases to D'_L. If wages are perfectly flexible, what is the effect on wages and employment? Show this in the diagram.
   b. Is there any involuntary unemployment in part a?
   c. Now suppose that wages can only adjust half as much as in part a—that is, wages are sticky. What is

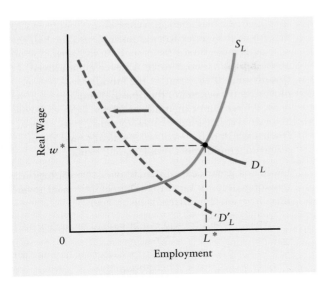

d. If wages and prices adjust only slowly to shocks, what happens to unemployment? Explain.

e. Explain why the key difference between New Keynesian and New Classical theories of unemployment involves the degree of wage and price flexibility.

6. The table below shows the percentage of the labour force accounted for by youths (15–24 years old) and older workers (25 years and older) over several years. Suppose that, due to their lower skills and greater turnover, youths have a higher unemployment rate than older workers (see Figure 30-3).

the effect on wages and employment in this case? Show this in the diagram.

d. Is there any involuntary unemployment in part **c**? How much?

5. Consider an economy that begins with real GDP equal to potential. There is then a sudden increase in the prices of raw materials, which shifts the *SRAS* curve up and to the left.

a. Draw the initial long-run equilibrium in an *AD/SRAS* diagram.

b. Now show the immediate effect of the supply shock in your diagram.

c. Suppose that wages and prices in this economy adjust instantly to shocks. Describe what happens to unemployment in this economy. Explain.

| | Percentage of Labour Force | |
Year	Youths	Older Workers
1.	20	80
2.	21	79
3.	22	78
4.	23	77
5.	25	75
6.	27	73
7.	29	71
8.	31	69

a. Suppose that in year 1 real GDP is equal to potential GDP, and the unemployment rate among older workers is 6% but is 14% among youths. What is the economy's NAIRU?

b. Now suppose that for the next eight years real GDP remains equal to potential. Compute the value of NAIRU for each year.

c. Explain why NAIRU rises even though output is always equal to potential.

DISCUSSION QUESTIONS

1. Interpret the following statements from newspapers in terms of types of unemployment.

a. "Recession hits local factory; 2000 laid off."

b. "Of course, I could take a job as a dishwasher, but I'm trying to find something that makes use of my high school training," says a local teenager in our survey of the unemployed.

c. "Retraining is the best reaction to the increased use of robots."

d. "Uneven upturn: Signs of recovery in Alberta, but Ontario is still in recession."

2. Discuss the following views. Is it possible that both views are right? Explain.

a. "Canadian workers should resist automation, which is destroying their jobs," says a labour leader.

b. "Given the fierce foreign competition faced by Canadian firms, it's a case of automate or die," says an industrialist.

3. "No one needs to be out of work if he or she really wants a job; just look at the Help Wanted signs in many fast-food businesses and retail shops." Does the existence of the unfilled vacancies suggested in the quotation

imply that there need be no cyclical unemployment as long as workers are not excessively fussy about the kinds of jobs they will take?

4. What differences in approach toward the problem of unemployment are suggested by the following facts?

   a. In the 1960s and 1970s, Britain spent billions of dollars on subsidizing firms that would otherwise have gone out of business in order to protect the jobs of the employees.

   b. Sweden has been a pioneer in spending large sums to retrain and to relocate displaced workers.

5. Advocates of discretionary fiscal policy often argue that the government can reduce unemployment by increasing spending on such things as highways, bridges, sewer systems, and so on. What do you think of such a policy to "create jobs"? Is such a policy equally likely to create jobs during a recession as when the economy is operating at potential output? Explain.

6. Consider two hypothetical countries. In Country A, 20 percent of the labour force is unemployed for half the time and employed for the other half; the remaining 80 percent of the labour force is never unemployed. In Country B, 100 percent of the labour force is unemployed for 10 percent of the time and employed for the other 90 percent of the time. Note that both countries have an overall unemployment rate of 10 percent. Discuss which of these countries seems to have the more serious unemployment problem, and explain why.

7. There is a great deal of debate over the appropriate level of generosity for Canada's unemployment insurance program (Employment Insurance).

   a. Explain what problem can be caused by having a UI system that is too generous.

   b. Explain what problem can be caused by having a UI system that is not generous enough.

   c. If UI generosity were reduced and the NAIRU declined as a result, is this necessarily a desirable outcome?

CHAPTER 31

Budget Deficits and Surpluses

(LO) *LEARNING OBJECTIVES*

1 Understand how the government's annual budget deficit (or surplus) is related to its stock of debt.

2 Explain the difference between the overall budget deficit and the primary budget deficit.

3 Explain the meaning of the cyclically adjusted budget deficit, and how it can be used to measure the stance of fiscal policy.

4 Understand Ricardian equivalence.

5 Explain how deficits crowd out investment and net exports.

6 Explain why a high stock of debt may hamper monetary and fiscal policy.

7 Discuss several different proposals for balancing the budget.

Until the late 1990s, no single measure associated with the government was the focus of more attention and controversy than the size of the government budget deficit. Some people argued that the deficit was an economic time bomb, waiting to explode and cause serious harm to our living standards. Others argued that the only real danger posed by deficits was from the dramatic policy changes proposed to eliminate them. By 1999, however, after nearly two decades of debate about the budget deficit, the focus had shifted abruptly to what the governments—federal and provincial—should do with their budget surpluses. Just as debates once raged over the harmful effects of high government budget deficits, debates currently rage about whether governments that are facing budget surpluses should increase spending, reduce taxes, or use the surpluses to reduce the outstanding stock of government debt.

In this chapter, we examine various issues surrounding the government budget. We begin by considering the simple arithmetic of government budgets. This tells us how the deficit or surplus in any given year is related to the outstanding stock of debt. We then explore why deficits and debt matter for the performance of the economy—as well as what changes we can expect over the near future if Canadian governments are successful in maintaining either balanced budgets or budget surpluses.

Facts and Definitions

There is a simple relationship between the government's expenditures, its tax revenues, and its borrowing.

The Government's Budget Constraint

Just like any individual, government expenditures must be financed either by income or by borrowing. The difference between individuals and governments, however, is that governments typically do not earn income by selling products or labour services; instead, they earn income by levying taxes. Thus, all government expenditure must be financed either by tax revenues or by borrowing. This point is illustrated by the following simple equation, which is called the government's *budget constraint:*

$$\text{Government Expenditure} = \text{Tax Revenue} + \text{Borrowing}$$

There are three broad components to government expenditures. The first is the government's purchases of goods and services, G. The second is transfers to individuals or firms, such as unemployment insurance or industrial subsidies, denoted TR. The third component is interest payments on the outstanding stock of debt. This is referred to as **debt-service payments**, denoted $i \times D$, where i is the interest rate and D is the stock of government debt. If we let T represent the government's tax revenues, we can rewrite the government's budget constraint as

debt-service payments   Payments which represent the interest owed on a current stock of debt.

$$G + TR + i \times D = T + \text{Borrowing}$$

or, subtracting T from both sides,

$$(G + TR + i \times D) - T = \text{Borrowing}$$

This equation simply says that any excess of total government spending over tax revenues must be financed by government borrowing.

The government's annual **budget deficit** is the excess of total government expenditure over total revenues in a given year. From the budget constraint above, this annual deficit is exactly the same as the amount borrowed by the government during the year. Since the government borrows by issuing bonds and selling them to lenders, borrowing by the government increases the government's outstanding stock of debt. Since D is the outstanding stock of government debt, ΔD is the *change* in the stock of debt during the course of the year. The budget deficit can therefore be written as

budget deficit   Any shortfall of current revenue below current expenditure.

$$\text{Budget Deficit} = \Delta D = (G + TR + i \times D) - T$$

The government's annual budget deficit is the excess of total expenditure over total tax revenues in a given year. It is also equal to the change in the stock of government debt during the year.

Notice two points about budget deficits. First, a change in the size of the deficit requires a change in the level of expenditures *relative* to the level of tax revenues.

For a given level of tax revenues, a smaller deficit can come about only through a reduction in government expenditures; conversely, for a given level of expenditures, a smaller deficit requires an increase in tax revenues. Second, since the deficit is equal to the amount of new government borrowing, the stock of government debt will rise whenever the budget deficit is positive. Even a drastic reduction in the size of the annual budget deficit is therefore not sufficient to reduce the outstanding stock of government debt; the stock of debt will fall only if the budget deficit becomes *negative*. In this case, there is said to be a **budget surplus**.

A deficit increases the stock of debt; a surplus reduces it.

budget surplus   Any excess of current revenue over current expenditure.

The Primary Budget Deficit

The total level of government expenditure comprises purchases of goods and services (G), transfer payments (TR), and debt-service payments ($i \times D$). Since at any point in time the outstanding stock of government debt—determined by *past* government borrowing—cannot be influenced by current government policy, the debt-service component of total expenditures is beyond the control of the government. In contrast, the other components of the government's budget are said to be *discretionary* because the government can choose to change the levels of G, TR or T. To capture the part of the total deficit that is attributable to discretionary expenditures and revenues, the government's **primary budget deficit** is defined as the difference between the total budget deficit and the debt-service payments:

primary budget deficit   The difference between the government's overall budget deficit and its debt-service payments.

$$\begin{array}{ll} \text{Primary} \\ \text{Budget Deficit} \end{array} = \begin{array}{ll} \text{Total} \\ \text{Budget Deficit} \end{array} - \begin{array}{ll} \text{Debt-Service} \\ \text{Payments} \end{array}$$

$$= (G + TR + i \times D - T) - i \times D$$

$$= (G + TR) - T$$

The government's primary budget deficit shows the extent to which tax revenues are able to finance the *discretionary* part of total expenditure. Another name for discretionary expenditure is the government's *program spending*.

It is possible that the government has an overall budget deficit but a *primary* budget surplus, indicating that tax revenues more than cover program spending but are insufficient to fully cover debt-service payments as well. For example, in the 1996–1997 fiscal year, the federal government had an overall budget deficit of $13.7 billion while debt-service payments were $45.2 billion. There was thus a primary budget *surplus* in that year of $31.5 billion—that is, total tax revenues exceeded program expenditures by $31.5 billion. By the next fiscal year, the federal government had eliminated the deficit and actually had an overall budget surplus of $3.2 billion. Debt-service payments were $44 billion, so the primary budget surplus was $47.2 billion.

The primary budget deficit is the difference between the overall budget deficit and the level of debt-service payments. In recent years, the federal government has had a primary budget surplus, indicating that tax revenues were more than sufficient to cover program expenditures.

For an illustration of the government's budget constraint, and of the distinction between overall budget deficits and primary budget deficits, see Figure 31-1. This distinction becomes very important when we examine changes in the debt-to-GDP ratio later in the chapter.

FIGURE 31-1   An Illustration of the Government's Budget Constraint

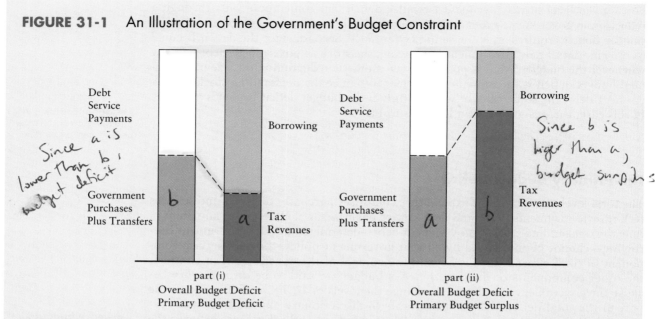

Since a is lower than b, budget deficit

Since b is bigger than a, budget surplus

part (i)
Overall Budget Deficit
Primary Budget Deficit

part (ii)
Overall Budget Deficit
Primary Budget Surplus

The sum of all expenditures by government must be financed either by tax collection or by borrowing. The deficit is the difference between total expenditures and total tax collection; it is also equal to the total level of borrowing. In both parts of the figure, the government's budget constraint is illustrated by the fact that the two bars are the same height, showing that total expenditures must be equal to tax revenues plus borrowing. In both parts there is an overall budget deficit because tax revenues are not sufficient to finance total expenditures (and so there is positive borrowing). In part (i), taxes are not even enough to cover government purchases and transfers, and so there is a primary budget deficit. In part (ii), taxes are more than enough to cover government purchases and transfers, and so there is a primary budget surplus (even though there is an overall budget deficit).

Deficits and Debt in Canada

Federal Government

For the most recent federal budget forecasts, see the website for the Department of Finance: www.fin.gc.ca.

In a growing economy, many macroeconomic variables such as the levels of government expenditure and tax revenue tend also to grow. As a result, rather than looking at the absolute size of the government deficit or debt, economists focus on government debt and deficits in relation to the overall size of the economy. Some budget deficits that would be unmanageable in a small country like New Zealand might be quite acceptable for a larger country like Canada, and trivial for a huge economy like the United States. Similarly, a government budget deficit that seemed crushing in Canada in 1899 might appear trivial in 1999 because the size of the Canadian economy is many times larger now than it was then.

The path of federal budget deficits since 1970 is shown in Figure 31-2. The top panel shows total federal spending and total federal tax revenues as percentages of GDP. The bottom panel shows the total federal deficit as a percentage of GDP. Persistent deficits began in the mid 1970s and lasted until the mid 1990s.

The substantial increase in the budget deficit in the early 1980s reflects the combined effects of the severe recession in 1982, some mild discretionary fiscal expansion, and increased interest payments on the government's debt. This last element was due in part to the higher real interest rates in the early 1980s and the accumulation of the deficits in the late 1970s which added to the stock of government debt. The effects of a strong economic recovery in the late 1980s, combined with active measures on the part of the federal government, then resulted in a reduction in the deficit. By 1989, at the beginning of a significant economic downturn, the deficit was just over 3 percent of GDP. The recession of 1991 again pushed up the deficit, but by then the large stock of federal government debt made the federal government reluctant to let the deficit rise considerably. As a result, by 1993, two years into a slow economic recovery, the federal budget deficit had increased only to about 5 percent of GDP. As the recovery progressed further, and the federal government continued its policy of reducing the deficit, the deficit fell rapidly until finally being eliminated in the 1997–98 fiscal year.

As we saw in the previous section, a deficit implies that the stock of government debt is rising. Thus, the persistent deficits that began in the 1970s have their counterpart in a steadily rising stock of government debt. Figure 31-3 shows the path of Canadian federal government debt since 1940. At the beginning of the Second World War, the stock of federal debt was equal to about 45 percent of GDP. The enormous increase in the debt-to-GDP ratio over the next five years reflects wartime borrowing used to finance military expenditures. From 1946 to 1974, however, there was a continual decline in the debt-to-GDP ratio. The economy was growing quickly during this period. But equally important was that the federal government in the post-war years typically ran significant budget surpluses. These two factors explain the dramatic decline in the debt-to-GDP ratio between 1946 and 1974.

By 1975 the federal debt was only 14 percent of GDP. The large and persistent budget deficits beginning in the mid 1970s, however, along with a general slowdown in the rate of economic growth, led to a significant upward trend in the debt-to-GDP ratio. The ratio climbed steadily from 1979 to 1996 and then, with the significant reductions in the deficit beginning in 1996, the debt-to-GDP ratio began to fall.

FIGURE 31-2 Federal Government Expenditures, Revenues, and Deficit, 1970–1998

(i) Revenues and expenditures

(ii) The budget deficit

The federal budget was in deficit every year between 1975 and 1997. In 1998, the federal government had a budget surplus of 0.4 percent of GDP. The graphs in part (i) show expenditures and revenues of the federal government, both as a percentage of GDP. The difference is the federal deficit, shown in part (ii).

(*Source: Economic Reference Tables*, Department of Finance. Recent data are available on the Department of Finance website: www.fin.gc.ca.)

Provincial Governments

Canada is relatively special among developed countries in the sense that its provincial governments are responsible for a significant fraction of total government revenues and expenditures. In many countries, sizable regional governments either do not exist, as in New Zealand, or are often required to run balanced budgets, as is the case for about two

The Canadian government ran very large budget deficits to fi-nance Canada's participation in the Second World War. As a result, Canada's debt increased to 110 percent of GDP by 1946.

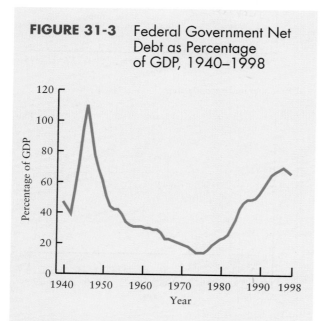

FIGURE 31-3   Federal Government Net Debt as Percentage of GDP, 1940–1998

The federal government's debt-to-GDP ratio fell dramatically after the Second World War and continued falling until 1975. It then increased markedly for the next two decades. In the late 1990s when government deficits were reduced and the economy was in a healthy recovery, the debt-to-GDP ratio began to fall.

(*Source:* Statistics Canada, CANSIM database.)

thirds of the fifty states in the United States. In contrast, the size of Canadian provincial governments—measured by their spending and taxing powers relative to that of the federal government—means that an examination of government debt and deficits in Canada would not be complete without paying attention to the provincial governments' fiscal positions.

For example, in the 1997–98 fiscal year, the federal government had $166 billion of tax revenues, representing 17 percent of GDP. In the same year, the combined provincial and territorial governments had only slightly less tax revenues—a total of $150 billion, or 16.9 percent of GDP.

When examining the size and effects of budget deficits or surpluses, it is important to consider all levels of government—federal, provincial, and municipal.

During the 1970s, the provincial governments were running budget deficits and so the stock of provincial government debt was increasing. But the deficits were small enough that this debt was not growing relative to GDP. During the 1980s and early 1990s, however, provincial deficits grew dramatically. The provincial debt grew from roughly 4 percent of GDP in 1980 to 20 percent in 1993. Since then, most provincial governments have reduced or eliminated their deficits, and some are operating small surpluses.

An International Perspective

Figure 31-4 shows how the size of government debt in Canada compares with those in the other major developed economies.[1] Canada's debt (combining all levels of government) is slightly above average among the G7 countries. The two high-debt countries are Japan and Italy. Italy, with a debt-to-GDP ratio of almost 120 percent, has been a high-debt country for many years. Japan, in contrast, has only recently become a high-debt country. In the late 1990s, in an attempt to stimulate its stagnant economy, Japan increased its government spending considerably. As a result of the fiscal expansion and a significant recession, Japan's debt-to-GDP ratio increased by 40 percentage points between 1995 and 2000.

---

[1]These data are not directly comparable with those in Figure 31-3 for two reasons. First, Figure 31-4 shows the debt of all levels of government combined, whereas Figure 31-3 shows just federal government debt. Second, Figure 31-4 shows *gross* debt whereas Figure 31-3 shows *net* debt. Gross debt is higher than net debt in Canada because some federal debt is held as an asset by provincial governments.

Some Analytical Issues

In the next section we discuss some potential effects of budget deficits and surpluses on the aggregate economy. Before doing this, however, we must examine some basic analytical issues: deficits and the stance of fiscal policy; changes in the debt-to-GDP ratio; and the relationship between government deficits and national saving.

The Stance of Fiscal Policy

In Chapters 23 and 25 we examined some basic issues surrounding **fiscal policy**, which is the use of government spending and tax polices to alter real GDP. We noted there that changes in expenditure and taxation normally lead to changes in the government's budget deficit or surplus. Thus, it is tempting to view changes in the government's budget deficit as the result of changes in fiscal policy. For example, we could interpret a decrease in the deficit as indicating a contractionary fiscal policy, since the fall in the deficit is associated with either a reduction in government expenditures or an increase in tax revenue (or both). Was the dramatic fall in the Canadian federal budget deficit between 1995 and 1999 *purely* the result of fiscal policy?

No. In general, only some changes in the deficit are due to discretionary changes in the government's expenditure or taxation policies. Other changes have nothing to do with explicit changes in policy, but instead are the result of changes in the level of economic activity that are outside the influence of government policy. If our goal is to judge the stance of fiscal policy, however, it is only the changes in the deficit *caused by changes in policy* that are relevant.

FIGURE 31-4   Consolidated Government Gross Debt, G7 Countries, 2000

(bar chart: Gross Debt as Percentage of GDP)

Canada's government debt is slightly above average by the standards of the richest developed countries. The debt-to-GDP ratios shown here are forecasts for the year 2000 made in 1999. The data are for all levels of government combined.

(Source: These data are available on the website for the Organization for Economic Cooperation and Development (OECD): www.oecd.org.)

fiscal policy The use of the government's tax and spending policies in an effort to influence the level of GDP.

The Budget Deficit Function

To see why the budget deficit can rise or fall even when there is no change in fiscal policy, recall the equation defining the government's budget deficit. Since government transfers are payments by the government to the private sector, and taxes are payments made by the private sector to the government, it is convenient to rewrite the government's budget deficit by combining taxes and transfers to get

$$\text{Budget Deficit} = (G + i \times D) - (T - TR)$$

The key point now is that the level of taxes and transfers typically depends on the level of national income, even with unchanged policy. For example, as income rises the level of revenue raised through income taxation also rises. Furthermore, as national income (real GDP) rises there are typically fewer transfers (such as welfare or unemployment insurance) made to the private sector. Thus, $(T - TR)$ increases when national income increases. In contrast, the level of government purchases and debt-service payments can

For macroeconomic data that are comparable across countries, see the OECD's website: www.oecd.org.

be viewed as more-or-less independent of the level of national income, at least over short periods of time. Thus, with no changes in expenditure or taxation policies, the budget deficit will tend to increase in recessions and fall in booms. That is, as national income rises, the government's budget deficit falls.

For a given spending and taxing policy, the budget deficit rises as real GDP falls, and falls as real GDP rises.

budget deficit function   A relationship which plots the government's budget deficit as a function of the level of real GDP.

Figure 31-5 plots this basic relationship, which is called the **budget deficit function**. When the government determines its expenditure and taxation polices, it determines the *position* of the budget deficit function. A more expansionary fiscal policy shifts the budget deficit function up. A more contractionary fiscal policy shifts the budget deficit function down. In contrast, a change in the level of real GDP in the absence of any policy change will represent a *movement along* the budget deficit function. Thus, for a given set of policies, the budget deficit will decrease when Y rises and increase when Y falls. Similarly, for a given level of Y, an expansionary fiscal policy shifts the function up and increases the budget deficit; a contractionary fiscal policy shifts the function down and reduces the budget deficit.

Fiscal policy determines the position of the budget deficit function. Changes in real GDP lead to movements along a given budget deficit function.

FIGURE 31-5   The Budget Deficit Function and Cyclical Adjustment

(i) The budget deficit function   (ii) Change in the measured deficit   (iii) Change in the cyclically adjusted deficit

The budget deficit can change either because of a change in fiscal policy or because of a change in real GDP. Parts (i) and (ii) illustrate the same budget deficit function, showing that the budget deficit declines (budget surplus rises) as real GDP rises. The budget deficit function is labelled B.

Part (ii) defines the cyclically adjusted deficit (CAD) as the budget deficit that would exist if real GDP were equal to Y^*. In the example, the CAD is a deficit. At a sufficiently high income Y_0, the actual budget would be in surplus by an amount S_0. At output lower than Y^*, such as Y_1, the actual budget would be in deficit by D', more than the amount of the CAD. Along the curve in part (ii), fiscal policy is unchanged. The deficit (and surplus) changes only because real GDP changes.

Part (iii) shows how the actual deficit (or surplus) might move in a different direction from the CAD. Suppose that the economy starts at Y_0, with fiscal policy given by B_0. If fiscal policy is made more restrictive, through some combination of higher taxes and lower government purchases, the budget deficit function shifts to B_1. At the same time, if output should fall to Y_1, the budget surplus of S will turn into a deficit of D'. By looking at the actual budget balance, one would see the budget move from surplus to deficit, suggesting, incorrectly, that fiscal policy had become more stimulative. Focusing on the CAD, however, the level of budget balance at Y^* makes it clear that B_1 is more restrictive than B_0; that is, the CAD is smaller with the fiscal policy given by B_1 than that given by B_0.

The Cyclically Adjusted Deficit

Given the problem of using the budget deficit to gauge the stance of fiscal policy, economists define the **cyclically adjusted deficit (CAD)** as the budget deficit that would exist with the current set of policies if real GDP were equal to potential GDP, Y^*. This is also called the *structural budget deficit* or the *full-employment budget deficit*. This is shown in parts (ii) and (iii) of Figure 31-5. All changes in the cyclically adjusted deficit reflect changes in the stance of fiscal policy, because they come only from shifts in the budget deficit function.

Figure 31-6 shows the cyclically adjusted deficit in Canada, and plots it together with the actual budget deficit. Both are expressed as percentages of GDP and represent the combined budget deficits of all levels of government. Unlike the actual budget deficit, which can be precisely measured, the cyclically adjusted deficit can only be estimated. The reason is that its value depends on the value of potential GDP, Y^*, which itself is not directly observable and hence must be estimated. Note from Figure 31-6 that the actual deficit is larger than the cyclically adjusted deficit during times of recessionary gaps such as 1981–1985 and 1990–1997. This relationship reflects the fact that during these periods actual GDP is less than potential GDP and thus actual tax revenues are *less than they would be if output were equal to potential*. Conversely, the actual budget deficit is less than the cyclically adjusted deficit during periods of inflationary gaps, such as 1986–1990, reflecting the fact that during these periods actual GDP is greater than potential and thus tax revenues are *greater than they would be if output were equal to potential*. In those years where the actual deficit is approximately equal to the cyclically adjusted deficit, such as 1985, 1990, and 1999, real GDP is approximately equal to potential.

The stance of fiscal policy is shown by the *changes* in the cyclically adjusted deficit. For example, the dramatic rise in the cyclically adjusted deficit from 1981 to 1985 reveals a considerable fiscal expansion; the decline from 1985 through 1988 reveals a fiscal contraction. From 1989 to 1995, the path of the cyclically adjusted deficit suggests that the stance of fiscal policy was roughly constant. Since 1995, the decline in the cyclically adjusted deficit reflects a very considerable fiscal contraction.

The stance of fiscal policy—that is, whether fiscal policy is expansionary or contractionary—is determined by changes in the cyclically adjusted deficit.

cyclically adjusted deficit (CAD) An estimate of what the government budget deficit would be if real GDP were at its potential level.

FIGURE 31-6   The Actual and Cyclically Adjusted Deficit, Combined Government, 1982–2000

The difference between the actual budget deficit and the cyclically adjusted budget deficit reveals the level of output compared to potential. The changes in the cyclically adjusted deficit show changes in the stance of fiscal policy. The actual budget deficit is above the cyclically adjusted budget deficit when output is below potential; the actual deficit is less than the cyclically adjusted deficit when output is above potential. An increase in the cyclically adjusted deficit reveals a fiscal expansion; a decrease reveals a fiscal contraction. The values for 1999 and 2000 are forecasts.

(*Source: OECD Economic Outlook*, June 1999)

The Debt-to-GDP Ratio

We discussed above that in order to gauge the importance of government deficits and debt they should be considered relative to the size of the economy. Public debate, however, is often couched in terms of the absolute size of the budget deficit. Here we examine the link between the overall budget deficit, the primary budget deficit, and changes in the debt-to-GDP ratio.

Changes in the Debt-to-GDP Ratio

With a little work, it is possible to write a simple expression that relates the government's primary budget deficit to the change in the debt-to-GDP ratio. (To see the complete derivation of this equation, see *Extensions in Theory 31-1*.) The equation is:

$$\Delta d = x + (r - g) \times d$$

where d is the debt-to-GDP ratio, x is the government's *primary* budget deficit as a percentage of GDP, r is the real interest rate, g is the growth rate of real GDP, and Δd is the *change* in the debt-to-GDP ratio.

This simple equation shows that there are two separate forces which tend to increase the debt-to-GDP ratio. First, if the real interest rate exceeds the growth rate of real GDP (if r exceeds g), then the debt-to-GDP ratio will rise, and Δd will be positive. Second, if the government has a *primary* budget deficit (if x is positive) then the debt-to-GDP ratio will rise.

The Importance of Real Interest Rates.

It is the *real* interest rate, and not the nominal interest rate, that is important for determining the change in the debt-to-GDP ratio. Many commentators argue that high nominal interest rates are largely responsible for increasing the government's debt-service requirements and thus pushing up the deficit and debt. But this view is only partly correct. Although it is the nominal interest rate that determines how a given stock of debt will accumulate over time, this view misses the point that it is the accumulation of the *real* stock of debt that matters in terms of the government's *real* financial liabilities. And as we saw in Chapter 29 when we discussed inflation, high nominal interest rates are often associated with high inflation. Thus, although high nominal interest rates increase the government's debt-service requirements, the accompanying high inflation reduces the real value of the government's debt. The accumulation of the government's stock of *real* debt therefore depends on the difference between the nominal interest rate and the rate of inflation. This difference is simply the real interest rate, r. It follows, therefore, that changes in the debt-to-GDP ratio (which is a *real* variable) depend on the difference between the growth rate of the real stock of debt, r, and the growth rate of real GDP, g.

The Role of the Primary Deficit.

If our focus is to be on the debt-to-GDP ratio, rather than on the absolute size of the debt, then tracking the behaviour of the overall budget deficit may be misleading. Suppose that $r = g$ and thus the second term in the equation above is zero. Further, suppose that the government is running a small primary surplus, so that total tax revenues more than cover program spending. In this case, the primary surplus (x is negative) implies that the debt-to-GDP ratio is *falling;* but it is entirely possible that the overall budget deficit is positive, revealing simply that the debt-service payments exceed the primary surplus.

Stabilizing the Debt-to-GDP Ratio

Suppose the government's goal is to prevent further increases in the debt-to-GDP ratio. If the real interest rate exceeds the growth rate of real GDP—a reasonable description of the Canadian economy over the past two decades—then a government with a positive stock of outstanding debt *must* run a primary surplus in order to stabilize the debt-to-

EXTENSIONS IN THEORY 31-1

Changes in the Debt-to-GDP Ratio

This box derives the simple equation in the text describing the change in the debt-to-GDP ratio. Let d be the debt-to-GDP ratio and let Δd be the amount by which d changes annually. Since d is a ratio, its change over time depends on the change in the numerator relative to the change in the denominator. That is, the debt-to-GDP ratio will increase if the stock of debt grows more quickly than GDP; it will decrease if the stock of debt grows less quickly than GDP. Representing the *percentage change* in d as $\Delta d/d$, we have*

$$\frac{\Delta d}{d} = \frac{\Delta D}{D} - \frac{\Delta GDP}{GDP}$$

Now think about each of these terms separately. As you will recall from the first section of this chapter, the change in the stock of debt, ΔD, is equal to the amount of new government borrowing—that is, it is equal to the budget deficit. From the government's budget constraint, this is equal to $(G + TR + i \times D - T)$. The second term in the equation above is the growth rate of GDP. Note that the growth rate of GDP depends on both the rate of growth of real output and the rate of inflation. If we let g be the rate of growth of *real* GDP and π be the rate of inflation, then $g + \pi$ is the growth rate of (nominal) GDP. We therefore rewrite the expression above to get

_____

*For any variable X that is equal to the ratio of two other variables, Y/Z, the percentage change in X is closely approximated by the percentage change in Y minus the percentage change in Z. The lower are the rates of change of Y and Z, the better is this approximation.

$$\frac{\Delta d}{d} = \frac{G + TR - T + i \times D}{D} - (g + \pi)$$

Now we multiply both sides by d to get an expression for the absolute change in the debt-to-GDP ratio:

$$\Delta d = \frac{G + TR - T + i \times D}{D} \times d - (g + \pi) \times d$$

Since d is equal to D/GDP, it follows that d/D is equal to $1/GDP$. Our equation can thus be simplified:

$$\Delta d = \frac{G + TR - T + i \times D}{GDP} - (g + \pi) \times d$$

Now recall that $(G + TR - T)$ is the primary budget deficit. Let x be this primary budget deficit *as a percentage of GDP* and express the debt-service payments also as a percentage of GDP. This gives

$$\Delta d = x + i \times d - (g + \pi) \times d$$

Finally, recall that the real interest rate is equal to the nominal interest rate minus the rate of inflation,

$$r = i - \pi$$

We now combine terms to get

$$\Delta d = x + (r - g) \times d$$

which is the equation shown in the text.

GDP ratio. Furthermore, the larger is the real interest rate relative to the growth rate of GDP, the larger is the primary surplus required to stabilize the debt-to-GDP ratio.

To see this, let x^* be the value of the primary budget deficit that is consistent with a stable debt-to-GDP ratio—that is, x^* is the value of x such that Δd equals zero. From our equation above, setting Δd equal to zero results in

$$x^* = -(r - g) \times d$$

This equation shows the basic point that if the debt-to-GDP ratio is being pushed up by a real interest rate which exceeds the real growth rate of GDP, then a stable debt-to-GDP ratio is only possible with a value of x which is negative—that is, a primary budget surplus.

If the real interest rate exceeds the growth rate of real GDP, then stabilizing the debt-to-GDP ratio requires a primary budget surplus.

For an illustration of this central point, consider some of the numbers facing the federal minister of finance at the time of the March 1999 budget. The real interest rate on government debt was about 4 percent while the real growth rate of the economy was about 2.8 percent. Given the existing debt-to-GDP ratio of about 0.65, these data implied a value of x^* equal to $-(0.040 - 0.028) \times (0.65) = -0.0078$. Thus, the federal government would have had to run a primary surplus of about 0.8 percent of GDP in order to keep the debt-to-GDP ratio constant. As it turned out, the actual primary surplus in 1999 was much bigger than necessary to stabilize the debt-to-GDP ratio. The primary surplus was about 5 percent of GDP (an overall surplus of 0.4 percent and debt-service payments of about 4.6 percent), so the debt-to-GDP ratio declined.

Government Deficits and National Saving

As we will see in the next section, the effects of government deficits on real GDP and interest rates depend in large part on the relationship between government deficits and national saving. We therefore examine this important issue now.

Defining Terms

As we saw in Chapter 22, private saving is the difference between disposable income and consumption. And as we saw in Chapter 23, government saving is the difference between government tax revenues and government purchases. That is, government saving is equal to the budget surplus. National saving is the sum of government saving and private saving:

$$\text{National Saving} = \text{Private Saving} + \text{Government Saving}$$

Since government saving is equal to the budget surplus, an increase in the budget deficit is a reduction in government saving.

$$\text{National Saving} = \text{Private Saving} - \text{Government Budget Deficit}$$

The effect of budget deficits on the level of national saving thus depends on the link between budget deficits and private saving. For example, suppose that the government budget deficit increases by $1 billion. If this *reduction* in government saving leads to an *increase* in private saving by exactly $1 billion, there will be no change in national saving. On the other hand, if private saving rises by less than $1 billion, national saving will fall as a result of the increase in the budget deficit.

What is the link between the government deficit and the level of private saving? The answer lies in recognizing that—eventually—all government expenditures must be paid for out of taxes. Earlier in the chapter we said that expenditures during any given year could be financed either by tax revenues or by borrowing. But money borrowed in one year must *eventually* be repaid. Thus, borrowing today means higher taxes in the future to repay that debt.

Government debt is a postponed tax liability. An increase in the deficit today must be matched by an increase in taxes at some point in the future.

The link between government deficits and private saving then rests on the extent to which the current population of taxpayers recognizes the requirement for higher future taxes when the government increases its current borrowing. For example, if the government decides to reduce taxes this year by $5 billion and issue $5 billion in new bonds, do the taxpayers recognize that those bonds will need to be repaid with higher taxes ($5 billion plus interest) in the future?

Ricardian Equivalence

The link between government deficits and private saving is associated with the idea of **Ricardian Equivalence,** named after the Classical economist David Ricardo (1772–1823), and brought back to prominence among modern-day economists through the work of Robert Barro, currently at Harvard University. The central proposition of Ricardian Equivalence is that consumers recognize government borrowing as a future tax liability and thus they view taxes as *equivalent* to government borrowing in terms of the effect on their own wealth. Therefore, a reduction in taxes and an increase in borrowing (or the reverse case) do not affect the wealth of the private sector and thus does not affect their consumption behaviour.

An example to help you understand the basic idea of Ricardian Equivalence is illustrated in Figure 31-7. Suppose that the government decides to reduce current taxes by $5 billion *with unchanged government expenditures,* and thus decides to increase its current borrowing by $5 billion. If current taxpayers recognize that an increase in government borrowing of $5 billion today represents an increase in their future taxes of

Ricardian Equivalence   The proposition that the method of financing government spending (taxes or borrowing) has no effect on national saving because private saving will just offset any government dissaving.

FIGURE 31-7   A Tax Reduction and Ricardian Equivalence

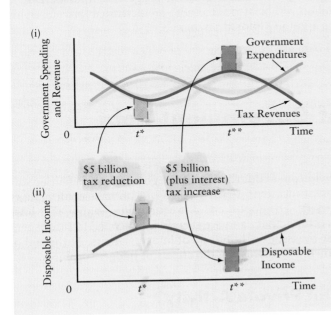

For an unchanged path of government expenditures, a reduction in taxes today must be matched with an increase in future taxes. **Ricardian consumers will not feel wealthier as a result.** Part (i) shows the initial path of government taxes and expenditures, with the associated deficits and surpluses. Part (ii) shows the initial path of disposable income for the private sector.

If the government reduces taxes by $5 billion in year t^*, the deficit will be increased by that amount. Disposable income at t^* will also increase by $5 billion. But in some future year, say t^{**}, the government will need to raise taxes by $5 billion (plus interest) to repay that debt. When this happens, the deficit will fall but so will disposable income. Ricardian consumers recognize that there is no change in their lifetime wealth and hence they do not spend more at t^* when their disposable income rises. Non-Ricardian consumers do not foresee the tax increase at t^{**} and thus *do* feel wealthier at t^*—they will increase their consumption at t^*.

$5 billion (plus interest), then the current generation of taxpayers will not feel any more or less wealthy as a result of the reduction in current taxes, and consequently will not change their level of current expenditure on goods and services. But, if their consumption is unchanged and their disposable income is higher by $5 billion, then their current saving must increase by the full amount of the reduction in government saving. Thus, "Ricardian" consumers faced with a change in the government deficit will adjust their private saving so as to keep national saving constant.

Now suppose that current taxpayers do perceive an increase in their wealth when their current taxes are reduced. There are several reasons why this might be so. One possibility is that individuals might be short-sighted and thus tend to place more emphasis on current tax reductions than on tax increases in the distant future. This would certainly be true if today's generation of taxpayers knew that the future tax increases would have to be paid by other people. Another possibility is that there may be a great deal of uncertainty about the government's future spending plans so that it is unclear whether the current tax reduction will be offset by future tax increases or matched by future expenditure reductions. Whatever the reason, suppose that the current generation *feels* wealthier as a result of the reduction in current taxes. We then expect them to increase their current expenditures on goods and services. As a result of the higher expenditures, private saving of such "non-Ricardian" individuals will therefore increase by less than the reduction in government saving, leading to an overall reduction in national saving.

"Ricardian" consumers will not feel wealthier as a result of the government borrowing because they recognize the increase in their future tax liabilities. "Non-Ricardian" consumers do not recognize this future liability and thus feel wealthier when the government borrows.

Whether taxpayers recognize the future tax liabilities associated with government deficits is ultimately an empirical question. Most evidence suggests that Ricardian Equivalence does not hold completely. That is, the evidence suggests that an increase in the government deficit by $5 billion will be associated with an increase in private saving by less than $5 billion and thus a fall in national saving.

Most evidence suggests that an increase in the government deficit leads to a decrease in the level of national saving.

The Effects of Government Debt and Deficits

Let's now examine why we should care about the size of the government deficit or surplus. We begin with the important idea that deficits *crowd out* private-sector activity and thereby harm future generations. The opposite idea is equally important—that budget surpluses *crowd in* private-sector activity and are therefore beneficial to future generations. In this section, we pose the issue as the effects of budget deficits. At the end of the section we review the arguments by discussing the effects of budget surpluses.

crowding out The offsetting reduction in private expenditure caused by the rise in interest rates that follows an expansionary fiscal policy.

Do Deficits Crowd Out Private Activity?

It is useful to make the distinction between closed and open economies. We consider the two cases separately.

Investment in Closed Economies

In a closed economy, the amount of national saving is exactly equal to the amount of domestic investment; after all, the only way that a closed economy can save is to accumulate physical capital. Suppose in a closed economy there is an increase in the budget deficit brought about by a reduction in taxes. What is the effect on domestic investment? As we saw in the previous section, the answer to this question depends on the degree to which taxpayers are Ricardian—that is, on the degree to which current taxpayers recognize that today's deficit must be financed by higher future taxes. If taxpayers are not purely Ricardian, then private saving will rise by less than the fall in government saving. This response implies a decrease in the supply of national saving. The resulting excess demand for funds will put upward pressure on the domestic real interest rate. But as the real interest rate increases, those components of aggregate demand that are sensitive to the interest rate—investment in particular—will fall. The result is what is called the **crowding out** of domestic investment; it is shown in Figure 31-8.

If government borrowing to finance the deficit drives up the interest rate, some private investment will be crowded out.

Net Exports in Open Economies

The effect of budget deficits in an open economy is a little different. Consider once again the possibility that the Canadian government reduces taxes and thus increases its budget deficit. Furthermore, suppose that taxpayers are not purely Ricardian so that private saving rises by less than the fall in government saving. What is the effect of such a fall in national saving in an open economy like Canada's? As real interest rates rise in Canada, foreigners are attracted to the higher-yield Canadian assets and thus foreign financial capital flows into Canada. But since Canadian dollars are required in order to buy Canadian interest-earning assets, this capital inflow increases the demand for Canadian dollars and thus increases the external value of the Canadian dollar (the Canadian dollar appreciates).

This appreciation makes Canadian goods more expensive relative to foreign goods, inducing an increase in imports and a reduction in exports, thereby reducing Canada's net exports. In an open economy like Canada, therefore, a rise in the government deficit leads to an appreciation of the currency and to a crowding out of net exports.

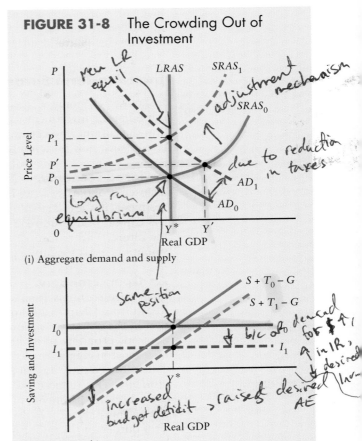

FIGURE 31-8   The Crowding Out of Investment

(i) Aggregate demand and supply

(ii) Saving and investment

For a closed economy whose real GDP equals potential, an increase in the budget deficit will cause a reduction in national saving and investment. Consider a closed economy that is in long-run equilibrium at Y^* and P_0 in part (i). The same position is shown in part (ii) as saving equal to investment at Y^* and I_0. Suppose that the government reduces its taxes from T_0 to T_1, thus increasing the budget deficit. This raises desired aggregate expenditure (and lowers desired national saving) at all levels of income. In part (i), the new short-run equilibrium is at Y' and P'. The adjustment mechanism will then cause factor prices to rise, shifting the SRAS curve from $SRAS_0$ to $SRAS_1$. The new long-run equilibrium will be at Y^* and P_1.

The effect of this change on saving and investment can be seen in part (ii). At the new long-run equilibrium, real income is unchanged at Y^*, but the price level is higher. This implies that the demand for money will have increased, causing a rise in interest rates. These higher interest rates will reduce desired investment expenditure, shown in the figure as a reduction from I_0 to I_1.

In an open economy, instead of driving up interest rates sufficiently to crowd out private investment, the government budget deficit tends to attract foreign financial capital, appreciate the domestic currency, and crowd out net exports.

The Long-Term Burden of the Debt

In a closed economy, a rise in the government deficit pushes up interest rates and crowds out domestic investment. In an open economy a rise in the government deficit appreciates the currency and crowds out net exports. Despite the apparent differences in these two effects, they both imply a *long-term burden of government debt*.

A Closed Economy.

The overall effect of the increase in the government deficit in a closed economy is a rise in the real interest rate and a fall in the level of domestic investment. But less current investment means that there will be a smaller stock of physical capital in the future, and thus a reduced ability to produce goods and services in the future. This reduction in future production possibilities, which implies lower consumption levels for future generations, is the long-term burden of the debt.

An Open Economy.

The overall effect of the increase in the government deficit in an open economy is an appreciation of the currency and a reduction in net exports. Recall from Chapter 23, however, that such a reduction in net exports implies a reduction in the country's *national asset formation*. This in turn increases the need for the domestic economy to make interest or dividend payments to foreigners in the future. Instead of having a smaller future capital stock as a result of the government's budget deficit, the country has an unchanged capital stock but *less of it is owned by domestic residents*. This reduced ownership lowers the domestic residents' future stream of income because payments must be paid to the foreign owners of the domestic capital stock. This reduction in the future stream of income for domestic residents is the long-term burden of the public debt in an open economy.

In both open and closed economies, the long-term burden of public debt takes the form of reduced consumption for future generations.

Does Government Debt Harm Future Generations?

The previous discussion reveals an important aspect of the costs of government debt and deficits:

Government deficits generate a redistribution of resources away from future generations toward the current generation.

After all, the government deficits are being used to finance goods and services that are provided to the current generation, but that will be financed by taxes levied on future generations.

This last sentence suggests that current government deficits are always financing goods and services that are provided to the current generation. Is this really true? Some government spending is on goods and services that will continue to be used well into the future. For example, if the government increases its current borrowing to finance the building of bridges or the expansion of highways, future generations will receive some of the benefits of this government spending. And, given that future generations will reap the benefits of some of these projects, it may be appropriate that future generations pay some of the taxes required to finance such projects.

Whether current government deficits impose a burden on future generations depends on the nature of the government goods and services being financed by the deficit. At one extreme, the government borrowing may finance a project that generates a return only to future generations, and thus the future generations may not be made worse off by today's budget deficit. An example might be the government's financing of long-term medical research projects that generate a return only in the distant future. At the other extreme, the government deficit may finance some government program that benefits only the current generation, and thus the future generations are inappropriately saddled with the future tax bill. An example might be the government's financing of a world's fair such as Expo '86 in Vancouver or a major sporting event, like the 1999 Pan Am Games in Winnipeg.

Budget deficits used to finance investment projects may not harm future generations because the future generations will benefit from the investment.

The concern that deficits may be inappropriately placing a financial burden on future generations has led some economists to advocate the idea of *capital budgeting* by the government. Under this scheme, the government would essentially classify all of its expenditures as either consumption or investment; the former would be spending that mostly benefits the current generation while the latter would be spending that mostly benefits future generations.

With capital budgeting, government deficits could be used to minimize the undesirable redistributions of income between generations. For example, the government might be committed to borrowing no more in any given year than the expenditures classified as investments. In this way, future generations would receive benefits from current government spending that are approximately equivalent to the future taxes they will pay.

Does Government Debt Hamper Economic Policy?

The costs imposed on future generations by government debt are very real. Unfortunately, the fact that these costs sometimes occur in the very distant future often leads us to ignore their importance. But other costs associated with the presence of government debt are more immediately apparent. In particular, government debt may make the conduct of monetary and fiscal policy more difficult.

Monetary Policy

To see how a large stock of government debt can hamper the conduct of monetary policy, consider a country that has a high debt-to-GDP ratio and that has a real interest rate above the growth rate of GDP. As we saw previously, the debt-to-GDP ratio will continue to grow in this situation unless the government starts running significant primary budget *surpluses*. But such primary surpluses require either increases in taxation or reductions in program spending, both of which are politically unpopular. If such primary surpluses look unlikely to be achieved in the near future, both foreign and domestic creditors may come to expect that the government will put pressure on the central bank to purchase—or *monetize*—an increasing portion of its deficit. Such monetization means that the money supply is increasing and will eventually be reflected in higher inflation. Any ensuing inflation would thus erode the real value of the bonds held by creditors. Such fears of future debt monetization will lead to expectations of future inflation and thus will put upward pressure on nominal interest rates and on some prices and wages. Thus, even in the absence of any actions by the central bank to increase the rate of growth of the money supply, a large government debt may lead to the *expectation* of future inflation, thus hampering the task of the central bank in keeping inflation and inflationary expectations low.

In December 1995, before the federal government had been successful in reducing its large annual budget deficits and thus slowing the rise of the debt-to-GDP ratio, the Governor of the Bank of Canada, Gordon Thiessen, appeared before the House of Commons Standing Committee on Public Accounts. His comments to that committee expressed this view that high levels of government debt generate concerns on the part of creditors.

> *. . . We would probably all agree . . . that our society needs to sort out its views about acceptable levels of taxation and the size of government, and those views can influence the amount of debt our society can afford to carry. However, when you reach a high debt-to-GDP ratio, what is sustainable is also very much influenced by the willingness of investors in financial markets to hold your debt.*
>
> *I do not mean to imply that financial markets might suddenly decide to stop lending to Canadian governments. What happens, as recent experience has shown, is that at very high levels of debt, there may be an increasing nervousness among lenders so that they would only continue to hold Canadian government debt at much higher interest rates.*[2]

Fiscal Policy

In Chapter 23 we saw that fiscal policy could potentially be used to stabilize aggregate demand and thereby stabilize real output. For example, in a recession the government might reduce tax rates or increase spending to stimulate aggregate demand; in a booming economy, the government might reduce spending or increase tax rates to prevent the economy from overheating. Having cyclically-adjusted budget deficits in recessions and cyclically-adjusted budget surpluses in booms is one obvious way of implementing *counter-cyclical fiscal policy*.

How does the presence of government debt affect the government's ability to conduct such counter-cyclical fiscal policy? Perhaps the easiest way to answer this question is to recall the equation that describes the change in the debt-to-GDP ratio:

$$\Delta d = x + (r - g) \times d$$

This equation shows that the size of the *change* in the debt-to-GDP ratio depends on the *level* of the debt-to-GDP ratio. For example, if the real interest rate exceeds the growth rate of real GDP, so that $r - g$ is positive, then the increase in the debt-to-GDP ratio (Δd) will be higher if d is already high than if it is low (for any given value of x).

With this relationship in mind, consider the dilemma faced during a recession by a government that is considering an expansionary fiscal policy. On the one hand, the short-run benefits in terms of raising the level of real GDP seem clear; on the other hand, the same government may be wary of taking actions that lead to large increases in the debt-to-GDP ratio.

If the stock of outstanding government debt is small relative to the size of the economy, then the government has a great deal of flexibility in conducting counter-cyclical fiscal policy. The small value of d implies that d will be rising only slowly in the absence of a primary deficit. Thus, there may well be room for the government to increase the primary deficit—either by increasing program spending or by reducing tax rates—without generating a large increase in the debt-to-GDP ratio. But the government has significantly less flexibility if the stock of outstanding government debt is already very large. In this case, the high value of d means that even in the absence of a primary budget deficit, d will be increasing quickly. Thus, any increase in the primary deficit brought

---

[2]Comments by Gordon Thiessen in the *Bank of Canada Review,* Winter 1995–1996.

about by the counter-cyclical fiscal policy runs the danger of generating increases in the debt-to-GDP ratio that may be viewed by creditors as unsustainable.

The idea that a large and rising stock of government debt could "tie the hands" of the government in times when it would otherwise want to conduct counter-cyclical fiscal policy was brought to the fore of Canadian economic policy by the late Douglas Purvis of Queen's University (and a coauthor on this textbook for many years). Purvis argued in the mid 1980s that Canadian government deficits must be brought under control quickly so that the debt would not accumulate to the point where the government would have no room left for fiscal stabilization policy. These warnings were not heeded. By the onset of the next recession in 1990, the federal government had added roughly $200 billion to the stock of debt and, predictably, the government felt unable to use discretionary fiscal policy to reduce some of the effects of the recession.

The Current "Fiscal Dividend"

We have been discussing the effects of government debt and deficits on the economy. As we saw earlier, government deficits were an important part of the Canadian economic environment for over twenty years from the early 1970s to the mid 1990s. But by 1998, after several years of devoted deficit fighting, the federal government had its first surplus in over twenty years, and most of the provinces had also eliminated their budget deficits.

By late 1999, it appeared that the federal government would be running significant budget surpluses for the next several years. According to forecasts made by the Department of Finance in November 1999, the projected surplus for the 1999–2000 fiscal year was $9.5 billion. Furthermore, *if the government maintained its 1999 fiscal stance*, the growth of the economy was expected to lead to an annual surplus of roughly $30 billion by the 2004–05 fiscal year. The *cumulative* surplus between 1999 and 2005 was projected to be roughly $100 billion. Such forecasts naturally sparked a considerable debate about how best to spend this "fiscal dividend"—a term used to describe the budget "return" from several years' "investment" in fiscal cutbacks.

Some people argued the need to restore spending in health care, education, and other social programs to the levels that existed in 1995, before the federal government reduced their transfer payments to the provinces. Others argued the need to reduce income-tax rates, in part to stem an alleged "brain drain"—the exodus of highly trained workers—from Canada to the United States. A third group advocated delaying any spending increases or tax reductions until after a few years' of budget surpluses could make a noticeable reduction in the stock of government debt. The Liberal government of Jean Chrétien advocated a so-called 50-50 rule whereby half of any projected surpluses would be used to boost spending and half would be used to finance some combination of tax reductions and debt repayment. For example, a projected surplus of $20 billion might be used to finance higher spending of $10 billion, lower taxes of $5 billion, and debt repayment of $5 billion. Note, however, that these actions would largely eliminate the projected surplus. In our example, the projected surplus of $20 billion becomes—after the 50-50 rule is imposed—an actual surplus of only $5 billion.

If this 50-50 rule is followed into the near future, with some part of each projected surplus being used to repay the debt, then the federal government will record a stream of budget surpluses, at least for the next few years. What will be the effect on the Canadian economy of such surpluses? To analyse the economic effects of budget surpluses, we need only to reverse the arguments that we have developed in this chapter. After all, an increase in the budget surplus is just the same as a reduction in the budget deficit. But it will be useful to review and summarize these arguments. If the Canadian federal and provincial governments succeed in running budget surpluses over the next few years, our economic theory tells us we should start to see the following things:

- Assuming that consumers are *not* fully Ricardian, the rise in the government budget surplus will raise the level of national saving.
- The rise in national saving will put downward pressure on interest rates and "crowd in" investment.
- The lower interest rates will lead to less capital inflow and thus the Canadian dollar will depreciate, leading to a rise in Canada's net exports.
- As the surpluses continue, the stock of government debt will actually be falling. Combined with a growing economy, this will make the debt-to-GDP ratio fall relatively sharply.
- The lower debt-to-GDP ratio will reduce bondholders' fears of future monetization and thus reduce inflation expectations.
- The lower debt-to-GDP ratio will restore the government's flexibility to use countercyclical fiscal policy if the economy enters another recession.

Balanced Budgets

As we have seen in this chapter, government budget deficits contribute to aggregate demand and thus have the potential to be used as an integral part of a fiscal policy designed to stabilize real GDP. However, we have also seen that government budget deficits crowd out private economic activity and impose a long-term burden, either through a reduced stock of physical capital or through greater foreign indebtedness. A tradeoff therefore appears to exist between the desirable short-run stabilizing role of deficits and the undesirable long-run costs of government debt. This tradeoff has been the source of constant debate. Here we examine some possible solutions involving different concepts of a balanced budget.

Before going on, however, note that not everyone agrees that the accumulation of government debt represents a problem. One argument often seen in the popular press is that debt itself is not a problem—the problem is that the debt is held by foreigners rather than by domestic residents. Foreign ownership of the debt is alleged to be undesirable because interest payments are made to foreigners, reducing the income available for Canadians. Such claims have even led to the proposal that the Canadian government issue new "Canada-only" bonds to Canadians and then use the newly raised funds to redeem foreign-held government debt. *Applying Economic Concepts 31-1* explains why such a policy would be unlikely to change Canadian national income.

We now go on to examine different concepts of balanced budgets.

See Chapter 31 of www.pearsoned.ca/lipsey for an interview with Paul Martin in which he discusses some of the political difficulties of reducing the budget deficit: "*Regaining Canada's Fiscal Levers,*" *World Economic Affairs.*

Annually Balanced Budgets

Much current rhetoric of fiscal restraint calls for the government budget to be balanced every year. Though there has clearly been a significant move toward deficit reduction in Canada over the past few years, both federally and among the provinces, there has been little emphasis placed on the idea that governments should be constrained to balance their budgets *every year*.

Balancing the budget on an annual basis would be extremely difficult to achieve. The reason is that a significant portion of the government budget is beyond the short-term control of the government, and a further large amount is hard to change quickly. For example, the entire debt-service component of government expenditures is determined by past borrowing and thus cannot be altered by the current government. In addition, as we saw in our discussion of the cyclically adjusted deficit, changes in real GDP that are beyond the control of the government lead to significant changes in tax revenues (and transfer payments) and thus generate significant changes in the budget deficit.

APPLYING ECONOMIC CONCEPTS 31-1
A Common Myth About Government Debt

In 1999 about one-quarter of the federal government's debt was held outside of Canada. Thus, of the $44 billion in interest payments made on the government debt in 1999, roughly $11 billion was paid to foreigners. This fact has led many commentators in the popular press to suggest that Canada "reclaim" its national debt and keep these "lost" interest payments. These observers seem to believe that if more of the Canadian government debt were held within Canada, then Canada would be a richer country.

How do we "reclaim" the debt? The federal government simply has to issue new debt to Canadians and use the proceeds of this borrowing to redeem existing debt held by foreigners. By so doing, the fraction of government debt held by Canadians would be increased and the fraction held by foreigners decreased. Advocates of this proposal argue that the result would be higher Canadian income in the long run as fewer interest payments are sent to foreign creditors.

Proponents of this view fail to recognize the importance of an *integrated* world capital market and the fact that government bonds are only one type of asset held by creditors. Suppose that the federal government issued $1 billion of new "Canadians-only" bonds to Canadians and used the proceeds to redeem an equal amount of existing foreign-held federal government debt. Two questions must be addressed: (1) What would make Canadians buy such bonds?; and (2) What would happen to Canada's net foreign indebtedness as a result? We deal with these two issues in turn.

In order to convince Canadians to buy $1 billion worth of these new bonds, these same Canadians must somehow be convinced to divert $1 billion from some other use. For example, they could give up $1 billion worth of consumption to buy these bonds or they could sell $1 billion worth of their holdings of private corporate bonds to buy these new government bonds. In the first case, the reduction in consumption implies an increase in private saving. But it is difficult to see why Canadians would be prepared to increase their private saving simply in response to a change in the ownership of the federal government debt. One thing that might convince them to increase their saving is if these new bonds offered a rate of return greater than that of other assets available on

the market. But, in this case, it is hard to see how the federal government can improve its fiscal position by issuing new high-interest-rate bonds to raise funds used to redeem existing lower-interest-rate bonds.

Suppose, then, that these new "Canadians-only" bonds are *not* successful in increasing the amount of total private saving. Instead, the issuance of these bonds simply leads some Canadians to sell $1 billion of their holdings of private corporate debt so that they can hold the new bonds. The government then takes the $1 billion raised by the selling of the new bonds and redeems $1 billion worth of foreign-held debt. The total amount of government debt is unchanged, but less of the total debt is held by foreigners. The story does not end there, however. Recall that Canadians were able to buy these new bonds only by selling off some of their current holdings of private corporate debt. But with an unchanged pool of Canadian savings, these corporate bonds *must* be bought by foreigners. Thus, total private corporate debt is unchanged, but *more* of it is held by foreigners. Now, while it is true that the federal government has $1 billion less foreign-held debt, the private sector has $1 billion *more* foreign-held debt. And, as the government will now be making fewer interest payments to foreign creditors, the Canadian economy as a whole—the private plus public sectors—will be making the same interest payments to foreigners as before. Thus, the issuing of "Canadians-only" bonds, and the reduction in foreign-held government debt, has no effect on the stream of income available to domestic residents.

Is there some way that the Canadian economy can reduce its foreign indebtedness? Yes, but with a highly integrated global capital market like the one that exists today, schemes like Canadians-only bonds will not work. The only way that the Canadian economy can reduce its indebtedness to foreign creditors is to increase its national saving rate. This requires either an increase in private saving or an increase in public saving (that is, a reduction in the deficit), or both. Thus, if the Canadian budget surpluses continue over the next few years, we should observe a gradual decline in Canadian foreign indebtedness.

Even if it were possible for the government to perfectly control its path of spending and revenues on a year-to-year basis, it would probably be *undesirable* to balance the budget every year. We saw above that government tax revenues (net of transfers) tend to fall in recessions and rise in booms. In contrast, the level of government purchases is more-or-less independent of the level of real GDP. As a result, fiscal policy contains a

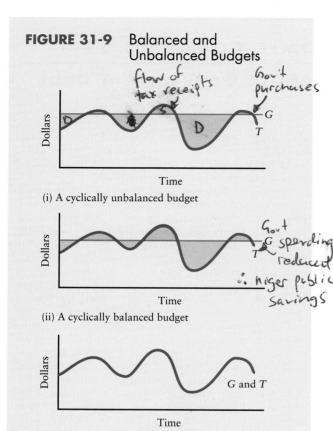

FIGURE 31-9   Balanced and Unbalanced Budgets

flow of tax receipts

Gov't purchases

(i) A cyclically unbalanced budget

Gov't G spending reduced

∴ higer public savings

(ii) A cyclically balanced budget

(iii) A constantly balanced budget

An annually balanced budget is a destabilizer; a cyclically balanced budget is a stabilizer. The flow of tax receipts (net of transfers) T is shown varying over the business cycle; in parts (i) and (ii), government purchases G is shown at a constant rate.

In part (i), deficits (red areas) are common and surpluses (green areas) are rare because the average level of expenditure exceeds the average level of taxes. Such a policy will tend to stabilize the economy against cyclical fluctuations, but public saving is negative, on average.

In part (ii), the level of government purchases have been reduced until it is approximately equal to the average level of tax receipts. The budget is now balanced cyclically. The policy still tends to stabilize the economy against cyclical fluctuations because of deficits in slumps and surpluses in booms. However, public saving is higher than in part (i).

In part (iii), a constantly balanced budget has been imposed. Deficits have been prevented, but the level of government purchases now varies over the business cycle, which tends to destabilize the economy by accentuating the cyclical swings in real GDP.

built-in stabilizer; in recessions, the increase in the budget deficit stimulates aggregate demand whereas in booms the budget surplus reduces aggregate demand.

But things would be very different with an annually balanced budget. With a balanced budget, government expenditures would be *forced* to adjust to the changing level of tax revenues. In a recession, when tax revenues naturally decline, a balanced budget would require either a *reduction* in government expenditures or an *increase* in tax rates, thus generating a major *destabilizing* force on real GDP. Similarly, as tax revenues naturally rise in an economic boom, the balanced budget would require either an increase in government expenditures or a reduction in taxes, thus risking an overheating of the economy.

An annually balanced budget would accentuate the swings in real GDP.

Cyclically Balanced Budgets

One alternative to the extreme policy of requiring an annually balanced budget is to require that the government budget be balanced over the course of a full economic cycle, as shown in Figure 31-9. Budget deficits would be permitted in recessions as long as they were matched by surpluses in booms. In this way, the built-in stabilizers could still perform their important role, but there would be no persistent build-up of government debt. In principle, this is a desirable treatment of the tradeoff between the short-run benefits of deficits and the long-run costs of debt.

Despite its appeal, the idea of cyclically balanced budgets has its problems as well. Perhaps the most important problem with a cyclically balanced budget is an operational one. In order to have a law that requires the budget to be balanced over the cycle, it is necessary to be able to *define* the cycle unambiguously. But there will always be disagreement about what stage of the cycle the economy is currently in, and thus there will be disagreement as to whether the current government should be increasing or reducing its deficit. Compounding this problem is the fact that politicians will have a stake in the identification of the cycle. Those who favour increased deficits will argue that this year is an unusually bad year and thus an increase in the deficit is justified; deficit "hawks," in contrast, will always tend to find this year to be unusually good, and thus a time to run budget surpluses.

Though a budget balanced over the course of the business cycle is in principle a desirable way of reconciling short-term stabilization with long-term prudence, the business cycle may not be well enough defined to make this policy operational.

A second problem is largely political. Suppose that one government runs large deficits for a few years and then gets replaced in an election. Would the succeeding government then be bound to run budget surpluses? What one government commits itself to in one year does not necessarily restrict what it (or its successor) does in the next year. It is this problem which leads many in the U.S. to suggest a Constitutional Amendment to deal with deficits; once the Constitution is altered, any government is bound by it until, through a very lengthy process, it is changed again.

Allowing for Growth

A further problem with any policy that requires a balanced budget—whether over one year or over the business cycle—is that the emphasis is naturally on the overall budget deficit. But, as we saw earlier in this chapter, what determines the change in the debt-to-GDP ratio is the growth of the debt *relative* to the growth of the economy. With a growing economy, it is possible to have positive overall budget deficits—and thus a growing debt—and still have a falling debt-to-GDP ratio. Thus, to the extent that the debt-to-GDP ratio is the relevant gauge of a country's debt problem, focus should be placed on the debt-to-GDP ratio rather than on the budget deficit itself.

Some economists view a stable (or falling) debt-to-GDP ratio as the appropriate indicator of fiscal prudence. Their view permits a deficit such that the stock of debt grows no faster than GDP.

By this standard, the deficits of the late 1990s have been "prudent" because they have led to a growth rate in the stock of debt smaller than the growth rate of real GDP, and thus a reduction in the debt-to-GDP ratio. For example, in 1996, the debt-to-GDP ratio reached its recent maximum of 70 percent. The combined effects of a rapidly growing economy and some planned expenditure reductions then led to a decline in the annual budget deficit from $32 billion in 1996 to $13.6 billion in 1997 and to a surplus of $3.2 billion in 1998. With the 1999 forecast of budget surpluses for the next 4 years, the debt-to-GDP ratio was estimated to reach 55 percent by the year 2004.

For some forecasts and analysis of the government's fiscal options, see the Royal Bank's website: www.royalbank.ca. Go to "corporate information" and then "economics".

S U M M A R Y

Facts and Definitions

⑩❶❷

- The government's budget deficit is equal to total government expenditure minus total government revenue. Since the government must borrow to finance any shortfall in its revenues, the annual deficit is equal to the increase in the stock of government debt during the course of a year. Whenever the deficit is positive, the stock of government debt is growing.
- The primary budget deficit is equal to the excess of the government's program spending over total tax revenues.

The difference between the total budget deficit and the primary deficit is the debt-service payments.
- In 1975, the Canadian federal government net debt was 14 percent of GDP. Large and persistent budget deficits beginning in the 1970s increased the stock of debt so that by 1996 the federal government net debt was equal to about 70 percent of GDP. By 2000, after several years of fiscal contraction, the budget was balanced and the debt was about 60 percent of GDP.

Some Analytical Issues

- Since taxes (net of transfers) tend to rise when real GDP rises, the overall budget deficit tends to rise during recessions and fall during booms. This tendency makes the budget deficit a poor measure of the stance of fiscal policy.
- The cyclically adjusted deficit is the budget deficit that would exist with the current set of fiscal policies if real GDP were equal to potential GDP. Changes in the cyclically adjusted deficit reflect changes in the stance of fiscal policy.
- The change in the debt-to-GDP ratio from one year to the next is given by

$$\Delta d = x + (r - g) \times d$$

where d is the debt-to-GDP ratio, x is the primary deficit as a percentage of GDP, r is the real interest rate, and g is the growth rate of real GDP. If r exceeds g, then a primary surplus is required to stabilize the debt-to-GDP ratio.

- National saving equals government saving plus private saving. An increase in the government budget deficit represents a fall in government saving. The link between budget deficits and private saving depends on the extent to which taxpayers recognize the future tax liabilities associated with current government deficits. When taxpayers are purely Ricardian, any change in government saving is exactly offset by an equal and opposite change in private saving, leaving national saving unchanged. Available evidence suggests that an increase in the government's budget deficit will not be fully offset by an increase in private saving and thus will decrease national saving.

The Effects of Government Debt and Deficits

- In a closed economy, an increase in the budget deficit leads to a reduction in national saving and a rise in real interest rates. This increase in interest rates reduces the amount of investment and leads to a long-term decline in the domestic capital stock.
- In an open economy, an increase in the budget deficit initially pushes up real interest rates. But this attracts foreign financial capital, which drives up the external value of the currency. As the currency appreciates, there is a reduction in net exports. The capital inflow implies an increase in the country's net foreign indebtedness.
- In either open or closed economies, the long-term burden of government debt is a redistribution of resources away from future generations and toward current generations.
- A large debt-to-GDP ratio may lead creditors to expect increases in inflation, as the government attempts to finance deficits through the creation of money. Such increases in inflationary expectations hamper the conduct of monetary policy.
- A large debt-to-GDP ratio also limits the extent to which the government can conduct counter-cyclical fiscal policy without risking large increases in the debt-to-GDP ratio which may be viewed by creditors as unsustainable.

Balanced Budgets

- Since tax revenues (net of transfers) naturally rise as real GDP increases, a policy to balance the budget on an annual basis forces either expenditures to rise or tax rates to fall during booms. This produces destabilizing fiscal policy.
- Cyclically balanced budgets, in principle, permit the short-run benefits of deficits to be realized without incurring the long-run costs of debt accumulation. Implementation of this policy is difficult, however, since the identification of the business cycle is very controversial.
- In a growing economy, it is more sensible to focus on changes in the debt-to-GDP ratio than on balancing the budget over some horizon.

KEY CONCEPTS

Government's budget constraint
Primary budget deficit
The relationship between deficits and
 the national debt
Debt-service payments

Debt-to-GDP ratio
National, government, and private
 saving
Ricardian Equivalence
Crowding out of investment

Crowding out of net exports
Long-term burden of the debt
Annually balanced budget
Cyclically balanced budget

STUDY EXERCISES

1. The table below shows government spending data over eight years in Debtland. All figures are in billions of dollars. The symbols used are as defined in the text.

Year	(1) G	(2) T	(3) TR	(4) iD	(5) Total Deficit	(6) Primary Deficit	(7) Stock of Debt
1995	150	175	25	25	—	—	—
1996	155	180	25	26	—	—	—
1997	160	185	25	27	—	—	—
1998	165	190	23	26	—	—	—
1999	165	195	20	25	—	—	—
2000	165	200	20	24	—	—	—
2001	160	205	20	23	—	—	—
2002	155	210	20	22	—	—	—

 a. Compute debtland's overall budget deficit in each year and complete column 5 in the table. (Since we are computing the deficit, a negative number indicates a surplus.)
 b. Compute Debtland's primary budget deficit in each year and complete column 6 in the table.
 c. Suppose the initial stock of debt (in 1994) was $400 billion. Noting that the deficit in 1995 adds to the stock of debt, what is the stock of debt by the end of 1995?
 d. Compute the stock of debt for each year and complete column (7) in the table.
 e. Suppose you know that Debtland's debt-to-GDP ratio was the same in 2002 as in 1994. How much did GDP grow between 1994 and 2002?

2. The figure below shows the budget deficit function for a country.

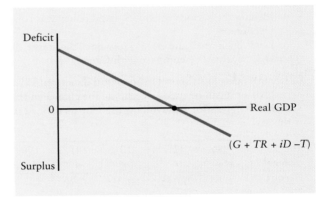

 a. Explain why the budget deficit function is downward sloping.
 b. If the government increases its level of purchases (G), what happens to the deficit at any level of real GDP? Show this in the diagram.
 c. If the government increases its level of tax revenues (T), what happens to the deficit at any level of real GDP? Show this in the diagram.
 d. Explain why a rise in the actual budget deficit does not necessarily reflect an expansionary fiscal policy. How would a fiscal expansion appear in the diagram? A fiscal contraction?

3. The U.S. government was slightly ahead of the Canadian government in reducing its budget deficit. The following table shows the actual budget deficit and the cyclically adjusted deficit (both as a percentage of GDP) for the United States from 1989 to 1997.

Year	Actual deficit	CAD
1989	2.8	2.9
1990	3.9	3.2
1991	4.6	3.4
1992	4.7	3.7
1993	3.9	3.7
1994	3.0	2.8
1995	2.3	2.6
1996	1.4	1.6
1997	0.3	1.0

a. On a scale diagram (with the year on the horizontal axis) graph the actual deficit and the cyclically adjusted deficit.

b. Identify the periods when U.S. fiscal policy was expansionary.

c. Identify the periods when U.S. fiscal policy was contractionary.

d. Look back at Figure 31-6. How does the stance of U.S. fiscal policy compare with Canada's?

4. The following table shows hypothetical data from 1995 to 2001 that can be used to compute the change in the debt-to-GDP ratio. The symbols used are as defined in the text.

Year	(1) x	(2) r	(3) g	(4) d	(5) Δd
1995	0.03	0.045	0.025	0.70	—
1996	0.02	0.04	0.025	—	—
1997	0.01	0.035	0.025	—	—
1998	0.00	0.035	0.025	—	—
1999	−0.01	0.03	0.025	—	—
2000	−0.02	0.03	0.025	—	—
2001	−0.03	0.025	0.025	—	—

a. Remember from the text that the change in the debt-to-GDP ratio (Δd) during a year is given by $\Delta d = x + (r - g)d$. Compute Δd for 1995.

b. Column 4 is the debt-to-GDP ratio. Note that d in 1996 is equal to d from 1995 plus Δd in 1995. Compute d in 1996.

c. Using the same method, compute d and Δd for each year, and complete columns 5 and 6.

d. Plot d in a scale diagram with the year on the horizontal axis. What discretionary variable was most responsible for the observed decline in d?

e. Note that as the primary deficit x falls between 1995 and 2001, there is also a downward trend in the real interest rate. Can you offer an explanation for this?

5. The diagram below shows an *AD/SRAS* diagram. The economy begins at E_0 with output equal to Y^*. Suppose the government in this closed economy increases its budget deficit by borrowing to increase the level of G, thus causing the *AD* curve to shift to the right.

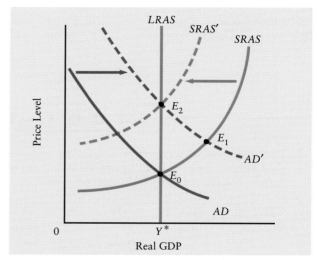

a. How does the interest rate at E_1 compare with that at E_0? Explain.

b. Given your answer to part **a**, how does investment at E_1 compare to investment at E_0?

c. Explain the economy's adjustment toward E_2. What happens to the interest rate and investment?

d. What is the long-run effect of the government deficit? How would this be reflected in the diagram?

6. The diagram below shows an *AD/SRAS* diagram. The economy begins at E_0 with output equal to Y^*. Suppose

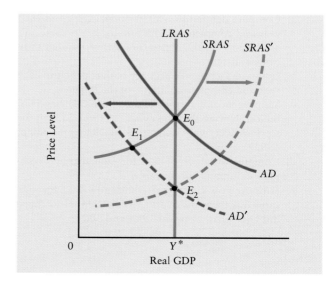

the government in this closed economy decreases its budget deficit by increasing T (and keeping G unchanged), thus causing the AD curve to shift to the left.

a. How does the interest rate at E_1 compare with that at E_0? Explain.
b. Given your answer to part **a**, how does investment at E_1 compare to investment at E_0?

c. Explain the economy's adjustment toward E_2. What happens to the interest rate and investment?
d. What is the long-run effect of the government deficit? How would this be reflected in the diagram?
e. Comparing the short-run and the long-run effects of this policy, what dilemma does the government face in reducing its deficit?

DISCUSSION QUESTIONS

1. Evaluate each of the following proposals to "control the deficit" in order to avoid the long-run burden of the debt.

   a. Maintain a zero cyclically adjusted deficit.
   b. Keep the debt-to-GDP ratio constant.
   c. Limit government borrowing in each year to some fixed percentage of national income in that year.

2. Judith Maxwell, former chairperson of the now disbanded Economic Council of Canada, warned in 1991 that "when interest rates are higher than the economic growth rate, the ratio of debt to GDP acquires dangerous upward momentum." Discuss why this is so. How does the primary deficit enter the analysis?

3. In the federal budget of 1995, the minister of finance announced some significant expenditure reductions which would reduce the deficit. In the budget of 1996, he announced no new expenditure cuts yet still predicted the deficit to fall. Explain how these statements by the minister of finance should be interpreted.

4. Paul Martin, the federal minister of finance who is credited with reducing Canada's budget deficit in the late 1990s, stressed the importance of using very conservative forecasts for economic growth. Explain the role of forecasts, and why Martin chose to use conservative ones.

5. In the text we discussed the effects of government budget deficits. In the past few years, however, the Canadian federal deficit has fallen markedly, from 3 percent of GDP in 1989 (the peak of the business cycle) to a *surplus* of 0.5 percent of GDP in 1999 (close to a peak in the business cycle). Discuss the likely short-term and long-term effects that you would expect to follow such a sustained *reduction* in the deficit.

6. A government official recently exclaimed, "The Prime Minister's policies are working! Lower interest rates combined with staunch fiscal policy have reduced the deficit significantly." What do interest rates have to do with government spending and taxes when it comes to deficit management?

CHAPTER 32

Economic Growth

The Centre for the Study of Living Standards is an Ottawa-based research institute that studies the determinants of economic growth. Visit their website at www.csls.ca.

Economic growth is the single most powerful engine for generating long-term increases in living standards. What happens to our material living standards over time depends largely on the growth in real GDP in relation to the growth in population—that is, it depends on the growth of real per capita GDP. Growth in real per capita GDP does not necessarily make *everybody* in Canada better off. But it does mean that the *average* standard of living is higher.

What determines the growth rate of per capita GDP in Canada? Is this something that is beyond our control, or are there some government policies that can stimulate economic growth? If there are, what are the costs of such policies, and are the benefits worth the costs?

In this chapter we examine this important issue of economic growth, beginning with some basic concepts and then moving on to explore the costs and benefits of growth. In the remainder of the chapter we consider various theories of economic growth, an area in which much new research is being done. Finally, we examine the idea that there may be *limits to growth*.

The Nature of Economic Growth

Over the past century, most residents of most countries in the industrialized world have become materially better off decade by decade. Children have typically been substantially better off than their parents were at the same age. Beginning in the mid 1970s, however, the engine of growth faltered. Growth rates fell, though they remained positive. Although we still live in a very wealthy society, many observers speak of the end of the dream that each generation can expect to be much better off than its predecessors.

Over the long run, the main cause of rising real GDP is **economic growth**—the increase in potential output due to changes in factor supplies (labour and capital) and in the productivity of factors (output per unit of factor input). The removal of a serious recessionary gap might cause a once-and-for-all increase in real GDP by, at the very most, 5 percent. However, a growth rate of 3 percent per year raises potential GDP by 10 percent in three years, doubles it in about 24 years, and quadruples it in 47 years. Even a 1 percent growth rate doubles potential GDP over one normal lifetime of about 70 years.

economic growth
Increases in real potential GDP.

Because growth can go on over very long periods, it is a much more powerful method of raising living standards than the removal of recessionary gaps.

Table 32-1 illustrates the cumulative effect of what you might think are very small differences in growth rates. Notice that if one country grows faster than another, the gap in their respective living standards will widen progressively. If, for example, Canada and France start from the same level of income but Canada grows at 3 percent per year while France grows at 2 percent per year, Canada's income will be twice France's in 72 years. [35] You may not think that it matters much whether the economy grows at 2 percent or 3 percent per year, but your children and grandchildren certainly will.

TABLE 32-1 The Cumulative Effect of Economic Growth

Year	Annual Growth Rate				
	1%	2%	3%	5%	7%
0	100	100	100	100	100
10	111	122	135	165	201
30	135	182	246	448	817
50	165	272	448	1 218	3 312
70	201	406	817	3 312	13 429
100	272	739	2 009	14 841	109 660

Small differences in growth rates make enormous differences in levels of potential GDP over a few decades. Let potential GDP be 100 in year 0. At a growth rate of 3 percent per year, it will be 135 in 10 years, 448 after 50 years, and over 2000 in a century. Notice the difference between 2 percent and 3 percent growth—even small differences in growth rates make big differences in future income levels.

Efficiency and Equity

Observing that sustained economic growth is the most important force for raising living standards over the long term in no way implies the unimportance of policies designed to increase economic efficiency or to redistribute income in the pursuit of greater equity.

Improving Efficiency

If, at any moment in time, real GDP could be increased by removing certain inefficiencies in the economy, such gains would be valuable. After all, as long as scarcity exists (and it always does), any increase in real GDP is welcome. Furthermore, inefficiencies may themselves act to reduce the growth rate. For example, government subsidies to failing firms that may be criticized on grounds of productive and allocative efficiency may also reduce growth rates by reducing the incentive to innovate.

Improving Equity

Economic growth has made the poor vastly better off than they would have been if they had lived 100 years ago. Yet that is little consolation when they see that they cannot afford many things that are currently available to citizens with higher incomes. After all, people compare themselves with others in their own society, not with their counterparts at other times or in other places. Because people care about relative differences among individuals, governments in most countries continue to have policies to redistribute income and to make such basic services as education and health care available to all people, regardless of their ability to pay for them.

Interrelationships Among the Goals

Economists once assumed that the goals of improving equity, increasing economic efficiency, and ensuring growth could each be treated independently. But it is now understood that equity, efficiency, and economic growth are interrelated. For example, policies that redistribute income to the poor in ways that provide large disincentives to work may adversely affect economic growth. It follows that policies designed to reduce inefficiencies or improve equity should be examined carefully for any effects that they may have on economic growth, and policies designed to influence growth need to be examined for their effects on economic efficiency and income distribution. A policy that reduces growth may be a bad bargain, even if it increases the immediate efficiency of the economy or creates a more equitable distribution of income. Similarly, a policy that increases growth may be a bad bargain if it achieves that higher growth only by misallocating resources or by redistributing income in ways that are deemed to be undesirable.

Benefits of Growth

Let's look in more detail, first, at the benefits of growth and then at its costs. *Applying Economic Concepts 32-1* and *32-2* outline some of the commonly heard arguments on both sides of the growth debate.

Average Living Standards

For all who share in it, economic growth is a powerful means of improving living standards. A family that is earning $35 000 today can expect an income of about $42 600 within 10 years (in constant dollars) if it shares in a 2 percent growth rate, $51 800 if the rate is 4 percent.

A family often finds that an increase in its income can lead to changes in the pattern of its consumption—extra money buys important amenities of life and also allows them to save more for the future. Similarly, economic growth that raises average income may change the whole society's consumption patterns. Not only do expanding markets in a rapidly growing country make it profitable to produce more cars, but the government is led to construct more highways and to provide more recreational areas for its affluent and mobile population.

One illustration of the basic point that patterns of demand change as a country becomes wealthier is to note the different attitudes toward environmental protection in rich and poor countries. In developing countries, most of the resources of the country are devoted to providing basic requirements of life such as food, shelter, and clothing. These countries typically do not have the "luxury" of being concerned about environmental degradation. Some may consider this a short-sighted view, but the fact is that the concerns associated with hunger *today* are much more urgent than the concerns associated with *future* environmental problems. In contrast, richer countries are wealthy enough that they can easily provide the basic requirements of life and devote significant resources to environmental protection.

Alleviation of Poverty

Not everyone benefits equally from growth. Many of the poorest are not even in the labour force and hence are unlikely to share in the higher wages that, along with profits,

APPLYING ECONOMIC CONCEPTS 32-1

An Open Letter from a Supporter of the "Growth Is Good" School

Dear Ordinary Citizen:

You live in the world's first civilization that is devoted principally to satisfying *your* needs rather than those of a privileged minority. Past civilizations have always been based on leisure and high consumption for a tiny upper class, a reasonable living standard for a small middle class, and hard work with little more than subsistence consumption for the great mass of people.

The continuing Industrial Revolution is based on mass-produced goods for you, the ordinary citizen. It ushered in a period of sustained economic growth that has dramatically raised consumption standards of ordinary citizens. Consider a few examples: travel, live and recorded music, art, good food, universal literacy, inexpensive books, and a genuine chance to be educated. Most important, there is leisure to provide time and energy to enjoy these and thousands of other products of the modern developed economy.

Would any ordinary family seriously prefer to go back to the world of 150 or 500 years ago in its same *relative* social and economic position? Surely the answer is no. However, for those with incomes in the top 1 or 2 percent of the income distribution, economic growth has destroyed much of their privileged consumption position. They must now vie with the masses when they visit the world's beauty spots and be annoyed, while lounging on the terrace of a palatial mansion, by the sound of charter flights carrying ordinary people to inexpensive holidays in faraway places. Many of the rich complain bitterly

about the loss of exclusive rights to luxury consumption, and it is not surprising that they find their intellectual apologists.

Whether they know it or not, the antigrowth economists are not the social revolutionaries they think they are. They say that growth has produced pollution and wasteful consumption of all kinds of frivolous products that add nothing to human happiness. However, the democratic solution to pollution is not to go back to the time when so few people consumed luxuries that pollution was trivial but rather to learn to control the pollution that mass consumption tends to create.

It is only through further growth that the average citizen can enjoy consumption standards (of travel, culture, medical and health care, and so on) now available only to people in the top 25 percent of the income distribution—which includes the intellectuals who earn large royalties from the books they write in which they denounce growth. If you think that extra income confers little real benefit, just ask those in the top 25 percent to trade incomes with average citizens.

Ordinary citizens, do not be deceived by disguised elitist doctrines. Remember that the very rich and the elite have much to gain by stopping growth and even more by rolling it back, but you have everything to gain by letting it go forward.

Onward!

A. N. Optimist

---

are the primary means by which the gains from growth are distributed. For this reason, even in a growing economy, redistribution policies will be needed if poverty is to be reduced.

A rapid growth rate makes the alleviation of poverty easier politically. If existing income is to be redistributed, someone's standard of living will actually have to be lowered. However, when there is economic growth and when the *increment* in income is redistributed (through government intervention), it is possible to reduce income inequalities without actually having to lower anyone's income. It is much easier for a rapidly growing economy to be generous toward its less fortunate citizens—or neighbours—than it is for a static economy.

Costs of Growth

Other things being equal, most people would probably regard a high rate of growth as preferable to a low one. However, we know that other things are seldom equal. There are some important costs associated with economic growth.

APPLYING ECONOMIC CONCEPTS 32-2

An Open Letter from a Supporter of the "Growth Is Bad" School

Dear Ordinary Citizen:

You live in a world that is being despoiled by a mindless search for ever-higher levels of material consumption at the cost of all other values. Once upon a time, men and women knew how to enjoy creative work and to derive satisfaction from simple activities. Today, the ordinary worker is a mindless cog in an assembly line that turns out more and more goods that the advertisers must work overtime to persuade the worker to consume.

Statisticians count the increasing flow of material output as a triumph of modern civilization. You wake to the hum of your air conditioner, watch the shopping channel while you dress for work, brew your chemically treated decaffinated coffee, and eat your bread baked from superrefined flour; you climb into your car to sit in vast traffic jams on exhaust-polluted highways.

Television commercials tell you that by consuming more, you are happier, but happiness lies not in increasing consumption but in increasing the ratio of *satisfaction of wants* to *total wants*. Because the more you consume, the more the advertisers persuade you that you want to consume, you are almost certainly less happy than the average citizen in a small town in 1900, whom we can visualize sitting on the family porch, sipping lemonade, and enjoying the antics of the children as they jump rope using pieces of old clothesline.

Today, the landscape is dotted with endless factories that produce the plastic trivia of modern society. They drown you in a cloud of noise, air, and water pollution. The countryside is despoiled by strip mines, petroleum refineries, acid rain, and dangerous nuclear power plants, producing energy that is devoured insatiably by modern factories and motor vehicles. Worse, our precious heritage of natural resources is being rapidly depleted.

Now is the time to stop this madness. We must end this mad rush to produce more and more output, reduce pollution, conserve our natural resources, and seek justice through a more equitable distribution of existing total income.

Many years ago, Thomas Malthus taught us that if we do not limit population voluntarily, nature will do it for us in a cruel and savage manner. Today, the same is true of output: If we do not halt its growth voluntarily, the halt will be imposed on us by a disastrous increase in pollution and a rapid exhaustion of natural resources.

Citizens, awake! Shake off the worship of growth, learn to enjoy the bounty that is yours already, and reject the endless, self-defeating search for increased happiness through ever-increasing consumption.

Upward!

I. Realvalues

If economic growth just means more of the truly "unnecessary" things in life, is it really that worthwhile?

The Opportunity Cost of Growth

In a world of scarcity, almost nothing is free. Growth requires heavy investment of resources in capital goods, as well as in activities such as education. Often these investments yield no immediate return in terms of goods and services for consumption; thus, they imply that sacrifices have been made by the current generation of consumers.

Growth, which promises more goods tomorrow, is achieved by consuming fewer goods today. For the economy as a whole, this sacrifice of current consumption is the primary cost of growth.

An example will suggest the importance of this cost. Suppose that a hypothetical economy is operating at potential output and is experiencing growth in real GDP at the rate of 2 percent per year. Its citizens consume 85 percent of the GDP and invest 15 percent. But suppose that if they immediately decrease their consumption to 77 percent of GDP (and increase investment to 23 percent), they will produce more capital and thus shift at once to a 3 percent growth rate. The new rate can be maintained as long as they keep saving and investing 23 percent of real GDP. Should they do it?

Figure 32-1 illustrates the choice in terms of time paths of consumption. With the assumed figures, it takes ten years for the actual amount of consumption to catch up to what it would have been had no reallocation been made. In the intervening 10 years, a good deal of consumption is lost, and the cumulative losses in consumption must be made up before society can really be said to have broken even. It takes an *additional* 9 years before total consumption over the whole period is as large as it would have been if the economy had remained on the 2 percent path. [36]

Over a longer period, however, the payoff from the growth policy becomes enormous. Thirty years on, real GDP in the more rapidly growing economy is 21 percent higher than in the slower-growing economy. After fifty years, it is 48 percent higher.

Social Costs of Growth

A growing economy is also a changing economy. Part of growth is accounted for by existing firms expanding and producing more output, hiring more workers, and using more equipment and intermediate goods. But another part of growth is accounted for by

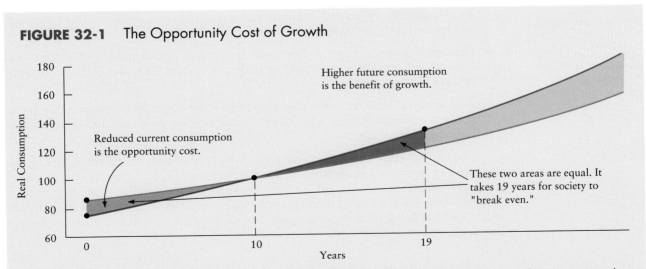

FIGURE 32-1   The Opportunity Cost of Growth

Transferring resources from consumption to investment lowers current consumption but raises future consumption. The example assumes that GDP in year 0 is 100 and that growth of 2 percent per year is possible when consumption equals 85 percent of GDP. It is further assumed that to achieve a 3 percent growth rate, consumption must fall to 77 percent of GDP. A shift from the red path to the blue path in year 0 decreases consumption for 10 years but increases it thereafter. By year 19 the gains in consumption have made up for the losses from the first 10 years.

existing firms' being overtaken and made obsolete by new firms, by old products' being made obsolete by new products, and by existing skills being made obsolete by new skills.

The process of economic growth renders some machines obsolete and also leaves some workers partly obsolete.

No matter how well-trained workers are at age 25, in another 25 years many will find that their skills are at least partly obsolete. A high growth rate usually requires rapid adjustments, which can cause much upset and misery to some of the people affected by it.

It is often argued that costs of this kind are a small price to pay for the great benefits that growth can bring. Even if this is true in the aggregate, these personal costs are borne very unevenly. Indeed, many of the people for whom growth is most costly (in terms of lost jobs or lowered incomes) share least in the fruits that growth brings.

Sources of Growth

We know that output is produced by combining the services of various factors of production such as labour, capital, and land. Furthermore, we know that the current state of our knowledge—or technology—limits our ability to get more and more output from a given set of factors of production. It follows, therefore, that we can account for growth in real GDP by increases in the *amount* of available factors of production, increases in the *quality* of the available factors of production, or increases in the state of *technology* that determines how much output we are able to get from a given set of factors of production.

The four fundamental determinants of growth of total output are:

human capital   The capitalized value of productive investments in persons; usually refers to value derived from expenditures on education, training, and health improvements.

1. *Growth in the labour force.* This may be caused by growth in population or by increases in the fraction of the population that chooses to participate in the labour force.

2. *Growth in human capital.* **Human capital** is the term economists use to refer to the set of skills that workers have. Human capital can increase through either formal education or on-the-job training.

3. *Growth in physical capital.* The stock of physical capital (such as factories, machines, transportation and communications facilities) increases only through the process of investment.

4. *Technological improvement.* This may be brought about by innovation that introduces new products, new ways of producing existing products, and new forms of business organization.

The various theories of economic growth that we explore in the remainder of this chapter can be viewed as theories of these different sources of growth. For example, some theories emphasize the role of increases in physical capital in explaining growth; others emphasize the role of increases in human capital; still others emphasize the importance of technological improvements. But all theories of economic growth take as a starting point these four fundamental determinants of growth.

Theories of Economic Growth

In this section we study some of the theories that economists use to understand economic growth. This is an exciting area. Ideas are changing rapidly as both theoretical and empirical research expands our knowledge. Our first step is to relate investment and saving, which we studied in detail in previous chapters, to economic growth.

Investment, Saving, and Growth

Both investment and saving affect the level and rate of growth of real GDP. To understand their influence, it is critical to distinguish between their short-run and long-run effects.

Short-Run and Long-Run Effects of Investment

The theory of output determination that we studied in Chapters 22 through 25 is a short-run theory. It takes potential output as constant and concentrates on the effects of shifts in aggregate demand brought about by changes in various types of desired expenditure, including investment. These shifts cause actual GDP to fluctuate around a given level of potential GDP. The short-term effects of changes in investment are shown by rightward shifts in the *AD* curve.

In the long run, by adding to the nation's capital stock, investment raises potential output. This effect is shown by rightward shifts in the *LRAS* curve.

The theory of economic growth is a long-run theory. It concentrates on the effects of investment in raising potential output and ignores short-run fluctuations of actual output around potential.

The contrast between the short- and long-run aspects of investment is worth emphasizing. In the short run, any activity that puts income into people's hands will raise aggregate demand. Thus, the short-run effect on real GDP is the same whether a firm spends by hiring workers to dig holes (and then hires more workers to refill them) or by building a new factory. But the long-run growth of potential GDP is affected only by the part of spending that *adds to a nation's productive capacity*—by the new factory but not by the refilled hole.

Similar observations hold for government purchases of goods and services. Any increase in purchases will add to aggregate demand and real GDP in the short run, but only some expenditures increase *potential* GDP and thus will increase GDP in the long run. Although public investment expenditure on such things as roads and health may increase potential GDP, expenditure that shores up a declining industry in order to create employment may have an adverse effect on potential GDP. The latter expenditure may prevent the reallocation of resources in response to shifts both in the pattern of world demand and in the country's comparative advantage. Thus, in the long run, the country's capacity to produce commodities that are demanded on world markets may be diminished.

Short-Run and Long-Run Effects of Saving

As we saw in Chapters 22 and 23, the short-run effect of an increase in saving is to reduce aggregate demand. If households or governments elect to save more, they must (by definition) decide to spend less. The resulting downward shift in the aggregate expenditure function lowers aggregate demand and thus lowers equilibrium real GDP.

Over the longer term, however, higher national saving is necessary for higher investment. Firms usually reinvest their own saving, and the saving of households passes to firms, either directly through the purchase of stocks and bonds or indirectly through financial intermediaries such as commercial banks and trust companies. In the long run, the higher the level of national saving, the higher the level of investment. And because of the accumulation of more and better capital equipment, the higher the level of investment, the higher the level of potential GDP.

In the long run, there is no paradox of thrift; societies with high rates of national saving have high investment rates and, other things being equal, high growth rates of real GDP.

Investment and Growth in Industrialized Countries

We said above that countries with high rates of investment are also countries with high rates of real GDP growth. To provide evidence in support of this claim, Figure 32-2 shows data from the most industrialized countries between 1970 and 1990. Each point in the figure corresponds to a single country and shows that country's annual average investment rate (as a percentage of GDP) plotted against the annual average growth rate in real per capita GDP. What is clear from the figure is a strong positive relationship between investment rates and growth rates, exactly as suggested by our discussion above.

Hong Kong is an example of an economy that has had very high rates of investment and also very high rates of real GDP growth.

Neoclassical Growth Theory

aggregate production function
The relation between the total amount of each factor of production employed in the nation and the nation's total GDP.

Recall the four fundamental sources of economic growth that we discussed at the beginning of this section. Much of what is referred to as *Neoclassical growth theory* is based on the idea that these four forces of economic growth can be connected by what is called the **aggregate production function**. This is an expression for the relation between the total amounts of labour (L) and physical capital (K) employed, the quality

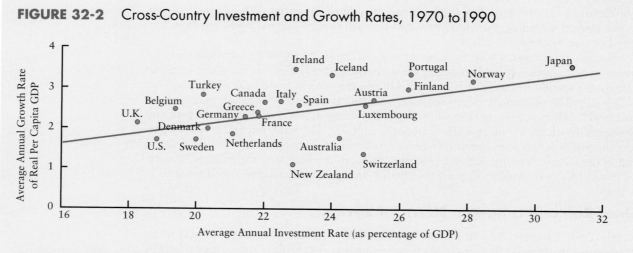

FIGURE 32-2   Cross-Country Investment and Growth Rates, 1970 to1990

There is a strong positive relationship between a country's investment rate (as a percentage of GDP) and its growth rate of real per capita GDP. For each of the countries, the annual averages for investment rates and per capita GDP growth rates are computed between 1970 and 1990. Each point represents the average values of these variables for a single country over this 20-year period. The line is the "line of best fit" between the growth rates and the investment rates. Countries with high investment rates tend to be countries with high rates of economic growth.

(*Source:* International Monetary Fund)

of labour's human capital (H), the state of technology (T), and the nation's total level of output (GDP). The aggregate production function can be expressed as:

$$GDP = F_T(L, K, H)$$

It is an *aggregate* production function because it relates the economy's *total* output to the *total* amount of the factors that are used to produce that output.[1] (Those who have studied microeconomics will recall that a micro production function, such as is discussed in Chapters 7 and 8, relates the output of *one firm* to the factors of production employed by *that firm*.)

The production function above—indicated by F_T—tells us how much GDP will be produced for given amounts of labour and physical capital employed, given levels of human capital and a given state of technology. Using the notation F_T is a simple way of indicating that the function relating L, K and H to GDP depends on the state of technology. For a given state of technology (T), changes in either L, K or H will lead to changes in GDP. Similarly, for given values of L, K and H, changes in T will lead to changes in GDP. [37]

When discussing economic growth, we focus on the changes in potential output and ignore short-term fluctuations of output around potential. Hence we can interpret GDP in the aggregate production function as potential output.

Early Neoclassical growth theory dealt with economic growth when technological knowledge remained unchanged. There were no innovations: no new ways of making things and no new products. As a result, the relation between inputs and output, as shown by the aggregate production function, did not change. Since T was assumed to be constant, the aggregate production function could simply be written as

$$GDP = F(L, K, H)$$

indicating that growth in GDP was due only to changes in labour, physical capital, or human capital.

Properties of the Aggregate Production Function

The key aspects of the Neoclassical model are that the aggregate production function displays *diminishing returns* when either factor is increased on its own and *constant returns* when all factors are increased together (and in the same proportion).

To understand these important concepts, let us simplify things slightly by combining physical and human capital together so that we can think of a single factor called "capital." Now suppose that the labour force grows while the stock of capital remains constant. More and more people go to work using a fixed quantity of capital. The amount that each new unit of input adds to total output is called its *marginal product*. The operation of the **law of diminishing returns** tells us that the employment of additional units of labour will eventually add less to total output than the previous unit. In other words, each additional unit of labour will sooner or later produce a diminishing marginal product. This famous relation is referred to as *diminishing returns to a single factor*, and it is illustrated in Figure 32-3.

law of diminishing returns The hypothesis that if increasing quantities of a variable factor are applied to a given quantity of fixed factors, the marginal product and average product of the variable factor will eventually decrease.

---

[1]Natural resources (including land, forests, mineral deposits, etc.) are also important inputs to the production process. We leave them out of this discussion only for simplicity.

FIGURE 32-3   Diminishing Returns to the Variable Factor

(1) Units of Variable Factor (Labour)	(2) Units of Total Output	(3) Average Product of Labour (2/1)	(4) Marginal Product of Labour ($\Delta2/\Delta1$)
1	12.0	12.0	
2	17.0	8.5	5.0
3	20.8	6.9	3.8
4	24.0	6.0	3.2
5	26.8	5.4	2.8
6	29.4	4.9	2.6
7	31.9	4.6	2.5
8	34.0	4.2	2.1
9	36.0	4.0	2.0
10	37.9	3.8	1.9

(i) Total product

(ii) Marginal and average product

With one input held constant, the marginal and average products of the variable factor eventually decline. We have assumed a hypothetical production function given by: output = $4\sqrt{KL}$; we have also assumed that K is constant and equal to 9. Column 2 shows total output as more of the variable factor, labour, is used with a fixed amount of capital. Total output is plotted in part (i) of the figure. Both the average product of labour and the marginal product of labour decline continuously. They are plotted in part (ii) of the figure.

The law of diminishing returns applies to any factor that is varied while the other factors are held constant. Hence, successive amounts of capital added to a fixed supply of labour will also eventually add less and less to GDP.

According to the law of diminishing returns, the increment to total production will eventually fall steadily whenever equal increases of a variable factor of production are combined with another factor of production whose quantity is fixed.

The other main property of the Neoclassical aggregate production function is called **constant returns to scale.** This says that if the amounts of labour and capital are both changed in equal proportion, total output will also change in that proportion. For ex-

constant returns to scale   A situation in which output increases in proportion to the change in all inputs as the scale of production is increased.

ample, 10 percent increases in the amounts of both labour and capital will lead to a 10 percent increase in GDP. [38]

Sources of Growth in the Neoclassical Model

Now consider each of the sources of growth on the list at the beginning of this section. To begin, we let each source operate with the others held constant.

Labour-Force Growth. Over the long term, we can associate labour-force growth with population growth (although in the short term, the labour force can grow if participation rates rise even though the population remains constant). As more labour is used, there will be more output produced. The law of diminishing returns tells us that sooner or later, each further unit of labour to be employed will cause smaller and smaller additions to GDP. Eventually, not only will the marginal product of labour be falling, but the average product will fall as well. Beyond that point, although economic growth continues in the sense that total output is growing, living standards are falling in the sense that average GDP *per person* is falling. If we are interested in growth in living standards, we are concerned with increasing real GDP per person.

In the Neoclassical growth model, whenever diminishing average returns applies, increases in population on their own are accompanied by increasing GDP but falling living standards.

Capital Accumulation. Growth in physical capital occurs whenever there is enough investment to make up for the capital that wears out during the production process. But how does the stock of human capital increase?

Human capital has several aspects. One involves improvements in the health and longevity of the population. Of course, these are desired as ends in themselves, but they also have consequences for both the size and the productivity of the labour force. There is no doubt that improvements in the health of workers have increased productivity per worker-hour by cutting down on illness, accidents, and absenteeism.

A second aspect of human capital concerns technical training—from learning to operate a machine to learning how to be a scientist. This training depends on the current state of knowledge, and advances in knowledge allow us not only to build more productive physical capital but also to create more effective human capital. Also, the longer a person has been educated, the more adaptable and, hence, the more productive in the long run that person is in the face of new and changing challenges.

The accumulation of capital—either physical or human—affects GDP in a manner similar to population growth. Eventually, each successive unit of capital will add less to total output than each previous unit of capital.

There is, however, a major contrast with the case of labour-force growth because it is output *per person* that determines living standards, not output per unit of capital. Thus, as the amount of physical or human capital increases, living standards increase because output is rising while the population is constant. However, because the increases in capital are subject to diminishing returns, successive additions to the economy's capital stock bring smaller and smaller increases in per capita output.

In the Neoclassical model, the operation of diminishing returns means that capital accumulation on its own brings smaller and smaller increases in real per capita GDP.

Balanced Growth with Constant Technology. Now consider what happens if labour and capital (both human and physical capital) grow at the same rate. In this case, the Neoclassical assumption of constant returns to scale means that GDP grows in proportion to the increases in inputs. As a result, per capita output remains constant. Thus, growth in labour and capital leads to growth in total GDP but unchanged per capita GDP.

This "balanced growth path" is not, however, the kind of growth that concerns people interested in explaining rising living standards. Since increases in living standards are determined largely by increases in *per capita* output, it is clear that this balanced growth path is unable to explain *rising* living standards.

If capital and labour grow at the same rate, GDP will increase. But in the Neoclassical growth model with constant returns to scale, this "balanced growth path" will not lead to improvements in living standards.

Technological Change

The Neoclassical model predicts that increases in the per capita stock of capital (physical or human) will improve living standards, but that such improvements will eventually stop due to diminishing returns. In contrast, if both capital and labour are growing at the same rate, the Neoclassical model predicts no improvements in living standards, as per capita GDP will be constant.

So how does the Neoclassical model explain the sort of ongoing long-term improvements in living standards that Canada and other countries have experienced over the past century or more? The answer is technological advance, including new knowledge and the improved technology contained within new plant and equipment.

New knowledge and inventions can contribute markedly to the growth of potential output, even without capital accumulation. To illustrate this point, suppose that the proportion of a society's resources devoted to the production of capital goods is just sufficient to replace capital as it wears out. If the old capital is merely replaced in the same form, the capital stock will be constant, and there will be no increase in the capacity to produce. However, if there is a growth of knowledge so that as old equipment wears out it is replaced by different and more productive equipment, then productive capacity will be growing.

embodied technical change Technical change that is intrinsic to the particular capital goods in use.

The increase in productive capacity created by installing new and better capital goods is called **embodied technical change**. Its historical importance is clear: The assembly line and automation transformed most manufacturing industries, the airplane revolutionized transportation, and electronic devices now dominate the information-technology industries. Innovations like these create new investment opportunities.

Less obvious but nonetheless important are technical changes that are embodied in *human* capital. These are changes that result from a better-educated, more experienced labour force; better management practices and techniques; improved design, marketing, and organization of business activities; and feedback from user experience leading to product improvement.

Many—perhaps most—innovations are embodied in either physical or human capital. These innovations cause continual changes in the techniques of production and in the nature of what is produced.

Looking back over the past century, firms produce very few products today in the same way that they did in the past, and much of what is produced and consumed is in the form of new or vastly improved products. Major innovations of the twentieth century include the development of such key products as telephones, radios, televisions, automobiles, airplanes, plastic, CD players, refrigerators, washing machines, coaxial cable, xerography, electron microscopes, telecommunications satellites, computers, transistors, and silicon chips. It is hard for us to imagine life without them.

We have been discussing the benefits of technological change in terms of raising overall living standards. Ever since the Industrial Revolution, however, some workers have feared the effects of technological change. Technological change, after all, is often responsible for workers' losing their jobs as employers replace less efficient labour with more efficient equipment. *Lessons from History 32-1* examines the relationship between technological progress and changes in employment. The main lesson we can learn is that technological change over the years has created far more jobs than it has destroyed.

Can We Measure Technological Change?

Technological change is obviously important. You need only look around you at the current products and production methods that did not exist a generation ago, or even ten years ago, to realize how the advance of technology changes our lives. The development of the Internet is an obvious example of such technological advance. But *how much* does technology change? Unfortunately, technology is not something that is easily measured and so it is very difficult to know just how important it is to the process of economic growth.

In 1957, Robert Solow, an economist at MIT who was awarded the Nobel prize 30 years later for his research on economic growth, attempted to measure the amount of technical change in the United States. He devised a way to infer from the data (under some assumptions about the aggregate production function) how much of the observed growth in real GDP was due to the growth in labour and capital, and how much was due to technical change. His method led to the creation of what is now called the "Solow residual." The Solow residual is the amount of growth in GDP that cannot be accounted for by growth in the labour force or by growth in the capital stock. Since Solow was thinking about changes in GDP as having only three possible sources—changes in capital, changes in labour, and changes in technology—the "residual" was naturally interpreted as a measure of technical change.

Today, economists do not view the Solow residual as a precise estimate of the amount of technical change. The main reason is that much technical change is known to be embodied in new physical and human capital. Thus, capital accumulation and technological change are inherently connected. For example, imagine a firm that replaces an old 286 PC with a new Pentium II PC. Both PCs might be considered one unit of capital, but clearly the Pentium embodies new technology that is completely absent in the old 286. In this case, even though the firm's total capital stock hasn't changed, the process of replacing the old capital with new capital also increased the firm's level of technology. Because capital accumulation and technological advance are so closely linked, Solow's method, which views the two processes as distinct, cannot provide a reliable estimate of technical change. Due to the amount of new technology embodied in new capital equipment, the Solow residual is, at best, an underestimate of the true amount of technical change.

Despite these problems, Solow's method of "growth accounting" and the Solow residual are still widely used by economists in universities and government. The Solow residual often goes by another name—the rate of growth of *total factor productivity (TFP)*.

See Chapter 32 of www.pearsoned.ca/lipsey for an interesting discussion of why the computer revolution has not yet appeared in measurements of productivity growth: Jeremy Leonard, "Computers and Productivity in the Information Economy," *World Economic Affairs*.

Endogenous Technological Change

In the Neoclassical model, innovation increases the amount of output producible from a given level of factor inputs. But this innovation is itself unexplained. The Neoclassical model thus views technological change as *exogenous*. It has profound effects on economic variables, such as GDP, but it is not itself influenced by economic causes. It just happens.

LESSONS FROM HISTORY 32-1

Should Workers Be Afraid of Technological Change?

From time immemorial people have observed that technological change destroys particular jobs and have worried that it will destroy jobs in general. Should they worry?

Technological change *does* destroy particular jobs. When water wheels were used to automate the fulling of cloth in 12th century Europe, there were riots and protests among the fullers who lost their jobs. A century ago, 50 percent of the labour force in North America and Europe was required to produce the required food. Today, less than 5 percent of the labour force is needed in the high-income countries to feed all their citizens. In other words, out of every 100 jobs that existed in 1900, 50 were in agriculture and 45 of those have been destroyed by technological progress over the course of the 20th century.

Just as technological change destroys some jobs, it also creates many new jobs. The displaced agricultural workers did not join the ranks of the permanently unemployed—although some of the older ones may have, their children did not. Instead they, and their children, took jobs in manufacturing and service industries and helped to produce the mass of new goods and services—such as automobiles, refrigerators, computers, and foreign travel—that have raised living standards over the century.

Worries that technological change will cause general unemployment have been recorded for at least 250 years but, so far at least, there is no sign that those displaced by technological change (or their children) are being forced into the ranks of the permanently unemployed. Over all of recorded history, technological change has created more jobs than it has destroyed.

But how about today? Aren't there good reasons to be more afraid of technological change now than in the past? Modern technologies have two aspects that worry some observers. First, they tend to be *knowledge intensive*. A fairly high degree of literacy and numeracy, as well as familiarity with computers, is needed to work with many but not all of these new technologies. Second, through the process of globalization, unskilled workers in advanced countries have come into competition with unskilled workers everywhere in the world. Both of these forces are decreasing the relative demand for unskilled workers in developed countries and may lead to falling relative wages for unskilled workers in countries like Canada. If labour markets are insufficiently flexible, this change in relative demand may also lead to some structural unemployment.

For these reasons, some people blame the high unemployment rates in Europe (and to a lesser extent, in Canada) on the new technologies. This is hard to reconcile, however, with the fact that the lowest unemployment rates in the industrialized countries are currently being recorded in the United States, the most technologically dynamic of all countries. This suggests that the cause of high European unemployment rates may be not enough technological change and too much government interference rather than too much technological change.

Yet recent research by many scholars has established that technological change is responsive to such economic signals as prices and profits; in other words, it is *endogenous* to the economic system. Though much of the earliest work on this issue was done in Europe, the most influential overall single study was by an American, Nathan Rosenberg, whose trailblazing 1982 book *Inside the Black Box: Technology and Economics* argued this case in great detail.

Technological change stems from research and development and from innovating activities that put the results of R&D into practice. These are costly and highly risky activities, undertaken largely by firms and usually in pursuit of profit. It is not surprising, therefore, that these activities respond to economic incentives. If the price of some particular input such as petroleum or skilled labour goes up, R&D and innovating activities will be directed to altering the production function to economize on these inputs. This process is not simply a substitution of less expensive inputs for more expensive ones within the confines of known technologies; rather, it is the *development of new technologies* in response to changes in relative prices.

There are several important implications of this new understanding that, to a great extent, growth is achieved through costly, risky, innovative activity that often occurs in response to economic signals.

Learning by Doing

The pioneering theorist of innovation, Joseph Schumpeter (1883–1950), developed a model in which innovation flowed in one direction, from a pure discovery "upstream" to more applied R&D, then to working machines, and finally to output "downstream."

In contrast, modern research shows that innovation involves a large amount of "learning by doing" at all of its stages. (We discuss this kind of learning in more detail in Chapter 34.) What is learned downstream then modifies what must be done upstream. The best innovation-managing systems encourage such "feedback" from the more applied steps to the purer researchers and from users to designers.

This interaction is illustrated, for example, by the differences that existed for many years between the Japanese automobile manufacturers and their North American competitors in the handling of new models. North American design was traditionally centralized: Design production teams developed the overall design and then instructed their production sections what to do, as well as asking for bids from parts manufacturers to produce according to specified blueprints. As a result, defects in the original design were often not discovered until production was under way, causing many costly delays and rejection of parts already supplied. In contrast, Japanese firms involved their design and production departments and their parts manufacturers in all stages of the design process. Parts manufacturers were not given specific blueprints for production; instead, they were given general specifications and asked to develop their own detailed designs. As they did so, they learned. They then fed information about the problems they were encountering back to the main designers while the general outlines of the new model were not yet finalized. As a result, the Japanese were able to design a new product faster, at less cost, and with far fewer problems than were the North American firms. In recent years, however, the North American automotive firms have adopted many of these Japanese design and production methods.

Knowledge Transfer

The *diffusion* of technological knowledge from those who have it to those who want it is not costless (as it was assumed to be in Schumpeter's model). Firms need research capacity just to adopt the technologies developed by others. Some of the knowledge needed to use a new technology can be learned only through experience by plant managers, technicians, and operators. We often tend to think that once a production process is developed, it can easily be copied by others. In practice, however, the diffusion of new technological knowledge is not so simple.

For example, some economists argue that most industrial technologies require technology-specific organizational skills that cannot be "embodied" in the machines themselves, instruction books, or blueprints. The needed knowledge is *tacit* in the sense that it cannot be taught through books and can only be acquired by experience—much like driving a car or flying an airplane. Acquiring tacit knowledge requires a deliberate process of building up new skills, work practices, knowledge, and experience.

The fact that diffusion is a costly and time-consuming business explains why new technologies take considerable time to diffuse, first through the economy of the originating country and then through the rest of the world. If diffusion were simple and virtually costless, the puzzle would be why technological knowledge and best industrial practices did not diffuse very quickly. As it is, decades can pass before a new technological process is diffused everywhere that it could be employed.

Market Structure and Innovation

Because it is highly risky, innovation is encouraged by strong rivalry among firms and discouraged by monopoly practices. Competition among three or four large firms often produces much innovation, but a single firm, especially if it serves a secure home market protected by trade barriers, seems much less inclined to innovate. The reduction in trade barriers over the past several decades and the increasing globalization of markets as a result of falling transportation and communication costs have increased international competition. Whereas one firm in a national market might have had substantial monopoly power three or four decades ago, today it is more likely to be in intense competition with firms based in other countries.

Government interventions that are designed to encourage innovation often allow the firms in an industry to work together as one. Unless great care is exercised and unless sufficient foreign competition exists, the result may be a national monopoly that will discourage risk taking rather than encourage it, as is the intention of the policy.

Shocks and Innovation

One interesting consequence of endogenous technical change is that shocks that would be unambiguously adverse to an economy operating with fixed technology can sometimes provide a spur to innovation that proves a blessing in disguise. A sharp rise in the price of one input can raise costs and lower the value of output per person for some time. But it may lead to a wave of innovations that reduce the need for this expensive input and, as a side effect, greatly raise productivity.

Sometimes individual firms will respond differently to the same economic signal. Sometimes those that respond by altering technology will do better than those that concentrate their efforts on substituting within the confines of known technology. For example, in *The Competitive Advantage of Nations,* Harvard economist Michael Porter tells the story of the consumer electronics industry, in which U.S. firms moved their operations abroad to avoid high, rigid labour costs. They continued to use their existing technology and went where labour costs were low enough to make that technology pay. Their Japanese competitors, however, stayed at home. They innovated away most of their labour costs and then built factories in the United States to replace the factories of U.S. firms that had gone abroad!

Theories Based on Increasing Returns

We saw earlier that Neoclassical theories of economic growth assume that investment is always subject to diminishing returns. New growth theories emphasize the possibility of *historical increasing returns to investment:* As investment in some new area, product, or production technology proceeds through time, each new increment of investment is more productive than previous increments. Economists have noted a number of sources of increasing returns. These fall under the two general categories of *fixed costs* and *knowledge*.

Fixed Costs

There are three reasons why there may be an important fixed-cost component to the amount of investment undertaken in an industry or region.

1. Investment in the early stages of development of a country, province, or town may create new skills and attitudes in the workforce that are then available to all subsequent firms, whose costs are therefore lower than those encountered by the initial

firms. (For those who have studied microeconomics, the early firms are conferring a positive *externality* on those who follow them, as described in Chapter 16.)

2. Each new firm may find the environment more and more favourable to its investment because of the infrastructure that has been created by those who came before.

3. The first investment in a new product will encounter countless production problems that, once overcome, cause fewer problems to subsequent investors.

More generally, many investments require fixed costs, the advantages of which are then available to subsequent firms; hence, the investment costs for "followers" can be substantially less than the investment costs for "pioneers." In short, doing something really new is difficult, whereas making further variations on an accepted and developed new idea becomes progressively easier.

Another important issue concerns the behaviour of customers. When a new product is developed, customers will often resist adopting it, both because they may be conservative and because they know that new products usually have teething troubles. Customers also need time to learn how best to use the new product—they need to do what is called "learning by using."

Slow acceptance of new products by customers is not necessarily irrational. When a sophisticated new product comes on the market, no one is sure if it will be a success, and the first customers to buy it take the risk that the product may subsequently turn out to be a failure. They also incur the costs of learning how to use it effectively. Many potential users take the not unreasonable attitude of letting others try a new product, following only after the product's success has been demonstrated. This makes the early stages of innovation especially costly and risky.

Successive increments of investment associated with an innovation often yield a range of increasing returns as costs that are incurred in earlier investment expenditure provide publicly available knowledge and experience and as customer attitudes and abilities become more receptive to new products.

The implications of these ideas have been the subject of intense study ever since they were first embedded in modern growth models by Paul Romer of Stanford University and Maurice Scott of Oxford University.[2] Probably the most important contrast between these new theories and the Neoclassical theory concerns investment and income. In the Neoclassical model, diminishing returns to capital implies a limit to the possible increase of per capita GDP. In the new models, investment alone can hold an economy on a "sustained growth path" in which per capita GDP increases without limit, provided that the investment embodies the results of continual advances in technological knowledge.

Knowledge

An even more fundamental aspect of the new growth theories is the shift from the economics of goods to the economics of *ideas*. Physical goods, such as factories and machines, exist in one place at one time. This has two consequences. First, when physical goods are used by someone, they cannot be used by someone else. Second, if a given labour force is provided with more and more physical objects to use in production, sooner or later diminishing returns will be encountered.

A computer is an "ordinary" good because if I own it then you cannot also own it. But the knowledge required to build the computer is a public good. And knowledge, unlike traditional factors of production, is not necessarily subject to the law of diminishing returns.

[2]As with so many innovations, these new views have many historical antecedents, including a classic article in the 1960s by Nobel Prize winner Kenneth Arrow of Stanford University.

Ideas have different characteristics. Once someone develops ideas, they are available for use by everyone simultaneously. Ideas can be used by one person without reducing their use by others. For example, if one firm uses a truck, another firm cannot use it at the same time; but one firm's use of a revolutionary design for a new suspension on a truck does not prevent other firms from using that design as well. Ideas are often not subject to the same use restrictions as goods. (For those that have studied microeconomics, some knowledge has aspects that make it a *public good,* as we discussed in Chapter 16.)

Ideas are also not necessarily subject to diminishing returns. As our knowledge increases, each increment of new knowledge does not inevitably add less to our productive ability than each previous increment. A year spent improving the operation of semiconductors may be more productive than a year spent improving the operation of vacuum tubes (the technology used before semiconductors).

The evidence from modern research is that new technologies are usually *absolutely factor-saving*—in other words, they use less of all inputs per unit of output. Furthermore, there is no evidence that from decade to decade the factor saving associated with increments of new knowledge is diminishing.

Modern growth theories stress the importance of ideas in producing what is called *knowledge-driven growth.* New knowledge provides the input that allows investment to produce increasing rather than diminishing returns. Because there are no practical limits to human knowledge, there need be no immediate boundaries to finding new ways to produce more output using less of all inputs.

Neoclassical growth theories gave economics the name "the dismal science" by emphasizing diminishing returns under conditions of given technology. The modern growth theories are more optimistic because they emphasize the unlimited potential of knowledge-driven technological change.

Are There Limits to Growth?

Many opponents of growth argue that sustained world growth is undesirable; some argue that it is impossible. The idea that economic growth is limited by nature is not new. In the early 1970s, a group called the "Club of Rome" focused on the limits to growth arising from the finite supply of natural resources. Extrapolating from the oil shortages caused by the OPEC cartel, the Club of Rome concluded that industrialized countries faced an imminent absolute limit to growth. Do such limits really exist? We discuss the two issues of resource exhaustion and pollution.

Resource Exhaustion

The years since World War II have seen a rapid acceleration in the consumption of the world's resources, particularly fossil fuels and basic minerals. World population has increased from under 2.5 billion to over 6 billion in that period; this increase alone has intensified the demand for the world's resources. Furthermore, as people attain higher incomes, they consume more resources. Thus, not only are there more people in the world, but many of those people are consuming increasing quantities of resources.

The technology and resources available today could not possibly support all of the world's population at a standard of living equal to that of the average Canadian family. It is evident that resources and our present capacity to cope with pollution and environmental degradation are insufficient to accomplish this rise in living standards with present technology.

See the United Nations' website for international data on economic development: www.un.org. Click on "Economic and Social Development" and then go to "Statistics."

Most economists, however, agree that absolute limits to growth, based on the assumptions of constant technology and fixed resources, are not relevant. As modern growth theory stresses, technology changes continually, as do stocks of resources. For example, 40 years ago, few would have thought that the world could produce enough food to feed its present population of 6 billion people, let alone the 10 billion at which the population is projected to stabilize sometime in the twenty-first century. Yet this task now seems feasible.

The future is always uncertain, and it is instructive to recall how many things that we accept as commonplace today would have seemed miraculous a mere 25 years ago.

Yet there is surely cause for concern. Although many barriers can be overcome by technological advances, such achievements are not instantaneous and are certainly not automatic. There is a critical problem of timing: How soon can we discover and put into practice the knowledge required to solve the problems that are made ever more imminent by the growth in the population, the affluence of the rich nations, and the aspirations of the billions who now live in poverty? There is no guarantee that a whole generation will not be caught in transition between technologies, with enormous social and political consequences.

Pollution

A further problem is how to cope with pollution. Air, water, and soil are polluted by a variety of natural activities and, for billions of years, the environment has coped with these. The earth's natural processes had little trouble coping with the pollution generated by its 1 billion inhabitants in 1800. But the 6 billion people who now exist put demands on pollution abatement systems that threaten to become unsustainable. Smoke, sewage, chemical waste, hydrocarbon and greenhouse-gas emissions, spent nuclear fuel, and a host of other pollutants threaten to overwhelm the earth's natural regenerative processes.

Conscious management of pollution was unnecessary when the world's population was one billion people, but such management has now become a pressing matter.

Conclusion

The world faces many problems. Starvation and poverty are the common lot of citizens in many countries and are not unknown even in countries such as Canada and the United States, where average living standards are very high. Growth has raised the average citizens of advanced countries from poverty to plenty in the course of two centuries—a short time in terms of human history. Further growth is needed if people in developing countries are to escape material poverty, and further growth would help advanced countries to deal with many of their pressing economic problems.

Rising population and rising per capita consumption, however, put pressure on the world's natural ecosystems, especially through the many forms of pollution. Further growth must be *sustainable* growth, which must in turn be based on knowledge-driven technological change. Past experience suggests that new technologies will use less of all resources per unit of output. But if they are dramatically to reduce the demands placed on the earth's ecosystems, price and policy incentives will be needed to direct technological change in more "environmentally friendly" ways. Just as present technologies are much less polluting than the technologies of a century ago, the technologies of the twenty-first century must be made much less polluting than today's.

There is no guarantee that the world will solve the problems of sustainable growth, but there is nothing in modern growth theory and existing evidence to suggest that such an achievement is impossible.

SUMMARY

The Nature of Economic Growth

- Sustained increases in real GDP are due mainly to economic growth, which continuously pushes the *LRAS* curve outward, thereby increasing potential output.
- Growth is frequently measured by using rates of change of potential real GDP per person. The cumulative effects of even small differences in growth rates become very large over periods of a decade or more.
- The most important benefit of growth lies in its contribution to the long-run struggle to raise living standards and to escape poverty. Growth also facilitates the redistribution of income among people.

- Growth, though often beneficial, is never costless. The opportunity cost of growth is the diversion of resources from current consumption to capital formation. For individuals who are left behind in a rapidly changing world, the costs are higher and more personal.
- There are four fundamental determinants of growth: increases in the labour force; increases in physical capital; increases in human capital; and improvements in technology.

Theories of Economic Growth

- Investment has short-term effects on real GDP through aggregate demand and long-term effects through growth in potential output. Saving reduces consumption and aggregate demand and therefore reduces real GDP in the short run, but in the long run, saving finances the investment that leads to growth in potential output.
- The Neoclassical theory of growth displays diminishing returns when one factor is increased on its own and constant returns when all factors are increased together. In a balanced growth path, the quantity of labour, the quantity of capital, and real GDP all increase at a constant rate. But since per capita output is constant, living standards are not rising.
- Changes in output that cannot be accounted for by changes in the levels of physical and human capital and in the size of the labour force are attributed to changes in what is called total factor productivity (TFP). Although it

is sometimes associated with technological change, TFP does not measure all of such change because much of it is embodied in new physical and human capital.
- In the Neoclassical growth model, technological change is assumed to be exogenous—unaffected by the size of the labour force, the size of the capital stock, or the level of economic activity.
- Recent growth theory treats technological change as an endogenous variable that responds to market signals. The diffusion of technology is also endogenous. It is costly and often proceeds at a relatively slow pace.
- Some modern growth theories display constant or increasing returns as investment increases on its own. This investment confers externalities such that successive increments of investment may add constant or even successively increasing amounts to total output.

Are There Limits to Growth?

- The critical importance of increasing knowledge and new technology to the goal of sustaining growth is highlighted by the great drain on existing natural resources that has resulted from the explosive growth of population and output in recent decades. Without continuing technological change, the present needs and aspirations of the world's population cannot come anywhere close to being met.

- Rising population and rising real incomes place pressure on resources. Although not all resources will be exhausted, particular resources, such as petroleum, will be.
- The increase in population has similar effects on pollution: The earth's environment could cope naturally with much of human pollution 200 years ago, but the present population is so large that pollution has outstripped nature's coping mechanisms.

KEY CONCEPTS

The cumulative nature of growth
Benefits and costs of growth
Short-run and long-run effects of investment and saving
The aggregate production function

Diminishing marginal returns
Constant returns to scale
Balanced growth
Total factor productivity

Endogenous technical change
Increasing returns to investment
The economics of goods and of ideas
Resource depletion and pollution

STUDY EXERCISES

1. In the text we said that, over many years, small differences in growth rates can have large effects on the level of income. This question will help you understand this important point. Consider an initial value of real GDP equal to Y_0. If real GDP grows at a rate of g percent annually, then after N years real GDP will be equal to $Y_0(1+g)^N$. Now consider the following table. Let the initial level of GDP in all cases be 100.

	Real GDP With Alternative Growth Rates					
	(1)	(2)	(3)	(4)	(5)	(6)
Year	1%	1.5%	2%	2.5%	3%	3.5%
0	100	100	100	100	100	100
1	—	—	—	—	—	—
3	—	—	—	—	—	—
5	—	—	—	—	—	—
10	—	—	—	—	—	—
20	—	—	—	—	—	—
30	—	—	—	—	—	—
50	—	—	—	—	—	—

a. Using the formula provided above, compute the level of real GDP in column 1 for each year. For example, in year 1, real GDP will equal $100(1+.01)^1 = 101$.
b. Now do the same for the rest of the columns.
c. In Year 20, how much larger (in percentage terms) is real GDP in the 3% growth case compared to the 1.5% growth case?
d. In Year 50, how much larger (in percentage terms) is real GDP in the 3% growth case compared to the 1.5% growth case?

2. The diagram below shows two paths for aggregate consumption. One grows at a rate of 3 percent per year; the other grows at 4 percent per year but begins at a lower level.

a. Suppose the economy jumps from Path 1 to Path 2 in year 0 because its rate of capital accumulation increases. What is the opportunity cost in this economy for this increase in capital accumulation?
b. Suppose the economy jumps from Path 1 to Path 2 in year 0 because its rate of R&D expenditures in-

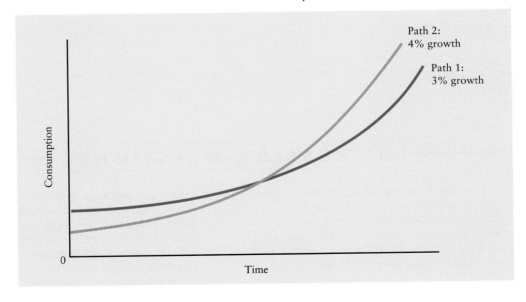

crease. The greater R&D leads to technological improvements that generate the higher growth rate. What is the opportunity cost to this economy for the increase in R&D expenditures?

c. Show in the figure the "breakeven" point for the economy after both of the changes described above. Explain.

3. In the text we discussed the short-run and the long-run effects of saving.

a. Explain why an increase in saving *reduces* real GDP in the short run.

b. Show the answer to part a in an *AD/SRAS* diagram.

c. Explain why an increase in saving *increases* real GDP in the long run.

d. Show the answer to part c in an *AD/SRAS* diagram.

4. The Neoclassical growth theory is based on the existence of an aggregate production function—showing the relationship between labour (*L*), capital (*K*), technology (*T*) and real GDP (*Y*). The table below shows various values for *L*, *K*, and *T*. In all cases, the aggregate production function is assumed to take the following form:

$$Y = T \times \sqrt{KL}$$

Labour (*L*)	Capital (*K*)	Technology (*T*)	Real GDP (*Y*)
10	20	1	—
15	20	1	—
20	20	1	—
25	20	1	—
10	20	1	—
15	30	1	—
20	40	1	—
25	50	1	—
20	20	1	—
20	20	3	—
20	20	4	—
20	20	5	—

a. Compute real GDP for each case and complete the table.

b. In the first part of the table, note that capital is constant but labour is increasing. What property of the production function is displayed? Explain.

c. In the second part of the table, note that capital and labour are increasing by the same proportion. What property of the production function is displayed? Explain.

d. What type of growth is being shown in the third part of the table?

5. In the early 1970s the Club of Rome, extrapolating from the rates of resource use at the time, predicted that the supply of natural resources (especially oil) would be used up within a few decades. Subsequent events appear to have proven them wrong.

a. What is predicted to happen to the price of oil (and other natural resources) as population and per capita incomes rise?

b. Given your answer to part a, what is the likely response by firms and consumers who use such resources?

c. Now explain why resource exhaustion should, through the workings of the price system, lead to technological developments that reduce the use of the resource.

DISCUSSION QUESTIONS

1. Economic growth is often studied in macroeconomic terms, but in a market economy, who makes the decisions that lead to growth? What kinds of decisions and what kinds of actions cause growth to occur? How might a detailed study of individual markets be relevant to understanding economic growth?

2. Discuss the following quote from a recent newspaper article: "Economics and the environment are not strange bedfellows. Environment-oriented tourism is one creative way to resolve the conflict between our desire for a higher standard of living and the realization that nature cannot absorb everything we throw at it. The growing demand for eco-tourism has placed a premium on

the remaining rain forests, undisturbed flora and fauna, and endangered species of the world."

3. "The case for economic growth is that it gives man greater control over his environment, and consequently increases his freedom." Explain why you agree or disagree with this statement by Nobel laureate W. Arthur Lewis.

4. Dr. David Suzuki, an opponent of further economic growth, has argued that despite the fact that "in the twentieth century the list of scientific and technological achievements has been absolutely dazzling, the costs of such progress are so large that negative economic growth may be right for the future." Policies to achieve this include "rigorous reduction of waste, a questioning and distrustful attitude toward technological progress, and braking demands on the globe's resources." Identify some of the benefits and costs of economic growth, and evaluate Suzuki's position. What government policies would be needed to achieve his ends?

5. In this chapter we discussed four fundamental determinants of growth in real output; increases in the labour force; increases in the stock of physical capital; increases in human capital; and improvements in technology. For each of the four, give an example of a government policy that is likely to increase growth. Discuss also the likely cost associated with each policy. Does one of your proposed policies appear better (in a cost-benefit sense) than the others?

6. The Solow residual has been called a "measure of our ignorance" of the causes of growth. Explain this viewpoint. Is the Solow residual a good measure of technical change?

CHAPTER 33

Challenges Facing the Developing Countries

LEARNING OBJECTIVES

1 Gain a general knowledge of the extent of world income inequality.

2 Understand some of the main challenges facing developing countries.

3 Understand the emergence of a new view of development, known as the "Washington consensus."

4 Understand the current debates about development policies.

In the comfortable urban life of today's developed countries, most people have lost sight of the fact that a short time ago—very short in terms of the life span of the earth—people were nomadic food gatherers, garnering an existence as best they could from what nature threw their way. It has been only about 10 000 years since the Neolithic agricultural revolution, when people changed from food gatherers to food producers. Throughout most of subsequent human history, civilizations have been based on a comfortable life for a privileged minority and unremitting toil for the vast majority. Only within the past two centuries have ordinary people become able to expect leisure and high consumption standards—and then only in the world's economically developed countries.

In this chapter we review some of the challenges faced by the world's developing countries—those countries that have not yet been fortunate enough to achieve the living standards that we, in Canada, all too often take for granted.

developed countries
The higher-income countries of the world, including the United States, Canada, Western Europe, Japan, Australia, and South Africa.

developing countries
The lower-income countries of the world, most of which are in Africa, Asia, and Latin America.

newly industrialized countries (NICs)
Countries that have industrialized and grown rapidly over the past 40 years.

The Uneven Pattern of Development

Over 6 billion people are alive today, but the wealthy parts of the world contain no more than 20 percent of the world's population. Many of the rest struggle for subsistence. Many exist on a level at or below that endured by peasants in ancient Egypt or Babylon.

The richest countries with the highest per capita incomes are referred to by the United Nations as **developed countries**. These include the United States, Canada, most of the countries of Western Europe, South Africa, Australia, New Zealand, Japan, and a few others. The poorer states are referred to by the UN as the **developing countries** and include a diverse set of nations. Some, such as Vietnam, Argentina, and China, are growing very rapidly, while others, such as Haiti, Rwanda, and Sierra Leone are actually experiencing negative growth rates of real per capita income. Between these two is another group of nations, called the **newly industrialized countries (NICs)**. They include South

Korea, Singapore, Taiwan, and Hong Kong. These countries grew rapidly in the three decades after 1960 and typically have per capita incomes close to 50 percent of those found in the developed nations. Several other countries in Southeast Asia are close behind the NICs. These include Indonesia, Malaysia, and Thailand. In 1997 and 1998, however, many of these NICs—especially Malaysia, Indonesia, Thailand, and South Korea—experienced sudden economic recessions brought on, to some extent, by the significant collapse in the external value of their currencies.

Viewing the problem of raising per capita income in a poorer country as one of economic *development* recognizes that the whole structure of its economy often needs to be altered to create economic growth. This is a complex task; many countries remain undeveloped today despite decades of effort by their governments (often assisted with aid from developed countries) to get them on a path of sustained growth.

Data on per capita incomes throughout the world (as shown in Table 33-1) cannot be accurate down to the last $100 because there are many problems in comparing national incomes across countries. For example, homegrown food is vitally important to living standards in developing countries, but it is excluded from or at best imperfectly included in the national income statistics of most countries. Nevertheless, the data reflect enormous real differences in living standards that no statistical inaccuracies can hide. The *development gap*—the discrepancy between the standards of living in countries at either end of the distribution—is real and large.

Figure 33-1 provides another way of looking at inequality. It shows the geographical distribution of per capita income. The map reveals why modern political discussions of income distribution often use the labels *North* and *South* to refer to the rich and the poor nations, respectively.

The consequences of low income levels can be severe. In rich countries like Canada and the United States, variations in rainfall are reflected in farm output and farm income. In poor countries, variations in rainfall are often reflected in the death rate. In these countries, many people live so close to a subsistence level that slight fluctuations in the food supply bring death by starvation to large numbers. Other, less dramatic characteristics of poverty include inadequate diet, poor health, short life expectancy, and illiteracy.

The North-South Institute is a Canadian research institute that focuses on economic development. See their website: www.nsi-ins.ca.

TABLE 33-1   Income and Population Differences Among Groups of Countries, 1996

GNP Per Capita (US$)	(1) Number of Countries	(2) GNP (US$ millions)	(3) Population (millions)	(4) GNP Per Capita (US$)	(5) Percentage of World Population	(6) Percentage of World GNP
Less than $785	63	1 596 837	3 236	493	56.2	5.4
$786 to $3115	63	1 962 719	1 125	1 745	19.6	6.6
$3116 to $9635	31	2 178 234	473	4 606	8.2	7.4
$9636 or more	53	23 771 825	919	25 867	16.0	80.6
World	210	29 509 615	5 754	5 129	100.0	100.0

There is considerable inequality in the distribution of world income. The unequal distribution of world income is shown in columns 5 and 6. The poorest half of the world's population earns just 5 percent of world income. The richest 16 percent earns over 80 percent of world income.

(*Source: World Bank Atlas, 1998.*)

FIGURE 33-1   Countries of the World, Classified by Per Capita GNP, 1996

Income group
U.S. dollars

| | Low
$785 or less | | Lower-middle
$786 – $3115 | | Upper-middle
$3116–$9635 | | High
$9636 or more |

There is a sharp geographical division between "North" and "South" in the level of income per capita. The nations of the world are classified here according to four levels of measured per capita GNP, as shown in Table 33-1. The poorest group, shown in brown, represents 56 percent of the world's population and just over 5 percent of world GNP. The wealthiest group, shown in orange, includes North America, Europe, Japan, and Australia and represents 16 percent of the world's population and over 80 percent of world GNP.

For these reasons, reformers in developing countries feel a sense of urgency not felt by their counterparts in rich countries. Yet, as Table 33-2 shows, some of the poorest countries in the world are among those with very low or negative growth rates of per capita GDP, with the following consequence:

The development gap has been widening for the very poorest countries.

As we shall see, this is a problem of both output and population. It is also an international political problem. What are the causes of underdevelopment, and how may they be overcome?

Impediments to Economic Development

Per capita income grows when aggregate income grows faster than population. Many forces can impede such growth. Here we study a number of possible impediments.

TABLE 33-2 The Relationship Between the Level and the Growth Rate of Per Capita Income, 1990–1996

Growth of GNP Per Capita, 1990–1996 (% per year)	Number of Countries	GNP (US$ million) 1996	Population (millions) 1996	GNP Per Capita (US$) 1996
Less than 0	69	2 152 165	832	2 587
0 to 0.9	21	6 037 894	342	17 655
1.0 to 1.9	25	15 772 567	1 043	15 122
2.0 to 2.9	20	1 399 561	488	2 868
3.0 or more	39	3 899 334	2 896	1 346

The very poorest countries spend much of their increase in income on a rising population. Hence, their increase in income per capita is less than half that of the countries that are already richer. The gap in income between rich and many of the very poor countries is not closing.

(*Source: World Bank Atlas*, 1998.)

Resources

A country's supply of natural resources is important. A country with infertile land and inadequate supplies of natural resources will find income growth more difficult to achieve than one that is richly endowed with such resources.

How these resources are managed also matters. When farmland is divided into many small parcels, it may be much more difficult to achieve the advantages of modern agricultural techniques than when the land is available in huge tracts for large-scale farming. Fragmented land holdings may result from a dowry or inheritance system or may be politically imposed. One of the populist policies following the Mexican Revolution early in the twentieth century was the redistribution of land from large landowners to ordinary peasants. Today, however, fragmented land ownership prevents Mexican agriculture from producing at costs low enough to compete in international markets. The Mexican government now faces an agonizing choice between allowing its populist land reforms to be reversed or continuing to protect a large agricultural sector whose inefficiency is increasing relative to competing suppliers.

Although abundant supplies of natural resources can assist growth, they are neither sufficient to ensure growth nor necessary for it. Some countries with large supplies of natural resources have poor growth performance because the economic structure encourages waste. Prime examples are the former Soviet Union, Argentina before the 1990s, and Uganda. In contrast, other countries have enjoyed rapid rates of economic growth based on human capital and entrepreneurial ability despite a dearth of natural resources. Prime examples are Switzerland in earlier centuries, Japan over the past 100 years (until its significant current economic malaise, beginning in the early 1990s), and Singapore, Hong Kong, and Taiwan since the end of World War II.

When we discuss inefficiency in resource use, it helps to distinguish between two kinds of economic inefficiency, which are studied in microeconomics. *Allocative inefficiency* occurs when factors of production are used to make an inefficient combination of goods. There are too many of some goods and too few of others, and thus the society is at the wrong point on its production possibility boundary. If resources are reallocated to produce less of some and more of other types of goods, some people can be made better off while no one is made worse off.

Productive inefficiency occurs when factors of production are used in inefficient combinations. Given the prices of capital and labour, some production processes use too much capital relative to labour, while others use too little. Productive inefficiency implies that the society is *inside* its production possibility boundary. If factor combinations are altered, more of all goods can be produced.

Monopolistic market structures, as well as taxes, tariffs, and subsidies, are some important sources of the distortions that lead to both allocative and productive inefficiencies.

A third kind of inefficiency, called *X-inefficiency*, occurs either when firms do not seek to maximize their profits or when owners of the factors of production do not seek to maximize their well-being. Like allocative and productive inefficiency, X-inefficiency also puts the economy inside its production possibility boundary.

Professor Harvey Liebenstein of the University of California, the economist who developed the concept, has studied X-inefficiency in developing countries. He cites psychological evidence to show that non-maximizing behaviour is typical of situations in which the pressure that has been placed on decision makers is either very low or very high. According to this evidence, if the customary living standard can be obtained with little effort, people are likely to follow customary behaviour and spend little time trying to make *optimal* decisions that would improve their well-being. When pressure builds up, so that making a reasonable income becomes more difficult, optimizing behaviour becomes more common. Under extreme pressure, however, such as very low living standards or a rapidly deteriorating environment, people become disoriented and once again do not adopt optimizing behaviour.

Human Capital

Numbers of people matter, and so do their training and experience. A well-developed entrepreneurial class, motivated and trained to organize resources for efficient production, is often missing in poor countries. The cause may be that managerial positions are awarded on the basis of family status or political patronage rather than merit, it may be the prevalence of economic or cultural attitudes that do not favour acquisition of wealth by organizing productive activities, or it may simply be an absence of the quantity or quality of education or training that is required.

In today's world, much production is knowledge-intensive, thus putting a premium on a well-educated workforce. The ability to read, do basic calculations, operate electronic equipment, and follow relatively complex instructions are important requirements for much modern labour. Failure to develop such essential labour skills can be an important cause of lack of growth.

Poor health is another source of inadequate human resources. When the labour force is healthy, less working time is lost, and more effective effort is expended.

Agriculture

A developing country whose labour force is mainly devoted to agriculture has little choice but to accept this basic allocation of resources. It can build up its industrial sector, and if its efforts are successful, the proportion of the population devoted to urban pursuits will rise. But the change will come slowly, leaving a large portion of the country's resources in rural pursuits for a long time to come.

It follows that policies to help the agriculture sector raise productivity are an important part of the development strategy in any agriculture-based poor country. These can fill the dual purposes of raising incomes of rural workers and reducing the cost of food for urban workers.

A developing country's government may choose to devote a major portion of its resources to stimulating agricultural production, say, by mechanizing farms, irrigating land, using new seeds and fertilizers, and promoting agricultural research and development. Modern developments of new crops and new growing techniques put a premium on agricultural research and development (R&D) so that a country can adopt, and usually adapt, other country's agricultural innovations. Also, nonfood agricultural and forest products are becoming increasingly important, and R&D expenditures are often needed if these are to become established products. If successful, the country will stave off starvation for its current population, and it may even develop an excess over current needs and thus have a crop available for export. A food surplus can earn foreign exchange to buy needed imports.

In many developing countries, the labour force is mainly devoted to agriculture. Increasing the efficiency of agriculture is an important part of a successful development strategy.

The gains from this strategy, while large at first, are subject to diminishing returns. Further gains in agricultural production have an ever-higher opportunity cost, measured in terms of the resources needed to irrigate land and to mechanize production. Critics of reliance on agricultural output argue that developing economies must start at once to develop other bases for economic growth.

Many developing countries (as well as many developed ones) suffer from misguided government intervention in the agriculture sector. In India, for example, the government—motivated by a desire to *diversify* agricultural production by increasing the number of crops under cultivation—has encouraged crops such as oilseeds and sugarcane, in which India has a comparative *dis*advantage, and discouraged crops such as rice, wheat, and cotton, in which India has a strong comparative advantage. It has subsidized food prices, thus giving large benefits to the urban population.

Population Growth

Population growth is one of the central problems of economic development. Some developing countries have population growth rates in excess of their GDP growth rates and therefore have *negative* growth rates of per capita GDP. Many developing countries have rates of population growth that are nearly as large as their rates of GDP growth. As a result, their standards of living are barely higher than they were 100 years ago. They have made appreciable gains in aggregate income, but most of the gains have been literally eaten up by the increasing population.

The critical importance of population growth to living standards was perceived early in the nineteenth century by Thomas Malthus (1766–1834). He asserted two relations concerning rates of increase. First, food production tends to increase in an *arithmetic* progression (e.g., 100, 103, 106, 109, 112, where the increments in this example are 3 *units* per period). Second, population tends to increase in a *geometric* progression (e.g., 100, 103, 106.09, 109.27, 112.55, where the increase in this example is 3 *percent* per period). Consequently, Malthus argued that under conditions of natural growth, population will always tend to outrun the growth in food supply. The difference in our example may not seem like much after only five periods. But after 20 periods, the arithmetic progression in food supply has increased it to 160, whereas the geometric progression in the population has increased it to 181.

Malthus's prediction helped to earn economics the label "the dismal science." And, in some poor areas of the world, the predictions ring all too true, even today. Where agricultural methods are fairly traditional so that food production increases only slowly, population tends to increase at more rapid rates. The result is subsistence living, with population held in check by low life expectancies and periodic famines.

Fortunately, over most of the world, Malthus's predictions have been proved false. Two reasons are paramount. First, Malthus underestimated the importance of technological

For a lot of good data about developing countries, see the UN's website: www.un.org. Click on "Economic and Social Development."

change, which has increased agricultural productivity at a *geometric* rate in many countries, a rate far higher than the rate at which the demand for food has been growing in most advanced countries. Second, he underestimated the extent of voluntary restrictions of population growth due both to the widespread use of birth control techniques and other changes in behaviour such as delayed marriages. As a result, population has grown more slowly than the production of food (and most other things) in developed countries. In these places, living standards have been rising rather than falling.

For the more advanced industrialized countries, Malthusian pressures are not a problem today. For many poor countries, where people subsist on what they grow for themselves, the tendency for the growth in population to outstrip the growth in the food supply makes Malthusian pressures a current threat.

Figure 33-2 illustrates actual and projected world population. By now, the population problem is almost completely limited to developing countries. About 97 percent of the expected growth in the world's population between now and 2050 will be in the developing countries of Africa, Asia, and Latin America.

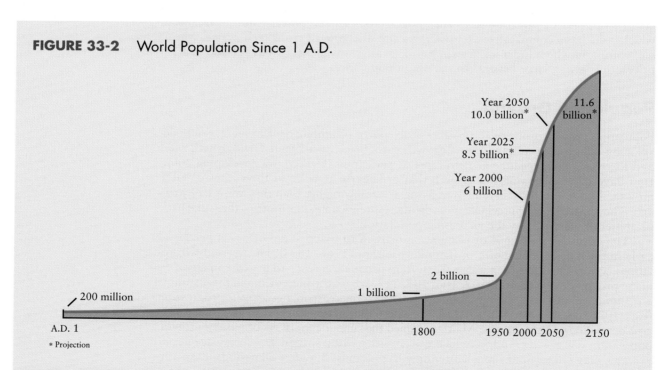

FIGURE 33-2   World Population Since 1 A.D.

World population was just over 6 billion in 2000 and is projected to rise to 10 billion by the middle of the 21st century. The population of industrialized countries has nearly stabilized. But, in developing countries, population is skyrocketing. Up to 97 percent of population growth between now and 2050 will occur in developing countries. By that time, total world population will have reached 10 billion. Birth and death rates among present populations allow estimates to be made up to about the middle of the next century with reasonable accuracy. The projection to 11.6 billion by 2150 is much more conjectural and highly uncertain.

(*Source:* United Nations Population Fund.)

Cultural Barriers

Traditions and habitual ways of doing business vary among societies, and not all are equally conducive to economic growth. In developing countries, cultural forces are often a source of inefficiency. Sometimes personal considerations of family, past favours, or traditional friendship or enmity are more important than market incentives in motivating behaviour. In a traditional society in which children are expected to stay in their parents' occupations, it is more difficult for the labour force to change its characteristics and to adapt to the requirements of growth than in a society in which upward mobility is a goal itself.

The fact that existing social, religious, or legal patterns may make growth more difficult does not imply that they are undesirable. Instead, it suggests that the benefits of these patterns must be weighed against the costs, of which the limitation on growth is one. When people derive satisfaction from a religion whose beliefs inhibit growth or when they value a society in which every household owns its own land and is more nearly self-sufficient than in another society, they may be quite willing to pay a price in terms of forgone growth opportunities.

Many critics argue that development plans, particularly when imposed by economists coming from developed countries, pay too little attention to local cultural and religious values. Even when they are successful by the test of increasing GDP, such success may be at too great a cost in terms of social upheaval for the current generation.

Cultural traditions in developing countries often stand in the way of increases in efficiency and economic growth.

A country that wants development must accept some alteration in traditional ways of doing things. However, a tradeoff between speed of development and amount of social upheaval can be made. The critics argue that such a tradeoff should be made by local governments and should not be imposed by outsiders who understand little of local customs and beliefs. An even more unfavourable possibility is that the social upheaval will occur without achieving even the expected benefits of GDP growth. If the development policy does not take local values into account, the local population may not respond as predicted by Western economic theories. In this case, the results of the development effort may be disappointingly small.

Domestic Saving

Although modern development strategies call in many instances for a large infusion of imported foreign capital, the rise of domestically owned firms, which will reap some of the externalities created by foreign technology, is one key to sustained development. This requires a supply of domestic saving to finance their growth.

If more domestic capital is to be created at home by a country's own efforts, resources must be diverted from the production of goods for current consumption. This reallocation of resources implies a reduction in *current* living standards. If living standards are already at or near the subsistence level, such a diversion will be difficult. At best, it will be possible to reallocate only a small proportion of resources to the production of capital goods.

Such a situation is often described as the *vicious circle of poverty:* Because a country has little capital per head, it is poor; because it is poor, it can devote few resources to creating new capital rather than to producing goods for consumption; because little new capital can be produced, capital per head remains low, and the country remains poor.

The vicious circle can be made to seem an absolute constraint on growth rates. Of course, it is not; if it were, we would all still be at the level of the early agricultural civilizations. The grain of truth in the vicious-circle argument is that some surplus must be available somewhere in the society to allow saving and investment. In a poor society with an even distribution of income, in which nearly everyone is at the subsistence level, saving may be very difficult. But this is not the common experience. Usually there is at least a small middle class that can save and invest if opportunities for the profitable use of funds arise.

Infrastructure

infrastructure The basic installations and facilities (especially transportation and communications systems) on which the commerce of a community depends.

Key services, called **infrastructure**, such as transportation and a communications network, are necessary for efficient commerce. Roads, bridges, railways, and harbours are needed to transport people, materials, and finished goods. Phone and postal services, water supply, and sanitation are essential to economic development.

The absence of a dependable infrastructure can impose severe barriers to economic development.

Many governments feel that money spent on a new steel mill shows more impressive results than money spent on such infrastructure investments as automating the telephone system. Yet private, growth-creating entrepreneurial activity will be discouraged more by the absence of good telephone communications than by the lack of domestically produced steel.

Foreign Debt

The 1970s and early 1980s witnessed explosive growth in the external debt of many developing nations. Since the mid 1980s, most of these countries have experienced difficulties in making the payments required to service their debt. "Debt rescheduling"—putting off until the future payments that cannot be made today—has been common, and many observers feel that major defaults are inevitable unless ways of forgiving the debt can be found.

The trend toward increased debt started when OPEC quadrupled the world price of oil in 1973. Because many developing nations relied on imported oil, their trade balances moved sharply into deficit. At the same time, the OPEC countries developed massive trade surpluses. Commercial banks helped to recycle the deposits of their OPEC customers into loans to the developing nations. These loans financed some necessary adjustments and some worthwhile new investment projects. However, a large part of the funds were used unwisely; wasteful government spending and lavish consumption splurges occurred in many of the borrowing countries.

A doubling of energy prices in 1979 led to a further increase in the debt of developing nations. The severe world recession that began in 1981 reduced demand for the exports of many of these countries. As a result, they were unable to achieve many benefits from the adjustments and investment expenditures that they had made. Furthermore, sharp increases in real interest rates (caused in part by the widespread fight against inflation) led to increased debt-service payments; as a result, many countries could not make their payments.

The lending banks had little choice but to reschedule the debt—essentially lending the developing nations the money to make interest payments while adding to the principal of the existing loans. The International Monetary Fund (IMF) played a central role in arranging these reschedulings by making further loans and concessions conditional on appropriate policies of adjustment and restraint. These conditions were intended to limit wasteful government expenditure and consumption and thus to increase the likelihood that the loans would eventually be repaid. Critics of the IMF's role argued that much of the restraint resulted in reduced investment and hence that the IMF's conditions were counterproductive.

During the mid 1980s, the world economy recovered, inflation fell, and real interest rates fell. As a result, the developing countries' export earnings grew, their debt-service obligations stabilized, and the crisis subsided. A sharp fall in the price of oil, which started in late 1985, further eased the problems of the oil-importing nations, but it also created a new debt problem.

Throughout the period of rising energy prices in the 1970s, a number of oil-exporting developing nations—including Mexico, Venezuela, and Indonesia—saw in those high prices new opportunities for investment and growth. Based on their high oil revenues, their ability to borrow improved. Their external debt grew, and they were able to avoid many of the adjustments that the oil-importing developing nations had been forced to undertake. When oil prices fell in the 1980s and 1990s, however, these oil exporters found themselves in difficult positions.

By the late 1990s, attention had focused on the so-called highly indebted poor countries (HIPCs). Figure 33-3 shows for 1997 the ratios of external debt to GNP for the ten most indebted of the HIPCs. In 1999, a meeting of the most industrialized countries (the G8 countries) agreed in principal to accelerate debt relief for the HIPCs. But the details of this plan have not yet been worked out.

FIGURE 33-3   External Debt in the Highly Indebted Poor Countries, 1997

The Highly Indebted Poor Countries (HIPCs) had external debts equal to $201 billion in 1997. The data shown here are the external debts of the ten most indebted of the HIPCs. The numbers shown for each country are that country's external debt as a percentage of its GNP. Angola, for example, had just over $10 billion in external debt in 1997, which was 232 percent of its GNP.

(*Source:* These data are available on the World Bank's website: www.worldbank.org.)

Development Policies

The past two decades have seen a remarkable change in the views of appropriate policies for industrial development. The views that dominated development policies during the period from 1945 to the early 1980s have given way to a new set of views that reflect the experience of the earlier period.

The Older View

The dominant approaches toward development strategies from 1945 to the early 1980s were inward-looking and interventionist.

The policies were inward-looking in the sense that replacing imports was the primary goal of fostering local industries. These local industries were usually protected with very high tariffs and supported by large subsidies and favourable tax treatment. The exchange rate was almost always pegged, usually at a level which overvalued the currency (that is, the exchange rate was pegged *below* its free-market value). As we will explain in detail in Chapter 36, fixing the exchange rate below its free-market level raises the domestic currency prices of exports and lowers the prices of imports, which leads to an excess demand for foreign exchange. The argument for keeping export prices high was that foreign demand for traditional exports was inelastic so that (as we saw in Chapter 4) raising their prices would raise the amount received by their sellers. The excess demand for foreign exchange caused by the overvaluation of the currency led to a host of import restrictions and exchange controls such as import licences and quotas issued by government officials.

Many governments were hostile to foreign investment and made it difficult for multinational firms to locate in their countries. For example, many had local ownership rules requiring that any foreign firm wanting to invest there must set up a subsidiary in which local residents would own at least half of the shares. Much new investment was undertaken by government-owned industries, while subsidization of privately owned local industries was often heavy and indiscriminate. Industrial activity was often controlled, with a license being required to set up a firm or to purchase supplies of scarce commodities. Much investment was financed by local savings, which were sometimes made voluntarily and sometimes forced by the state.

This whole set of measures is often referred to as being *inward-looking* and based on *import substitution*. Strictly, import substitution refers to the attempt to build local industries behind protectionist walls to replace imports. Often, however, the term is used more generally to refer to the entire battery of related measures just described.

These interventionist measures gave great power to government officials and, not surprisingly, corruption was rife. Bribes were needed to obtain many things, including state subsidies, licences, and quotas. As a result, many resources were allocated to those who had the most political power and were willing to pay the highest bribes, rather than to those who could use the resources most efficiently.

Heavy subsidization of private firms and state investment in public firms required much money, and the tax structures of many poor countries could not provide sufficient funds. As a result, such expenditures were often financed by borrowing from the central bank which, as we saw in Chapters 28 and 29, ultimately leads to inflation. Persistent inflation was a major problem in many of these countries. Inflation was almost always in the double-digit range and quite often soared to several hundred percent per year.

Most of the economies where these policies were employed fell short of full central planning and full state ownership of resources. As a result, there was still some private initiative and some profit seeking through normal market means. But the overall policy thrust was inward-looking and interventionist.

The Rise of the New View

During the 1980s, four important events contributed to a reappraisal of this development model. First, developing countries that had followed these policies most faithfully had some of the poorest growth records. Second, the GDP growth rates of the more industrialized countries of Eastern Europe and the Soviet Union that had followed interventionist approaches to their own growth were visibly falling behind those of the market-based economies. Third, Taiwan, Singapore, South Korea, and Hong Kong, which had departed from the accepted model by adopting more market-based policies, were prospering and growing rapidly. Fourth, the globalization of the world's economy led to an understanding that countries could no longer play a full part in world economic growth without a substantial presence of multinational corporations within their boundaries. Given the size of developing countries, this meant the presence of foreign-owned multinationals. We now discuss each of these four events in more detail.

Experience of the Developing Countries

Highly interventionist economies fared poorly in the 1950s, 1960s, and 1970s. Economies as varied as Argentina, Myanmar (then Burma), Tanzania, Ethiopia, and Ghana were all interventionist and all grew slowly, if at all. In Ethiopia, the emperor was overthrown, and the new government adopted rigid Soviet-style policies. Attempts to collectivize agriculture led, as they had 50 years previously in the Soviet Union, to widespread famine. Some countries, such as Ghana, Nigeria, and Myanmar, started from relatively strong economic positions when they first gained their independence but later saw their GDPs and living standards shrink. Other countries, such as India and Kenya, sought a middle way between capitalism and socialism. They fared better than their more highly interventionist neighbours, but their development was still disappointingly slow.

Experience of the Socialist Countries

Earlier in this century, many observers were impressed by the apparent success of planned programs of "crash" development, of which the Soviet experience was the most remarkable and the Chinese the most recent. Not surprisingly, therefore, many of the early development policies of the poorer countries sought to copy the planning techniques that appeared to underlie these earlier socialist successes.

In recent decades, however, the more developed socialist countries began to discover the limitations of their planning techniques. Highly planned government intervention seems most successful in providing infrastructure and developing basic industries, such as electric power and steel, and in copying technologies developed in more market-oriented economies. However, it is now seen to be much less successful in providing the entrepreneurial activity, risk taking, and adaptivity to change that are key ingredients to *sustained* economic growth and technological change.

The discrediting of the Soviet approach to development was given added emphasis when the countries of Eastern Europe and the former Soviet Union abandoned their system *en masse* and took the difficult path of rapidly introducing market economies. Although China, the last major holdout, posted impressive growth figures in the 1990s, two "nonsocialist" reasons are important in explaining its performance. First, over 90 percent of the population is engaged in basically free-market agriculture—because that sector has long been free of the central-planning apparatus that so hampered agriculture in the former Soviet Union. Second, while the state-controlled industries suffer increasing inefficiencies, a major investment boom took place in China's Southeast coastal provinces. Here foreign investment, largely from Japan and the Asian NICs, introduced a rapidly growing and highly efficient industrialized market sector.

See Chapter 33 of www.pearsoned.ca/lipsey for a discussion of socialist Cuba's recent process of economic reform: Archibald Ritter, "Is Cuba's Economic Reform Process Paralyzed?" *World Economic Affairs.*

Experience of the NICs

South Korea, Taiwan, Hong Kong, and Singapore—the so-called Asian Tigers—have turned themselves from relative poverty to relatively high income in the course of less than 40 years.

During the early stages of their development, they used import restrictions to build up local industries and to develop labour forces with the requisite skills and experiences. In the 1950s and early 1960s, however, each of the four abandoned many of the interventionist aspects of the older development model. They created market-oriented economies with less direct government intervention than other developing economies, who stuck with the accepted development model.

Korea and Singapore did not adopt a laissez faire stance. Instead, both followed quite strong policies that targeted specific areas for development and encouraged those areas with various economic incentives. In contrast, Hong Kong and Taiwan have had somewhat more laissez faire attitudes toward the direction of industrial development.

After local industries had been established, all four adopted outward-looking, market-based, export-oriented policies. This approach tested the success of various policies to encourage specific industries by their ability to compete in the international marketplace. With industries designed to serve a sheltered home market, it is all too easy to shelter inefficiency more or less indefinitely. With export-oriented policies *not based on subsidies,* the success of targeted firms and industries is tested in international markets, and unprofitable firms fail.

Not far behind the NICs is a second generation of Asian and Latin American countries that have also adopted more market-oriented policies and have seen substantial growth follow. Indonesia, Thailand, the Philippines, Mexico, Chile, and Argentina are examples. Even Vietnam and Laos are liberalizing their economies as communist governments come to accept that a market economy is a necessary condition for sustained economic growth.

Several Southeast Asian economies fell into significant recessions that began in late 1997 and continued throughout 1998 and early 1999. As of late 1999, however, it appears that these recessions, though very significant, will not lead to a return of interventionist policies in these countries. Of course, only time will tell.

Globalization

At the heart of globalization lies the rapid reduction in transportation costs and the revolution in information and communication technology that has characterized the past two decades. One consequence has been that the internal organization of firms is changing to become less hierarchical and rigid and more decentralized and fluid. Another consequence is that the strategies of transnational corporations (TNCs), which span national borders in their organizational structures, are driving globalization and much of economic development. Because most trade, and much investment, is undertaken by TNCs, no country can develop into an integrated part of today's world economy without a substantial presence of TNCs within its borders. The importance of TNCs is now recognized, and most aspiring developing countries generally put out a welcome mat for them.

Historically, only a few countries, notably Japan and Taiwan, have industrialized without major infusions of foreign direct investment (FDI). Moreover, these cases took place before the globalization of the world's economy. It is doubtful that many (or any) of today's poor countries could achieve sustained and rapid growth paths without a substantial amount of FDI brought in by foreign-owned transnationals. Without such FDI, both the transfer of technology and foreign networking would be difficult to achieve.

Developing countries have gradually come to accept the advantages of FDI. First, FDI often provides somewhat higher-paying jobs than might otherwise be available to local residents. Second, it provides investment that does not have to be financed by local saving. Third, it provides training in worker and management skills that come from working with large firms linked into the global market. Fourth, it can provide advanced technology that is not easily transferred outside of the firms that are already familiar with its use.

Today, virtually all developing economies encourage foreign TNCs to locate within their borders. Where governments used to worry that their countries had too much FDI, they now worry that there may be too little.

The Washington Consensus

As a result of these various experiences, a new consensus on development policy has emerged. The revised model calls for a more outward-looking, international-trade-oriented, and market-based route to development. It calls for accepting market prices as an instrument for the allocation of resources. This means abandoning both the heavy subsidization and the pervasive regulations that characterized the older approach. But it also calls for a careful use of government policy in providing basic infrastructure, public goods, and dealing with market failures.

This consensus is often referred to as the "Washington Consensus." It describes the conditions that are believed to be necessary for a poorer country to get itself on a path of sustained development. These views are accepted by a number of international agencies, including the World Bank, the IMF, and several UN organizations. The main elements of this consensus are as follows:

1. Government should adopt sound fiscal policies that avoid large budget deficits. In particular, persistent *structural* deficits should be avoided.

2. Government should adopt sound monetary policies, with the goal of maintaining low and stable inflation rates. Exchange rates should be determined by market forces rather than being pegged by central banks.

3. The tax base should be broad, and marginal tax rates should be moderate.

4. Markets should be allowed to determine prices and the allocation of resources. Trade liberalization is desirable, and import licencing, with its potential for corruption, should be avoided.

5. Targeted protection for specific industries and a moderate general tariff, say, 10 to 20 percent, may provide a bias toward widening the industrial base of a developing country. But such protection should be for a specified period that is not easily extended.

6. Industrial development should rely to an important extent on local firms and on attracting FDI and subjecting it to a minimum of local restrictions that discriminate between local and foreign firms. (Of course, restrictions will be required for such things as environmental policies, but these should apply to all firms, whether foreign-owned or locally owned.)

7. An export orientation (as long as exports do not rely on permanent subsidies) provides competitive incentives for the building of skills and technologies geared to world markets, permits realization of scale economies, and provides access to valuable information flows from buyers and competitors in advanced countries.

8. Education, health (especially for the disadvantaged), and infrastructure investment are desirable forms of public expenditure. Because future demands are hard to predict and subject to rapid change, a balance must be struck between training for specific skills and training for generalized and adaptive abilities.

Visit the World Bank's website at: www.worldbank.org.

Visit the IMF's website at:
www.imf.org.

9. Finally, emphasis needs to be placed on poverty reduction for at least two reasons. First, poverty can exert powerful antigrowth effects. People in poverty will not develop the skills to provide an attractive labour force, and they may not even respond to incentives when these are provided. Malnutrition in early childhood can affect a person's capacities for life. Second, although economic growth tends to reduce the incidence of poverty, it does not eliminate it.

Debate Beyond the Washington Consensus

The basic Washington consensus on outward-looking, market-oriented economic policies provides what many people believe are necessary conditions for a country to achieve a sustained growth path in today's world.

The policies suggested by the Washington consensus relate primarily to the behaviour of governments themselves.

Sufficient or Just Necessary?

There is substantial debate around one crucial issue: Are the conditions of the Washington consensus *sufficient* to encourage the kinds and volumes of both domestic and foreign investment needed to develop comparative advantages in higher-value-added industries, or are they merely *necessary*?

Some observers believe that these conditions are sufficient. In their view, all a country needs to do is to meet these conditions. Domestic saving will finance domestic investments, FDI will flow in, and a sustained growth path will be established. Other economists worry that many countries may have only limited ability to attract FDI, to benefit from it, and to create sufficient domestic investment, even after fulfilling the conditions of the Washington consensus. The latter set of economists point to the experience of some African countries where TNCs operated extractive industries that despoiled the countryside and produced little permanent benefit for the host country; they merely extracted the available resources and then left. Others point out that there is a major difference between pure extractive enterprises and manufacturing enterprises, the latter having more potential spillovers to the local economy than the former.

What does happen after the conditions of the consensus are fulfilled will depend in part on the existing endowments of the country in question. If large supplies of natural resources or cheap, well-educated labour are available, fulfilling these conditions may be sufficient. Commentators who call for policies beyond those of the Washington consensus argue that for some countries, a past history of nongrowth, plus the absence of positive externalities that go with a reasonably developed industrial sector, may require that the government adopt a more active set of *integrated* trade, technology-transfer, and innovation policies. This set of policies would be aimed at encouraging the development of human and technological capabilities.

Policies that go beyond the Washington consensus are directed at the interactions between governments and the private sector, particularly as represented by TNCs.

Implications of Modern Growth Theory

What is at issue in the debate just described is related to the newer views on economic growth that were discussed in Chapter 32. The key new view is that *endogenous* technological innovation is the mainspring of economic growth. Things emphasized by economists for centuries, such as aggregate saving and investment, are still essential, but technological change is now considered to lie at the core of the growth process.

As we saw in Chapter 32, technological change is a costly process that is undertaken mainly by firms in pursuit of profit. Research and development are by their nature risky and uncertain activities. The technological path followed by firms and industries is evolutionary in the sense that it develops as experiments and errors are made.

For developing countries, one of the most important of the many new insights stemming from research into the growth process is that adopting someone else's technology is often not a simple, costless task. Substantial R&D capacity is needed to adapt other people's technology to one's own purposes and to learn how to use it—except where the technology uses only very simple machines that can be operated by unskilled labour. For one reason, much of the knowledge required to use a technology is tacit; it can be obtained only from learning by doing and by using. This creates difficulties in imitating the knowledge, as well as uncertainty regarding which modifications will work in any new situation. It is true even when technology moves from one firm to another in the same industry and the same country. The problems are greater when technology moves across industrial or national borders. The difficulties of adopting new technologies also become more difficult the more complex and information-intensive the technology becomes.

It follows that all knowledge is not freely tradable. Neither a firm nor a government can go out and buy it ready-to-use. Acquiring *working* technological knowledge requires both investment and the experience that allows workers and management slowly to acquire the needed tacit knowledge.

Usable new knowledge comes to a developing country through a slow and costly diffusion process.

See Chapter 33 of www.pearsoned.ca/lipsey for an interview with Harvard's Jeffrey Sachs on the Asian crisis of 1997–98 and the need for reform of the IMF and World Bank: "The Devil's in the Details," *World Economic Affairs.*

What May Be Needed

The foregoing view of technological change suggests to some economists a major reason why active government policies that go beyond the Washington consensus may be needed.

Protection of the Domestic Market.
Such policies can work at the early stages by establishing a protected domestic market through tariffs and other import restrictions. Virtually every country that has moved to a sustained growth path in the past, including the United States, Canada, Japan, and all of the NICs, has used import substitution in its early stages of industrialization. A protected home market provides a possible solution to the problem of coping with the enormous externalities involved in building up an infrastructure of physical and human capital as well as the required tacit knowledge and abilities. Even if all the specific young industries that are protected by the import substitution policy do not grow into self-sufficient mature industries, the externalities may still be created and become available for a second generation of more profitable firms.

Protection of the home market from international competition can, however, pose serious problems unless it is selective and temporary. Investment may occur mainly in areas where comparative advantage never grows. High costs of protected industries may create a lack of competitiveness in other domestic industries whose inputs are the outputs of the protected industries. Some potential comparative advantages may not be exploited because of the distorting effects of existing tariffs, and—as always—consumers bear much of the cost in terms of high prices of protected outputs.

Innovation Policies.
Trade restrictions do not provide the only route to building industrial and R&D capacity by encouraging technological diffusion and creating structural competitiveness. Other methods include the much-needed public investment in infrastructure and in human capital and many other things such as the provision of adequate financial schemes to favour investment in physical and intangible assets, procurement and tax

incentives, provision of technical and marketing information, consulting services for assisting firms in industrial restructuring and in the adoption of new technologies and organizational techniques, support services in design, quality assurance and standards, schemes for training and retraining personnel, and facilities for start-up companies.

Advocates of such a policy package stress the importance of having these incentives as part of a more general innovation and competition policy in order to encourage technological transfer to the local economy (such transfers are riddled with market failures arising from their externalities). Linkages among firms, and between firms and universities and research institutions, both within the country and with the rest of the world, are also important.

Policies that encourage the development of small- and medium-size enterprises are important to any development strategy. These tend to be locally owned and tend to be the vehicle by which know-how and best practices are transferred from TNCs to the local economy. They are also the sector most vulnerable to excessive red tape, rules and regulations, profit taxes, and other interferences that raise the cost of doing business.

A Cautionary Note.   There is no doubt that the governments of many poor countries have been highly interventionist—and some still are. Hence, a good first strategy is often to diminish the government's place in the economy. There is no point in adopting a new, relatively rational technology-promotion strategy if existing government interventions are irrational and heavy. The unproductive interventions must be cleared away first. This does not mean, however, that if a government were starting from scratch, the best objective would be to minimize its place in the economy.

Whatever methods are chosen, selective intervention is a delicate instrument, highly dangerous in inept hands; in fact, even when in practiced hands, much damage can be done.

The intervention needs to be carefully tailored to get specific results and to reduce the opportunities for small groups to gain at the expense of others. To meet these objectives, most assistance should, as a rule, be terminated after specified periods of time. It is also important to leave room for the market to generate, and support, unforeseen opportunities.

Conclusion

According to the World Bank, approximately 1.2 billion of the world's people subsist on less than one dollar (U.S.) per day. Despite the fact that one U.S. dollar buys much more in Addis Ababa than it does in New York, Toronto, or Paris, there is still a significant fraction of the world's population that is—by any reasonable standard—very poor.

What can be done? The World Bank's prescriptions fall into two broad categories:

1. Create new economic opportunities for the poor. Because the poor's main source of income is what they are paid for their labour, this means promoting labour-intensive economic growth.

2. Equip the poor to grasp these opportunities. This step calls for adequate provision of basic social services such as primary education, health, and family planning.

The World Bank also points out that one of the most damaging economic distortions in many developing countries is excessive taxation of farming. This hits the very part of the economy on which most of the poor depend for their livelihood.

The World Bank suggests that a major reduction in poverty is possible worldwide. What is needed is the acceptance of the new consensus on the importance of market determination and of reducing state control and state ownership of business activity. This, in addition to a large dose of enlightened policies to bring education, health, and jobs to ordinary people and improved technology to the nations' firms, could pay enormous dividends in reducing poverty and suffering. Only time will tell how much of that hopeful potential will be realized over the next decade or so.

S U M M A R Y

The Uneven Pattern of Development

LO 1

- About one-quarter of the world's population still exists at a level of bare subsistence, and nearly three-quarters are poor by Canadian standards. Although some poorer societies have grown rapidly, the gap between the very richest and very poorest appears to be increasing.

Impediments to Economic Development

LO 2

- Impediments to economic development include excessive population growth; resource limitations; inefficient use of resources; inadequate infrastructure; excessive government intervention; and institutional and cultural patterns that make economic growth difficult.

Development Policies

LO 3 4

- The older model for development policies included heavy tariff barriers and a hostility to foreign direct investment (FDI) to protect the home market for local firms; many government controls over, and subsidization of, local activities; and exchange rates pegged at excessively low values (overvalued currencies) with imports regulated by licences.
- The new view is given in the Washington consensus, which calls for sound fiscal and monetary policies; broad-based taxes levied at moderate rates; market determination of prices and quantities; discriminating use of infant industry protection for moderate time periods; an acceptance of FDI and the presence of TNCs; active government provision of education, health care, and infrastructure; and antipoverty programs to help in human resource development and to aid citizens who are left behind by the growth process.
- An active debate turns on whether the conditions of the Washington consensus are sufficient, or just necessary, to establish a country on a sustained growth path. Analysts who regard it as sufficient feel that once unleashed, natural market forces will create sustained growth.
- Analysts who regard the conditions of the Washington consensus as necessary but not sufficient point to substantial externalities and pervasive market failures in the diffusion of technological knowledge from developed to developing nations. These economists call for active government innovation policies to augment investment and to assist the transfer of technological know-how and practice to the local economy.

KEY CONCEPTS

The development gap
Impediments to economic development
The vicious circle of poverty

The NICs
TNCs and FDI
The Washington consensus

Externalities and market failures in the diffusion of technology

STUDY EXERCISES

1. Go to the website for the United Nations (www.un.org). From the home page go to "Economic and Social Development." Then click on "Statistics" and search for "Social Indicators." Then answer the following questions.

   a. List the average rate of population growth for:

Albania	Canada	Iceland
Angola	Czech Republic	India
Bangladesh	Guatemala	Rwanda

   b. Explain why, *ceteris paribus*, high rates of population growth make it more difficult for a country to increase its average living standards. What role in your answer is played by the diminishing marginal returns to labour?

2. Go to the website for the United Nations (www.un.org). From the home page go to "Economic and Social Development." Then click on "Statistics" and search for "Social Indicators." Then answer the following questions.

   a. List the level of per capita GDP (US$) for the same group of countries as in Question 1, part a.
   b. Which country listed by the U.N. has the highest per capita GDP?
   c. Which country listed by the U.N. has the lowest per capita GDP?

3. Go to the World Bank's website (www.worldbank.org). Search for "Data" and then select "Data by Topic". Choose "Growth in Consumption and Investment" and then answer the following questions.

   a. List the amounts of gross saving and gross investment (as percentages of GDP) for:

Algeria	Côte d'Ivoire	Malaysia
Bolivia	Ecuador	Nigeria
Canada	Latvia	Tanzania

   b. On a scale diagram, with the investment rate on the horizontal axis and the saving rate on the vertical axis, plot the data for each of the chosen countries. Do you see any relationship?
   c. Based on what you have learned (perhaps especially from Chapter 32), explain why high investment rates are typically associated with high growth rates of GDP.
   d. In this chapter, we argued that some countries face a growth challenge because of their small pool of domestic saving. Based on your diagram from part a, explain the importance of domestic saving.

4. Go to the World Bank's website (www.worldbank.org). Search for "Data" and then select "Data by Topic." Choose "Agricultural Output and Productivity" and then answer the following questions.

   a. List the agricultural value added per worker for the following countries:

Australia	Dominican Republic	Netherlands
Botswana	Haiti	Niger
Chile	India	Paraguay

   b. Can you offer some possible explanations for the greater productivity in agriculture in the developed countries?

5. In the text we discussed that an adequate infrastructure is important to economic development. Go to the website for the United Nations (www.un.org). From the home page go to "Economic and Social Development." Then click on "Statistics" and search for "Social Indicators." Then answer the following questions.

   a. List the percentage of the population with access to safe water and to sanitation (both urban and rural populations) for:

Afghanistan   Norway
Bahrain   South Africa
Colombia   Thailand
Indonesia

b. According to the "Washington Consensus," should the public or the private sector be providing water and sanitation in developing countries?

c. Can you provide a reason why public expenditures in sanitation (and health care, more generally) may lead to increases in long-run productivity?

DISCUSSION QUESTIONS

1. In his *Essay on the Principle of Population as it Affects the Future Improvement of Society,* first published in 1789, Thomas Malthus wrote:

   > This natural inequality of the two powers of population and of production in the earth . . . [forms] the great difficulty that to me appears insurmountable in the way to perfectibility of society. All other arguments are of slight and subordinate consideration in comparison of this. I see no way by which man can escape from the weight of this law which pervades all animated nature. No fancied equality, no agrarian revolutions in their utmost extent, could remove the pressure of it even for a single century.

   Discuss Malthus's "insurmountable difficulty" in view of the events of the past 100 years.

2. To what extent does the vicious circle of poverty apply to poor families that are living in the richest developed countries? Consider carefully, for example, the similarities and differences facing a poor family living in Vancouver and one living in Ghana, where per capita income is less than $400 per year. Did it apply to Canadian immigrants who arrived at the turn of the century with $10 in their pockets?

3. Would removing all restrictions on immigration into the advanced countries help to improve living standards in the developing nations? How might such a policy affect living standards in the advanced countries?

4. "High coffee prices bring hope to impoverished Latin American peasants," reads the headline. Mexico, Kenya, and Burundi, among other developing countries, have the right combination of soil and climate to increase their coffee production greatly. Discuss the benefits and risks to them if they pursue coffee production as a major avenue of their development.

5. History has shown that rapid development of poor countries is often accompanied by some measure of devastation of the country's natural resources. Can you provide some examples? Must this outcome always occur? How can the developed countries help to stem the devastation? Why don't they help more than they do at present?

PART ELEVEN

International Economics

Does a country always benefit from free trade? If so, why do many people appear to believe the opposite? Can government policy influence a country's pattern of comparative advantage? Is there any connection between the government's budget deficit and the country's current account deficit? How is Canada's exchange rate determined? Should Canada maintain a flexible exchange rate or should it peg the value of its currency to the U.S. dollar? These are the sorts of questions you will be able to answer after reading the final three chapters of this book.*

Chapter 34 explores the gains from trade, and how these gains are based on the important concept of comparative advantage. We discuss the reasons why a country might have a comparative advantage in a particular product, and how some government policies can have the effect of changing a country's pattern of comparative advantage. We will also examine a country's terms of trade, the relative prices at which a country trades with the rest of the world.

In Chapter 35, the focus is on trade policy. We explore the case for free trade as well as the case for protection (we also examine some common but fallacious arguments for protection). We then discuss some methods of protection, such as tariffs, quotas, and nontariff barriers. The chapter then examines current trade policy in Canada, with an emphasis on the North American Free Trade Agreement.

Chapter 36 discusses the exchange rate and the balance of payments. We examine the foreign-exchange market and why the balance of payments accounts are always in balance. The important distinction between fixed exchange rates and flexible exchange rates will be discussed in detail, and we will explore the kinds of events that lead to an appreciation or a depreciation of the Canadian dollar. Finally, we explore three "hot" policy debates, including the cases for and against Canada's adopting a fixed exchange rate.

---

*Chapter 36 does not appear in *Microeconomics*.

CHAPTER 34

The Gains from International Trade

LO *LEARNING OBJECTIVES*

❶ Understand why the gains from trade depend on comparative advantage and not on absolute advantage.

❷ Explain the gains from trade due to economies of scale and learning-by-doing.

❸ Understand how factor endowments and climate can influence a country's comparative advantage.

❹ Explain the law of one price.

❺ Explain why countries export some goods and import other goods.

❻ Understand what is meant by a country's terms of trade.

Canadian consumers buy cars from Germany, Germans take holidays in Italy, Italians buy spices from Africa, Africans import oil from Kuwait, Kuwaitis buy Japanese cameras, and the Japanese buy Canadian lumber. *International trade* refers to the exchange of goods and services that takes place across international boundaries.

The founders of modern economics were concerned with foreign trade problems. The great eighteenth-century British philosopher and economist David Hume (1711–1776), one of the first to work out the theory of the price system as a control mechanism, developed his concepts mainly in terms of prices in foreign trade. Adam Smith (1723–1790) in his *Wealth of Nations* attacked government restriction of international trade. David Ricardo (1772–1823) developed the basic theory of the gains from trade that is studied in this chapter. The repeal of the Corn Laws—tariffs on the importation of grains into the United Kingdom—and the transformation of that country during the nineteenth century from a country of high tariffs to one of complete free trade were to some extent the result of agitation by economists whose theories of the gains from international trade led them to condemn tariffs.

International trade is becoming increasingly important, not just for Canada but for the world as a whole. As Figure 34-1 shows, the volume of world trade has grown much faster than has world real GDP over the past half-century. Since 1950, the world's real GDP has increased by six times, an average annual growth rate of 3.6 percent. Over the same period, however, the volume of world trade has increased by *seventeen* times, an average annual growth rate of 5.8 percent.

Figure 34-2 shows some data for Canadian trade in 1998. The figure shows the value of Canadian exports and imports in several broad industry groupings. There are three important points to note from the figure. First, international trade is very important for Canada. In 1998, Canada exported and imported over $300 billion in goods—if we added trade in services, the value would rise to over $360 billion. This amounts to over 40 percent of Canada's GDP. Second, exports and imports are roughly the same size, so that the *volume* of trade is much larger than the *balance* of trade—the value of exports equal minus the value of imports. Third, in most of the industry groupings there are significant amounts of both imports and exports. Such *intra-industry trade* will be discussed later in the chapter. Canada does not just export resource products and import manufactured goods; it also imports many resource products and exports many manufactured goods.

In this chapter, we inquire into the gains to living standards that result from such international trade. We find that the source of the gains from trade lies in differing cost conditions among geographical regions. World income is maximized when countries specialize in the products in which they have the lowest opportunity costs of production. These costs are partly determined by natural endowments (geographical and climatic conditions), partly by public policy, and partly by historical accident. We then go on to discuss the terms on which international trade takes place—this refers to the amount that must be exported to obtain a given amount of imports.

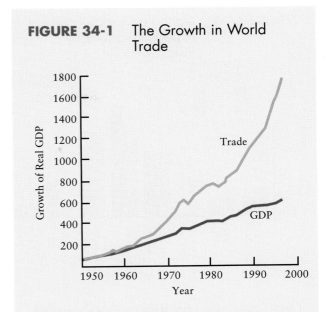

FIGURE 34-1   The Growth in World Trade

The volume of world trade has grown much faster than world GDP over the past fifty years. The figure shows the growth of real GDP and the volume of trade since 1950. Both are expressed as index numbers, set equal to 100 in 1950. Real world GDP has increased six times since 1950; world trade volume has increased seventeen times.

(*Source:* World Trade Organization.)

Sources of the Gains from Trade

An economy that engages in international trade is called an **open economy;** one that does not is called a **closed economy.** A situation in which a country does no foreign trade is called one of *autarky.*

The benefits of trade are easiest to visualize by considering the differences between a world with trade and a world without it. Although politicians often regard foreign trade differently from domestic trade, economists from Adam Smith on have argued that the causes and consequences of international trade are simply an extension of the principles governing domestic trade. What is the advantage of trade among individuals, among groups, among regions, or among countries?

For information on world trade, see the World Trade Organization's website: www.wto.org.

open economy   An economy that engages in international trade.

closed economy   An economy that has no foreign trade.

Interpersonal, Interregional, and International Trade

To begin, consider trade among individuals. Without trade, each person would have to be self-sufficient; each would have to produce all the food, clothing, shelter, medical services, entertainment, and luxuries that he or she consumed. A world of individual self-sufficiency would be a world with extremely low living standards.

Trade among individuals allows people to specialize in activities they can do well and to buy from others the goods and services they cannot easily produce. A good doctor who

FIGURE 34-2   Canadian Exports and Imports of Goods by Industry, 1998

Canada exports and imports large volumes of goods in most industries. The data show the value of goods exported and imported by industry in 1998 (trade in services is not shown). The total value of goods exported was $322.2 billion; the total value of goods imported was $303.4 billion.

(*Source:* These data are available on Statistics Canada's website: www.statcan.ca.)

is a bad carpenter can provide medical services not only for her own family but also for an excellent carpenter without the training or the ability to practice medicine. Thus, trade and specialization are intimately connected.

Without trade, everyone must be self-sufficient; with trade, people can specialize in what they do well and satisfy other needs by trading.

The same principle applies to regions. Without interregional trade, each region would be forced to be self-sufficient. With trade, each region can specialize in producing products for which it has some natural or acquired advantage. Plains regions can specialize in growing grain, mountain regions in mining and forest products, and regions with abundant power in manufacturing. Cool regions can produce wheat and other crops that thrive in temperate climates, and hot regions can grow such tropical crops as bananas, sugarcane, and coffee. The living standards of the inhabitants of all regions will be higher when each region specializes in products in which it has some natural or acquired advantage and obtains other products by trade than when all regions seek to be self-sufficient.

This same basic principle also applies to nations. A national boundary seldom delimits an area that is naturally self-sufficient. Nations, like regions and individuals, can gain from specialization. More of some goods are produced domestically than residents wish to consume, while residents would like to consume more of other goods than is produced domestically. International trade is necessary to achieve the gains that international specialization makes possible.

With trade, each individual, region, or nation is able to concentrate on producing goods and services that it produces efficiently while trading to obtain goods and services that it does not produce efficiently.

Specialization and trade go hand in hand because there is no motivation to achieve the gains from specialization without being able to trade the goods produced for goods desired. Economists use the term **gains from trade** to embrace the results of both.

We will examine two sources of the gains from trade. The first is differences among regions of the world in climate and resource endowment that lead to advantages in producing certain goods and disadvantages in producing others. These gains occur even though each country's costs of production are unchanged by the existence of trade. The second source is the reduction in each country's costs of production that results from the greater scale of production that specialization brings.

gains from trade
The increased output due to the specialization according to comparative advantage that is made possible by trade.

The Gains from Trade with Constant Costs

In order to focus on differences in countries' conditions of production, suppose that each country's average costs of production are constant. We will use an example below involving only two countries and two products, but the general principles apply as well to the case of many countries and many products.

Absolute Advantage

One region is said to have an **absolute advantage** over another in the production of good X when an equal quantity of resources can produce more X in the first region than in the second. Total production can be increased if each country specializes in producing the product for which it has an absolute advantage.

The gains from specialization make the gains from trade possible. If consumers in both countries are to get the goods they desire in the required proportions, each must export some of the commodity in which it specializes and import commodities in which other countries are specialized.

absolute advantage The situation that exists when a given amount of resources can produce more of some commodity in one country than in another.

Comparative Advantage

When each product has an absolute advantage over others in a product, the gains from trade are obvious. But what if one country can produce all commodities more efficiently than other countries? This was the question English economist David Ricardo (1722–1823) posed nearly 200 years ago. His answer underlies the theory of *comparative advantage* and is still accepted by economists today as a valid statement of the potential gains from trade.

The gains from specialization and trade depend on the pattern of comparative, not absolute, advantage.

An example will help to make the point. Let us assume that there are two countries, Canada and the European Union. Both countries produce the same two goods, wheat and cloth, but the opportunity costs of producing these two products differ between countries. Recall from Chapter 1 that the opportunity cost is given by the slope of the production-possibility curve, and it tells us how much of one good we have to give up in order to produce one more unit of the other. For the moment we assume that this opportunity cost is constant in each country at all combinations of outputs.

For the purposes of our example we assume that the opportunity cost of producing one kilogram of wheat is 0.60 metres of cloth in Canada, while in the European Union it is 2.0 metres of cloth. These data are summarized in Table 34-1. The second column of this table gives the same information again but expressed as the opportunity cost of one metre of cloth (so the numbers there are reciprocals of the numbers in the first column).

The sacrifice of cloth involved in producing wheat is much lower in Canada than it is in the EU. World wheat production can be increased if Canada rather than the EU produces it. Looking at cloth production, we can see that the loss of wheat involved in producing one unit of cloth is lower in the EU than in Canada. World cloth production can therefore be increased if the EU rather than Canada produces it. The gains from a Canadian shift towards wheat production and an EU shift towards cloth production are shown in Table 34-2.

TABLE 34-1 Opportunity Cost of Wheat and Cloth in Canada and the European Union (EU)

	Wheat (kg)	Cloth (m)
Canada	0.60 m of cloth	1.67 kg of wheat
EU	2.0 m of cloth	0.5 kg of wheat

Comparative advantages reflect opportunity costs that differ between countries. The first column expresses opportunity cost for a kilogram of wheat. The second column expresses the same information for a metre of cloth. Canada has a comparative advantage in wheat production, the EU in cloth.

TABLE 34-2 The Gains from Specialization

	Changes from each country producing one more unit of the product in which it has the lower opportunity cost	
	Wheat (kg)	Cloth (m)
Canada	+1.0	−0.6
EU	−0.5	+1.0
Total	+0.5	+0.4

Whenever opportunity costs differ between countries, specialization can increase the production of both products. These calculations show that there are gains from specialization given the opportunity costs of Table 34-1. To produce one more kilogram of wheat, Canada must sacrifice 0.6 m of cloth. To produce one more metre of cloth, the EU must sacrifice 0.5 kg of wheat. Making both changes increases world production of both wheat and cloth.

FIGURE 34-3　Gains from Trade with Constant Opportunity Costs

(i) Canada　　　　　　　　　(ii) European Union

International trade leads to specialization in production and increased consumption possibilities. The purple lines in parts (i) and (ii) represent the production possibility boundaries for Canada and the EU, respectively. In the absence of any international trade these also represent each country's consumption possibilities.

The difference in the slopes of the production possibility boundaries reflects differences in comparative advantage, as shown in Table 34-1. In each part the opportunity cost of increasing production of wheat by the same amount (measured by the distance *ba*) is the amount by which the production of cloth must be reduced (measured by the distance *bc*). The relatively steep production possibility boundary for Canada thus indicates that the opportunity cost of producing wheat in Canada is less than that in the European Union.

If trade is possible at some relative prices between the two countries' opportunity costs of production, each country will specialize in the production of the good in which it has a comparative advantage. In each part of the figure, production occurs at *S* (for specialization); Canada produces only wheat, and the EU produces only cloth.

Consumption possibilities are given by the green line that passes through *S* and has a slope equal to the with-trade relative prices. Consumption possibilities are increased in both countries; consumption may occur at some point such as *d* that involves a combination of wheat and cloth that was not obtainable in the absence of trade.

The gains from trade arise from differing opportunity costs in the two countries.

The slope of the production possibility boundary indicates the opportunity costs, and the existence of different opportunity costs implies comparative advantages that can lead to gains from trade. Figure 34-3 illustrates how two countries can both gain from trade when they have different opportunity costs in production and those opportunity costs are independent of the level of production. An alternative diagrammatic illustration of the gains from trade appears in *Extensions in Theory 34-1* where the production possibility boundary is concave (which means that the opportunity cost for each good is higher when more of that good is being produced).

The conclusions about the gains from trade arising from international differences in opportunity costs are summarized below.

1. Country A has a comparative advantage over Country B in producing a product when the opportunity cost of production in Country A is lower. This implies, however, that it has a comparative *dis*advantage in the other product.

2. Opportunity costs depend on the relative costs of producing two products, not on absolute costs.

3. When opportunity costs are the same in all countries, there is no comparative advantage and there is no possibility of gains from specialization and trade.

4. When opportunity costs differ in any two countries and both countries are producing both products, it is always possible to increase production of both products by a suitable reallocation of resources within each country.

The Gains from Trade with Variable Costs

So far, we have assumed that unit costs are the same whatever the scale of output, and we have seen that there are gains from specialization and trade as long as there are interregional differences in opportunity costs. If costs vary with the level of output, or as experience is acquired via specialization, *additional* gains are possible.

Scale and Imperfect Competition

Real production costs, measured in terms of resources used, generally fall as the scale of output increases. The larger the scale of operations, the more efficiently large-scale machinery can be used and the more a detailed division of tasks among workers is possible. Small countries, such as Switzerland, Belgium, and Israel, whose domestic markets are not large enough to exploit economies of scale would find it prohibitively expensive to become self-sufficient by producing a little bit of everything at very high cost.

Trade allows small countries to specialize and produce a few products at high enough levels of output to reap the available economies of scale.

Wine is a good example of an industry in which there is much intra-industry trade. Canada, for example, imports wine from many countries but also exports Canadian-made wine to the same countries.

Very large countries, such as the United States, have markets large enough to allow the production of most items at home at a scale of output great enough to obtain the available economies of scale. For them, the gains from trade arise mainly from specializing in products in which they have a comparative advantage. Yet, even for such countries, a broadening of their markets permits achieving scale economies in subproduct lines, such as specialty steels or certain lines of clothing.

One of the important lessons learned from patterns of world trade since World War II has concerned imperfect competition and product differentiation. Virtually all of today's manufactured consumer goods are produced in a vast array of differentiated product lines. In some industries, many firms produce this array; in others, only a few firms produce the entire array. In either case, they do not exhaust all available economies of scale. Thus, an increase in the size of the market, even in an economy as large as the United States, may allow the exploitation of some previously unexploited scale economies in individual product lines.

These possibilities were first dramatically illustrated when the European Common Market (now known as the European Union or EU) was set up in the late 1950s. Economists had expected that specialization would occur according to the theory of comparative advantage, with one country specializing in cars, another in refrigerators, another in fashion clothes, another in shoes, and so on. This is not the way it worked out. Instead, much of the vast growth of trade was in *intra-industry* trade—that is, trade of goods or services within the same broad industry. Today, one can buy French, English, Italian, and German fashion goods, cars, shoes, appliances, and a host of other products in London, Paris, Berlin, and Rome. Ships loaded with Swedish furniture bound for London pass ships loaded with English furniture bound for Stockholm, and so on.

EXTENSIONS IN THEORY 34-1

The Gains From Trade More Generally

Examining the gains from trade is relatively easy in the case where each country's production possibilities boundary is a straight line. What happens in the more realistic case where the production possibilities boundary is concave? As this box shows, the same basic principles of the gains from trade apply to this more complex case.

International trade leads to an expansion of the set of goods that can be consumed in the economy in two ways:

1. by allowing the bundle of goods consumed to differ from the bundle produced; and,

2. by permitting a profitable change in the pattern of production.

Without international trade, the bundle of goods produced is the bundle consumed. With international trade, the consumption and production bundles can be altered independently to reflect the relative values placed on goods by international markets.

Fixed Production

In each part of the figure, the purple curve is the economy's production possibility boundary. In the absence of interna-

tional trade, the economy must consume the same bundle of goods that it produces. Thus, the production possibility boundary is also the consumption possibility boundary. Suppose that the economy produces and consumes at point a, with x_1 of good X and y_1 of good Y, as in part (i) of the figure.

Next suppose that with production point a, good Y can be exchanged for good X internationally. The consumption possibilities are now shown by the line tt drawn through point a. The slope of tt indicates the quantity of Y that exchanges for a unit of X on the international market.

Although production is fixed at point a, consumption can now be anywhere on the line tt. For example, the consumption point could be at b. This could be achieved by exporting y_2y_1 units of Y and importing x_1x_2 units of X. Because point b (and all others on line tt to the right of a) lies outside the production possibility boundary, there are potential gains from trade. Consumers are no longer limited by their own country's production possibilities. Let us suppose that they prefer point b to point a. They have achieved a gain from trade by being allowed to exchange some of their production of good Y for some quantity of good X and thus to consume more of good X than is produced at home.

The same increase in intra-industry trade happened with Canada-U.S. trade over successive rounds of tariff cuts, the most recent being the 1989 Canada-U.S. Free Trade Agreement, and its 1994 expansion into the North American Free Trade Agreement that included Mexico. In several broad industrial groups, including automotive products, machinery, textiles, and forestry products, both imports and exports increased in each country.

What free trade in Europe and North America did was to allow a proliferation of differentiated products, with different countries each specializing in different subproduct lines. Consumers have shown by their expenditures that they value this enormous increase in the range of choice among differentiated products. As Asian countries have expanded into North American and European markets with textiles, cars, and electronic goods, North American and European manufacturers have increasingly specialized their production and now export textiles, cars, and electronic equipment to Asia even while importing similar but differentiated products from Asia.

Learning by Doing

The discussion so far has assumed that costs vary only with the *level* of output. But they may also vary with the *accumulated experience* in producing a product over time.

Variable Production

There is a further opportunity for the expansion of the country's consumption possibilities: With trade, the production bundle may be profitably altered in response to international prices. The country may produce the bundle of goods that is most valuable in world markets. That is represented by the bundle *d* in part (ii). The consumption possibility set is shifted to the line *t't'* by changing production from *a* to *d* and thereby increasing the country's degree of specialization in good *Y*. For every point on the original consumption possibility set *tt*, there are points on the new set *t't'* that allow

more consumption of both goods—for example, compare points *b* and *f*. Notice also that, except at the zero-trade point *d*, the new consumption possibility set lies *everywhere above the production possibility curve.*

The benefits of moving from a no-trade position, such as *a*, to a trading position such as *b* or *f* are the *gains from trade* to the country. When the production of good *Y* is increased and the production of good *X* decreased, the country is able to move to a point such as *f* by producing more of good *Y*, in which the country has a comparative advantage, and trading the additional production for good *X*.

(i) Fixed production

(ii) Variable production

Early economists placed great importance on a concept that is now called **learning by doing**. They believed that as countries gained experience in particular tasks, workers and managers would become more efficient in performing them. As people acquire expertise, costs tend to fall. There is substantial evidence that such learning by doing does occur. It is particularly important in many of today's knowledge-intensive high-tech industries.

The distinction between this phenomenon and the gains from economies of scale is illustrated in Figure 34-4. It is one more example of the difference between a movement along a curve and a shift of the curve.

Recognition of the opportunities for learning by doing leads to an important implication: Policymakers need not accept *current* comparative advantages as given. Through such means as education and tax incentives, they can seek to develop new comparative advantages.[1] Moreover, countries cannot complacently assume that their existing comparative advantages will persist. Misguided education policies, the wrong tax incentives, or policies that discourage risk taking can lead to the rapid erosion of a country's comparative advantage in particular products.

learning by doing
The increase in output per worker that often results as workers learn through repeatedly performing the same tasks. It causes a downward shift in the average cost curve.

---

[1]They can also foolishly use such policies to develop industries in which they do not have and will never achieve comparative advantages.

FIGURE 34-4 Gains from Trade Due to Scale and Learning Effects

(i) Economies of scale

(ii) Learning by doing

Specialization may lead to gains from trade by permitting economies of larger-scale output, by leading to downward shifts of cost curves, or both. Consider a country that wishes to consume the quantity q_0. Suppose that it can produce that quantity at an average cost per unit of c_0. Suppose further that the country has a comparative advantage in producing this product and can export the quantity q_0q_1 if it produces q_1. This may lead to cost savings in two ways.

As shown in part (i), the increased level of production of q_1 compared to q_0 permits it to *move along* its cost curve from a to b, thereby reducing costs per unit to c_1. This is an economy of scale.

As shown in part (ii), as workers and management become more experienced, they may be able to produce at lower costs. This is learning by doing. The downward *shift*, shown by the arrows, lowers the cost of producing every unit of output. At output q_1, costs per unit fall to c_2. The movement from a to b' incorporates both economies of scale and learning by doing.

Sources of Comparative Advantage

We have seen that comparative advantage is the source of the gains from trade. But why do comparative advantages exist? Since a country's comparative advantage depends on its opportunity costs, we could also ask: Why do different countries have different opportunity costs?

Different Factor Endowments

The traditional answer to this question was provided early in the twentieth century by two Swedish economists, Eli Heckscher and Bertil Ohlin. Ohlin was subsequently awarded the Nobel Prize in economics for his work in the theory of international trade. Their explanation for international differences in opportunity costs is now incorporated in the Heckscher-Ohlin model. According to their theory, the international cost differences that form the basis for comparative advantage arise because factor endowments differ across countries. This is often called the *factor endowment theory of comparative advantage.*

To see how this theory works, consider the prices for various types of goods in countries *in the absence of trade.* A country that is well endowed with fertile land but has a small population (like Canada) will find that land is cheap but labour is expensive. It will therefore produce land-intensive agricultural goods cheaply and labour-intensive goods, such as machine tools, only at high cost. The reverse will be true for a second country that is small in size but possesses abundant and efficient labour (like Japan). As a result, the first country will have a comparative advantage in agricultural production and the second in goods that use much labour and little land.

According to the Heckscher-Ohlin theory, countries have comparative advantages in the production of goods that use intensively the factors of production with which they are abundantly endowed.

For example, Canada is abundantly endowed with forests relative to most other countries. According to the Heckscher-Ohlin theory, Canada has a comparative advantage in goods that use forest products intensively, such as newsprint, paper, raw lumber, and wooden furniture. In contrast, relative to most other countries, Canada is sparsely endowed with labour. Thus, Canada has a comparative disadvantage in goods that use labour intensively, such as cotton or many other textile products.

Different Climates

The factor endowment theory has considerable power to explain comparative advantage but it does not provide the whole explanation. One additional influence comes from all those natural factors that can be called *climate* in the broadest sense. If you combine land, labour, and capital in the same way in Nicaragua and in Iceland, you will not get the same output of most agricultural goods. Sunshine, rainfall, and average temperature also matter. If you seek to work with wool or cotton in dry climates, you will get different results than when you work in damp climates. (You can, of course, artificially create any climate you wish in a factory, but it costs money to create what is freely provided elsewhere.)

Canada is extremely well endowed with forests. It is no surprise, therefore, that it has a comparative advantage in a whole range of forestry products.

Climate affects comparative advantage.

Of course, if we consider "warm weather" a factor of production, then we could simply say that countries like Nicaragua are better endowed with that factor than countries like Iceland. In this sense, explanations of comparative advantage based on different climates are really just a special case of explanations based on factor endowments.

Acquired Comparative Advantage

Today it is clear that many comparative advantages are *acquired*. Further, they can change. Thus, comparative advantage should be viewed as being *dynamic* rather than static. New industries are seen to depend more on human capital than on fixed physical capital or natural resources. The skills of a computer designer, a videogame programmer, or a sound mix technician are acquired by education and on-the-job training. Natural endowments of energy and raw materials cannot account for Silicon Valley's leadership in computer technology, for Canada's prominence in communications technology or for Switzerland's prominence in private banking. When countries find their former dominance (based on comparative advantage) in such smokestack industries as cars and steel declining, their firms need not sit idly by. Instead, they can begin to adapt by developing new areas of comparative advantage.

Contrasts

This modern view is in sharp contrast with the traditional assumption that cost structures based largely on a country's natural endowments lead to a given pattern of international comparative advantage. The traditional view suggests that a government interested in maximizing its citizens' material standard of living should encourage specialization of production in goods where it currently has a comparative advantage. If all countries follow this advice, the theory predicts, each will be specialized in a relatively narrow range of distinct products. The British will produce engineering products, Canadians will be producers of resource-based primary products, Americans will be farmers and factory workers, Central Americans will be banana and coffee growers, and so on.

There are surely elements of truth in both extreme views. It would be unwise to neglect resource endowments, climate, culture, social patterns, and institutional arrangements. But it would also be unwise to assume that all of them were innate and immutable.

To some extent, these views are reconciled by the theory of human capital, which is a topic we discussed in *Microeconomics*. Comparative advantages that depend on human capital are consistent with traditional Heckscher-Ohlin theory. The difference is that this type of capital is acquired through conscious decisions relating to such matters as education and technical training.

The Determination of Trade Patterns

Comparative advantage has been the central concept in our discussion about the sources of the gains from trade. If Canada has a comparative advantage in lumber and Italy has a comparative advantage in shoes, then the total output of lumber and shoes could be increased if Canada specialized in the production of lumber and Italy specialized in the production of shoes. With such patterns of specialization, Canada would naturally export lumber to Italy and Italy would export shoes to Canada.

It is one thing to discuss the potential gains from trade if countries specialized in the production of particular goods and exported these to other countries. But do *actual* trade patterns occur along the lines of comparative advantage? In this section of the chapter we use a simple demand-and-supply model to examine why Canada exports some products and imports others. We will see that comparative advantage, whether natural or acquired, does indeed play a central role.

There are some products, such as coffee and mangos, that Canada does not produce (and will probably never produce). Any domestic consumption of these product must therefore be satisfied by imports from other countries. At the other extreme, there are some products, such as nickel or potash, where Canada is one of the world's major suppliers, and demand in the rest of the world must be satisfied partly by exports from Canada. There are also some products, such as houses, that are so expensive to transport that every country produces approximately what it consumes.

Our interest in this section is in the many intermediate cases in which Canada is only one of many producers of an internationally traded product, as with beef, oil, copper, wheat, lumber, and newsprint. Will Canada be an exporter or an importer of such products? And what is the role played by comparative advantage?

For data on Canadian trade by industry and by country, see Statistics Canada's website: www.statcan.ca. Go to "Canadian Statistics" and then "Trade."

The Law of One Price

Whether Canada imports or exports a product for which it is only one of many producers depends to a great extent on the product's price. This brings us to what economists call the *law of one price*.

The law of one price states that when a product which can be cheaply transported is traded throughout the entire world, it will tend to have a single worldwide price.

Many basic products, such as copper wire, steel pipe, iron ore, and computer RAM chips, fall within this category. The world price for each good is the price that equates the quantity demanded worldwide with the quantity supplied worldwide.

The world price of an internationally traded product may be influenced greatly, or only slightly, by the demand and supply coming from any one country. The extent of one country's influence will depend on how important its demands and supplies are in relation to the worldwide totals.

The simplest case for us to study arises when the country, which we will take to be Canada, accounts for only a small part of the total worldwide demand and supply. In this case, Canada does not itself produce enough to influence the world price significantly. Similarly, Canadian purchases are too small a proportion of worldwide demand to affect the world price in any significant way. Producers and consumers in Canada thus face a world price that they cannot influence by their own actions.

Notice that in this case, the price that rules in the Canadian market must be the world price (adjusted for the exchange rate between the Canadian dollar and the foreign currency). The law of one price says that this must be so. What would happen if the Canadian domestic price diverged from the world price? If the Canadian price were below the world price, no supplier would sell in the Canadian market because more money could be made by selling abroad. The absence of supply to the Canadian market would thus drive up the Canadian price. Conversely, if the Canadian domestic price were above the worldwide price, no buyers would buy from a Canadian seller because money could be saved by buying abroad. The absence of demand on the Canadian market would thus drive down the Canadian price.

The Pattern of Foreign Trade

Let us now see what determines the pattern of international trade in such circumstances.

An Exported Product

To determine the pattern of Canadian trade, we first show the Canadian domestic demand and supply curves for some product, say, lumber. This is done in Figure 34-5. The intersection of these two curves tells us what the price and quantity would be *if there were no foreign trade.* Now compare this no-trade price with the world price of that product.[2] If the world price is higher, the actual price in Canada will exceed the no-trade price. In this situation there will be an excess of Canadian supply over Canadian demand. Domestic producers want to sell q_2 units of lumber but domestic consumers want to buy only q_1 units. If Canada were a closed economy, such excess supply would drive the price down to p_d. But in an open economy with a world price of p_w, this excess supply gets exported to Canada's trading partners.

Countries export products whose world price exceeds the price that would exist domestically if there were no foreign trade.

What is the role of comparative advantage in this analysis? We have said that Canada will export lumber if the world price exceeds Canada's no-trade price. Note that in a competitive market the price of the product reflects the product's marginal cost, which in turn reflects the opportunity cost of producing the product. That Canada's no-trade price for lumber is lower than the world price reflects the fact that the opportunity cost of producing lumber in Canada is less than the opportunity cost of producing it in the rest of the world. Thus, by exporting goods which have a low no-trade price, Canada is exporting the goods in which it has a comparative advantage.

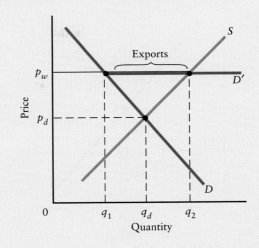

FIGURE 34-5   An Exported Good

Exports occur whenever there is excess supply domestically at the world price. The domestic demand and supply curves are D and S, respectively. The domestic price in the absence of foreign trade is p_d, with q_d produced and consumed domestically. The world price of p_w is higher than p_d. At p_w, q_1 is demanded while q_2 is supplied domestically. The excess of the domestic supply over the domestic demand is exported.

The Export Development Corporation is a crown corporation devoted to improving Canada's export prospects. For information about Canada's exports, check out its website: www.edc—see.ca.

[2]If the world price is stated in terms of some foreign currency (as it often is), then the price must be converted into Canadian dollars using the current exchange rate between the foreign currency and Canadian dollars.

FIGURE 34-6   An Imported Good

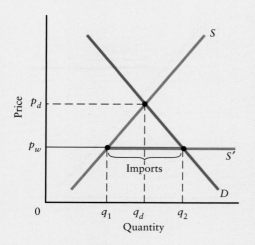

Imports occur whenever there is excess demand domestically at the world price. The domestic demand and supply curves are D and S, respectively. The domestic price in the absence of foreign trade is p_d, with q_d produced and consumed domestically. The world price of p_w is less than p_d. At the world price q_2 is demanded, whereas q_1 is supplied domestically. The excess of domestic demand over domestic supply is satisfied through imports.

Countries export the goods for which they are low-cost producers. That is, they export goods in which they have a comparative advantage.

An Imported Product

Now consider some other product—for example, computer RAM chips. Once again, look first at the domestic demand and supply curves, shown this time in Figure 34-6. The intersection of these curves determines the no-trade price that would rule if there were no foreign trade. The world price of RAM chips is below the Canadian no-trade price so that, at the price ruling in Canada, domestic demand is larger and domestic supply is smaller than if the no-trade price had ruled. The excess of domestic demand over domestic supply is met by imports.

Countries import products whose world price is less than the price that would exist domestically if there were no foreign trade.

Again, this analysis can be restated in terms of comparative advantage. The high Canadian no-trade price of RAM chips reflects the fact that RAM chips are more costly to produce in Canada than elsewhere in the world. This high cost means that Canada has a comparative disadvantage in RAM chips. So Canada imports goods for which it has a comparative disadvantage.

Countries import the goods for which they are high-cost producers. That is, they import goods for which they have a comparative disadvantage.

Is Comparative Advantage Obsolete?

In the debate preceding the signing of both the Canada-U.S. Free Trade Agreement and the North American Free Trade Agreement (NAFTA), some opponents argued that the agreements relied on an outdated view of the gains from trade based on comparative advantage. The theory of comparative advantage was said to be obsolete.

In spite of such assertions, comparative advantage remains an important economic concept. At any one time—because comparative advantage is reflected in international relative prices, and these relative prices determine what goods a country will import and what it will export—the operation of the price system will result in trade that follows the current pattern of comparative advantage. For example, if Canadian costs of producing steel are particularly low relative to other Canadian costs, Canada's price of steel will be low by international standards, and steel will be a Canadian export (which it is). If Canada's costs of producing textiles are particularly high relative to other Canadian costs, Canada's price of textiles will be high by international standards, and Canada will import textiles (which it does). Thus, there is no reason to change the view that Ricardo long ago expounded: *Current comparative advantage is a major determinant of trade under free-market conditions.*

What has changed, however, is economists' views about the *determinants* of comparative advantage. It now seems that current comparative advantage may be more open to change by private entrepreneurial activities and by government policy than used to be thought. Thus, what is obsolete is the belief that a country's current pattern of comparative advantage, and hence its current pattern of imports and exports, must be accepted as given and unchangeable.

The theory that comparative advantage determines trade flows is not obsolete, but the theory that comparative advantage is completely determined by forces beyond the reach of public policy has been discredited.

It is one thing to observe that it is *possible* for governments to influence a country's pattern of comparative advantage. It is quite another to conclude that it is *advisable* for them to try. The case in support of a specific government intervention requires that (1) there is scope for governments to improve on the results achieved by the free market, (2) the costs of the intervention be less than the value of the improvement to be achieved, and (3) governments will actually be able to carry out the required interventionist policies (without, for example, being sidetracked by considerations of electoral advantage).

The Terms of Trade

We have seen that world production can be increased when countries specialize in the production of the products in which they have a comparative advantage and then trade with one another. We now ask: How will these gains from specialization and trade be shared among countries? The division of the gain depends on what is called the **terms of trade,** which relate to the quantity of imported goods that can be obtained per unit of goods exported. They are measured by the ratio of the price of exports to the price of imports.

terms of trade The ratio of the average price of a country's exports to the average price of its imports, both averages usually being measured by index numbers.

A rise in the price of imported goods, with the price of exports unchanged, indicates a *fall in the terms of trade*; it will now take more exports to buy the same quantity of imports. Similarly, a rise in the price of exported goods, with the price of imports unchanged, indicates a *rise in the terms of trade*; it will now take fewer exports to buy the same quantity of imports. Thus, the ratio of these prices measures the amount of imports that can be obtained per unit of goods exported.

Because actual international trade involves many countries and many products, a country's terms of trade are computed as an index number:

$$\text{Terms of Trade} = \frac{\text{Index of Export Prices}}{\text{Index of Import Prices}} \times 100$$

A rise in the index is referred to as a *favourable* change in a country's terms of trade (sometimes called a terms of trade *improvement*). A favourable change means that fewer goods have to be exported per unit of goods imported than was previously the case. For example, if the export price index rises from 100 to 120 while the import price index rises from 100 to 110, the terms-of-trade index rises from 100 to 109. At the new terms of trade, a unit of imports will require approximately 9 percent fewer exports than at the old terms of trade.

A decrease in the index of the terms of trade, called an *unfavourable* change (or a terms of trade *deterioration*), means that the country can import less in return for any given amount of exports, or, equivalently, it must export more to pay for any given

FIGURE 34-7   Canada's Terms of Trade, 1970–1998

Canada's terms of trade have been quite variable over the past 30 years, but they have also displayed a long-term improvement. The data shown are Canada's terms of trade—the ratio of an index of Canadian export prices to an index of Canadian import prices. As the relative prices of lumber, oil, wheat, electronic equipment, textiles, fruit, and other products change, the terms of trade naturally change. Especially notable are the sharp increases in 1973 and 1980, caused by the OPEC oil shocks. The decline in the late 1990s is due to the reduction in world commodity prices following the Asian crisis in 1997-1998.

(Source: Economic Reference Tables, Department of Finance, and Bank of Canada.)

amount of imports. For example, the sharp rise in oil prices in the 1970s led to large unfavourable shifts in the terms of trade of oil-importing countries. When oil prices fell sharply in the mid 1980s, the terms of trade of oil-importing countries changed favourably. The converse was true for oil-exporting countries.

Canada's terms of trade since 1970 are shown in Figure 34-7. As is clear, the terms of trade are quite variable, reflecting frequent changes in the relative prices of different products. Also clear from the figure is that Canada's terms of trade have displayed a long-term improvement over the past 30 years.

Note the deterioration in Canada's terms of trade in the late 1990s. Deep recessions in several Southeast Asian countries contributed to a dramatic fall in world commodity prices between the middle of 1997 and the end of 1998. Many of these commodities—copper, gold, oil, newsprint, lumber, pork—are important Canadian exports. Thus, a decline in their price implies a deterioration in Canada's terms of trade.

S U M M A R Y

Sources of the Gains from Trade

- One country (or region or individual) has an absolute advantage over another country (or region or individual) in the production of a specific product when, with the same input of resources in each country, it can produce more of the product than can the other.
- Comparative advantage is the relative advantage one country enjoys over another in the production of various products. It occurs whenever countries have different

opportunity costs of producing particular goods. World production of all products can be increased if each country transfers resources into the production of the products in which it has a comparative advantage.

- The most important proposition in the theory of the gains from trade is that trade allows all countries to obtain the goods in which they do not have a comparative advantage at a lower opportunity cost than they would face if they were to produce all products for themselves; specialization and trade therefore allow all countries to have more of all products than they could have if they tried to be self-sufficient.

- As well as gaining the advantages of specialization arising from comparative advantage, a nation that engages in trade and specialization may realize the benefits of economies of large-scale production and of learning by doing.

- Classical theory regarded comparative advantage as largely determined by natural resource endowments that are difficult to change. Economists now believe that some comparative advantages can be acquired and consequently can be changed. A country may, in this view, influence its role in world production and trade. Successful intervention leads to a country's acquiring a comparative advantage; unsuccessful intervention fails to develop such an advantage.

The Determination of Trade Patterns

- The law of one price says that internationally traded goods that are inexpensive to transport must sell at the same price in all countries. Economists call this the world price.
- Countries will export a good when the world price exceeds the price that would exist in the country if there were no trade. The low no-trade price reflects a low opportunity cost and thus a comparative advantage in that

good. Thus, countries export goods for which they have a comparative advantage.
- Countries will import a good when the world price is less than the price that would exist in the country if there were no trade. The high no-trade price reflects a high opportunity cost and thus a comparative disadvantage in that good. Thus, countries import goods for which they have a comparative disadvantage.

The Terms of Trade

- The terms of trade refer to the ratio of the prices of goods exported to the prices of those imported. This determines the quantity of imports that can be obtained per unit of exports. The terms of trade determine how the gains from trade are shared.

- A favourable change in the terms of trade—a rise in export prices relative to import prices—means that a country can acquire more imports per unit of exports, and vice versa.

K E Y   C O N C E P T S

Interpersonal, interregional, and international specialization
Absolute advantage and comparative advantage

Opportunity cost and comparative advantage
The gains from trade: specialization, scale economies, and learning by doing

The sources of comparative advantage
Factor endowments
Acquired comparative advantage
The law of one price
The terms of trade

STUDY EXERCISES

1. The following diagram shows the production possibilities boundary for Arcticland, a country that produces two goods, ice and fish. Labour is the only factor of production.

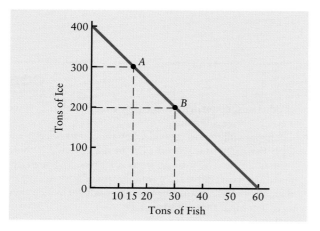

   a. Beginning at any point on Arcticland's production possibilities boundary, what is the opportunity cost of producing 10 more tons of fish?
   b. Beginning at any point on Arcticland's production possibilities boundary, what is the opportunity cost of producing 100 more tons of ice?

2. The following table shows the production of wheat and corn in Brazil and Mexico. Assume that both countries have one million acres of arable land.

	Brazil	Mexico
Wheat	90 bushels per acre	50 bushels per acre
Corn	30 bushels per acre	20 bushels per acre

   a. Which country has the absolute advantage in wheat? In corn? Explain.
   b. Which country has the comparative advantage in wheat? In corn? Explain.
   c. Explain why one country can have an absolute advantage in both goods but cannot have a comparative advantage in both goods.
   d. On a scale diagram with wheat on the horizontal axis and corn on the vertical axis, draw each country's production possibilities boundary.
   e. What is shown by the slope of each country's production possibilities boundary? Be as precise as possible.

3. The following diagrams show the production possibilities boundaries for Canada and France, both of which produce two goods, wine and lumber.

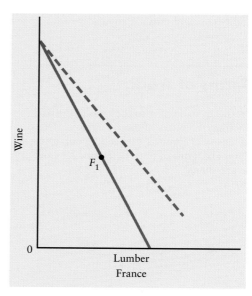

   a. Which country has the comparative advantage in lumber? Explain.
   b. Which country has the comparative advantage in wine? Explain.
   c. Suppose that Canada and France are initially not trading with each other and are producing at points C_1 and F_1, respectively. Suppose when trade is introduced, the free-trade relative prices are shown by the dashed line. Which combination of goods will each country now produce?
   d. In this case, what will be the pattern of trade for each country?

4. The diagrams below show the Canadian markets for newsprint and machinery, which we assume to be competitive.

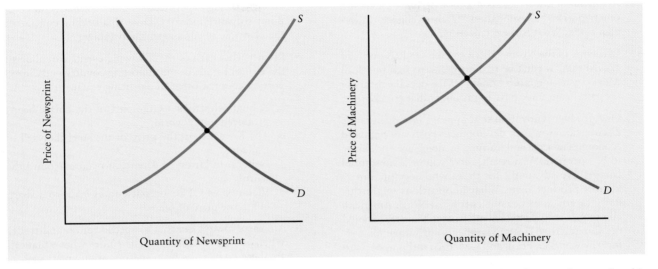

a. Suppose there is no international trade. What would be the equilibrium price and quantity in the Canadian newsprint and machinery markets?

b. Now suppose that Canada is open to trade with the rest of the world. If the world price of newsprint is *higher* than the price of newsprint from part **a**, what will happen to the levels of domestic production and consumption? Explain.

c. If the world price of machinery is lower than the price of machinery from part **a**, what happens to the levels of domestic consumption and production? Explain.

5. The table below shows indexes for the prices of imports and exports over several years for a hypothetical country.

Year	Import Prices	Export Prices	Terms of Trade
1996	90	110	—
1997	95	87	—
1998	98	83	—
1999	100	100	—
2000	102	105	—
2001	100	112	—
2002	103	118	—

a. Compute the terms of trade in each year for this country and fill in the table.

b. In which years does the terms of trade improve?

c. In which years does the terms of trade deteriorate?

d. Explain why a terms of trade "improvement" is good for the country.

6. For each of the following events, explain the likely effect on Canada's terms of trade. Your existing knowledge of Canada's imports and exports should be adequate to answer this question.

a. A hurricane damages much of Brazil's coffee crop.

b. OPEC countries succeed in significantly restricting the world supply of oil.

c. Several new large copper mines come into production in Chile.

d. A major recession in Southeast Asia reduces the world demand for pork.

DISCUSSION QUESTIONS

1. Adam Smith saw a close connection between the wealth of a nation and its willingness "freely to engage" in foreign trade. What is the connection?

2. One critic of the North American Free Trade Agreement argued that "it can't be in our interest to sign this deal; Mexico gains too much from it." What does the theory of the gains from trade have to say about that criticism?

3. One product innovation that appears imminent is the electric car. However, development costs are high and economies of scale and learning by doing are both likely to be operative. As a result, there will be a substantial competitive advantage for those who develop a marketable product early. What implications might this have for government policies toward North American automobile manufacturers' activities in this area? Should the Canadian or U.S. governments encourage joint efforts by Chrysler, Ford, and GM, even if this appears to lessen competition between them?

4. Studies of Canadian trade patterns have shown that industries with high wages are among the largest and fastest-growing export sectors. One example is the computer software industry. Does this finding contradict the principle of comparative advantage?

5. Predict what each of the following events would do to the terms of trade of the importing country and the exporting country, other things being equal.

   a. A blight destroys a large part of the coffee beans produced in the world.
   b. The Koreans cut the price of the steel they sell to Canada.
   c. General inflation of 4 percent occurs around the world.
   d. Violation of OPEC output quotas leads to a sharp fall in the price of oil.

6. Are there always benefits to specialization and trade? When are the benefits greatest? Under what situations are there *no* benefits from specialization and trade?

CHAPTER 35

Trade Policy

LEARNING OBJECTIVES

1. Understand the various situations in which a country may rationally choose to protect some industries.

2. Recognize the most common fallacious arguments in favour of protection.

3. Explain the effects of placing a tariff or a quantity restriction on an imported good.

4. Recognize that trade-remedy laws are sometimes just thinly disguised protection.

5. Explain the difference between trade creation and trade diversion.

6. Know the main features of the North American Free Trade Agreement.

Conducting business in a foreign country is not always easy. Differences in language, in local laws and customs, and in currency often complicate transactions. Our concern in this chapter, however, is not with these complications but with government policy toward international trade, which is called **trade policy.** At one extreme is a policy of free trade—that is, an absence of any form of government interference with the free flow of international trade. Any departure from free trade designed to protect domestic industries from foreign competition is called **protectionism.**

We begin by briefly restating the case for free trade and then go on to study various valid and invalid arguments that are commonly advanced for some degree of protection. We then explore some of the methods that are commonly used to restrict trade, such as tariffs and quotas. Finally, we examine the many modern institutions designed to foster freer trade on either a global or a regional basis. Of central importance to Canada is the North American Free Trade Agreement (NAFTA).

trade policy
A government's policy involving restrictions placed on international trade.

protectionism Any government policy that interferes with free trade in order to give some protection to domestic industries against foreign competition.

Free Trade or Protection?

Today, most governments accept the proposition that a relatively free flow of international trade is desirable for the health of their individual economies. But heated debates still occur over trade policy. Should a country permit the completely free flow of international trade, or should it sometimes seek to protect its local producers from foreign competition? If some protection is desired, should it be achieved by tariffs or by nontariff barriers? **Tariffs** are taxes designed to raise the price of foreign goods. **Nontariff barriers (NTBs)** are devices other than tariffs that are designed to reduce the flow of imports;

tariff A tax applied on imports of goods or services.
nontariff barriers (NTBs) Restrictions other than tariffs designed to reduce the flow of imported goods or services.

examples are quotas and customs procedures that are deliberately more cumbersome than necessary.

The Case for Free Trade

The case for free trade was presented in Chapter 34. Comparative advantages arise whenever countries have different opportunity costs. Free trade encourages all countries to specialize in producing products in which they have a comparative advantage. This in turn maximizes world production and hence maximizes average world living standards (as measured by the world's per capita GDP).

Free trade does not necessarily make *everyone* better off than they would be in its absence. For example, reducing an existing tariff often results in individual groups receiving a smaller share of a larger world output so that they lose even though the average person gains. If we ask whether it is *possible* for free trade to improve everyone's living standards, the answer is "yes." But, if we ask whether free trade always does so, the answer is "not necessarily."

Given that all countries can be better off by specializing in those goods in which they have a comparative advantage, it is puzzling that most countries of the world continue in some way to restrict the flow of trade. Why do tariffs and other barriers to trade continue to exist two centuries after Adam Smith and David Ricardo stated the case for free trade? Is there a valid case for some protection?

The Case for Protection

Two kinds of arguments for protection are commonly offered. The first concerns national objectives *other than* maximizing total income; the second concerns the desire to increase one country's national income, possibly at the expense of the national incomes of other countries.

Objectives Other than Maximizing National Income

It is possible to believe that a country's national income is maximized with free trade and yet rationally oppose free trade because of a concern with other policy objectives.

Noneconomic Advantages of Diversification.   Comparative advantage might dictate that a small country should specialize in producing a narrow range of products. However, there may be social advantages in a more diverse economy. Citizens would be given a wider range of occupations, and the social and psychological advantages of diversification may more than compensate for the reduction in per capita output.

Countries whose economies are based on the production of only a few goods face risks from fluctuations in world prices. For this reason, protection to promote diversification may be viewed as desirable.

Risks of Specialization.   For a very small country, specializing in the production of only a few products—though dictated by comparative advantage—might involve risks that the country does not wish to take. One such risk is that technological advances may render its basic product obsolete. Another risk, especially for countries specialized in producing a small range of agricultural products, is that swings in world prices lead to large swings in national income. Everyone understands these risks, but there is debate about what governments can do about it. The pro-tariff argument is that the government can encourage a more diversified economy by protecting industries that otherwise could not compete. Opponents argue that governments, being naturally influenced by political motives, are poor judges of which industries can be protected in order to produce diversification at a reasonable cost.

Protection of Specific Groups.   Although free trade—and specialization according to comparative advantage—will maximize per capita GDP over the whole economy, some specific groups may have higher incomes under protection than under free trade. Of particular interest in Canada and the United States has been the effect that greater international trade has on the incomes of unskilled workers.

Consider the ratio of skilled workers to unskilled workers. There are plenty of both types throughout the world. Compared to much of the rest of the world, however, Canada has more skilled and fewer unskilled people. When trade is expanded because of a reduction in tariffs, Canada will tend to export goods made by its abundant skilled workers and import goods made by unskilled workers. (This is the basic prediction of the *factor endowment theory* of comparative advantage that we discussed in Chapter 34.) Because Canada is now exporting more goods made by skilled labour, the domestic demand for such labour rises. Because Canada is now importing more goods made by unskilled labour, the domestic demand for such labour falls. This specialization according to comparative advantage raises average Canadian living standards, but it will also tend to raise the wages of skilled Canadian workers relative to the wages of unskilled Canadian workers.

If increasing trade has these effects, then reducing trade by raising trade barriers can have the opposite effects. Raising trade barriers may raise the incomes of unskilled Canadian workers, giving them a larger share of a smaller total GDP. The conclusion is that trade restrictions can improve the earnings of one group whenever the restrictions increase the demand for that group's services. This is done, however, at the expense of a reduction in *overall* national income and hence the country's average living standards.

This analysis is important because it reveals both the grain of truth and the dangers that lie behind the resistance to reductions in trade restrictions on the part of some labour groups and some organizations whose main concern is with the poor.

Social and distributional concerns may lead to the rational adoption of protectionist policies. But the cost of such protection is a reduction in the country's average living standards.

Economists cannot say that it is irrational for a society to sacrifice some income to achieve other goals. But economists can do three things when presented with such arguments for adopting protectionist measures. First, they can ask if the proposed measures really do achieve the ends suggested. Second, they can calculate the cost of the measures in terms of lowered living standards. Third, they can see if there are alternative means of achieving the stated goals at lower cost in terms of lost national income.

Maximizing One Country's National Income

Next we consider several arguments for the use of tariffs when the objective is to maximize a country's national income.

To Alter the Terms of Trade.   Tariffs can be used to change the terms of trade in favour of a country that makes up a large fraction of the world demand for some product that it imports. By restricting its demand for that product through a tariff, it can force down the price that foreign exporters receive for that product. The price paid by domestic consumers will probably rise but as long as the increase is less than the tariff, foreign suppliers will receive less per unit. For example, a 20 percent U.S. tariff on the import of

Canadian softwood lumber might raise the price paid by U.S. consumers by 12 percent and lower the price received by Canadian suppliers by 8 percent (the difference between the two prices being received by the U.S. treasury). This reduction in the price received by the foreign suppliers of a U.S. import is a terms-of-trade improvement for the United States (and a terms-of-trade deterioration for Canada).

To Protect Against "Unfair" Actions by Foreign Firms and Governments.
Tariffs are used to prevent foreign industries from harming domestic industries by employing predatory practices. Two common practices are subsidies paid by foreign governments to their exporters and price discrimination by foreign firms, which is called *dumping* when it is done across international borders. These practices are typically countered by levying tariffs called *countervailing duties* and *antidumping duties*. The circumstances under which dumping and foreign subsidization provide a valid argument for such tariffs are considered in detail later in this chapter.

infant industry argument The argument that new domestic industries with potential for economies of scale or learning by doing need to be protected from competition from established, low-cost foreign producers so that they can grow large enough to achieve costs as low as those of foreign producers.

To Protect Infant Industries.
The oldest valid argument for protection as a means of raising living standards concerns economies of scale. It is usually called the **infant industry argument**. An infant industry is nothing more than a new, small industry. If such an industry has large economies of scale, costs will be high when the industry is small but will fall as the industry grows. In such industries, the country first in the field has a tremendous advantage. A developing country may find that in the early stages of development, its industries are unable to compete with established foreign rivals. A trade restriction may protect these industries from foreign competition while they grow up. When they are large enough, they will be able to produce as cheaply as foreign rivals and thus be able to compete without protection.

Most of the now industrialized countries developed their industries initially under quite heavy tariff protection. (In Canada's case, the National Policy of 1876 established a high tariff wall behind which many Canadian industries developed and thrived for many years.) Once the industrial sector was well developed, these countries moved to reduce their levels of protection, thus moving a long way toward freer trade.

To Encourage Learning by Doing.
Learning by doing, which we discussed in Chapter 34, suggests that the pattern of comparative advantage can be changed. If a country learns enough by producing products for which it currently has a comparative *dis*advantage, it may gain in the long run by specializing in those products, developing a comparative advantage as the learning process lowers their costs.

Learning by doing is an example of what in Chapter 34 we called *dynamic* comparative advantage. The success over the past three decades of such newly industrializing countries (NICs) as Hong Kong, South Korea, Singapore, Taiwan, Indonesia, and Thailand seemed to many observers to be based on acquired skills and government policies that created favourable business conditions. These successes gave rise to the theory that comparative advantages can change and that they can be developed by suitable government policies, which can, however, take many forms other than restricting trade.

Some countries have succeeded in developing strong comparative advantages in targeted industries, but others have failed. One reason such policies sometimes fail is that protecting local industries from foreign competition may make the industries unadaptive and complacent. Another reason is the difficulty of identifying the industries that will be able to succeed in the long run. All too often, the protected infant grows up to be a weakling requiring permanent protection for its continued existence, or else the rate of learning is slower than for similar industries in countries that do not provide protection from the chill winds of international competition. In these instances, the anticipated comparative advantage never materializes. The NICs mentioned above avoided these problems by insisting that the protected industries serve the export market. If they could not succeed within a few years in the tough world of international competition, they lost their domestic support.

To Earn Pure Profits.   Another argument for tariffs or other trade restrictions is to help create an advantage in producing or marketing some new product that is expected to generate pure profits. To the extent that all lines of production earn normal profits, there is no reason to produce goods other than ones for which a country has a comparative advantage. Some goods, however, are produced in industries containing a few large firms where economies of scale provide a natural barrier to entry. Firms in these industries can earn high profits even over long periods of time. If protection of the domestic market can increase the chance that one of the protected domestic firms will become established and thus earn high profits, the protection may pay off. This is the general idea behind the concept of *strategic trade policy*.

Opponents of strategic trade policy argue that it is nothing more than a modern version of age-old and faulty justifications for tariff protection. Once all countries try to be strategic, they will all waste vast sums trying to break into industries in which there is no room for most of them. Domestic consumers would benefit most, they say, if their governments let other countries engage in this game. Consumers could then buy the cheap, subsidized foreign products and export traditional nonsubsidized products in return. The opponents of strategic trade policy also argue that democratic governments that enter the game of picking and backing winners are likely to make more bad choices than good ones. One bad choice, with all of its massive development costs written off, would require that many good choices also be made in order to make the equivalent in profits that would allow taxpayers to break even overall.

An ongoing dispute between Canada and Brazil illustrates how strategic trade policy is often difficult to distinguish from pure protection. The world's two major producers of regional jets are Bombardier, based in Montreal, and Embraer SA, based in Brazil. For several years, each company has accused their competitor's government of using illegal subsidies to help their domestic company sell jets in world markets. Brazil's Pro-Ex program provides Embraer's customers with low-interest loans with which to purchase Embraer's jets. The Canadian government's Technology Partnerships program is a $300 million annual fund that subsidizes research and development activities in high-tech aerospace and defence companies. As the leading Canadian aerospace company, Bombardier benefits significantly from this program.

In 1999, the World Trade Organization (WTO) ruled that both the Brazilian and Canadian governments were using illegal subsidy programs to support their aerospace firms. Both countries, however, naturally view their respective programs as necessary responses to the other country's subsidization. Many economists believe that an agreement to eliminate both programs would leave a "level playing field" while saving Brazilian and Canadian taxpayers a considerable amount of money. By the end of 1999, the two countries had not reached an agreement involving reductions in their subsidy programs.

See Chapter 35 of www.pearsoned.ca/lipsey for an interview with Bombardier's Laurent Beaudoin on the need for subsidies in the aerospace industry: "Trade and Subsidies in the Air," *World Economic Affairs*.

The Importance of Competition

In today's world, a country's products must stand up to international competition if they are to survive. Over time, this requirement demands that they hold their own in competition for successful innovations. Over even so short a period as a few years, firms that do not develop new products and new production methods fall seriously behind their competitors in many industries. Protection, by reducing competition from foreign firms, reduces the incentive for industries to fight to succeed internationally. If any one

For a list and discussion of many ongoing trade disputes, see the WTO's website: www.wto.org.

country adopts high tariffs unilaterally, its domestic industries will become less competitive. Secure in its home market because of the tariff wall, its protected industries are likely to become less and less competitive in the international market. As the gap between domestic and foreign industries widens, any tariff wall will provide less and less protection. Eventually, the domestic industries will succumb to the foreign competition. Meanwhile, domestic living standards will fall relative to foreign ones as an increasing productivity gap opens between domestic protected industries and foreign, internationally oriented ones.

Although restrictive trade policies have sometimes been pursued following a rational assessment of the approximate cost, such policies are often pursued for political objectives or on fallacious economic grounds, with little appreciation of the actual costs involved.

Fallacious Arguments for Protection

We have seen that there are generally gains from trade, although trade does not necessarily make everyone in a country better off. We have also seen that there are some situations in which there are valid arguments for restricting trade. For every valid argument, however, there are many fallacious arguments—many of these are based, directly or indirectly, on the misconception that in every transaction there is a winner and a loser. Here we review a few such arguments that are frequently advanced in political debates concerning international trade.

Keep the Money at Home

This argument says that if I buy a foreign good, I have the good and the foreigner has the money, whereas if I buy the same good locally, I have the good and our country has the money, too. This argument is based on a common misconception. It assumes that domestic money actually goes abroad physically when imports are purchased and that trade flows only in one direction. But when Canadian importers purchase Japanese goods, they do not send dollars abroad. They (or their financial agents) buy Japanese yen and use them to pay the Japanese manufacturers. They purchase the yen on the foreign-exchange market by giving up dollars to someone who wishes to use them for expenditure in Canada. Even if the money did go abroad physically—that is, if a Japanese firm accepted a shipload of Canadian $100 bills—it would be because that firm (or someone to whom it could sell the dollars) wanted them to spend in the only country where they are legal tender—Canada.

Canadian currency, or any other national currency, ultimately does no one any good except as purchasing power. It would be miraculous if Canadian money could be exported in return for real goods. After all, the Bank of Canada has the power to create as much new Canadian money as it wishes (at almost zero direct cost). It is only because Canadian money can buy Canadian products and Canadian assets that others want it.

Protect Against Low-Wage Foreign Labour

This argument says that the products of low-wage countries will drive Canadian products from the market, and the high Canadian standard of living will be dragged down to that of its poorer trading partners. Arguments of this sort have swayed many voters over the years.

As a prelude to considering this argument, think what the argument would imply if taken out of the international context and put into a local one, where the same principles govern the gains from trade. Is it really impossible for a rich person to gain by trading with a poor person? Would the local millionaire be better off if she did all her own typing, gardening, and cooking? No one believes that a rich person gains nothing by trading with those who are less rich.

Why, then, must a rich group of people lose when they trade with a poor group? "Well," some may say, "the poor group will price its goods too cheaply." Does anyone believe that consumers lose from buying in discount houses or supermarkets just because the prices are lower there than at the old-fashioned corner store? Consumers gain when they can buy the same goods at a lower price. If Mexican or Malaysian firms pay low wages and sell their goods cheaply, workers in those countries may suffer, but Canadians will gain by obtaining imports at a low cost in terms of the goods that must be exported in return. The cheaper our imports are, the better off we are in terms of the goods and services available for domestic consumption.

As we said earlier in this chapter, *some* Canadians may be better off if Canada places high tariffs on the import of Mexican goods. In particular, if the Mexican goods compete with goods made by unskilled Canadian workers, then those unskilled workers will be better off if a Canadian tariff protects their firms and thus their jobs. But Canadian income overall—that is, average per capita real income—will be higher when there is free trade.

See Chapter 35 of www.pearsoned.ca/lipsey for an interview with MIT's Paul Krugman, who explains why countries do not "compete" against each other: Paul Krugman, "Fresh Thoughts from a Saltwater Economist," *World Economic Affairs*.

Exports Are Good; Imports Are Bad

Exports create domestic income; imports create income for foreigners. Thus, other things being equal, exports tend to increase our total GDP, and imports tend to reduce it. Surely, then, it is desirable to encourage exports by subsidizing them and to discourage imports by taxing them. This is an appealing argument, but it is incorrect.

Exports raise GDP by adding to the value of domestic output, but they do not add to the value of domestic consumption. The standard of living in a country depends on the goods and services available for consumption, not on what is produced.

If exports really were "good" and imports really were "bad," then a fully employed economy that managed to increase exports without a corresponding increase in imports ought to be better off. Such a change, however, would result in a reduction in current standards of living because when more goods are sent abroad but no more are brought in from abroad, the total goods available for domestic consumption must fall.

The living standards of a country depend on the goods and services consumed in that country. The importance of exports is that they provide the resources required to purchase imports, either now or in the future.

Create Domestic Jobs

It is sometimes said that an economy with substantial unemployment, such as Canada during much of the 1990s, provides an exception to the case for freer trade. Suppose that tariffs or import quotas cut the imports of Japanese cars, Korean textiles, German kitchen equipment, and Polish vodka. Surely, the argument maintains, this will create more employment in Canadian industries producing similar products. This may be true but it will also *reduce* employment in other industries.

The Japanese, Koreans, Germans, and Poles can buy from Canada only if they earn Canadian dollars by selling their domestically produced goods and services to Canada (or by borrowing dollars from Canada).[1] The decline in their sales of cars, textiles,

---

[1]They can also get dollars by selling to other countries and then using their currencies to buy Canadian dollars. But this intermediate step only complicates the transaction; it does not change its fundamental nature. Other countries must have earned the dollars by selling goods to Canada or borrowing from Canada.

kitchen equipment, and vodka will decrease their purchases of Canadian lumber, cars, software, banking services, and holidays. Jobs will be lost in Canadian export industries and gained in industries that formerly faced competition from imports. The major long-term effect is that the same total employment will merely be redistributed among industries. In the process, living standards will be reduced because employment expands in inefficient import-competing industries and contracts in efficient exporting industries.

A country that imposes tariffs in an attempt to create domestic jobs risks starting a "trade war" with its trading partners. Such a trade war can easily leave every country worse off, as world output (and thus income) falls significantly. An income-reducing trade war followed the onset of the Great Depression in 1929 as many countries increased tariffs to protect their domestic industries in an attempt to stimulate domestic production and employment. Most economists agree that this trade war made the Great Depression worse than it otherwise would have been.

There are several fallacious arguments for protection that are often heard in political debate. These arguments suffer from a misunderstanding of the sources of gains from trade or from the misbelief that protection can increase total employment.

Methods of Protection

We now go on to explore the various tools that governments use to provide protection to domestic industries.

Two main types of protectionist policy are illustrated in Figure 35-1. Both cause the price of the imported good to rise and its quantity demanded to fall. They differ, however, in how they achieve these results. The caption to the figure analyses these two types of policy.

Policies that Directly Raise Prices

The first type of protectionist policy directly raises the price of the imported product. A tariff, also often called an *import duty*, is the most common policy of this type. Other such policies are any rules or regulations that fulfill three conditions: They are costly to comply with; they do not apply to competing, domestically produced products; and they are more than is required to meet any legitimate purpose other than restricting trade.

As shown in part (i) of Figure 35-1, tariffs affect both foreign and domestic producers, as well as domestic consumers. The initial effect is to raise the domestic price of the imported product above its world price by the amount of the tariff. Imports fall. As a result, foreign producers sell less and must transfer resources to other lines of production. The price received on domestically produced units rises, as does the quantity produced domestically. On both counts, domestic producers earn more. However, the cost of producing the extra production at home exceeds the price at which it could be purchased on the world market. Thus, the benefit to domestic producers comes at the expense of domestic consumers. Indeed, domestic consumers lose on two counts: First, they consume less of the product because its price rises, and second, they pay a higher price for the amount that they do consume. This extra spending ends up in two places: The extra that is paid on all units produced at home goes to domestic producers, and the extra that is paid on units still imported goes to the government as tariff revenue.

FIGURE 35-1   Tariffs and Quotas to Protect Domestic Producers

(i) Free trade

(ii) Restricted trade

The same reduction in imports and increase in domestic production can be achieved by using either a tariff or a quantity restriction. In both parts of the figure, D and S are the domestic demand and supply curves, respectively, and p_w is the world price of some product that is both produced at home and imported.

Part (i) of the figure shows the situation under free trade. Domestic consumption is q_1, domestic production is q_0, and imports are $q_0 q_1$.

Part (ii) shows what happens when protectionist policies restrict imports to the amount $q_3 q_2$. When this is done by levying a tariff of T per unit, the price in the domestic market rises by the full amount of the tariff to p_d. Consumers reduce consumption from q_1 to q_2 and pay an extra amount, shown by the shaded areas 1, 2, and 4, for the q_2 that they now purchase. Domestic production rises from q_0 to q_3. Because domestic producers receive the domestic price, their receipts rise by the three light-shaded areas, labelled 1, 2, and 3. Area 3 is revenue that was previously earned by foreign producers under free trade, while areas 1 and 2 are now paid by domestic consumers because of the higher prices they now face. Foreign suppliers of the imported good continue to receive the world price, so the government receives as tariff revenue the extra amount paid by consumers for the $q_3 q_2$ units that are still imported (shown by the dark shaded area, 4).

When the same result is accomplished by a quantity restriction, the government—through either a quota or a voluntary export restriction (VER)—reduces imports to $q_3 q_2$. This drives the domestic market price up to p_d and has the same effect on domestic producers and consumers as the tariff. Since the government has merely restricted the quantity of imports, both foreign and domestic suppliers get the higher price in the domestic market. Thus, foreign suppliers now receive the extra amount paid by domestic consumers (represented by the shaded area labelled 4) for the units that are still imported.

Policies that Directly Reduce Quantities

The second type of protectionist policy directly restricts the quantity of an imported product. A common example is the **import quota,** by which the importing country sets a maximum of the quantity of some product that may be imported each year. Another measure is the **voluntary export restriction (VER),** an agreement by an exporting country to limit the amount of a product that it sells to the importing country.

Figure 35-1 shows that a quantity restriction and a tariff have similar effects on domestic consumers and producers—they both raise domestic prices, increase domestic

import quota   A limit set by the government on the quantity of a foreign commodity that may be shipped into that country in a given time period.

voluntary export restriction (VER)   An agreement by an exporting country to limit the amount of a good exported to another country.

production, and reduce domestic consumption. But a quantity restriction is actually *worse* than a tariff for the importing country because the effect of the quantity restriction is to raise the price received by the foreign suppliers of the good. In contrast, a tariff leaves the foreign suppliers' price unchanged and instead generates tariff revenue for the government of the importing country.

Canada, the United States, and the European Union have used VERs extensively, and the EU makes frequent use of import quotas. Japan has been pressured into negotiating several VERs with Canada, the United States, and the EU in order to limit sales of some of the Japanese goods that have had the most success in international competition. For example, in 1983, the United States and Canada negotiated VERs whereby the Japanese government agreed to restrict total sales of Japanese cars to these two countries for three years. When the agreements ran out in 1986, the Japanese continued to restrict their automobile sales by unilateral voluntary action. Japan's readiness to restrict its exports to North America reflects the high profits that Japanese automobile producers were making under the system of VERs, as explained in Figure 35-1. In recent years, such VERs have become less important because Japan's major automobile producers, Honda and Toyota, both have established manufacturing plants in Canada.

Trade-Remedy Laws and Nontariff Barriers

As tariffs were lowered over the years since 1947, countries that wished to protect domestic industries began using, and often abusing, a series of trade restrictions that came to be known as nontariff barriers (NTBs). The original purpose of some of these barriers was to remedy certain legitimate problems that arise in international trade and, for this reason, they are often called *trade-remedy laws*. All too often, however, such laws are misused to become potent means of simple protection.

Dumping

Selling a product in a foreign country at a lower price than in the domestic market is known as **dumping**. Dumping is a form of price discrimination studied in the theory of monopoly. Most governments have antidumping duties designed to protect their own industries against what is viewed as unfair foreign pricing practices.

Dumping, if it lasts indefinitely, can be a gift to the receiving country. Its consumers get goods from abroad at less than their full cost of production.

Dumping is more often a temporary measure, designed to get rid of unwanted surpluses, or a predatory attempt to drive competitors out of business. In either case, domestic producers complain about unfair foreign competition. In both cases, it is accepted international practice to levy antidumping duties on foreign imports. These duties are designed to eliminate the discriminatory elements in their prices.

Unfortunately, antidumping laws have been evolving over the past three decades in ways that allow antidumping duties to become barriers to trade and competition rather than to provide redress for unfair trading practices.

Several features of the antidumping system that is now in place in many countries make it highly protectionist. First, any price discrimination between national markets is classified as dumping and is subject to penalties. Thus prices in the producer's domestic market become, in effect, minimum prices below which no sales can be made in foreign markets, whatever the nature of demand in the domestic and foreign markets. Second, following a change in the U.S. law in the early 1970s, many countries' laws now calculate the "margin of dumping" as the difference between the price that is

dumping The practice of selling a commodity at a lower price in the export market than in the domestic market for reasons unrelated to differences in costs of servicing the two markets.

charged in that country's market and the foreign producer's average cost. Thus when there is a global slump in some industry so that the profit-maximizing price for all producers is below average cost, foreign producers can be convicted of dumping. This gives domestic producers enormous protection whenever the market price falls temporarily below average cost. Third, law in the United States (but not in all other countries) places the onus of proof on the accused. Facing a charge of dumping, a foreign producer must prove within the short time allowed for such a defence that the charge is unfounded. Fourth, U.S. antidumping duties are imposed with no time limit, so they often persist long after foreign firms have altered the prices that gave rise to them.

Governments have often been persuaded that low-price competition from foreign firms is "unfair" competition, and have levied antidumping duties on the imported goods. A recent example in Canada was an alleged case of dumping by Gerber, a U.S.-based producer of jarred baby food. In 1997, Heinz, the only Canadian producer, claimed that Gerber was pricing its products in Canada below costs, causing Heinz to lose sales. Heinz pushed for antidumping duties to be imposed on Gerber imports, and in April of 1998 the Canadian government agreed and imposed a 69 percent duty on Gerber imports. This duty was high enough to cause Gerber to reconsider the value of selling in the Canadian market. Later in the same year, however, consumer groups and the federal Competition Bureau argued that the very high duties on Gerber's products effectively left Heinz as a monopolist in the Canadian market. They urged a reluctant Canadian government to repeal the duty so that consumers could benefit from the competition between Gerber and Heinz.

Countervailing Duties

Countervailing duties, which are commonly used by the U.S. government but much less so elsewhere, provide another case in which a trade-remedy law can sometimes become a covert method of protection. The countervailing duty is designed to act, not as a tariff barrier, but rather as a means of creating a "level playing field" on which fair international competition can take place. Privately owned domestic firms rightly complain that they cannot compete against the seemingly bottomless purses of foreign governments. Subsidized foreign exports can be sold indefinitely at prices that would produce losses in the absence of the subsidy. The original object of countervailing duties was to counteract the effect on price of the presence of such foreign subsidies.

If a domestic firm suspects the existence of such a subsidy and registers a complaint, its government is required to make an investigation. For a countervailing duty to be levied, the investigation must determine, first, that the foreign subsidy to the specific industry in question does exist and, second, that it is large enough to cause significant injury to competing domestic firms.

There is no doubt that countervailing duties have sometimes been used to counteract the effects of unfair competition that are caused by foreign subsidies. Many governments complain, however, that countervailing duties are often used as thinly disguised protection. At the early stages of the development of countervailing duties, only subsidies whose prime effect was to distort trade were possible objects of countervailing duties. Even then, however, the existence of equivalent domestic subsidies was not taken into account when decisions were made to put countervailing duties on subsidized imports. Thus the United States levies some countervailing duties against foreign goods even though the foreign subsidy is less than the domestic subsidy. This does not create a level playing field.

Over time, the type of subsidy that is subject to countervailing duties has evolved until almost any government program that affects industry now risks becoming the object of a countervailing duty. Because all governments, including most U.S. state governments,

Canada's supply-management programs such as those in the dairy industry have been a perpetual source of friction in international trade negotiations.

have programs that provide direct or indirect assistance to industry, the potential for the use of countervailing duties as thinly disguised trade barriers is enormous.

Current Trade Policy

In the remainder of the chapter, we discuss trade policy in practice. We start with the many international agreements that govern current trade policies and then look in a little more detail at the NAFTA.

Before 1947, any country was free to impose tariffs on its imports. However, when one country increased its tariffs, the action often triggered retaliatory actions by its trading partners. The 1930s saw a high-water mark of world protectionism as each country sought to raise its employment and output by raising its tariffs. The end result was lowered efficiency, less trade, but no more employment or income. Since the end of World War II, much effort has been devoted to reducing tariff barriers, both on a multilateral and on a regional basis.

The GATT and the WTO

One of the most notable achievements of the post-World War II era was the creation of the General Agreement on Tariffs and Trade (GATT). The GATT has since been replaced by the World Trade Organization (WTO). The principle of the GATT was that each member country agreed not to make unilateral tariff increases. This prevented the outbreak of "tariff wars" in which countries raised tariffs to protect particular domestic industries and to retaliate against other countries' tariff increases.

The Uruguay Round—the final round of trade agreements under GATT—was completed in 1994 after years of negotiations. It reduced world tariffs by about 40 percent. But a significant failure of these talks was not getting a major liberalization of trade in agricultural goods. Such an agreement was resisted by the EU and Canada. The EU has a scheme called the Common Agricultural Policy (CAP) that provides general support for most of its agricultural products, many of which are exported. The EU's position as a subsidized net exporter causes major harm to agricultural producers in developing countries whose governments are too poor to compete with the EU in a subsidy war.

Canada, which has free trade in many agricultural commodities, was concerned to maintain its supply management over a number of industries including poultry, eggs, and dairy products. These schemes are administered by the provinces who restrict domestic production and thus push domestic prices well above world levels. The federal government made them possible by imposing quotas on imports of these products at the national level.

Canada, the EU, and a number of other countries that lavishly protect some or all of their domestic agricultural producers were finally forced to agree to a plan to end all import quotas on agricultural products. In a process called "tariffication," these quotas have been replaced by "tariff equivalents"—tariffs that restrict trade by the same amount as the quotas did. Canadian tariff equivalents are as high as several hundred percent in some products, showing just how restrictive the Canadian policy is. The hope among countries that are pushing for freer trade in agricultural commodities is that pressure will build to reduce these very high tariffs over the next few decades.

Despite the failure to achieve free trade in agricultural products, the Uruguay Round is generally viewed as a success. Perhaps its most significant achievement was the creation of the World Trade Organization (WTO) to replace the GATT. An important part of the WTO is its formal dispute-settlement mechanism. This mechanism allows countries to take cases of alleged trade violations—such as illegal subsidies or tariffs—to the WTO for a formal ruling, and also obliges member countries to follow the ruling. The WTO's dispute-settlement mechanism is thus a significant step toward a "rules based" global trading system.

The WTO, however, does have its opponents. In December 1999, trade ministers from the WTO member countries met in Seattle to set the agenda for a proposed new round of trade talks. (Not surprisingly, there were difficulties establishing the agenda—not least were the familiar problems in dealing with subsidies to agriculture.) The Seattle meetings were delayed and interrupted by massive protests from environmental and labour groups, among others, who argued that the WTO's process of negotiating trade agreements pays insufficient attention to environmental and labour standards, especially in the developing countries. Many WTO officials and trade ministers, including those from the developing countries, recognized the importance of environmental and labour issues but questioned the wisdom of formally including these concerns in trade agreements. Reaching agreement on trade issues among the 134 member countries of the WTO is difficult enough—it would be almost impossible if the issues were bundled with the even more contentious environmental and labour issues. The result would be an overall agreement that achieved very little in terms of either trade liberalization, environmental protection, or establishing labour standards. Instead, many trade officials argued that the existing International Labour Organization should be strengthened and a separate international organization like the WTO should be created to promote environmental issues. These organizations could then push ahead to achieve in their respective domains the same success that the GATT achieved over fifty years of negotiations.

For further progress to be made on trade liberalization, environmental and labour issues will probably have to be addressed. Either domestic political pressures will push individual member countries to insist that these issues be included within the WTO negotiations, or other organizations like the WTO will be developed and/or strengthened to address the concerns. Whatever approach is followed, it appears that these will surely continue to be hot policy issues into the 21st century.

Despite the obstacles, many economists and policy makers now see multilateral free trade in goods and services as an attainable goal. After notable success in liberalizing trade in goods and services, attention in recent years has swung toward accomplishing the same thing for foreign direct investment (FDI). *Applying Economic Concepts 35-1* discusses the attempt to negotiate a Multilateral Agreement on Investment (MAI), and the political difficulties that were encountered along the way.

For more information on the WTO, see its website at www.wto.org.

Regional Trade Agreements

Regional agreements seek to liberalize trade over a much smaller group of countries than the WTO membership. Three standard forms of regional trade-liberalizing agreements are *free trade areas, customs unions,* and *common markets.*

A **free trade area (FTA)** is the least comprehensive of the three. It allows for tariff-free trade among the member countries, but it leaves each member free to levy its own trade policy with respect to other countries. As a result, members must maintain customs points at their common borders to make sure that imports into the free trade area do not all enter through the member that is levying the lowest tariff on each item. They must also agree on *rules of origin* to establish when a good is made in a member country and hence is able to pass tariff-free across their borders and when it is imported from outside the FTA and hence is subject to tariffs when it crosses borders within the FTA.

free trade area (FTA)
An agreement among two or more countries to abolish tariffs on all or most of the trade among themselves while each remains free to set its own tariffs against other countries.

APPLYING ECONOMIC CONCEPTS 35-1

The Multilateral Agreement on Investment

The view that free flows of foreign direct investment (FDI) are necessary to the efficient functioning of the world economy led governments of many developed countries to seek international rules on the treatment of foreign investment. In the absence of such rules, firms and investors face a great deal of uncertainty about how their foreign-located assets will be treated by the government in the host country, especially in regard to expropriation and discriminatory taxation. This kind of uncertainty leads firms to invest less than they otherwise would, thereby reducing the benefits that would otherwise accrue to both host and source countries.

Under the auspices of the Organization for Economic Cooperation and Development (OECD), Canada joined other countries in negotiations toward a Multilateral Agreement on Investment, popularly known as the MAI. The underlying principle of the MAI is that signatory governments would commit themselves to treat foreign-owned firms no differently from domestically owned firms. The proposed MAI also includes a mechanism for the settlement of disputes caused by alleged violations of the agreement.

By early in 1998, the MAI negotiations had stalled for two main reasons. First, many countries (including Canada and France) pushed strongly for some industries to be exempt from the agreement. These countries wanted the ability to discriminate against foreign firms in politically sensitive "cultural" industries, such as publishing and broadcasting. Many other countries argued that such exemptions defeat the purpose of the agreement and were reluctant to grant them. Further, exemptions greatly increase the complexity of the agreement, in part because it

becomes necessary to provide a precise industrial classification for every unit of foreign investment.

The second and probably more important difficulty encountered by the MAI was that many interest groups around the world began expressing their concerns about the MAI's impact on environmental standards and social programs. Environmental lobby groups argued that the MAI would weaken any country's ability to set environmental standards different from those of its trading partners. Grassroots citizens' movements expressed their concerns about a country's ability to continue providing generous social programs. Though these criticisms received considerable attention in the popular press, a careful examination of the proposed MAI suggests that many of the criticisms are baseless.

The text of the proposed MAI clearly specifies that a country party to the agreement is not restricted in its design and implementation of policies, provided the policies treat foreign and domestic firms equally. If Canada, for example, wished to toughen its environmental standards by requiring firms to install better scrubbers in smokestacks, this policy would not contravene the MAI as long as the new policy applied equally to foreign-owned and domestically owned firms.

By the summer of 1998, the member countries of the OECD decided to delay further negotiations of the MAI. But failure in this set of negotiations will not make the issue go away. With over $300 billion of FDI flowing *annually* between many countries of the world, foreign investment has become too important to be ignored. A widespread set of rules for FDI is surely in our future.

---

customs union
A group of countries who agree to have free trade among themselves and a common set of barriers against imports from the rest of the world.

common market
A customs union with the added provision that factors of production can move freely among the members.

A **customs union** is a free trade area in which the member countries agree to establish a common trade policy with the rest of the world. Because they have a common trade policy, the members need neither customs controls on goods moving among themselves nor rules of origin. Once a good has entered any member country it has met the common rules and regulations and paid the common tariff and so it may henceforth be treated the same as a good that is produced within the union. An example of a customs union is Mercosur, an agreement linking Argentina, Brazil, Paraguay, and Uruguay.

A **common market** is a customs union that also has free movement of labour and capital among its members. The European Union is by far the most successful example of a common market. Indeed, the EU is now moving toward a full *economic union* in which all economic policies in the member countries are harmonized. The adoption of the euro as the common currency of 11 EU countries in 1999 was a significant step in this direction.

Trade Creation and Trade Diversion

A major effect of regional trade liberalization is to reallocate resources. Economists divide these effects into two categories, *trade creation* and *trade diversion*. These concepts were first developed by Jacob Viner, a Canadian-born economist who taught at the University of Chicago and Princeton University and was a leading economic theorist in the first half of the 20th century.

Trade creation occurs when producers in one member country find that they can export to another member country as a result of the elimination of the tariffs. For example, when the North American Free Trade Agreement (NAFTA) eliminated most cross-border tariffs between Mexico, Canada, and the United States, some U.S. firms found that they could undersell their Canadian competitors in some product lines, and some Canadian firms found that they could undersell their U.S. competitors in other product lines. As a result, specialization occurred, and new international trade developed. This trade, which is based on (natural or acquired) comparative advantage, is illustrated in Table 35-1.

Trade creation represents efficient specialization according to comparative advantage.

Trade diversion occurs when exporters in one member country replace foreign exporters as suppliers to another member country. For example, trade diversion occurs when U.S. firms find that they can undersell competitors from the rest of the world in the Canadian market, not because they are the cheapest source of supply, but because their tariff-free prices under NAFTA are lower than the tariff-burdened prices of imports from other countries. This effect is a gain to U.S. firms and Canadian consumers of the product but a loss to Canada overall, which now has to export more goods for any given amount of imports than before the trade diversion occurred. Table 35-1 also illustrates trade diversion.

From the global perspective, trade diversion represents an inefficient use of resources.

The History of Free Trade Areas

The first important free trade area in the modern era was the European Free Trade Association (EFTA). It was formed in 1960 by a group of European countries that were unwilling to join the European Common Market (the forerunner of the European Union) because of its all-embracing character. Not wanting to be left out of the gains from trade, they formed an association whose sole purpose was tariff removal. First, they removed all tariffs on trade among themselves. Then each country signed a free-trade-area agreement with the EU. This made the EU-EFTA market the largest tariff-free market in the world (over 300 million people). In recent years almost all of the EFTA countries have entered the EU.

In 1989, a sweeping agreement between Canada and the United States instituted free trade on almost

trade creation
A consequence of reduced trade barriers among a set of countries whereby trade within the group is increased and trade with the rest of the world remains roughly constant.

trade diversion
A consequence of reduced trade barriers among a set of countries whereby trade within the group replaces trade that used to take place with countries outside the group.

TABLE 35-1 Trade Creation and Trade Diversion

Producing Country	Canadian Delivered Price Without Tariffs (dollars)	Canadian Delivered Price with a 10 Percent Tariff (dollars)
Trade creation		
Canada	40.00	40.00
United States	37.00	40.70
Trade diversion		
Taiwan	20.00	22.00
United States	21.50	23.65

Regional tariff reductions can cause trade creation and trade diversion. The table gives two cases. In the first case, a U.S. good, which could be sold for $37.00 in Canada, has its price increased to $40.70 by a 10 percent Canadian tariff. The Canadian industry, which can sell the good for $40.00 with or without a tariff on imports, is protected against the more efficient U.S. producer. When the tariff is removed by the NAFTA, the U.S. good wins the market by selling at $37.00. Trade is created between Canada and the United States by eliminating the inefficient Canadian production.

In the second case, Taiwan can undersell the U.S. in the Canadian market for another product when neither is subject to a tariff (column 1) and when both are subject to a 10 percent tariff (column 2). But after the NAFTA, the U.S. good enters Canada tariff-free and sells for $21.50, whereas the Taiwanese good, which is still subject to the Canadian tariff, continues to sell for $22.00. The U.S. good wins the market, and Canadian trade is diverted from Taiwan to the U.S. even though Taiwan is the lower-cost supplier (excluding the tariff).

all goods and most nongovernment services and covered what is the world's largest flow of international trade between any two countries. In 1994, this agreement was extended into the North American Free Trade Agreement (NAFTA) by renegotiating the Canada-U.S. agreement to include Mexico. Provision is made within the NAFTA for the accession of other countries with the hope that it may eventually evolve into an agreement linking all countries of the western hemisphere.

The possible expansion of NAFTA is being examined. Indeed, the first accession was to have been Chile. But the negotiations for its entry into NAFTA were held up by domestic political considerations in the United States. The first few years of the 21st century may well see a significant push for expansion of NAFTA.

Australia and New Zealand have also entered into an association that removes restrictions on trade in goods and services between their two countries. The countries of Latin America have been experimenting with free trade areas for many decades. Most earlier attempts failed but, in the past few years, more durable FTAs seem to have been formed, the most successful of which is Mercosur, which includes Argentina, Brazil, Uruguay, and Paraguay. Whether these will remain stand-alone agreements or evolve into a broader continental agreement remains to be seen.

In early 1998, the negotiations for the Free Trade Area of the Americas (FTAA) were formally launched in Santiago, Chile. These negotiations will take many years and will involve discussions of rules of origin, environmental concerns, the treatment of foreign direct investment, agricultural policy, and how best to integrate the many regional agreements into a single comprehensive agreement. Only time will reveal the eventual outcome of these negotiations.

The North American Free Trade Agreement

The NAFTA is an extension of the 1989 Canada-U.S. Free Trade Agreement (FTA) with some important improvements based on the experience of the earlier agreement. It is a free trade area and not a customs union; each country retains its own external trade policy, and rules of origin are needed to determine when a good is made within the NAFTA and thus allowed to move freely among the members.

National Treatment

The fundamental principle that guides the NAFTA is the principle of *national treatment*. The principle of national treatment means that countries are free to establish any laws they wish and that these can differ as much as desired among member countries, with the sole proviso that these laws must not discriminate on the basis of nationality. Canada can have tough environmental laws or standards for particular goods, but it must enforce these equally on Canadian, Mexican, and U.S. firms and on domestically produced and imported goods. The idea of national treatment is to allow a maximum of policy independence while preventing national policies from being used as barriers to trade and investment.

Other Major Provisions

There are several other major provisions in NAFTA. First, all tariffs on trade between the United States and Canada were eliminated by 1999. Canada-Mexico and Mexico-U.S. tariffs are to be phased out over a 15-year period that started in 1994. Also, a number of nontariff barriers are eliminated or circumscribed.

Second, the agreement guarantees national treatment to foreign investment once it enters a country while permitting each country to screen a substantial amount of inbound foreign investment before it enters.

Third, all existing measures that restrict trade and investment that are not explicitly removed by the agreement are "grandfathered," a term referring to the continuation of a practice that predates the agreement and would have been prohibited by the terms of the agreement were it not specifically exempted. This is probably the single most important departure from free trade under the NAFTA. Under it, a large collection of restrictive measures in each of the three countries are given indefinite life. An alternative would have been to "sunset" all of these provisions by negotiating dates at which each would be eliminated. From the point of view of long-term trade liberalization, even a 50-year extension would have been preferable to an indefinite exemption.

Fourth, a few goods remain subject to serious nontariff trade restrictions. In Canada, the main examples are supply-managed agricultural products, beer, textiles, and the cultural industries. Restrictions for the Canadian supply-managed agricultural products may be short-lived because of their tariffication under the Uruguay round of GATT. Textile restriction in both the United States and Canada comes under the Multifiber Agreement, which is being phased out over a 15-year period under the Uruguay round. In the United States, textiles, shipping between U.S. ports, and banking were shielded from free trade in good and services.

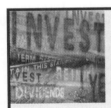

APPLYING ECONOMIC CONCEPTS 35-2

Canadian Wine: A Free-Trade Success Story

Before the Canada-U.S. FTA was signed in 1989, great fears were expressed over the fate of the Canadian wine industry, located mainly in Ontario and British Columbia. It was heavily tariff protected and, with a few notable exceptions, concentrated mainly on cheap, low-quality products. Contrary to most people's expectations, rather than being decimated, the industry now produces a wide variety of high-quality products, some of which have won international competitions in Europe.

Why did this surprising result occur? The high Canadian tariff was levied on a per unit rather than on an *ad valorem* basis. For example, the tariff was expressed as so many dollars per litre rather than as a specific percentage of the price. Charging a tariff by the litre gave most protection to the low quality wines with low value per litre. The higher the per-litre value of the wine, the lower the percentage tariff protection. For example, a $5-per-litre tariff would have the following effects. A low-quality imported wine valued at $5 per litre would have its price raised to $10, a 100 percent increase in price, whereas a higher quality imported wine valued at $25 per litre would have its price increased to $30, only a 20 percent increase in price.

Responding to these incentives, the Canadian industry concentrated on low-quality wines. The market for these wines was protected by the nearly prohibitive tariffs on competing low-quality imports, and also by the high prices charged for high-quality imports. In addition, protection was provided by many hidden charges that the various provincial governments' liquor monopolies levied in order to protect local producers.

When the tariff was removed, the incentives were to move up-market, producing much more value per acre of land. Fortunately, much of the Canadian wine-growing land in the Okanagan Valley in BC and the Niagara Peninsula in Ontario is well-suited for growing the grapes required for good wines. Within a very few years, and with some government transitional assistance, Canadian wines were competing effectively with imported products in the medium-quality range. BC and Ontario wines do not yet reach the quality of major French wines in the $40-$70 (per bottle) range but they compete very effectively in quality with wines in the $10-$25 range, and sometimes even higher up the quality scale.

The success of the wine industry is a fine example of how tariffs can distort incentives and push an industry into a structure that makes it dependent on the tariff. Looking at the pre-FTA industry, very few people suspected that it would be able to survive, let alone produce a world-class product.

APPLYING ECONOMIC CONCEPTS 35-3

Headline Trade Disputes Between Canada and the United States

The flow of goods and services across the Canada-U.S. border is the largest flow of trade between any two countries. In 1998, approximately $500 billion worth of goods and services crossed this border. Although more than 95 percent of this trade passes between the two countries without dispute or hindrance, some items have been beset by persistent disputes. Here is a brief discussion of three of the most contentious areas in U.S.-Canadian trade.

Softwood Lumber

Canada exports large amounts of softwood lumber to the United States. And U.S. producers have persistently claimed that Canadian provincial government policies provide a concealed subsidy that should be evened out with a countervailing duty. The main bone of contention is *stumpage,* which is the royalty that governments charge the logging companies for cutting timber on government-owned land. In the United States, stumpage fees are set by open auction. In Canada, the fees are set in private negotiations between logging companies and the government. U.S. critics argue that the much lower Canadian stumpage fees that emerge from this negotiation process are a subsidy from the government to the lumber industry. Canadians argue that the higher U.S.

stumpage fees reflect the higher services that U.S. governments provide for their lumber companies by way of infrastructure that Canadian lumber companies must provide for themselves.

Just before the Canada-U.S. FTA was finalized, the Canadian government imposed an export tax on lumber going to the United States, to forestall the imposition of a U.S. countervailing duty. When this tax expired, Canada did not renew it and the United States imposed a countervailing duty. Two dispute-settlement panels found in Canada's favour, but largely on the grounds of narrow technicalities. The United States then changed its laws to remove what they saw as the loopholes that the Canadians had used. In 1996, the Canada-U.S. Softwood Lumber Agreement was signed. This agreement restricts the volume of duty-free exports of Canadian softwood lumber to the United States until 2001, with the Canadian government imposing export taxes on any exports that exceed the limit.

Supply-Managed Agricultural Industries

Several of the Canadian provinces use supply-management systems to support farm incomes. Such systems typically involve issuing quotas to farmers to restrict output. The result

---

For information about NAFTA, go to the website for the NAFTA Secretariat: www.nafta-sec-alena.org.

Fifth, trade in most nongovernmental services is liberalized by giving service firms the right of establishment in all member countries and the privilege of national treatment. There is also a limited opening of the markets in financial services to entry from firms based in the NAFTA countries.

Finally, a significant minority of government procurement is opened to cross-border bids.

Dispute Settlement

From Canada's point of view, by far the biggest setback in the negotiations for the Canada-U.S. FTA was the failure to obtain agreement on a common regime for countervailing and antidumping duties. In view of that failure, no significant attempt was made to deal with this issue in the NAFTA negotiations. The U.S. Congress has been unwilling to abandon the unilateral use of these powerful weapons.

In the absence of such a multilateral regime, a dispute-settlement mechanism was put in place. Under it, the domestic determinations that are required for the levying of antidumping and countervailing duties are subject to review by a panel of Canadians, Americans, and Mexicans. This international review replaces appeal through the domestic courts. Panels are empowered to uphold the domestic determinations or refer the decision to the domestic authority—which in effect is a binding order for a new in-of such quotas is to substantially raise the prices paid by Canadian consumers. For years, the Canadian government had supported these policies by imposing import quotas on the managed products, without which their prices would be driven down to world levels. The Canadian government successfully negotiated exemptions for these quotas under the Canada-U.S. FTA. In the Uruguay round of GATT negotiations, despite spirited resistance, the Canadian government was forced to agree to "tariffication" of these quotas. The United States then took the position that although the quotas had been exempt under the FTA, their tariff equivalents were not. After all, the U.S. argued, all tariffs without exception are to be removed by 1999 under the FTA. At the time of writing, the debate continues without an obvious resolution.

Cultural Industries

Canada has always sought to support its magazines, book sellers, film distributors, and other cultural industries from U.S. competition. Although there was never any pressure to prevent governments on both sides of the border from subsidizing the performing arts, such as music and drama, protection of the cultural industries more widely defined was a serious bone of contention during the FTA negotiations. In the end, Canada got exemption for all of its broadly defined cultural industries.

In the mid 1990s, the Canadian government became concerned over the presence of Canadian editions of U.S. split-run magazines. These magazines, such as *Time* and *Sports Illustrated*, contain mostly U.S. content but also include a few pages of Canadian editorial content. Because the fixed costs of the magazine are covered by the U.S. sales of the magazine, the Canadian advertising rates can be lower than those of Canadian-based magazines. The Canadian government and Canadian magazine publishers argued that the presence of such split-run magazines would make it more difficult for Canadian magazines to sell advertising space, thus putting them in an untenable financial position. Failure of Canadian magazines would then damage an important part of Canadian culture. In 1995, the Canadian government imposed an 80 percent tax on advertising expenditures in the Canadian editions of U.S. split-run magazines.

The U.S. government and U.S. magazine publishers argued that the Canadian government's attempts to protect Canadian culture by protecting their magazines were nothing more than simple trade protection. On this basis, they saw no difference between aid to Canadian magazines and aid to textiles firms or the aerospace industry. The United States brought their complaint to the World Trade Organization and, in 1997, the WTO ruled against Canada—that is, it ruled that Canada's tax on split-run advertising contravened international trade agreements.

The Canadian government then attempted to write new legislation that would be consistent with WTO rules but would still have the effect of preventing the U.S. split-run magazines. This prompted the United States to threaten the imposition of duties on a whole range of Canadian exports if the Canadian government did not drop its attempts to prevent the split-runs. Finally, in 1999, the Canadian and U.S. governments reached an agreement to provide limited access to the Canadian market for the U.S.-based split-run magazines.

vestigation. The referral can be repeated until the panel is satisfied that the domestic laws have been correctly and fairly applied.

This is pathbreaking: For the first time in its history, the United States has agreed to submit the administration of its domestic laws to *binding* scrutiny by an international panel that often contains a majority of foreigners.

Results

The Canada-U.S. FTA aroused a great debate in Canada. Indeed, the Canadian federal election of 1988 was fought almost entirely on the issue of free trade. Supporters looked for major increases in the security of existing trade from U.S. protectionist attacks and for a growth of new trade. Detractors predicted a flight of firms to the U.S., the loss of Canadian competitiveness, and even the loss of Canada's political independence.

By and large, however, both the Canada-U.S. FTA and NAFTA agreements have worked out just about as expected by their supporters. Industry has clearly restructured in the direction of greater export orientation in all three countries, and trade creation has occurred. All three countries are importing more from and exporting more to each other. This trend is particularly true between Canada and the United States. As the theory of trade predicts, specialization has occurred in many areas, resulting in more U.S. imports of some product lines from Canada and more U.S. exports of other

See Chapter 35 of www.pearsoned.ca/lipsey for an interesting discussion of the results of FTA and NAFTA: Richard Lipsey, "Free Trade—Real Results Versus Unreal Expectations," *World Economic Affairs*.

See Chapter 35 of www.pearsoned.ca/lipsey for an interview with former Prime Minister Brian Mulroney on the political aspects of FTA and NAFTA: "Standing Firm on Free Trade," *World Economic Affairs*.

See the website for the Department of Foreign Affairs and International Trade for information on the dispute-settlement mechanism: www.dfait-maeic.gc.ca.

goods to Canada. In 1988, before the Canada-U.S. FTA took effect, Canada exported $85 billion in goods and services to the United States, and imported $74 billion from the United States. By 1998, the value of Canada-U.S. trade had almost quadrupled—Canadian exports to the United States had increased to $271 billion and imports from the United States had increased to $234 billion.

It is hard to say how much trade diversion there has been and will be in the future. The greatest potential for trade diversion is with Mexico, which competes in the U.S. and Canadian markets with a large number of products produced in other low-wage countries. South-East Asian exporters to the United States and Canada have been worried that Mexico would capture some of their markets by virtue of having tariff-free access denied to their goods. Most estimates predict, however, that trade creation will dominate over trade diversion.

Most transitional difficulties were initially felt in each country's import-competing industries, just as theory predicts. An agreement such as the NAFTA brings its advantages by encouraging a movement of resources out of protected but inefficient import-competing industries, which decline, and into efficient export industries, which expand because they have better access to the markets of other member countries. Southern Ontario and parts of Quebec had major problems as some traditional exports fell and resources had to be moved to sectors where trade was expanding. Eight years after the agreement, however, southern Ontario was booming again and its most profitable sectors were those that exported to the United States.

There were also some pleasant surprises resulting from free trade. Two Canadian industries that many economists expected to suffer from the FTA and NAFTA were wine-making and textiles. Yet both of these industries have prospered as Canadian firms have improved quality, productivity, and benefited from increased access to the huge U.S. market. *Applying Economic Concepts 35-2* discusses the success of the Canadian wine industry after the tariffs on wine were eliminated.

Finally, the dispute-settlement mechanism seems to have worked well. A large number of disputes have arisen and have been referred to panels. Panel members have usually reacted as professionals rather than as nationals. Most cases have been decided on their merits; allegations that decisions were reached on national rather than professional grounds have been rare.

With over $500 billion annually in two-way trade between Canada and the United States, however, it is inevitable that some disputes arise. *Applying Economic Concepts 35-3* discusses three of the most contentious trade disputes that still disturb the generally tranquil state of Canada-U.S. trade.

S U M M A R Y

Free Trade or Protection?

- The case for free trade is that world output of all products can be higher under free trade than when protectionism restricts regional specialization.

- Protection for an individual country can be urged as a means to ends other than maximizing that country's living standards. Examples of such ends are to produce a diversified economy, to reduce fluctuations in national income and to retain distinctive national traditions.

- Protection can also be urged on the grounds that it may lead to higher living standards for the protectionist country than would a policy of free trade. Such a result might come about by using a monopoly position to influence the terms of trade or by developing a dynamic comparative advantage by allowing inexperienced or uneconomically small industries to become efficient enough to compete with foreign industries.

- Some fallacious protectionist arguments are that (a) mutually advantageous trade is impossible because one trader's gain must always be the other's loss; (b) buying abroad sends our money abroad, while buying at home keeps our money at home; (c) our high-paid workers must be protected against the competition from low-paid foreign workers; and (d) imports are to be discouraged because they lower national income and cause unemployment.

Methods of Protection

- Trade can be restricted by policies that either directly raise prices, such as tariffs, or operate in the first instance on quantities, such as import quotas and voluntary export restrictions.
- As tariff barriers have been reduced over the years, they have been replaced in part by nontariff barriers. The two most important are antidumping and countervailing duties which, although providing legitimate restraints on unfair trading practices, are also used as serious nontariff barriers to trade.

Current Trade Policy

- The General Agreement on Tariffs and Trade (GATT), under which countries agree to reduce trade barriers through multilateral negotiations and not to raise them unilaterally, has greatly reduced world tariffs since its inception in 1947.
- The World Trade Organization (WTO) was created in 1995 as the successor to GATT. It has 134 member countries and contains a formal dispute-settlement mechanism.
- Regional trade-liberalizing agreements such as free trade areas and common markets bring efficiency gains through trade creation and efficiency losses through trade diversion.

- The North American Free Trade Agreement (NAFTA) is the world's largest and most successful free trade area, and the European Union is the world's largest and most successful common market.
- NAFTA is based on the principle of "national treatment". This allows Canada, the United States, and Mexico to implement whatever social, economic, or environmental policies it chooses providing that such policies treat foreign and domestic firms (and their products) equally.

K E Y   C O N C E P T S

Free trade and protectionism
Tariffs and import quotas
Voluntary export restrictions (VERs)
Countervailing and antidumping duties

The General Agreement on Tariffs and
  Trade (GATT)
The World Trade Organization (WTO)
Common markets, customs unions,
  and free trade areas

Trade creation and trade diversion
Nontariff barriers
The North American Free Trade
  Agreement (NAFTA)

STUDY EXERCISES

1. Canada produces steel domestically and also imports it from abroad. Assume that the world market for steel is competitive and that Canada is a small producer, unable to affect the world price. Since Canada imports steel, we know that in the absence of trade, the Canadian equilibrium price would exceed the world price.

   a. Draw a diagram showing the Canadian market for steel, with imports at the world price.
   b. Explain why the imposition of a tariff on imported steel will increase the price of *both* domestic and imported steel.
   c. Show the effects of such a tariff in the diagram.
   d. Who benefits and who is harmed by such a tariff?

2. The diagram below shows the Canadian market for leather shoes, which we assume to be competitive. The world price is p_w. If the Canadian government imposes a tariff of t dollars per unit, the domestic price then rises to $p_w + t$.

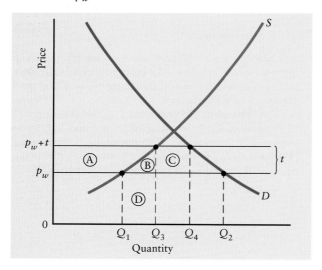

   a. What quantity of leather shoes is imported before the tariff is imposed? After the tariff?
   b. What is the effect of the tariff on the Canadian production of shoes? Which areas in the diagram show the increase in domestic producers' revenue?
   c. With the tariff in place, Canadian shoe producers are earning higher revenues. Which areas in the diagram show how much of this increased revenue is attributed to the higher price paid by Canadian consumers?
   d. The Canadian government earns tariff revenue on the imported shoes. Which area in the diagram shows this tariff revenue?

3. Use the diagram from Question 2 to analyse the effects of imposing an import quota instead of a tariff to protect domestic shoe producers. Draw the diagram as in Question 2 and answer the following questions.

   a. Explain why an import quota of Q_3Q_4 raises the domestic price to $p_w + t$.
   b. With import quotas, the Canadian government earns no tariff revenue. Who gets this money now?
   c. Is the import quota better or worse than the tariff for Canada as a whole? Explain.

4. Under pressure from the Canadian and U.S. governments in the early 1980s, Japanese automobile producers agreed to restrict their exports to the North American market. After the formal agreement ended, the Japanese producers decided unilaterally to continue restricting their exports. Carefully review Figure 35-1 and then answer the following questions.

   a. Explain why such Voluntary Export Restrictions (VERs) are "voluntary."
   b. Explain why an agreement to export only 100 000 cars to North America is better for the Japanese producers than a North American tariff that results in the same volume of Japanese exports.
   c. Who is paying for these benefits to the Japanese producers?

5. Go to Statistics Canada's website: www.statcan.ca. Find the data on "the economy" and then on "international trade," and answer the following questions.

   a. For the most recent year shown, what was the value of Canada's exports to the United States? To the European Union?
   b. For the same year, what was the value of Canada's imports from the United States? From the European Union?
   c. Compute what economists call the "volume of trade" (the sum of exports and imports) between Canada and the United States. How has the volume of trade grown over the past five years? Has trade grown faster than national income?

6. The table below shows the prices *in Canada* of cotton towels produced in the United States, Canada, and Malaysia. All cotton towels are identical.

Producing Country	Canadian Price (in $) without tariff	Canadian Price (in $) with 20% tariff
Canada	4.75	4.75
United States	4.50	5.40
Malaysia	4.00	4.80

a. Suppose Canada imposes a 20 percent tariff on imported towels from any country. Assuming that Canadians purchase only the lowest-price towels, from which country will Canada buy its towels?

b. Now suppose that Canada eliminates tariffs on towels from all countries. Which towels will Canada now buy?

c. Canada and the United States now negotiate a free-trade agreement that eliminates all tariffs between the two countries, but Canada maintains the 20 percent tariff on other countries. Which towels now get imported into Canada?

d. Which of the situations described above is called trade creation and which is called trade diversion?

DISCUSSION QUESTIONS

1. Some Canadians opposed Canada's entry into NAFTA on the grounds that Canadian firms could not compete with the goods produced by cheap Mexican labour. Comment on the following points in relation to the above worries:

   a. "Mexicans are the most expensive cheap labour I have ever encountered"—statement by the owner of a Canadian firm who is moving back from Mexico to Canada.

   b. The theory of the gains from trade says that a high-productivity, high-wage country can gain from trading with a low-wage, low-productivity country.

   c. Technological change is rapidly reducing labour costs as a proportion of total costs in many products; in many industries that use high-tech production methods this proportion is already well below 20 percent.

2. Should Canada and the United States trade with countries with poor human rights records? If trade with China is severely restricted because of its lack of respect for human rights, who will be the gainers and who the losers? Argue the cases that this policy will help, and that it will hinder, human rights progress in China.

3. Import quotas and voluntary export restrictions are often used instead of tariffs. What real difference, if any, is there between quotas, voluntary export restrictions (VERs), and tariffs? Explain why lobbyists for some import-competing industries (cheese, milk, shoes) support import quotas while lobbyists for others (pizza manufacturers, soft drink manufacturers, retail stores) oppose them. Would you expect labour unions to support or oppose quotas?

4. Over the past several years, many foreign automobile producers have built production and assembly facilities in Canada and in the United States. What are some advantages and disadvantages associated with shifting production from, for example, Japan to Canada? Will these cars still be considered "imports"? What is beginning to happen to the definitions of "foreign made" and "domestic made"?

5. Consider a mythical country called Forestland, which exports a large amount of lumber to a nearby country called Houseland. The lumber industry in Houseland has convinced its federal government that it is being harmed by the low prices being charged by the lumber producers in Forestland. You are an advisor to the government in Forestland. Explain who gains and who loses from each of the following policies.

   a. Houseland imposes a tariff on lumber imports from Forestland

   b. Forestland imposes a tax on each unit of lumber exported to Houseland

   c. Forestland agrees to restrict its exports of lumber to Houseland

   d. Which policy is likely to garner the most political support in Houseland? In Forestland?

6. In March 1999, the Canadian government imposed antidumping duties of up to 43 percent on hot-rolled steel imports from France, Russia, Slovakia, and Romania. The allegation was that these countries were dumping steel into the Canadian market.

   a. Who benefits from such alleged dumping? Who is harmed?

   b. Who benefits from the imposition of the antidumping duties? Who is harmed?

   c. Is Canada as a whole made better off by the imposition of the duties? Explain.

CHAPTER 36

Exchange Rates and the Balance of Payments

🔵 *LEARNING OBJECTIVES*

1 Explain the various components of Canada's balance of payments.

2 Understand why the balance of payments accounts always balance.

3 Understand the determinants of the demand for and the supply of foreign currency.

4 Explain the various factors that cause changes in the exchange rate.

5 Explain why a current account deficit is not necessarily undesirable.

6 Understand the theory of purchasing power parity, as well as its limitations.

7 Explain how flexible exchange rates can dampen the effects of terms-of-trade shocks on output and employment.

As we saw in Chapter 19, the external value of the Canadian dollar has fluctuated considerably over the past 25 years. It fell sharply between 1983 and 1988, and then increased until 1992 when it was back at the level of the early 1980s. Between 1992 and 1999, it fell again, by over 20 percent.

In this chapter, we ask what it means to speak of the "external value of the dollar," what causes this value to change, and the implications that such changes have for the economy. We examine the important difference between *flexible* and *fixed* exchange rates, and the Bank of Canada's role under each system. The discussion will bring together material on three topics studied elsewhere in this book: the theory of supply and demand (Chapter 3), the nature of money (Chapter 26), and international trade (Chapter 34).

We begin, however, by examining a country's balance of payments—the record of transactions in goods, services, and assets with the rest of the world. We examine what is meant by a balance of payments deficit or surplus, and what role the central bank plays in determining it.

The Balance of Payments

balance-of-payments accounts *A summary record of a country's transactions with the rest of the world, including the buying and selling of goods, services, and assets.*

To know what is happening to the course of international trade, government statistical agencies (like Statistics Canada) keep track of the transactions between countries. The record of such transactions is made in the **balance-of-payments accounts.** For computing Canada's balance of payments, each transaction, such as the exports or imports of goods, or the purchase or sales of assets, is classified according to whether the transaction generates a *payment* or a *receipt* for Canada.

Table 36-1 shows the major items in the Canadian balance-of-payments accounts for 1998. Transactions that represent a receipt for Canada, such as the sale of a product or asset to foreigners, are recorded in the balance-of-payments accounts as a *credit* item. Transactions that represent a payment for Canada, such as the purchase of a product or asset from foreigners, are recorded as a *debit* item.

There are three main categories to the balance of payments: the *current account*, the *capital account*, and the *official financing account*. We examine each account in turn.

The Current Account

The **current account** records transactions arising from trade in goods and services. It also includes net investment income that residents of one country earn from assets issued to them by foreigners. The current account is divided into two main sections.

The first section, called either the **trade balance** or the *balance of trade*, records payments and receipts arising from the import and export of goods, such as computers and cars, and services, such as legal or architectural services. (Tourism constitutes a large part of the trade in services.) Canadian imports of goods and services require a payment to foreigners and thus are entered as debit items on the trade account; Canadian exports of goods and services generate a receipt to Canada and thus are recorded as credit items.

The second section, called **capital-service account,** records the payments and receipts that represent income on assets. When Canadians pay income to the foreign owners of Canadian-located assets, this requires a payment to foreigners and thus is entered as a debit item. Income Canadians receive that is earned from their assets located abroad is a receipt from foreigners and thus enters as a credit item.

As shown in Table 36-1, Canadian exports of goods and services were just under $370 billion in 1998, and Canadian imports of goods and services were just under $360 billion. The trade account had a surplus of $11 billion—in other words, in 1998 Canada sold $11 billion more worth of goods and services to the world than it bought from the world. But in terms of the capital-service account, things were the other way around. The table shows that Canadians paid $29.4 billion more to foreigners in investment income than they received from foreigners. The current account balance (the sum of the trade and capital-service accounts) thus had a deficit of $18.4 billion.

TABLE 36-1 Canadian Balance of Payments, 1998 (billions of dollars)

CURRENT ACCOUNT	
Trade Account	
Merchandise exports	+323.4
Service exports	+43.7
Merchandise imports	−304.0
Service imports	−52.1
Trade balance	+11.0
Capital-Service Account	
Net investment income (including unilateral transfers)	−29.4
Current Account balance	−18.4
CAPITAL ACCOUNT	
Net change in Canadian investments abroad [capital outflow (−)]	−33.6
Net change in foreign investments in Canada [capital inflow (+)]	+52.1
Capital Account balance	+18.5
OFFICIAL FINANCING ACCOUNT	
Changes in reserves [increases (−)]	−7.4
Statistical Discrepancy	+7.3
Official Financing balance	−0.1
Balance of Payments	0.0

The overall balance of payments always balances, but the individual components do not have to. In 1998, Canada had an overall trade surplus (including trade in goods and services) of $11.0 billion. There was a deficit of $29.4 billion on the capital-service account. There was thus a $18.4 billion deficit on current account. There was also a surplus on the capital account because capital imports exceeded capital exports. The capital plus current account surplus is what is sometimes referred to as the balance of payments, and in 1998, there was an overall surplus of just $0.1 billion. This is exactly offset by the official financing balance plus the statistical discrepancy. The statistical discrepancy entry compensates for the inability to measure some items accurately.

(*Source: Bank of Canada Review,* Spring 1999.)

The Capital Account

The second main division in the balance of payments is the **capital account,** which records international transactions in assets. The purchase of foreign assets by Canadians is treated just like the purchase of foreign goods. Since purchasing a foreign asset requires a payment from Canadians to foreigners, it is entered as a debit item in the Canadian capital account. Note that when Canadians purchase foreign assets, financial capital is leaving Canada and going abroad, and so this is called a *capital outflow.*

The sale of Canadian assets to foreigners is treated just like the sale of Canadian goods to foreigners. Since selling a Canadian asset abroad generates a receipt for Canada, it is entered as a credit item in the Canadian capital account. Note that when Canadians sell assets to foreigners, financial capital is entering Canada from abroad, and so this is called a *capital inflow.*

As shown in Table 36-1, in 1998, Canadians increased their holdings of assets abroad by \$33.6 billion, resulting in a capital outflow of that amount. At the same time, foreigners increased their holdings of assets in Canada by \$52.1 billion, resulting in a capital inflow of that amount. The net capital inflow resulted in a surplus in the capital account of \$18.5 billion.

Though not shown in Table 36-1, the capital account is divided into direct investment and portfolio investment. **Direct investment** (also called *foreign direct investment*) relates to changes in foreign ownership of domestic firms and domestic ownership of foreign firms. One form of direct investment in Canada is capital investment in a branch plant or a subsidiary corporation in Canada in which the investor has voting control. Another form is a takeover, in which a controlling interest in a firm, previously controlled by residents, is acquired by foreigners. **Portfolio investment** is investment in bonds or a minority holding of shares that does not involve legal control.

The Official Financing Account

The final section in the balance of payments represents transactions in the official reserves that are held by the central bank and is called the *official financing account* or sometimes the *official settlements account.* The central banks of most countries, including Canada, hold financial reserves in the form of gold, foreign currencies, and bonds denominated in foreign currencies.

The Bank of Canada can intervene in the market for foreign currency to influence the Canadian dollar's exchange rate. For example, to prevent the external value of the dollar from falling, the Bank of Canada must purchase Canadian dollars and sell foreign currency. It can do so only if it holds reserves of foreign currency. When the Bank of Canada wishes to stop the value of the dollar from rising, it enters the market and sells dollars. In this case, the Bank purchases foreign currency, which it then adds to its reserves.

Since foreign currency is an asset for the Bank of Canada, it follows that when the Bank of Canada enters the foreign-exchange market to buy or sell foreign currency, it is simply buying or selling an asset. We deal with that transaction in the same way we deal with the other asset transactions in the capital account. Specifically, when the Bank purchases foreign currency (and sells Canadian dollars) this transaction represents the purchase of an asset from abroad, and thus it enters as a debit item in the balance of payments. Conversely, when the Bank sells foreign currency (and purchases Canadian dollars), this transaction represents the sale of an asset to foreigners, and thus it enters as a credit item in the balance of payments.

Table 36-1 shows that in 1998 the Bank of Canada *increased* its reserves of foreign exchange by $7.4 billion; it therefore purchased more foreign exchange during the year than it sold.

For balance of payments statistics for many countries, see the IMF's website: www.imf.org.

The Meaning of Payments Balances and Imbalances

We first examine why the overall balance of payments *always* balances. We then explore what is meant by the often-used terms "balance of payments deficit" or "balance of payments surplus."

The Balance of Payments Must Balance

The balance of payments accounts are based on the important idea of *double-entry bookkeeping*. Since any transaction involves something being sold and something being received, each transaction has two entries in the balance of payments. The value of the good or asset that is *sold* appears as a credit item in the balance of payments accounts. The value of the good or asset that is *received* in the transaction appears as a debit item in the balance of payments accounts. Since the dollar value of what is sold obviously equals the dollar value of what is received, these two entries clearly offset each other. Thus the balance of payments must always balance. In some cases, the different entries will appear on different accounts; in other cases both entries will appear on the same account. Some examples will help to illustrate how this works.

Suppose that a Canadian software company sells some computer software to a customer in Germany for $1 million. The sale of the software is an export of a good for Canada and thus enters as a credit item in Canada's current account. In return, the Canadian firm receives $1 million cash, which is clearly an asset. This is essentially a "purchase" of assets for Canada and appears as a debit item in Canada's capital account. Thus, as a result of this transaction, the $1 million credit on current account is offset by the $1 million debit on the capital account. The balance of payments, as always, is in balance.

Now consider a wealthy Canadian investor who sells a Canadian government bond to a Swiss citizen for $5 million. The sale of the bond appears as a credit item in Canada's capital account. In return, suppose that the Canadian investor receives the $5 million cash directly into his Swiss bank account. This is the accumulation of an asset for Canada and thus appears as a debit item in Canada's capital account. Thus, as a result of this transaction, the $5 million credit on capital account is offset by the $5 million debit on capital account. The current account is not affected by this transaction. And, as always, the balance of payments is in balance.

Double-entry bookkeeping in the balance of payments means that any transaction leads to both a credit item and an equal-value debit item. The balance of payments must therefore always balance.

This accounting result is important. It is not based on assumptions about behaviour or any other theoretical reasoning—it is an *accounting identity*. Many people nonetheless find the idea of double-entry bookkeeping confusing. *Applying Economic Concepts 36-1* discusses an individual student's balance of payments with the rest of the world, and illustrates why any individual's balance of payments must always balance.

The Relationships Among Various Balances

Two important implications follow directly from our observation that the overall payments must balance:

APPLYING ECONOMIC CONCEPTS 36-1

A Student's Balance of Payments with the Rest of the World

Many students find a country's balance of payments confusing, especially the idea that the balance of payments *must always* balance. Why, they often ask, can't Canada export more goods and services to the world than it imports, and at the same time have a net sale of assets to the rest of the world? The connection between the current-account transactions and the capital-account transactions is not always obvious.

Perhaps the easiest way to see this connection is to consider an individual's "balance of payments" with the rest of the world. Of course, most individuals would not normally compute their balance of payments, but by doing so we can recognize the everyday concepts involved and also see the necessary connection between any individual's "current account" and "capital account." The reason why Canada's balance of payments must always balance is exactly the same reason why an individual's balance of payments must always balance.

The table shows the balance of payments for Stefan, a university student. Stefan is fortunate in several respects. First, his parents are able to provide some of the funds needed to fi-

Stefan's Balance of Payments

Current Account (Income and Expenditure)	
Labour income ("exports")	+$10 000
Purchase of goods and services ("imports")	−$17 000
Interest income	+$ 500
Transfers (from his parents)	+$10 000
Current Account Balance	+ $3 500

Capital Account (Changes in Assets) (− denotes an increase)	
Financial Assets	
Purchase of Canada Savings Bonds	−$1 500
Change in Savings Account Deposits	−$2 000
Capital Account Balance	−$3 500
BALANCE OF PAYMENTS	$0

1. The terms *balance-of-payments deficit* and *balance-of-payments surplus* must refer to the balance on some part of the payments accounts. The terms make no sense if they are applied to the overall balance of payments.

2. A deficit on any one part of the accounts implies an offsetting surplus on the rest of the accounts.

We now consider two important applications of these statements. The first application concerns the balance on the official financing account and the combined balance on the current plus capital accounts; the second concerns the separate balances on current and capital accounts. Keep in mind that we use the word *overall* when referring to the balance of payments *including the official financing account.*

Official Financing and the Rest of the Accounts.　We know that the term "balance-of-payments deficit" does not strictly make sense since the balance of payments must always balance overall. But such a term is nonetheless often used in the nance his education. Second, he has a summer job which pays well. Third, he was given some Canada Savings Bonds when he was born that provide him with some interest income every year.

The top part of the table shows Stefan's income and expenditures for a single year. This is his current account. The bottom part shows the change in Stefan's assets over the same year. This is his capital account. (Note that, for Stefan as well as for any country, the capital account does not show the overall stock of assets—it only shows the *changes* in the stock of assets during the year.)

Let's begin with his current account. Stefan has a good summer job that earns him $10 000 after taxes. This $10 000 represents Stefan's "exports" to the rest of the world—he earns this income by selling his labour services to a tree-planting company. Over the year, however, he spends $17 000 on tuition, books, clothes, beer, pizza, photocopying, and other goods and services. These are Stefan's "imports" from the rest of the world. Stefan clearly has a "trade deficit" equal to $7000—he "imports" more than he "exports."

There are two other sources of income shown in Stefan's current account. First, he earns $500 in interest income. Second, his parents give him $10 000 to help pay for his education—a *transfer* in the terminology of balance of payments accounting. The interest income and transfer together make up Stefan's "capital-service account"—Stefan has a surplus of $10 500.

Stefan's overall current account shows a surplus of $3500. This means he receives $3500 more in total income than he spends on goods and services. But where does this $3500 go?

Now let's consider Stefan's capital account, the bottom part of the table. The $3500 surplus on current account *must* end up as increases in Stefan's assets. He increases his holdings of Canada Savings Bonds by $1500 and increases his saving-account deposits by $2000. Note that since Stefan must make a "payment" to purchase these assets, they appear as a debit item in his capital account. Stefan's capital account balance is a deficit of $3500.

Finally, note that Stefan's current account and capital account *must* sum to zero. There is no way around this fact. Any surplus of income over expenditures (on current account) must show up as an increase in his assets (or a decrease in his debts) on capital account. Conversely, any excess of expenditures over income must be financed by reducing his assets (or by increasing his debts). Stefan's balance of payments *must* balance.

What is true for Stefan is true for any individual and also true for any accounting unit you choose to consider. Saskatoon's balance of payments with the rest of the world must balance. Saskatchewan's balance of payments with the rest of the world must balance. Western Canada's balance of payments with the rest of the world must balance. And so must Canada's, and any other country's.

press and even by some economists. What does this mean? Most often the term is used carelessly—a balance of payments deficit is mentioned when what is actually meant is a current account deficit. There are also occasions when people speak of a country as having a balance-of-payments deficit or surplus when they are actually referring to the balance of all accounts *excluding* official financing—that is, to the combined balance on current and capital accounts.

For example, consider a situation in which Canada has a current account deficit of $20 billion—Canada is buying $20 billion more in goods and services from the rest of the world than it is selling to the world. At the same time, suppose the capital account surplus is only $15 billion—Canada is selling $15 billion more in assets to the rest of the world than it is buying in return. In this case, some people would say that Canada has a "balance of payments deficit" of $5 billion. But what is really true is that the Bank of Canada, on the official financing account, is selling $5 billion of foreign currency reserves. The $5 billion surplus on the official financing account is exactly "financing" the "balance of payments deficit."

In the opposite situation, where the current account and capital account together are in surplus, some people would say there is a "balance of payments surplus." But the Bank of Canada is in this case purchasing foreign-currency reserves. The overall balance of payments balances.

A "balance of payments deficit" refers to a situation where the Bank of Canada is selling foreign currency. A "balance of payments surplus" refers to a situation where the Bank of Canada is buying foreign currency. In both cases, as always, the balance of payments is actually in balance.

What we have just said implies that the balance of payments can be in deficit or surplus *only if* the central bank changes its foreign-exchange reserves. If the central bank does not participate in the foreign-exchange market, however, its foreign currency reserves will be unchanged and so the official financing balance must be zero. In this case, there can be no deficit or surplus in the balance of payments.

The Current and Capital Account Balances.   Suppose that the Bank of Canada does not engage in any foreign-exchange transactions. The official financing account is thus zero. Now any deficit or surplus on the current account must be matched exactly by an equal and opposite surplus or deficit on the capital account.

For example, if Canada has a current account deficit of $10 billion, then there *must* be a capital account surplus of $10 billion. The intuition is straightforward. If Canada has a $10 billion deficit on current account, then it is importing more goods and services (including debt service) than it is exporting. But how does it finance these "extra" imports? Some individual or firm or government in Canada must sell some Canadian assets to (or borrow from) some individual or firm or government in the rest of the world—that is, Canada must have a capital account surplus.

Similarly, suppose Canada has a current account surplus of $10 billion, reflecting more earnings from exports than expenditures on imports. What does Canada do with the "extra" earnings? It must acquire some assets from the rest of the world—that is, Canada must have a capital account deficit.

If the central bank does not change its holdings of foreign-currency reserves, the current account and capital account must sum to zero.

This brings us to the end of our discussion of the balance of payments. Keep in mind that this is just an exercise in accounting. Though at times you may find it difficult to keep the various credits and debits in the various accounts straight in your mind, remember that the structure of the accounting system is quite simple. Here is a brief review:

1. The current account shows all transactions in goods and services between Canada and the rest of the world (including investment income and transfers).

2. The capital account shows all transactions in assets between Canada and the rest of the world.

3. The official financing account shows the change in the Bank of Canada's holding of foreign-currency reserves (including gold).

4. All transactions involving a payment from Canada appear as a debit item. All transactions involving a receipt to Canada appear as a credit item.

5. The balance of payments—the sum of the current account, capital account, and official financing account—must always be zero.

We now go on to explore how exchange rates are determined in the foreign-exchange market. We will see that a knowledge of the various categories in the balance of payments will help in our understanding of why changes in exchange rates occur.

The Bank of Canada holds millions of dollars worth of gold as part of its official reserves.

The Foreign-Exchange Market

Money is vital in any sophisticated economy that relies on specialization and trade. Yet money as we know it is a *national* matter. If you live in Argentina, you earn pesos and spend pesos; if you operate a business in Austria, you borrow schillings and pay your workers in schillings. The currency of a country is acceptable within the border of that country, but usually it will not be accepted by firms and households in another country. Just try buying your next pair of jeans in Canada with British pounds sterling or Japanese yen!

Trade between countries normally requires the exchange of the currency of one country for that of another.

The exchange of one currency for another is called a *foreign-exchange transaction*. The **exchange rate** is the rate at which one currency exchanges for another. In Canada's case, the exchange rate is the price of one unit of foreign currency in terms of Canadian dollars. Put another way, it is the Canadian-dollar price of one unit of foreign currency. For example, in August 1999, the price of one U.S. dollar was 1.52 Canadian dollars. Thus, the Canada-U.S. exchange rate was 1.52.

We could just as easily define the exchange rate in the opposite way. We could define it as the number of units of foreign currency that could be purchased with one Canadian dollar. In our example from August 1999, the exchange rate between the Canadian and U.S. dollars would then be 1/1.52 = 0.657. One Canadian dollar would purchase 65.7 U.S. cents.

In this book, however, we *always* define the exchange rate in the way Canadian economists usually do—as the Canadian-dollar price of one unit of foreign currency. This definition makes it clear that foreign currency, like any good or service, has a price expressed in Canadian dollars. In this case, the price of the "good" has a special name— the exchange rate.

A rise in the external value of the Canadian dollar—an **appreciation** of the Canadian dollar—means that it takes fewer Canadian dollars to purchase one unit of foreign currency. For example, if the Canadian dollar appreciates against the U.S. dollar from 1.52 to 1.45, it takes 7 fewer Canadian cents to purchase one U.S. dollar. Thus, an appreciation of the Canadian dollar implies a *fall* in the exchange rate. Conversely, a decline in the external value of the Canadian dollar—a **depreciation** of the Canadian dollar— means that it takes more Canadian dollars to purchase one unit of foreign currency. Thus, a depreciation of the Canadian dollar means a *rise* in the exchange rate.

The external value of a currency is the inverse of the exchange rate. Thus, an appreciation of the Canadian dollar is a fall in the exchange rate; a depreciation of the Canadian dollar is a rise in the exchange rate.

We now go on to build a simple model of the foreign-exchange market. This will allow us to analyse the determinants of the exchange rate. To keep things simple, we use an example involving trade between Canada and Europe, and thus we examine the determination of the exchange rate between the two currencies, the Canadian dollar and the euro. But, in this example, Europe is just a shorthand for "the rest of the world" and the euro is just a shorthand for "all other currencies." (It would be more natural to think in terms of Canada-U.S. trade since 80 percent of Canadian trade is with the United States, but this quickly becomes confusing because both country's currencies are called the dollar.)

Because dollars are traded for euros in the foreign-exchange market, it follows that a demand for euros implies a supply of dollars and that a supply of euros implies a demand for dollars.

exchange rate   The number of units of domestic currency required to purchase one unit of foreign currency.

more commonly used.
← rather than

appreciation   A rise in the external value of the domestic currency in terms of foreign currencies; a fall in the exchange rate.

depreciation   A fall in the external value of domestic currency in terms of foreign currency; that is, a rise in the exchange rate.

For this reason, a theory of the exchange rate between dollars and euros can deal either with the demand and supply of dollars or with the demand and supply of euros; both need not be considered. We will concentrate on the demand, supply, and price of euros. Thus, the market we will be considering (in general terms) is the foreign-exchange market—the "product" is foreign exchange (euros in our case) and the "price" is the exchange rate (the Canadian-dollar price of euros).

We develop our example in terms of the demand and supply analysis first encountered in Chapter 3. To do so, we need only to recall that in the market for foreign exchange, transactions that generate a receipt for Canada in its balance of payments represent a *supply* of foreign exchange (foreign exchange is being supplied by the foreigners who purchase Canadian goods or assets). Conversely, transactions that are a payment from Canada in the balance of payments represent a *demand* for foreign exchange (foreign exchange is being demanded by the Canadians who are purchasing foreign goods or assets).

We begin by focusing only on the demand and supply of foreign exchange arising from the current and capital accounts. Later we turn to the important role of official financing by the Bank of Canada. But, for now, suppose that the Bank of Canada makes no transactions in the foreign-exchange market.

The Supply of Foreign Exchange

The supply of foreign exchange in the foreign-exchange market arises from all international transactions that represent a receipt in Canada's balance of payments.

Canadian Exports

One important source of supply of foreign exchange is foreigners who do not currently hold Canadian dollars but who wish to buy Canadian-made goods and services. A Japanese importer of lumber is such a purchaser; an Austrian couple planning a vacation in Canada is another; the Russian government seeking to buy Canadian steel is a third. All are sources of supply of foreign exchange, arising out of international trade. Each potential buyer wants to sell its own currency in exchange for Canadian dollars that it can then use to purchase Canadian goods and services.

Capital Inflows

A second source of supply of foreign exchange comes from foreigners who wish to purchase Canadian assets, such as government or corporate bonds, or plant and equipment currently located in Canada. To buy Canadian assets, holders of foreign currencies must first sell their foreign currency and buy Canadian dollars. In recent years, foreign households and firms have invested tens of billions of dollars in Canadian securities and real estate. This has required the conversion of foreign currencies into Canadian dollars. The resulting transactions are called *long-term capital flows*.

In Chapter 28 we discussed how the Bank of Canada's efforts to reduce inflation in the early 1990s pushed Canadian interest rates well above those in other countries. With the increase in Canadian rates, floods of "foreign money" came into Canada to buy short-term treasury bills and notes, certificates of deposit, and other securities. The buyers were seeking a high return on their liquid assets, but first these buyers had to convert their U.S. dollars, yen, guilder, marks, and francs into Canadian dollars in the foreign-exchange market. When people sell financial assets in one country for foreign exchange that they then use to buy short-term financial assets in another country, the transactions are called *short-term capital flows*.

Reserve Currency

Firms, banks, and governments often accumulate and hold foreign-exchange reserves, just as individuals maintain savings accounts. These reserves may be in several different currencies. For example, the government of Nigeria may decide to increase its reserve holdings of Canadian dollars and reduce its reserve holdings of euros; if it does so, it will be a supplier of euros (and a demander of Canadian dollars) in foreign-exchange markets.

The Total Supply of Foreign Exchange

The supply of foreign exchange (or the demand for Canadian dollars) by holders of foreign currencies is the sum of the supplies for all of the purposes just discussed—for purchases of Canadian exports, for capital inflow to Canada and for the purchase of Canadian dollars to add to currency reserves.

Furthermore, because people, firms, and governments in all countries purchase goods and assets from many other countries, the demand for any one currency will be the aggregate demand of individuals, firms, and governments in a number of different countries. Thus, the total supply of foreign exchange (or the demand for Canadian dollars) may include Germans who are offering euros, Japanese who are offering yen, Argentinians who are offering pesos, and so on. For simplicity, however, we go back to our two-country example and use only Canada and Europe.

The Supply Curve for Foreign Exchange

The supply of foreign exchange on the foreign-exchange market is represented by a positively sloped curve, such

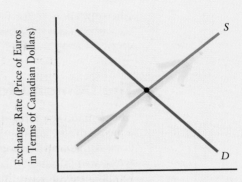

FIGURE 36-1   The Market for Foreign Exchange

The demand for foreign exchange is negatively sloped, and the supply of foreign exchange is positively sloped, when plotted against the exchange rate, measured as the Canadian-dollar price of one unit of foreign currency. The demand for foreign exchange is given by the negatively sloped blue line *D*. It represents the sum of transactions on both current and capital accounts that require payments to foreigners.

The supply of foreign exchange is given by the positively sloped red line *S*. It represents the sum of transactions on both current and capital accounts that represent receipts from foreigners.

A depreciation of the Canadian dollar is a rise in the exchange rate (moving up the vertical axis); an appreciation of the dollar is a fall in the exchange rate (moving down the vertical axis).

as the one shown in Figure 36-1. This figure plots the Canadian-dollar price of euros (the exchange rate) on the vertical axis and the quantity of euros on the horizontal axis. Moving up the vertical scale, more dollars are needed to purchase one euro—the dollar is depreciating. Moving down the vertical scale, fewer dollars are needed to purchase one euro—the dollar is appreciating.

Why is the supply curve for foreign exchange positively sloped? Consider the supply of foreign exchange derived from foreign purchases of Canadian exports. If the Canadian dollar depreciates, it takes fewer euros to purchase one Canadian dollar. Thus, for a given Canadian-dollar price of the product the euro price has fallen. European consumers will therefore buy more of the cheaper Canadian goods and will thus supply more foreign exchange for this purpose. In the opposite case, when the dollar appreciates, the euro price of Canadian exports rises. European consumers will buy fewer Canadian goods and thus supply less foreign exchange.[1]

---

[1]We have assumed here that the foreign price elasticity of demand for Canadian exports is greater than one, so that a price change leads to a proportionately larger change in quantity demanded. This is a common assumption in the analysis of international trade. In the case of Canada (and other small countries) it is common to go further and make the "small open economy" assumption—that the country faces *given world prices* for both its exports and imports. In this case, the foreign price elasticity of demand for exports is infinite.

Similar considerations affect other sources of supply of foreign exchange. When the Canadian dollar depreciates (a high exchange rate), Canadian assets and securities become attractive purchases, and the quantity purchased will rise. With this rise, the amount of foreign exchange supplied to pay for the purchases will increase.

The supply curve for foreign exchange is positively sloped when it is plotted against the exchange rate; a depreciation of the Canadian dollar (a rise in the exchange rate) increases the quantity of foreign exchange supplied.

The Demand for Foreign Exchange

The demand for foreign exchange arises from all international transactions that represent a payment in Canada's balance of payments. What sort of international transactions generate a demand for foreign exchange (and a supply of Canadian dollars)? Canadians seeking to purchase foreign products will be supplying Canadian dollars and demanding foreign exchange for this purpose. Holders of Canadian securities may decide to sell their Canadian holdings and shift them into foreign assets. If they do, they will supply Canadian dollars and demand foreign exchange. Similarly, a country with reserves of Canadian dollars may decide to sell them in order to demand some other currency.

The Demand Curve for Foreign Exchange

When the Canadian dollar depreciates, the Canadian-dollar price of European goods rises. Because it takes more dollars to buy the same European good, Canadians will buy fewer of the now more expensive European goods. The amount of foreign exchange being demanded by Canadians in order to pay for imported European goods will fall.[2] In the opposite case, when the Canadian dollar appreciates, European goods become cheaper, more are sold, and more dollars are spent on them. Thus, more foreign exchange will be demanded to pay for the extra imports. This same argument applies in exactly the same way to the purchases of foreign assets. Figure 36-1 shows the demand curve for foreign exchange.

The demand curve for foreign exchange is negatively sloped when it is plotted against the exchange rate; an appreciation of the Canadian dollar (a fall in the exchange rate) increases the quantity of foreign exchange demanded.

The Determination of Exchange Rates

The demand and supply curves in Figure 36-1 do not include official financing transactions (the demands or supplies for foreign exchange by the Bank of Canada). To complete our analysis, we must incorporate the role of official financing transactions. We need to consider three important cases:

---

[2]As long as the price elasticity of demand for imports is greater than one, the fall in the volume of imports will exceed the rise in price, and hence fewer dollars will be spent on them. This condition (and the one in the previous footnote) is related to a famous long-standing issue in international economics, called the *Marshall-Lerner condition*. In what follows, we take the standard approach of assuming that both the price elasticity of demand for imports and the price elasticity of the demand for Canadian exports exceeds one. This guarantees that the slopes of the curves are as shown in Figure 36-1.

1. When the central bank makes no transactions in the foreign-exchange market, the exchange rate is determined by the equality between the supply and demand for foreign exchange arising from the capital and current accounts. In this situation there is said to be a purely **flexible exchange rate**.

2. When the central bank intervenes in the foreign-exchange market to "fix" the exchange rate at a particular value, there is said to be a **fixed exchange rate** or *pegged exchange rate*.

3. Between these two "pure" systems are a variety of possible intermediate cases, including the *adjustable peg* and the *managed float*. In the **adjustable peg system,** governments set and attempt to fix specific values for their exchange rates, but they explicitly recognize that circumstances may arise in which they will change that value. In a **managed float,** the central bank seeks to have some stabilizing influence on the exchange rate but does not try to fix it at some publicly announced value.

Most countries today operate a mostly flexible exchange rate. It is mostly market determined but the central bank sometimes intervenes to offset short-run fluctuations. There are, however, some important exceptions. The countries of the European Union (EU), for example, had a system of fixed exchange rates (relative to each other's currencies) between 1979 and 1999. In 1999 the EU introduced a common currency—the euro—that was adopted by most of the EU member countries (an important exception being the United Kingdom). Thus, they now have fixed exchange rates relative to each other (since they have the same currency) but have a flexible exchange rate (with some short-term interventions) relative to countries outside the EU. The United States, Japan, the United Kingdom, Australia, and most other major industrialized countries have flexible exchange rates with relatively small amounts of foreign-exchange intervention by their central banks.

Canada used flexible exchange rates (with limited intervention) throughout most of the period following the Second World War. Even when most countries pegged their currencies to the U.S. dollar under the Bretton Woods system, Canada had a flexible exchange rate. Later in the chapter we examine the issues involved in choosing a flexible or fixed exchange-rate system. For now, let's explore how the various systems operate.

flexible exchange rate   An exchange rate that is left free to be determined by the forces of demand and supply on the free market, with no intervention by the monetary authorities.

fixed exchange rate   An exchange rate that is maintained within a small range around its publicly stated par value by the intervention in the foreign-exchange market by a country's central bank.

adjustable peg system   A system in which exchange rates are fixed in the short term but are occasionally changed in response to persistent payments imbalances.

managed float   A situation in which the central bank intervenes in the foreign exchange market to smooth out some of the large, short-term fluctuations in a country's exchange rate, while still leaving the market to determine the exchange rate in the longer term.

Flexible Exchange Rates

Consider an exchange rate that is set in a freely competitive market, with no intervention by the central bank. Like any competitive price, the exchange rate fluctuates according to the conditions of demand and supply.

Suppose the current exchange rate is so high (say, e_1 in Figure 36-2) that the quantity of foreign exchange supplied exceeds the quantity demanded. There is thus an abundance of foreign exchange and a shortage of Canadian dollars. This excess supply of foreign exchange, just as in our analysis in Chapter 3, will cause the price of foreign exchange (the exchange rate) to fall. As the exchange rate falls—an appreciation of the Canadian dollar—the euro price of Canadian goods rises, and this leads to a reduction in the quantity of foreign exchange supplied. Also, as the exchange rate falls, the Canadian-dollar price of European goods falls, and this fall leads to an increase in the quantity of foreign exchange demanded. Thus, the excess supply of foreign exchange leads to a fall in the exchange rate which in turn reduces the amount of excess supply. Where the two curves intersect, quantity demanded equals quantity supplied, and the exchange rate is at its equilibrium value.

In 1999, eleven countries of the European Union adopted a common currency—the euro. Early in 2000, the exchange rate was 1.05 euros per U.S. dollar, or 0.71 euros per Canadian dollar.

FIGURE 36-2   Fixed and Flexible Exchange Rates

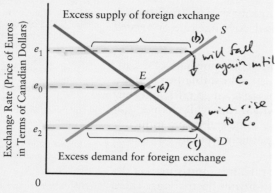

Excess supply of foreign exchange

Excess demand for foreign exchange

Quantity of Foreign Currency (Euros)

In the absence of official financing by the central bank, the exchange rate adjusts to clear the foreign-exchange market. The demand for and supply of foreign exchange are as in Figure 36-1. If official financing is zero, there is a flexible exchange rate. It will adjust to equate the demand and supply of foreign exchange; this occurs at E with an exchange rate of e_0.

If the exchange rate is higher than that, say at e_1, the supply of foreign exchange will exceed the demand. The exchange rate will fall (the dollar will appreciate) until it reaches e_0, where balance is achieved at E. If the exchange rate is below e_0, say at e_2, the demand for foreign exchange will exceed the supply. The exchange rate will rise (the dollar will depreciate) until it reaches e_0, where balance is achieved at E.

The central bank can fix the exchange rate by using its official financing transactions to meet the excess demands or supplies that arise at the fixed value of the exchange rate. For example, if it chooses to fix the exchange rate at e_1, there will be an excess supply of foreign exchange because receipts (on current and capital accounts) will exceed payments. The central bank will thus purchase foreign exchange (and sell dollars) to meet the excess supply. Alternatively, if the central bank chooses to fix the exchange rate at e_2, there will be an excess demand for foreign exchange because receipts (on current and capital accounts) will be less than payments. The central bank will thus sell foreign exchange (and buy dollars) to meet the excess demand.

What happens when the exchange rate is below its equilibrium value? The quantity of foreign exchange demanded will exceed the quantity supplied. With foreign exchange in excess demand, its price will naturally rise, and as it does the amount of excess demand will be reduced until equilibrium is re-established.

A foreign-exchange market is like other competitive markets in that the forces of demand and supply lead to an equilibrium price at which quantity demanded equals quantity supplied.

Recall that we have been assuming that there is no official financing by the central bank, so that demand and supply in the foreign-exchange market represent transactions only on the current or capital account. We now consider a system of fixed exchange rates in which official financing plays a central role in the analysis.

Fixed Exchange Rates

When official financing transactions are used to fix the exchange rate at a particular value, the current account and the capital account do not necessarily sum to zero. The balance on the official financing account has to be whatever is necessary to offset the excess demand or supply of foreign exchange that arises. This is also shown in Figure 36-2.

The gold standard that operated for much of the nineteenth century and the early part of the twentieth century was a fixed exchange-rate system. The Bretton Woods system, established by international agreement in 1944 and operated until the mid 1970s, was a fixed exchange-rate system that provided for circumstances under which the external value of the currency could be lowered (a *devaluation*) or raised (a *revaluation*). It was thus an adjustable peg system; the International Monetary Fund (IMF) has its origins in the Bretton Woods system, and one of its principal tasks was approving and monitoring exchange-rate changes. The European Exchange Rate Mechanism (ERM) of the early 1990s was also a fixed exchange-rate system for the countries in the European Union; their exchange rates were fixed to each other but floated as a block against the U.S. dollar and other currencies. As mentioned earlier, this system of separate currencies with fixed exchange rates was replaced in 1999 when most of the countries of the EU adopted a common currency—the euro.

Applying Economic Concepts 36-2 examines how a fixed exchange-rate system operates. It shows why a central bank that chooses to fix its exchange rate must give up some control of its foreign-exchange reserves. This presents some problems, as it did for Thailand in the summer of 1997, at the beginning of the 1997-1998 Asian Crisis.

We now go on to study the workings of a flexible exchange-rate system, the system used in Canada and most major countries.

Changes in Flexible Exchange Rates

What causes exchange rates to vary? The simplest answer to this question is changes in demand or supply in the foreign-exchange market. Anything that shifts the demand curve for foreign exchange to the right or the supply curve for foreign exchange to the left leads to a rise in the exchange rate—a depreciation of the Canadian dollar. Conversely, anything that shifts the demand curve for foreign exchange to the left or the supply curve for foreign exchange to the right leads to a fall in the exchange rate—an appreciation of the Canadian dollar. These points are nothing more than a restatement of the laws of supply and demand, applied now to the market for foreign exchange; they are illustrated in Figure 36-3.

What causes the shifts in demand and supply that lead to changes in exchange rates? There are many causes, some transitory and some persistent. We mention several of the most important ones.

FIGURE 36-3   Changes in Exchange Rates

(i) Demand shifts

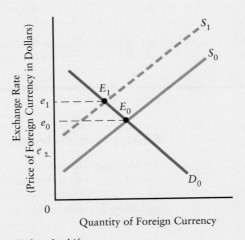
(ii) Supply shifts

An increase in the demand for foreign exchange or a decrease in the supply will cause the dollar to depreciate (the exchange rate to rise); a decrease in the demand or an increase in supply will cause the dollar to appreciate (the exchange rate to fall). The initial demand and supply curves D_0 and S_0 are as in Figures 36-1 and 36-2. Equilibrium is at E_0 with an exchange rate of e_0. An increase in the demand for foreign exchange as shown by a rightward shift in the demand curve from D_0 to D_1 in part (i), or a decrease in the supply of foreign exchange as shown by a leftward shift in the supply curve from S_0 to S_1 in part (ii), will cause the dollar to depreciate. In both parts, the new equilibrium is at E_1, and the dollar depreciation is shown by the rise in the exchange rate from e_0 to e_1. Conversely, a decrease in the demand for foreign exchange or an increase in the supply of foreign exchange will cause the dollar to appreciate.

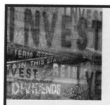

APPLYING ECONOMIC CONCEPTS 36-2

Managing Fixed Exchange Rates

This box provides some details on how a central bank operates a regime of fixed exchange rates. Though Canada has a flexible exchange rate (with occasional foreign-exchange intervention by the Bank of Canada), we will imagine a situation where the Bank of Canada pegs the Canadian-U.S. exchange rate.

Suppose that the Bank of Canada fixed the exchange rate between the narrow limits of, say, C$1.47 to C$1.53 to the U.S. dollar. The Bank then stabilizes the exchange rate in the face of seasonal, cyclical, and other fluctuations in demand and supply, entering the market to prevent the rate from going outside the permitted band. At the price of $1.47, the Bank offers to buy any amount of U.S. dollars; at the price of $1.53, the Bank offers to sell any amount of U.S. dollars. When the Bank buys U.S. dollars, its exchange reserves rise; when it sells U.S. dollars, its reserves fall.

We make the following observations:

1. If the demand curve cuts the supply curve in the range 1.47 to 1.53, as D_0 does in the accompanying figure, then the Bank need not intervene in the market.

2. If the demand curve shifts to D_1, then the Bank must sell U.S. dollars from its reserves to the extent of $q_4 q_1$

in order to prevent the price of U.S. dollars from rising above 1.53.

3. If the demand curve shifts to D_2, the Bank must buy U.S. dollars to the extent of $q_2 q_3$ in order to prevent the price of U.S. dollars from falling below 1.47.

If, on average, the demand and supply curves intersect in the range 1.47 to 1.53, then the Bank's foreign-exchange reserves will be relatively stable, with the Bank buying U.S. dollars when the demand is abnormally low and selling them when the demand is abnormally high. Over a long period, the average level of reserves will then be fairly stable.

If conditions change, the Bank's foreign-exchange reserves will rise or fall more or less continuously. For example, suppose that the average level of demand becomes D_1, with fluctuations on either side of this level. The average drain on the Bank's foreign-exchange reserves will then be $q_4 q_1$ *per period*. But this situation cannot continue indefinitely because the Bank only has a limited amount of foreign-exchange reserves. In this situation, the Bank has two alternatives: It can change the fixed exchange rate so that the band of permissible prices straddles the new equilibrium price, or it can try to shift the curves so that the intersection is in the band 1.47 to 1.53. To accomplish this goal, it must restrict demand for

A Supply-Side Increase in the Domestic Price of Exports

Suppose that some event on the supply side of the paper market results in an increase in the Canadian-dollar price of Canadian paper. For example, the government may impose a new pollution tax on paper producers. What this will do to the supply of foreign exchange depends on the price elasticity of foreign demand for the Canadian product. If the demand for Canadian paper is elastic, perhaps because other countries supply the same product in world markets, the total amount spent on Canadian paper will decrease and hence less foreign exchange will be supplied to purchase Canadian paper. Thus, the supply curve for foreign exchange will shift to the left and the Canadian dollar will depreciate. This is illustrated in part (ii) of Figure 36-3. If the demand is inelastic (say, because Canada is the only country that produces this particular kind of paper), then more will be spent, the supply of foreign exchange to pay the bigger bill will shift the supply curve to the right, and the Canadian dollar will appreciate.

A Rise in the Foreign Price of Imports

Suppose that the euro price of European automobiles increases sharply. Suppose also that Canadian consumers have an elastic demand for European cars because they can easily switch to Canadian-made substitutes. Consequently, they spend fewer euros for

Exchange Rate (Canadian dollars per U.S. dollar)

Quantity of Foreign Exchange (U.S. Dollars)

the curve is shifted exactly to S' where it intersects D_1 at q_1 units of foreign exchange, the inflow of short-term capital just covers the potential shortfall, and the exchange reserves are not run down. Provided the Bank guessed correctly that the demand was abnormally high, the policy will work. If the demand now falls to produce a free-market rate within the permitted range, the Bank can lower interest rates, as it no longer needs to attract short-term capital to cover the excess demand for foreign exchange at the maximum permitted exchange rate.

Thailand in 1997 provides an example of an exchange rate fixed at a level that led to a persistent excess demand for foreign exchange. Thailand's central bank had fixed the value of its currency, the baht, to the U.S. dollar. When an excess demand for foreign currency developed in Thailand, the central bank began to deplete its stock of foreign-exchange reserves as it purchased the baht in an attempt to support its external value. By July of 1997, however, the central bank's stock of foreign-exchange reserves had been depleted to such an extent that it could no longer fix the exchange rate. With an excess demand for foreign exchange and a central bank that could no longer fix the exchange rate, depreciation was the natural result. The baht depreciated dramatically and Thailand then moved away from a fixed exchange-rate system. This event is generally viewed as the beginning of the 1997-1998 Asian Crisis during which several countries, including Malaysia, Indonesia, and South Korea, experienced similar declines in their foreign-exchange reserves and were forced to abandon their fixed exchange rates.

foreign exchange: It can impose import quotas and foreign-travel restrictions, or it can seek to increase the supply of U.S. dollars by encouraging Canadian exports.

The Bank can induce movements of short-term capital to assist in its policy of fixing the exchange rate in spite of fluctuations in the demand for and supply of foreign exchange. Suppose, for example, in the figure that the demand for U.S. dollars is D_1 and the supply S, so that there is a potential loss of reserves of q_4q_1 per period. The Bank of Canada can raise the short-term rate of interest and attract short-term capital, thus shifting the supply of U.S. dollars to the right. If

European automobiles than they did before and hence demand less foreign exchange. The demand curve for foreign exchange shifts to the left, and the Canadian dollar will appreciate. If the demand for European cars were inelastic, total spending on them would rise, and the demand for foreign exchange would shift to the right, leading to a depreciation of the Canadian dollar. This is illustrated in part (i) of Figure 36-3.

Changes in the Overall Price Levels

Suppose that instead of a change in the price of a specific export, such as cars or paper, there is a change in *all* prices because of a general inflation. We consider separate cases, each corresponding to a different pattern of Canadian relative to foreign inflation.

Equal Inflation in Both Countries.
Suppose that inflation is running at 5 percent in both Canada and Europe. In this case, the euro prices of European goods and the dollar prices of Canadian goods both rise by 5 percent. At the *existing* exchange rate, the dollar prices of European goods and the euro prices of Canadian goods will each rise by 5 percent, and hence the relative prices of imports and domestically produced goods will be unchanged in both countries. Since there is no reason to expect a change in either

country's demand for imports at the original exchange rate, the inflation in the two countries leaves the equilibrium exchange rate unchanged.

Inflation in Only One Country.   What will happen if there is inflation in Canada while the price level remains stable in Europe? The dollar price of Canadian goods will rise, and they will become more expensive in Europe. This increase will cause the quantity of Canadian exports, and therefore the amount of foreign exchange supplied by European importers, to decrease. Thus, the supply curve for foreign exchange shifts to the left.

At the same time, European goods in Canada will have an unchanged Canadian-dollar price, while the price of Canadian goods sold in Canada will increase because of the inflation. Thus, European goods will be more attractive compared with Canadian goods (because they have become relatively cheaper), and thus more European goods will be bought in Canada. At any exchange rate, the amount of foreign exchange demanded to purchase imports will rise. Thus, the demand curve for foreign exchange shifts to the right.

Canadian inflation that is unmatched in Europe will therefore cause the supply curve for foreign exchange to shift to the left and the demand curve for foreign exchange to shift to the right. As a result, the equilibrium exchange rate *must* rise—there is a depreciation of the Canadian dollar relative to the euro.

Inflation at Unequal Rates.   The two foregoing examples are, of course, just limiting cases of a more general situation in which the price levels change in both countries. The arguments can readily be extended when we realize that it is the *relative* size of the changes in prices in two countries that determines whether home goods or foreign goods look more or less attractive. If country A's inflation rate is higher than country B's, country A's exports are becoming relatively expensive in B's markets while imports from B are becoming relatively cheap in A's markets. This causes the price of A's currency to fall—A's currency depreciates relative to B's.

If the price level in one country is rising relative to that in another country, the equilibrium value of its currency will be falling relative to that of the other country.

Capital Movements

Capital flows can exert strong influences on exchange rates. For example, an increased desire by Canadians to purchase European assets (a capital export for Canada) will shift the demand curve for foreign exchange to the right, and the dollar will depreciate. This process is illustrated in part (i) of Figure 36-3.

A movement of financial capital has the effect of appreciating the currency of the capital-importing country and depreciating the currency of the capital-exporting country.

This statement is true for all capital movements, short-term or long-term. Because the motives that lead to large capital movements are likely to be different in the short and long terms, however, it is worth considering each separately.

Short-Term Capital Movements.   An important motive for short-term capital flows is a change in interest rates. International traders hold transactions balances just as do domestic traders. These balances are often lent out on a short-term basis rather than being left idle. Naturally, the holders of these balances will tend to lend them, other things being equal, in markets where interest rates are highest. Thus, if one country's short-term interest rate rises above the rates in other countries (say, because that country undertakes a contractionary monetary policy), there will tend to be a large inflow of short-term capital into that country in an effort to take advantage of the high rate. This inflow of financial capital will increase the demand for the domestic currency and cause it to appreciate. If the short-term interest rate should fall in one country (say, because of a monetary expansion in that country), there will tend to be a shift in capital away from that country and its currency will tend to depreciate.

A second motive for short-term capital movements is speculation about the *future value* of a country's exchange rate. If foreigners expect the Canadian dollar to appreciate in the near future, they will rush to buy assets that pay off in Canadian dollars, such as Canadian stocks or bonds; if they expect the Canadian dollar to depreciate in the near future, they will be reluctant to buy or to hold Canadian securities.

Long-Term Capital Movements.   Long-term capital movements are largely influenced by long-term expectations about another country's profit opportunities and the long-run value of its currency. A French firm would be more willing to purchase a Canadian factory if it expected that the dollar profits would buy more euros in future years than the profits from investment in a French factory. This could happen if the Canadian firm earned greater profits than the French firm, with exchange rates remaining unchanged. It could also happen if the profits were the same but the French firm expected the Canadian dollar to appreciate relative to the euro.

Structural Changes

An economy can undergo structural changes that alter the equilibrium exchange rate. *Structural change* is an all-purpose term for a change in cost structures, the invention of new products, changes in preferences between products, or anything else that affects the pattern of comparative advantage. Consider three examples.

Suppose that the reluctance of firms in one country to adopt technological innovations results in that country's products not improving as rapidly as those produced in other countries. Consumers' demand (at fixed prices) will shift slowly away from the first country's products and toward those of its foreign competitors. This shift will cause a gradual depreciation in the first country's currency because fewer people want to buy that country's goods and thus fewer people want to buy that country's currency.

A second example relates to the discovery of valuable mineral resources. Prominent examples are the development of natural gas in The Netherlands in the early 1960s, the development of North Sea oil in the United Kingdom in the 1970s, and the recent discovery of large diamond mines in the Northwest Territories. If firms in one country make such a discovery and begin selling these resources to the rest of the world, then the foreign purchasers must supply their foreign currency in order to purchase the currency of the exporting country. The result is an appreciation of the currency of the exporting country.

Anything that leads to changes in the pattern of trade, such as changes in costs or changes in demand, will generally lead to changes in exchange rates.

A final example relates to changes in demand for a country's exports. For many countries, including Canada, the prices of the goods that it sells to other countries are determined in world markets. Examples include commodities such as oil, copper, pulp, lumber, wheat, coffee, cocoa, zinc, tin, aluminum, and gold. Changes in the world demand or supply for these commodities typically have significant effects on exchange rates. For example, if there is a reduction in the world demand for these products there will be an accompanying reduction in demand for the currencies of those countries that export these products. Their currencies will depreciate. In 1997 and 1998, for example, there was a notable decline in many commodity prices, and the currencies of major commodity exporters such as Australia, New Zealand, Canada, and South Africa depreciated significantly.

The Volatility of Exchange Rates

We have discussed several variables that can lead to changes in the exchange rate, including changes in relative prices, changes in interest rates, and changes in the pattern of trade. Since these variables are changing at different times by different amounts and often in different directions, it should not be surprising that exchange rates are constantly changing. Indeed, exchange rates are one of the most volatile of all macroeconomic variables. One reason for this volatility that we have not yet discussed is that foreign-exchange traders, when they are deciding whether to buy or sell foreign currency, respond to all sorts of "news" that they think will influence economic conditions, both currently and in the future. Since such news is constantly becoming available, the exchange rate is continuously changing as this new information leads traders to change their demand and supply decisions. *Applying Economic Concepts 36-3* discusses in more detail how news affects the volatility of exchange rates.

Three Policy Issues

This chapter has so far been devoted to explaining how the balance of payments accounts are constructed and how exchange rates are determined. It is now time to use this knowledge to explore some important and interesting policy issues. We examine three policy issues that are commonly discussed in the popular press. As we will see, these discussions are not always as well-informed as they could be. We pose the three policy issues as questions:

1. Is a current account deficit bad for Canada?

2. Is there a "correct" value for the Canadian dollar?

3. Should Canada fix its exchange rate with the U.S. dollar?

Current Account Deficits

In recent years, Canada has had a current account deficit. Canada usually has a significant trade surplus since it exports more goods and services to the world than it imports. But because it makes more investment payments (both interest and dividends) to foreigners than it receives from foreigners, it has a deficit on the capital-service portion of the current account. The overall current account balance in recent years has been a deficit, usually between $15 billion and $25 billion.

As we have learned, Canada's balance of payments must always balance, so the current account deficit is matched by a capital account surplus of the same size (the balance on the official financing account is usually very small). This capital account surplus means that Canada sells more assets to the rest of the world—both bonds and equity—than it buys from the rest of the world.

Is it undesirable for Canada to have a current account deficit and, therefore, a capital account surplus? It is certainly common for TV anchors to report negatively upon a

APPLYING ECONOMIC CONCEPTS 36-3

News and the Exchange Rate

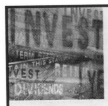

Foreign-exchange markets are different from markets for consumer goods in that the vast bulk of trading takes place between professional foreign-exchange traders working for banks, mutual-fund companies, and pension funds. These traders do not meet each other face to face. Rather, they do their transactions over the telephone, and the other party to the transaction could be anywhere in the world. The structure of this market has one interesting implication: exchange rates respond to news. Let's see why this is and what this means.

Deals done by the professional traders are all on a large scale, typically involving sums no smaller than $1 million and often very much larger. Each trader tends to specialize in trades between a small number of currencies, say the Canadian and the U.S. dollars, or the U.S. dollar and the Japanese yen. But the traders for all currencies for each bank sit close together in a trading room so they can hear what is going on in the other markets. When a big news event breaks, anywhere in the world, this will be shouted out simultaneously to all traders in the room.

Each trader is also faced with several computer screens and many buttons that connect him or her quickly by telephone to other traders. Speed of transaction can be very important if you are dealing with large amounts of money in a market that is continuously changing the prices quoted. The most recent price quotes from around the world appear on the screens. However, contracts are agreed over the telephone (and are recorded in case of a disagreement) and the paperwork follows within two days.

As exchange rates are closely related to expectations and to interest rates, the foreign-exchange traders have to keep an eye on all major news events affecting the economic environment. Since all the players in the foreign-exchange markets are professionals, they are well-informed, not just about what has happened but also about forecasts of what is likely to happen. Accordingly, the exchange rate at any point in time reflects not just history but also current expectations of future events.

As soon as some future event comes to be expected—such as the central bank's plans to tighten monetary policy—it will be reflected in the current exchange rate. Events expected to happen soon will be given more weight than those events expected to happen in the more distant future. The fact that expectations of future events get incorporated quickly into the exchange rate has an interesting implication: the only component in today's news that will cause the exchange rate to change is what was *not expected* to happen. Economists attribute the unforecastable component of news to a random error. It is random in the sense that it has no detectable pattern and it is unrelated to the information available before it happened.

Some events are clearly unforecastable, like an earthquake in Japan or a head of state having a heart attack. Others are the production of economic statistics for which forecasts have generally been published. In the latter case it is the deviation of announced figures from their forecast value which tends to move exchange rates.

So, exchange rates are moved by news. And since news is random and unpredictable, changes in exchange rates will tend to be random. Some people, observing the volatility of exchange rates, conclude that foreign-exchange markets are inefficient. However, with well-informed professional traders who have forward-looking expectations, new information is rapidly transmitted into prices. The volatility of exchange rates, therefore, largely reflects the volatility of relevant, but unexpected, events around the world.

---

rise in the current account deficit and positively upon its decline. But are current account deficits really a problem? We address this issue in three parts.

Mercantilism

Many people argue that a current account deficit is undesirable because it means that Canada is buying more goods and services from the world than it is selling to the world. Central to this view is the belief that exports are "good" and imports are "bad." We discussed this belief, and argued why it was incorrect, in Chapter 35 when we explored some of the fallacious arguments for trade protection.

As a carryover from a long-discredited eighteenth-century doctrine called *mercantilism*, a current account surplus is sometimes called a "favourable balance," and a current account deficit is sometimes called an "unfavourable balance." Mercantilists, both ancient and modern, believe that a country's gains from trade arise only from having a "favourable" balance of trade—that is, by exporting more goods and services than it imports. But this belief misses the central point of comparative advantage that we explored in Chapter 34—that countries gain from trade because trade allows each country to specialize in the production of those products in which its opportunity costs are low. The gains from trade have *nothing* to do with whether there is a trade deficit or a trade surplus.

Lessons from History 36-1 discusses the doctrine of mercantilism. The lesson to be learned is that the gains from trade depend on the *volume* of trade (both imports and exports) rather than the *balance* of trade. There is nothing inherently bad about having a current account deficit.

International Borrowing

If Canada has a current account deficit, then it also has a capital account surplus. It is a net seller of assets to the rest of the world. These assets are either bonds, in which case Canadians are borrowing from foreigners, or they are shares in firms (equities) in which case Canadians are selling their capital stock to foreigners.

LESSONS FROM HISTORY 36-1
Mercantilism, Then and Now

Media commentators, politicians, and much of the general public often appear to believe that a nation should secure a current-account surplus. They believe that the benefits derived from international trade are measured by the size of that surplus.

This view is related to the *exploitation doctrine* of international trade: One country's surplus is another country's deficit. Hence, one country's gain, judged by its surplus, must be another country's loss, judged by its deficit.

People who hold such views today are echoing an ancient economic doctrine called *mercantilism*. The mercantilists were a group of economists who preceded Adam Smith. They judged the success of trade by the size of the trade balance. In many cases, this doctrine made sense in terms of their objective, which was to use international trade as a means of building up the political and military power of the state, rather than as a means of raising the living standards of its citizens. A current account surplus allowed the nation (then and now) to acquire assets. (In those days, the assets took the form of gold. Today, they are mostly claims on the currencies of other

countries.) These assets could then be used to pay armies, to purchase weapons from abroad, and to finance colonial expansions.

If the objective is to promote the welfare and living standards of ordinary citizens, however, the mercantilist focus on the balance of trade makes no sense. The principle of comparative advantage shows that average living standards are maximized by having individuals, regions, and countries specialize in the things that they can produce comparatively best and then trading to obtain the things that they can produce comparatively worst. The more specialization there is, the more trade occurs.

For the country as a whole, therefore, the gains from trade are to be judged by the *volume* of trade rather than by the *balance* of trade. A situation in which there is a large volume of trade even though each country has a zero balance of trade can thus be regarded as satisfactory. Furthermore, a change in policy that results in an equal increase in both exports and imports will generate gains because it allows for specialization according to comparative advantage, even though it causes no change in either country's trade balance.

It follows that the question "Should Canada have a current account deficit?" is the same as the question "Should Canadians be net sellers of assets to foreigners?" It is not immediately clear that the answer to this question should be: No. It is true that by selling bonds to foreigners, Canadians increase their indebtedness to foreigners and will eventually have to redeem the bonds as well as pay interest. And by selling income-earning equities to foreigners, Canadians give up a stream of income that they would otherwise have. But, in both cases, they get a lump-sum of funds that can be used for any type of consumption or investment. Is it obviously "better" to have a lower debt or a higher future income stream than to have a lump-sum of funds right now? If it were better, no family would ever borrow money to buy a house or a car, and no firm would ever borrow money to build a factory.

A country that has a current account deficit is either borrowing from the rest of the world or selling its ownership of some of its capital stock to the rest of the world. This is not necessarily undesirable.

To argue that it is undesirable for Canada to have a current account deficit is to argue that Canadians as a whole should not borrow from (or sell physical assets to) the rest of the world. But surely the wisdom of borrowing depends on *why* Canadians are borrowing. It is therefore important to know *why* there is a current account deficit.

Causes of Current Account Deficits

There are several possible causes of a current account deficit. This can be seen most clearly by recalling some national-income accounting from Chapter 20. Recall that GDP is equal to the sum of actual consumption, investment, government purchases and net exports,

$$GDP = C_a + I_a + G_a + NX_a$$

where the subscript "a" denotes *actual* expenditure rather than desired expenditure. Next, note that GNP is equal to GDP plus the net investment income received from abroad, which we call R.

$$GNP = GDP + R = C_a + I_a + G_a + NX_a + R$$

Note the current account balance is simply the trade balance, NX_a, plus the net investment income, R. We denote the actual current account balance CA_a. If CA_a is positive, there is a current account surplus; if CA_a is negative, there is a current account deficit. The equation now becomes

$$GNP = C_a + I_a + G_a + CA_a \qquad (36\text{-}1)$$

Now consider how a given amount of GNP that accrues to households can be spent. There are only three ways to dispose of income. It can be consumed, saved, or paid in taxes. That is,

$$GNP = C_a + S_a + T_a \qquad (36\text{-}2)$$

By equating Equations 36-1 and 36-2, and by omitting the "a" subscripts for simplicity, we derive an interesting relationship between national saving, investment, and the current account balance:

$$C + I + G + CA = C + S + T$$
$$\Rightarrow CA = S + (T-G) - I$$

This equation says that the current account balance in any year is exactly equal to the excess of national saving, $S + (T - G)$, over domestic investment. If Canadians (and their governments) decide to save more than is needed to finance the amount of domestic investment, where do the excess funds go? They are used to acquire foreign assets, and thus Canada has a current account surplus ($CA>0$). In contrast, if Canadians do not save enough to finance the amount of domestic investment, the balance must be financed by foreign funds. Thus, Canada has a current account deficit ($CA<0$). Finally, we can rearrange this equation very slightly to get

$$CA = (S - I) + (T - G) \qquad (36\text{-}3)$$

which says that the current account balance is equal to the government budget surplus plus the excess of private saving over investment.

Equation 36-3 shows that there are three separate reasons for any given increase in the current account deficit (a fall in CA). First, a reduction in private saving, other things equal, will lead to a rise in the current account deficit. Second, a rise in domestic investment, other things equal, will increase the current account deficit. Finally, other things equal, a rise in the government's budget deficit (a fall in the budget surplus) will raise the current account deficit. This third case is often referred to as a situation of *twin deficits*. That is, a rise in the government's budget deficit will also have the effect (if S and I remain constant) of increasing the current account deficit.

An increase in the level of investment, a decrease in the level of saving, and an increase in the government's budget deficit are all possible causes of an increase in a country's current account deficit.

In the end, it makes little sense to discuss the desirability of a change in the current account deficit without first knowing the *cause* of the change. Knowing the cause is crucial to knowing whether the change in the current account deficit is undesirable. The following two examples illustrate this important point.

First, suppose that investment opportunities in Canada are very promising and, as a result, there is an increase in the level of investment. Most people would consider such an investment boom desirable because it would increase current output and employment and, by increasing the country's capital stock, it would also increase the level of potential output in the future. But as is clear from Equation 36-3, the immediate effect of the rise in Canadian investment is an increase in the Canadian current account deficit. In this case, it would be difficult to argue that Canada's current account deficit is undesirable.

For a second example, suppose the domestic economy begins to slow and households and firms are pessimistic about the future. In such a situation, we expect households to increase their saving and firms to reduce their investment, thus increasing the value of $(S - I)$. As the economy slows we would also expect the government's tax revenues to fall, thus decreasing the value of $(T - G)$. But it is easy to imagine a situation where the first effect dominates the second effect, thus leading to an increase in the current account surplus. Is the increase in Canada's current account surplus desirable? Most people would probably agree that the onset of a recession as described above is surely undesirable, involving a loss of output and employment.

A country's current account deficit can increase for a number of reasons. Whether the rise in the current account deficit is desirable depends on its underlying cause. A rise in the current account deficit may reflect a positive economic development; a decline in the current account deficit may reflect a negative economic development.

Is There a "Correct" Value for the Canadian Dollar?

From the summer of 1997 to the end of 1999, the external value of the Canadian dollar fell from about 72 to 65 U.S. cents. It was common to hear financial commentators discuss how the Canadian dollar was "undervalued." Opposite statements were heard a few years earlier in 1991 when, as a result of high Canadian interest rates caused by a significant monetary contraction, foreign financial capital flowed into Canada and the Canadian dollar appreciated enormously (its external value increased to about 90 U.S. cents). At that time many financial commentators argued that the Canadian dollar was "overvalued." In both cases, the observers appeared to believe that there was some "correct" value for the Canadian dollar. Is there?

As we saw in the previous section, a country that chooses to use a flexible exchange rate has its exchange rate determined by competitive forces in the foreign-exchange market. In Canada, and other countries as well, fluctuations in exchange rates have many causes. Some changes may be good for Canada, such as a world-wide shortage of wheat that drives up the world price of wheat, a major Canadian export. Others may be bad for Canada, such as the discovery of new copper mines in Chile that drives down the price of copper, also a major Canadian export. But the various supply and demand forces are coming together in the foreign-exchange market to determine the equilibrium value of the exchange rate. Changes in this value may reflect positive or negative events for Canada, but it makes little sense to think of this equilibrium value as being either too high or too low.

With a flexible exchange rate, the market determines the value of the exchange rate. With respect to the forces of demand and supply, the equilibrium exchange rate is the "correct" exchange rate.

In saying that the current equilibrium exchange rate is the "correct" rate in no way suggests that it will necessarily be the correct exchange rate in the future. Indeed, foreign-exchange markets are so large, with so many participants in so many countries, each responding to a slightly different set of events and expectations, that the equilibrium exchange rate is constantly changing. In other words, as various forces lead to frequent changes in the demand and supply for the Canadian dollar in foreign-exchange markets, the "correct" value of the Canadian exchange rate is constantly changing.

Some economists accept that the current exchange rate, as determined by the foreign-exchange market, is indeed the correct rate, but they make a distinction between the immediate value of the exchange rate and its long-run value. These economists argue that, whereas various shocks may cause the exchange rate to rise or fall in the short run, there does exist some "fundamental" level to which it will return. This brings us to the theory of *purchasing power parity*.

Purchasing Power Parity

The theory of **purchasing power parity** (**PPP**) holds that over the long term, the value of the exchange rate between two currencies depends on the two currencies' relative purchasing power. The theory holds that a currency will tend to have the same purchasing power when it is spent in its home country as it would have if it were converted to foreign exchange and spent in the foreign country. Another way to say the same thing is that the price of *identical baskets of goods* should be the same in the two countries when

purchasing power parity (PPP)   The theory that over the long term, the exchange rate between two currencies adjusts to reflect relative price levels (relative purchasing power).

the price is expressed in the same currency. If we let P_C and P_E be the price levels in Canada and Europe, respectively, and let e be the price of euros in terms of Canadian dollars (the exchange rate), then the theory of purchasing power parity can be expressed as

$$P_C = e \times P_E \qquad (36\text{-}4)$$

This equation simply says that if a basket of goods costs 1000 euros in Europe and the exchange rate is 1.2 (that is, 1.2 Canadian dollars per euro), then that same basket of goods should cost 1200 dollars in Canada ($1.2 \times 1000 = 1200$).

According to the theory of purchasing power parity, the exchange rate between two country's currencies is determined by the relative price levels in the two countries.

The idea behind PPP is a simple one. Suppose that Equation 36-4 did *not* hold—specifically, suppose that P_C was greater than $e \times P_E$, so that Canadian-dollar prices in Canada exceed the Canadian-dollar prices of the same goods in Europe. In this case, people would increase their purchases of European goods and reduce their purchases of Canadian goods. These actions would have the effect of depreciating the Canadian dollar (a rise in e); and this would continue until the equality was reestablished.

The *PPP exchange rate* is the value of the exchange rate that makes Equation 36-4 hold. That is, the PPP exchange rate (between the Canadian dollar and the euro) is given by

$$e^{PPP} \equiv P_C/P_E \qquad (36\text{-}5)$$

Note that the PPP exchange rate is itself not constant. If inflation is higher in Canada than in Europe, for example, then P_C will be rising faster than P_E and so the PPP exchange rate will be rising. Conversely, if inflation is lower in Canada than in Europe, then P_C will be rising more slowly than P_E and the PPP exchange rate will be falling.

For *The Economists'* Big Mac Index that uses the idea of PPP, see its website: www.economist.com.

A Caveat About PPP

Should we expect the *actual* exchange rate to equal the PPP exchange rate? The theory of purchasing power parity predicts that if the actual exchange rate (e) does not equal the PPP exchange rate (e^{PPP}), then demands and supplies of Canadian and European goods will change until $e = e^{PPP}$. Thus, the theory of PPP predicts that the actual exchange rate will eventually equal the PPP exchange rate.

Recall from Equation 36-4 that P_C and P_E were defined as the prices of *identical baskets of goods* in Canada and Europe, respectively. Given that the goods are the same, the argument that the prices should (eventually) be equated across the two countries is sensible—if the prices are not equated across the two countries, then there would be an incentive to purchase in the cheaper country rather than in the more expensive country, and this would lead to changes in the exchange rate until Equation 36-4 *did* hold.

One problem, however, when we apply the theory of purchasing power parity to *national price indices*, such as the Consumer Price Index or the Implicit GDP Deflator, is that the two baskets of goods are typically *not* the same—for two reasons.

Different Countries Produce Different Goods.   Suppose we apply the theory of PPP to the Canada-Europe exchange rate and we use the GDP deflators from the two countries as the measures of prices. Recall from Chapter 20 that the GDP deflator is an index of prices *of the goods produced within the country*. But Canada and Europe clearly produce very different goods. The price of forest products will have a large weight in the Canadian GDP deflator, but less weight in the European GDP deflator; in contrast, the price of wine will have a much larger weight in the European GDP deflator than in the Canadian one.

The implication of these differences for the theory of PPP is important. As long as changes in the *relative* prices of goods occur, such as a change in the price of forest products relative to wine, then P_C (the Canadian GDP deflator) will change relative to P_E (the European GDP deflator) *even though the prices of individual goods might be equated across the two countries.* Thus, differences in the structure of the price indices between two countries mean that using a PPP exchange rate computed on the basis of Equation 36-5 will be misleading. In other words, in the presence of changing relative prices, there is no reason to expect the actual exchange rate to equal the PPP exchange rate as defined in Equation 36-5.

Nontraded Goods Are Important.   The previous discussion emphasized that the *baskets* of goods across two countries might differ even though the products in the baskets were the same. But even if Canada and Europe produced exactly the same range of goods, so that the various weights in the GDP deflators were the same, there is still a reason why the basket of goods in Canada differs from the basket of goods in Europe. Some of the goods produced in Canada are *nontraded goods*, such as haircuts and restaurant meals. Nontraded goods are also produced in Europe. But, since nontraded goods cannot be traded (by definition), there is nothing that will force their prices to be equal across the two countries. If haircuts are more expensive in Paris than in Toronto (as they are), we do not expect people to shift their consumption of haircuts away from Paris toward Toronto, and thus we should not expect the actual exchange rate to move to make Equation 36-4 hold.

The conclusion of this discussion is that we must be very careful in selecting the price indices we use when we apply the theory of purchasing power parity. We know that countries have different patterns of production and thus have different structures to their national price indices. Thus, in the presence of changes in relative prices of various products, the national price indices can change in ways that will not lead to changes in the exchange rate. Similarly, the presence of nontraded goods implies that some differences in prices across countries will not lead to changes in the location of demand and thus changes in the exchange rate.

Should Canada Have a Fixed Exchange Rate?

In recent years, some economists have suggested that Canada peg the value of its currency to the U.S. dollar. Advocates of a fixed Canadian exchange rate see this policy as a means of avoiding the significant fluctuations in the Canadian exchange rate that would otherwise occur—fluctuations such as the 15 percent appreciation that occurred between 1989 and 1991, and the 10 percent depreciation that occurred between 1997 and 1998. They argue that exchange-rate fluctuations generate uncertainty for importers and exporters and thus increase the costs associated with trade.

Others have gone further in suggesting that Canada actually abandon its currency altogether and simply adopt the U.S. dollar. They point to the European Union, which introduced the euro as its common currency in 1999. If a common currency is acceptable to most of Europe, why should Canada and the United States be any different? Note that if Canada and the United States were to share a common currency, the exchange rate between the two countries would, of course, be fixed.

These are contentious suggestions that have attracted a great deal of public attention in recent years. We examine this issue by comparing the main benefits of flexible and fixed exchange rates. Whereas flexible exchange rates dampen the effects on output and employment from shocks to a country's terms of trade, fixed exchange rates reduce the uncertainty faced by traders. The benefits and costs of having a common currency between two regions is examined in *Extensions in Theory 36-1*, which explains the theory of "optimal currency areas."

EXTENSIONS IN THEORY 36-1

Optimal Currency Areas

In 1961, Canadian economist Robert Mundell, now at Columbia University, developed the theory of "optimal currency areas." In 1999 he was awarded the Nobel Prize in economics, partly for this work. He examined the conditions under which it is optimal for two countries to have a common currency, and the conditions under which the countries would be better off maintaining separate currencies with a flexible exchange rate. Mundell's conclusions can be summarized as follows.

1. Other things equal, the more the two countries trade with one another, the larger are the benefits from having a common currency (and the lower are the benefits from having separate currencies with a flexible exchange rate).

2. Other things equal, the less correlated are the two countries' terms of trade, the smaller are the benefits from having a common currency (and the larger are the benefits from having separate currencies with a flexible exchange rate).

The Basic Theory

The accompanying diagram illustrates the situation that Mundell describes. Our example is that of Canada and the United States. The green arrows represent the trade of goods, services, and assets between the two countries. The red arrows represent the various shocks to each country's terms of trade. Mundell's central result is that, other things equal, the more important the green arrows are, the better it is to have a common currency. On the other hand, the "less similar" each country's red arrows are, the worse it is to have a com-

mon currency. By "less similar" we mean that the changes in one country's terms of trade are different, or occur at different times, than the changes in the other country's terms of trade.

To understand Mundell's arguments, we must understand how the green and red arrows relate to the costs and benefits of having a common currency (rather than separate currencies with a flexible exchange rate).

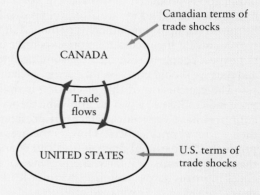

The main benefit of the two regions having a common currency is that importers and exporters in each country can save on the costs associated with having a flexible (and perhaps volatile) exchange rate. There are two types of costs. The first is the *uncertainty* that is generated by having a volatile exchange rate. The more uncertainty there is surrounding the price of foreign currency, the less likely are firms to enter contracts that involve foreign exchange. This reduc-

Flexible Exchange Rates as "Shock Absorbers"

See Chapter 36 of www.pearsoned.ca/lipsey for a debate on the appropriate exchange rate regime for Canada: Pierre Fortin, "What Can We Do About Exchange Rates that Move Too Much?" and Bill Robson, "Resisting the Lure of Fixed Exchange Rates," *World Economic Affairs*.

For most of the years following the Second World War, Canada has used a flexible exchange rate. Even when most other major countries chose to peg the value of their currencies to the U.S. dollar (and to gold) under the Bretton Woods system, Canada usually chose a flexible exchange rate (there were a few short periods in which Canada fixed its exchange rate). For all of its history Canada's economy has been dependent on the export of resource-based products, the prices of which are determined in world markets and are often highly variable from year to year. Changes in these prices constitute changes in Canada's terms of trade and, as we saw earlier in this chapter, changes in a country's terms of trade are an important reason why exchange rates are so variable.

tion in trade leads to a reduction in the gains from trade. The second cost is the *transaction cost* of converting one currency into another. If the two countries have separate currencies, then every time some good or service is traded between the two countries, someone (either the importer or the exporter) must spend the time and resources necessary to convert currencies. Given that such costs are incurred every time goods are traded, it follows that the greater is the volume of trade between the two regions, the greater are the benefits (that is, the costs avoided) from having a common currency.

The main benefit from each country's maintaining a separate currency with a flexible exchange rate is that the exchange rate can act as a "shock absorber," dampening the effects on the country's output and employment from shocks to its terms of trade. For example, consider what would happen if there were a reduction in the world price of copper. Copper is a major Canadian export but a U.S. import. When the price of copper falls due to a reduction in world copper demand, Canada's terms of trade deteriorate but the U.S. terms of trade improve. The fall in the price of copper leads to a contraction in the Canadian copper industry. If Canada shares a common currency with the United States, the result of the shock will simply be a reduction in output and employment in Canada's copper industry. The contraction in that sector will eventually reduce wages, and the economy will eventually return to potential output. But the adjustment may be long and painful.

In contrast, if Canada and the United States have separate currencies, then the reduction in the world price of copper will tend to depreciate the Canadian dollar relative to the U.S. dollar. The Canadian copper industry will still be in recession, for there has been a reduction in demand for its products, but the overall Canadian downturn will be dampened by the depreciation of the Canadian dollar. In other words, even though the copper industry is in recession, other sectors of the Canadian economy will actually *expand* as a result of the depreciation because their products are now more competitive in world markets. The overall result is that, with

a separate currency and flexible exchange rate, the deterioration in Canada's terms of trade leads to a less severe Canadian recession than if Canada shared a currency with the United States.

Mundell said that two countries constitute an *optimal currency area* if by adopting a common currency the two countries together save more in uncertainty and transactions costs than they incur by sacrificing the output-dampening effects of a flexible exchange rate.

What Is the Optimal Currency Area?

Some economists have recently advocated that Canada adopt the U.S. dollar as its currency. Do they believe that Canada and the United States constitute an optimal currency area? Probably not, but that is also not quite the right policy question. The provinces and territories of Canada already use a common currency even though they may not satisfy Mundell's condition for being an optimal currency area. Similarly, the U.S. states use a common currency and may not constitute an optimal currency area. Thus, the relevant policy question from Canada's perspective is whether Canada and the United States together form a *better* currency area than Canada by itself.

Some economists think this is probably true. They point to the massive and growing volume of trade between the two countries as the best reason for Canada and the United States to share a currency. Other economists stress the importance of exchange rates as shock absorbers. They point to the 1997-1998 decline in world commodity prices as an ideal example of a situation in which Canada benefited from having a flexible exchange rate. Canada's resource sector contracted sharply in response to this deterioration in Canada's terms of trade. Especially hard hit was British Columbia's forestry industry. But the depreciation of the Canadian dollar (by roughly 10 percent against the U.S. dollar) led to expansions in manufacturing industries in Ontario and Quebec that significantly reduced the overall effect of the terms of trade shock.

That the exchange rate adjusts in response to shocks is actually the main advantage of a flexible (rather than fixed) exchange rate. A flexible exchange rate acts as a "shock absorber", dampening the effects on the country's output and employment from shocks to its terms of trade. To understand how this happens, consider a simple example.

Suppose a reduction in world demand leads to a reduction in the world price of newsprint. Newsprint is a major Canadian export, and so when the world price of newsprint falls, Canada's terms of trade deteriorate. The fall in the price of newsprint leads to a leftward shift in the Canadian aggregate demand curve, as shown in part (i) of Figure 36-4. Canadian GDP declines, caused by the reduction in output in the newsprint industry. If Canada has a fixed exchange rate, that is pretty much the end of the story.

Canadian wages will eventually fall and output will eventually return to potential, but the recession may be slow and painful.

In contrast, if Canada has a flexible exchange rate, the deterioration in the terms of trade will lead to a reduction in the supply of foreign exchange and thus to a depreciation of the Canadian dollar. The aggregate demand curve will still shift to the left, reducing Canada's GDP. The newsprint industry will still be in recession, for there has been a reduction in demand for its products. But the overall Canadian downturn will be dampened by the depreciation of the Canadian dollar. Other sectors of the Canadian economy will actually *expand* as a result of the depreciation because their products are now more competitive in world markets. Thus, as shown in part (ii) of Figure 36-4, the leftward shift of the aggregate demand curve will not be as large as in the case of the fixed exchange rate. The overall result is that, with a flexible exchange rate, the deterioration in Canada's terms of trade leads to a less severe Canadian recession than if Canada had a fixed exchange rate.

One of the advantages of flexible exchange rates is that, in response to shocks to the terms of trade, the exchange rate can act as a shock absorber, dampening the effects of the shock on output and employment.

FIGURE 36-4   Flexible Exchange Rates as a Shock Absorber

(i) Foreign-exchange market   (ii) AD and SRAS

Flexible exchange rates adjust to terms of trade shocks and thus dampen the effect on output and employment. The economy begins with the exchange rate equal to e_0 in part (i) and GDP equal to Y^* in part (ii). A reduction in the world's demand for Canadian exports causes a reduction in the supply of foreign exchange, shifting S_0 to S_1 in part (i).

With a fixed exchange rate, the Bank of Canada maintains the exchange rate at e_0, satisfying the excess demand for foreign exchange by selling its foreign-currency reserves. The reduction in the demand for Canada's exports is a negative aggregate demand shock. AD_0 shifts to the left to AD_1 in part (ii), causing GDP to fall to Y_1. The recessionary gap eventually pushes wages down, the $SRAS$ curve shifts to the right over time, and the economy moves along AD_1 to Y^*. The adjustment, however, may be protracted.

With a flexible exchange rate, the Bank of Canada allows the Canadian dollar to depreciate. The exchange rate rises to e_1 in part (i). The reduction in demand for Canadian exports still causes the AD curve to shift to the left in part (ii), but the shift is dampened by the depreciation of the dollar, which makes Canadian products more competitive in world markets. The AD curve shifts only to AD_2 and so GDP falls only to Y_2. There is a still a recession, but smaller than in the case with a fixed exchange rate.

The Asian crisis of 1997–1998 provides an excellent example of how Canada's flexible exchange rate dampened the effects of a negative terms of trade shock. When the Asian countries of Malaysia, Indonesia, Thailand, and South Korea experienced their large recessions in 1997 and 1998, their demand for many raw materials declined sharply. As they are major users of raw materials, the effect was felt on world markets. The average prices of raw materials fell by roughly 30 percent from the summer of 1997 to the end of 1998. Many of these raw materials, of course, are important exports for Canada, and so the decline in their world prices implied a terms of trade deterioration for Canada.

Especially hard hit was British Columbia's forestry sector, where output fell dramatically in many paper and lumber mills due to the lack of sales in Asia. As expected, there was also a significant depreciation of the Canadian dollar, just as described in Figure 36-4. But as the Canadian dollar depreciated, the Canadian manufacturing sector, concentrated mainly in Ontario and Quebec, was given a large boost. The 10 percent depreciation of the Canadian dollar meant that Canadian machinery, furniture, telecommunications equipment, and a whole range of other products were now more competitive in world markets. Thus, the boom in the central Canadian manufacturing sector offset to some extent the significant recession that was going on in British Columbia. If Canada had had a fixed exchange rate, the 10 percent depreciation would not have occurred. But the initial shock from the Asian crisis would still have taken place. The net result would have been lower output and higher unemployment than actually occurred.

For much analysis of the Asian Crisis, see Nouriel Roubini's website: www.stern.nyu.edu/~nroubini.

Note that having a fixed exchange rate does not prevent a country from being subjected to shocks. Many advocates of fixed exchange rates, however, seem to think that by fixing the value of a country's currency, the country is shielding itself from undesirable fluctuations. But shocks to a country's terms of trade will always occur. As long as there are changes in the demand and supply for various products around the world, there will also be changes in a country's terms of trade. What Figure 36-4 shows, however, is that by fixing the exchange rate and thus avoiding the fluctuations in the value of the currency, the effects of the shock merely show up as increased volatility in output and employment.

A country will always experience shocks in its terms of trade. A flexible exchange rate absorbs some of the shock, reducing the effect on output and employment. A fixed exchange rate simply redistributes the effect of the shock—the exchange rate is smoother but output and employment are more volatile.

Trade, Transactions Costs, and Uncertainty

See Chapter 36 of www.pearsoned.ca/lipsey for an interview with Milton Friedman on the desirability of flexible exchange rates: "Confirmed Convictions," *World Economic Affairs*.

Despite the benefits of international trade, there are costs involved in exporting and importing goods and services. The *transactions costs* of international trade involve the costs associated with converting one currency to another, as must be done either by the importer or the exporter of the product that is traded. For example, if you have an import-export business in Canada and want to import some bicycles from Japan, then you will probably have to purchase Japanese yen at a bank or foreign-exchange dealer and, with those yen, pay the Japanese seller for the bicycles. Even if the Japanese seller accepts Canadian dollars for the bicycles, and this often is the case, he will be required to convert those Canadian dollars into yen before he can use that money in Japan to pay his workers or pay for other costs of production.

The greater is the volume of trade between two countries, the higher are the aggregate transaction costs associated with international trade.

Note that such transactions costs exist even if trade takes place between two countries with fixed exchange rates. For example, if Canada pegged the value of the Canadian dollar to the U.S. dollar, any trade between the two countries would still require the costly conversion of one currency to the other. Thus, the existence of transactions costs cannot be used as an argument in favour of fixed exchange rates and against flexible exchange rates. As long as there are two currencies, the transactions costs must be borne by one party or the other. These transactions costs could only be avoided if the two countries shared a common currency. *Extensions in Theory 36-1* examines the theory of "optimal currency areas" in which these transactions costs play a central role.

Many economists believe, however, that the volatility of flexible exchange rates generates another type of cost for importers and exporters. Specifically, the unpredictability of the exchange rate leads to *uncertainty* in the profitability of any specific international transaction. Such uncertainty, given risk-averse firms, can be expected to lead to a smaller volume of international trade and thus to fewer benefits from such trade.

For example, suppose that a Canadian appliance manufacturer enters into a contract to purchase a specified amount of steel from a Japanese producer for a specified yen price in one year's time. In this case, the Japanese producer bears no *foreign-exchange risk* because the price is specified in yen. But the Canadian appliance manufacturer bears considerable risk. If the yen depreciates relative to the dollar over the coming year, fewer Canadian dollars will be required to pay for the steel. But if the yen appreciates relative to the dollar over the coming year, more Canadian dollars will be required to pay for the steel. The Canadian buyer therefore faces a risk in terms of the Canadian-dollar cost of the steel. If the firm is *risk averse*, meaning simply that it would be prepared to pay a cost to avoid the risk, then the presence of the risk may lead to fewer international transactions of this type. Perhaps to avoid the foreign-exchange risk, the Canadian buyer will decide instead to buy Canadian-made steel, even though it may be slightly more expensive or not quite the right type that is needed.

If the presence of foreign-exchange risk leads to less international trade, there will be a reduction in the gains from trade.

Many of the people who advocate Canada's move to a fixed exchange rate point to the avoidance of this foreign-exchange risk as the main benefit. They argue that if the Canadian dollar were pegged in value to the U.S. dollar, both importers and exporters would face less uncertainty on the most important part of their trade—that between Canada and the United States. With the greater certainty, they argue, would come greater trade flows and thus an increase in the overall gains from trade.

But many economists disagree. While accepting the basic argument regarding the risks created by flexible (and volatile) exchange rates, they note that importers and exporters already have the means to avoid this uncertainty. In particular, traders can participate in *forward markets* in which they can buy or sell foreign exchange *in the future* at prices specified today. For example, the Canadian appliance manufacturer could enter into a contract to purchase the required amount of yen in one year's time at a price of 100 yen per Canadian dollar. In this case, no matter what happened to the yen-dollar exchange rate in the intervening year, the uncertainty regarding the Canadian-dollar price of the steel would be entirely eliminated.

Summing Up

So, should Canada give up its flexible exchange rate and instead peg the value of the Canadian dollar to the U.S. dollar? Advocates of this policy emphasize the foreign-exchange risk faced by importers and exporters, and the gains from increased trade that would result from a fixed exchange rate. Opponents to the policy emphasize the shock-absorption benefits from a flexible exchange rate, and the greater volatility in output and employment that Canada would have if it were to fix its exchange rate.

This debate will surely go on for a while, partly because it is difficult to quantify the costs and benefits of a flexible exchange rate. Economists on both sides of the debate understand and accept the logic of the arguments from the other side. But researchers have so far been unable to determine how much of a shock is absorbed by a flexible exchange rate, and thus to estimate how much more volatile output and employment would be with a fixed exchange rate. Similarly, it is very difficult to estimate just how much more trade would take place if the foreign-exchange risk faced by traders was eliminated by means of a fixed exchange rate. Without convincing empirical evidence supporting the move to a fixed exchange rate, however, the status quo will probably remain. It is probably safe to assume that Canada will continue to have a flexible exchange rate, at least for the next several years.

SUMMARY

The Balance of Payments

- Actual transactions among the firms, households, and governments of various countries are reported in the balance-of-payments accounts. In these accounts, any transaction that represents a receipt for Canada (Canadians sell goods or assets to foreigners) is recorded as a credit item. Any transaction that represents a payment from Canada (Canadians purchase goods or assets from foreigners) is recorded as a debit item.

- If all transactions are recorded in the balance of payments, the sum of all credit items necessarily equals the sum of all debit items. Thus, the balance of payments must always balance.

- Major categories in the balance-of-payments accounts are the trade account, the capital-service account, the current account (which is equal to the trade account plus the capital-service account), the capital account, and the official financing account.

- When a country is said to have a "balance of payments deficit" (or surplus), what is usually meant is that the sum of current and capital accounts is a deficit (or surplus). That is, it excludes the transactions on the official financing account. If official financing is zero, a balance on current account must be matched by a balance on capital account of equal magnitude but opposite sign.

The Foreign-Exchange Market

- The exchange rate between the Canadian dollar and some foreign currency is defined to be the number of Canadian dollars required to purchase one unit of the foreign currency. A rise in the exchange rate is a depreciation of the Canadian dollar; a fall in the exchange rate is an appreciation of the Canadian dollar.

- The supply of foreign exchange (or the demand for Canadian dollars) arises from Canadian exports of goods and services, capital flows into Canada, and the desire of foreign banks, firms, and governments to use Canadian dollars as part of their reserves.

- The demand for foreign exchange (or the supply of Canadian dollars to purchase foreign currencies) arises from Canadian imports of goods and services, capital flows from Canada, and the desire of holders of Canadian dollars to decrease the size of their holdings.

- A depreciation of the Canadian dollar lowers the foreign price of Canadian exports and increases the amount of foreign exchange supplied (to purchase Canadian exports). Thus, the supply curve for foreign exchange is positively sloped when plotted against the exchange rate.

- A depreciation of the Canadian dollar raises the dollar price of imports from abroad and hence lowers the amount of foreign exchange demanded to purchase foreign goods. Thus, the demand curve for foreign exchange is negatively sloped when plotted against the exchange rate.

The Determination of Exchange Rates

LO 4

- When the central bank does not intervene in the foreign exchange market, there is a flexible exchange rate. Under fixed exchange rates, the central bank intervenes in the foreign-exchange market to maintain the exchange rate at an announced value. To do this, the central bank must hold sufficient stocks of foreign-exchange reserves.
- Under a flexible, or floating, exchange rate, the exchange rate is determined by supply and demand for the currency.
- The Canadian dollar will appreciate in foreign-exchange markets if there is an increase in the supply of foreign exchange (an increase in demand for Canadian dollars) or if there is a reduction in demand for foreign exchange (a reduction in supply of Canadian dollars). The opposite changes will lead to a depreciation of the Canadian dollar.
- Changes in the exchange rate are caused by changes in such things as the rate of inflation in different countries, capital movements, structural conditions, and expectations about the future exchange rate.

Three Policy Issues

LO 5 6 7

- The view that current account deficits are undesirable is usually based on the mercantilist notion that exports are "good" and imports are "bad." But the gains from trade have nothing to do with the balance of trade—they depend on the volume of trade.
- From national income accounting, the current account surplus is given by

$$CA = (S - I) + (T - G)$$

An increase in investment, a decrease in saving, and an increase in the government budget deficit can each be the cause of a rise in the current account deficit.
- With a flexible exchange rate, supply and demand in the foreign-exchange market determine the "correct" value of the exchange rate. But this "correct" value is constantly changing as market conditions vary.
- The theory of purchasing power parity (PPP) predicts that exchange rates will adjust so that the purchasing power of a given currency is the same in different countries. That is, the price of an identical basket of goods will be equated in different countries (when expressed in the same currency).
- If price indices from different countries are used as the basis for computing the PPP exchange rate, differences in the structure of price indices across countries, together with the presence of nontraded goods, can be responsible for persistent deviations of the actual exchange rate from this measure of the PPP exchange rate.
- An important benefit of a flexible exchange rate is that it acts as a shock absorber, dampening the effects on output and employment from shocks to a country's terms of trade.
- An important benefit of fixed exchange rates is that it reduces transactions costs and foreign-exchange risk faced by importers and exporters.

K E Y   C O N C E P T S

Balance-of-payments accounts
Current and capital accounts
Changes in official reserves
Foreign exchange and exchange rates
Appreciation and depreciation

Sources of the demand for and supply of foreign exchange
Fixed and flexible exchange rates
Mercantilist views on the balance of trade and volume of trade
Purchasing power parity

PPP exchange rate
PPP and nontraded goods
Exchange rate overshooting
Flexible exchange rates as shock absorbers
Foreign-exchange risk
Optimal currency areas

STUDY EXERCISES

1. The table below shows Deborah's financial details for 1999. Answer the following questions about her "balance of payments."

Deborah's Financial Details, 1999	
Income from babysitting	$2500
Income from newspaper route	$3500
Gift from grandparents	$1000
Interest from bank deposits	$ 150
Expenditure on coffee and pastry	$1000
Expenditure on tuition	$3500
Purchase of mutual funds	$1200
Bank balance at end of year	$3500
Increase in bank balance	$1450

   a. What is Deborah's "trade balance"? Explain.
   b. What is Deborah's overall current account balance? Explain.
   c. What is Deborah's capital account balance? Explain.
   d. There is one (and only one) piece of information shown above that is not needed to compute Deborah's balance of payments. What is it? Explain why it is not needed.

2. The diagram below shows the demand for foreign currency (the supply of Canadian dollars) and the supply of foreign currency (the demand for Canadian dollars). The equilibrium exchange rate is e^*. Assume that Canada has a flexible exchange rate.

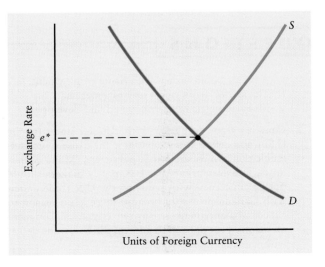

   a. Show in the diagram the effect of a general inflation in Canada (when there is no inflation in the rest of the world). Explain.
   b. Show what happens to the exchange rate if there is an increase in foreign demand for Canadian telecommunications equipment. Explain.
   c. Show the effect of an increase in Canadian investors' demand for Japanese government bonds. Explain.

3. The diagram below shows the demand for foreign currency (the supply of Canadian dollars) and the supply of foreign currency (the demand for Canadian dollars). The equilibrium exchange rate is e^*.

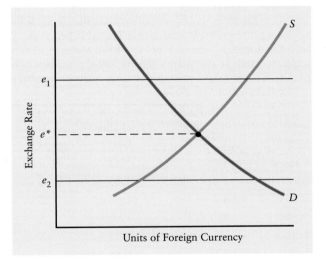

   a. Suppose the Bank of Canada decides to fix the exchange rate at e_1. What must the Bank do to accomplish its goal?
   b. In part **a**, do the current and capital accounts sum to zero? Explain.
   c. Now suppose the Bank of Canada decides to fix the exchange rate at e_2. What must the Bank do to accomplish this goal?
   d. With the exchange rate fixed at e_2, do the current and capital accounts sum to zero? Explain.

4. Suppose the Canadian economy is at potential output with a stable price level. There is then an upturn in the world demand for construction materials, especially lumber.

   a. Draw a diagram of the foreign-exchange market. Assuming that Canada has a flexible exchange rate, show the likely effect on the external value of the Canadian dollar.

b. Explain the Bank of Canada's participation in the foreign-exchange market if Canada has a fixed exchange rate.

c. Now draw an *AD/SRAS* diagram for the Canadian economy. What is the likely effect of the shock on Canadian GDP under the conditions in part **a**?

d. What would be the effect of the shock on Canadian GDP under the conditions of part **b**?

e. Explain how a flexible exchange rate acts as a shock absorber, insulating the economy from both positive and negative shocks.

5. Every few months, *The Economist* publishes its "Big Mac Index." Using the current exchange rates, it compares the U.S.-dollar price of Big Macs in several countries. It then concludes that countries in which the Big Mac is cheaper (in U.S. dollars) than in the United States have "undervalued" currencies. Similarly, countries with Big Macs more expensive than in the United States have "overvalued" currencies. The table below shows the domestic-currency prices of Big Macs in various countries. It also shows the exchange rate, expressed as the number of units of domestic currency needed to purchase one U.S. dollar.

Country	Domestic Currency Price	Current Exchange Rate	U.S. Dollar Price
Canada	$ 2.75 (Cdn.)	1.52	$ —
Australia	$ 3.50 (Aus.)	1.85	$ —
U.S.A.	$ 2.25	1.00	$ —
Japan	375 yen	125	$ —
France	3.6 euros	1.15	$ —
U.K.	1.50 pounds	0.80	$ —

a. For each country, use the exchange rate provided to convert the domestic-currency price to the U.S.-dollar price.

b. By the logic used in *The Economist*, which currencies are overvalued and which are undervalued relative to the U.S. dollar?

c. Are Big Macs traded goods? If not, does this present a problem for *The Economist*? Explain.

d. Which of the following goods do you think would be a better candidate for this exercise? Explain your choice.
i) cement
ii) diamonds
iii) fresh fruit
iv) computer RAM chips

6. A former Canadian Prime Minister once suggested that Canada should try to have balanced trade, industry by industry.

a. Do you think this makes sense? Explain.

b. How about the idea of balanced trade, country by country? Explain whether this makes sense.

DISCUSSION QUESTIONS

1. What is the probable effect of each of the following on the exchange rate of a country, other things being equal?

a. The quantity of oil imports is greatly decreased, but the value of imported oil is higher due to price increases.

b. The country's inflation rate falls well below that of its trading partners.

c. Rising labour costs of the country's manufacturers lead to a worsening ability to compete in world markets.

d. The government greatly expands its gifts of food and machinery to developing countries.

e. A major boom occurs with rising employment.

f. The central bank raises interest rates sharply.

g. More domestic oil is discovered and developed.

2. Canada's trade surplus with the United States (or the U.S. trade deficit with Canada) is the cause of considerable concern to some U.S. politicians. Many economists, however, argue that U.S. policy makers should not be concerned with reducing the U.S. trade deficit with Canada primarily because there is no reason to expect a balance between any two countries. Comment on the need for policies to address the U.S. trade deficit with Canada.

3. Outline the reasoning behind the following 1989 newspaper headline: "Loonie strengthens as Bank of Canada raises rates."

4. "Under a flexible exchange rate system, no country need suffer unemployment, for if its prices are low enough, there will be more than enough demand to keep its factories and farms fully occupied." The evidence suggests that flexible exchange rates have not generally eliminated unemployment. Can you explain why? Can changing exchange rates ever cure unemployment?

5. On November 27, 1995, a letter to *The Globe and Mail* said that "the economy of this once wonderful country is in the sewer and the politicians keep on tinkering, not knowing how to fix it." The letter proposed a 20 percent depreciation of the Canadian dollar, and argued that the immediate effects would be (among other things):

   - a dramatic rise in exports
   - a dramatic fall in imports
   - a large net inflow of new foreign investment

   What do you think of the proposal? What would the Bank of Canada have to do to achieve a 20 percent depreciation of the Canadian dollar? If such a depreciation were to take place, is it possible to have the effects claimed by the author of the letter? Explain.

6. Many commentators are perplexed when they observe a depreciation of the Canadian dollar but not a reduction in the Canadian current account deficit. Explain why there is not a precise relationship between the value of the dollar and the current account balance. Give one example of an event that would give rise to each of the following:

   a. appreciation of the Canadian dollar and a fall in Canada's current account surplus.
   b. depreciation of the Canadian dollar and a fall in Canada's current account surplus.

7. Every few months, *The Economist* publishes its "Big Mac Index." Using the current exchange rates, it compares the U.S.-dollar price of Big Macs in several countries. It then concludes that countries in which the Big Mac is cheaper (in U.S. dollars) than in the United States have "undervalued" currencies. Similarly, countries with Big Macs more expensive than in the United States have "overvalued" currencies.

   a. Explain how the logic of this approach is based on the "law of one price."
   b. Are Big Macs traded goods? If not, does this present a problem for *The Economist*? Explain.

MATHEMATICAL NOTES

1. Because one cannot divide by zero, the ratio $\Delta Y/\Delta X$ cannot be evaluated when $\Delta X = 0$. However, as ΔX *approaches* zero, the ratio $\Delta Y/\Delta X$ increases without limit:

$$\lim_{\Delta X \to 0} \frac{\Delta Y}{\Delta X} = \infty$$

Therefore, we say that the slope of a vertical line (when $\Delta X = 0$ for any ΔY) is equal to infinity.

2. Many variables affect the quantity demanded. Using functional notation, the argument of the next several pages of the text can be anticipated. Let Q^D represent the quantity of a commodity demanded and

$$T, \overline{Y}, N, \hat{Y}, p, p_j$$

represent, respectively, tastes, average household income, population, income distribution, the commodity's own price, and the price of the jth other commodity.

The demand function is

$$Q^D = D(T, \overline{Y}, N, \hat{Y}, p, p_j), \qquad j = 1, 2, \ldots, n$$

The demand schedule or curve is given by

$$Q^D = d(p) \,\Big|\, T, \overline{Y}, N, \hat{Y}, p_j$$

where the notation means that the variables to the right of the vertical line are held constant.

This function is correctly described as the demand function with respect to price, all other variables being held constant. This function, often written concisely as $q^d = d(p)$, shifts in response to changes in other variables. Consider average income: if, as is usually hypothesized, $\partial Q^D/\partial \overline{Y} > 0$, then increases in average income shift $q^d = d(p)$ rightward and decreases in average income shift $q^d = d(p)$ leftward. Changes in other variables likewise shift this function in the direction implied by the relationship of that variable to the quantity demanded.

3. Quantity demanded is a simple and straightforward but frequently misunderstood concept in everyday use, but it has a clear mathematical meaning. It refers to the dependent variable in the demand function from note 2:

$$Q^D = D(T, \overline{Y}, N, \hat{Y}, p, p_j)$$

It takes on a specific value whenever a specific value is assigned to each of the independent variables. The value of Q^D changes whenever the value of any independent variable is changed. Q^D could change, for example, as a result of a change in any one price, in average income, in the distribution of income, in tastes, or in population. It could also change as a result of the net effect of changes in all of the independent variables occurring at once.

Some textbooks reserve the term *change in quantity demanded* for a movement along a demand curve, that is, a change in Q^D as a result *only* of a change in p. They then use other words for a change in Q^D caused by a change in the other variables in the demand function. This usage is potentially confusing because it gives the single variable Q^D more than one name.

Our usage, which corresponds to that in more advanced treatments, avoids this confusion. We call Q^D *quantity demanded* and refer to any change in Q^D as a *change in quantity demanded*. In this usage it is correct to say that a movement along a demand curve is a change in quantity demanded, but it is incorrect to say that a change in quantity demanded can occur *only because of* a movement along a demand curve (because Q^D can change for other reasons, for example, a *ceteris paribus* change in average household income).

4. Similar to the way we treated quantity demanded in note 2, let Q^S represent the quantity of a commodity supplied and

$$C, X, p, w_i$$

represent, respectively, producers' goals, technology, the product's price, and the price of the ith input.

The supply function is

$$Q^S = S(C, X, p, w_i), \qquad i = 1, 2, \ldots, m$$

The supply schedule or curve is given by

$$Q^S = s(p) \,\Big|\, C, X, w_i$$

This is the supply function with respect to price, all other variables being held constant. This function, often written concisely as $q^s = s(p)$, shifts in response to changes in other variables.

5. Equilibrium occurs where $Q^D = Q^S$. For *specified values of all other variables,* this requires that

$$d(p) = s(p) \qquad [5.1]$$

Equation 5.1 defines an equilibrium value of p; hence, although p is an *independent* or *exogenous* variable in each of the supply and demand functions, it is an *endogenous* variable in the economic model that imposes the equilibrium condition expressed in Equation 5.1. Price is endogenous because it is assumed to adjust to bring about equality between quantity demanded and quantity supplied. Equilibrium quantity, also an endogenous variable, is determined by substituting the equilibrium price into either $d(p)$ or $s(p)$.

Graphically, Equation 5.1 is satisfied only at the point where the demand and supply curves intersect. Thus, supply and demand curves are said to determine the equilibrium values of the endogenous variables, price and quantity. A shift in any of the independent variables held constant in the d and s functions will shift the demand or supply curves and lead to different equilibrium values for price and quantity.

6. The definition in the text uses finite changes and is called *arc elasticity.* The parallel definition using derivatives is

$$\eta = \frac{dq}{dp} \cdot \frac{p}{q}$$

and is called *point elasticity.* Further discussion appears in the Appendix to Chapter 4.

7. The propositions in the text are proved as follows. Letting *TE* stand for total expenditure, we can write

$$TE = p \cdot q$$

It follows that the change in total expenditure is

$$dTE = q \cdot dp + p \cdot dq \qquad [7.1]$$

Multiplying and dividing both terms on the right-hand side of Equation 7.1 by $p \cdot q$ yields

$$dTE = \left[\frac{dp}{p} + \frac{dq}{q} \right] \cdot (p \cdot q)$$

Because dp and dq are opposite in sign as we move along the demand curve, dTE will have the same sign as the term in brackets on the right-hand side that dominates—that is, on which percentage change is largest.

A second way of arranging Equation 7.1 is to divide both sides by dp to get

$$\frac{dTE}{dp} = q + p \cdot \frac{dq}{dp} \qquad [7.2]$$

From the definition of point elasticity in note 6, however,

$$q \cdot \eta = p \cdot \frac{dq}{dp} \qquad [7.3]$$

which we can substitute into Equation 7.1 to obtain

$$\frac{dTE}{dp} = q + q \cdot \eta = q \cdot (1 + \eta) \qquad [7.4]$$

Because η is a negative number, the sign of the right-hand side of Equation 7.4 is negative if the absolute value of η exceeds unity (elastic demand) and positive if it is less than unity (inelastic demand).

Total expenditure is maximized when dTE/dp is equal to zero. As can be seen from Equation 7.4, this occurs when elasticity is equal to -1.

8. The axis reversal arose in the following way. Alfred Marshall (1842–1924) theorized in terms of "demand price" and "supply price," these being the prices that would lead to a given quantity being demanded or supplied. Thus,

$$p^d = d(q) \qquad [8.1]$$
$$p^s = s(q) \qquad [8.2]$$

and the condition of equilibrium is

$$d(q) = s(q)$$

When graphing the behavioural relationships expressed in Equations 8.1 and 8.2, Marshall naturally put the independent variable, $q,$ on the horizontal axis.

Leon Walras (1834–1910), whose formulation of the working of a competitive market has become the accepted one, focused on quantity demanded and quantity supplied *at a given price.* Thus,

$$q^d = d(p)$$

$$q^s = s(p)$$

and the condition of equilibrium is

$$d(p) = s(p)$$

Walras did not use graphical representation. Had he done so, he would surely have placed p (his independent variable) on the horizontal axis.

Marshall, among his other influences on later generations of economists, was the great popularizer of graphical analysis in economics. Today, we use his graphs, even for Walras's analysis. The axis reversal is thus one of those historical accidents that seem odd to people who did not live through the "perfectly natural" sequence of steps that produced it.

9. The distinction made between an incremental change and a marginal change is the distinction for the function $Y = Y(X)$ between $\Delta Y/\Delta X$ and the derivative dY/dX. The latter is the limit of the former as ΔX approaches zero. We shall meet this distinction repeatedly—in this chapter in reference to marginal and incremental *utility* and in later chapters with respect to such concepts as marginal and incremental *product, cost,* and *revenue.* Where Y is a function of more than one variable—for example, $Y = f(X, Z)$—the marginal relationship between Y and X is the partial derivative $\partial Y/\partial X$ rather than the total derivative, dY/dX.

10. The hypothesis of diminishing marginal utility requires that we can measure utility of consumption by a function

$$U = U(X_1, X_2, \ldots, X_n)$$

where $X_1, \ldots, X_n$ are quantities of the n goods consumed by a household. It really embodies two utility hypotheses: first,

$$\partial U/\partial X_i > 0$$

which says that the consumer can get more utility by increasing consumption of the commodity; second,

$$\partial^2 U/\partial X_i^2 < 0$$

which says that the utility of *additional* consumption of some good declines as the amount of that good consumed increases.

11. Because the slope of the indifference curve is negative, it is the absolute value of the slope that de-clines as one moves downward to the right along the curve. The algebraic value, of course, increases. The phrase *diminishing marginal rate of substitution* thus refers to the absolute, not the algebraic, value of the slope.

12. The relationship between the slope of the budget line and relative prices can be seen as follows. In the two-good example, a change in expenditure (ΔE) is given by the equation

$$\Delta E = p_C \cdot \Delta C + p_F \cdot \Delta F \qquad [12.1]$$

Expenditure is constant for all combinations of F and C that lie on the same budget line. Thus, along such a line we have $\Delta E = 0$. This implies

$$p_C \cdot \Delta C + p_F \cdot \Delta F = 0 \qquad [12.2]$$

and thus

$$-\Delta C/\Delta F = p_F/p_C \qquad [12.3]$$

The ratio $-\Delta C/\Delta F$ is the slope of the budget line. It is negative because, with a fixed budget, one must consume less C in order to consume more F. In other words, Equation 12.3 says that the negative of the slope of the budget line is the ratio of the absolute prices (i.e., the relative price). Although prices do not show directly in Figure 6A-3, they are implicit in the budget line: Its slope depends solely on the relative price, while its position, given a fixed money income, depends on the absolute prices of the two goods.

13. *Marginal product,* as defined in the text, is really *incremental* product. More advanced treatments distinguish between this notion and marginal product as the limit of the ratio as ΔL approaches zero. Marginal product thus measures the rate at which total product is changing as one factor is varied and is the partial derivative of the total product with respect to the variable factor. In symbols,

$$MP = \frac{\partial TP}{\partial L}$$

14. We have referred specifically both to diminishing *marginal* product and to diminishing *average* product. In most cases, eventually diminishing marginal product implies eventually diminishing average product. This is, however, not necessary, as the accompanying figure shows.

In this case, marginal product diminishes after v units of the variable factor are employed. Because marginal product falls toward, but never quite reaches, a value of m, average product rises continually toward, but never quite reaches, the same value.

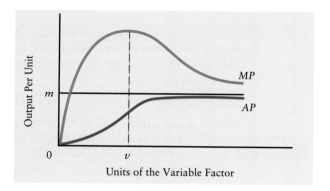

Output Per Unit

m

MP

AP

0

v

Units of the Variable Factor

15. Let q be the quantity of output and L the quantity of the variable factor. In the short run,

$$TP = q = f(L) \qquad [15.1]$$

We now define

$$AP = \frac{q}{L} = \frac{f(L)}{L} \qquad [15.2]$$

$$MP = \frac{dq}{dL} \qquad [15.3]$$

We are concerned with the relationship between these two. Where average product is rising, at a maximum, or falling is determined by its derivative with respect to L:

$$\frac{d(q/L)}{dL} = \frac{L \cdot (dq/dL) - q}{L^2} \qquad [15.4]$$

This may be rewritten

$$\frac{1}{L} \cdot \left[\frac{dq}{dL} - \frac{q}{L} \right] = \frac{1}{L} \cdot (MP - AP) \qquad [15.5]$$

Clearly, when MP is greater than AP, the expression in Equation 15.5 is positive and thus AP is rising. When MP is less than AP, AP is falling. When they are equal, AP is neither rising nor falling.

16. The text defines *incremental cost*. Strictly, marginal cost is the rate of change of total cost with respect to output, q. Thus,

$$MC = \frac{dTC}{dq}$$

From the definitions, $TC = TFC + TVC$. Fixed costs are not a function of output. Thus, we may write $TC = Z + f(q)$, where $f(q)$ is total variable costs and Z is a constant. From this we see that $MC = df(q)/dq$. MC is thus independent of the size of the fixed costs.

17. This point is easily seen if a little algebra is used:

$$AVC = \frac{TVC}{q}$$

but note that $TVC = L \cdot w$ and $q = AP \cdot L$, where L is the quantity of the variable factor used and w is its cost per unit. Therefore,

$$AVC = \frac{L \cdot w}{AP \cdot L} = \frac{w}{AP}$$

Because w is a constant, it follows that AVC and AP vary inversely with each other, and when AP is at its maximum value, AVC must be at its minimum value.

18. A little elementary calculus will prove the point:

$$MC = \frac{dTC}{dq} = \frac{dTVC}{dq} = \frac{d(L \cdot w)}{dq}$$

If w does not vary with output,

$$MC = \frac{dL}{dq} \cdot w$$

However, referring to note 15 (Equation 15.3), we see that

$$\frac{dL}{dq} = \frac{1}{MP}$$

Thus,

$$MC = \frac{w}{MP}$$

Because w is fixed, MC varies negatively with MP. When MP is at a maximum, MC is at a minimum.

19. Strictly speaking, the marginal rate of substitution refers to the slope of the tangent to the isoquant at a particular point, whereas the calculations in Table 8A-1 refer to the average rate of substitution between two distinct points on the isoquant. Assume a production function

$$Q = Q(K,L) \qquad [19.1]$$

Isoquants are given by the function

$$K = I(L, \overline{Q}) \qquad [19.2]$$

derived from Equation 19.1 by expressing K as an explicit function of L and Q. A single isoquant relates to a particular level of output, Q. Define Q_K and Q_L as an alternative, more compact notation for $\partial Q/\partial K$ and $\partial Q/\partial L$, the marginal products of capital and labour. Also, let Q_{KK} and Q_{LL} stand for $\partial^2 Q/\partial K^2$ and $\partial^2 Q/\partial L^2$, respectively. To obtain the slope of the isoquant, totally differentiate Equation 19.1 to obtain

$$dQ = Q_K \cdot dK + Q_L \cdot dL$$

Then, because we are moving along a single isoquant, set $dQ = 0$ to obtain

$$\frac{dK}{dL} = -\frac{Q_L}{Q_K} = MRS$$

Diminishing marginal productivity implies $Q_{LL} < 0$ and $Q_{KK} < 0$, and hence, as we move down the isoquant of Figure 8A-1, Q_K is rising and Q_L is falling, so the absolute value of MRS is diminishing. This is called the *hypothesis of a diminishing marginal rate of substitution*.

20. Formally, the problem is to maximize

$$Q = Q(K,L)$$

subject to the constraint

$$p_K \cdot K + p_L \cdot L = C$$

To do this, form the Lagrangean,

$$\mathcal{L} = Q(K, L) - \lambda(p_K \cdot K + p_L \cdot L - C)$$

The first-order conditions for this maximization problem are

$$Q_K = \lambda \cdot p_K \qquad [20.1]$$
$$Q_L = \lambda \cdot p_L \qquad [20.2]$$
$$p_K \cdot K + p_L \cdot L = C \qquad [20.3]$$

Dividing Equation 20.1 by Equation 20.2 yields

$$\frac{Q_K}{Q_L} = \frac{p_K}{p_L}$$

That is, the ratio of the marginal products, which is -1 times the MRS, is equal to the ratio of the factor prices, which is -1 times the slope of the isocost line.

21. Marginal revenue is mathematically the derivative of total revenue with respect to output, dTR/dq. Incremental revenue is $\Delta TR/\Delta q$. However, the term *marginal revenue* is used loosely to refer to both concepts.

22. For notes 22 through 24, it is helpful first to define some terms. Let

$$\pi_n = TR_n - TC_n$$

where π_n is the profit when n units are sold.

If the firm is maximizing its profits by producing n units, it is necessary that the profits at output q_n be at least as large as the profits at output zero. If the firm is maximizing its profits at output n, then

$$\pi_n \geq \pi_0 \qquad [22.1]$$

The condition says that profits from producing must be greater than profits from not producing. Condition 22.1 can be rewritten as

$$TR_n - TVC_n - TFC_n \geq TR_0 - TVC_0 - TFC_0 \qquad [22.2]$$

However, note that by definition

$$TR_0 = 0 \qquad [22.3]$$
$$TVC_0 = 0 \qquad [22.4]$$
$$TFC_n = TFC_0 = Z \qquad [22.5]$$

where Z is a constant. By substituting Equations 22.3, 22.4, and 22.5 into Condition 22.2, we get

$$TR_n - TVC_n \geq 0$$

from which we obtain

$$TR_n \geq TVC_n$$

This proves Rule 1.

On a per-unit basis, it becomes

$$\frac{TR_n}{q_n} \geq \frac{TVC_n}{q_n} \qquad [22.6]$$

where q_n is the number of units produced.

Because $TR_n = q_n \cdot p_n$, where p_n is the price when n units are sold, Condition 22.6 may be rewritten as

$$p_n \geq AVC_n$$

23. Using elementary calculus, we may prove Rule 2.

$$\pi_n = TR_n - TC_n$$

each of which is a function of output q. To maximize π, it is necessary that

$$\frac{d\pi}{dq} = 0 \qquad [23.1]$$

and that

$$\frac{d^2\pi}{dq^2} < 0 \qquad [23.2]$$

From the definitions,

$$\frac{d\pi}{dq} = \frac{dTR}{dq} - \frac{dTC}{dq} = MR - MC \quad [23.3]$$

From Equations 23.1 and 23.3, a necessary condition for attaining maximum π is $MR - MC = 0$, or $MR = MC$, as is required by Rule 2.

24. To prove that for a negatively sloped demand curve, marginal revenue is less than price, let $p = p(q)$. Then

$$TR = p \cdot q = p(q) \cdot q$$

$$MR = \frac{dTR}{dq} = q \cdot \frac{dp}{dq} + p$$

For a negatively sloped demand curve, dp/dq is negative, and thus MR is less than price for positive values of q.

25. The equation for a downward-sloping straight-line demand curve with price on the vertical axis is

$$p = a - b \cdot q$$

where $-b$ is the slope of the demand curve. Total revenue is price times quantity:

$$TR = p \cdot q = a \cdot q - b \cdot q^2$$

Marginal revenue is

$$MR = \frac{dTR}{dq} = a - 2 \cdot b \cdot q$$

Thus, the MR curve and the demand curve are both straight lines, and the (absolute value of the) slope of the MR curve ($2b$) is twice that of the demand curve (b).

26. The marginal revenue produced by the factor involves two elements: first, the additional output that an extra unit of the factor makes possible and, second, the change in price of the product that the extra output causes. Let Q be output, R revenue, and L the number of units of labour hired. The contribution to revenue of additional labour is $\partial R / \partial L$. This, in turn, depends on the contribution of the extra labour to output $\partial Q / \partial L$ (the marginal product of the factor) and $\partial R / \partial Q$ (the firm's marginal revenue from the extra output). Thus,

$$\frac{\partial R}{\partial L} = \frac{\partial Q}{\partial L} \cdot \frac{\partial R}{\partial Q}$$

We define the left-hand side as marginal revenue product, MRP. Thus,

$$MRP = MP \cdot MR$$

27. The proposition that the marginal labour cost is above the average labour cost when the average is rising is essentially the same proposition proved in note 15. Nevertheless, let us do it again, using elementary calculus.

The quantity of labour supplied depends on the wage rate: $L^s = f(w)$. Total labour cost along the supply curve is $w \cdot L^s$. The average cost of labour is $(w \cdot L^s) / L^s = w$. The marginal cost of labour is

$$\frac{d(w \cdot L^s)}{dL^s} = w + L^s \cdot \frac{dw}{dL^s}$$

Rewrite this as

$$MC = AC + L \cdot \frac{dw}{dL^s}$$

As long as the supply curve slopes upward, $dw/dL^s > 0$; therefore, $MC > AC$.

28. In general, for any growth rate per unit of time, g, and starting value, P_0, the price level at time t will be $P_0(1 + g)^t$. This is the formula for *compound* growth at rate g per unit of time. For small values of g, $(1 + g)^t$ will be very close to $(1 + tg)$. But as g gets larger, so does the difference. For example, if prices are growing at 2 percent per month, the annual growth will be $(1.02)^{12} = 1.268$, yielding a growth rate of 26.8 percent per year. This is considerably more than 24 percent, which is just the monthly rate times 12. Generally, annual rates of growth are calculated by compounding rates of growth that are measured over shorter or longer periods than one year.

29. In the text, we define MPC as an incremental ratio. For mathematical treatment, it is sometimes convenient to define all marginal concepts as derivatives: $MPC = dC/dY_D$, $MPS = dS/dY_D$, and so on.

30. The basic relationship is

$$Y_D = C + S$$

Dividing through by Y_D yields

$$\frac{Y_D}{Y_D} = \frac{C}{Y_D} + \frac{S}{Y_D}$$

and thus

$$1 = APC + APS$$

Next, take the first difference of the basic relationship to get

$$\Delta Y_D = \Delta C + \Delta S$$

Dividing through by ΔY_D gives

$$\frac{\Delta Y_D}{\Delta Y_D} = \frac{\Delta C}{\Delta Y_D} + \frac{\Delta S}{\Delta Y_D}$$

and thus

$$1 = MPC + MPS$$

31. The total expenditure over all rounds is the sum of an infinite series. If we let A stand for autonomous expenditure and z for the marginal propensity to spend, the change in autonomous expenditure is ΔA in the first round, $z \cdot \Delta A$ in the second, $z^2 \cdot \Delta A$ in the third, and so on. This can be written as

$$\Delta A \cdot (1 + z + z^2 + \ldots + z^n)$$

If z is less than 1, the series in parentheses converges to $1/(1 - z)$ as n approaches infinity. The total change in expenditure is thus $\Delta A/(1 - z)$. In the example in the box, $z = 0.80$; therefore, the change in total expenditure is five times ΔA.

32. This is easily proved. The banking system wants sufficient deposits (D) to establish the target ratio (v) of deposits to reserves (R). This gives $R/D = v$. Any change in D of size ΔD has to be accompanied by a change in R of ΔR of sufficient size to restore v. Thus, $\Delta R/\Delta D = v$, so $\Delta D = \Delta R/v$ and $\Delta D/\Delta R = 1/v$. This can be shown also in terms of the deposits created by the sequence in Table 26-7.

Let v be the reserve ratio and $e = 1 - v$ be the excess reserves per dollar of new deposits. If X dollars are initially deposited in the system, the successive rounds of new deposits will be X, eX, e^2X, e^3X, ... The series

$$X + eX + e^2X + e^3X + \ldots$$
$$= X \cdot [1 + e + e^2 + e^3 + \ldots]$$

has a limit of $X \cdot \dfrac{1}{1 - e}$

$$= X \cdot \frac{1}{1 - (1 - v)} = \frac{X}{v}$$

This is the total new deposits created by an injection of \$$X$ of new reserves into the banking system. For example, when $v = 0.20$, an injection of \$100 into the system will lead to an overall increase in deposits of \$500.

33. Suppose that the public wishes to hold a fraction, c, of deposits in cash, C. Now suppose that X dollars are injected into the system. Ultimately, this money will be held either as reserves by the banking system or as cash by the public. Thus, we have

$$\Delta C + \Delta R = X$$

From the banking system's reserve behaviour, we have $\Delta R = v \cdot \Delta D$, and from the public's cash behaviour, we have $\Delta C = c \cdot \Delta D$. Substituting into the above equation, we get the result that

$$\Delta D = \frac{X}{v + c}$$

From this we can also relate the change in reserves and the change in cash holdings to the initial injection:

$$\Delta R = \frac{v}{v + c} \cdot X$$

$$\Delta C = \frac{c}{v + c} \cdot X$$

For example, when $v = 0.20$ and $c = 0.05$, an injection of \$100 will lead to an increase in reserves of \$80, an increase in cash in the hands of the public of \$20, and an increase in deposits of \$400.

34. Let $L(Y,r)$ give the real demand for money measured in purchasing power units. Let M be the

supply of money measured in nominal units and P the price level, so that M/P is the real supply of money. Now the equilibrium condition requiring equality between the demand for money and the supply of money can be expressed in real terms as

$$L(Y, r) = \frac{M}{P} \qquad [36.1]$$

or in nominal terms by multiplying through by P,

$$P \cdot L(Y, r) = M \qquad [36.2]$$

In Equation 36.1, a rise in P disturbs equilibrium by lowering M/P, and in Equation 36.2, it disturbs equilibrium by raising $P \cdot L(Y, r)$.

35. This is based on what is called the "rule of 72". Any sum growing at the rate of X percent per year will double in approximately $72/X$ years. For two sums growing at the rates of X percent and Y percent per year, the *difference* between the two sums will double in approximately $72/(X - Y)$ years.

36. The time taken to break even is a function of the *difference* in growth rates, not their *levels*. Thus, if 4 percent and 5 percent or 5 percent and 6 percent had been used in the example, it still would have taken the same number of years. To see this quickly, recognize that we are interested in the ratio of two growth paths:

$$\frac{e^{r_1 t}}{e^{r_2 t}} = e^{(r_1 - r_2)t}$$

37. A simple example of a production function is GDP $= z(LK)^{1/2}$. This equation says that to find the amount of GDP produced, multiply the amount of labour by the amount of capital, take the square root, and multiply the result by the constant z. This production function has positive but diminishing marginal returns to either factor. This can be seen by evaluating the first and second partial derivatives and showing the first derivatives to be positive and the second derivatives to be negative.

For example,

$$\frac{\partial \text{GDP}}{\partial K} = \frac{z \cdot L^{1/2}}{2 \cdot K^{1/2}} > 0$$

and

$$\frac{\partial^2 \text{GDP}}{\partial K^2} = -\frac{z \cdot L^{1/2}}{2 \cdot K^{3/2}} < 0$$

38. The production function GDP $= z(LK)^{1/2}$ displays contant returns to scale. To see this, multiply both L and K by the same constant, θ, and see that this multiplies the whole value of GDP by θ:

$$z(\theta L \cdot \theta K)^{1/2} = z(\theta^2 \cdot LK)^{1/2} = \theta z(LK)^{1/2} = \theta \cdot \text{GDP}$$

Time Line of Great Economists

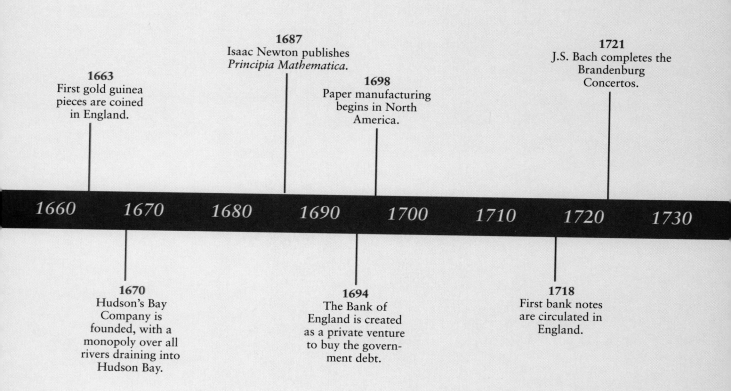

1663
First gold guinea pieces are coined in England.

1687
Isaac Newton publishes *Principia Mathematica*.

1698
Paper manufacturing begins in North America.

1721
J.S. Bach completes the Brandenburg Concertos.

1660 1670 1680 1690 1700 1710 1720 1730

1670
Hudson's Bay Company is founded, with a monopoly over all rivers draining into Hudson Bay.

1694
The Bank of England is created as a private venture to buy the government debt.

1718
First bank notes are circulated in England.

A D A M   S M I T H *(1723–1790)*

Adam Smith was born in 1723 in the small Scottish town of Kirkcaldy. He is perhaps the single most influential figure in the development of modern economics, and even those who have never studied economics know of his most famous work, *The Wealth of Nations*, and of the terms *laissez faire* and the *invisible hand*, both attributable to Smith. He was able to describe the workings of the capitalist market economy, the division of labor in production, the role of money, free trade, and the nature of economic growth. Even today, the breadth of his scholarship is considered astounding.

Smith was raised by his mother, as his father had died before his birth. His intellectual promise was discovered early, and at age 14 Smith was sent to study at Glasgow and then at Oxford. He then returned to an appointment as professor of moral philosophy at University of Glasgow, where he became one of the leading philosophers of his day. He lectured on natural theology, ethics, jurisprudence, and political economy to students who traveled from as far away as Russia to hear his lectures.

In 1759, Smith published *The Theory of Moral Sentiments*, in which he attempted to identify the origins of moral judgment. In this early work, Smith writes of the motivation of self-interest and of the morality that keeps it in check. After its publication, Smith left his post at the University of Glasgow to embark on a European tour as the tutor to a young aristocrat, the Duke of Buccleuch, with whom he traveled for two years. In exchange for this assignment Smith was provided with a salary for the remainder of his life. He returned to the small town of his birth and spent the next 10 years alone, writing his most famous work.

An Inquiry into the Nature and Causes of the Wealth of Nations was published in 1776. His contributions in this book (generally known as *The Wealth of Nations)* were revolutionary, and the text became the foundation of much of modern economics. It continues to be reprinted today. Smith rejected the notion that a country's supply of gold and silver was the measure of its wealth—rather, it was the real incomes of the people that determined national wealth. Growth in the real incomes of the country's citizens—that is, economic growth—would result from specialization in production, the division of labor, and the use of money to facilitate trade. Smith provided a framework for analyzing the questions of income growth, value, and distribution.

Smith's work marked the beginning of what is called the Classical period in economic thought, which continued for the next 75 years. This school of thought was centered on the principles of natural liberty (laissez faire) and the importance of economic growth as a means of bettering the conditions of human existence.

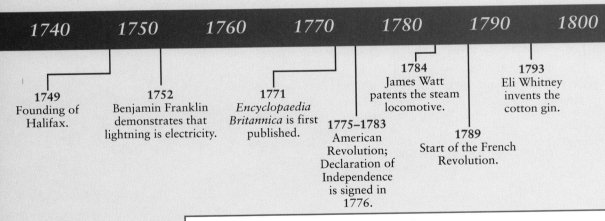

1740   **1750**   **1760**   **1770**   **1780**   **1790**   **1800**

1749
Founding of
Halifax.

1752
Benjamin Franklin
demonstrates that
lightning is electricity.

1771
*Encyclopaedia
Britannica* is first
published.

1775–1783
American
Revolution;
Declaration of
Independence
is signed in
1776.

1784
James Watt
patents the steam
locomotive.

1789
Start of the French
Revolution.

1793
Eli Whitney
invents the
cotton gin.

T H O M A S   M A L T H U S *(1766–1834)*

Thomas Malthus was born into a reasonably well-to-do English family. He was educated at Cambridge and from 1805 until his death he held the first British professorship of political economy in the East India Company's college at Haileybury. In 1798 he published *An Essay on the Principle of Population as It Affects the Future Improvement of Society*, which was revised many times in subsequent years until finally he published *A Summary View of the Principle of Population* in 1830.

It is these essays on population for which Malthus is best known. His first proposition was that population, when unchecked, would increase in a geometric progression such that the population would double every 25 years. His second proposition was that the means of subsistence (i.e. the food supply) cannot possibly increase faster than in arithmetic progression (increasing by a given number of units every year). The result would be population growth eventually outstripping food production, and thus abject poverty and suffering for the majority of people in every society.

Malthus's population theory had tremendous intellectual influence at the time and became an integral part of the Classical theory of income distribution. However, it is no longer taken as a good description of current or past trends.

DAVID RICARDO *(1772–1823)*

David Ricardo was born in London to parents who had immigrated from the Netherlands. Ricardo's father was very successful in money markets, and Ricardo himself had earned enough money on the stock exchange that he was very wealthy before he was 30. He had little formal education, but after reading Adam Smith's *The Wealth of Nations* in 1799, he chose to divide his time between studying and writing about political economy and increasing his own personal wealth.

Ricardo's place in the history of economics was assured by his achievement in constructing an abstract model of how capitalism worked. He built an analytic "system" using deductive reasoning that characterizes economic theorizing to the present day. The three critical principles in Ricardo's system were (1) the theory of rent, (2) Thomas Malthus's population principle, and (3) the wages-fund doctrine. Ricardo published *The Principles of Political Economy and Taxation* in 1817, which dominated Classical economics for the following half-century.

Ricardo also contributed the concept of comparative advantage to the study of international trade. Ricardo's theories regarding the gains from trade had some influence on the repeal of the British Corn Laws in 1846—tariffs on the importation of grains into Great Britain—and the subsequent transformation of that country during the nineteenth century from a country of high tarrifs to one of completely free trade.

1814
British forces burn
Washington, D.C., in the
War of 1812.

1831
The first horse-
drawn buses
appear in
New York.

1837
Victoria becomes
Queen of England
(until 1901).
Rebellions in
Upper and Lower
Canada.

1800   1810   1820   1830

1805
Admiral Horatio
Nelson's victory
(and death)
at Trafalgar.

1815
Napoleon
defeated at Waterloo
and exiled to
St. Helena;
Corn Laws passed
in Britain.

1822
First textile
mills are built
in Lowell,
Massachusetts.

JOHN STUART MILL *(1806–1873)*

John Stuart Mill, born in London, was the son of James Mill, a prominent British historian, economist, and philosopher. By age 12 he was acquainted with the major economics works of the day, and at 13 he was correcting the proofs of his father's book, *Elements of Political Economy*. J. S. Mill spent most of his life working at the East India Company—his extraordinarily prolific writing career was conducted entirely as an aside. In 1848 he published his *Principles of Political Economy*, which updated the principles found in Adam Smith's *The Wealth of Nations* and which remained the basic textbook for students of economics until the end of the nineteenth century. In *Principles*, Mill made an important contribution to the economics discipline by distinguishing between the economics of production and of distribution. He pointed out that economic laws had nothing to do with the distribution of wealth, which was a societal matter, but had everything to do with production.

Previous to Mill's *Principles* was his *System of Logic* (1843), which was the century's most influential text on logic and the theory of knowledge. His essays on ethics, contemporary culture, and freedom of speech, such as *Utilitarianism* and *On Liberty*, are still widely studied today.

KARL MARX *(1818–1883)*

Karl Marx was born in Trier, Germany (then part of Prussia), and studied law, history, and philosophy at the universities of Bonn, Berlin, and Jena. Marx traveled between Prussia, Paris, and Brussels, working at various jobs until finally settling in London in 1849, where he lived the remainder of his life. Most of his time was spent in the mainly unpaid pursuits of writing and studying economics in the library of the British Museum. Marx's contributions to economics are intricately bound to his views of history and society. *The Communist Manifesto* was published with Friedrich Engels in 1848, his *Critique of Political Economy* in 1859, and in 1867 the first volume of *Das Kapital*. (The remaining volumes, edited by Engels, were published after Marx's death.)

For Marx, capitalism was a stage in an evolutionary process from a primitive agricultural economy toward an inevitable elimination of private property and the class structure. Marx's "labor theory of value," whereby the quantity of labor used in the manufacture of a product determined its value, held the central place in his economic thought. He believed that the worker provided "surplus value" to the capitalist. The capitalist would then use the profit arising from this surplus value to reinvest in plant and machinery. Through time, more would be spent for plant and machinery than for wages, which would lead to lower profits (since profits arose only from the surplus value from labor) and a resulting squeeze in the real income of workers. Marx believed that in the capitalists' effort to maintain profits in this unstable system, there would emerge a "reserve army of the unemployed." The resulting class conflict would become increasingly acute until revolution by the workers would overthrow capitalism.

1859
Charles Darwin publishes *On the Origin of Species*.

1846
Britain repeals the Corn Laws.

1867
British North America Act establishes the Dominion of Canada. Alfred Nobel invents dynamite.

1840   1850   1860   1870

1844
Electric telegraph opens between Washington and Baltimore.

1861–1865
The U.S. Civil War; Abraham Lincoln is assassinated in 1865.

1869
Opening of the Suez Canal.

1840
Act of Union unites Upper and Lower Canada.

LEON WALRAS *(1834–1910)*

Leon Walras was born in France, the son of an economist. After being trained inauspiciously in engineering and performing poorly in mathematics, Walras spent some time pursuing other endeavors, such as novel writing and working for the railway. Eventually he promised his father he would study economics, and by 1870 he was given a professorship in economics in the Faculty of Law at the University of Lausanne in Switzerland. Once there, Walras began the feverish activity that eventually led to his important contributions to economic theory.

In the 1870s, Walras was one of three economists to put forward the marginal utility theory of value (simultaneously with William Stanley Jevons of England and Carl Menger of Austria). Further, he constructed a mathematical model of general equilibrium using a system of simultaneous equations that he used to argue that equilibrium prices and quantities are uniquely determined. Central to general equilibrium analysis is the notion that the prices and quantities of all commodities are determined simultaneously because the whole system is interdependent. Walras's most important work was *Elements of Pure Economics*, published in 1874. In addition to all of Walras's other accomplishments in economics (and despite his early poor performance in mathematics!), we today regard him as the founder of mathematical economics.

Leon Walras and Alfred Marshall are regarded by many economists to be the two most important economic theorists who ever lived. Much of the framework of economic theory studied today is either Walrasian or Marshallian in character.

CARL MENGER (1840–1921)

Carl Menger was born in Galicia (then part of Austria), and he came from a family of Austrian civil servants and army officers. After studying law in Prague and Vienna, he turned to economics and in 1871 published *Grundsatze der Volkswirtschaftslehre* (translated as *Principles of Economics*), for which he became famous. He held a professorship at the University of Vienna until 1903. Menger was the founder of a school of thought known as the "Austrian School," which effectively displaced the German historical method on the continent and which survives today as an alternative to mainstream Neoclassical economics.

Menger was one of three economists in the 1870s who independently put forward a theory of value based on marginal utility. Prior to what economists now call the "marginal revolution," value was thought to be derived solely from the inputs of labor and capital. Menger developed the marginal utility theory of value, in which the value of any good is determined by individuals' subjective evaluations of that good. According to Menger, a good has some value if it has the ability to satisfy some human want or desire, and *utility* is the capacity of the good to do so. Menger went on to develop the idea that the individual will maximize total utility at the point where the last unit of each good consumed provides equal utility—that is, where marginal utilities are equal.

Menger's emphasis on the marginal utility theory of value led him to focus on consumption rather than production as the determinant of price. Menger focused only on the demand for goods and largely ignored the supply. It would remain for Alfred Marshall and Leon Walras to combine demand and supply for a more complete picture of price determination.

1871
The Great Fire destroys much of Chicago.

1876
Alexander Graham Bell invents the telephone and founds Bell Telephone Co.

1880
Thomas Edison invents the electric light bulb.

1885
The last spike is driven on the Canadian Pacific Railway. Louis Riel is hanged.

1870   1875   1880   1885

ALFRED MARSHALL (1842–1924)

Alfred Marshall was born in Clapham, England, the son of a bank cashier, and was descended from a long line of clerics. Marshall's father, despite intense effort, was unable to steer the young Marshall into the church. Instead, Marshall followed his passion for mathematics at Cambridge and chose economics as a field of study after reading J. S. Mill's *Principles of Political Economy*. His career was then spent mainly at Cambridge, where he taught economics to John Maynard Keynes, Arthur Pigou, Joan Robinson, and countless other British theorists in the "Cambridge tradition." His *Principles of Economics,* published in 1890, replaced Mill's *Principles* as the dominant economics textbook of English-speaking universities.

Marshall institutionalized modern marginal analysis, the basic concepts of supply and demand, and perhaps most importantly the notion of economic equilibrium resulting from the interaction of supply and demand. He also pioneered partial equilibrium analysis—examining the forces of supply and demand in a particular market provided that all other influences can be excluded, *ceteris paribus.*

Although many of the ideas had been put forward by previous writers, Marshall was able to synthesize the previous analyses of utility and cost and present a thorough and complete statement of the laws of demand and supply. Marshall refined and developed microeconomic theory to such a degree that much of what he wrote would be familiar to students of this textbook today.

It is also interesting to note that although Alfred Marshall and Leon Walras were simultaneously expanding the frontiers of economic theory, there was almost no communication between the two men. Though Marshall chose partial equilibrium analysis as the appropriate method for dealing with selected markets in a complex world, he did acknowledge the correctness of Walras's general equilibrium system. Walras, on the other hand, was adamant (and sometimes rude) in his opposition to the methods that Marshall was putting forward. History has shown that both the partial and the general equilibrium approaches to economic analysis are required for understanding the functioning of the economy.

THORSTEIN VEBLEN (1857–1929)

Thorstein Veblen was born on a farm in Wisconsin to Norwegian parents. He received his Ph.D. in philosophy from Yale University, after which he returned to his father's farm because he was unable to secure an academic position. For seven years he remained there, reading voraciously on economics and other social sciences. Eventually, he took academic positions at the University of Chicago, Stanford University, the University of Missouri, and the New School for Social Research (in New York). Veblen was the founder of "institutional economics," the only uniquely North American school of economic thought.

In 1899, Veblen published *The Theory of the Leisure Class,* in which he sought to apply Charles Darwin's evolutionism to the study of modern economic life. He examined problems in the social institutions of the day, and savagely criticized Classical and Neoclassical economic analysis. Although Veblen failed to shift the path of mainstream economic analysis, he did contribute the idea of the importance of long-run institutional studies as a useful complement to short-run price theory analysis. He also reminded the profession that economics is a *social* science, and not merely a branch of mathematics.

Veblen remains most famous today for his idea of "conspicuous consumption." He observed that some commodities were consumed not for their intrinsic qualities but because they carried snob appeal. He suggested that the more expensive such a commodity became, the greater might be its ability to confer status on its purchaser.

1896
First modern Olympic Games are held in Athens. Klondike Gold Rush begins.

1898
Spanish-American War.

1900
J.P. Morgan buys out Andrew Carnegie, forming the biggest business in the world, U.S. Steel.

1890   1895   1900   1905

1889
Gustave Eiffel designs the Eiffel Tower for the Paris World Exposition.

1903
The Wright Brothers' first successful flight.

VILFREDO PARETO (1848–1923)

Vilfredo Pareto was an Italian, born in Paris, and was trained to be an engineer. Though he actually practiced as an engineer, he would later succeed Leon Walras to the Chair of Economics in the Faculty of Law at the University of Lausanne.

Pareto built upon the system of general equilibrium that Walras had developed. In his *Cours d'économie politique* (1897) and his *Manuel d'économie politique* (1906) Pareto set forth the foundations of modern welfare economics. He showed that theories of consumer behavior and exchange could be constructed on assumptions of ordinal utility, rather than cardinal utility, eliminating the need to compare one person's utility with another's. Using the indifference curve analysis developed by F. Y. Edgeworth, Pareto was able to demonstrate that total welfare could be increased by an exchange if one person could be made better off without anyone else becoming worse off. Pareto applied this analysis to consumption and exchange, as well as to production. Pareto's contributions in this area are remembered in economists' references to *Pareto optimality* and *Pareto efficiency*.

JOSEPH SCHUMPETER *(1883–1950)*

Joseph Schumpeter was born in Triesch, Moravia (now in the Czech Republic). He was a university professor and later a Minister of Finance in Austria. In 1932, he emigrated to the United States to avoid the rise to power of Adolf Hitler. He spent his remaining years at Harvard University.

Schumpeter, a pioneering theorist of innovation, emphasized the role of the entrepreneur in economic development. The existence of the entrepreneur meant continuous innovation and waves of adaptation to changing technology. He is best known for his theory of "creative destruction," where the prospect of monopoly profits provides owners the incentive to finance inventions and innovations. One monopoly can replace another with superior technology or a superior product, thereby circumventing the entry barriers of a monopolized industry. He criticized mainstream economists for emphasizing the static (allocative) efficiency of perfect competition—a market structure that would, if it could ever be achieved, retard technological change and economic growth.

Schumpeter's best known works are *The Theory of Economic Development* (1911), *Business Cycles* (1939), and *Capitalism, Socialism and Democracy* (1943).

1908
Henry Ford introduces
the Model-T.

1912
Titanic sinks on her
maiden voyage, killing
1,513 people.

1914
Opening of the
Panama Canal.
World War I begins.

1917
Bolshevik Revolution
in Russia brings
V. I. Lenin to power.

1918
Treaty of Versailles ends
World War I.

1905   *1910*   *1915*   *1920*

JOHN MAYNARD KEYNES *(1883–1946)*

John Maynard Keynes was born in Cambridge, England. His parents were both intellectuals, and his father, John Neville Keynes, was a famous logician and writer on economic methodology. The young Keynes was educated at Eton and then at Kings College, Cambridge, where he was a student of Alfred Marshall and Arthur Pigou. His career included appointments to the Treasury in Britain during both World Wars I and II, a leading role in the establishment of the International Monetary Fund (through discussions at Bretton Woods, New Hampshire, in 1944), and editorship of the *Economic Journal* from 1911 to 1945, all in addition to his academic position at Kings College.

Keynes published extensively during his life but his most influential work, *The General Theory of Employment, Interest, and Money,* appeared in 1936. This book was published in the midst of the Great Depression when the output of goods and services had fallen drastically, unemployment was intolerably high, and it had become clear to many that the market would not self-adjust to achieve potential output within an acceptable period of time. Fluctuations in economic activity were familiar at this point, but the failure of the economy to recover rapidly from this depression was unprecedented. Neoclassical economists held that during a downturn both wages and the interest rate would fall low enough to induce investment and employment and cause an expansion. They believed that the persistent unemployment during the 1930s was caused by inflexible wages and they recommended that workers be convinced to accept wage cuts.

Keynes believed that this policy, though perhaps correct for a single industry, was not correct for the entire economy. Widespread wage cuts would reduce the consumption portion of aggregate demand, which would offset any increase in employment. Keynes argued that unemployment could be cured only by manipulating aggregate demand, whereby increased demand (through government expenditure) would increase the price level, reduce real wages, and thereby stimulate employment.

Keynes's views found acceptance after the publication of his *General Theory* and had a profound effect on government policy around the world, particularly in the 1940s, 1950s, and 1960s. As we know from this textbook, Keynes's name is attached to much of macroeconomics, from much of the basic theory to the Keynesian short-run aggregate supply curve and the Keynesian consumption function. His contributions to economics go well beyond what can be mentioned in a few paragraphs—for, in effect, he laid the foundations for modern macroeconomics.

E D W A R D   C H A M B E R L I N   *(1899–1967)*

Edward Chamberlin was born in La Conner, Washington, and received his Ph.D. from Harvard University in 1927. He became a full professor at Harvard in 1937 and stayed there until his retirement in 1966. He published *The Theory of Monopolistic Competition* in 1933.

Before Chamberlin's book (which appeared more or less simultaneously with Joan Robinson's *The Economics of Imperfect Competition*), the models of perfect competition and monopoly had been fairly well worked out. Though economists were aware of a middle ground between these two market structures and some analysis of duopoly (two sellers) had been presented, it was Chamberlin and Robinson who closely examined this problem of imperfect markets.

Chamberlin's main contribution was explaining the importance of product differentiation for firms in market structures between perfect competition and monopoly. Chamberlin saw that though there may be a large number of firms in the market (the competitive element), each firm created for itself a unique product or advantage that gave it some control over price (the monopoly element). Specifically, he identified items such as copyrights, trademarks, brand names, and location as monopoly elements behind a product. Though Alfred Marshall regarded price as the only variable in question, Chamberlin saw both price and the product itself as variables under control of the firm in monopolistically competitive markets.

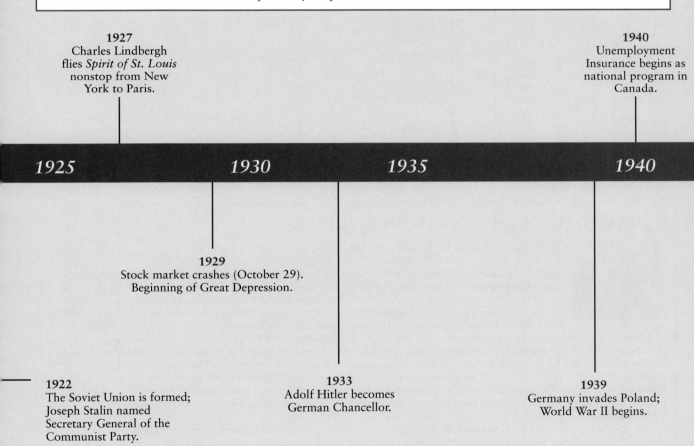

1927
Charles Lindbergh
flies *Spirit of St. Louis*
nonstop from New
York to Paris.

1940
Unemployment
Insurance begins as
national program in
Canada.

1925   1930   1935   1940

1929
Stock market crashes (October 29).
Beginning of Great Depression.

1922
The Soviet Union is formed;
Joseph Stalin named
Secretary General of the
Communist Party.

1933
Adolf Hitler becomes
German Chancellor.

1939
Germany invades Poland;
World War II begins.

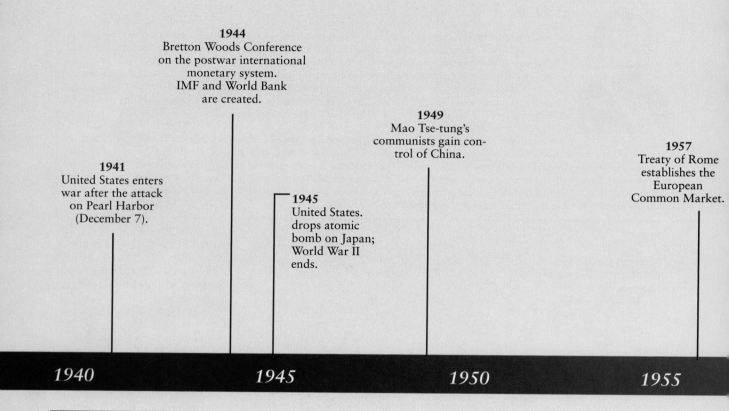

1944
Bretton Woods Conference
on the postwar international
monetary system.
IMF and World Bank
are created.

1949
Mao Tse-tung's
communists gain con-
trol of China.

1957
Treaty of Rome
establishes the
European
Common Market.

1941
United States enters
war after the attack
on Pearl Harbor
(December 7).

1945
United States.
drops atomic
bomb on Japan;
World War II
ends.

1940   *1945*   *1950*   *1955*

FRIEDRICH AUGUST VON HAYEK (1899–1992)

Friedrich von Hayek was born in Vienna and studied at the University of Vienna, where he was trained in the Austrian tradition of economics (a school of thought originating with Carl Menger). He held academic positions at the London School of Economics and the University of Chicago. He returned to Europe in 1962 to the University of Freiburg in what was then West Germany and the University of Salzburg in Austria. He was awarded the Nobel Prize in Economics in 1974.

Hayek contributed new ideas and theories in many different areas of economics, but he is perhaps best known for his general conception of economics as a "coordination problem." His observation of market economies suggested that the relative prices determined in free markets provided the signals that allowed the actions of all decision makers to mesh—even though there was no formal planning taking place to coordinate these actions. He emphasized this "spontaneous order" at work in the economy as the subject matter for economics. The role of knowledge and information in the market process became central to Hayek, an idea that has grown in importance to the economics profession over the years.

Hayek's theory of business cycles provided an example of the breakdown of this coordination. A monetary disturbance (e.g., an increase in the money supply) would distort the signals (relative prices) by artificially raising the return to certain types of economic activity. When the disturbance disappeared, the boom caused by these distorted signals would be followed by a slump. Although Hayek's business-cycle theory was eclipsed by the Keynesian revolution, his emphasis on economics as a coordination problem has had a major influence on contemporary economic thought.

Hayek was also prominent in advocating the virtues of free markets as contributing to human freedom in the broad sense as well as to economic efficiency in the narrow sense. His *The Road to Serfdom* (1944) sounded an alarm about the political and economic implications of the then-growing belief in the virtues of central planning. His *Constitution of Liberty* (1960) is a much deeper philosophical analysis of the forces, economic and otherwise, that contribute to the liberty of the individual.

1959
Fidel Castro
overthrows
Fulgencio Batista
in Cuba.

INDEX

The page on which a key term is defined is printed in boldface.

Photo Credits

Chapter 1 Canapress/Associated Press/Lionel Cironneau – 2, 6; Tony Stone Images/Daniel Bosler – 1, 9; PhotoDisc, Inc. – 15

Chapter 2 Tony Stone Images/Steven Peters – 28; Dick Hemingway - 1, 24, 31

Chapter 3 Tony Stone Images/Chris McCooey – 50; Saskatchewan Travel – 47, 48, 57; Canapress/Jacques Boissinot – 65

Chapter 4 Imperial Oil Limited – 47, 70, 77; Dick Hemingway – 87

Chapter 5 PhotoDisc, Inc. – 47, 98, 113; Saskatchewan Wheat Pool/Frank Fohr – 120; Ontario Ministry of Agriculture and Food – 102

Chapter 6 Tony Stone Images/Frank Siteman – 127, 128, 135

Chapter 7 Courtesy MacMillan Bloedel Limited – 160; PhotoEdit/Vic Bider – 127, 157, 170

Chapter 8 PhotoDisc, Inc. – 127, 184, 185; Corbis-Bettmann – 192

Chapter 9 Alberta Government Services – 211; Tony Stone Images – 205, 206, 223; Barrett & McKay Photographers – 218

Chapter 10 Dick Hemingway – 205, 230, 237; PhotoDisc, Inc. – 239

Chapter 11 Dick Hemingway – 256; Canadian Press Archives/AP Photo/Miller Brewing Co. – 205, 253, 270

Chapter 12 CRTC – 289; Canapress/Associated Press/Shuji Kajiyama – 205, 279, 297

Chapter 13 The Stock Market/Blaine Harrington III – 313; Canapress/John Lehmann – 303, 304, 324

Chapter 14 Abitibi-Price Inc. – 303, 330, 341; Foote Collection Manitoba Archives/N2762 – 344; Boeing Commercial Airplane Group – 346

Chapter 15 Canapress/Mike Ridewood – 354; Imperial Oil Limited – 303, 352, 362

Chapter 16 Canapress/Nick Procaylo – 371, 372, 382; Dick Hemingway – 387; CP Archive Photo/Roy Antal – 395

Chapter 17 British Columbia Forest Service/Barbara Davies Photo – 408; The Slide Farm/Al Harvey – 412; CP Archive Photo/Red Deer Advocate/Randy Fiedler – 371, 405, 417

Chapter 18 Tony Stone Images/Christopher Bissell – 425; CP Archive Photo/Paul Chiasson – 371, 423, 437; Dick Hemingway – 439

Chapter 19 Marko Shark – 458; Canadian Pacific – 449, 450, 468

Chapter 20 Dick Hemingway – 477; Toyota Motor Manufacturing Canada Inc. – 484; FPG International LLC/Michael Goldman – 449, 475, 488

Chapter 21 Corbis Digital Stock Images – 449, 494, 496

Chapter 22 Dick Hemingway – 507, 508, 513; The Slide Farm/Al Harvey – 516

Chapter 23 Ontario Ministry of Tourism and Recreation – 507, 534, 548

Chapter 24 PhotoEdit/Myrleen Ferguson – 558; British Columbia Forest Service/Ray Wormald Photo – 507, 557, 565

Chapter 25 Dick Hemingway – 507, 579, 581; Impact Visuals Photos & Graphics Inc./Donna Binder – 587

Chapter 26 Corbis - 610; Tony Stone Images/Alan Klehr – 605, 606; Dick Hemingway – 624

Chapter 27 Leucar Photo – 605, 635, 636; Dick Hemingway – 636; Dick Hemingway – 640

Chapter 28 CP Archive Photo/Tom Hanson – 679; CP Archive Photo/Fred Chartrand – 605, 659

Chapter 29 CP Archive Photo/Ryan Remiorz – 691, 692, 701; PhotoDisc, Inc. – 715

Chapter 30 PhotoEdit/Spencer Grant – 691, 722, 734; Prentice Hall, Inc. – 737

Chapter 31 National Archives of Canada/Donald I. Grant/PA115568 – 754; PhotoDisc, Inc. – 691, 749, 765

Chapter 32 AP Wide World Photos – 691, 776, 780; PhotoDisc, Inc. – 784; PhotoDisc, Inc. – 793

Chapter 33 Hamilton Wright Organization Inc. – 805; United Nations Photo – 691, 800, 807

Chapter 34 PhotoDisc, Inc. – 827; British Columbia Forest Service/R.J. Challenger Photo – 821, 822, 831

Chapter 35 Superstock, Inc./Ping Amranand – 821, 841, 842; Agriculture Quebec – 856

Chapter 36 CP Archive Photo – 821, 864, 870; Tony Stone Images – 875

Study Material

Study Skills Tips   S-3

Self-Test Questions   S-31

Answers to Self-Test Questions   S-75

Practice Exams   S-97

Answers to Practice Exams   S-133

National Library of Canada Cataloguing in Publication

Lipsey, Richard G., 1928-
    Economics / Richard G. Lipsey, Christopher T.S. Ragan, Paul N. Courant. – 10th Canadian ed., study ed.

ISBN 0-321-12591-6

1. Economics. I. Ragan, Christopher II. Courant, Paul N. III. Title.

HB171.5.L733 2003   330   C2002-901956-7

Special thanks to Ingrid Kristjanson, Sam Fefferman, and Scott Cawfield for their contributions to this Study Edition.

0-321-12591-6

Vice President, Editorial Director: Michael J. Young
Executive Editor: Dave Ward
Marketing Manager: Deborah Meredith
Developmental Editor: Maurice Esses
Production Editor: Mary Ann McCutcheon
Production Coordinator: Andrea Falkenberg
Page Layout: Carol Magee
Permissions and Photo Research: Susan Wallace-Cox
Art Director: Mary Opper
Interior Design: Anthony Leung
Cover Design and Image: Artville LLC

1 2 3 4 5   07 06 05 04 03

Printed and bound in United States.

Study Skills Tips

The Six Keys to Success in Study Skills

Striving for success in university or college is no easy task. It requires motivation, commitment, initiative, responsibility, positive thinking, and a willingness to face your fears. In combination, these six keys will keep you in motion toward new knowledge and opportunities.

1. Get Motivated

The people who want to achieve and win … motivate themselves.

—Mike Ditka

Motivation is the energy that fuels your drive to achieve, and a motivator is anything that motivates you. There are at least as many motivators as there are people, and what motivates any given person can change from situation to situation or even from day to day. For example, some potential motivators for attending school could be supporting a family, learning a marketable skill, gaining earning potential, impressing others, or improving yourself.

It's nearly impossible to remain motivated continually. Motivation can slip away when you least expect to lose it. Everyone has energy highs and lows, and sometimes you don't feel like accomplishing anything. How can you renew lost motivation?

- **Spend time reflecting on why your goal is meaningful to you.**
  Remind yourself of what you wanted.

- **Make a decision to take one step toward your goal.**
  Sometimes feeling overwhelmed by a goal immobilizes you. Focus on the step you can take today.

- **After you take the first step, reward yourself for a job well done.**
  Rewards can be material (a new CD) or they can be more internal (a walk outside, time spent with a friend).

- **Examine and deal with your obstacles.**
  What's getting in your way? Maybe your health or finances have been troubling you. Whatever it is, make a commitment to deal with your problems as soon as they arise. They'll be more manageable that way.

- **Begin, or begin again.**
  If you can just get yourself started, you'll feel better as you continue working toward your goals. A law of physics, Newton's first law of motion, says that things in motion tend to stay in motion, and that things at rest tend to stay at rest. Be a thing in motion.

For example, to pass an early-morning class that you've already failed once, you decide to implement two strategies. First, you promise yourself that you will go to every class and turn in your work on time. Second, you make a commitment to write daily in a journal. Your motivation: Passing this course is necessary to continue your education, and the skills you learn will help you get a good job when you graduate. Plus, you promise yourself a reward: If you get at least a B– in the course, you will buy yourself that mobile phone you've been wanting.

To reach your goal, you remove obstacles to success. Instead of staying up late and being too tired to go to class, you start going to bed earlier. As a first step to getting up early, you put your alarm clock across the room so that you have to get up to shut it off. If you keep it up, your motivation should pay off. Even so, follow-through may be difficult for you. If you discover this is the case, you may want to shift to another strategy, such as trying to schedule afternoon classes in order to compensate for your sleep habits.

2. Make a Commitment

Formulate a goal, not a fuzzy, vague goal, but sharp, defined, and specific. Put that goal in your conscious mind, holding it tenaciously until it sinks into the unconscious, and when it does, you will have it, because it has you …

—Norman Vincent Peale, *You Can If You Think You Can*

How do you focus the energy of motivation? Make a commitment. Commitment means that you do what you say you will do. It requires honesty and trustworthiness. When you honour a commitment, you prove to others as well as yourself that your words and intentions can be trusted. A committed person follows through on a promise.

Commitment doesn't just refer to a personal relationship. You can apply the tasks of commitment—and the rewards—to academic goals, professional relationships, your working life, career goals, and self-improvement. Commitment often stretches over a period of time. You may commit to finishing school in six semesters. Not only have you made a promise, but you hold yourself to that promise for as long as the commitment demands.

Commitment requires you to focus your energy on something specific. In order to remain successfully committed, you need to break goals into manageable pieces, setting your specific goal and naming the steps of the process you will use to achieve it.

How do you go about making and keeping a commitment?

- **State your commitment concretely.**
  It's hard to commit to something like "I'm going to pass this Economics course," because you haven't set yourself clear tasks. Commit to something specific such as "I plan to pass this Economics course with an A grade."

- **Get started and note your progress.**
  Looking for improvements on the way, no matter how small, can keep you going.

- **Renew your commitment regularly.**
  How many times have you committed to making a change in your life, only to find that your resolve fades away in a few weeks—or even a few days? You're not a failure if you lose momentum—it's normal. Review your goal, commit to it, and get back on track.

- **Keep track of your commitment.**
  Find ways to make sure you don't forget the commitments you have made. Make a list of commitments to keep in your date book. If commitments involve events or projects that take place on specific dates, be sure to note them on the calendar. Post notes to yourself on your refrigerator, your wall, or your mirror. Talk about your commitments with friends and family. Sometimes, just having someone supporting you and your goals helps you remain more accountable.

For example, you might make this specific commitment: "I will write goals and review them in my journal every night before going to sleep."

Making and keeping your commitments helps you keep a steady focus on your most important goals. It gives you a sense of accomplishment as you experience gradual growth and progress.

3. Take Initiative

You have to expect things of yourself before you can do them.

—Michael Jordan

When you take initiative, you push yourself to take that first difficult step. Initiative helps to get the pursuit of your goals off the ground. It jump-starts your journey and helps to renew motivation along the way. It enables you to respond continually to changes that occur.

When you use initiative, you take the first step *on your own* instead of waiting for someone else to fix the problem or having to be dragged into it by people, rules, or requirements. You take initiative when you go to a counsellor for help with a personal problem, talk to a friend about something he or she said that upset you, raise your hand to speak in a classroom, come up with a better way to do a job at work, or start on an exercise program.

Initiative requires you to keep on top of your goals and to listen to your instincts. You may discover that you want to do more than what is expected, which can be positive both at school and in the workplace. Initiative is a spark plug. It ignites the fuel of your motivation and powers your passions and commitment.

4. Be Responsible

Take responsibility for yourself ... without blaming the other person.

—Robert Alberti and Michael Emmons,
Your Perfect Right: A Guide to Assertive Living

Being responsible is all about living up to your obligations, both those that are imposed on you and those that you impose on yourself. It means that you can address situations and challenges that arise in your daily life. Through action, you prove that you are responsible, or "response-able," able to respond. When something needs to be done, a responsible person does the work—as efficiently as possible, on time, and to the best of his or her ability.

Responsibility can take enormous effort. However, being responsible has definite benefits. For one, you make a crucial impression on others. You earn the trust of your instructors, supervisors, relatives, and friends. When others trust you, they may give you increasing responsibility and opportunities for growth. Trust builds relationships, which in turn feed progress and success.

When you are trusted you are also respected, and respect brings its own rewards. Supervisors promote employees they respect. Even more important is the self-respect that emerges when you prove that you can live up to your promises. Responsible people are given power and opportunity because they have shown they are capable of making the best of both.

For example, when you complete class assignments on time, you demonstrate responsibility. When you correct errors and work on problem areas, you demonstrate a commitment to doing well. An instructor who sees these patterns of behaviour is likely to trust your judgment. You don't have to take on the world to show how responsible you can be. Responsibility shows in basic everyday actions: attending class, fulfilling requirements, turning in work on time, and being true to your word.

5. Think Positively

The world is moving so fast that the man who says it can't be done is interrupted by someone doing it.

—Norman Vincent Peale, *You Can If You Think You Can*

Attitude is everything in reaching success. Many people believe that what happens in your life can be linked to how you feel about yourself and your place in the world. Ask yourself whether you see a glass as half empty or half full. You may not create instant success by seeing it as half full, but you can create a mindset that helps you seize opportunity and make the most of it.

Your attitudes influence your choices and affect how you perceive and relate to others. A positive attitude can open your mind to learning experiences and inspire you to take action. On the other hand, a negative attitude can hinder learning and stifle initiative. For example, say you are enrolled in a Humanities course unrelated to your program or major. If you adopt the attitude that the course is a waste of time, chances are you won't learn much. If, however, you keep an open mind, the course might teach you something valuable or introduce you to a new area of interest.

One of the ways you can create a positive attitude is with positive self-talk. When you hear negative thoughts in your mind (I'm not very smart/I can't make it through this Economics course/I'm not good enough), replace them with positive ones (I have a lot to offer/It won't be easy, but I'm smart enough to figure it out/I am talented). Talk to yourself as if you were talking to another person, someone you care a lot about. You would probably never talk to a friend as harshly as you talk to yourself at times. Take that to heart and be kind to yourself. The following hints will help you put positive self-talk into action.

Stop negative talk in its tracks and change it to positive talk.
If you catch yourself thinking, "I can never write a decent Economics paper," stop and say to yourself, "I can do better than that and next time I will." Then think over how you plan to do it.

Take a moment to pay yourself a general compliment.
"I am a terrific, valuable, and powerful person." Or be specific. "I have really improved in my Economics and Accounting classes." Some people use word calendars with daily affirmations. These are great reminders of positive self-talk.

Replace words of obligation, which take power from you, with words of personal intent.

I should	becomes	I choose to
I have to	becomes	I want to
I'll try	becomes	I will
I mean to	becomes	I promise to

Words of intent give you power and control because they imply a personal decision to act. When you say, "I have to be in class by 9," you're saying that someone else has power over you and has handed you a required obligation. When you say, "I want to be in class by 9 because I don't want to miss anything I need to learn about," you're saying that the choice is yours.

Build on your successes.

Even when you don't think you are at your best, don't let that diminish your victories. Congratulate yourself when you take any positive steps. Whether you do well on a paper, write in your journal for a week straight, get to class on time all week, or have fewer mistakes on this week's assignment than last week's, each success helps you believe in yourself. Every step is a step in the right direction, no matter how small. Try keeping a list of your successes in a notebook.

It can be very difficult to think positively. If you have a deep-rooted feeling of unworthiness, you may want to see a counsellor. Many people have benefited from skilled professional advice.

6.   Face Your Fears

Two great forces operate in the world … fear and faith. Fear is very powerful, but faith is more powerful.

—Norman Vincent Peal, *You Can If You Think You Can*

Everyone experiences fear. Even when you are excited about a change, new experiences often feel frightening. The changes involved in pursuing an education can inspire fear. You wonder if you can handle the work and if you have chosen the right school or program.

The successful pursuit of an education demands a willingness to push your limits and face your fears. Only when you identify and confront your fears can you start to work through challenges.

Let's review, and comment on these six steps to success:

1. **You Need Motivation.** Motivation is the energy that drives you, connects you, to your goal. With it, barring a major life crisis, you will achieve your goal. Without it, you will be perennially at the bottom of the ski-hill, watching all the others going up and coming down the slopes successfully. With motivation, you can move mountains of the mind. There are many clues in our material about how to foster motivation: set down in writing what you want, take small steps every day toward what you want, reward yourself from time to time along the way, and resolve any obstacle to success. Keep on going when you get going, and start planning now.

2. **You Need Commitment.** Be specific about what you want. "I needed something to do" won't cut it. Formulate these kinds of statements, "I want to graduate from Carleton

University, or the University of Calgary in June, 2005 with at least a B+ average." Include in every goal statement **what** you want, **when** you want it, and at **what standard**.

3. **You Need Initiative.** Michael Jordan says that you have to expect things of *yourself*. That's not your parents' expectations, nor those of your friends, nor even those created by your always being an "A" level student. **State your expectations, and state objectives.** It may take some time, and you may want to consult a professional counsellor, for example, through the Counselling Centre at your college or university. When you have decided what you want, don't just look at it, be active … seize it!

4. **You Need Responsibility.** Your professors, as will your managers at work, look for your sense of responsibility. People who promise things and don't follow through are not high achievers. Also, don't rest on past laurels; in college or university you are in an entirely different ballpark from secondary schools. Self-reliance and personal accountability are required at the post-secondary level; secondary school may have been a more leisurely jaunt for you.

   You will need strong time and stress management skills, and you should expect to trade off some of your personal freedom to succeed.

5. **You Need Positive Thinking.** Positive thinking is the essence of effective motivation. If you think you can, you very likely can. Without it, you "need a life." Avoid the negative, especially negative people. In *You Can If You Think You Can*, Norman Vincent Peale said, "Associate with positive, exciting people, and let their excitement rub off on you. Keep thinking, keep moving, keep participating."[1] Join all the business associations you can, and when you do, find there the most enthusiastic winners, and try to get their business cards. You may get a job offer; most certainly you will get new business ideas. Offer your card to them, even if it says only that you are a Business student. Find people who love life, and associate with them.

6. **You Need to Overcome Fears.** Everyone has fears; it's how you deal with them that matters. If they immobilize you, they are dangerous. If you name them, face them, overcome them, then they were just another obstacle for you to jump over. Florence Griffith Joyner, perhaps American's best black female athlete of all time, said, "When anyone tells me I can't do anything, I'm just not listening anymore." And read Norman Vincent Peale's *You Can If You Think You Can*, or any of Mark Twain's works such as *The Adventures of Tom Sawyer*, if you need a positive energy boost, or a good laugh.

---

[1] Norman Vincent Peale, *You Can If You Think You Can* (Pawling, New York: Foundation for Christian Living and Prentice-Hall, 1984), p. 144.

How Can You Manage Your Time?

Time is one of your most valuable and precious resources. Unlike money, or opportunity, or connections, time doesn't discriminate—everyone has the same 24 hours in a day, every day. *Your responsibility—and your potential for success—lies in how you use yours.* You cannot manipulate or change how time passes, but you can spend it taking steps to achieve your goals. Efficient time management helps you achieve your goals in a steady, step-by-step process.

In all careers, as well as in economic studies, efficient time management will be crucial to your career longevity and academic success. If you do not hand in assignments on time, or if you disappear for a few months, your instructor will notice and likely lose confidence in your ability to finish the course successfully. Likewise, if you are chronically late for work, or showing at work that you are more interested in chatting than helping achieve results, you may well not make it through the probationary period. All these behaviours may be related to poor management of time, and instructors and managers consider this aspect of work as important, sometimes more important, than your formal educational credentials.

We are going to show you in this section how to take control of your time through the use of schedules and calendars, priority-setting, and various other strategies.

Time management, like physical fitness, is a lifelong pursuit. Both are great for you! No one can plan a perfect schedule or build a terrific physique and then be "done." You'll work at time management throughout your life, and it can be tiring. Your ability to manage your time will vary with your mood, your stress level, how busy you are, and other factors. Do your best, given your constraints. Time management involves taking responsibility for how you spend your time, building a schedule, and making your schedule work through lists and other strategies.

Taking Responsibility for How You Spend Your Time

Being in control of how you manage your time is a key factor in taking responsibility for yourself and your choices. When you plan your activities with an eye to achieving your most important goals, you are taking personal responsibility for how you live.

Building a Schedule

Just as a road map helps you travel from place to place, a schedule is a time-and-activity map that helps you get from the beginning of the day (or week, or month) to the end as smoothly as possible. A written schedule helps you gain control of your life. Schedules have two major advantages: They allocate segments of time for the fulfillment of your daily, weekly, monthly, or longer-term goals; and they serve as a concrete reminder of tasks, events, responsibilities, and deadlines. Few moments are more stressful than suddenly realizing you have forgotten a key project or test.

Keep a Date Book

Gather the tools of the trade: a pen or pencil and a date book (sometimes called a planner). Some of you already have date books and may have used them for years. Others may have had no luck with them or have never tried. Even if you feel you are not the type of person who would use one, give it a try. A date book is indispensable for keeping track of your time. Paul Timm says, "Most time management experts agree that rule number one in a thoughtful planning process is: Use some form of a planner where you can write things down."

There are two major types of date books. The day-at-a-glance version devotes a page to each day. While it gives you ample space to write the day's activities, this version makes it difficult to see what's ahead. The week-at-a-glance book gives you a view of the week's plans, but has less room to write per day. If you write out your daily plans in detail, you might like the day-at-a-glance version. If you prefer to remind yourself of plans ahead of time, try the book that shows a week's schedule all at once. Some date books contain additional sections that allow you to note plans and goals for the year as a whole and for each month. You can also create your own sheets for yearly and monthly notations in a notepad section, if your book has one, or on plain paper that you can then insert into the book.

Another option to consider is an electronic planner. These are compact mini-computers that can hold a large amount of information. You can use them to schedule your days and weeks, make to-do lists, and create and store an address book. Electronic planners are powerful, convenient, and often fun. On the other hand, they certainly cost more than the paper version, and you can lose a lot of important data if something goes wrong with the computer inside. Evaluate your options and decide what you like best.

Set Weekly and Daily Goals

The most ideal time management starts with the smallest task and builds to bigger ones. Setting short-term goals that tie in to your long-term goals gives you the following benefits:

- Increased meaning for your daily activities
- Shaping your path toward the achievement of your long-term goals
- A sense of order and progress

For college and university students as well as working people, the week is often the easiest unit of time to consider at one glance. Weekly goal-setting and planning allows you to keep track of day-to-day activities while giving you the larger perspective of what is coming up during the week. Take some time before each week starts to remind yourself of your long-term goals. Keeping long-term goals in mind will help you determine related short-term objectives you can accomplish during the week to come.

Link Daily and Weekly Goals With Long-Term Goals

After you evaluate what you need to accomplish in the coming year, semester, month, week, and day in order to reach your long-term goals, use your schedule to record those steps. Write down the short-term goals that will enable you to stay on track. Here is how a student might map out two different goals over a year's time.

This year: Complete enough courses to graduate in 6 semesters.
                   Improve my physical fitness.

This semester: Complete my Economics class with a B average or higher.
                   Lose 10 pounds and exercise regularly.

This month:	Set up study-group schedule to coincide with quizzes.
	Begin walking and weight lifting.
This week:	Meet with Economics study group; go over material for Friday's class.
	Go for a fitness walk three times; go to weight room twice.
Today:	Go over Chapter 3 in Economics text.
	Walk for 40 minutes.

Prioritize Goals

Prioritizing enables you to use your date book with maximum efficiency. On any given day, your goals will have varying degrees of importance. Record your goals first, and then label them according to level of importance, using these categories: Priority 1, Priority 2, and Priority 3. Identify these categories using any code that makes sense to you. Some people use numbers, as above. Some use letters (A, B, C). Some write activities in different colours according to priority level. Some use symbols (*, +, −).

Priority 1

Activities are the most important things in your life. They may include attending class, preparing an Economics assignment, or meeting with a friend to discuss your progress in Accounting.

Priority 2

Activities are part of your routine. Examples include grocery shopping, working out, or cleaning. Priority 2 tasks are important but more flexible than Priority 1's.

Priority 3

Activities are those you would like to do but can reschedule without much sacrifice. Examples might be a trip to the mall, a visit with a friend, or a social phone call. As much as you would like to accomplish them, you don't consider them urgent. Many people don't enter Priority 3 tasks in their date books until they are sure they have time to get them done.

Prioritizing your activities is essential for two reasons. First, some activities are more important than others, and effective time management requires that you focus most of your energy on Priority 1 items. Second, looking at all your priorities helps you plan when you can get things done. Often, it's not possible to get all your Priority 1 activities done early in the day, especially if these activities involve scheduled classes or meetings. Prioritizing helps you set Priority 1 items and then schedule Priority 2 and 3 items around them as they fit.

Keep Track of Events

Your date book also enables you to schedule events. Rather than thinking of events as separate from goals, tie them to your long-term goals just as you would your other tasks. Being aware of quiz dates, due dates for assignments, and meeting dates will aid you in your goals to achieve in school and become involved.

Note events in your date book so that you can stay aware of them ahead of time. Write them in daily, weekly, monthly, or even yearly sections, where a quick look will remind you that they are approaching. Writing them down will help you see where they fit in the context of your other activities. For example, if you have three big tests and a presentation all in one week, you'll want to take time in the weeks before to prepare for them all.

Following are some kinds of events worth noting in your date books:

- Due dates for papers, projects, presentations, and tests
- Important meetings, medical appointments, or due dates for bill payments
- Benchmarks for steps toward a goal, such as due dates for sections of a project.

List Low-Priority Goals Separately

Priority 3 tasks can be hard to accomplish. As the least important tasks, they often get put off from one day to the next. You may spend valuable time rewriting these items day after day in your date book instead of getting them done. One solution is to keep a list of Priority 3 tasks in a separate place in your date book. That way, when you have an unexpected pocket of free time, you can consult your list and see what you have time to accomplish. Keep this list current by crossing off items as you accomplish them and writing in new items as soon as you think of them. Rewrite the list when it gets too messy.

Time Management Strategies

Managing time takes thought and energy. Here are some additional strategies to try.

1. **Plan your schedule each week.** Before each week begins, note events, goals, and priorities. Look at the map of your week to decide where to fit activities such as studying and Priority 3 items. For example, if you have a test on Thursday, you can plan study sessions on the days up until then. If you have more free time on Tuesday and Friday than on other days, you can plan workouts or Priority 3 activities at those times. Looking at the whole week will help you avoid being surprised by something you have forgotten was coming up.

2. **Make and use to-do lists.** Use a to-do list to record the things you want to accomplish. If you generate a daily or weekly to-do list on a separate piece of paper, you can look at all tasks and goals at once. This will help you consider time frames and priorities. You might want to prioritize your tasks and transfer them to appropriate places in your date book. Some people create daily to-do lists right on their date book pages. This kind of specific to-do list can help you prioritize and accomplish an unusually large task load.

3. **Make thinking about time a priority.** Devote a minimum of 10 to 15 minutes a day to planning your schedule. Although making a schedule takes time, it can mean hours of saved time later. Say you have two errands to run, both on the other side of town. Not planning ahead could result in your driving across town twice in one day. The extra driving time is far more than it would have taken to plan the day in advance.

4. **Refer to your schedule.** Many people make detailed schedules, only to forget to look at them. Carry your date book wherever you go and check it throughout the day. Find a date book size you like—there are books that fit into your briefcase, bag, or even your pocket.

5. **Post monthly and yearly calendars at home.** Keeping a calendar on your desk, or on the wall will help you stay aware of important events. You can purchase one or draw it yourself, month by month, on plain paper. Use a yearly or a monthly version and keep it where you can refer to it often.

6. **Schedule downtime.** When you're wiped out from too much activity, you don't have the energy to accomplish much with your time. A little downtime will refresh you and improve your attitude. Even half an hour a day will help. Fill the time with whatever

relaxes you—having a snack, reading, watching TV, playing a game or sport, walking, writing, or just doing nothing. Make downtime a priority.

7. **Be flexible.** Since priorities determine the map of your day, week, month, or year, any priority shift can jumble your schedule. Be ready to reschedule your tasks as your priorities change. On Monday, a homework assignment due in a week might be Priority 2. By Saturday, it has become Priority 1. On some days a surprise priority such as a medical emergency or a family situation may pop up and force you to cancel everything else on your schedule. Other days a class may be cancelled and you will have extra time on your hands. Adjust to whatever each day brings.

8. **Leave unscheduled time in your schedule whenever possible.** Just when you think you have control over your schedule, something inevitably comes along that will alter your plan. Try to keep some of your time unscheduled in case you have to shift tasks around. For example, if you get stuck working overtime, you may have to reschedule a meeting with a counsellor for later in the day.

Here is a review for you of our main points which emphasizes the areas in which you are most likely to waste your time:

1. **You Need a Time Planner.** Keep a planning book, or calendar, or both preferably. Schedule in your planning book, or electronic calendar, every major task, appointment, or deadline. Use it every day. Keep it with you nearly all the time, especially in class and while studying. Take it to bed with you, and use it to plan the next day carefully. You will get up with objectives, rather than a list of "maybe's."

2. **You Need to Set Overall Goals and Objectives.** Set goals for the week, month, year as well as your short-term objectives. Goals will be such things as, "Achieving a B+ or A in Economics 120," or "Graduating from Centennial College's Business Management Program by June, 2004." Objectives will be things like "I need to improve my graphing skills this semester," or "I want to improve my fitness level by getting a job in that area this summer."

3. **You Need a Priority Management System for Your Goals and Objectives.** For example, your goal "To graduate from Centennial's Business Management Program by June, 2004" will be Priority Level 1;

   Your goal to "Join the local Chamber of Commerce so that I can get and network with business contacts," could also be Priority Level 1, especially if you are in your final year of studies;

   Your goal to "Join a local Fitness and Hiking Association so that I can look and feel good," would likely be a Priority Level 2;

   Your goal to "Schedule an evening clubbing with my friends at the Mighty Moose," will be Priority Level 3.

4. **Don't Procrastinate or Be Too Leisurely!** It's very important to schedule leisure into your daily and weekly schedule, but also be totally straightforward and even urgent about your major goals and objectives.

If you can, do it now; if you can't do it now, plan!

5. **Be a Realistic Planner.** If you schedule five hours a night for studying, but you know from experience that your effective study schedule is only about two hours, then go with the two hours per night only. Do two hours per night four times a week, for example, rather than scheduling a blockbuster evening. Your study efficiency may well drop to next to nothing in the third or fourth hour of concentrated study. Do the two hours, and go for a walk, or run, or listen to some music for the third and fourth hour instead.

6. **Learn to Say "NO" as much as "YES."** Saying "Yes!" at the right time is often the key to clinching a deal in business, or in your planning. But if you want to take control of your time and stress, learn to say "No!" to unreasonable demands on your precious time. Drop the optional night course which interferes with your nightly study schedule, learn to say "No!" to television programs which you know are a waste of time, and say "No!" to certain social events which interfere with your schedule.

7. **Avoid the Time Wasters!** A good thing about keeping track of your time is that you will be able to identify your time wasters. Watching too much television, clubbing too often, spending too much time on the phone, working too much, are examples of time wasters. You may be surprised at "working too much" as a time waster! If your part-time job is wreaking havoc with your grades, then discuss this with your supervisor to find a reasonable compromise. If you can't find a compromise, put your education first. The long-term returns of education will be far greater than the short-term gains at work. Remember your Priority 1 goal!

How Can You Take Notes Effectively? How Does Note Taking Help You?

Notes help you learn when you are in class, doing research, or studying. Since it is virtually impossible to take notes on everything you hear or read, the act of note taking encourages you to decide what is worth remembering.

Recording Information in Class

Your notes have two purposes: First, they should reflect what you heard in class; and second, they should be a resource for studying, writing, or comparing with your text material.

Preparing to Take Class Notes

Taking good class notes depends on good preparation, including the following:

- If your instructor assigns reading on a lecture topic, you may choose to complete the reading before class so that the lecture becomes more of a review than an introduction.

- Use separate pieces of letter-size paper for each class. If you use a three-ring binder, punch holes in papers your instructor hands out and insert them immediately following your notes for that day.

- Choose a comfortable seat where you can easily see and hear, and be ready to write as soon as the instructor begins speaking.

- Choose a note-taking system that helps you handle the instructor's speaking style. While one instructor may deliver organized lectures at a normal speaking rate, another may jump from topic to topic or speak very quickly.

- Set up a support system with a student in each class. That way, when you are absent, you can get the notes you missed.

What to Do During Class

Because No one has the time to write down everything he or she hears, the following strategies will help you choose and record what you feel is important, in a format that you can read and understand later.

- Date each page. When you take several pages of notes during a lecture, add an identifying letter or number to the date on each page: 11/27 A, 11/27 B … or 11/27—1 of 3, 11/27—2 of 3.

- Add the specific topic of the lecture at the top of the page.
  For example: 11/27A—Public Expenditure

- If your instructor jumps from topic to topic during a single class, try starting a new page for each topic.

- Ask yourself critical-thinking questions as you listen: Do I need this information? Is the information important or is it just a digression? Is the information fact or opinion? If it is opinion, is it worth remembering?

- Record whatever an instructor emphasizes.

- Continue to take notes during class discussions and question-and-answer periods. What your fellow students ask the instructor about may help you as well.

- Leave one or more blank spaces between points. This white space will help you review your notes, because information will appear in self-contained sections.

- Draw pictures and diagrams that help illustrate ideas.

- Indicate material that is especially important with a star, with underlining, using a highlighter pen, or by writing words in capital letters.

- If you cannot understand what the instructor is saying, leave a space and place a question mark in the margin. Then ask the instructor to explain the idea again after class, or discuss it with a classmate. Fill in the blank when the idea is clear.

- Take notes until the instructor stops speaking. Students who stop writing a few minutes before the class is over may miss critical information.

- Make your notes as legible, organized, and complete as possible. Your notes are useful only if you can read and understand them.

Make Notes a Valuable After-Class Reference

Class notes are a valuable study tool when you review them regularly. Try to begin your review within a day of the lecture. Read over the notes to learn the information, clarify abbreviations, fill in missing information, and underline or highlight key points. Try to review each week's notes at the end of that week. Think critically about the material, in writing, study group discussions, or quiet reflective thought, using the following questions:

- What do these ideas mean? What examples support or negate them?
- How do I evaluate these ideas? Why are they important?
- How do these ideas, facts, and statements fit together? Is there any missing information?

Summarizing your notes is another important review technique. Summarizing involves critically evaluating which ideas and examples are most important and writing them in a condensed form. You may prefer to summarize as you review your notes, although you might also try summarizing your notes from memory after you review them.

You can take notes in many ways. Different note-taking systems suit different people and situations. Explore each system and choose what works for you.

What Note-Taking System Should You Use?

You will benefit most from the system that feels most comfortable to you. The most comfortable note-taking systems include outlines, the Cornell system, and think links.

Taking Notes in Outline Form

When a reading assignment or lecture seems well organized, you may choose to take notes in outline form. Outlining shows the relationships among ideas and their supporting examples through the use of line-by-line phrases set off by varying indentations.

Formal outlines indicate ideas and examples using Roman numerals, capital and lowercase letters, and numbers. When you are pressed for time, such as during class, you can use an informal system of consistent indenting and dashes instead. Formal outlines also require at least two headings on the same level—that is, if you have a II A you must also have a II B.

Guided Notes

From time to time, an instructor may give you a guide, usually in the form of an outline, to help you take notes in class. This outline may be on a page that you receive at the beginning of the class, on the board, or an a projector.

Although guided notes help you follow the lecture and organize your thoughts during class, they do not replace your own notes. Because they are more of a basic outline of topics than a comprehensive coverage of information, they require that you fill in what they do not cover in detail. If you "tune out" in class because you think that the guided notes are all you need, you will most likely miss important information.

When you receive guided notes on paper, write directly on the paper if there is room. If not, use a separate sheet and write on it the outline categories that the guided notes suggest. If the guided notes are on the board or an overhead, copy them down, leaving plenty of space in between for your own notes.

Using the Cornell Note-Taking System

The Cornell note-taking system, also known as the T-note system, was developed more than 45 years ago by Walter Pauk at Cornell University. The system is successful because it is simple—and because it works. It consists of three sections on ordinary note paper:

- Section 1, the largest section, is on the right. Record your notes here in informal outline form.

- Section 2, to the left of your notes, is the cue column. Leave it blank while you read or listen, then fill it in later as you review. You might fill it with comments that highlight main ideas, clarify meaning, suggest examples, or link ideas and examples. You can even draw diagrams.

- Section 3, at the bottom of the page, is the summary area, where you summarize the notes on the page. When you review, use this section to reinforce concepts and provide an overview.

When you use the Cornell system, create the note-taking structure before class begins. Picture an upside-down letter T. Make the cue column about 7 centimetres wide and the summary area 5 centimetres tall.

Creating a Think Link

A think link, also known as a mind map, is a visual form of note taking. When you draw a think link, you diagram ideas using shapes and lines that link ideas and supporting details and examples. The visual design makes the connections easy to see, and the use of shapes and pictures extends the material beyond mere words. Many learners respond well to the power of visualization. You can use think links to brainstorm ideas for paper topics as well.

One way to create a think link is to start by circling your topic in the middle of a sheet of unlined paper. Next, draw a line from the circled topic and write the name of the first major idea at the end of that line. Circle the idea as well. Then jot down specific facts related to the idea, linking them to the idea with lines. Continue the process, connecting thoughts to one another using circles, lines, and words.

A think link may be difficult to construct in class, especially if your instructor speaks quickly. In this case, use another note-taking system during class. Then make a think link as you review.

Once you choose a note-taking system, your success will depend on how well you use it. Personal shorthand will help you make the most of whatever system you choose.

How Can You Write Faster When Taking Notes?

When taking notes, many students feel they can't keep up with the instructor. Using some personal shorthand (not standard secretarial shorthand) can help to push the pen faster. Shorthand is writing that shortens words or replaces them with symbols. Because you are the only intended reader, you can misspell and abbreviate words in ways that only you understand.

The only danger with shorthand is that you might forget what your writing means. To avoid this problem, review your shorthand notes while your abbreviations and symbols are fresh in your mind. If there is any confusion, spell out words as you review.

Here are some suggestions that will help you master this important skill:

1. Use the following standard abbreviations in place of complete words:

w/	with	cf	compare, in comparison to
w/o	without	ff	following
→	means; resulting in	Q	question
←	as a result of	p.	page
↑	increasing	*	most importantly
↓	decreasing	<	less than
∴	therefore	>	more than
∵	because	=	equals
≈	approximately	%	per cent
+ or &	and	Δ	change
—	minus; negative	2	to; two; too
No. or #	number	vs	versus; against
i.e.	that is	eg	for example
etc.	and so forth	c/o	care of
ng	no good	kg	kilogram

2. Shorten words by removing vowels from the middle of words:

prps	=	purpose
Crvtte	=	Corvette (as on a vanity licence plate for a car)

3. Substitute word beginnings for entire words:

assoc	=	associate; association
info	=	information

4. Form plurals by adding s:

prblms	=	problems
prntrs	=	printers

5. Make up your own symbols and use them consistently:

b/4	=	before
2thake	=	toothache

6. Learn to rely on key phrases instead of complete sentences ("German—nouns capitalized" instead of "In the German language, all nouns are capitalized").

Effective notes are a measure of your ability to listen—a life skill as well as an academic skill. Your notes will provide material that will help you study and prepare for tests.

When you take notes, you become an active learner rather than being passive, with its danger of your possibly panicking a few weeks out from exams because you realize that you don't have time to carefully study all the texts. Further, some of the material presented in class will likely be coming from the professor's knowledge base and experience; it may not be in any text.

Note taking helps you think critically and organize material effectively. Having notes will help you learn efficiently because you are not taking up valuable class time with personal learning questions. Note taking will likely be essential in your job later, especially if you will be called upon to prepare frequent reports.

How Can You Do Better on Tests?

Many people don't look forward to taking tests. If you are one of those people, try thinking of exams as preparation for life. When you volunteer, get a job, or work on your family budget, you'll have to apply what you know. This is exactly what you do when you take a test.

Like a runner who prepares for a marathon by exercising, eating right, taking practice runs, and getting enough sleep, you can take steps to master your exams. Your first step is to study until you understand the material that will be on the test. Your next step is to use the following strategies to become a successful test taker: Identify test type and material covered, use specific study skills, prepare physically, and conquer test anxiety.

Identify Test Type and Material Covered

Before you begin studying, try to determine the type of test you will face and what it will cover:

- Will it be a short-answer test with true/false and multiple-choice questions, an essay test, or a combination?

- Will the test cover everything you studied since the semester began or will it be limited to a narrow topic?

- Will the test be limited to what you learned in class and in the text or will it also cover outside readings?

Your instructors may answer these questions for you. Even though they may not tell you the specific questions that will be on the test, they might let you know what blocks of information will be covered and the question format. Some instructors may even drop hints throughout the semester about possible test questions. While some comments are direct ("I might ask a question on the subject of _____ on your next exam"), other clues are subtle. For example, when instructors repeat an idea or when they express personal interest in a topic ("One of my favourite theories is …"), they are letting you know that the material may be on the test.

Often, the questions you write and ask yourself when you read assigned materials may be part of the test. In addition, any textbook study questions are good candidates for test material.

If you know people who took the instructor's course before, ask them about class tests.

Try to find out how difficult the tests are and whether the test focuses more on assigned readings or class notes. Ask about instructor preferences. If you learn that the instructor pays close attention to graphs, plan your work accordingly. Examine old tests if instructors make them available in class or on reserve in the library. If you can't get copies of old tests, use clues from the class to predict test questions. After taking the first exam in the course, you will have a lot more information about what to expect in the future.

Use Specific Study Skills

Certain study skills are especially useful for test taking. They include choosing study materials, setting a study schedule, critical thinking, taking a pre-test, and becoming organized.

Choose Study Materials

Once you have identified as much as you can about the subject matter of the test, choose the materials that contain the information you need to study. You can save yourself time by making sure that you aren't studying anything you don't need to. Go through your notes, your texts, any primary source materials that were assigned, and any handouts from your instructor. Set aside any materials you don't need so they won't take up your valuable time.

Set a Study Schedule

Use your time-management skills to set a schedule that will help you feel as prepared as you can be. Consider all the relevant factors—the materials you need to study, how many days or weeks until the test date, and how much time you can study each day. If you establish your schedule ahead of time and write it in your date book, you will be much more likely to follow it.

Schedules will vary widely according to situation. For example, if you have only three days before the test and no other obligations during that time, you might set two 2-hour study sessions for yourself during each day. On the other hand, if you have two weeks before a test date, classes during the day, and work three nights a week, you might spread out your study sessions over the nights you have off work during those two weeks.

Prepare Through Critical Thinking

Approach your test preparation critically, working to understand rather than just to pass the test by repeating facts. As you study, try to connect ideas to examples, analyze causes and effects, establish truths, and look at issues from different perspectives. Although it takes work, critical thinking will promote a greater understanding of the subject and probably a higher grade on the exam. Using critical thinking is especially important for essay tests. Prepare by identifying potential essay questions and writing your responses.

Take a Pre-test

Use questions from the ends of textbook chapters to create your own pre-test. Choose questions that are likely to be covered in the test, then answer them under testlike conditions—in quiet, with no books or notes to help you, and with a clock telling you when to quit. Try to duplicate the conditions of the actual test.

Become Organized

Get organized and stay on track as you prepare for each test.

Prepare Physically

When taking a test, you often need to work efficiently under time pressure. If your body is tired or under stress, you will probably not think as clearly or perform as well. If you can, avoid working through the night. Get some sleep so that you can wake up rested and alert. If you are someone who presses the snooze button in the morning, try setting two alarm clocks and placing them across the room from your bed. That way, you'll be more likely to get to your test on time.

Eating right is also important. Sugar-laden snacks will bring your energy up only to send it crashing back down much too soon. Similarly, too much caffeine can add to your tension and make it difficult to focus. Eating nothing will leave you drained, but too much food can make you want to take a nap. The best advice is to eat a light, well-balanced meal before a test. When time is short, grab a high-energy snack such as a banana, some orange juice, or a granola bar.

Conquer Test Anxiety

A certain amount of stress can be a good thing. Your body is on alert, and your energy motivates you to do your best. For many students, however, the time before and during an exam brings a feeling of near-panic known as test anxiety. Described as a bad case of nerves that makes it hard to think or remember, test anxiety can make your life miserable and affect how you do on tests. When anxiety blocks performance, here are some suggestions.

- **Prepare so you'll feel in control.** The more you know about what to expect on the exam, the better you'll feel. Find out what material will be covered, the format of the questions, the length of the exam, and the percentage of points assigned to each question.

- **Put the test in perspective.** No matter how important it may seem, a test is only a small part of your educational experience and an even smaller part of your life. Your test grade does not reflect the kind of person you are or your ability to succeed in life.

- **Make a study plan.** Divide the plan into a series of small tasks. As you finish each one, you'll feel a sense of accomplishment and control.

- **Practise relaxation.** When you feel test anxiety coming on, take some deep breaths, close your eyes, and visualize positive mental images related to the test, like getting a good grade and finishing confidently with time to spare.

Test Anxiety and the Returning Adult Student

If you're returning to school after a layoff of five, ten, or even twenty years, you may wonder if you can compete with younger students or if your mind is still able to learn new material. To counteract these feelings of inadequacy, focus on how your life experiences have given you skills you can use. For example, managing work and a family requires strong time management, planning, and communication skills that can help you plan your study time, juggle school responsibilities, and interact with students and instructors.

In addition, your life experiences give you examples with which you can understand ideas in your courses. For example, managing your finances may help you understand economics or accounting practices; and work experience may give you a context for what you learn in a business management course. If you let yourself feel positive about your knowledge and skills, you may improve your ability to achieve your goals.

Coping with Math Anxiety

For many students there is a special anxiety associated with math.

Students who believe they are no good at math probably won't do well on numerical or algebraic problems, even if they study. Their attitude creates a huge obstacle to their success. If you are one of these students, here are some steps you can take to begin thinking about math—and math tests—in a different way.

- **See the value in learning to use your mind in a mathematical way.** Mathematical thinking is another type of critical thinking. It can help you solve the little and big problems that are part of your world, including how to measure the amount of wallpaper you need in a room, how to compare interest rates on student loans, and even how to analyze the stock market.

- **Think of math as a tool that will help you land a good job.** In fields such as engineering, accounting, and banking, the ability to solve numerical problems is at the heart of the work. In real estate, retail sales, medicine, and publishing, you may use math for tasks such as writing budgets and figuring mortgage rates.

- **Turn negative self-talk into positive self-talk.** Instead of telling yourself that a problem is too hard, tell yourself that if you take small, logical steps, you will succeed.

- **Don't believe that women can't do math.** Sheila Tobias says that when male students fail a math quiz, they don't think they worked hard enough; however, when female students fail, they are three times more likely to feel that they just don't have what it takes. Whether you are a man or a woman, work to overcome this stereotype.

- **Use the people and resources around you.** Get to know your math instructor so you're comfortable asking for help. Join a math study group and make building confidence a group goal. Have a pep meeting right before a big test. Look for math-anxiety workshops. Seek out a tutor who can help you improve your skills and build your confidence.

- **Become comfortable in the world of math.** Find a computer program with math games or buy a paperback book with math puzzles. Do percentages and estimations in your head. Have fun with problems and enjoy solving them. Then transfer these feelings to class work and tests.

- **Understand math's relationship to your life success.** Being at ease with numbers can serve you in day-to-day functions. Percentages can help you compare the financial benefits of different loan programs; addition and subtraction will allow you to balance a chequebook, and fractions will help you compare costs at work. Furthermore, working with numbers helps to develop general thinking skills. The precise calculation and problem solving involved in math help you develop precision, a focus on detail, patience, and a sense of order.

When you have prepared using the strategies that work for you, you are ready to take your exam. Focus on methods that can help you succeed when the test begins.

What Strategies Can Help You Succeed on Tests?

Even though every test is different, there are general strategies that will help you handle almost all tests, including short-answer and essay exams.

Write Down Key Facts

Before you even look at the test, write down any key information—including formulas, rules, and definitions—that you studied recently or even right before you entered the test room. Use the back of the question sheet or a piece of scrap paper for your notes (make sure it is clear to your instructor that this scrap paper didn't come into the test room already filled in!). Recording this information right at the start will make forgetting less likely.

Begin With an Overview of the Exam

Even though exam time is precious, spend a few minutes at the start of the test to get a sense of the kinds of questions you'll be answering, what kind of thinking they require, the number of questions in each section, and the point value of each section. Use this information to schedule the time you need to spend on each section. For example, if a two-hour test is divided into two sections of equal point value—a multiple-choice section with 60 questions and a short-answer section with ten questions—you can spend an hour on the multiple-choice section (one minute per question) and an hour on the short-answer question (six minutes per question).

As you make your calculations, think about the level of difficulty of each section. If you think you can handle the multiple-choice questions in less than an hour and that you'll need more time for the short-answer questions, rebudget your time in a way that works for you.

Know the Ground Rules

A few basic rules apply to any test. Following them will give you an advantage.

- **Read test directions.** While a test made up of 100 true/false questions and one essay may look straightforward, the directions may tell you to answer eighty, or that the essay is an optional bonus. Some questions or sections may be weighted more heavily than others. Try circling or underlining key words and numbers that remind you of the directions.

- **Begin with the parts or questions that seem easiest to you.** Starting with what you know best can boost your confidence and help you save time to spend on the harder parts.

- **Watch the clock.** Keep track of how much time is left and how you are progressing. You may want to plan your time on a scrap piece of paper, especially if you have one or more essays to write. Wear a watch or bring a small clock with you to the test room. A wall clock may be broken, or there may be no clock at all! Take your time too. Rushing is almost always a mistake, even if you feel you've done well. Stay until the end so you can refine and check your work.

- **Master the art of intelligent guessing.** When you are unsure of an answer, you can leave it blank or you can guess. In most cases, guessing will benefit you. First eliminate all the answers you know—or believe—are wrong. Try to narrow your choices to two possible answers; then, choose the one that makes more sense to you. When you recheck your work, decide if you would make the same guesses again, making sure there isn't a qualifier or fact that you hadn't noticed before.

- **Follow directions on machine-scored tests.** Machine-scored tests require that you use a special pencil to fill in a small box on a computerized answer sheet. Use the right pencil (usually, a number 2) and mark your answer in the correct space. Neatness counts on these tests, because the computer can misread stray pencil marks or partially erased answers. Periodically, check the answer number against the question number to make sure they match. One question skipped can cause every answer following it to be marked as incorrect.

Use Critical Thinking to Avoid Errors

When the pressure of a test makes you nervous, critical thinking can help you work through each question thoroughly and avoid errors. Following are some critical-thinking strategies to use during a test.

- **Recall facts, procedures, rules, and formulas.** You base your answers on the information you recall. Think carefully to make sure you recall it accurately. If you don't know how to attack a question or problem, consider any similar questions or problems that you have worked on in class or while studying. Especially with objective questions, items that seem different from what you have studied may indicate answers you can eliminate.

- **Think through causes and effects.** For a numerical problem, think through how you plan to solve it and see if the answer—the effect of your plan—makes sense. For an essay question that asks you to analyze a condition or situation, consider both what caused the condition and what effects it has.

- **Find the best idea to match the example or examples given.** For a numerical problem, decide what formula (idea) best applies to the example or examples (the data of the problem). For an essay question, decide what idea applies or relates to the examples given.

- **Support ideas with examples.** When you put forth an idea in an answer to an essay question, be sure to back up your idea with an adequate number of examples that fit.

- **Evaluate each test question.** In your initial approach to any question, evaluate what kinds of thinking will best help you solve it. For example, essay questions often require cause-and-effect and idea-to-example thinking, while objective questions often benefit from thinking through similarities and differences.

The general strategies you have just explored can also help you address specific types of test questions.

Master Different Types of Test Questions

Although the goal of all test questions is to discover how much you know about a subject, every question type has its own way of asking what you know. Objective questions, such as multiple choice or true/false, test your ability to recall, compare, and contrast information and to choose the right answer from among several choices. Subjective questions, usually essay questions, demand the same information recall but ask that you analyze the mind actions and thinking processes required, then organize, draft, and refine a written response. The following guidelines will help you choose the best answers to both types of questions.

Multiple-Choice Questions

Multiple-choice questions are the most popular type on standardized tests. The following strategies can help you answer these questions:

- **Read the directions carefully.** While most test items ask for a single correct answer, some give you the option of marking several choices that are correct.

- **Read each question thoroughly.** Then look at the choices and try to answer the question.

- **Underline key words and phrases in the question.** If the question is complicated, try to break it down into small sections that are easy to understand.

- **Pay special attention to qualifiers such as only, except, etc.** For example, negative words in a question can confuse your understanding of what the question asks ("Which of the following is not …").

- **If you don't know the answer, eliminate those answers that you know or suspect are wrong.** Your goal is to narrow down your choices. Here are some questions to ask:

  - Is the choice accurate in its own terms? If there's an error in the choice—for example, a term that is incorrectly defined—the answer is wrong.

  - Is the choice relevant? An answer may be accurate, but it may not relate to the essence of the question.

  - Are there any qualifiers, such as always, never, all, none, or every? Qualifiers make it easy to find an exception that makes a choice incorrect. For example, the statement that "children always begin talking before the age of two" can be eliminated as an answer to the question, "When do children generally start to talk?"

  - Do the choices give you any clues? Does a puzzling word remind you of a word you know? If you don't know a word, does any part of the word (prefix, suffix, or root) seem familiar to you?

- **Look for patterns that may lead to the right answer, then use intelligent guessing.** Test-taking experts have found patterns in multiple-choice questions that may help you get a better grade. Here is their advice:

  - Consider the possibility that a choice that is more general than the others is the right answer.

  - Look for a choice that has a middle value in a range (the range can be from small to large, from old to recent). This choice may be the right answer.

  - Look for two choices with similar meanings. One of these answers is probably correct.

- **Make sure you read every word of every answer.** Instructors have been known to include answers that are correct except for a single word.

  Here are some examples of the kinds of multiple-choice questions you might encounter in an Introduction to Macroeconomics course (the correct answer follows each question):

  1. The term "investment" in macroeconomics means
     a. the total amount of capital goods in the country.
     b. the total amount of money invested in bonds and stocks.

   c. the same thing as profits.

   d. the production of goods not for immediate consumption use such as factories, machines, residential housing, and changes in inventories.

   e. the production of goods for immediate consumption.

   (The correct answer is d.)

2. Suppose that the steel industry has a total output of $63.8 billion and purchases $49.0 billion in intermediate inputs. Then the value added in billions of the steel industry in that period is

   a. $112.8

   b. $63.8

   c. $49.0

   d. $14.8

   e. −$49.0

   (The correct answer is d.)

True/False Questions

True/false questions test your knowledge of facts and concepts. Read them carefully to evaluate what they truly say. Try to take these questions at face value without searching for hidden meaning. If you're really stumped, guess (unless you're penalized for wrong answers).

Look for qualifiers in true/false questions, such as *all, only, always, because, generally, usually,* and *sometimes,* that can turn a statement that would otherwise be true into one that is false, or vice versa. For example, "The grammar rule, 'I before E except after C,' is *always* true" is false, whereas "The grammar rule, 'I before E except after C,' is *usually* true," is true. The qualifier makes the difference. Here are some examples of the kinds of true/false questions you might encounter in an Introduction to Macroeconomics course.

Are the following statements true or false?

1. An increase in the foreign exchange value of the Canadian dollar will increase aggregate demand in Canada.

   (The correct answer is False.)

2. If interest rates increase, the quantity of real money demanded decreases.

   (The correct answer is True.)

Essay Questions

An essay question allows you to use your writing skills to demonstrate your knowledge and express your views on a topic. Start by reading the questions and deciding which to tackle (sometimes there's a choice). Then focus on what each question is asking, the mind actions you will have to use, and the writing directions. Read the question carefully and do everything you are asked to do. Some essay questions may contain more than one part.

Watch for certain action verbs that can help you figure out what to do. Underline these words as you read any essay question and use them as a guide.

Next, budget your time and begin to plan. Create an informal outline of think link to map your ideas and indicate examples you plan to cite to support those ideas. Avoid spending too much time on introductions or flowery prose. Start with a thesis idea or statement that states in a broad way what your essay will say. As you continue to write your first paragraph, introduce the essay's points, which may be sub-ideas, causes and effects, or examples. Wrap up the essay with a concise conclusion.

Use clear, simple language in your essay. Support your ideas with examples, and look back at your outline to make sure you are covering everything. Try to write legibly: If your instructor can't read your ideas, it doesn't matter how good they are. If your handwriting is messy, try printing, skipping every other line, or writing on only one side of the paper.

Do your best to save time to reread and revise your essay after you finish getting your ideas down on paper. Look for ideas you left out and sentences that might confuse the reader. Check for mistakes in grammar, spelling, punctuation, and usage. No matter what subject you are writing about, having a command of these factors will make your work all the more complete and impressive. Here are some examples of essay questions you might encounter in your Introduction to Macroeconomics course. In each case, notice the action verbs.

Essay Questions:

1. Some politicians and economists argue that tax cuts are beneficial for the economy in the short run *and* the long run. Describe, explain, and evaluate their arguments.

2. "Unemployment is a more serious economic and social problem than inflation. Therefore, it is worthwhile to increase inflation by a small amount in order to lower unemployment." Evaluate this statement. Do you agree or disagree with it? Give your reasons.

Use Specific Techniques for Math Problems

Mathematical test problems present a special challenge to some students, especially those who suffer from math anxiety. These strategies may help you overcome any difficulties you might have.

Analyze problems carefully.

Make sure that you take all the "givens" into account as you begin your calculations. Focus also on what you want to find or prove.

Write down any formulas, definitions, or theorems that apply to the problem.

Do this before you begin your calculations.

Before you begin, make an estimate to come up with a "ballpark" solution.

Then work the problem and check the solution against your estimate. The two answers should be close. If they're note, recheck your calculations. You may have made a simple calculation error.

Break the calculation into the smallest possible pieces.

Go step by step and don't move on to the next step until you are clear about what you've done so far.

Recall how you solved similar problems.

Past experience can give you valuable clues as to how to solve a particular problem.

Draw a picture to help you see the problem.

This can be a graph, a diagram, a chart, or any other visual image that relates to the problem at hand.

Take your time.

Precision demands concentration and focus. Also, if you're using a calculator, one wrong keystroke can mean the difference between a right and wrong answer.

Be neat.

When it comes to numbers, mistaken identity can mean the difference between a right and a wrong answer. A 4 that looks like a 9 or a 1 that looks like a 7 can make trouble.

Use the opposite operation to check your work.

When you come up with an answer, work backwards to see if you are right. Use subtraction to check your addition; use division to check multiplication; and so on. Try to check every problem before you hand in your paper.

Look back at the questions to be sure you did everything that was asked.

Did you answer every part of the question? Did you show all the required work? Be as complete as you possibly can.

How Can You Learn From Test Mistakes?

The purpose of a test is to see how much you know, not merely to achieve a grade. The knowledge that comes from attending class and studying should allow you to correctly answer test questions. Knowledge also comes when you learn from your mistakes. If you don't learn from what you get wrong on a test, you are likely to repeat the same mistake again on another test and in life. Learn from test mistakes just as you learn from mistakes in your personal and professional life.

Try to identify patterns in your mistakes by looking for:

- careless errors—In your rush to complete the exam, did you misread the question or directions, blacken the wrong box, skip a question, or use illegible handwriting?

- conceptual or factual errors—Did you misunderstand a concept or never learn it in the first place? Did you fail to master certain facts? Did you skip part of the assigned text or miss important classes in which ideas were covered?

You may want to rework the questions you got wrong. Based on the feedback from your instructor, try rewriting an essay, recalculating a problem, or redoing the questions that follow a reading selection. As frustrating as they are, remember that mistakes show that you are human, and they can help you learn. If you see patterns of careless errors, promise yourself that next time you'll try to budget enough time to double-check your work. If you pick up conceptual and factual errors, rededicate yourself to better preparation.

When you fail a test, don't throw it away. First, take comfort in the fact that a lot of students have been in your shoes and that you are likely to improve your performance. Then recommit to the process by reviewing and analyzing your errors. Be sure you understand why you failed. You may want to ask for an explanation from your instructor. Finally, develop a plan to really learn the material, if you didn't understand it in the first place.

How Can You Cope with Life Challenges?

Think Positively About Failure

When you feel you have failed, how can you boost your outlook?

Stay aware of the fact that you are a capable, valuable person.

People often react to failure by becoming convinced that they are incapable and incompetent. Fight that tendency by reminding yourself of your successes, focusing your energy on your best abilities, and knowing that you have the strength to try again. Realize that your failure isn't a setback as long as you learn form it and rededicate yourself to excellence. Remember that the energy you might expend on talking down to yourself would be better spent on trying again and moving ahead.

Share your thoughts and disappointment with others.

Everybody fails. Trading stories will help you realize you're not alone. People refrain from talking about failures out of embarrassment, often feeling as though no one else could have made as big a mistake as they did. When you open up, though, you may be surprised to hear others exchange stories that rival your own. Be careful not to get caught in a destructive cycle of complaining, however. Instead, focus on the kind of creative energy that can help you find ways to learn from your failures.

Look on the bright side.

At worst, you have at least learned a lesson that will help you avoid similar situations in the future. At best, there may be some positive results of what happened. If your romance flounders, the extra study time you suddenly have may help you boost your grades. If you fail a class, you may discover that you need to focus on a different subject that suits you better. What you learn from a failure may, in an unexpected way, bring you around to where you want to be.

Dealing With Success

Success isn't reserved for the wealthy, famous people you see glamourized in magazines and newspapers. Success isn't money or fame, although it can bring such things. Success is being who you want to be and doing what you want to do. Success is within your reach.

Pay attention to the small things when measuring success. You may not feel successful until you reach an important goal you have set for yourself. However, along the way each step is a success. When you are trying to drop a harmful habit, each time you stay on course is a success. When you are juggling work, school, and your personal life, just coping with what every new day brings equal success. If you received a C on a paper and then earned a B on the next one, your advancement is successful.

Remember that success is a process. If you deny yourself the label of "success" until you reach the top of where you want to be, you will have a much harder time getting there. Just moving ahead toward improvement and growth, however fast or slow the movement, equals success.

Here are some techniques to handle your successes.

First, appreciate yourself.

You deserve it. Take time to congratulate yourself for a job well done—whether it be a good grade, an important step in learning a new language, a job offer, a promotion or graduation, or a personal victory over substance abuse. Bask in the glow a bit. Everybody hears about his or her mistakes, but people don't praise themselves (or each other) enough when success happens. Praise can give you a terrific vote of confidence. Praise inspires us to action.

Take that confidence on the road.

This victory can lead to others. Based on this success, you may be expected to prove to yourself and others that you are capable of growth and of continuing your successes and building upon them. Show yourself and others that the confidence is well-founded. Confidence fights, and beats, fear. You can build your confidence by reading books on optimism and positive thinking.

Stay sensitive to others.

There could be people around you who may not have been so successful. Remember that you have been in their place, and they in yours, and the positions may change many times over in the future. Enjoy what you have, work to build on it and not to take it for granted, and support others as they need it. Use every opportunity to meet new people.

Staying sensitive to others is an important goal always, whether you are feeling successful or less than successful. Giving what you can of your time, energy, and resources to the community and the world is part of being aware of what others need. Your contributions can help to bring success to others.

Self-Test Questions

Chapter 1

1. Economics can be best described as
   (a) the study of how a society ought to allocate its resources.
   (b) the study of the use of scarce resources to satisfy unlimited human wants.
   (c) the application of sophisticated mathematical models to address social problems.
   (d) a normative science.
   (e) the study of how to reduce inflation and unemployment.

2. Scarcity exists because there are limited resources. For this reason, all economic choices involve
   (a) a value judgment.
   (b) pride.
   (c) an opportunity cost.
   (d) complementary ends.
   (e) greed.

3. If the government of Ontario chooses to build a school, those resources are no longer available to build a hospital. This illustrates the concept of:
   (a) equalization.
   (b) normative economics.
   (c) opportunity cost.
   (d) marginal decisions.
   (e) the circular flow.

4. The production possibilities boundary is a diagram demonstrating that
   (a) when a society combines its resources efficiently, it cannot produce more of one good without producing less of the other good.
   (b) when a society combines its resources inefficiently, it cannot produce more of one good without producing less of the other good.
   (c) some resources are always idle in a democratic society.
   (d) all points inside the curve are preferred to all points on the curve.
   (e) the demand for goods always exceeds the supply.

5. Suppose a new law required all Canadian workers to retire at age 50. The effect on the Canadian economy would be to move
   (a) it along its production possibility boundary.
   (b) its production possibility boundary inward.
   (c) it beyond its production possibility boundary.
   (d) its production possibility boundary outward.
   (e) There would be no change in Canada's production possibilities boundary.

Figure 1-1 shows two production possibilities boundaries for a country that produces two types of goods—military goods and civilian goods. Refer to this figure to answer questions 6 and 7.

FIGURE 1-1

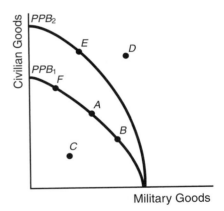

6. Refer to Figure 1-1. If this country is constrained by the production possibility boundary PPB_1 and is currently producing the combination of goods indicated at point A, it can produce more military goods by moving to point
   (a) F.
   (b) E.
   (c) B.
   (d) C.
   (e) D.

7. Refer to Figure 1-1. A shift of the production possibility boundary from PPB_1 to PPB_2 implies
    (a) a movement from full employment to some unemployment.
    (b) that if point C is the new choice of outputs, productivity has increased in the civilian goods industries.
    (c) that technology in the civilian goods industries has improved.
    (d) an inevitable decrease in total output.
    (e) that technology in the military goods industries has improved.

8. The distinction between private and public sector production is
    (a) an economic one, depending upon whether the output is sold on the market or not.
    (b) a distinction between efficient and inefficient production.
    (c) a legal one, depending upon the ownership of the producing organization.
    (d) subsidiary to the question of whether the output is marketed or not.
    (e) a financial one, depending on whether the producing firm is listed on a public stock exchange.

9. Generally, economists agree that
    (a) the mix of price and command principles that exists in Canada is the best.
    (b) the optimal mix of price and command systems remains constant over time.
    (c) most production and consumption decisions are more efficiently coordinated by the price system than by central planning.
    (d) government intervention in the economy is only justified in time of war.
    (e) command economies have been very successful in distributing income in socially just ways.

10. If some income earned by households is not spent on the output of firms, this will cause the circular flow of income to
    (a) stop.
    (b) run over.
    (c) expand.
    (d) contract.
    (e) explode.

Chapter 2

1. Which of the following is a normative statement?
    (a) The higher is the level of taxes, the lower is consumption spending.
    (b) The higher is the level of taxes, the higher are wage demands.
    (c) A reduction in exports taxes on petroleum would result in higher workers' wages.
    (d) Tuition fees at universities should be waived for low-income students.
    (e) A free-trade agreement between two countries will result in an increase in trade.

2. Which of the following statements provides the best example of the law of large numbers?
    (a) More people will make large errors than small errors in estimating the number of people in a crowd.
    (b) The larger the number of people making a measurement, the smaller the average of their errors.
    (c) More people will underestimate the number of people in a room than will overestimate the number of people.
    (d) The larger the number of people, the smaller the number of people making measurement errors.
    (e) The larger the number of people making a measurement, the more accurate will be their measurements.

3. Suppose an ice cream shop's revenue is influenced, in part, by the region's average daily temperature. When examining the determinants of the firm's revenue, the average daily temperature is a(n) _____ variable.
    (a) endogenous
    (b) exogenous
    (c) flow
    (d) dependent
    (e) induced

4. Approaching any economic issue via the scientific method involves
    (a) formulating normative statements about it.
    (b) finding the correct data to validate the theory.
    (c) seeking agreement from colleagues regarding the correctness of the theory.
    (d) considering stock and flow variables.
    (e) setting up a theory that will explain it and then seeing if the theory can be refuted by evidence.

5. The statement that an increase in average per capita income will lead to an increase in the demand for new cars is an example of a(n)
   - (a) prophecy.
   - (b) prediction.
   - (c) normative statement.
   - (d) theory.
   - (e) economic law.

6. Of the following, which is the most important characteristic of a successful theory?
   - (a) The theory provides a basis for facts about economic behaviour.
   - (b) The theory should never be refuted.
   - (c) The theory adequately explains all economic behaviour.
   - (d) All assumptions on which it is based are true.
   - (e) The theory allows us to predict behaviour reasonably accurately.

7. Choose the answer that best explains why economists build models that abstract from the complexities of reality.
   - (a) Because the complexities of reality are unimportant.
   - (b) Because they believe they gain a greater understanding of reality.
   - (c) Because economists are not interested in reality.
   - (d) Because economists don't understand the real world.
   - (e) Because the scientific method is wrong.

8. It is only reasonable to reject an economic hypothesis when
   - (a) one or more of the assumptions on which it is based fails to conform with reality.
   - (b) it is shown to be wrong with certainty by empirical observation.
   - (c) the probability that it is wrong, based on empirical observation, is judged to be unacceptably high.
   - (d) an empirical observation is encountered in which its predictions fail.
   - (e) the possibility of error has been completely eliminated.

9. In a co-ordinate graph with Y on the vertical axis and X on the horizontal axis, suppose point A represents co-ordinates ($X=3$, $Y=12$) and point B represents co-ordinates ($X=9$, $Y=24$). Then the slope of the straight line joining points A and B is
   - (a) −2.
   - (b) 2.
   - (c) 2/3.
   - (d) −3.
   - (e) 3.

10. Different observations of one variable all taken in different places at the same point in time are called
    - (a) cross-sectional data.
    - (b) time-analysis data.
    - (c) logarithmic data.
    - (d) topographic data.
    - (e) time-series data.

Chapter 3

1. Quantity demanded of a given commodity can be represented by
   - (a) a demand curve.
   - (b) a demand schedule.
   - (c) a point on a demand curve.
   - (d) the money value of the stock of the commodity held by households.
   - (e) the slope of the demand curve.

2. Consider hot dog wieners and hot dog buns. When the price of hot dog wieners increases, the demand for buns is likely to
   - (a) remain unchanged, although the price of buns is likely to fall.
   - (b) remain unchanged, although the price of buns is likely to rise.
   - (c) remain unchanged.
   - (d) increase.
   - (e) decrease.

3. Consider the following two statements. (1) An increase in the price of popsicles will cause a decrease in the demand for popsicles. (2) An increase in the price of popsicles will cause an increase in the demand for fudgsicles. In which of these two statements is the term "demand" used correctly?

   (a) neither statement
   (b) the first statement
   (c) the second statement
   (d) both statements

4. The term "quantity supplied" refers to the amount of a commodity that

   (a) producers actually sell during a given period of time at a given price.
   (b) households wish producers to sell during a given period of time at a given price.
   (c) is exchanged between producers and consumers at all possible prices.
   (d) producers wish to sell at a given price during a given period of time.

5. The positive slope of the supply curve indicates that

   (a) as price goes up, quantity supplied will decrease.
   (b) consumers will want to buy less at higher prices.
   (c) as price goes up, quantity supplied will increase.
   (d) if the costs of production increase, the quantity supplied will have to increase also.
   (e) as price goes up, quantity supplied will remain constant.

6. Suppose that fertilizer is necessary to produce wheat. If the price of fertilizer falls

   (a) the supply curve of fertilizer shifts to the left.
   (b) the supply curve of wheat shifts to the right.
   (c) the supply curve of wheat shifts to the left.
   (d) there is a movement along the supply curve of wheat.
   (e) the supply curve of fertilizer shifts to the right.

Table 3-1 lists the supply and demand schedule for dozens of roses. Refer to this table to answer questions 7 and 8.

TABLE 3-1

Price	Quantity Supplied per period	Quantity Demanded per period
$10	200	500
$20	300	450
$30	400	400
$40	500	350
$50	600	300

7. In Table 3-1, the equilibrium price for a dozen roses is _____.

   (a) $10
   (b) $20
   (c) $30
   (d) $40
   (e) $50

8. In Table 3-1, how many dozens of roses would actually be purchased if the price were $10?

   (a) 200
   (b) 300
   (c) 350
   (d) 400
   (e) 500

FIGURE 3-1

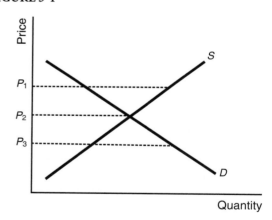

9. In Figure 3-1, if the price were P_3 there would be _____ of this good.

   (a) excess supply.
   (b) excess demand.
   (c) an equilibrium price and quantity of this good.
   (d) a surplus.

10. Movie theatre prices are less during the daytime than in the evening. If the supply of movies does not change between daytime and evening, then the most likely explanation for this difference in price is
    (a) the evening demand curve is to the left of the daytime demand curve.
    (b) the evening demand curve is to the right of the daytime demand curve.
    (c) the evening supply curve is to the left of the daytime supply curve.
    (d) the evening supply curve is to the right of the daytime supply curve.

Chapter 4

1. When the percentage change in quantity demanded (resulting from a price change) is less than the percentage change in price, demand is said to be
    (a) elastic.
    (b) zero elastic.
    (c) perfectly elastic
    (d) unit elastic.
    (e) inelastic

2. Which of the following statements would you expect to be true about T-shirts and clothing?
    (a) Compared with clothing, T-shirts have a lower price elasticity of demand because they are specifically defined.
    (b) Because T-shirts are clothing, but not all clothing is T-shirts, T-shirts would have a lower price elasticity than clothing.
    (c) Clothing has a higher price elasticity of demand because it is a necessity.
    (d) Because T-shirts are clothing, T-shirts would have the same price elasticity of demand as clothing.
    (e) Clothing has a lower price elasticity of demand because it is more broadly defined.

3. Suppose that the quantity demanded of paperback novels rises from 80 000 to 120 000 units when the price falls from $11 to $9 per unit. The price elasticity of demand for this product is
    (a) 1/3.
    (b) 1.
    (c) 2/3.
    (d) 3/2.
    (e) 2.

4. If the total expenditure on perfume increases when the price of perfume falls, the price elasticity of demand is
    (a) greater than one (demand is elastic).
    (b) less than one (demand is inelastic).
    (c) unity (demand is unit elastic).
    (d) not determinable from the information given.
    (e) exactly zero.

5. The elasticity of supply for some product will tend to be smaller
    (a) the higher is the elasticity of demand for the product.
    (b) the lower is the elasticity of demand for the product.
    (c) the harder it is for firms to shift from the production of one product to another product.
    (d) the easier it is for firms to shift from the production of one product to another product.

6. Because the elasticity of supply adjusts over time, a shift in demand will, in the short run, generally cause
    (a) the price to overshoot its long-run equilibrium value.
    (b) the price to undershoot its long-run equilibrium value.
    (c) the quantity exchanged to overshoot its long-run equilibrium value.
    (d) both price and quantity exchanged to overshoot their long-run equilibrium values.
    (e) none of the above.

7. Producers will bear a larger burden of a sales tax if
    (a) demand is relatively elastic and supply is relatively inelastic.
    (b) demand is relatively inelastic and supply is relatively elastic.
    (c) both demand and supply are relatively inelastic.
    (d) both demand and supply are relatively elastic.
    (e) the tax is collected by firms rather than remitted directly to the government by consumers.

8. The imposition of a sales tax will cause the least burden on consumers when demand is
    (a) elastic.
    (b) unitary elastic.
    (c) perfectly inelastic.
    (d) perfectly elastic.
    (e) vertical.

9. If the income elasticity of demand for a good is 1.25, a 10 percent increase in income results in
   (a) a 12.5 percent increase in the quantity demanded.
   (b) a 12.5 percent decrease in the quantity demanded.
   (c) a 125 percent increase in the quantity demanded.
   (d) a decrease in quantity demanded.
   (e) not enough information to answer this question.

10. Suppose the cross-elasticity of demand for two goods, domestic beer and imported beer, is positive. If the price of imported beer falls, then quantity demanded will
   (a) rise for both domestic and imported beer.
   (b) fall for both domestic and imported beer.
   (c) rise for domestic beer and fall for imported beer.
   (d) fall for domestic beer and rise for imported beer.
   (e) not enough information to answer this question.

Chapter 5

1. An increase in the price of rubber can be expected to increase the price of automobile tires because
   (a) consumers view the two goods as substitutes.
   (b) the cost of producing tires will rise and thus the supply of tires will fall.
   (c) the cost of producing tires will fall and thus the supply of tires will rise.
   (d) tires are inferior goods.
   (e) tires are normal goods.

2. One reason why the price of cement in Florida may be relatively insensitive to changes in the price of cement in British Columbia is that
   (a) cement is an inferior good.
   (b) cement is a normal good.
   (c) not very many consumers travel back and forth between Florida and British Columbia.
   (d) cement is very costly to transport.
   (e) cement is easily produced in both regions.

3. In free markets, surpluses are eliminated by
   (a) government price controls.
   (b) rationing.
   (c) black markets.
   (d) price increases.
   (e) price decreases.

4. If the equilibrium price of some good is $1000, a price ceiling of $800 will bring about
   (a) the same general effects as a price ceiling of $1200.
   (b) the same general effects as an equilibrium price of $1000.
   (c) the same general effects as a price ceiling of $200.
   (d) massive surpluses of the good.
   (e) no change in the market

FIGURE 5-1

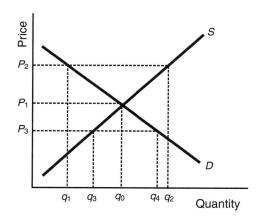

5. Refer to Figure 5-1. P_2 represents a price imposed by the government. What is the quantity of this good that would be exchanged in the market?
   (a) q_0
   (b) q_1
   (c) q_2
   (d) q_3
   (e) q_4

6. Refer to Figure 5-1. P_3 represents a price imposed by the government. The result would be
   (a) excess supply of q_3q_4.
   (b) excess supply of q_3q_0.
   (c) excess demand of q_0q_2.
   (d) excess demand of q_1q_2.
   (e) excess demand of q_3q_4.

7. Assuming that the long-run supply of housing is relatively elastic, the imposition of binding rent controls will
   (a) lead to a reduction in the housing shortage over time.
   (b) lead to a worsening of the housing shortage over time.
   (c) lead to no significant change in the housing shortage.
   (d) lead to only a temporary housing shortage.
   (e) lead the price of rental housing to revert back to its equilibrium level.

8. Who are likely to be the biggest beneficiaries of rent controls?
   (a) landlords
   (b) prospective tenants
   (c) current tenants
   (d) construction companies
   (e) no group will benefit from the controls

9. If the government's goal is to protect farmers from fluctuating incomes, it must make the demand curve facing the farmers
   (a) elastic.
   (b) inelastic.
   (c) perfectly inelastic.
   (d) horizontal.
   (e) unit elastic.

10. Suppose a Canadian farmer is able to sell his product at a given world price that is unaffected by his own volume of sales. This farmer would
   (a) increase his income with each unit he sold.
   (b) restrict his supply to maintain his income.
   (c) restrict his supply to maintain his income.
   (d) store his output and wait for a better price.
   (e) cause the world market supply curve to shift to the right, thereby causing the price to fall.

Chapter 6

1. If a good has a positive marginal utility, then consumption of an additional unit would mean
   (a) that total utility is also zero.
   (b) that total utility would not change.
   (c) that total utility would be increasing.
   (d) that total utility would be decreasing.
   (e) that the consumer would no longer receive any satisfaction from any consumption of this good.

2. Given the assumption of utility maximization, Karen will allocate her expenditures in such a way that
   (a) her total utility from each good is equal.
   (b) the total number of dollars she spends on each good is equal.
   (c) her utility received from the last unit of each good is equal.
   (d) her utility received per dollar spent on the last unit of each good is equal.
   (e) the marginal utility of all goods consumed is zero.

3. If a consumer is maximizing his utility between a pair of products (X and Y) then the following is true:
   (a) $P_X(MU_X) = P_Y(MU_Y)$.
   (b) $MU_X = MU_Y$.
   (c) $MU_X/P_X = MU_Y/P_Y$.
   (d) $MU_X/P_Y = MU_Y/P_X$.
   (e) $P_X = P_Y$.

4. Consumer surplus
   (a) is the sum of the marginal values to the consumer.
   (b) is the total value that a consumer receives from a purchase of a particular good.
   (c) is a measure of the gains a consumer receives in the market.
   (d) is the difference between what the consumer is willing to pay and what he/she actually pays.
   (e) is the consumption of a commodity above and beyond the amount required by the consumer.

FIGURE 6-1

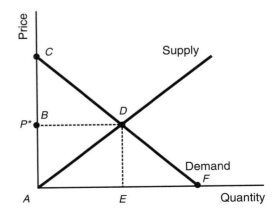

5. In Figure 6-1, suppose the market price is P^*. In this case, consumer surplus is outlined by the area
   (a) *ACDE*.
   (b) *ABDF*.
   (c) *ACF*.
   (d) *BCD*.
   (e) *ADE*.

6. Consider a scarce, necessary commodity that is provided to households by the government at a price of zero. Economic theory tells us that
   (a) the commodity is equitably distributed.
   (b) there will be an excess supply of this commodity.
   (c) households will consume more of this good than they would in a free market.
   (d) consumer surplus is zero.

7. Since there is a plentiful supply of water in Canada (this is not true in many parts of the world), the consumption of water in Canada
   (a) takes place at relatively low marginal value.
   (b) takes priority over some other good.
   (c) takes place at relatively high marginal value.
   (d) should be regulated by the government.
   (e) has a total utility of zero.

8. The paradox of value refers to the
   (a) confusion between total and marginal values.
   (b) belief that goods with high total values should command high prices.
   (c) belief that goods with low total values should command low prices.
   (d) belief that the price of something necessary to sustain life is "more valuable" than a decorative, luxury item.
   (e) all of the above.

9. The real purchasing power of an individual will NOT be affected if
   (a) money income is cut in half and the prices of all goods and services fall by fifty percent.
   (b) money income falls and the price of one good falls.
   (c) money income doubles and the prices of all goods and services are cut in half.
   (d) money income doubles and the prices of all goods and services remain constant.
   (e) none of the above.

10. Suppose a consumer can purchase only two goods, beef and chicken. If the price of beef falls, and the consumption of chicken increases, we can conclude that the increased consumption of chicken is due to
    (a) neither the income effect nor the substitution effect.
    (b) both the income effect and the substitution effect.
    (c) the income effect only.
    (d) the substitution effect only.

Chapter 7

1. The opportunity cost of any factor of production is
   (a) the benefit forgone by not using it in its worst alternative.
   (b) its accounting cost.
   (c) the money actually paid to the factor of production.
   (d) the benefit forgone by not using it in its best alternative.
   (e) none of the above.

2. If the owner of a firm uses his own inputs in the firm, then economists refer to the opportunity cost of these inputs as
   (a) direct production costs.
   (b) accounting costs.
   (c) sunk costs.
   (d) imputed costs.
   (e) inverted costs.

3. Normal profits are
   (a) the difference between economic profits and accounting profits.
   (b) the imputed returns to capital and risk taking just necessary to prevent owners from withdrawing from the industry.
   (c) the same as accounting profits.
   (d) the excess of revenue over full economic costs including imputed returns to capital and risk taking.
   (e) profits that are not considered to be excessive by society's norms.

4. If increasing quantities of a variable factor are applied to a given quantity of fixed factors, then the law of diminishing returns tells us that
   (a) the marginal product and the average product of the variable factor will eventually decrease.
   (b) the marginal product will eventually decrease with constant average product.
   (c) the average product will eventually decrease with constant marginal product.
   (d) the average product will eventually decrease, but only if total product is held constant.
   (e) total product will eventually begin to fall.

5. Marginal productivity has reached the point of diminishing marginal returns when
   (a) marginal product has reached a maximum.
   (b) average product has reached a maximum.
   (c) the marginal product begins to fall at an increasing rate.
   (d) the total product begins to fall.
   (e) the marginal product curve lies below the average product curve.

6. Average product is at its maximum when
   (a) total product is maximized.
   (b) marginal product is maximized.
   (c) the maximum quantity of the variable input is employed.
   (d) diminishing returns cease to operate.
   (e) average product equals marginal product and marginal product is falling.

7. Marginal cost is
   (a) the change in total cost resulting from an additional unit of output.
   (b) the change in fixed cost resulting from an additional unit of output.
   (c) the difference between average total cost and average variable cost.
   (d) the cost per unit when the firm is operating at capacity.
   (e) the cost of an additional unit of a variable factor of production.

8. Short-run cost curves are eventually upward sloping because of the effects of
   (a) the increasing price of variable inputs.
   (b) diminishing marginal product.
   (c) increasing fixed costs.
   (d) increasing marginal productivity of the variable inputs.
   (e) all of the above.

9. If marginal cost is rising, then
   (a) the average fixed cost must be rising.
   (b) the average variable cost must be rising.
   (c) the average total cost must be rising.
   (d) marginal product must be zero.
   (e) marginal product must be falling.

10. Which of the following is true of a plant that is operating at its capacity?
   (a) Average fixed cost is at a minimum.
   (b) Marginal cost is at a minimum.
   (c) Average variable cost is at a minimum.
   (d) Average total cost is at a minimum.
   (e) More of the variable factor of production should be employed.

Chapter 8

1. In the long run, a profit-maximizing firm produces any given level of output by choosing the production method that
   (a) minimizes costs.
   (b) maximizes the marginal product of all factors.
   (c) maximizes the marginal product of labour.
   (d) shows a flat total cost curve.
   (e) all of the above.

2. Assuming two inputs, labour (L) and capital (K), cost minimization requires
   (a) $P_K MP_K = P_L MP_L$
   (b) $MP_L = MP_K$
   (c) $MP_K/P_K = MP_L/P_L$
   (d) $MP_K/P_L = MP_L/P_K$
   (e) $P_K = P_L$

3. If a firm is using labour and capital such that the MP of labour is two times the MP of capital, and the price of labour is four times the price of capital, the firm should
   (a) increase capital and decrease labour.
   (b) decrease capital and labour.
   (c) decrease capital and increase labour.
   (d) increase both labour and capital.
   (e) not substitute away from its present factor mix.

4. Suppose that capital costs $6 per unit and labour costs $3 per unit. For a profit-maximizing firm operating at its optimal factor mix, if the marginal product of capital is 80, the marginal product of labour is _____.
   (a) 10
   (b) 20
   (c) 40
   (d) 90
   (e) 120

5. Suppose that capital costs $5 per unit and labour costs $2 per unit. If the marginal product of capital is 40 and the marginal product of labour is 40, the firm should
   (a) employ more capital and labour.
   (b) employ less capital and labour.
   (c) employ more capital and less labour.
   (d) employ less capital and more labour.
   (e) not change its current factor use.

6. The long-run average cost (*LRAC*) curve shows
   (a) the lowest unit cost at which the firm can produce a given output.
   (b) the highest unit costs of producing a given output.
   (c) the operation of the law of diminishing returns.
   (d) what happens to the fixed costs in the long run.
   (e) the same as the short-run average cost curve.

7. A short-run average total cost curve and a long-run average cost curve are tangent
   (a) where the short-run cost curve is downward sloping.
   (b) where the short-run cost curve is upward sloping.
   (c) when the quantity of the fixed factor being employed is at the optimal level for that level of output.
   (d) where the short-run cost curve is downward-sloping and the quantity of the fixed factor is optimal.
   (e) by coincidence.

8. Assume a firm is using 10 units of capital and 10 units of labour to produce 10 carpets. Now it doubles both inputs resulting in a new total of 25 carpets being produced. This firm is experiencing
   (a) decreasing returns to scale.
   (b) increasing returns to scale.
   (c) constant returns to scale.
   (d) diseconomies of scale.
   (e) increasing costs.

9. In the very long run, the production function could be changed by
   (a) rising costs of the factors of production.
   (b) increasing returns to scale of operation.
   (c) increasing education of labour.
   (d) diminishing returns.
   (e) none of the above.

10. If there is an improvement in technology available to the firm,
   (a) the firm will move to a lower point on both its long-run and short-run average cost curves.
   (b) the firm will move to a lower point on its long-run average cost curve only.
   (c) both the long-run and short-run average cost curves will shift downward.
   (d) there will be a downward shift in the long-run average cost curve but not in the short- run average cost curve.
   (e) there will be no change in the cost curves in the long run.

Chapter 9

1. One assumption made in the theory of perfect competition is that
   (a) the individual firm can affect the price of the product it sells.
   (b) the individual firm can influence demand by advertising.
   (c) each firm must earn economic profits to remain in the industry.
   (d) any firm can easily enter or leave the industry.
   (e) there are few producers of an identical product.

2. The short-run supply curve of a perfectly competitive firm is
   (a) the entire marginal-cost curve.
   (b) the rising portion of the average-variable-cost curve.
   (c) the average-revenue curve.
   (d) the marginal-cost curve above the average-variable-cost curve.
   (e) the industry supply curve.

3. Consider a firm that is producing where price equals average total cost and average total cost is less than marginal cost. If this is a perfectly competitive firm it should
   (a) reduce output.
   (b) expand output.
   (c) shut down.
   (d) increase the market price.
   (e) not change output.

Consider the following cost curves for a perfectly competitive firm. Refer to this figure to answer questions 4-6.

FIGURE 9-1

4. In Figure 9-1, if the current market price is $22 the profit-maximizing output of this firm is
   (a) 100 units.
   (b) 200 units.
   (c) 250 units.
   (d) 270 units.
   (e) 300 units.

5. In Figure 9-1, if the price is $30 and the firm is producing at its profit-maximizing output, then total costs for the firm are
   (a) $300.
   (b) $360.
   (c) $6000.
   (d) $6600.
   (e) $9000.

6. In Figure 9-1, the short-run supply curve for this firm is its
   (a) *SRATC* curve at or above $20.
   (b) *SRAVC* curve at or above $10.
   (c) marginal cost curve.
   (d) marginal cost curve at or above $20.
   (e) marginal cost curve at or above $10.

7. If all firms in a perfectly competitive market are producing where each firm has $P > SRATC$, we can predict that
   (a) individual firms in the industry will increase their output.
   (b) new firms will enter the market because existing firms are earning economic profits.
   (c) the market supply curve will become less elastic.
   (d) existing firms will continue to earn economic profits in the long run.
   (e) all of the above.

8. Long-run equilibrium in a perfectly competitive industry is characterized by
   (a) internal economies of scale.
   (b) an output level at which firms' *SRATC* curves are tangent to the downward sloping portion of their *LRAC* curves.
   (c) falling costs.
   (d) rising costs.
   (e) each firm producing at the minimum point on its *LRAC* curve.

9. If a competitive firm is producing where its $MR = MC$, but is operating to the left of the minimum point of its *LRAC* curve,
   (a) it cannot be producing its present output efficiently.
   (b) it can reduce its average costs by building a larger plant.
   (c) it can still be in long-run equilibrium as long as $P = SRATC$.
   (d) its profits will decrease if it builds a larger plant.
   (e) none of the above

10. Consider a perfectly competitive industry in which demand for the product is in steady decline over time. Economic theory predicts that in the long run
    (a) newer, more efficient firms will enter the industry and earn normal profits.
    (b) existing firms will modernize plant and equipment in order to increase efficiency.
    (c) existing firms will expand output as a means of recovering losses.
    (d) firms will begin advertising in order to increase demand for their product.
    (e) plant and equipment will not be replaced, and capacity in the industry will gradually shrink.

Chapter 10

1. If a monopolist is producing a level of output that maximizes its profits, then the
    (a) price always exceeds average total cost.
    (b) price equals marginal cost.
    (c) price exceeds marginal cost.
    (d) price equals marginal revenue.
    (e) price is below marginal revenue.

2. A firm can be described as a natural monopoly when
    (a) there are no competing firms.
    (b) it holds an exclusive charter from the government.
    (c) the *ATC* curve is upward sloping.
    (d) the *MC* curve is downward sloping.
    (e) it can supply the entire market and be the most efficient size.

3. A monopolistic firm will be earning zero economic profits when
    (a) average total cost is minimized.
    (b) marginal revenue equals marginal cost.
    (c) marginal revenue equals price.
    (d) price equals marginal cost.
    (e) average total cost equals price.

4. If a monopolist's marginal revenue is $MR = 25 - 3Q$ and marginal cost is $MC = 10$, then the profit-maximizing quantity that the monopolist should produce is
    (a) 0.
    (b) 5.
    (c) 7.
    (d) 10.
    (e) 25.

5. When firms in an industry join together to form a cartel, then
    (a) member firms have agreed to cooperate in reducing costs.
    (b) member firms have agreed to reduce their joint output.
    (c) the demand curve facing the industry must be inelastic.
    (d) the demand curve facing the industry must be elastic.
    (e) member firms have agreed to reduce investment

6. Consider a cartelized industry where output has been restricted and the price of the product has been raised. An individual firm (X) can benefit most from the existence of the cartel if
    (a) all firms, including X, cooperate and restrict output.
    (b) firm X restricts output, while the other firms do not.
    (c) all firms, except X, cooperate and restrict output.
    (d) no firms restrict output.
    (e) all firms revert back to their competitive outputs.

7. A monopolist is able to increase profits by practising price discrimination because
    (a) the cost curves facing the monopolist shift downward.
    (b) the price of the output is raised above the competitive price.
    (c) different prices can be charged according to the willingness to pay of each consumer.
    (d) the market price is raised above the competitive price.
    (e) different prices can be charged according to the different marginal cost on each unit produced.

8. Which of the following equations are true for a perfectly price discriminating monopolist?
    (a) $MR = P$
    (b) $MR = 1/2P$
    (c) $AR = ATC$
    (d) $MC = 1/2MR$
    (e) none of the above

Suppose a monopolist faces the demand curve and cost curves shown below in Figure 10-1. Refer to this figure to answer questions 9 and 10.

FIGURE 10-1

Part (A)

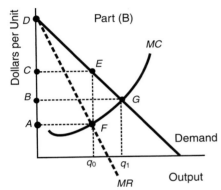

Part (B)

9. In Figure 10-1, part (A), a perfect price discriminating monopolist produces the quantity

   (a) q_0.
   (b) q_1.
   (c) q_2.
   (d) q_3.

10. In Figure 10-1, part (B), if the monopolist practises perfect price discrimination, the consumer surplus is represented by the area

   (a) *CDE*.
   (b) *BDG*.
   (c) *BCEG*.
   (d) *ABGF*.
   (e) zero—there is no consumer surplus.

Chapter 11

1. Imperfectly competitive markets are characterized by

   (a) inelastic market demand curves.
   (b) similar cost conditions facing each individual firm.
   (c) non-price competition among firms.
   (d) economies of scale.
   (e) all of the above.

2. The excess-capacity theorem predicts

   (a) that when price-taking firms maximize their profits by setting price equal to marginal cost, each firm operates with some excess capacity.
   (b) that long-run equilibrium in a monopolistically competitive industry occurs with all firms producing at a lower output level than that at which average total costs are minimized.
   (c) that profit-maximizing firms will always choose to operate with some degree of excess capacity, in order to be flexible in the face of shifts in demand.
   (d) that monopolistic firms will achieve positive economic profits by restricting output below the economically efficient level at which average total costs are minimized.

3. A good example of a monopolistically competitive firm is:

   1. The Gap clothing store
   2. Dairy Queen
   3. a Prince Edward Island potato farmer

   (a) 1 only
   (b) 2 only
   (c) 3 only
   (d) 1 and 2 only
   (e) 2 and 3 only

4. If firms are able to freely enter and exit a monopolistically competitive industry, then we can predict

   (a) a negatively sloped demand curve for the industry.
   (b) strategic behaviour with regard to other firms in the industry.
   (c) brand proliferation.
   (d) zero profits in long-run equilibrium.
   (e) excess capacity in the industry.

5. An oligopolist is different from a perfect competitor or a monopolist in that it

   (a) operates where $MR = MC$.
   (b) takes account of its competitors' reactions to its output decisions.
   (c) always makes positive profits.
   (d) always operates with the protection of entry barriers.
   (e) earns zero profits in the long run.

6. Which of the following is an incorrect statement about a Nash equilibrium?

   (a) A Nash equilibrium is an example of a non-cooperative equilibrium.
   (b) In a Nash equilibrium, all players are maximizing their payoffs given the current behaviour of the other players.
   (c) In a Nash equilibrium, all players are better off than they would be with any other combination of strategies.
   (d) A Nash equilibrium is a self-policing equilibrium.

7. Collusion is advantageous to the oligopolist because

   (a) it removes much of the uncertainty about rivals' reactions.
   (b) it makes all firms more efficient.
   (c) it leads to greater product differentiation.
   (d) it reduces the cost of advertising.

8. Which of the following is an example of a firm-created barrier to entry?

   (a) *LRAC* curve negatively sloped over large range of output
   (b) large set-up costs
   (c) brand proliferation
   (d) heavy advertising
   (e) C and D

9. If an oligopolistic firm is producing a product with a short product life then it is likely that it will never be able to exhaust its scale economies because

   (a) input prices are continually rising.
   (b) it will always be operating at the minimum *LRAC*.
   (c) it will operate on the upward-sloping portion of its *LRAC* curve.
   (d) it will remain on the downward-sloping portion of its *LRAC* curve.

10. Empirical evidence and everyday observation suggest that oligopolies contribute to economic growth in the very long run by

    (a) achieving allocative efficiency.
    (b) consistently producing at full-capacity output.
    (c) achieving technological improvements and innovations through research and development.
    (d) decreasing minimum efficient scale.
    (e) employing large numbers of people.

Chapter 12

1. The condition for allocative efficiency is that

   (a) goods are allocated equitably.
   (b) there are no idle resources in the economy.
   (c) $MC = P$ for all goods.
   (d) $MRP = P$ for all inputs.
   (e) price equals average cost for all goods.

2. Consider two firms, A and B, that are producing the same product but with different marginal costs. In this case,

   (a) a reallocation of output between the firms can lower the industry's total cost.
   (b) neither firm is producing its output at the lowest attainable cost.
   (c) some resources must be unemployed.
   (d) each firm is being wasteful.
   (e) one firm is not maximizing profits.

3. Choose the statement that best compares the long-run equilibrium of a competitive industry and that in a monopolized industry.

   (a) Resources will be allocated efficiently in both the competitive and monopolized industries.
   (b) Allocative efficiency will be achieved in the competitive, but not the monopolized industry.
   (c) Allocative efficiency is not possible in either industry.
   (d) Allocative efficiency will be achieved in the monopolized, but not the competitive industry.

4. The deadweight loss of monopoly is

   (a) its fixed cost.
   (b) any negative profit due to cyclical decreases in demand.
   (c) the forgone surplus due to the allocatively inefficient monopoly output level.
   (d) the cost of maintaining effective barriers to entry.
   (e) the extra administrative costs of operating a large firm.

Refer to Figure 12-1 to answer questions 5–8.

FIGURE 12-1

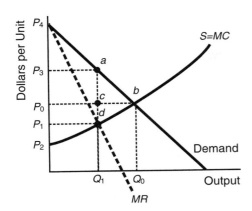

5. Refer to Figure 12-1. If the diagram depicts a perfectly competitive industry, the equilibrium price and quantity is
   (a) P_1 and Q_1.
   (b) P_3 and Q_1.
   (c) P_0 and Q_0.
   (d) P_1 and Q_2.

6. Refer to Figure 12-1. The area representing consumer surplus at the monopoly equilibrium is outlined by
   (a) dcb.
   (b) P_4aQ_1.
   (c) P_3adP_1.
   (d) P_3P_4a.

7. Refer to Figure 12-1. Comparing the monopoly equilibrium to the perfectly competitive equilibrium, the area representing the gain in producer surplus due to monopoly is outlined by
   (a) P_1P_3ad less cbd.
   (b) P_0P_3ac less cbd.
   (c) P_0P_3ab less abc.
   (d) P_3P_4a less abc.

8. Refer to Figure 12-1. Comparing the perfectly competitive equilibrium to the monopoly equilibrium, the deadweight loss of monopoly is
   (a) Q_1abQ_0.
   (b) cbd.
   (c) dab.
   (d) abc.

9. Consider a natural monopoly that is operating at a level of output with falling average costs. If the regulator sets the price equal to MC
   (a) the firm would operate at a loss and eventually go out of business.
   (b) shortages would result.
   (c) the demand curve would shift to the left.
   (d) the firm would earn economic profits.
   (e) the demand curve would shift to the right.

10. The regulator can reduce the profits of a natural monopoly by imposing a per-unit output tax (rather than directly regulating price). Such a tax would cause the monopolist's
    1. average total cost curve shifts upward.
    2. marginal cost curve shifts upward.
    3. demand curve shifts to the left.

    (a) 1 only
    (b) 2 only
    (c) 3 only
    (d) 1 and 2 only
    (e) 2 and 3 only

Chapter 13

1. Suppose all Canadians earned equal incomes. In this case, Canada's Lorenz curve would be
   (a) close to the horizontal axis.
   (b) the diagonal line.
   (c) a curve close to the diagonal line.
   (d) a curve substantially below the diagonal line.
   (e) non-existent.

2. Which of the following is the best definition of the marginal revenue product (MRP) of a factor of production?
   (a) the average product of the factor multiplied by the price of the output
   (b) the change in revenue caused by the sale of an additional unit of output
   (c) the increase in output resulting from the use of an additional unit of the factor multiplied by the cost of that factor
   (d) marginal revenue multiplied by total product
   (e) the change in revenue generated by the sale of the product produced by an additional unit of input

Consider Table 13-1 for a firm producing hockey sticks. Refer to this table to answer questions 3 and 4.

TABLE 13-1

Total Number of Units of the Factor (hours worked)	Total Number of Hockey Sticks Produced
2	100
3	110
4	128
5	148
6	162
7	170
8	166

3. Refer to Table 13-1. The marginal physical product of the 7th hour worked is _____.
   (a) -8
   (b) 0
   (c) 8
   (d) 162
   (e) 170

4. Refer to Table 13-1. Suppose the firm is a perfect competitor and faces a given market price for hockey sticks equal to $2 per stick. The marginal revenue product of the 5th hour worked is

   _____.
   (a) $128
   (b) $148
   (c) $20
   (d) $40
   (e) $2

5. An increase in the supply of labour will result from all of the following changes EXCEPT:
   (a) an increase in immigration.
   (b) an increase in female labour-force participation rates.
   (c) an increase in the retirement age.
   (d) an increase in wages.

6. Factors of production (land, labour and capital) shift between uses such that
   (a) distribution of wealth is equalized.
   (b) the amount of industry in separate regions of the country are balanced.
   (c) the net advantages to the owners of the factors are maximized.
   (d) the ratio of capital to labour increases.
   (e) only the monetary advantages to the owners of the factors are maximized.

7. Suppose the government decides, in the interest of "fairness," to impose a policy prohibiting factor-price differentials. The likely result would be
   (a) a horizontal factor supply curve.
   (b) a decrease in net factor demands.
   (c) an increase in factor mobility.
   (d) a shortage of factors in uses with low net advantage.
   (e) all of the above.

8. Choose the statement that best describes the difference between "economic rent" and other factor payments.
   (a) Economic rent is unearned income of the factor whereas other payments are earned.
   (b) Economic rent is not a cost to the firm but other payments are.
   (c) A reduction in economic rent will not reduce the availability of the factor whereas reducing other payments of factors will reduce their availability.
   (d) There is no difference between economic rent and other factor payments.

9. Suppose Jacques Villeneuve earns $2 million per year on the race-car circuit. Suppose that if he weren't racing his best alternative would be to earn $200 000 per year selling cars. By race-car driving, Jacques Villeneuve
   (a) is earning economic rent of $2 200 000 per year.
   (b) is earning economic rent of $2 000 000 per year.
   (c) is earning economic rent of $1 800 000 per year.
   (d) is earning economic rent of $200 000 per year.
   (e) is not earning economic rent.

10. If the supply curve for a factor is perfectly inelastic, the payment to the factor would be
    (a) partly economic rent and partly transfer earnings.
    (b) neither economic rent or transfer earnings.
    (c) wholly transfer earnings.
    (d) wholly economic rent.

Chapter 14

1. Human capital exists in the form of all of the following EXCEPT:
   (a) education.
   (b) training.
   (c) gender.
   (d) health.
   (e) experience.

2. If you choose to remain in school beyond the compulsory minimum period then you are
   (a) realizing the benefits of your investment in human capital.
   (b) delaying your investment in human capital.
   (c) refusing to invest in your human capital.
   (d) investing further in your human capital.

3. Wages differ due to differences in human capital. Such wage differentials
   (a) are not justifiable on efficiency grounds.
   (b) will persist in competitive equilibrium.
   (c) are not an important source of observed wage differentials.
   (d) are an example of economic distortions due to monopoly power.
   (e) are only due to distortions in labour markets.

4. The following statements describe the adverse effects suffered by groups subject to labour-market discrimination. Which of the statements is false?
   (a) They will be more likely to experience spells of unemployment.
   (b) Their children's ability and willingness to invest in human capital will be less on average than those of children of other groups.
   (c) They will receive lower wages on average than other groups.
   (d) Their human capital will increase.

5. If there is discrimination against some workers in market A but no discrimination in market B, then all of the following effects are predicted EXCEPT:
   (a) a decrease in supply and higher wages in the A occupations.
   (b) more employment in the A occupations.
   (c) an increase in supply and lower wages in the B occupations.
   (d) more unemployment in the B occupations if there is a binding minimum wage.

6. If we compare the wage rate and the level of employment achieved in a competitive labour market versus a monopsonistic labour market, the latter will generate
   (a) lower level of employment and a lower wage.
   (b) higher level of employment and a lower wage.
   (c) higher level of employment and a higher wage rate.
   (d) lower level of employment and a higher wage rate.
   (e) level of employment and wage rate equivalent to those generated by competitive conditions.

7. If a labour market that is currently in competitive equilibrium has a binding minimum wage imposed on it, then
   (a) wages will increase and employment will increase.
   (b) wages will increase but employment will decrease.
   (c) wages will increase and there will be no unemployment.
   (d) all of these are possible.

8. A legislated minimum wage is likely to have which of the following effects?
   (a) In competitive labour markets, an effective minimum wage increases wages but decreases employment.
   (b) In a monopsonistic labour market a binding minimum wage may increase both wage rates and employment.
   (c) In a monopsonistic labour market, a minimum wage set equal to the competitive wage will increase wages but not employment.
   (d) The wage and employment effects of a minimum wage will be the same in competitive and monopsonistic labour markets.
   (e) Both A and B.

9. Suppose that the professional association of plumbers reduced entry into their profession by lengthening its training program. The likely effect is that
   (a) the supply curve of plumbers will shift to the left.
   (b) the supply curve of plumbers will shift to the right.
   (c) both the demand and supply curves for plumbers will shift to the left.
   (d) the demand curve of plumbers will shift to the right.
   (e) there will be an increase in the quantity of plumbers supplied.

10. Some people are concerned that "good" manufacturing jobs are being replaced by "bad" service jobs. Why is this not necessarily a problem?
   (a) Despite the decline in manufacturing employment real disposable income has continued to rise.
   (b) The decline in manufacturing employment is partly due to increasing productivity in that sector.
   (c) Productivity increases in the service sector are likely underestimated.
   (d) Consumers have an increased demand for services as real income increases.
   (e) All of the above.

Chapter 15

1. *Present value* refers to the
   (a) value that a capital good will have in the future.
   (b) current interest rate.
   (c) current purchase price of a capital good.
   (d) value today of a payment to be made or received in the future.
   (e) value in the future of a payment made today.

2. The present value of $100 to be received one year from now, with an interest rate of 8 percent, is
   (a) $85.73.
   (b) $94.34.
   (c) $92.59.
   (d) $102.13.
   (e) $108.00

3. If the interest rate if 10 percent, the present value of $200 paid 3 years from now is
   (a) $20.00.
   (b) $40.00.
   (c) $56.45.
   (d) $150.26.
   (e) $165.28.

4. Suppose a piece of capital will produce an *MRP* of $1000 per year for the next three years (beginning one year from now). What is the maximum price a firm will pay to purchase it today if the interest rate is 7 percent?
   (a) $816.37
   (b) $1,649.81
   (c) $2,584.37
   (d) $3,210.00

5. In general, a profit-maximizing firm will purchase a piece of capital if
   (a) the present value of the stream of future *MRPs* exceeds the purchase price.
   (b) the present value of the stream of future *MRPs* falls below the purchase price.
   (c) the simple sum of the future *MRPs* exceeds the purchase price.
   (d) the simple sum of the future *MRPs* falls below the purchase price.
   (e) the future value of the stream of *MRPs* exceeds the purchase price.

6. Choose the best reason for a rightward shift in the demand for capital curve over the very long run.
   (a) diminishing returns to capital
   (b) changes in technology improve the productivity of capital
   (c) a decrease in the interest rate
   (d) an increase in the interest rate
   (e) a fall in the *MC* of capital

7. The socially optimal rate of extraction of any nonrenewable resource is such that
   (a) no extraction takes place.
   (b) the price of the resource is constant over time.
   (c) the price of the resource increases at a rate less than the interest rate.
   (d) the price of the resource increases at a rate greater than the interest rate.
   (e) the price of the resource increases at a rate equal to the interest rate.

8. The rate of extraction of nonrenewable resources is predicted to _____ if the interest rate rises, causing their current prices to _____.
   (a) increase; rise
   (b) increase; fall
   (c) decrease; rise
   (d) decrease; fall

9. "Common property" nonrenewable resources tend to
   (a) not be extracted.
   (b) be extracted at the socially optimal rate.
   (c) be extracted more slowly than is socially optimal.
   (d) be extracted more rapidly than is socially optimal.
   (e) be extracted optimally since all agents agree "commonly" on the optimal extraction rate.

10. An example of a nonrenewable resource that can have some characteristics of common property is
    (a) coal.
    (b) iron ore.
    (c) forest products.
    (d) land.
    (e) petroleum products.

Chapter 16

1. Which of the following statements about free-market economies is false?
   (a) An efficiently functioning market economy will correct temporary shortages and surpluses.
   (b) Markets tend to be impersonal and to decentralize economic power.
   (c) The government has a role to play in correcting market failures.
   (d) In a free-market economy there is no role for government intervention.
   (e) The existence of profits and losses provide signals to other economic agents.

2. Economists use the term *market failure* to refer to those market situations where
   (a) income is not distributed equitably.
   (b) the outcome is not allocatively efficient.
   (c) externalities are present in the economy.
   (d) the economy is not in equilibrium.
   (e) the government has intervened in the economy.

3. The reason that externalities prevent an efficient market outcome is
   (a) the discrepancy between private and social costs.
   (b) asymmetric information.
   (c) the inability of a firm in an industry characterized by increasing returns to scale to make positive profits if it sets price equal to marginal cost.
   (d) a failure of the market to generate socially valued outcomes such as a given degree of vertical equity.
   (e) pollution.

4. An efficient level of provision of a public good is achieved when
   (a) the cost of providing an extra unit of the good is equal to the valuation of each consumer of the extra unit.
   (b) the cost of providing an extra unit of the good is equal to the sum of all consumers' valuations for that unit.
   (c) the cost of providing an extra unit of the good is equal to the price of the good.
   (d) the valuation of each consumer for the last unit of the good produced is zero.
   (e) voters are satisfied that an adequate amount of the good is being produced.

5. Why would it be inefficient for the government to charge a price for consuming a public good such as national defence?
   (a) Too much defence will be provided.
   (b) The price cannot be set to cover all defence costs.
   (c) No one will be willing to pay to consume any national defence.
   (d) The marginal cost of providing national defence is zero.

6. In which area are we likely to encounter the problem of moral hazard?
   (a) home insurance
   (b) dental insurance
   (c) medical services
   (d) legal services
   (e) all of the above

7. The problem of adverse selection will arise when an individual
   (a) is not able to take advantage of another individual.
   (b) has the incentive to and is able to shift costs to another individual.
   (c) selects a product with adverse externalities associated therewith.
   (d) purchases a lot of insurance because the individual knows he is at high risk.
   (e) all of the above.

8. The development of Canada's national park system is an example of government intervention through
   (a) public provision.
   (b) redistribution.
   (c) regulation.
   (d) restructuring of economic incentives.
   (e) subsidization.

9. Attempts by farm lobbyists in Ottawa to influence agricultural subsidies represent
   (a) an inefficient public choice.
   (b) the government acting like a monopolist.
   (c) rent seeking.
   (d) an externality.
   (e) asymmetric information.

10. Economists generally agree that government intervention in the economy is called for
   (a) whenever there is market failure.
   (b) whenever the costs of market failure are greater than the benefits of the existence of markets.
   (c) whenever the benefits of the correction of the market failure through intervention are greater than the costs of the intervention.
   (d) only when the market fails to provide a socially useful good.
   (e) whenever the costs of the intervention are greater than the value of the correction of the market failure.

Chapter 17

1. What is the condition for allocative efficiency?
   (a) marginal social cost equals marginal social benefit
   (b) marginal private cost equals marginal private benefit
   (c) average social cost equals average social benefit
   (d) marginal social cost equals marginal private benefit
   (e) firms are maximizing profits

2. When a private firm is abating pollution such that the marginal cost and marginal benefit of abatement are equal,
   (a) any further reduction in pollution will lower net social benefits.
   (b) pollution has been eliminated.
   (c) any further reductions in pollution will continue to increase net social benefits.
   (d) then the firm is likely to increase output.
   (e) then the firm is likely to decrease output.

3. When considering an entire industry, the marginal benefit of reducing pollution is expected
   (a) to rise as the level of pollution gets closer to zero.
   (b) to remain constant for all levels of pollution control.
   (c) to exceed the marginal cost of pollution control for all positive levels of pollution.
   (d) to fall as the amount of pollution control undertaken rises.
   (e) to be always greater than the marginal cost of pollution reduction.

4. When an external cost is said to have been internalized, it means that
   (a) the opportunity cost of production is passed on to the consumer.
   (b) the private cost of production is borne by the producer.
   (c) the producer must bear the external costs that he imposes.
   (d) the consumer must bear the net social benefits imposed by the producer.

5. Pollution abatement is being achieved at a socially optimal level when
   (a) governments have strong anti-pollution legislation in effect.
   (b) the marginal cost of reducing pollution is just equal to the marginal benefit from doing so.
   (c) the marginal cost of reducing pollution is just equal to the profit of the polluting firm.
   (d) all pollution has been abated.
   (e) none of the above; there is no optimal abatement.

6. Pollution externalities can be internalized by which of the following methods?
   (a) emission limits
   (b) fines for "over-polluters"
   (c) emissions taxes
   (d) direct pollution controls
   (e) moral suasion

7. The use of emissions taxes as a method of reducing pollution
   (a) does not solve the problem of firms facing differing cost schedules for pollution abatement.
   (b) is less efficient than direct controls.
   (c) allows firms to select the most efficient abatement techniques.
   (d) forces the firm to internalize the pollution externality.
   (e) both C and D.

8. If emissions permits are traded freely between polluting firms in the private market,
   (a) there will be more than the optimal amount of pollution.
   (b) the amount of pollution abatement will be identical to that which the firms would have undertaken willingly on their own.
   (c) each firm will face identical costs of pollution abatement.
   (d) all firms will use identical pollution abatement technologies.
   (e) marginal abatement costs will be equalized across firms.

In Figure 17-1, firms X and Y have the following marginal cost of pollution abatement curves. Refer to this figure to answer questions 9 and 10.

FIGURE 17-1

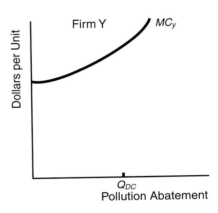

9. Refer to Figure 17-1. Suppose the government imposes direct controls on pollution such that each firm is required to abate pollution to the level Q_{DC}. The result will be
   (a) fair and just because both firms are facing the same requirements.
   (b) economically inefficient because Firm X is not producing as much pollution as Firm Y and therefore should not be faced with the same controls.
   (c) economically efficient because even though their MCs of abatement differ, the MC of abatement for the last unit of pollution abated is equal.
   (d) economically inefficient because Firm Y is abating pollution at a much higher marginal cost than Firm X.

10. Refer to Figure 17-1. An economically efficient method of controlling pollution from Firms X and Y would be to
    (a) impose direct controls such that Firms X and Y are each abating equal amounts of pollution, Q_{DC}.
    (b) levy a uniform emissions tax such that Firm X would choose to abate more pollution than Firm Y.
    (c) levy a uniform emissions tax such that Firms X and Y were each abating equal amounts of pollution.
    (d) allow Firms X and Y to choose their own optimal level of pollution control, depending on their private costs.

Chapter 18

1. An example of a tax expenditure is
   (a) the salary paid to a Revenue Canada employee.
   (b) a household's income-tax payment to Revenue Canada.
   (c) the deductibility of a portion of charitable contributions in determining taxable income.
   (d) the direct burden of a tax that is borne by the household.
   (e) the excess burden of a tax that is borne by the household.

2. Suppose taxes are levied in the following way: for an income of $25 000 the tax is $5000; for an income of $50 000 the tax is $20 000; for an income of $100 000 the tax is $50 000. Such a tax is
   (a) regressive.
   (b) progressive.
   (c) indexed.
   (d) proportional.
   (e) unrealistic.

3. Consider a monopolist that is earning profits in the long run. If the government imposes a lump-sum tax on this monopolist (that is less than its profits), then
   (a) output would decrease and price to consumers would increase.
   (b) neither output nor price would change.
   (c) the output would remain the same while price increased.
   (d) the monopolist would cease production.
   (e) new firms would enter the industry.

4. Some important taxes are regressive. In an effort to achieve proportionality in the overall tax system it is therefore necessary to impose
   (a) substantial progressivity in income taxes.
   (b) a negative income tax.
   (c) a flat-rate tax.
   (d) consumption taxation.
   (e) efficiency in the tax system.

5. The excess burden of a tax
   (a) is the incidence of a tax.
   (b) is the additional costs that result from the induced changes in behaviour due to the tax.
   (c) increases economic efficiency by eliminating distortions in the economy.
   (d) is always progressive.
   (e) is always regressive.

6. The relevant objective for tax policy is the design of a system
   (a) that minimizes inefficiency, holding constant the amount of revenue to be raised.
   (b) that maximizes the amount of revenue raised, holding constant the inefficiencies created in the economy.
   (c) that raises the maximum possible revenue.
   (d) that does not interfere with the market economy because this only causes inefficiencies.
   (e) either B or C.

7. Which of the following areas of spending account for the largest portion of Canadian federal government expenditures?
   (a) equalization payments
   (b) defence spending
   (c) subsidies to Canadian businesses
   (d) transfer payments to individuals and other levels of government
   (e) interest payments on the national debt

8. Canada's system of fiscal federalism is based on the basic principle that
   (a) only provinces that are "federalist" should receive fiscal assistance from the federal government.
   (b) each province is an independent fiscal entity.
   (c) the tax base should be approximately equal in each of the provinces and territories.
   (d) the true cost of provision of public goods to the various provinces should be recovered in tax revenue from the province receiving the benefit.
   (e) individuals should have approximately the same access to public goods no matter where they live.

9. Welfare recipients are faced with a withdrawal of welfare benefits and an increase in income tax as their income rises. This creates a problem because
   (a) firms become unwilling to hire people that are currently unemployed.
   (b) of the powerful disincentives to work for low-income individuals.
   (c) of the incentives for workers to shirk and/or retire early.
   (d) of the incentives for firms to lay off workers more frequently for short periods.
   (e) none of the above.

10. The design of social policy often involves a tradeoff between efficiency and equity because
   (a) income redistribution through social policy increases incentives for efficient behaviour of economic units.
   (b) economic units who are efficient completely dislike equity.
   (c) income redistribution through social policy often reduces incentives for efficient behaviour of economic units.
   (d) the economy can achieve an efficient allocation of resources by starting with an unequal allocation of resources.

Chapter 19

1. Macroeconomics is mainly concerned with the behaviour of
   (a) individual households and how they deal with such problems as inflation and unemployment.
   (b) large economic units such as the Canadian government or General Motors.
   (c) economic disaggregates.
   (d) economic aggregates.
   (e) governments and their intervention in individual markets.

2. What is the output gap?
   (a) It is the difference between potential and actual national income.
   (b) It is the difference between real and nominal national income.
   (c) It is the difference between output in the current year and output in the base year.
   (d) It is the difference between GNP and GDP.
   (e) It is the difference between output and employment.

3. The term "potential income" usually refers to
   (a) the maximum GDP that an economy actually achieves throughout its entire history.
   (b) GDP achieved during periods when 100 percent of the labour force is employed.
   (c) a goal that can never be achieved by the economy.
   (d) the GDP that would be produced if the economy's resources were employed at a normal intensity of use.
   (e) the GDP that could be produced if the economy's resources were employed at their maximum intensity of use.

4. When we study short-run fluctuations in national income, we usually assume that potential income is
   (a) be rising.
   (b) constant.
   (c) non-existent.
   (d) falling at its long-run average growth rate.
   (e) equal to actual income.

5. If a country's labour force is 20 million people, and 1 million are unemployed, the country's unemployment rate is
   (a) 2.5 percent.
   (b) 5 percent.
   (c) 3.5 percent.
   (d) 4 percent.
   (e) 0.5 percent.

6. As telephone directory assistance becomes more fully automated, telephone operators find themselves with unneeded skills at the same time that computer programmers and telephone banking specialists are in high demand. Such unemployed telephone operators would be classified as
   (a) structurally unemployed.
   (b) frictionally unemployed.
   (c) cyclically unemployed.
   (d) naturally unemployed.
   (e) underemployed.

7. Choose the correct equation for determining the inflation rate from period 1 to period 2.
   (a) $(P_2 - P_1) \times 100$
   (b) $(P_2 / P_1) \times 100$
   (c) $[(P_2 - P_1)/P_1] \times 100$
   (d) $(P_1 / P_2) \times 100$
   (e) $[(P_1 - P_2)/P_2] \times 100$

8. Suppose a union and a firm agree on a nominal wage contract specifying a wage increase of 3 percent but the price level is expected to rise by 5 percent over the course of the contract. In this case,
   (a) the employees'purchasing power will rise.
   (b) the employees' purchasing power will fall.
   (c) the employer will experience a smaller increase in purchasing power than would have occurred if the price level had held steady.
   (d) both employer and employees will benefit in increased purchasing power.

9. Under which circumstance will there be no real effects from inflation?
   (a) no on realizes that it is happening
   (b) the inflation is fully anticipated and no one changes their behaviour
   (c) the anticipated rate of inflation is more than the actual rate of inflation
   (d) the anticipated rate of inflation is less than the actual rate of inflation
   (e) the actual rate of inflation is less than 5 percent

10. Choose the best definition of the exchange rate.
    (a) The exchange rate is a term for foreign currencies or claims on foreign currencies.
    (b) The exchange rate is a system of quotas imposed on the international exchange of goods.
    (c) The exchange rate is the value of one Canadian dollar in terms of foreign currencies.
    (d) The exchange rate is the number of Canadian dollars needed to buy one unit of foreign currency.

Chapter 20

1. Suppose national-income accounting was done by adding up the market values of all outputs of all firms. This approach would
   (a) accurately reflect the value of production in the economy.
   (b) obtain gross domestic product.
   (c) obtain gross national product.
   (d) underestimate the production in the economy.
   (e) overestimate the production in the economy.

2. Choose the correct equation for determining GDP from the expenditure side.
   (a) $GDP = C_a + I_a + G_a + (IM_a - X_a)$.
   (b) $GDP = C_a + I_a + G_a -$ net exports.
   (c) $GDP = C_a + I_a + G_a + (X_a - IM_a)$.
   (d) $GDP = C_a + I_a + G_a$.
   (e) $GDP = C_a + I_a +$ net exports.

3. In macroeconomics the term "investment" means something different than in popular use. In macroeconomics, it refers to
   (a) the total amount of capital goods in the country.
   (b) the production of goods for immediate consumption.
   (c) the same thing as profits.
   (d) the production of goods not for immediate consumption use.
   (e) money invested in financial capital markets.

4. When calculating GDP from the expenditure side, why do we not include transfer payments in G_a?
   (a) Transfer payments do not represent a payment for a good or a service.
   (b) Transfer payments are not counted as income by any economic agent.
   (c) Transfer payments include imports and thus are not included in G_a.
   (d) It is difficult to assess the market value of a transfer payment.
   (e) Transfer payments are small enough to ignore when computing the national accounts.

5. Suppose a Canadian firm imports $5000 worth of frisbees and sells them for $10 000. The effect on GDP would be
   (a) to decrease the value of GDP by $15 000.
   (c) to increase the value of GDP by $10 000.
   (b) to increase the value of GDP by $15 000.
   (d) to increase the value of GDP by $5000.
   (e) no effect on GDP since the frisbees were produced outside of Canada.

Table 20-1 shows total output for an economy over 2 years. Use this table to answer questions 6-8.

TABLE 20-1

2000	Price	Quantity
coconuts	$1.00	100 units
bananas	$3.00	200 units
pineapples	$6.00	100 units

2001	Price	Quantity
coconuts	$2.00	120 units
bananas	$4.00	200 units
pineapples	$8.00	90 units

6. Refer to Table 20-1. The nominal Gross Domestic Product in 2001 was
   (a) $1760.
   (b) $1500.
   (c) $1300.
   (d) $1260.
   (e) $410.

7. Refer to Table 20-1. The real GDP in 2001, expressed in 2000 dollars, was
   (a) $1760.
   (b) $1500.
   (c) $1300.
   (d) $1260.
   (e) $410.

8. Refer to Table 20-1. The implicit GDP deflator in 2001 (using 2000 as the base year) is
   (a) 71.59.
   (b) 100.
   (c) 103.4
   (d) 114.6
   (e) 139.7

9. An increase in which of the following variables would be the best indicator of an increase in labour productivity?
   (a) national income
   (b) real national income
   (c) real GDP per hour worked
   (d) real GDP per capita
   (e) national output

10. Current measures of GDP tend to overstate economic welfare because
    (a) the benefits of increased leisure time are ignored.
    (b) the non-market activity of work in the home is ignored.
    (c) the economic "bads" associated with production, such as pollution, are ignored.
    (d) transactions such as teenage babysitting services are ignored.
    (e) the tips that waiters receive are ignored.

Chapter 21

1. In the long run, some economists argue that money is neutral because it has no effect on
   (a) nominal GDP and nominal interest rates.
   (b) real GDP and employment.
   (c) nominal interest rates and inflation.
   (d) the price level or the rate of inflation.

2. Changes in factor supply are generally considered to be a long run concept because
   (a) wages increase rapidly in the short run, thus dampening the growth of employment.
   (b) only aggregate demand is observed in the short run.
   (c) additions to the labour force and capital stock happen only gradually over time.
   (d) observed changes to the capital stock are almost impossible to make in the short run.

3. The textbook suggests that in the short run, the
   (a) output gap opens or closes as the economy moves through the phases of the business cycle.
   (b) output gap is constant because the capital stock cannot change.
   (c) actual GDP is always less than potential GDP.
   (d) actual GDP is always greater than potential GDP.
   (e) actual GDP is always equal to potential GDP.

4. Decreases in real GDP may be caused by a(n)
   (a) decrease in factor utilization rates.
   (b) decrease in exchange rates.
   (c) decrease in unemployment rates.
   (d) increase in factor productivity.
   (e) all of the above.

5. In the equation GDP = $L \times [E/L] \times [GDP/E]$ where (L) is the labour force and (E) is the level of employment, the term $[GDP/E]$ represents
   (a) output per unit of capital.
   (b) the ratio of population to the number of people unemployed.
   (c) one minus the unemployment rate.
   (d) a simple measure of the productivity of labour.

6. A former Governor of the Bank of Canada argued that when inflation and interest rates are high a policy aimed at lowering both inflation and interest rates must *first* raise interest rates. This apparent contradiction is explained by the fact that

    (a) the Governor of the Bank of Canada is typically a patronage appointment with little formal training or knowledge of economic theory.
    (b) higher interest rates inhibit saving which increases the supply of funds for lending and, other things constant, drives the "price" of borrowing down.
    (c) interest rates move in cycles and therefore tend to rise before they fall.
    (d) higher interest rates in the short run reduce economic activity, put downward pressure on inflation, and eventually reduce the nominal interest rate.
    (e) what goes up must come down.

7. If the economy is operating at an output level where actual GDP is greater than potential GDP, then we can conclude that

    (a) there is excess capacity in the economy.
    (b) some factors of production are idle.
    (c) there is a high level of unemployment.
    (d) factor utilization rates are above their normal levels.
    (e) this is an impossibility since an economy cannot produce more than its potential.

8. GDP can be represented by the equation: $GDP = F \times (F_E/F) \times (GDP/F_E)$. The term (F_E/F) represents

    (a) factor supply per level of output.
    (b) output per capita.
    (c) the factor utilization rate.
    (d) productivity.
    (e) income per person.

9. On the basis of both theory and empirical evidence, most economists believe that changes in monetary policy

    (a) are neutral in the long run but do affect nominal variables such as wages, prices and the rate of inflation.
    (b) have no effect in the short run.
    (c) affect GDP, investment and employment in both the long and short runs.
    (d) have only long run effects on GDP.

10. Long-run changes in GDP usually involve changes in

    (a) actual GDP but no changes in potential GDP.
    (b) both potential GDP and actual GDP, but no change in the output gap.
    (c) potential GDP with changes in the output gap.
    (d) potential GDP with no change in the output gap.
    (e) the output gap.

Chapter 22

1. If the $MPC = 0.75$, an increase in household income causes consumption expenditure to

    (a) rise by more than the increase in income.
    (b) rise by the full increase in income.
    (c) rise by less than the full increase in income.
    (d) fall, as an increase in income will increase saving.
    (e) remain constant, because the $MPC < 1$.

2. If a family's annual disposable income rose from $60 000 to $65 000 and their desired consumption expenditures rose from $50 000 to $54 000, it can be concluded that the

    (a) marginal propensity to consume is $800.
    (b) average propensity to consume is 0.8.
    (c) marginal propensity to consume is 0.8.
    (d) average propensity to save is 0.8.
    (e) marginal propensity to save is 0.8.

3. The aggregate expenditure (*AE*) function is an upward-sloping curve that describes

    (a) the amount spent on an economy's output at each national income.
    (b) what firms and households would like to spend at each level of national income.
    (c) what an economy would like to spend, in the absence of income constraints, at each level of output.
    (d) what is actually spent on an economy's output at each level of output.
    (e) what is actually spent at each level of national income.

Consider Table 22-1, which describes a closed economy with no government. Refer to this table to answer questions 4 and 5.

TABLE 22-1

1. equilibrium condition is $Y = C + I$
2. $MPS = 0.20$
3. the autonomous part of C is $50
4. Investment is autonomous and equals $25

4. Refer to Table 22-1. The equilibrium level of national income will be
   (a) $375.
   (b) $249.
   (c) $155.
   (d) $93.75.
   (e) $75.

5. Refer to Table 22-1. At the equilibrium level of national income, the level of saving will be
   (a) equal to consumption expenditures.
   (b) $375.
   (c) $50.
   (d) $25.
   (e) $15.

6. Suppose the level of actual national income is less than desired aggregate expenditure. In this case,
   (a) inventories will build up, causing national income to rise.
   (b) national income will fall, because desired expenditures are less than actual expenditures.
   (c) shortages of goods and reductions in inventories will cause producers to increase output and national income to rise.
   (d) national income may increase or decrease, depending on the relative sizes of the average propensity to consume and the average propensity to save.
   (e) there will be no change in national income because only actual expenditure is relevant.

7. Consider a simple macro model with no government or foreign trade, and a given price level. The requirement for equilibrium is that
   (a) desired saving equals desired investment.
   (b) desired saving equals zero.
   (c) consumption equals desired investment.
   (d) desired investment equals zero.
   (e) desired investment equals actual saving.

Refer to this figure to answer questions 8–10.

FIGURE 22-1

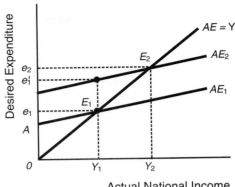

8. In Figure 22-1, assuming AE_1 to be the prevailing aggregate expenditure function, the distance 0A is a measure of
   (a) aggregate expenditure at equilibrium national income level 0C.
   (b) autonomous expenditures.
   (c) induced expenditures.
   (d) income not spent on domestic output.

9. In Figure 22-1, the simple multiplier could be measured by the ratio
   (a) $Y_1 Y_2 / e_1 e_2$.
   (b) $Y_1 Y_2 / e_1 e_1'$.
   (c) $e_2 e_1 / Y_1$.
   (d) Y_2 / e_2.

10. According to Figure 22-1, if national income is Y_1, and desired aggregate expenditure is AE_2, then desired aggregate expenditure
    (a) exceeds income and income will rise.
    (b) exceeds income and income will fall.
    (c) is less than income and income must rise.
    (d) is less than income and income must fall.
    (e) is equal to income and will not change.

Chapter 23

1. Suppose $G = 500$ and T = 0.2Y. When $Y = 2000$, public saving is _____, denoting a budget _____.
   (a) 100; surplus
   (b) 100; deficit
   (c) −100; surplus
   (d) −100; deficit
   (e) 0; balance

2. An increase in domestic national income, other things being equal, causes
   (a) the net export curve to shift upward.
   (b) the net export curve to pivot upward.
   (c) a move downward along the net export curve.
   (d) the net export curve to pivot downward.
   (e) no effect on net exports.

3. We have the following macro model: $C = 200 + .76Y$, $I = 300$, $G = 450$, $T = 0$, $X = 120$, $IM = .06Y$. Equilibrium national income is _____.
   (a) 1050
   (b) 3500
   (c) 3566.67
   (d) 7935
   (e) 17,250.

4. We have the following macro model: $C = 200 + .76Y$, $I = 300$, $G = 450$, $T = 0$, $X = 120$, $IM = .06Y$. The marginal propensity to spend on national income, z, is _____.
   (a) 0.76
   (b) 0.82
   (c) 0.7728
   (d) 0.70
   (e) 0.65

5. We have the following macro model: $C = 200 + .76Y$, $I = 300$, $G = 450$, $T = 0$, $X = 120$, $IM = .06Y$. Consumption expenditure at equilibrium national income is _____.
   (a) 1675.44
   (b) 2910.67
   (c) 4980
   (d) 2860
   (e) 4830

6. We have the following macro model: $C = 200 + .76Y$, $I = 300$, $G = 450$, $T = 0$, $X = 120$, $IM = .06Y$. The trade balance at equilibrium national income is
   (a) a deficit of 171.6.
   (b) a deficit of 94.
   (c) a surplus of 15.28.
   (d) a surplus of 125.
   (e) a deficit of 460.

7. Which of the following changes can cause a decrease in the value of the multiplier?
   (a) an increase in the marginal propensity to consume
   (b) a decrease in the marginal propensity to import
   (c) a decrease in income-tax rates
   (d) an increase in the marginal propensity to save
   (e) an increase in the marginal propensity to spend

8. In an open-economy macro model with government, an increase in the equilibrium level of GDP could be caused by
   (a) an increase in taxes at all levels of income.
   (b) a decrease in the desired level of saving at all levels of income.
   (c) a decrease in desired consumption at all levels of income.
   (d) an increase in the desired level of imports at all levels of income.
   (e) a decrease in government spending.

9. If the marginal propensity to spend on domestic income is 0.75, a $2 billion increase in government purchases will cause equilibrium national income to _____ by _____.
   (a) increase; $2.67 billion
   (b) decrease; $2.67 billion
   (c) increase; $8 billion
   (d) decrease; $8 billion

10. In a simple macro model with government, an increase in the income-tax rate (t) causes the AE curve to
    (a) shift parallel downward.
    (b) shift parallel upward.
    (c) pivot downward.
    (d) pivot upward.
    (e) remain stationary.

Chapter 24

1. When the price level rises, the real value of money holdings _____; when the price level falls, the real value of money holdings _____.
   (a) rises; falls
   (b) falls; is not affected
   (c) falls; rises
   (d) is not affected; falls
   (e) is not affected; rises

2. On a graph that shows the derivation of the *AD* curve, a change in the price level causes
   (a) a shift in the *AE* curve and a movement along the *AD* curve.
   (b) a shift in both the *AE* and *AD* curves.
   (c) a movement along the *AE* curve and a shift in the *AD* curve.
   (d) a movement along the *AE* curve but not along the *AD* curve.

3. Points on the aggregate demand curve
   (a) show only changes in relative prices and quantities.
   (b) correspond to a particular point on industry demand curves for a particular product.
   (c) relate total demand for a given level of real GDP to a particular price level.
   (d) show the direct relationship between the price level and net exports.
   (e) show the direct relationship between the price level and the demand for consumer goods.

4. The short-run aggregate supply *(SRAS)* curve is drawn with which variables on the axes of the graph?
   (a) the price level on the vertical axis and *MPC* on the horizontal axis.
   (b) national income on the vertical axis and total desired consumption on the horizontal axis.
   (c) the price level on the vertical axis and real national income on the horizontal axis.
   (d) national income on the vertical axis and marginal cost on the horizontal axis.
   (e) the price level on the vertical axis and real disposable income on the horizontal axis.

5. A leftward shift in the *SRAS* curve implies that
   (a) at any given price level, a higher level of national output will be supplied.
   (b) there is an increase in aggregate supply.
   (c) the same national output will be produced, but at a lower price level.
   (d) there is a demand shock.
   (e) at any given price level, a lower level of national output will be supplied.

6. Why do we believe that the *SRAS* curve tends to be relatively flat at low levels of output?
   (a) Consumer demand is price-inelastic when output is low.
   (b) Firms are faced with unused capacity, and thus can increase output without increasing costs.
   (c) Profits are normally high in this section of the *SRAS* curve, so firms are willing to expand output.
   (d) Output is fixed.
   (e) All of the above.

7. Suppose the level of real GDP is such that the value of aggregate output exceeds the value of desired aggregate expenditures. In this case, we can say that
   (a) an inflationary gap exists.
   (b) national income will fall.
   (c) inventories will fall.
   (d) a shortage of national output will exist.
   (e) national income will rise.

8. Suppose there is an increase in autonomous consumption and there is no change in the price level. The result is
   (a) the *AE* curve shifts downward and the *AD* curve shifts to the left.
   (b) the *AE* curve shifts downward and the *AD* curve shifts to the right.
   (c) the *AE* curve shifts upward and the *AD* curve shifts to the left.
   (d) the *AE* curve shifts upward and the *AD* curve shifts to the right.

9. A rightward shift of the *SRAS* curve can be brought about by
   (a) a decrease in productivity.
   (b) an increase in productivity.
   (c) a decrease in input prices.
   (d) an increase in output prices.
   (e) B or C.

10. Consider the economy in a short-run equilibrium where the *SRAS* curve is vertical. If there is an increase in aggregate demand, the aggregate expenditure *(AE)* curve will
    (a) shift to a higher level and stay there.
    (b) shift to a higher level, but then shift part of the way down to its original position.
    (c) shift to a higher level but then return to its original position.
    (d) shift to a lower level and stay there.
    (e) shift to a lower level, but then return to its original position.

Chapter 25

1. When an inflationary gap exists, all of the following things are happening EXCEPT:
   (a) Increases in unit costs are rising faster than productivity.
   (b) The *SRAS* curve is shifting leftward.
   (c) The output gap is causing shifts in the *SRAS* curve that drive up the price level.
   (d) The *AD* curve is shifting leftward more rapidly than is the *SRAS* curve.
   (e) There is upward pressure on wages.

2. Which of the following adjustments describe what will happen when the economy is in an inflationary gap?
   (a) wages do not adjust, but the *AD* curve shifts to the right
   (b) wages fall, unit costs fall and the *AD* curve shifts rightward
   (c) wages rise, unit costs rise and the *SRAS* curve shifts leftward
   (d) wages fall, unit costs rise and the *SRAS* curve shifts leftward
   (e) wages fall, unit costs fall, and the *SRAS* curve shifts rightward

Refer to this figure to answer questions 3-6.

FIGURE 25-1

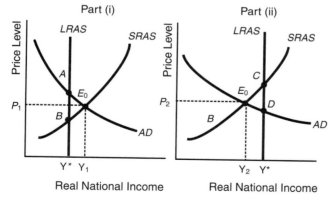

3. If the economy in Figure 25-1 part (ii) is currently producing Y_2, at this level of real national income the economy is experiencing
   (a) a recessionary gap.
   (b) an inflationary gap.
   (c) a labour shortage.
   (d) a long-run equilibrium.
   (e) potential output.

4. If the economy in Figure 25-1 part (i) is currently producing Y_1 and if it can automatically adjust to the full-employment level of production Y^*, then
   (a) the *SRAS* curve will shift to the left and intersect the *AD* curve at A.
   (b) the LRAS curve will shift to the right until it intersects the *SRAS* curve and *AD* curve at Y_1 output level.
   (c) the *AD* curve will shift to the left and intersect the *SRAS* curve at point B.
   (d) the economy will stay at Y_1 level of production.
   (e) the economy is in long-run equilibrium and will not adjust further.

5. If the economy in Figure 25-1 part (ii) is currently producing Y_2 level of output and wages are sticky downward, then
   (a) the economy will eventually self-adjust to point C.
   (b) the economy will only slowly move toward point D as wages slowly adjust.
   (c) the level of output will decrease below Y_2.
   (d) the economy will quickly self-adjust to point C.
   (e) *AD* will eventually increase and return the economy to full-employment level of output.

6. Assume that in Figure 25-1 part (i) the economy is currently producing Y_1 level of output and the government initiates an expansionary fiscal policy. The result will likely be
   (a) the *LRAS* curve will shift to the left, intersecting the *SRAS* and *AD* curves at Y^* level of output.
   (b) no change in either price level or output, since expansionary fiscal policy is ineffective.
   (c) the *SRAS* curve will shift to the left, intersecting the *LRAS* and *AD* curves at point A.
   (d) the *SRAS* curve and the *AD* curve will shift left simultaneously until the new equilibrium occurs at potential national income.
   (e) the *AD* curve will shift to the right, intersecting the *SRAS* at a point that exacerbates the inflationary gap.

7. The *LRAS* curve shows the relationship between the price level and real national income
   (a) in the short run.
   (b) when wages are in adjustment but prices are unstable.
   (c) when national income is at less than potential income.
   (d) when technology is allowed to change.
   (e) after factor prices have fully adjusted to eliminate output gaps.

8. Beginning at potential output, a permanent increase in aggregate demand will have its effect on real national income reversed in the long run with a _____ shift in _____.
   (a) rightward; *SRAS*
   (b) rightward; *AD*
   (c) leftward; *SRAS*
   (d) leftward; *AD*
   (e) none of the above.

9. Suppose policymakers implement an expansionary fiscal policy in an effort to eliminate a recessionary gap. If the *SRAS* curve then shifts unexpectedly to the right, the fiscal policy ends up being _____, and national income _____ potential GDP.
   (a) too weak; stays below
   (b) too weak; rises above
   (c) too strong; stays below
   (d) too strong; rises above
   (e) appropriate; equals

10. Income taxes act as an automatic stabilizer by _____ the marginal propensity to spend, thus _____ the multiplier.
    (a) raising; raising
    (b) raising; lowering
    (c) lowering; raising
    (d) lowering; lowering

Chapter 26

1. In order for paper currency to be considered money it must be
   (a) convertible into a precious metal.
   (b) impossible to counterfeit.
   (c) acceptable as a medium of exchange.
   (d) issued by a government agency.
   (e) issued by a commercial bank.

2. Money serves all of the following functions in an economy EXCEPT:
   (a) eliminate the necessity for a double coincidence of wants.
   (b) solve the problem of inflation.
   (c) solve the problem of trading indivisible commodities such as live animals.
   (d) allow better use of specialization and division of labour.
   (e) provide a convenient way for people to think about "value".

3. The currency that is in circulation in Canada today is
   (a) fully backed by gold held at the Bank of Canada.
   (b) backed by the U.S. dollar.
   (c) backed by the euro.
   (d) fractionally backed by gold.
   (e) not officially backed by anything.

4. A commercial bank's target reserve ratio is the
   (a) fraction of its deposit liabilities that it wishes to holds as reserves, either as cash or as deposits with the Bank of Canada.
   (b) fraction of its deposit liabilities that it actually holds as cash in its own vaults.
   (c) fraction of its deposit liabilities that are backed by gold.
   (d) ratio of Canadian dollars to foreign currencies that the commercial banks hold on their books.
   (e) ratio of chequable deposits to term deposits that the commercial banks hold on their books.

5. A central bank creates money by
   (a) selling some of its foreign-currency reserves for domestic currency.
   (b) issuing its own Central Bank bonds.
   (c) increasing the rate of inflation.
   (d) selling government treasury bills to the commercial banks.
   (e) purchasing government bonds on the open market.

6. If the target reserve ratio in the banking system is 10 percent, there is no cash drain and all excess reserves are lent out, then a new deposit of $1 will lead to an expansion of the money supply of
   (a) $20.
   (b) 10 cents.
   (c) $1.10.
   (d) $10.
   (e) $1.

Refer to the following passage to answer questions 7–9.

The Bank of Canada purchases $2 million worth of government securities from an investment dealer with a cheque drawn on the Bank of Canada. The dealer deposits this cheque at the IB&T Bank. The target reserve ratio of all commercial banks is 25 percent. Assume all commercial banks are operating with no excess reserves and there is no cash drain.

7. The IB&T Bank is immediately in a position to expand its loans by
   (a) $500 000.
   (b) $1.25 million.
   (c) $1.5 million.
   (d) $2 million.
   (e) $8 million.

8. If the IB&T Bank increases its loans to the maximum extent possible with its new excess reserves, the second generation banks will be able to expand their loans by
   (a) $3.75 million.
   (b) $1.125 million.
   (c) $1.5 million.
   (d) $.94 million.
   (e) $1 million.

9. The maximum creation of new deposits by the banking system, including the dealer's original deposit in the IB&T Bank, is
   (a) $2 million.
   (b) $8 million.
   (c) $10 million.
   (d) $12 million.
   (e) $20 million.

10. Suppose your mother deposits $1000 in cash in her chequing account with a local bank. This transaction alone would
    (a) decrease the money supply.
    (b) not change the money supply.
    (c) increase the money supply.
    (d) none of the above

Chapter 27

1. If the annual market rate of interest is 5 percent, an asset that promises to pay $1000 in two years has a present value of
   (a) $800.
   (b) $907.03.
   (c) $833.30.
   (d) $1200.
   (e) $909.00.

2. The term "demand for money" usually refers to
   (a) the average person's desire to hold cash.
   (b) the sum of all desired holdings of cash.
   (c) the sum of all desired assets, including cash, bond, and real property.
   (d) the aggregate demand for cash and demand deposits.
   (e) the cash and deposits actually held by firms.

3. If the economy experiences a decrease in real national income we can expect
   (a) an increase in the speculative demand for money.
   (b) an increase in the total demand for money.
   (c) a decrease in transactions demand for money.
   (d) an increase in transactions demand for money.
   (e) an increase in precautionary demand for money.

4. Beginning when the economy is in monetary equilibrium, an increase in the money supply will
   (a) not change the equilibrium.
   (b) cause a reduction in the demand for money, leading to a higher rate of interest.
   (c) cause an excess demand for money and a decrease in the rate of interest.
   (d) cause an increase in the demand for money, leading to a lower rate of interest.
   (e) lead to a movement down the money demand curve to a lower rate of interest.

5. The predicted effects of a decrease in the money supply are
   (a) a fall in the rate of interest and an increase in investment expenditure.
   (b) a rise in the rate of interest and in increase in investment expenditure.
   (c) a fall in the rate of interest and a decrease in investment expenditure.
   (d) a rise in the rate of interest and a decrease in investment expenditure.

6. A rise in the price level activates the transmission mechanism by
   (a) causing an increased demand for money balances, leading people to sell bonds, which in turn leads to a rise in the interest rate.
   (b) causing a decreased demand for money balances, leading people to sell bonds, which in turn leads to a rise in the interest rate.
   (c) causing an increased demand for money balances, leading people to buy bonds, which in turn leads to a fall in the interest rate.
   (d) causing a decreased demand for money balances, leading people to buy bonds, which in turn leads to a fall in the interest rate.
   (e) causing an increased demand for money balances, leading people to sell bonds, which in turn leads a fall in the interest rate.

7. What is the sequence of events by which an inflationary gap is eliminated by the economy's automatic adjustment mechanism?
   (a) interest rates rise, investment falls, and aggregate expenditure increases
   (b) interest rates rise, investment rises, and aggregate expenditure increases
   (c) interest rates rise, investment falls, and we move leftward along the *AD* curve
   (d) interest rates rise, investment falls, and the *AD* curve shifts rightward
   (e) interest rates rise, investment falls, and the *AD* curve shifts leftward

8. Which of the following correctly describes the way in which a change in the money supply affects aggregate demand?
   (a) a shift of the investment demand function and a movement along the aggregate expenditure curve
   (b) a movement along the investment demand function and a shift of the aggregate expenditure curve
   (c) a shift of both the investment demand function and the aggregate expenditure curve
   (d) movements along the investment demand function and the aggregate expenditure curve
   (e) a movement along the aggregate expenditure curve

9. A very steep investment demand curve and a relatively flat liquidity-preference schedule
   (a) make it impossible for the Bank of Canada to change the money supply.
   (b) increase the effectiveness of monetary policy.
   (c) imply that large increases in the money supply have little effect on aggregate expenditure.
   (d) make the money supply a particularly powerful policy variable.
   (e) are believed by many monetarists to be realistic descriptions of the economy.

10. An increase in the money supply will lead to the largest increase in aggregate demand when there is
   (a) an elastic demand for money and inelastic investment demand.
   (b) an inelastic demand for money and inelastic investment demand.
   (c) an elastic demand for money and elastic investment demand.
   (d) an inelastic demand for money and elastic investment demand.

Chapter 28

1. Suppose the Bank of Canada purchases government bonds on the open market. Commercial banks will find that they have
   (a) inadequate cash reserves.
   (b) increased net worth.
   (c) reduced deposits.
   (d) a decreased value of loans.
   (e) excess cash reserves.

2. The sale of government bonds by the Bank of Canada is predicted to
   - (a) decrease reserves of the commercial banks, and eventually lead to an expansion of the money supply.
   - (b) increase reserves of the commercial banks, and eventually cause a contraction of the money supply.
   - (c) decrease reserves of the commercial banks, and eventually cause a contraction of the money supply.
   - (d) increase reserves of the commercial banks, and eventually cause an expansion of the money supply.

3. Suppose a household sells $25 000 worth of government securities to the Bank of Canada and puts the cash it receives in a cookie jar. As a result of this transaction
   - (a) the nation's money supply will increase by $25 000.
   - (b) the nation's money supply will stay constant.
   - (c) the nation's money supply will decrease by $25 000.
   - (d) deposits will increase by a multiple of $25 000 depending on the target reserve ratio.
   - (e) loans will increase by a multiple of $25 000 depending on the value of the target reserve ratio.

4. If the Bank of Canada were conducting an expansionary monetary policy they would be
   - (a) buying government bonds.
   - (b) re-imposing a reserve requirement.
   - (c) selling government bonds.
   - (d) using moral suasion to reduce commercial bank loans.
   - (e) conducting open-market operations to increase the rate of interest.

5. Monetary policy is directed toward which of the following variables?
   - (a) an equitable distribution of income
   - (b) real national income and the price level
   - (c) the efficient use of resources
   - (d) the share of national income going to the owners of capital
   - (e) the slope of the *SRAS* curve

6. The most important attribute of an intermediate target as a guide to implementing monetary policy is
   1. that its changes directly add to aggregate demand.
   2. that information about it must be available on a frequent basis.
   3. that its movements must be closely correlated to those of the policy variable.
   - (a) both 1 and 2
   - (b) both 2 and 3
   - (c) both 1 and 3
   - (d) 1 only
   - (e) 2 only

7. If the economy is experiencing a recessionary gap, an appropriate monetary policy by the Bank of Canada could include
   - (a) increasing the discount rate.
   - (b) the purchase of government securities by the Bank of Canada.
   - (c) the sale of government securities to the public.
   - (d) increasing reserve requirements.
   - (e) increasing the tax rate.

8. If investment spending is very responsive to changes in interest rates,
   - (a) aggregate expenditures will rise when the supply of money decreases.
   - (b) an expansionary monetary policy will not succeed in increasing aggregate expenditures.
   - (c) an expansionary monetary policy will succeed in increasing aggregate expenditures.
   - (d) banks will have no excess reserves.

9. A Bank of Canada policy of maintaining a constant money supply would end up being expansionary if
   - (a) the currency appreciated.
   - (b) the demand for money decreased sharply.
   - (c) the demand for money increased sharply.
   - (d) interest rates rose.
   - (e) both A and B.

10. Bank of Canada policy since the late 1980s has been dominated by the goal of
    - (a) zero cyclical unemployment.
    - (b) "price stability".
    - (c) low interest rates.
    - (d) a stable external value of the Canadian dollar.
    - (e) full employment.

Chapter 29

1. Suppose the Bank of Canada imposes a monetary policy that is designed to stabilize the economy. According to the theory of "rational expectations" this policy will fail unless
   (a) the government is operating with a balanced budget.
   (b) labour unions agree to no increase in wage contracts.
   (c) the Bank of Canada always validates an inflationary gap.
   (d) any change in the money supply is unexpected.
   (e) any change in the money supply is fully anticipated.

2. If the NAIRU is 8 percent and the actual unemployment rate is 5 percent,
   (a) there is no pressure on the *SRAS* curve to shift.
   (b) there is a recessionary gap.
   (c) demand forces put upward pressure on wages.
   (d) the *SRAS* curve will shift downward.
   (e) it will get permanently stuck there.

3. Why might a central bank decide to validate a negative supply shock?
   (a) There is no other mechanism for returning the economy to full employment.
   (b) The economy might suffer a long slump before wages and prices fall enough to restore full employment.
   (c) Central banks tend to pay little heed to inflation.
   (d) By so doing, it can both forestall the rise in the price level and the temporary fall in national income.
   (e) There are no negative effects from this policy action.

4. In the absence of any monetary validation, a single negative supply shock will
   (a) eventually be self-correcting as wages slowly fall.
   (b) never be self-correcting without government policy to expand the money supply.
   (c) be self-correcting only if the aggregate demand curve shifts.
   (d) result in a permanent output gap.
   (e) have no short-run or long-run effects.

5. If repeated negative supply shocks are responded to with monetary validations by the central bank, the economy will be faced with
   (a) a one-time increase in prices.
   (b) continuous inflation.
   (c) alternating periods of inflation and deflation.
   (d) steady reductions in real output.
   (e) both B and D

6. Which of the following statements is the most accurate interpretation of the phrase: "inflation is a monetary phenomenon"?
   (a) The price level cannot rise without an increase in the money supply.
   (b) A sustained rise in prices is possible only with sustained increases in the money supply.
   (c) Only an increase in the money supply can start a period of inflation.
   (d) Repeated supply shocks cannot drive up prices if there is no monetary validation.
   (e) Increases in the price level are always associated with increases in the money supply.

7. Assume the economy is in long-run equilibrium with real national income at Y^*. Suppose there is a one-time decrease in *SRAS* causing the price level to rise in the short run. If, in the long run, the economy moves back to Y^* without any change in aggregate demand, the price level will be
   (a) equal to what it was before the supply shock.
   (b) higher than it was in short-run equilibrium.
   (c) lower than it was before the supply shock.
   (d) lower than it was in the short-run equilibrium but higher than it was originally.

8. Suppose a sustained inflation is in place. The central bank could reduce this inflation by
   (a) shifting the *SRAS* curve upward.
   (b) shifting the *SRAS* curve downward.
   (c) increasing the outward shift of the *AD* curve.
   (d) stopping the outward shift of the *AD* curve.

9. Attempts to remove a sustained inflation often produce stagflation. This is because inflationary expectations cause
   (a) the *AD* curve to shift too far to the right.
   (b) the *AD* curve to shift too far to the left.
   (c) the *SRAS* curve to continue shifting upward.
   (d) the *SRAS* curve to continue shifting downward.

10. What is the argument put forward by economists who support a zero-inflation policy?
    (a) The likelihood of achieving potential output is greater if the central bank gives full priority to maintaining a stable price level.
    (b) It is never possible to achieve potential output and the Bank of Canada has better control over price level as a policy variable.
    (c) It is not possible to achieve potential output and zero inflation simultaneously.
    (d) Achieving full employment output is not a worthwhile policy goal.

Chapter 30

1. Suppose that in a given year 60 000 existing jobs in the economy are eliminated and 80 000 new jobs are created. The unemployment rate will rise over that year
    (a) under no circumstances.
    (b) if less than 20 000 people join the labour force.
    (c) if more than 20 000 people join the labour force.
    (d) if more than 20 000 people drop out of the labour force.
    (e) if less than 20 000 people drop out of the labour force.

2. In theories of national-income determination, changes in real GDP are typically associated with changes in
    (a) voluntary unemployment.
    (b) frictional unemployment.
    (c) structural unemployment.
    (d) cyclical unemployment.
    (e) all of the above

3. Full employment means that there exists
    (a) zero unemployment.
    (b) no job vacancies at the time.
    (c) only structural and/or frictional unemployment.
    (d) only involuntary unemployment.
    (e) an unemployment rate of less than 5 percent.

4. If all labour markets had perfectly flexible wages (as suggested by New Classical theories), involuntary unemployment
    (a) would not exist.
    (b) would rise when the labour demand curve shifts to the left.
    (c) would rise when the labour demand curve shifts to the right.
    (d) would rise when the labour supply curve shifts to the left.
    (e) would rise when the labour supply curve shifts to the right.

5. A central argument of New Keynesian theories of unemployment is that
    (a) monetary policy is never effective at reducing unemployment.
    (b) all unemployment is caused by government intervention in the economy.
    (c) competitive labour markets cannot be relied upon to immediately eliminate involuntary unemployment.
    (d) all markets clear quickly, including labour markets, and unemployment will be quickly eliminated.
    (e) all unemployment arises from workers being unwilling to supply labour.

6. Efficiency wages
    (a) provide workers with a good reason to quit.
    (b) provide firms with a good reason to dismiss workers.
    (c) are wages that unions are able to extract from firms.
    (d) allow firms to pay workers less than the market-clearing wage.
    (e) are wages paid in excess of the market-clearing level in order to induce workers to be productive.

7. Which of the following statements about frictional unemployment is true?
    (a) The only possible cure comes from shifting the aggregate demand curve to the left.
    (b) The only possible cure comes from shifting the aggregate demand curve to the right.
    (c) There are no jobs for the unemployed people in the economy.
    (d) There is a occupational mismatch between the job vacancy and the unemployed worker.
    (e) The job vacancy and the unemployed worker have not yet found each other.

8. Suppose that a total ban on fishing is imposed on the Atlantic provinces at the same time that new oil fields come into production in Alberta. This is bound to cause some _____ unemployment in Canada's economy.
   (a) frictional
   (b) structural
   (c) cyclical
   (d) efficiency-wage
   (e) natural

9. A decline in the importance of unions would probably put _____ pressure on the NAIRU.
   (a) upward
   (b) downward
   (c) no observable
   (d) any of the above

10. It is possible that high unemployment insurance benefits can have the effect of
   (a) lowering structural unemployment.
   (b) lowering frictional unemployment.
   (c) raising structural unemployment.
   (d) raising frictional unemployment.
   (e) There would be no effect on unemployment.

Chapter 31

1. A simple equation describing the government's budget constraint is
   (a) government expenditure = tax revenue – borrowing.
   (b) government expenditure = tax revenue + debt-service payments.
   (c) tax revenue = government expenditure + borrowing.
   (d) government expenditure = tax revenue + borrowing.
   (e) tax revenue = borrowing – government expenditure.

2. The ratio of national debt to GDP is
   (a) not a useful statistic; we are essentially "dividing apples by oranges".
   (b) a useful statistic; we see how much of the national debt is owed by each individual citizen.
   (c) a useful statistic; we see the burden of the debt more clearly than using the national debt figure alone.
   (d) a useful statistic; we see the part of the year's GDP that has to be sacrificed every year to repay the national debt.
   (e) not a useful statistic; the GDP is not a meaningful measure of the well-being of the economy.

3. The budget deficit function is graphed with the budget deficit on the vertical axis and _____ on the horizontal axis, and is therefore _____ sloping.
   (a) real GDP; downward
   (b) real GDP; upward
   (c) the interest rate; downward
   (d) the interest rate; upward

4. The cyclically adjusted deficit is the budget deficit that would exist
   (a) with taxes and expenditures measured at the equilibrium level of GDP.
   (b) if the economy were at potential national income.
   (c) if tax rates were set to maximize tax revenues.
   (d) if there were no discretionary fiscal interventions in the economy.
   (e) if policy were changed to eliminate the business cycle.

5. If the government wants to maintain a stable debt-to-GDP ratio and if the growth rate of real GDP exceeds the real rate of interest, then
   (a) the government must have a primary budget surplus.
   (b) the government must implement an expansionary fiscal policy.
   (c) nominal interest rates must be constant.
   (d) the money supply should be increased at a constant rate.
   (e) the government must have a primary budget deficit.

6. The distinction between financing government expenditure through levying taxes or by issuing debt is largely irrelevant to those who believe in "Ricardian Equivalence" because
   (a) both will increase the money supply.
   (b) both will increase unemployment.
   (c) individuals' expenditure patterns will react the same way in either case.
   (d) both means have the same effect on the government's budget in the short run.
   (e) neither will have any real effects in the economy.

7. Consider an open economy with exports and imports. The idea that net exports are crowded out by government deficits assumes that
   (a) the pressure for higher interest rates attracts an inflow of capital that causes the currency to appreciate.
   (b) much government expenditure is typically directed towards imported goods and services.
   (c) government demand for labour tends to create manpower shortages in export industries.
   (d) the rise in private-sector wealth associated with the rising stock of government bonds leads to a fall in the savings rate.
   (e) both A and D.

8. In a closed economy the long-term burden of government debt occurs when
   (a) it is no longer possible to find individuals in the private sector willing to finance the debt.
   (b) the burden of the debt is being borne by the current generation rather than future generations.
   (c) the stock of physical productive capital is reduced because of past crowding-out.
   (d) foreign owners of Canadian debt demand repayment.
   (e) none of the above

9. What are the likely effects of imposing an annually balanced budget?
   (a) Swings in national income that accompany changes in autonomous expenditure flows would be reduced.
   (b) Swings in national income that accompany changes in autonomous expenditure flows would be accentuated.
   (c) National income would decrease in response to changes in autonomous expenditure flows.
   (d) National income would increase in response to changes in autonomous expenditure flows.
   (e) National income would be reduced in all circumstances.

10. If the government was able to operate a cyclically balanced budget (consistent with fiscal policy being stabilizing), then the budget would
    (a) have deficits during recessionary periods.
    (b) have deficits during inflationary periods.
    (c) never have surpluses.
    (d) be balanced every four years.
    (e) be balanced every year.

Chapter 32

1. In the long run the major effect on real GDP is exerted by
   (a) upward shifts of the *SRAS* curve.
   (b) rightward shifts of the *LRAS* curve.
   (c) rightward shifts of the *AD* curve.
   (d) upward shifts of the *AE* curve.
   (e) leftward shifts of the *AD* curve.

2. Choose the variable below that best measures a nation's standard of living.
   (a) nominal GDP
   (b) real GDP
   (c) per capita real GDP
   (d) per capita nominal GDP
   (e) nominal GNP

3. *Ceteris paribus*, an economy with high population growth will experience
   (a) an increase in per capita national income.
   (b) a decrease in the capital-output ratio.
   (c) a decrease in per capita output.
   (d) an increasingly ageing population.
   (e) an inward shift of the production possibilities curve.

4. An economy with a low national saving rate is likely to experience
   (a) a high growth rate because aggregate expenditure will be high out of any given income.
   (b) either a high or low growth rate depending on the investment schedule.
   (c) a *SRAS* curve moving continually to the right.
   (d) trouble achieving potential real national income in the short run.
   (e) a low growth rate because sustained high investment is not possible with low saving.

5. A central theme of the Neoclassical growth model is that
   (a) growth arises from correcting market failures.
   (b) there are constant returns to investment.
   (c) there are increasing returns to capital investment
   (d) growth arises only from technological innovation.
   (e) there are diminishing marginal returns to a single factor.

6. Which of the following situations describes an aggregate production function with constant returns to scale? A one percent increase in labour input
   (a) produces a one percent increase in output.
   (b) along with a one percent increase in capital produces the same amount of output.
   (c) along with a one percent decrease in capital produces the same amount of output.
   (d) along with a one percent increase in capital produces one percent more output.
   (e) induces a one percent increase in capital input.

7. Economics at one time came to be referred to as the "dismal science" because Neoclassical theories of growth emphasized
   (a) a growing inequality of income.
   (b) increasing government intervention in the economy.
   (c) increasing damage to the environment.
   (d) the immoral behaviour of firms.
   (e) diminishing returns in production.

8. Modern growth theory is based on which two of the following assumptions?
   (a) Technological change is mainly exogenous to an economy and investment yields diminishing returns.
   (b) Technological change is mainly exogenous to an economy and investment yields increasing returns.
   (c) Technological change is mainly endogenous to an economy and investment yields diminishing returns.
   (d) Technological change is mainly endogenous to an economy and investment yields increasing returns.

9. Models of endogenous growth
   (a) ignore the role of technology.
   (b) assume that the growth rate of technology is exogenous.
   (c) stress the role of knowledge and learning in the economy's rate of growth.
   (d) incorporate factors such as central-bank behaviour.
   (e) assume that the rate of growth of the economy is equal to the rate of population growth.

10. It will not be possible to meet the present needs and aspirations of the world's growing population without
   (a) enormous increases in financial capital.
   (b) increasing knowledge and technical change.
   (c) reductions in the world's capital stock, as a means of controlling the exhaustion of natural resources.
   (d) co-ordination of fiscal and monetary policies.

Chapter 33

1. The development gap refers to
   (a) the difference between actual and potential GDP in developing countries.
   (b) the difference between actual GDP in capitalist countries and communist countries.
   (c) the difference in living standards between wealthy and poor countries.
   (d) the difference in living standards between poor countries and the world average.

2. If a developing country stresses agricultural production as a source of economic development, then the economic gains from this policy will eventually fall because of
   (a) lack of innovation.
   (b) diminishing returns.
   (c) falling world food prices.
   (d) productive inefficiency.
   (e) allocative inefficiency.

3. Per capita income in a developing country will increase if aggregate income
   (a) grows faster than the population.
   (b) grows at the same rate as the population.
   (c) grows more slowly than the population.
   (d) does not change when the population increases.

4. Thomas Malthus's predictions about food supply and population have proved false (over most of the world) for which of the following reasons?
   (a) Malthus underestimated the amounts of income redistribution that would take place.
   (b) Population grew more quickly than Malthus predicted.
   (c) Malthus underestimated the importance of technical change in agriculture.
   (d) Malthus underestimated the voluntary restrictions on population growth.
   (e) Both C and D.

5. With respect to developing countries, what is the meaning of the "vicious cycle of poverty"?
   (a) Exploitation of the developing countries by the developed countries.
   (b) The exports of the developing countries have been subject to significant price decreases in the last decade.
   (c) Exploitation of the poor within a developing country by other citizens who are wealthy and powerful.
   (d) Most developing countries are too poor to generate the saving needed for sustained economic growth.
   (e) The need to increase the role of government to stimulate growth in the economy in the face of bureaucratic inefficiency.

6. From the Second World War until the early 1980s most of the developing countries in the world followed development strategies with which of the following characteristics?
   (a) low tariffs, few subsidies to industry, pegged exchange rates.
   (b) high tariffs, few subsidies to industry, flexible exchange rates.
   (c) high tariffs, many subsidies to industry, pegged exchange rates.
   (d) low tariffs, many subsidies to industry, flexible exchange rates.
   (e) low tariffs, few subsidies to industry, flexible exchange rates.

7. With respect to developing countries, it is generally believed that import substitution will
   (a) allow for rapid growth in the long run.
   (b) allow developing countries to benefit from their comparative advantage.
   (c) lead away from appropriate specialization.
   (d) tend to increase the growth of global trade.
   (e) reduce the chances of government corruption.

8. According to the more modern views of economic growth and development, the variable considered to lie at the core of the growth process is
   (a) domestic saving and investment.
   (b) labour force productivity.
   (c) natural resource endowments.
   (d) endogenous technological innovation.
   (e) well-designed fiscal policy.

9. According to most contemporary economists, long-term development of an economy is least likely to be promoted by which of the following development strategies
   (a) an agricultural strategy.
   (b) a partial restraint on population growth.
   (c) the development of export commodities.
   (d) import substitution policies.
   (e) policies that allow for foreign direct investment.

10. One of the main reasons that developing countries are now more welcoming of transnational corporations (TNCs) than in the past is
   (a) the establishment of TNCs within the borders of the developing country makes it easier for the country to isolate itself from the world economy.
   (b) TNCs pay higher tax rates than locally owned corporations.
   (c) TNCs can provide a transfer of technology and know-how to the developing country.
   (d) TNCs now allow 50 percent domestic government ownership upon location in a developing country.

Chapter 34

1. We refer to one region having an absolute advantage over a second region in the production of a particular good when
    (a) the first region has a more educated labour force than the second.
    (b) the first region has a larger supply of the raw materials required to produce that good.
    (c) an equal quantity of resources can produce more of that good in the first region than in the second.
    (d) there is no demand for that good in the second region.

2. Under what circumstances will there be no gains from specialization and trade between two countries?
    (a) Neither country has an absolute advantage in the production of any good.
    (b) Neither country has a comparative advantage in the production of any good.
    (c) Opportunity costs differ between the two countries.
    (d) There are no economies of scale.
    (e) One country has an absolute advantage in the production of all goods.

3. Consider two countries that are each producing beer and cola. We know that the country with the lower opportunity cost for cola (in terms of beer) will also have
    (a) an absolute advantage in the production of beer.
    (b) a comparative advantage in the production of cola.
    (c) a comparative advantage in the production of beer.
    (d) an absolute advantage in the production of cola.
    (e) an absolute advantage in the production of both beer and cola.

4. Canada exports electronic equipment to Asian countries and Asian countries export electronic equipment to Canada. This is a(n)
    (a) violation of the law of comparative advantage.
    (b) obvious failure to take advantage of specialization.
    (c) likely result of economies of scale and product differentiation.
    (d) general conclusion of the Heckscher-Ohlin theory.
    (e) example of the inefficiency of trade patterns.

5. International trade permits a country to
    (a) produce and consume beyond its production possibilities boundary.
    (b) shift its production possibilities boundary outward.
    (c) lower the per-unit production costs of all goods which it is producing.
    (d) expand its production possibilities while holding constant its consumption possibilities.
    (e) consume beyond its production possibilities boundary.

Table 34-1 shows the quantities of mangoes and pineapples that can be produced in Brazil and Mexico with one unit of equivalent resources. Refer to this table to answer questions 6-9.

TABLE 34-1

	Mangoes	Pineapples
Brazil	30	5
Mexico	12	4

6. The opportunity cost of one pineapple in Brazil is
    (a) .1667 mangoes.
    (b) 1.2 pineapples.
    (c) 6 mangoes.
    (d) .8 pineapples.

7. The opportunity cost of one mango in Mexico is
    (a) 3 pineapples.
    (b) 1/3 of a pineapple.
    (c) lower than the opportunity cost of mangoes in Brazil.
    (d) indicative of Mexico's comparative advantage in mango production.

8. Brazil has an absolute advantage in the production of
    (a) mangoes.
    (b) pineapples.
    (c) neither mangoes nor pineapples.
    (d) both mangoes and pineapples.

9. If Brazil were to transfer 1/2 unit of resources from pineapples to mangoes and Mexico were to transfer one unit of resources from mangoes to pineapples, the effect on the total output of the two countries would be as follows:
   (a) Mango production would increase by 15.
   (b) Mango production would increase by 3 and pineapple production would increase by 1.5.
   (c) Mango production would increase by 18 and pineapple production would decrease by 1.
   (d) Pineapple production would increase by 4.

10. We say that a country's terms of trade have deteriorated whenever its
    (a) import prices rise more than its export prices.
    (b) export prices rise more than its import prices.
    (c) import prices fall while its export prices remain constant.
    (d) export prices rise while its import prices remain constant.

Chapter 35

1. The reasoning behind protectionist policies is to
   (a) create a level playing field.
   (b) promote exports.
   (c) raise government revenues through tariffs.
   (d) maximize world production.
   (e) shield local producers from foreign competition.

2. One argument for protectionism is called the infant-industry argument, whereby a new small industry
   (a) must be protected even if it will never have a comparative advantage.
   (b) must be protected permanently to provide for a diversified economy.
   (c) will need protection once it has exploited available economies of scale.
   (d) may need protection temporarily until it can exploit economies of scale.
   (e) must be protected in order to provide a domestic supply.

3. If wages in Mexico are lower than those in Canada,
   (a) tariffs should be imposed on imports from Mexico to protect Canadian workers.
   (b) Canadian consumers may benefit by purchasing low-cost goods from Mexico.
   (c) Canada may have a comparative advantage in all products.
   (d) Mexico may have a comparative advantage in all products.
   (e) Mexico probably has an absolute advantage in all products due to its low labour costs.

4. It is not possible for one country to sell all products more cheaply than other countries for any length of time because the
   (a) importing countries will react by constructing severe trade barriers.
   (b) exporting country will find its cost of production increasing relative to the importing country.
   (c) depreciation of the importing countries' currencies ensures that trade will flow in both directions.
   (d) depreciation of the exporting country's currency will lead to trade in both directions.
   (e) the principle of absolute advantage would then be violated.

Refer to this figure to answer questions 5–8.

FIGURE 35-1

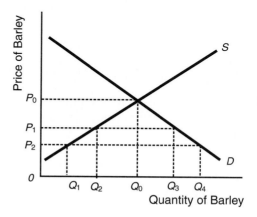

5. In Figure 35-1, at the price P_2, the Canadian domestic supply of barley is
   (a) Q_1.
   (b) Q_2.
   (c) Q_3.
   (d) Q_4.
   (e) Q_5.

6. In Figure 35-1, at the price P_2, the quantity of barley imported into the Canadian market is
   (a) Q_0Q_4.
   (b) Q_1Q_0.
   (c) Q_2Q_4.
   (d) Q_2Q_3.
   (e) Q_1Q_4.

7. In Figure 35-1, if Canada imposes a tariff causing the price of barley in Canada to rise from P_2 to P_1, the consequence would be that
   (a) both domestic production and domestic consumption would decrease by equal amounts.
   (b) domestic production will increase from Q_1 to Q_2 and domestic consumption will fall from Q_4 to Q_3.
   (c) domestic production will increase from Q_1 to Q_3 and domestic consumption will fall from Q_4 to Q_3.
   (d) domestic production will exceed domestic consumption.
   (e) both domestic production and domestic consumption would increase by equal amounts.

8. In Figure 35-1, suppose the initial no-tariff price is P_2 and then the Canadian government responded to political pressure from domestic barley growers and imposed a tariff high enough that all imports were eliminated. As a result, the price and quantity of barley in Canada would be, respectively,
   (a) P_1 and Q_3.
   (b) P_2 and Q_4.
   (c) P_0 and Q_4.
   (d) P_1 and Q_2.
   (e) P_0 and Q_0.

9. Trade diversion
   (a) represents a benefit of creating a free-trade area.
   (b) is inefficient trade that follows the establishment of a regional trading bloc.
   (c) is always larger than trade creation.
   (d) is always smaller than trade creation.
   (e) occurs in theory, but it has never been observed in practice.

10. The fundamental principle that guides the NAFTA is the principle of national treatment. The basic idea is that
   (a) member countries have complete autonomy over their own laws and the way in which they are applied to any firm, domestic or foreign, operating on their soil.
   (b) member countries cannot establish new laws which harm the domestic environment.
   (c) any new laws being considered by a member country must first be subject to a cross-border judicial panel.
   (d) member countries can establish new laws as they wish, as long as these laws are interpreted to apply equally to domestic and foreign-owned firms.

Chapter 36

1. When a Canadian purchases a foreign asset (such as a Japanese government bond) it is considered a
   (a) capital inflow and is recorded as a credit on the current account.
   (b) capital outflow and is recorded as a debit on the capital account.
   (c) capital outflow and is recorded as a debit on the current account.
   (d) capital inflow and is recorded as a credit on the capital account.

2. Which one of the following transactions would appear as a debit in the current account of Canada's balance of payments?
   (a) A Dutch bank makes a loan to a Canadian firm.
   (b) A Canadian subsidiary exports raw materials to its Japanese parent company.
   (c) Canadians receive dividends on Canadian investment in Europe.
   (d) Canadian tourists in Italy visit fine Italian restaurants.
   (e) The Bank of Canada purchases U.S. dollars to hold in its official reserves.

3. Suppose the current account of the balance of payments is in deficit. In this case, we can be sure that
   (a) the capital account is in surplus.
   (b) the capital account is also in deficit.
   (c) the combination of the capital account and the official financing account must be in surplus.
   (d) total debts exceed total credits.
   (e) the official financing account must be in surplus.

4. A rise in the Canadian-dollar price of foreign currency is
   (a) an appreciation of the Canadian dollar.
   (b) a depreciation of the Canadian dollar.
   (c) a decrease in the exchange rate.
   (d) a gain in the relative value of the Canadian dollar.
   (e) a rise in the external value of the Canadian dollar.

5. If the Canadian dollar depreciates, there will be a _____ in the demand for imports, and the number of Canadian dollars offered in the foreign-exchange market will _____.
   (a) rise; rise
   (b) rise; fall
   (c) fall; rise
   (d) fall; fall

6. Consider a country that is operating under a fixed-exchange-rate system. The balance of payments will always show total debits equal to total credits because
   (a) fluctuations in exchange rates will bring debits and credits into equality.
   (b) official financing will offset any deficit or surplus in current and capital accounts.
   (c) short-term capital flows will always offset any deficit or surplus in current accounts and long-term capital accounts.
   (d) the capital account will always offset a deficit or surplus in the current account.
   (e) none of the above

7. Consider a country that is operating under a flexible-exchange-rate system. Any balance-of-payments deficit will be eliminated by
   (a) an increase in the value of the country's currency.
   (b) an increase in the demand for foreign exchange.
   (c) a decrease in the supply of foreign exchange.
   (d) an appreciation of the country's currency.
   (e) a depreciation of the country's currency.

8. If the balance-of-payments accounts do not include any official financing, then it is likely that
   (a) the central bank has pegged the exchange rate so that the current and capital accounts sum to zero.
   (b) the exchange rate is being determined freely in the foreign-exchange market.
   (c) this country must not be engaging in international trade.
   (d) there must be a disequilibrium in the foreign-exchange market.
   (e) none of the above

9. Suppose two countries, A and B, are trading with each other. Suppose also that inflation in B is higher than in A. There will be
   (a) an increase in the demand for Country B's currency in the foreign-exchange market.
   (b) an increase in the supply of Country B's currency in the foreign-exchange market.
   (c) an increase in Country B's exports.
   (d) a decrease in Country B's imports.
   (e) no effect on the foreign-exchange market.

10. What is purchasing power parity?
   (a) It is an index of the average value of exchange rates.
   (b) It is a theory that says price levels in two countries are equal when measured in a common currency.
   (c) It is a theory that allows for both countries' currencies to appreciate at their own rates of inflation.
   (d) It is a situation that tends to cause those currencies with lower inflation rates to depreciate.
   (e) It is a condition that holds exactly in the short run but not in the long run.

Answers to Self-Test Questions

Chapter 1

1. B
Scarcity is central to all of economics—there are only so many resources but generally unlimited wants or desires.

2. C
Because of scarcity, choosing more of item A means choosing less of some other item B. This is the opportunity cost associated with the choice.

3. C
With scarcity comes the need for choice. And with choice there is opportunity cost. The cost of choosing X is that the next best alternative, Y, is unavailable. The opportunity cost of building a school is that some other government spending, such as on hospitals, cannot take place.

4. A
The production possibilities boundary shows the concepts of scarcity, choice, and opportunity cost. Opportunity cost is reflected by the negative slope—that producing more of one item requires producing less of another, as long as we are using resources efficiently.

5. B
The new law would reduce the available labour—an important factor of production. With less of this factor available, the maximum amount of production is reduced, so the *PPB* shifts inward.

6. C
With PPB_1, points D and E are infeasible. Point B has more military goods than point A and is feasible since it is on PPB_1.

7. C
Technology has not improved in the military goods industry, otherwise the horizontal intercept of the *PPB* would have shifted to the right. The movement of the vertical intercept reflects the improvement in technology in civilian goods production.

8. C
Private-sector firms are owned by individuals. Public-sector firms are owned by the government.

9. C
Though most economists agree that there is a role for some government intervention (for reasons discussed in detail in later chapters), there is a broad consensus that the vast majority of decisions are best left to individual consumers and producers to be coordinated by the price system.

10. D
Any increase in saving—whether by firms or households—is a withdrawal from the circular flow, and such a withdrawal leads to a contraction of the circular flow.

Chapter 2

1. D
A positive statement is one that states what is (or will be): All of the choices except the one about tuition fees are positive (though they may be incorrect). A normative statement describes what ought to be, and this involves a value judgement.

2. B
Every individual will make an error in measurement. But the more people there are, the more likely it is that the errors of one will offset the errors of another, thereby reducing the average error.

3. B
Since the average daily temperature is not influenced by people's incomes or actions, it is determined outside the theory in question, and is thus an exogenous variable.

4. E
Essential to the scientific method is the construction of theories and the confrontation of theories by evidence.

5. D
Put crudely, a theory states that X leads to Y. This is the form of statement made.

6. E
If a theory is unable to predict behaviour accurately, either the theory will be discarded or it will be modified. Only theories that predict reasonably accurately will be retained.

7. B

The most important reason for making "unrealistic" assumptions is to simplify the scope of analysis. Highly realistic assumptions may make the model so complicated that no insights are generated.

8. C

Nothing gets proven with certainty. But we reject a hypothesis when the empirical evidence suggests that the probability that it is wrong is very high.

9. B

Slope equals $\Delta Y / \Delta X$. In this case, $\Delta Y = 12$ and $\Delta X = 6$. Therefore, slope equals 2.

10. A

This is the definition of cross-sectional data.

Chapter 3

1. C

Quantity demanded depends on price, income, tastes, prices of other products and several other factors. It refers to a particular point on a demand curve, rather than the entire curve (or entire demand schedule).

2. E

Wieners and buns are complements. Thus an increase in the price of wieners leads to fewer buns being purchased. This decreases the demand for film.

3. C

Statement (1) should really say "... cause a decrease in the *quantity of popsicles demanded*". Statement (2) is correct and reflects the fact that popsicles and fudgsicles are substitutes.

4. D

This is the definition of "quantity supplied"—the amount producers want to sell at a particular price in a given period of time.

5. C

By the definition of the supply curve, its positive slope indicates that quantity supplied increases as the price increases.

6. B

Since fertilizer is used to wheat, the fertilizer influences the position of the supply curve for wheat. A fall in the price of fertilizer increases the profitability of producing wheat and thus shifts the supply curve for wheat to the right.

7. C

Equilibrium price is the price where quantity demanded equals quantity supplied—$30 in this case.

8. A

At a price of $10, consumers would want to purchase 500 dozen, but producers would only be prepared to sell 200 dozen. Thus the amount *actually* purchased would be 200 dozen.

9. B

At P_2, quantity demanded equals quantity supplied, so this is the equilibrium price. Below P_2, there is excess demand. Above P_2, there is excess supply.

10. B

The supply curve is stable. Thus, changes in price must be explained by shifts in the demand curve. The higher evening price therefore suggests that the evening demand curve is to the right of the daytime demand curve.

Chapter 4

1. E

Price elasiticity is equal to the percentage change in quantity demanded divided by the percentage change in price. Demand is said to be *inelastic* whenever elasticity is less than one.

2. E

The degree of substitutability is the key determinant of elasticity. Since clothing has fewer substitutes than does T-shirts (since clothing is a much broader category), the demand for clothing will be less elastic than the demand for T-shirts.

3. E

Elasticity is equal to $(\Delta q/q)/(\Delta p/p)$ where q and p are the average quantity and price. Thus elasticity in this case is $(40\,000/100\,000)/(2/10)$, which is $(0.40)/(0.2) = 2$.

4. A

Since total expenditure rises, the percentage decrease in price must be smaller than the percentage increase in quantity demanded. Thus the elasticity of demand is greater than one—demand is elastic.

5. C

The key determinant of supply elasticity is the ease with which firms can take resources away from producing one good and use them to produce another. If such reallocations are difficult, supply is less elastic.

6. A
Long-run supply is more elastic than short-run supply. Thus an increase in demand will cause a larger price increase in the short run than in the long run. This is the "overshooting" of the long-run equilibrium price.

7. A
Consumers bear more of the burden if demand is inelastic (for a given supply curve). Producers bear more of the burden if supply is inelastic (for a given demand curve).

8. D
If demand is perfectly elastic (horizontal demand curve), then consumers can easily substitute away to other goods when a tax pushes up the price. In this extreme case, consumers will bear none of the burden.

9. A
Income elasticity is the percentage change in quantity demanded divided by the percentage change in income. Thus, an income elasticity of 1.25 means that a 10 percent increase in income increases quantity demanded by 12.5 percent.

10. D
As the price of imported beer falls, quantity demanded for imported beer naturally rises. If the two beers are substitutes (as is reasonable) then the quantity demanded of domestic beer should fall.

Chapter 5

1. B
As rubber becomes more expensive, the cost of producing rubber tires increases. This increase in cost shifts the supply curve of tires to the left, thus driving up the equilibrium price of tires.

2. D
Cement is very costly to transport relative to its price. So there is only limited mobility of the supply of cement between these two regions. As a result, the market for cement is regionally segmented.

3. E
A surplus (excess supply) in a free market will generally lead producers to cut prices, thus pushing the price down to the equilibrium level.

4. C
If the price ceiling is set *below* the equilibrium price, excess demand will result. This is true for a very low price ceiling ($200) or a relatively high one ($800), as long as both are below the equilibrium price.

5. B
At any disequilibrium price, the quantity exchanged is equal to the *lesser of* quantity demanded and quantity supplied. So q_1 is the answer.

6. E
At P_3 there is clearly excess demand of the amount $q_3 q_4$. Only q_3 will actually be exchanged.

7. B
The short-run supply of rental housing is very inelastic. Only over the long run will the quantity supplied of rental housing change significantly. So whatever shortage is caused in the short run will be *worsened* as time goes by.

8. C
Landlords do not benefit. Future tenants are harmed because of the shortage of housing. The real beneficiaries are the *current* tenants who benefit from the low-priced housing.

9. E
If the demand curve facing farmers is unit elastic, then fluctuations in quantity supplied will still cause price fluctuations, but farmer's total incomes will be constant.

10. A
The individual farmer has no effect on the world price so he would never benefit by restricting his own output. In this case, each unit sold increases his income by the world price.

Chapter 6

1. C
If marginal utility is positive, then the consumption of one more unit adds to total utility.

2. D
Utility maximization requires that MU/P is equal for *all* goods. If this is not true, then some reallocation of the consumer's budget will increase total utility.

3. C
Utility maximization requires that MU/P is equal for *all* goods. If this is not true, then some reallocation of the consumer's budget will increase total utility.

4. D
This is the definition of consumer surplus. It is the "bargain" that a consumer gets for having to pay less than the amount they were willing to pay.

5. D
Consumer surplus is the area below the demand curve above the price line. It is therefore shown by the area *BCD*.

6. C
If the demand curve is downward sloping, then the administered price of zero suggests that households will increase their quantity demanded. (Since it is a scarce good, its free-market price would be greater than zero.) In this case, the government provision is satisfying what would in a free market be an excess demand.

7. A
The abundance of water makes its price low. This increases quantity demanded and leads consumers to use it to the point where its *marginal* value is low (though its total value is high).

8. E
The paradox comes from the confusion of total and marginal values and the failure to recognize that supply (as well as demand) determines price.

9. A
If money income and *all* prices change by the same percentage, then real income (purchasing power) is unchanged.

10. C
In this case, the *relative* price of chicken has increased, so the substitution effect is to reduce chicken consumption. If we observe that chicken consumption increases, it must be from the income effect. (There is more real income because of the reduction in the price of beef.)

Chapter 7

1. D
The opportunity cost for *anything* is the benefit forgone by not using it in its best alternative.

2. D
Since there is no market transaction for the inputs, the opportunity cost must be imputed. It is equal to the benefits of using the input in the next best use.

3. B
If there are only normal profits—economic profits are zero—then owners will keep their capital in the firm, but no new capital will be attracted to the industry. Owners will be earning just what is available to them in their next best alternative uses.

4. A
The law is most appropriately called the law of *eventually* diminishing returns. As the marginal product falls below the average product, the average product will begin to fall.

5. A
The point of diminishing marginal returns is *defined* to be the point where marginal product reaches a maximum.

6. E
MP intersects *AP* at its maximum point. Whenever *MP* is below *AP*, *AP* is falling.

7. A
This is the definition of marginal cost: $MC = \Delta TC/\Delta Q$.

8. B
Because *MP* eventually declines, marginal costs eventually rise. This ultimately makes *AVC* and *ATC* upward sloping as well.

9. E
A rising *MC* curve does not imply a rising *ATC* curve, since *AFC* could be falling significantly. But a rising *MC* curve does imply that *MP* is falling (indeed, this is why *MC* does rise).

10. D
The capacity of a plant is defined to be the level of output where *ATC* is minimized.

Chapter 8

1. A
With all factors of production variable, a profit-maximizing firm chooses the production method to minimize costs.

2. C
For any level of output, costs are minimized if $MP_K/P_K = MP_L/P_L$. If this equality does not hold, the production method can be altered in a manner that reduces costs.

3. A
Cost minimizing requires $MP_L/MP_K = P_L/P_K$. In this example, $MP_L/MP_K < P_L/P_K$ and so the firm is using too much labour and not enough capital. By using more capital, MP_K would fall; by using less labour, MP_L would rise.

4. C
Cost minimizing requires $MP_L/MP_K = P_L/P_K$. Since the firm has the optimal factor mix, $3/6 = MP_L/80$, so the missing MP_L is 40.

5. D
Cost minimization requires $MP_L/MP_K = P_L/P_K$. In this example, $MP_L/MP_K = 40/40 > P_L/P_K = 2/5$ and so the firm is using too much capital (MP_K is too low) and not enough labour (MP_L is too high).

6. A
The *LRAC* curve is defined as the lower envelope of the *SRATC* curves. It shows the lowest possible cost of producing any given level of output (for the current state of technology).

7. C
Each *SRATC* curve is drawn for a different plant size. The only point where the *SRATC* curve touches the *LRAC* curve is at that level of output for which the plant size (fixed factor) is optimal. For all other levels of output, that plant size is either too small or too large for long-run cost minimization.

8. B
If all inputs increase by X percent and output increases by *more than* X percent, then there are increasing returns to scale. This is the declining-cost portion of the *LRAC* curve.

9. C
A change in the production function means a change in the relationship between the *quantity* of factors and the *quantity* of output. This could be caused by improved *quality* of inputs, as would occur with greater education for labour.

10. C
Changes in technology shift the short-run and long-run cost curves: downward for improvements and upward for deteriorations.

Chapter 9

1. D
The assumption of free entry and exit is central to the theory of perfect competition—as are the assumptions of price-taking behaviour and homogeneous products.

2. D
The firm takes price (marginal revenue) as given and adjusts output until price equals marginal cost. As price rises, output rises along the *MC* curve. For prices below the minimum of *AVC*, the firm shuts down.

3. A
To maximize profits, output should be adjusted until $P = MC$. Since the firm is currently producing where $P = ATC$, and since $MC > ATC$, it must be that $P < MC$. So the firm is producing too much.

4. D
Profit maximization requires $P = MC$ (as long as $P > AVC$). At $P = \$22$, Q should be 270 units.

5. D
For $P = \$30$, profit maximization requires $Q = 300$. At $Q = 300$, $SRATC = \$22$. Thus, total cost must be $\$22 \times 300 = \$6600$.

6. E
The short-run supply curve for a competitive firm is the *MC* curve above the *AVC* curve. When price is less than *AVC*, the firm shuts down.

7. B
With $P = SRATC$, existing firms are making positive economic profits (since costs include the opportunity cost of the owner's capital). Thus new firms will enter the industry in pursuit of these "excess" profits.

8. E
The industry is in long-run equilibrium only when no firm has the incentive to either leave the industry or expand its plant size (to take advantage of further scale economies). Thus each firm is at the minimum of both its *SRATC* and *LRAC* curve.

9. B
As long as the firm is to the left of the minimum of its *LRAC* curve, it can benefit by expanding its plant size and reducing its average costs.

10. E
As demand steadily falls, so too will the market price. This leads to losses, which eventually leads firms to leave the industry. Capacity to produce this product will fall.

Chapter 10

1. C
Profit maximization requires that *MR* equals *MC*. But for a monopolist, *MR* is less than price (the *MR* curve is below the demand curve). Thus price exceeds *MC*.

2. E
A natural monopoly means that if firms produce at capacity output (minimum efficient scale), there is only room for one firm in the industry. It is "natural" because the monopoly is not created by artificial entry barriers but by natural technological considerations.

3. E
For any firm, including a monopolist, economic profits are determined by the difference between price and average total cost. Zero economic profit implies $P = ATC$.

4. B
Profit maximization requires $MR = MC$. This implies $25 - Q = 10$, which implies $-3Q = -15$, which implies $Q = 5$.

5. B
The whole purpose of a cartel is to restrict industry output and thus increase price. This is independent of demand elasticity (although the less elastic is demand, the more price will be increased for a given reduction in output).

6. C
This is the basic dilemma of a cartel. All firms *together* have the incentive to restrict output so as to increase price. But any *individual* firm has the incentive to increase output as long as the other firms are restricting theirs.

7. C
The essence of price discrimination is that different prices are charged depending on the consumers' willingness to pay. If the price differences reflect *cost* differences, this is not price discrimination.

8. A
Perfect price discrimination means that each unit is sold at a different price—the most consumers will pay. This price is equal to marginal revenue since reducing the price for the next unit does not require reducing the price for any other units.

9. C
For perfect price discrimination, the demand curve is also the marginal revenue curve. Thus profit maximization requires $MR = MC$, which occurs at the level of output equal to q_2.

10. E
With perfect price discrimination, output is equal to q_1, the competitive output level. But each unit is sold at the price given by the height of the demand curve—the consumer's maximum willingness to pay. So consumer surplus is zero.

Chapter 11

1. C
Central to imperfectly competitive market structures is *product differentiation*. This permits much non-price competition—through advertising, quality, service and so on.

2. B
Long-run equilibrium in a monopolistically competitive industry has each firm with zero profits, $P = ATC$. Since each firm faces a downward sloping demand curve, this means each firm produces where the demand curve is tangent to *ATC*, which means at an output level *below* the firm's capacity (where *ATC* is minimized).

3. D
The Gap and DQ are both monopolistic competitors. There are other (similar, but not identical) clothing stores and fast food joints. But the individual potato farmer's product is identical to the product of hundreds of other farmers, and so he is a perfect competitor.

4. D
Free entry and exit is what ensures zero profits in the long run (in both perfect competition and monopolistic competition). If existing firms are profitable, entry occurs; if existing firms are making losses, exit occurs.

5. B
Central to oligopoly is the notion of *strategic behaviour*—that is, firms think about how other firms will respond to changes in their behaviour. Perfect competitors are so small (relative to the industry) that they don't worry about such strategy. Monopolists have no competitors to think about.

6. C
A Nash equilibrium is a non-cooperative equilibrium in which each player does its best given the actions of the other players. But all players are *not necessarily* better off than in a different outcome. The Prisoner's Dilemma is the obvious counterexample.

7. A

If oligopolistic firms can successfully collude, they can behave—collectively—as a monopolist. In this case, the strategic considerations are removed (although each firm still has the incentive to cheat).

8. E

Firm-created entry barriers are not related to economies of scale (declining *LRAC* and set-up costs). But producing many brands of a similar product (for example, breakfast cereals) and heavy advertising can successfully deter entry.

9. D

With a short product life, the firm may not be producing the good long enough for it to work its way down the *LRAC* curve by expanding its plant size. Thus it may never fully realize the available economies of scale.

10. C

Oligopolies use their economic profits to finance research and development, in the hope that they can continue earning economic profits (by staying ahead of their competitors). Such research and development contributes to technological progress and long-term economic growth.

Chapter 12

1. C

Since price reflects the marginal benefit of the good to society, $P = MC$ in all industries means that the "right amount" of each good is being produced. This is allocative efficiency.

2. A

If marginal cost is not the same at the two firms, then output can be reduced at the high-*MC* firm and increased at the low-*MC* firm. This will reduce total costs for a given level of output.

3. B

In the competitive industry $P = MC$, and so allocative efficiency is achieved. In the monopolized industry $P > MC$ and so it is not allocatively efficient.

4. C

The deadweight loss of monopoly is defined to be the consumer and producer surplus that is not realized because the monopolist restricts output below the competitive level.

5. C

In perfect competition the industry supply curve is the summation of all the *MC* curves. Thus the equilibrium price is P_0 and the quantity is q_0.

6. D

Consumer surplus is equal to the area under the demand curve but above the price line. With the monopoly price of P_3 (output where $MC = MR$), consumer surplus is the area P_3P_4a.

7. B

Producer surplus in the competitive equilibrium is the area above the *MC* curve and below the price line (price $= P_0$). In the monopoly equilibrium, the gain in producer surplus is the area P_0P_3ac, but the area *cbd* is lost. Thus the net gain is P_0P_3ac less *cbd*.

8. C

The deadweight loss of monopoly is defined to be the consumer and producer surplus that is *not* realized because the monopolist restricts output below the competitive level. In this case it is the area *dab*.

9. A

Since *ATC* is falling, *MC* must be *below ATC*. So with $P = MC$, price will be below average costs. The firm will be making economic losses. If this regulation persists, the firm will eventually go out of business.

10. D

A per-unit tax increases *MC* by the amount of the tax. This also increases average total costs, but it does nothing to the demand curve.

Chapter 13

1. B

The Lorenz curve shows how the cumulative total income changes with the cumulative percentage of the number of households. If all households have equal incomes, the Lorenz curve would be exactly the diagonal line.

2. E

This is the definition of *MRP*.

3. C

The marginal physical product (*MPP*) of the factor is the change in total output when the factor input changes by one unit. For the 7th unit of labour, output rises from 162 to 170 units, so the *MPP* is 8.

4. D

The marginal revenue product (*MRP*) of the factor is the change in total revenue when the factor input is changed by one unit. Since the output price is always $2, total revenue is equal to $2 times total output. For the 5th unit of the factor, total revenue rises from $256 to $296 and so the *MRP* is $40.

5. D

An increase in wages will likely increase the quantity of labour supplied (a movement along the supply curve). All of the other choices are likely to shift the supply curve to the right.

6. C

Owners of factors of production shift the factors between uses until net advantage is maximized. Recall that net advantage includes both monetary and non-monetary rewards to the factor.

7. D

If the government requires all factors to receive the same price, then factors will naturally avoid the undesirable jobs. There will be many shortages in such low-net-advantage uses.

8. C

The total payment to any factor can be divided into transfer earnings—the amount required to keep the factor in its present use—and economic rent—anything else. Reductions in factor payments will not cause the factor to leave its current use as long as there is still positive rent.

9. C

His actual earnings are $2 million. His transfer earnings are $200 000. So his economic rent is his earnings in excess of the transfer earnings—in this case, $1 800 000.

10. D

Perfectly inelastic supply means that the same quantity of the factor will be supplied no matter how low the price goes. In this case, there are no transfer earnings and so the whole of the payment is economic rent.

Chapter 14

1. C

Human capital is the term economists use for the *quality* of labour gained through education, training, experience and health. Gender is not relevant.

2. D

Any schooling beyond the legal minimum is investment in human capital that is voluntarily undertaken. The benefits of this investment are only realized in the future.

3. B

Wage differentials due to differences in human capital will persist as long as the human-capital differences exist. These are *equilibrium* differentials.

4. D

It is highly unlikely that workers who are unemployed, or underemployed, because of labour-market discrimination will experience an increase in human capital.

5. B

Discrimination against some workers in market A essentially removes some workers from the supply in that market, reducing employment and raising wages there. These discriminated-against workers move to market B, driving down the wage there. If wages cannot fall (due perhaps to a minimum wage), then unemployment will rise in market B.

6. A

A monopsonist in the labour market is a single buyer of labour, and thus faces an upward-sloping supply curve. It restricts employment below the competitive level and pays a wage below the competitive level. Employment is such that $MRP_L = MC_L$ (> wage).

7. B

A binding minimum wage must be above the free-market equilibrium wage. There is thus excess supply of labour. Wages will rise but (because the demand for labour is negatively sloped) employment will fall.

8. E

In a competitive labour market a binding minimum wage must raise the wage and reduce employment. In a monopsonistic labour market, however, the monopsonist has restricted employment and pushed down the wage. A *moderate* increase in the wage due to a binding minimum wage may raise both wages and employment.

9. A

By increasing the length of the training program, plumbing school is made more costly and this reduces the number of entrants. This will shift the supply curve of plumbers to the left and raise the wages of plumbers.

10. E

All of these are reasons why the observed switch from manufacturing to service jobs is not necessarily undesirable.

Chapter 15

1. D
The value *today* of a receipt or payment in the future is called the *present value*.

2. C
With an interest rate of 8 percent (per year), the present value of $100 in one year is $100/(1.08) = $92.59.

3. D
At an interest rate of 10 percent per year, the present value of $200 in 3 years is $200/(1.10)^3$ which equals $150.26.

4. C
The present value of the stream of *MRP*s is equal to $1000/(1.07) + \$1000/(1.07)^2 + \$1000/(1.07)^3$. This sum is $2584.37, and is the most any firm would be prepared to pay today to acquire this piece of capital.

5. A
It will be profitable to buy a piece of capital equipment as long as the *PV* of the stream of *MRP*s exceeds the purchase price. If the price exceeds the *PV* of the stream of *MRP*s, the capital is not worthwhile investment.

6. B
A change in the interest rate is a *movement along* the demand curve for capital. A rightward shift in the demand for capital is caused by an improvement in capital's productivity, which makes it a more profitable investment for firms.

7. E
This is Hotelling's Rule—that the optimal rate of extraction is such that the price of the resource rises at a rate equal to the interest rate.

8. B
If interest rates rise now, then extracting the resource becomes more attractive now. Thus the current rate of extraction rises, pushing down the current price.

9. D
The problem with common property is that individuals have the incentive to overuse it, not recognizing that they may impose costs on others. Such nonrenewable resources thus tend to be extracted more quickly than is optimal.

10. E
Coal, iron ore, forest products and land are all generally *not* problems of common property because the benefits of the resource are usually confined to the land on or below which they lie (the ownership of which can be clearly defined). To the extent that underground petroleum reservoirs are interconnected, however, oil (and natural gas) may have common property aspects.

Chapter 16

1. D
In a free-market economy there is still a need for government—to correct market failures and to alter the distribution of income.

2. B
The term *market failure* is used to refer to situations where the free market does not produce an allocatively efficient outcome. One example is monopoly, another is an externality.

3. A
The differences between private and social marginal costs leads to externalities and an inefficient free-market outcome. Production which generates pollution as a by-product is an example.

4. B
Since all consumers can use the public good at the same time (non-rivalrous consumption), the social marginal benefit of the good is the *sum* of everyone's private marginal benefits. For the optimal provision, this sum of *MB*s should be equal to the *MC*.

5. D
Once national defence is provided in any reasonable amount, the cost of providing it to *an extra person* is zero. Since *MC* is zero, efficient allocation requires that consumers pay zero. Any positive price would lead to too little of the public good being consumed.

6. E
Moral hazard exists whenever one party to a transaction has both the ability and the incentive to shift costs onto the other party. All of the examples potentially involve moral hazard—on the part of the consumer for insurance, and on the part of the doctor or lawyer for their services.

7. D
Adverse selection occurs whenever particularly high-risk individuals are more likely to purchase insurance.

8. A

Canada's system of national parks is an example of the government providing public goods (at prices well below the average cost of provision).

9. C

Rent seeking occurs whenever individuals or firms try to influence policymakers to direct the allocation of resources in their favour.

10. C

Market failure is *not* a sufficient condition for government intervention. If the cost of intervention is smaller than the cost of the market failure, then the intervention is justified.

Chapter 17

1. A

Allocative efficiency requires that each good be produced such that the marginal social cost equals the marginal social benefit.

2. A

Suppose that *MC* is upward sloping and *MB* is downward sloping. If the *MC* of abatement equals the *MB* of abatement, then further abatement will cost more to society than it will generate in benefits. Society will be worse off.

3. D

For the first units of pollution reduction, the marginal benefit will be high. As more and more pollution is eliminated, however, the benefit from *additional* pollution control falls. Thus the *MB* curve of pollution reduction is downward sloping.

4. C

If the act of production generates *external* costs, then those costs are internalized to the firm only when the firm must bear those costs. An emissions tax equal to the marginal external cost is one method of internalizing the externality.

5. B

Pollution abatement is a "good" like any other. Its optimal amount (for society) is where the *MB* of abatement equals its *MC*. This will almost certainly occur when some pollution remains.

6. C

In order to internalize pollution externalities, polluting firms must be made to bear the marginal external cost of their production. Emissions taxes can do this. Another choice is to directly control the *quantity* of output—but this does not change the firm's marginal costs.

7. E

Emissions taxes (of the right amount) fully internalize the exernality. And since the price system is still in use, firms have the incentive to minimize the costs of abatement.

8. E

With tradable emissions permits, firms who can abate at low cost will want to sell permits; high-cost-abatement firms will buy permits. The market price for the permits is the marginal abatement cost, and this will be the same for all firms.

9. D

Efficiency requires that a given amount of abatement be done at least cost. This requires that the *MC* of abatement be equated across all firms. With different abatement technologies, direct controls typically result in inefficiency.

10. B

Efficiency requires that a given amount of abatement be done at least cost. This requires that the *MC* of abatement be equated across all firms. With different abatement technologies, direct controls typically result in inefficiency. A uniform emissions tax, however, will make each firm face the same "marginal benefit" of abatement and will thus equate their *MC* of abatement. But Firm X will abate more than Firm Y.

Chapter 18

1. C

A tax expenditure is an exemption from taxation or a tax deduction that reduces the government's tax revenue. The deductability of a portion of charitable contributions is a classic example.

2. B

Progressive and regressive taxes are defined as such according to the behaviour of the average tax rate as income rises. The average tax rate in this example increases from 20 percent to 40 percent to 50 percent as income rises. This tax is clearly progressive.

3. B

A lump-sum tax changes neither the marginal costs or revenues faced by the monopolist, and thus the profit-maximizing level of output is unchanged. As long as the tax is less than the firm's profits, output will remain at the pre-tax level.

4. A

If the goal of tax policy is to have an overall tax system that is proportional, then progressivity must occur in some part of the system to offset the regressivity of sales and excise taxes. Income taxes would be the obvious choice for a progressive tax.

5. B

The excess burden of a tax is the loss in consumer or producer surplus that results from the changes in behaviour caused by the tax. If a tax on good X leads to no change in the quantity of good X exchanged, there is no excess burden of the tax (but there will be a direct burden).

6. A

The practical consideration for designing a tax system is that a certain amount of revenue must be raised to finance government expenditure. Given this revenue requirement, the tax system should be designed to minimize the inefficiencies.

7. D

Transfer payments are payments to individuals or firms *not* in exchange for goods or services, such as UI and welfare payments. These are the most important components of federal spending (some being given to provincial governments who then give them to individuals).

8. E

Provinces of different sizes have different tax bases. To the extent that there are scale economies in the provision of public goods, equal access to public goods across provinces requires intergovernmental transfers.

9. B

A poverty trap exists whenever very-low-income people have no incentive to increase their earned income because such increases would disqualify them from income-support payments and leave them financially no better off than before.

10. C

Redistribution of income invariably involves introducing inefficiencies into the economy, and thus there is a trade-off in the design of social policy.

Chapter 19

1. D

Macroeconomics is concerned with the behaviour and determination of economic aggregates such as the price level, national income and the unemployment rate.

2. A

The output gap (or GDP gap) is *defined* to be the difference between actual GDP and potential GDP, $Y - Y^*$.

3. D

Potential GDP is *not* the maximum that the economy can produce. It is the level of GDP produced when factors of production are employed at their normal utilization rate.

4. B

When studying short-run fluctuations, economists focus on the deviations of actual output from potential output. They usually take potential output to be given.

5. B

The unemployment rate is the number of unemployed expressed as a fraction of the labour force. In this case, it is 1/20 = 0.05, or 5 percent.

6. A

Structural unemployment occurs when the skills or location of the available workers do not match the skill requirements or location of the firms with job vacancies.

7. C

The rate of inflation from year t to $t+1$ is $((P_{t-1} - P_t)/P_t) \times 100$. For example, if the price level rises from 120 to 132, the rate of inflation is $((132 - 120)/120) \times 100$ which is equal to 10 percent.

8. B

With nominal wages rising by 3 percent and the price level rising by 5 percent, real wages will fall by 2 percent. Employees' purchasing power will fall.

9. B

In general, the effects of anticipated inflation are less than unanticipated inflation. If the inflation is fully anticipated, and as a result nobody changes their behaviour, then there will clearly be no real effects.

10. D

The exchange rate is *defined* to be the number of Canadian dollars required to purchase one unit of foreign exchange. Its inverse is the external value of the Canadian dollar.

Chapter 20

1. E

Since production usually occurs in stages, with one firm's output being another firm's input—this approach would suffer from *double counting*. It would badly overstate the value of production.

2. C

GDP from the expenditure side is the sum of total expenditure on *domestic output*. We add actual consumption, investment, government purchases, and exports. We then subtract imports (which represent expenditure on foreign output).

3. D

Investment is a flow variable, representing the production of capital goods (in a given time period) that are used for future production rather than current consumption.

4. A

Transfer payments do not represent income *generated by production*. They are income for the recipients but not for the economy as a whole. All other statements are correct.

5. D

Using the expenditure approach, consumption expenditures increased by $10 000 but imports increased by $5000, thereby increasing GDP by $5000. Using a value-added approach, the firm bought $5000 worth of inputs and sold them for $10 000, thereby adding $5000 to value (and thus to GDP).

6. A

Nominal GDP is the money value of production. This is $240 + $800 + $720 = $1760.

7. D

Real GDP in 2001 (expressed in 2000 dollars) is the money value of 2001 production *using 2000 prices*. This is $120 + $600 + $540 = $1260.

8. E

The implicit price deflator is (nominal GDP/real GDP) × 100. Nominal GDP in 2001 is $1760. Real GDP in 2001 (using 2000 prices) is $1260. So the implicit deflator is ($1760/$1260) × 100 = 139.7.

9. C

Productivity is output per unit input. The best measure of labour productivity is real GDP per hour worked.

10. C

The presence of pollution and other "bads" that are not included (as negative items) in GDP implies that GDP overstates economic welfare. (There are other reasons, such as the unmeasured value of leisure, that GDP understates economic welfare.)

Chapter 21

1. B

Money is said to be neutral when a change in the money supply has no effect on real variables such as real GDP, employment, and real interest rates. Most economists agree that money is not neutral in the short run but is neutral over the long run.

2. C

Sudden changes in demand are commonplace in the short run. But such sudden changes in supply æ coming from changes in the labour force, capital stock, or productivityæare rare. Most changes in factor supply occur only gradually with the passage of time.

3. A

The short run in macroeconomics is often defined in terms of a constant level of potential output but a changing level of actual GDP. As real GDP changes over the course of the business cycle, so too does the output gap.

4. A

Real GDP will decrease if factors of production are used less intensively, if productivity falls, or if employment falls (which often means that unemployment rises).

5. D

GDP is gross domestic product. E is the level of employment, measured either in terms of workers or worker-hours. So GDP/E is output per unit of employment, a simple measure of labour productivity.

6. D

A tightening of monetary policy (a reduction in the growth rate of the money supply) raises interest rates and reduces the flow of economic activity. This reduction in activity leads to an excess supply of factors of production, and in turn puts downward pressure on inflation. As inflation eventually falls, so too do nominal interest rates.

7. D
Potential output is defined to be the level of real GDP that exists when factors of production are being used at their normal rates. Actual output can exceed potential output when factors of production are used more intensively than normal. This is a situation of an inflationary output gap æ there is excess demand for factors and pressure for factor prices to rise.

8. C
F is the total supply of factors. Fe is the employment of factors. Therefore, Fe/F is the fraction of available factors that are employed æ the factor utilization rate.

9. A
Money is said to be neutral when a change in the money supply has no effect on real variables such as real GDP, employment, and real interest rates. Most economists agree that money is not neutral in the short run but is neutral over the long run. Even when money is neutral, however, it will have an effect on nominal variables such as nominal wages, prices, and the rate of inflation.

10. B
In the long run, changes in real GDP are due mostly to supply-side considerations such as population growth, capital accumulation, and productivity growth. These all change the level of potential GDP. Changes in the output gap æ the difference between actual GDP and potential GDP æ are more determined by demand-side factors in the short run.

Chapter 22

1. C
The *MPC* is the amount of each additional dollar of income that gets consumed. Thus for *MPC* = 0.75, an increase in income of ΔY causes consumption to rise by $0.75 \times \Delta Y$.

2. C
The *MPC* is defined to be $\Delta C/\Delta Y$ as we move along the consumption function. In this case $MPC = \$4000/\$5000 = 0.8$. (Note that the *average* propensity to consume, *APC*, = C/Y. In this case it falls slightly from 0.833 to 0.831.)

3. B
The *AE* function shows the level of *desired* aggregate expenditure at each level of actual national income.

4. A
Given points 2 and 3, the consumption function is $C = 50 + 0.8Y$. Thus the *AE* function is $AE = 75 + 0.8Y$. Applying the equilibrium condition, we get $Y = 75 + 0.8Y$ which we can re-arrange to get $Y = 75/(1 - 0.8) = 75/0.2 = 375$.

5. D
Given points 2 and 3, the consumption function is $C = 50 + 0.8Y$. Thus the *AE* function is $AE = 75 + 0.8Y$. Applying the equilibrium condition, we get $Y = 75 + 0.8Y$ which we can re-arrange to get $Y = 75/(1 - 0.8) = 75/0.2 = 375$. At $Y = 375$, consumption is equal to $50 + 0.8(375)$ which is 350. Thus saving is $Y - C = 375 - 350 = 25$. Equivalently, note that equilibrium also requires desired saving to equal desired investment, $S = I$. Since I is equal to 25, we know that in equilibrium S must equal 25.

6. C
When actual income is less than desired aggregate expenditure, there is excess demand. Inventories will be depleted. Producers will increase production and so national income will rise. This is the process that moves the economy toward equilibrium GDP.

7. A
There are two equivalent ways to think of the equilibrium condition. One is that desired aggregate expenditure equals actual output. The other is that desired investment equals desired saving.

8. B
Autonomous expenditure is the amount of desired expenditure that does not depend on national income. It is the vertical intercept of the *AE* function.

9. B
The multiplier is the change in equilibrium income divided by the change in autonomous expenditure that brings it about. If autonomous expenditures shift AE_1 to AE_2, then the multiplier is Y_1Y_2/e_1e_1'.

10. A
With Y_1 and AE_2, desired aggregate expenditure exceeds actual income (by the amount e_1e_1'). This excess demand will deplete inventories and cause producers to increase output. National income will rise.

Chapter 23

1. D
With $Y = 2000$, tax revenue (T) is $0.2(2000) = 400$. So with $G = 500$ and $T = 400$, public saving is -100, denoting a budget deficit.

2. C
Exports are autonomous and so do not depend on domestic income. But imports rise as domestic income rises, and so the NX function is downward sloping. A rise in domestic income thus leads to a movement down along the NX curve.

3. C
The AE function is $AE = (200 + 0.76Y) + 300 + 450 + (120 - 0.06Y)$. This can be simplified to be $AE = 1070 + 0.7Y$. The equilibrium condition is that $Y = AE$. This yields $Y = 1070 + 0.7Y$ which implies that equilibrium is $Y = 1070/0.3 = 3566.67$.

4. D
The AE function is $AE = (200 + 0.76Y) + 300 + 450 + (120 - 0.06Y)$. This can be simplified to be $AE = 1070 + 0.7Y$. The marginal propensity to spend on national income is the slope of the AE function, which in this case is 0.7.

5. B
The AE function is $AE = (200 + 0.76Y) + 300 + 450 + (120 - 0.06Y)$. This can be simplified to be $AE = 1070 + 0.7Y$. The equilibrium condition is that $Y = AE$. This yields $Y = 1070 + 0.7Y$ which implies that equilibrium is $Y = 1070/0.3 = 3566.67$. Substituting this value of income into the consumption function we get $C = 200 + 0.76(3566.67) = 2910.67$.

6. B
The AE function is $AE = (200 + 0.76Y) + 300 + 450 + (120 - 0.06Y)$. This can be simplified to be $AE = 1070 + 0.7Y$. The equilibrium condition is that $Y = AE$. This yields $Y = 1070 + 0.7Y$ which implies that equilibrium is $Y = 1070/0.3 = 3566.67$. Substituting this value into IM we get $IM = 0.06(3566.67) = 214$. With $X = 120$ the trade balance is $120 - 214 = -94$.

7. D
The steeper is the AE curve, the larger is the multiplier. The slope of the AE curve is given by the marginal propensity to spend on domestic income. Of the choices offered, only an increase in the marginal propensity to save would reduce the slope of the AE curve and thus reduce the multiplier.

8. B
An increase in equilibrium GDP will be caused by an upward shift of the AE curve. Of the choices given, only a decrease in desired saving (at any level of Y) will achieve this.

9. C
If $z = 0.75$, the simple multiplier is $1/(1 - z)$ which is 4.0. Thus if G increases by \$2 billion, equilibrium GDP will rise by \$8 billion.

10. C
The marginal propensity to spend on domestic income, z, is the slope of the AE curve. $Z = MPC(1 - t) - MPI$. A rise in t thus reduces z and flattens the AE curve.

Chapter 24

1. C
The *real* value of money is its purchasing power. Thus as the price level rises, the real value of a given amount of money falls (and vice versa).

2. A
A change in P causes a change in wealth and thus a shift of the AE curve. This is a *movement along* the AD curve.

3. C
The AD curve shows how real equilibrium national income (from the 45-degree line diagram) changes as the price level changes.

4. C
The $SRAS$ curve shows how much real output firms would like to produce at different price levels (holding factor prices and technology fixed).

5. E
When the $SRAS$ curve shifts left, firms are prepared to provide less output at any given price level. This is a *decrease* in aggregate supply.

6. B
When output is low, firms usually have unused capacity. In this case, firms may be able to increase output without driving up unit costs. Hence they don't require higher prices in order to produce more output.

7. B
If actual output exceeds desired aggregate expenditure, then this is a situation of excess supply. The unplanned accumulation of inventories will lead firms to reduce output. National income will fall.

8. D
The increase in autonomous expenditure shifts the *AE* curve up. The increase in equilibrium GDP with a constant price level means that the *AD* curve has shifted to the right.

9. E
Any event that decreases the price of factor inputs or improves technology is a positive supply shock—a rightward shift of the *SRAS* curve.

10. C
The increase in aggregate demand implies an upward shift in *AE*. But as the price level rises, the subsequent reduction in wealth shifts the *AE* curve back down. Since *SRAS* is vertical, we know there will be no change in equilibrium GDP, so the *AE* curve is shifting back to its starting point.

Chapter 25

1. D
An inflationary gap exists when $Y > Y^*$. In this situation, there is excess demand for factors of production that drives wages (and other factor prices) up. These factor-price increases shift the *SRAS* curve to the left, causing the price level to rise.

2. C
An inflationary gap means that $Y > Y^*$. Excess demand in factor markets pushes up wages (and other factor prices). This pushes up unit labour costs and shifts the *SRAS* up and to the left.

3. A
The output gap is $Y - Y^*$. When the output gap is negative, as in the figure, it is referred to as a recessionary gap. This will be a situation of excess supply of factors.

4. A
With $Y_1 > Y^*$, there is an inflationary gap. There is excess demand for factors that will push factor prices up. This will cause the *SRAS* curve to shift to the left until the economy is in long-run equilibrium at point *A*.

5. B
With $Y_2 < Y^*$, there is a recessionary gap. There is excess supply of factors. But if wages and other factor prices are slow to fall then the *SRAS* will shift only slowly to the right, bringing the economy (eventually) to point *D*.

6. E
The expansionary fiscal policy increases equilibrium output at any price level—that is, it shifts the *AD* curve to the right. The complete macroeconomic equilibrium therefore has higher output and price level, making the existing inflationary gap even larger.

7. E
The *LRAS* curve is vertical at Y^*. It shows the relationship between the price level and real GDP after input prices have fully adjusted to excess demands or supplies.

8. C
A rightward shift in the *AD* curve causes *Y* to rise above Y^* temporarily. The inflationary gap causes factor prices to rise, shifting the *SRAS* curve to the left. *Y* falls back to Y^*.

9. D
This is a potential problem with "fine tuning" a fiscal policy to the current output gap. If the environment changes suddenly, the fiscal policy may end up being inappropriate—in this case pushing output above Y^*.

10. D
Income taxes reduce the marginal propensity to spend on domestic income (*z* in Chapters 22 and 23) and thus reduce the multiplier. They therefore permit GDP to fluctuate less in response to shocks than it otherwise would.

Chapter 26

1. C
"Money is what money does." Since the most important function of money is as a medium of exchange—to facilitate transactions—paper money (or anything else, for that matter) must be acceptable as a medium of exchange in order to be considered money.

2. B
Money really is quite remarkable. It facilitates transactions by eliminating the double coincidence of wants. Because it makes trade so much easier, it promotes specialization and all of the efficiencies created by it. It also provides a simple yardstick for assessing value.

3. E
Canada's currency was, in the past, backed by gold but it has for many years been backed by nothing. Its value comes only from the fact that it is legal tender and is widely accepted.

4. A

The target reserve ratio is defined to be the ratio of cash reserves (vault cash or at the central bank) to deposits that the commercial banks try to maintain. This target ratio changes as the economic environment changes.

5. E

By purchasing government securities with cash, the central bank increases its holdings of securities (assets) and also increases the amount of outstanding currency (liabilities). This increases the monetary base.

6. D

With a target reserve ratio of v, the change in deposits will equal $1/v$ times the change in reserves. In this case v = 10 percent so the deposits (and hence the money supply) will expand by $10 ($1/0.10 = 10$).

7. C

The cheque for $2 million is a new deposit into the IB&T Bank. IB&T puts 25 percent—$500 000—into reserves and thus has $1 500 000 available to expand its loans.

8. B

The cheque for $2 million is new deposit into the IB&T Bank. IB&T puts 25 percent—$500 000—into reserves and thus has $1 500 000 available to expand its loans. The second generation banks then get $1 500 000 of new deposits and put 25 percent —$375 000—into reserves, leaving $1 125 000 available for lending.

9. B

With a target reserve ratio of v, the change in deposits equals $1/v$ times the change in reserves. In this case, reserves increase by $2 million. Thus deposits increase by $(1/0.25) \times (2 \text{ million}) = \$8 \text{ million}$.

10. B

This $1000 may be a new deposit for your mother's bank, but it is not for the banking system as a whole. The money supply is unchanged. (Unless, for example, the $1000 came from your mother selling a bond to the Bank of Canada, in which case the monetary base will have increased by $1000.)

Chapter 27

1. B

The present value of the asset is $\$1000/(1.05)^2$ which is $907.03.

2. D

By "money," economists usually mean cash and demand deposits. Thus the demand for money refers to households' and firms' demand for cash and demand deposits.

3. C

As real GDP falls, so too does the volume of transactions for which money is needed. Thus we expect a decline in the transactions demand for money.

4. E

Suppose there is an increase in the supply of money. As people try to rid themselves of excess money balances, they bid up the price of bonds and thus drive down interest rates. Only at the lower interest rate are they content to hold the larger stock of money. This will be a movement down along the money demand (LP) curve.

5. D

A decrease in the money supply leads to excess demand for money. As people try to sell bonds to replenish their money holdings, interest rates rise. This leads to a reduction in desired investment expenditure.

6. A

A rise in P leads to an increase in (nominal) money demand. This pushes up interest rates as people try to sell bonds to satisfy their greater demand for money.

7. C

Consider the economy's adjustment as the SRAS curve shifts to the left (because factor prices rise in response to the inflationary gap). As prices rise, the demand for money rises and thus interest rates are pushed up. As interest rates rise, desired investment falls, equilibrium GDP falls and we move up along the AD curve.

8. B

A change in the money supply leads to a change in interest rates and a movement along the investment curve. But the change in desired investment implies a *shift* of the AE curve.

9. C

A relatively flat LP schedule implies that a given change in the money supply has only a small effect on interest rates. Then a steep investment demand curve implies a small change in desired investment. This combination is one of relatively *ineffective* monetary policy.

10. D

For the most effective monetary policy we need a change in the money supply to cause a large change in the interest rate and a large change in desired investment. Thus, we need a relatively inelastic LP curve and a relatively elastic investment demand curve.

Chapter 28

1. E
When the Bank buys bonds, it uses currency to complete the transaction, which gets deposited into the commercial banking system. This is a new deposit and will create excess reserves which can then be loaned out by commercial banks.

2. C
When the Bank sells bonds, it receives currency in return. This leads to a reduction in deposits and reduces reserves in the commercial banking system. The commercial banks then must call in existing loans; the money supply is reduced.

3. A
The $25 000 does *not* become a new deposit to the banking system and so the process of deposit creation does not take place. In this case, the money supply increases only by the amount of the initial open-market purchase, $25 000.

4. A
An expansionary monetary policy is one where the Bank *purchases* government securities; in this case reserves in the banking system increase and the money supply increases.

5. B
Monetary policy is used to avoid (or reverse) undesirable swings in real GDP caused by shocks to the economy. In the long run, however, when money is neutral, monetary policy is directed at influencing the price level.

6. B
The Bank's policy variables are real GDP in the short run and the price level in the long run. An intermediate target, to be effective, must have a reasonably stable relationship with these policy variables. It must also be frequently observable so that the central bank can know that adjustments in its policy have had the desired effect on the intermediate target.

7. B
In a recessionary gap, presumably the Bank wants to design an expansionary policy. An open-market purchase of government bonds would increase reserves in the banking system, reduce interest rates, and stimulate investment and net exports.

8. C
If desired I is sensitive to changes in interest rates, then monetary policy will be relatively effective—an increase in the money supply will reduce interest rates and stimulate desired expenditure.

9. B
If a change in the money market leads to lower interest rates, desired investment will increase and real GDP will rise. It matters not whether the fall in interest rates comes from an increase in money supply or a decline in money demand. Thus if money supply is constant and money demand declines, interest rates would fall and desired expenditures would increase.

10. B
The Bank of Canada announced a goal of "price stability" in January 1988. Though this was never precisely defined, the clear goal (that has been achieved) was to keep inflation at very low levels.

Chapter 29

1. D
According to this theory, in order for any change in monetary policy to have real effects, it must be *unanticipated*. Any anticipated policy will be built into future price expectations and will therefore cause the *SRAS* to shift, offsetting the effect of the *AD* shift on output.

2. C
With $U < U^*$, there is an inflationary gap ($Y > Y^*$). This creates excess demand for factors, pushes up factor prices and causes *SRAS* to shift to the left.

3. B
With a negative *SRAS* shock, Y will fall and P will rise. But because wages may be slow to fall in response to excess supply, the recessionary gap may persist. To avoid this, the Bank may validate the shock by expanding the money supply, shifting *AD* to the right.

4. A
With a negative *SRAS* shock, Y will fall and P will rise. But because wages may be slow to fall in response to excess supply, the recessionary gap may persist. But eventually wages will fall and the *SRAS* curve will shift back to the right, returning Y to Y^*.

5. B
If the central bank validates every leftward shift of *SRAS*, then both *AD* and *SRAS* will be shifting up—there will be continuous inflation.

6. B

Many shocks can lead to one-time changes in the price level. But *sustained* inflation can only exist if there is sustained growth in the money supply. (If the *AD* curve is stable, the effects of any shock will eventually disappear as output returns to Y^* with a stable price level.)

7. A

The negative *SRAS* shock reduces Y and raises P. The recessionary gap causes excess supply of factors and (eventually) factor prices fall. As this occurs, the *SRAS* curve shifts back and P returns to its initial level.

8. D

To reduce any sustained inflation, the *AD* curve must either stop shifting out or the rate at which it is shifting out must be reduced. This requires reducing the growth rate of the money supply.

9. C

Slowly adjusting inflationary expectations mean that *SRAS* continues to shift up even after the tight monetary policy has been introduced. Ending a sustained inflation, therefore, invariably involves creating a significant recessionary gap.

10. A

Most zero-inflation advocates argue that the economy will achieve Y^* in the long run (long-run money neutrality) and that attempts to stabilize output will simply stand in the way of the economy's adjustment process. Thus, the Bank should focus on its long-run policy variable, the price level.

Chapter 30

1. C

The unemployment rate is $(1 - E/LF)$, where E is employment and LF is the labour force. Employment has increased by 20 000. So the unemployment rate will fall if the labour force increases by fewer than 20 000 people. If the labour force increases by more than 20 000, the unemployment rate will rise.

2. D

As Y fluctuates around Y^*, U fluctuates around U^*. These are changes in *cyclical* unemployment.

3. C

When unemployment is only frictional or structural, we say there is full employment—the unemployment rate equals the natural rate, U^*. $U^* > 0$, and is currently thought by many economists to be about 7 percent in

Canada.

4. A

With perfectly flexible wages, labour markets would always clear. In this case, there would never be involuntary unemployment (because wages would fall to eliminate it).

5. C

The essence of New Keynesian theories is that wages and/or prices are *not* fully flexible and thus markets do not clear immediately. Thus wages cannot be relied upon to quickly eliminate involuntary unemployment.

6. E

If worker effort, or productivity, increases with a higher wage, firms may find it profitable to keep wages above the market-clearing level. Such *efficiency* wages are a New Keynesian explanation for some unemployment.

7. E

The reason for frictional unemployment is that it takes time for jobs and workers to find each other. (Occupational or locational mismatch is *structural* unemployment.)

8. B

Structural unemployment occurs when there is an occupational or locational mismatch between unemployed workers and firms with vacancies. The unemployed fishermen in Atlantic Canada are mismatched with the oilfield vacancies in Alberta. But there may be no *deficient demand* in the country as a whole.

9. B

To the extent that unions raise wages (by restricting the supply of labour) and thus increase unemployment, a reduction in unionization will reduce U^* (and raise Y^*).

10. D

A UI system makes it less costly for unemployed workers to remain unemployed and continue searching for an appropriate job. By lengthening job-search spells, the UI system probably increases frictional unemployment, and increases it more the higher are the UI benefits.

Chapter 31

1. D

All government expenditure (including transfers and debt-service payments) must somehow be financed. There are only two methods—tax revenue and borrowing (issuing debt).

2. C

The debt-to-GDP ratio is a useful statistic even though it is the ratio of a stock to a flow. The flow (GDP) is the tax base available to the government; the stock is proportional to the annual debt-service payments that must be made. So the ratio gives an indication of the importance of the debt-service payments relative to the size of the economy.

3. A

Real GDP is on the horizontal axis. As real GDP rises (for unchanged fiscal policy), tax revenues rise, transfers fall, and so the budget deficit falls. The budget deficit function is therefore downward sloping.

4. B

The cyclically adjusted deficit (CAD) is *defined* to be the budget deficit that would exist if $Y = Y^*$ and fiscal policy remained at its current level. Changes in fiscal policy lead to changes in the CAD.

5. E

Recall that the change in the debt-to-GDP ratio, d, is given by $\Delta d = x + (r - g)d$, where x is the primary deficit as a fraction of GDP, r is the real interest rate and g is the growth rate of real GDP. To keep $\Delta d = 0$, $x = -(r - g)d$. If $r < g$, x must be positive which means a primary budget deficit.

6. C

Ricardian Equivalence is the proposition that for a given pattern of G, the *method* of finance (current taxation vs borrowing) makes no difference to the economy. It is based on the idea that current government borrowing is recognized by taxpayers as an increase in *future* taxes and thus leaves their wealth—and hence their spending patterns—unchanged.

7. E

If Ricardian Equivalence holds, there is never crowding out due to government deficits. But if Ricardian Equivalence does not hold, then the deficit will push up interest rates because national saving falls. In an open economy this will attract foreign capital, appreciate the currency, and crowd out net exports.

8. C

If the government deficit reduces national saving and thus pushes up interest rates, some domestic private investment will be crowded out. The reduced future capital stock is the long-term burden of the debt.

9. B

Real GDP will always be subject to shocks. With an annually balanced budget, taxes would have to rise (or expenditures fall) when real GDP is falling. Such a fiscal policy would accentuate existing fluctuations rather than stabilizing them.

10. A

Most economists recognize the problems associated with the long-term accumulation of debt, but they also recognize the benefits of short-run countercyclical fiscal policy. A cyclically balanced budget would display deficits when $Y < Y^*$ and surpluses when $Y > Y^*$. There would be no long-term build-up of debt.

Chapter 32

1. B

The economy's adjustment mechanism eventually returns output to potential, Y^*. Thus long-run increases in real GDP come from increases in Y^*—rightward shifts in the *LRAS* curve.

2. C

Standard of living is difficult to measure. But the best "output-based" measure is per capita real GDP—it shows how much *real* output is available per person (on average).

3. C

High population growth will mean high labour-force growth and thus high growth in real GDP. But because of the diminishing marginal product of labour, real GDP per capita will fall (holding the capital stock and technology constant).

4. E

With low saving, it is difficult to finance such domestic investment. And lower investment generally leads to lower growth rates of real GDP.

5. E

Central to the Neoclassical growth model is the idea of diminishing marginal (and average) returns to both labour and capital.

6. D

A production function displays constant returns to scale when an X percent increase in *all* factors leads to an X percent increase in output.

7. E

Central to the Neoclassical growth model is the idea of diminishing marginal (and average) returns to both labour and capital. This implies (in the absence of technological change) that increases in population will cause output per capita—and thus living standards—to fall even though total output continues to rise.

8. D

Endogenous technical change and increasing returns to investment are two central themes in modern growth theory. The Neoclassical growth theory, in contrast, assumes exogenous technical change and diminishing returns to investment.

9. C

Endogenous growth models stress the importance of knowledge and learning—especially the way in which the incentives for such acquisition of human capital are influenced by the economic environment.

10. B

Given the diminishing returns to labour, the growth of population with a fixed supply of world resources implies that ongoing improvements in technology and knowledge will be needed to keep per capita output—and thus average living standards—from declining.

Chapter 33

1. C

This is the definition of the development gap.

2. B

Improving productivity in the agricultural sector (or elsewhere) is always welcome, for example, but there is generally a cost involved. After basic irrigation and pest-control systems are designed, the opportunity cost of further improvements may be so high as to make it not worthwhile.

3. A

Per capita income is GDP/population. Thus it will increase only if GDP rises faster than the population.

4. E

Malthus overestimated population growth (because he did not foresee the rise of birth control) and vastly underestimated the significance of technological change.

5. D

A poor country generally does not have enough people who can afford to save. A small pool of national saving thus makes it difficult to finance investment, which retards long-term growth. This is why FDI is so important to many developing countries (including Canada in its early years).

6. C

Many older development policies were based on growth through import substitution—producing the goods that they would otherwise import. This involved high tariffs and subsidies, and often exchange rates were pegged to make domestic industries more competitive.

7. C

Many older development policies were based on growth through import substitution—producing the goods that they would otherwise import. This involved high tariffs and subsidies. But such policies lead away from specialization according to comparative advantage and in most cases will hinder long-run growth.

8. D

Modern views of growth are based on the importance of innovation and the accumulation of knowledge.

9. D

Many older development policies were based on growth through import substitution—producing the goods that they would otherwise import. This involved high tariffs and subsidies. But such policies lead away from specialization according to comparative advantage and in most cases will hinder long-run growth.

10. C

A poor country generally does not have enough people who can afford to save. A small pool of national saving thus makes it difficult to finance investment, which retards long-term growth. TNCs, through the process of FDI, can thus play an important role in financing investment as well as bringing new technology to the developing country.

Chapter 34

1. C

Let X be the number of units of resources required to produce the good. If X is less in the first country than the second, the first country has an absolute advantage in the production of that good.

2. B
There are gains from trade *only* if countries have a comparative advantage in some goods. If countries have the same pattern of opportunity costs, then there is no comparative advantage and so no gains from trade.

3. B
Comparative advantage is about opportunity cost. If one country can produce a good with lower opportunity cost (i.e., fewer other goods forgone) then can the other country, the first country has a comparative advantage in the production of that good.

4. C
With product differentiation and economies of scale in the production of each product variety, two-way trade of similar products is consistent with the theory of comparative advantage. Here, the comparative advantage comes from the scale economies. Such trade is called intra-industry trade.

5. E
By specializing in production (and thus taking advantage of other countries' low-opportunity-cost industries), trade allows a country to consume outside of its own production possibility boundary.

6. C
One unit of Brazilian resources can produce 30 mangoes or 5 pineapples. Thus each Brazil pineapple "costs" 6 mangoes.

7. B
One unit of Mexican resources can produce 12 mangoes or 4 pineapples. Thus each Mexican pineapple "costs" 3 mangoes, or each mango "costs" 1/3 of a pineapple.

8. D
Since one unit of resources can produce more of both mangoes and pineapples, Brazil has an absolute advantage in both goods.

9. B
By transferring 1/2 unit toward mangoes, Brazil's production of mangoes would rise by 15 and pineapples would fall by 2 1/2. A one-unit transfer in Mexico toward pineapples would increase pineapples by 4 and decrease mangoes by 12. Thus, overall, mangoes would rise by 3 and pineapples would rise by 1 1/2.

10. A
The terms of trade is the ratio of export prices to import prices. A deterioration means that import prices rise relative to export prices—a decline in the terms of trade.

Chapter 35

1. E
Protectionist policies—tariffs, subsidies or voluntary export restraints—are implemented primarily to protect domestic producers (and their employees) from foreign competition.

2. D
The basis of the infant-industry argument is that new firms need protection until they can compete on their own. There is either economies of scale or learning by doing at the heart of the argument.

3. B
Low wages in Mexico contribute to low prices of Mexican goods. Canadian consumers benefit from having access to low–price products.

4. C
If Canada exports *all* products initially, then the Canadian dollar will appreciate (and other countries currencies will depreciate) until Canada begins to import some goods.

5. A
At price P_2, the Canadian production is Q_1. (Q_4 is demanded and so imports will be Q_1Q_4.)

6. E
At price P_2, the Canadian production is Q_1. Q_4 is demanded and so imports will be Q_1Q_4.

7. B
At price P_2, the Canadian production is Q_1. Q_4 is demanded and so imports will be Q_1Q_4. If a tariff pushes the price up to P_1, there will still be excess *domestic* demand and so imports will exist. But domestic production rises to Q_2, domestic consumption falls to Q_3, and so imports fall to Q_2Q_3.

8. E
To eliminate all imports (which are equal to Q_1Q_4 when price = P_2) the domestic price must rise so that there is no excess demand *domestically*. Domestic price would be P_0 and quantity would be Q_0.

9. B
Trade diversion occurs when Country A imports from Country B (after forming a trading bloc with them) even though imports from an "outside" country C are lower priced. It is inefficient trade and is a major concern regarding the formation of trading blocs.

10. D

National treatment offers each country complete autonomy in its design and implementation of policy as long as such policies apply equally to domestic and foreign firms and to both imports and domestically produced goods.

Chapter 36

1. B

The purchase of the asset implies an outflow of money from Canada. This is a capital outflow and, like all outflows of money, is recorded as a debit item (in this case on the capital account).

2. D

A debit item on the current account is either an import or the remittance of debt-service payments abroad. The Canadians in Italy are "importing" tourist services.

3. C

The balance of payments must always balance. Thus if the current account has a deficit, the remainder of the balance of payments—capital account plus official financing account—must be in surplus.

4. B

The exchange rate, *e*, is the number of Canadian dollars required to purchase one unit of foreign currency. A rise in *e* is a *depreciation* of the Canadian dollar.

5. D

A depreciation of the Canadian dollar makes Canadian goods cheaper relative to foreign goods. The ensuing substitution will *decrease* the demand for foreign goods and reduce the quantity of foreign currency demanded. This is why the demand curve for foreign currency is downward sloping.

6. B

The balance of payments must *always* balance. In a fixed-exchange-rate system, the current and capital accounts usually do not balance—the difference must be offset by the central bank's official financing.

7. E

With a pure flexible exchange rate, the official financing account is zero. Thus a balance of payments deficit must reflect excess demand for foreign currency that will lead to a depreciation of the domestic currency. This depreciation will eliminate the balance of payments deficit.

8. B

If there is no official financing, then the central bank is not intervening in the foreign-exchange market. In this case the exchange rate is being determined freely in the market.

9. B

With higher inflation in B, the prices in B are rising relative to those in A. This shifts demand toward A's goods and away from B's goods. People in B will supply more foreign exchange in order to purchase the cheaper goods from A.

10. B

PPP is based on the law of one price—that the prices of goods in different places should be the same when measured in a common currency. PPP becomes a problem, however, when it is applied to broad price indexes rather than just individual traded goods.

Microeconomics Practice Exam #1

This one-hour exam consists of 40 multiple-choice questions and 5 short-answer questions. The exam is worth 60 marks.

Part I: Multiple-Choice Questions

(40 marks)

Choose the best answer for each of the following:

1. The fundamental problem of economics is, in short,
   - (a) the existence of too many poor people.
   - (b) the difficulty in finding jobs for all.
   - (c) the scarcity of resources relative to wants.
   - (d) constantly rising prices.
   - (e) None of the above.

2. Opportunity cost measures the
   - (a) different opportunities for spending money.
   - (b) the monetary cost of purchasing a commodity.
   - (c) alternative means of producing output.
   - (d) amount of one good forfeited to obtain a unit of another good.
   - (e) none of the above

3. Which of the following is not one of the main characteristics of a market economy?
   - (a) Individuals pursue their own self-interest.
   - (b) Private property.
   - (c) Sellers compete to sell their wares to potential buyers.
   - (d) Firms seek to meet production quotas.
   - (e) People respond to incentives.

4. A theory may contain all *but* which of the following?
   - (a) Predictions about behaviour that are deduced from the assumptions.
   - (b) A set of assumptions defining the conditions under which the theory is operative.
   - (c) A normative statement expressed as a functional relation
   - (d) Hypotheses about how the world behaves.
   - (e) Hypothesized relationships among variables.

5. If goods A and B are complements, an increase in the price of good A will lead to
   - (a) an increase in the price of good B.
   - (b) a decrease in the quantity demanded of good B.
   - (c) a decrease in demand for good B.
   - (d) no change in demand for good B because A and B are not substitutes.
   - (e) a rightward shift in the demand for good B.

6. Assuming a downward-sloping demand curve, an improvement in production technology for some good is predicted to lead to
   - (a) a decrease in equilibrium price and an increase in equilibrium quantity exchanged.
   - (b) an increase in both equilibrium price and quantity exchanged.
   - (c) a decrease supply.
   - (d) a decrease in equilibrium price but no change in equilibrium quantity exchanged.
   - (e) an increase in equilibrium price and a decrease in equilibrium quantity

7. Comparative statics
   - (a) is the analysis of market equilibria under different sets of conditions.
   - (b) is the analysis of demand without reference to time.
   - (c) refers to constant equilibrium prices and quantities.
   - (d) describes the path by which equilibrium price changes.
   - (e) refers to disequilibrium prices and quantities.

8. An increase in the price of a good and a decrease in total expenditure on this good are associated with

   (a) inferior goods.
   (b) substitute goods.
   (c) normal goods.
   (d) elastic demand.
   (e) inelastic demand.

9. Suppose that the short-run demand for a good is relatively more inelastic than its long-run demand. A given rightward shift in the supply curve will lead to a

   (a) smaller decrease in price in the long-run than in the short-run.
   (b) smaller increase in quantity in the long-run than in the short-run.
   (c) larger decrease in price in the long-run than in the short-run.
   (d) smaller decrease in both price and quantity in the long-run than in the short-run.
   (e) larger decreases in both price and quantity in the long-run than in the short-run.

10. Suppose the market supply curve for some good is upward sloping. If the imposition of a sales tax causes no change in the equilibrium quantity sold in the market, the good's demand curve must be _____, meaning that the burden of the tax has fallen completely on the _____.

    (a) vertical, firms.
    (b) vertical, consumers.
    (c) horizontal, firms.
    (d) horizontal, consumers.
    (e) not enough information to answer this question.

11. Partial equilibrium analysis refers to

    (a) shifts in the demand curve only.
    (b) shifts in the supply curve only.
    (c) short-run changes in equilibrium.
    (d) the study of all markets together.
    (e) the study of a single market in isolation.

12. Holding a product's price below its equilibrium level will

    (a) ensure that everyone obtains the quantity they desire to purchase.
    (b) encourage an increased production of the good.
    (c) result in less of the good being consumed.
    (d) eliminate the incentive for black-market profiteering.
    (e) result in an excess supply of the good.

13. The total value Mr. Wimpy places on his consumption of hamburgers equals

    (a) the amount he pays for them.
    (b) price times marginal value.
    (c) marginal value multiplied by quantity demanded.
    (d) price multiplied by quantity demanded.
    (e) his total expenditure on hamburgers plus his consumer surplus.

14. At the point where the budget line is tangent to an indifference curve,

    (a) equal amounts of goods give equal satisfaction.
    (b) the ratio of prices of the goods must equal the marginal rate of substitution.
    (c) the prices of the goods are equal.
    (d) a household cannot be maximizing its satisfaction.
    (e) the marginal rate of substitution is zero.

15. Normal profits refer to

    (a) what all firms, on average, obtain as a return on investment.
    (b) the base used by Revenue Canada to levy business taxes.
    (c) the imputed return to capital and risk-taking required to keep firms in the industry.
    (d) the level of profits necessary to ensure that the firm covers its day-to-day operating expenses.
    (e) a return to capital that is comparable to rates of return earned on bank deposits.

16. The law of diminishing returns states that

   (a) as output increases, the rate of increase in costs will eventually decrease.

   (b) as output increases, profits will eventually decline.

   (c) the incremental output achieved by increases in a variable factor will eventually decrease.

   (d) as more labour is employed, the wage rate will increase and thereby increase costs.

   (e) as more labour is employed, the total product curve eventually has a negative slope.

17. The cost-minimizing factor mix is obtained when

   (a) the marginal products of all factors are equalized.

   (b) the marginal product per dollar expended on each factor is equalized.

   (c) the marginal product of each factor divided by total expenditure on that factor is equalized across all factors.

   (d) the cost of employing an additional unit of each factor is equalized across all factors.

   (e) each factor's marginal cost is equalized.

18. If the long run average cost curve is upward sloping, the firm is experiencing

   (a) long run decreasing returns.

   (b) diseconomies of scale.

   (c) increasing costs.

   (d) All of the above.

   (e) None of the above.

19. A profit-maximizing firm, regardless of market structure, should shut down production and suffer a short run loss equal to its fixed cost if

   (a) average revenue is less than average variable cost.

   (b) average revenue is less than average total cost but greater than average variable cost.

   (c) total revenue is less than total cost but greater than total variable cost.

   (d) its economic profits are negative and smaller in absolute value than total fixed cost.

   (e) profits are negative.

20. Long run equilibrium in a perfectly competitive industry is characterized by

   (a) each firm in the industry earning maximum attainable profits.

   (b) each firm in the industry making zero economic profits.

   (c) no firm desiring to enter or exit this industry.

   (d) no firm desiring to alter its plant size.

   (e) All of the above.

21. Since the profit-maximizing monopolist produces that output where marginal cost equals marginal revenue, we can conclude that

   (a) P equals MC.

   (b) P equals MR.

   (c) P exceeds MC.

   (d) P exceeds ATC.

   (e) P equals ATC.

22. Natural barriers to entry

   (a) include patent laws and exclusive franchises.

   (b) most commonly arise through economies of scale.

   (c) result from an increasing long run average cost curve.

   (d) imply that small firms have lower ATC curves than larger firms.

   (e) must be sustained by government regulation.

23. Economic theory predicts cartels to be unstable because

   (a) there is an incentive for individual firms to produce beyond their quota.

   (b) governments will invariably dismantle them.

   (c) although industry profits increase, the profits of individual firms decrease.

   (d) individual firms have an incentive to produce less than the restrictions imposed on them by the cartel.

   (e) the industry output that maximizes joint profits for the cartel tends to exceed that of a competitive market.

24. Firms that sell a differentiated product (such as Burger King and Harvey's) each

   (a) face a downward-sloping demand curve.
   (b) have some ability to administer price.
   (c) receive information on market conditions through changes in quantity sold at the set price.
   (d) tend to absorb transitory fluctuations in demand by changing output and holding prices constant.
   (e) All of the above.

25. Which of the following forms of *competitive behaviour* is observed in imperfectly competitive markets?

   (a) Offering of product guarantees.
   (b) Advertising.
   (c) Offering competing product standards.
   (d) Creating barriers to entry.
   (e) All of the above.

26. Which of the following is NOT consistent with the "excess capacity theorem" in monopolistic competition

   (a) these firms will be producing at an output level that exceeds the minimum average total cost output level.
   (b) the trade-off for product variety is a higher unit production cost.
   (c) the assumptions of freedom of entry and downward-sloping demand curves result in an "excess capacity" situation.
   (d) is a characteristic of long run equilibrium in this market structure.
   (e) these firms will not be producing at minimum average total cost in the long run equilibrium.

27. Allocative efficiency holds when

   (a) price equals marginal cost.
   (b) the consumer valuation of the last unit produced equals the value of resources used to produce this unit.
   (c) the sum of consumers' and producers' surplus is maximized.
   (d) it is impossible to reallocate resources in such a way as to make one individual better off, without making someone else worse off.
   (e) All of the above.

28. Productive efficiency holds

   (a) when $P = MC$ for perfect competition.
   (b) only for perfect competition and monopolistic competition where long run profits are zero.
   (c) when firms produce that output where the *ATC* curve is at a minimum.
   (d) throughout the market economy where the objective of firms is to maximize profits.
   (e) for natural monopolies where diseconomies of scale are fully exploited.

29. A perfectly competitive, profit-maximizing firm hires a factor up to the point at which

   (a) the factor's price equals its marginal revenue product.
   (b) the marginal cost of hiring the factor equals the additional revenue obtained from that factor's marginal contribution to output.
   (c) the factor's price equals its marginal physical product times the product's price.
   (d) All of the above.
   (e) None of the above.

30. Which of the following is not an example of an equilibrium differential in a factor price?

   (a) Land in downtown Toronto is more expensive than land in the suburbs.
   (b) Wages in the Alberta construction trades are higher than elsewhere in the country because of a booming Albertan economy.
   (c) Individuals working in isolated communities tend to be paid more than their counterparts in the more accessible cities.
   (d) A dentist is paid more than a dental hygienist.
   (e) Certain workers receive higher wages because of greater working hazards.

31. If discrimination prevented a certain group of people from entering labour market E but not labour market O,

   (a) the wage rate would be lower than the competitive level in both markets.
   (b) the labour supply curve is farther to the left than it would otherwise be in both markets.
   (c) wage rates will tend to be higher in market E and lower in market O than they would be with no discrimination.
   (d) individuals in labour market E would benefit only if the demand curve for labour is elastic.
   (e) None of the above.

32. The "efficiency wage hypothesis" suggests that

    (a) competitive firms pay more than the competitive wage in order to induce workers to be more productive.
    (b) transfer wages are very high if workers are paid more than the competitive wage.
    (c) quit rates from jobs that pay more than the competitive wage are very high.
    (d) wages rates across industries always will be equalized.
    (e) unions always increase workers' productivity.

33. The rental price of capital for a given period

    (a) is always equal to its purchase price.
    (b) will be equated with the capital's marginal revenue product in that period as a result of profit maximization.
    (c) is zero if the firm owns its capital.
    (d) is the rate of return on capital for each dollar invested in that capital.
    (e) is always equal to the interest rate, as a result of profit maximization.

34. The present value of a capital asset will increase if

    (a) the *MRP* values per period decrease.
    (b) *MRP* values are received farther into the future.
    (c) the interest rate decreases.
    (d) the purchase price of the capital asset decreases.
    (e) None of the above.

35. Consider a negative externality such as cigar smoking in a room of one smoker and one non-smoker. According to the *Coarse Theorem*, if property rights to the air are given to the _____, then _____ can be obtained.

    (a) smoker; compensation.
    (b) non-smoker; tax revenue.
    (c) non-smoker; justice.
    (d) smoker; moral hazard.
    (e) smoker or non-smoker; allocative efficiency.

36. Which of the following is the best example of a good that is excludable and non-rivalrous in consumption.

    (a) Pay-per-view television.
    (b) The cod fishery.
    (c) A lighthouse.
    (d) Police protection.
    (e) A radio broadcast.

37. A profit-maximizing competitive firm

    (a) always produces in excess of the output that is allocatively efficient.
    (b) always generates pollution as a by-product of production.
    (c) produces more than the allocatively efficient output when it ignores external costs associated with its production.
    (d) automatically considers external costs in making production decisions.
    (e) internalizes all external costs.

38. A firm currently emitting pollutants would have an incentive to reduce emissions if

    (a) an emissions tax per unit of discharge were imposed.
    (b) private citizens were able to sue for pollution damages.
    (c) it were forced to purchase emissions permits.
    (d) a tax on output were designed to internalize the externality.
    (e) Any of the above actions were taken.

39. If the income tax is progressive, the marginal tax rate must be

    (a) less than the average tax rate.
    (b) the same as the average tax rate.
    (c) greater than the average tax rate.
    (d) continuously increasing with income.
    (e) constant.

40. Horizontal equity refers to

    (a) the East-West distribution of income.
    (b) the treatment of individuals with identical incomes but different circumstances.
    (c) the treatment of households of similar composition but with different incomes.
    (d) the flat-rate tax scheme.
    (e) changes in the marginal tax rate across income levels.

Part II: Short-Answer Questions

(20 marks)

For each of the following questions, explain your answer.

1. Economic theory predicts that rent control policies are an effective method of redistributing income and promoting equity in general. Do you agree? Explain.

2. If Product A is twice the price of Product B, this necessarily implies that the total consumer value derived form consuming Product A is twice that of Product B. Is this correct? Explain.

3. Fully explain the following statement. "Perfect competition will typically, but not always, promote allocative efficiency.

4. The competitive nature of the labour market will affect the consequences of a binding minimum wage law. Explain the previous statement.

5. Identify and explain the "two burdens" of a tax. In your answer make sure that you explain how the degree of elasticity of demand affects the size of these two burdens.

Microeconomics Practice Exam #2

This two-hour exam consists of 100 multiple-choice questions and 5 short-answer questions. The exam is worth 110 marks.

Part 1: Multiple-Choice Questions

(100 marks)

1. An increase in quantity demanded refers to
   (a) rightward shifts in the demand curve only.
   (b) a movement up along a demand curve.
   (c) a greater willingness to purchase at each price.
   (d) an increase in actual purchases.
   (e) a movement down along a demand curve

2. An increase in the price of an input will
   (a) decrease quantity supplied.
   (b) decrease quantity supplied at each price.
   (c) decrease supply.
   (d) cause the supply curve to shift to the left.
   (e) (b), (c) and (d) are correct

3. Excess demand exists whenever
   (a) price exceeds the equilibrium price.
   (b) quantity supplied is greater than quantity demanded.
   (c) the equilibrium price is above the existing price.
   (d) there is downward pressure on price.
   (e) there is surplus production.

4. The "laws of demand and supply" are
   (a) federal statutes and are therefore enforced by the RCMP.
   (b) enshrined in the Canadian Constitution.
   (c) irrefutable propositions concerning economic behaviour.
   (d) basic assumptions in economic theory.
   (e) predictions of economic behaviour that have tended to withstand much, but not all, empirical testing.

5. An increase in both equilibrium price and quantity exchanged is consistent with
   (a) an increase in supply.
   (b) a decrease in supply.
   (c) a decrease in quantity supplied.
   (d) an increase in demand.
   (e) a decrease in demand.

Questions 6 and 7 refer to the following diagram.

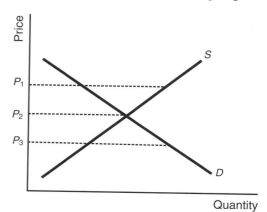

6. At a price of P_1,

   (a) there is upward pressure on price.
   (b) demand will rise to restore equilibrium.
   (c) quantity supplied is greater than quantity demanded.
   (d) the market has reached an equilibrium price.
   (e) a shortage exists.

7. When price equals P_3,

   (a) quantity exchanged equals quantity demanded.
   (b) there is excess supply.
   (c) there is a tendency for price to rise.
   (d) the market is in equilibrium.
   (e) a surplus exists.

8. The price elasticity of demand is measured by the

   (a) change in quantity demanded divided by the change in price.
   (b) change in price divided by the change in quantity demanded.
   (c) slope of the demand curve.
   (d) percentage change in quantity demanded divided by the percentage change in price.
   (e) average quantity demanded divided by the average price.

9. If the percentage change in price is greater than the percentage change in quantity demanded, demand

   (a) is elastic.
   (b) is inelastic.
   (c) is unit-elastic.
   (d) shifts outward to the left.
   (e) shifts to the right.

10. If a 10 percent increase in the price of ski lift tickets causes a 5 percent decrease in total expenditure on lift tickets, then demand is

   (a) elastic.
   (b) inelastic.
   (c) perfectly inelastic.
   (d) normal.
   (e) inferior.

11. Which of the following commodities is more likely to have an elastic demand?

   (a) Toothpicks.
   (b) Cigarettes.
   (c) Heart pacemakers.
   (d) Broccoli.
   (e) Vegetables.

12. "Tax incidence" refers to

   (a) who is legally responsible for paying the tax revenue to the government.
   (b) the legislative process taxes must pass through.
   (c) the economic costs of avoiding taxes.
   (d) who ultimately bears the burden of the tax.
   (e) None of the above.

13. Consumers bear a greater share of the burden of the tax, the more

   (a) inelastic is supply.
   (b) elastic is supply.
   (c) inelastic is demand.
   (d) elastic is demand.
   (e) Both (b) and (c) are correct.

14. If the price elasticity of demand for a good is 2 and price increases by 2 percent, the quantity demanded

   (a) decreases by 4 percent.
   (b) decreases by 1 percent.
   (c) decreases by 2 percent.
   (d) does not change.
   (e) is indeterminable with data provided.

15. The market for public transportation in Winnipeg is likely to be linked to which of the following markets?

   (a) Mass transit in Toronto.
   (b) Winnipeg Stock Exchange.
   (c) Mortgage rates in Canada.
   (d) Parking in downtown Winnipeg.
   (e) World market for wheat.

16. Suppose Vancouver gets a professional baseball team. One would predict that the market for _____ would be impacted through a _____ linkage.

   (a) housing; input-output.
   (b) restaurant meals; supply-side resource constraint.
   (c) Vancouver Grizzlies basketball tickets; regional mobile demand.
   (d) Vancouver Canucks hockey tickets; demand-side resource constraint.
   (e) movies; regional mobile supply.

17. Supply management schemes use quotas to

   (a) help export Canadian agricultural products.
   (b) reduce the cost of becoming a producer.
   (c) provide producers with a unit elastic demand curve.
   (d) increase the price of output and stabilize annual farm receipts.
   (e) compete with imports.

18. If the marginal utility from consuming a good is zero, total utility is

   (a) also zero.
   (b) constant.
   (c) negative.
   (d) decreasing.
   (e) increasing.

19. Sally is allocating her expenditure between movies and cappuccinos in such a way that she maximizes her utility. If the price of admission to the movies increases, Sally will reallocate her expenditure such that

   (a) the marginal utility of a movie increases.
   (b) her movie attendance will increase.
   (c) her cappuccino consumption will decrease.
   (d) the marginal utility of cappuccino increases.
   (e) the marginal utility per dollar spent on movies will exceed that for cappuccinos.

20. The hypothesis of diminishing marginal utility states that

   (a) the less of a commodity one is consuming, the less the additional utility obtained by an increase in its consumption.
   (b) the more of a commodity one is consuming, the more the additional utility obtained by an increase in its consumption.
   (c) the more of a commodity one is consuming, the less the additional utility obtained by an increase in its consumption.
   (d) the more of a commodity one is consuming, the less will be total utility.
   (e) marginal utility cannot be measured, but total utility can.

21. According to utility theory, a consumer will maximize total utility when goods A and B are consumed in quantities such that MU_A/MU_B

   (a) equals the ratio of the price of A to the price of B.
   (b) equals the ratio of total utility of A to that of B.
   (c) equals the ratio of the price of B to the price of A.
   (d) equals the ratio of the quantities demanded.
   (e) always equals unity.

22. A firm has total revenues of $100 000, total monetary outlays of $75 000, and an opportunity cost of capital of $25 000. It is correct to say that

   (a) economic profits are $25 000.
   (b) normal profits are $25 000.
   (c) accounting profits are zero.
   (d) profits are negative.
   (e) economic profits are zero.

23. Which of the following is an example of a short run production decision?

   (a) A firm decides to relocate.
   (b) A contractor decides to work its crew overtime to finish a job.
   (c) A railway decides to eliminate all passenger service.
   (d) A paper company installs antipollution equipment.
   (e) An airline expands its fleet of aircraft.

24. If marginal product is falling, marginal product

   (a) is always less than average product.
   (b) is always equal to average product.
   (c) is always greater than average product.
   (d) can be greater than, equal to, or less than average product.
   (e) is negative.

25. If no raw materials are used in production, a firm's wage bill in the short run equals its

   (a) short run total costs.
   (b) total variable costs.
   (c) total fixed costs.
   (d) marginal costs.
   (e) average total cost multiplied by output.

26. Suppose a firm doubles employment of all of its factors and, as a result, output increases from 100 units to 300 units. This firm is operating under

    (a) diseconomies of scale.
    (b) long run decreasing returns.
    (c) decreasing costs.
    (d) decreasing total cost.
    (e) increasing costs.

27. A firm experiencing long run increasing returns that decides to increase output should do so by

    (a) substituting more labour and less capital.
    (b) employing a new technology.
    (c) employing less of each factor.
    (d) building smaller plants.
    (e) building larger plants.

28. An upward shift in the family of short run cost curves as well as the long run average cost curve could be explained by

    (a) economies of scale.
    (b) an increase in the fixed factor such as plant size.
    (c) an increase in a factor price.
    (d) a larger capital-labour ratio.
    (e) technological improvement.

29. Which of the following characteristics is true of a perfectly competitive industry that is subject to continuous technological change?

    (a) Only plants of recent vintage and thus greater efficiency will operate.
    (b) The market price equals the minimum average total cost of the most efficient plants.
    (c) The market price equals the minimum average total cost of the least efficient plant still in use.
    (d) Plants with a greater than average level of efficiency will make positive profits.
    (e) Any plant without the most recent and efficient technology will be closed immediately.

30. In which of the following situations should a profit-maximizing firm leave its output unaltered?

    (a) $MR > MC$ and $TR > TC$.
    (b) $MR = MC$ and $TR > TC$.
    (c) $MR > MC$ and $TR = TC$.
    (d) $MR < MC$ and $TR < TC$.
    (e) $MR = MC$ and $TR < TC$.

31. If a competitive industry faced a steady decrease in demand, economic theory predicts that in the long run

    (a) firms will gradually leave the industry, thereby shrinking its productive capacity.
    (b) firms will modernize plant and equipment in order to increase efficiency.
    (c) existing firms will expand output levels as a means of recovering losses.
    (d) the industry will expand with newer, more efficient firms entering.
    (e) Both (b) and (d) are correct.

32. Suppose the following data are observed for a perfectly competitive firm: output = 5000 units, market price = $1, fixed costs = $2000, total variable costs = $1000, and marginal cost = $1.25. To maximize profits the firm should

    (a) reduce output.
    (b) expand output.
    (c) shut down.
    (d) increase the market price.
    (e) not change output.

33. At its current level of output, a perfectly competitive firm's average variable cost is $8.00, average total cost is $10.00, and marginal cost is $9.00. If the market price is $10.00, this firm can increase profits by

    (a) shutting down production.
    (b) decreasing output.
    (c) increasing output.
    (d) increasing the market price.
    (e) not changing output. This firm is at its profit-maximizing position.

34. If a perfectly competitive firm is producing where price equals average total cost and average total cost is greater than marginal cost, the firm should

    (a) reduce output.
    (b) expand output.
    (c) shut down.
    (d) increase the market price.
    (e) not change output.

35. Natural barriers to entry

    (a) include patent laws and exclusive franchises.
    (b) most commonly arise through economies of scale.
    (c) result from an increasing long run average cost curve.
    (d) imply that small firms have lower *ATC* curves than larger firms.
    (e) must be sustained by government regulation.

36. The process of "creative destruction" refers to

    (a) the threat of price-cutting behaviour.
    (b) the inherent instability of cartels.
    (c) an early declaration of bankruptcy as a means of avoiding debts.
    (d) the takeover of a competitive industry by a monopoly.
    (e) the replacement of one monopoly by another through invention and innovation.

37. A cartel increases the industry's profits by

    (a) fully capturing all economies of scale.
    (b) ceasing all active competitive behaviour with respect to price.
    (c) agreeing to sell all current output at an agreed-upon fixed price.
    (d) decreasing industry output and thereby increasing market price.
    (e) agreeing to produce more, but sell at a higher price.

38. Which of the following is not a problem associated with enforcement of a successful cartel?

    (a) Entry of new firms.
    (b) Government restrictions on output.
    (c) Preventing cartel members from violating the agreed-upon production level.
    (d) Convincing other firms to join the cartel.
    (e) Monitoring the output of cartel members.

39. Economic theory predicts cartels to be unstable because

    (a) there is an incentive for individual firms to produce beyond their quota.
    (b) governments will invariably dismantle them.
    (c) although industry profits increase, the profits of individual firms decrease.
    (d) individual firms have an incentive to produce less than the restrictions imposed on them by the cartel.
    (e) the industry output that maximizes joint profits for the cartel tends to exceed that of a competitive market.

40. Which of the following is the best example of price discrimination?

    (a) Some air travellers pay lower air fares as standby passengers.
    (b) A telephone company charges lower rates for long-distance calls after midnight than during the day.
    (c) A local transit company allows senior citizens, the unemployed, and children to ride at reduced fares.
    (d) The London underground charges each individual according to the distance travelled.
    (e) A cinema charges lower prices on Tuesdays than on Fridays or Saturdays.

41. The key difference between oligopolists and firms that operate in all other market structures is that oligopolists

    (a) are guaranteed long run profits.
    (b) produce an identical product but administer prices.
    (c) take explicit account of the impact of their decisions on competing firms.
    (d) do not engage in strategic behaviour.
    (e) do not engage in tacit collusion.

42. The cooperative, joint profit-maximizing outcome in oligopoly

    (a) is a long run equilibrium so long as there are barriers to entry.
    (b) will be unstable because each firm has an incentive to produce more output to increase profits.
    (c) results in allocative efficiency.
    (d) maximizes the output of each firm.
    (e) is an equilibrium so long as collusion is explicit as opposed to tacit.

43. Cooperation among oligopolistic firms that affects prices

 (a) is an effective agreement because it is a legal contract.
 (b) results in long run joint profit-maximizing equilibrium and stability in the industry.
 (c) tends to break down through strategic behaviour and technological innovation.
 (d) is more likely the greater the number of firms in the industry.
 (e) is more likely the weaker are the industry's barriers to entry.

44. Advertising expenditures can create a barrier to entry by

 (a) increasing costs for new entrants.
 (b) raising the minimum efficient scale of production.
 (c) allowing existing firms to announce to potential entrants the intention to engage in predatory pricing.
 (d) making a market contestable.
 (e) Both (a) and (b).

45. The equilibrium payoffs in the Prisoner's Dilemma

 (a) are a Nash equilibrium.
 (b) result from noncooperative behaviour.
 (c) are such that no individual prisoner can do better by changing its plea.
 (d) All of the above.
 (e) None of the above.

46. The observation that some oligopolistic firms sometimes sell at below cost is explained as

 (a) non-maximizing behaviour.
 (b) predatory pricing.
 (c) administered pricing.
 (d) non-price competition.
 (e) tacit cooperation.

47. Resources are allocated efficiently when

 (a) there are no unemployed resources.
 (b) all firms are producing at the lowest attainable cost.
 (c) prices are as low as possible.
 (d) no alternative allocation of resources makes at least one household better off without making another household worse off.
 (e) profits are maximized.

48. If two firms are producing the same product with different marginal costs, then

 (a) a reallocation of output between the firms can lower the industry's total cost.
 (b) neither firm is producing its output at the lowest attainable cost.
 (c) some resources must be unemployed.
 (d) each firm is being wasteful.
 (e) one firm is not maximizing profits.

49. Allocative efficiency holds when

 (a) price equals marginal cost.
 (b) the consumer valuation of the last unit produced equals the value of resources used to produce this unit.
 (c) the sum of consumers' and producers' surplus is maximized.
 (d) it is impossible to reallocate resources in such a way as to make one individual better off, without making someone else worse off.
 (e) All of the above.

50. Productive efficiency holds

 (a) when $P = MC$ for perfect competition.
 (b) only for perfect competition and monopolistic competition where long run profits are zero.
 (c) for natural monopolies where economies of scale are fully exploited.
 (d) throughout the market economy where the objective of firms is to maximize profits.
 (e) when firms produce that output where the ATC curve is at a minimum.

51. Producers' surplus is defined as

 (a) profits.
 (b) retained earnings.
 (c) total revenue less total costs.
 (d) total revenue less total variable costs.
 (e) total revenue less total fixed costs.

52. The deadweight loss of monopoly is

 (a) its fixed cost.
 (b) any negative profit due to cyclical decreases in demand.
 (c) the forgone total surplus due to the allocatively inefficient monopoly output level.
 (d) the cost of maintaining effective barriers to entry.
 (e) the extra administrative costs of operating a large firm.

53. The marginal revenue product of a factor is

    (a) the change in revenue from selling the extra output produced by an additional unit of a factor.
    (b) average physical productivity of the factor multiplied by product price.
    (c) the change in revenue from selling one more unit of output.
    (d) equal to the market price of the product that is produced by the factor.
    (e) its marginal physical product times the factor's price.

54. The marginal physical product of labour is

    (a) total output divided by total labour in use.
    (b) the change in output divided by the change in labour use.
    (c) total labour in use divided by total output.
    (d) the change in labour use divided by the change in output.
    (e) None of the above.

55. A perfectly competitive, profit-maximizing firm hires a factor up to the point at which

    (a) the factor's price equals its marginal revenue product.
    (b) the marginal cost of hiring the factor equals the additional revenue obtained from that factor's marginal contribution to output.
    (c) the factor's price equals its marginal physical product times the product's price.
    (d) All of the above.
    (e) None of the above.

56. Perfectly competitive, profit-maximizing firms that employ any factor until marginal revenue product equals its price will hire

    (a) additional units of the factor if its price falls, other things equal.
    (b) more of the factor if the price of the product it produces falls, other things equal.
    (c) less of the factor if technology changes such that factor productivity rises, other things equal.
    (d) additional units of the factor if the factor's price exceeds its marginal revenue product.
    (e) the same quantities of all factors.

57. Which of the following explains why a profit-maximizing, competitive firm's demand curve for labour slopes downward? As the quantity of labour employed rises,

    (a) the marginal physical product of labour eventually falls.
    (b) the firm's marginal revenue declines as output increases.
    (c) the marginal cost of hiring another unit of labour increases.
    (d) All of the above.
    (e) None of the above.

58. If the quantity demanded for a factor of production decreases by 10 percent when its price increases by 8 percent, the elasticity of demand for the factor is

    (a) −18.0.
    (b) 1.25 percent.
    (c) −0.80.
    (d) −2.00.
    (e) −1.25.

59. Evidence for Canada indicates that

    (a) the growth in union membership was low in the immediate post-war era (late 1940s and early 1950s).
    (b) the growth in union membership was low in the 1980s and early 1990s.
    (c) unionization rates in the public sector are lower than those in the private sector.
    (d) unions have not been able to create a union wage premium.
    (e) unions have taken no role in lobbying for legislation that applies to all workers.

60. Featherbedding practices by unions

    (a) shift the supply curve of labour to the right.
    (b) if successful will increase the demand for labour.
    (c) increase the loss in employment to union members when union wage premiums are increased.
    (d) increase the productivity of workers.
    (e) None of the above are correct.

61. If the interest rate is 5 percent, the present value of $500 received two years from now is

   (a) $453.51.
   (b) $525.
   (c) $467.19.
   (d) $551.25.
   (e) $510.

62. The formula for the present value of $10 received three years from now and an interest rate of 10 percent is

   (a) $10/(.1)^3$.
   (b) $10/3(1.1)$.
   (c) $(1.1)^3/10$.
   (d) $10/(1.1)^3$.
   (e) $10^3/(1.1)^3$.

63. A profit-maximizing firm will hire a unit of capital as long as its rental price is

   (a) less than the marginal revenue product.
   (b) equal to the marginal revenue product.
   (c) greater than the marginal revenue product.
   (d) less than its purchase price.
   (e) less than its present value.

64. The _____ is the rate of interest and the _____ distant the payment date, the lower will be the present value of a future payment.

   (a) higher; more.
   (b) higher; less.
   (c) lower; more.
   (d) lower; less.
   (e) None of the above.

65. The firm's demand curve for capital shows
   (a) the relationship between interest rates and present value.
   (b) an asset's present value for the current period only.
   (c) how the firm's desired stock of capital varies with changes in *MRP*.
   (d) how the firm's *MRP* changes with the interest rate.
   (e) how the firm's desired stock of capital varies with the interest rate.

66. In the very-long run, the demand for capital curve shifts to the right as

   (a) diminishing returns to capital becomes evident.
   (b) technological improvements increase the productivity of captial.
   (c) the interest rate decreases.
   (d) more capital is employed.
   (e) the present value of capital falls.

67. If the current price of oil is $20.00 per barrel and the annual interest rate is 7 percent, it pays to

   (a) produce less now if next year's price is less than $21.40.
   (b) have the same extraction rate every year regardless of what happens to oil prices in the future.
   (c) produce more now if next year's price is less than $21.40.
   (d) produce more next year if oil prices rise less than 7 percent from today's prices.
   (e) None of the above.

68. A profit-maximizing firm will leave a nonrenewable resource in the ground when its price is

   (a) uncertain in the future.
   (b) expected to rise.
   (c) expected to rise at a rate less than the rate of interest.
   (d) expected to rise at a rate greater than the rate of interest.
   (e) constant over time.

69. The likely result in a market economy if the government taxed away all profits would be

   (a) a more rapid shift of resources to expanding industries.
   (b) the removal of the most important incentive for resource allocation.
   (c) improved market signals and responses.
   (d) improved information about temporary shortages and surpluses.
   (e) enhanced efficiency in resource allocation.

70. Which of the following is *not* an argument for increased reliance on markets for allocating resources?

    (a) The market system coordinates millions of independent economic decisions automatically.
    (b) Profits in a market economy provide a stimulus for innovation and growth.
    (c) Markets function best when external benefits are associated with consumption or production.
    (d) Market forces provide an effective means of adapting to changing economic conditions.
    (e) In a market system relative prices reflect relative costs.

71. If a ton of newspaper costs $350 to produce and in the process causes $10 worth of pollution damage to the environment,

    (a) the private cost is $360 per ton.
    (b) the social cost is $10 per ton and the private cost is $350 per ton.
    (c) the private cost is $350 per ton and the social cost is $340 per ton.
    (d) the social cost is $360 per ton and the private cost is $350 per ton.
    (e) the social cost is $10 per ton and the private cost is $360 per ton.

72. If there are costly externalities associated with an economic activity and that activity is carried out until the private marginal benefit equals the private marginal cost,

    (a) this activity should be subsidized.
    (b) the social marginal net benefit is positive.
    (c) private costs exceed social costs.
    (d) too many resources are being allocated to this activity.
    (e) output of this activity should increase.

73. The presence of external benefits associated with production implies that

    (a) private output exceeds the socially optimal output.
    (b) private output is less than the socially optimal output.
    (c) private output corresponds to the socially optimal output.
    (d) Any of the above, depending on the relative magnitude of social and private benefits.
    (e) Any of the above, depending upon whether social benefits exceeds external benefits.

74. A market economy is unlikely to provide a sufficient amount of a public good like national defence because

    (a) national defence does not benefit everyone to the same degree.
    (b) private firms produce national defence less efficiently than does the government.
    (c) consumers are poorly informed about the benefits of national defence.
    (d) it is impossible to withhold national defence from people who don't pay for it.
    (e) Both (a) and (b) are correct.

75. Which of the following best describes the reason for overfishing in Canada's offshore fisheries?

    (a) Fishing has depleted fish stocks, leading to smaller catches.
    (b) The private marginal cost incurred by fishermen is less than the social marginal cost.
    (c) The private marginal cost incurred by future generations of fishermen is greater than the private marginal cost incurred by current fishermen.
    (d) Canadian governments explicitly encourage fishing through subsidies to fishermen.
    (e) Fishing is a non-rivalrous activity.

76. The market for "lemons" is an example of market failure due to

    (a) public goods.
    (b) externalities.
    (c) monopoly power.
    (d) asymmetric information.
    (e) pursuit of social goals other than allocative efficieny.

77. Arthur Okun's comparison of the economy to a "leaky bucket" refers to the

    (a) loss of efficiency due to imperfect competition in the economy.
    (b) forgone tax revenues resulting from an inefficient tax system.
    (c) costs involved in the regulation of the economy.
    (d) the efficiency costs involved in the redistribution of income.
    (e) the reduction in tax revenues due to tax evasion.

78. With multiple firms emitting pollutants, economic efficiency requires that

    (a) all emitters reduce pollution by the same percentage.
    (b) marginal costs of abatement be equal for all emitters.
    (c) all emitters reduce pollution by the same absolute amount.
    (d) there be zero emissions.
    (e) firms reduce emissions in proportion to their size.

79. The requirement that all pollution sources adopt a specific pollution control technique when there are many methods for controlling a certain type of pollution

    (a) is likely to be the most efficient way to achieve a certain amount of pollution abatement.
    (b) is likely to be less efficient than either emissions taxes or tradable emissions permits in achieving a given amount of abatement.
    (c) is more efficient the more divergent the abatement costs of different firms.
    (d) eliminates the need for monitoring and enforcement by the regulatory agency.
    (e) is likely to minimize total costs of achieving a given level of abatement in the industry.

80. Which of the following is *not* true of direct pollution controls?

    (a) They minimize total abatement costs for a given level of pollution.
    (b) They are slow to adopt improved abatement technology.
    (c) They are costly to monitor and enforce.
    (d) They require the government to direct firms on how to abate.
    (e) All of the above are true.

81. When we say that a firm has internalized an externality, we mean

    (a) production takes place indoors.
    (b) production occurs without any external damage.
    (c) the firm takes into account all costs associated with production.
    (d) the firm is complying with all regulatory standards.
    (e) pollution has been eliminated.

82. Complete abatement would be optimal, only if

    (a) the marginal benefit of abatement is always positive.
    (b) the marginal benefit of abatement were positive and constant.
    (c) the marginal benefit of abatement were positive and increasing.
    (d) the marginal cost of abatement were zero.
    (e) None of the above.

83. If the plastics industry has been disposing of its wastes free of charge, government regulation to ensure a more efficient use of resources would affect the industry's output and product price in which of the following ways?

    (a) Both output and price would decrease.
    (b) Output would decrease, but there would be no change in price.
    (c) Output would be unchanged, but price would increase.
    (d) Price would increase and output would decrease.
    (e) There would be no change in either price or output.

84. Internalizing a production externality will

    (a) shift the demand curve for the good to the left.
    (b) shift the supply curve (*MC* for a monopoly) for the good to the left.
    (c) shift both the demand and supply curves to the left.
    (d) increase the size of external costs.
    (e) have no effect on either demand or supply.

85. Which of the following groups purchased SO_2 emissions permits but did not use them?

    (a) Coal-burning electric power plants.
    (b) The Environmental Protection Agency.
    (c) Power plants with high abatement costs.
    (d) Power plants with low abatement costs.
    (e) Environmentalists.

86. Which of the following is *not* an example of a direct pollution control?

    (a) Bans on household fireplaces in some cities.
    (b) Automobile pollution controls.
    (c) A bag fee for garbage removal.
    (d) A requirement that scrubbers be installed on factory chimneys.
    (e) Laws against littering.

87. If rich people and poor people smoke the same amount, a sales tax on cigarettes is regressive because

    (a) everyone spends the same proportion of income on cigarettes.
    (b) the demand for cigarettes is inelastic.
    (c) the tax paid per person represents a larger proportion of a poor person's income.
    (d) the rich are better informed about the health hazards of smoking.
    (e) the poor pay more taxes.

88. If a tax takes the same amount of money from everyone regardless of individual income, the tax is

    (a) a flat-rate tax.
    (b) proportional.
    (c) regressive.
    (d) horizontally inequitable.
    (e) All of the above.

89. If an individual's average tax rate is 30 percent and marginal tax rate is 50 percent, an additional $100 income would imply additional tax payments of

    (a) $50.
    (b) $30.
    (c) $80.
    (d) $20.
    (e) Indeterminable without income level.

90. Tax expenditures refer to

    (a) how the government spends its tax revenues.
    (b) an individual's annual tax payments.
    (c) tax concessions that are made to influence the behaviour of taxpaying units.
    (d) intergovernmental transfers.
    (e) expenditures of future tax revenues.

91. The more elastic is demand, the greater will be the

    (a) tax revenue raised from a given excise tax.
    (b) horizontal equity of a particular tax.
    (c) progressivity of a tax.
    (d) excess burden of a tax.
    (e) direct burden of a tax.

92. The judgment concerning whether a tax is regressive, proportional, or progressive is based on a comparison of the amount of tax with the

    (a) tax base.
    (b) value of the item being taxed.
    (c) taxpayer's income.
    (d) distribution of income.
    (e) level of government expenditures.

93. A marginal tax rate of 58 percent on taxable income of $200 000 implies

    (a) that a person with $200 000 of taxable income pays $116 000 in taxes.
    (b) that the tax system is progressive.
    (c) that the tax system is vertically equitable.
    (d) that a dollar of income above $200 000 increases one's tax liability by $0.58.
    (e) All of the above.

94. Which of the following is an example of a tax expenditure?

    (a) Registered Retirement Savings Plans.
    (b) Old Age Security.
    (c) Canada Pension Plan.
    (d) Guaranteed Income Supplement.
    (e) Employment Insurance.

95. In a two-country and two-good model, gains from trade would not exist if

    (a) one country had an absolute advantage in the production of both goods.
    (b) a given amount of resources produced more of both goods in one country.
    (c) one country was endowed with far more resources than the other.
    (d) the countries had the same opportunity costs in the production of both goods.
    (e) only one country had a comparative advantage in the production of one good.

96. Which of the following statements is not true about opportunity cost?

    (a) Equal opportunity costs for pairs of commodities between two countries lead to gains from trade.
    (b) Opportunity costs depend on relative production costs.
    (c) Differences in opportunity costs across countries can enhance total output of both goods through trade and specialization.
    (d) Comparative advantage can be expressed in terms of opportunity costs.
    (e) Opportunity cost can be read as the slope of a tangent to a country's production possibility curve.

97. If production of each unit of wool in country *A* implies that beef production must be decreased by four units, while in country *B* each additional unit of beef decreases wool output by four units, the gains from trade

    (a) are maximized if country *A* specializes in wool production and country *B* in beef.
    (b) are maximized if country *A* specializes in beef production and country *B* in wool.
    (c) are maximized if country *A* allocates 80 percent of its resources to wool and the remainder to beef, while country *B* does the opposite.
    (d) are maximized if country *A* allocates 20 percent of its resources to wool and the remainder to beef, while country *B* does the opposite.
    (e) cannot be realized because opportunity costs in the two countries are the same.

98. A country may favourably alter its terms of trade by restricting domestic

    (a) demand and thereby reduce the price of imports for domestic consumers.
    (b) demand and thereby reduce the price of imports received by foreign producers.
    (c) supply and thereby reduce the price of imports for domestic consumers..
    (d) supply and thereby reduce the price of imports for domestic consumers.
    (e) demand and supply and thereby reduce imports.

99. _____ serve to raise a country's standard of living only to the extent that they raise national income to permit the purchase of more

    _____.

    (a) Tariffs; imports.
    (b) Exports; imports.
    (c) Imports; strategic subsidies.
    (d) Imports; non-traded goods.
    (e) Exports; domestically produced goods.

100. A large country, accounting for a significant share of world demand for an imported product, can increase its national income by

    (a) encouraging domestic production.
    (b) restricting domestic demand for the product, thereby decreasing its price and improving the terms of trade.
    (c) imposing import quotas on the product.
    (d) subsidizing imports of the good and thereby monopolize world consumption.
    (e) negotiating voluntary export restrictions.

Part II: Short-Answer Questions

(10 marks)

For each of the following questions, explain your answer.

1. In the short-run, all profit-maximizing companies produce at a level of output that satisfies two rules. What are they?

2. In the short run, what is the point, in terms of costs, at which a company will cease production?

3. What does a microeconomist mean by saying that a company has positive accounting profits, but zero economic profits?

4. Identify three kinds of taxes that are levied by Canadian governments. Suggest how they could be made more efficient and progressive.

5. Distinguish between a country having an absolute advantage in trade and having a comparative advantage.

Macroeconomics Practice Exam #1

This one-hour exam consists of 40 multiple-choice questions and 5 short-answer questions. The exam is worth 60 marks.

Part I: Multiple-Choice Questions

(40 marks)

Choose the best answer for each of the following:

1. Which of the following is not a macroeconomic issue?
   (a) Changes in the unemployment rate.
   (b) A fall in the Consumer Price Index.
   (c) Historical trends in the growth of real per capita national income.
   (d) Short-term fluctuations in national income around its long-run trend.
   (e) The change in the price of VCR machines relative to the price of movie theatre tickets.

2. Changes in real national income reflect only changes in output, whereas changes in current-dollar national income reflect
   (a) only price changes.
   (b) only changes in potential output.
   (c) changes in neither output nor price.
   (d) changes in both price and output.
   (e) only changes in real purchasing power.

3. Full employment in Canada
   (a) implies that the measured unemployment rate is zero.
   (b) occurs when the natural rate of unemployment is zero.
   (c) occurs when the output gap is positive.
   (d) has never been achieved in Canada.
   (e) occurs when the only existing unemployment is structural and frictional.

4. Estimating final output (GDP) by adding the sales of all firms
   (a) will overstate total output because it counts the output of intermediate goods more than once.
   (b) will understate the total value of national output.
   (c) is a measure of income accruing to Canadian residents.
   (d) provides the same value as net national income.
   (e) is the best measure of economic activity.

5. Disposable personal income is
   (a) always the same as personal income.
   (b) income that is used only for consumption.
   (c) personal income remaining after net income taxes.
   (d) exclusive of transfer payments such as unemployment insurance payments.
   (e) personal income minus capital consumption allowances.

6. If do-it-yourself homeowners stopped building their backyard decks and instead hired self-employed university students, then national income would
   (a) be reduced as now measured.
   (b) be unaffected if the students reported their earnings.
   (c) increase if the students reported their earnings.
   (d) be unaffected since the students are not wage earners.
   (e) include only the costs of materials, but not wages.

7. Changes in national income in the short run

   (a) are primarily supply determined.
   (b) are primarily due to changes in factor productivity.
   (c) must equal changes in its potential level according to the GDP Accounting Equation.
   (d) are primarily caused by changes in aggregate demand.
   (e) will reflect price and wage adjustments.

8. The consensus among economists is that monetary policy

   (a) affects real macroeconomic variables only in the long run.
   (b) involves taxation and government expenditure programs.
   (c) affects potential GDP in the short run.
   (d) affects nominal macroeconomic variables in the long run.
   (e) affects both real and nominal macroeconomic variables in the long run.

9. Which of the following will shift the *AE* function upward?

   (a) A decrease in autonomous consumption.
   (b) An increase in real national income.
   (c) The real rate of interest falls.
   (d) The marginal propensity to spend increases.
   (e) None of the above is correct.

10. At a level of national income where aggregate desired expenditure falls short of actual national income, there will be a tendency for

    (a) national income to rise.
    (b) national income to be in equilibrium.
    (c) inventories to unexpectedly increase.
    (d) prices to rise.
    (e) None of the above.

11. An upward shift of the saving function causes equilibrium income to

    (a) fall.
    (b) rise.
    (c) remain constant but consist of more consumption and less investment.
    (d) remain constant but consist of less consumption and more investment.
    (e) remain constant but it does not affect desired aggregate expenditure.

12. The multiplier is larger

    (a) the higher the level of autonomous expenditures.
    (b) the lower the level of autonomous expenditures
    (c) the flatter the slope of the *AE* function.
    (d) the steeper the slope of the saving function.
    (e) the higher the value of the marginal propensity to consume.

13. An increase in the tax rate would

    (a) increase disposable income.
    (b) decrease the multiplier.
    (c) shift the *AE* function downward in a parallel fashion.
    (d) shift the *AE* function upward in a parallel fashion.
    (e) None of the above.

14. National income is likely to increase as the result of increases in all but which of the following, assuming other autonomous or exogenous variables remain constant?

    (a) Autonomous Imports.
    (b) Autonomous Exports.
    (c) Autonomous Government purchases.
    (d) Autonomous Investment.
    (e) Autonomous consumption.

15. The balanced budget multiplier (where an increase in government spending is paid for with an equal increase in taxes) is likely to be

    (a) equal to the multiplier for an increase in *G* without tax increases.
    (b) zero under all circumstances.
    (c) greater than the multiplier for an increase in *G* without tax increases.
    (d) less than the multiplier for an increase in *G* without tax increases.
    (e) infinitely large.

16. All other things being equal, a fall in the domestic price level causes

    (a) the aggregate expenditure curve to shift upward and hence leads to a movement downward and to the right along the *AD* curve.
    (b) the aggregate expenditure curve to shift upward and hence leads to a movement upward and to the left along the *AD* curve.
    (c) the *AD* curve to shift to the right and a movement upward and to the right along the *AE* curve.
    (d) the *AD* and the *AE* curves to shift upward.
    (e) the *SRAS* curve to shift downward.

17. Assume that the *SRAS* curve slopes upward. After an economic shock, we observe that the equilibrium price level is lower than before but real equilibrium output has increased. Which one of the following events, by itself, could explain this observation?

    (a) An increase in input prices.
    (b) An increase in factor productivity.
    (c) An increase in exports.
    (d) A reduction in investment expenditure.
    (e) A decrease in the tax rate.

18. Under what circumstances would an expansionary demand shock result in virtually no increase in real income but a large increase in the price level?

    (a) If the demand shock occurred in the flat range of the *SRAS* curve.
    (b) If the demand shock occurred in the intermediate range of the *SRAS* curve.
    (c) If the demand shock occurred in the steep portion of the *SRAS* curve.
    (d) If unit costs were constant before and after the demand shock.
    (e) If input prices decreased.

19. The appropriate fiscal policy to eliminate a recessionary gap, from a short-run point of view, would be to

    (a) increase taxes.
    (b) increase the budget deficit.
    (c) decrease transfer payments.
    (d) increase the budget surplus.
    (e) decrease government purchases of goods and services.

20. Assuming wage rates are flexible, the long-run effect of a contractionary demand shock is

    (a) a restoration of potential GDP as the *SRAS* curve shifts up and to the left.
    (b) the creation of a permanent recessionary gap.
    (c) a permanent decrease in potential GDP.
    (d) permanently higher unemployment levels.
    (e) a restoration of potential GDP as the *SRAS* curve shifts down and to the right.

21. The value of money depends primarily on

    (a) the gold backing of the currency alone.
    (b) the gold backing of both currency and deposits.
    (c) its purchasing power.
    (d) who issues it.
    (e) a government decree.

22. The reserve ratio is the fraction of a bank's

    (a) deposits that it must hold in the form of currency.
    (b) deposits that it holds as reserves either in currency or as deposits with the Bank of Canada.
    (c) assets that it holds in the form of reserves.
    (d) reserves that it is required to hold in the form of deposits with the Bank of Canada.
    (e) None of the above.

23. The process of creating deposit money by banks

    (a) is possible because of a fractional reserve system.
    (b) is consciously undertaken by each bank.
    (c) must occur if there are excess reserves.
    (d) permits only small, gradual changes in the money supply.
    (e) None of the above.

24. If the Bank of Canada increases the money supply, we would expect the
    (a) interest rate to fall, the *AE* curve to shift upward, and the *AD* curve to shift to the left.
    (b) interest rate to fall, the *AE* curve to shift downward, and the *AD* curve to shift to the right.
    (c) interest rate to rise, the *AE* curve to shift upward, and the *AD* curve to shift to the left.
    (d) interest rate to fall, the *AE* curve to be unaffected, and the *AD* curve to become flatter.
    (e) interest rate to fall, the *AE* curve to shift upward, and the *AD* curve to shift rightward.

25. If Canadian interest rates rise relative to those in other countries,
    (a) the demand for Canadian dollars in international exchange markets will increase.
    (b) the demand for Canadian dollars in international exchange markets will fall.
    (c) the exchange rate will rise.
    (d) the external value of the Canadian dollar will rise.
    (e) Both (a) and (d).

26. If the Bank of Canada sold $10 million of securities to the public in the open market,
    (a) reserves and securities in banks would each rise by $10 million.
    (b) deposits and reserves of banks would initially fall by $10 million.
    (c) the money supply would eventually increase by $1/v$ times the value of the sale (v is the reserve ratio).
    (d) deposits in the banking system would initially rise by $10 million.
    (e) the price of bonds would rise.

27. If the Bank of Canada purchases government bonds in the open market,
    (a) an excess supply of money balances is created, higher bond prices will prevail, and aggregate expenditure will be higher than before.
    (b) an excess demand for money balances is created, higher bond prices will prevail, and aggregate expenditure will be lower than before.
    (c) an excess supply of money balances is created, lower bond prices will prevail, and aggregate expenditure will be lower than before.
    (d) an excess demand for money balances is created, lower bond prices will prevail, and aggregate expenditure will be higher than before.
    (e) None of the above.

28. The acceleration hypothesis holds that
    (a) inflation will accelerate even if the central banks do not engage in validation.
    (b) inflation rates will increase without expectational inflation.
    (c) the *AD* and *SRAS* curves shift by a constant amount over time.
    (d) when the central bank engages in whatever rate of monetary expansion is needed to hold the inflationary gap constant, the rate of actual inflation will accelerate.
    (e) the percentage change in nominal wealth must be equal to the inflation rate.

29. The duration of the recession that develops when a central bank stops validating a sustained inflation
    (a) depends on inflationary expectations and wage momentum.
    (b) is determined by coincidental leftward shifts of the *AD* curve.
    (c) will typically be very short according to Keynesians.
    (d) will typically be very long according to monetarists.
    (e) must be extremely short if expectations are backward looking.

30. New Keynesian theories about the persistence of involuntary unemployment

    (a) stress the importance of adverse supply shocks.
    (b) start with the observation that wage rates do not respond quickly to changes in demand and supply in labour markets.
    (c) imply that most unemployment is caused by fluctuations in the willingness of people to supply labour.
    (d) are based on the premise that all unemployment workers cannot be retrained.
    (e) None of the above is correct.

31. Which of the following would be appropriate for reducing structural unemployment in the long run?

    (a) effective job training programs.
    (b) Increases in the minimum wage in all provinces.
    (c) Policies designed to promote more labour-saving technological change.
    (d) Strongly enforced interprovincial agreements to restrict labour migration.
    (e) Increasing government subsidies to declining industries.

32. The "crowding out" effect of a larger government budget deficit refers to the outcome of

    (a) higher interest rates and less private investment.
    (b) higher interest rates and more saving.
    (c) lower interest rates and more investment.
    (d) lower interest rates and less saving.
    (e) no change in national saving.

33. Ricardian equivalence states that if the government decides to borrow $7 million dollars to finance a tax cut of $7 million, then

    (a) current taxpayers do not believe that current borrowing will affect their future tax liabilities.
    (b) financing government deficits with foreign capital is equivalent to financing the deficits domestically.
    (c) private saving will increase by $7 million since consumers believe that the current borrowing will translate into future increased tax liabilities of $7 million.
    (d) national saving must increase.
    (e) the growing public debt always increases permanent disposable income.

34. In terms of aggregate demand and aggregate supply, economic growth refers to

    (a) rightward shifts of the LRAS curve.
    (b) rightward shifts of the AD curve.
    (c) leftward shifts of the SRAS curve.
    (d) simultaneous rightward shifts of the AD curve and the SRAS curve.
    (e) the elimination of a recessionary gap.

35. Which of the following is not a feature of the increasing returns theory of economic growth?

    (a) Firms that first develop new investment opportunities receive low initial rates of return because of high fixed costs.
    (b) Investors who follow "pioneer" investors face higher investment costs and therefore decreasing rates of return.
    (c) Once a technological breakthrough has been made, new investors garner high rates of return since this technology is usually available to them.
    (d) The acceptability of new products takes a learning-by-using process by consumers.
    (e) Both (b) and (d).

36. The Washington Consensus regarding the appropriate policies for developing countries to pursue includes all but which of the following items?

    (a) Limiting government budget deficits in order to avoid the need for inflationary finance or higher interest rates.
    (b) Relying on market-determined exchange rates.
    (c) Applying protection to infant industries in selected cases for a limited period of time.
    (d) Maximizing economic growth without regard to its effect on the distribution of income.
    (e) Education, health, and infrastructure investment are desirable forms of public expenditure.

37. Comparative advantage is said to exist whenever

   (a) one country can produce a given level of output with fewer resources compared to another country.

   (b) a given amount of resources produces more output in one country compared to another.

   (c) one country has an absolute advantage over another country in the production of all goods.

   (d) different countries have different opportunity costs in production.

   (e) two countries are of different sizes.

38. Countervailing duties are attempts to maintain "a level playing ground" by

   (a) retaliating against foreign tariffs.

   (b) raising or lowering tariffs multilaterally.

   (c) establishing a common tariff wall around a customs union.

   (d) assessing tariffs that will offset foreign government subsidies.

   (e) subsidizing exports.

39. If the Bank of Canada does not engage in any foreign-exchange transactions, then

   (a) any deficit in Canada' current account must be matched by an equal and opposite surplus on Canada's capital account.

   (b) any surplus on Canada's capital account must be matched by an equal and opposite surplus on Canada's current account.

   (c) any deficit in Canada's current account must be matched by Canadians buying more foreign assets.

   (d) any deficit in Canada's capital account must be matched by an equal and opposite deficit on Canada's current account.

   (e) the combined balance of Canada's current and capital accounts could be either in a deficit or surplus position.

40. Which of the following is not likely to cause an appreciation of the external value of the Canadian dollar under a flexible exchange rate?

   (a) An increase in interest rates in Canada relative to rates elsewhere.

   (b) A lower inflation rate in Canada relative to foreign rates, assuming all internationally traded goods are price elastic.

   (c) Lower earnings expectations on Canadian assets relative to those elsewhere.

   (d) Economic expansion in the economies of Canada's major trading partners.

   (e) A higher propensity to buy Canadian-produced goods in international markets.

Part II: Short-Answer Questions

(20 marks)

For each of the following questions, explain your answer.

1. Identify and explain four reasons why Real GDP per Capita does NOT accurately measure changes in human well-being over time or differences in human well-being between nations.

2. Frequently one observes the government practising budgetary restraint (reducing deficits, increasing surpluses) after the economy begins a recessionary period. Moreover, the government often urges households to "tighten their belts" and increase their savings as a precaution in the face of "tough times ahead." Use the aggregate expenditure model (Keynesian theory) to evaluate the governments' response to recessions, as described above.

3. What policy instruments (specific actions) might the Bank of Canada use to combat Canadian inflation? Explain, using the aggregate demand model, how these Bank of Canada actions would operate to reduce Canadian inflation.

4. Evaluate the common belief that increased government debt necessarily harms future generations.

5. Explain the advantages and disadvantages of a flexible exchange rate policy, when compared to a fixed exchange rate policy.

Macroeconomics Practice Examination #2

This two-hour exam consists of 100 multiple-choice questions and 5 short-answer questions. The exam is worth 110 marks.

Part 1: Multiple-Choice Questions

(100 marks)

1. The term *quantity demanded* refers to the
   - (a) amount of a good that consumers are willing to purchase at some price during some given time period.
   - (b) amount of some good that consumers would purchase if they only had the income to afford it.
   - (c) amount of a good actually purchased during a given time period.
   - (d) minimum amount of a good that consumers require and demand for survival.
   - (e) amount of a good that consumers are willing to purchase regardless of price.

2. An increase in quantity demanded refers to
   - (a) rightward shifts in the demand curve only.
   - (b) a movement up along a demand curve
   - (c) a greater willingness to purchase at each price
   - (d) an increase in actual purchases
   - (e) a movement down along a demand curve.

3. The demand curve and demand schedule
   - (a) each reflect the relationship between quantity demanded and price, ceteris paribus
   - (b) are both incomplete in that neither can incorporate the impact of changes in income or tastes
   - (c) are constructed on the assumption that price is held constant
   - (d) illustrate that in economic analysis, only two variables are taken into account at any time
   - (e) characterize the relationship between price and actual purchases.

4. An increase in demand means that
   - (a) consumers actually buy more of the good
   - (b) at each price, consumers desire a greater quantity
   - (c) consumers' tastes have necessarily changed
   - (d) price has decreased
   - (e) all of the above are correct.

5. If goods A and B are complements, an increase in the price of good A will lead to
   - (a) an increase in the price of good B
   - (b) a decrease in the quantity demanded of good B
   - (c) a decrease in demand for good B
   - (d) no change in demand for good B because A and B are not substitutes
   - (e) a rightward shift in the demand for good B.

6. The price elasticity of demand refers to a measure that shows the
   - (a) responsiveness of quantity demanded of a good to changes in its price
   - (b) variation in prices due to a change in demand
   - (c) size of price changes caused by a shift in demand
   - (d) degree of substitutability across commodities
   - (e) magnitude of the shifts in a demand curve.

7. The price elasticity of demand is measured by the
   - (a) change in quantity demanded divided by the change in price
   - (b) change in price divided by the change in quantity demanded
   - (c) slope of the demand curve
   - (d) percentage change in quantity demanded divided by the percentage change in price
   - (e) average quantity demanded divided by the average price.

8. If the percentage change in price is greater than the percentage change in quantity demanded, demand
   - (a) is elastic
   - (b) is inelastic
   - (c) is unit-elastic
   - (d) shifts outward to the left
   - (e) shifts to the right.

9. An increase in the price of a good and a decrease in total expenditure (or total revenue) on this good are associated with

    (a) inferior goods
    (b) substitute goods
    (c) normal goods
    (d) elastic demand
    (e) inelastic demand.

10. The elasticity of supply for a product will tend to be larger

    (a) the higher is the elasticity of demand for the product
    (b) the lower is the elasticity of demand for the product
    (c) the harder it is for firms to shift the production of 1 product to another product
    (d) the easier it is for the firms to shift from the production of 1 product to another product
    (e) the shorter the time period involved.

11. If real potential GDP is 893 billion and current real GDP is 890 billion, then

    (a) there is an inflationary gap of 3 billion
    (b) unemployment consists only of structural and frictional unemployment
    (c) there is a recessionary gap of 3 billion
    (d) the GDP gap is positive
    (e) both (a) and (b)

12. If a particular index number in 1999 is 149 and the base year is 1996, then the index shows an increase of

    (a) 4.9% between 1996 and 1999
    (b) 149% between 1996 and 1999
    (c) 49% between 1996 and 1999
    (d) .49% between 1996 and 1999
    (e) an indeterminable percent, since the value of the index in 1996 is unknown.

13. Suppose that the steel industry has a total output of $63.8 billion and purchases $49.0 billion in intermediate inputs. Hence, the value added in billions of the steel industry in that period is

    (a) $112.8
    (b) −$14.8
    (c) $63.8
    (d) $14.8
    (e) $49.0.

14. Changes in national income in the short run

    (a) are primarily supply determined
    (b) are primarily due to changes in factor productivity
    (c) must equal changes in its potential level according to the GDP Accounting Equation
    (d) are primarily caused by changes in aggregate demand
    (e) will reflect price and wage adjustments.

15. A short-run increase in the interest rate is likely to lead to

    (a) adjustments in prices and wages
    (b) increases in planned expenditures
    (c) decreases in GDP and employment
    (d) an increase in potential GDP
    (e) an inflationary gap.

16. The marginal propensity to consume (*MPC*) is expressed as

    (a) the change in autonomous consumption
    (b) the change in consumption divided by disposable income
    (c) consumption divided by disposable income
    (d) the change in consumption divided by the change in disposable income
    (e) consumption divided by the change in disposable income.

17. Total saving divided by total income is called the

    (a) marginal propensity to save
    (b) saving function
    (c) average propensity to save
    (d) marginal propensity not to consume
    (e) total propensity to save.

18. Public saving is equal to

    (a) net tax revenues minus government purchases
    (b) disposable income minus consumption expenditure
    (c) government purchases minus net tax revenues
    (d) private saving plus government saving
    (e) *I* plus *NX*.

19. The slope of the budget surplus curve is

    (a) equal to the marginal propensity to consume
    (b) equal to the marginal propensity to save
    (c) equal to the income tax rate
    (d) equal to the value of the multiplier
    (e) flat since all components are autonomous.

20. The aggregate demand (AD) curve relates
    - (a) real national income to desired expenditure for a given price level
    - (b) nominal national income to the price level
    - (c) equilibrium real national income to the price level
    - (d) consumption expenditure to the price level
    - (e) real national income to inflation rates.

21. A rightward shift in the SRAS curve is brought about by
    - (a) an increase in factor prices
    - (b) decreases in productivity
    - (c) increases in productivity and/or decreases in factor prices
    - (d) decreases in factor supplies
    - (e) increases in real wealth.

22. If an inflationary gap currently exists, an appropriate fiscal policy would be to
    - (a) increase taxes
    - (b) increase government purchases of goods and services
    - (c) decrease taxes
    - (d) increase transfer payments
    - (e) reduce the budget surplus.

23. The appropriate fiscal policy to eliminate a recessionary gap would be to
    - (a) increase taxes
    - (b) increase government purchases of goods and services
    - (c) decrease transfer payments
    - (d) increase the budget surplus
    - (e) decrease government purchases of goods and services.

24. The classical view of the neutrality of money states that
    - (a) the allocation of resources is independent of the distribution of income.
    - (b) the real part of the economy cannot affect relative prices.
    - (c) the supply of money has no effect on the real part of the economy.
    - (d) money is neutral in its effect on absolute prices in the economy.
    - (e) money consists only of paper notes issued by a neutral central bank.

25. According to the classical view, a 50% reduction in the money supply will, in the long run,
    - (a) reduce real GDP by 50 percent.
    - (b) lower all money prices by 50%.
    - (c) lower all money prices by 100%.
    - (d) lower all relative prices by 50%.
    - (e) have no effect on either relative or money prices.

26. Most modern economists believe that
    - (a) money is neutral in the long run.
    - (b) changes in money and changes in prices are closely linked over long periods of time.
    - (c) changes in money supply may have impacts on the real GDP in the short run.
    - (d) All of the above are correct.
    - (e) None of the above are correct.

27. For money to serve as an efficient medium of exchange, it must have all but which of the following characteristics?
    - (a) General acceptability.
    - (b) Convertibility into gold or silver.
    - (c) High value relative to its weight.
    - (d) Divisibility.
    - (e) Very difficult to counterfeit.

28. If you deposited your $2000 paycheque at your bank, the bank's balance sheet would change by
    - (a) +$2000 in deposits only.
    - (b) +$2000 in loans only, since you're lending the bank $2000.
    - (c) +$2000 in deposits and +$2000 in loans and securities.
    - (d) +$2000 in deposits and +$2000 in reserves.
    - (e) +$2000 in reserves only.

29. If a bank sells $2000 in securities to replenish its reserves, the bank's balance sheet would change by
    - (a) −$2000 in loans and securities and −$2000 in deposits.
    - (b) −$2000 in loans and securities and −$2000 in reserves.
    - (c) +$2000 in reserves only.
    - (d) +$2000 in loans and securities and +$2000 in reserves.
    - (e) −$2000 in loans and securities and +$2000 in reserves.

30. If a bank makes a loan of $2000 to a Harry Smit, a local donut shop owner, and credits $2000 to his chequing account, the bank's balance sheet would change by

    (a) −$2000 in reserves and +$2000 in deposits.
    (b) +$2000 in loans and securities and +$2000 in deposits.
    (c) −$2000 in reserves and +$2000 in loans in securities.
    (d) +$2000 in loans and securities only.
    (e) +$2000 in deposits only.

31. In equilibrium, the market price of a bond will be

    (a) the present value of the income stream it produces.
    (b) unaffected by changes in the interest rate.
    (c) the sum of the annual returns, compounded to their value at the end of the asset's useful life.
    (d) positively related to its yield.
    (e) must be the same as its face value, or its principal value.

32. A rise in the market price of a bond with a given income stream

    (a) will have no effect on the bond's interest rate.
    (b) is equivalent to a reduction in the present value of the bond.
    (c) is equivalent to an increase in the bond's rate of return.
    (d) will not affect the present value of the bond.
    (e) is equivalent to a decrease in the bond's rate of return.

33. A bond promises to pay $1000 one year from now. At an interest rate of 8 percent, the bond's present value is $_____. If the interest rate were 10 percent, the market value of the bond would be $_____.

    (a) $926; $909.
    (b) $1000; $1000.
    (c) $920; $900.
    (d) $1080; $1100.
    (e) $556; $500.

34. A bond that promises to pay $100 two years from now has a market price given by the formula

    (a) $PV = \dfrac{\$100}{(1 + i)}$

    (b) $PV = \dfrac{\$100}{(1 + i)^2}$

    (c) $PV = \$100(1 + i).$
    (d) $PV = \$100(1 + i)^2.$
    (e) $PV = \$100/i^2.$

35. An asset that pays the same dollar annual value forever is called a

    (a) perpetuity.
    (b) preferred share.
    (c) fixed-term bond.
    (d) treasury bill.
    (e) a junk bond.

36. The opportunity cost to firms and households of holding money balances is

    (a) zero, since all economic transactions require the use of money.
    (b) the foregone nominal interest that could have been earned on other assets.
    (c) low when nominal interest rates are high.
    (d) the nominal interest rate received on chequing accounts.
    (e) zero, since the Bank of Canada pays no interest for holding commercial bank reserves.

37. Suppose that the real and nominal supply of and demand for M1 was $16.7 billion in 1975 and that prices doubled between 1975 and 1983. What would be the nominal value of M1 in 1983 that maintains a constant real supply of money over this period?

    (a) $8.35 billion.
    (b) $33.4 billion.
    (c) $16.7 billion.
    (d) $41.75 billion.
    (e) None of the above.

38. Open-market operations are:

    (a) purchases and sales by the Bank of Canada of government securities in financial markets.
    (b) purchases and sales among the commercial banks of securities in financial markets.
    (c) sales of government securities by chartered banks to their customers.
    (d) total purchases and sales of government securities in the bond market.
    (e) switching government deposits between the banks and the Bank of Canada.

39. Which one of the following is *not* a policy instrument of the Bank of Canada?

    (a) Raising the tax rate on interest income received from government bonds.
    (b) Buying bonds from the commercial banks.
    (c) Switching government deposits between itself and the banking system.
    (d) Sale of bonds to the commercial banks.
    (e) Changes in the bank rate by influencing the level or range of the "overnight" rate.

40. If the Bank of Canada purchases bonds in the open market,

    (a) bank reserves will be reduced.
    (b) bank reserves will be increased.
    (c) the money supply will fall by a maximum of $1/v$ times the value of the purchase (v is the reserve ratio).
    (d) interest rates are likely to rise.
    (e) bond prices are likely to fall.

41. If the Bank of Canada sold $10 million of securities to the public in the open market,

    (a) reserves and securities in banks would each rise by $10 million.
    (b) deposits and reserves of banks would initially fall by $10 million.
    (c) the money supply would eventually increase by $1/v$ times the value of the sale (v is the reserve ratio).
    (d) deposits in the banking system would initially rise by $10 million.
    (e) the price of bonds would rise.

42. If the Bank of Canada purchases bonds in the open market, it is likely that

    (a) the price of bonds would fall and the interest rate would rise.
    (b) both the price of bonds and the interest rate would rise.
    (c) both the price of bonds and the interest rate would fall.
    (d) the price of bonds would rise and the interest rate would fall.
    (e) reserves in the banks would fall.

43. To eliminate an inflationary gap, the Bank of Canada might

    (a) sell bonds in the open market.
    (b) purchase bonds in the open market.
    (c) transfer government deposits into the banking system.
    (d) increase the monetary base.
    (e) lower the bank rate.

44. The bank rate is defined as the interest rate

    (a) charged on preferred-customer loans by a bank.
    (b) charged by banks for overdrafts of large corporations.
    (c) on credit card accounts.
    (d) on three-month treasury bills.
    (e) at which the Bank of Canada makes loans (advances) to the banks.

45. When the measured unemployment rate is below the *NAIRU* rate,

    (a) current national income is less than potential national income.
    (b) there is a recessionary gap.
    (c) frictional and structural unemployment are zero.
    (d) there will be pressure for factor prices to increase.
    (e) the Phillips curve analysis predicts negative percentage changes in wage rates.

46. Expectations of inflation will influence workers' demands for money wage changes. Hence, an expectation of future inflation will cause

    (a) the *AD* curve to shift up and to the right.
    (b) the *SRAS* curve to shift down and to the right.
    (c) the *AD* curve to shift down and to the left.
    (d) an inflationary gap in which measured unemployment is less than the *NAIRU*.
    (e) a recessionary gap as the *SRAS* curve shifts up and to the left and away from potential GDP.

47. Which of the following is not a characteristic or implication of backward-looking expectations?

    (a) Backward-looking expectations tend to change slowly.
    (b) If inflation has been 5 percent for several years in the past, people will expect it to be 5percent next year.
    (c) People revise their expectations in light of the mistakes that they made in estimating inflation in the past.
    (d) People will not continue to make persistent, systematic errors in forming expectations.
    (e) None of the above.

48. If there is no supply-shock inflation, expectations of future inflation are 1.5 percent, and excess-demand inflation is 4 percent then the predicted overall change in actual wages and prices is

    (a) 1.5 percent.
    (b) 4.0 percent.
    (c) 5.5 percent.
    (d) 2.5 percent.
    (e) 62.5 percent.

49. An inflationary process is said to be validated when

    (a) at least two federal government departments agree on the magnitude of price increases.
    (b) the initial cause of the inflation was an expansion of government expenditure.
    (c) the Bank of Canada maintains a constant nominal money supply during the inflationary process.
    (d) the central bank increases the money supply at such a rate that the expectations of inflation end up being correct.
    (e) the SRAS curve shifts leftward because of inflationary expectations.

50. A constant inflation rate is produced when

    (a) actual inflation is equal to a constant expectation of inflation.
    (b) excess-demand inflation is zero.
    (c) the economy operates at its potential level of GDP.
    (d) the central bank increases the money supply at the same rate as the expected and actual inflation rates.
    (e) All of the above are correct.

51. The measured unemployment rate will rise if

    (a) the percentage increase in employment is greater than the percentage increase in the labour force.
    (b) the percentage increase in total unemployment is less than the percentage change in the labour force.
    (c) with a constant labour force, the number of new jobs created is less than the number of jobs lost.
    (d) actual income rises temporarily from its potential level.
    (e) more discouraged, unemployed workers leave the labour force.

52. Which of the following is a potential cost of unemployment?

    (a) The potential output of valuable resources is wasted.
    (b) Workers who would like to work at prevailing wages may stay out of the labour force.
    (c) The unemployed contribute to social unrest in some societies.
    (d) Workers who are unemployed for prolonged periods miss job training opportunities.
    (e) All or any of the above.

53. Involuntary unemployment

    (a) occurs when there is a job available but the unemployed person is unwilling to accept it at the existing wage.
    (b) will tend to increase during booms.
    (c) will tend to increase as the costs of searching for a job increase, other things equal.
    (d) occurs when a person is willing to accept a job at the going wage rate but no such job can be found.
    (e) occurs when highly skilled jobs are available but an unskilled worker is not qualified to be hired.

54. Unemployment that occurs as a result of the normal turnover of labour as people move from job to job is called

    (a) involuntary unemployment.
    (b) structural unemployment.
    (c) cyclical unemployment.
    (d) frictional unemployment.
    (e) real-wage unemployment.

55. The existence of structural unemployment means that

    (a) there is an inadequate number of jobs in the economy.
    (b) the building trades workers, particularly those in structural steel, are suffering high rates of unemployment.
    (c) the composition of the demand for labour does not match the composition of available supply.
    (d) cyclical unemployment must also be present.
    (e) all unemployment is voluntary.

56. Search unemployment

    (a) may be a form of voluntary frictional unemployment.
    (b) will tend to increase if search costs are low.
    (c) occurs when members of the labour force look for more suitable jobs.
    (d) occurs because workers do not have perfect knowledge of job availability.
    (e) All of the above.

57. Which of the following does *not* usually explain the creation of structural unemployment?

    (a) Economic adjustments created by changes in input mixes.
    (b) Changes in the composition of the labour force.
    (c) The pattern of the demand for goods changes.
    (d) Contractionary monetary policy.
    (e) New labour force entrants having inadequate training or skills for available jobs.

58. If an economy has achieved its *NAIRU*, it follows that

    (a) the measured unemployment rate is necessarily zero.
    (b) the economy operates in a recessionary gap.
    (c) the value of the output gap is zero.
    (d) there is neither structural nor frictional unemployment in the economy.
    (e) all unemployment is involuntary.

59. The value of the Canadian federal (government net) debt as a share of GDP in the 1990s was

    (a) somewhere between 60 and 70 percent.
    (b) lower than its value in the 1960s.
    (c) greater than its value during World War II.
    (d) equal to the value of the federal government deficit as a share of GDP.
    (e) slightly less than 90 percent.

60. Which one of the following statements is true?

    (a) An overall budgetary deficit implies a primary budget deficit.
    (b) A budgetary deficit means that government borrowing does not change.
    (c) Higher real interest rates imply lower debt-service payments.
    (d) A budgetary deficit necessitates an increase in government borrowing.
    (e) Transfer payments are excluded from the category program spending.

61. The primary federal deficit is defined as

    (a) the total federal deficit minus the value of outstanding debt.
    (b) the total federal deficit generated by transfer payments to primary industries.
    (c) the total federal deficit excluding debt-service payments.
    (d) the deficit that exists at potential national income.
    (e) the federal deficit attributable to debt-service payments.

62. With a decrease in current taxes, "non-Ricardian" consumers are likely to

  (a) cause the *AD* curve to shift up and to the right in the short run since national saving decreases.
  (b) have no effect on the *AD* curve since national saving is unaffected.
  (c) cause the *AD* curve the shift down and to the left as they increase private saving by more than the decrease in government saving.
  (d) have no effect on either the *AD* curve or real interest rates.
  (e) cause the *SRAS* curve to shift down and to the right.

63. The "crowding out" effect of a larger government budget deficit in a closed economy refers to the outcome of

  (a) higher interest rates and less private investment.
  (b) higher interest rates and more saving.
  (c) lower interest rates and more investment.
  (d) lower interest rates and less saving.
  (e) no change in national saving.

64. The "crowding out" of a larger government budget deficit in an open economy refers to the outcome of

  (a) higher interest rates, an appreciation of the domestic currency, and increased net exports.
  (b) higher interest rates, lower capital inflows and net exports.
  (c) lower interest rates, more capital inflows, lower net exports.
  (d) a depreciation of the domestic currency and an increase in net exports.
  (e) higher interest rates, an appreciation of the domestic currency, and reduced net exports.

65. If a larger government budget deficit reduces the capital stock in the long run, then

  (a) the current standard of living is likely to decline, but the future standard of living will improve.
  (b) the future standard of living is likely to decline.
  (c) the current generation bears the burden of the debt.
  (d) the concept of Ricardian "equivalence" holds.
  (e) future generations will be unaffected so long as consumption expenditure increases offset the effects of the deficit.

66. Some economists are concerned that policies that result in a large and growing budget deficit

  (a) reduce the government's flexibility to use fiscal policy as a stabilization tool.
  (b) create high interest payments, leaving less revenue for other public needs.
  (c) may lead to a growing foreign indebtedness.
  (d) will erode the competitiveness of the export sector as the exchange rate depreciates.
  (e) All of the above.

Use the following table for questions 67-71.

Labour	Capital	Output
10.0	10	10.0
10.0	15	11.8
10.0	20	13.2
15.0	15	15.0
22.5	15	19.1

67. The marginal product of capital (extra output per extra unit of capital input, other inputs unchanged)

  (a) is 1.8 when capital rises from 10 to 15.
  (b) is .14 when capital rises from 15 to 20.
  (c) rises when progressively more capital is used.
  (d) demonstrates the principle of increasing returns to scale.
  (e) is 0.36 when capital rises from 10 to 15.

68. The marginal product of labour (extra output per extra unit of labour input, other inputs unchanged)

  (a) is 0.55 (approximately) when labour rises from 15 to 22.5.
  (b) is 4.1 when labour rises from 15 to 22.5.
  (c) is 1.8 when labour rises from 10 to 15.
  (d) cannot be estimated in this table.
  (e) demonstrates the principle of increasing returns to scale.

69. This economy operates under constant returns to scale because

  (a) increasing capital inputs has a constant positive effect on output.
  (b) increasing labour and capital inputs by 50 percent increases output by 50 percent.
  (c) increasing labour inputs has a constant positive effect on output.
  (d) both marginal productivities are positive and constant.
  (e) of the law of diminishing returns.

70. When labour (workers) increases from 15.0 to 22.5 and capital remains at 15,

    (a) living standards per worker increase because marginal productivity is positive.
    (b) output per worker stays constant because capital is constant.
    (c) living standards per worker decrease even though marginal productivity is positive.
    (d) the average productivity of labour (workers) is 0.55 approximately.
    (e) living standards per worker increase because average productivity of labour increases.

71. Suppose that two countries have the same per capita output. Country A has an annual economic growth rate of 6 percent, while country B grows at 3 percent per year. According to the rule of 72, country A will have a per capita output four times as large as country B's in

    (a) 12 years.
    (b) 36 years.
    (c) 24 years.
    (d) 48 years.
    (e) 72 years.

72. Economic growth is best defined as

    (a) a rise in real national income as unemployment is reduced.
    (b) fluctuations of GDP around its potential level.
    (c) a rise in real per capita GDP (living standard) over time.
    (d) increases in current real GDP as structural unemployment decreases.
    (e) a reduction in the inequality of income distribution.

73. Theories of economic growth stress

    (a) ways of reducing income inequalities.
    (b) the elimination of short-term inefficiencies.
    (c) the factors that increase potential real GDP over time.
    (d) the need to increase consumption and decrease saving over time.
    (e) the need for countries to become self-sufficient in food production.

74. According to the "rule of 72," a growth in population of 2 percent per year means that population will double in approximately

    (a) 2 years.
    (b) 144 years.
    (c) 72 years.
    (d) 260 years.
    (e) 36 years.

75. The development gap is defined as

    (a) the discrepancy between the standards of living in countries at either end of the world income distribution.
    (b) the difference between output growth rates in developed and developing countries.
    (c) the difference in the degree of allocative efficiency in developed countries and developing countries.
    (d) the discrepancy between the savings rates in developed countries compared with those in developing countries.
    (e) None of the above.

76. The group of nations, called the newly industrialized countries (NICs),

    (a) grew rapidly in terms of real per capita GDP rapidly in the three decades after 1960.
    (b) typically have per capita incomes close to 50 percent of those found in developed nations.
    (c) include countries such as South Korea and Singapore.
    (d) generally followed outward-looking and market-based policies.
    (e) All of the above are correct.

77. Increases in real GDP in developing countries do not necessarily lead to economic advancement if

    (a) growth in productivity is greater than real GDP growth.
    (b) population growth exceeds real GDP growth.
    (c) market-oriented processes replace command-economy decision making.
    (d) foreign capital is the major source of the expansion in real GDP.
    (e) None of the above.

78. Which one of the following would *not* be considered a barrier to economic development of particular countries?

    (a) Rapid population growth.
    (b) Inefficient use of resources.
    (c) International trade.
    (d) Inadequate human resources.
    (e) Inadequate services such as communications and transportation.

79. Which of the following is the best example of *allocative inefficiency*?

    (a) Some productive processes use too much labour relative to capital.
    (b) Society is at the "wrong" point on its production possibility boundary.
    (c) Firms do not seek to maximize their profits.
    (d) Owners of factors of production do not seek to maximize their material welfare.
    (e) Some productive processes use too much capital relative to labour.

80. The vicious circle of poverty

    (a) refers to insufficient domestic savings generated at low levels of income to finance economic growth.
    (b) applies to countries that borrow from abroad and spend the proceeds on consumer goods.
    (c) results from the failure of policies in developing countries to hold population growth to zero percent.
    (d) describes a situation in which savings out of domestic income are invested abroad, lowering the domestic rate of capital accumulation.
    (e) implies that a widening of income-distribution inequality is an inevitable aspect of economic development.

81. What factors contributed to the growth of external debt of many developing nations?

    (a) OPEC substantially increased oil prices in 1973 and 1979.
    (b) Increases in real interest rates in the 1980s increased debt-servicing charges for governments in these countries.
    (c) High export sales of developing nations were financed by large capital outflows.
    (d) High saving rates in these countries translated into large capital inflows from developed countries.
    (e) Both (a) and (b) are correct.

82. Country X has an absolute advantage over country Y in the production of widgets if

    (a) fewer resources are required in X to produce a given quantity of widgets than in Y.
    (b) a given amount of resources in X produces more widgets than the same amount of resources in Y.
    (c) relative to Y, more widgets can be produced in X with fewer resources.
    (d) All of the above.
    (e) None of the above.

83. If, given the same amount of inputs, Canadian farmers produce 2 tons of rice per acre while Japanese farmers produce 1 ton of rice per acre, we can be certain that

    (a) Canada should export rice to Japan.
    (b) Canada has a comparative advantage in rice production.
    (c) Canada has an absolute advantage in rice production.
    (d) Japanese rice farmers must be paid twice as much as Canadian farmers.
    (e) Both (a) and (b) are correct.

84. Comparative advantage is said to exist whenever

    (a) one country can produce a given level of output with fewer resources compared to another country.
    (b) a given amount of resources produces more output in one country compared to another.
    (c) one country has an absolute advantage over another country in the production of all goods.
    (d) different countries have different opportunity costs in production.
    (e) two countries are of different sizes.

85. If there are two countries A and B, and two goods X and Y, and if A has a comparative advantage in the production of X, it necessarily follows that

    (a) A has an absolute advantage in the production of X.
    (b) B has an absolute advantage in the production of X.
    (c) A has a comparative disadvantage in the production of Y.
    (d) B has an absolute advantage in the production of Y.
    (e) B has a comparative disadvantage in the production of Y.

86. Which of the following is *not* a source of comparative advantage?

   (a) Factor endowments.
   (b) Climate.
   (c) Country size.
   (d) Acquiring human capital.
   (e) None of the above.

87. Gains from specialization can arise when

   (a) countries have different opportunity costs in production.
   (b) there are economies of scale in production.
   (c) experience gained via specialization lowers cost through learning by doing.
   (d) trading partners have a different comparative advantage.
   (e) All of the above.

88. Free trade within the European Community led to

   (a) each member country specializing in specific products (e.g., furniture, cars, etc.).
   (b) a large increase in product differentiation, with countries tending to specialize in subproduct lines (e.g., office furniture, household furniture, etc.).
   (c) no perceptible alteration in production patterns.
   (d) less trade among EC members.
   (e) less product diversity.

89. Which of the following national objectives is a valid argument for some degree of protectionism?

   (a) Concentration of national resources in a few specialized products.
   (b) Increases in average incomes.
   (c) Diversification of a small economy in order to reduce the risk associated with cyclical fluctuations in price.
   (d) Ability of domestic firms to operate at minimum efficient scale.
   (e) Maximization of the national standard of living.

90. A country may favourably alter its terms of trade by restricting domestic

   (a) demand and thereby reduce the price of imports for domestic consumers.
   (b) demand and thereby reduce the price of imports received by foreign producers.
   (c) supply and thereby reduce the price of imports for domestic consumers..
   (d) supply and thereby reduce the price of imports for domestic consumers.
   (e) demand and supply and thereby reduce imports.

91. _____ serve to raise a country's standard of living only to the extent that they raise national income to permit the purchase of more _____.

   (a) Tariffs; imports.
   (b) Exports; imports.
   (c) Imports; strategic subsidies.
   (d) Imports; non-traded goods.
   (e) Exports; domestically produced goods.

92. A large country, accounting for a significant share of world demand for an imported product, can increase its national income by

   (a) encouraging domestic production.
   (b) restricting domestic demand for the product, thereby decreasing its price and improving the terms of trade.
   (c) imposing import quotas on the product.
   (d) subsidizing imports of the good and thereby monopolize world consumption.
   (e) negotiating voluntary export restrictions.

93. The problem with restricting imports as a means of reducing domestic unemployment is that

   (a) it merely redistributes unemployment from import-competing industries to our export industries when trading partners retaliate.
   (b) Canadians would rather do without than have to buy Canadian-produced goods.
   (c) Our import-competing industries are not labour-intensive.
   (d) Our import-competing industries are always fully employed.
   (e) Both (c) and (d) are correct.

94. A central difference in the effects of a tariff and a voluntary export restriction (VER)—set at the same quantity as under the tariff—is that

    (a) the VER yields a higher price for consumers than the tariff.
    (b) the tariff pushes the consumer price beyond the price associated with the VER.
    (c) government tariff revenue becomes suppliers' revenue with a VER.
    (d) as the quantity sold decreases under the VER, the revenue of producers decreases.
    (e) Both (a) and (c) are correct.

95. Which of the following international transactions would be recorded as a credit in Canada's balance of payment accounts?

    (a) Canadians buy U.S. bonds.
    (b) Canadians send cash gifts to their relatives in Italy.
    (c) Canadians receive dividend income from Germany.
    (d) Canadian firms pay New York consulting companies for their services.
    (e) The Bank of Canada purchases foreign currency (and sells Canadian dollars).

96. Which international transaction would be recorded in France's current account?

    (a) French banks receive interest payments associated with their holdings of bonds issued by the German government.
    (b) French investors purchase stocks issued by Canadian companies.
    (c) A French investment group buys a mining company located in Bolivia.
    (d) The central bank of France adds to its holdings of U.S. dollars.
    (e) None of the above are correct.

97. Which international transaction would be recorded in Canada's capital account as a credit?

    (a) Canadian sales of agricultural products to China.
    (b) Germans buy farm land in Saskatchewan.
    (c) Canadian investors receive interest payments from their U.S. bond holdings.
    (d) Japanese families book skiing tours to British Columbia.
    (e) The Bank of Canada increases its holdings of gold and/or foreign-currency reserves.

98. If the Bank of Canada decreases its holdings of a foreign currency, then

    (a) this transaction would be recorded as a debit in Canada's capital account.
    (b) this probably represents the Bank's effort to prevent an appreciation of the external value of the Canadian dollar.
    (c) the combined balance of Canada's current and capital accounts must be in a deficit position.
    (d) this transaction would be recorded as a credit in Canada's Official Financing Account.
    (e) Both (c) and (d) are correct.

99. If the Bank of Canada does *not* engage in any foreign-exchange transactions, then

    (a) any deficit in Canada' current account must be matched by an equal and opposite deficit on Canada's capital account.
    (b) any surplus on Canada's capital account must be matched by an equal and opposite surplus on Canada's current account.
    (c) any deficit in Canada's current account must be matched by Canadians buying more foreign assets.
    (d) any deficit in Canada's capital account must be matched by an equal and opposite surplus on Canada's current account.
    (e) the combined balance of Canada's current and capital accounts could be either in a deficit or surplus position.

100. If the Bank of Canada increases its holdings of foreign reserves, then

    (a) this transaction is analogous to a capital inflow to Canada.
    (b) the combined balance of Canada's current and capital accounts must be in a deficit position.
    (c) it may be trying to prevent a depreciation of the external value of the Canadian dollar.
    (d) a deficit on the current account is being matched by an equal and opposite surplus on the capital account.
    (e) None of the above are correct.

Part 2: Short-Answer Questions

(10 marks)

1. There are two basic methods for measuring national income. Name them.

2. Define Net Domestic Income at factor cost.

3. To calculate GDP using the expenditure approach, name the four components that we add together.

4. What is the consumption function?

5. What does the marginal propensity to consume measure?

6. Define equilibrium national income in two ways.

7. What is the present value of $100, to be received two years from now, if the interest rate is 5%. Show the formula and your work.

8. When the Bank of Canada buys securities from the open market, what happens to the money supply?

9. When the Bank of Canada sells securities to the open market, what happens to the money supply?

Answers to Practice Exams

Microeconomics Practice Exam #1

Part I: Multiple Choice

1. c
2. d
3. d
4. c
5. c
6. a
7. a
8. d
9. a
10. b
11. e
12. c
13. e
14. b
15. c
16. c
17. b
18. d
19. a
20. e
21. c
22. b
23. a
24. e
25. e
26. a
27. e
28. c
29. d
30. b
31. c
32. a
33. b
34. c
35. e
36. a
37. c
38. e
39. c
40. b

Part II: Short Answer

1. In the short run, to the extent that the "true rental price" paid by renters is below the equilibrium price, rent controls will end up redistributing income from landlords to renters. Assuming that renters earn, on average, lower incomes than landlords, this policy will redistribute income from rich to poor. Also, by keeping rent prices at a lower level than the equilibrium price level, those at or close to the poverty level can better afford rental housing, a necessity.

In the long run, shortages of "liveable" rental housing will result, as landlords reduce new apartment construction and convert rental units to condominiums or simply do not maintain the rental units that they continue to rent—leading to more slum housing. These shortages particularly hurt "potential future tenants" who simply will not have rental housing units available to them. In addition, these shortages typically lead to black markets, where landlords may require hidden "large entry fees" which can result in higher than equilibrium prices being charged. Now, instead of rental housing being cheaper for lower income renters, it will be more expensive. This policy will now tend to conflict with the goal of "more equitable distribution of income."

As far as promoting equity in general, rent controls, by creating shortages, will lead to alternate allocation schemes. Landlords may decide to allocate the scarce rental space according to "sellers' preferences" which can lead to very unfair criteria being used to decide who becomes and who does not become tenants in their buildings.

2. Because the market price of a product depends on both demand and supply, there can be products on which consumers place a high total value (such as water) that sell for a low price, because the last unit of the product consumed yields a relatively low marginal value (due to its relatively high supply). In other words, since relative prices reflect relative marginal values (of the last unit consumed) and NOT total values, the statement in question 2 is false.

3. In cases where "market failures" are absent, perfect competition promotes allocative efficiency by maximizing the sum of producer and consumer surplus. However, if externalities relate to the product being provided by perfect competition, allocative efficiency will not be achieved. More specifically, in product situations where external costs exist, a perfectly competitive market will tend to over-allocate resources. Conversely, in product situations where external benefits exist, a perfectly competitive market will tend to under-allocate resources.

4. If a binding minimum wage law is imposed on a competitive labour market, this will reduce the quantity of labour demanded and will increase the quantity of labour supplied. This will result in a decline in employment and an increase in unemployment in this competitive labour market.

However, if a binding minimum wage law is imposed in labour markets where the employers have monopsony power, the minimum wage law can actually result in an increase in wages and an increase in employment. Only to the extent that the minimum wage ends up being set above the competitive wage will employment start to fall.

5. The "two burdens" of a tax refer to both the direct burden and the excess burden. The direct burden is the visible amount of tax actually paid by the taxpayers to the government. The excess burden is the loss in consumer surplus resulting from the imposition of the tax. The excess burden reflects the allocative inefficiency of the tax.

In general, the more elastic the demand for the product is, the greater will be the excess burden resulting from a tax on this product. This implies that the excess burden can be minimized by imposing taxes on goods with the lowest elasticities. However, this often results in a conflict with equity, as inelastic products are often necessity items that the poor spend a larger portion of their income on.

Microeconomics Practice Exam #2

Part 1: Multiple Choice

1. e
2. e
3. c
4. e
5. d
6. c
7. c
8. d
9. b
10. a
11. d
12. d
13. e
14. a
15. d
16. d
17. d
18. b
19. a
20. c
21. a
22. e
23. b
24. d
25. b
26. c
27. e
28. c
29. b
30. b
31. a
32. a
33. c
34. b
35. b
36. e
37. d
38. b
39. a
40. c
41. c
42. b
43. c
44. a
45. d
46. b
47. d
48. a
49. e
50. d
51. d
52. c
53. a
54. b
55. d
56. a
57. a
58. e
59. b
60. b
61. b
62. a
63. b
64. a
65. e
66. b
67. c
68. d
69. b
70. c
71. d
72. d
73. b
74. d
75. b
76. d
77. d
78. b
79. b
80. a
81. c
82. d
83. d

84. b
85. e
86. c
87. c
88. c
89. a
90. c
91. d
92. c
93. d
94. a
95. d
96. a
97. b
98. b
99. b
100. b

In order to be efficient and progressive, Canadian governments would have to change the current mix of taxes. This would require joint government planning of types of tax, levels of tax, incidence of burden on the taxpayer. Such governmental planning does not take place at present.

5. Absolute advantage: A country is able to produce more of a good with a given level of resources than another country.

   Comparative advantage: A country is able to produce a particular good at a lower opportunity cost than another country.

Part 2: Short Answer

(10 marks)

1. First rule: Price is greater than average variable cost.

   Second rule: Marginal cost of the output equals marginal revenue.

2. It is that point of sales at which revenues do not cover the variable costs of production.

3. In calculating economic profit, economists take into account total revenue minus all costs of production, including the opportunity costs of an owner's capital. Accountants do not take into account opportunity costs in their calcuation of a firm's costs.

4. Kinds of taxes in Canada include:

   Personal income tax
   Corporate income tax
   Excise taxes
   Federal sales taxes
   Provincial sales taxes
   Capital gains taxes

Macroeconomics Practice Exam #1

Part I: Multiple Choice

1. e
2. d
3. e
4. a
5. c
6. c
7. d
8. d
9. c
10. c
11. a
12. e
13. b
14. a
15. d
16. a
17. b
18. c
19. b
20. e
21. c
22. b
23. a
24. e
25. e
26. b
27. a
28. d
29. a
30. b
31. a
32. a
33. c
34. a
35. b
36. d
37. d
38. d
39. a
40. c

Part II: Short Answer

1. Real GDP per capita omits changes or differences in leisure time, underground activity, home production, pollution and congestion.

   If, as real GDP increases over time, leisure time increases, real GDP understates the true increase in standard of living. Two countries could have the same real GDP per capita, but Country A could have additional economic activity in the form of home production, and underground activities. These non-market activities mean that in Country A, real GDP per capita understates the true degree of human well-being. Finally, a rapid increase in real GDP per capita may be accompanied by a significant increase in pollution and congestion. In this case, the increase in real GDP per capita overstates the true increase in human well-being.

2. When the government practises restraint by reducing their deficit or increasing their surplus, this means that either current government expenditures are being reduced or current taxes are being increased or both. This will decrease aggregate expenditures and, as a result, equilibrium real GDP will decline, which will only worsen the recession. In addition, if households take the government's advice and increase their savings, this will reduce current consumption expenditure, which will also decrease aggregate expenditures and cause a multiplied decrease in equilibrium GDP. Needless to say, in the short run, the government's actions serve to worsen the recession.

3. The Bank of Canada could either sell government bonds, through open market operations, or switch some federal government deposits from the chartered banks into the Bank of Canada in order to reduce chartered bank reserves and increase Canadian interest rates. The increased Canadian interest rates will decrease investment spending, which, in turn, will reduce aggregate demand and Canadian inflation. As well, higher Canadian interest rates will tend to increase the external value of the Canadian dollar (appreciate the Canadian exchange rate) and this will reduce net exports and cause an addition reduction in aggregate demand and inflation.

4. Whether or not government debt places a burden on future generations depends on the effect that the government debt has on the mix of capital goods versus consumption goods produced in the economy. If the government debt reduces private capital (due to the crowding out effect, etc.) and does not replenish the capital stock through increased public capital goods, one could argue that there is a burden on future generations. As an example, if the monies collected by incurring additional government debt are used to fund consumption goods such as Expo 86 in Vancouver, then this will likely incur a burden on future generations. On the other hand, if the monies used from the government debt are used to fund long-term medical research projects, which mainly benefit future generations, then one cannot say that the debt placed a burden on future generations.

5. The key advantage of a flexible exchange rate is that, in response to shocks to Canada's terms of trade, the flexible exchange rate can act as a "shock absorber", dampening the effects of the shock on Canadian aggregate demand, output and employment. As an example, if the world demand for pulp and paper declined, this will cause a depreciation of the Canadian dollar. This depreciation will mean that the decline in world demand will not cause such a large decrease in Canadian aggregate demand (compared to what would happen under a fixed exchange rate).

The key disadvantage of a flexible exchange rate is that, since the exchange rate typically fluctuates daily, this imposes risks to Canadian importers and/or exporters that would be absent under a fixed exchange rate. For example, if a Canadian firm imports Japanese cars quoted in Japanese yen, and the yen appreciates relative to the Canadian dollar before payment is made, the importer will pay more, in Canadian dollars, than expected for the imported cars. This flexible exchange rate risk can therefore scare away trade and the gains that would accompany this trade.

Macroeconomics Practice Exam #2

Part 1: Multiple Choice

1. a
2. e
3. a
4. b
5. c
6. a
7. d
8. b
9. d
10. d
11. c
12. c
13. d
14. d
15. c
16. d
17. c
18. a
19. c
20. c
21. c
22. a
23. b
24. c
25. b
26. d
27. b
28. d
29. e
30. b
31. a
32. e
33. a
34. b
35. a
36. b
37. b
38. a
39. a
40. b
41. b
42. d
43. a
44. e
45. d
46. e
47. d
48. c
49. d
50. e
51. c
52. e
53. d
54. d
55. c
56. e
57. d
58. c
59. a
60. d
61. c
62. a
63. a
64. e
65. b
66. e
67. e
68. a
69. b
70. c
71. d
72. c
73. c
74. e
75. a
76. e
77. b
78. c
79. b
80. a
81. e
82. d
83. c
84. d

85. c
86. c
87. e
88. b
89. c
90. b
91. b
92. b
93. a
94. c
95. c
96. a
97. b
98. e
99. d
100. e.

Part 2: Short Answer

1. Two basic measures of national income are the expenditure approach and the income approach.

2. Net Domestic Income at factor cost is the sum of all wages and salaries in the economy, all interest payments, and all profits.

3. The four components of the expenditure approach are

   Consumption
   Investment
   Government purchases
   Net exports

4. The consumption function is the relationship between disposable income and desired consumption.

5. The marginal propensity to consume measures a change in desired consumption divided by a change in disposable income. It can be expressed as $\Delta C / \Delta Y_d$.

6. Equilibrium national income is defined as a) national income and b) the point where desired saving equals desired investment.

7. The present value of this asset is
   $$PV = R / (1 + i)^2$$
   $$= \$100(1.05)^2$$
   $$= \$90.70$$

8. When the Bank of Canada buys securities on the open market, the reserves of the commercial banks are increased. The banks can lend more money, thus increasing the money supply.

9. When the Bank of Canada sells securities on the open market, the reserves of the commercial banks are decreased. The commercial banks can then lend less money, decreasing the money supply.

Common Abbreviations Used in Tex

Greek Letters	η	(eta)	Elasticity
	Δ	(delta)	Change in

Abbreviations

Microeconomics

ATC	Average Total Cost
AVC	Average Variable Cost
D	Demand
i	Rate of Interest
MC	Marginal Cost
MP	Marginal Product
MR	Marginal Revenue
MRP	Marginal Revenue Product
S	Supply
TC	Total Cost
TR	Total Revenue

Macroeconomics

AD	Aggregate Demand
AS	Aggregate Supply
AE	(Desired) Aggregate Expenditure
C	Aggregate Consumption Expenditure
CPI	Consumer Price Index
G	Government Purchases
GDP	Gross Domestic Product
GNP	Gross National Product
I	Aggregate Investment Expenditure
i	Nominal Interest Rate
IM	Aggregate Imports of Goods and Services
LRAS	Long-Run Aggregate Supply
M	Money Supply
M1, M2, M2+	Measures of Money Supply
P	Price Level
r	Real Interest Rate
S	Aggregate Private Saving
SRAS	Short-Run Aggregate Supply
T	Government Tax Revenue (Net of Transfers)
TR	Government Transfer Payments
U	Unemployment Rate
U^*	Natural Rate of Unemployment (NAIRU)
X	Aggregate Exports of Goods and Services
X-IM or NX	Net Exports of Goods and Services
Y	Real GDP
Y^*	Potential GDP
Y_D	Disposable Income

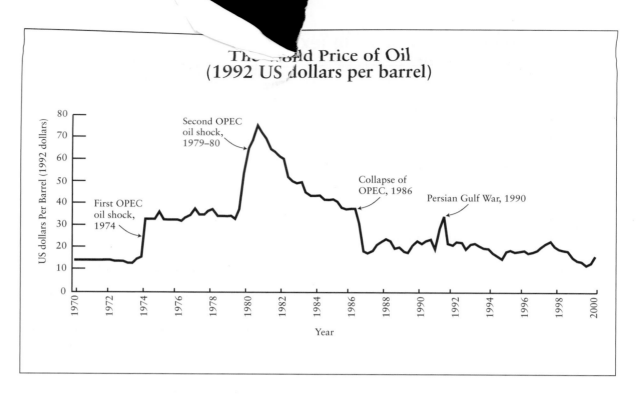

The World Price of Oil
(1992 US dollars per barrel)

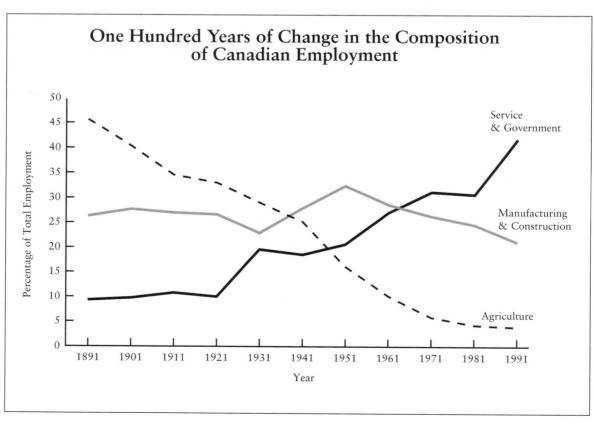

One Hundred Years of Change in the Composition
of Canadian Employment

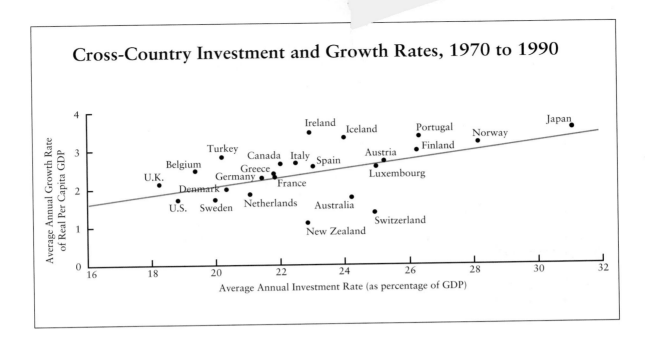

Cross-Country Investment and Growth Rates, 1970 to 1990

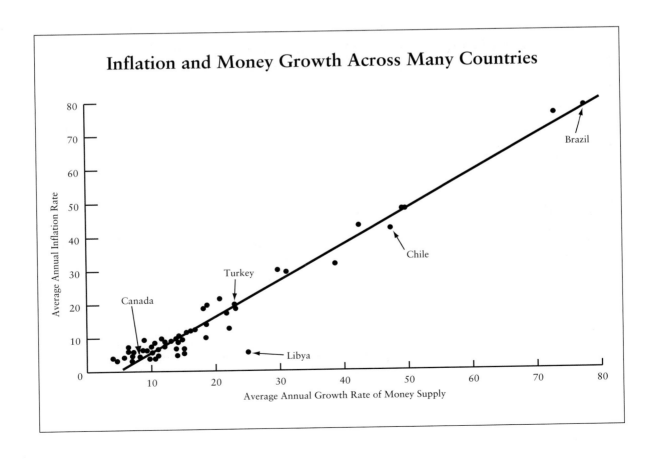

Inflation and Money Growth Across Many Countries

Economists on K

On the economic problem...

The peculiar character of the problem of a rational economic order is determined precisely by the fact that the knowledge of the circumstances of which we must make use never exists in concentrated or integrated form, but solely as the dispersed bits of incomplete and frequently contradictory knowledge which all the separate individuals possess. The economic problem of society is thus not merely a problem of how to allocate "give" resources—if "given" is taken to mean given to a single mind which deliberately solves the problem.... It is rather a problem of how to secure the best use of resources known to any of the members of society, for ends whose relative importance only these individuals know. Or, to put it briefly, it is a problem of the utilization of knowledge not given to anyone in its totality.

Friedrich Hayek, 1974 Nobel Laureate
"The Use of Knowledge in Society," *American Economic Review*, September 1945

On 'balance' in economics...

There is a long-standing tension in economics between belief in the advantages of the market mechanism and awareness of its imperfections.... There is a large element of Rohrschach test in the way each of us responds to this tension. Some of us see Smithian virtues as a needle in a haystack, as an island of measure zero in a sea of imperfections. Others see all the potential sources of market failure as so many fleas on the thick hide of an ox, requiring only an occasional flick of the tail to be brushed away. A hopeless eclectic without any strength of character, like me, has a terrible time of it.... I need only listen to Milton Friedman talk for a minute and my mind floods with thoughts of increasing returns to scale, oligopolistic interdependence, consumer ignorance, environmental pollution, intergenerational inequity, and on and on. There is almost no cure for it, except to listen for a minute to John Kenneth Galbraith, in which case all I can think of are the discipline of competition, the large number of substitutes for any commodity, the stupidities of regulation, the Pareto optimality of Walrasian competition, the importance of decentralizing decision making to where the knowledge is, and on and on. Sometimes I think it is only my weakness of character that keeps me from making obvious errors.

Robert Solow, 1987 Nobel Laureate
"On Theories of Unemployment," *American Economic Review,* March 1980

On choosing between theories...

... any theory has implications ... and it is true that most of us would not value the theory if we did not think these implications corresponded to happenings in the real economic system. But a theory is not like an airline or bus timetable. We are not interested simply in the accuracy of its predictions. A theory also serves as a base for thinking. It helps us to understand what is going on by enabling us to organise our thoughts. Faced with a choice between a theory which predicts well but gives us little insight into how the system works and one which gives us this insight but predicts badly, I would choose the latter, and I am inclined to think that most economists would do the same.

... Testable predictions are not all that matters. And realism in our assumptions is needed if our theories are ever to help us understand why the system works in the way it does. Realism in assumptions forces us to analyse the world that exists, not some imaginary world that does not. It is, of course, true that our assumptions should not be completely realistic. There are factors we leave out because we do not know how to handle them. There are others we exclude because we do not feel the benefits of a more complete theory would be worth the costs involved in including them.... There are good reasons why the assumptions of our theories should not be completely realistic, but this does not mean that we should lose touch with reality.

Ronald Coase, 1991 Nobel Laureate
"How Should Economists Choose?" in *Essays on Economics and Economists*
(Chicago: The University of Chicago Press, 1994)